MW00522873

Introducing

Updated Edition

Bring the American Dream to Life in Your Classroom.

WEST'S AMERICAN GOVERNMEN

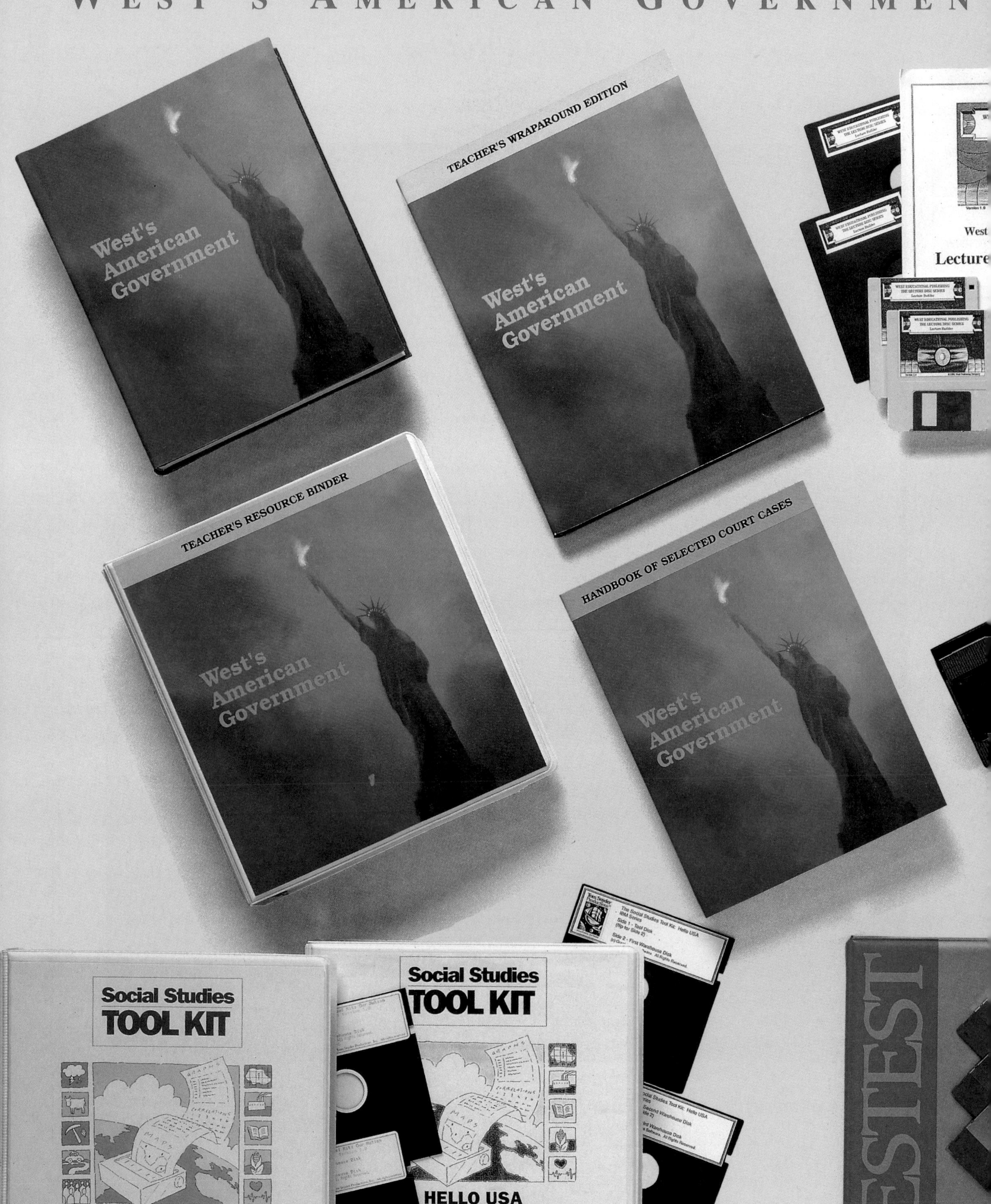

WEST EDUCATIONAL PUBLISHING offers you a new choice for your American government classroom. This new choice is a multi-faceted, visually outstanding program for teaching American government in the 1990s and beyond. This new choice will engage students in a comprehensive study of American government, from lessons in historical analysis to lessons in community involvement. This new choice is **WEST'S AMERICAN GOVERNMENT.**

WEST'S AMERICAN GOVERNMENT is an integrated instructional program offering a complete learning experience. This exciting, up-to-date, comprehensive study of American government includes an in-depth examination of the institutions, processes, politics, and policies that are vital parts of our system of government.

WEST'S AMERICAN GOVERNMENT will help you and your students keep pace with our American government and its ever-changing role in the global community. **WEST'S AMERICAN GOVERNMENT** gives your students the perspective necessary to understand and cope with the extraordinary international events occurring almost daily. This text further helps you and your students keep pace with the rapid political and social changes here at home. **WEST'S AMERICAN GOVERNMENT** encourages students to understand and appreciate our diverse, multicultural nation.

WEST'S AMERICAN GOVERNMENT encourages students to look closely at the American dream. They examine how it was conceived, how it is presently defined, where it is going, and perhaps most importantly, what it means to the students themselves. In this careful investigation of the American dream, **WEST'S AMERICAN GOVERNMENT** asks students to analyze, question, evaluate and forge their own opinions. Beyond this, **WEST'S AMERICAN GOVERNMENT** stresses that students have a responsibility to participate actively in American government.

WEST'S AMERICAN GOVERNMENT is a fresh, new program that provides a wealth of teaching options designed for today's classroom. This exciting program is described in the following pages of this brochure. For any additional information, please contact your local WEST representative or call our main office at 612-687-7482. In Texas, call 1-800-432-6201.

WEST'S AMERICAN GOVERNMENT

WEST'S AMERICAN GOVERNMENT is an integrated instructional program beginning with an exciting and up-to-date student textbook.

The nine units of this text offer a comprehensive study of the content areas of American government, from the precepts set down by our founding fathers to federalism as it exists today; from the nature and functions of Congress and the Supreme Court to the struggle for civil rights and current domestic and foreign policy issues; and from the presidency to an important overview of state and local government systems and more.

Visually striking and written in an accessible and enjoyable style, **WEST'S AMERICAN GOVERNMENT** has been created to meet the needs of today's students.

WEST'S AMERICAN GOVERNMENT has features designed to bring the study of American government to life and to show it in action. Other features work to develop citizenship skills and build social studies and other important skills.

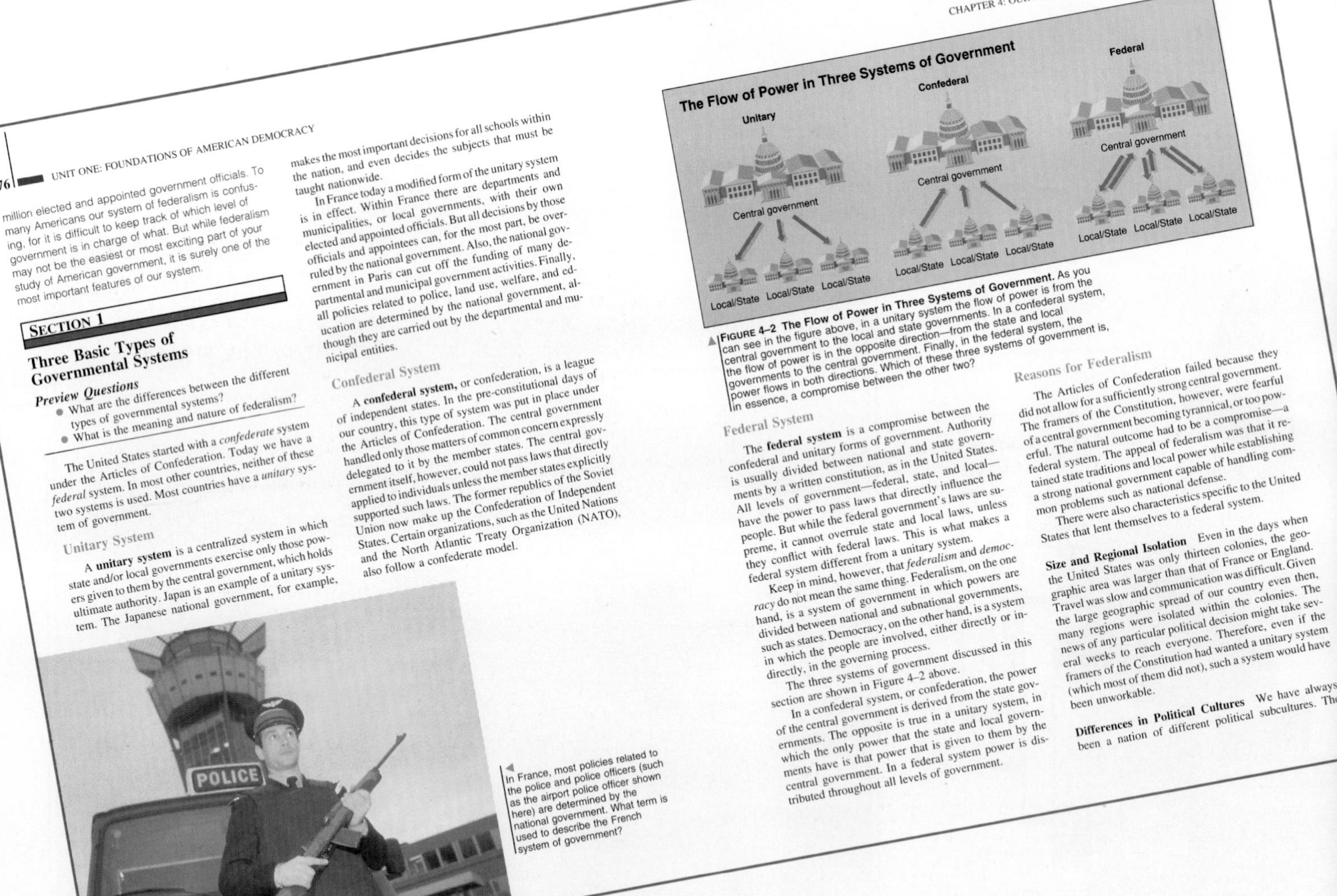

76 UNIT ONE: FOUNDATIONS OF AMERICAN DEMOCRACY

million elected and appointed government officials. To many Americans our system of federalism is confusing, for it is difficult to keep track of which level of government is in charge of what. But while federalism may not be the easiest or most exciting part of your study of American government, it is surely one of the most important features of our system.

SECTION 1

Three Basic Types of Governmental Systems

Preview Questions

- What are the differences between the different types of governmental systems?
- What is the meaning and nature of federalism?

The United States started with a *confederate* system under the Articles of Confederation. Today we have a *federal* system. In most other countries, neither of these two systems is used. Most countries have a *unitary* system of government.

Unitary System

A **unitary system** is a centralized system in which state and/or local governments exercise only those powers given to them by the central government, which holds ultimate authority. Japan is an example of a unitary system. The Japanese national government, for example, makes the most important decisions for all schools within the nation, and even decides the subjects that must be taught nationwide.

In France today a modified form of the unitary system is in effect. Within France there are departments and municipalities, or local governments, with their own elected and appointed officials. But all decisions by those officials and appointees can, for the most part, be overruled by the national government. Also, the national government in Paris can cut off the funding of many departmental and municipal government activities. Finally, all policies related to police, land use, welfare, and education are determined by the national government, although they are carried out by the departmental and municipal entities.

Confederal System

A **confederal system,** or confederation, is a league of independent states. In the pre-constitutional days of our country, this type of system was put in place under the Articles of Confederation. The central government handled only those matters of common concern expressly delegated to it by the member states. The central government itself, however, could not pass laws that directly applied to individuals unless the member states explicitly supported such laws. The former republics of the Soviet Union now make up the Confederation of Independent States. Certain organizations, such as the United Nations and the North Atlantic Treaty Organization (NATO), also follow a confederate model.

In France, most policies related to the police and police officers (such as the airport police officer shown here) are determined by the national government. What term is used to describe the French system of government?

CHAPTER 4: OUR SYSTEM OF FEDERALISM 77

FIGURE 4–2 The Flow of Power in Three Systems of Government. As you can see in the figure above, in a unitary system the flow of power is from the central government to the local and state governments. In a confederal system, the flow of power is in the opposite direction—from the state and local governments to the central government. Finally, in the federal system, the power flows in both directions. Which of these three systems of government is, in essence, a compromise between the other two?

Federal System

The **federal system** is a compromise between the confederal and unitary forms of government. Authority is usually divided between national and state governments by a written constitution, as in the United States. All levels of government—federal, state, and local—have the power to pass laws that directly influence the people. But while the federal government's laws are supreme, it cannot overrule state and local laws, unless they conflict with federal laws. This is what makes a federal system different from a unitary system.

Keep in mind, however, that *federalism* and *democracy* do not mean the same thing. Federalism, on the one hand, is a system of government in which powers are divided between national and subnational governments, such as states. Democracy, on the other hand, is a system in which the people are involved, either directly or indirectly, in the governing process.

The three systems of government discussed in this section are shown in Figure 4–2 above.

In a confederal system, or confederation, the power of the central government is derived from the state governments. The opposite is true in a unitary system, in which the only power that the state and local governments have is that power that is given to them by the central government. In a federal system power is distributed throughout all levels of government.

Reasons for Federalism

The Articles of Confederation failed because they did not allow for a sufficiently strong central government. The framers of the Constitution, however, were fearful of a central government becoming tyrannical, or too powerful. The natural outcome had to be a compromise—a federal system. The appeal of federalism was that it retained state traditions and local power while establishing a strong national government capable of handling common problems such as national defense.

There were also characteristics specific to the United States that lent themselves to a federal system.

Size and Regional Isolation Even in the days when the United States was only thirteen colonies, the geographic area was larger than that of France or England. Travel was slow and communication was difficult. Given the large geographic spread of our country even then, many regions were isolated within the colonies. The news of any particular political decision might take several weeks to reach everyone. Therefore, even if the framers of the Constitution had wanted a unitary system (which most of them did not), such a system would have been unworkable.

Differences in Political Cultures We have always been a nation of different political subcultures. The

Art and Photo Program

The quality of the art and photo program is exceptional. The teaching captions contain questions to check student comprehension of key facts and concepts as well as to stimulate critical thinking.

CHAPTER 1

Government and the People—The Global Connection

Keynote

"But what is government itself, but the greatest of all reflections on human nature? If men were angels, no government would be necessary."

—— James Madison
(1751–1836) Fourth President of the United States

CHAPTER OBJECTIVES

To learn and understand

- The meaning of politics and government and the purposes that government serves.
- The different types of government and the main principles of democracy.
- The challenge of interdependence with other nations.

Unit and Chapter Openers

The spectacular art created especially for this text features symbols and images that relate to unit and chapter content. *Keynote* quotes and *Chapter Objectives* are included for each chapter.

Architect of the American Dream

Multi-faceted portraits of certain Americans who were instrumental in the inspiration and advancement of the American dream are presented in *Architect of the American Dream*.

Biographical information and original source materials combine to encourage students to analyze and evaluate the roles and contributions of these important figures. These two-page features include a likeness of a famous American, a brief biography, background information, a sample of his or her own words, and questions designed to develop critical thinking.

ARCHITECT OF
The American Dream

George Washington

Even though George Washington was born more than two and a half centuries ago, he remains one of the foremost architects of the American dream. He was a central figure during the events that shaped the founding of our nation.

George Washington was born in Bridges Creek, Westmoreland County, Virginia, on February 22, 1732. After his father's death in 1743 he lived chiefly at Mount Vernon and worked as a surveyor. He served as a lieutenant colonel in the French and Indian Wars from 1754 to 1758 and in 1759 entered the Virginia colonial legislature, the House of Burgesses. He was a leader in the movement for independence and a delegate to the First and Second Continental Congresses. On June 15, 1775, he was chosen to be general and commander in chief of the Army of the United Colonies. He persevered through the long and difficult years of the Revolution until his secret and rapid march from the Hudson River to the Chesapeake Bay. This resulted in the surrender of British General Cornwallis at Yorktown in 1781, thus ending the war. When he resigned his commission in 1783, he said he was through with public life, but his retirement did not last.

Returning to public life, he supported the movement for a more effective union and presided over the Philadelphia Convention in 1787 that adopted the Constitution. Even though he did not design the Constitution, many believe it would not have taken the shape it did without his commanding presence and leadership.

The framers of the Constitution respected George Washington and wanted him to be the first president. They created the office with him in mind. He had the qualities they thought a chief executive should have: honesty, fairness, wisdom, dignity, natural leadership, and the ability to balance executive authority with the rights of citizens. He was elected unanimously as the first president. George Washington knew the importance of being the first to hold the office. He wrote: "I walk on untrodden ground. . . . There is scarcely any part of my conduct that may not hereafter be drawn into precedent." He did indeed set precedents, including establishing a cabinet and holding regular cabinet meetings. He thought of the United States as "an experiment entrusted to the hands of the American people" and knew that it was his responsibility to give that experiment proper direction. During his two terms, he helped to set the new nation on a solid foundation and organized the machinery of government. He declined a third term of office, which set the precedent of limiting the number of presidential terms to two.

HIS WORDS

Farewell Address, September 17, 1796

"The great rule of conduct for us in regard to foreign nations is, in extending our commercial relations to have with them as little *political* connection as possible. So far as we have already formed engagements let them be fulfilled with perfect good faith. Here let us stop.

Europe has a set of primary interests which to us have none or a very remote relation. Hence she must be engaged in frequent controversies, the causes of which are essentially foreign to our concerns. Hence, therefore, it must be unwise in us to implicate ourselves by artificial ties in the ordinary

This painting by Howard Chandler Christy depicts the scene at the signing of the Constitution of the United States on September 17, 1787. Why do you think George Washington was chosen to preside over the convention?

HIS WORDS–*continued*

vicissitudes of her politics or the ordinary combinations and collisions of her friendships or enmities.

Our detached and distant situation invites and enables us to pursue a different course. If we remain one people, under an efficient government, the period is not far off when we may defy material injury from external annoyance; when we may take such an attitude as well cause the neutrality we may at any time resolve upon to be scrupulously respected; when belligerent nations, under the impossibility of making acquisitions upon us, will not lightly hazard the giving us provocation; when we may choose peace or war, as our interest, guided by justice, shall counsel.

It is our true policy to steer clear of permanent alliances with any portion of the foreign world, so far, I mean, as we are now at liberty to do it; for let me not be understood as capable of patronizing infidelity to existing engagements. I hold the maxim no less applicable to public than to private affairs that honesty is always the best policy. I repeat, therefore, let those engagements be observed in their genuine sense. But in my opinion it is unnecessary and would be unwise to extend them."

DEVELOPING CRITICAL THINKING SKILLS

1. Washington states that "Europe has a set of primary interests which to us have none or a very remote relation." How has our relationship with Europe changed since the days of George Washington?
2. What do you think Washington meant when he said, "the period is not far off when we may defy material injury from external annoyance"?
3. At what point in history did our nation begin to stray from Washington's advice to "steer clear of permanent alliances with any portion of the foreign world"?

FOR FURTHER READING

Cunliffe, Marcus. *George Washington: Man and Monument.* Boston: Little Brown, 1958.

Davis, Burke. *George Washington and the American Revolution.* New York: Random House, 1975.

Eaton, Jeanette. *Leader by Destiny: George Washington, Man and Patriot.* New York: Harcourt Brace, 1938.

43

Building Social Studies Skills

WEST'S AMERICAN GOVERNMENT's skill building program ranges from basic skills, to social studies and citizenship skills, to critical thinking skills.

An integral part of the skill building program is *Building Social Studies Skills*. A different skill is covered in each chapter, such as: how to use the features in the text and government publications; how to analyze primary sources, political cartoons and political commercials; how to work with statistics; and how to distinguish between fact and opinion.

BUILDING SOCIAL STUDIES SKILLS

Using Government Publications

Every year the government prints hundreds of publications, many of which can be useful in understanding American government and politics. Listed below are several government publications that may prove useful in your studies.

The *Statistical Abstract of the United States* is published by the Bureau of the Census. It contains hundreds of tables that give statistics on the social, political, and economic status of government and business in the United States. Its hundreds of charts, graphs, and tables cover topics such as population, law enforcement, immigration, and much more.

The *Book of States* is published by the Council of State Governments. It contains information on state governments, economies, taxes, constitutions, and many other subjects.

The *Congressional Record* is published for every

of Congress, lists of committees and committee assignments, statistics for recent congressional elections, and maps of congressional districts.

The *United States Government Manual* is a guide to the federal government. It contains information about the legislative, executive, and judicial branches of government and federal agencies and commissions. Addresses and telephone numbers of government offices are also included.

PRACTICING YOUR SKILLS

Go to your local library and use the sources listed above to find the following items and information.

Citizenship Skills and Responsibilities

One per chapter, *Citizenship Skills and Responsibilities* encourage students to be productive, informed citizens and to participate in government. Topics vary from community involvement to being conscious of waste in the environment.

CITIZENSHIP SKILLS AND RESPONSIBILITIES

The Duties of Citizenship

Americans are citizens of a democracy. As you have learned, democracy is government by the people, and citizen involvement is at the heart of democracy. If only a few people decided to become involved in government, public decisions would be left to those few. Such a government would no longer be an effective democracy. Being a citizen in a democratic society requires learning certain skills, some of

tween fact and opinion, recognize their own biases and values, see both sides of an issue, and identify irrelevant and ambiguous information.

4. **Communicating.** Citizens must be able to express their views and communicate their ideas effectively, both in writing and in speaking.
5. **Cooperating.** Citizens must be able to work together to achieve common goals.

Government in Action

Government in Action helps students understand the day-to-day functioning of the American government and the people involved. These features vary in format: often a case study, sometimes a profile, sometimes a day in the life of an important government official, and sometimes a focus on personal law.

There are at least two *Government in Action* features in every chapter. At the end of each *Government in Action* are *Think About It* questions to stimulate critical thinking.

GOVERNMENT IN ACTION

CASE STUDY

The Bill of Rights Was Not a Foregone Conclusion

Many state ratifying conventions had been assured that a bill of rights would be discussed at the first session of the new Congress. Nonetheless, James Madison could not get his proposed constitutional amendments considered each time he stood up in the House of Representatives to present them. At the time Madison was attempting to get the House to consider his amendments, the new Congress was in the midst of creating a new structure for government. It was involved in debates on issues such as import and tonnage duties. Madison kept asserting that a bill of rights was more important business, but to no avail. House members believed the discussion would take up more time than the House could then spare. Moreover, most of the Fed-

points.'' A person looking back today might wonder how this could be.

Madison countered these objections by reminding the Congress that North Carolina and Rhode Island had not yet ratified the new Constitution and that the amendments had been promised to the people. He suggested that if Congress took action on the amendments, it might cause those who were opposed to the Constitution in the first place to change their minds. Although the House listened to Madison's plea, the members still postponed any consideration of the amendments for a month. After frequent reminders by Madison, work by a select committee, and several postponements, the Bill of Rights was finally approved by the House on August 24,

Challenge to the American Dream

This feature near the end of every chapter concerns an issue, often current and controversial. Students examine political issues that must be addressed for the American dream to continue into the coming century. At the end of each *Challenge to the American Dream* are critical thinking questions titled *You Decide*. Students consider a key issue and evaluate approaches for dealing with it.

CHALLENGE TO THE AMERICAN DREAM

Do Our Representatives Represent Too Many People?

Everybody accepts the notion that direct democracy as practiced in ancient Greece would not work in a nation of over 250 million people. Even if a small percentage of the total adult population wanted to participate in direct democracy, the result would be a mass

of the continued rate of population growth. Others poi out that this nation will probably reach its maximu stable population sometime between the years 2020 a 2040. While the population will probably increase about 300 to 330 million, it will not be significantly larg than it is now. In other words, if representative demc racy is working today, even with all of its faults, it w certainly work with 50 to 80 million more people. T two senators from each state will represent an avera of 6 million people; for representatives, the average w be about 690,000 people. Certainly, the effect and inf ence any individual citizen has on his or her elect officials will not markedly change with a population th is 25 percent larger.

Chapter Review

The main concepts in each chapter are reinforced in the *Key Terms* (listed with page references), *Summary*, *Review Questions*, and *Questions for Thought and Discussion*. *Improve Your Skills* exercises develop basic communication, writing and social studies skills. *Activities and Projects* are also included for extension assignments. **WEST'S AMERICAN GOVERNMENT** also includes a comprehensive glossary.

CHAPTER 4 REVIEW

Key Terms

act of admission 88
alien 85
child custody 83
common-law marriage 82
concurrent majority 93
concurrent powers 83
confederal system 76
cooperative federalism 95
decentralization 90
Dennison rule 86
division of powers 78
dual federalism 94
elastic clause 80
enabling act 88
exports 80
expressed or enumerated powers 78
extradition 86
federal system 77
fugitive 86
full faith and credit clause 86
horizontal federalism 85
implied powers 80
inherent powers 80
interstate compacts 86
intrastate commerce 94
legal tender 80
loose constructionists 92
monopoly 92
necessary and proper clause 80
New Deal 95
new federalism 95
privileges and immunities clause 85
republican form of government 86
reserved powers 81
resulting powers 80
revenue-sharing program 95
secession 94
strict constructionists 92
supremacy clause 89
unitary system 76

Summary

1. The Constitution created a federal system—one based on the division of powers between the federal government and the states. Other forms of governmental systems are a unitary system, in which state and/or local governments exercise only those powers given to them by the central government, and a confederal system, which is a league of independent states.

2. Under the U.S. Constitution, the federal government has three types of powers: expressed or enumerated powers, implied powers, and inherent powers. Some powers are expressly denied to the federal government and some powers are reserved to the states. Local governments are created by their states and have no legal existence apart from them. Concurrent powers are those simultaneously held by both the federal and state governments.

3. Horizontal federalism defines relations among the states. Under this system, states may not discriminate against citizens of other states, and are obligated to give full faith and credit to the laws and activities of other states. They must also agree to extradite persons accused of crimes elsewhere. Many states have settled differences among themselves by entering into interstate compacts. The Constitution obligates the federal government to provide the state with a republican form of government, to protect each state against foreign invasion and domestic violence, and to respect each state's territorial integrity.

4. The supremacy clause of the Constitution makes the federal government the supreme governing body of the land. The Supreme Court's decision in *McCulloch* v. *Maryland* (1819) became the basis for strengthening the federal government's power. Since the Supreme Court decision in *Gibbons* v. *Ogden* (1824), the federal government has used the commerce clause to increase its authority over virtually all areas of economic activity.

5. The practice of federalism has changed throughout the years. Historically, we can view the changing model of federalism in the United States as having three eras: dual federalism, cooperative federalism, and new federalism.

Review Questions

1. Explain the differences between the three different types of governmental systems.
2. Explain how federalism creates a two-way system of government.
3. Why did the framers of our Constitution choose a federal framework?
4. What is the source of the national government's expressed powers? What is the source of its implied powers?
5. How has the necessary and proper clause enabled the national government to expand its powers?
6. On what basis does the Constitution deny certain powers to the national government?

CHAPTER 4 REVIEW—Continued

7. Explain the concept of concurrent powers.
8. What does the privileges and immunities clause prevent?
9. Why is the concept of full faith and credit so important to interstate relationships?
10. What is the importance of the interstate compact?
11. What obligations does the Constitution impose upon the federal government with regard to the states?
12. What is the significance of the supremacy clause in our federal system?
13. What was the outcome of the case *McCulloch* v. *Maryland*?
14. Have there been any changes in the balance of political power between the state and national governments throughout the years?

Questions for Thought and Discussion

1. What do you think our government would be like if there were no division of powers between the national government and the states?
2. Should states be given greater power, less power, or do they currently have enough power?
3. Why do you think the powers to wage war and to relate to foreign nations belong to the national government?
4. What factors do you think have been responsible for the national government's growth of power?

Improving Your Skills

Communication Skills

Asking Effective Questions

Asking questions is one of the most important ways for us to learn facts, share ideas, and become informed. Asking effective questions will help you become a better-informed and more responsible citizen. Effective questions are designed to obtain specific information.

To ask effective questions requires preparation. When we don't obtain the information we seek from questions we ask, it is usually because we are asking the wrong source, asking the wrong questions, or asking them in the wrong way. Before you ask questions:

1. Determine the exact information you want to obtain.
2. Determine the best sources of that information.
3. Decide what questions will best draw out the information.
4. Decide how you should ask the questions. Remember that questions that can be answered with only a *yes* or a *no* will not give you much information.

Writing

Follow the four steps above to plan a class interview with a city or county official concerning a current issue in your community.

1. As a group, discuss the kinds of information you would like to obtain from the official. Write down ideas as they occur. Then narrow your ideas to a few specific issues.
2. Decide which city or county official would be the best source for that information.
3. Using the ideas you generated in Step 1, create a formal list of questions for the interview. Have your teacher approve your questions.

Social Studies Skills

Map Reading

Look at the map on page 91 (Federal Ownership of Land in the United States) to answer the following questions.

1. How is federally owned land identified?
2. Do any states have no federally owned land?
3. List the states in which the federal government owns 50 percent or more of the land.

Activities and Projects

1. Stage a debate on the following issue: Federal aid in the form of categorical grants gives the national government too much control over the states and should be abolished.
2. Call or write the district office of your local school district. Find out what kinds of state and federal aid your school district receives. Interview as many school officials as possible (principals, school board members, teachers, etc). Ask them to describe how they feel the aid (or lack of it) affects your school. Report your findings to the class.

The Resource Center

This collection of important resource materials found at the end of the text is conveniently available to students:

- The Constitution, including the Amendments with full and extensive annotations
- Original source documents
- How to read a court case
- Annotated table of court cases
- Extended case studies expand text material and allow students to investigate the important issues in greater depth. Extended case studies provide additional original source material and pose questions for critical analysis.
- Presidents and vice presidents of the United States
- Supreme Court chief justices and associate justices
- Atlas of the states
- United States and world maps

THE RESOURCE CENTER

CONTENTS

The Teacher's Wraparound Edition is the centerpiece of the **WEST'S AMERICAN GOVERNMENT** integrated instructional program. A wealth of strategies, activities and supplements are at your fingertips. From the *Chapter Preview and Planning Guide* to the lesson plan material presented in innovative and convenient wraparound format, the **WEST'S AMERICAN GOVERNMENT Teacher's Wraparound Edition** is designed to maximize the value of your preparation time and enrich and expand your classroom presentation.

"Finally you and your students can be on the same page!"

The Teacher's Wraparound Edition has been designed for the way you read and work. The entire Student Edition is contained in the Teacher's Wraparound Edition. Each page from the Student Edition is slightly reduced and surrounded by a wide variety of teaching materials developed for today's classroom. Finally you and your students can be on the same page!

The core lesson plan material is right there surrounding the student text pages. Complete lesson plan instructions begin with pre-teaching assessment and range through cooperative learning, reteaching, evaluation, and extension.

The *Chapter Preview and Planning Guide* found at the front of the Teacher's Wraparound Edition includes *Teacher Background Information*, *Resources*, and *Pacing Suggestions*.

The Teacher's Wraparound Edition includes specific teaching strategies for each and every special feature found in the student text.

The Teacher's Wraparound Edition also shows you how to use all the exciting teaching supplements that are part of WEST'S integrated instructional program. For example, explanatory material and bar codes for the **WEST'S AMERICAN GOVERNMENT** videodisc are included in the Teacher's Wraparound Edition for each unit.

•Reteaching and evaluation strategies are stated clearly for each section, as well as for chapter evaluation strategies.

•Complete chapter and section introductory material features *Kickoff Activities*, *Section Previews*, *Points to Stress*, *Using the Keynotes* instructions, and more.

Critical Thinking Skills Encourage students to analyze the statement that "the American way of life is, in many respects, the result of the American way of governing." How would you define the American way of life?

Reteaching Strategies
1. Allow small groups of students to review and discuss the notes they took while reading this section.
2. Have the students work with partners to write their own definitions of these terms: *limited government; representative government.*

Evaluation Strategies
1. Have the students write their answers to the first three questions of the Section 1 Review.
2. Have the students work in groups to discuss their responses to the final Section 1 Review question. Check on each discussion group to be sure all the students are contributing.
3. Have the students take the Section 1 Quiz found in the TRB.

Figure Answer The British felt that a colony on Roanoke Island would be an advantage in their conflict with Spain.

Section 1 Review (Answers)
1. The concept that government is not all-powerful and that it may do only those things the people have given it the power to do. The American way of government follows this concept by limiting the power of government and of those who govern.
2. A system in which public policies are made by officials who are selected by the people and held accountable through elections.
3. John Locke argued that people were born free, equal, and independent and that all persons had a natural right to life, liberty and property. Thomas Hobbes contributed to the idea that government was not based on power, but on an agreement negotiated between the rulers and the ruled. Montesquieu was the first political writer to speak of dividing government into three separate branches. Rousseau argued that the people alone had the right to determine how they should be governed.
4. Answers will vary, e.g., the rights of those accused of a crime such as the right to a trial.

SECTION 2

Points to Stress
• The first British outpost in North America and its history.
• The manner of government proposed by the Plymouth Company in the Mayflower Compact.
• Fundamental Orders of Connecticut and the principles it enumerated.
• The role of the early colonial legislatures.

Kick-Off Activity
Have the students list at least eig[ht] words or phrases that come to mind when they think of the Pilgrims. Then have the students share, compare, and discuss thei[r] lists.

Working with the Preview Questions
Ask the students to read these study questions and briefly discus[s] their responses before they read

26 ■ CHAPTER 2

26 ■ UNIT ONE: FOUNDATIONS OF AMERICAN DEMOCRACY

Montesquieu, but wanted to ensure that the American form of government had an even more distinct separation of powers. In this way, they hoped that liberty would be safer in the United States than in England.

As you shall see, the ideas of these philosophers are clearly embodied in the documents that outline the American philosophy of government.

The American way of life is, in many respects, the result of the American system of government, which resulted from many struggles against nature, England, and ourselves. In order to fully understand this system, we must trace its roots back to our nation's beginnings. Between 1600 and 1750, Americans, as we would later be called, developed a **political philosophy**, which is a set of notions or ideas about how people should be governed.

SECTION 1 REVIEW

1. What is the concept of limited government? How did the American way of government evolve out of this concept?
2. What is the system of representative government?
3. How did the theories of European philosophers influence American political thinking?
4. **For critical analysis:** What are some common restrictions on government in the United States that follow the principle of limited government?

SECTION 2

The First British Settlements

Preview Questions
- What was the first British settlement in North America? What were some of the changes that this settlement went through?
- How was the Plymouth Company set up to be governed?
- What was the nation's first written constitution? What kind of government did it establish?

During the 1590s, Britain and Spain were constantly at war. Government officials in Britain decided that their war efforts against Spain would be improved by having British ships along the shores of North America. These ships could then harass the Spanish treasure fleets, which consisted of fast ships that took gold and other precious metals from the New World to Spain. Sir Walter Raleigh, the adventurer and writer, convinced England's queen, Elizabeth I, to allow him to establish the first British outpost in North America. He did this by sending a ship of settlers in 1585 to Roanoke Island off the coast of North Carolina in an unsuccessful attempt to create a settlement.

The Many British Attempts at Settlement

In 1607 another group from London, the Virginia Company, established a trading post in Virginia, which they called Jamestown. In the first year of its existence, over 60 percent of the colony's 105 inhabitants had died. In 1609, England sent over 800 new arrivals. By the spring of the following year only 60 were left. The survivors, admitting defeat, decided to return to England. Just as they were planning to depart, new supplies and more settlers arrived on three ships. The original 60 colonists changed their plans; together, the colonists all

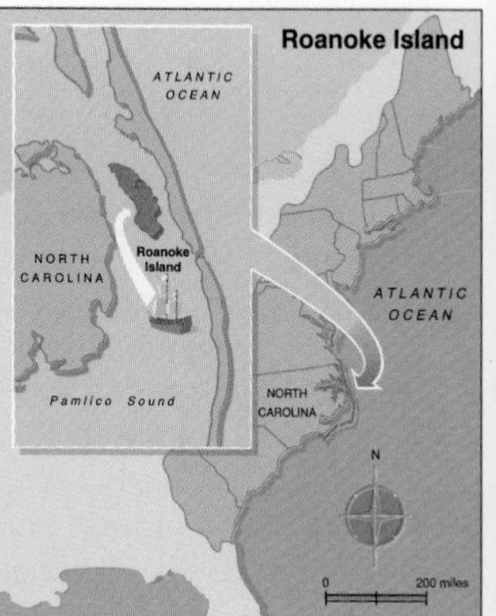

▲ FIGURE 2–1 **Roanoke Island.** The first British outpost in North America was established by Sir Walter Raleigh on Roanoke Island in 1585. Why did Britain want to establish a settlement in North America?

TEACHER'S WRAPAROUND

•You are offered a variety of interesting teaching strategies, including discussion starter questions, enrichment activities, extension activities, critical thinking skills activities, and cooperative learning activities.

•*Discussion Starters* help to stimulate exchange of ideas within your classroom.

•Answers for photo and art captions are conveniently placed at your fingertips.

•*Critical Thinking Skills* activities help your students to analyze, compare, contrast and synthesize.

•Special teaching features such as *Multidiscipline Strategies, Developing Skills for the Information Age* activities, and *FYI* sections can expand and enrich teaching presentations.

the section. Tell the students that they should be prepared to answer these questions more fully when they have finished reading the section.

Teaching Strategies

Introduction
After the students have read the section introduction, encourage them to discuss the establishment and disappearance of the Roanoke colony. Ask volunteers to read more about this settlement and its mysterious fate and then to share their findings with the rest of the class.

Enrichment
Have several volunteers research the early history of St. Augustine, Florida, and share their findings with the rest of the class.

Discussion Starter
Ask the students: What importance do you think this charter must have had for the colonists? How might it have affected their attitudes and actions? What effect do you think it had on the importance of Jamestown to future colonists?

Vocabulary
Ask the students: What is the difference between a charter and a compact? What does this difference imply about differences between the Jamestown settlers and the Pilgrims?

Caption Answer The English colonists at Jamestown found life to be very harsh as 60% of the colony's 105 inhabitants died during the first year of the colony.

Critical Thinking Skills
Ask the students to write a one-paragraph answer to the following: Why were women not included in these activities? What does this exclusion tell you about the society in which the Pilgrims lived?

Multidiscipline Strategies

Math Have the students work in groups to analyze the figures given for the survival of settlers in the Jamestown colony. In each group mentioned in the text, what percentage survived? If those percentages were applied to the population of the school, how many students would survive? Then encourage the group members to collect data on other settlements, including perhaps Roanoke and Plymouth. Have each group prepare a chart or graph showing the survival rates they have collected and calculated.

This 19th century engraving depicts the arrival of the first English colonists at Jamestown, Virginia in May, 1607. What happened to these colonists?

rebuilt Jamestown, which became the first permanent British settlement in North America.[1]

Of the six thousand people who left England for Virginia between 1607 and 1623, four thousand died. Those who lived established a type of government that would serve as a model for later colonial adventures.

Representative Assembly The king of England gave the Virginia Company of London a **charter,** a written grant of authority, to make laws "for the good and welfare" of the Jamestown settlement. Jamestown's colonists used this charter to institute a **representative assembly,** a law-making body that is composed of individuals who represent the population. A representative assembly is different from a *direct democracy,* which was discussed in Chapter 1—a type of government in which citizens collectively make the decision.

Pilgrims and the Mayflower Compact The Plymouth Company established the first New England colony in 1620. A group of English Protestants, calling themselves Pilgrims, sailed to North America on the *Mayflower,* a 180-ton, 90-foot (27-meter) ship with three masts and two decks. They landed at what is now Provincetown Harbor, at the tip of Cape Cod in Massachusetts. (They later moved the ship to Plymouth, Massachusetts, which became their new home.) Even before the Pilgrims went ashore, the adult males drew up the **Mayflower Compact,** or agreement, in which they set up a government and promised to obey its laws. (See the Resource Center.) It was signed by 41 of the 44 men aboard on November 21, 1620. No women were allowed to sign it, nor did they have any direct part in developing it, because women at that time did not have any political status. The Pilgrims felt obligated to establish a written document for self-government because their leaders believed that they needed a set of rules to govern themselves. They also wanted to create a government based on the consent of the governed.

The Mayflower Compact, although often referred to as a constitution, was in fact a *social contract,* of the type that Locke had described—an agreement among individuals to establish a government and to abide by its rules. This particular social contract had great historical significance because it served as a **prototype**—a model—for similar compacts in American history.

By 1639 a number of Pilgrims were being persecuted for their religious beliefs, and decided to leave

1. It was not the first permanent *European* settlement in North America. That honor goes to St. Augustine, Florida—a city that still exists—which was founded on September 8, 1565, by the Spaniard Pedro Menéndez de Áviles.

•*Critical Thinking Skills* activities to foster your students' higher order thinking skills are found throughout the Teacher's Wraparound Edition.

•Helpful, innovative *Reteaching Strategies* are included for each and every section of the student text.

•Separate teaching strategies are offered for each special feature found in the student book, created to help your students read, discuss, analyze, apply, and review the feature content.

On this page from the Teacher's Wraparound Edition is sufficient material on this *Government in Action* feature to help develop a complete lesson.

The *Think About It* questions from the student text are also answered right here on the corresponding Teacher's Wraparound page.

TEACHING GOVERNMENT IN ACTION

Read
Before the students begin reading, encourage them to share their ideas about the Bill of Rights: Do you think that most people today consider the Bill of Rights an integral part of our Constitution? How do you imagine people considered the Bill of Rights 200 years ago? After a brief discussion, ask volunteers to take turns reading the Case Study aloud to the class.

Discuss
Stimulate a class discussion by asking questions such as these: How would you describe the situation in the House of Representatives during this time? How would you compare that situation to the situation that exists in the House of Representatives today? Do citizens still feel that many representatives are more interested in setting up a taxation system and in collecting taxes than in defending the rights of individuals?

Analyze and Apply
Have the students write a 200-word essay explaining why Maine's assertion that the Bill of Rights are "amendments on comparatively unimportant points" was incorrect.

Review
Ask the students these review questions: Who continued to urge the Congress to approve the Bill of Rights? Why did he have to work so long and hard to get these ten amendments approved?

Think About It (Answers)
1. The Federalists were in favor of a strong national government.
2. Like many Federalists, he believed that the existing Constitution already had sufficient protection of individual freedoms.

Critical Thinking Skills
Guide the students in considering the Bill of Rights as a protection of the fundamental rights of individuals: In what sense are the rights protected by the Bill of Rights fundamental? Do you consider that individuals have other fundamental rights not addressed by these ten amendments? If so, what are they and how are they protected?

Reteaching Strategies
1. Have small groups of students work together to write five sentences beginning "You ought. . . ." Then ask the group members to rewrite their sentences, replacing *ought* with *should*. Ask the group members: How are the sentences different? How do these differences help you understand Madison's attitudes and intentions?
2. Work with groups of students to prepare a simple time line, showing main events in the proposal, drafting, and adoption of the Bill of Rights.

Evaluation Strategies
1. Have the students write their responses to the Preview Questions found at the beginning of the section.

GOVERNMENT IN ACTION

CASE STUDY

The Bill of Rights Was Not a Foregone Conclusion

Many state ratifying conventions had been assured that a bill of rights would be discussed at the first session of the new Congress. Nonetheless, James Madison could not get his proposed constitutional amendments considered each time he stood up in the House of Representatives to present them. At the time Madison was attempting to get the House to consider his amendments, the new Congress was in the midst of creating a new structure for government. It was involved in debates on issues such as import and tonnage duties. Madison kept asserting that a bill of rights was more important business, but to no avail. House members believed the discussion would take up more time than the House could then spare. Moreover, most of the Federalist members of Congress believed that they were in the process of solving more urgent problems. Indeed, the notes of many representatives at the time showed that they were more interested in setting up a system of levying and collecting taxes, rather than worrying about the rights of individuals. In 1886, legal scholar Sir Henry Maine referred to the American Bill of Rights as a "certain number of amendments on comparatively unimportant points." A person looking back today might wonder how this could be.

Madison countered these objections by reminding the Congress that North Carolina and Rhode Island had not yet ratified the new Constitution and that the amendments had been promised to the people. He suggested that if Congress took action on the amendments, it might cause those who were opposed to the Constitution in the first place to change their minds. Although the House listened to Madison's plea, the members still postponed any consideration of the amendments for a month. After frequent reminders by Madison, work by a select committee, and several postponements, the Bill of Rights was finally approved by the House on August 24, 1789.

THINK ABOUT IT

1. Why would the Federalist members of the new Congress not be very concerned about considering a bill of rights?
2. How could Sir Henry Maine believe that the Bill of Rights was unimportant?

are used to seeing "Congress shall make no law . . ." "no soldier shall . . ." and "the accused shall. . . ." But the *oughts* and *ought nots* were typical of the language contained in the English Bill of Rights and in the Virginia Declaration of Rights.

Consider one constitutional amendment proposed by the state of Virginia's ratifying convention: "That excessive bail *ought* not to be required, nor excessive fines imposed, nor cruel and unusual punishments inflicted." Madison changed that wording to read, "Excessive bail *shall* not be required, nor excessive fines imposed, nor cruel and unusual punishments inflicted." Wishful thinking was not good enough or bold enough for Madison. Madison required the language of *command.*

Ten Amendments Are Ratified

On December 15, 1791, the Bill of Rights was adopted when Virginia agreed to ratify the ten amendments. The basic structure of American government had already been established. After 1791, the fundamental rights of individuals were protected, at least in theory, at the *national* level.

The Bill of Rights ensures constitutional guarantees of freedom of expression and belief, of individual security, and of equal and fair treatment before the law. The Tenth Amendment spells out the reserved powers of the states, covered in the next chapter on our federal system of government.

EACHER'S WRAPAROUND

•Answers are provided for all content questions found in the student text.

•*Kickoff Activities*, *Points to Stress* and instructions for *Working with the Preview Questions* precede each section and help you acquaint students with the upcoming material.

2. Have the students write their answers to the Section 3 Review.
3. Have the students take the Section 3 Quiz found in the TRB.

Section 3 Review (Answers)

1. He sorted through more than two-hundred recommendations and drafted what was to become the Bill of Rights.
2. The word "ought" sounded weak to Americans, while the word "shall" sounded more authoritative.
3. Answers will vary, e.g., without the Bill of Rights, governmental power would gradually increase over the years. Individual rights would not be as respected by government officials.

SECTION 4

Points to Stress

- The methods for proposing and ratifying amendments to the Constitution.
- The factors that have limited the number of amendments.

Kickoff Activity

Ask the students to write, in their own words, definitions of the verb *amend* and of the noun *amendment*. When they have finished writing, let them share their definitions.

Working with the Preview Questions

Ask a volunteer to read these study questions aloud. Let the students briefly discuss their ideas in response to the questions; then have them read the section to find more complete answers.

Teaching Strategies

Introduction

After the students have read the section introduction, help them discuss its content and their reactions: Why do you think the framers provided four possible ways for an amendment to become law?

Discussion Starter

Encourage the students to discuss these two methods of proposing an amendment: What are the most important differences between the two methods?

FYI

One Person, One Vote

"One person, one vote" refers to the principle that all citizens, regardless of where in a state they reside, are entitled to equal legislative representation. This principle was laid down by the Supreme Court in the case of *Reynolds* v. *Simms* (1964). The Court ruled that a state's apportionment plan for both houses of a bicameral state legislature must allocate seats on a population basis so that voting power is as equal as possible for all segments of the population. This concept is discussed in detail in Chapter 21 of this text.

•*FYI* features appear throughout the Teacher's Wraparound Edition, providing you with important and interesting facts and anecdotes related to chapter content.

Caption Answer The Twenty-first Amendment, passed in 1933, repealed Prohibition.

CHAPTER 3: THE CONSTITUTION 63

SECTION 3 REVIEW

1. What role did James Madison play in developing the Bill of Rights?
2. Why was the distinction between the words *ought* and *shall* so critical in the final version of the Bill of Rights?
3. **For critical analysis:** What do you think our government would be like without these ten amendments?

SECTION 4

The Formal Process of Amending the Constitution

Preview Questions

- What are the processes by which formal changes can be made in the Constitution?
- Why are so few amendments accepted?

Our Constitution has endured for over two hundred years with only twenty-seven added amendments. The framers, in Article V, made the formal amendment process extremely difficult. There are two ways to propose an amendment and two ways to ratify one. The result is only four possible ways for an amendment to become law.

Methods of Proposing an Amendment

The two methods of proposing an amendment are:

1. A two-thirds vote in the Senate and in the House of Representatives is required. All of the twenty-seven existing amendments have been proposed this way.
2. If two-thirds of the state legislatures request a national amending convention, then Congress must call one. A simple majority of the convention could then propose amendments to the states for ratification. There has yet to be a successful amendment proposal using this method.

The notion of an amendment convention is exciting to many people. In two separate years, calls for a national amendment convention almost became reality. Between 1963 and 1969, thirty-three state legislators (out of the necessary thirty-four) attempted to call a convention to amend the constitution to eliminate the Supreme Court's "one person, one vote" decisions. Between 1975 and 1990, thirty-two states asked for a national convention to propose an amendment requiring that the federal government balance its budget—that it spend no more than it receives in revenues.

Methods of Ratifying an Amendment

There are two methods of ratification:

1. Three-fourths of the state legislatures can vote in favor of the proposed amendment. This method is

"I CANNOT TELL A LIE—I DID IT WITH MY LITTLE HATCHET!"

◀ This American newspaper cartoon from 1901 shows Prohibition supporter Carrie Nation on the warpath in Kansas. Carrie Nation, who was one of the early crusaders against alcohol, was famous for storming into taverns and using a hatchet to break up beer kegs and liquor bottles. The work by Nation and others led to the Eighteenth Amendment, which prohibited the manufacture, sale, or transportation of intoxicating liquors. Which amendment to the Constitution repealed the Eighteenth Amendment?

SECTION 4 ■ 63

West's American Government Multimedia Program

The **West's American Government** fully integrated instructional program uses media as never before to help make the study of American government dynamic and enriching.

Created especially for **West's American Government**, the videodisc, videotape and software enable you to effectively and easily integrate today's technology into your classroom presentations. The Teacher's Wraparound Edition includes instructions and suggestions for using these exciting multimedia components.

West's American Government Videodisc

The videodisc includes motion video segments for each unit, plus a dazzling array of still images including charts, maps, graphs, and tables. Among the motion segments are top-of-the-line news and public affairs presentations from some of today's most respected broadcasters. Both the motion segments and the high quality still images are especially effective when used with West's Lecture Builder Software. For your convenience, bar codes for each motion segment are included in the Teacher's Wraparound Edition.

Additionally, a second narrative sound track in Spanish is accessible on the videodisc.

The nine segments of the disc are as follows:
Part 1 Foundations of American Democracy
Part 2 The Rights of All Citizens
Part 3 The Politics of Democracy
Part 4 The Federal Legislative Branch
Part 5 The Federal Executive Branch
Part 6 The Federal Judicial Branch
Part 7 American Policy in a Changing World
Part 8 State and Local Governments
Part 9 Other Nations

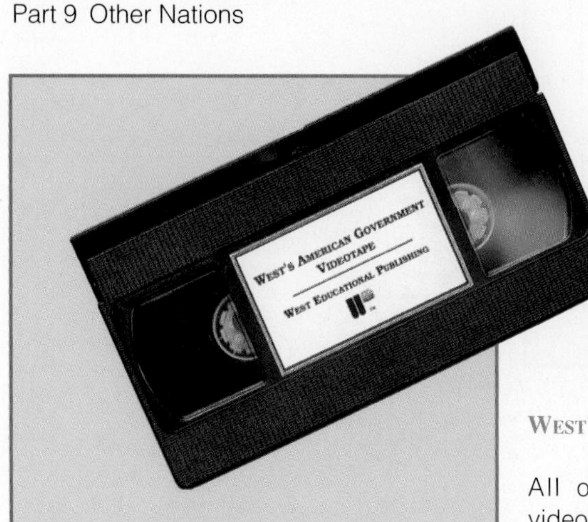

West's American Government Video

All of the motion segments on the videodisc are also available on videotape.

MULTIMEDIA PACKAGE

WEST'S AMERICAN GOVERNMENT LECTURE BUILDER SOFTWARE

This user-friendly authoring software developed specifically for use with West videodiscs allows you to customize your lectures or disc presentations prior to class and deliver the lectures without the use of the hand-held remote control.

Customizing allows you to select and order items from any section on the disc. You can also edit video clips and still-frame sequences.

To deliver the lecture stored on the computer, you simply press the return key on the computer and advance to the next image. This process eliminates the need to enter codes with the remote control while lecturing.

Macintosh
(The Macintosh version requires Hypercard 2.0, provided.)
IBM PC and Compatibles
(The IBM version requires Windows 3.0, not provided.)

WEST'S AMERICAN GOVERNMENT SOCIAL STUDIES TOOL KIT: HELLO USA SOFTWARE

This teacher-friendly software package includes a binder containing software disks and documentation with specific applications for **WEST'S AMERICAN GOVERNMENT**.

Students explore political data analysis with computers to aid in the study of American government.

The Social Studies Tool Kit Software can be used in your classroom with a projection panel (for use on an overhead), in the computer lab, or on personal computers for individual projects.

The user can call up data files directly related to chapter content. For example, while studying voter apathy in Chapter 1, you might use the file on voter turnout.

State-to-state statistical comparisons can be charted, graphed, or mapped. Student activity sheets are available in the Teacher's Resource Binder. These files include data from the 1991 U.S. Statistical Abstract.

IBM PC and Compatibles (*Hello USA*)
Apple IIe/GS (*Our Nation*)

WESTEST COMPUTERIZED TESTING

WEST'S AMERICAN GOVERNMENT includes a computerized test bank of over 3300 questions. WESTEST 2.0™ allows you to create, edit, store, and print exams. The system is menu driven with a desktop format and offers the options of using keystrokes or a mouse, accelerator keys, and function keys.

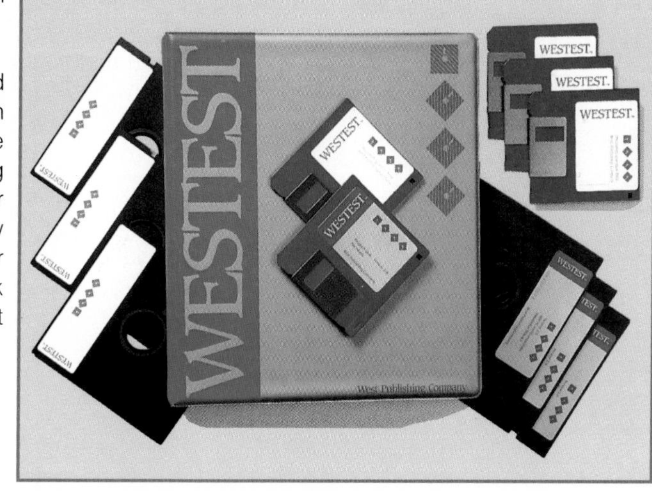

All of this makes the program quick and easy to use. WESTEST 2.0 users can randomly generate or selectively choose questions, add new or edit existing questions, view summaries of the exam or test bank chapters, set up and preview their pages, and print (the exam, answer sheet, answer key, or the entire test bank chapter). This software also makes it possible for you to import graphics.

IBM PC/Compatibles
Macintosh

THE TEACHER'S RESOURCE BINDER contains:

Test Bank

The Test Bank was written by an expert in both American government and test preparation. In addition to the computerized WESTEST Test Bank of over 3300 questions described on the previous page, there are:

- A Pretest, consisting of 100 multiple-choice questions.
- Two printed tests for each chapter consisting of 30 multiple-choice questions, a matching set of 10 items and several essay questions.
- A Unit Test for each unit, consisting of 40 multiple-choice questions and several essays.
- Two Half-Year Exams, one for Chapters 1 through 14, and one for Chapters 15 through 26 consisting of 100 multiple-choice questions and several essays.
- A Final Exam consisting of 100 multiple-choice questions and several essays.

Worksheets

Three levels of student activity sheets include reteaching, on-level, and enrichment. Two levels of Spanish worksheets are also available.

Acetate Transparencies

These color transparencies include some of the figures from the text itself as well as additional material to enrich lessons. The Teacher's Wraparound Edition indicates where and how the transparencies can best be used.

Original Source Documents

These are in addition to the original source documents included in the *Resource Center* in the back of the text.

Mock Trial

This stimulating classroom activity includes all the information necessary for preparing and carrying out a mock trial in your classroom. As your students participate in this mock trial they gain a greater appreciation and understanding of our judicial system.

WEST'S AMERICAN GOVERNMENT HANDBOOK OF SELECTED COURT CASES

Your students can experience the actual language of the court for themselves as they read the excerpts from more than 30 significant court cases, all of which are mentioned in the text. This is a useful and interesting resource for both you and your students.

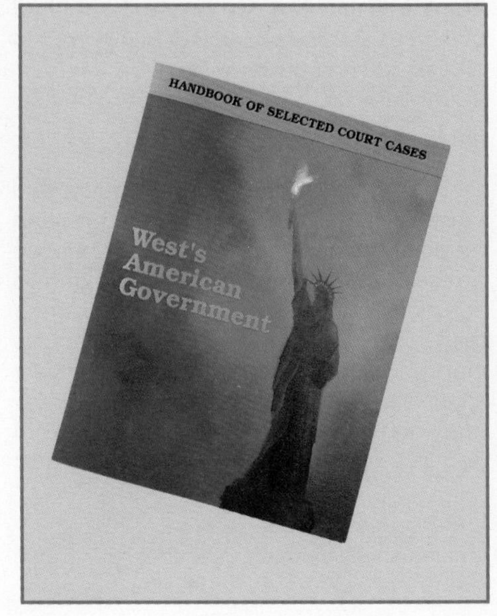

To Conclude

A Cohesive Program

West's American Government is a carefully assembled and integrated teaching program designed to work well for you, the teacher.

Understandable

The Student Edition is written for student comprehension and enjoyment, and the Teacher's Wraparound Edition offers an abundance of teaching suggestions to enhance the learning experience for students of all ability levels.

Skill Development

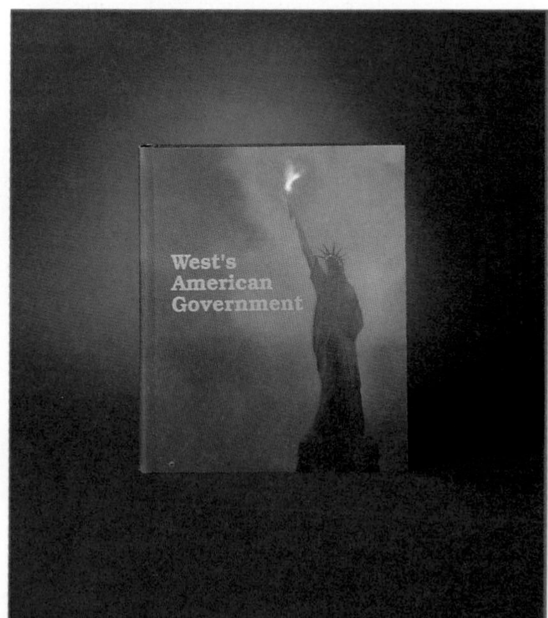

West's American Government stresses skill development throughout the Student Edition features and in the Teacher's Wraparound Edition.

Skill building features in the Teacher's Wraparound Edition include basic communication, writing, math, and social studies skills. More complex skills are stressed in the *Multidiscipline Strategies*, *Law Related Activities*, *Developing Skills for the Information Age*, and more.

To develop students' social studies skills, there is one *Building Social Studies Skills* feature in each chapter of the student text. A *Citizenship Skills and Responsibilities* feature in every chapter helps build the skills and understanding your students need to effectively participate in our government at the community, state, and national levels.

Critical thinking skills are stressed throughout the Student Edition and Teacher's Wraparound Edition.

West's American Government helps students understand our system of government and the American dream. The program further challenges students to fully understand and accept their responsibilities and privileges as members of our complex, multicultural society. **West's American Government** fosters appreciation and understanding.

Motivational

West's American Government is designed to excite your students about studying American government and politics. From the spectacular art program to an engaging writing style, from thought-provoking *Think About It* questions to media components, from meaningful activities to original source documents and real court cases, this is a program specifically created for today's American government classroom.

West's American Government Contents

WEST'S AMERICAN GOVERNMENT *Updated Edition*

TEACHER'S WRAPAROUND EDITION

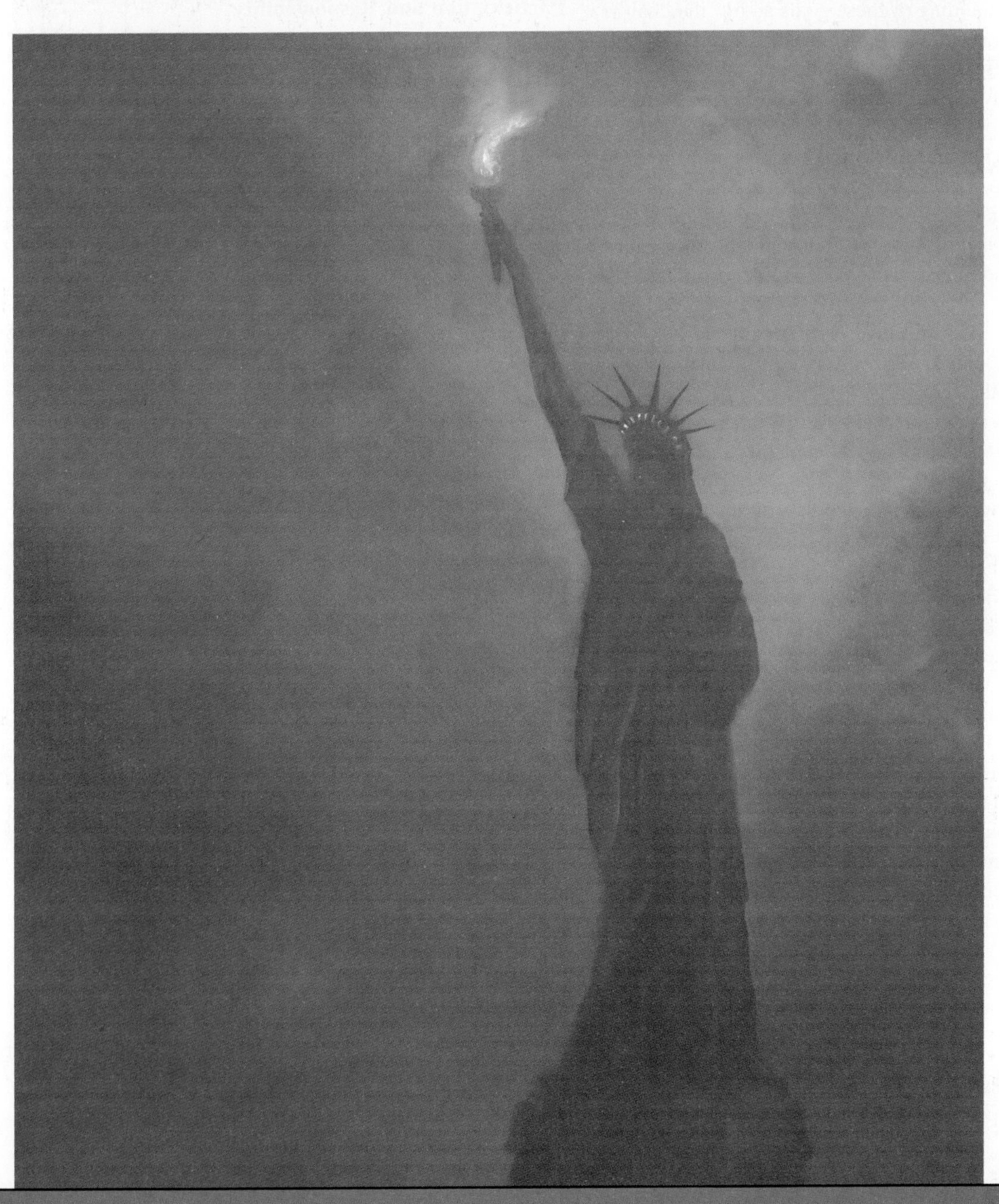

Preface to the Teacher's Wraparound Edition

The story of American democracy is an exciting one. America is a great country and has a great deal of which to be proud. Still, its citizens must continue to strive toward the goals expressed in our Constitution and embodied in the American dream. *West's American Government* has been designed to provide you and your students with an analysis and understanding of these goals and of the challenges, both new and old, that Americans must confront in order to maintain and improve our democracy.

In addition to providing students with an understanding of the heritage of our democracy, *West's American Government* provides thoughtful, comprehensive, and up-to-date coverage. All of the core materials necessary for a thorough understanding of American government and politics are provided. Specifically, the philosophical, political, and historical foundations of the American form of government are clearly laid out in the first few chapters of the Student Edition. Politics, political parties, campaigns, and voting are then presented, followed by an examination of the institutions of the federal government. A particularly complete section on state and local government comes next, and the final chapter permits your students to compare America's government with that of other countries.

The current changes taking place in our American democracy, as well as in politics and governments around the world, underscore how exciting and challenging the study of American government and politics today can be. The *West's American Government* program is designed to help you make this excitement come alive in the classroom. The centerpiece of the *West's American Government* instructional program is the Teacher's Wraparound Edition you hold in your hands. Because we understand that your teaching task is not an easy one, features are included in this wraparound edition that are designed to help you plan your daily lessons, enhance your course presentations, and create a teaching environment that meets both your needs and those of your students.

American government and politics are subjects that cannot be taught in a vacuum; they must be presented along with important underlying principles. We believe that citizen participation and responsibility, cultural diversity, the American dream and America's role in the global community are important themes that should be interwoven with the teaching of American government. Each of these themes is stressed in *West's American Government.*

Participation and Responsibility

American democracy cannot function without a participating electorate. Therefore, *West's American Government* stresses throughout the book the theme of citizen participation and the responsibilities of citizenship.

Participation is further stressed in the Teacher's Wraparound Edition. Here you will find many suggestions for enrichment, extension, and service-learning activities that will actively involve your students in the political process.

Cultural Diversity

While the notion of American society as a melting pot has been with us for a long time, the concept of cultural diversity and multiculturalism is still relatively new. Rather than force all residents of this nation into one cultural mode, today's view of our society is one in which different cultures can and should be encouraged to flourish. The theme of cultural diversity is an important aspect of the Student Edition of *West's American Government.* In Chapter 7 critical emphasis is placed on the understanding and appreciation of this diversity.

Additionally, you will find teaching suggestions in this Teacher's Wraparound Edition designed to help your students explore their own perceptions of cultural diversity.

Global Community

Global political changes are occurring at an astounding rate. Empires have fallen and democracy has taken hold in nations that had long struggled under totalitarian systems. *West's American Government* recognizes these changes and discusses their impact upon America's role in the global community.

The Emphasis is on Skills

We believe that your students will master the course content in American government better if they acquire improved social studies and communication skills. Additionally, we believe that such skills will help them in their other classes, and in being well-informed American citizens and voters. We have devoted many parts of the *West's American Government* instructional program to student skills development. Throughout the text, an emphasis is placed on problem solving and critical thinking. You will also find extensive skills enrichment materials at the end of each chapter. These include communication skills—all with a writing assignment—as well as additional social studies skills activities.

This Teacher's Wraparound Edition further emphasizes skill building. It is filled with helpful skill building suggestions including critical thinking skills activities, law related activities, observable mastery activities, and innovative multidiscipline strategies.

The Major Features of *West's American Government*

When you glance through *West's American Government* you will find numerous features that have been included to build and broaden your students' understanding of important course concepts. All of these features are designed to make the teaching and learning experience more meaningful.

These features are also made teacher friendly in this Wraparound Edition, which includes distinct teaching suggestions—conveniently highlighted with colored titles—for each and every feature found in the student book.

The Unit and Chapter Openers

Special illustrations have been developed for each unit and chapter opener. This art is not used simply for visual impact, but can also be used as a teaching tool. The chapter openers also present a Keynote quote that serves as the starter for the chapter materials and is tied into the chapter content via the chapter introduction. There is also a list of chapter objectives, which the student should be able to master by the end of his or her study of that particular chapter. Both features are supported in this Wraparound Edition with additional teaching notes.

The Overall Photo and Art Program

Your students will discover a wealth of exhibits, drawings, maps, portraits, and the like to pique their interest in the subject material on each page. Photos and other art features have been especially chosen to enhance the content. As a part of our overall program of stressing student comprehension and critical thinking skills, most of the photos and figures have content comprehension and/or critical-thinking questions at the end of the captions. The answers to all of these questions are included in this Wraparound Edition.

Building Social Studies Skills

This feature is a critical part of the skills enhancement program for your students. Each chapter covers a new skill such as Using Government Publications, Analyzing Primary Sources, Analyzing Political Cartoons, and Evaluating Political Commercials. Each Building Social Studies Skills feature ends with a section called Practicing Your Skills, which requires the student to apply the skills that he or she has just learned. Additional social studies skills activities are included at the end of each chapter.

Citizenship Skills and Responsibilities

This important feature stresses student participation and responsibility by providing important information on both the whys and hows of citizen participation. All of these skills sections end with Taking Action, which encourages your students to begin to take an active role in our democratic processes.

Government in Action

Every chapter includes Government in Action features. Each of these features ends with a section, called Think About It, which requires the student to assess his or her own views. There are four types of Government in Action features.

- **Case Study** These factual case studies enhance the student's understanding through the use of real-world examples of how government works.
- **Profile** Many important political figures in government, both past and present, are presented in these biographical sketches that appear throughout this book.
- **Personal Law** At selected points in the text, your students are introduced to relevant aspects of personal law that will affect them throughout their lives.

- **A Day in the Life** What do politicians do? Your students will learn the inside answer to this question through this exciting feature. Several key American public figures, including President George Bush, have made available, for use in *West's American Government,* schedules from a typical day in their lives. In each Day in the Life feature, these schedules are combined with informative biographical sketches and photographs.

Architect of the American Dream

George Washington, Martin Luther King, Jr., and Susan B. Anthony are just three of the towering historical figures profiled as Architects of the American Dream. Each of these two-page features includes biographical information, original source excerpts from the architect's speeches or writings, photographs and/or artwork, critical-thinking questions, and a list of additional readings.

Challenge to the American Dream

Every chapter ends with this feature, dealing with a thought provoking issue. These features are designed to stimulate controversy, discussion, and critical thinking. At the end of each Challenge to the American Dream the student is asked to make a decision about what should or should not be done in the political arena concerning the issue discussed.

Wraparound Edition Support

As stated earlier, each of these features is supported in the Teacher's Wraparound Edition with distinct teaching suggestions which include prereading tips, discussion-starter questions, analyze-and-apply activities, suggested review questions, and answers for all content-related questions found in the student feature.

Chapter-Ending Materials

Each chapter ends with two or three pages of important review materials. They are as follows:

- **Key Terms**—each listed with the appropriate page reference.
- **Summary**—each summary section conveniently numbered to correspond to the appropriate chapter.
- **Review Questions**—cover each section in the chapter, including feature content.
- **Questions for Thought and Discussion**—can be used by you or can be assigned to your students.
- **Improving Your Skills**—this section is always subdivided into:
  - **Communication Skills** with a writing exercise.
  - **Social Studies Skills.**
- **Activities and Projects.**
- **Answers**—this Teacher's Wraparound Edition includes complete answers for all content questions in the student text chapter-ending materials.

The Resource Center

Found at the end of both the student text and this Teacher's Wraparound Edition, the *West's American Government* Resource Center is filled with a wealth of important, interesting and useful resources.

- **Original Source Documents**—No modern text on American Government would be complete without a serious sampling of original source documents. Such a sampling, including the Declaration of Independence, *Federalist Papers Numbers 10* and *51*, the Preamble to the Charter of the United Nations, and more, are included in this Resource Center. Also included in this Resource Center is a fully annotated U.S. Constitution designed to enable your students to understand this cornerstone of our American political system.
- **Legal Cases**—This section of the Resource Center focuses on legal cases by giving your students detailed, understandable instructions on how to read legal case citations and find court decisions. Also included here is a Table of Court Cases featuring a short summary of the court cases discussed in the text or in footnotes throughout the Student Edition.
- **Extended Case Studies**—To provide your students with an extended issue-centered look at government in action, we have selected a number of important topics from the text and created these extended case studies. Each of these case studies includes background information, original source materials, and critical-thinking questions.
- **Additional Resouce Center Materials**—The Resource Center also includes a complete listing of the presidents and vice presidents of the United States, a complete listing of the Supreme Court justices, state atlas materials, and maps of the United States and the World.

About the Teacher's Wraparound Edition

With an innovative new design, the Teacher's Wraparound Edition of *West's American Government* is structured to be the ideal teaching tool for today's American Government classroom. Here a wealth of teaching information is provided at your fingertips. *West's American Government Teacher's Wraparound Edition* includes:

- Complete chapter and section introductory material featuring Kickoff Activities, Section Previews, Points to Stress, and more.
- A variety of interesting teaching strategies, including Discussion Starter questions, Enrichment activities, Extension activities, Critical Thinking Skills activities, and Cooperative Learning activities.
- Reteaching and Evaluation Strategies for each section as well as Chapter Evaluation Strategies.
- Distinct teaching strategies for each special feature found in the Student Edition.
- Answers for all content questions found in the Student Edition.
- Answers for photo and art caption questions.
- Special features designed to enhance course presentations, such as, Multidiscipline Strategies, Developing Skills for the Information Age activities, and FYI background sections.
- Instructional Objectives that correspond with each section in each chapter of the book.
- A complete Chapter Preview and Planning Guide, which immediately follows this Preface, including helpful teacher background material, designed to place each chapter in context for the instructor.

Additionally, this Teacher's Wraparound Edition acts as your guide for using the many exciting supplemental components that complete the *West's American Government* instructional program.

West's American Government Laser Videodisc

One of the most recent advances in technology for presenting educational concepts and ideas is the laser videodisc. West Publishing Company is proud to make available with this text a videodisc that includes the following:

- Introductory remarks about the videodisc itself, as well as about each segment, by Professor Roger LeRoy Miller of the Center for Policy Studies at Clemson University and General Editorial Consultant/Program Coordinator for *West's American Government.* These remarks, in print form, are included on the unit opener pages of this Teacher's Wraparound Edition.
- Full-motion video segments from a variety of sources including the U.S. State Department, the Public Broadcasting System, C-SPAN, and many others.
- Over 300 still-frame images adapted from art throughout the Student Edition.

Our videodisc is usable on any standard laser videodisc player and can be controlled either by a hand controller or by a bar code wand.

On each unit opening spread in the Teacher's Wraparound Edition, you will find Professor Miller's introductory remarks for the appropriate videodisc motion segment, as well as the bar code necessary to access the motion segment. To use the bar code, simply turn on the videodisc player and monitor, insert the videodisc, and pass the wand over the bar code while pressing the button on the side of the wand. The videodisc will automatically find the correct motion segment and display it on the video monitor. The videodisc also includes many still-frame exhibits adapted from the Student Edition. Additionally, the videodisc can be controlled with a remote controller using the frame numbers provided.

The videodisc also includes a Spanish language sound track.

To provide maximum flexibility, all motion segments from the videodisc are available on video tape.

Lecture Builder Software

To further maximize the value of the videodisc in your classroom, our user-friendly authoring software allows you to customize your media presentations prior to class and deliver the stored presentation on the computer by simply pressing the return key to advance to the next image. Customizing allows you to select and order items from any section on the disc. You can also edit video clips and still-frame sequences.

Using Other Program Components

The Student Edition and the Teacher's Wraparound Edition are only two components of the *West's American Government* complete instructional program for you and your students. Every program component in this system is designed to be easy to use, to simplify your preparations, and to make your teaching job easier and the learning process more effective.

The Teacher's Resource Binder (TRB)

- Test Bank—includes over 3,300 questions written specifically for *West's American Government.* For your convenience, the following reproducible tests are available:
  pretest
  two tests for each chapter
  a test for each unit
  an exam for each half of the text
  one final exam
- Worksheets—reteaching, on-level, and enrichment worksheets are provided for each chapter. Spanish language worksheets are also available in two levels.
- Acetate Transparencies—these color transparencies are designed to enrich classroom presentations and include some figures adapted from art in the text as well as additional material. The Teacher's Wrap-around Edition indicates where the transparencies can best be used.
- Mock Trial—complete instructions and materials for staging a mock trial in your classroom are also included.
- Resource Lists—in addition to the Resource List found in the Chapter Preview and Planning Guide of the Teacher's Wraparound Edition, supplementary lists of useful print and media resources for each chapter are included in the TRB.
- Original Source Documents—these reproducible documents are in addition to the documents found in the text and in the Resource Center.

WESTEST 2.0

This computerized testing software, available for the IBM PC, Compatibles, and Macintosh, includes the complete test bank of over 3,300 questions. WESTEST 2.0 allows you to create, edit, store, and print tests. The system is menu-driven with a desktop format and offers the options of using key strokes or a mouse, accelerator keys and function keys. You can randomly generate or selectively choose questions, add new questions, or edit existing questions.

West's Handbook of Selected Court Cases

This includes a summary, as well as excerpted language of the court, for more than 30 significant court cases, all of which are mentioned in the text.

Social Studies Tool Kit Software

This software package, available for IBM PC, Compatibles, and Apple IIe/GS computers, consists of a wide variety of data that will enhance the study of American government. Suggested activities utilizing the Social Studies Tool Kit Software are also provided.

PREVIEW AND PLANNING GUIDE

CHAPTER 1
Government and the People—The Global Connection

Begins on page 2

Background Material

The nature of government has been debated since the origin of government itself. Philosophers like Plato believed that government could only be as good as those who ruled, and for that reason only the intellectually, morally, and physically elite should rule through an aristocracy. The nature of government in a democracy, reasoned Plato, was a prescription for anarchy administered by an inferior and unqualified mob.

Although writing at a later date, Hobbes shared Plato's pessimistic view toward man's ability for self-determination. Hobbes wrote in the *Leviathan* that living in the "state of nature," man existed in a condition that was savage and brutish as a consequence of each person trying to have and master the other person's possessions. The only way to check this self-destructive competition was by agreeing to enter a "covenant," a voluntary act by which free men would pass "incommunicable and inseparable" power to a strong yet fair monarchical form of government.

Locke and Hobbes both theorized that originally man lived in a state of nature, but Locke described it as a more rational and peaceful place. Like Plato, Locke's ideas about the nature of man colored his perceptions about the nature of government. Unlike Plato or Hobbes, Locke had an optimistic view of man and hence concluded that man should rule by self-determination, and that the state is needed only for marginal violations of the law and reason. Locke wrote in the *Second Treatise* that "government by consent" with "the right to rebel" was an adequate formula to guard against rebellion. Locke's view of the social contract was that the sole legitimate basis of limited government was popular consent. Revolution under particular conditions was a justifiable and natural remedy in defense of liberty. Thus he reserved for the people the right to change their government if it threatened liberty.

Rousseau in *The Social Contract* brings a different perspective to the role of a citizen in government. Locke's concept of liberty emphasizes the absence of restraint by government, while Rousseau's emphasis is on the positive results of participation in public affairs. According to Rousseau's theory, a citizen's obligation to community is derived from his own individual consent. The body politic is possessed of a "general will." "The general will is always right and tends to public advantage . . . ." Sovereign authority is derived only from the general will. "The passage from the state of nature to the civil state produces a very remarkable change in man, by substituting justice for injustice in his conduct and giving his actions the morality they had formerly lacked." In acting through the authority of the state, the people act under the obligation to consider only the good of all—the common interest.

The democratic basis of government described by Locke and Rousseau did not replace theories based on a more pessimistic view of human nature. Such a view of government, by definition, discounts the primacy of the individual and replaces it with the primacy of the state in the form of a dictator, political party, or royal family.

Considering the realities of the global connection mentioned in the chapter, it is of great importance that students consider the types of governmental systems under which people are ruled and the fundamental values of the leaders of those systems. Interdependence, modern technology, and a shared environment demand that people become aware of and involved with their political systems. What is the nature of American government? What is the nature of the people who rule and of those who are ruled? Can this government and its people face the challenges of our third century? These are questions that all students should be asked.

Pacing Chart

Full Year Course: Six days
One Semester Course: Two to three days. For Semester courses that are not of a survey nature, this chapter could be omitted.

Selected Print and Media Resources

Animal Farm. Animated film based on the novel, Phoenix Films.

Race to Save the Planet. A multiple-part video, PBS Video.

Roskin, Michael, *Countries and Concepts: An Introduction to Comparative Politics.* Prentice Hall.

Soe, Christian (ed.). *Comparative Politics.* Annual publication, Dushkin.

NOTE: For additional resources, see *West's American Government Teacher's Resource Binder (TRB).*

PREVIEW AND PLANNING GUIDE

CHAPTER 2
Forging the American Dream

Begins on page 22

Background Material

"A government of our own is our natural right." So wrote Thomas Paine in *Common Sense.* The Navigation Acts, the Proclamation of 1763, and the Stamp Acts in their aggregate made it clear to colonists that if they wished for representative and limited government by consent, then a struggle for independence was the final solution. Ironically, it was not so much revolution that Americans wanted as it was perpetuating the status quo, a situation which saw extensive individual liberties granted by colonial legislatures under a lengthy period of British indifference to enforcement of British law. Only when Britain began a policy of firm control over the political and economic life of the colonies by force did revolution become the outcome.

Americans soon found out that acquiring independence was easier than setting up a government that would safeguard the freedoms for which they fought. The new nation's first government under the Articles of Confederation proved feeble in meeting the challenges of military reverses and needs for revenue. The national government required the consent of the state legislatures and near unanimous agreement among them in order to take action, leaving Congress virtually impotent. The British were fomenting trouble west of the Appalachians. The states would not ratify a treaty that John Jay negotiated with Spain, presumably concerning navigation along the Mississippi River, and there was the embarrassment of not being able to deal with pirates along the Barbary Coast. The economy was impaired by states who ignored their tax obligations to Congress, printed too much money to finance their own debt, and by a federal government that did not have the authority to regulate interstate commerce. These factors, coupled with Shay's rebellion, spurred the call for a national convention.

Many of the framers were not so much motivated by the high ideals of democracy as they were by pragmatic politics. In fact, there was a fundamental fear of unchecked democracy. Delegate Sherman argued that the people should not elect House members saying the people should have as little as possible to say about government. Delegate Gerry stated, "The evils we experience flow from the excess of democracy." There were those who disagreed with this sentiment, among them George Mason, who said that a popularly elected legislature "was to be the grand depository of the democratic principle of the Government." Madison agreed with James Wilson that no government could survive without the confidence of the people.

It is not surprising given the diversity of opinion on such matters that the Constitution has been called a "bundle of compromises." Indeed there were some integral compromises, but there were elements to which all delegates were dedicated: separation of powers, checks and balances, popular sovereignty, representative government, and a strong central government. When about to adjourn, Benjamin Franklin said, "From such an assembly can a perfect production be expected? It therefore astonishes me to find this system approaching so near perfection as it does." If the framers forged the American dream, teachers can help students keep the dream alive.

Pacing Chart

Full Year Course: Six days
One Semester Course: Four days

Selected Print and Media Resources

Collier, Christopher and James Collier. *Decision in Philadelphia.* Ballantine, 1987.

Constitution. Quarterly Journal, Foundation for the United States Constitution, New York, New York.

Farrand, Max. *The Records of the Federal Convention of 1787.* Yale University Press, 1966.

The Federalist Papers. Mentor.

Lindop, Edmond. *Birth of the Constitution.* Enslow, 1987.

Morris, Richard. *Witnesses at the Creation.* Mentor, 1989.

Patrick, John and Clair Keller. *Lessons on the Federalist Papers; Supplements to High School Courses in Government and Civics.* May be ordered from the Social Studies Development Center, Indiana University.

1787: A Simulation Game of the Constitutional Convention. Olcott Forward.

We the People . . . Constitution for the United States of America. Center for Civic Education, Calabasas, Ca. Student and teacher workbooks on constitutional themes.

Creating the Constitution. Apple Computer Simulation, Educational Activities, 1987.

Crisis of Democracy, a videocassette with Bill Moyers that explores whether the U.S. has lost sight of the ideals set forth by the Founders. Mystic Fire, 1989.

Note: For additional resources, see *West's American Government Teacher's Resource Binder (TRB).*

PREVIEW AND PLANNING GUIDE

CHAPTER 3
The Constitution *Begins on page 52*

Background Material

Limited government and popular sovereignty are cornerstones of our constitutional government. The Constitution as supreme law offers protection against abuses of civil rights and liberties by government officials. However, as our troubled experience with the weak central government under the Articles of Confederation revealed, it was necessary to create a national government strong enough to "enable the government to control the governed: and in the next place oblige it to control itself." (Madison, *Federalist No. 51.*) Our Constitution was the framers' attempt to resolve the dilemma by counterbalancing the powers of the three branches of government and by placing limits on those powers in order to preserve individual freedoms. An excellent source of information on this subject is *The Federalist.*

The first step was to strengthen and clarify the practice of separation of powers. The threat of too much power in any one branch was articulated by Madison in *Federalist No. 47* when he wrote, "No political truth is certainly of greater intrinsic value . . . than that . . . the accumulation of all powers legislative, executive, and judiciary, in the same hands . . . may justly be pronounced the very definition of tyranny."

Although separating powers was necessary, it was not sufficient to ensure protection of liberties. Madison mentions in *Federalist No. 51* that, "The great security against a gradual concentration of the several powers in the same department consists in giving to those who administer each department the necessary constitutional means . . . to resist encroachment on the others." According to Madison, checks and balances would work because, "Ambition must be made to counteract ambition."

In response to important societal changes which have taken place throughout our history, the debate over the relevance of our Constitution is often renewed. Does the structure of our government as it is spelled out in the Constitution allow us to successfully respond to current challenges? Have the formal and informal methods of amending the Constitution been adequate? There is ample reason for optimism.

Although the formal methods of amending the Constitution have been infrequently utilized, this is a reflection of stability rather than paralysis. An examination of the amendments shows the ability of the society and its government to make significant changes. A more serious threat would be the capricious formal amending of the Constitution to advance short-term political or social agendas. Perhaps this was the case with the Eighteenth Amendment and proposed amendments to ban flag desecration. As vital as the formal amending process is, it is the informal methods of amendment and interpretation that maintain the stability of our system.

Congress, the president, the Supreme Court, political parties, and custom, have all combined to provide flexibility in a manner that allows the original goals of the framers to be adapted to current conditions. These informal methods have allowed us to cope with social, technological, and international change with a vitality that is impossible by formal methods alone. As Wilson stated, the informal amending methods provide us with "a constitutional convention in continuous session."

Pacing Chart

Full Year Course: 5 days
One Semester Course: 3 days

Selected Print and Media Resources

Bill of Rights. Posters, Knowledge Unlimited.

Padover, Saul K. and Jacob Landynski. *The Living Constitution.* Mentor, 2nd ed.

Rodney Holder, Angela. *The Meaning of the Constitution.* Barron's, 2nd ed., 1987

The Constitution; A Framework to Govern the Nation. 28 minute videocassette, Close-Up Foundation, 1985

The Constitution: Relevant for Today? 57 minute video, Close-Up Foundation, 1987.

Democracy and Rights: One Citizen's Challenge. Videocassette, Close-Up Foundation/Smithsonian.

Government Keyword Series. Computer Software, Focus Media.

The U.S. Constitution in Action. 8-part filmstrip series, Random House Media.

Note: For additional resources, see *West's American Government Teacher's Resource Binder (TRB).*

CHAPTER 4
Our System of Federalism

Begins on page 74

Background Material

Federalism is defined as the distribution of governmental powers between the national government and the state governments. Unlike confederations where the states have final authority over public policy or unitary systems where the national level has direct authority over the local agencies of government, federalism allows simultaneous national and state power within their own realms. It is the dynamic nature of the type and degree of power given to the national government and states that makes the study of federalism essential.

The framers established this system of two levels of independent government and further established the supremacy of the national government in the supremacy clause of Article VI of the Constitution. Court interpretations of this and other constitutional grants of power have further defined and expanded the supremacy of the national government.

Chief Justice Marshall set forth the doctrine of national supremacy in *McCulloch* when speaking for a unanimous Court. He wrote, "The government of the Union is emphatically and truly a government of the people . . . and all means which are appropriate, which are plainly adapted to that end, which are not prohibited . . . are constitutional." The *formal* powers of the national government are basically the same as were outlined in 1787, but the loose constructionist view of Marshall has prevailed, even through the period of dual federalism. Abraham Lincoln once declared in a speech that, "We all declare for liberty, but in using the same word we do not all mean the same thing." He correctly could have substituted the word *federalism* for *liberty,* because it was the continued conflict over what federalism ought to be that precipitated the forced ratification process that was our Civil War. From that point on, like it or not, everyone realized that the national level of government would be paramount.

As important as the structure and powers of federalism outlined in the Constitution and Supreme Court cases are, the informal, often unanticipated, consequences of federalism are just as vital. Federalism allows for unity without consensus on every issue. Our political party organization reflects this reality, since diverse interests can be accommodated under a national party banner even though there exist serious state or regional differences. Federalism diffuses power and hence makes it difficult for a faction, or even the majority, to assume too much power. But perhaps the best feature of federalism is that it provides these functions while keeping government close to the people.

Federalism has undergone dual federalism, cooperative federalism, creative federalism, horizontal federalism, and the various "new" federalisms. Despite these changes, federalism is going to continue to be an important foundation of American politics, with both the national government and the state governments playing integral roles. The challenge to federalism is partly in finding qualified people to operate at each of the two levels of government, not in restructuring the levels of government or rearranging their respective powers.

Pacing Chart

Full Year Course: 5 days
One Semester Course: 3 days

Selected Print and Media Resources

Bernotas, Bob. *The Federal Government: How it Works.* Chelsea House, 1990.

Beyle, Thad L. (ed.). *State Government: CQ's Guide to Current Issues and Activities.* Congressional Quarterly, 1990.

Block Grant: A Simulation of Lobbying and Decision Making. DAC Educational Publications, 1990.

Elazar, Daniel. *American Federalism.* Harper and Row, 3rd ed., 1984.

Encyclopedic Dictionary of American Government. Dushkin, 4th ed., 1991.

Plano, Jack and Milton Greenberg. *The American Political Dictionary.* Holt, Rinehart, Winston, 8th ed., 1989.

Stinebricker, Bruce (ed.). *State and Local Government.* Dushkin, 5th ed., 1991.

American Government II. Disk for Apple, covers federalism, Intellectual Software.

Federalism: The National Government vs. the States. 16 mm film, Public Media Incorporated.

McCulloch v. *Maryland.* VHS from filmstrip, Guidance Associates, 1989.

The U.S. Constitution: Nationalism and Federalism. Three Apple Computer programs, Focus Media, 1991.

Note: For additional resources, see *West's American Government Teacher's Resource Binder (TRB).*

PREVIEW AND PLANNING GUIDE

CHAPTER 5
Personal Freedoms

Begins on page 102

Background Material

In *Federalist No. 84,* Hamilton states, ''(T)ruth is, after all the declamation we have heard, that the Constitution is itself, in every rational sense . . . A BILL OF RIGHTS.'' He made few converts. A bill of rights was the price paid for ratifying the new Constitution. In its first session, Congress promulgated ten amendments that were ratified in 1791 and became our Bill of Rights. The Bill of Rights restricted the national government, because at the time the states had legislatures that would either abide by the will of the people or follow a Bill of Rights in state constitutions.

So it was fear of the national government that spawned the explicit articulation of our most precious civil liberties. This has created an interesting paradox, because that same national government that we wanted to check is now the arbiter of what constitutes a violation of civil liberty. Problems arise when we go from general themes, such as, ''Congress shall make no law respecting the establishment of religion,'' to specific legislation, such as allowing a state sponsored moment of silence in a public school. Controversy surrounding the interpretation of the First Amendment remains intense.

With regard to most First Amendment protections, there is a clear division between *belief* and *practice,* with people being free to believe whatever they wish. What constitutes proper practice, however, has proven to be a conundrum. In the case of religion, the *Lemon* test—that legislation have a secular purpose, neither advance nor inhibit religion, and avoid excessive government entanglement with religion—was an attempt to provide standards that legislatures could follow. For the most part it has helped, but the government itself changes emphasis over time. Today, the Rehnquist Court is shifting toward an accommodationist view of religion, one that does not prohibit government from encouraging religion as long as there is no religious favoritism.

The rest of the guarantees of the First Amendment have also raised significant questions when put into practice. It is believed that *speech,* especially political speech, was granted a preferred position and that *conduct* was subject to government restriction. This perception was contradicted in *Texas* v. *Johnson,* which stated that burning the American flag was constitutionally protected. As jealous as we are of press freedom, about the only thing that is clear is the belief that prior restraint is unconstitutional, as purported in *Near* v. *Minnesota.* Does the press have the right to withhold information from a court of law? Can the materials and files of a newspaper be legally searched by law enforcement officials? No, and yes. Do the media have a constitutional right to cover trials? Do the media have a constitutional right to film an execution? Yes, and no. Advocates on both sides of these issues have valid points of view, but there can be only one majority from the Supreme Court.

What needs to be remembered is that often it is not any test, position, or precedent that decides these issues: Congress and judges do. For that reason the process of adjudicating First Amendment disputes will continue for as long as we possess and value our Constitution and the civil liberties and civil rights that it guarantees.

Pacing Chart

Full Year Course: 7 days
One Semester Course: 4 days

Selected Print and Media Resources

Alderman, Ellen and Caroline Kennedy. *In Our Defense; The Bill of Rights in Action.* Morrow, 1991.

Bartholomew, Paul and Joseph Menez. *Summaries of Leading Cases on the Constitution.* Helix Books, 1990.

Evans, Edward. *Freedom of Speech.* Lerner, 1990.

Fenwick, Lyndon. *Should the Children Pray? A Historical, Judicial, and Political Examination of Public School Prayer.* Baylor University Press, 1990.

Friendly, Fred and Martha Elliott. *The Constitution; That Delicate Balance.* McGraw-Hill, 1984.

Hentoff, Nat. *The First Freedom; The Tumultuous History of Free Speech in America.* Delacorte Press, 1988.

The Constitution: That Delicate Balance. Series of 16 mm films, Public Media Incorporated.

Constitutional Law. Intellectual Software.

God and the Constitution. 60 minute video, PBS Video.

Our Constitutional Rights: Landmark Supreme Court Decisions. Films Inc. and BFA Educational Media, distributed by Random House.

Supreme Court Decision. Computer software simulation, Queue.

Witt, Elder (ed.). *CQ's Guide to the U.S. Supreme Court.* CQ Press, 1990.

Note: For additional resources, see *West's American Government Teacher's Resource Binder (TRB).*

PREVIEW AND PLANNING GUIDE

CHAPTER 6
Equality Under the Law

Begins on page 128

Background Material

Civil liberties and civil rights are interpreted and defined by the Supreme Court. The Supreme Court itself is not static, often defining a civil right in one manner only to overturn or redefine the right at a later date. This has happened in many notorious instances. In 1896 the Court in *Plessy* v. *Ferguson* upheld Louisiana law requiring segregation in rail cars. In 1954 the Court reversed itself in *Brown* v. *Board of Education of Topeka* by unanimously stating, ". . . segregation of children in public schools solely on the basis of race . . . may affect their hearts and minds in a way unlikely ever to be undone . . . We conclude that in the field of public education . . . 'separate but equal' has no place."

In 1942 the Court had an opportunity to expand civil liberties for the accused. The case was *Betts* v. *Brady,* which said indigent criminal defendants were not guaranteed the right to counsel. Justice Hugo Black dissented. Twenty-one years later Black's dissent became the majority in *Gideon.* Was the Court wrong in 1942 or 1963? Either position can be defended.

These changes are best exemplified in the area of Fourth Amendment rights. Beginning with *Weeks* in 1914 and culminating with *Mapp* in 1961, a liberal minoritarian Supreme Court drafted the controversial exclusionary rule. With new conservative justices appointed to the bench and a concurrent mood of conservativism in society at large, the Supreme Court has narrowed and redefined the rule. An "inevitable discovery" exception was added in 1984 in *Nix* v. *Williams,* meaning that tainted evidence could be used if it ultimately would be found by legal means. Another 1984 case, *U.S.* v. *Leon,* declared the "good faith" exception, which allows evidence to be used in trials as long as officers *thought* they were acting legally. *Maryland* v. *Garrison,* 1987 added the "honest mistake" exception, which allowed officers to use evidence for conviction even though it was obtained after they had gone into the wrong apartment. Advocates of law and order such as Chief Justice Rehnquist are as pleased with the trend as civil libertarians are critical.

The exception of "in plain sight" was upheld and expanded in 1990, *Horton* v. *California,* when illegal weapons were seized by police who had a warrant to search for jewelry. The Court also ruled that the Constitution protects people and their possessions, not places, in *California* v. *Ciraolo,* 1986 when low-flying police planes saw evidence of illegality in a backyard. Sobriety checkpoints, too, are allowed even with no evidence that any particular motorist is intoxicated, as spelled out in *Michigan* v. *Sitz,* 1990.

In 1991, with Justice Souter replacing Justice Brennan, the Court ruled that suspects could be held up to 48 hours without a warrant, as opposed to 24 or 36 hours used by some states. With Justice Marshall's subsequent departure from the bench the new majority's reinterpretation of civil liberties is likely to continue.

Pacing Chart

Full Year Course: 10 days
One Semester Course: 6 days

Selected Print and Media Resources

America's Conscience: The Constitution in Our Daily Life. Reproducible activities, Anti-Defamation League, 1987.

Blauner, Bob. *Black Lives, White Lives: Three Decades of Race Relations in America.* University of California Press, 1989.

Citizens and the Legal System. Student workbook with masters, Scholastic, 1990.

Corwin, Edward and J. W. Peltason. *Understanding the Constitution.* Holt, Rinehart and Winston, 11th ed., 1988.

Lewis, Anthony. *Gideon's Trumpet.* Random House, 1964.

McKenna, George and Stanley Feingold. *Taking Sides: Clashing Views on Controversial Political Issues.* Dushkin, 7th ed., 1991.

Price, Janet and Alan Levine and Eve Cary. *The Rights of Students.* Southern Illinois Press, 1988.

We The Jury. Simulation kit, Constitutional Rights Foundation, 1987.

You Decide: Applying the Bill of Rights to Real Cases. Reproducible materials, Midwest Publications, 1991.

Blacks and the Constitution. 60 minute video, PBS Video, 1987.

Brown v. *Board of Education.* 10 minute video, Guidance Associates, 1989.

Gideon v. *Wainwright, Miranda* v. *Arizona.* 14 minute video, Guidance Associates, 1989.

The Road To Brown. 50 minute video, California Newsreel, 1989.

Student Rights. Filmstrip, cassette, Educational Enrichment Materials, 1982.

PREVIEW AND PLANNING GUIDE

CHAPTER 7
Citizenship and Responsibilities

Begins on page 156

Background Material

It is within each American citizen, not just within elected and appointed officials, that political power resides. For that reason a clear understanding of citizenship is essential. America is a nation whose history is shared by over 50 million immigrants. Prior to the 1880s, states encouraged immigration due to the strength and vitality it added. Early immigrants were Northern or Western Europeans who blended easily with the existing population. New immigrants were Eastern or Southern European, and later Chinese. Congress responded to the intolerance of society by passing the Chinese Exclusion Act of 1882, and other restrictive immigration acts based on nationality.

In the 1920s the concept of limiting certain nationalities culminated in the Quota Act of 1921. The Immigration Act of 1924 along with the National Origins Act of 1929 established a new quota system plus limits on the total number of immigrants to be admitted. Country-by-country quotas were eliminated in 1965, but there was still a cap of 20,000 for each nation. Changes were made in the 1980s for refugees in the Refugee Act of 1980, and for illegal immigrants in the Immigration Reform and Control Act of 1986. The biggest change in policy came in 1990. The Immigration Act of 1990 increased levels by 40 percent annually to 700,000. It also tripled the number of visas to skilled and professional immigrants.

An unknown number of people who come to this country each year live as illegal aliens. This causes many problems, including, but not limited to, deportation policies, the rights of illegal aliens to hold jobs, the rights of their employers, and the rights of their children. Part of the 1986 law dealt with an amnesty program that allowed aliens who could prove that they had been in the country for at least five years to apply for temporary legal residency status. They could then apply for permanent residency and eventually citizenship. The efficacy of the amnesty program is still the subject of heated debate.

All countries have guidelines that dictate who is a citizen of that nation, to whom all rights and responsibilities of citizenship apply. The manner in which citizenship is acquired, retained, and lost is of major consequence. People can become citizens by being born anywhere considered to be United States soil, by being born of a parent who is a citizen, or through naturalization. There are three ways for naturalization to take place: by act of Congress, by treaty, and by individual initiative. Although not as common as acquisition, citizenship can also be taken away. The basic ways Americans lose citizenship are through punishment for a crime, expatriation, and denaturalization.

The rights of all people, citizens or not, were greatly enhanced through the nationalization of the Bill of Rights, a process which began with the *Gitlow* case in 1925. The rights of citizens are well known, but citizen responsibilities are also part of the formula. These include voting, paying taxes, attending school, serving in the military, and serving as a juror or witness, among others. But perhaps the prime responsibility of all people is to display tolerance and open-mindedness in our diverse, multicultural society.

Pacing Chart

Full Year Course: 4 days
One Semester Course: 2–3 days. Depending on the thrust of the course this chapter could be excluded.

Selected Print and Media Resources

Basic Citizenship Skills Reviews. Reproducible masters, Educational Masterprints, 1980.

Deutsch, Howard David. *Getting Into America: The United States Visa and Immigration Handbook.* Random House.

Loescher, Gil and John Scanlan. *Calculated Kindness: Refugees and America's Half-Open Door, 1945 to Present.* Free Press, 1986.

Real Life Citizenship: Understanding Citizenship. Workbook, masters, and transparencies, Scholastic, 1990.

Taki, Ronald. *Strangers from a Different Shore: A History of Asian Americans.* Little, Brown, 1989.

The Constitution: That Delicate Balance: Immigration Reform. 16 mm film, Public Media Incorporated.

The Dred Scott Decision. 15 minute video, Guidance Associates, 1989.

European Immigration to the U.S. Disk for Apple, map and graph skills, Focus Media.

Immigration: Growth of a Nation. Sound filmstrip, 2 parts, Random House Media.

Refugee Road. 16 mm film, Foglight Films.

Note: For additional resources, see *West's American Government Teacher's Resource Binder (TRB).*

PREVIEW AND PLANNING GUIDE

CHAPTER 8
Political Parties *Begins on page 180*

Background Material

Americans have mixed emotions when it comes to political parties. Cynics charge that parties work to get their candidates elected and then proceed to forget the voters. They argue that there is no real choice between the two parties. Others argue that party influence is on the decline, the role of parties is not as crucial as it was in the past, and parties are being replaced by other institutions. Yet the vast majority of citizens still identify with one of the two major parties and favor the two-party system. Which position is correct? Each position has a degree of truth.

In decades past, the textbook definition of political parties, ''individuals who organize outside of government to win elections, operate government, and determine public policy,'' was as nearly valid as possible. Today, that definition is lacking. In reality, the two party system is in danger, particularly for Democrats in suburban areas and for Republicans in large cities and the south. Even where there is a legitimate two-party struggle, problems exist. In the spring of 1991 a *Chicago Tribune* article said this about Democratic National Chairman Ron Brown: ''When Ron Brown . . . became chairman of the Democratic National Committee . . . he probably thought he was going to head up an organized political party. He was wrong. He got the Democrats.'' The quote accentuates the fact that parties are loose confederations rather than tightly controlled organizations. Perhaps it gives weight to the notion that we might be seeing a dealignment in our party system, or perhaps a realignment toward the Republicans.

The Republicans are not much better off. Although they do keep winning the White House, they slip further and further from garnering a majority at any other level of the political process, be it Congress, state legislatures, or gubernatorial mansions. The Republicans have their own internal problems, which were represented by the fight over reapportionment in the early 1990s. Ironically, Republican National Chairman Clayton Yeutter was in favor of amendments to the Voting Rights Act that would have guaranteed minority representation at the Republican Convention in the hopes that Republicans might fare better in districts of traditional Democratic strength. This precipitated a negative response from other Republicans, such as William Bennett, who believed that such a policy was an endorsement of racial quotas, long the antithesis of the Republican platform.

All of this presupposes that parties matter, that parties work. There is no question that the traditional power of parties has been eroded by Supreme Court rulings outlawing patronage, by the media, by campaign consultants, and by a constituency that is growing ever more apathetic toward politics. Nevertheless, it would be a mistake to conclude parties are irrelevant. Parties still make nominations, and still conduct elections. Political parties still run government, acting as a mortar for branches of government and for federalism. Very simply, political parties provide valuable, albeit changed, functions; parties work.

Pacing Chart

Full Year Course: 7 days
One Semester Course: 3 to 4 days

Selected Print and Media Resources

Dalton, Russell. *Citizen Politics in Western Democracies.* Chatham House Publishers, 1988.

Keefe, William. *Parties, Politics, and Public Policy in America.* Congressional Quarterly, 1988.

Lindop, Edmund. *All About Republicans.* Enslow, 1985.

Lindop, Edmund and Joy Crane Thornton. *All About Democrats.* Enslow, 1985.

Maisel, L. Sandy (ed.). *The Parties Respond: Developments in the American Party System.* Westview Press, 1990.

Martis, Kenneth. *The Historical Atlas of Political Parties in the U.S. Congress 1789–1989.* Macmillan, 1989.

Sabato, Larry. *The Party's Just Begun: Shaping Political Parties for America's Future.* Little, Brown, 1988.

Schattschneider, E. E. *Party Government.* Holt, Rinehart and Winston, 1942.

Scott, Ruth and Ronald Hrebenar. *Parties in Crisis: Party Politics in America.* John Wiley and Sons, 1984.

Sunquist, James L. *Dynamics of the Party System.* Brookings Institution, 1983.

Teaching the Excitement of Politics in America. Taft Institute for Two-Party Government, 1985.

Anatomy of U.S. Political Parties. Filmstrip, Guidance Associates.

Understanding Editorial Cartoons. Filmstrip, Knowledge Unlimited, 1989.

Note: For additional resources, see *West's American Government Teacher's Resource Binder (TRB).*

PREVIEW AND PLANNING GUIDE

CHAPTER 9
Public Opinion and Interest Groups

Begins on page 206

Background Material

Public opinion and special interest groups are essential to American politics. Although we speak of public opinion, there are, in fact, many elements that comprise the public, each with differing sets of opinions. Those public opinions may be fluid over time or may be very stable. Not all public opinion on the same issue is equal, for some people manifest very intense feelings while others possess latent or mild opinions. Finally, opinions are not evenly prioritized; some people may have very strong feelings about an issue while others are indifferent. Self-interest is a great motivator of public opinion!

It is the task of pollsters to measure public opinion. Public opinion polls are not perfect measures of what the people want, but even their detractors concede they are the best tool we have. Although polls are used judiciously and can be accurate when done by professionals, there has been a proliferation in the use of polls used in campaigns that can distort reality. They are often used as if an election is a horse race. Perhaps the best way to work for what one believes is by supporting a special interest group.

Madison warned in *The Federalist, No. 10,* that the challenge to government is to control the "various and interfering interests." People still have negative perceptions of interest groups, at least about the other guy's interest groups! The biggest fear of factions is that they will thwart the public interest while advancing some individual's or group's self-interest. The discussion is not that simple, for there is a maze of conflicting special interests in our system which act as a check to any single group's control. However, the potential for the special interest domination is the price we pay for the constitutionally protected freedom of assembly and the right to petition government.

Special interest groups have to compete for the time and resources of their members because people belong to many groups simultaneously. Special interests try to overcome overlapping membership and a lack of resources by employing various techniques, both formal and informal. These techniques include lobbying, election support, grassroots pressure, litigation, and demonstrations. There has been an enormous growth in the number and kinds of interest groups, and the easiest explanation is that they work! This is best exemplified in the area of PACs, which wield power by raising large amounts of money that in turn is used to influence the outcome of elections and legislation. Although this type of spending was upheld by the Supreme Court in the *Buckley* v. *Valeo* decision, there are numerous proposals to restrict and reform the activities of PACs. With or without reform, special interest groups and the opinions they represent will continue to be an integral part of the political process.

Pacing Chart

Full Year Course: 7 days
One Semester Course: 4 days

Selected Print and Media Resources

Asher, Herbert. *Polling and the Public: What Every Citizen Should Know.* CQ Press, 1987.

Crespi, Irving. *Public Opinion, Polls, and Democracy.* Westview Press, 1989.

Dionne, E. J. Jr. *Why Americans Hate Politics.* Simon & Schuster, 1991.

Hrebenar, Ronald and Ruth K. Scott. *Interest Group Politics in America.* Prentice Hall, 2nd ed., 1990.

Mahood, H. R. *Interest Group Politics in America: A New Intensity.* Prentice Hall, 1990.

Public Opinion. American Enterprise Institute for Public Policy Research, Bimonthly periodical.

Sabato, Larry. *PAC Power.* Norton, 1985.

Stern, Philip. *The Best Congress Money Can Buy.* Pantheon, 1988.

Wolpe, Bruce. *Lobbying Congress: How the System Works.* Congressional Quarterly, 1990.

Congressional Bill Simulator. Computer program, Focus Media, 1985.

Interest Groups and Lobbying: A Look at the Third House of Congress. Two filmstrips, Multimedia Productions, Inc.

Lobbying and Political Action Committees. 60 minute video, Close-Up Foundation, 1985.

The Lobbying Game. Simulation, Gamed Simulations.

Polls and Politics. Apple Computer, Minnesota Educational Computing Corporation.

The Power Game: The Unelected. 60 minute video, PBS Video, 1988.

Note: For additional resources, see *West's American Government Teacher's Resource Binder (TRB).*

PREVIEW AND PLANNING GUIDE

CHAPTER 10
Campaigns, Elections, and the Media

Begins on page 232

Background Material

Ours is a limited government where those who possess power acquire and retain it directly or indirectly by election. This emphasizes the importance of nominations and campaigns prior to the election. There has been a constant desire to reform the system to make it more democratic.

It did not take political parties long to dominate the nominating process. By the end of the 18th century, New York City political campaigns were organized in a fashion that would be clearly recognizable to us today, including fundraising, ward organization, and election day transportation for voters. The method of choosing nominees for the ballot was the party caucus, a method that allowed party elites to control the selection process. Although still used today in various forms, caucuses gave way to the nominating convention.

The primary was the next step. A primary was more democratic because it allowed all party members to vote for the selection of candidates. It is inaccurate to speak of a primary as if it always means the same thing. Among the states there is a vast array of types of primaries: Proportional primaries, open and closed primaries, direct delegate primaries, preference primaries, binding primaries, blanket primaries, runoff primaries, nonpartisan primaries, and combinations of the above!

Party endorsement used to be enough to insure a solid campaign organization. Today, however, money seems to be the most vital, yet controversial, element of campaigns. On average, Congressmen must raise over $5,000 a week in campaign contributions to get re-elected, and senators must raise over $20,000 a week! This raises a second problem—the source of campaign money.

One cannot talk about campaign finance without examining the role of PACs and the impact of the Federal Election Campaign Act of 1974. PACs have an incredible amount of influence, and to date calls to reform them have not been successful. The Federal Election Campaign Act receives mixed reviews. The biggest criticism is its failure to include congressional campaigns under its spending limits. The highlight of the act has been controlling the financing of presidential elections.

The media have altered the way that presidential politics take place. During the nominating phase the media focus on personalities and the "horse race" aspect because this gains reader and viewer interest. The media's record in the general election is somewhat better, but there is still media manipulation, a focus on negative campaigning, and extensive use of propaganda techniques, especially during presidential debates.

The controversy concerning presidential elections extends to the electoral college. Most Americans do not understand exactly how the Electoral College operates, but they hate it. The biggest objection is the undemocratic and indirect nature of a system that institutionalizes a buffer between the will of the people and the White House.

Pacing Chart

Full Year Course: 7 days
One Semester Course: 5 days

Selected Print and Media Resources

Abrahamson, Jeffrey and Christopher Arterton and Gary Orren. *The Electronic Commonwealth: The Impact of New Media Technologies on Democratic Politics.* Basic Books, 1988.

Abramson, Paul R., *et al. Change and Continuity in the 1988 Elections.* CQ Press, 1990.

Asher, Herbert. *Presidential Elections and American Politics.* Dorsey, 4th ed., 1988.

Jackson, Brooks. *Broken Promises: Why the Federal Election Commission Failed.* Brookings, 1990.

Jewell, Malcolm and David Olsen. *American State Political Parties and Elections,* 3rd. ed., Dorsey Press, 1988.

Nelson, Michael. *The Elections of 1988.* CQ Press, 1989.

Polsby, Nelson and Aaron Wildavsky. *Presidential Elections: Strategies of American Electoral Politics.* Scribner, 7th ed., 1988.

Speaks, Larry. *Speaking Out: Inside the Reagan White House.* Scribner's, 1988.

The Classics of Political TV Advertising. 2 videos, 1986.

Elect III. Computer program on elections with user input, MECC, 1982.

The Media and Presidential Politics: Here and Now. Video, Hound's Head Productions, 1988.

The Power Game: The Unelected. Video, PBS Video, 1988.

Note: For additional resources, see *West's American Government Teacher's Resource Binder (TRB).*

CHAPTER 11
Voters and Voting Behavior

Begins on page 260

Background Material

American electoral behavior is a paradox. Over the last 200 years, the franchise has expanded to include landless males, African Americans, Native Americans, women, eighteen-year olds, and Hispanics. As the number of potential voters increased, the percentage of the electorate who actually voted went down.

Shunning the ballot box is becoming a national pastime. Some argue that restrictive registration is to blame, but easing requirements would bring fewer than 10% of those who do not vote to the polls. There is something fundamentally wrong, something that transcends registration requirements, the length of ballots, or the number of polling places. Curtis Gans, director of the Committee for the Study of the American Electorate says, "More and more people are losing faith in the efficacy of their vote. The will to participate and the faith that such participation will be meaningful is atrophying."

There are various causes. Party identification among voters is less important than it used to be, especially in primaries, and there are fewer people who classify themselves as strong party identifiers. There is a reliance on television over newspapers as a source of political information. Television might bring the world into your living room, but it also keeps you there.

Less citizen involvement makes it easier for special interests in the form of corporations, labor, or single-issue lobbies, to dominate the political agenda. Voter turnout for state and local elections is even smaller than for national elections. Voters appear to ask very little: Candidates should indicate how they differ on important issues; and candidates' performance when in office should be driven more by the issues than by concerns for reelection or by the influence of special interest groups.

There has been a lot of discussion about electoral reform. Bills have been introduced both in Congress and in state legislatures that would negate many registration restrictions. Some have called for mail-in registration, while others have proposed registration up until the time of the election. There have been proposals for automatic registration upon driver's license renewal and upon the completion of change-of-address requests given to the Post Office. Reform and reform proposals have not been limited to the registration process. Some states allow for voting prior to the election date, while others are searching for ways to shorten ballots in an effort to end so-called ballot fatigue. Finally, there have been numerous attempts by partisan and non-partisan groups alike to educate the electorate as to how, when, and where to vote.

There is no evidence that an increase in the quantity of voters will equate with a corresponding increase in quality of our democracy. America seems destined to be a nation which "will cross an ocean to fight for freedom but, will not cross the street to vote in an election."

Pacing Chart

Full Year Course: 7 days
One Semester Course: 4 days

Selected Print and Media Resources

Campaigns and Elections. Magazine published seven times a year by Campaigns & Elections, Inc.

Conway, M. Margaret. *Political Participation in the United States.* CQ Press, 2nd ed., 1990.

Dunham, Pat. *Electoral Behavior in the United States.* Prentice Hall, 1991.

Lindop, Edmund. *By a Single Vote! One-Vote Decisions that Changed American History.* Stackpole Books, 1987.

Lyons, Schley and Theodore Arrington. *Who Votes and Why.* The Taft Institute for Two-Party Government, 1988.

Piven, Francis F. and Richard A. Cloward. *Why Americans Don't Vote.* Pantheon, 1989.

Salmore, Stephen A. and Barbara G. Salmore. *Candidates, Parties, and Campaigns: Electoral Politics in America.* CQ Press, 2nd ed., 1989.

Let's Vote. Five filmstrips, Universal Education.

The Right to Vote: Our Democratic Privilege. Four filmstrips, Random House.

Taking Action: America Works. 20 minute video, AFL-CIO.

Votes. Simulation, Interact Company.

Voting—As If Your Life Depended On It. Two Filmstrips, Multimedia Productions, Inc.

The Voting Machine. Computer program, Career Publishing, 1987.

Note: For additional resources, see *West's American Government Teacher's Resource Binder (TRB).*

PREVIEW AND PLANNING GUIDE

CHAPTER 12
The Organization of Congress

Begins on page 282

Background Material

The Constitutional Convention was deadlocked on the issue of representation between small and large states. The usually placid deliberations were slipping toward acrimonious debate when Doctor Franklin spoke: "When a broad table is to be made, and the edges of the planks do not fit, the artist takes a little from both and makes a good joint. In like manner here both sides must part with some of their demands . . ." Thus Congress was born of compromise and continues to receive sustenance through compromise.

After bicameralism and the nature of representation were agreed upon, the framers had to settle on the correct number of representatives, another contentious issue. Though there are now 435 members in the House of Representatives, this is approximately only one representative for every 600,000 people, as compared to the 65 members in 1789 who each represented about 60,000.

Although Article I of the Constitution has been amended only slightly, there is little resemblance between today's Congress and that of two hundred years ago. In the evolution of Congress, powerful committee and leadership organizations have developed that act as miniature legislatures within Congress. The complexity and quantity of legislation that necessitates large staffs and an enormous operating budget has been another major development. Nevertheless, many things remain unchanged. Qualifications for Congress are the same and its primary powers and responsibilities remain the same.

Members of Congress are still indicted in the press for being too generous in giving themselves pay raises and for having too many privileges. Congress, too, is accused of representing parochial district interests over those of the nation, and at the same time putting national interests over those of individual citizens who deserve representation. Opinion surveys show that Americans believe that Congress as a whole is inefficient and disorganized, but believe that their own legislators do a fine job.

What we may sometimes forget is that Congress was intended to be a deliberative body. It was intended to be against swift or capricious government.

Pacing Chart

Full Year Course: 5 days
One Semester Course: 3 days

Selected Print and Media Resources

Bailey, Christopher. *The U.S. Congress.* Blackwell, 1989.

Barone, Michael and Grant Ujifusa. *The Almanac of American Politics, 1990.* National Journal, 1989.

Committee: A Simulation of the Congressional Committee System. Role-Playing, Interact.

Congressional Directory. Government Printing Office, Biennial.

Dodd, Lawrence and Bruce Oppenheimer, (eds.). *Congress Reconsidered,* 4th ed. CQ Press, 1989.

Hutson, James H. *To Make All Laws: Perspectives on Representation in American Government.* Houghton Mifflin, 1990.

Jigsaw Politics: Shaping the House After the 1990 Census. Congressional Quarterly Books, 1990.

Miller, James. *Running in Place: Inside the Senate.* Simon and Schuster, 1986.

Orstein, Norman, *et al. Vital Statistics on Congress, 1989–1990.* Congressional Quarterly, 1989.

Congress: How it Works—And Sometimes Doesn't. 59 minute video, Guidance Associates.

Congress: Reflecting the Public Will. 30 minute video, Close Up Foundation.

Congress: Representing the Will of the People. 28 minute video, Close Up Foundation.

Congress: What It Is, How It Works, and How It Affects You. 3 videos *Time* Magazine guide, 60 minutes total, Guidance Associates.

Inside Government: Congressman. 16 minute video, Churchill Films, Inc.

The Legislative Branch. 16 mm film, 22 minutes, National Geographic.

The Power Game: The Congress. 60 minute video, PBS Video.

U.S. Government in Action: The House of Representatives. 20 minute video, New York Times/Teaching Resources Films.

U.S. Government in Action: The Senate. 18 minute video, New York Times/Teaching Resources Films.

Note: For additional resources, see *West's American Government Teacher's Resource Binder (TRB).*

PREVIEW AND PLANNING GUIDE

CHAPTER 13
The Powers of Congress

Begins on page 312

Background Material

By April of 1789, the Senate and House had acquired a quorum, and it set out to define the powers enumerated in Article I. They had to verify the electoral college ballots so the executive branch could begin its work. The new Congress began to create our judicial system. The issue of primacy was the manner in which they would raise money.

Congress had other powers articulated in Article I that needed attention. Raising an army, establishing a capital, regulating commerce, and creating a postal system were just a few. However, Article I did not specify the particulars of these expressed powers. Congress also had to develop its own institutional rules by which to function. Compared to today's standards Congress progressed rapidly, despite Madison's declaration that, "Scarcely a day passes without some striking evidence of . . . delays . . . merely from the want of precedents." Within relatively few years, Congress passed the Judiciary Act, determined that the capital would be today's Washington, D.C., approved the Bill of Rights, created three departments for the executive branch, set up ways to pay off debt and collect money through taxes, tariffs, and duties, set up the U.S. Census Bureau, and authorized the patent office.

Two landmark Supreme Court cases allowed Congress to expand its ability to exercise power. *McCulloch* v. *Maryland* endorsed the implied powers doctrine allowing for what has been called a loose interpretation of the Constitution. Loose constructionists were further buttressed by the Marshall Court's ruling in *Gibbons* v. *Ogden* with its broad interpretation of the commerce clause. Today, that same clause is used to regulate banking, television, minimum wage and a host of other commercial matters, at times even including questions of civil rights. As long as the "elastic" powers of Congress are derived from one of the expressed powers, Congress will be able to do whatever it deems "necessary and proper."

The non-legislative powers of Congress can be as important or more important than the legislative powers. Although rarely used, the power of impeachment is in the hands of Congress and must be taken seriously by all branches of government, as Nixon's resignation revealed. The powers to propose amendments and choose presidents may have been used less than the framers anticipated, although the potential of each is enormous. A constant function of Congress is its responsibility to provide advice and consent. Recent Supreme Court and Executive Department appointments reveal the competition between the branches and political parties. This non-legislative power will remain important as Congress and the president vie to preserve and expand their constitutional powers.

The complexities of modern society have blurred the lines between legislative, judicial, and executive operations, and for that reason the investigative and oversight functions of Congress are essential. We know that Congress can provide excellent investigation and oversight, as the Watergate and CIA experiences demonstrated, but we also know that Congress can lack the will to vigorously pursue its investigatory powers. Perhaps the Iran-Contra and savings and loan scandals demonstrated this.

Pacing Chart

Full Year Course: 6 to 7 days
One Semester Course: 4 days

Selected Print and Media Resources

Aberbach, Joel D. *Keeping a Watchful Eye: The Politics of Congressional Oversight.* Brookings, 1990.

Fisher, Louis. *Constitutional Conflicts Between Congress and the President.* Princeton University Press, 1985.

Fisher, Louis. *The Politics of Shared Power: Congress and the Executive.* CQ Press, 2nd ed., 1987.

Mezey, Michael L. *Congress, the President, and Public Policy.* Westview Press, 1989.

Turner, Stansfield. *Secrecy and Democracy: The CIA in Transition.* Houghton Mifflin, 1985.

The Committee: Taxation with Representation. 58 minute video, PBS Video.

Summer of Judgment: The Impeachment Hearings. 60 minute video, PBS Video.

Summer of Judgment: The Watergate Hearings. 2-part, 120 minute video, PBS Video.

The U.S. Congress and the Constitution. 57 minute video, Close Up Foundation.

Note: For additional resources, see *West's American Government Teacher's Resource Binder (TRB).*

PREVIEW AND PLANNING GUIDE

CHAPTER 14
How Congress Makes Laws

Begins on page 332

Background Material

The primary function of Congress is to be the supreme lawmaking body of the nation, but when the specifics of the lawmaking are examined, controversy erupts. Some political observers believe that Congress does not have the power to fulfill its lawmaking duties given the influence of the president, media, and special interest groups, but a weak Congress was not the fear of the framers. In *Federalist, No. 51* Madison wrote, "In a republican government the legislative authority necessarily predominates. The remedy for this . . . is to divide the legislature into different branches; and to render them . . . as little connected with each other as . . . their common functions . . . will admit." Madison and his peers may have done a better job than they realized. In their quest to check the legislature, the framers gave us a Constitution against efficient government. It is curious that we expect the opposite.

In addition to the constitutional remedy of bicameralism, numerous institutional changes in Congress since 1789 have added to legislative lethargy. Political parties used to be so powerful that they could pass or thwart legislation regardless of the people's will. Party predominance has been modified since then. Members of Congress have electoral independence today, so lawmaking can be done with less concern about party loyalty.

The large number of agenda items places a pressure on Congress that the framers could only have imagined. There is serious need for expertise on a myriad of subjects, and the committee system is the best way to facilitate that expertise. If Madison were alive today, he might well fear power in the hands of the president rather than Congress. In order to compete with the president and to keep up with its increasing and technically demanding workload, Congress expanded the authority and scope of its committees. Along with committee specialization have come increased obstacles to legislation and inevitable battles over turf, money, and power. A trade bill, for example, might have to go through ten different subcommittees before it makes it to the floor, each step an additional opportunity to alter or block the original legislation.

The House is expected to advance a national agenda. This can become difficult or even impossible if the president advances a contrary agenda in his State of the Union address. Party caucuses have been utilized to help organize Congress, but regional and ideological differences can keep caucuses from helping beyond selecting committee assignments, chairmanships, and leadership positions.

Congress has shown a growing reliance on conference committees, which until the 1970s were dominated by secrecy and the seniority system. Conference committees are temporary committees made up of members from both the House and the Senate to iron out the differences between each House's version of a particular bill. Does the rise of conference committee power reflect an inability of Congress to work otherwise, or is it prudent management by chamber leaders? Representative Dicks's (Dem. Wash.) comment, "Let's face it, the conference committee is where it all happens", may help to answer the question.

All bills must clear the presidential veto hurdle. It is difficult to go against a popular president, especially by gaining a two-thirds vote in both houses of Congress. It is easy for the president to depict Congress as a bunch of bickering, pork-barrel motivated politicians. It is a wonder our lawmakers don't get more sympathy.

Pacing Chart

Full Year Course: 7 or 8 days
One Semester Course: 5 days

Selected Print and Media Resources

Huitt, Ralph. *Senate Politics: Operating Within the System.* Pergamon Books, 1987.

Kingdom, John W. *Congressmen's Voting Decisions.* 2nd ed., Harper and Row, 1981.

Oleszek, Walter J. *Congressional Procedures and the Policy Process.* CQ Press, 3rd. ed., 1988.

Smith, Steven S. *Call to Order: Floor Politics in the House and Senate.* Brookings, 1989.

West, Darrel M. *Congress and Economic Policy Making.* University of Pittsburgh, 1987.

House of Representatives Simulation. Students write and vote on legislation, DAC Educational Publications.

How a Bill Becomes a Law. Computer Program, Queue.

How a Bill Becomes a Law. 15 minute video, Associated Press.

How a Bill Becomes a Law: Wall Chart. 3 posters combine into one, Perfection Form.

Note: For additional resources, see *West's American Government Teacher's Resource Binder (TRB).*

PREVIEW AND PLANNING GUIDE

CHAPTER 15
The Presidency

Begins on page 354

Background Material

A paradoxical model of government created by the framers is represented by the executive branch outlined in Article II. On the one hand, there is incredible potential for power, yet on the other hand, there are the checks of the legislature, courts, and the people. There was fear that tyranny would result if the executive was given too much power, but a countervailing fear was present among those who felt a weak executive would be unable to prohibit rule by the mob, thus threatening security and property.

Hamilton took such a position in *Federalist, No. 70.* "There is an idea . . . that a vigorous executive is inconsistent with the genius of republican government . . . Energy in the executive is a leading character in the definition of good government. It is essential to the protection of the community against foreign attacks; . . . to the protection of property . . . ; to the security of liberty against . . . faction, and of anarchy."

The framers were versed in the writings of Locke, which declared an executive should be removed from office by the legislature and the people if he violated the limits of power granted to him. However, Locke was cognizant that during crisis a president should be allowed to "act according to the discretion of the executive, for the public good without the prescription of law, and sometimes even against it." The framers set up an executive branch that would correct the weaknesses experienced under the Articles of Confederation while not being able to possess the absolute power of a monarch.

As in the past, we struggle with what constitutes the proper degree and scope of executive power, especially in light of the trend that has seen the president's power grow relative to the power of the other branches.

The size of the executive branch has grown along with its influence. The cabinet has gone from four to fourteen departments, while the size of the executive office helps make it possible for the president to administer the functions demanded of him. These functions are diverse and extend well beyond those listed in the Constitution. New positions have emerged such as the chief of staff and the press secretary. New positions correspond with duties related to the budget, national security, the economy, the environment, science, and other areas.

Many factors restrict and constrain a president. Congress is the primary check on the president provided in the Constitution. Fear of losing the next election, domestic and international opinion, the media, the courts, the other political party, and members of their own executive branch are other factors that thwart and frustrate presidents.

Pacing Chart

Full Year Course: 10 days
One Semester Course: 4 or 5 days

Selected Print and Media Resources

Cronin, Thomas E. (ed.). *Inventing the American Presidency.* University Press of Kansas, 1989.

DiClerico, Robert E. *The American President.* Prentice Hall, 3rd. ed., 1990.

Diller, Daniel C. and Stephan L. Robertson. *The Presidents, First Ladies, and Vice Presidents.* CQ Press, 1989.

Germond, Jack W. and Jules Witcover. *Whose Broad Stripes and Bright Stars? The Trivial Pursuit of the Presidency 1988.* Warner, 1989.

Milkis, Sydne M. and Michael Nelson. *The American Presidency. Origins and Development, 1776–1990.* CQ Press, 1990.

Branches of Government: The Executive Branch. Video, National Geographic Educational Series.

The Challenge of the Presidency. 60 minute video, PBS Video.

Meet the Presidents. Computer program, Versa Computing.

The Power Game: The Presidency. 60 minute video, PBS Video.

The Presidency, the Press and the People. 120 minute video, PBS Video.

The Presidency Series. Computer program, Social Studies School Services.

Style and the Presidents. 65 minute video, ABC News.

Television and the President. 98 minutes, On the Air.

U.S. Government in Action: The Cabinet. 18 minute video, New York Times/Teaching Resources Film.

U.S. Government in Action: The Presidency. 17 minute video, New York Times/Teaching Resources Films.

Note: For additional resources, see *West's American Government Teacher's Resource Binder (TRB).*

PREVIEW AND PLANNING GUIDE

CHAPTER 16
The President at Work

Begins on page 376

Background Material

The president is the most powerful individual in the world. What makes that fact more incredible is that his powers are constrained by groups in and out of government.

As chief executive, the president sees that the laws of the nation are administered. The size of the government demands that this be done by relying on personal staff and the cabinet. Presidential aides in the executive office often fulfill the wishes of the president with a passion that threatens the separation of powers.

Although ceremonial, the chief of state role is important, especially in the age of television. Welcoming ceremonies and dedications are good opportunities to enhance public approval while buttressing public morale. The president is our number one political celebrity.

Commander in chief is the most serious constitutional role. The responsibility for controlling millions of military personnel during times of peace and war has been heavy for all presidents. Truman's atomic bomb, Johnson's Vietnam War, and Bush's Desert Storm are examples of this enormous responsibility.

Foreign affairs has traditionally been the venue for expansion of presidential authority. Although aided by the Department of State and the National Security Council, it is the president who ultimately decides. The Senate may have the power to ratify treaties, but executive agreements give the president a great deal of latitude.

As the power of the president has grown, so has his influence as chief legislator. The president offers new initiatives and attempts to set agendas for both domestic and foreign policy. White House dispatches sent to Capitol Hill do not guarantee that the president's wishes will be followed, but they often define the limits of the legislative process and frequently contain drafts. Presidential lobbying is difficult to ignore. The threat of veto is also used to influence the type of legislation that Congress passes.

Even though he has no formal party position, the president is the head of his political party. Presidents who can retain control of the campaign finance and patronage potential offered by their office, as Reagan did, can wield considerable clout. Being president is no guarantee that the party will heed commands, as Carter found out in 1980. Much of the political success presidents experience is due to personal style within the party.

The Constitution and its separation of powers restrict the president. The Senate can reject nominees, as with Judge Bork, and can fail to ratify treaties, as with Salt II. The Supreme Court can restrain the president and interpret his responsibilities, as in *U.S.* v. *Nixon.* There are other checks as well: public opinion, the media, the other party, interest groups, and bureaucratic resistance are some. Are there sufficient constraints on the president? This is a good question to ask students.

Pacing Chart

Full Year Course: 7 days
One Semester Course: 3 days

Selected Print and Media Resources

Barnet, Richard J. *The Rocket's Red Glare: When America Goes to War—The Presidents and the People.* Simon & Schuster, 1990.

Beard, Charles A. and Detlev Vagts. *The Presidents in American History.* Messner, 1989.

Bond, John R. and Richard Fleisher. *The President in the Legislative Arena.* University of Chicago Press, 1990.

DiClerico, Robert E. (ed.). *Analyzing the Presidency.* Dushkin, 2nd ed., 1990.

Kellerman, Barbara and Ryan J. Barilleaux. *The President as World Leader.* St. Martin's Press, 1990.

Missiles in Cuba: A Decision-Making Game. Simulation, Social Studies School Service.

Tebbel, John and Sarah Miles Watts. *The Press and the Presidency: From George Washington to Ronald Reagan.* Oxford Press, 1985.

Five Presidents on the Presidency. 16 mm film, BFA.

Gerald Ford: The Healing of the Presidency. 60 minute video, PBS Video.

Jimmy Carter: The Moralist President. 60 minute video, PBS Video.

Ronald Reagan: The Presidency in Affirmation. 60 minute video, PBS Video.

The Presidency Series. 5 part computer series, Focus Media.

Note: For additional resources, see *West's American Government Teacher's Resource Binder (TRB).*

PREVIEW AND PLANNING GUIDE

CHAPTER 17
The Bureaucracy in Action

Begins on page 400

Background Material

The federal bureaucracy is the least popular governmental institution. Degrading the bureaucracy by both politicians and everyday citizens is as American as apple pie. Presidents campaign against bureaucracy, the very institution they are responsible to administer. Carter, in criticizing a particular agency in the federal bureaucracy, said it was, "disorganized, wasteful, has no purpose, and its policies are incomprehensible or devised by special interest groups with little regard for the welfare of the average citizen." Reagan said, "Government is not the solution to our problem; government is the problem."

Liberals see the bureaucracy as a bastion of the status quo, while conservatives believe it to be too intrusive in private life. The rest simply think it is too big, unaccountable, and not fulfilling its charge. Cynics think that bureaucrats are paid too much and work too little, as shown in *Washington Post* polls. At the same time, bureaucrats are accused of being too powerful and manipulative. Our misgivings about the bureaucracy are further confused when the same poll reveals the vast majority of us are pleased with the individual service we received from a bureaucrat. Finally, with over 5 million people employed directly by the government, it is difficult not to have a personal contact with a worker in the bureaucracy.

Behind the campaign and political rhetoric is the reality that the bureaucracy is the creature of Congress or the Constitution, and the servant of the president. The key issues are whether or not the bureaucracy is accountable to the president and Congress, and whether bureaucrats serve the interests of their clientele.

The bureaucratization of America is a direct result of the Great Depression and World War II. There is a popular attitude that the bureaucracy functions as an automaton, dictating policy at its whim. This oversimplifies reality. The number of bureaucrats has nothing directly to do with the degree of their power. When their task is clearly delineated by Congress, as with Social Security laws for example, the will of the people is met. When room for discretion is left to an agency, as in the case of military procurement, then the bureaucracy has more power. Our government needs agencies and their personnel to carry out its programs and policies. The truth is that both Congress and the president have the authority and capability to control the bureaucracy if they choose to do so. Congress has the responsibility to watch the president to ensure economy and accountability. Individual members of Congress as committee chairs and members are not so vigilant.

Pacing Chart

Full Year Course: 7 days
One Semester Course: 3 days

Selected Print and Media Resources

Burke, John P. *Bureaucratic Responsibility.* Johns Hopkins University Press, 1986.

The Capital Source: Who's Who, What, Where in Washington. National Journal, annual.

Eccles, James. *The Hatch Act and the American Bureaucracy.* Vantage Press, 1981.

Goodsell, Charles T. *The Case for Bureaucracy.* Chatham House, 2nd ed., 1985.

Hummel, Ralph P. *The Bureaucratic Experience.* St. Martin's Press, 2nd ed., 1982.

Kaufman, Herbert. *Time, Chance, and Organizations.* Chatham, 1986.

Rourke, Francis. *Bureaucracy, Politics, & Public Policy.* Little, Brown, & Co., 1984.

Strausman, Jeffery D. *Public Administration.* Longman, 2nd ed., 1990.

Agencies That Protect the Consumer. 6 filmstrips, Universal Education.

American Government V. Computer program, Intellectual Software.

Federal Bureaucracy. Filmstrip, Social Studies School Service.

The Power Game: The Pentagon. 60 minute video, PBS Video.

The Power Game: The Unelected. 60 minute video, PBS Video.

U.S. government in Action: The Regulatory Agencies. 15 minute video, New York Times/Teaching Resources Films.

Note: For additional resources, see *West's American Government Teacher's Resource Binder (TRB).*

PREVIEW AND PLANNING GUIDE

CHAPTER 18
The Federal Courts

Begins on page 430

Background Material

''(T)he judiciary, from the very nature of its functions, will always be the least dangerous to the political rights of the Constitution . . . the judiciary is beyond comparison the weakest of the three departments of power.'' Thus spoke Hamilton in *Federalist, No. 78.* The Marshall Courts ruling in *Marbury* v. *Madison* would enable the judicial branch over time to become an equal partner, at least in terms of possessing a check against the legislative and executive branches of government. Judicial review determined what some had thought to be true all along—that the judicial branch could declare laws unconstitutional. This initiative did much to dispel notions about being the weakest branch of government.

It is understandable that so many felt underwhelmed by the judicial branch. Montesquieu, after all, had said in *Spirit of Laws* that the ''judiciary is next to nothing.'' Also, Article III is the shortest and least descriptive, not even taking the time to articulate qualifications for office! The powers of the judicial branch were straightforward, except for Section 2, which stated, ''judicial Power shall extend to all Cases in Law and Equity.'' This can rightly be called the judicial branch's elastic clause. Why the lack of foresight on the part of the framers? Of all the mechanisms prescribed by the Constitution, the judicial branch, especially the Supreme Court, was uniquely American. Never before or since has a valid attempt at an *independent* judiciary been tried.

As the Supreme Court demonstrated dominance of the national government over the states, the indirect recipient of power was the president. Although conflict with Jackson and Lincoln took place, it was not until the latter half of the 20th century that the judicial branch checked the executive. Initially, as cases like *Worcester* v. *Georgia* and *Ex parte Merryman* demonstrated, the Court had no power of enforcement, a situation still true. In most instances the Supreme Court is joined by some combination of Congress, public opinion, and the executive branch, which is sufficient power of enforcement.

Truman found out during the Korean War, as did Nixon in opinions concerning his possession of tape recordings of White House conversations, that the Supreme Court would limit executive privilege. It would be difficult today to mount a credible argument that the judicial branch was ''nothing.'' Rather it is a unique and powerful part of our system of checks and balances.

Pacing Chart

Full Year Course: 8 days
One Semester Course: 5 days

Selected Print and Media Resources

Abraham, Henry J. *The Judicial Process.* Oxford, 5th ed., 1986.

Bernstein, Richard B. and Jerome Agel. *Into The Third Century: The Supreme Court.* Walker and Co., 1989.

Choper, Jesse H. *The Supreme Court and Its Justices: The Best of the ABA Journal.* The American Bar Association, 1987.

Lawson, Don. *Landmark Supreme Court Cases.* Enslow, 1987.

O'Brien, David M. *Storm Center; The Supreme Court in American Politics.* Norton, 1987.

Rehnquist, William H. *The Supreme Court: How It Was, How It Is.* Morrow & Co., 1987.

The Supreme Court at Work. CQ Press, 1990.

Tribe, Laurence H. and Michael Dorf. *On Reading the Constitution.* Harvard University Press, 1991.

Woodward, Bob and Scott Armstrong. *The Brethren: Inside the Supreme Court.* Avon, 1976.

Weiss, Ann E. *The Supreme Court.* Enslow, 1987.

Witt, Elder (ed.). *Guide to the U.S. Supreme Court.* CQ Press, 1990.

For the People. 60 minute video, PBS Video.

This Honorable Court: A History of the Court. 60 minute video, PBS Video.

This Honorable Court: Inside the Supreme Court. 60 minute video, PBS Video.

Justice For All. 60 minute video, PBS Video.

Justice Sandra Day O'Connor. 60 minute video, PBS Video.

The Supreme Court: Guardian of the Constitution. 28 minute video, Close-Up Foundation.

U.S. Government in Action: The Supreme Court. 19 minute video, New York Times/Teaching Resources Films.

Note: For additional resources, see *West's American Government Teacher's Resource Binder (TRB.)*

PREVIEW AND PLANNING GUIDE

CHAPTER 19
Economic Policy, Poverty, and the Environment

Begins on page 458

Background Material

To the framers of the Constitution, politics could not be separated from economics. It was fear of losing property that quickened the call to the Constitutional Convention, and the desire to protect property which caused tensions among the delegates. Doctor Franklin was quoted as saying, "If proportional representation takes place, the small States contend their liberties will be in danger. If the equality of votes is put into place, the large States say their money will be in danger."

The pursuit of property in a stable economy is of even greater importance today, because we have a yet-to-be-realized goal that all are to take part in America's prosperity. The government has always been involved with the economy, but as technology advanced and the nation industrialized, government intervention became indispensable.

The Great Depression revealed that only the federal government had adequate resources to tame the business cycle. The tools of monetary and fiscal policy can work, but the reality is that individuals and businesses are free to exercise economic choices, even poor ones. Congress seldom has the will to raise taxes and cut spending when needed to battle inflation, although it takes stimulative economic measures with amazing rapidity. Deficit spending seems to have become a permanent aspect of the budget process. The Fed is free of direct political pressure, but politics still intervene. Even good monetary policy has to be complemented by prudent fiscal policy and corresponding good judgment by consumers and business.

Despite periods of recession and inflation, our economy continues to be the most dynamic and prosperous in the world. Unfortunately, not everyone takes part in the riches. Single-parent families, the young, and minorities are disproportionately among the ranks of the poor. Despite devoting enormous resources to combat the problem over the decades, there is no significant reduction in the percentage of poor; in fact, their numbers have grown considerably.

The government has been an active participant in trying to protect the environment. People may disagree with the direction and degree of government policy, but for the last century the federal government has produced some effective legislation, culminating with the 1990 Clean Air Act. As with all social problems, the environment cannot be preserved by government power alone.

Pacing Chart

Full Year Course: 6 days
One Semester Course: 4 days

Selected Print and Media Resources

Alt, James E. and K. Alec Chrystal. *Political Economics.* Wheatsheaf, 1983.

Birnbaum, Jeffery and Alan Murray. *Showdown at Gucci Gulch: Lawmakers, Lobbyists, and the Unlikely Triumph of Tax Reform.* Vintage, 1988.

Economic Report of the President. United States Government Printing Office, annual.

Heilbroner, Robert L. *The Worldly Philosophers.* Simon & Schuster, 6th ed., 1986.

Kiewiet, D. Roderick. *Macroeconomics and Micropolitics.* University of Chicago Press, 1983.

McKenzie, Richard B. *Competing Visions: The Political Conflict Over America's Economic Future.* Cato Institute, 1985.

Shuman, Howard. *Politics and the Budget,* 2nd ed., Prentice Hall, 1988.

World Eagle: The Monthly Social Studies Resource. World Eagle, Inc.

Big Government and Private Enterprise. Filmstrip, Current Affairs Films.

The Committee: Taxation with Representation. 58 minute video, PBS Video.

Conservation and the Balance in Nature. 16 mm film, International Film Bureau.

Extinction. Environmental problems simulation, Sinauer.

Food for the World—A Series. Filmstrip, National Geographic.

The Greenhouse Effect. 17 minute video, Focus Media.

The Ozone Layer: How Important Is It? 22 minute video.

The Rising Seas. 28 minute video, Focus Media.

Understanding the American Economy. 45 minute video, Focus Media.

The Vanishing Forest: The Crisis of Tropical Deforestation. Filmstrip, Knowledge Unlimited.

Note: For additional resources, see *West's American Government Teacher's Resource Binder (TRB).*

CHAPTER 20
Defense and Foreign Policy

Begins on page 488

Background Material

Defense and foreign policy were important priorities to the framers. Spain precluded our use of the Mississippi, Britain excluded us from the St. Lawrence, and Barbary pirates committed acts of terrorism against our vessels off the coast of Tripoli. John Jay expressed the particulars needed for adequate national defense against foreign nations in *The Federalist No. 4*. "If they see that our national government is efficient and well administered, our trade prudently regulated, our militia properly organized and disciplined, our resources and finances discreetly managed, and our credit reestablished, our people free, contented, and united, they will be much more disposed to cultivate our friendship than provoke our resentment." It was left to the Constitution, Congress, presidents, and history to make Jay's prescription for peace a reality.

Article II, Section I empowers the president as commander-in-chief, a position some presidents have used with more discretion than others. In 1789 Congress established the Department of State, and in 1947 it combined the Departments of War and Navy into a new organized Department of Defense. The Secretary of State is the formal head of foreign policy, but as Kissinger in Nixon's first term showed, at times the National Security Advisor better represents the president.

Article I gives Congress the authority to declare war, approve Defense and State Department appointments as well as ambassadors, and reject or approve treaties. The War Powers Act was passed in order for Congress to regain foreign policy influence, but its efficacy is still being debated.

At times America's foreign policy goals seem contradictory or nonexistent. Presidents Reagan and Nixon were accused of supporting right-wing dictators who violated human rights as long as they helped contain communism. Carter was charged with weakening the CIA to the point that it was incapable of dealing with the Iran hostage crisis, and Bush committed thousands of troops to free Kuwait while at the same time granting most favored nation status to China. Old alliances like NATO might seem less relevant, and new alignments of nations and resources to stop regional conflicts and terrorism are yet to be refined. The best that can be said is that perhaps our foreign policy is evolving and taking shape for the "new world order" President Bush talks about.

Adding to the complexity is the United Nations, a body with idealistic goals thwarted by realistic parochialism of member nations. Under Reagan, the U.S. withheld funds from the U.N. because third world nations aligned to reject our initiatives, yet with Desert Storm it seemed an ideal mechanism of cooperation against Saddam Hussein and Iraq.

Pacing Chart

Full Year Course: 8 days
One Semester Course: 4 days

Selected Print and Media Resources

Brown, L. Carl (ed.). *Centerstage: American Diplomacy Since World War II.* Holmes & Meier, 1989.

Hastedt, Glenn P. *American Foreign Policy: Past, Present, Future.* Prentice Hall, 2nd ed., 1991.

Hughes, Barry B. *Continuity and Change in World Politics.* Prentice Hall, 1991.

Kaufman, William W. *A Reasonable Defense.* Brookings Institution, 1986.

Kissinger, Henry. *White House Years.* Little, Brown, 1979.

McNamara, Robert S. *Out of the Cold War: New Thinking for American Foreign and Defense Policy in the 21st Century.* Simon & Schuster, 1989.

Spanier, John. *Games Nations Play.* CQ Press, 7th ed., 1990.

Stoessinger, John G. *The Might of Nations: World Politics in Our Time.* McGraw-Hill, 9th ed., 1990.

American Foreign Policy: How It Works. Filmstrip, Prentice Hall.

Fighting Terrorism: Inside the National Security Council. 60 minute video, PBS Video.

The Power Game: The Pentagon. 60 minute video, PBS Video.

Profiles in Diplomacy: The U.S. Foreign Service. 60 minute video, PBS Video.

Secret Intelligence. Four part video series, PBS Video.

To What End? 60 minute video, PBS Video.

Youth Looks at the CIA. Filmstrip, Multimedia Productions, Inc.

Note: For additional resources, see *West's American Government Teacher's Resource Binder (TRB).*

CHAPTER 21
State Constitutions and Legislative Processes

Begins on page 520

Background Material

Our system of federalism consists of a national government and fifty states. States have been important to the politics of our nation long before the Constitutional Convention. People, accustomed, if not attached, to their states, were suspicious of attempts to make them subordinate to a national government.

Subordination to the central government did not negate states as powerful governmental bodies. States connect with people more directly than the national government connects with people. States are free to experiment with legislation. If their policies succeed, other states, or even the national government, may wish to emulate the legislation. If the policies fail, then the damage is contained to one state. It would be a mistake to conclude that the states are microcosms of the national government. Political scientist James Q. Wilson wrote, "State governments are not miniature versions of the federal government, and municipal governments are not miniature versions of the state ones. There is almost as much variation in the forms and operations of government *within* the United States as among the United States and other democratic nations.

Free to establish any system of republican government, the states all chose a system with a chief executive, and none denied the judiciary the power of judicial review. The general structure and enumeration of powers in state constitutions are also very similar. Even with these similarities in structure, there is great variety in policy and governmental administration among the states.

Most state constitutions have the same unwieldy structure and are excessively long, often the result of a healthy suspicion of state government combined with the inability to separate constitutional law from statutory law. States can amend their constitutions through the legislature and by constitutional initiative. Legislative organization and the lawmaking process are also similar among the states.

The most striking distinction between the U.S. Constitution and the state constitutions is the potential for direct democracy at the state level. The initiative allows citizens to circulate petitions in order to get an issue placed on the ballot. The referendum, an issue placed on the ballot by the legislature, is another opportunity for direct democracy. The recall allows citizens to circulate petitions in order to seek a recall election. The recall has been used infrequently but exists as a legitimate threat.

Pacing Chart

Full Year Course: 5 days
One Semester Course: 2 or 3 days. Note: The time allocated to the teaching of state and local government concepts in this unit might need to be tailored to meet individual needs and curricula.

Selected Print and Media Resources

Begle, Thad L. (ed.). *State Governments: CQ's Guide to Current Issues and Activities.* CQ Press, Annual.

Berman, David R. *State and Local Politics.* 5th ed. Allyn and Bacon, 1987.

The Book of the States, 1990–1991. The Council of State Governments, 1990.

Cornwell, Elmer E. Jr., Jay S. Goodman, and Wayne R. Swanson. *State Constitutional Conventions: The Politics of the Revision Process in Seven States.* Praeger, 1975.

Cronin, Thomas E. *Direct Democracy: The Politics of Initiative, Referendum, and Recall.* Harvard Press, 1989.

Jacob, Herbert, *et al. Politics in the American States.* Scott, Foresman, 5th ed., 1990.

Press, Charles and Kenneth VerBerg. *State and Community Governments in a Dynamic Federal System.* Harper Collins, 3rd ed., 1991.

Saffel, David C. *State and Local Government: Politics and Public Policies.* McGraw-Hill, 4th ed., 1990.

State Elective Officials and the Legislatures. The Council of State Governments, 1985.

Government in the United States. Filmstrip, National Geographic.

State and Local Government in Action. Filmstrip, New York Times.

State Government. 16 mm film/video, Britannica Learning Materials.

Statehood. Simulation, Interact Company.

Your Vote Counts: States and Local Government. Filmstrip, Guidance Associates.

Note: For additional resources, see *West's American Government Teacher's Resource Binder (TRB).*

PREVIEW AND PLANNING GUIDE

CHAPTER 22
Governors and State Administrators

Begins on page 544

Background Material

The British crown appointed royal governors who were responsible to and acted under the authority of the crown. As a consequence, state legislative actions were at times overridden and individual due process was often denied. Following the American Revolution, the states had a healthy and justified distrust of governors. Governors under the Articles of Confederation were given few powers, were elected by state legislatures, and served terms of only one or two years. Delegate Wilson was quoted in the Constitutional Convention as saying, ''All the 13 States, tho' agreeing in scarce any other instance, agree in placing a single magistrate at the head of the Government.'' Delegate Sherman responded, ''It was so . . . but then it should be also remarked that in all the States there was a Council of advice, without which the first magistrate could not act.'' Gradually the demands for executive leadership lead to the current environment where governors can exercise extensive authority and power.

Governors continue to be a source of national leadership. Fifteen presidents were at one time governors, and in this century over 120 governors have been elected to the U.S. Senate. A major difference between the offices of president and governor is that the president is the *chief* executive, while the governor shares the duties of the executive branch with a variety of other elected executive officials. Both must fulfill formal and informal qualifications for office, win a partisan nomination and election process, and carry out those duties specified in their respective constitutions. Along with the expansion of power for governors was a lengthening of terms of office and an increase in salary and benefits commensurate with the office.

Governors have many roles to fulfill, from chief legislator to chief spokesperson. The powers of the governor include appointment and removal of agency officials, administering laws, proposing budgets, power over the militia, and other legislative and judicial powers. The most important legislative powers come in setting the agenda and the power to veto legislative acts. The power of line-item veto found in 43 states enhances the power of an executive. Pardons, parole, and reprieves constitute the main judicial powers, although they are sparingly exercised.

Forty-seven states elect executive branch officers in addition to a governor. The lieutenant governor is usually elected and may be from a different party. The lieutenant governor usually has very little power, and at best waits for an opportunity to run for governor. The attorney general acts as the state's legal advisor. An attorney general has the power to write law through opinions. This high-visibility position is often a stepping stone to the governorship. Forty-seven states have a secretary of state who is the official records keeper. The power of the secretary of state varies greatly from state to state. Financial functions are carried out by a treasurer and state comptroller, positions which are basically that of money manager.

Conflict between the governor and these other elected offices can be partisan, personal, or issue based. Consequently, governors rely more on their own staffs and attempt to limit the other officers to their constitutionally prescribed roles.

Pacing Chart

Full Year Course: 5 or 6 days
One Semester Course: 2 days

Selected Print and Media Resources

Beyle, Thad L. (ed.). *State Government: CQ's Guide to Current Issues and Activities, 1990–91.* CQ Press, 1990.

Jewel, Malcolm E. *Parties and Primaries: Nominating State Governors.* Praeger, 1984.

Osborne, David. *Laboratories of Democracy.* Harvard Business School Press, 1988.

Real Life Citizenship: Citizens and Their Local and State Governments. Student workbook, transparencies. Scholastic.

Rosenthal, Alan. *Governors and Legislatures: Contending Powers.* CQ Press, 1990.

Sabato, Larry. *Goodbye to Good-Time Charlie: The American Governorship Transformed.* CQ Press, 2nd ed., 1983.

Schulze, William. *State and Local Government.* West, 1988.

State Government. 16 mm, Britannica Learning Materials.

State and Local Government in Action. 6 Filmstrips, 12 duplicating masters, guide, New York Times.

Statehood. Simulation, Interact Company.

Note: For additional resources, see *West's American Government Teacher's Resource Binder (TRB).*

CHAPTER 23
The State Courts

Begins on page 562

Background Material

Of the two distinct court systems in the United States, federal and state, the state courts hear the vast majority of cases. The primary function of state courts is to adjudicate disputes between private persons—civil cases—and disputes between government and private persons—criminal cases. The 28,000 state and municipal judges are yeomen of the judicial labor force as their legal pronouncements and interpretations have the effect of making law. State judges often interpret national law, and of the hundreds of thousands of such cases only a handful get reviewed by the Supreme Court.

Each state has a unique judicial system, but it is fair to generalize that state courts reflect the following structure: minor courts of limited jurisdiction, general jurisdiction trial courts, and appellate courts. With the advent of issues like abortion and the right to die being adjudicated in our courts, judges have become visibly embroiled in the controversy. This makes the selection of judges important.

Judges may be appointed, elected by the legislature, elected by the people, or selected by a plan that uses a combination of the three. Selection of judges is contentious, and there is little empirical evidence to indicate that the method of selection alters the outcome of decisions.

According to public opinion polls, crime is a major fear of Americans. The primary responsibility for protecting life and property falls on the state. As Americans demand a get-tough approach to crime, some legislatures have enacted mandatory sentencing and victim compensation laws. These politically popular laws have some drawbacks. Judges lose some discretion in sentencing even in the face of mitigating circumstances or court-mandated rulings concerning overcrowded prisons. Often, state budgets or civil courts cannot take the strain of victim compensation laws.

District attorneys have discretion in determining who should be charged with a crime. In many states, D.A.s present evidence to grand juries, which in turn can hand down indictments. If a state does not use grand juries, the D.A. submits evidence to a judge who then issues an indictment (sometimes called an information). A suspect is then arraigned and faces a preliminary hearing. A trial by judge or jury, at the defendant's option, is next. After the trial comes the verdict and the sentence. Over 90% of suspects brought to trial are convicted, not because the courts are stacked, but because D.A.s do not usually bring frivolous cases to already crowded courts. Of all convictions only 5% to 10% come as a result of a trial verdict; the rest are the result of plea bargaining. John Langbein in "Torture and Plea Bargaining," *The Public Interest* (Winter, 1980), wrote that plea bargaining results in "condemnation without adjudication." But plea bargaining has its defenders who argue that it approximates the results of a trial yet swiftly and cheaply.

Sentencing varies from state to state, but the general goals of imprisonment are the same. States demand retribution, individual and general deterrence, and/or rehabilitation. Budget problems of states are making alternatives like halfway houses, work release programs, and community corrections facilities more appealing.

Pacing Chart

Full Year Course: 4 to 5 days
One Semester Course: 2 to 3 days

Selected Print and Media Resources

Baum, Lawrence. *American Courts: Process and Policy.* Houghton Mifflin, 2nd ed., 1990.

Carp, Robert A. and Ronald Stidham. *Judicial Process in America.* CQ Press, 1989.

DuBois, Philip L. *From Bench to Ballot.* University of Texas Press, 1980.

Gates, John B. and Charles A. Johnson. *American Courts: A Critical Assessment.* CQ Press, 1990.

Litwak, Mark. *Courtroom Crusaders.* Morrow, 1989.

People v. *Haines.* Court simulation, Constitutional Rights Foundation.

Small Claims Court: Everyday Justice for Ordinary People. 28 photocopy masters, Weston Walch.

Wice, Paul. *Judges and Lawyers.* Harper Collins, 1991.

Ethics on Trial. 58 minute video, WETA.

Juvenile Justice. Filmstrip, Color Educational Enrichment Materials.

The Legal Process: A Teen's Experience. Four filmstrips, United Learning.

The Rule of Law: The Struggle for Democracy. 58 minute video, Democracy Films Ltd.

Note: For additional resources, see *West's American Government Teacher's Resource Binder (TRB).*

PREVIEW AND PLANNING GUIDE

CHAPTER 24
Local Government

Begins on page 584

Background Material

There are over 82,000 units of local government in the United States. Illinois alone has over 6,000 units, while Hawaii has but 18. Local government has existed longer than state or national government, and continues to provide fundamental daily services. Ironically, although local government has the greatest and most immediate impact on citizens, it is the level of government that receives the least attention. This is illustrated by low voter turnout for local elections.

Local governments vary greatly in such matters as size, structure, function, and constituency, yet they all share the attribute of being creatures of the state. State government is unitary, with all power vested in the state. Local units of government exist at the discretion of the state. Some state constitutions have home-rule amendments that afford cities and counties more power and place greater restrictions against interference by state officials.

Regardless of charter type, local units of government must provide services. These include education, police and fire protection, public welfare, city planning and zoning, and recreation and cultural services. The manner in which these services are delivered depends in large part on the operation and structure of the local unit.

Counties are the primary unit used to assist the state in administering its laws. The size of counties, both in territory and population, varies enormously. Counties are usually involved with record keeping for births, deaths, marriages, voting, and property ownership. They also constitute a primary element of the judicial systems, administer licenses, collect taxes, develop transportation systems, and maintain parks.

Counties may be structured with a county-manager plan, where a board retains power and the county manager executes the policies of the board. The chief-administrator plan gives more power to the executive, power that is shared with the board. The elected-chief-executive plan allows the voters to choose the executive and grants the executive the most power.

Cities may be ruled by the mayor-council plan, with either a strong or weak mayor. The commission plan has popularly elected commissioners jointly control the government. The council-manager plan has the council appointing a professional executive. The mayor-administrator plan has a strong mayor appointing an administrative executive officer. Each plan has its pros and cons, but the mayor-council plan is the oldest and most widely used. The methods and means of governing cities have undergone important reforms over time—reforms that have seen the demise of machine-style patronage. For the most part, the administration of city government has become professionalized.

The addition of townships and special districts to the government mix causes some political observers to conclude that wasteful duplication of services demands consolidation of local government units. This is easier said than done given the vested political and economic interests of those who would have to turn power over to the new consolidated government unit.

Pacing Chart

Full Year Course: 4 or 5 days
One Semester Course: 1 or 2 days

Selected Print and Media Resources

Ackerman, Barbara. *You the Mayor? The Election of a City Politician.* Auburn House, 1989.

Bingham, Richard D. *State and Local Government in an Urban Society.* Random House, 1986.

Gray, Virginia and Peter K. Eisinger. *American States and Cities.* Harper Collins, 1991.

Houseman, Gerald L. *State and Local Government: The New Battlefield.* Prentice-Hall, 1986.

Stouffer, William B., *et al. State and Local Relations: The Individual and the Governments.* Harper Collins, 1991.

City Government—Closest to the People. 16mm/videocassette, Coronet Films.

City Government in the United States. 16mm/videocassette, Educational Media.

Council: A Simulation of Problem-Solving at the Community Level. Simulation, Interact.

Our Town Meeting: A Lesson in Civic Responsibility. Computer program, Tom Snyder.

Poletown Lives! 16mm film, Information Factory.

Rainbow Bay. Simulation, Interact.

Who Runs Your Town? Filmstrip, Multimedia Productions.

Your Vote Counts: State and Local Government. 40 minute video, Guidance Associates.

Note: For additional resources, see *West's American Government Teacher's Resource Binder (TRB).*

PREVIEW AND PLANNING GUIDE

CHAPTER 25
Paying for State and Local Government

Begins on page 606

Background Material

Financing state and local government has never been so controversial or important as it is in the 1990s. State legislatures, as in Illinois and Connecticut, have allowed budget deadlines to pass, placing state services in jeopardy. The political compromises between legislators and governors are sometimes creative attempts to raise revenues while still providing services. This is difficult to do. Inflation, increased demands and expectations from citizens, reduced funds from Washington, and competition from other taxing bodies all combine to create problems which may not have solutions.

The historic sources of revenue for state and local government, sales taxes and property taxes, have for the most part reached their maximums. As state lotteries, increased user fees, and legalized gambling demonstrate, state and local governments are in a quest for new sources of revenue. Non-tax revenues continue to be vital, but only represent a small percentage of revenues. Borrowing has increased among the states, usually by issuing bonds. Government bonds are like loans from citizens to the government. Before the bonds mature, citizens receive interest, and at maturity the citizens receive the price of the bond. State bonds are exempt from federal income tax, which, along with the security of the investment, explains their appeal. Revenue bonds are backed by the money for the specific project for which they were issued, while general obligation bonds can depend on the credit rating of the government that issues them. This is why governments do not wish to see a drop in their credit ratings.

The job of financing services by state and local governments has been made more difficult by the reduction in the amount of federal funds provided to the states. Although there are cries to restore levels of federal funding to pre-1980 levels, the economic realities of the federal budget are likely to preclude this. As for the federal aid that still exists, Congress often attaches significant requirements and restrictions. Categorical aid programs may have matching funds stipulations. Project grants allow Congress to bypass the state government and give money directly to local units of government.

Although nobody enjoys paying taxes, the expectation is that there will be a high level of service received for each tax dollar. The state and local governments spend most of their money on education, public welfare, highways, and hospitals. Growing sources of expenditures are education and correctional facilities. Most states employ an executive budget process that mirrors the federal budget-making process. The governor prepares the budget, and, once voted on by the legislature, administers the funds.

Financing state and local governments should receive more attention from the electorate than ever. Taxation and expenditures relate to politics almost as much as they relate to economics. By exercising their right to vote, citizens have an opportunity to guarantee that tax strategies and spending policies reflect their needs and wishes. If they do not exercise this right, they have no legitimate basis for complaint.

Pacing Chart

Full Year Course: 4 days
One Semester Course: 2 days

Selected Print and Media Resources

Burns, James M., Jack Peltason, and Thomas E. Cronin. *State and Local Politics.* Prentice Hall, 6th ed., 1990.

Facts and Figures on Government Finance, 1989. Tax Foundation, 1990.

Maxwell, James A. and Richard Aaronson. *Financing State and Local Governments.* Brookings Institute, 4th ed., 1986.

Pagano, Michael and Richard Moore. *Cities and Fiscal Choices.* Duke University Press, 1985.

U.S. Bureau of the Census: State Government Finances in 1989. Government Printing Office, 1990.

Van Horn, Carl E. (ed.), *The State of the States.* CQ Press, 1989.

American Taxpayers in Revolt. Filmstrip, Current Affairs Films.

Block Grant: A Simulation of Lobbying and Decision Making. Simulation, Interact.

The Judicial Branch. 16mm film, National Geographic.

Taxes: Who Needs Them. 16mm film, Handel Film Corporation.

Note: For additional resources, see *West's American Government Teacher's Resource Binder (TRB).*

PREVIEW AND PLANNING GUIDE

CHAPTER 26
Comparing Governments and Economic Systems

Begins on page 626

Background Material

This text has concentrated on American government, but Americans are not isolated from the rest of the world. An emerging reality is that the world is a global community, which directly and indirectly has an impact on our daily lives.

Although there are important exceptions, the trend in this global community is toward democratic reform. For that reason, it is imperative to have a basic understanding of the various democratic institutions around the world. Britain is a constitutional monarchy. It has a unitary structure of government under a parliamentary democracy. The parliament is bicameral, but legislative power rests with the House of Commons. The prime minister and cabinet are elected by the majority party in the House of Commons, so executive power is fused with, as opposed to separated from, legislative power.

Unlike Britain, Japan has a written constitution created at the direction of the United States after World War II. Like Britain, Japan has a ceremonial head of state in the Emperor. Legislative power rests with the Diet, with the lower house (the House of Representatives) holding most of the power. It chooses the prime minister and the cabinet. A unique feature in the Japanese constitution is a U.S. imposed antimilitary provision, a feature that is coming under attack both at home and abroad.

France has had a different fate. The unitary, mixed parliamentary-presidential system was created in 1958 to repair the flaw of a weak executive provided for in the previous constitution. The president now dominates as the only nationally elected official who has the unique power to choose the prime minister and the cabinet. The prime minister has combined legislative and executive powers, initiating and administering the policies of the president. Like the U.S., Britain, Japan, and France are well established democracies.

In 1991 the Soviet Union collapsed and splintered into a number of more or less independent republics. These countries are now loosely joined together as the Commonwealth of Independent States. Among the problems that now face the United States is how best to define and further its interests by providing help to the newly emerging governments and economies.

Pacing Chart

Full Year Course: 6 days
One Semester Course: 4 or 5 days

Selected Print and Media Resources

Aganbegyan, Abel. *Inside Perestroika: The Future of the Soviet Economy.* Harper & Row, 1990.

Barry, Donald, D. *Contemporary Soviet Politics.* Prentice Hall, 2nd ed., 1991.

Budge, Ian and David McKay. *The Changing British Political System: Into the 1990s.* Longman, 2nd ed., 1990.

Campbell, Colin, *et al. Politics and Government in Europe Today.* Harcourt Brace Jovanovich, 1990.

Hammer, Darrell P. *The USSR: The Politics of Oligarchy.* Westview Press, 3rd ed., 1990.

Ishida, Takeshi and Ellis S. Krauss. *Democracy in Japan.* University of Pittsburgh Press, 1989.

Milner, Henry. *Sweden: Social Democracy in Practice.* Oxford, 1989.

Safran, William. *The French Polity.* Longman, 3rd ed., 1991.

Sakwa, Richard. *Gorbachev and His Reforms.* Prentice Hall, 1991.

Comparative Political Systems: The United States, The United Kingdom, and the Soviet Union. 3 filmstrips, Social Studies School Service.

An Introduction to Capitalism, Socialism, and Communism. Filmstrips, National Geographic.

Japan. 76 minute video, Focus Media.

Living With Glasnost and Perestroika: Understanding the USSR Today. 60 minute video, Focus Media.

Our Economy: How It Works. 6 separate 18 minute videos, Focus Media.

Simpolicon: Simulation of Political and Economic Development. Computer simulation, Cross Cultural Software.

Understanding the American Economy. 45 minute video, Focus Media.

U.S./Soviet Relations. 4 segments, 30 minutes each, Close Up Foundation.

Note: For additional resources, see *West's American Government Teacher's Resource Binder (TRB).*

WEST'S AMERICAN GOVERNMENT *Updated Edition*

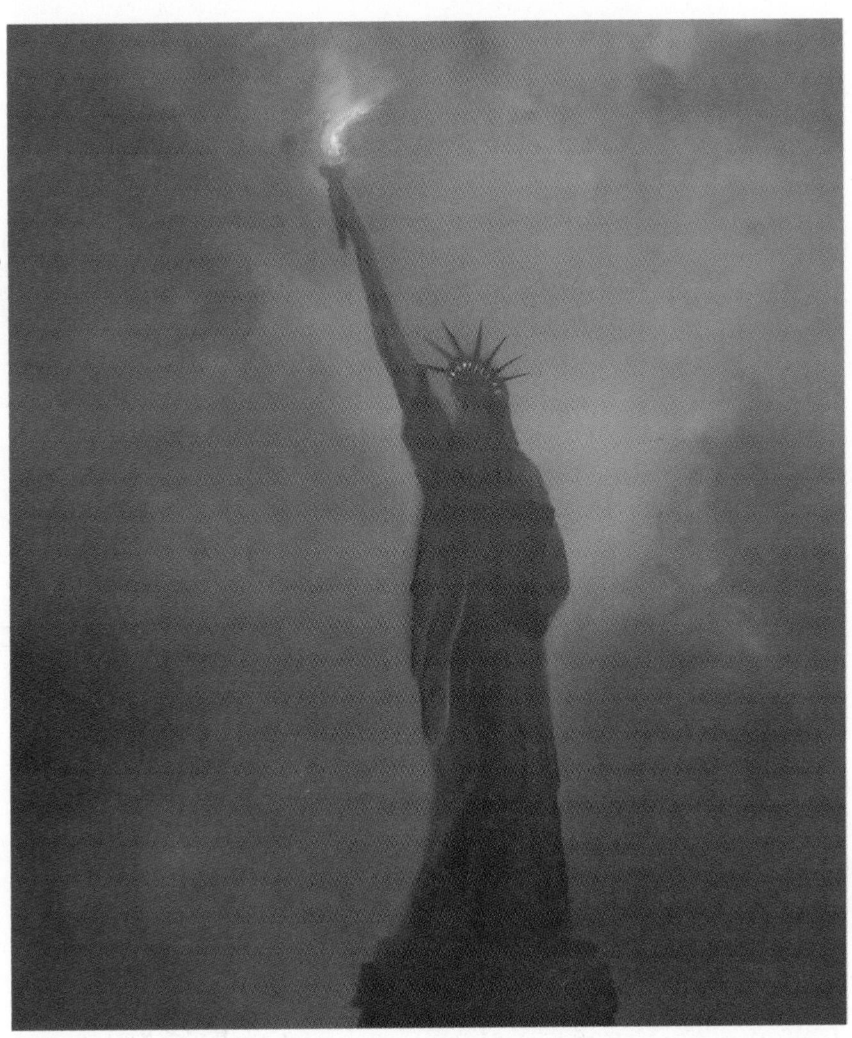

WEST'S AMERICAN GOVERNMENT

ABOUT THE COVER

This 7′×4′ oil painting ''Sweet Liberty'' by George Sumner was created in an effort to raise money for the restoration and centennial celebration of the Statue of Liberty. The artist's interpretation of our symbol of freedom, the torch burning brightly in a world of turmoil, reflects his optimism that peace and freedom will prevail.

Only three contemporary works of art are permanently installed in the museum at the base of the Statue. Sumner was deeply honored to enshrine ''Sweet Liberty'' there as part of the celebration on July 4, 1986.

In his environmental impressionist style, George Sumner continues to strive for the conservation and protection of our planet. He has dedicated ''Sweet Liberty'' to the people of America—in honor of a country and its soul.

West Publishing Company

St. Paul New York San Francisco Los Angeles

WEST'S COMMITMENT TO THE ENVIRONMENT

In 1906, West Publishing Company began recycling materials left over from the production of books. This began a tradition of efficient and responsible use of resources. Today, up to 95 percent of our legal books and 70 percent of our college texts are printed on recycled, acid-free stock. West also recycles nearly 22 million pounds of scrap paper annually—the equivalent of 181,717 trees. Since the 1960s, West has devised ways to capture and recycle waste inks, solvents, oils, and vapors created in the printing process. We also recycle plastics of all kinds, wood, glass, corrugated cardboard, and batteries, and have eliminated the use of styrofoam book packaging. We at West are proud of the longevity and the scope of our commitment to our environment.

610 Opperman Drive
P.O. Box 64526
St. Paul, MN 55164-0526

Printed in the United States of America

99 98 97 96 95 94 93 92 8 7 6 5 4 3 2 1

Library of Congress Cataloging-in-Publication Data

West's American government.
p. cm.
Includes index.
1. United States—Politics and government. I. Title.
JK274.M59 1992
320.973—dc20 91-30900
Student Edition (Updated Edition): 0-314-02373-9
Teacher's Wraparound Edition (Updated Edition): 0-314-02374-7

ART: Miyake Illustration and Design
COMPOSITION: Parkwood Composition Service, Inc.
COVER IMAGE: "Sweet Liberty . . . in honor of a country and its soul" by George Sumner. Original oil 4′×7′ (miniprints available—please contact Sumner Fine Arts, Sausalito, CA).

Acknowledgments

Unit/Chapter Art Credits

Unit One Independence Hall/Bettmann; Trucks/Image Bank; **Chapter 1** Statue of Liberty/Bettmann; **Chapter 2** Independence Hall/Bettmann; **Chapter 4** Trucks/Image Bank; Soldiers/Bettmann; **Unit Two** Martin Luther King/Bettmann; Man on Strike/Black Star/Steve Leonard; Flag Burning/Bettmann; **Chapter 5** Strikers/Black Star/Steve Leonard; Flag Burning/Bettmann; **Chapter 6** Martin Luther King/Bettmann; Indian Woman/Bettmann; **Unit Three** Convention/Black Star/Rick Friedman; Theodore Roosevelt/The Granger Collection, New York; Money/FPG; Ellis Island Immigrants/Bettmann; **Chapter 7** Statue of Liberty/Bettmann; Immigrants/Bettmann; **Chapter 8** Donkey/Bettmann; Elephant/Bettmann; Convention/Black Star/Rick Friedman; Teddy Roosevelt/The Granger Collection, New York; **Chapter 9** National Organization for Women/Black Star/John Troha; Gray Panthers/Black Star/Tom Sobolik; Money/FPG; **Chapter 10** TV/Sony Corporation; Nixon/Kennedy Debate/Bettmann; Campaign Signs/Stock Boston; **Chapter 11** Voting Booth/Bettmann; Suffragettes/Bettmann; **Unit Four** Congress in Session/House of Representatives; Attendance Board/House of Representatives; Man giving speech/Black Star/Dennis Brack; TV/Sony Corporation; **Chapter 12** Foley presiding over House/Sygma/Ron Sachs; New Jersey District Map/State of New Jersey; **Chapter 13** Man giving speech/Black Star/Dennis Brack; Budget meeting/Black Star/Dennis Brack; Impeachment Ticket/The Granger Collection, New York; **Chapter 14** Sample Bill/House of Representatives; Hopper Box/House of Representatives; Attendance Board/House of Representatives; Congress in Session/House of Representatives; TV/Sony Corporation; **Unit Five** Five Presidents/Bettmann; Shuttle Launch/UPI/Bettmann Newsphotos; Nixon's visit to China/UPI/Bettmann; Helicopter/Black Star/Dennis Brack; **Chapter 15** Lincoln Memorial/The Granger Collection, New York; Five Presidents/Bettmann; **Chapter 16** Bush/State of the Union/House of Representatives; Helicopter/Black Star/Dennis Brack; Carter and Panamanian President/Sygma/Tom Zimberoff; Nixon in China/UPI/Bettmann; **Chapter 17** Postal Worker/Black Star/Dennis Brack; Shuttle Launch/UPI/Bettmann Newsphotos; Park Ranger/David Hanover; **Unit Six** Supreme Court Justices/Sygma; John Marshall/Collection of the Curator/Supreme Court; **Chapter 18** John Marshall/Collection of the Curator/Supreme Court; Supreme Court Justices/Sygma; Thurgood Marshall/Supreme Court Historical Society/National Geographic Society; **Unit Seven** United Nations/United Nations/Y. Nagata; Exxon Valdez/Sygma/Alain Keler; Stealth/Sygma; Troops/Reuters/Bettmann—Phillipe Wojazer; Berlin Wall/Sygma/J. Langevin; CIA Seal/Central Intelligence Agency; **Chapter 19** Exxon Valdez/Sygma/Alain Keler; Homeless person/Stock Boston/J. Dunn; **Chapter 20** Troops/Reuters/Bettmann—Phillippe Wojazer; United Nations/United Nations/Y. Nagata; Stealth/Sygma; Berlin Wall/Sygma/J. Langevin; CIA Seal/Central Intelligence Agency; **Unit Eight** Capitol Building/State of Nebraska/Nebraska Land Magazine; Flag/State of Alaska; Flag/State of Illinois; Seal/State of Texas; Court House/Texas Department of Highways and Public Transportation; City Hall & Mayor Dinkins/Sygma/A. Tannenbaum; Mario Cuomo/Office of the Governor of New York; School Children/Black Star/James Suger; Firefighter/Stock Boston/Martin Rogers; **Chapter 21** Capitol (tall one on left)/State of Nebraska/Nebraska Land Magazine; Flag and Seal/State of Nebraska/Nebraska Land Magazine; Flag/State of Illinois; Flag/State of Alaska; State office building/State of Alaska; Constitution and Capitol Building/State of Texas; Texas Flag/Austin American

(Acknowledgments continued following index)

Contents in Brief

PREFACE

You are fortunate to be living in one of the most exciting and challenging periods in history. Political, social, technological, and economic changes are occurring at a faster pace than ever before. Recent events have dramatically altered the face of Europe, Asia, and the world. The empire once called the Soviet Union no longer exists. It has been replaced by a collection of independent republics, some only loosely tied together. Today, news stories are almost instantaneously broadcast around the world, and you can buy computing power in a laptop computer that only 20 years ago would have required equipment that filled an entire room. The impact of these changes has been immediate and wide-ranging, and will undoubtedly have long-lasting effects.

The book you hold in your hands, WEST'S AMERICAN GOVERNMENT, is new. It has been developed to help you understand the fast-changing world in which we all live. It is not just a book of facts, although facts are important. It is not a book of current events, although many of them are used as examples. Rather, you are beginning to read a book that examines the *process* of government and politics. Current events may not remain current for long, but the political process in this country changes very slowly. An understanding of the American political system will serve you well as a point of reference as you strive to understand what is happening elsewhere in the world.

Being informed allows you to enjoy the privileges and understand the responsibilities of citizenship. Knowledge of the Constitution, understanding of how our governmental institutions and the American political system function, and awareness of today's issues are necessary in order for you to make the most of your role as a participant in our living democracy.

In addition to learning about American government and politics, it is also important for you to understand the underlying themes and ideas that are an important part of our American heritage. When the founders, in the Declaration of Independence, stated that all people are created equal and all have the right to life, liberty, and the pursuit of happiness, they were stating the underlying ideals of the American dream. How this dream has changed, been shaped, and expanded is an important theme of this text. Over the course of history, the American dream was forged out of the experiences and hopes of a wide diversity of ethnic groups and cultures. In recent years, this cultural diversity has even been further expanded as America has welcomed many new groups. Incorporating this expanded cultural diversity into American life and making sure that all people have a chance to share the American dream is a challenge for the America of today and certainly of tomorrow.

CONTENTS

Congress of the United States,

OFFICIAL BALLOT

H. RES.

UNIT SIX
The Federal Judicial Branch 428

UNIT SEVEN
American Policy in a Changing World 456

ILLINOIS
WEST
EAST
INTERSTATE
80
INTERSTATE
80
LIMIT

The Daily Press
Trade Gap Widens

THE RESOURCE CENTER

FEATURES

ARCHITECT OF THE AMERICAN DREAM

GOVERNMENT IN ACTION

Citizenship Skills and Responsibilities

Building Social Studies Skills

Challenge to the American Dream

Challenge to the American Dream—Continued

Charts, Tables, Graphs, and Maps

*Unnumbered illustrations appearing in boxed features.

CHARTS, TABLES, GRAPHS, AND MAPS—Continued

WEST'S AMERICAN GOVERNMENT *Updated Edition*

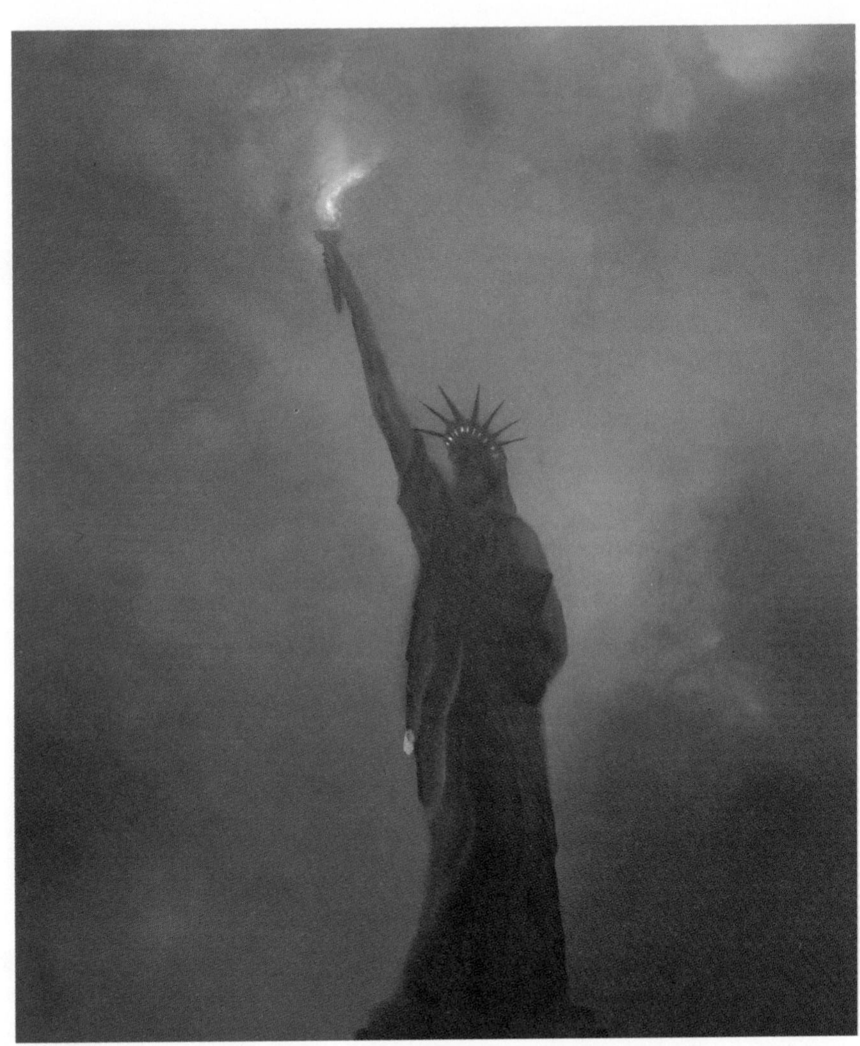

Working with the Videodisc

The text below is from Professor Roger LeRoy Miller's introduction for the motion segment for Unit 1:

Certainly no video, however long, could do justice to explaining the foundations of American democracy. For those foundations date back to early European philosophers who influenced the writers of the Declaration of Independence and of the Constitution. Those foundations date back to the way the average citizen was treated in England prior to the formation of the United States of America. Those foundations also include the political, social, and economic setting of the American colonies, the failure of the Articles of Confederation, and the importance of federalism as it was outlined not only in the Constitution but as it evolved in the years that followed.

To access this segment, use the bar code below or the videodisc index found in the *TRB*.

Frame 3600

UNIT ONE

Foundations of American Democracy

Unit Contents

CHAPTER INTRODUCTION

Instructional Objectives
By the end of this chapter students should be able to:
• Define politics and government and recognize the purposes of government.
• Differentiate between autocracy and democracy.
• Describe the primary principles of democracy.
• Discuss the role of interdependence among nations.

Using the Keynote
Help the students discuss the James Madison quotation by posing questions such as these: What aspects of human nature does government reflect? In what sense are human beings not angels? Why would government be unnecessary if humans were angels? Do you agree with the ideas expressed by Madison? Why or why not?

Introducing the Chapter
Before the students begin reading the Introduction, write this statement on the chalkboard: You must have rules in order to be free. Do the students agree or disagree with this thesis? Why? How can rules make people free? How can rules keep people from being—or feeling—free? Encourage students to share and discuss their responses.

After the students have read the Introduction, help them discuss it by asking questions such as these: In what sense is life in Prosperville chaotic? What specific problems do the people of Prosperville face? How could government help the people solve these problems?

Previewing the Sections

Section 1 Ask the students to find and read the five main headings in this section. Then help students begin to consider the section by asking questions such as these: In your opinion, who should study government and politics? Why should those people study them? What are the benefits of learning about government and politics?
Section 2 Have volunteers find and read aloud the three main headings in Section 2. Help them anticipate what they will read by asking questions such as these: What do you already know about the differences between autocracy and democracy?
Section 3 Ask the students to find and read the three main headings in this section. Then pose questions such as these: How do you think our nation's economy, technology, and environment are related to our form of government? How do you think our economy, technology, and environment affect our nation's relationships to other nations?

CHAPTER 1

Government and the People—The Global Connection

CHAPTER OBJECTIVES

To learn and understand

- The meaning of politics and government and the purposes that government serves.
- The different types of government and the main principles of democracy.
- The challenge of interdependence with other nations.

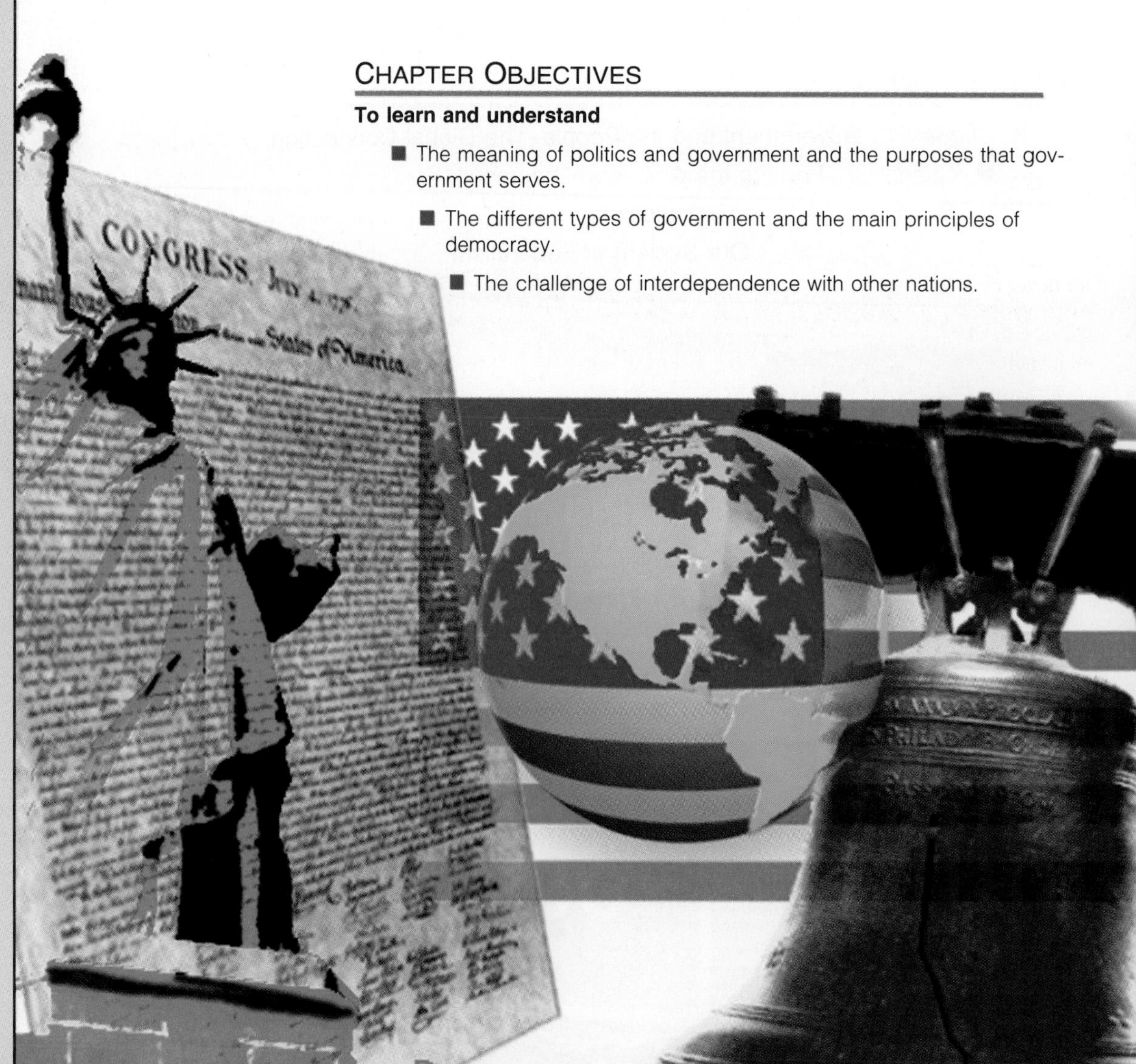

West's American Government Assignment Guide

Activity Sheets
Basic Concepts 1 *TRB* (Reteaching)
Enrichment Activity 1 *TRB*
Building Social Studies Skills 1 *TRB*
Quizzes
Chapter 1 Section 1 Quiz *TRB*
Chapter 1 Section 2 Quiz *TRB*
Chapter 1 Section 3 Quiz *TRB*

Tests
Chapter 1 Test A *TRB*
Chapter 1 Test B *TRB*
Chapter 1 Test Bank *TRB*
Chapter 1 WESTEST Computerized Testing
Social Studies Tool Kit Software
Chapter 1 Activity

SECTION 1

Points to Stress
- The role of social conflict as it relates to politics.
- A definition of politics.
- The characteristics of government.
- The importance of being politically involved.
- List the major purposes of government.
- The salient characteristics of the nation-state.
- The four major theories on the origin of government.

Kickoff Activity
Have students write one or two sentences explaining what they think government is. Then have volunteers read their responses aloud to the rest of the class, and encourage students to discuss the various explanations.

Working with the Preview Questions
Ask volunteers to read the questions aloud, and encourage students to share their responses to these questions before reading the section. Tell students that they should be prepared to answer these questions when they have finished reading the section.

Keynote

"But what is government itself, but the greatest of all reflections on human nature? If men were angels, no government would be necessary."

—— **James Madison**
(1751–1836) Fourth President of the United States

INTRODUCTION

Even at the time James Madison made the above statement over 200 years ago, he was observing what had been apparent for many centuries. People need an organized form of government and a set of rules by which to live. None of us is an angel. As Madison recognized, human nature requires us to have a form of government.

If someone said that you must have rules in order to be free, what would you say? You might disagree. But imagine for a moment what life might be like if there were no government. Consider this news story of an *imaginary* town called Prosperville that grew up almost overnight after the discovery of gold in the early 1900s:

> Many Prosperville citizens have become virtual prisoners in their own homes. Because there are no courts of law in Prosperville, land and property ownership disputes have become impossible to settle. People have begun to take over one another's land by force. Last week there were seven shootings over such disputes. Dishonest people have moved into town; robberies and violent crimes are committed against citizens almost every day. There is no police force to protect the citizens, so people are becoming frightened to walk in the streets. They have begun to carry weapons. Suspected criminals are being lynched by groups of vigilantes. Through fear and misunderstandings, many innocent people have been hanged. There are no schools for the children of Prosperville, and no postal service for its citizens. Because there are no child labor laws, the owners of some of the gold mines are working the children of the poorer families for fourteen hours a day, at ten cents an hour. Because there is no public health officer, plague is spreading throughout the town. There are rumors that a band of desperadoes is riding toward Prosperville to take it over. One citizen, who owns most of the gold mines, has decided to form his own army and name himself mayor. He wants to outlaw all churches except his own and impose a tax on all citizens to build himself a mansion. He has spies in the town working for him to seek out his opponents. People have become suspicious of one another; they have stopped caring about what happens to anyone but themselves.

As you can see from the story of Prosperville, life without government would be chaotic. In fact, government is one of humanity's oldest and most universal institutions. History records very few societies that have existed with no government. In order to live together, people need some form of authority and organization. Thus, as the earliest societies developed, so did the need for government.

SECTION 1

The Meaning of Politics and Government

Preview Questions

- What purposes does government serve?
- What is a nation?
- What are the characteristics of a nation?
- What are the theories regarding the origins of the state?

Politics means many things to many people. To some, politics is an expensive and extravagant game played at election time in Washington, D.C., in state capitols, and in city halls. To others, politics involves all the tactics and maneuvers carried out by the president and Congress. Most formal definitions of politics begin with the notion of **social conflict**—the idea that people in a society disagree over beliefs, values, and what the society's priorities should be. It also includes the idea that conflicts will arise over how the society should use its scarce resources. This conflict is seen as inevitable and

Teaching Strategies

Introduction

Have the students read this section introduction to themselves. Then encourage discussion by posing these questions: What is the difference between politics and government? Can politics exist without government? Why or why not? Can government exist without politics? Why or why not?

Discussion Starter

Help the students discuss politics as "a sideshow on the circus of life." What is a sideshow? Who participates in a sideshow, and who observes it? How significant is a sideshow to the participants? to the observers?

Cooperative Learning

Have students work in groups to brainstorm lists of ways in which they—and others their age—can participate in the political process. Each group should create a poster that summarizes their ideas. Encourage the students to decorate their posters. Hang the posters around the room.

Extension

Help students identify and discuss the policies advocated by blacks, whites, Hispanics, women, and the elderly. What are the particular concerns of each group? How do members of each group express their concerns and work to have their policies adopted? You may also want to have volunteers research and report on special interest organizations formed by members of each group.

natural in any social system. It is not inherently bad. In fact, the process of resolving these conflicts provides good opportunities for positive change.

Political scientist Harold D. Laswell offered a brief but useful definition of **politics:** the process that determines "who gets what, when, and how" in a society. Another political scientist, David Easton, defines politics as "the authoritative allocation of values." Both definitions imply that a set of procedures is needed to resolve the questions of who receives which benefits from society. These benefits may include wealth, status, health care, and higher education. Politics, in this case, encompasses all the activities involved in that process.

There are also many different notions about the meaning of government. A political scientist would define **government** as the individuals and processes that make society's rules about who gets what, and that possess the power and authority to enforce those rules. You might view government as a distant group of politicians who campaign loudly for reelection in your hometown and who debate issues in Washington, D.C. A citizen who has broken the law might view government as an interference, while another elderly citizen might view government as a "rescuer" that provides public services such as transportation, health care, and protection from crime in her neighborhood. Perhaps the best way to understand both politics and government is by understanding how they affect you.

Why Study Government and Politics?

One student of politics maintained that to most Americans politics is "a sideshow on the circus of life." Generally, thinking about government and politics ranks well below family, work, romance, and many other activities. Most of us, however, will at some time in our lives enter the political world. People usually enter that world through many different forms of **political participation.** Voting, the most common form, is only one among many. Discussing politics or watching news programs about the government are other forms.

More and more people with common interests are joining together to participate in politics because they see how government affects their own interests. Blacks, whites, Hispanics, women, and the elderly all advocate policies concerning equality in America. Consumers, farmers, small business owners, and corporation managers all want government to make economic and political decisions that favor their interests. These groups have become involved in politics because they realize how far reaching and long lasting government action can be. They see how profoundly politics touches their everyday lives.

▼ Voter registration drives such as the one shown here encourage citizens to participate in our government through voting. What are some other forms of political participation?

Caption Answer Answers will vary, but might include discussing politics, watching news programs, circulating petitions, serving on juries, etc.

Vocabulary
Ask students: What is apathy? (indifference; lack of interest and commitment) What signs of apathy do you see in your school's government? in your local government? What are the specific results of apathy in school and local government?

Cooperative Learning
Have a group of volunteers work together to explore the government decisions that affect the students' school. How have businesses, parent groups, and others tried to influence those decisions? How effective were their efforts? The group should present its findings in a short oral report.

Discussion Starter
Encourage students to identify and discuss specific examples of political conflict within their school and their local community.

Vocabulary
Focus students' attention on the definitions of power and authority. Then ask: What is the difference between power and authority? What other organizations and individuals have power? How can you tell that they have power? How do they use their power? Which of those organizations and individuals have authority? What is the source of their authority?

▲ Government in its many forms touches our lives on a daily basis. For example, these government inspectors work to ensure that the meat we purchase in supermarkets is safe and of high quality. What are some other ways that government touches our daily lives?

Caption Answer Student answers will vary. You might wish to point out to students that they are currently being affected by government, which requires them to attend school and be educated.

Yet there are many people who say they do not want to be involved in government and politics. These people do not realize that they already are involved. Apathy, or indifference, is as much a political statement as active participation—both positions influence who gets what in society. Good school systems, safe communities, and adequate health standards are the results of political decisions that are influenced by who participates, who is prevented from participating, and who chooses not to participate in government and politics.

Every day of our lives is affected by someone's political choices. The quality of the food you had for breakfast was regulated by a government agency. The cost of the eggs and milk were probably influenced by the government's decisions concerning economic aid to farmers, as well as the farmers' ability to influence government to grant that aid. The quality of the school you attend and the public transportation (or lack of it) in your community are the results of how the government decided to allocate its resources to your city or state.

Thus, the question is not *whether* to become involved in politics and government, but *how* to become involved. The choice is not whether politics and government affect us. They do, and will continue to do so throughout our lives. The choice is how aware we want to be, and how we want to affect politics.

Purposes of Government

The first step in understanding how government works is to understand what it actually does for people and society. Government serves five major purposes: (1) it solves conflicts; (2) it provides public services; (3) it provides for the national security and common defense; (4) it sets goals for public policies; and (5) it preserves culture.

Solving Conflicts Even though people have lived together in groups since the beginning of time, we have not learned how to do so without political conflict—disputes over how to distribute the society's valued resources. These valued resources, such as property, are limited, while people's wants are unlimited. This imbalance creates conflict, and as a result, people need ways to determine who wins and who loses, and how to get the losers to accept that decision. Who has the legitimate power and authority to make these decisions? This is where government steps in.

Governments decide how conflicts will be resolved so that public order can be maintained. Governments have **power**—the ability to influence the behavior of others. Power is getting someone to do something he or she would not do otherwise. Power may involve force

Critical Thinking Skills
Guide students in analyzing the quotation from Abraham Lincoln: What main idea did Lincoln express? In what context do you imagine Lincoln was speaking? Is his idea as relevant today as it was when he expressed it? Why or why not?

Discussion Starter
Ask students why defense has become so expensive and complex. How has the United States responded to the new demands on our national defense structure? How have other major world powers responded? How have other, less powerful countries responded?

Enrichment
Ask students to work in pairs or small groups to research the societal goals set by the governments of other countries. You might wish to assign a country to each group. Then allow students to share their findings in short oral reports. Students can use the world map found in the Resource Center in choosing their nations.

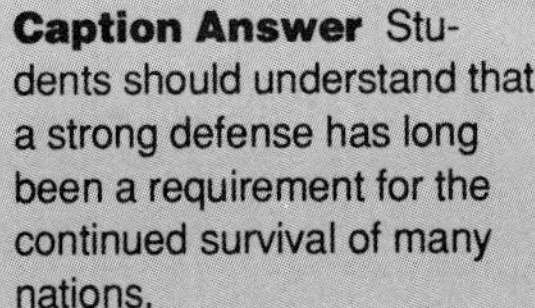

Caption Answer Students should understand that a strong defense has long been a requirement for the continued survival of many nations.

Providing for the common defense can be very expensive. For instance, a great deal of money is required to buy military hardware such as this vehicle used by the United States Army during Operation Desert Storm in 1991. Why do you think defense matters have been given such a high priority throughout history?

(often called coercion), or persuasion, or reward. Governments also have **authority**—legitimate power. In this case, legitimate means even more than legal—it implies moral correctness and a collective recognition and acceptance of this authority. Power and authority are central to government's ability to resolve conflicts by making and enforcing laws, placing limits on what people can do, and developing court systems to make final decisions.

Providing Public Services Another purpose of government is to distribute benefits and provide essential services that people cannot carry out alone. Governments undertake projects that individuals usually would not or could not do on their own, such as building and maintaining roads, providing welfare programs, operating public schools, and preserving national parks. Governments also provide such services as law enforcement, fire protection, and public health and safety programs. As Abraham Lincoln once said:

> The legitimate object of government is to do for a community of people whatever they need to have done but cannot do at all, or cannot so well do for themselves in their separate and individual capacities. But in all that people can individually do for themselves, government ought not to interfere.

Providing for National Security and Common Defense Governments also provide for a nation's security and for common defense against attack from other nations. Historically, defense matters have always been given high priority by governments and have demanded considerable time, effort, and expense. In the twentieth century, however, national defense has become an especially expensive and complex activity for almost every government in the world.

The government of the United States provides for common defense and security with its Army, Navy, Air Force, Marines, and Coast Guard. The State Department, Defense Department, Central Intelligence Agency (CIA), and other agencies also contribute to this defense network. As part of an ongoing policy of national security, many departments and agencies in the federal government are constantly dealing with other nations. The Constitution gives our national government exclusive power over relations with foreign nations. No individual state can negotiate a treaty with a foreign nation.

Setting Goals for Public Policies Governments set goals meant to improve the lives of their citizens. These goals may affect the people on a local, state, or national scale. Upon setting these goals, governments design plans of action, known as **public policies,** to support or achieve these goals.

There are many issues on which government must make public policy choices. These public policy goals may be short term, such as improving a city's education system by adding new classes, or long term, such as discovering new energy sources. Political and social goals for the United States might include decisions to launch an orbiting space station by the year 2000, to eliminate discrimination against Americans with disabilities, or to clean up the environment in the 1990s.

Preserving Culture A nation's culture includes the customs, language, beliefs, and values of its people.

Critical Thinking Skills
Help students consider the particular problems faced by the government of the United States in preserving the nation's culture. What differences in customs, language, beliefs, and values can you identify? How do those differences affect daily life? What decisions does our government appear to have made regarding those differences?

Enrichment
Have a group of volunteers research and report on the specific form of government in your city or town. Ask the group to present their finding in a poster that explains the form of government.

Comprehension
Ask students to distinguish between the government of a nation and the government of a city or a state. Then ask students to distinguish between the government of a nation and the government of an international body, such as the United Nations.

Enrichment
Ask a volunteer to read the footnote at the bottom of this page. Have a group of volunteers research the distinction between this definition of nation and a second definition, which defines a *nation* as "a group of like people." The volunteers should identify several nations that include more than one group of like people; they should also be prepared to discuss the problems and special situations such nation may face. Ask the volunteers to share the results of their research with the entire class.

Extension
Help students consider what can happen when a group of people without territory attempts to form its own nation. Students should be able to identify specific groups that have made such an attempt: What motivated these people? How did existing nation-states react? Why?

Governments have worked to preserve their nation's culture in ways that citizens cannot. For example, the observance of Independence Day and Thanksgiving in the United States helps carry on a tradition that celebrates our history. In France, Bastille Day is celebrated every July 14th. In the People's Republic of China, National Day is celebrated October 10. Perhaps the ultimate way that governments preserve their national culture and way of life is through defending it against force or attack by other nations that wish to impose their wills on others.

The Nation

Governments exist to serve citizens in the many ways outlined above, but where are governments actually found? You probably have a student government in your school that helps make decisions and rules for your student body. Your city has a government that makes decisions for its local residents. The largest group of people served by a government is the body of people living within a nation. A **nation** is a particular geographic boundary within which an organized government makes and enforces laws *without the approval of a higher authority.*[1]

Characteristics of Nations

Today there are over 170 different nations in the world and no two are the same. Each one has its unique geographical, economic, cultural, and linguistic features. To be a nation, however, they must have four fundamental characteristics: territory, population, sovereignty, and government.

Territory Obviously, a nation must start out with some land on which its people can live and the boundaries of the state must be recognized by other nations. The total area of the United States is 3,615,122 square miles (9,363,123 square kilometers). The People's Republic of China covers 3,691,502 square miles (9,560,990 square kilometers). Both the United States and China have expanded their territory since they were first established. Other nations, such as Mexico, have diminished in size since their beginning.

Recognizing the location of political boundaries between nations is often a source of conflict and has led to many wars throughout history. Wars have also resulted when nations have attempted to take over the territory of other nations. Sometimes stronger nations come to the aid of weaker ones who are invaded. This is what happened when the United States sent troops to the Middle East in reaction to the Iraqi invasion of Kuwait in 1990.

Population A nation contains people who occupy its territory. The number of persons living within each nation varies, ranging from several thousand in Luxembourg to over a billion in the People's Republic of China. The population of the United States is over 250 million.

▼ Indonesia, shown here, is one of over 170 different nations in the world today. What are the four fundamental characteristics of a nation?

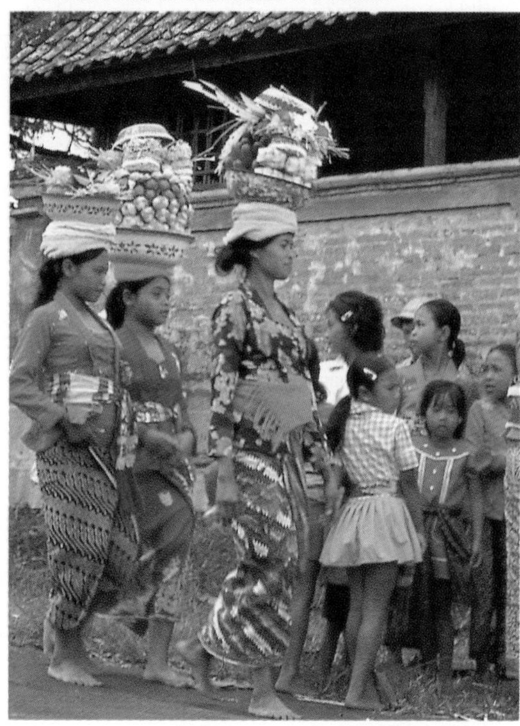

Caption Answer The four fundamental characteristics of a nation are territory, population, sovereignty, and government.

1. Note that the word *state* and the word *nation* are commonly interchanged in conventional usage. *Webster's Ninth New Collegiate Dictionary* defines *state* as "a politically organized body of people usually occupying a definite territory; especially one that is sovereign," and defines *nation* as "a community of people composed of one or more nationalities and possessing a more or less defined territory and government." For the purposes of clarity we will use *nation* to refer to sovereign nations, such as Mexico or Japan, and use *state* only to refer to states in the United States of America, such as Oregon or Texas.

Enrichment
Have volunteers identify the wars in which the United States (including the original colonies) has been engaged throughout its history. What questions of sovereignty were raised in these wars? How were those questions of sovereignty resolved?

Discussion Starter
What does Otto von Bismark's statement mean? What did he mean by "blood and iron"? How do you imagine the German people reacted to Bismark's idea? How do you imagine the people in neighboring countries reacted?

Caption Answer Students should understand that a British painter might not have depicted the signers of the Declaration of Independence in the same heroic light as did Trumbull. At this point you might wish to discuss with the students the fact that popular art and culture often reflect the prevailing mood of the country. As an extension assignment, you might ask several students to research and report on the similarities and differences between art from the American Revolution and art from the Russian Revolution of 1917.

Observable Mastery
Compile a long list of nations and organizations, such as Brazil, the U.N., Sudan, the PLO, Poland, the IRA, Japan, GM, etc. Have students demonstrate that they can classify each as a nation or not using the criteria from the text.

Cooperative Learning
Have students work in small groups to consider the two major forms of government. Assign each group one government form, and have group members brainstorm the advantages of that kind of government. Then have all the students share and discuss their ideas.

Critical Thinking Skills
Guide students in considering the theories proposed to explain the existence of states: How do you think these theories were developed? What facts might be used to support each theory? Do you imagine that a single theory will ever be proved? widely accepted? Why or why not?

Vocabulary
Ask students to recall the most familiar definition of *evolution.* How does this definition help explain the meaning of the term *evolutionary theory?*

This painting of the signers of the Declaration of Independence was done by John Trumbull. Trumbull, who served as a soldier in the Continental Army during the War for Independence, was known as "The Patriot Painter." How might a British painter of the same period have depicted this scene?

Sovereignty The essential feature that determines a nation is **sovereignty**—the right, power, and authority to govern its own people. A nation has complete authority to determine its form of government, its economic and legal systems, and its foreign policy. The United States claimed sovereignty in 1776 through the Declaration of Independence, when it severed any dependence or ties with Great Britain.

Where the sovereignty is located—who holds the power within a nation—is extremely important. Some nations are ruled by one person or a small group of people. As you will learn, in a democratic government the people hold the power and are sovereign.

Government Every nation has some form of political organization through which public policies are made and enforced. Most nations have several levels of government, which operate according to an overall plan. Most governments today have either a unitary or federal system of government. A **unitary government** is one in which all authority is vested in the central government. A **federal government,** such as in the United States, divides its powers and authority between national and state governments. A third type of government is a confederate government made up of a group of independent states. You will learn more about these systems in Chapter 4.

How Did Government Begin?

What factors first brought about the existence of governments? This question has been examined and debated for many centuries by political thinkers and historians. Over the years, many theories have been proposed, but none provides conclusive answers. Nonetheless, several of these theories have been widely discussed.

Evolutionary The **evolutionary theory** holds that government developed gradually, step by step. The first stage of human political development was the primitive family, usually headed by the father. Over a period of many years, families joined together and worked cooperatively for protection. The units gradually grew from clans to tribes. Usually one of the older males (or a group of males) led the tribe and was looked upon to make decisions and resolve conflicts between members. As the years went by, the number of families involved grew and the ''government'' became larger and more formalized. These groups eventually gave up the nomadic life and settled down to an agricultural existence.

Force According to the **force theory,** governments first originated when strong persons or groups conquered territories, and then forced everyone living in those territories to submit to their will. Then, **institutions**—police, courts, and tax collectors—were created to make people work and to collect all or part of what they produced for the conquerors. The first leader of the German Empire, Otto von Bismark, said in 1862 that ''the great questions of our day cannot be solved by speeches and majority votes . . . but by blood and iron.'' Obviously, Bismark was a strong proponent of the force theory of government.

Divine Right Prior to the eighteenth century, the theory of divine right was widely accepted in Europe (and in ancient Egypt, China, Greece, and Rome). The **divine right theory** held that God gave those of royal birth the unlimited right to govern other men and women—the ''divine right'' to rule. According to this theory, only God could judge those of royal birth. Thus, all citizens

TEACHING GOVERNMENT IN ACTION

Read
Introduce this Case Study by asking students to share their ideas about the definition of *revolution.* Then have a volunteer read the Case Study aloud to the rest of the class.

Discuss
Encourage students to share and discuss their responses to these questions: What made the events of 1776 a revolution? Do you think that the United States (as we know it) could have been created without a revolution? If so, how? If not, why not?

Analyze and Apply
Ask students to imagine discussions among colonists considering whether or not to support and participate in the American Revolution of 1776. Encourage students to discuss ideas that might be presented to support both sides. Then have each student write a scene in which three or more colonists talk about what they plan to do and why they made those decisions.

Review
Help students review the Case Study by posing these questions: What distinguishes a revolution from other changes in government? What usually causes groups of people to support and participate in a revolution? Where and when did two of the important revolutions of the Western world take place?

Think About It (Answers)
1. Answers will vary, e.g., a revolution of ideas might mean a drastic rethinking of a situation. A revolution of ideas might begin in a large group of people in a country with serious economic or social problems or inequalities (such as the former Soviet Union). Such a revolution of ideas by a large group in a nation's population might lead to a revolution for political change.
2. Answers will vary, e.g., revolutions occur when the people are repressed and no methods are provided for expression or change. The United States is a democracy and governed by the will of the people. If the people want change, our government was designed to be flexible and responsive to these demands. While there have been drastic changes in the U.S. government that can only be described as revolutionary (e.g., the end of slavery, the women's movement, the civil rights movement, etc.), they have been accomplished without overthrowing the structure or system of government.

CASE STUDY

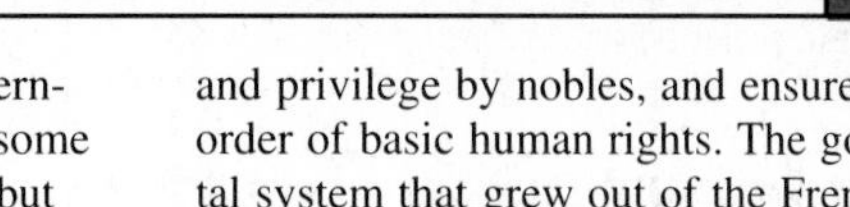

The French Revolution

GOVERNMENT IN ACTION

Not all countries have as stable a government as we do in the United States. And some countries that do were not always stable, but in fact were created out of revolutions.

A drastic change in a government can be a **revolution.** In a revolution, a government is overthrown by force and a new government is established. Revolutions often occur when many people in a society believe that the government and economy are not meeting their needs.

One of the most important revolutions in the Western world was the French Revolution, which began as a popular uprising in 1789. The result was the overthrow of the monarchy (rulership by a king or queen) of Louis XVI. The causes for the popular uprising were excessively high taxes on the working classes relative to the exceedingly low taxes on the nobility and the Church. In Paris, rebels armed themselves heavily and stormed the Bastille, a prison that had formerly held many famous political dissidents, on July 14, 1789. The uprising was successful and a new constitution was written in 1791. It eliminated the old order, which had created inequality and privilege by nobles, and ensured a new order of basic human rights. The governmental system that grew out of the French Revolution is credited with being the model of popular sovereignty and civil equality that rapidly spread throughout Europe.

As you know, the United States was created by a revolution in 1776. Americans have disagreed sharply over many issues since then. We have even suffered through a nearly devastating civil war. But we have never had to face another revolution. We are fortunate that our government was designed to be flexible and responsive to the demands of its citizens.

THINK ABOUT IT

1. Sometimes journalists and social commentators talk about a revolution in *ideas.* Does the term *revolution* in such a phrase have anything to do with the term *revolution* as applied to political change?
2. Why is a revolution virtually impossible in the United States today?

The United States' War for Independence is often credited as being an inspiration for the French Revolution. What is one way in which the French Revolution, as depicted in this painting, differed from our War for Independence?

Caption Answer Student answers will vary but should reflect an understanding of the fact that the War for Independence basically involved battles to free the colonists from the authority of the government in Britain. As such, there were no mass executions of those in power as occurred in the French Revolution.

Enrichment
Have each student research the life and works of John Locke, Thomas Hobbes, or Jacques Rousseau. Ask students to share their findings in written or oral reports.

Comprehension
Have students discuss or write their responses to these questions: What is a social contract? When and how do people enter into a social contract?

and that possess the power and authority to enforce those rules. Government (1) resolves conflicts (2) provides public services (3) provides for national security and the common defense (4) sets goals for public policies (5) preserves culture.
2. Territory, population, sovereignty, and government.
3. Evolutionary theory holds that government developed gradually. Force theory holds that strong persons conquered territories and forced others living in those territories to submit to their will. Divine right theory holds that God gave those of royal birth the unlimited right to govern. Social Contract theory holds that people are born with natural rights and would form a sort of social contract with government to voluntarily give up some of their freedoms in order to gain the benefits of orderly government.
4. Answers will vary, e.g., education, medical services, recycling, parcel delivery.

SECTION 2

Points to Stress
- Explain the meaning of autocracy.
- The types of monarchies; the types of dictatorships.
- The differences between monarchy and dictatorship.

Figure Answer Absolute monarchs built their power around the divine right theory that God gave those of royal birth the unlimited right to rule.

This figure content is also featured on *West's American Government Videodisc* (see the index found in the *TRB*) and is available in the transparency package.

Reteaching Strategies
1. Have the students work with partners to list (from the text) five major purposes of government. Then ask the partners to list at least two specific actions a government might take in fulfilling each purpose.
2. Work with groups of students to discuss the following places: British Columbia, the Southwest, Mexico, Central America, Japan, Hawaii, the Middle East. Which are nation-states? What makes them nation-states? Which are not nation-states? Why?

Evaluation Strategies
1. Have the students write their answers to the Section 1 Review questions.
2. Have the students take the Section 1 Quiz found in the *TRB*.

Section 1 Review (Answers)
1. Government consists of the individuals and processes that make society's rules about who gets what,

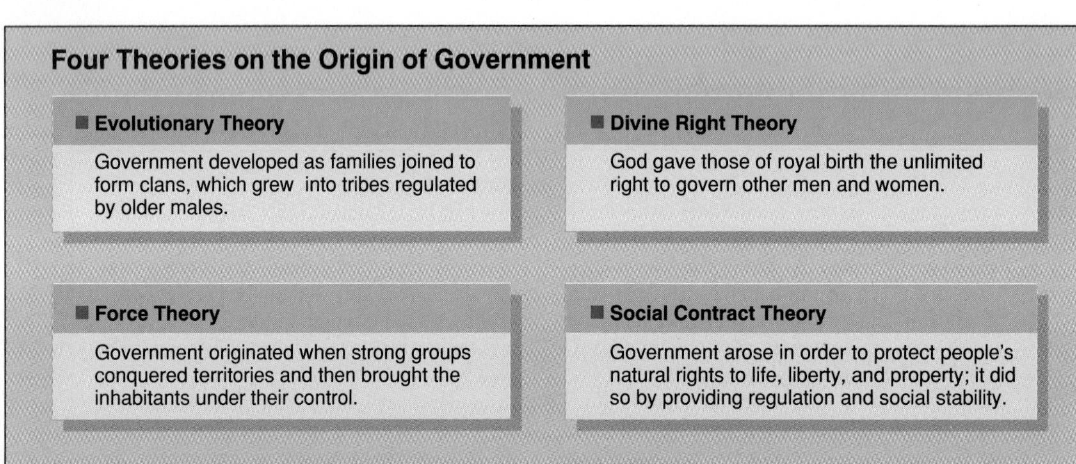

Four Theories on the Origin of Government
Evolutionary Theory
Government developed as families joined to form clans, which grew into tribes regulated by older males.
Divine Right Theory
God gave those of royal birth the unlimited right to govern other men and women.
Force Theory
Government originated when strong groups conquered territories and then brought the inhabitants under their control.
Social Contract Theory
Government arose in order to protect people's natural rights to life, liberty, and property; it did so by providing regulation and social stability.

▲ **FIGURE 1–1 Four Theories on the Origin of Government.** The figure above lists four widely discussed theories of how government developed. Which theory would an absolute monarch be most likely to support?

were bound to obey their monarchs, no matter how unfair or unjust they seemed to be.

Social Contract The **social contract theory** was developed in the seventeenth and eighteenth centuries by philosophers such as John Locke and Thomas Hobbes in England, and Jean-Jacques Rousseau in France. According to this theory, individuals voluntarily agree with one another to create a government and in so doing give to that government adequate power to secure the mutual protection and welfare of all individuals. John Locke, one writer who particularly influenced the American colonists, argued that people are born with **natural rights** to life, liberty, and property that no government can take away. He theorized that the purpose of government was to protect natural rights and that any government that abused its power by interfering with those rights should not be obeyed. Human beings, he asserted, would voluntarily give up some of their freedoms in order to gain the benefits of orderly government. The unwritten means by which they did this was a social contract.

Locke's theories greatly influenced many of the leaders in the American Revolution. Benjamin Franklin, James Madison, and Thomas Jefferson were all followers of Locke. His thoughts and even some of his exact words were used in the Declaration of Independence and in the Constitution. Locke's thoughts also influenced many people in France. Like the leaders of the American Revolution, these people found that they had to fight to win popular sovereignty. (See the case study on page 9.)

Section 1 Review

1. What is government and what purposes does it serve?
2. What are the characteristics of a nation?
3. What are the theories regarding the origin of government?
4. **For critical analysis:** Government in the United States provides many services. What are some services that are currently provided both by government and by business and industry? (Hint: One example is medical care.)

Section 2

How Do Governments Differ from One Another?

Preview Questions
- What are the main differences among the various types of government?
- What is the difference between a direct and an indirect democracy?

Through the centuries, governments have been organized in many different ways. A government's structure is influenced by a number of factors such as history, customs, values, geography, climate, resources, and human experiences and needs. No two nations have exactly

- Explain the meaning of democracy.
- The various types of democracies.
- The differences between direct and indirect democracy.
- The major principles of democracy.

Kickoff Activity

Write these questions on the chalkboard: Who makes the rules and laws in this country? Who makes the rules and laws in other countries? Have students write their responses, including as much detail as possible. Then encourage students to share and discuss their ideas.

Working with the Preview Questions

Have a volunteer read the study questions aloud. Ask the students to keep a simple chart as they read the section, noting the main differences between the different types of government.

Teaching Strategies

Introduction

After the students have read the section introduction, encourage them to discuss their responses to these questions: Why do no two nations have exactly the same form of government? What factors might cause similarities among forms of government? What factors might cause differences among forms of government?

Cooperative Learning

Have students work in small groups to identify specific monarchs about whom they have read or heard. Within a limited period of time (such as five minutes) have group members work together to list as many kings, queens, emperors, empresses, and tsars as possible. Then let group members review the list and identify each individual as an absolute monarch or a constitutional monarch.

Enrichment

Ask volunteers to collect news articles and photographs depicting the activities of modern constitutional monarchs. Have the volunteers share their collection with the rest of the class, and encourage students to draw conclusions about the functions and responsibilities of modern monarchs.

Vocabulary

Ask students to recall and define other words that come from the Greek root *demos* or the Greek root *kratia.*

Observable Mastery

Make two columns on a blackboard or transparency with the titles "Autocratic" and "Democratic." Provide a list of nations that students must correctly place in one of the two columns. If students disagree allow them to discuss their rationale.

Discussion Starter

What is the most important difference between an absolute monarch and a dictator? Would the life of an average citizen be more comfortable under the rule of an absolute monarch or the rule of a dictator? Encourage students to explain and discuss their responses.

the same form of government. Over time, however, political analysts have developed different descriptions designed to classify different systems of governments. One of the most meaningful ways of classifying governments is according to *who* governs. Who has the power to make the rules and laws that all must obey?

Rule By One: Autocracy

In an **autocracy,** the power and authority of the government is in the hands of a single person. In ancient times, autocracy was one of the most common forms of government (and still exists in some parts of the world). These autocrats usually obtained their power either by inheriting it (as in the divine right theory of monarchy) or by using force.

Monarchy One form of autocracy, known as a **monarchy,** is government by a king, queen, emperor, empress, or tsar. The monarch, usually acquiring his or her power through inheritance, is the highest authority in the government. Historically, most monarchies have been **absolute monarchies,** in which rulers held complete and unlimited power. They claimed that their right to absolute power came from God. Challenging this power meant not only treason against the government, but was regarded as a sin against God.

Most modern monarchies, however, are **constitutional monarchies,** in which kings or queens share governmental power with elected lawmakers. Their power is limited, or checked, by other government leaders and by constitutions. In most cases, the people themselves elect these leaders to office. Constitutional monarchs, such as those in Great Britain, Denmark, and Sweden, serve mainly as *ceremonial* leaders of their governments.

Dictatorship Another form of autocracy is a **dictatorship,** in which a single leader rules, although *not* through inheritance. Dictatorships are **authoritarian,** meaning the dictator can use arbitrary power and is not subject to constitutional limitations. He or she is also not responsible to voters or to their elected representatives. Changes in leadership can only come about by voluntary resignation, death, or forcible overthrow.

Dictatorships can also be **totalitarian,** which means the leader (or group of leaders) seeks to control almost all aspects of social and economic life. The needs of the nation come before the needs of individuals and all citizens must work for the common goals established by the government. Examples of this form of government include Adolf Hitler's government in Nazi Germany from 1933 to 1945, Benito Mussolini's rule in Italy from 1922 to 1943, and Josef Stalin's rule in the Soviet Union from 1929 to 1953. More contemporary examples include Saddam Hussein in Iraq and Fidel Castro in Cuba.

BENT OFFERINGS By Don Addis

ABSOLUTE MONARCHY MEANS NEVER HAVING TO SAY YOU'RE SORRY
© 1991 Creators Syndicate, Inc.
don addis
10-1

Rule by Many: Democracy

The most familiar form of government to Americans is **democracy,** in which the supreme political authority rests with the people. The word democracy comes from the Greek *demos,* meaning "the people," and *kratia,* meaning "rule." The main idea of democracy is that government exists only by the consent of the people, and reflects the will of the majority.

The Athenian Model of Direct Democracy Democracy as a form of government began long ago. In its purest form, direct democracy was practiced in Athens and other ancient Greek city-states about 2,500 years ago. **Direct democracy** exists when the will of the people is directly translated into public policy. While some consider the Athenian form of direct democracy ideal because it demanded a high degree of participation, others point out that only nonslave males were allowed to participate.

Clearly, direct democracy is possible only in small communities in which citizens can meet in a chosen place

Critical Thinking Skills
Guide the students in analyzing direct democracy as an ideal form. How does direct democracy as practiced in ancient Athens compare to democracy as practiced in our communities? Do citizens of the United States still consider direct democracy an ideal? Why or why not?

Enrichment
Ask groups of volunteers to read about nations with presidential democracies and nations with parliamentary democracies. Where are the two forms of representative democracy practiced? What are the most important differences between the two forms? Have the volunteers share their findings in oral reports to the class.

Critical Thinking Skills
Have students discuss and analyze the quotation from Abraham Lincoln: What does this concept imply about the duties and responsibilities of citizens within a democracy? What can happen if citizens do not accept those duties and responsibilities?

Caption Answer The Athenian model of direct democracy is often lauded as the ideal form of democracy because it required each citizen to participate in the governing process.

Discussion Starter
Have students discuss their responses to these questions: Can you cite any examples of direct democracy within your school or local government? If so, how does the direct democracy function? How effective is it? What examples of representative democracy can you cite within your school or local government? How are the representatives selected? To whom are they responsible? How effective do the students or citizens consider their representatives?

▲ The New England town meeting is a form of direct democracy. Why was direct democracy in Athens considered to have been an ideal form of democracy?

and decide key issues and policies. Some New England town meetings and a few of the smaller political subunits, or cantons, of Switzerland still use a modified form of direct democracy.

Representative Democracy Although our founders were aware of the Athenian model and agreed with the idea of government based on the consent of the governed, many feared that a pure, direct democracy would deteriorate into mob rule. They believed that large groups of people meeting together would ignore the rights and opinions of people in the minority, and would lead to decisions being made without careful thought. For this reason, they thought that a representative democracy would enable public decisions to be made in a calmer and more fair manner.

In a **representative democracy** (also called **indirect democracy**), the will of the majority is expressed through a smaller group of individuals elected by the people to act as their representatives. These representatives are elected by the people, are responsible to the people for their conduct, and can be voted out of office. Our founders preferred to use the term **republic,** which is essentially the same as a representative democracy. As our population has grown, this republic has become increasingly removed from the Athenian model, as you will learn by reading Challenge to the American Dream on page 18.

Presidential and Parliamentary Democracy In the modern world there are two forms of representative democracy: presidential and parliamentary. A **presidential democracy** is one in which the law-making and law-implementing branches of government are separate. For example, in the United States, Congress is charged with the power to make laws and the president is charged with the power to carry them out. In a **parliamentary democracy** the law-making and law-implementing branches of government overlap. In England, for example, the Prime Minister and the Cabinet are members of the legislature and enact the laws as well as carry them out.

Principles of Democracy

> This country, with all its institutions, belongs to the people who inhabit it. Whenever they shall grow weary of the existing government, they can exercise their constitutional right of amending it, or their revolutionary right to dismember or overthrow it.

With these words, Abraham Lincoln underscored the most fundamental concept of American government: that the people, not the government, are ultimately in control.

Extension

Have the students study figure 1–2, Forms of Government. Then have students make their own version of this figure on poster paper. Have students add to their forms of government chart by providing real world examples for each form of government. For example, under Historical Absolute Monarchy, students might list King Henry VIII (England) 1500s. Each should include a name, country, and approximate date for each example. After the students have completed their charts, allow the students to present and explain their work to the class.

This figure content is also featured on *West's American Government Videodisc* (see the index found in the *TRB*) and is available in the transparency package.

Figure Answer The United States government is a presidential democracy in which the people elect representatives and a president.

FIGURE 1–2 Forms of Government. While no two nations have exactly the same form of government, most governments can be described by one of the models in the figure below. Which of the models best describes the United States government?

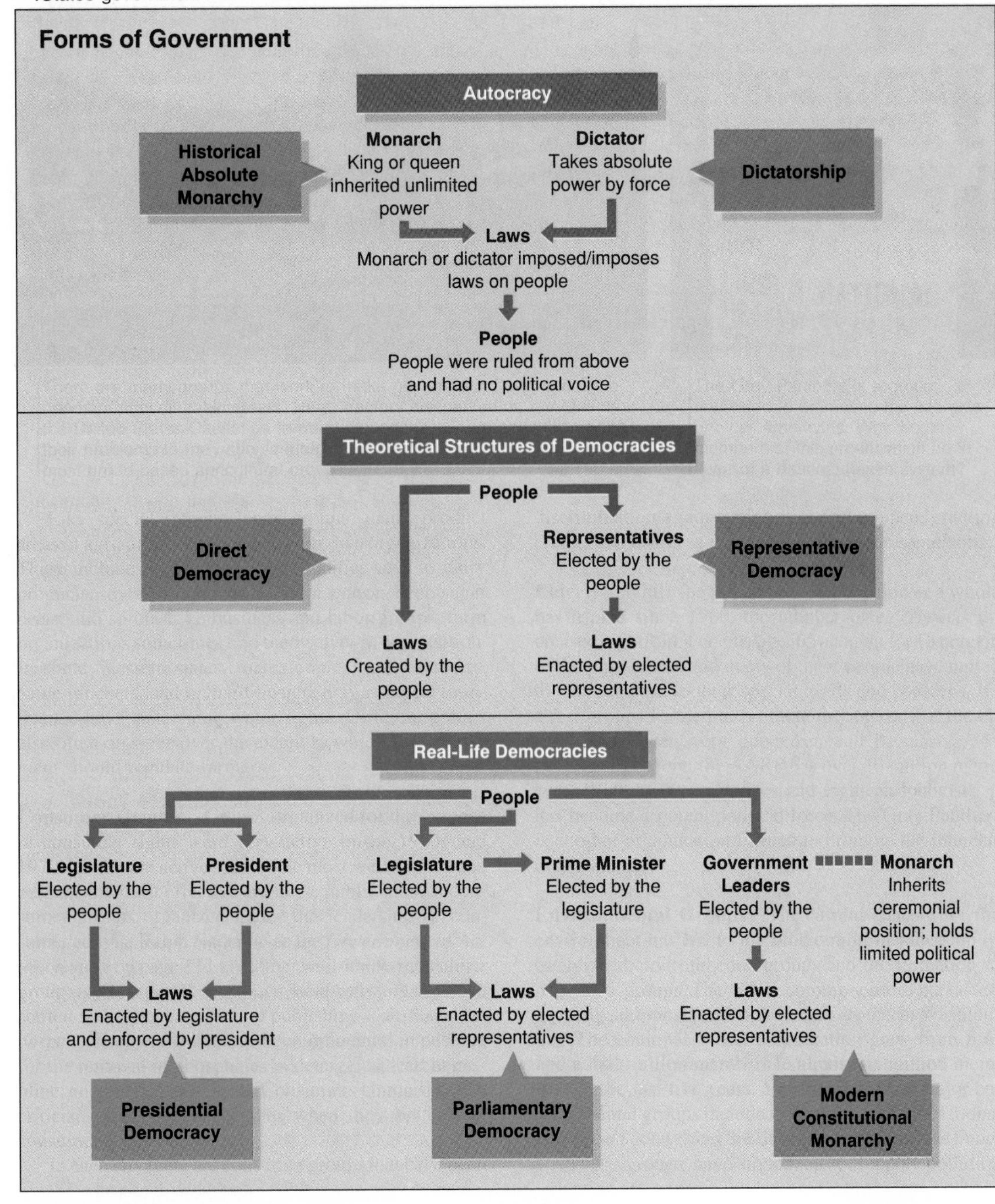

Service Learning Activity

The popular phrase "think globally, act locally" has immediate political ramifications for students.

Have students visit or interview people in agencies who are responsible for the implementation or enforcement of environmental standards (i.e., municipal sanitation officials or the nearest branch of the state or federal EPA). Have students discover the various local environmental challenges that these people face, and have students acquire information concerning the level of citizen participation in these matters. Students could evaluate the degree to which people use the skills listed in the "Citizenship Skills and Responsibilities" activity.

TEACHING CITIZENSHIP SKILLS AND RESPONSIBILITIES

Read
Begin by asking the students to share their ideas about citizenship: What does it mean? What rights does it bestow? What responsibilities does it involve? Then have the students read the Citizenship Skills section to themselves.

Discuss
Pose these questions for class discussion: Do you think most people in this country value their citizenship? What signs do you see that people do—or do not—value their citizenship? What benefits do you think people gain from learning and practicing citizenship skills?

Analyze and Apply
Have students work in groups to list at least ten specific actions they can take to learn and practice citizenship skills.

Review
Help students review Citizenship Skills by posing these questions: Who should learn and practice citizenship skills? Why is it important for all citizens to become involved in government? Which citizenship skill do you consider most important? Why?

Reteaching Strategies
1. Have the students bring to class short articles or news stories about life in autocracies. Let students discuss these articles in small groups: What details show that the government is an autocracy? How does this form of government seem to affect the citizens?
2. Have students imagine that their class is about to form its own government. How would the government be set up if it were to be a direct democracy? How would the government be set up if it were to be a representative democracy? Let each student write short descriptions of the two processes.

Evaluation Strategies
1. Have the students write their answers to the Section 2 Review questions.
2. Have the students take the Section 2 Quiz found in the *TRB.*

Section 2 Review (Answers)
1. In a monarchy, the monarch acquires his or her power through inheritance. In a dictatorship, a single leader rules but *not* through inheritance. Dictatorships are authoritarian, meaning the dictator gains power by using force, either through a military victory or by overthrowing another dictator.
2. Direct democracy exists when the will of the people is directly translated into public policy at mass meetings. Our founders agreed with the idea of government based on the consent of the governed, but believed that direct democracy would deteriorate into mob rule. They believed that the rights and opinions of people in the minority would be ignored.
3. In an indirect or representative democracy the will of the majority is expressed through a smaller group

CITIZENSHIP SKILLS AND RESPONSIBILITIES
The Duties of Citizenship

Americans are citizens of a democracy. As you have learned, democracy is government by the people, and citizen involvement is at the heart of democracy. If only a few people decided to become involved in government, public decisions would be left to those few. Such a government would no longer be an effective democracy. Being a citizen in a democratic society requires learning certain skills, some of which include:

1. **Acquiring and using information.** Citizens must know how to find answers to important questions. They do this by reading books, magazines, and government publications, and by using radio and television media. They must know how to ask questions, write letters, and make telephone calls to obtain the information they need. Throughout this book, you will be learning how to gather and use various types of information.
2. **Making decisions.** Citizens need to recognize that there may be more than one solution to any given problem. They must be able to evaluate alternatives and be familiar with the decision-making process.
3. **Making sound judgments.** In order to make sound judgments, citizens must distinguish between fact and opinion, recognize their own biases and values, see both sides of an issue, and identify irrelevant and ambiguous information.
4. **Communicating.** Citizens must be able to express their views and communicate their ideas effectively, both in writing and in speaking.
5. **Cooperating.** Citizens must be able to work together to achieve common goals.

These and many other specific citizenship skills are reviewed throughout this book.

TAKING ACTION

1. Choose a current issue facing your community, such as how to solve the homeless problem or how to reduce illegal drug use. Read as much as you can about the issue for two weeks. Put together a file of the newspaper and magazine articles that you have rëad about the subject.
2. Over the same period, watch TV or listen to the radio for news on the same topic. Take notes on what you learn.
3. Decide what you think must be done to solve the problem you have chosen. Make a list of your conclusions.

Democracy is based on five principles, all of which will be discussed throughout this text:

- **Equality in voting.** Citizens need equal opportunities to express their preferences about policies or leaders.
- **Individual freedom.** All individuals must have the greatest amount of freedom possible without interfering with the rights of others.
- **Equality of all persons.** The law must entitle all persons to equal treatment within the society.
- **Majority rule and minority rights.** The majority should rule, while guaranteeing minorities' rights.
- **Voluntary consent to be governed.** The people who make up a democracy must agree voluntarily to be governed by the rules laid down by their representatives.

SECTION 2 REVIEW

1. What is the difference between a monarchy and a dictatorship?
2. What is direct democracy and why did our founders oppose it?
3. What is the difference between a direct democracy and an indirect, or representative, democracy?
4. What are the principles of democracy?
5. **For critical analysis:** How do you think your life would be different if you were living in a country ruled by a monarch?

of individuals elected by the people to act as their representatives.

4. Equality in voting, Individual freedom, equality of all persons, majority rule and minority rights, and voluntary consent to be governed.

5. Answers will vary, e.g., ceremonial occasions in which the royal family were involved would have much more importance in my life.

SECTION 3

Points to Stress

- A definition and examples of interdependence.
- The major reasons for growing interdependence.
- The role of the global economy, technology, and our shared environment.

Kickoff Activity

Write the following statement on the chalkboard: *The world is getting smaller.* Ask the students to list at least five facts that support this idea. Then encourage students to share and discuss their lists.

Working with the Preview Questions

Go over the two study questions with the class. Ask students to read Section 3, taking notes in response to these questions.

Teaching Strategies

Introduction

Ask the students to restate the definition of *interdependence* in their own words. Encourage them to discuss other contexts in which the word is used.

Cooperative Learning

Have students work in groups to list the imported products that they—or their family members—purchase. When group members have listed as many products as possible, have them discuss the reasons they or other consumers select imported products over those produced in the United States.

Enrichment

Ask volunteers to learn about American laws or regulations that restrict imports. When and why were these laws or regulations enacted? Who is trying to change these laws and regulations? Why? Have the volunteers share and discuss their findings with the rest of the class.

Vocabulary

Ask students to share their own definitions of the term *technology* and to give examples of technological developments. Which of these developments increase interdependence? Are there any new technologies that decrease interdependence?

Caption Answer Interdependence.

SECTION 3

The Challenge of Interdependence

Preview Questions

- What does interdependence mean?
- What are the reasons for this growing interdependence?

You have read about how each nation is sovereign, with its own population, territory, and government. This does not mean that each nation is a world in itself. Each nation is one among many nations in the world, all sharing the same planet and the same environment. When you hear people say that "the world is getting smaller," they mean that through increased communications and transportation, people around the world have become more aware of and affected by the goals and problems of others. All of us are becoming more and more interdependent. **Interdependence** means that nations rely on each other for many different reasons. There are several important reasons for this currently increasing interdependence.

The Global Economy

One of the most important ways in which nations are becoming interdependent is through world trade. Nations depend on one another for the products they cannot make or cannot grow for themselves. They also depend on each other for natural resources not found within their own borders. Economic policies in one country can strongly affect the economy and well-being of another. In the United States, for example, we buy cars from Germany, Italy, and Japan; videocassette recorders from Korea and Japan; wool shirts from Scotland; and shoes and other leather goods from Italy, Spain, and Argentina. Other countries buy our cars, our computers, and our agricultural products. If another country's government decides that it wants to prohibit its citizens from purchasing American goods, that decision affects us economically. If we decide to do the same thing, our government's action affects citizens in other countries.

When McDonald's went into business in Moscow, Russian citizens were able to see how it is possible to receive a high quality product at a low price with friendly service. This has had an effect on what they expect from other businesses in their country. The same has happened in the United States. When Americans saw that the Japanese could make cars of higher quality, on average, than American-made cars, American auto makers felt pressured to improve the quality of domestically produced cars.

The Role of Technology

Interdependence has also increased because of the improvements in communication and transportation technologies. Satellites, computers, airplanes, and facsimile (fax) machines have linked nations and their peoples in ways that were only dreamed of years ago. Americans with television satellite dishes can watch news broadcasts from many countries. Radio broadcasts allow people around the world to hear news from other nations. In 1989, when Chinese students demonstrated for democracy in Beijing's Tiananmen Square, the world watched the daily events on television. The Chinese government tried to cut off the world news media, but news continued to flow through long-distance telephone links and satellite broadcasts. When the Iraqis invaded Kuwait in 1990, everyone knew it immediately throughout the world. As Iraqi soldiers carried much of Kuwait's wealth into Iraq, the world knew quickly that Iraq's ruler, Saddam Hussein, was not telling the truth about his

▼ The first McDonald's Restaurant in Moscow is an example of the globalization of business. Such globalization increases the amount that nations rely on each other. What word is used to describe the increasing reliance of nations on one another?

Teaching Social Studies Skills

Read

Introduce this feature by pointing out that a textbook is designed to be a tool for learning and, like any tool, will be most effective if used properly. Then ask the students to read this feature silently.

Discuss

Encourage students to share and discuss their responses to these questions: Do you think following the guidelines presented here will help you get more from this textbook than if you were to use it in a less systematic manner? Can these guidelines help you in other courses?

Analyze and Apply

Allow the students some time to go through the steps outlined under "How to Use this Textbook." Then assign the Practicing Your Skills items at the end of this feature.

Review

Help students to review the guidelines by asking a volunteer to write the headings for each guideline on the board or on a transparency.

Practicing Your Skills (Answers)

1. 760. Loose monetary policy.
2. (a) George Washington, Martin Luther King, Jr., Susan B. Anthony, Abraham Lincoln, John Marshall, and Franklin Delano Roosevelt. (b) Nine units and 26 chapters. (c) Government in Action features named will vary.
3. Architect of the American Dream, Government in Action, Citizenship Skills and Responsibilities, Building Social Studies Skills, and Challenge to the American Dream.
4. 19.
5. The Constitution, as presented in the Resource Center, is annotated.
6. Admission dates will vary according to your state.

Multidiscipline Strategies

Math, Geography, Research This exercise will strengthen students' math, geography, and research skills. Give each student six or seven countries to research with the task of determining if those nations are democratic or autocratic. Have students combine their lists to compile a total list. Then have them work together to calculate the percentage of democratic versus nondemocratic governments on the total list. Mention the trends in Latin America and Eastern Europe, which have added to the number of democracies in the world today, as well as other areas with democratic struggles. Sources such as *The World Factbook,* and *The World Almanac* can assist students in their research.

Building Social Studies Skills

Using the Features of This Textbook

Within any textbook there is a vast amount of information that you can make your own. To help you, this textbook is divided into many parts, each of which has its own function. Some parts prepare you for information; other parts help you study that information. Using a textbook and its parts wisely is an important first move toward mastering its contents.

How to Use this Textbook

To get the most from this textbook, use the following guidelines.

1. **Study the table of contents to locate information.** Here you can find where each chapter, section, feature, map, graph, and table can be found.
2. **Examine the chapter- and unit-opening pages.** Read the titles and objectives, and ask yourself questions about the photos, such as how each relates to the chapter title. Read the introduction and familiarize yourself with the theme.
3. **Skim the chapter.** Preview the chapter, noting each section title and the subheadings. These will give you clues about how the chapter will progress. Note the maps, photographs, and other visuals to get a feel for the chapter. Read the section guide questions that start each section.
4. **Read the chapter carefully.** Use the headings and subheadings to get clues about the main and supporting ideas. Reread any paragraph that is unclear until you understand what it says. Pay attention to the boldfaced words—they are highlighted because they are important terms. Review the illustrations and relate them to the content of your reading. Use the review questions at the end of the sections to check your understanding.
5. **Read the special features.** Each chapter has special features that will add to your knowledge of government. You will recognize them easily because they will appear in boxes. You may prefer to read them as you go along, which is often a good idea, because many of the features directly relate to the surrounding information. Or you may prefer to read them as part of the previewing step, or before reviewing the section. When you read them is not as important as being sure you do read them.
6. **Summarize and review the chapter.** Each chapter ends with a summary that will help you recap the main ideas. Each chapter also has a set of review questions, questions for thought and discussion, activities and projects, a communication skill exercise and a social studies skill exercise. All of these review features are designed to help you master the material.
7. **Look at the glossary.** The glossary includes definitions for the important new words found in this book.
8. **Use the Resource Center.** The Resource Center found in the back of this book is loaded with useful material including original source documents and more.

Remember, no textbook can teach you this course. A textbook cannot be a substitute for your instructor's skills and experience. This book, like all textbooks, is a tool. When used properly, it can enhance your knowledge and broaden your understanding.

Practicing Your Skills

1. Turn to the glossary and answer these questions: (a) On what page(s) in the glossary is the term *veto* found? (b) What is the last entry under L?
2. Turn to the table of contents and answer the following questions: (a) Who are the Americans profiled under "Architects of the American Dream"? (b) How many units and chapters does the book have? (c) Name three "Government in Action" features found in the book.
3. List all of the special features used in the textbook.
4. How many individuals are featured in the profiles and the "Architects of the American Dream" combined?
5. What is special about the Constitution as it is presented in the Resource Center?
6. Find your state in the State Atlas in the Resource Center. When was it admitted to the Union?

Observable Mastery
Have students bring in a list of products from home which demonstrates the global connection of products and technology. You could also have them research local firms in order to see where major suppliers come from in order to demonstrate economic interdependence. Plot the various suppliers on a world map.

Enrichment
Have several students research how the war news was communicated in the United States during World War I and during World War II. What technological changes occurred between the two world wars? How did those changes affect the coverage of the wars? How did the changes affect the involvement and response of citizens in the United States?

Extension
Ask students to write about or discuss specific international news events that they have seen broadcast on TV. How did actually seeing the event affect you? How did seeing the event seem to affect others in this country? Do you believe the coverage of the event affected the response of our government to the event? Why or why not?

Reteaching Strategies
1. Have students work in small groups to brainstorm as many endings as possible for the following sentence: *The nations of the world are interdependent because . . .*
2. Help the students discuss the information presented in the photograph on page 15. Then have them write their own statements of the ideas communicated by the photograph.

Evaluation Strategies
1. Have the students write their answers to the Section 3 Review questions.
2. Have the students take the Section 3 Quiz found in the *TRB.*

Section 3 Review (Answers)
1. Interdependence means that nations rely on each other for many different reasons.
2. Countries are becoming more interdependent through increased world trade, because of improvements in communications and transportation, and because nations must work together to protect an environment shared by all.
3. Answers will vary, e.g., growing interdependence will have a positive effect on the United States because we can gain from the technological and medical knowledge of other countries. Increased world trade and less trade barriers will also benefit the United States through lower prices and access to a larger variety of goods.

Caption Answer Students should understand that all of us, regardless of nationality or citizenship, share the same air, the same water, and that we all live on the same planet. Therefore, protecting the environment should be viewed as a global issue rather than as a national issue.

▲ When Iraq's leader, Saddam Hussein, dumped oil into the Persian Gulf it was an environmental disaster. Why should Americans be concerned with environmental disasters that take place in other parts of the world?

intentions in Kuwait. In 1991, an attempted coup against the government of Mikhail Gorbachev in the Soviet Union was viewed by hundreds of millions of world citizens. Throughout that vast country, citizens immediately responded against the attempted coup. When the popularly elected president of Russia, Boris Yeltsin, stood on top of an army tank in front of the Russian Parliament and told his people to resist, the image was seen by people all over the world.

Virtually no events can go unknown and unseen in the political world today, no matter where they take place. Indeed, some political analysts believe that the worldwide spread of relatively inexpensive telecommunications has been a principal reason why nondemocratic countries have had to change—their citizens know that better forms of government exist elsewhere in the world because they hear about them on the radio or see them on TV or in movie houses.

Our Shared Environment

Nations of the world are also interdependent because they share the same air and water. Pollution in one nation can affect the people and environment of other nations. As a result, the world's nations must depend on each other to protect an environment that knows no national boundaries.

An accident at a nuclear power plant in one country can affect the lives of millions of people thousands of miles away. The clear-cutting of the Brazilian rain forest might affect all of us if the world's oxygen level is severely reduced. In the United States, many of our electric utility plants generate pollution that spreads hundreds of miles into Canada and creates the problem of acid rain, which has a high acid content that harms Canadian forests and lakes.

The depletion of the earth's ozone layer is a global problem. One of the major causes is thought to be the release of chlorofluorocarbons into the atmosphere. Some countries have banned the use of chlorofluorocarbons, for example, in the making of refrigerator coolant. But what happens if one country continues to produce numerous products that cause more and more chlorofluorocarbons to be released into the air? Clearly, there is an interdependence among countries here that cannot be ignored.

Nor can we ignore the problem of dangerous pesticides and chemicals. A country may ban pesticide use domestically, but still allow its manufacturer to sell it to countries where it is not banned. This occurred with the chemical DDT. The same is true with respect to medicines that may not be approved in the country in which they are manufactured, but can be sold elsewhere in the world. What if those pesticides and medicines have dangerous side effects?

The United States is truly part of a global society. Decision makers must always be aware of this fact of modern life.

Section 3 Review

1. What does interdependence mean?
2. Why is the world becoming more interdependent?
3. **For critical analysis:** Do you think this growing interdependence will have a positive or negative effect on the United States? Explain your answer.

TEACHING CHALLENGE TO THE AMERICAN DREAM

Read
Introduce this material by asking students to remeber that direct democracy as practiced in ancient Greece, is considered an ideal form of democracy, but one that is not practical for our population. Then ask volunteers to read aloud this feature to the class.

Discuss
Encourage students to share and discuss their responses to these questions: How has the growth of our population affected political representation in this country? Has it created any problems? Does modern communications technology help to lessen the impact of these problems? What else might be done?

Developing Skills for the Information Age:

Interdependence among nations manifests itself in numerous ways and is covered by the media in contrasting themes. The global economy and technology are topics for many stories in publications like *Fortune, Business Week,* and *Forbes.* Our shared environment is regularly featured in periodicals such as *Time, U.S. News and World Report, National Geographic,* and *International Wildlife.* Students should be directed to these and similar sources in order to witness how the topic of global interdependence is treated. While reading students should be aware of the conflicting types of coverage that these issues receive from sources and consider the reasons for the different media presentations.

Analyze and Apply
Ask students to do some research regarding federal representation in your state. How many people does each senator from your state represent? Is there an office for that senator in your city? Have students list their federal representatives and how each of these representatives can most easily be contacted.

Review
Help students review this material by asking them to write a 100-word essay on the topic of adequate representation in our growing population.

You Decide
1. Answers will vary, e.g., representative democracy worked better because each representative had fewer interests to represent. The makeup of the country was not as diverse.
2. Anwers will vary, e.g., if there were more representatives in the House or Senate the length of time it would take to pass a bill would greatly increase.
3. Answers will vary, e.g., there are no alternatives that might work better.
4. Answers will vary, e.g., this technology would increase participation

CHALLENGE TO THE AMERICAN DREAM

Do Our Representatives Represent Too Many People?

Everybody accepts the notion that direct democracy as practiced in ancient Greece would not work in a nation of over 250 million people. Even if a small percentage of the total adult population wanted to participate in direct democracy, the result would be a mass meeting that could not be held in even the largest structure in the world. Representative democracy is therefore the most practical democratic system we can use in this country.

Our representative democracy took on a distinct form in 1788 with the ratification of the U.S. Constitution. The first president, George Washington, took office in 1789 when the population numbered about 4 million. During the first election, twenty-two senators and fifty-nine representatives were elected. Therefore, the two senators from each state represented an average of 180,000 citizens. The average member of the House of Representatives represented about 68,000 citizens. The situation in 1789 was, of course, a far cry from the Athenian model of direct democracy.

Consider now the current situation. The population in the United States has grown to over 250 million. There is still one president. The number of senators has increased to 100, however, and the number of representatives to 435. That means that the two senators from every state represent an average of 5 million Americans. The average member of the House represents about 575,000 Americans. At the extreme, the two senators from California represent almost 30 million Americans.

This is a nation of diverse cultures, needs, desires, demands, preferences, and religious beliefs. Is it possible for any one representative to truly reflect the "will of the people" when each congressional official in our government represents so many Americans?

Some have begun to question whether representative democracy can still work in the United States because of the continued rate of population growth. Others point out that this nation will probably reach its maximum, stable population sometime between the years 2020 and 2040. While the population will probably increase to about 300 to 330 million, it will not be significantly larger than it is now. In other words, if representative democracy is working today, even with all of its faults, it will certainly work with 50 to 80 million more people. The two senators from each state will represent an average of 6 million people; for representatives, the average will be about 690,000 people. Certainly, the effect and influence any individual citizen has on his or her elected officials will not markedly change with a population that is 25 percent larger.

The challenge to the American dream is, nonetheless, to improve the representative nature of our democracy in spite of an increasing population. This can be done by more voter participation, a greater understanding among all Americans (particularly young people) of the political process, and more limits on the degree to which our representatives are allowed to act in their own best interests rather than in those of the people they represent.

You Decide

1. Do you think that representative democracy worked better at the beginning of our nation's history, when each senator and representative represented fewer Americans? Explain.
2. Some have argued that each member of the House now represents too many Americans and that therefore the number of representatives should be increased. What problems would arise if that occurred?
3. If, indeed, representative democracy is in danger because of an increase in population, what alternatives might work better?
4. Some people look to technology that will allow electronic voting from the home as a way of meeting this challenge. Do you think such technology would increase political participation among Americans? Do you think this would adequately meet the challenge to the American dream just presented?

and provide representatives with clear mandates from those with the time and interest to participate.

Chapter Evaluation

To evaluate student mastery of chapter material, you might:

1. Use Chapter Test A from the *TRB* or Chapter Test B from the *TRB*.

2. Use Chapter Test B from the *TRB*.

3. Construct your own test using items from the *West American Government Test Bank* found in the *TRB*.

4. Use the accompanying computerized test software to construct and print a customized chapter test.

Review Questions (Answers)

1. People need some form of government to provide authority and organization.

2. Voting, discussing politics, watching a news program, and joining together to form groups with like interests in governmental decisions.

3. Solving conflicts, providing public services, providing for national security and the common defense, setting goals for public policies, and preserving culture.

4. Territory is the land on which people can live with recognized boundaries. Population refers to the people living within each nation and their demographic characteristics. Sovereignty is the nation's right, power, and authority to govern its people. Government is the political organization through which public policies are made and enforced.

5. Evolutionary theory is that government developed gradually in stages. According to the force theory, governments first originated when strong persons or groups conquered territories, and then forced everyone living in those territories to submit to their will. The theory of divine right is that God gave those of royal birth the unlimited right to govern other men and women. The social contract theory holds that human beings would voluntarily give up some of their freedoms in order to gain the benefits of orderly government.

6. Autocracies; rule by one, either monarchy or dictatorship and democracies; rule by many.

7. A monarch acquires his or her power through inheritance. A dictator acquires power through force.

8. Authoritarianism, which means the dictator gains supreme power through force.

9. Representative democracy best describes the government of the United States.

10. The people hold the supreme political authority in a democracy.

CHAPTER 1 REVIEW

Key Terms

absolute monarchies 11
authoritarian 11
authority 6
autocracy 11
constitutional monarchies 11
democracy 11
dictatorship 11
direct democracy 11
divine right theory 8
evolutionary theory 8
federal government 8
force theory 8
government 4
institutions 8
interdependence 15
majority rule 14
monarchy 11
nation 7
natural rights 10
parliamentary democracy 12
political participation 4
politics 4
power 5
presidential democracy 12
public policies 6
representative democracy (indirect democracy) 12
republic 12
revolution 9
social conflict 3
social contract theory 10
sovereignty 8
totalitarian 11
unitary government 8

Summary

1. Government consists of the individuals and processes that make society's rules, and that possess the power to enforce the rules about resolving conflicts over the allocation of resources. Politics is the process that determines ''who gets what, when, and how'' in society. Government serves several major purposes: solving conflicts, providing public services, providing for the national security and common defense, setting political and social goals, and preserving culture. The nation is the basic political unit in the world today. A nation is a political community with its own population, territory, sovereignty, and government. The force theory of government holds that governments first originated when one person or group conquered a given territory and forced everyone living in that territory to submit to their will. The evolutionary theory holds that government developed gradually, beginning with the family. The divine right theory holds that God gave those of royal birth the ''divine right'' to rule. The social contract theory holds that government rose out of the voluntary act of free individuals to serve the will of the people.

2. Although all governments carry out the same basic functions, there are tremendous differences in the ways governments can be organized and operated. In an autocracy, power is concentrated in the hands of an individual. In a democracy, the supreme political authority rests with the people. Direct democracy, as practiced in ancient Greek city-nations, exists when the will of the people is directly translated into public policy at mass meetings. In a representative democracy, popular will is expressed through individuals elected by the people to act as representatives. The basic democratic principles include equality in voting, individual freedom, social equality for all persons, and majority rule and minority rights.

3. Interdependence means that nations rely on each other for many different reasons. One of the most important ways in which nations rely on each other is through world trade. Interdependence has also increased because of the improvements in the technologies of communications and transportation. Nations are also interdependent because they share the same environment.

Review Questions

1. Why do people living in groups need some form of government?
2. What are several forms of political participation?
3. What are the purposes of government?
4. List and explain the characteristics of a nation.
5. List and explain the four major theories of the origins of government.
6. Into what types can governments be classified?
7. How does a monarchy differ from a dictatorship?
8. What is the primary characteristic of any dictatorship?
9. Which form of government best describes the government of the United States?
10. Who holds the supreme political authority in a democracy?

11. In a direct democracy, the will of the people is directly translated into public policy at mass meetings. In a representative democracy, the will of the majority is expressed through a smaller group of individuals elected by the people to act as their representatives. *Representative democracy* best describes the government of the United States.

12. Equality of voting is important because citizens need equal opportunities to express preferences. Individual freedom and equality are important because each person must have the greatest amount of freedom possible without infringing on the rights of others. Majority rule and minority rights are important because the majority should rule but the rights of minorities should be guaranteed in order that they might sometimes become majorities through fair and lawful means. Voluntary consent to be governed is important because the people must voluntarily agree to be governed by the rules laid down by their representatives.

13. Because of increasing world trade, advancements in communications and transportation, and because nations must depend on each other to protect the world's shared environment.

14. Acquiring and using information; making decisions, making sound judgments, communicating, and cooperating.

15. Each representative must represent many more citizens with many diverse cultures, needs, desires, and preferences.

CHAPTER 1 REVIEW—Continued

11. Explain the differences between a direct democracy and an indirect, or representative, democracy. Which type best describes the system used in the United States?
12. What are the basic concepts of democracy and why are they important?
13. Explain why there is a growing interdependence between nations.
14. Name at least four skills required to be a good citizen.
15. How has population growth weakened the representative nature of our democracy?

Questions for Thought and Discussion

1. Give three examples of why you must have rules in order to be free.
2. Historians have speculated that at one time humans lived without a form of organized government. Why do you think early peoples decided to devise laws and governments? What is your own theory of the origin of government?
3. In your opinion, should our democracy be direct or representative? Give reasons for your answer.
4. Compare the three types of government outlined in this chapter and describe what your life might be like living under each one.
5. Consider the decision-making process in your city. Can you identify certain individuals or social groups that seem to control the decision making? How are such "elite" groups controlled by the voters?
6. There are many reasons why nations are becoming more interdependent. The reasons discussed in this chapter were increased international trade, better and less expensive communications technology, and world environmental problems. Can you think of at least one other reason why nations are becoming more interdependent? Develop your answer.

Improving Your Skills
Communication Skills

Listening

Have you ever heard someone talking to you, but couldn't remember anything that he or she said five minutes later? The person was probably insulted because you weren't really listening. Many individuals don't really listen to half of what they hear in life. We may hear the words but don't turn them into understandable and useful information. We consciously or unconsciously sort through what we've heard, and focus on only *part* of the information. You may easily remember the scores of every football game last year, or the top five MTV videos for the past six months, but when it comes to remembering what your teacher said in yesterday's class, you draw a blank.

You can become an effective listener at school, at work, and with family and friends by understanding the listening process:

- You hear what's being said.
- You make a decision as to its importance.
- You react to it.
- You file the information or discard it.

To become a more effective listener, you must gain more control over this process. Follow these guidelines:

1. ***Tell yourself that you want to retain what you are hearing.*** Concentrate on the speaker and tune out outside interferences such as music, telephones, other conversations, and anything else about which you might be thinking. You must discipline yourself to become an active, involved listener because it is easy to be distracted.
2. ***Try to organize what you hear by listening to clues from the speaker.*** For example, "The main point here is that . . . ; The three reasons this happened are . . . ."
3. ***If you know that a lecture or discussion is going to be based on something you have previously heard or learned, review that information ahead of time.*** It is much easier to relate new information to knowledge that you already have.
4. ***Try to relate what you hear to your own knowledge and experience.*** Coming up with concrete examples of what is being explained may help you understand. For example, if you are learning about the concepts of democracy, think of specific situations in which they apply to you.
5. ***Ask questions if you don't understand or need more information.*** If you need a point repeated or clarified, don't hesitate to ask the speaker.

Questions for Thought and Discussion (Answers)

1. Answers will vary, e.g., to provide laws that contribute to safety so I may walk the streets freely. To provide rules that give me the freedom to operate a profitable business.

2. Answers will vary, e.g., people decided to devise laws and governments to bring organization to chaos. My own theory is that government began with strong and wise leaders who convinced others that organization and authority were necessary. Most people had the need to be led and so agreed with what these strong leaders proposed.

3. Answers will vary, e.g., we should have a representative government because our population has grown far too much for a direct democracy to be possible.

4. Answers will vary, e.g., under a monarchy I would be much more in awe of the king or queen and ceremony would be more important to me. Under a dictatorship I would have fewer freedoms such as voting and expressing my opinions.

5. Answers will vary, e.g., in my city the mayor and a close group of his assistants seem to make most of the decisions. This "elite" group is still subject to the voters judgment at the next election. Voters also put pressure on the mayor's office by calls, visits, letters to the editor, and generally letting their approval or disapproval be known publicly.

6. Answers will vary, e.g., the need to share technology in other areas such as medical knowledge in order to alleviate disease and sickness throughout the world. The need to stop nuclear weapons from falling into dangerous irresponsible hands.

Social Studies Skills (Answers)

1. Both are shown to be forms of autocracy.

2. With direct democracy, no representatives exist to carry out the will of the people in passing legislation.

3. With a presidential democracy, both the president and legislature are elected by the people. With a parliamentary democracy, only the legislature is elected directly by the people. It then chooses a prime minister.

4. There is a nominal, or ceremonial, leader who exists with a constitutional monarchy.

5. Because there is no true power that passes to the monarch.

CHAPTER 1 REVIEW—Continued

Writing

On a sheet of paper, complete the following statements.

1. The qualities most important for a high-ranking government policymaker are . . .
2. The best things about the United States are . . .
3. The president should work toward . . .

Get into teams with three or four of your classmates. Take turns reading your responses to each other. Then take turns trying to repeat exactly how the others in your team have completed the statements.

Social Studies Skills

Learning About Forms of Government

Use Figure 1–2 on page 13 to answer the following questions. This figure shows the forms of government. It simplifies the many complex forms that governments have taken since the beginning of organized society.

1. How does the upper panel on autocracy relate an absolute monarchy with a dictatorship?
2. In the middle panel, what is the distinction between laws developed under direct democracy and those developed under representative democracy?
3. In the bottom panel, what is the distinction between a presidential democracy and a parliamentary democracy?
4. In the bottom panel, what distinguishes a modern constitutional monarchy from a parliamentary democracy?
5. In the bottom panel, why do you think the arrow pointing towards ''monarch'' is a broken line?

Activities and Projects

1. Divide the class into groups of five or six. Assume that each group has founded a new town that is growing quickly but as yet has no form of government. Each group should devise a plan of government for each town. Decide what the town goals will be, how a leader will be chosen, and what rules will be made and enforced.
2. Prepare a series of posters that illustrate each form of government described in this chapter. Use pictures and words.
3. Stage a debate or class forum on one of the following topics:
   (a) People could provide public services better without government interference.
   (b) Representative democracy cannot work because the people don't take enough time to learn about important political issues.
   (c) A dictatorship may be better than a democracy if the dictator is a smart and kind person.
   (d) The United States should only worry about its own problems, not those in any other country.

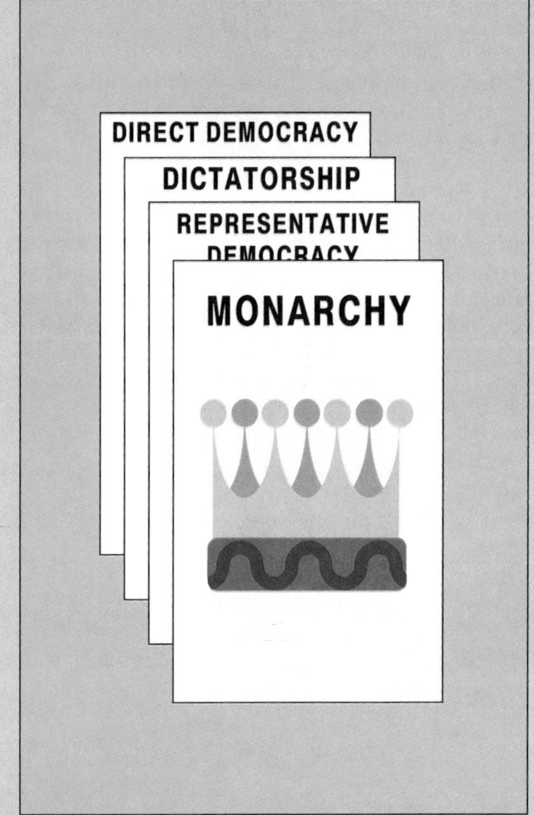

CHAPTER INTRODUCTION

Instructional Objectives
At the end of the chapter students should be able to
- Describe the British heritage on which our government is based.
- Summarize the development of the American governmental system as it was influenced by early British settlements.
- List the events that culminated with independence for the colonies.
- Differentiate between the govermental arrangement under the Articles of Confederation and that of the Constitutional Convention.
- Point to the major events and compromises that took place during the drafting and ratification of the Constitution.

Using the Keynote
Have the students read and discuss the quotation from Stephen Hopkins: If Hopkins had been speaking at the end of the twentieth century, rather than at the end of the eighteenth century, how would his language have been different? How would his arguments for the independence of the colonies have been different?

Continue the discussion by posing these questions about Stephen Hopkins: How do you imagine his success in business affected his ideas about independence for the colonies? How do you think his political views may have been influenced by his experience as governor of Rhode Island and chief justice of the Rhode Island superior court?

Introducing the Chapter
After the students have read the Introduction, encourage discussion by posing questions such as these: What were the means of communication and travel during the 1770s? What are they today? Why are those differences important? Do you think more modern means of communication and travel would have been more likely to increase the power the British Crown was able to exert over the colonies or more likely to increase the speed and vehemence with which the colonists were able to rebel against the Crown? Why? Encourage the students to express and support differing points of view.

Previewing the Sections

Section 1 Ask the students to look through Section 1, noting the three main headings and glancing at the photographs. Then encourage the students to share their ideas about what they expect to learn in this section.
Section 2 Have volunteers read aloud the three main headings in this section. Then help the students begin to consider the contents of the section by asking questions such as these: What are the early British settlements in North America with which you are already familiar? What do you know about the fate of those settlements?
Section 3 Ask the students to find and read the seven main

CHAPTER 2

Forging the American Dream

CHAPTER OBJECTIVES

To learn and understand

- The European origins of the American governmental system.
- The development of the American governmental system through the first British settlements.
- The colonies' push for independence.
- The governmental arrangements set up by the Articles of Confederation.
- The Constitutional Convention and the ratification of the Constitution of the United States.

headings within this section. Then ask: What do these headings tell you about the efforts of the colonies to band together?
Section 4 Have the students skim through this section, noting the charts and the four main headings. Then encourage them to discuss what they already know about the Articles of Confederation.
Section 5 Have volunteers find and read aloud the four main headings in Section 5. Then help the students anticipate what they will read by asking questions such as these: What do you already know about the Constitutional Convention?
Section 6 Ask the students to look through Section 6, finding and reading the three main headings. Encourage them to discuss the meaning of the section title itself and of the term *battle lines* used in the first main heading.

West's American Government Assignment Guide

Activity Sheets
Basic Concepts 2 *TRB* (Reteaching)
Enrichment Activity 2 *TRB*
Building Social Studies Skills 2 *TRB*
Quizzes
Chapter 2 Section 1 Quiz *TRB*
Chapter 2 Section 2 Quiz *TRB*
Chapter 2 Section 3 Quiz *TRB*
Tests
Chapter 2 Test A *TRB*
Chapter 2 Test B *TRB*
Chapter 2 Test Bank *TRB*
Chapter 2 Computerized Testing WESTEST
Software
Chapter 2 Activity

Keynote

"The Colonies are at so great a distance from England that the members of Parliament can generally have but little knowledge of their business, connections, and interests but what is gained from people who have been there; the most of these have so slight a knowledge themselves that the information they can give are very little to be dependent on, though they may pretend to determine with confidence on matters far above their reach."

—— **Stephen Hopkins (1721–1785) Member of First and Second Continental Congresses**

INTRODUCTION

Most people know that the United States first started out as English colonies. As the opening quote makes clear, the distance between the colonies and England was vast. The rulers in Great Britain had difficulty keeping current on what was happening in America and consequently knew little about the colonists' activities or needs. This does not mean that if satellite communications had been available in the 1770s, the American Revolution never would have happened. But perhaps that revolution would have started later had the British Crown known how life really was across the Atlantic.

In spite of our revolutionary break with England in 1776, much of the political thought that has formed the way our nation governs itself has its origins in the theories of European philosophers.

SECTION 1

European Origins of Our Governmental System

Preview Questions

- What is limited government? Where did the concept of limited government come from?
- What is the system of representative government? Where did this system come from?
- What were some early influences on American political philosophy?

The American colonies were settled by individuals from many nations, including France, Spain, Holland, Sweden, and Norway. Nonetheless, the majority of American settlers came from England. The English colonists brought with them the two principles of *limited government* and *representative government,* which became important factors in forming the American political system.

Limited Government

For many years under the British monarchy, the king or queen had virtually unrestricted powers. This changed in 1215, when King John was forced by his nobles to sign the **Magna Carta,** or great charter. (See the Resource Center at the back of this book.) This monumental document provided for a trial by jury of one's **peers** (equals). It prohibited the taking of life, liberty, and property without due process of law. Additionally, the Magna Carta forced the king to obtain the nobles' approval of any taxes he imposed on his royal subjects. Government became a contract between the king and his subjects.

The Magna Carta's importance to England cannot be overemphasized, for it clearly established the principle of **limited government**—a government on which strict limits are placed, usually by a constitution. Hence, the Magna Carta signaled the end of the monarch's absolute power. While it is true that the rights provided under the Magna Carta originally applied only to the nobility, it formed the basis of the future constitutional government for all individuals in England and eventually in the United States.

The principle of limited government was expanded 400 years later, in 1628, when Charles I was forced to sign the Petition of Rights. Among other things, this petition prohibited the king from imprisoning political critics without a jury trial. Perhaps more importantly, the

SECTION 1

Points to Stress
• The definition of limited government and its origin.
• The system of representative government and its derivation.
• Early influences that shaped the American political philosophy.
• Political philosophers who influenced the framers' attitudes.

Kickoff Activity
Give the students five minutes in which to list as many British influences on our lives as possible. At the end of the allotted time, encourage the students to share and discuss their lists.

Working with the Preview Questions
Have volunteers read the study questions aloud. Then ask each student to prepare a note page with headings based on these questions. As they read Section 1, have the students fill in notes under the appropriate headings.

Teaching Strategies

Introduction
Instruct the students to read the section introduction and then discuss their responses to questions such as these: Who was already in North America when the settlers arrived? What role did those people play in establishing the colonies? From what countries—other than England—did settlers arrive? How do you think the colonists dealt with the diversity of the population? How do you think the colonists' actions and attitudes may affect the way people in our country deal with the diversity in the current population?

Caption Answer Students should understand that the Magna Carta formed the basis for constitutional government in England and was, therefore, a part of the political background that the colonists brought with them from England.

Cooperative Learning
Ask a group of volunteers to learn more about the Magna Carta. These students should work together to research the history, the contents, and the significance of this document. Then let the volunteers share their findings with the rest of the class.

Vocabulary
Ask the students to explain this use of the word *absolute.* (without limitation) In what sense was the king's power absolute? What is the opposite of absolute power? (limited power)

Discussion Starter
Help students discuss each of these ideas from the English Bill of Rights: How do you think this was important to the American British colonists in the 1600s? How is it relevant to the government of our country today?

Comprehension
Have the students name as many specific examples of representative government as possible. (They should consider school, city, state, and federal governments.) How can you recognize each as a representative government? Who are your representatives in each of these governments?

Critical Thinking Skills
Ask the students to compare the English parliament with what they know about the American Congress: How are the two governing bodies alike? What are the most important differences? What do you think accounts for those differences?

▲ When King John signed the Magna Carta, the principle of limited government was established. Why do you think the Magna Carta was important to the formation of the United States Constitution?

petition declared that even the king or queen had to obey the law of the land.

In 1689, the English government passed the English Bill of Rights, which further extended the concept of limited government. Several important ideas were included in this document:

- The king or queen could not interfere with parliamentary elections.
- The king or queen must have Parliament's approval to levy (collect) taxes or to maintain any army.
- The king or queen must rule with the consent of the people's representatives in Parliament.
- The people could not be subject to cruel or unusual punishment or to excessive fines.

Because the British colonists in North America were also British citizens, the English Bill of Rights of 1689 applied to them. Because of this, virtually all the major concepts in the English Bill of Rights became part of the American system of government.

Representative Government

A system of **representative government** is one in which the people, by whatever means, choose a limited number of individuals to make governmental decisions for all citizens. Those chosen by the citizens are called **representatives.** Usually, these representatives are elected to office for a specific period of time.

In England, this group of representatives is called **Parliament.** As it did in the eighteenth century, Parliament consists of an upper chamber, called the House of Lords, and a lower chamber, called the House of Commons, which was mostly made up of merchants and property owners. Members of the House of Commons were elected by other merchants and property owners. Thus in England, the concept of government by and for the people became reality. It later became a model by which the thirteen American colonies would govern themselves as well. (A more complete explanation of Parliament can be found in Chapter 26.)

Early Philosophical Influences

It may seem obvious to you that government without the **consent** (permission and agreement) of the governed should not exist. Such a notion, however, was still very new and revolutionary in the 1600s. An important English political philosopher, John Locke, who wrote *Two Treatises of Government* in 1689, argued that neither custom nor tradition, nor the fact of being born in a certain society, were sufficient reasons to obey rulers. He stated that "No one could be subjected to the political power of another, without his [or her] own consent." Government, therefore, was only legitimate as long as the people continued to consent to it. Locke further argued that all persons were born free, equal, and independent, and all persons had a **natural right** to life, liberty, and property—rights that everyone possessed even before governments existed. He argued that the primary purpose of government was to protect those natural rights, and believed that government was really a social contract between the people and their government.

Both John Locke and another English philosopher, Thomas Hobbes, theorized that before government existed, people lived in "a state of nature" in which they had unlimited freedom and the right to do as they wished. Hobbes argued that this situation led to chaos and violence because the weak could not protect themselves against the strong. Rights could only be won through force. Life in this "free" state of nature, therefore, was essentially, as Hobbes put it, "nasty, brutish, and short."

Enrichment
Have volunteers research the lives and works of John Locke, Thomas Hobbes, Jean-Jacques Rousseau, and Charles Louis de Montesquieu. What were the most important ideas developed by each of these philosophers? How were their ideas alike? How were they different? How can the influence of each be seen in the Declaration of Independence and the U.S. Constitution? Ask the volunteers to prepare written or oral presentations of their findings.

Caption Answer Locke believed that the primary purpose of government was to protect each citizen's natural right to life, liberty, and property.

▲ English political philosopher John Locke argued that "No one could be subjected to the political power of another without his [or her] own consent." What did Locke see as the primary purpose of government?

According to Hobbes in his landmark political study *Leviathan,* which was published in 1651, human beings voluntarily agreed to create a powerful government in order to establish security and safety. In exchange for this, they gave up the freedoms they had won in the state of nature, and owed their complete loyalty to the government that protected them. He believed that a government in which a ruler enjoyed absolute authority over the people would end the conflicts waged in the natural state. Although few political thinkers agreed that the individual owed total loyalty to the government, Hobbes' writings contributed to the growing idea that government was based on a negotiated agreement between the rulers and the ruled, rather than on raw force and power.

Like Hobbes and Locke, Jean-Jacques Rousseau, a French philosopher, also believed that people had once lived in a state of nature and freedom, but had many years ago entered into a contractual agreement with their government. He wrote that many governments in more recent times had come under the control of unjust rulers who ruled at the expense of their citizens' personal freedom. He argued that the people alone had the right to determine how they should be governed. In *The Social Contract,* published in 1762, he wrote that "man is born free, yet everywhere he is found in chains." Rousseau was referring to the large number of people on the European continent living under oppressive governments. He proposed that because all human beings in a state of nature were born free, the main duty of government should be to maintain as much freedom as possible in a civilized society.

A French philosopher, Charles de Secondat, the Baron of Montesquieu, was the first political writer to speak about the idea of dividing government into three separate branches with different duties and the ability to check on each other's power. In his book *The Spirit of the Laws,* published in 1748, Montesquieu pointed out in an examination of English government that no one person was allowed to make the laws, enforce the laws, and interpret the laws. This partial separation of governmental responsibilities helped to prevent the abuse of power and to protect the liberties of the English people. The framers of our Constitution agreed with

▲ In 1762 French political philosopher Jean-Jacques Rousseau commented on the large number of Europeans living under oppressive governments by stating that "Man is born free, yet everywhere he is found in chains." What did Rousseau feel was the main duty of government?

Caption Answer Rousseau felt that the main duty of government should be to maintain as much freedom as possible in a civilized society.

Critical Thinking Skills
Encourage students to analyze the statement that "the American way of life is, in many respects, the result of the American way of governing." How would you define the American way of life?

Reteaching Strategies
1. Allow small groups of students to review and discuss the notes they took while reading this section.
2. Have the students work with partners to write their own definitions of these terms: *limited government; representative government.*

Evaluation Strategies
1. Have the students write their answers to the first three questions of the Section 1 Review.
2. Have the students work in groups to discuss their responses to the final Section 1 Review question. Check on each discussion group to be sure all the students are contributing.
3. Have the students take the Section 1 Quiz found in the *TRB*.

Figure Answer The British felt that a colony on Roanoke Island would be an advantage in their conflict with Spain.

Section 1 Review (Answers)
1. The concept that government is not all-powerful and that it may do only those things the people have given it the power to do. The American way of government follows this concept by limiting the power of government and of those who govern.
2. A system in which public policies are made by officials who are selected by the people and held accountable through elections.
3. John Locke argued that people were born free, equal, and independent and that all persons had a natural right to life, liberty and property. Thomas Hobbes contributed to the idea that government was not based on power, but on an agreement negotiated between the rulers and the ruled. Montesquieu was the first political writer to speak of dividing government into three separate branches. Rousseau argued that the people alone had the right to determine how they should be governed.
4. Answers will vary, e.g., the rights of those accused of a crime such as the right to a trial.

SECTION 2

Points to Stress
• The first British outpost in North America and its history.
• The manner of government proposed by the Plymouth Company in the Mayflower Compact.
• Fundamental Orders of Connecticut and the principles it enumerated.
• The role of the early colonial legislatures.

Kickoff Activity
Have the students list at least eight words or phrases that come to mind when they think of the Pilgrims. Then have the students share, compare, and discuss their lists.

Working with the Preview Questions
Ask the students to read these study questions and briefly discuss their responses before they read

Montesquieu, but wanted to ensure that the American form of government had an even more distinct separation of powers. In this way, they hoped that liberty would be safer in the United States than in England.

As you shall see, the ideas of these philosophers are clearly embodied in the documents that outline the American philosophy of government.

The American way of life is, in many respects, the result of the American system of government, which resulted from many struggles against nature, England, and ourselves. In order to fully understand this system, we must trace its roots back to our nation's beginnings. Between 1600 and 1750, Americans, as we would later be called, developed a **political philosophy,** which is a set of notions or ideas about how people should be governed.

Section 1 Review

1. What is the concept of limited government? How did the American way of government evolve out of this concept?
2. What is the system of representative government?
3. How did the theories of European philosophers influence American political thinking?
4. **For critical analysis:** What are some common restrictions on government in the United States that follow the principle of limited government?

Section 2

The First British Settlements

Preview Questions

- What was the first British settlement in North America? What were some of the changes that this settlement went through?
- How was the Plymouth Company set up to be governed?
- What was the nation's first written constitution? What kind of government did it establish?

During the 1590s, Britain and Spain were constantly at war. Government officials in Britain decided that their war efforts against Spain would be improved by having British ships along the shores of North America. These ships could then harass the Spanish treasure fleets, which consisted of fast ships that took gold and other precious metals from the New World to Spain. Sir Walter Raleigh, the adventurer and writer, convinced England's queen, Elizabeth I, to allow him to establish the first British outpost in North America. He did this by sending a ship of settlers in 1585 to Roanoke Island off the coast of North Carolina in an unsuccessful attempt to create a settlement.

The Many British Attempts at Settlement

In 1607 another group from London, the Virginia Company, established a trading post in Virginia, which they called Jamestown. In the first year of its existence, over 60 percent of the colony's 105 inhabitants had died. In 1609, England sent over 800 new arrivals. By the spring of the following year only 60 were left. The survivors, admitting defeat, decided to return to England. Just as they were planning to depart, new supplies and more settlers arrived on three ships. The original 60 colonists changed their plans; together, the colonists all

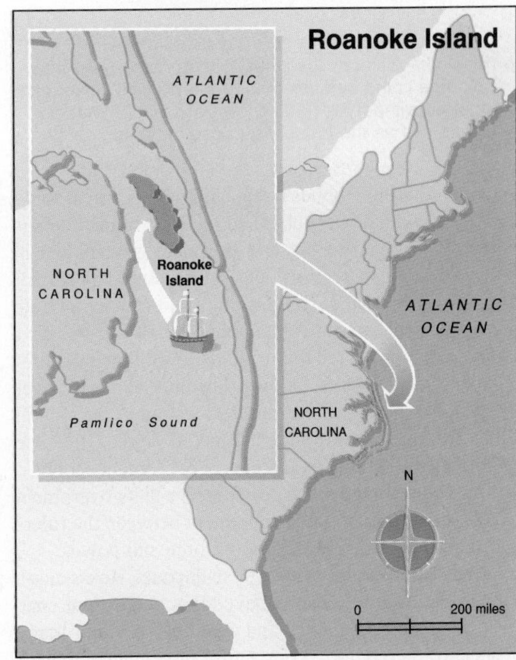

▲ **FIGURE 2–1 Roanoke Island.** The first British outpost in North America was established by Sir Walter Raleigh on Roanoke Island in 1585. Why did Britain want to establish a settlement in North America?

the section. Tell the students that they should be prepared to answer these questions more fully when they have finished reading the section.

Teaching Strategies

Introduction

After the students have read the section introduction, encourage them to discuss the establishment and disappearance of the Roanoke colony. Ask volunteers to read more about this settlement and its mysterious fate and then to share their findings with the rest of the class.

Enrichment

Have several volunteers research the early history of St. Augustine, Florida, and share their findings with the rest of the class.

Discussion Starter

Ask the students: What importance do you think this charter must have had for the colonists? How might it have affected their attitudes and actions? What effect do you think it had on the importance of Jamestown to future colonists?

Vocabulary

Ask the students: What is the difference between a charter and a compact? What does this difference imply about differences between the Jamestown settlers and the Pilgrims?

Caption Answer The English colonists at Jamestown found life to be very harsh as 60 percent of the colony's 105 inhabitants died during the first year of the colony.

Critical Thinking Skills

Ask the students to write a one-paragraph answer to the following: Why were women not included in these activities? What does this exclusion tell you about the society in which the Pilgrims lived?

Multidiscipline Strategies

Math Have the students work in groups to analyze the figures given for the survival of settlers in the Jamestown colony. In each group mentioned in the text, what percentage survived? If those percentages were applied to the population of the school, how many students would survive? Then encourage the group members to collect data on other settlements, including perhaps Roanoke and Plymouth. Have each group prepare a chart or graph showing the survival rates they have collected and calculated.

This 19th century engraving depicts the arrival of the first English colonists at Jamestown, Virginia in May, 1607. What happened to these colonists?

rebuilt Jamestown, which became the first permanent British settlement in North America.[1]

Of the six thousand people who left England for Virginia between 1607 and 1623, four thousand died. Those who lived established a type of government that would serve as a model for later colonial adventures.

Representative Assembly The king of England gave the Virginia Company of London a **charter,** a written grant of authority, to make laws "for the good and welfare" of the Jamestown settlement. Jamestown's colonists used this charter to institute a **representative assembly,** a law-making body that is composed of individuals who represent the population. A representative assembly is different from a *direct democracy,* which was discussed in Chapter 1—a type of government in which citizens collectively make the decision.

Pilgrims and the Mayflower Compact The Plymouth Company established the first New England colony in 1620. A group of English Protestants, calling themselves Pilgrims, sailed to North America on the *Mayflower,* a 180-ton, 90-foot (27-meter) ship with three masts and two decks. They landed at what is now Provincetown Harbor, at the tip of Cape Cod in Massachusetts. (They later moved the ship to Plymouth, Massachusetts, which became their new home.) Even before the Pilgrims went ashore, the adult males drew up the **Mayflower Compact,** or agreement, in which they set up a government and promised to obey its laws. (See the Resource Center.) It was signed by 41 of the 44 men aboard on November 21, 1620. No women were allowed to sign it, nor did they have any direct part in developing it, because women at that time did not have any political status. The Pilgrims felt obligated to establish a written document for self-government because their leaders believed that they needed a set of rules to govern themselves. They also wanted to create a government based on the consent of the governed.

The Mayflower Compact, although often referred to as a constitution, was in fact a *social contract,* of the type that Locke had described—an agreement among individuals to establish a government and to abide by its rules. This particular social contract had great historical significance because it served as a **prototype**—a model—for similar compacts in American history.

By 1639 a number of Pilgrims were being persecuted for their religious beliefs, and decided to leave

1. It was not the first permanent *European* settlement in North America. That honor goes to St. Augustine, Florida—a city that still exists—which was founded on September 8, 1565, by the Spaniard Pedro Menéndez de Áviles.

Discussion Starter
Help students discuss the fact that women were not allowed to help develop or to sign the Mayflower Compact: Why were women not included in these activities? What does this exclusion tell you about the society in which the Pilgrims lived? Are women included in all political decision-making activities today? Encourage the students to explain their responses.

Cooperative Learning
Divide the class into 13 small groups, and assign each group one of the 13 colonies: Connecticut, Delaware, Georgia, Maryland, Massachusetts Bay, New Hampshire, New Jersey, New York, North Carolina, Pennsylvania, Rhode Island, South Carolina, Virginia. Have the group members work together to learn about the history of their assigned colony, particularly its political documents and its legislature.

Reteaching Strategies
1. Help groups of students act out the process of making an important decision as it might have taken place in Jamestown and in the Plymouth colony. How are the processes alike? Why are they different?
2. Guide groups of students in discussing the Fundamental Orders of Connecticut: Why is this document important? How are its provisions similar to those of the U.S. Constitution?

Evaluation Strategies
1. Have the students write their responses to the Preview Questions at the beginning of the section.
2. Have the students write their answers to the Section 2 Review questions.

Extension
Ask volunteers to research the settlements and claims in North America established by these countries: Spain, France, Holland, Sweden, Finland. Let the volunteers share their findings with the rest of the class, and encourage students to discuss how these other settlements may have affected the development of colonial governments.

Caption Answer At that time women were not considered to have any political status or power. Therefore, they had no direct involvement in writing or developing the Mayflower Compact and were not allowed to sign it.

Figure Answer The first written constitution was the Fundamental Orders of Connecticut, which called for a representative assembly and the popular election of the governor and judges.

▲ In 1620 the Pilgrims sailed aboard the Mayflower to establish a colony in New England. Before going ashore, the Pilgrims drew up the Mayflower Compact, which established a set of rules under which they would govern themselves. Why were no women allowed to sign the Mayflower Compact?

the Massachusetts Bay Colony. They colonized the area that is now Connecticut and in the process developed America's first written constitution—the **Fundamental Orders of Connecticut.** This written document called for a representative assembly, made up of elected representatives from each town to serve in that assembly and to make laws. It also called for the popular election of a governor and judges.

By 1732, all thirteen colonies had been established, each with its own political documents and constitutions. For example, the Massachusetts Body of Liberties was adopted in 1641. It supported protection of individual rights and became part of colonial law. In 1683 the Pennsylvania Frame of Government was passed. This document, along with the 1701 Pennsylvania Charter of Privileges, established at least part of the basis for the U.S. Constitution and the Bill of Rights.

Early Legislatures

Not only did the colonies have constitutions, they also had law-making bodies, called **legislatures.** The first one was the Virginia House of Burgesses, established in 1619. The first laws that this colonial legislature passed were to aid farmers and to impose fines for public idleness and improper dress.

By the time the colonies declared independence from England in 1776, each colony had its own representative government, and most governments had been operating for over one hundred years. These colonial legislative bodies were the schooling grounds for many of the leaders who later wrote the U.S. Constitution in 1787. The representative legislatures provided leaders with experience in self-government and provided a model for our later political framework.

These colonial groups and their individual members also had extensive contact with the governing methods

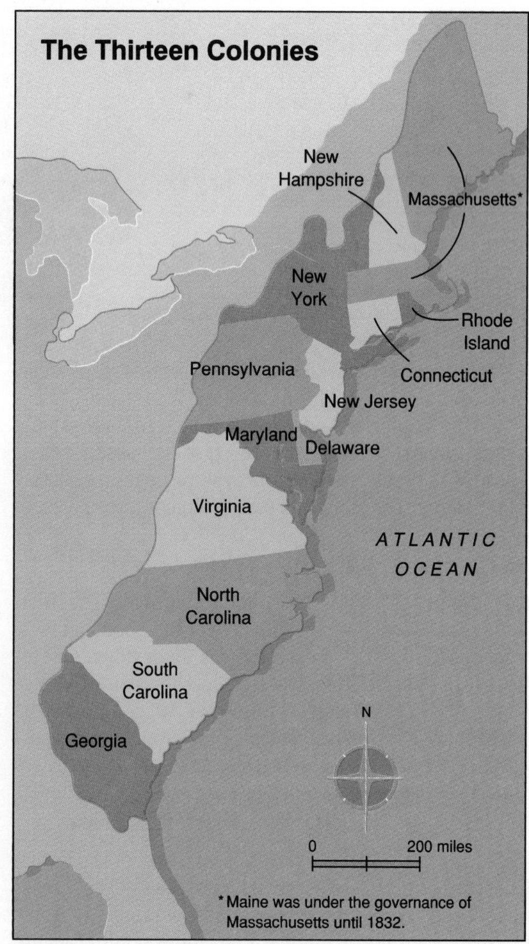

▲ **FIGURE 2–2 The Thirteen Colonies.** Georgia, the last of the thirteen colonies, was established in 1732. By this time, each of the thirteen colonies had developed its own political system complete with necessary political documents and a constitution. Which colony had the first written constitution and what was it called?

3. Have the students take the Section 2 quiz found in the *TRB.*

Section 2 Review (Answers)

1. The idea of a representative assembly, popular election, lawmaking bodies called legislatures, and the idea of a written constitution.

2. An assembly made up of elected representatives. The role of the people was to elect a governor and judges.

3. Answers will vary, e.g., it was the colonies' first example of representative democracy.

SECTION 3

Points to Stress

- Restrictions placed on the colonies by the British, and the reaction of the colonists.
- The need for and the objectives of the First Continental Congress.
- The accomplishments of the Second Continental Congress.
- Events and conflicts that precipitated the Declaration of Independence.
- The role of Natural Rights Philosophy on the Declaration of Independence.
- Perceptions of the citizens of the first states toward government.

Kickoff Activity

Have the students read the section title and then write their responses to this question: What differences in attitudes and interests may have made it difficult for the colonies to work together? After the students have finished writing, ask several volunteers to share their ideas with the rest of the class.

Working with the Preview Questions

Go over the study questions with the class. Then have the students read the section, taking notes in response to these questions.

Teaching Strategies

Introduction

After the students have read the section introduction, encourage them to discuss their responses to these questions: What was the significance of the three main responsibilities that the government in London maintained toward the colonies? Whom did those responsibilities serve?

Discussion Starter

Ask the students about the effects of the Navigation Acts: Who do you think benefited from these acts? How? Who suffered because of them? Why?

Caption Answer There were two primary reasons for the colonists' objections to the Stamp Act. One, the taxes were very severe. Two, the colonists had no elected official to represent their interests in Parliament. Therefore, the Stamp Act exemplified "taxation without representation."

of the native peoples. It was out of a rich Native American democratic tradition that some of the distinctive political beliefs of American life emerged.

Section 2 Review

1. What were the major political concepts brought to America by early English settlers?
2. What kind of governing body did the Fundamental Orders of Connecticut establish? What was the role of the people under this constitution?
3. **For critical analysis:** Describe the historical significance of the Fundamental Orders of Connecticut. How do we still see its principles in operation today?

SECTION 3

The Colonies Rebel

Preview Questions

- What were some of the restrictions that Britain placed on the colonies? How did the colonists react?
- Why was the First Continental Congress called into existence? What was decided at that meeting?
- What did the Second Continental Congress accomplish?
- What arguments and events led to the Declaration of Independence?
- What concerns did the citizens of the first states have toward their governments?

Even though the thirteen colonies had each been formed differently and were governed differently, they were all under the rulership of the British monarchy. Britain wanted the colonies to act in England's best interest, but the British government did little to manage its outposts in the colonies. After all, they were located more than three thousand miles (4831 kilometers) away and it took almost two months to sail across the Atlantic. Therefore, the colonies gradually became self-governing even though they were still officially ruled by the British Crown in London.

By the mid-1770s the government's responsibilities were limited to the defense of the colonies, a uniform system of money and credit, and a common market for colonial trade (that would benefit England). Otherwise, the colonies were free to do what they wanted. There was little taxation of the colonies to pay for the government in London.

Increasing British Restrictions

This period of limited taxation did not last. The British increased restrictions on the colonists in 1651 when the **Navigation Acts** were passed by the English Parliament. These acts required that only English ships (including ships of its colonies) could be used for trade within the British empire. Similar acts were passed until 1750.

In the early 1760s George III was crowned king of England. More restrictions were applied to colonial trade. The Proclamation of 1763 declared that no colonial settlement could be established west of the Appalachian Mountains. In 1764 the Sugar Act, which raised taxes, was passed to pay for wars that the British had waged. These taxes were also used to support British troops in North America, who were there to protect the colonists from the Indians and the French.

Taxation Without Representation

Further legislation soon followed. In 1765 the British Parliament passed the **Stamp Act,** placing the first direct tax on the colonies. The Stamp Act required the use of tax stamps on all legal documents, newspapers,

▲ This reproduction of a 19th century engraving shows American colonists protesting the Stamp Act by burning the English tax stamps in a bonfire in 1765. Why did the American colonists object to the Stamp Act?

Extension
Let several volunteers read about King George III and share their findings with the rest of the class. Then help the students discuss the effects of this particular king on the movement toward colonial independence: How do you think George III's personality and concept of the monarchy influenced the actions of the colonists during his reign?

Discussion Starter
Encourage the students to discuss their responses to these questions: Why did the participants in the Boston Tea Party dress as Mohawk Indians? What were the implications of their disguise?

Vocabulary
As they discuss the Coercive Acts, have the students review the definitions of *coercive* and *intolerable.*

Comprehension
Ask the students to identify the form of government the colonists were initiating by having each colony hold a convention to select delegates for the First Continental Congress.

Critical Thinking Skills
Help the students analyze and evaluate the committees by posing questions such as these: Do you think the formation of local committees to spy on the conduct of friends and neighbors was legal at the time? Do you think it was the right thing to do? Imagine that your town formed such a committee? Do you think it would be legal? Under what conditions, if any, do you think it would be the right thing to do?

Discussion Starter
Encourage the students to discuss the attitudes and aims of the British

Extension
Ask a group of students to assume the roles of delegates to the Stamp Act congress and to discuss these questions: What rights do we want to declare? What are our most important grievances? What can we accomplish by sending our declaration of rights and grievances to the king? What might we lose by sending such a declaration?

pamphlets, playing cards, and certain business agreements. The colonists denounced the new taxes, not only because the taxes were so severe, but also because they felt it was unfair to be taxed without having an elected official to represent their interests in Parliament. The colonists claimed this was ''taxation without representation.''

In October of 1765, nine of the thirteen colonies sent **delegates** (representatives) to the Stamp Act Congress held in New York City. The delegates prepared a declaration of rights and **grievances** (complaints) against the new British actions, which was sent to King George III. This action marked the first time that a majority of the colonies joined together to oppose British rule. As a result of the colonists' grievances, the British Parliament repealed the Stamp Act.

The British Crown passed new laws, however, designed to bind the colonies more tightly to the central government in London. Laws that imposed taxes on glass, paint, lead, and many other items were passed in 1767. The colonists protested the taxes by **boycotting**—refusing to purchase—all English goods. In 1773 anger over taxation reached a powerful climax at the famous Boston Tea Party, in which colonists dressed as Mohawk Indians dumped almost 350 chests of British tea into the Boston Harbor as a gesture of tax protest.

The British Parliament was quick to respond to the Tea Party. It passed the Coercive Acts (sometimes called the ''Intolerable Acts'') in 1774, which closed the harbor and placed the government of Boston under direct British control.

The First Continental Congress

In response to the ''Intolerable Acts,'' Rhode Island, Pennsylvania, and New York proposed the meeting of a colonial congress. The Massachusetts House of Representatives requested that all colonies select delegates to send to Philadelphia for such a congress.

On September 5, 1774, the **First Continental Congress** was held at Carpenters Hall in Philadelphia. Of the thirteen colonies, Georgia was the only one that did not send delegates. The First Continental Congress decided that the colonies should send a petition to King George III to explain their grievances. Other resolutions were passed to continue boycotting British trade and to require that each colony start an army. Almost immediately after receiving the petition, the British government condemned the congress' actions as open acts of rebellion.

The congressional delegates declared that every county and city in the colonies should form a committee whose mission was to spy on people's actions, and to report to the press the names of those who violated the trade boycott against Britain. The list of names was then printed in the local papers and the individuals so named were harassed and ridiculed. Over the next several months all colonial legislators supported this and other actions taken by the First Continental Congress.

The Second Continental Congress

Britain reacted to the resolution passed by the First Continental Congress with even more strict and repressive measures. On April 19, 1775, British soldiers, called Redcoats, fought with colonial citizen soldiers, called Minutemen, in the towns of Lexington and Concord in Massachusetts. The battle at Concord was the ''shot heard around the world,'' the first battle of the American Revolution. Less than a month later, delegates from twelve colonies (Georgia's delegates did not arrive until the fall) gathered in Pennsylvania for the **Second Continental Congress,** which immediately assumed the powers of a central government. It declared that the militiamen who had gathered around Boston were now a full army. It also named George Washington—a delegate to the Second Continental Congress who had some military experience—as its commander-in-chief.

The delegates to the Second Continental Congress still intended to reach a peaceful settlement with the British Parliament. As one declaration stated, ''we [the congress] have not raised armies with ambitious designs of separating from Great Britain, and establishing independent States.''

Independence

Public debate raged bitterly about the problems with Great Britain, but the stage was set for independence. One of the most rousing arguments in favor of independence was presented by a former English corsetmaker,[2] Thomas Paine, who wrote a brilliant pamphlet called *Common Sense.* In that pamphlet he mocked King George III, and attacked every argument that favored loyalty to the king. He wanted the developing colonies to become a model nation for democracy, in a world in

2. Corsets are close-fitting undergarments that were worn at the time by both men and women to give the appearance of having a smaller waist. Whalebone was inserted in the corsets to make them stiff, and lacing was used to tighten them around the body.

as reflected in their reaction to the colonists' petition describing their grievances.

Discussion Starter
Encourage the students to discuss the actions of the Second Continental Congress: By what right did the Congress assume the powers of a central government? Do you think that colonists who disagreed with this assumption of power had the right to protest? Why or why not?

Vocabulary
Ask the students: What does the term *near poetry* as applied to *Common Sense* mean? Do you consider the short selection from *Common Sense* "near poetry"? Why or why not?

Enrichment
Ask two groups of volunteers to research the lives and contributions of Samuel Adams and Richard Henry Lee. Have both groups plan and use an original method of presenting their information to the rest of the class.

Vocabulary
Ask the students to consider the use of the word *states* in the Resolution of Independence. What is the meaning of the word as it is used here? What does this imply about the intentions of the colonists?

COMMON SENSE;

ADDRESSED TO THE

INHABITANTS

OF

AMERICA,

On the following interesting

SUBJECTS.

I. Of the Origin and Design of Government in general, with concise Remarks on the English Constitution.

II. Of Monarchy and Hereditary Succession.

III. Thoughts on the present State of American Affairs.

IV. Of the present Ability of America, with some miscellaneous Reflections.

Man knows no Master save creating HEAVEN,
Or those whom choice and common good ordain.
THOMSON.

PHILADELPHIA;
Printed, and Sold, by R. BELL, in Third-Street.
MDCCLXXVI.

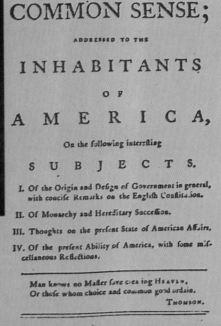

▶ Thomas Paine's pamphlet, *Common Sense,* went through 25 editions and sold over 120,000 copies in early 1776. How original were the arguments presented?

which other nations were oppressed by strong central governments.

None of Paine's arguments were new; in fact, most were commonly heard in tavern debates throughout the land. The reason that Paine's *Common Sense* was so effective was because of the near poetry of his words:

> A government of our own is our natural right: and when a man seriously reflects on the precariousness [uncertainty] of human affairs, he will become convinced, that it is infinitely wiser and safer, to form a constitution of our own in a cool and deliberate manner, while we have it in our power, than to trust such an interesting event to time and chance.

The Resolution of Independence Many colonists began to call for independence. Samuel Adams, a patriot from Massachusetts, asked "Is not America already independent? Why not then declare it?" In June of 1776, after more than a year of fighting, Richard Henry Lee of Virginia introduced the Resolution of Independence to the Second Continental Congress. By this time, the congress had already voted for free trade at all American ports for all countries except England. Congress had also suggested that all colonies establish state governments separate from Britain. On July 2 of that year, the congress adopted the Resolution of Independence:

> RESOLVED, That these United Colonies are, and of right ought to be free and independent States, that they are absolved from allegiance to the British Crown, and that all political connection between them and the state of Great Britain is, and ought to be, totally dissolved.

Although it was not a legally binding document, the Resolution of Independence was one of the first necessary steps to establish the **legitimacy**—legal authority—of a new nation in the eyes of foreign governments. The new nation required supplies for its armies and commitments of foreign military aid. Unless officials of foreign nations believed that this new land was truly

Caption Answer While the ideas were not really that original, *Common Sense* was popular for two main reasons. The first was the popularity of Paine's sentiments toward freedom for the colonies. The second was Paine's writing style, which used dynamic and forceful language beautifully.

Multidiscipline Strategies

Language Arts Ask a group of students to work together in reading and analyzing Thomas Paine's *Common Sense.* Have these students write an outline of the pamphlet. Then ask them to discuss their responses to these questions: Why do you think this pamphlet was considered so stirringly persuasive when it was first published? Why do you think people continue to read this pamphlet today?

Cooperative Learning
Have the students work in groups to learn more about Thomas Jefferson. Each group member should research aspects of Jefferson's life and contributions, and the entire group should share and discuss the information.

Enrichment
Ask the students to write short essays on the elimination of any condemnation of slavery in the Declaration of Independence: Why was such a condemnation eliminated? Do you consider its elimination justified? What might have happened—then and in the future—had the condemnation of slavery been retained in the Declaration?

Discussion Starter
Help the students discuss King George III's diary entry for July 4, 1776: Could the king have known about the Declaration of Independence when he wrote that diary entry? Why or why not? What kind of entry do you imagine the king might have written after learning about the Declaration? What attitude did he seem to have toward the colonists?

Extension
You might wish to have students read the Declaration of Independence for themselves. A copy of the Declaration of Independence can be found in the Resource Center at the back of this book as well as the student text. You might also wish to have the students work in small groups to outline the Declaration.

IN CONGRESS, JULY 4, 1776.

The unanimous Declaration of the thirteen united States of America,

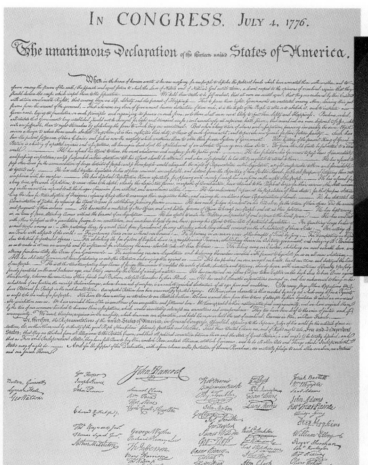

The Declaration of Independence, which was drafted by Thomas Jefferson, proclaimed to the world that Americans had been mistreated under British rule and were therefore severing their political ties with Britain. What did Jefferson, in the Declaration of Independence, name as an individual's inalienable rights?

Caption Answer The Declaration of Independence states "that all men are created equal, that they are endowed by their Creator with certain unalienable rights, that among these are life, liberty and the pursuit of happiness." You might have students compare this passage from the Declaration of Independence with the material earlier in the chapter on John Locke who stated that each citizen has a natural right to life, liberty, and property.

independent from Britain, they would not support its new leaders.

The Declaration of Independence Soon after Richard Henry Lee proposed the Resolution of Independence, Thomas Jefferson, a tall redheaded Virginia planter, began writing the draft of the Declaration of Independence. Jefferson worked alone on the document for the last two weeks in June. On June 28, he asked John Adams and Benjamin Franklin to look over his draft. They made few changes.

Immediately after adopting the Resolution of Independence, the congress was ready to pass Jefferson's declaration. Some of his work was amended so that all the delegates would accept it. For example, his condemnation of slavery was eliminated to satisfy delegates from Georgia and North Carolina, where slaves were held on many farms and plantations. On July 4, 1776, one of the world's most famous documents, the Declaration of Independence, was adopted. On that day King George III, unaware of events 3,000 miles away, wrote in his diary, "Nothing of importance happened today."

Minor changes were made in the following two weeks. On July 19, the modified draft became the "unanimous declaration of the thirteen United States of America." On August 2, the members of the Continental Congress signed it. The first official printed version carried only the signatures of the congress' president, John Hancock, and of its secretary, Charles Thompson.

TEACHING GOVERNMENT IN ACTION

Read
Before the students begin reading, encourage them to share their responses to these questions: How do you react to the often-used term founding fathers? What roles do you imagine women played in establishing the independence and developing the government of our country? Then have the students read the Case Study to themselves.

Discuss
Guide the students in discussing the Case Study by posing these questions: What do you consider the most important contributions made by the founding mothers? If the War of Independence were being fought today, what roles do you think women would play? Why would at least some of those roles be different from the work done by the women of the eighteenth century? What questions and conflicts might arise over the role of women in a twentieth-century war?

Analyze and Apply
Have each student interview at least three adults, asking what they consider the appropriate roles for women during times of war. Then have the students compare and discuss their findings.

Review
Have the students write their answers to these questions: What was the purpose of the Daughters of Liberty? How did Mercy Ottis Warren contribute to the movement toward independence and the establishment of a new government?

Think About It (Answers)
1. Answers will vary, e.g., women were not allowed to own property so they had no economic status. Without economic status, they would be given little opportunity to participate in any type of political affair.
2. Answers will vary, e.g., with each decade, women were allowed more significant roles in society. As these changes came about, women were allowed to participate more fully in political affairs, including wartime activities. It was also recognized in World Wars I and II that the help of women was vital.

GOVERNMENT IN ACTION

CASE STUDY

The Founding Mothers

There is always talk about America's founding fathers, but few of the books written about the colonial era ever mention our country's "founding mothers." While it may be true that no women were present at the Constitutional Convention, women nonetheless contributed significantly to the political changes of those times.

In the years prior to the American Revolution, many women encouraged opposition to the British. Small groups of women who called themselves "Daughters of Liberty" helped spread the boycott of British goods. Some women wrote political pamphlets, which helped turn public opinion in favor of independence. Mercy Ottis Warren (1728–1814) of Massachusetts was one of the first people to urge the Massachusetts delegates to the Second Continental Congress to vote for independence from England. Warren expressed her political ideas in written correspondence with John Adams and Thomas Jefferson, and wrote a three-volume history of the American Revolution called *The History of the Rise, Progress, and Determination of the American Revolution,* which was published in 1805. She also helped encourage pro-revolutionary sentiments by making fun of the British colonial government in her plays, *The Adulateur* (1773), *The Defeat* (1773), and *The Group* (1775).

During the War for Independence, many women served as nurses, seamstresses, and cooks. A few even disguised themselves as men and fought in battle. One such female soldier is buried in West Point Cemetery.

After independence was won many women remained politically active, including Mercy Warren. She campaigned against the proposed constitution because she did not think it allowed people to participate enough in the affairs of government.

THINK ABOUT IT

1. How do you think women's economic status over 200 years ago in this country may have prevented them from participating as actively as men did in the American Revolution?
2. How do you think the roles of women in World War I or World War II might have differed from their roles in the Revolutionary War?

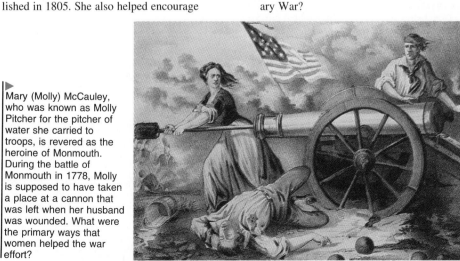

Mary (Molly) McCauley, who was known as Molly Pitcher for the pitcher of water she carried to troops, is revered as the heroine of Monmouth. During the battle of Monmouth in 1778, Molly is supposed to have taken a place at a cannon that was left when her husband was wounded. What were the primary ways that women helped the war effort?

Caption Answer Student answers will vary, but might include caring for the sick and wounded, cooking, mending clothes, etc. Women also helped by scavenging the battlefield for clothes and equipment. Women helped to bury the dead. One group of women in New York converted the lead from a statue of King George III, which had been torn down by New Yorkers, into cartridges for American rifles. Additionally, women helped to maintain the homes and the society for which the battles were being fought. On another note, you might wish to point out to students that there is some argument among historians regarding the validity of the stories that have grown up about Molly Pitcher.

Cooperative Learning
Have students work in groups to consider the meaning of this statement from the Declaration: "It is the Right of the People to alter or abolish [the government], and to institute a new government." Who are "the People"? Which group of people were the signers of the Declaration considering? How might other groups of people interpret this statement? Under what conditions do you think it would be appropriate for the people of our country to consider altering or abolishing their government? Can you imagine those conditions existing today? Why or why not?

Discussion Starter
Ask the students to discuss the form of government established in Pennsylvania and Georgia: Do you think this government could provide effective protection for the people? Why or why not?

Reteaching Strategies
1. Let the students work with partners to review and revise the notes they have taken on this section.
2. Have students work in groups to debate the signing of the Declaration of Independence. Assign some of the group members to support signing, and others to oppose it. Provide guidance as necessary, to be sure both sides of the issue are presented.

Evaluation Strategies
1. Have the students write their answers to the Section 3 Review questions.
2. Have the students take the Section 3 Quiz found in the *TRB*.

Section 3 Review (Answers)
1. The colonies were officially governed by the British Crown but were gradually becoming selfgoverning. This was mainly due to the distance between the colonies and the British government.
2. The colonists denounced the Act and sent delegates to the Stamp Act Congress, which prepared a declaration of rights and grievances.
3. A resolution that the colonies should send a petition to King George III to explain their grievances.
4. In 1773 the famous Boston Tea Party took place in which colonists dressed as Mohawks and dumped chests of British tea into the harbor to protest British taxes. There was a growing attitude that the colonies were indeed independent and should therefore declare their independence. In July of 1776, the Second Continental Congress adopted the Resolution of Independence.
5. Answers will vary, e.g., yes, the experiences of the colonists caused them to rally together against the British, but also made them fearful of a strong central government.

SECTION 4

Points to Stress
• The provisions articulated in the Articles of Confederation.
• Weaknesses of the Articles of Confederation.
• The importance of the 1780s to American history.

Natural Rights and the Consent of the Governed

The second paragraph of the Declaration of Independence begins with this sentence:

> We hold these Truths to be self-evident, that all Men are created equal, that they are endowed by their Creator with certain inalienable Rights, that among these are Life, Liberty, and the Pursuit of Happiness. . . .

The inalienable—or natural—rights referred to in the Declaration of Independence are the same rights that Locke presented in his political philosophy. Natural rights are *inherent* rights, meaning they cannot be taken away from a person, and are beyond the power of governments to grant or deny.

According to the Declaration of Independence, government exists to protect individuals' natural rights. In a democratic society, government derives its power from the **consent of the governed,** which means that the people give government the power to rule. Because government is based on the will of the people, it can also be abolished by the people. The Declaration of Independence declares that whenever any form of government "becomes destructive to these ends, it is the Right of the People to alter or abolish it, and to institute a new government." (See the Resource Center.)

The American Creed The ideals and standards set forth in the Declaration of Independence have become known as the **American Creed,** a set of political beliefs that most analysts agree exists in the United States. The American Creed stresses natural rights, limited government, equality under the law, and government by consent of the governed. In some ways, the Declaration of Independence defines the American sense of right and wrong. It presents a challenge to anyone who might wish to overthrow our democratic processes, or deny our citizens their natural rights to life, liberty, and the pursuit of happiness. (See the Resource Center.)

From Colonies to States

Even prior to the Declaration of Independence, some of the colonies had transformed themselves into sovereign states, with their own permanent governments. In May of 1776, the Second Continental Congress had directed each of the colonies to form "such governments as shall . . . best be conducive to the happiness and safety of their constituents [voters]." Before then all thirteen colonies had constitutions. Eleven of the colonies had newly drafted their constitutions; the other two, Rhode Island and Connecticut, made minor modifications to old royal charters. Seven of the new constitutions contained bills of rights that defined the personal liberties of all state citizens. All constitutions called for limited governments.

Many citizens were fearful of a strong central government because of their experience under the British Crown. They opposed any form of government that even seemed like monarchy, such as a strong **executive authority**—a person with wide-reaching administrative powers. Consequently, wherever such anti-royalist sentiment was strong, the legislature itself became all powerful. In Pennsylvania and Georgia, **unicameral** (one-house) **legislatures** were unchecked by executive authority. Indeed, anti-royalist sentiment was so strong that the executive branch was weak in most states. This situation would continue until the ratification of the U.S. Constitution.

Section 3 Review

1. What kind of relationships had developed between the British Crown and the colonies by the mid-1700s? Why?
2. How did the thirteen colonies respond to the Stamp Act of 1765?
3. What type of resolution did the First Continental Congress pass?
4. Describe the major events and common attitudes that led to the signing of the Declaration of Independence.
5. **For critical analysis:** Do you think the experiences under English rule made it difficult for Americans to form a strong national government? Explain your answer.

Section 4

The Articles of Confederation

Preview Questions

- What are the basic provisions and weaknesses of the Articles of Confederation?
- Why were the 1780s a critical period in American history?
- What major events and popular sentiments led to the Constitutional Convention of 1787?

• The events, conflicts, and sentiments that eventually led to the Constitutional Convention of 1787.

Kickoff Activity
Write these three terms on the board: *articles, confederation, Articles of Confederation.* Ask the students to use prior knowledge and/or guesswork to write definitions (in their own words) of the first two terms. Then have them write a definition of the third term, based on what they have already written. After the students have finished writing, encourage them to share and compare their responses.

Working with the Preview Questions
Allow volunteers to read these study questions aloud to the class. Remind the students to look for answers to these questions as they read, instructing them to be prepared to write complete answers when they have finished Section 4.

TEACHING SOCIAL STUDIES SKILLS

Read
Begin by letting the students name government publications with which they are familiar. For each kind of publication mentioned, ask: What kind of information does this publication present? Have you ever used this publication? How? Then have volunteers read the Building Social Studies Skills section aloud.

Discuss
Have the students discuss each publication: Who do you imagine uses this publication most frequently? How and why might you use it?

Analyze and Apply
Ask the students to work in pairs or small groups to locate each government publication in a local (or school) library. Have the students browse through a current copy of each and write a one- or two-sentence description of what they find.

Review
Have each student write this statement, filling in the blanks: I expect . . . will be the most useful government publication for me this year because. . . .

Teaching Strategies

Introduction
After the students have read the section introduction, stimulate discussion by asking these questions: How does the association of states in this early period of American history compare to what you know about our current government? Encourage the students to explain and support their ideas.

Vocabulary
Ask the students to define *ambassadors* and to explain the significance of using this term for the assembly representatives.

Comprehension
Have the students restate the quote from Articles of Confederation in their own words. Students may write their definitions or discuss it in small groups.

BUILDING SOCIAL STUDIES SKILLS
Using Government Publications

Every year the government prints hundreds of publications, many of which can be useful in understanding American government and politics. Listed below are several government publications that may prove useful in your studies.

The *Statistical Abstract of the United States* is published by the Bureau of the Census. It contains hundreds of tables that give statistics on the social, political, and economic status of government and business in the United States. Its hundreds of charts, graphs, and tables cover topics such as population, law enforcement, immigration, and much more.

The *Book of States* is published by the Council of State Governments. It contains information on state governments, economies, taxes, constitutions, and many other subjects.

The *Congressional Record* is published for every day that Congress is in session. It contains everything that is said and done on the floors of both houses. It is bound and indexed annually.

The *Congressional Directory* is a publication of the Congressional Joint Committee on Printing. It contains autobiographical accounts of the members of Congress, lists of committees and committee assignments, statistics for recent congressional elections, and maps of congressional districts.

The *United States Government Manual* is a guide to the federal government. It contains information about the legislative, executive, and judicial branches of government and federal agencies and commissions. Addresses and telephone numbers of government offices are also included.

PRACTICING YOUR SKILLS

Go to your local library and use the sources listed above to find the following items and information.

1. A map of your congressional district
2. An autobiographical account of one of the senators in your state
3. The name of the state judicial agency that can give you information about your state's handgun law

Anti-royalist sentiments influenced the thinking of the delegates to the Continental Congress, who formed a committee to draft a plan of confederation. A **confederation** is a voluntary association of *independent* states. In a confederation, the member states agree to let the central government undertake a limited number of activities, such as forming an army. But the member states themselves do not allow many restrictions on their own actions. They typically can still govern most state affairs as they see fit.

On November 15, 1777, the Second Continental Congress agreed on a draft of the plan, which was finally signed by all thirteen colonies on March 1, 1781. The Articles of Confederation, the result of this plan, served as this nation's first national constitution. They represent an important step in the creation of our governmental system. (See the Resource Center.)

The Government of the Confederation

The Congress of the Confederation was the central governing body for all the states. This congress was a unicameral assembly of ambassadors, as they were called, from the various states. Although the states could send between two and seven ambassadors each to the congress, each state, no matter what the size, had only one vote. The issue of sovereignty was an important part of the Articles of Confederation:

> Each State retains its sovereignty, freedom and independence, and every power, jurisdiction, and right, which is not by this Confederation expressly delegated to the United States in Congress assembled.

The structure of our government under the Articles of Confederation is shown in Figure 2–3 on page 36.

The Powers of Congress Under the Articles

Congress had several powers under the Articles of Confederation:

- To enter into treaties and alliances
- To establish and control armed forces

Cooperative Learning
Divide the class into small groups to consider figure 2–3, Our Government Under the Articles of Confederation: What essential information is presented about each section of the government? How does that government compare to the government later established and still in use today?

Discussion Starter
Ask the students: What is the importance of each power granted to Congress? Which powers—or aspects of powers—seem to be missing from this list? How do you think this allocation of power affected both the central government and the state governments?

Discussion Starter
Help the students discuss the development of the stature of the Congress of the Confederation within the community of nations: What was the particular significance of Congress's ability to negotiate and sign a peace treaty? How would the other nations of the world need to treat the colonies in the future?

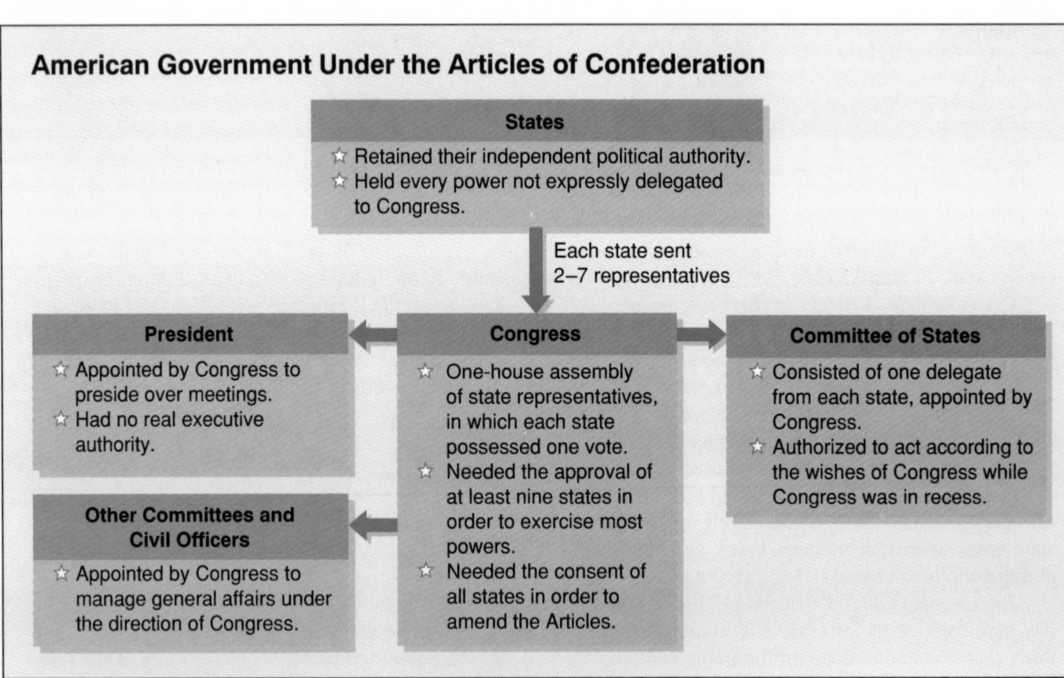

American Government Under the Articles of Confederation
States
Retained their independent political authority.
Held every power not expressly delegated to Congress.
Each state sent 2–7 representatives
President
Appointed by Congress to preside over meetings.
Had no real executive authority.
Congress
One-house assembly of state representatives, in which each state possessed one vote.
Needed the approval of at least nine states in order to exercise most powers.
Needed the consent of all states in order to amend the Articles.
Committee of States
Consisted of one delegate from each state, appointed by Congress.
Authorized to act according to the wishes of Congress while Congress was in recess.
Other Committees and Civil Officers
Appointed by Congress to manage general affairs under the direction of Congress.

FIGURE 2–3 American Government Under the Articles of Confederation. As you can see from looking at the figure above, the individual states were supreme in power under the Articles of Confederation. Under the Articles of Confederation, how was a president chosen? Was the president very powerful?

Figure Answer Under the Articles of Confederation, the president who was appointed by Congress, had a position similar to that of a chairperson in a meeting. The president under the Articles of Confederation had no real executive authority. Students should understand that this weak presidential role grew out of the colonists' mistrust of a strong central government and their fear of a tyrannical leader.

This figure content is also featured on *West's American Government Videodisc* (see the index found in the *TRB*) and is available in the transparency package.

- To declare war and make peace
- To regulate coinage (but not paper money)
- To borrow money from the people
- To create a postal system
- To regulate Indian affairs
- To set standards of weights and measures
- To create courts for problems related to ships at sea
- To settle disputes between the states under certain circumstances
- To guarantee that citizens visiting other states would have the same rights and privileges as the state's resident

Under the Articles, a number of accomplishments were made. Certain states' claims to western land were settled with the **Northwest Ordinance.** It established a basic pattern for how states should govern new territories north of the Ohio River. Additionally, and perhaps most importantly, the United States under the Articles of Confederation won the Revolutionary War. Congress was then able to negotiate a peace treaty with Great Britain that was signed in 1783. Under the treaty, Britain not only recognized American independence, but also granted the United States all of the territory from the Atlantic Ocean to the Mississippi River, and from the Great Lakes and Canada to what is now northern Florida.

The Articles of Confederation proved to be a good "first draft" for the Constitution of the United States, which was soon to follow. They were an unplanned experiment that tested some of the principles of government set forth earlier in the Declaration of Independence. Some argue that without the experience of government under the Articles of Confederation, it would have been difficult, if not impossible, to arrive at the compromises that were put into the Constitution several years later.

Weaknesses of the Government of the Confederation

In spite of its accomplishments, the government created by the Articles was in fact weak. Due to its lack of power, the central government had a difficult time coping with the problems that the growing nation was facing.

Critical Thinking Skills
Guide the students in analyzing the significance of the experience of the Articles of the Confederation: What do you think the leaders of the new nation learned from this experience? Why were those lessons significant in the further development of the government? Do you think the Constitution could have been so successful if it had not been preceded by the Articles of Confederation? Why or why not?

Cooperative Learning
Let the students work in groups to examine and discuss figure 2–4, Weaknesses in the Articles of Confederation. Have the members of each group identify the causes of each weakness and then discuss the result of that weakness. Encourage all the students in each group to contribute.

FIGURE 2–4 Weaknesses in the Articles of Confederation. The lack of a strong central government and the fierce independence of the states under the Articles of Confederation led to several problems. Each of these problems was due to a weakness in the Articles of Confederation. Which weakness led to financial problems for the central government?

Weaknesses in the Articles of Confederation

Weakness	Result
Congress could not force the states to meet military quotas.	They could not draft soldiers to form a standing army.
Congress could not regulate commerce between the states or with other nations.	Each state was free to set up its own system of taxes on goods imported from other states. Economic quarrels among the states broke out. There was difficulty in trading with other nations.
Congress could enter into treaties, but could not enforce its power or control foreign relations.	The states were not forced to respect treaties. Many states entered into treaties independent of Congress.
Congress could not directly tax the people.	It had to rely on the states to collect and forward taxes, which the states were reluctant to do. The central government was always short of money.
Congress had no power to enforce its laws.	The central government depended on the states to enforce its laws, which they rarely did.
Nine states had to approve any law before it was enacted.	Most laws were difficult, if not impossible, to enact.
Any amendment to the Articles required all 13 states to consent.	The powers of the central government could not be changed in practice.
There was no national judicial system.	Most disputes among the states could not be settled by the national government.
There was no executive branch.	Coordinating the work of the central government was almost impossible.

Figure Answer Because Congress could not directly tax the people and had to rely on the states to collect and forward taxes, the central government faced constant money problems.

This figure content is also featured on *West's American Government Videodisc* (see the index found in the *TRB*).

TEACHING CITIZENSHIP SKILLS AND RESPONSIBILITIES

Read
Introduce this section by asking the students these questions: Who makes decisions about government matters? What kinds of decisions do they make? What processes do you think they use—or should use—in making such decisions? Encourage the students to express and discuss a variety of ideas. Then have the students independently read Citizenship Skills and Responsibilities.

Discuss
Help the students discuss the section by asking these questions: Which steps in the decision-making process do you consider most important? Why? Which do you consider most difficult? Why? Which steps do you think could be left out of the process without affecting the outcome? Why? Encourage the students to present and support differing points of view.

Analyze and Apply
Have the students work in groups to select a local problem involving their class, their school, or their neighborhood. Then have the group members work through the decision-making process to reach a decision; on what should be done regarding the issue selected.

Review
Have each student write an evaluation of the process his or her group used in making a decision.

Comprehension
To check the students' understanding, ask them to write short answers to these questions: Why did the Articles of Confederation create a weak government? Why were the states so intent on maintaining their own sovereignty?

Reteaching Strategies
1. Have the students work with partners to write a one-paragraph summary of the information presented in figure 2–3, Our Government under the Articles of Confederation, page 36.
2. Work with groups of students to discuss the importance of the end of the War for Independence: What status did the signing of the peace treaty grant to the new nation?

Evaluation Strategies
1. Have the students write their responses to the Preview Questions at the beginning of the section.
2. Have the students write their answers to the Section 4 Review questions.
3. Have the students take the Section 4 Quiz found in the *TRB*.

CITIZENSHIP SKILLS AND RESPONSIBILITIES

Making Decisions

Think of a serious problem facing your community, such as crime, pollution, overpopulation, lack of educational facilities, or inadequate transportation systems. Although everyone might agree there is a problem, chances are everyone does not agree on the same solution.

One vital citizenship skill is making thoughtful decisions about such government matters. Also, some day you may want to make a decision about which candidate to elect for governor, state representative, or school board chair. You may need to decide what to do about one of the problems mentioned above. Remember that there is almost always more than one solution to any problem. To make the best decision, you need to identify all possible alternatives and choose the one that will be the most effective for yourself and others. Doing this means knowing what goals or values are involved in each alternative, and what the consequences of each choice will be.

The process outlined below can help you make wise decisions:

1. **Define what you need or want.** Try to pinpoint what it is you are trying to accomplish or what you need or want from your decision.
2. **Look carefully at your resources.** Be aware of all the resources available to you.
3. **Identify your choices.** There are at least two choices, and usually more, for every decision. Sometimes you need to gather information and do research in order to identify your choices. Try to come up with as many possibilities as you can without eliminating any.
4. **Sort through your choices.** After you've listed all your choices, take a good look at each one. Consider their advantages and disadvantages. Be sure that each option you are considering is legal and ethical.
5. **Compare your choices.** Use the information you have found to evaluate each possible choice. Compare them and see which one makes the most sense.
6. **Make the decision.**
7. **Make a plan to carry out your decision.**

TAKING ACTION

1. Think of a decision you have made recently. Name two options you had and name the advantages and disadvantages of each.
2. Think of a problem facing your community. Recommend a possible solution to the problem by using the decision-making process outlined above. Then send your recommendation to the council, commission, or official in charge of making such decisions.
3. Do you think the founding fathers used any part of this decision-making process while they were drafting the Declaration of Independence or the Articles of Confederation? Explain your answer.

The Articles of Confederation also had other major weaknesses, which are listed in Figure 2–4 on page 37. These weaknesses stemmed from the fact that the government under the Articles was made up of independent states that had no intention of giving up their sovereignty.

As you can see from the figure on page 37, much of the functioning of the government under the Articles basically depended on the goodwill of the states. Article 3, for example, simply established a ''league of friendship'' among the states, with no central government intended.

A Time of Crisis—the 1780s

The Revolutionary War ended on October 18, 1781. The Treaty of Paris, which confirmed the colonies' independence from Britain, was signed in 1783. Peace with the British may have been won, but peace within the new nation was hard to find. The states bickered among themselves, and refused to support the new central government in almost every way.

As George Washington stated, ''We are one nation today and thirteen tomorrow. Who will treat us on such

Caption Answer Shays' Rebellion is credited with being a catalyst for change. Many political and business leaders saw Shays' Rebellion as final proof that a strong central government was needed.

Section 4 Review (Answers)

1. The power to enter into treaties and alliances, establish and control armed forces, declare war and make peace, to create coinage, to borrow money, to regulate Indian affairs, to create courts for problems related to ships at sea, to settle disputes between states under certain circumstances, to create a postal system, and to guarantee that citizens visiting other states would have the same rights and privileges as the state's residents.
2. Congress was made up of one branch and each state could send two to seven representatives, but only had one vote per state. The exercise of most powers required approval of at least nine states.
3. Congress could not force states to meet military quotas and could not regulate commerce between the states or with other nations. Congress could enter into treaties, but could not enforce its powers or control foreign relations. **Congress could not directly tax the people. Congress had no power to enforce its own laws. There was no national judicial system and no executive branch. As a result the states came into conflict with each other and resisted the central government's decisions.**
4. States had begun to battle with each other over many issues. They started printing their own money and taxing each other's goods.
5. Answers will vary, e.g., it became apparent to these people that without a strong central government, the nation was in danger of deteriorating into disorganized competing factions.

terms?'' States started printing their own money at dizzying rates, which lead to inflated prices. The states also increasingly taxed each other's goods and at times even prevented trade altogether. The intensity of the states' squabbles reached a boiling point in a well-known event that occurred in August, 1786.

Shays' Rebellion In western Massachusetts, angry farmers protested the state legislature's decision not to issue cheap paper money, as well as the state court's decision to throw debtors in jails. Finally, in 1786, former revolutionary captain Daniel Shays, along with approximately two thousand armed farmers, seized county courthouses and disrupted the debtors' trials. Shays' men then launched an attack on the national government arsenal in Springfield. The rebellion continued to grow into the winter when it was finally stopped by the Massachusetts militia.

Despite the upheaval, the revolt had actually done something important. It had scared American political and business leaders, and caused more and more Americans to realize that a *true* national government had to be created. That central government had to be strong enough to cope with the serious economic problems facing the nation.

▼ This 19th century engraving depicts the battle between Daniel Shays' rebels and the government troops at the arsenal at Springfield, Massachusetts. Why was Shays' Rebellion so important?

The Annapolis Meeting Unhappy members of the Confederation Congress jumped at the Virginia legislature's call for a meeting of all states at Annapolis, Maryland, on September 11, 1786. Five of the thirteen states sent delegates, two of whom were Alexander Hamilton of New York and James Madison of Virginia. Both of these men favored a strong central government. Thus, they were called **nationalists.** They persuaded the other delegates to issue a report calling on the states to hold a constitutional convention in Philadelphia in May of the following year.

The Confederation Congress at first was reluctant to give its approval to the Philadelphia convention. By mid-February of 1787, however, seven of the states had named delegates to the Philadelphia meeting. Finally, on February 21, the Congress called upon the states to send delegates to Philadelphia ''for the sole and expressed purpose of revising the Articles of Confederation.'' That Philadelphia meeting became the Constitutional Convention.

Section 4 Review

1. What were the powers of Congress under the Articles of Confederation?
2. Describe the government set up by the Articles.
3. What were the major weaknesses of the Articles and what were the results of those weaknesses?
4. What did George Washington mean when he stated, ''We are one nation today and thirteen tomorrow. Who will treat us on such terms?''
5. **For critical analysis:** Why do you think Shays' Rebellion scared American business and political leaders?

Section 5

Creating The Constitution

Preview Questions

- What basic concepts did the delegates agree upon?
- What compromises were necessary and why?
- What were the final compromises reached?

Although the Philadelphia convention was supposed to start on May 14, 1787, few of the delegates had actually

SECTION 5

Points to Stress

- The delegates to the Constitutional Convention as framers.
- Basic precepts upon which the delegates to the Constitutional Convention agreed.
- The compromises that were necessary and the rationale behind the compromises.
- The actual final compromises that were reached.

Kickoff Activity

Have each student list at least three questions he or she would like to have answered about the Constitutional Convention. Ask the students to compare and discuss their questions, and encourage students to provide answers for one another's questions whenever possible. Tell students that they should return to their lists of questions after they have read the section.

Working with the Preview Questions

Ask a volunteer to read the three study questions aloud. Then have each student prepare a note-taking sheet with three headings based on these three questions. Ask the students to take notes on these sheets as they read Section 5.

Teaching Strategies

Introduction

After the students have read the section introduction, help them discuss the attendance at the Philadelphia convention: Why do you imagine so few delegates arrived by the starting date? Why do you think the convention commenced before all the delegates had arrived? What statement do you think Rhode Island was trying to make by not sending any delegates?

Law Related Activity

As stated here over half of the delegates to the 1787 Constitutional Convention were in the legal profession. Students should be encouraged to contact the local bar association with the intent to interview an attorney on the advantages and disadvantages of such a demographic composition. Students can compare responses from various attorneys in order to see if there are any trends. The attorney should also be asked if such an imbalance ought to be retained if there were to be another Constitutional Convention.

Cooperative Learning

Have the students work in groups to research the lives and works of George Washington, Benjamin Franklin, or James Madison. What experiences helped each man prepare for the Constitutional Convention? What were his most significant contributions to the convention? What did he accomplish in the years after the convention?

FYI

As mentioned in the chapter, the proceedings of the 1787 Convention were secret, and we may never know what actually happened in complete detail due to the sketchy and paultry notes taken of the proceedings. William Jackson was appointed official secretary and his notes constituted the official *Journal*. After destroying "all the loose scraps of paper" that he felt were unimportant, Jackson handed the *Journal* over to Washington, who was charged by the Convention to "retain the *Journal* and other papers subject to the orders of Congress, if ever formed under the Constitution." Washington handed the notes over to the Department of State in 1796 where they remained unpublished until 1818. More well known are the semi-official notes Madison kept on the proceedings, eventually published in 1840 under *The Papers of James Madison.* Although respected for his efforts, Madison too made many errors. At times he revised his notes to reflect incorrect information in the *Journal*. He also revised his notes to reflect accounts from other delegates' notes.

arrived in Philadelphia on that date. It formally opened in the East Room of the Pennsylvania State House (later named Independence Hall), on May 25th. Fifty-five of the seventy-four delegates had arrived. Only Rhode Island, where feelings were strong against creating a more powerful central government, did not send any delegates.

Who Were the Founding Fathers?

The 55 delegates were relatively young by today's standards. James Madison was 36, Alexander Hamilton was 32, and Jonathan Dayton of New Jersey was 26. Thirty-three were members of the legal profession. Fifty percent were college graduates in a country in which less than 1 percent finished college. Seven were former chief executives of their respective states; eight were important businessmen; six were large plantation owners; and three were physicians.

Several men stood out as leaders. George Washington, who served as commander-in-chief during the war for independence, was already a national hero. Among all the prominent men assembled at the Philadelphia convention, Washington was immediately recognized as the leader of the leaders. Benjamin Franklin was a world-famous scientist and diplomat. At 81 years old he played an active role in the debates (even though he had to be carried in on a portable chair held by four prisoners from the local jail). Virginia had sent James Madison, a brilliant supporter of a strong central government. Madison's carefully taken notes are our primary source of information about what happened at the Constitutional Convention. He is often called the "Father of the Constitution" because he authored the basic plan of government that was ultimately adopted by the convention. Thomas Jefferson, unfortunately, could not be at the convention because he was serving as Ambassador to France. John Adams was serving as Ambassador to Great Britain and could not attend either.

Working Conditions

The founding fathers worked for 116 days (of which they actually met on 89) in a room where the windows were usually shut. None of the framers of the Constitution wanted anybody to hear what they were doing, because they did not want rumors spread about the form of government upon which they would ultimately decide. Besides, if they opened the windows, hordes of flies would descend upon them. The air became humid and hot by noon of each day. At the end of each session they retired to the nearby tavern, the Indian Queen.

George Washington was chosen to preside over the meetings. Each state had one vote on all questions and a simple majority rule was used. The **quorum**—the number of members necessary to legally transact business for a group—consisted of delegates from at least seven states. All of the delegates present agreed on a number of basic concepts. They wanted the powers of the national government to be divided among three branches: legislative, executive, and judicial. They wanted the central government to limit the power of the states to make their own money. And they all wanted, in varying degrees, a more powerful central government. The debates within the convention were, therefore, not over these fundamental issues, but rather over how to put them into practice.

The Compromises

James Madison had spent months reviewing European political theory before he went to the Philadelphia Convention. When his Virginia delegation arrived before anybody else, he put them to work immediately. On the first day of the convention, governor Edmond Randolph of Virginia was able to present fifteen resolutions. This was a masterful political stroke on the part of the Virginia delegation. It immediately set the **agenda**—plan of things to be done—for the remainder of the convention.

The Virginia Plan The fifteen resolutions under the Virginia Plan proposed an entirely new national government under a constitution. The plan, which favored large states such as Virginia, called for the following:

- A **bicameral** (two-house) **legislature.** The lower house was to be chosen by the people. The smaller upper house was to be chosen by the elected members of the lower house. The number of representatives would be in proportion to the state's population (the larger states would have more representatives). The legislature could void any state laws.
- A national executive branch, elected by the legislature.
- A national court system, created by the legislature.

The smaller states immediately complained because they would have less representation in the legislature. After two weeks of debate they offered their own plan.

Discussion Starter
Encourage the students to discuss the attitude the founding fathers displayed toward the work of the convention.

Vocabulary
Reinforce the students' learning by asking: What other organizations use a quorum? How does each of those organizations define its quorum?

Comprehension
Help the students review by asking these questions: On what major issues did the delegates agree? Why did they agree on those issues? What was the major point of difference among the delegates?

Discussion Starter
Encourage discussion by asking questions such as these: Why are the actions of the Virginia delegation considered a masterful political stroke? What do you imagine the motivation for those actions was? What effect do they appear to have had?

Comprehension
Ask the students these questions: Which branch of government was dominant in the Virginia Plan? Why did the delegates from Virginia and from other large states support this plan?

Reinforcement
Ask the students to compare the Virginia Plan and the New Jersey Plan: In what respects were the two plans alike? What were the most significant differences between the two plans?

Discussion Starter
Encourage the students to discuss the possible consequences of the break-up of the Convention: What might have happened if the Great Compromise had not been proposed?

Vocabulary
Ask the students to share their own definitions of the word *compromise* and then to find a dictionary definition. Encourage the students to discuss familiar examples of compromise.

Critical Thinking Skills
Encourage the students to analyze the Three-Fifths Compromise: What attitudes are indicated by the acceptance of this compromise? How are the implications of those attitudes seen even today in this country?

Caption Answer The Three-Fifths Compromise helped to appease both Southerners and Northerners on the issues of taxation and representation. It, along with the compromise which allowed Congress to limit the number of slaves imported to the country after 1808 but allowed the South twenty years of unrestricted slave trade, worked to keep the nation from looking at the larger issue of the inhumanity of slavery. It also enabled the country to avoid confronting the issue in order to obtain the political compromise necessary to win ratification of the Constitution.

The New Jersey Plan William Paterson of New Jersey presented an alternate plan favorable to the smaller states. He argued that under the Articles of Confederation all states had equality and that therefore the convention had no power to change this arrangement. He suggested the following:

- That Congress be able to regulate trade and impose taxes.
- That each state have only one vote.
- That acts of Congress be the supreme law of the land.
- That an executive office of more than one person be elected by Congress.
- That the executive office appoint a national supreme court.

The Connecticut Plan, or the Great Compromise As the summer grew hotter, so did the tempers of the delegates. Most were unwilling to consider the New Jersey Plan. When the Virginia Plan was brought up again, delegates from the smaller states threatened to leave, and the convention was in danger of dissolving. The Convention was deadlocked. On July 16, Roger Sherman of Connecticut proposed a plan for the legislature that has become known as the Connecticut Compromise, or the Great Compromise:

- A two-house legislature in which the number of state representatives from the lower house (the House of Representatives) would be determined by the number of people in each state.
- An upper house, called the Senate, which would have two members from each state elected by the state legislatures.

The Connecticut Compromise broke the deadlock and, like any good compromise, it gave something to both sides. It resolved the small-state versus large-state controversy.

The Three-Fifths Compromise A second compromise settled a disagreement over how to count slaves for the purposes of determining how many representatives each state would have in the House. Although slavery was legal everywhere except in Massachusetts, most slaves and slaveowners lived in the South. The Southern states wanted slaves to be counted equally in determining representation in Congress, but not in determining taxation. Because they did not have many slaves, the Northern states took the opposite position. They wanted slaves counted for tax purposes but not for representation. The **Three-Fifths Compromise** settled this deadlock.

▲ Despite the fact that the War for Independence was fought for such ideals as the equality of all persons, some 500,000 African Americans were held as enslaved persons in 1776. How did the Three-Fifths Compromise help to continue this exploitation of enslaved people?

Three-fifths of the slaves were to be counted for both tax purposes and for representation. This part of the Constitution was eventually changed by the Thirteenth Amendment, which abolished slavery in 1865.

The Slavery Question Continued The Three-Fifths Compromise did not satisfy everyone present. Many delegates wanted slavery banned completely in the United States. The delegates compromised on this question by agreeing that Congress could limit the number of slaves imported into the country after 1808, but the issue of slavery itself was never addressed. The South won twenty years of unrestricted slave trade and a requirement that escaped slaves in free states be returned to their owners in slave states.

Those delegates who strongly believed that slavery should be banned had to face reality. The Southern states would never accept the Constitution if it interfered with the slave trade. A *tradeoff* was therefore accepted. In order to create a new and stronger government, the

TEACHING ARCHITECT OF THE AMERICAN DREAM

Read
Before the students begin to read this Architect of the American Dream feature on George Washington, ask them to list on a piece of paper ten adjectives that have been applied to George Washington. After the students have completed their lists, allow volunteers to share and explain their lists. The class then should work together to agree upon the ten adjectives they feel best fit George Washington. After completing this activity, allow volunteers to take turns reading this feature aloud to the class.

Discuss
Stimulate a class discussion of the Architect of the American Dream feature by asking the following questions: Was George Washington an important figure prior to the Revolutionary War? Why? What types of political experience did Washington have prior to the Revolutionary War? What role did Washington play in the War for Independence? What role did Washington play at the Constitutional Convention? How did Washington's actions as the first president affect the office of president today? What was the main point of this excerpt from Washington's Farewell Address? How did Washington feel about international interdependence?

Analyze and Apply
Divide the class into two groups for the purposes of staging a debate centered on the message of the excerpt from George Washington's Farewell Address. The debate topic should be proposed: George Washington's ideas about isolation-

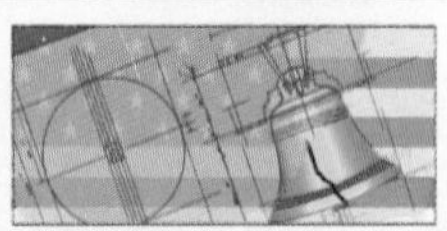

ARCHITECT OF The American Dream

Even though George Washington was born more than two and a half centuries ago, he remains one of the foremost architects of the American dream. He was a central figure during the events that shaped the founding of our nation.

George Washington was born in Bridges Creek, Westmoreland County, Virginia, on February 22, 1732. After his father's death in 1743 he lived chiefly at Mount Vernon and worked as a surveyor. He served as a lieutenant colonel in the French and Indian Wars from 1754 to 1758 and in 1759 entered the Virginia colonial legislature, the House of Burgesses. He was a leader in the movement for independence and a delegate to the First and Second Continental Congresses. On June 15, 1775, he was chosen to be general and commander in chief of the Army of the United Colonies. He persevered through the long and difficult years of the Revolution until his secret and rapid march from the Hudson River to the Chesapeake Bay. This resulted in the surrender of British General Cornwallis at Yorktown in 1781, thus ending the war. When he resigned his commission in 1783, he said he was through with public life, but his retirement did not last.

Returning to public life, he supported the movement for a more effective union and presided over the Philadelphia Convention in 1787 that adopted the Constitution. Even though he did not design the Constitution, many believe it would not have taken the shape it did without his commanding presence and leadership.

The framers of the Constitution respected George Washington and wanted him to be the first president. They created the office with him in mind. He had the qualities they thought a chief executive should have: honesty, fairness, wisdom, dignity, natural leadership, and the ability to balance executive authority with the rights of citizens. He was elected unanimously as the first president. George Washington knew the importance of being the first to hold the office. He wrote: "I walk on untrodden ground. . . . There is scarcely any part of my conduct that may not hereafter be drawn into precedent." He did indeed set precedents, including establishing a cabinet and holding regular cabinet meetings. He thought of the United States as "an experiment entrusted to the hands of the American people" and knew that it was his responsibility to give that experiment proper direction. During his two terms, he helped to set the new nation on a solid foundation and organized the machinery of government. He declined a third term of office, which set the precedent of limiting the number of presidential terms to two.

HIS WORDS

Farewell Address, September 17, 1796

"The great rule of conduct for us in regard to foreign nations is, in extending our commercial relations to have with them as little *political* connection as possible. So far as we have already formed engagements let them be fulfilled with perfect good faith. Here let us stop.

Europe has a set of primary interests which to us have none or a very remote relation. Hence she must be engaged in frequent controversies, the causes of which are essentially foreign to our concerns. Hence, therefore, it must be unwise in us to implicate ourselves by artificial ties in the ordinary ism are still approproate today. Each debate team should use what they know about our current world situation and what they know about George Washington to support or oppose this proposition: Are these ideas still appropriate? If Washington were alive today would he still support these ideas?

Review

To review this feature content and check student comprehension, ask the following questions: What type of legislative experience did George Washington have prior to the War for Independence? What role did George Washington play in the War for Independence and in the establishment of the United States Constitution? What role did George Washington play in shaping our modern presidency? What foreign policy recommendations did George Washington include in his Farewell Address?

Developing Critical Thinking Skills

1. Since George Washington's presidency, our relationship with Europe has changed dramatically as we have become increasingly interdependent with the countries of Europe. We now have strong political, social, and economic ties not only with the countries of Europe, but also with other countries throughout the world.

2. Washington referred to his belief that the nation would soon be both economically self sufficient and politically and militarily strong enough to stand alone without the need, or fear, of other nations.

3. Answers will vary, but students should understand that isolationism truly began to wane and global interdependence to rise in the early twentieth century with the onset of World War I.

Caption Answer Washington had proven himself to be a great leader during the War for Independence and was, therefore, the natural choice. Washington was a genuinely popular hero and had emerged from the War for Independence as a symbol of the new nation.

George Washington

This painting by Howard Chandler Christy depicts the scene at the signing of the Constitution of the United States on September 17, 1787. Why do you think George Washington was chosen to preside over the convention?

HIS WORDS–*continued*

vicissitudes of her politics or the ordinary combinations and collisions of her friendships or enmities.

Our detached and distant situation invites and enables us to pursue a different course. If we remain one people, under an efficient government, the period is not far off when we may defy material injury from external annoyance; when we may take such an attitude as well cause the neutrality we may at any time resolve upon to be scrupulously respected; when belligerent nations, under the impossibility of making acquisitions upon us, will not lightly hazard the giving us provocation; when we may choose peace or war, as our interest, guided by justice, shall counsel.

It is our true policy to steer clear of permanent alliances with any portion of the foreign world, so far, I mean, as we are now at liberty to do it; for let me not be understood as capable of patronizing infidelity to existing engagements. I hold the maxim no less applicable to public than to private affairs that honesty is always the best policy. I repeat, therefore, let those engagements be observed in their genuine sense. But in my opinion it is unnecessary and would be unwise to extend them."

DEVELOPING CRITICAL THINKING SKILLS

1. Washington states that "Europe has a set of primary interests which to us have none or a very remote relation." How has our relationship with Europe changed since the days of George Washington?
2. What do you think Washington meant when he said, "the period is not far off when we may defy material injury from external annoyance"?
3. At what point in history did our nation begin to stray from Washington's advice to "steer clear of permanent alliances with any portion of the foreign world"?

FOR FURTHER READING

Cunliffe, Marcus. *George Washington: Man and Monument.* Boston: Little Brown, 1958.

Davis, Burke. *George Washington and the American Revolution.* New York: Random House, 1975.

Eaton, Jeanette. *Leader by Destiny: George Washington, Man and Patriot.* New York: Harcourt Brace, 1938.

Discussion Starter
Guide the students in discussing the ban on export taxes: Why does the United States still not tax exports? How does this ban affect our economy? When and by whom is interest in export taxes still expressed?

Reteaching Strategies
1. Have the students work in small groups to review and revise the notes they took while reading this section.
2. Have the students work with partners to list the specific problems solved by the Great Compromise.

Evaluation Strategies
1. Have the students write their answers to the first two Section 5 Review questions.
2. Have the students work in small groups to discuss their responses to the final Section 5 Review question. Then have each student write a one-paragraph response.
3. Have the students take the Section 5 Quiz found in the *TRB.*

Section 5 Review (Answers)
1. The Virginia Plan called for a bicameral legislature. The lower house was to be chosen by the people and the smaller upper house by elected members of the lower house. The number of representatives would be proportional to the state's population, therefore benefitting the larger states. The major point of difference in the New Jersey plan was that each state would have only one vote.
2. The Great Compromise called for a two-house legislature in which state representatives from the lower house would be determined by the number of people in each state. An upper house, called the Senate, would have two members from each state elected by the state legislatures. The Three-Fifths compromise settled the argument over how to count slaves for the purposes of determining how many representatives each state would have in the House.
3. Answers will vary. One possibility is a unicameral legislature that would require a three-fourths majority to pass any bill. In that way, the small states could be protected, knowing that they could effectively stop any legislation in spite of their small number of representatives.

SECTION 6

Points to Stress
• Anti-Federalist objections to ratification of the Constitution.
• The advantages that the Federalists had relative to the Anti-Federalists.
• The chronology of ratification.

Kickoff Activity
Write these questions on the board, and have each student write answers to them: What does the word *ratify* mean? What kinds of things are ratified? Then ask the students to compare and discuss their responses.

Working with the Preview Questions
Have a volunteer read the two study questions aloud. Ask

founding fathers compromised on the slavery question. It was not until after the Civil War, over seventy years later, that the conflict ultimately was settled.

Banning Export Taxes The South's economic health depended in large part on its exports of agricultural products. (**Exports** are sales of goods to other countries.) The South feared that the Northern majority in Congress might pass taxes on these exports. Yet another compromise was reached. The South agreed to let Congress have the power to regulate **interstate commerce**—commerce among the states—as well as commerce with other nations. In exchange, the South was guaranteed that no export taxes would ever be imposed on their products. Today the United States is one of the few countries that does not tax exports.

Other Points of Debate Many other issues were debated. They included issues concerning the actual structure of commerce, the court system, the duration of the presidency, and the way the president should be elected.

The Final Document

The Connecticut Compromise was reached by mid-July. Still to be determined was the makeup of the executive branch and the judiciary. A five-man Committee of Detail undertook the remainder of this work and on August 6 presented a rough draft to the convention. On September 8, a committee was named to "revise the stile [style] of, and arrange the Articles which had been agreed to" by the convention. The Committee of Stile was headed by Gouverneur Morris of Pennsylvania.[3] On September 17, 1787 the final draft of the Constitution was approved by thirty-nine of the remaining forty-two delegates.

Section 5 Review

1. Describe the Virginia and New Jersey plans. What was the major difference between the two?
2. What were other major compromises reached by the convention delegates?
3. **For critical analysis:** What alternative compromises can you think of to the Connecticut Plan? Explain your ideas.

3. Morris was partly of French descent, which is why his first name may seem strange. Note, though, that naming one's child *Gouverneur* was not common at the time in any language, even French.

Section 6

Ratifying the Constitution

Preview Questions

- Why did the Anti-Federalists object to ratifying the Constitution?
- What were the Federalists' advantages over the Anti-Federalists?

The delegates' approval and signature of the Constitution did not mean that the Constitution was put into effect automatically. It had to be **ratified**—approved—by a majority of the states. The delegates to the convention agreed that each state should hold its own convention at which elected representatives would discuss and vote on the Constitution. The delegates also agreed that as soon as nine states approved it, it would take effect. Congress would then begin to organize the new government.

Look at Figure 2–5 on the next page. You can see that the process of getting all the states to ratify the Constitution took nearly two and a half years.

The Battle Lines Are Drawn—Federalists versus Anti-Federalists

Ratifying the Constitution was a tough battle, fought chiefly by two opposing groups. Those who favored a strong central government and the new Constitution—called the **Federalists**—and those who wanted to prevent the Constitution in its then current form from being ratified—called the **Anti-Federalists.**

The Federalists had several advantages to help their position. In the first place, they assumed a positive name, leaving their opposition with a negative label. The Federalists had also attended the Constitutional Convention, and knew about all of the discussions that had taken place. The Anti-Federalists had no actual knowledge of those discussions because they had been privately held; thus, they had no information about the Constitution itself. The Federalists also had time, money, and prestige on their side. Their impressive list of political thinkers and writers included Alexander Hamilton, John Jay, and James Madison. Federalists could communicate with each other more easily, because they were mostly bankers, lawyers, and merchants who lived in urban areas, where communication was better. The Federalists organized a quick and effective ratification campaign in order to elect themselves as delegates to each state's whether these questions suggest other questions. (Who and what were the Federalists and the Anti-Federalists?) Remind the students to keep these questions in mind as they read, and ask them to be prepared to answer the two study questions when they have finished Section 6.

Teaching Strategies

Introduction

Have the students read the section introduction, and guide them in considering figure 2–5, Ratification of the Constitution: In what order did the states ratify? What significance—if any—do you find in the order of ratification? Judging by these dates, which states seemed hesitant to ratify the Constitution? What reasons do you think they may have had for waiting? Which states had unanimous votes for ratification? Which did not? How important do you think these differences are?

Vocabulary

Have the students examine and discuss the terms *Federalist* and *Anti-Federalist:* What is the root of both words? What is the meaning of that root? What suffix has been added to form both words? What prefix—with what meaning—has been added to form *Anti-Federalist?*

Enrichment

Ask students to read and write short reports on the selected *Federalist Papers* found in the Resource Center at the back of this book.

Figure Answer New Hampshire became the ninth state to ratify the Constitution on June 21, 1788 at which point the Constitution was formally put into effect. It was still important, however, to have the big states of New York and Virginia ratify the Constitution because without them it would have little true power.

Ratification of the Constitution

State	Date	Vote For–Against
Delaware	Dec. 7, 1787	30–0
Pennsylvania	Dec. 12, 1787	46–23
New Jersey	Dec. 18, 1787	38–0
Georgia	Jan. 2, 1788	26–0
Connecticut	Jan. 9. 1788	128–40
Massachusetts	Feb. 6, 1788	187–168
Maryland	Apr. 28, 1788	63–11
South Carolina	May 23, 1788	149–73
New Hampshire	June 21, 1788	57–46
Virginia	June 25, 1788	89–79
New York	July 26, 1788	30–27
North Carolina	Nov. 21, 1789*	194–77
Rhode Island	May 29, 1790	34–32

* Ratification was originally defeated on August 4, 1788, by a vote of 184 to 84; the numbers here represent the second vote.

◀ **FIGURE 2–5 Ratification of the Constitution.** This table lists the dates on which each of the new states ratified the Constitution. When was the Constitution formally in effect?

ratifying conventions. The only point in favor of the Anti-Federalists is that they stood for the **status quo**—the way things were at the time. Usually it is more difficult to change than to stay with what is already known, experienced, and understood.

A national debate of unprecedented size arose over the ratification issue. During that debate a series of papers was published by the Federalists, which are collectively known as *The Federalist Papers.*

The Federalist Papers Alexander Hamilton, a leading Federalist, started answering the critics of the Constitution in New York by writing newspaper columns. He used the signature "Caesar." The Caesar letters appeared to have little effect, so Hamilton switched his signature to "Publius," and had John Jay and James Madison help him write the papers. In a period of less than a year, the three men wrote a series of eighty-five essays in defense of the Constitution. These essays were not only printed in New York newspapers, but were reprinted in other papers throughout the states. Hamilton was responsible for about two-thirds of the essays, but Madison's *Federalist Paper No. 10* is considered a classic in political theory. It deals with the nature of self-interested groups, or **factions,** as he called them. (You can read *Federalist Paper No. 10* in the Resource Center of this book.)

While not everyone agrees about how important *The Federalist Papers* were in securing ratification, all admit to their lasting value as an authoritative explanation of the Constitution.

The Anti-Federalists Respond The Anti-Federalists published their own replies using the names of "Montezuma" and "Philadelphiensis." They also wrote brilliantly, attacking nearly every part of the new document. Many contended that the Constitution was a document written by aristocrats that would lead the nation to aristocratic tyranny. The Anti-Federalists argued that the Constitution would lead to an overly powerful cen-

Developing Skills for the Information Age

That our "information age" is not limited to those things modern and high-tech, is well reflected by the continuing importance of *The Federalist Papers.* Have students read *Federalist #10* that is found in the Resource Center. Students can write in their own words what Madison was trying to say, updating the material. Some students might wish to write a newspaper article, editorial, or review of Madison's work. By doing a quick survey of current news stories students can find examples of what Madison meant by factions and the difference between a pure democracy and a republic.

Cooperative Learning
Have the students work in groups to find out about the background and significance of the names chosen by Federalist and Anti-Federalist columnists: Caesar, Publius, Montezuma, Philadelphiensis. Why do you think each name was chosen? What effect did the writers hope to achieve by publishing under these names? Have each group research one of the names and present its findings to the class in an oral report.

Comprehension
To check their comprehension, ask the students to identify and discuss the strongest argument presented by the Anti-Federalists. (The Constitution lacked a Bill of Rights.)

Enrichment
Ask two small groups of volunteers to research the lives and accomplishments of Patrick Henry and Samuel Adams. Have these groups present their findings to the rest of the class.

Discussion Starter
Encourage the students to discuss the decisions that resulted in ratification of the constitution: What promise led to ratification? Why was this promise important at the time? What lasting significance did it have?

Discussion Starter
Guide the students in discussing the stages of ratification of the Constitution: How effective was the formal ratification before New York and Virginia assented? Why? What might have happened if New York and Virginia had decided not to ratify the Constitution?

Caption Answer *The Federalist Papers,* especially Number 10 which is included in the Resource Center of this book, are outstanding explanations of what the United States Constitution is designed to do. Political scientist James Q. Wilson summed up the importance of *The Federalist Papers* thusly, "Though written for political purposes, *The Federalist* has become the single most important piece of American political philosophy ever produced."

Alexander Hamilton, James Madison, and John Jay were responsible for *The Federalist Papers,* a series of essays originally printed in New York newspapers and reprinted in other papers throughout the states arguing for the ratification of the new Constitution. Why are these essays still considered important?

tral government that would limit personal freedom. The Anti-Federalists' strongest argument, however, was that the Constitution lacked a bill of rights. They warned that without a bill of rights, a strong national government might take away the political rights won during the American Revolution. They demanded that the new Constitution clearly guarantee personal freedoms.

Among the Anti-Federalists were such patriots as Patrick Henry and Samuel Adams. They argued in favor of the leading view of the time in which small societies either governed themselves by direct democracy or by a large legislature with small districts. In actuality, much of *The Federalist Papers* argued a position that was unpopular at the time. As Patrick Henry said of the proposed Constitution, "I look upon that paper as the most fatal plan that could possibly be conceived to enslave a free people."

The Constitution Is Ratified

To gain necessary support, the Federalists finally promised to add a bill of rights to the Constitution as the first order of business under the new government. This promise turned the tide in favor of the Constitution. The contest for ratification was close in several states, but the Federalists finally won in all of them.

Ratification was unanimous in Delaware, New Jersey, and Georgia. Pennsylvania voted in favor by a margin of 2 to 1 and Connecticut by 3 to 1. Even though the Anti-Federalists were perhaps the majority in Massachusetts, a brilliant political campaign by the Federalists led to ratification on February 6, 1788. On June 21, 1788, by a 57 to 46 margin, New Hampshire became the ninth state to ratify; thus the Constitution was formally put into effect. New York and Virginia had not yet ratified, however, and without them the Constitution would have no true power. Virginia ratified on June 25 and New York on July 26, 1788. North Carolina waited until November 21 of the following year and Rhode Island waited until May 29, 1790, after the new government had taken office.

The New Government Starts

On September 13, 1788, the Congress of the Confederation chose New York as the temporary capital. On March 4, 1789, the new Congress convened in Federal Hall on Wall Street in New York City. On April 6, the first president of the United States, George Washington, was elected by unanimous vote. His vice president, John Adams, was also elected. The first oath of the office for a president of this country was taken on April 30 in New York City.

Although it is impossible to know for sure, we can imagine that the founding fathers, as well as our first

Reinforcement
Encourage the students to identify and discuss current signs that the U.S. Constitution is a living document.

Reteaching Strategies
1. Have the students work in small groups to list the central positions of the Federalists and of the Anti-Federalists.
2. Work with small groups of students, helping them discuss the significance of the ratification of the Constitution.

Evaluation Strategies
1. Have the students write their responses to the Preview Questions at the beginning of the section.
2. Have the students write their answers to the Section 6 Review questions.
3. Have the students take the Section 6 Quiz found in the *TRB.*

Section 6 Review (Answers)
1. There was a fairly large group known as the Anti-Federalists who strongly opposed the ratification.
2. The Anti-Federalists opposed the Constitution because they believed it would lead to an overly powerful central government that would limit personal freedom. They also argued that the Constitution lacked a bill of rights. The Federalists promised to add a Bill of Rights.
3. Answers will vary, e.g., a group today would have difficulty fighting the status quo. It would have to confront the present Constitutional requirements for change and the power of Congress and the states over this process. They would have difficulty with those who would argue that the present Constitution is working better than any other in history.

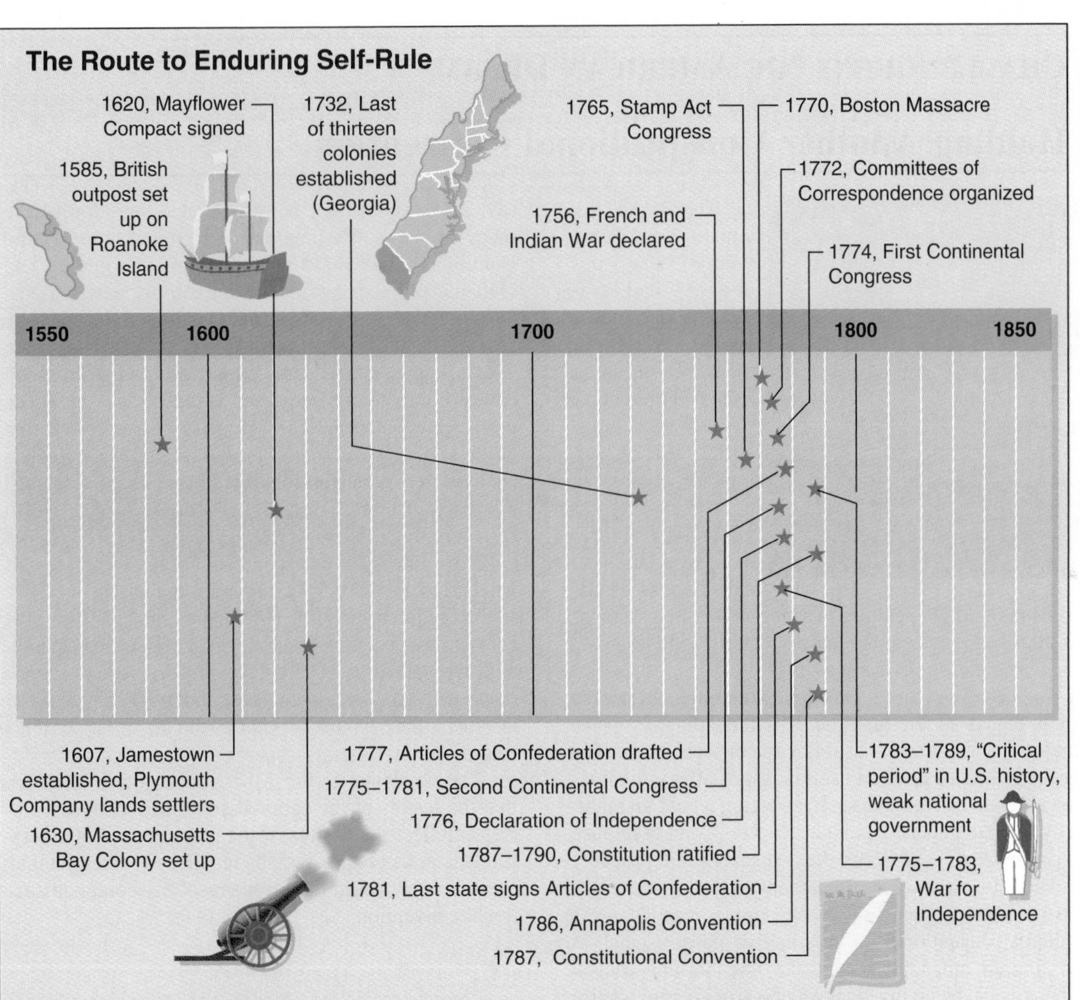

Figure 2–6 The Route to Enduring Self-Rule. The above time line chronicles the important events that took place from 1585 through the ratification of the Constitution in 1790. Which of these dates do you think most Americans would think are the most important?

Figure Answer Most Americans would probably say that July 4, 1776 is the most important of these dates.

elected officials under the new Constitution, could never have dreamed that over two hundred years later, the U.S. Constitution would be the oldest living government framework document in the world. Nor could they have understood the truly global significance of what happened when the first president of the United States was elected. Through the years the political system of democracy and the freedoms enjoyed by Americans have become the standard by which other countries' systems measure themselves.

Section 6 Review

1. Why did it take two and a half years for the states to ratify the Constitution?
2. What were the Anti-Federalists' objections to the Constitution? How did the Federalists respond to these objections?
3. **For critical analysis:** If a group today wanted to give the United States a new constitution, what problems would it encounter?

TEACHING THE CHALLENGE TO THE AMERICAN DREAM

Read
Begin by asking students to recall what they have learned about the Philadelphia Convention in 1787. Who were the delegates? How was the agenda set? How did they feel about privacy? Then ask volunteers to take turns reading aloud "Holding Another Constitutional Convention" to the rest of the class.

Discuss
Have the students discuss the following questions: What issues might be likely to come up during a second Constitutional Convention? Which interest groups would press to have their issues considered? How would the media react to a second Constitutional Convention? Could secrecy be maintained? How might the rest of the world react to a second Constitutional Convention? Do you think such a Convention would have any affect on our nation's economy? Would the stock market have a reaction?

Analyze and Apply
Ask the students to work in small groups to write an amendment they would wish to propose if a Constitutional Convention were held today. Groups should be ready to argue convincingly for their amendment. Each group should also come up with a proposal for who should chair the Constitutional Convention. Possible nominees for Chair might include the president, Speaker for the House of Representatives, a famous military leader, or other nationally known leader.

Review
Have each student choose one of the two "You Decide" questions and write a short essay answering that question.

CHALLENGE TO THE AMERICAN DREAM

Holding Another Constitutional Convention

The first and last constitutional convention that this country had was over two hundred years ago. Since then, many changes have occurred in the political, economic, social, and technological arenas of our society. Not surprisingly, a number of individuals have called for a second constitutional convention, to incorporate such changes as allowing prayer in the public schools and outlawing the burning of the American flag.

A second constitutional convention might follow the same pattern as the first one in Philadelphia, in which major changes to the basic document were made. But because the Constitution itself does not offer guidelines for a second convention, such a meeting would undoubtedly operate under rules laid down by Congress. Once it got under way, however, the delegates could probably modify those rules or interpret them according to the will of the majority. Let's say, for example, that Congress called a convention for a very narrow purpose, such as passing an amendment to make flag burning illegal. There would be no practical way for Congress to control the convention once it was under way. Who knows what additional proposals might be introduced?

Imagine some of the outrageous possibilities: Tampering with the structure of the executive branch by calling for a plural presidency (say with three individuals holding equal power); eliminating the office of vice president; repealing the right to freedom of speech. Such proposals are of course possible, though highly improbable. The potential for such drastic proposals being incorporated into the Constitution would depend upon the representatives present at the convention.

When all is said and done, the comparison between what happened at the Philadelphia Convention in 1787 and what might occur at a constitutional convention in, say, 2000, should not be exaggerated. We don't have many Franklins, Washingtons, Jeffersons, Madisons, and Hamiltons in our midst who are going to articulate and craft the political outlines of an entirely new national constitution. Moreover, it would be difficult to duplicate the secrecy with which the Philadelphia Convention met. The prying eyes and ears of the media would make it unlikely that major surprises would be sprung on an unsuspecting nation. The openness of the convention might even prevent any proposals for truly radical changes in the constitutional status quo. Finally, the rest of the world would be watching—something that wasn't happening in 1787.

But a limited convention still is a possibility, and, if it occurred, it could make important changes in our lives, such as requiring that the federal government raise taxes every time it wants to increase spending, or that schoolchildren start every school day with a moment of silence or prayer. To some, such changes would be welcome; to others, they would be seen as threats to the nation's future.

The challenge to the American dream is to ensure that the results of the national and state legislative processes reflect the desires of the majority of Americans. If this is in fact happening, there will be less reason than ever to worry about the problems of a second constitutional convention.

You Decide

1. If there were a second constitutional convention, which special interest groups might be the most powerful and why?
2. The United States Constitution is a model of brevity. Do you think that a new constitution would be as short as the original? Explain.
3. If you were a delegate to a second constitutional convention, what changes to the Constitution would you suggest? Why?

You Decide (Answers)

1. Interest groups that had the most to gain from the issues being determined at the Constitutional Convention would spend the most money and effort to influence it. For example, if it were possible to change the Constitution to give more rights to women, women's groups might be a powerful force at the Convention. However, there is no necessary reason why the group offered as an example—women—would be able to raise the most money to influence change. In reality, a multitude of groups would try to dominate the process, but chaos would be the likely result.

2. Answers will vary, e.g., a new Constitution would be much longer than the original because there are so many new issues today. Also, many of the difficult issues that the Supreme Court has faced in the last few decades would be made into Constitutional law in order to avoid ambiguities in the future.

3. Answers will vary, e.g., I would suggest that the president be elected by popular vote rather than by the electoral college.

Chapter Evaluation

To evaluate student mastery of chapter material, you might:

1. Use Chapter Test A from the *TRB*.

2. Use Chapter Test B from the *TRB*.

3. Construct your own test using items from the *West American Government Test Bank* found in the *TRB*.

4. Use the accompanying computerized test software to construct and print a customized chapter test.

CHAPTER 2 REVIEW

Key Terms

agenda 40
American Creed 34
Anti-Federalists 44
bicameral legislature 40
boycott 30
charter 27
confederation 35
consent 24
consent of the governed 34
executive authority 34
exports 44
delegates 30
factions 45
Federalists 44
First Continental Congress 30
Fundamental Orders of Connecticut 28
grievances 30
interstate commerce 44
legislatures 28
legitimacy 31
limited government 23
Magna Carta 23
Mayflower Compact 27
nationalists 39
natural right 23
Navigation Acts 29
Northwest Ordinance 36
Parliament 24
peers 23
political philosophy 26
prototype 27
quorum 40
ratified 44
representative assembly 27
representative government 24
representatives 24
Second Continental Congress 30
Stamp Act 29
status quo 45
Three-Fifths Compromise 41
unicameral legislature 34

Summary

1. The English colonists brought with them to North America political ideas that had been developing for centuries. Among these was the idea of limited government that derived from the Magna Carta and from the English Bill of Rights. Other important influences were the English system of representative government and the political philosophy of John Locke.

2. Jamestown became the first permanent British settlement in North America. Jamestown colonists instituted a representative assembly. The Plymouth Company established the first New England colony in 1620. Some of the Pilgrims developed a document called the Fundamental Orders of Connecticut, which provided for an assembly of elected representatives and the popular election of a governor and judges. By 1732, all thirteen colonies had been established, each with its own constitution and legislature.

3. The American colonies banded together against Britain to win independence. Oppressive economic practices imposed by the British heightened the colonists' desire for independence. At the First Continental Congress in 1774, the colonists passed a resolution that banned trade with Britain or purchase of British goods. The British treated the resolution as an open act of rebellion and attacked colonial militiamen at Lexington and Concord in 1775. This signaled the start of the American Revolution. A Second Continental Congress issued the Declaration of Independence in 1776. Even prior to the Declaration of Independence, some of the colonies had already transformed themselves into states.

4. The Articles of Confederation represented an important step in the creation of a national government and our current system. Despite its accomplishments, the national government established under the Articles of Confederation was weak. Financial conflicts, a lack of cooperation among the states, and an armed rebellion of farmers led by Daniel Shays led to a call for a convention to revise the Articles.

5. Our founders replaced the Articles with a new Constitution at a meeting in Philadelphia that lasted from May to September, 1787. Many of the provisions of the Constitution were arrived at through a series of compromises.

6. When the Constitution was submitted to the states for ratification, conflict between the Federalists and Anti-Federalists developed. The Federalists' promise to add the Bill of Rights helped resolve the conflict. On March 4, 1789, the new Congress convened in the Federal Hall on Wall Street in New York City. George Washington was elected president on April 6.

Review Questions (Answers)

1. The principles of limited government and representative government.

2. Americans used many of the principles used by British parliament.

3. In 1607, the Virginia Company established a trading post called Jamestown. The Plymouth Company established the first New England colony in 1620.

4. They drew up the Mayflower Compact, which was a form of social contract, an agreement among individuals to establish a government and abide by its rules. They developed America's first written constitution—the Fundamental Orders of Connecticut.

5. The British began placing more restrictions on the colonists' trade. They began taxing the colonies and the colonists claimed this was taxation without representation because they had no elected official to represent their interests in Parliament.

6. First, the Continental Congress of 1774 required that each colony start an army; this action was condemned by the British government. The British then instituted repressive measures. On April 19, 1775 British Red Coats fought with minutemen at Lexington and Concord.

7. The first was called in response to the "intolerable acts" which closed the Boston Harbor and placed the government of Boston under direct British control. The Second Continental Congress was called when British soldiers fought with colonial citizens as they tried to enforce even more strict and repressive measures.

8. It was a unanimous declaration of the thirteen United States of America formally establishing a new nation independent from Great Britain.

9. It established that natural rights are inherent and cannot be taken away by government. It established that government exists to protect individuals' natural rights and that government derives its power from the consent of the governed.

10. Government under the Articles was made up of independent states that had no intention of giving up their sovereignty.

11. States were at odds with each other and refused to support the new central government in every way. George Washington realized that these problems were tearing the nation apart.

12. The Connecticut Compromise was necessary to appease both the small and large states who had proposed plans to benefit themselves. It proposed a two-house legislature in which state representatives from the lower house would be determined by the number of people in each state. An upper house would have two members from each state elected by state legislatures.

13. The Federalists stressed the weakness of the Articles and argued that many of the difficulties facing the nation could be over-

CHAPTER 2 REVIEW—Continued

Review Questions

1. What two aspects of English government most strongly influenced the American style of government?
2. How did the British Parliament affect the way American government was organized?
3. What were the first British settlements?
4. What contribution did the Pilgrims make to the development of American government?
5. Explain the major reasons for the colonists' revolt against Great Britain.
6. Describe the events that led up to the American Revolution.
7. Why were the First and Second Continental Congresses called?
8. Why is the Declaration of Independence important?
9. What is significant about the second paragraph of the Declaration of Independence?
10. How did the Articles of Confederation fail to create a strong central government?
11. What led George Washington to say "We are one nation today and thirteen tomorrow. Who will treat us on such terms?"
12. Explain what the Connecticut Compromise stated and why it was necessary.
13. What major arguments did the Federalists offer in favor of the Constitution? Why did the Anti-Federalists oppose the Constitution?
14. What promise turned the tide in favor of ratifying the Constitution?
15. List and describe the steps that one should normally take to reach an intelligent decision.
16. What are some problems that might be encountered if Congress allows a second constitutional convention?

Questions for Thought and Discussion

1. If you had been a participant at the Constitutional Convention, would you have ended up a Federalist or an Anti-Federalist afterward? Explain why.
2. The Constitution has been described as a "bundle of compromises." When do you think political compromise is justifiable? When is it not justifiable? Support your answers with recent examples of political compromises.
3. Do you think it was right for the delegates to the Constitutional Convention to have met in secret? Would it be right for this to happen today?

Improving Your Skills

Communication Skills

Note Taking

The skills of listening and note taking are closely related. You must listen well in order to take good notes, and you must take notes—either mentally or on paper—in order to gain the most from listening. If you haven't done so already, read the section in Chapter 1 on listening.

There are many methods of note taking. Regardless of the method that you choose, the following guidelines will help you get the most from your note taking.

The Mechanics

1. ***Use a loose-leaf binder with notepaper.*** This way you can reorganize your notes or insert other materials. If you buy a spiral notebook instead, make sure it has pockets for handouts. Use a pen for easy readability.
2. ***Always indicate the date, class, and name of your topic at the top of your notes.***
3. ***Divide each page so that you have a 2 1/2-inch column on the right or left.*** Use this space to make sketches to illustrate important points, or to write helpful comments such as "T" for possible test question, "see textbook," or "use for term paper."

Prepare Your Mind

1. ***Read any assigned work before going to class.*** The lecture will make more sense and you will be able to relate the ideas to what you have read.
2. ***Review notes from the previous class a few minutes before class starts.***
3. ***Reflect for a few minutes on any personal experiences or previous learning that relates to the subject.*** New learning "sticks" most readily when it fits into a meaningful context.

come by the proposed Constitution. The Anti-Federalists argued that it would lead to an overly powerful central government. They also objected to the lack of a bill of rights.

14. The needed support was gained by the promise to add a bill of rights to the Constitution.

15. (1) Define what you need or want. (2) Look carefully at your resources. (3) Identify your choices. (4) Sort through your choices. (5) Compare your choices. (6) Make the decision. (7) Make a plan to carry out your decision.

16. Since the Constitution does not provide for rules for such a convention, Congress would probably provide rule. Once the convention was underway, however, there would be no practical way for Congress to control additional proposals from being introduced.

Questions for Thought and Discussion (Answers)

1. Answers will vary, e.g., I would have been an Anti-Federalist because I agree that a bill of rights is necessary to ensure that an overly powerful government does not interfere with individual freedoms.

2. Answers will vary, e.g., political compromise is justifiable when both sides can prove the merit of their arguments or when an impasse is reached which, if not reconciled, will prevent a problem from being solved. For example, certain compromises might have to be made by both sides during a nuclear arms summit. Some progress would be better than none, which is what might happen if both sides refused to compromise. Political compromise is not justifiable when it would dilute the end result to the point where it is useless. For example, if Congress were to pass an environmental law which, after many compromises were made, would make very little difference but would still be expensive.

3. Answers would vary, e.g., the delegates should not have met in private. The meetings should have been open to the public because in a democracy, the people have the right to know of the decisions of their governmental representatives.

Social Studies Skills (Answers)

1. About 1,100 miles between Georgia and Maine (which was governed by Massachusetts at the time).

2. The largest colony would have to be Massachusetts because it was governing Maine at the time.

3. Rhode Island and Delaware.

4. Pennsylvania has no coastline.

CHAPTER 2 REVIEW—Continued

Be a Keen Listener

1. ***Get interested.*** Rousing interest in the subject matter helps sharpen your attention and concentration, and heightens your learning and remembering. It also helps you shut out distractions.
2. ***Sort out the important points and significant details.*** Listen for key phrases such as:
   - *Contrast:* "on the one hand . . ." "on the other hand . . ." "but," "on the contrary"
   - *Additional points:* "in addition to," "as well as," "another"
   - *Conclusion:* "in summary," "as a result," "finally"
   - *Phrases that introduce main points:* "Thus, the important point is . . .," "What is essential to understand is . . .," "The three conditions are . . ."
3. ***Be mentally alert.*** Listen to changes in a speaker's volume or tone. Pay attention to his or her voice and actions.

Record

1. ***Take notes in your own words unless the subject is very technical.*** Write in block, paragraph, or outline form, whichever you can manage most accurately and quickly.
2. ***Skip a line whenever the lecturer moves on to another topic.***
3. ***Keep your notes brief, using words or phrases rather than sentences.*** Use common abbreviations and symbols such as:

   w = with
   w/o = without
   + = and
   vs. = versus
   def. = definition
   ex. = example

   Abbreviations can also be used for words that are used consistently. For example:

   SC = Supreme Court
   C. = Congress
   H.R. = House of Representatives
   gov. = government

Review

1. ***Review your notes as soon as possible after the class.*** Fill in missing words and flesh out the concepts based on what you remember. Underline the most important ideas. Make corrections, summaries, and additions in the margin.

Writing

1. Watch an evening news program, taking notes as you watch. Check to see if you have followed the note-taking guidelines listed above.
2. Take notes during a lecture. Afterward, compare your notes with a classmate, and exchange suggestions and tips for improving each other's notes.

Social Studies Skills

Map Reading

Use Figure 2–2 (The Thirteen Colonies) on page 28 to answer the following questions.

1. Approximately what is the distance between the northernmost colony and the southernmost colony?
2. Which is the largest colony?
3. Which are the two smallest colonies?
4. Which colony doesn't have any coastline?

Activities and Projects

1. Divide the class into groups of three or four. Have each group study one of the influential leaders of this period, such as Benjamin Franklin, James Madison, George Washington, Samuel Adams, Thomas Paine, Alexander Hamilton, Thomas Jefferson, Gouverneur Morris, or Patrick Henry. Each group should prepare a short oral report on how the leaders they researched contributed to the development of American government.
2. Prepare a wall chart that lists the major weaknesses of the Articles of Confederation and shows how those matters were remedied by the Constitution.
3. Stage a class Federalist/Anti-Federalist debate on this statement: *A strong federal government leads to violations of personal freedoms.* In the course of the debate, discuss how the issue of balance between a strong central government and people's rights continues to be a major factor in American politics.

CHAPTER INTRODUCTION

Instructional Objectives

By the end of this chapter students should be able to:

- Describe the structure of the Constitution.
- Discuss the Constitution's major principles on government.
- Define the Bill of Rights and discuss its origin.
- Differentiate between formal and informal amending methods.

Using the Keynote

Ask a volunteer to read aloud the quotation from Henry Clay. Then have several other volunteers restate the same idea in their own words. Encourage discussion by asking questions such as these: Do you think it is reasonable for human beings to try to create a document that can be used for countless generations? Why or why not? Do you think the Constitution has served the people well for the past two centuries? Do you imagine it will be serving the people well two centuries from now? Encourage all the students to contribute to the discussion, presenting and supporting their own points of view.

Introducing the Chapter

Ask the students to read the chapter introduction to themselves. Then ask these discussion questions: What do you think is meant by the term *living, breathing document?* How do you think the Constitution affected families 200 years ago? How do you think it affects you and your family today?

Previewing the Sections

Section 1 Have the students look through Section 1. What is the section title? What are the three main headings in the section? How do those headings relate to the section title?
Section 2 Ask the students to scan Section 2, noting the six main headings, the two features, and the chart. What to you expect to learn about the Constitution from reading this section?
Section 3 Ask a volunteer to find and real aloud the three main headings in this section. Encourage the students to discuss the photographs here and to speculate on their relationship to the section title.
Section 4 Have the students look through Section 4, noting the three main headings and the flow chart. Let the students suggest several questions they expect to have answered as they study Section 4.
Section 5 Let the students glance through this section. What do the headings, the vocabulary words, and the artwork indicate about this section?

CHAPTER 3

The Constitution

CHAPTER OBJECTIVES

To learn and understand

- The structure of the Constitution.
- The Constitution's major principles of government.
- The Bill of Rights and how it was formulated.
- The formal and informal processes of amending the Constitution.

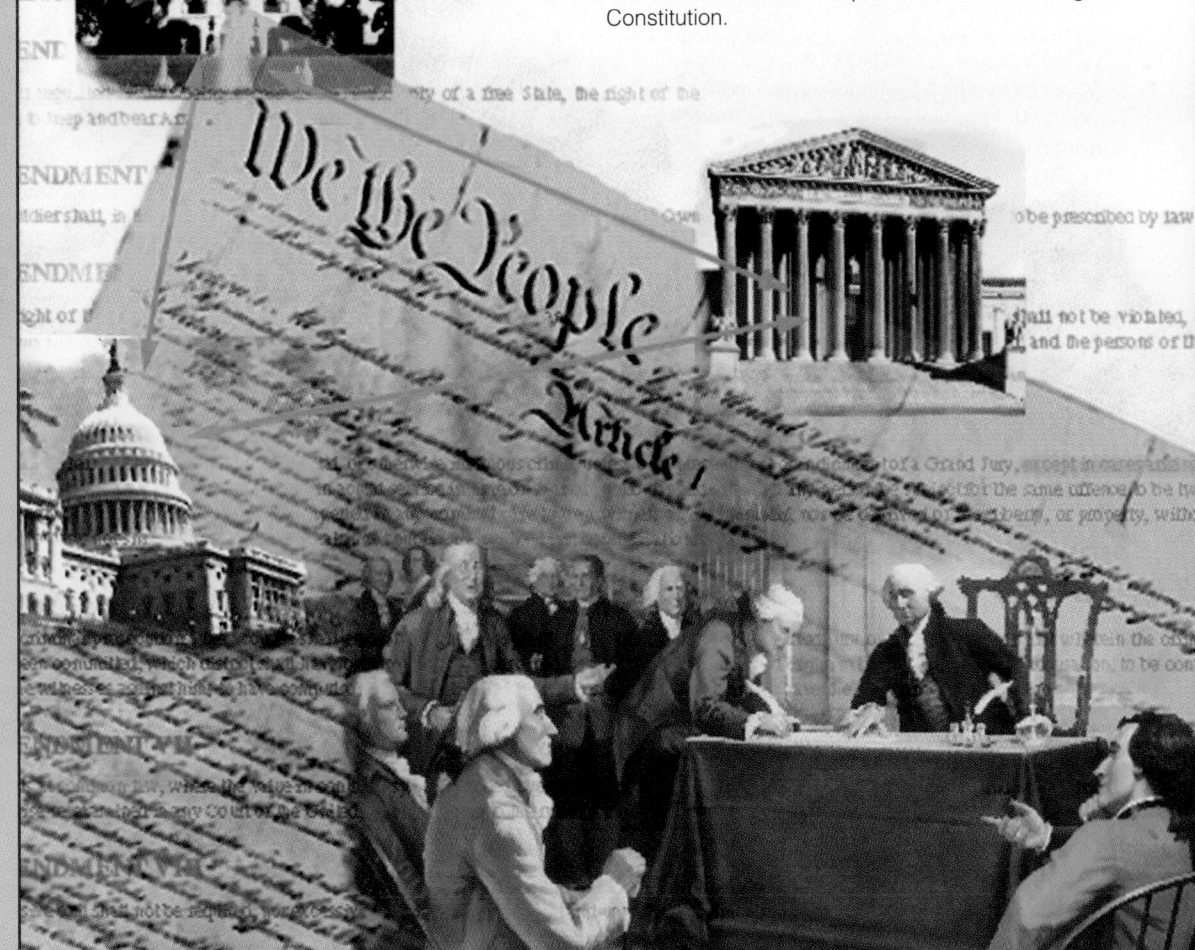

West's American Government Assignment Guide

Activity Sheets
Basic Concepts 3 *TRB* (Reteaching)
Enrichment Activity 3 *TRB*
Building Social Studies Skills 3 *TRB*
Quizzes
Chapter 3 Section 1 Quiz *TRB*
Chapter 3 Section 2 Quiz *TRB*
Chapter 3 Section 3 Quiz *TRB*
Chapter 3 Section 4 Quiz *TRB*
Chapter 3 Section 5 Quiz *TRB*
Tests
Chapter 3 Test A *TRB*
Chapter 3 Test B *TRB*
Chapter 3 Test Bank *TRB*
Chapter 3 WESTEST Computerized Testing
Social Studies Tool Kit Software
Chapter 3 Activity

SECTION 1

Points to Stress
• The Constitution is a framework of government that articulates ideals.
• After more than 200 years our lives are still influenced by the Constitution.
• The preamble enumerates the goals of our government.
• The federal system of government is outlined in the articles.
• Amendments allow for needed constitutional change.

Kickoff Activity
Ask the students to list ten words or phrases that come to mind when they think of the U.S. Constitution. Then encourage the students to compare and discuss their lists.

Working with the Preview Questions
Ask volunteers to read the three study questions aloud. Encourage students to answer the questions as fully as they can before reading. Then have the students read the section, looking for complete answers to the questions.

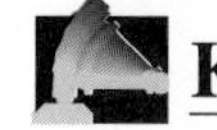

Keynote

"The Constitution of the United States was made not merely for the generation that then existed, but for posterity—unlimited, undefined, endless, perpetual posterity."

—— **Henry Clay**
(1777–1852) United States Senator

INTRODUCTION

If you take the time to sit down and actually read the Constitution, you might be amazed. It is not a dreary and obsolete relic of history that has nothing to do with your life today. It may not be written in a way you are normally accustomed to, but if you look beyond what seems to be its old-fashioned language to the thoughts and convictions of its framers, you might discover how this document relates to your life.

As Henry Clay's quote above states, the Constitution was not written for one generation, but for perpetual posterity. Certainly Clay understood the concept of change. He had served as a U.S. Senator for no less than four separate terms, the first starting in 1806 and the last ending in 1852. He had also served in the House of Representatives for six terms, during which he was Speaker of the House three times and then later became President John Q. Adams' secretary of state.

Clay recognized, along with others, that the framers of the Constitution had the foresight to know that this nation would constantly change. So they made the document general enough for each of the many generations that would follow to interpret it according to their needs and values. This is why our Constitution is often called a living, breathing document, created by people with a vision.

The Constitution serves today as the plan for government in the United States and is the supreme law of the land. It outlines the ideals of American government and describes how they should be achieved. It outlines the rules by which your government must carry out its actions and imposes limits on the powers of government. It tells you what your rights and privileges are. The Constitution affects you, your family, and your friends as much as it affected those who wrote it over 200 years ago.

SECTION 1

The Structure of Our Constitution

Preview Questions

- What are the three major parts of the Constitution?
- What is the purpose of the Preamble?
- What are the purposes of the seven articles in the Constitution?

In its original form, the United States Constitution contained only about five thousand words. Today, after twenty-seven amendments were added, there are still only about seven thousand words. Compared to virtually all state constitutions and to constitutions in other nations, ours is brief and to the point. The founding fathers did not attempt to spell out in detail exactly how the government should operate. Rather, they gave us a general

▼ The United States Constitution, which is on display at the National Archives in Washington, D.C., is visited by thousands of people who want to see the document that is the supreme law of the land. Why do you think the U.S. Constitution still works today, even though it was written over two hundred years ago?

Caption Answer The framers of the Constitution knew that the nation would constantly change and, therefore, drew up a document that was general enough to be interpreted according to the needs and values of each generation.

Teaching Strategies

Introduction
After the students have read the section introduction, help them discuss the content: Why is the brevity of our constitution so important? Why do you think the framers prepared a short, general framework for government, rather than a detailed explanation? What does this choice indicate about the aims and the attitudes of the framers?

Figure Answer Freedom of speech is one of the guarantees included in the First Amendment to the Constitution.

Multidiscipline Strategies

Health The "promote the general welfare," in the preamble has many applications today. Students should research the public health service agencies in order to see exactly how the government tries to ensure public health. The duties and tactics of the Centers for Disease Control; Food and Drug Administration; and Alcohol, Drug Abuse, and Mental Health Administration could all be examined.

Math "Promoting the general welfare" is not cheap, especially in light of current budget problems. Have students compare the budget of the Department of Health and Human Services over a five year period. Students should note the percentage change in the budget along with variables such as inflation and the number of citizens requiring care.

Structure of the U.S. Constitution

The Constitution	
The Preamble	
Article I	**Legislative Branch**
Section 1	Legislative Powers
Section 2	House of Representatives
Section 3	Senate
Section 4	Congressional Elections: Time, Place, and Manner
Section 5	Powers and Duties of the Houses
Section 6	Rights of Members
Section 7	Legislative Powers: Bills and Resolutions
Section 8	Powers of Congress
Section 9	Powers Denied to Congress
Section 10	Powers Denied to the States
Article II	**Executive Branch**
Section 1	Nature and Scope of Presidential Power
Section 2	Powers of the President
Section 3	Duties of the President
Section 4	Impeachment
Article III	**Judicial Branch**
Section 1	Judicial Powers, Courts, and Judges
Section 2	Jurisdiction
Section 3	Treason
Article IV	**Relations Among the States**
Section 1	Full Faith and Credit
Section 2	Treatment of Citizens
Section 3	Admission of States
Section 4	Republican Form of Government
Article V	**Method of Amendment**
Article VI	**National Supremacy**
Article VII	**Ratification**

▲ FIGURE 3–1 **Structure of the U.S. Constitution** The figure above and on the next page provides an outline for the structure of the United States Constitution. Where in the Constitution would you look to find the guarantee of freedom of speech?

framework for governing the nation. (This is why those who devised the U.S. Constitution are also called its framers.) The framework they provided has lasted for more than two hundred years—it is the world's oldest single-document written constitution.

The Constitution consists of three major parts: a preamble, seven articles, and twenty-seven amendments. You can see an overview of the structure of our Constitution in Figure 3–1 above and on the following page.

The Preamble

A **preamble** is an introductory statement. When this introductory statement is put at the beginning of a

Cooperative Learning
Have students work in groups to restate the preamble in the students' own words. Group members should work together, being sure each student understands the meaning and intent of this paragraph.

Discussion Starter
Encourage the students to discuss their responses to these questions about the preamble: Why is it not law? In what ways is it important to the laws established in other sections of the Constitution?

The complete text of the United States Constitution including the Bill of Rights and all other amendments is included with annotations in the Resource Center found at the back of both the student text and this Teacher's Wraparound Edition.

Structure of the U.S. Constitution (continued)

Amendments to the Constitution		
Bill of Rights	First Amendment	Religion, Speech, Assembly, and Petition (1791)
	Second Amendment	Militia and the Right to Bear Arms (1791)
	Third Amendment	Quartering of Soldiers (1791)
	Fourth Amendment	Searches and Seizures (1791)
	Fifth Amendment	Grand Juries, Self-Incrimination, Double Jeopardy, Due Process, and Eminent Domain (1791)
	Sixth Amendment	Criminal Court Procedures (1791)
	Seventh Amendment	Trial by Jury in Civil Cases (1791)
	Eighth Amendment	Bail, Cruel and Unusual Punishment (1791)
	Ninth Amendment	Rights Retained by the People (1791)
	Tenth Amendment	Reserved Powers of the States (1791)
Pre-Civil War Amendments	Eleventh Amendment	Suits Against States (1795)
	Twelfth Amendment	Election of the President (1804)
Civil War/ Reconstruction Amendments	Thirteenth Amendment	Prohibition of Slavery (1865)
	Fourteenth Amendment	Citizenship, Due Process, and Equal Protection of the Laws (1868)
	Fifteenth Amendment	Right to Vote (1870)
Twentieth-Century Amendments	Sixteenth Amendment	Income Taxes (1913)
	Seventeenth Amendment	Popular Election of Senators (1913)
	Eighteenth Amendment	Prohibition (1919)
	Nineteenth Amendment	Women's Right to Vote (1920)
	Twentieth Amendment	Lame Duck Amendment (1933)
	Twenty-first Amendment	Repeal of Prohibition (1933)
	Twenty-second Amendment	Limitation of Presidential Terms (1951)
	Twenty-third Amendment	Presidential Electors for the District of Columbia (1961)
	Twenty-fourth Amendment	Anti-Poll Tax Amendment (1964)
	Twenty-fifth Amendment	Presidential Disability and Vice Presidential Vacancies (1967)
	Twenty-sixth Amendment	Eighteen-Year-Old Vote (1971)
	Twenty-seventh Amendment	Congressional Compensation Changes (1992)

This figure content is also featured on *West's American Government Videodisc* (see the index found in the *TRB*).

document, it is used to set forth the reasons and intentions for what follows it. Hence, the Preamble of the U.S. Constitution sets forth the general purposes of American government.

> We the People of the United States, in Order to form a more perfect Union, establish Justice, insure domestic Tranquility, provide for the common defence, promote the general Welfare, and secure the Blessings of Liberty to ourselves and our Posterity, do ordain and establish this Constitution for the United States of America.

The Preamble lists the major goals that American government should strive for. Rather than being law

Discussion Starter
Let the students respond to these questions: Why is the division of the government into three branches important? Why do you think the founders were insistent upon this kind of division? Why is it important to citizens today? In what other levels of government do you see similar separations of power?

Critical Thinking Skills
Encourage students to consider what could have happened if nine—and only nine—states ratified the Constitution: Would the other four states have been governed by the laws of the Constitution? If not, would the nine signing states actually have been governed by those laws? Why do you think this provision for ratification—rather than a requirement of unanimous affirmation—was included in the Constitution?

Reteaching Strategies
1. Let students work with partners to write short outlines of this section. Check to be sure the outlines include all the main ideas presented in the section and do not indicate a confusion between details and main ideas.
2. Work with small groups of students to review and discuss the division of the government into three separate branches.

Evaluation Strategies
1. Have the students write their answers to the Section 1 Review.
2. Have the students take the Section 1 Quiz found in the *TRB.*

Section 1 Review (Answers)
1. The preamble, the articles, and the amendments.
2. The Preamble sets forth the reasons for what follows and the major goals of the document, namely that the authority of the new document comes from the people.
3. Answers will vary, e.g., the general nature of the rules allows for flexibility enabling the Constitution to adapt to changing times and situations.

SECTION 2

Points to Stress
• Creating a government under the control of the people.
• The principle of *rule of law* in the Constitution.
• The basic underlying principles of the Constitution-limited government, popular sovereignty, separation of powers, checks and balances, judicial review, and federalism.

Kickoff Activity
Ask each student to write a one- or two-sentence definition of the noun principles. Then encourage the students to compare their definitions; explain that, in this section, they will be reading about the basic principles outlined in the Constitution.

Working with the Preview Questions
Have the students read these two study questions. Then ask each

itself, in the sense that the rest of the Constitution is, it explains what the founders hoped the new government would accomplish. It shows that they wanted our government to provide law, order, and stability for this new country. They also wanted our government to serve the citizens while at the same time ensuring the liberty of each individual.

The Articles

There are seven articles in the Constitution, identified by the Roman numerals I through VII. The first three articles establish the structure and explain the functions of the three branches of government: the legislative, the executive, and the judicial. Article I, for example, outlines the legislative powers that are given to Congress and describes how laws should be made.

Article II, in a similar manner, tells how the executive branch—the presidency—is empowered to carry out the laws passed by Congress. It also tells us how the president is elected.

Article III establishes the judicial branch of the federal government. Article III states that there shall be one Supreme Court, and gives Congress the power to create lower courts. It also defines what kinds of cases the courts can hear.

The relations among states are described in Article IV, which describes how state governments and the federal government are linked together. The amendment process, or how to change the Constitution, is described in Article V. Article VI makes the Constitution, laws passed by Congress, and treaties of the United States the "supreme law of the land." This is called the **supremacy clause.** The supremacy clause means that all U.S. citizens, as well as the state and local governments, grant ultimate authority to federal laws, treaties, and the Constitution. Finally, Article VII indicates that the Constitution goes into effect after nine states ratify it.

The Amendments

The third part of the Constitution consists of twenty-seven **amendments**—formal changes to the basic document to date. These range from the first ten, known as the Bill of Rights, which were all passed in 1791, to the twenty-seventh amendment, passed in 1992, which requires an intervening congressional election before any changes in congressional compensation may be instituted.

Later in this chapter you will read about the amendments in more detail, as well as about how the amendment process actually works. Before you do that, though, you need to examine the major principles of government that are included in the U.S. Constitution.

Section 1 Review

1. What are the three major parts of the Constitution?
2. How does the Preamble set the tone of the document?
3. **For critical analysis:** What is the relationship between the very general nature of the rules of government found in the United States Constitution and the fact it is the world's oldest single-document written constitution?

Section 2

The Constitution's Major Principles of Government

Preview Questions
- What are the basic principles upon which the Constitution of the United States is built?
- How does the system of checks and balances operate?

While the Constitution may seem filled with many details about how our nation should be governed, these details fall under at least six broad principles of government. Many of these details relate to how the government itself should be controlled. As James Madison (1751–1836) once said, after you have given the government the ability to control its citizens, you have to "oblige it to control itself."

In keeping with this concept of controlling the government, the first basic governing principle of the Constitution is *limited government,* which was discussed in Chapters 1 and 2. The others are popular sovereignty, separation of powers, checks and balances, judicial review, and federalism.

Limited Government

The framers were all fearful of the powerful English monarchy, against which they had so recently rebelled. They therefore included in the Constitution the principle of limited government, which means that government can only do what the people allow it to do. This principle can be found in many parts of the Constitution. For student to prepare a note sheet with headings based on the study questions. Have the students fill in their note sheets as they read the section.

Teaching Strategies

Introduction

Have the students read the section introduction. Then help them consider the Madison quotation by posing questions such as these: How can a government control itself? How is it possible to "oblige" a government to control itself? Do you agree that it is necessary to oblige a government to control itself? Why or why not?

Discussion Starter

Encourage the students to discuss their responses to these questions: Should the president and/or presidential appointees ever be above the law? If so, under what circumstances? If not, why not? You may want to have volunteers organize and present a debate on the rule of law.

Critical Thinking Skills

Help the students analyze the link between the principle of popular sovereignty and the principle of limited government: In what respects are these two principles similar? Would it be possible to have popular sovereignty without limited government, or limited government without popular sovereignty? Why or why not?

Vocabulary

Encourage the student to consider and discuss the definition of *tyranny.* Ask volunteers to give definitions in their own words; ask others to suggest examples of tyranny.

Extension

Encourage interested volunteers to read more about Montesquieu, who was the first political writer to speak about the idea of separation of powers. The volunteers should share their findings in an oral report to the class.

example, while Articles I, II, and III indicate what the federal government *can* do, the first nine amendments to the Constitution list ways that government *cannot* limit certain individual freedoms.

The idea of limited government is often called the **rule of law,** which states that government officers themselves are never above the law. Government, which refers to the *individuals* who form it, must always obey the principal laws that are found in the Constitution. Otherwise stated, no person is above the law.

Popular Sovereignty

Popular sovereignty means that the people are the ultimate source of any power given to the government. Remember that the phrases that frame the Preamble to the Constitution are "We the People of the United States . . . do ordain and establish this Constitution for the United States of America." In other words, it is the people who form the government.

The principle of popular sovereignty can be closely linked to the principle of limited government. According to both principles, the people are the ultimate source of governmental authority.

Separation of Powers

The framers of the Constitution wanted to construct a government that would prevent the rise of **tyranny** (absolute and unlimited power and authority). To this end, James Madison devised a scheme, the **Madisonian Model,** in which the powers of the government were separated into different branches: the executive, legislative, and judicial.[1] By separating powers, no one branch would have enough power to dominate the other. This principle of separation of powers is laid out in Articles I, II, and III. Congress, or the legislative branch, passes laws; the president, or the executive branch, carries them out and administers them; and the courts, or the judicial branch, interpret them.

Checks and Balances

Even with the separation of powers, the framers feared that one branch of government could dominate the other two. In order to prevent this, the principle of

1. The concept of the separation of powers is generally credited to French political philosopher Charles de Secondat, Baron de Montesquieu (1689–1755), who included it in his monumental two-volume work entitled *Spirit of The Laws,* published in 1748.

▼ Independence Hall in Philadelphia, where the framers met to create the Constitution, is shown here at a celebration honoring the 200th anniversary of the signing of the Constitution. Why did the framers want to include the concept of limited government in the Constitution?

Caption Answer Students should understand that the framers were fearful of the abuses of power that took place under the English monarchy and therefore, included the concept of limited government in the Constitution to guard against these abuses.

Discussion Starter
Help the students discuss the framers' fear that one branch of government might dominate the other two: What was the basis of this fear? Was the fear well founded? Why or why not? Is that fear still relevant in modern government? What examples can you cite?

Cooperative Learning
Let students work in small groups to examine and discuss figure 3–2, Checks and Balances. Ask group members to consider specific examples of each kind of power listed in the chart.

Enrichment
Have a group of volunteers research recent uses of the presidential veto. Then ask those volunteers to present their information either in a display chart or in a brief oral report.

Critical Thinking Skills
Ask students to analyze the relationship between independence and cooperation among the branches of government as developed by the Constitution. Have each student write a paragraph describing this relationship.

Discussion Starter
Ask these questions to help the students discuss the opinion of constitutional scholars that the framers *meant* the federal courts to have the power of judicial review: How would you defend—or attack—this opinion? If the framers intended the federal courts to have that power, why didn't they include an explicit statement of that power in the Constitution?

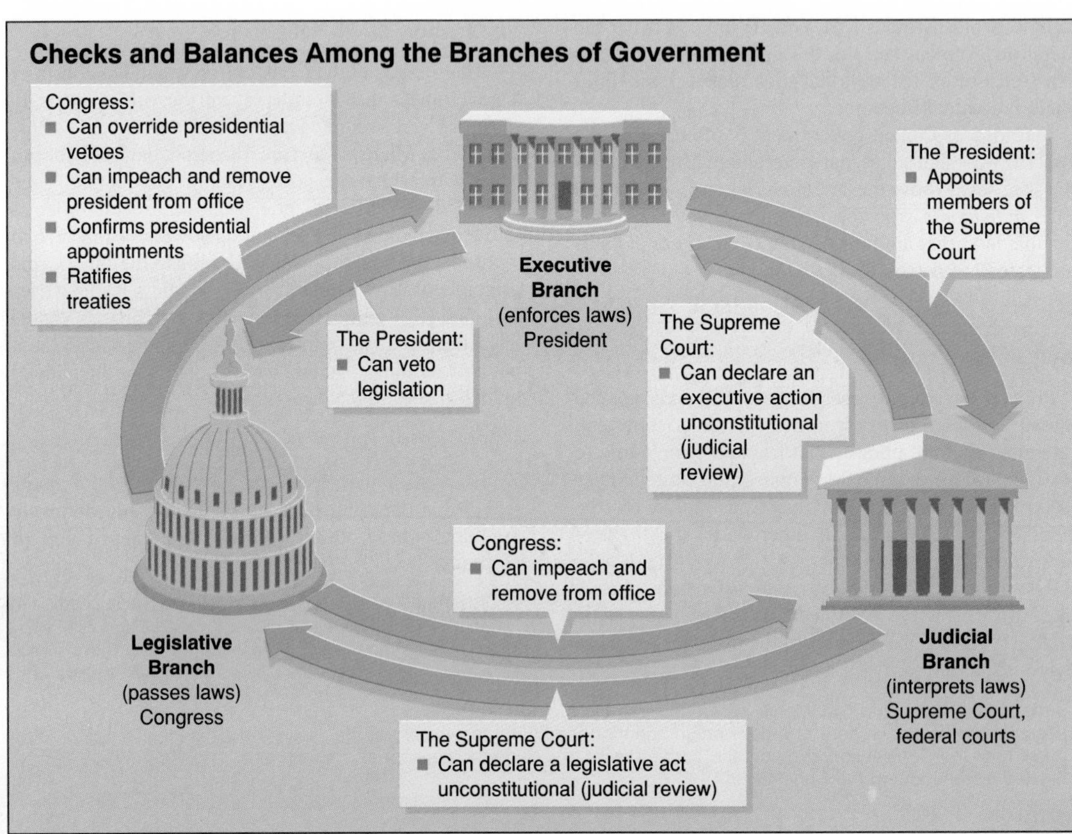

Checks and Balances Among the Branches of Government
Congress:
Can override presidential vetoes
Can impeach and remove president from office
Confirms presidential appointments
Ratifies treaties
Executive Branch
(enforces laws)
President
The President:
Appoints members of the Supreme Court
The President:
Can veto legislation
The Supreme Court:
Can declare an executive action unconstitutional (judicial review)
Congress:
Can impeach and remove from office
Legislative Branch
(passes laws)
Congress
Judicial Branch
(interprets laws)
Supreme Court, federal courts
The Supreme Court:
Can declare a legislative act unconstitutional (judicial review)

FIGURE 3–2 Checks and Balances Among the Branches of Government The above figure details the system of checks and balances among the branches of the United States government. As you can see, each branch of government has some authority over the actions of each other branch. Why did the framers include a system of checks and balances in the Constitution?

Figure Answer The system of checks and balances was included so that one branch of government would not be able to dominate the other two.

This figure content is also featured on *West's American Government Videodisc* (see the index found in the *TRB*) and is available in the transparency package.

checks and balances was introduced into the Constitution. Under this principle, each branch of government is independent of the others, but also exercises power over the actions of the others. Look at Figure 3–2 above and you can see how this is done.

As the figure shows, the president checks Congress by holding **veto power,** which is the ability to refuse to sign congressional bills into law. Congress, in turn, controls taxes and spending and the Senate must approve presidential appointments. For example, the president can appoint justices to the Supreme Court, but only after the advice and consent of the Senate.

Under the system of checks and balances, each branch's independence is protected, yet at the same time the Constitution forces cooperation between at least two branches at a time, which thereby fosters dependence. For example, Congress can pass a law, but the executive branch must approve, administer, and enforce it.

Judicial Review

Judicial review refers to the court's ability to decide whether an act of a legislature does or does not violate the Constitution. In actual cases that come before the Supreme Court, if the justices find that a federal or state law violates the U.S. Constitution, that law is declared **unconstitutional.** Such a law no longer has any validity or legitimacy—it is as if it did not exist. For example, if your state passes a law that specifically allows the state police to monitor telephone conversations (wiretapping)

Comprehension
Check the students' comprehension by asking this question: How did the Supreme Court become part of the system of checks and balances?

Discussion Starter
Encourage the students to discuss the relationship between the endurance of the principle of federalism and the origin of that principle in compromise: Do you think that arising out of compromise made the principle of federalism more—or less—durable? How would you explain and support your opinion?

Reteaching Strategies
1. Have the students work in small groups to compare and revise the notes they took while reading this section.
2. Work with small groups of students to discuss the rule of law: What is it? Why is it important? Then have each student write a paragraph summarizing the group discussion.

Evaluation Strategies
1. Have the students write their answers to the first two Section 2 Review questions.
2. Have the students work with partners to discuss and then write their responses to the final question of the Section 2 Review.
3. Have the students take the Section 2 Quiz found in the *TRB.*

In our system of checks and balances, the United States Supreme Court, which meets in the Supreme Court Building in Washington, D.C. (shown here) has the power of judicial review. How would you describe judicial review?

Caption Answer Judicial review is the court's ability—in cases which come before it—to review legislation to determine whether or not it is in violation of the U.S. Constitution. For an example of judicial review at work, please see the Government in Action case study *Marbury* v. *Madison* in this section.

without formally obtaining permission from a judge, the U.S. Supreme Court might strike down that law as unconstitutional because it violates the Fourth Amendment to the Constitution. If you had been convicted of a crime based on evidence obtained through the illegal wiretapping of your phone lines, your conviction would probably be overturned because of the unconstitutional nature of the law that justified tapping your phones without formal permission from a court.

The Constitution does not *explicitly* state that the principle of judicial review should be put into practice. Most constitutional scholars do believe, however, that the framers *meant* that the federal courts should have that power. In the 1803 case of *Marbury* v. *Madison,* judicial review became part of the United States' system of government. The Supreme Court ruled for the first time that part of an act that Congress had passed was unconstitutional. Chief Justice John Marshall declared that it is "the province and duty of the Judiciary department to say what the law is." (See next page.)

After this important case, the Supreme Court became part of the checks and balances system through its power of judicial review. It now had the right in related court cases to declare the policies of the other two branches of government unconstitutional.

Federalism

In a federal system of government, the national, or federal, government coexists with various state governments. Because the states feared too much centralized control, the Constitution granted states' rights. This **principle of federalism,** which means that some powers belong to the federal government while others belong to the states, has lasted for over two hundred years. This principle was a compromise between delegates to the Philadelphia convention who had strong federalist views and those who felt that the states should retain most of their rights. In the next chapter you will read about the federal system in more detail.

TEACHING GOVERNMENT IN ACTION

Read
Ask the students to read this Case Study to themselves. Then have volunteers review the specifics of the *Marbury* v. *Madison* case so that all the students understand the situation clearly.

Discuss
Encourage the students to discuss the Case Study: How do you imagine Chief Justice Marshall must have felt when this case came before the Supreme Court? What problems might either decision have created for Marshall and the Supreme Court? Do you imagine that this dilemma affected the decision Marshall helped make?

Think About It (Answers)
1. Answers will vary, e.g., it is the duty of the executive branch to see that the Supreme Court's decisions are put into practice. Also, journalists report Supreme Court decisions and follow up on how they are implemented so that the public knows. Those who are affected positively by Supreme Court decisions will let politicians and the public know when the Supreme Court's decisions are not being implemented.
2. By using the power of judicial review to declare part of the Judiciary Act of 1789 unconstitutional, Marshall established the power of the Supreme Court to rule on the constitutionality of acts of Congress and actions of the executive branch. This brought the Court into more of an equal status with Congress and the president.

Analyze and Apply
Ask the students to work in groups to research other laws that have been deemed "repugnant to the Constitution" and thus "void." Have each group select a specific case and present it to the rest of the class.

Review
Use these questions to help the students review the Case Study: What decision did the Supreme Court make regarding Jefferson and Madison's refusal to deliver the commission intended for Marbury? What other, more far-reaching, decision did Marshall express for the Supreme Court?

Section 2 Review (Answers)
1. Limited government, popular sovereignty, separation of powers, checks and balances, and federalism.
2. The principles of popular sovereignty and limited government are linked because, according to both principles, the people are the only source of governmental authority. The principles of checks and balances, separation of powers, judicial review, and federalism are all

GOVERNMENT IN ACTION

CASE STUDY

Marbury v. *Madison* (1803)

John Adams was president from 1797 to 1801. He supported the idea of a strong national government. In 1800 he lost his bid for presidential reelection to Thomas Jefferson. Adams thought that Jefferson's supporters would weaken the power of the national government by asserting states' rights. He also feared that Jefferson's supporters would be anti-business. So during the final hours of Adams' presidency, he worked feverishly to "pack" the judiciary with loyal supporters who favored a strong national government. He made what became known as "midnight appointments" just before Jefferson took office.

All of Adams' judicial appointments had to be certified and delivered. The task of delivery fell on Adams' secretary of state, John Marshall. Out of the fifty-nine midnight appointments, Marshall delivered only forty-two. He assumed that the remaining seventeen would be delivered by Jefferson's new secretary of state, James Madison. Of course, the new administration refused to cooperate in packing the judiciary: Jefferson refused to have Madison deliver the remaining commissions.

William Marbury—who was to be a judge—along with three other Federalists to whom the commissions had not been delivered, decided to sue. The suit was brought directly to the Supreme Court seeking a **writ of mandamus** (an order issued by a court to force a government official to act), authorized by the Judiciary Act of 1789.

Coincidentally, the man responsible for the lawsuit, John Marshall, had stepped down as Adams' secretary of state only to become chief justice of the Supreme Court. He was now in a position to decide the case for which he was responsible.* Marshall was faced with a dilemma: If he ordered the commissions delivered, the new secretary of state could simply refuse. The Court had no way to enforce its decisions because it had no police force. Also, Congress was controlled by the Jeffersonian Republicans, who might impeach Marshall for such an action.** But if Marshall simply allowed Secretary of State Madison to do as he wished, the Court's power would be severely eroded.

Marshall stated for the unanimous Court that Jefferson and Madison had acted incorrectly in refusing to deliver Marbury's commission. Marshall also stated, however, that the Supreme Court did not have the authority to hear this particular case, because the section of the law that gave it such authority was unconstitutional. The Judiciary Act of 1789 specified that the Supreme Court could issue writs of mandamus as part of its authority. Marshall didn't agree and pointed out that Article III of the Constitution, which spells out the Supreme Court's authority, did not mention writs of mandamus. In other words, Congress did not have the right to expand the Court's jurisdiction, so this section of the Judiciary Act of 1789 was unconstitutional and hence void.

With this decision, the power of the Supreme Court was enlarged when it stated that "A law repugnant [offensive] to the Constitution is void."

THINK ABOUT IT

1. If the Supreme Court has no way to compel action because it has no police force, then how are its decisions put into practice?
2. How did Marshall's use of judicial review prevent the Supreme Court's power from being eroded?

* Today any justice who previously has been involved in the issue before the Court would probably disqualify himself or herself because of a conflict of interest.

** In fact, in 1805, Congress did impeach Supreme Court Justice Samuel Chase, a Federalist, though he was not convicted.

related to the concept that different branches of government act independently and can serve to check the powers of the other branches and levels.

3. Answers will vary, e.g., these principles allowed for both a strong central government and protections against governmental tyranny. The "supremacy clause" of Article VI gave the national government an advantage over state governments. The "necessary and proper" clause in Article I Section 8 did as well.

SECTION 3

Points to Stress

- Protection of individual rights at the *national* level resulting in a written bill of rights.
- The role of James Madison in writing the Bill of Rights.
- The difference between *ought to* and *shall* in the Bill of Rights.

Kickoff Activity

Have the students list at least five facts that relate to the Bill of Rights. Then encourage the students to compare and discuss their lists. Point out to the students that they will learn more about the Bill of Rights as they study this section.

Working with the Preview Questions

Ask the students to read these two study questions and to think about them while reading the section. Tell the students that they will be expected to answer these questions when they have finished Section 3.

Teaching Strategies

Introduction

After the students have read the section introduction, ask them to recall the process of compromise by which the Constitution was ratified: Why was the Bill of Rights especially important to this compromise?

Caption Answer The decision in *Marbury* v. *Madison* established the precedent for judicial review when the Supreme Court struck down a section of the Judiciary Act of 1789 as unconstitutional.

Caption Answer Students should understand that Rockwell was pointing out that, in the United States, not only the rich and powerful enjoy freedom of speech, but all men have this right thanks to the First Amendment of the Constitution.

Section 2 Review

1. List the basic principles upon which the Constitution was built.
2. How do these principles relate to each other?
3. **For critical analysis:** How does the inclusion of these principles make the Constitution stronger than the Articles of Confederation discussed in Chapter 2?

Section 3

The Bill of Rights

Preview Questions

- Why was the Bill of Rights drafted?
- What events led to the ratification of the Bill of Rights?

In order for the Constitution to be ratified in several important states, the Federalists had to provide assurances that amendments would be passed to protect individual liberties against violations by the national government. At the state ratifying conventions, protection of many specific rights was recommended. James Madison considered these recommendations as he labored to draft what became the Bill of Rights (see the *Government in Action* feature on page 62).

Madison's Difficult Job

Ironically, a year earlier Madison had told Jefferson, "I have never thought the omission [of the Bill of Rights] a material defect" of the Constitution. But Jefferson's enthusiasm for a Bill of Rights apparently influenced Madison, as did his own desire to gain popular support for election to Congress. Madison promised in his campaign letter to voters that once they elected him, he would force Congress to "prepare and recommend to the States for ratification, the most satisfactory provisions for all essential rights."

After sorting through more than two hundred state recommendations, the final number of amendments that Madison came up with was sixteen. Congress tightened the language somewhat and eliminated four of the amendments. Of the remaining twelve, two—one dealing with the apportionment of representatives and one on the compensation (payment) of the members of Congress—were rejected by the states. The remaining ten are what now form our Bill of Rights.

▲ The landmark case of *Marbury* v. *Madison* arose when William Marbury (pictured above) sued Secretary of State James Madison. Why is this case important?

The Difference Between *Ought* and *Shall*

Madison worked with the suggested proposals that the state ratifying conventions had provided. All of these proposals were framed in terms of the words *ought* and *ought not.* Those words sound weak to Americans who

▲ This famous painting entitled "Freedom of Speech" was painted by American artist Norman Rockwell, who was known for his moving portraits of American life. Look at how the man who is standing and speaking is dressed. What point do you think Rockwell was trying to make?

TEACHING GOVERNMENT IN ACTION

Read
Before the students begin reading, encourage them to share their ideas about the Bill of Rights: Do you think that most people today consider the Bill of Rights an integral part of our Constitution? How do you imagine people considered the Bill of Rights 200 years ago? After a brief discussion, ask volunteers to take turns reading the Case Study aloud to the class.

Discuss
Stimulate a class discussion by asking questions such as these: How would you describe the situation in the House of Representatives during this time? How would you compare that situation to the situation that exists in the House of Representatives today? Do citizens still feel that many representatives are more interested in setting up a taxation system and in collecting taxes than in defending the rights of individuals?

Analyze and Apply
Have the students write a 200-word essay explaining why Maine's assertion that the Bill of Rights are "amendments on comparatively unimportant points" was incorrect.

Review
Ask the students these review questions: Who continued to urge the Congress to approve the Bill of Rights? Why did he have to work so long and hard to get these ten amendments approved?

Think About It (Answers)
1. The Federalists were in favor of a strong national government.
2. Like many Federalists, he believed that the existing Constitution already had sufficient protection of individual freedoms.

Critical Thinking Skills
Guide the students in considering the Bill of Rights as a protection of the fundamental rights of individuals: In what sense are the rights protected by the Bill of Rights fundamental? Do you consider that individuals have other fundamental rights not addressed by these ten amendments? If so, what are they and how are they protected?

Reteaching Strategies
1. Have small groups of students work together to write five sentences beginning "You ought. . . ." Then ask the group members to rewrite their sentences, replacing *ought* with *should.* Ask the group members: How are the sentences different? How do these differences help you understand Madison's attitudes and intentions?
2. Work with groups of students to prepare a simple time line, showing main events in the proposal, drafting, and adoption of the Bill of Rights.

Evaluation Strategies
1. Have the students write their responses to the Preview Questions found at the beginning of the section.

GOVERNMENT IN ACTION

CASE STUDY

The Bill of Rights Was Not a Foregone Conclusion

Many state ratifying conventions had been assured that a bill of rights would be discussed at the first session of the new Congress. Nonetheless, James Madison could not get his proposed constitutional amendments considered each time he stood up in the House of Representatives to present them. At the time Madison was attempting to get the House to consider his amendments, the new Congress was in the midst of creating a new structure for government. It was involved in debates on issues such as import and tonnage duties. Madison kept asserting that a bill of rights was more important business, but to no avail. House members believed the discussion would take up more time than the House could then spare. Moreover, most of the Federalist members of Congress believed that they were in the process of solving more urgent problems. Indeed, the notes of many representatives at the time showed that they were more interested in setting up a system of levying and collecting taxes, rather than worrying about the rights of individuals. In 1886, legal scholar Sir Henry Maine referred to the American Bill of Rights as a "certain number of amendments on comparatively unimportant points." A person looking back today might wonder how this could be.

Madison countered these objections by reminding the Congress that North Carolina and Rhode Island had not yet ratified the new Constitution and that the amendments had been promised to the people. He suggested that if Congress took action on the amendments, it might cause those who were opposed to the Constitution in the first place to change their minds. Although the House listened to Madison's plea, the members still postponed any consideration of the amendments for a month. After frequent reminders by Madison, work by a select committee, and several postponements, the Bill of Rights was finally approved by the House on August 24, 1789.

THINK ABOUT IT

1. Why would the Federalist members of the new Congress not be very concerned about considering a bill of rights?
2. How could Sir Henry Maine believe that the Bill of Rights was unimportant?

are used to seeing "Congress shall make no law . . ." "no soldier shall . . ." and "the accused shall. . . ." But the *oughts* and *ought nots* were typical of the language contained in the English Bill of Rights and in the Virginia Declaration of Rights.

Consider one constitutional amendment proposed by the state of Virginia's ratifying convention: "That excessive bail *ought* not to be required, nor excessive fines imposed, nor cruel and unusual punishments inflicted." Madison changed that wording to read, "Excessive bail *shall* not be required, nor excessive fines imposed, nor cruel and unusual punishments inflicted." Wishful thinking was not good enough or bold enough for Madison. Madison required the language of *command.*

Ten Amendments Are Ratified

On December 15, 1791, the Bill of Rights was adopted when Virginia agreed to ratify the ten amendments. The basic structure of American government had already been established. After 1791, the fundamental rights of individuals were protected, at least in theory, at the *national* level.

The Bill of Rights ensures constitutional guarantees of freedom of expression and belief, of individual security, and of equal and fair treatment before the law. The Tenth Amendment spells out the reserved powers of the states, covered in the next chapter on our federal system of government.

2. Have the students write their answers to the Section 3 Review.
3. Have the students take the Section 3 Quiz found in the *TRB.*

Section 3 Review (Answers)

1. He sorted through more than two-hundred recommendations and drafted what was to become the Bill of Rights.
2. The word "ought" sounded weak to Americans, while the word "shall" sounded more authoritative.
3. Answers will vary, e.g., without the Bill of Rights, governmental power would gradually increase over the years. Individual rights would not be as respected by government officials.

SECTION 4

Points to Stress

- The methods for proposing and ratifying amendments to the Constitution.
- The factors that have limited the number of amendments.

Kickoff Activity

Ask the students to write, in their own words, definitions of the verb amend and of the noun *amendment.* When they have finished writing, let them share their definitions.

Working with the Preview Questions

Ask a volunteer to read these study questions aloud. Let the students briefly discuss their ideas in response to the questions; then have them read the section to find more complete answers.

SECTION 3 REVIEW

1. What role did James Madison play in developing the Bill of Rights?
2. Why was the distinction between the words *ought* and *shall* so critical in the final version of the Bill of Rights?
3. **For critical analysis:** What do you think our government would be like without these ten amendments?

SECTION 4

The Formal Process of Amending the Constitution

Preview Questions

- What are the processes by which formal changes can be made in the Constitution?
- Why are so few amendments accepted?

Our Constitution has endured for over two hundred years with only twenty-seven added amendments. The framers, in Article V, made the formal amendment process extremely difficult. There are two ways to propose an amendment and two ways to ratify one. The result is only four possible ways for an amendment to become law.

Methods of Proposing an Amendment

The two methods of proposing an amendment are:

1. A two-thirds vote in the Senate and in the House of Representatives is required. All of the twenty-seven existing amendments have been proposed this way.
2. If two-thirds of the state legislatures request a national amending convention, then Congress must call one. A simple majority of the convention could then propose amendments to the states for ratification. There has yet to be a successful amendment proposal using this method.

The notion of an amendment convention is exciting to many people. In two separate years, calls for a national amendment convention almost became reality. Between 1963 and 1969, thirty-three state legislators (out of the necessary thirty-four) attempted to call a convention to amend the constitution to eliminate the Supreme Court's "one person, one vote" decisions. Between 1975 and 1990, thirty-two states asked for a national convention to propose an amendment requiring that the federal government balance its budget—that it spend no more than it receives in revenues.

Methods of Ratifying an Amendment

There are two methods of ratification:

1. Three-fourths of the state legislatures can vote in favor of the proposed amendment. This method is

LUNCH
"I CANNOT TELL A LIE--I DID IT WITH MY LITTLE HATCHET!"
Mrs. Nation's Reform Crusade in Kansas, as the Globe Artist Understands It From the Press Dispatches.

This American newspaper cartoon from 1901 shows Prohibition supporter Carrie Nation on the warpath in Kansas. Carrie Nation, who was one of the early crusaders against alcohol, was famous for storming into taverns and using a hatchet to break up beer kegs and liquor bottles. The work by Nation and others led to the Eighteenth Amendment, which prohibited the manufacture, sale, or transportation of intoxicating liquors. Which amendment to the Constitution repealed the Eighteenth Amendment?

Teaching Strategies

Introduction

After the students have read the section introduction, help them discuss its content and their reactions: Why do you think the framers provided four possible ways for an amendment to become law?

Discussion Starter

Encourage the students to discuss these two methods of proposing an amendment: What are the most important differences between the two methods?

FYI

One Person, One Vote

"One person, one vote" refers to the principle that all citizens, regardless of where in a state they reside, are entitled to equal legislative representation. This principle was laid down by the Supreme Court in the case of *Reynolds* v. *Simms* (1964). The Court ruled that a state's apportionment plan for both houses of a bicameral state legislature must allocate seats on a population basis so that voting power is as equal as possible for all segments of the population. This concept is discussed in detail in Chapter 21 of this text.

Caption Answer The Twenty-first Amendment, passed in 1933, repealed Prohibition.

TEACHING GOVERNMENT IN ACTION

Read

Before assigning this Government in Action profile, write the word *suffrage* on the board. Ask student volunteers to define this term using their own words. Students should understand that *suffrage* refers to the right to vote. Explain to students that this Government in Action feature is a profile of Elizabeth Cady Stanton, one of the leaders of the women's suffrage movement during the mid 1800s. Then allow volunteers to read this feature aloud to the rest of the class.

Discuss

Stimulate a class discussion of this feature by asking the following questions: Who was Elizabeth Cady Stanton? Why do you think she has been included in this textbook? What contributions did she make toward American government? Why is the Seneca Falls Convention important?

Analyze and Apply

Have students go to the library and research other important leaders in the fight for women's rights. Each student should write a profile of the leader they have chosen, similar to this profile of Elizabeth Cady Stanton. You might want to allow students to choose leaders both from the mid 1800s and from more recent times. Allow students to share their profiles with the rest of the class.

Review

Use the following questions to review the content of this Government in Action feature. What was the first political issue with which Elizabeth Cady Stanton got involved? What happened to the women who attended the London Anti-Slavery Convention in 1840? What was the result of this event? What grievances are listed in this excerpt from the Womens' Declaration of Independence drafted at the women's rights convention at Seneca Falls, New York, in 1848? What was the *Revolution?*

Think About It (Answers)

1. Answers will vary, e.g., women were treated with so little respect because they had so little power due to the fact that men owned most of the property and businesses.

2. Women were not granted the right to vote until the ratification of the Nineteenth Amendment in 1920.

3. There are many similarities, from the similar wording in the first line to the concept of listing grievances as an explanation for actions.

GOVERNMENT IN ACTION

PROFILE

Elizabeth Cady Stanton

Elizabeth Cady Stanton, one of the prominent female reformers of the mid-1800s, was born in New York City on November 12, 1815. She graduated from the Troy Female Seminary in New York and in 1840 married lawyer and reformer Henry Brewster Stanton.

Elizabeth Cady Stanton became involved first in the antislavery movement. While attending a London antislavery convention in 1840, she and other American women delegates were refused admission because of their sex. When American men refused to participate in the convention, a compromise was reached. The women were allowed to sit in a balcony—as long as they kept a curtain drawn in front of them so they wouldn't distract the men by their presence. The outrage of Stanton and other women against this treatment led to the Women's Rights Convention at Seneca Falls, New York, in 1848. The Women's Declaration of Independence was drafted there by Stanton. It said in part:

> We hold these truths to be self-evident: that all men and women are created equal . . . The history of mankind is a history of repeated injuries and usurpation on the part of man toward woman, having in direct object the establishment of absolute tyranny over her . . . He has endeavored in every way that he could to destroy woman's confidence in her own powers, to lessen her self-respect and to make her willing to live a dependent and abject life . . . Now, in view of this entire disfranchisement of one half of the people of this country, their social and religious degradation . . . and because women feel themselves aggrieved, oppressed and fraudulently deprived of their most sacred rights, we insist that they have immediate admission to all the rights and privileges which belong to them as citizens of the United States.

This gathering, along with Stanton's powerful speech, ushered in the modern feminist movement. After 1851, Stanton worked in close cooperation with Susan B. Anthony in their struggle for women's right to vote. She was president of the National Woman Suffrage Association and its successor body, and was coeditor of *The Revolution,* a publication of the feminist movement.

THINK ABOUT IT

1. Why do you think women were treated with so little respect in the 1840s?
2. How long did it take for women to obtain the right to vote after the Women's Rights Convention at Seneca Falls?
3. What similarities exist between the Women's Declaration of Independence and the United States Declaration of Independence of 1776?

Discussion Starter
Help the students compare the two methods of ratification: How are the two methods similar? What are the most important differences? Why do you think the first method has been used so much more than the second?

Extension
Ask volunteers to research Prohibition: How was it started? How long did it last? How did people respond to it? How was it ended? Then have the volunteers share their findings with the rest of the class.

Critical Thinking Skills
Ask the students to share their ideas, either in discussions or in paragraphs, to these questions: What purpose do the difficulties of the ratification process serve? What do you think the intent of the framers might have been in establishing such a difficult ratification process?

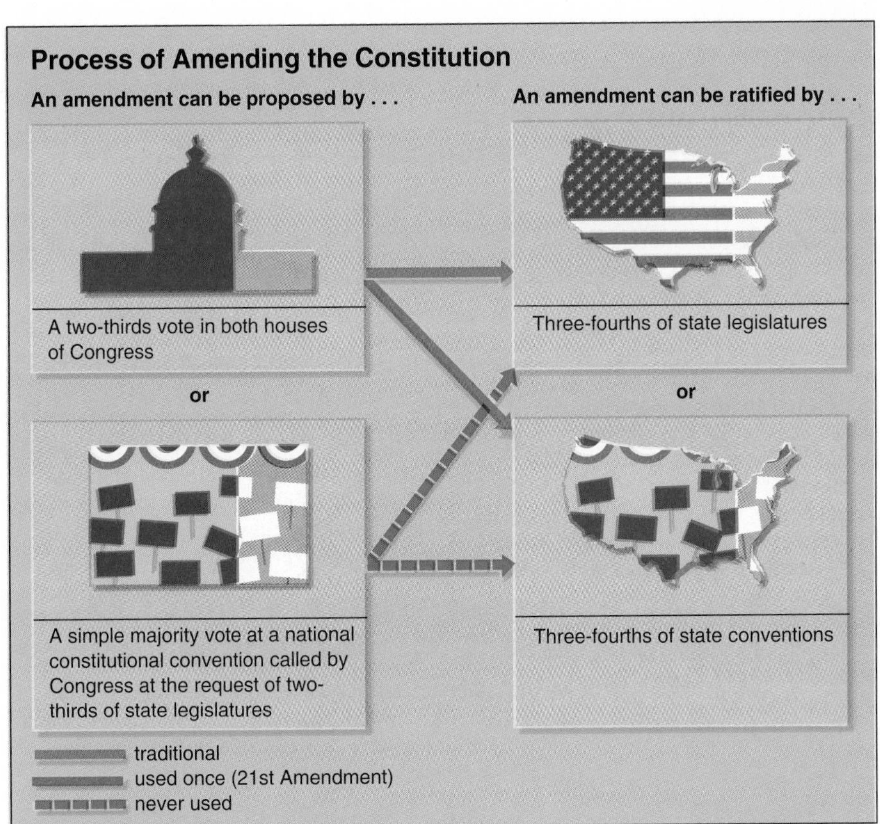

Process of Amending the Constitution
An amendment can be proposed by . . .
An amendment can be ratified by . . .
A two-thirds vote in both houses of Congress
or
A simple majority vote at a national constitutional convention called by Congress at the request of two-thirds of state legislatures
Three-fourths of state legislatures
or
Three-fourths of state conventions
traditional
used once (21st Amendment)
never used

▲ **FIGURE 3–3 Process of Amending the Constitution** As you can see from the figure above, amending the Constitution is a two-step process of proposal and ratification. What are the two methods for proposing amendments to the Constitution?

considered the ''traditional'' ratification method and has been used twenty-six times.

2. The states can call special conventions to ratify the proposed amendment. If three-fourths of the states approve, the amendment is ratified.

The second method was used only once in 1933 to **repeal**—to make void—the Eighteenth Amendment, which prohibited the ''manufacture, sale, or transportation of intoxicating liquors'' in this country. The era in which this amendment was operative, from 1920 to 1933, is commonly known as Prohibition. In 1933, state ratifying conventions were necessary to ratify the Twenty-first Amendment, which repealed the Eighteenth Amendment, because those who favored its repeal knew that the ''pro-dry'' legislatures in the more conservative states would never have passed such a measure.

You can see the four methods for proposing and ratifying amendments in Figure 3–3 above.

Why So Few Amendments Accepted?

More than seven thousand amendments to the Constitution have been formally proposed. Indeed, several are proposed every year in Congress, but only thirty-three that were submitted by the states have been passed. Of those, only twenty-seven have been ratified. The process, therefore, must be more difficult than Figure 3–3 seems to indicate.

The competing social and economic interests in this nation guarantee one thing: The two-thirds approval required from both the House and Senate to propose an amendment is difficult to achieve. Seventeen sparsely populated states, which nevertheless have thirty-four of

Caption Answer An amendment may be proposed by a two-thirds vote in both houses of Congress, or by a national convention called by Congress at the request of two-thirds of the states. A proposed amendment may be ratified by the legislatures of three-fourths of the states or by conventions of three-fourths of the states.

This figure content is also featured on *West's American Government Videodisc* (see the index found in the *TRB*).

Multidiscipline Strategies

Math Have the students work in groups to figure out the number of votes necessary to propose and ratify an amendment by each method. Group members should begin by determining what facts they need to gather and what calculations they need to make. After they have compiled and calculated the numbers, have them plan and draw graphs to display the figures. Let the groups share and compare their graphs: Which different types of graphs were used? Which show the figures most effectively?

TEACHING CITIZENSHIP SKILLS AND RESPONSIBILITIES

Read
Introduce this Citizenship Skills and Responsibilities section by asking the students to define *cooperation* and *compromise*. What does each involve? How are they alike, and how are they different? After this discussion, have the students read the section to themselves.

Discuss
Help the students discuss what they have read: What makes the negotiation process necessary? Why is it helpful to have a disinterested person sit in during negotiation? Which step in the negotiation process do you consider most difficult? Why?

Analyze and Apply
Have the students form several groups, and ask the members of each group to choose—or make up—an issue that might engender conflict. Let the group members first act out a conflict over this issue and then act out a negotiated compromise. Be sure each group's negotiation proceeds through all four steps.

Review
To help the students review Citizenship Skills and Responsibilities, ask each student to write an essay describing how compromise and negotiation can be used in everyday life.

Discussion Starter
Encourage the students to share their responses to these questions: Do you consider seven years a "reasonable time limit" for the ratification process? Why or why not? If not, what time limit would you suggest as more reasonable? Why?

Enrichment
Have an interested student research *Dillon* v. *Gloss* and share the most important features of the case with the rest of the class.

Reteaching Strategy
1. Work with small groups of students to examine and discuss the flow chart on page 65. Then have each student write a one-paragraph summary of the information presented in the chart. Make sure that students understand the difference between proposing and ratifying.

Evaluation Strategies
1. Have the students write their answers to the first three questions of the Section 4 Review.
2. Encourage the students to discuss their ideas about the final question in the Section 4 Review with partners or in small groups. Then have each student write a short essay in response to the question.
3. Have the students take the Section 4 Quiz found in the *TRB*.

Section 4 Review (Answers)
1. A two-thirds vote in the Senate and in the House of Representatives. If two-thirds of the state legislatures request a national amendment convention, then Congress must call one; at the convention, a simple majority vote is required to propose an amendment.

CITIZENSHIP SKILLS AND RESPONSIBILITIES
Compromise and Negotiation

Compromise

In order to achieve goals and to benefit everyone in a society, citizens must work together. Cooperation, the process of working together, involves being both a leader and a follower. It also involves coping with conflict in a group and learning how to reach a compromise. In every conflict situation there are at least two strong positions. Compromise is the political process through which the potential and real conflicts between the opposing groups are resolved.

In order for a compromise to be effective, all sides must agree to certain points. First, each opposing party must be willing to accept less than what it actually wants. One party is usually willing to accept less if the other party or parties will also accept less. Compromise means that no side wins entirely, but no side loses completely either. A compromise carries with it the promise of some benefit to all parties involved.

Negotiation

Often, the issues are so important to all sides that it is hard for anyone to see room for a compromise. Agreement becomes difficult, and a negotiation process must take place. Usually, a third-party person who is not in favor of either side sits in on these negotiations.

There are four steps to the negotiation process:

1. *Each side must state what it wants.*
2. *Each side must state what it views as an unacceptable outcome.*
3. *Each side must state the minimum of what it will accept.*
4. *All sides must agree to the terms laid out in the negotiation.*

TAKING ACTION

1. Choose an issue that is presently dividing your school, or imagine one that might: for instance, a difference of opinion between students and faculty regarding a certain rule; differences between groups of students regarding a new dress code; the banning of personal cassette players; or the requirement that all students learn to use computers. Poll your classmates on the issues to find out where they stand. Then divide students into two groups according to their opinions. Form a third group to act as a student task force to mediate between the two opposing groups. Meanwhile, groups should select students to act as their representatives. Use the four steps of the negotiation process to reach a compromise.
2. Watch a debate on one of your local stations or on C-SPAN in which lawmakers argue the pros and cons of pending legislation. Take notes about the positions of the opposing sides and then determine where the opponents have decided to compromise in order to get the legislation passed.

the one hundred senators, can block any amendment proposal.

The ratification process is even more difficult. After approval of Congress, three-fourths (thirty-eight) of the state legislatures must then approve the amendment in one of the two manners described previously. As you can imagine, any amendment must have wide popular support within both parties and in all regions of the country.

The Time-Limit Problem The Constitution does not specify any time limit for ratification. It was not until the 20th century that Congress, in a Supreme Court case, placed a "reasonable time limit" on the ratification process. It set a seven-year deadline in 1917 for what was to become the Eighteenth Amendment (Prohibition). In 1921, the Supreme Court ruled in favor of Congress on the constitutionality of this time limit in the case of *Dillon* v. *Gloss*. Congress wrote the ratification time limit into the amendment proposal itself. It also did this in the Twentieth, Twenty-first, and Twenty-second Amendments. In the Twenty-third through the Twenty-sixth Amendments, seven-year deadlines were included as part of separate congressional resolutions.

2. Three-fourths of state legislatures can vote in favor of a proposed amendment, or states can call special conventions to ratify the proposed amendment. The mode of ratification is determined by Congress.
3. The two-thirds approval required from House and Senate to propose an amendment is difficult to achieve because of the diverse social and economic interests in the nation. Ratification by three-fourths of the state legislatures is equally or more difficult to obtain, particularly if there is any controversy over the amendment.
4. Answers will vary, e.g., the essence of federalism is the distribution and sharing of power between the national and state governments. State representatives are elected to represent even when dealing with amendments.

SECTION 5

Points to Stress

- The Constitution is very flexible and has adapted to the growth and changes of our government.
- The Constitution has been informally amended through Congressional legislation, presidential actions, and judicial review.
- Political parties and custom and usage have also informally amended the Constitution.

Kickoff Activity

Ask the students to write short answers in response to this question: How is an informal process different from a formal process? After they have finished writing, encourage the students to share their responses.

Working with the Preview Questions

Go over these study questions with the students. Ask the students to take notes in response to these questions as they read. When the students have finished Section 5, have them share and discuss their notes.

SECTION 4 REVIEW

1. By what two methods may amendments to the Constitution be proposed?
2. By what two methods may they be ratified?
3. Why have so few amendments been accepted?
4. **For critical analysis:** In the state-legislature ratifying procedure, it is legislators who ratify the amendment. Discuss the criticism of this process, which is based on the fact that state legislators are not voted into office initially because of their stand on any proposed amendment.

SECTION 5

The Informal Amending Process

Preview Questions

- What is meant by the informal amending process?
- What are the methods by which the Constitution has been informally amended?

For the most part, the Constitution provides a skeleton of how our system of government should work. The details of that system have been fleshed out over the years as the various branches of government have fulfilled their duties. Formal amendments have played an important role in making the Constitution a living document. The Constitution, however, has kept pace with the times and grown as an instrument of government through informal changes as well. It has proved itself to be a remarkably flexible document, adapting itself time and again to new events and concerns.

The methods by which the Constitution has been informally amended are numerous. They include:

- Congressional legislation
- Presidential actions
- Judicial review
- Political parties
- Custom and usage

Congressional Legislation

One might say that the Constitution gave Congress the ball and Congress carried it. For example, the Constitution gives Congress the power to regulate foreign and interstate commerce (business dealings that cross national and state boundaries) in Article I, Section 8, Clause 3. But there is no clear definition of what foreign commerce is, nor of what interstate commerce is. Under the **commerce clause,** Congress has passed thousands of laws, which by their nature have defined the meaning of foreign and interstate commerce. In so doing, Congress has informally added to the Constitution.

Consider another example. In Article III, Section 1, the Constitution dictates that our national judiciary shall consist of one supreme court and "such inferior courts, as Congress may from time to time ordain and establish." Through a series of acts, Congress has indeed established a federal court system, one that you will study in Chapter 13.

The Constitution does not provide for specific executive departments and agencies, such as the Department of Defense or the Federal Communications Commission. Congress has created them in its legislation.

Presidential Actions

Nowhere in the Constitution does it indicate that the president should propose bills or even budgets to Congress. Yet since the time of Woodrow Wilson (who served as president from 1913 to 1921) each year the president proposes hundreds of bills to Congress.

The Constitution states that while Congress may declare war, the president is commander in chief of the armed forces. At times our president has sent American forces into conflict without a declaration of war by Congress. President Lincoln did this in the Civil War. President Truman did this during the Korean conflict (1950–1953). Presidents Kennedy and Johnson sent military personnel to Vietnam during the 1960s. President Reagan sent armed forces to the tiny Caribbean island of Grenada in 1983 without congressional approval. President Bush sent troops to Panama in 1989 and to the Middle East in 1990.

Presidents have also conducted foreign affairs by the use of **executive agreements,** made between the president and a foreign chief of state. Although these agreements are made without the approval of Congress, they do serve as legally binding agreements.

Judicial Review

Another way of informally changing the Constitution is through the power of judicial review. Through judicial review the Supreme Court adapts the Constitution to current-day situations. For example, electronic technology did not exist when the Constitution was ratified. Nonetheless, the Supreme Court used the Fourth Amendment guarantees against unreasonable searches and seizures to place limits on wiretapping and other electronic

Teaching Strategies

Introduction

Before the students read this section introduction, ask them to define the adjective flexible and to discuss the importance of flexibility.

Vocabulary

Ask the students to define *inferior* as it is used here *(inferior courts).* Have volunteers use dictionaries to find the appropriate definition, if necessary.

Cooperative Learning

Divide the class into six groups, and assign each group one of these recent uses of presidential power to send American forces into combat (Truman, Kennedy, Johnson, Reagan, Bush in Panama, Bush in the Middle East). Have the members of each group work together to find out the causes and outcome of the assigned conflict, as well as the reactions of Congress and citizens. Each group should present its findings in an oral report to the class.

Vocabulary
Ask the students to define the words *judicial* and *review* and then the term *judicial review.*

Discussion Starter
Ask the students to explain what they think Woodrow Wilson meant when he said "the Supreme Court is a constitutional convention in continuous session." Encourage students to present, discuss, and support various ideas.

Discussion Starter
Encourage the students to share what they know about American political parties: What are the two major parties? What are the main purposes of these parties?

Vocabulary
Ask the students to define the terms *custom* and *usage.* How are the two alike? How are they different? How do you image custom and usage can affect the Constitution?

eavesdropping methods by government officials in the twentieth century.

The Supreme Court has changed its interpretation of the Constitution in accordance with changing times. A good example of this change has to do with a ruling in 1896, when the Court said that separate-but-equal public facilities for African Americans were constitutional. By 1954 the times had changed and the Supreme Court reversed that decision. It ruled that separate-but-equal facilities for blacks and whites could never truly be equal if they were separate. Woodrow Wilson summarized the Supreme Court's work quite accurately when he once described it as ''a constitutional convention in continuous session.''

Political Parties

The activities of political parties have had a profound effect on the American political system. Political parties today are responsible for nominating candidates, and for organizing campaigns, and placing employees in our government. Political parties provide the government with ideological and political direction. Members of both the Senate and the House of Representatives often conduct their work on the basis of the party with which they identify. The president often makes key appointments with an eye to party politics.

One can say the government of the United States is a government organized by political parties. The Constitution does not, however, make explicit reference to those parties. The Constitution specifies the requirements a candidate must have to hold office. It says when elections shall be held, but does not explain how our leaders should be chosen. The national conventions for the Republican and Democratic parties that occur every four years are not mentioned in the Constitution.

Custom and Usage

Through time a certain number of unwritten customs have taken on the strength of written laws. Today, for example, we accept the existence of a presidential **cabinet**, the heads of the departments in the executive branch, as an official organization within the presidency. The Constitution, however, does not mention a cabinet.

This soldier, shown here against the backdrop of burning oil well fires in Kuwait, was one of about 500,000 U.S. troops sent to the Middle East in 1990 by President Bush. How is this action an example of the informal amending process?

Caption Answer President Bush sent troops to the Middle East for Operation Desert Storm without formal declaration of war. This shows how presidential actions can work to informally amend the Constitution. Unlike other modern presidents though, President Bush received a vote of authority to use force by both houses of Congress, following dramatic televised debates.

TEACHING SOCIAL STUDIES SKILLS

Read

Before the students begin reading, ask if they know what primary sources are. Have volunteers offer definitions and examples. If the students are familiar with primary sources, encourage them to explain the differences between a primary source and a secondary source. Have a volunteer read the speech excerpt aloud; then have the students read the rest of the Building Social Studies Skills section to themselves.

Discuss

Help the students discuss what they have read: What specific works can you cite as examples of primary sources? Why are all primary sources not equally reliable? Why might a newspaper editorial be less reliable than a diary or a journal? What factors might make a diary or journal relatively unreliable? Why might a photograph be more reliable than a political cartoon?

Analyze and Apply

Have the students work with partners or in small groups to select a specific decade of this century. Ask the partners or group members to work together to gather at least five different primary sources with information about that decade; then have them analyze and discuss the reliability of each source.

Review

Pose these questions for review: What is a primary source? What are the three essential steps in analyzing a primary source?

There are more original source documents included in the Resource Center and in the *TRB*.

Practicing Your Skills (Answers)

1. President Yeltsin of Russia survived the attempted coup.
2. Answers will vary, but students generally should read significant credibility into information printed in the *Wall Street Journal.*
3. The main idea is that those who attempted the coup in Moscow failed. One supporting idea is that Yeltsin ended up the most powerful political figure in the nation.

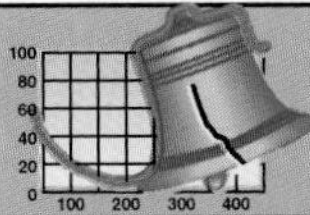

BUILDING SOCIAL STUDIES SKILLS

Analyzing Primary Sources

> Well, I wanted to report to the American people on some of the latest developments related to the situation in the Soviet Union.
>
> I spoke at length this morning to President Boris Yeltsin. The call began at about 8:30 and I also talked to Ambassador Strauss, who is now in our embassy in Moscow, in position and I also talked in the last 20 hours to President Menem in Argentina, Prime Minister Mulroney, Prime Minister Major, and I will continue these kinds of consultative calls.
>
> President Yeltsin was clearly encouraged by the fact that he had survived another night in the Russian Parliament building without a major assault by the forces supporting this coup. He told me that tens of thousands of Muscovites had turned out to help guard the building from attack.
>
> Yeltsin said he was encouraged by indications that more and more military units and their commanders were abandoning support of the coup.

The above quotation, from a speech by President George Bush on August 21, 1991, is a primary source. A primary source is an original document, record, or account of an event in history. There are many types of primary sources besides speeches. Some primary sources include the following:

- legal documents
- letters
- diaries
- journals
- ships' logs
- newspapers
- movies
- drawings
- magazines
- editorials
- tax rolls
- voting lists
- business ledgers
- sound recordings
- photographs
- advertisements
- poetry and songs
- collections of oral history
- political cartoons
- minutes of meetings

Some primary sources are more reliable than others for factual information. For example, a newspaper editorial about someone may be less reliable than a diary or journal. A photograph taken in 1942 may be more reliable than a political cartoon drawn in the same year.

Analyzing primary sources is much the same as analyzing information from other sources. Use the following steps:

1. **Determine the reliability of the source.** Consider the background of your source, and how the source got its information. Is it direct, firsthand knowledge? Does the information seem to be believable, unbiased, and accurate? Consider how your source is using the information: Is it to inform or to persuade?
2. **Read the information carefully.** Look for the main ideas and the supporting ideas.
3. **Ask yourself questions.** Ask who and what is involved and when and where the action is taking place. Ask how the events occurred, if that question hasn't already been answered, and always ask why the source is making the information available.

PRACTICING YOUR SKILLS

1. What is the main idea of the excerpt from the above speech by President Bush?

Read the following excerpt from page one of the *Wall Street Journal* on August 22, 1991.

> In a dramatic climax to the coup in Moscow, the hard-liners who took power Monday were forced to capitulate yesterday by defiant protesters and a determined Russian parliament that held firm against tanks and threats. Boris Yeltsin, the president of the Russian republic, led that resistance from the embattled parliament building in Moscow and seemed to tower over the hard-liners during the tense standoff. He now emerges as easily the most powerful force in the nation.

2. How reliable do you think this source is?
3. What is the main idea of the article? What are the supporting ideas?

Reteaching Strategies
1. Have the students work with partners to list five informal methods by which the Constitution has been amended and one example of each method.
2. Let the students form five groups, each focused on one of the methods by which the Constitution has been informally amended. Ask the group members to discuss that method and then to work together to write an explanation of it.

Evaluation Strategies
1. Have the students write their answers to the Section 5 Review questions.
2. Have the students take the Section 5 Quiz found in the *TRB.*

Section 5 Review (Answers)
1. Congressional legislation, presidential actions, judicial review and other court rulings, political parties, and through custom and usage.
2. This informal process illustrates the flexibility of the Constitution and its ability to keep up with the changing times. However, it has also led to times of "crisis" at such times as the Watergate scandal and the Iran-Contra scandal.
3. Answers will vary, e.g., when Franklin Roosevelt broke the "no third-term" tradition, the Twenty-second Amendment was added to the Constitution.

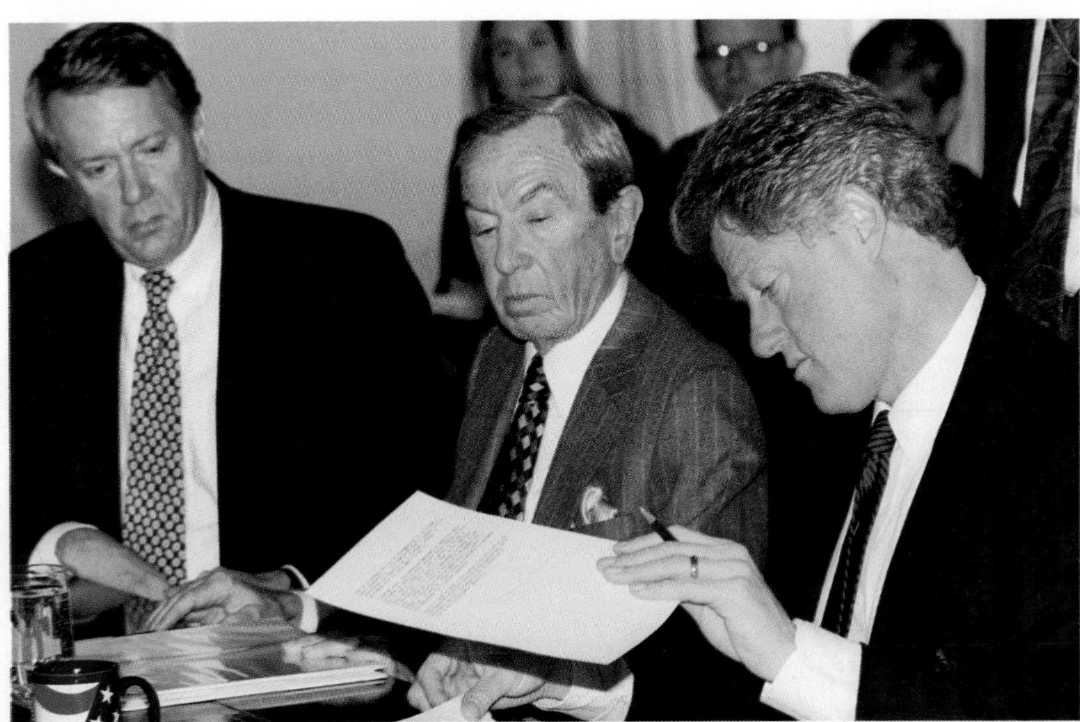

▲ The president's group of closest advisors is known as the cabinet. Here President Clinton is meeting with Secretary of the Interior Bruce Babbitt and Secretary of State Warren Christopher. Where in the Constitution is the existence of a cabinet explained?

Caption Answer There is no formal mention of the Cabinet in the Constitution. The Cabinet has come about over time through customs set down since George Washington appointed the first Cabinet members during his first term.

For many years there was a tradition that no president would run for a third term. This tradition was started by George Washington. Franklin D. Roosevelt defied this tradition by running for office and winning a third presidential term in 1940, and then winning a fourth term in 1944. Many politicians and ordinary citizens believed that Roosevelt was creating a permanent presidency, almost as if he were setting himself up as a king. As a result, the Twenty-second Amendment was added, which limits the duration of presidential **tenure** (the period of holding office) to two four-year terms. In this way, tradition evolved to become law.

Until the Twenty-fifth Amendment was passed in 1967, the Constitution said nothing about the vice president assuming the office of president in the event of the president's death. Yet on eight occasions that is exactly what happened. The Constitution, though, only conferred the powers and duties of the president, rather than the office itself, to a vice president in such instances (Article II, Section 1, Clause 6).

The Constitution, with its formal and informal amendments, has gone from serving the needs of a small rural republic with no international prestige to providing a political framework for a major world government with immense geographic, natural, and human resources.

Section 5 Review

1. How can the Constitution be informally amended?
2. Why is this process important to understanding constitutional change?
3. **For critical analysis:** If custom and usage generate informal amendments to the Constitution, explain how a violation of custom and usage by, say, a president, can lead to a formal change in the Constitution. Give an example.

TEACHING CHALLENGE TO THE AMERICAN DREAM

Read

Begin by asking the students to share and discuss what they know about the ERA: What do the letters stand for? Were your parents or their friends involved in the ERA movement? If so, how? After this introductory discussion, ask volunteers to take turns reading the Challenge to the American Dream feature aloud.

Discuss

To encourage the students to discuss this section, pose questions such as these: Why do you think the Equal Rights Amendment was not even given a hearing in Congress for nearly 50 years? Why do you think this amendment aroused such strong feelings, both pro and con? Do you think the Equal Rights Amendment might still be ratified? Why or why not?

Analyze and Apply

Have the students form small groups, and ask the members of each group to organize a debate on the ratification of the Equal Rights Amendment. (If necessary, remind the students that debating in opposition to their beliefs is good practice and can improve their understanding of the issue.)

Review

Ask the students these review questions: What specific rights would the Equal Rights Amendment guarantee? To whom would it guarantee those rights? Who was the leading organizer of the opposition to the ERA? What central argument did she and her followers present?

You Decide (Answers)

1. Answers will vary but students should understand that many viewed the ERA as essential for women's rights while others viewed it as a threat to their way of life.
2. The ERA was an attempt to establish full, legal, and constitutional equality for women. Discrimination in employment, property ownership, educational opportunities, and marriage have been commonplace.

CHALLENGE TO THE AMERICAN DREAM

The Equal Rights Amendment

The Equal Rights Amendment, or ERA, was the proposed Twenty-seventh Amendment to the U.S. Constitution. Although the problems it meant to solve were (and are) complex, the wording of the amendment was very simple: *Equality of rights under the law shall not be denied or abridged by the United States or by any state on account of sex.*

The ERA was first introduced in Congress in 1923 by leaders of the National Women's Party, which felt that women's obtaining the right to vote was not enough to change women's status in society. After almost fifty years, during which the amendment was not even given a hearing in Congress, it was finally approved by both the House and Senate in 1972.

As noted in this chapter, any constitutional amendment must be ratified by the legislatures (or conventions) in three-fourths of the states before it can become law. Since the early 1900s, most proposed amendments have required that ratification occur within seven years after Congress approves it. Supporters of the ERA initially had until March 22, 1979, to obtain ratification by thirty-eight states.

The ERA had tremendous popular support, especially among those who saw it as a way to invalidate numerous existing state laws that continue to discriminate against women and hold them in inferior status. By March 22, 1973, the ERA had been ratified by thirty states—eight fewer than were needed. At the same time forces opposing the ERA were becoming more organized and militant.

Much of the responsibility for the defeat of the ERA rests with the efforts of Phyllis Schlafly, a housewife from Alton, Illinois, and a law school graduate. Emphasizing the positive and unique qualities of the traditional roles women have played in society, Schlafly mobilized the sentiments of many women and men against the ERA through the Stop-ERA and the Eagle Forum organizations. Schlafly claimed that pro-ERA groups were hostile to all the values women had traditionally held and to the general welfare of women.

Other opponents of the ERA felt that past instances of discrimination against women were adequately dealt with in Supreme Court rulings, state court rulings, and new legislation at both state and federal levels. Therefore, these opponents felt that the ERA was no longer necessary and would simply "clutter" the Constitution. Some religious groups also came out strongly against the ERA.

The opponents' campaign was effective. The necessary thirty-eight states failed to ratify the amendment within the seven-year period, in spite of the support given to the ERA in numerous national platforms and by six presidents and both houses of Congress. The National Organization for Women (NOW), the principal women's organization in support of the ERA, boycotted states that did not ratify the amendment. A number of pro-ERA associations refused to hold their conventions in Las Vegas, Miami Beach, Atlanta, Chicago, Kansas City, and New Orleans because their states were among those that turned down the amendment. As the 1979 deadline neared, five approvals were still lacking, and three states rescinded their ratification. Although Congress decided to extend the deadline to June 30, 1982, the ERA again failed to receive the required number of ratifications by that deadline.

The challenge to the American dream is whether women need the Equal Rights Amendment to be on equal footing with men throughout society, or whether Congress and state legislatures will pass enough effective legislation to obtain the same result.

You Decide

1. Why do you think such a simply worded amendment would arouse such heated debate?
2. What arguments can be used to support the ERA?

Chapter Evaluation
To evaluate student mastery of chapter material, you might:
1. Use Chapter Test A from the *TRB.*
2. Use Chapter Test B from the *TRB.*
3. Construct your own test using items from the *West American Government Test Bank* found in the *TRB.*
4. Use the accompanying computerized test software to construct and print a customized chapter test.

Review Questions (Answers)
1. It is made up of the Preamble which lists the major goals, the Articles which outline powers, and the Amendments.
2. The Supremacy Clause is Article VI which makes the Constitution, laws passed by Congress, and treaties of the United States the "supreme law of the land."
3. Limited government is the idea that government is not all-powerful and may do only those things the people have given it the power to do. Popular sovereignty means that the people are the ultimate sources of any power given to the government. Separation of powers means that governmental powers are separated into different branches. Checks and balances is the idea that each branch is independent but also exercises power over the action of others. Judicial review refers to the court's power to determine the constitutionality of the actions of the legislative and executive branches of government. Federalism means that some powers belong to the national government, while others belong to the states.
4. This principle is found in many parts of the Constitution. The basic limitations come from the manner in which separate branches of government have overlapping powers. The Bill of Rights also guarantees certain individual rights and places procedural restrictions on the government.
5. Under the principle of checks and balances, each branch is independent of the others, but also exercises power over the actions of the others.
6. In order for the Constitution to be ratified in several important states, the Federalists had to provide assurances that amendments would be added to protect individual liberties against violations by the national government.
7. A two-thirds vote in the Senate and in the House or a simple majority vote at a national convention called by Congress at the request of two-thirds of the state legislatures.
8. Three-fourths of state legislatures can vote in favor of the proposed amendment or the states can call special conventions to ratify the proposed amendment.
9. The approval required to ratify an amendment is difficult because of the diverse economic and social interests in the nation.
10. Congressional legislation such as the laws Congress passes to interpret and build on the commerce clause. Presidential actions such as a president sending American forces into a conflict without a declaration of war by Congress. Judicial review refers to situations where the court has adapted the Constitution to current-day situations. Political parties are responsi-

CHAPTER 3 REVIEW

Key Terms

amendments 56
cabinet 68
checks and balances 58
commerce clause 67
executive agreements 67
judicial review 58
Madisonian Model 57
preamble 54
principle of federalism 59
repeal 65
rule of law 57
supremacy clause 56
tenure 70
tyranny 57
unconstitutional 58
veto power 58
writ of mandamus 60

Summary

1. The Constitution is this nation's fundamental law. It is made up of three parts: the Preamble, the articles, and twenty-seven amendments. In brief, concise language, it establishes the basic organization of the nation's government and the powers of its various branches.

2. The Constitution sets forth the six basic principles upon which the American system of government rests. These are limited government, popular sovereignty, separation of powers, checks and balances, judicial review, and federalism.

3. On December 15, 1791, the Bill of Rights was adopted. It set out the constitutional guarantees of freedom of expression and belief, of security for each individual, and of equal and fair treatment before the law. Additionally, it provided in the Tenth Amendment for the concept of the reserved powers of the states in the federal system of government.

4. The formal amendment process is set out in Article V. It provides for four methods, two of which have never been used. To date, twenty-seven amendments have been added. One reason why only twenty-seven amendments have been added to the Constitution is that passage of an amendment requires widespread support among lawmakers and the public.

5. Informal amendments have also broadened the Constitution. Although informal amendments do not change the written words of the document, they have influenced the way we have interpreted the Constitution in light of new events and concerns. Informal amendments have been brought about through congressional legislation, presidential actions, judicial review, political parties, and custom and usage.

Review Questions

1. Describe the basic structure of the Constitution.
2. What is the Supremacy Clause and why is it important?
3. Identify and briefly describe the six basic principles of the Constitution.
4. How does the Constitution provide for limited government?
5. How does the system of checks and balances work?
6. Explain how the Bill of Rights was added to the Constitution.
7. What are the two methods of proposing an amendment to the Constitution?
8. What are the two methods of ratifying an amendment?
9. Why have only twenty-seven amendments been added to the Constitution?
10. What are the methods by which the Constitution has been informally amended? Give an example of each.
11. What are the four steps to the negotiation process outlined in *Citizenship Skills and Responsibilities* in this chapter? Why is each step an important part of this process?
12. How was the Equal Rights Amendment defeated?

Questions for Thought and Discussion

1. The principle of checks and balances was built into the American system of government. In what ways do you think this system has created conflict between the branches? In what ways has it avoided conflict?
2. Think of an amendment you would like to add to the Constitution. Develop and present an argument, either

ble for nominating candidates and for organizing and staffing our government. Custom and usage such as the tradition that presidents would not run for third terms.

11. (1) Each side states what they want. (2) Each side states what it views as an unacceptable outcome. (3) Each side states the minimum it will accept. (4) All sides must agree to terms laid out in the negotiation. Each step is important because, in order to compromise, each side must be willing to accept less than they actually want.

12. Opposing forces became organized and militant in order to defeat the amendment. They linked the amendment with a broader range of controversial social issues.

Questions for Thought and Discussion (Answers)

1. The system of checks and balances could cause conflict between the executive branch and the legislative branch when the Senate refuses to approve presidential nominations or when Congress overrides a presidential veto. It may cause conflict between the judicial branch and the legislative branch when a law that Congress has passed is found unconstitutional by the Supreme Court. The system of checks and balances has minimized some conflicts because it provides a set of rules that must be followed by each branch.

2. Answers will vary, e.g., the Equal Rights Amendment should be added to the Constitution because it is the only way to invalidate all the existing state laws that continue to maintain the inferior status of women by discriminating against them.

3. The adaptability of the Constitution has come about through the formal amendment process and through the informal amendment process.

4. Answers will vary, e.g., the founders made the amendment process difficult so that the document could not be changed impulsively. The founders provided two ways to propose amendments and two ways to ratify them. Both methods require a serious majority and deter impulsive action while allowing the document to remain a "living Constitution" which can be adapted.

5. Answers will vary, e.g., an amendment to the Constitution becomes a part of the Constitution which brings it under the Supremacy clause. If a law passed by Congress comes into conflict with the amendment, the Constitution prevails. The processes by which an amendment is adopted and law is passed by Congress are also different.

Social Studies Skills (Answers)

1. The drawing shows the capitol physically colored two-thirds of the way by a different color than the other third of the way. This indicates that a two-thirds vote in both houses is necessary.

2. A national constitutional convention has never been called.

3. Ratification by three-fourths of state conventions.

CHAPTER 3 REVIEW—Continued

orally or in writing, on why your amendment should be added.

3. What characteristics of the Constitution have enabled it to survive and adapt to the growth and change of our nation?
4. The Constitution has been amended only twenty-six times in over two hundred years, although many more amendments have been proposed. Why do you think the founders made the amendment process so difficult? Develop and present arguments either for or against the present amendment process.
5. What is the difference between a law passed by Congress and an amendment to the Constitution?

Improving Your Skills

Communication Skills

Learning from What You Read:

One of the most common assignments made in high school and college is to study a chapter in a textbook. Yet many students do not know how to read effectively in order to learn. They "read blindly," and when they have finished reading the chapter, they can't remember most of what they read.

Do you want to know how to use your brain for learning? First, you "turn it on" by *wanting* to learn. Second, you become a detective searching for meaning by using the following approach in reading your textbook:

1. ***Survey.*** Survey the assigned material for an overview of the content. Pay attention to the title, the section heads, the first paragraphs, and the last paragraphs. Read the introduction, the chapter summary, and the chapter objectives.
2. ***Question.*** Questions create curiosity, improve concentration, give purpose to your search, and make important ideas more visible—all of which improve comprehension. Rephrase the main headings and subheadings into questions. Jot down questions that occur to you while surveying the chapter. Read the review questions at the ends of the sections and the chapter.
3. ***Read.*** Read each section carefully, actively searching for answers to your questions as you read. You are a detective with a purpose, absorbing ideas more quickly as a result of surveying the chapter and asking questions.
4. ***Recite.*** At the end of each section, look away from the book for a few seconds. Think about what you've learned and recite it out loud. This makes a deeper impression on your mind. Answer the review questions out loud. Hearing your answers will help you put the information into long-term memory.
5. ***Review.*** After you've followed the above steps with each section, you're ready to look at the whole chapter and see how all the parts relate to each other. This total review is the final step for organizing the information to understand and remember it.

This method of learning is called the SQRRR (or SQ3R) approach, which stands for *survey, question, read, recite,* and *review.*

Writing

1. Write an explanation of the SQRRR study approach, defining the purpose of each step in your own words.
2. Begin studying the next chapter of this textbook, applying the techniques of surveying and questioning only.

Social Studies Skills

Interpreting a Diagram

Use Figure 3–3 (The Process of Amending the Constitution) on page 65 to answer the following questions.

1. How does the drawing in the upper left-hand corner of the diagram relate to the words directly underneath it about the necessary vote in both houses of Congress for a proposed amendment to pass?
2. Which amendment procedure has never been used?
3. Which amendment procedure has been used only once?

Activities and Projects

1. With a group, make a scrapbook of articles and political cartoons from newspapers and magazines that illustrate the underlying principles of the Constitution: limited government, popular sovereignty, and so on. Write a brief description for each item, explaining how it shows the Constitution in action.
2. Prepare a class report on the reasons and events that led to the adoption of one of the twenty-six amendments. Present the report in class.

CHAPTER INTRODUCTION

Instructional Objectives

By the end of the chapter, students should be able to:

- Differentiate among the three types of governmental systems.
- Specify how the division of powers operates in the American federal system.
- Characterize interstate relations and what the national government must do for the states.
- Define the Supremacy Clause.
- Discuss the role of the Supreme Court in the development of the federal system.

Previewing the Sections

Section 1 Have the students look through Section 1, noting the four main headings and the figure. Have the students list at least five questions they expect to have answered as they read this section.

Section 2 Have volunteers find and read aloud the five main headings in Section 2; also ask all the students to find the figure on page 81. Then help the students begin to consider the section by asking questions such as these: Among which groups is governmental power divided? Why do you think such divisions of power are important?

Section 3 Ask the students to glance through Section 3, noting the main headings, the photographs, and the figure. Then encourage the students to discuss what they expect to learn about relations among the states as they read this section.

Section 4 Have the students read and discuss the title of Section 4: What do you think this title means? Then have the students look through the section, find-

West's American Government Assignment Guide

Activity Sheets
Basic Concepts 4 *TRB* (Reteaching)
Enrichment Activity 4 *TRB*
Building Social Studies Skills 4 *TRB*
Quizzes
Chapter 4 Section 1 Quiz *TRB*
Chapter 4 Section 2 Quiz *TRB*
Chapter 4 Section 3 Quiz *TRB*
Chapter 4 Section 4 Quiz *TRB*
Chapter 4 Section 5 Quiz *TRB*
Tests
Chapter 4 Test A *TRB*
Chapter 4 Test B *TRB*
Chapter 4 Test Bank *TRB*
Chapter 4 WESTEST Computerized Testing
Social Studies Tool Kit Software
Chapter 4 Activity

CHAPTER 4

Our System of Federalism

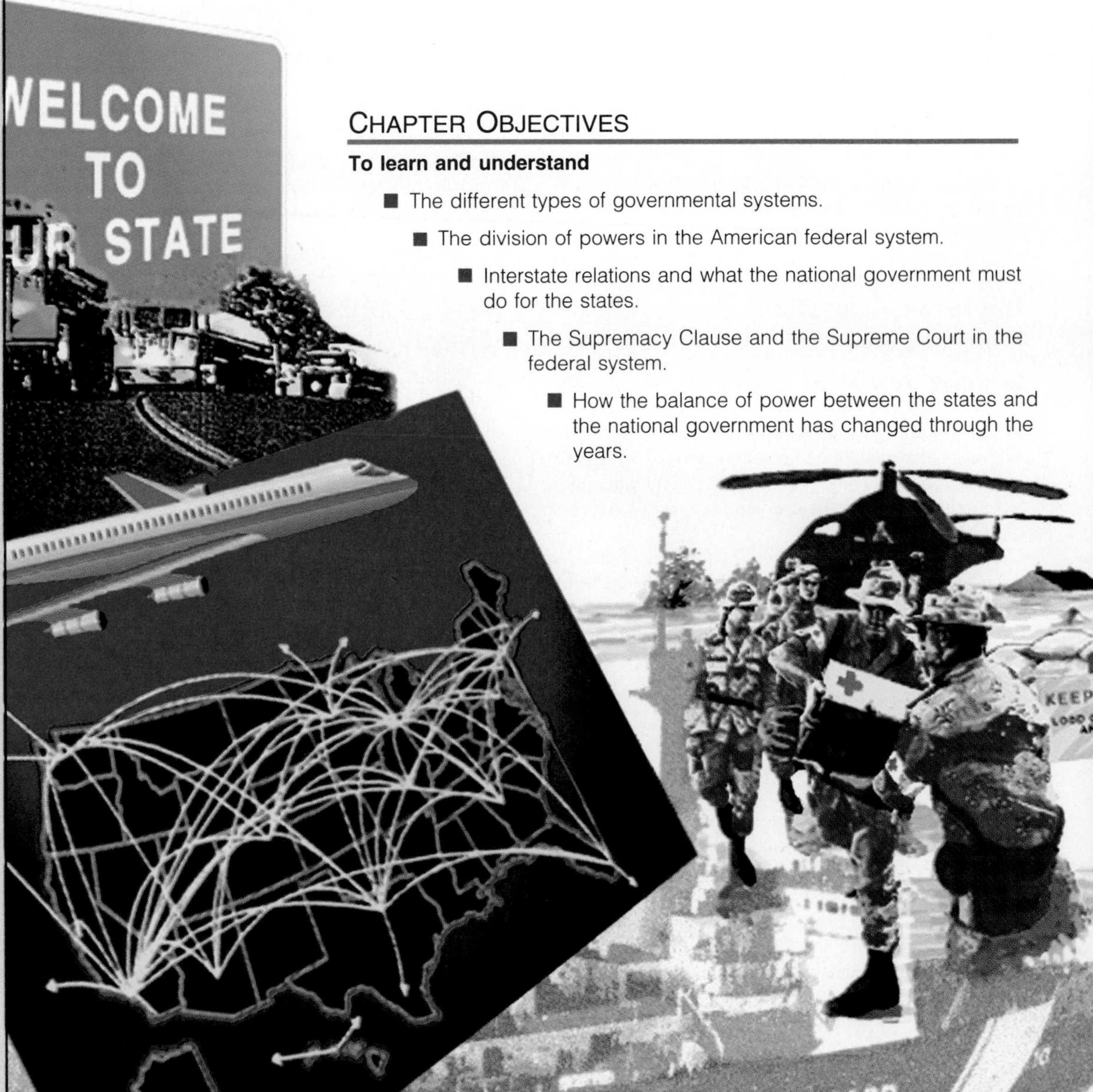

CHAPTER OBJECTIVES

To learn and understand

- The different types of governmental systems.
- The division of powers in the American federal system.
- Interstate relations and what the national government must do for the states.
- The Supremacy Clause and the Supreme Court in the federal system.
- How the balance of power between the states and the national government has changed through the years.

ing the main headings. Ask: What methods do you think were used to answer the question posed in the section title?

Section 5 Have volunteers read aloud the title and the main headings in Section 5. Encourage the students to discuss what they anticipate learning from this section.

Using the Keynote

Have a volunteer read aloud the quotation from *The Southern Manifesto.* Encourage the students to discuss the intent and the language of the quotation: How would you make this same statement in your own words? What specific words in this quotation have particularly strong connotations? *(decry, encroachments)* What are the connotations of those words? Do you think this quotation might express the opinion held by at least some states during all periods of our history? Why or why not?

Introducing the Chapter

Have the students read the chapter introduction. Then encourage discussion by posing questions such as these: What did you learn about the opening quotation? Were you surprised by its source? Why or why not? Why do you think the matter of identifying and separating federal and state matters has continued to be such a complex issue?

Keynote

"We decry the Supreme Court's encroachments on rights reserved to the states and to the people, contrary to established law, and to the Constitution."

The Southern Manifesto: A Declaration of Constitutional Principles (1956)

INTRODUCTION

As was discussed in the previous chapter, one of the basic principles upon which the authors of the Constitution based their plan was the concept of federalism. They invented an arrangement that gives the federal government certain powers and reserves others for the states. In addition, there are some powers that are shared by the federal and state governments. Finally, there are powers the Constitution denies to each level of government: local, state, and federal. The authors of the Constitution developed a federal system because they wanted to limit the powers of government and assure that the rights of the people would be protected. They recognized that the federal and state governments serve different purposes.

Identifying and separating federal and state matters, however, has not always been easy. In fact, throughout American history there has been much disagreement over the proper limits of federal and state jurisdictions, or areas of authority. As recently as 1956, 19 senators and 77 representatives from Southern states who were opposed to the Supreme Court's decision concerning desegregation of schools (*Brown* v. *Board of Education,* 1954) signed *The Southern Manifesto: A Declaration of Constitutional Principles,* in which they made the above statement.

Thus, the American federal system of government has been as controversial as it is complex. It consists of over eighty thousand separate governmental units, as Figure 4–1 illustrates. Those more than eighty thousand separate governments are run by over half a

Governmental Units in the United States Today

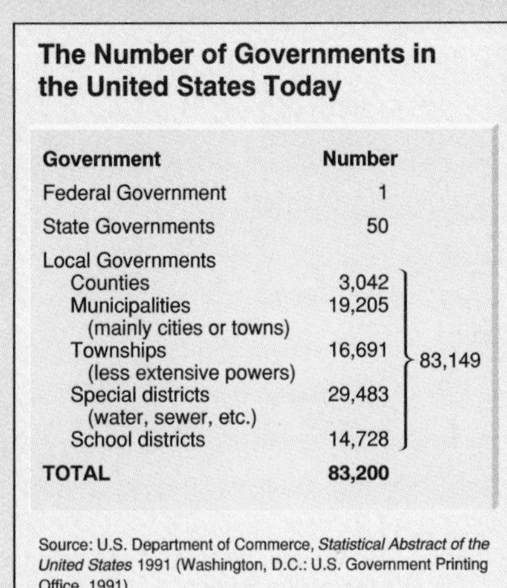

The Number of Governments in the United States Today

Government	Number	
Federal Government	1	
State Governments	50	
Local Governments		
Counties	3,042	83,149
Municipalities (mainly cities or towns)	19,205	
Townships (less extensive powers)	16,691	
Special districts (water, sewer, etc.)	29,483	
School districts	14,728	
TOTAL	**83,200**	

Source: U.S. Department of Commerce, *Statistical Abstract of the United States* 1991 (Washington, D.C.: U.S. Government Printing Office, 1991).

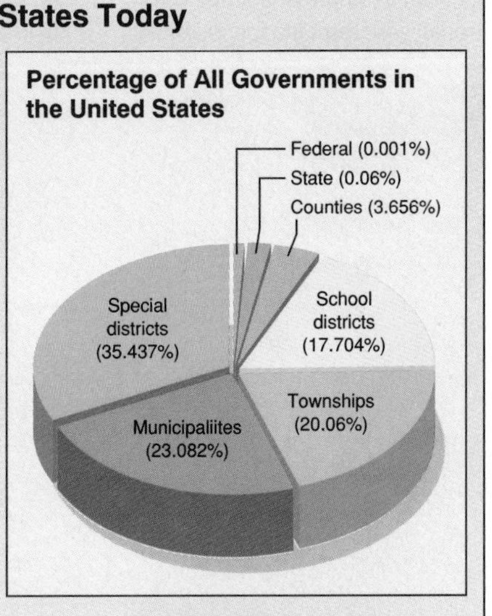

FIGURE 4–1 Governmental Units in the United States Today. There are 83,200 existing governmental units. What percentage of this total do municipalities and townships form?

Figure Answer Municipalities and townships combined account for 43.142 percent of the total number of governments in the United States. It would help to further emphasize the importance of this figure by asking the following: Does the federal government make up a large percentage of the total number of governments in the United States? Does this figure accurately reflect the importance of the federal government? How about state governments?

SECTION 1

Points to Stress
- The differences among confederal, federal, and unitary systems.
- Federalism's definition and characteristics.
- The reasons for federalism in America.

Kickoff Activity
Give the students five minutes in which to list as many different countries as they can. At the end of the allotted time, encourage the students to share and compare their lists. Then, as the students read Section 1, have them refer back to their lists, trying to identify the type of governmental system in each country.

Working with the Preview Questions
Have volunteers read the study questions aloud. Ask several students to share their ideas for note-taking in this section, based on these study questions. Then have the students take notes as they read Section 1.

Teaching Strategies

Introduction
After the students have read the section introduction, help them discuss what they already know about the three governmental systems identified here. Then explain to the students that they will be reading detailed explanations of these systems in the rest of Section 1.

Caption Answer The modern French government is a modified form of the unitary system of government—a centralized system in which state or local governments exercise only those powers given to them by the national government. Under this system, the national government holds ultimate authority in nearly all matters.

Vocabulary
Ask the students to identify the word *(unit)* from which *unitary* is formed. What is the Latin word from which that word developed? What is the meaning of that Latin word? How do these word meanings help explain the concept of a unitary system?

Enrichment
Ask several students to work together to learn more about the French system of government. Then ask those students to share their findings with the rest of the class.

Comprehension
Have the students briefly review and discuss the government established under the Articles of Confederation. What identifies that government as a confederal system?

Enrichment
Ask a group of students to research examples of state and local laws and actions that have been overruled because they conflict with the national government. Have these students prepare a visual display to present their findings to the rest of the class.

million elected and appointed government officials. To many Americans our system of federalism is confusing, for it is difficult to keep track of which level of government is in charge of what. But while federalism may not be the easiest or most exciting part of your study of American government, it is surely one of the most important features of our system.

SECTION 1

Three Basic Types of Governmental Systems

Preview Questions
- What are the differences between the different types of governmental systems?
- What is the meaning and nature of federalism?

The United States started with a *confederate* system under the Articles of Confederation. Today we have a *federal* system. In most other countries, neither of these two systems is used. Most countries have a *unitary* system of government.

Unitary System

A **unitary system** is a centralized system in which state and/or local governments exercise only those powers given to them by the central government, which holds ultimate authority. Japan is an example of a unitary system. The Japanese national government, for example, makes the most important decisions for all schools within the nation, and even decides the subjects that must be taught nationwide.

In France today a modified form of the unitary system is in effect. Within France there are departments and municipalities, or local governments, with their own elected and appointed officials. But all decisions by those officials and appointees can, for the most part, be overruled by the national government. Also, the national government in Paris can cut off the funding of many departmental and municipal government activities. Finally, all policies related to police, land use, welfare, and education are determined by the national government, although they are carried out by the departmental and municipal entities.

Confederal System

A **confederal system,** or confederation, is a league of independent states. In the pre-constitutional days of our country, this type of system was put in place under the Articles of Confederation. The central government handled only those matters of common concern expressly delegated to it by the member states. The central government itself, however, could not pass laws that directly applied to individuals unless the member states explicitly supported such laws. The former republics of the Soviet Union now make up the Confederation of Independent States. Certain organizations, such as the United Nations and the North Atlantic Treaty Organization (NATO), also follow a confederate model.

In France, most policies related to the police and police officers (such as the airport police officer shown here) are determined by the national government. What term is used to describe the French system of government?

Critical Thinking Skills
Ask the students to analyze the differences between federalism and democracy: How can federalism exist without democracy? How can democracy exist apart from federalism?

Comprehension
To encourage a review, ask the students: Why were the framers fearful of a strong central government? Why was a compromise necessary in establishing our federal system?

Discussion Starter
Ask the students to consider the factors of size and regional isolation: Why were they so important during the framing of the Constitution? How have those factors changed for our country today? Do you think this difference might have affected the outcome if the Constitution were being framed today?

The Flow of Power in Three Systems of Government

Unitary	Confederal	Federal
Central government	Central government	Central government
Local/State Local/State Local/State	Local/State Local/State Local/State	Local/State Local/State Local/State

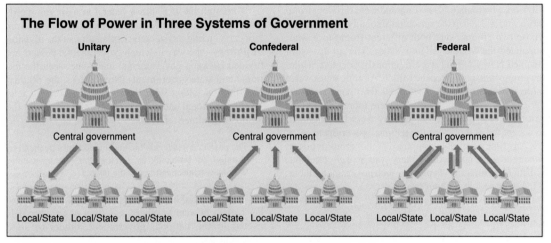

FIGURE 4–2 The Flow of Power in Three Systems of Government. As you can see in the figure above, in a unitary system the flow of power is from the central government to the local and state governments. In a confederal system, the flow of power is in the opposite direction—from the state and local governments to the central government. Finally, in the federal system, the power flows in both directions. Which of these three systems of government is, in essence, a compromise between the other two?

Federal System

The **federal system** is a compromise between the confederal and unitary forms of government. Authority is usually divided between national and state governments by a written constitution, as in the United States. All levels of government—federal, state, and local—have the power to pass laws that directly influence the people. But while the federal government's laws are supreme, it cannot overrule state and local laws, unless they conflict with federal laws. This is what makes a federal system different from a unitary system.

Keep in mind, however, that *federalism* and *democracy* do not mean the same thing. Federalism, on the one hand, is a system of government in which powers are divided between national and subnational governments, such as states. Democracy, on the other hand, is a system in which the people are involved, either directly or indirectly, in the governing process.

The three systems of government discussed in this section are shown in Figure 4–2 above.

In a confederal system, or confederation, the power of the central government is derived from the state governments. The opposite is true in a unitary system, in which the only power that the state and local governments have is that power that is given to them by the central government. In a federal system power is distributed throughout all levels of government.

Reasons for Federalism

The Articles of Confederation failed because they did not allow for a sufficiently strong central government. The framers of the Constitution, however, were fearful of a central government becoming tyrannical, or too powerful. The natural outcome had to be a compromise—a federal system. The appeal of federalism was that it retained state traditions and local power while establishing a strong national government capable of handling common problems such as national defense.

There were also characteristics specific to the United States that lent themselves to a federal system.

Size and Regional Isolation Even in the days when the United States was only thirteen colonies, the geographic area was larger than that of France or England. Travel was slow and communication was difficult. Given the large geographic spread of our country even then, many regions were isolated within the colonies. The news of any particular political decision might take several weeks to reach everyone. Therefore, even if the framers of the Constitution had wanted a unitary system (which most of them did not), such a system would have been unworkable.

Differences in Political Cultures We have always been a nation of different political subcultures. The

Figure Answer The federal system is a compromise between the unitary system and the confederal system of government.

This figure content is also featured on *West's American Government Videodisc* (see the index found in the *TRB*) and is available in the transparency package.

FYI

"There are two ways to empty a room in Washington: Hold a fund raiser for a defeated candidate or a debate on federalism." This quote by Charles Robb, then Governor of Virginia, reflects the negative image federalism receives. As the chapter states, although federalism is not the most exciting part of government, it is important. A vital role of federalism is its capacity for testing new ideas on a small geographical basis before it is determined that they are fit for the nation as a whole.

Many states outlawed capital punishment long before *Furman* v. *Georgia.* States have different gun control laws, as well as different pollution control laws. The point is that federalism allows the states to experiment in ways that satisfy local concerns while providing a testing ground for possible solutions to nationwide problems.

Reteaching Strategies

1. Let the students work in small groups to compare and revise their notes on Section 1. Encourage group members to refer back to the section, adding to and correcting their notes.

2. Work with small groups of students to review the information presented in the figure on page 77, The Three Systems of Government. Then have the group members work together to write a summary of the information presented in the figure.

Evaluation Strategies

1. Have the students write their answers to the first three questions in the Section 1 Review.

2. Divide the students into groups, and have each group discuss their responses to the final question in the Section 1 Review. Then have each student write a one- or two-paragraph response.

3. Have the students take the Section 1 Quiz found in the *TRB.*

Section 1 Review (Answers)

1. A unitary system is a centralized system in which state and local governments exercise only those powers given to them by the central government. A confederal system is a league of independent states. A federal system is a compromise between the two systems, in which authority is shared between national and state governments.

2. Federalism is a system in which powers are divided between the national and subnational government. Democracy, on the other hand, is a system in which all the people are involved, either directly or indirectly, in the governmental process.

3. The government under the Articles of Confederation was weak, but the framers feared a too powerful central government that might come with a unitary system. The outgrowth was a compromise—the federal system.

4. Answers will vary, e.g., in order to ensure that all persons are treated equally throughout the United States.

SECTION 2

Points to Stress

- The three powers delegated to the national government.
- Powers that are denied to the national government.
- Powers that are reserved to the states.
- Powers that are prohibited from the states.
- The concurrent powers.

Kickoff Activity

Write these questions on the chalkboard: POWER—What is it? Who has it? Give the students five minutes in which to write their answers, expanding their ideas as fully as possible within that time limit. Then let volunteers share their responses with the rest of the class. Explain that, as they read this section, the students will be learning about the powers of governments.

Pilgrims who founded New England were different from those who worked in the agricultural society of the South. Those two groups were both different from those who populated the Middle Atlantic states. The groups who founded New England were religiously oriented, while the groups who populated the Middle Atlantic states were more business oriented. And those who populated the agricultural society of the South were more individualistic than other groups; that is, they were less inclined to accept the authority of the national government.

Any time a nation is composed of numerous political subcultures, the notion of a unitary system of government is difficult to imagine. Typically, such governments have ruled their people with an iron fist.

Section 1 Review

1. Describe confederal and unitary systems. How do they differ from a federal system?
2. Why doesn't a federalist system necessarily have to be democratic?
3. Why did the framers create a federal system of government for the United States?
4. **For critical analysis:** Increasingly, the federal government has attempted to make laws that apply to the whole of the United States rather than to specific states. For example, by threatening to withhold federal funding to help rebuild highways, the federal government forced all of the states to raise their minimum age for buying and consuming alcoholic beverages to 21. Why do you think the national government is pushing toward more uniformity in state laws?

Section 2

Dividing Governmental Power

Preview Questions

- What are the three kinds of powers delegated to the national government?
- What powers are denied to the national government?
- What powers are reserved for the states? What powers are prohibited?
- What are the concurrent powers?

Although the U.S. has a federal system, the words *federal system* cannot be found in the U.S. Constitution. Nor can you find a systematic explanation of the **division of powers**—the way in which governmental powers are divided between governmental units—between the national and state governments. Nonetheless, the original Constitution, along with the Tenth Amendment, tells what the national and state governments can do. As the Tenth Amendment states:

> The powers not *delegated* to the United States by the Constitution, nor prohibited by it to the States, are reserved to the States respectively, or to the people.

The key word here is *delegated,* which means ''giving certain powers to others.'' Certain powers are delegated to the national government, others to state governments.

The Powers of the National Government

The national government in this country has powers delegated, or granted to it, only by the Constitution. There are three types of delegated powers: *expressed* (or *enumerated*), *implied,* and *inherent.*

The Expressed, or Enumerated, Powers Most of the powers explicitly delegated to the national government are enumerated, or clearly listed, in Article I, Section 8. These are called **expressed,** or **enumerated, powers.** There are eighteen separate clauses enumerating twenty-seven different powers specifically given to Congress. These include:

- Coining money
- Regulating interstate commerce
- Levying and collecting taxes
- Declaring war
- Establishing post offices

Some of the amendments give expressed powers, too. The Sixteenth Amendment, for example, gives Congress the power to impose a federal income tax. Other parts of the Constitution grant expressed powers to the executive branch. Article II, Section 2 enumerates certain powers of the president, which include:

- Making treaties
- Appointing certain federal office holders
- Granting pardons

Working with the Preview Questions

Ask volunteers to read the study questions aloud. Then have the students set up note-taking sheets, with five heads based on these four questions. Remind the students to fill in their note-taking sheets as they read the section.

Teaching Strategies

Introduction

After the students have read the section introduction, encourage them to discuss the importance of dividing powers between the national and state governments: Why were clear divisions important at the end of the eighteenth century?

TEACHING SOCIAL STUDIES SKILLS

Read

Introduce this topic by asking students to describe what they think of when they hear the word "cartoon." (Most students will probably list animated children's cartoons or comic strips.) Explain to students that in this feature, they will be looking at political cartoons, designed to put forth a point of view on political issues. Then allow a volunteer to read the Building Social Studies Skills feature aloud to the class.

Discuss

Help the students discuss this feature by asking these questions: Why do you think cartoons are an effective way to express a point of view? How are symbols used in political cartoons? How are caricatures used? Why is it important that the reader understand the background of the issue in order to appreciate the point of a political cartoon?

Analyze and Apply

Have the students work in small groups to answer the questions listed in Number 1 under Practicing Your Skills. Then, as a homework assignment, ask each student to complete Practice Activity Number 2. Have students share both their clipped cartoons and their original cartoons with the rest of the class.

Review

To evaluate students' understanding of the concepts presented in this feature, ask students to write short essays on one of the following topics: (1) to understand a political cartoon, one must understand the issue discussed, (2) the use of symbols or caricatures in political cartoons.

Practicing Your Skills (Answers)

1. Answers will vary, but students should point to the use of the donkey as a symbol of the Democratic Party.

2. Students' cartoons will vary but should reflect an understanding of the point of view in their clipped cartoons.

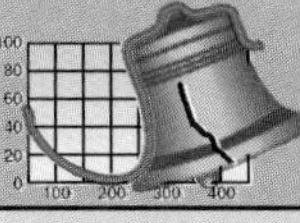

BUILDING SOCIAL STUDIES SKILLS
Analyzing Political Cartoons

Political or editorial cartoons have appeared in the editorial sections of newspapers and magazines throughout our nation's history. They are often funny, but can also communicate serious messages. Their simplicity, directness, and humor can make them a powerful tool for influencing public opinion. They sometimes present a positive point of view, but more often are critical of a person, group, or issue. Cartoons are an effective way to express a point of view on often complex political issues. Although they may present an issue in simple terms, the reader still must understand the background of the issues to appreciate the cartoon.

Political cartoons often use one of two techniques: *symbolism* and *caricature.* Symbols are objects that are used to stand for something else. Some common symbols in political cartoons are the donkey for Democrats, the elephant for Republicans, Uncle Sam for the government, a dove for peace, the White House for the president, the Capitol for Congress, an eagle for the United States, and a bear for the former Soviet Union. Caricatures are distortions or exaggerations of the physical features of someone or something. Cartoonists will take a slightly prominent feature, such as big teeth or a long nose, and make it more enlarged or comical.

Labels are sometimes used to identify the important features. Captions are also used to either hint at the main idea of the cartoon or to represent the words of the character in the cartoon.

When reading a political cartoon, first examine the entire cartoon to determine the general topic. Then identify the symbols or caricatures used and what they identify. Read all the labels and the caption. Determine the tone of the cartoonist—are the figures presented in a positive or a negative light? Also, try to determine the quality of the humor—is it harsh and angry or is it gently mocking? Then determine whose viewpoint is being expressed. Remember that a political cartoon is an editorial in picture form and the cartoonist is expressing only one point of view. Try to imagine what the other side of the issue would look like in cartoon form.

PRACTICING YOUR SKILLS

1. Study the cartoon below and answer the following questions.
   - What is the cartoonist's point of view?
   - What is the tone of the cartoon?
   - Does the cartoonist use symbols or caricatures? If so, identify them.
2. Find and clip out a political cartoon. Interpret the cartoon to the class by using the criteria listed above. Then design a cartoon of your own that would express an alternative point of view.

By Marlette for New York Newsday

"Sometimes, Doctor, I get the feeling nobody's listening!"

Comprehension
Ask the students to restate this quotation from the Constitution in their own words.

Discussion Starter
Ask the students to consider the key words, *necessary* and *proper.* Who determines what is necessary and proper? When and how might problems of interpretation arise? How could such problems be resolved?

Discussion Starter
Help the students discuss examples of the national government's exercise of its implied powers: Why has the national government paid for an interstate highway system, involved itself in disputes between workers and managers, and waged a war against certain drugs? What groups might object to the exercise of such powers? On what basis could objections be raised? How would the objections be overcome?

Comprehension
Have the students answer these questions: Why are inherent powers so important? Why did the framers not enumerate those powers in the Constitution?

Discussion Starter
Encourage discussion by posing these questions: Why do you imagine the framers denied certain powers to the national government? How have these provisions of the Constitution affected the development of our government during the past two centuries?

Discussion Starter
Guide the students in discussing their responses to these questions: How does the establishment of national education standards differ from the creation of a national public school system? Why is one considered constitutional while the other is not? Do you think this difference is open to interpretation? Why or why not?

Caption Answer Most of those powers that are expressly denied to the national government can be found in Article I, Section 9 and in the First through Eighth Amendments to the U.S. Constitution. You might want to instruct students that they will learn more about the freedoms listed here in Chapter 5.

Implied Powers Certain powers are given to the national government even though they are not expressly presented in the Constitution. They are *reasonably implied* (suggested or indicated), however, and are therefore called **implied powers.** Their constitutional basis is found in Article I, Section 8, Clause 18, which states that Congress shall have the power

> To make all Laws which shall be necessary and proper for carrying into Execution the foregoing Powers, and all other Powers vested by this Constitution in the Government of the United States, or in any Department or Officer thereof.

The key words in that clause are *necessary and proper.* For this reason it is often called the **necessary and proper clause.** Others have named it the **elastic clause** because it gives elasticity to our constitutional system. The necessary and proper clause gives Congress all those powers that can be reasonably inferred, but are not expressly stated, in the brief wording of the Constitution. Through exercising the power vested in it by this clause, the national government has strengthened the scope of its authority to meet many problems that the founding fathers did not or could not anticipate.

There are thousands of examples of the national government's exercise of implied powers. The Constitution does not expressly state that the national government is responsible for the construction of an interstate highway system. Yet our government has paid money for precisely this purpose. Certainly nowhere in the Constitution is it expressly stated that the national government should involve itself in the disputes between workers and their managers. But Congress does involve itself in such disputes through one of its agencies. Nowhere in the Constitution does it state that Congress should pass laws prohibiting the manufacture, sale, and consumption of certain drugs. Nonetheless, Congress has done so.

Sometimes several expressed powers are added together, and are then called **resulting powers.** As an example, consider the printing of paper money as **legal tender**—legitimate currency for trade and purchasing. The Constitution gives Congress the expressed power to coin money, as well as to borrow money and to regulate interstate commerce. The resulting power gives our national government the authority to designate the money it produces legal tender for the payment of debts.

Inherent Powers The last category of powers is **inherent powers,** the powers that governments have simply because governments exist. Any government of a sovereign nation has to have certain powers or it could not be considered a government.

The inherent powers are few, but important. Each nation's government must clearly have the ability to act in its own interest within the community of nations. Therefore, each national government must have the inherent ability to make treaties, to regulate immigration, to acquire territory, to wage war, and to create peace.

Prohibited Powers

The Constitution prohibits or denies a number of powers to the national government. It does this in several distinct ways.

Expressly Denied Most of the powers expressly denied to the national government can be found in Article I, Section 9, and in the First through the Eighth Amendments. The national government cannot, for example, impose duties (taxes) on **exports**—goods sold to other countries. Moreover, the national government cannot deny freedom of religion, speech, press, or assembly. It cannot conduct illegal searches or seizures.

Demonstrations, such as this anti-war rally held in Austin, Texas, are protected under the Constitution, which bars the government from interfering with freedom of religion, speech, press, or assembly. Where in the Constitution can you find which powers are expressly denied to the national government?

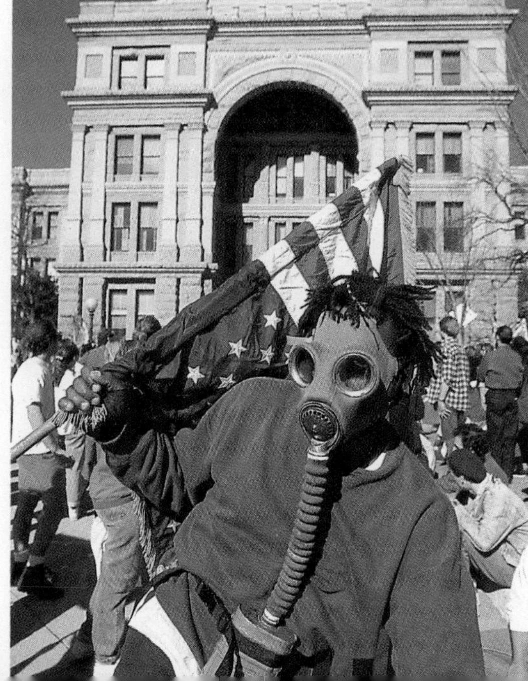

Enrichment
Have the students research their own state militia. What is its history? What functions does it now serve?

Critical Thinking Skills
Help the students analyze the manner in which all states were led to increase the legal drinking age to 21: What level of government actually exerted the power to raise the legal age of drinking? Is this an abuse of power by the federal government? Why or why not?

Cooperative Learning
Have the students form groups in which to examine and discuss the chart, Powers Granted by the Constitution.

Figure Answer The Constitution grants the power to establish courts to both the federal and state governments. Therefore, it is a concurrent power. Note that Article III establishes the Supreme Court. All other federal courts are established by acts of Congress.

This figure content is also featured on *West's American Government Videodisc* (see the index found in the *TRB*) and is available in the transparency package.

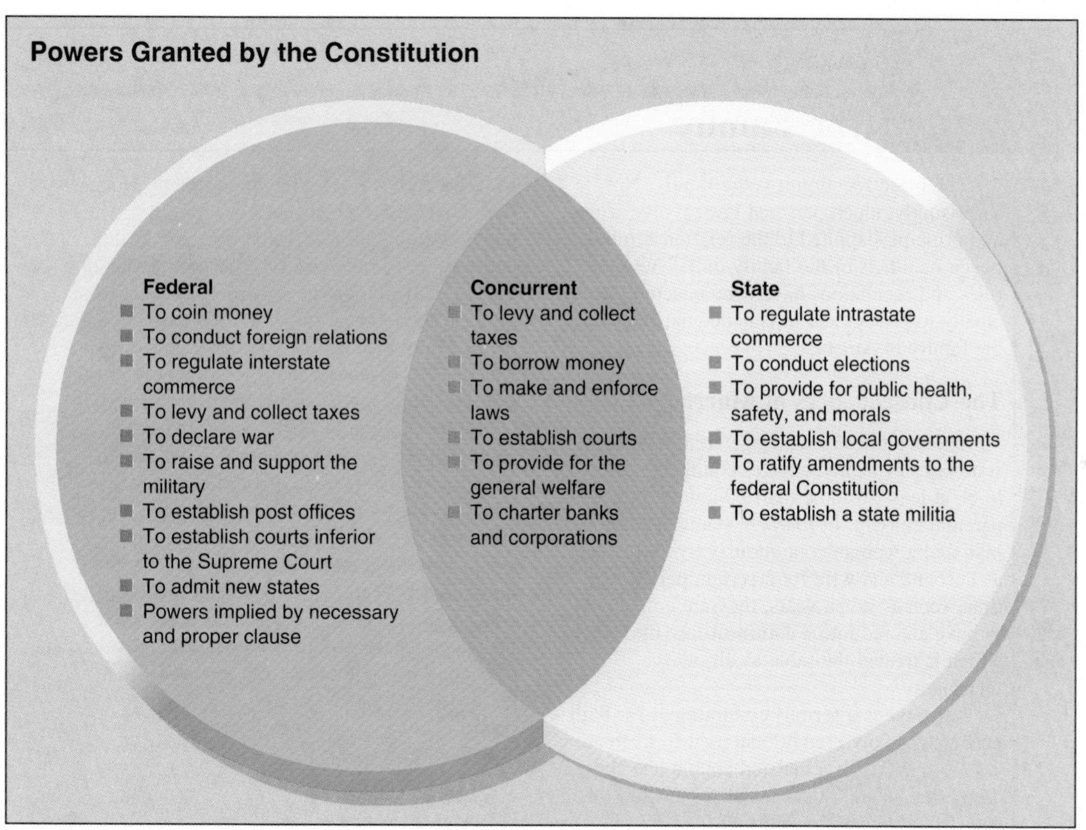

Powers Granted by the Constitution
Federal
To coin money
To conduct foreign relations
To regulate interstate commerce
To levy and collect taxes
To declare war
To raise and support the military
To establish post offices
To establish courts inferior to the Supreme Court
To admit new states
Powers implied by necessary and proper clause
Concurrent
To levy and collect taxes
To borrow money
To make and enforce laws
To establish courts
To provide for the general welfare
To charter banks and corporations
State
To regulate intrastate commerce
To conduct elections
To provide for public health, safety, and morals
To establish local governments
To ratify amendments to the federal Constitution
To establish a state militia

▲ **FIGURE 4–3 Powers Granted by the Constitution.** The figure above outlines the powers granted by the Constitution to the federal government and to the state governments, and to both the federal and state governments concurrently. According to the Constitution, which level of government is entitled to create and administer courts?

Not Delegated Our national government is one that has only those powers given to it by the Constitution. Any power not delegated, either expressly or implicitly, to it by the Constitution in one of the ways discussed above is prohibited to it. The Constitution does not, for example, give the national government the power to create a national public school system; as a result, our country does not have one. The Constitution does not expressly give the national government the power to create a uniform system of criminal sentencing, which we do not have either.

The Powers of the States

Through the Tenth Amendment, the Constitution reserves certain powers to the states. These **reserved powers** are not given to the national government, nor can they be taken away by it. At the same time, they are not denied to the state governments.

Some of these reserved powers are each state's right to regulate commerce within its borders and to provide for a state militia. In essence, states have the authority over all their internal affairs and over the health, safety, and welfare of their people. The states exercise their reserved powers when they create public school systems and regulate such family law issues as marriage, divorce and child support. They also exercise their reserved powers when they set age limits on purchasing and drinking alcoholic beverages and driving an automobile. The federal government can, however, influence state governments. For example, under the threat of withholding federal highway funds in the 1980s, all states were forced to increase the legal age of drinking to 21.

Multidiscipline Strategies

Health
Review with the students the fact that the federal government forced all the states to raise the legal age of drinking to 21. Have the students work in groups to research the facts and statistics that probably motivated that action. What are the effects of alcohol? How are those effects influenced by a person's age? What do statistics show about the relationship between alcohol consumption and traffic-accident injuries and deaths? Let each group choose its own focus and then present its findings to the rest of the class.

TEACHING GOVERNMENT IN ACTION

Read
Introduce this Government In Action feature by asking students to define the term *family.* Allow students to share their various definitions. Explain to students that the U.S. Census Bureau defines family as a "group of two or more persons who are related by birth, marriage, or adoption, and who live together." Then, allow student volunteers to read this Government In Action feature aloud to the rest of the class.

Discussion Starter
Guide the students in discussing powers that are explicitly prohibited to the states: What is the purpose of forbidding states to tax imports and exports? What is the purpose of forbidding states to enter into treaties with other countries? What might happen if states attempted to exert such powers?

Discuss
Guide the students in discussing this feature: Why should the government be interested in marriages? (Students should understand that marriage is a legal contract and, therefore, is governed by laws.) Which do you think has more legal consequences, a marriage or a divorce? Why do you think the federal child abuse and prevention act was not passed until 1984? Were there laws to protect children prior to the passage of this act? (Students should understand that many states had laws to protect the children prior to the passage of this act, but that this act was designed to encourage all states to adopt laws to prevent child abuse.) What happens if a divorced parent refuses to pay child support?

Analyze and Apply
Have groups of volunteers look into the laws in your state that relate to the topics discussed in this feature. One of the groups could look into whether or not your state treats common law marriages as legal. Another group could research and report on your state's child abuse and prevention treatment laws. Finally, a group of volunteers might also look into state and local laws concerning delin-

GOVERNMENT IN ACTION

PERSONAL LAW

The Family

The basic social unit is the family. Not surprisingly, much personal law involves rules and principles applied to the relationship between members of the family unit. These rules and regulations have been enacted principally to protect and to enhance marriage and the family in America.

The Consequences of Marriage

The legalities of marriage are regulated by state law. Typically, a state requires a person to be at least 18 to be married unless there is parental consent. In fourteen states, when a man and a woman continuously live together as husband and wife for a certain period of time, such as seven years, they are considered to have entered into a **common-law marriage** which is treated the same as all other marriages.

Marriage is a serious commitment for both parties. It involves emotional as well as financial obligations. If a married couple has children, then an additional set of responsibilities enters into the arrangement.

Protecting the Rights of Children

To a large extent parents have a right to rear their children any way they want, free from interference from the government. Nonetheless, the government intrudes into the parent-child relationship whenever the health and welfare of the child is threatened. Even at the federal level, the government has tried to give children more rights. In 1984 the Federal Child Abuse Prevention and Treatment Act was passed. This act encourages the fifty states to adopt laws to prevent child abuse.

Some children have no proper parental care or have no home and are without the necessities of life. They typically fall under the jurisdiction of the juvenile court system, a system used to handle the laws as they apply to minors (those under 18). When this occurs, these minors become ''dependents'' of the court, which may then order their care, supervision, and support. In some cases, a dependent child may be taken from the custody of its lawful parents and placed in a foster home or in the home of a relative.

Rights of Children After a Divorce

Divorce is a common fact of life in the United States. Half of all marriages end in divorce. Consequently, many minors find themselves in a so-called broken-home environ-

Powers Prohibited to the States

Just as the Constitution denies certain powers to the national government, it also denies some to the state governments. The explicit prohibitions are found in Article I, Section 10, as well as in the Thirteenth, Fourteenth, Fifteenth, Nineteenth, Twenty-fourth, and Twenty-sixth Amendments.

One power explicitly prohibited to the states is the taxation of imports or exports to and from other states or with foreign countries. Another denied power concerns treaties: No state is allowed to enter into a treaty on its own with another country.

Because the Constitution lays out a federal system, no state is allowed to endanger that system. Therefore, states are not allowed to tax activities and agencies of the federal government.

What About Local Governments?

As you know by now, the federal system involves a federal government and fifty state governments. But what quent child support payments. What is done to collect such payments in your state? What agreement does your state have with other states to collect delinquent support payments?

Review
As a review exercise, you might ask students to write an essay in response to one of the three Think About It topics.

Think About It (Answers)
Student answers to Think About It questions will vary, i.e.:
1. Advocates such as social workers, or marriage and family counselors, should be assigned to represent minor children in divorce proceedings.
2. The legal age for drinking is higher due to high incidence of accidents and deaths related to drunk driving among teens.
3. The interests of the children should be of primary importance to those determining custody because it is the children who will be most affected by any custody decisions.

Discussion Starter
Encourage the students to share and discuss what they know about their local government: What form does it take? What specific issues are of particular concern to the local government? What is the relationship of the local government to the state government?

Vocabulary
Ask the students to define *concurrent.* What is the meaning of the prefix *con-*? How does understanding this prefix help you understand the word?

ment. The courts award **child custody** and visitation rights when a divorce occurs. If both parents demand custody of a child or argue about visitation rights, the court decides what is best for the child. Most states (44) follow the Uniform Marriage and Divorce Act. It specifies how a court should determine custody arrangements in the best interests of the child.

Child Custody and Support Courts granting divorces must also issue orders to provide for the future support of children. Even when such support is provided, the parent who has the child, most or even all of the time, may have difficulty collecting child support payments. The fact is that such payments are not often made after the first several years. If the parent not making the support payments lives in the same state, the other parent can use that state's judicial system to attempt to collect. In contrast, if the parent not making the support payment lives in another state, a more serious problem arises. How can the parent with the child enforce child support payments in another state? Until the late 1960s, this task was almost impossible. In 1968, though, the Uniform Reciprocal Enforcement of Support Act was passed. Under this law the prosecutor in the local state can cause a formal legal proceeding to be initiated in the state in which the delinquent parent lives. The court in the other state will enter the child support order and enforce it under that state's laws.

THINK ABOUT IT

1. In divorce proceedings, both spouses usually have the help of a lawyer to protect the rights of each. Minor children in divorce proceedings typically do not have anyone arguing their interests in courts, however. Should the situation be altered and if so, how?
2. At the age of 18, in most states, minors legally become adults and therefore can vote, get married without parental consent, join the military, etc. Nonetheless, in no state today can anyone under the age of 21 legally purchase or consume alcoholic beverages. Why does this inconsistency exist?
3. As you have learned, most states follow the Uniform Marriage and Divorce act for determining custody issues. Whose interests should be of primary importance to those determining custody? Explain your answer.

about the over eighty thousand local government units? How are they governed? You will examine this question in more detail in Part 8 of this book. For now, you should understand that nothing in the Constitution refers explicitly to the powers of local government, and that the relationship between state and local governments is unitary; that is, local governments exist at the will of the states. No local government exists independently of its parent state. Through the constitutions and laws of each state, these local units have been created and are allowed to continue to function. When local governmental units act, they are acting with the power of the state government. That means anything that the states cannot constitutionally do, local government also cannot do.

Concurrent Powers

In certain areas the Constitution gives national and state governments equal rights to pass legislation and to regulate specific activities. These are called **concurrent powers.** Concurrent powers are held separately but equally by both state and national governments. By

Discussion Starter
Guide the students in discussing concurrent powers: Why does it make sense that certain powers should be held concurrently by both the state and national governments? Which kinds of powers might appropriately be concurrent powers?

Observable Mastery
Place the three forms of governmental systems, Unitary, Confederal, and Federal, on the board. Have students complete a diagram or chart depicting the flow of power between the two branches of government for each system. Next, have students define and give an example for each of the three. Finally, under the Federal model that students have completed, have them list examples of powers delegated to the national government and powers reserved for the states.

Figure Answer The power to grant titles of nobility is denied by the Constitution to any government in the United States.

This figure content is also featured on *West's American Government Videodisc* (see the index found in the *TRB*).

Reteaching Strategies
1. Encourage the students to compare their note-taking sheets with partners. Have the partners work together to revise and improve their work, referring to the text as often as necessary.
2. Work with small groups of students to review the meaning of expressed powers, implied powers, and inherent powers, with examples of each.

Evaluation Strategies
1. Have the students write their answers to the Section 2 Review.
2. Have the students take the Section 2 Quiz found in the *TRB*.

Section 2 Review (Answers)
1. The way in which governmental powers are divided between governmental units.
2. Expressed or enumerated, which are listed in the Constitution, primarily in Article I, Section 8, such as the power to regulate interstate commerce. Implied powers are those reasonably implied by the enumerated powers, or the "legitimate ends" of the Constitution. Inherent powers, which are those naturally associated with the national government, such as the power to conduct foreign policy.
3. The necessary and proper clause gives Congress power to make all the laws it finds necessary for carrying out its enumerated powers. It is the basis for the so-called "implied powers" doctrine enunciated in *McCulloch* v. *Maryland.*
4. By expressly denying certain powers and by not delegating powers.
5. States have the authority over all their internal affairs and over the health, safety, and welfare of people within their state.
6. Local governments are not referred to in the Constitution. Local governments are created through the laws and constitutions of each state.

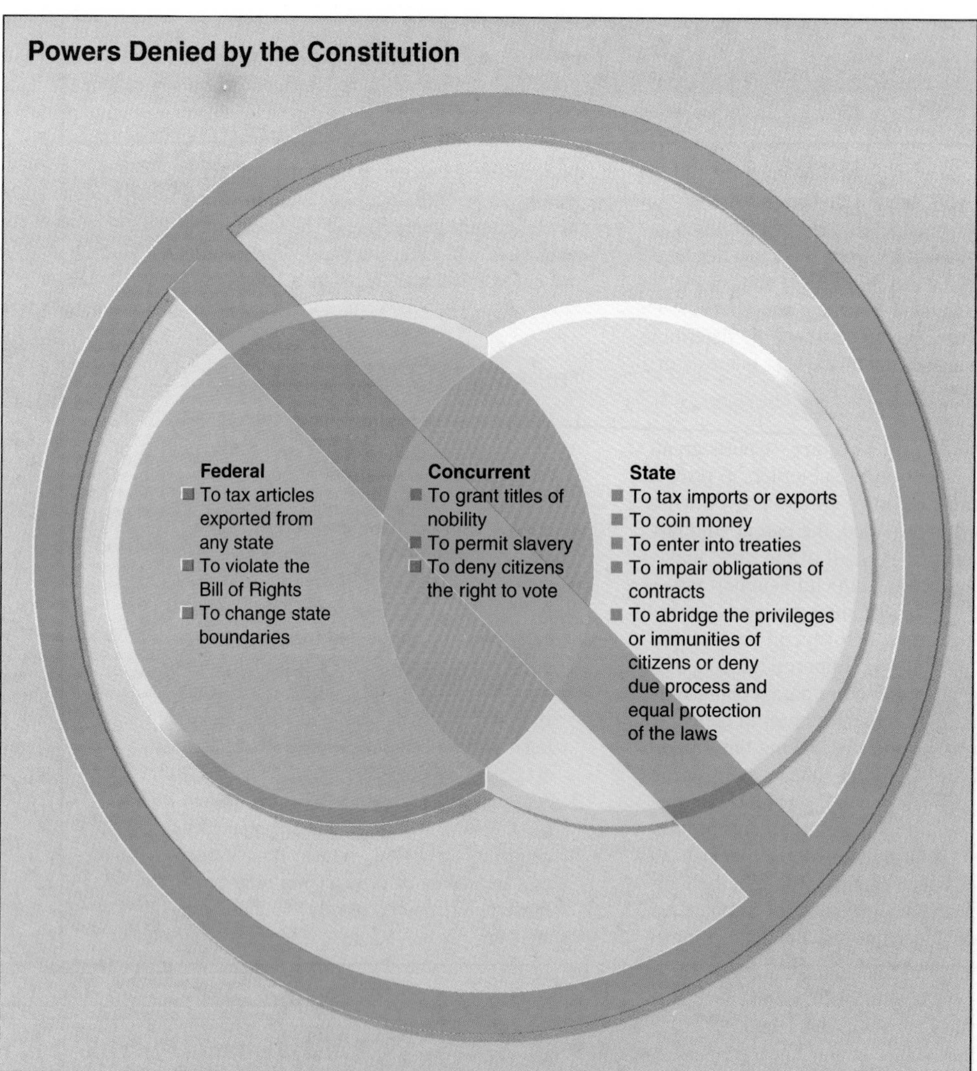
Powers Denied by the Constitution
Federal
To tax articles exported from any state
To violate the Bill of Rights
To change state boundaries
Concurrent
To grant titles of nobility
To permit slavery
To deny citizens the right to vote
State
To tax imports or exports
To coin money
To enter into treaties
To impair obligations of contracts
To abridge the privileges or immunities of citizens or deny due process and equal protection of the laws

▲ FIGURE 4–4 **Powers Denied by the Constitution.** The figure above lists the powers denied to the federal government, to state governments, and to both levels of government. According to this, can either the federal government or a state government grant titles of nobility?

definition, all concurrent powers are neither granted exclusively to the national government nor denied to the states.

For example, both state and federal governments have the power to tax. The types of taxation, however, are divided between the levels of government. States may not levy taxes on imported goods, but the federal government may. In addition, neither level of government can tax the facilities of the other. For example, Texas cannot tax the federal government on the fees it charges people to use the federal court building located in Texas.

Certain concurrent powers are implied rather than stated expressly. They include the power to borrow

7. The areas in which national and state governments possess equal rights to pass legislation and regulate certain activities.
8. Answers will vary, e.g., the problem is so important nationwide, that it requires federal legislation and oversight. The states cannot handle the problem by themselves. The states may have wanted the federal government to take over the responsibility.

Section 3

Points to Stress

- Characteristics of horizontal federalism.
- The constitutional provisions pertaining to relations among the states.
- The duties of the national government relative to the states under the Constitution.

Kickoff Activity
Ask the students to write short answers to these questions: What do you think our state contributes to the well-being of other states? How do you think our state benefits from other states? Then encourage the students to share and discuss their responses.

Working with the Preview Questions
Ask the students to read the study questions and then to make plans for taking notes on this section: What definition should you include in your notes? What list of constitutional provisions should you include? What list of duties should you include? Have the students take notes, based on these study questions, as they read the section.

money, to establish courts, and to charter banks. Both the national and state governments share these powers.

SECTION 2 REVIEW

1. What is meant by the phrase "division of powers"?
2. What are the three types of powers delegated to the national government? Explain and give examples of each one.
3. What is the significance of the necessary and proper clause?
4. What are the two ways in which the Constitution denies powers to the national government?
5. What are some powers that the Constitution reserves to the states?
6. Where do local governments fit into the federal system?
7. What are the concurrent powers?
8. **For critical analysis:** The Tenth Amendment reserves to the states all those powers not delegated to the national government nor prohibited to the state governments. How can you explain the national government's legislation with respect to the construction of an interstate highway system not mentioned in the Constitution?

SECTION 3

The Relations Among the States

Preview Questions

- What is horizontal federalism?
- What are the constitutional provisions that relate to relations among the states?
- What are the duties of the national government with respect to the states under the Constitution?

So far we have dealt with the relationship between the federal and state governments. The states also have social, commercial, and other dealings among themselves. The citizens of one state travel to other states, and buy various items from other states. All activities, problems, and policies that pass between states make up what is called **horizontal federalism.** The rules of horizontal federalism laid out in the U.S. Constitution prevent any one state from setting itself apart from all the others. The Constitution has three important provisions that relate to horizontal federalism, each of which was taken almost directly from the Articles of Confederation.

Privileges and Immunities

Article IV, Section 2 indicates that:

> The Citizens of each State shall be entitled to all Privileges and Immunities of Citizens in the several States.

The **privileges and immunities clause** prevents states from discriminating against citizens of other states. A resident of one state cannot be treated as an **alien**—a foreigner—when in another state. Each state is required to extend to all U.S. citizens from any other state the protection of that state's laws, the right to work, access to the courts, and any other privileges they may grant their own citizens. A resident of Texas cannot be treated as an alien when that person is in New York. She or he must have access to the courts of each state, the right to travel, and the right to own property.

There are certain instances, however, of "discrimination" against out-of-state residents. For example, at most state universities, out-of-state residents have to pay higher fees than do in-state residents at those universities. In some states a certain amount of residency time is

▼ The privileges and immunities clause of the United States Constitution prevents states from discriminating against citizens of other states. However, there are certain areas where citizens from other states are treated differently. Out-of-state travelers entering into the State of Arizona must stop at agriculture inspection stations (such as the one shown here) so that inspectors can verify that no banned agricultural products are being brought into the state. Why do you think certain agricultural products would be banned?

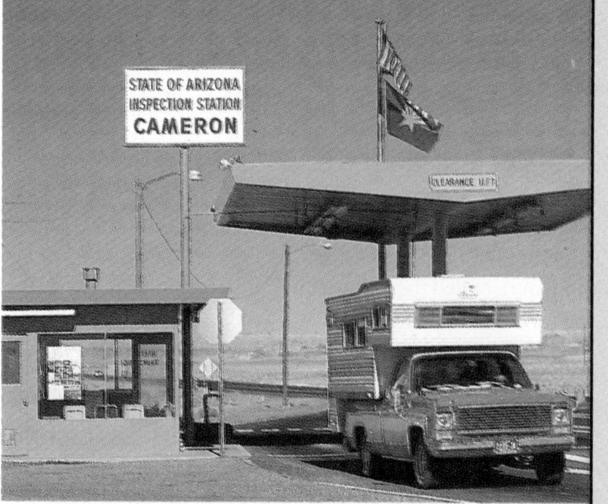

Teaching Strategies

Introduction
Have the students read the section introduction to themselves. Then help them discuss what they have read: Why are the relations among the states so important? What is horizontal federalism? How does it affect the states?

Enrichment
Ask some of the students to research the rights that their state grants to aliens: Who has access to the courts of the state? Who has the right to travel and the right to own property? What specific rights are not granted to resident aliens? To tourists? Then have these students share their findings with the rest of the class.

Caption Answer Many states ban certain agricultural products from being imported into the state not because of the crop itself, but because of certain insects which can be harbored in these products. Generally speaking, these insects pose a great threat to agricultural production.

Discussion Starter
Encourage the students to share their own ideas and experiences about the unity of American citizens as fostered by the full faith and credit clause.

Comprehension
Ask the students to work in pairs or small groups to recast Article IV, Section 2 in their own words.

Discussion Starter
Encourage the students to discuss the Dennison Rule: How do you think this decision could have been considered constitutional? Do you think the Dennison Rule was fair? Why or why not?

Enrichment
Ask a volunteer to research and then explain to the class the status of Puerto Rico within the United States.

Cooperative Learning
Have the students work in groups to research and discuss problems and concerns that involve their own state and its neighboring states.

Law Related Activity
Have students research their state for interstate compacts. What are they? Why were they done? How do they continue to help their state? Students should be encouraged to contact the attorney general, secretary of state, various state legislators, or appropriate state agencies. Students should also research areas of tension or conflict between their state and another state to determine the reasons and to explore possible solutions.

Comprehension
Have the students review the definition of a *republican form of government.* What federal responsibilities are involved in this form of government? What responsibilities do the states undertake?

Discussion Starter
Guide the students in discussing the action taken by congress after the Civil War: What issues are addressed in the Thirteenth, Fourteenth, and Fifteenth Amendments? Why did southern states delay ratifying those amendments? What statement were those southern states making to the national government? Why did Congress refuse to admit senators and representatives from those states until they had ratified the amendments? What statement was Congress making to those states?

Discussion Starter
Have the students review what they have researched about state militias: If it is the responsibility of the national government to defend any state, what are the responsibilities of the states' militias? Whom do they serve? How?

Critical Thinking Skills
Guide the students in analyzing the president's power to keep peace within a state: Why do you think

required before public assistance benefits, such as welfare, are obtainable. Some states do not recognize common-law marriages that are recognized in other states.

The Full Faith and Credit Clause

Article IV, Section 1 states that:

> Full Faith and Credit shall be given in each State to the public Acts, Records, and judicial Proceedings of every other State.

The **full faith and credit clause** requires states to recognize one another's laws and court decisions. That means that rights that are established, say under a deed of property, will be honored in another state. If you own property in Florida, your ownership rights are valid in Texas, where you may wish to sell the property to a local resident. As another example, if you are legally married in the state of Missouri that marriage will be honored in Montana.

The full faith and credit clause was originally included in the Articles of Confederation in order to promote mutual friendship among the people of the different colonies. As part of the U.S. Constitution this clause has contributed to the unity of American citizens because it allows all Americans to move from state to state without worrying about losing any rights that they have.

Interstate Extradition

The term **extradition** refers to transporting a **fugitive**—an individual wanted for committing a crime—from one state to another. Article IV, Section 2 of the Constitution states that:

> A Person charged in any State with Treason, Felony, or other Crime, who shall flee from Justice, and be found in another State, shall on Demand of the executive Authority of the State from which he fled, be delivered up, to be removed to the State having Jurisdiction [authority] of the Crime.

Although the language of this section seems clear, until 1987 state governors were not required by law to extradite fugitives. An 1861 ruling by the U.S. Supreme Court, called the **Dennison Rule,** upheld the right of the governor of Ohio to refuse an extradition request by the governor of Kentucky for a "free man of color," on charges that he had helped a slave escape to freedom.

The Dennison Rule stood for 126 years. Then in 1987 the U.S. Supreme Court reversed itself in a case involving an Iowan, Ron Calder, who was supposed to stand trial in Puerto Rico for alleged homicide in a traffic mishap. The governor of Iowa refused to extradite Calder but was forced to do so after the Supreme Court ruled in favor of the extradition.

In many cases today, the question of extraditing fugitives has little meaning. Congress has made it a federal crime to flee across state lines to avoid prosecution for certain serious crimes. That means that agents of the national government will arrest fugitives regardless of what state they are in. Fugitives are usually turned over to the state from which they fled.

Interstate Compacts

Adjoining states often have common problems and concerns that relate to shared resources and territory. They have to worry about water use, environmental standards, and air-traffic control. States therefore often enter into mutual agreements called **interstate compacts.** One of the best-known examples of an interstate compact was the establishment of the Port of New York Authority. The states of New York and New Jersey entered into this agreement in 1921 to develop and operate the harbor facilities in the area. A number of states in the Southwest entered into the Interstate Oil and Gas Compact in 1935.

What the National Government Must Do for the States

The national government has certain duties with respect to the fifty states. Most of these are listed in Article IV, Section 4:

> The United States shall guarantee to every State in this Union a Republican Form of Government, and shall protect each of them against Invasion; and on Application of the Legislature, or of the Executive (when the Legislature cannot be convened) against domestic Violence.

Guarantee of a Republican Form of Government A **republican form of government** is one in which the people are governed by elected representatives. Our national government therefore has had to ensure that each state government was formed according to the will of the majority of its citizens.

The only time that the republican guarantee became truly important was after the Civil War, when a number of Southern states had not ratified the Thirteenth, Fourteenth, and Fifteenth Amendments, nor had they changed their laws to recognize voting rights and other rights of African Americans. As a result, Congress refused to admit senators and representatives from those states until they had made the appropriate reforms.

the president has the power to intervene without being asked? Under what circumstances do you think the president can—or should—intervene without a state request? Under what circumstances do you think the president would not be justified in intervening? Encourage the students to explain and defend differing points of view.

Cooperative Learning
Ask the students to work in groups to research these examples of national intervention to keep the peace within states: Detroit, 1967; Chicago and Baltimore, 1968; Little Rock, 1957; University of Mississippi, 1962; University of Alabama, 1963. Group members should read about the situation that led to unrest in each case, the acts of violence involved, the efforts and intentions of state leaders, and the efforts and effectiveness of national intervention.

Comprehension
Ask the students to identify legal means by which a state might be divided into two or more states.

Reteaching Strategies
1. Work with small groups of students to review the privileges and immunities clause, Article IV, Section 2: What does the clause mean? How does it affect the states? Then have the group members work together to rewrite the clause in their own words.
2. Have the students work with partners to review and revise the notes they have taken on the section contents. Encourage the students to refer to the text for corrections and additions.

Evaluation Strategies
1. Have the students write their answers to the Section 3 Review questions.
2. Have the students take the Section 3 Quiz found in the *TRB*.

Protection Against Foreign Invasion Today, an attack launched against any one state is an attack against all fifty states. While everybody today takes that concept for granted, it was not so well accepted in the 1780s. At that time, the states were not sure if they would stand together if one of them were attacked. Each state agreed, therefore, to give its war-making powers to the national government, only if the government pledged in turn to protect each of the states.

Protection Against Domestic Violence Each state is obliged to keep the peace within its own geographical boundaries. If for some reason a state cannot do so, the national government may provide help. On a number of occasions presidents have had to send in federal troops, called the National Guard, to control upheavals within various states. For example, in 1967 President Lyndon Baines Johnson sent federal troops to Detroit at the request of Michigan's governor, George Romney. Local and state police personnel were unable to stop riots and looting that were happening in the inner city during that summer. Similarly, President Johnson sent federal troops to the cities of Chicago and Baltimore to help control violent outbreaks that followed the assassination of Dr. Martin Luther King, Jr. in April of 1968.

In all three instances, the president sent the National Guard at the request of local and state officials. The president is not legally bound to wait for such a request, however. Whenever federal property is endangered or federal law is violated, the president can act. Indeed, in 1894, President Grover Cleveland sent federal troops to Illinois, in spite of the objections of Governor William Altgeld, to stop the rioting in the Chicago rail yards that year. The rioters had threatened federal property and had slowed down the flow of mail and interstate commerce.

President Dwight D. Eisenhower sent federal troops to Little Rock, Arkansas in 1957, as did President John F. Kennedy to the University of Mississippi in 1962 and to the University of Alabama in 1963. In each of these instances, these two presidents acted to stop the unlawful obstruction of school integration orders that had been issued by the federal courts.

Territorial Integrity Under the Constitution, the federal government must guarantee the territorial integrity of each state; that is, it must recognize each state's legal existence and physical boundaries. It must also guarantee the number of votes each state has in Congress. Article IV, Section 3 prevents the national government from geographically dividing a state to make a new state, or from changing boundaries between states. If it wants to do this, both the states involved and Congress have to agree on the changes.

Some argue that the admission of West Virginia to the United States in 1863 violated this guarantee. West Virginia was formed from the forty western counties that had broken away from Virginia during the Civil War. At the time the new state was formed, less than 50 percent of the Virginia legislators agreed to its formation. Congress legitimized the legislators' decision by claiming that they were the only legislators legally capable of acting for the people of Virginia.

When rioting broke out in Baltimore, Maryland in April, 1968, President Lyndon Baines Johnson (shown below) sent in federal troops to help control the disturbance. Under what conditions can the President use federal troops to help keep the peace in individual states?

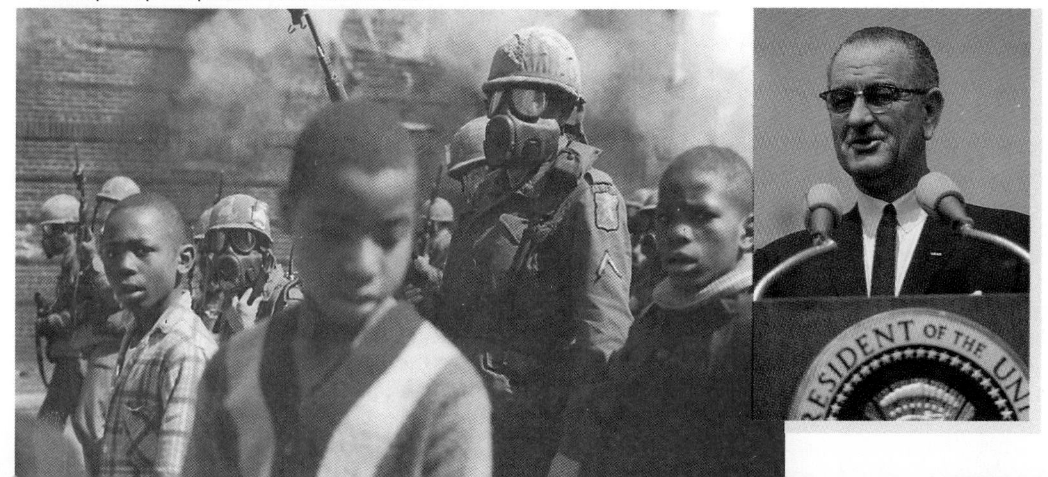

Caption Answer The president can send in troops at the request of local and state officials (as was the case in Baltimore, Maryland in 1968) or whenever federal property is endangered or federal law is violated.

TEACHING CITIZENSHIP SKILLS AND RESPONSIBILITIES

Read
Introduce this section by encouraging the students to talk about the problems of hunger: Who faces problems of hunger? What role do you think the government should take in helping the hungry? What role do you think individuals should take? Encourage the students to express and support varying points of view. Then ask a volunteer to read the Citizenship Skills and Responsibilities section aloud to the rest of the class.

Discuss
Let the students share their responses to the section: How do you feel about the ideas suggested here? Which approach presented in this section seems most effective to you? Why?

Analyze and Apply
Have the students work together to gather as much information about hunger groups as possible. Following the suggestions in this section, the students should compile a complete list of local hunger groups, as well as information from national groups. Encourage the students to publish this information—perhaps in posters, flyers, or newsletters—to be shared with the rest of the school and with the local residents. Also encourage the students not just to volunteer individually but also to organize groups of students to volunteer goods and services on a regular basis.

Review
Ask the following questions to help the students review: Where are people dying of starvation and malnutrition? What are the short-term solutions to the problem of hunger? What are the long-term solutions?

Section 3 Review (Answers)
1. The privileges and immunities clause; the full faith and credit clause (see Article IV, Sections 1 and 2).
2. The full faith and credit clause requires states to recognize one another's laws and court decisions.
3. The federal government must guarantee to each state a republican form of government. It also must protect states against foreign invasion, must protect states against domestic violence if the state is unable to do so, and must respect the territorial integrity of each state.
4. Both states benefitted from having large transportation centers that affected both areas. It would have been more costly to have two separate governing authorities in such a highly populated and concentrated area. An alternative would have been two separate regulation systems for transportation centers.

SECTION 4

Points to Stress
- The supremacy clause.
- *McCulloch* v. *Maryland* and its impact on relations between the national government and the states.
- The importance of *Gibbons* v. *Ogden* and the impact it had on our economic system.
- Issues that precipitated the Civil War.

CITIZENSHIP SKILLS AND RESPONSIBILITIES
Community Action Project—Helping the Hungry

Hunger is one of the most heartbreaking and urgent problems facing the world today. Although it is difficult to believe that people are actually dying of starvation and malnutrition every few seconds, hunger haunts us everywhere—outside our homes, in our own cities, and in faraway countries.

Hunger is being fought by people on many fronts—from short-term solutions, such as providing a hot meal to someone who doesn't know where to turn, to long-term solutions, such as supporting new legislation to alter our policies of food distribution. Helping to feed the hungry in your own community is always a good starting point. Listed below are some actions that can help you begin.

TAKING ACTION

1. Locate the local hunger groups in your area. Start by calling your church, synagogue, or the mayor's office, or look in the Yellow Pages under "Social Service Agencies." If you don't have any luck, there are many national organizations that can help you locate a group. A few of them are listed below:

   National Student Campaign Against Hunger
   29 Temple Place, Boston, MA 02111
   617-292-4823

   The Salvation Army
   799 Bloomfield Avenue, Verona, NJ 07044
   201-239-0606

   Seeds
   222 East Lake Drive, Decatur, GA 07044
   404-378-3566

2. Offer to help out in the office of a local hunger project by answering phones, writing letters, or raising funds.
3. Donate food to a food bank. If you can't locate the food bank nearest you, contact:

   Second Harvest
   116 South Michigan Avenue, Suite 4
   Chicago, IL 60603
   312-263-2303

   Consider volunteering to work in the warehouse sorting contributed food, or assisting with pickups or deliveries.
4. Volunteer two or three hours a week in a soup kitchen that cooks and serves food for homeless people.

If you are interested in starting your own group to fight hunger, order a copy of Seeds' *Hunger Action Handbook—What You Can Do and How to Do It.* It's available from Seeds at the above-listed address.

If you are interested in volunteering to work on a project to end hunger around the world, order Seeds' magazine *Volunteer Opportunities Guide.*

The process of admitting a state to the Union involves several steps. First, people residing in a geographic area desiring statehood apply to Congress for admission. If Congress agrees, it passes an **enabling act,** which directs the proposed state to form a constitution. The state then holds a constitutional convention and obtains approval of the constitution by popular vote. If Congress agrees to statehood when the proposed state constitution is submitted, it passes an **act of admission**. Once a state has entered the Union, it is automatically equal in status to all other states.

Information on when each state was admitted to the Union is included in the Resource Center.

SECTION 3 REVIEW

1. What are the Constitutional provisions that relate to horizontal federalism?
2. What does the full faith and credit clause require?
3. Under the Constitution, what responsibilities does the federal government have toward the states?
4. **For critical analysis:** Two or more states enter into interstate compacts only if all parties benefit. How do you think both New Jersey and New York benefited from the Port of New York Authority Interstate Compact? What would have been an alternative to such an agreement?

• The difference between loose and strict constructionists.

Kickoff Activity
Write these questions on the chalkboard: What is supremacy? In what kinds of situations is it important? Have the students write their responses and then share and discuss their ideas.

Working with the Preview Questions
Ask volunteers to read the study questions aloud, and encourage the students to share their responses to these questions before reading the section. Then tell the students that they should be prepared to answer these questions when they have finished reading Section 4.

Teaching Strategies

Introduction
After the students have read the section introduction, encourage discussion by posing questions such as these: Why do you think the states and the national government continue to struggle for power? Do you think this struggle is appropriate? Do you think it is helpful? Why or why not?

Discussion Starter
Pose these questions for discussion: Why do you think states opposed actions of the national government so frequently during the first decades after the Constitution was ratified? You might wish to remind students of the authority enjoyed by the states under the Articles of Confederation. What do you imagine the states learned from these conflicts? What do you imagine the national government learned? Do you think the frequency of such conflicts increased or decreased as time passed? Why?

SECTION 4

Who Shall Reign Supreme?

Preview Questions

- What is the supremacy clause?
- What decision did the Supreme Court make in *McCulloch* v. *Maryland*? Why was it important?
- What was the issue before the Supreme Court in the case of *Gibbons* v. *Ogden*?
- What issue was at the heart of the controversy that led to the Civil War?

The **supremacy clause,** Article VI, Paragraph 2, gives the federal government supremacy over all state and local governments, and implies that states cannot use their reserved or concurrent powers to counter national policies. Every time a state or local officer, such as a judge or sheriff, takes office, he or she becomes bound by an oath to support the U.S. Constitution. National governmental power always takes precedence over any conflicting state action. For example, when President Eisenhower sent the National Guard to Little Rock High School in Arkansas in 1957, he did so to make sure that the desegregation plan ordered by the federal courts was carried out.

Much of the legal history of the United States has involved conflicts between the supremacy of the national government and the desires of the states to remain independent. The most extreme example of this conflict was the Civil War in the 1860s.

Through the years, because of the Civil War and several key Supreme Court decisions, the national government has increased its power. The first important Supreme Court decision involved a state trying to impose its will on the national government.

McCulloch v. *Maryland*

For several decades after the Constitution was ratified, the states opposed many actions of the national government. When Congress chartered two banks—the First and Second Banks of the United States (1791 and 1816)—and provided part of the money necessary to get them started, a number of states complained. They claimed that the existence of these nationally chartered banks presented unfair competition against state banks. Maryland was one such state to hold this view. The government of Maryland imposed a tax on the Baltimore branch of the Second Bank of the United States. The branch's chief cashier, James McCulloch, decided not to pay the Maryland tax. The state of Maryland took the conflict to its state court, which ruled that McCulloch had to pay the tax. The federal government appealed the case to the U.S. Supreme Court, then headed by Chief Justice John Marshall.

In 1957, when governor Orval Faubus tried to block integration of Central High School in Little Rock, Arkansas, President Dwight D. Eisenhower pressed the Arkansas National Guard into federal service and sent in 1,000 National Guard paratroopers to ensure that the desegregation plan ordered by the United States Federal Court was carried out. The photo here shows the school's first African-American students walking up the steps to the school's entrance flanked by federal troops armed with rifles and bayonets. What Constitutional provision granted Eisenhower the power to make this move?

Caption Answer Article VI, Paragraph 2, otherwise known as the Supremacy Clause, gives the federal government supremacy over state and local governments. Therefore, states cannot use their powers to oppose national policies. It is the president's responsibility to make sure that the laws are "faithfully executed." He may call state militias into the service of the United States. See Article II, Sections 2 and 3.

TEACHING GOVERNMENT IN ACTION

Read
Introduce this Case Study by telling the students that the federal government owns 80 percent of Nevada. It also owns large portions of the land in Alaska, Utah, Idaho, Oregon, Wyoming, and California. Ask the students to speculate about the kinds of problems that might be raised by this land ownership. Then have volunteers read the Case Study aloud to the rest of the class.

Discuss
Encourage the students to discuss the Case Study: What does the map show? What do you consider the most effective arguments made by proponents of the Sagebrush Rebellion? Why do you find those arguments persuasive? What do you consider the most effective arguments of the opponents? Why do you find those arguments persuasive? Which side do you think is right? Why?

Analyze and Apply
Have the students work in groups to find out about federal land ownership in their state: How much land does the federal government own? What use is being made of that land? What are the attitudes of local and state leaders toward that land ownership? Are there proponents of the Sagebrush Revolution in their state? Have the group members work together to write a summary of their findings.

Review
Ask the students these review questions: What is the Sagebrush Rebellion? What does it hope to achieve? Who argues against the Sagebrush Rebellion? What arguments do those opponents make?

Think About It (Answers)
1. Answers will vary, e.g., the states do not have the right to claim ownership over lands currently owned by the United States because the federal government takes precedence over state governmental power. States must send their representatives to Congress in order to change laws.
2. Answers will vary, e.g., the state governments should have control over the land management within their own borders. The federal government should step in only when the lands are important on the national level, such as a national park.

GOVERNMENT IN ACTION

CASE STUDY

The Sagebrush Rebellion

A federal system, no matter how well thought out, is always going to run into problems. States like to have control over as much as possible. But so do the bureaucrats running the national government. Nowhere has this conflict been more obvious than with the ownership of land in the United States. Look at the map on the next page.

In the Western states, the federal government owns a remarkably high proportion of all land. In Nevada this figure is 80 percent.

Advocates of **decentralization**—a shift of power from federal to state or local governments—argue that states must be allowed to make their own decisions about how their land should be used. The controversy over who should own land in much of the West has been called the Sagebrush Rebellion. It began a number of years ago when the Nevada legislature passed a law declaring that 49 million acres of federal land properly belonged to that state. This idea caught the attention of other Western states, because the federal government owns most of Alaska and Nevada, the bulk of Utah, Idaho, and Oregon, and nearly half of Wyoming and California. A movement began to reclaim lands from federal ownership. The movement united an otherwise maverick group of state activists and rugged individualists with a sense of common cause.

Certain groups in the Western states claimed that the federal government was acting as a powerful absentee landlord, imposing a lot of regulations but never present to deal with their problems. They saw Washington, D.C., as ''Big Brother'' (referred to in George Orwell's book *1984*) and the Eastern states as unsympathetic to their region's unique vital concerns. As Nevada Attorney General Rich Bryan asserted, ''We're tired of being pistol-whipped by the bureaucrats and dry-gulched by federal regulations.'' Nevada Senator Norm Glaser added: ''We're not just a bunch of wild-eyed cowboys out to lynch some federal officials. We're serious people asking for a serious look at the unfair treatment the West is receiving.''

Those individuals who prefer the current situation claim that despite the complaints, from meat import quotas to vital water reclamation projects, Westerners often come out quite well under a big federal government. They argue that the West is living in a fantasy if it thinks it can survive without the federal government. ''If you pulled the federal presence out of Colorado, the state would collapse,'' said then Senator Gary Hart from Colorado. Eastern and Western environmentalists argue that if the federal government hadn't stepped in, the West would have sold out and exploited its rare environmental resources. The Idaho Environmental Council said that federal management for the most part ''has been far superior to that of the various land boards of the Western states managing state-owned public lands.''

Although the Sagebrush Rebellion seemed to subside in the 1980s during President Reagan's administration, it was rekindled in 1990 under President Bush's administration. Fearful of losing control over their own land, and of losing access to natural resources on the West's public lands, a group of ranchers, miners, loggers, and others who rely on the millions of acres of those public lands met in Las Vegas in 1990 to develop a strategy. The Sagebrush Rebellion may be in the headlines again soon.

THINK ABOUT IT

1. To what extent do you think the states, particularly in the West, have the right to claim ownership over lands currently owned by the federal government?
2. What role should the federal government play in land management in this country?

3. Answers will vary, e.g., the federal government should not turn lands over to private individuals because much of this land needs to be environmentally protected by the federal government.

4. Answers will vary, e.g., the Sagebrush Rebellion illustrates the problem that state governments will sometimes resent and resist federal intervention. While each state naturally wants the benefits provided by the federal government, they want to be able to act in their own best interests. When two levels of government operate over the same people and the same territory, the arrangement becomes complex and tensions, conflicts, and competition are bound to arise.

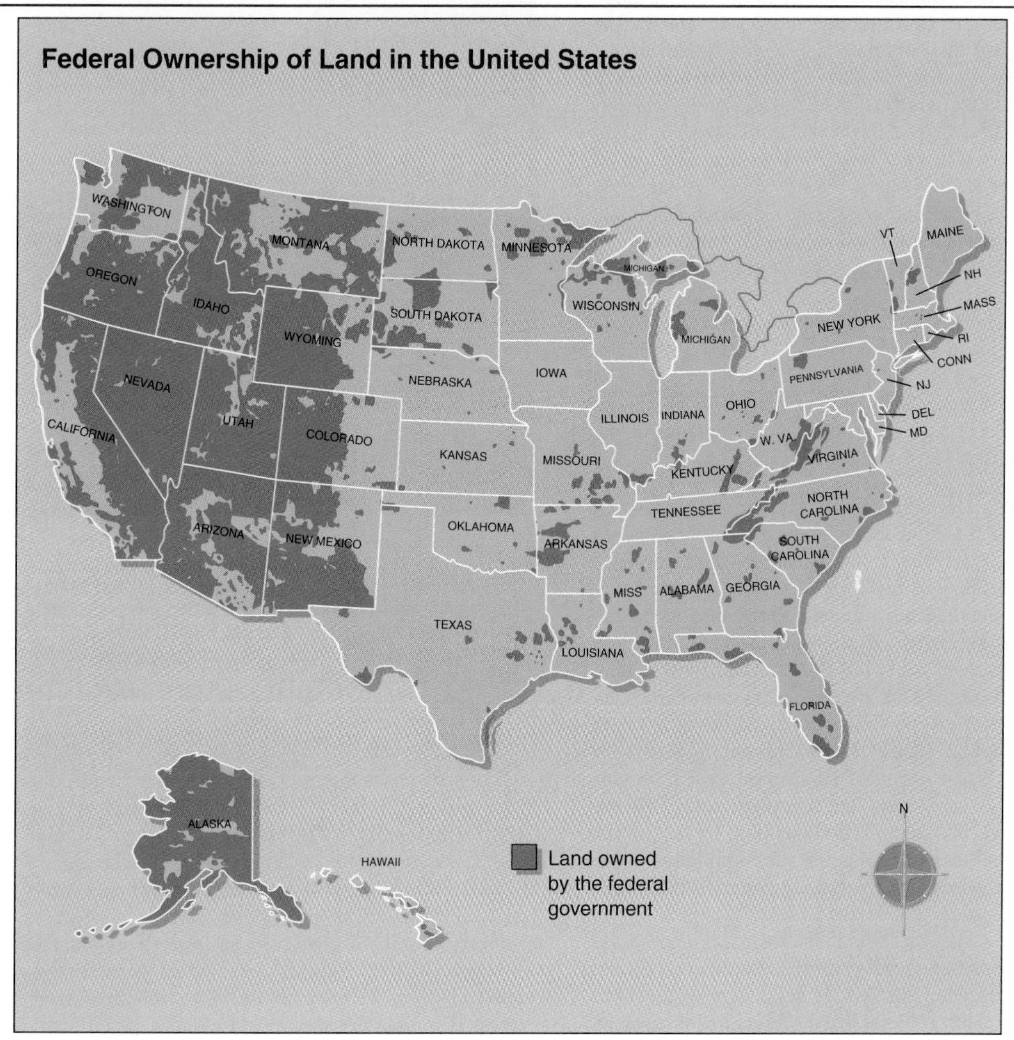

This figure content is also featured on *West's American Government Videodisc* (see the index found in the *TRB*) and is available in the transparency package.

What role should the state governments play?

3. Should the federal government turn federal lands over to private individuals, such as cattle raisers and oil drillers? Explain.
4. What does the Sagebrush Rebellion tell us about the problems that are a part of our system of federalism today?

Discussion Starter
Encourage the students to discuss both sides of this legal issue: Did Congress have the authority to charter and contribute capital to the Second Bank of the United States? Ask the students to consider the most persuasive arguments presented on both sides of this question.

Comprehension
Ask several of the students to use their own words in defining *strict constructionist* and *loose constructionist.*

Vocabulary
Ask the students to consider and discuss Marshall's statement that the necessary and proper clause included "all means which are appropriate" to carry out "the legitimate ends" of the Constitution. Which words in Marshall's statement might be considered open to interpretation? ("which are appropriate") What questions might be raised by this decision?

Discussion Starter
Encourage the students to discuss the importance of Marshall's decision in *McCulloch* v. *Maryland.* How does that decision affect our lives today?

Vocabulary
Ask the students to define *commerce* in their own words and then to check the definitions given in a dictionary.

Cooperative Learning
Have students work in small groups to learn more about monopolies: What examples of monopolies can they find? Under what circumstances are monopolies legal today? What major monopolies have been broken up? By whom? Why?

Caption Answer This decision clearly favored the loose constructionists.

The Legal Issue The issue before the Supreme Court was not simply a question of whether the Second Bank had to pay Maryland's tax. It also had to do with whether Congress had the authority to charter and contribute capital to the Second Bank of the United States. The question was whether the Constitution's necessary and proper clause granted this authority. Those who sided with the state of Maryland were called **strict constructionists.** They wanted the words of the Constitution to be interpreted literally. They thought the words *necessary and proper* referred to only those powers that were *indispensable* for the designated powers of the national government. The Constitution gave the national government the power to coin money and regulate its value. Nothing was specifically stated in the Constitution about the creation of a national bank.

Those who sided with the national government were considered **loose constructionists.** They did not think the words *necessary and proper* should be examined in their strictest sense. They argued that literal interpretation of the necessary and proper clause would mean that it would have no effect at all.

The Court's Decision Some say that John Marshall had made up his mind about the outcome of *McCulloch* v. *Maryland* (1819) even before he heard the arguments. Marshall decided in favor of McCulloch, who represented the national government. Marshall pointed out that there is no expressed provision in the Constitution to form a national bank, but that if establishing such a bank helped the national government to exercise its designated (expressed) powers, then the authority to do so could be implied. Marshall also said that the necessary and proper clause included "all means which are appropriate" to carry out "the legitimate ends" of the Constitution. He could not find anything in the Constitution "which excludes incidental or implied powers; and which requires that everything granted shall be expressly and minutely described."

From that day on, Marshall's decision became the basis for strengthening our national government's power. Marshall's decision enabled the national government to grow and to meet problems that the founding fathers were unable to foresee. Indeed, today practically every implied power of the national government has been explained by the use of the necessary and proper clause.

Another way that the national government's power has been expanded is through the Court's interpretation of the *commerce clause.* Chief Justice John Marshall was asked to examine an important conflict involving this clause five years after *McCulloch* v. *Maryland.*

▲ Supreme Court Chief Justice John Marshall in his opinion on *McCulloch* v. *Maryland* (1819) stated that the necessary and proper clause of the United States Constitution included "all means which are appropriate to carry out the legitimate ends of the Constitution." Did this decision favor the strict constructionists or the loose constructionists?

Gibbons v. *Ogden*

The states have the reserved power to regulate commerce within their borders. But Article I, Section 8 gives Congress the power to "regulate commerce with foreign nations, and among the several States. . . ." The framers of the Constitution did not define the word *commerce.* Strict constructionists had a very narrow view of its meaning, loose constructionists an expanded view. Did commerce include travel by steamboat between two states? That was the issue before the court in the famous case of *Gibbons* v. *Ogden.*

Controlling Steamboat Travel In 1803 Robert Fulton, the inventor of the steamboat, and the American minister to France, Robert Livingston, obtained from the New York State Legislature the exclusive right, called a **monopoly,** to use steamboats on the waters of New York State. Using this monopoly right, they licensed Aaron Ogden to operate steamboats between New York

Discussion Starter
Encourage the students to share and discuss their personal responses to these regulations by the federal government: Do you think such regulations are fair? Whom do they help? Whom—if anyone—do they hurt? Do you think our federal government should impose and enforce more regulations, or fewer regulations? Why?

Discussion Starter
Before the students begin reading The Battleground of the Civil War, ask them to discuss what they already know and think about the Civil War: What were the major causes of the war? What were the most important results? Then encourage the students to re-evaluate their thinking as they read this section.

Discussion Starter
Encourage the students to discuss the Tariff Acts: What purpose were these taxes intended to serve? Why do you think the Southern states object to these tariffs while the Northern states did not? Do you believe that South Carolina had any valid justification for its attempt to nullify the tariffs? If so, what was its justification? If no, why not?

In the famous case of *Gibbons* v. *Ogden* (1824) a steamboat monopoly granted by the State of New York was challenged by a competing ferry service operating in the waterways between New York and New Jersey (which are shown as they look today). How did the decision in this case strengthen the power of Congress to regulate interstate commerce?

Caption Answer The decision in *Gibbons* v. *Ogden* expanded the definition of commerce and increased Congress' power to regulate interstate commerce when Marshall's decision said, in essence, the only limitations on Congress' power to regulate interstate commerce were those limitations specifically found in the Constitution.

and New Jersey. Thomas Gibbons also operated steamboats between the two states, but did so without permission from the state of New York. As a result, Ogden sued Gibbons in the New York state courts. Ogden won, and Gibbons issued an appeal to the U.S. Supreme Court.

The Court Decides The Supreme Court and its Chief Justice Marshall were loose constructionists. They expanded the definition of *commerce* to include all business dealings, such as steamboat travel. The court ruled against the monopoly that Ogden had obtained through license from Fulton and Livingston. Gibbons had to be allowed to compete. Marshall not only used this opportunity to expand the definition of commerce, but also to increase the national government's power to regulate it. He said,

> "What is this power? It is the power . . . to prescribe [set down] the rule by which commerce is to be governed. This power, like all others vested in Congress, is complete in itself."

In other words, Marshall said that the national government's power to regulate commerce had only those limitations specifically found in the Constitution and no others.

Since that decision in 1824, the national government has invoked the commerce clause to increase its authority over virtually all areas of economic activity. Few economic activities (even those that take place entirely *within* a state) are outside the regulatory power of the national government. When you buy meat in the supermarket, it is graded according to federal government regulations, which are determined by the U.S. Department of Agriculture. When you ride in a car, many of the safety features in that car were required to be there by an agency of the federal government. When a door-to-door salesperson sells you something, many of the rules governing that sale come from the Federal Trade Commission (FTC). Even when a death occurs in your family, the information you are given about the cost of preparing and burying the body is now regulated by the federal government.

The Battleground of the Civil War

It is easy to think of the Civil War only as a fight to free the slaves. The war, however, can also be viewed as a power struggle between the states and the national government. At the heart of the controversy that led to the Civil War was the issue of national versus state supremacy. That debate was brought to a bloody climax between 1860 and 1865.

In 1824, 1828, and 1832 the national government passed tariff acts, which imposed higher taxes on goods imported into the United States. The Southern states believed that such taxes were against their best interest. One Southern state, South Carolina, attempted to *nullify* the tariffs, or to make them void. It claimed that in cases of conflict between state and national governments, the state should have the ultimate authority to determine the welfare of its citizens. Additionally, some Southerners believed that democratic decisions could only be made when all the segments of society that were affected by those decisions were in agreement. In other words, a **concurrent majority** had to agree. Without that, a decision should not be binding on those whose interest it violates.

Developing Skills for the Information Age

The division of powers between our national and state governments and the supremacy of the national government vis-a-vis the states is manifest in the media. Have students read a major metropolitan newspaper and view major network news, CNN, and/or national PBS news coverage. Students should keep track of how many stories and how much space or time are devoted to state compared to national issues.

The type of story as it relates to the various types of powers should also be recorded. A summary of the above material should be expressed in written form that provides a description and analysis of the results.

Comprehension
Ask these questions to check the students' comprehension: In what sense did the Civil War result from the South's desire for increased states' rights? In what sense did the Civil War reduce states' rights?

Caption Answer The end of the Civil War brought an increase in the political power of the national government.

As an extension exercise, you might allow volunteers to research and report on Matthew Brady, the photographer who took this photograph. Volunteers should relate Brady's efforts with those of television war correspondents today in the form of an oral report to the class.

Reteaching Strategies
1. Work with small groups of students to go over the central issues of *McCulloch* v. *Maryland* and *Gibbons* v. *Ogden.* Then have the group members work together to write a one-sentence summary of the importance of each case.
2. Have the students work with partners to review and discuss the Civil War as a fight over states' rights versus the power of the national government. Then let the partners write short summaries of their discussions.

Evaluation Strategies
1. Have the students write their responses to the Preview Questions from the beginning of the section.
2. Have the students write their answers to the Section 4 Review questions.
3. Have the students take the Section 4 Quiz found in the *TRB.*

Section 4 Review (Answers)
1. Under the supremacy clause of Article VI, federal laws normally take precedence.
2. The case established that the federal government has sovereign power and that the Constitution gives Congress the power to do whatever was "necessary and proper" to carry out any of its specific powers. The decision became an important basis for strengthening the power of the national government because it enabled Congress to act beyond the literal language of the Constitution.
3. The decision greatly broadened the definition of interstate commerce and paved the way for later federal control of such areas of interstate commerce as telegraph, telephone, radio, and television communication.
4. The issue of national versus state supremacy was at the heart of the controversy that led to the Civil War. Many Southerners believed that democratic decisions should only be made when all the segments of society that were affected by those decisions were in agreement. Supporters of this concurrent majority concept used it to justify the secession of the Southern states from the union.
5. Answers will vary. The evidence may be to the contrary in that the federal government is increasing its power over the states. For example, it forced a uniform speed limit on the states by threatening to withhold interstate highway funds.

▲ The American Civil War was fought over many issues including the conflict between national supremacy and states' rights. Did the end of the Civil War bring increased states' rights or increased power for the national government?

Supporters of this concurrent majority concept used it to justify the **secession**—withdrawal—of the Southern states from the union. When the South was defeated in the war, however, the idea that a state can successfully claim its right to secede was defeated with it. We live in an indestructible union of separate states. While the Civil War occurred because of the South's desire for increased states' rights, the result was just the opposite—an increase in the political power of the national government.

Section 4 Review

1. If a state law conflicts with a national law, which side must yield?
2. How did the Supreme Court's decision in *McCulloch* v. *Maryland* expand the power of the federal government?
3. How was the Supreme Court's decision in *Gibbons* v. *Ogden* significant?
4. How was the controversy that led to the Civil War related to the concept of federalism?
5. **For critical analysis:** The milestone events discussed in this section—*McCulloch* v. *Maryland, Gibbons* v. *Ogden,* and the Civil War—form part of the trend toward complete supremacy of the national government. What evidence, if any, do you see today that the trend is changing?

Section 5

The Changing Face of American Federalism

Preview Questions

- What is the concept of dual federalism?
- Why has the era since 1937 been labeled cooperative federalism?
- What is the concept of new federalism?

The balance of political power between the states and the national government has changed through the years. The milestones in the trend toward national government supremacy, described in the previous section, do not tell the full story. There are hundreds, if not thousands, of other court cases and other political actions that both the states and the national government have undertaken. Historically, we can see that the changing model of federalism in our country has passed through three eras: dual federalism, cooperative federalism, and new federalism.

The Era of Dual Federalism

When John Marshall died in 1835, the trend toward national supremacy fostered by him and the loose constructionists on the Court came to an end. During Andrew Jackson's presidency, from 1829 to 1837, he nudged the nation again toward states' rights. At this time in our history political participation increased, particularly among farmers and working men and women. Those individuals were involved in their own local economy. They appealed directly to their state governments for economic benefits. The states as a result took on an increasing sphere of authority over business activities.

The concept of **dual federalism** emphasizes the distinction between national and state spheres of authority, particularly in the area of economic regulation. The Constitution reserves to the states the ability to regulate all **intrastate commerce**—business done wholly within the state. Examples of intrastate commerce include selling fruit from one part of the state to the other, or rendering services within a local region. Under dual federalism, the Supreme Court simply becomes the referee between the national and state governments, which maintain diverse but sovereign powers.

From 1835 to 1864, John Marshall's replacement, Chief Justice Roger B. Taney, allowed the states to increase their power. As he stated in *Abelman* v. *Booth* (1859), he wanted to make sure that the Supreme Court

SECTION 5

Points to Stress
- The concept of dual federalism.
- The era since 1937 that has been called cooperative federalism.
- New federalism.

Kickoff Activity
As preparation for learning about different eras of federalism, have the students write their answers to these questions: What is federalism? How is federalism related to democracy? After the students have finished writing, allow volunteers to share their responses.

Working with the Preview Questions
Have the students read the study questions aloud and discuss how they can organize their notes on Section 5. Remind the students to use these questions as they read and take notes on the section.

Teaching Strategies

Introduction
Have the students read the section introduction on their own. Then encourage discussion by asking questions such as these: Why do you think the balance of political power between the states and the national government has continued to change? Why do you think it is important to understand the changes and their implications?

Enrichment
Have several students work together to research the life and accomplishments of Andrew Jackson: What was the basis of his interest in states' rights? How did he influence the concept of the presidency? What were his major political accomplishments? Then ask these students to prepare and present a report of their findings.

helped to "guard the states from any encroachment upon their reserved rights by the general [national] government."

Except for the period of the Civil War, the doctrine of dual federalism prevailed. For example, in *Hammer* v. *Dagenhart* (1918) the U.S. Supreme Court ruled that a 1916 federal law banning child labor was unconstitutional. It reasoned that child labor was a local problem and the power to deal with it was reserved to the states.

The era of dual federalism came to an end around 1937, when the United States was in the depths of the greatest depression it had ever experienced.

The Era of Cooperative Federalism

In the view of **cooperative federalism,** the national and state governments are seen as complementary parts of a single governmental mechanism, designed to promote the well-being of all of the nation's inhabitants. All of the powers of that mechanism are to be used to solve the problems facing the entire United States. Certainly the Great Depression, which began in 1929, can be described as a period of tremendous national problems. By the depths of the Great Depression in 1933, over five thousand banks had failed. One-fourth of the people willing to work could not find jobs. During the first three years of the Great Depression, the federal government did very little to solve the nation's economic misery.

▲ When Andrew Jackson was elected to the presidency in 1828, he began to push the nation towards states' rights. This led to the practice of "dual federalism." The system of dual federalism emphasized the distinction between national powers and states' rights. What was the role of the Supreme Court under this system?

A new administration headed by Franklin D. Roosevelt took office in 1933. The first hundred days of FDR's administration ushered in the **New Deal,** a program designed to help the U.S. out of the Depression. It included many government spending and public assistance programs, in addition to thousands of regulations of economic activity. For four years the U.S. Supreme Court, abiding by the doctrine of dual federalism, rejected virtually all of Roosevelt's federal regulation of business as unconstitutional. Then in 1937 Roosevelt threatened to "pack" the Supreme Court by adding new justices. The Supreme Court began to rule in his favor. National laws regulating agricultural prices, general wages, and the relationship between unions and business were passed again and withstood constitutional challenges.

The era since 1937 has been described as an era of cooperative federalism because the state and federal governments cooperated in solving complex mutual problems. It also marked the real beginning of the era of national supremacy, which continues into the present. It is true that today Congress can regulate almost any kind of economic activity no matter where that activity is located. For example, consider a manufacturing business that is located in one state, hires workers only from that state, and sells the products only within that state. The national government, nonetheless, can regulate the hours of work and wages paid to the workers, the safety conditions under which they work, the labeling on the product manufactured, the standards to which the product adheres, and, during certain periods in our history, even the price at which the product can be sold.

During the 1970s and 1980s, several government administrations attempted to revitalize the doctrine of dual federalism, which they renamed new federalism.

The New Federalism

One of the policies of President Richard M. Nixon's administration (1968–1974) was a reduction in the restrictions attached to federal grants to local and state governments. He called this policy the **new federalism.** He wanted local officials themselves to decide how tax revenues should be spent. The centerpiece of this new federalism was a **revenue-sharing program,** which gave local and state officials more freedom in making their spending decisions. The Nixon Administration

Vocabulary
Ask the students to define the word *dual.* How does this definition help make clear the meaning of *dual federalism?*

Vocabulary
Help the students review the meanings of the prefixes *intra-* and *inter-*. Then ask them to explain the difference between intrastate commerce and interstate commerce.

Discussion Starter
Encourage the students to discuss *Hammer* v. *Dagenhart.* Does this ruling make sense to you? Why or why not? What decision do you think would be made in a similar case now? Why? What has changed that might affect the decision of the Supreme Court?

Discussion Starter
Ask the students to consider why an economic depression would lead to an end of dual federalism. Encourage the students to share and discuss their ideas.

Caption Answer During the years of dual federalism, the Supreme Court acted as a referee between the national government and state governments and generally tended to favor a position of states' rights.

Comprehension
Ask the students these comprehension questions: What was the intent of the Nixon administration in establishing a revenue-sharing program? Why did the Reagan administration oppose the program?

Reteaching Strategies
1. Have the students work in groups to compare and discuss their section notes. Encourage them to refer to the text as they revise and clarify their notes.
2. Work with small groups of students to review the distinctions between dual federalism, cooperative federalism, and new federalism. Then let the group members work together to write a short explanation of the distinctions.

Caption Answer The era since 1937 has been labeled "the Era of Cooperative Federalism" since the federal government and states cooperate in solving difficult and complex mutual problems.

Evaluation Strategies
1. Have the students write their answers to the Section 5 Review questions.
2. Have the students take the Section 5 Quiz found in the *TRB*.

Section 5 Review (Answers)
1. Historically, the nation has passed through three eras: dual federalism, in which the national and state governments maintain diverse but sovereign powers; cooperative federalism, in which state and national governments are seen as complimentary parts of a single governmental mechanism; and new federalism, which involved a reduction in restrictions attached to federal grants to local and state governments.
2. Dual federalism emphasizes the distinction between national and state spheres of authority, particularly in the area of economic regulation. States regulate intrastate commerce and the federal government stays within its realm of interstate commerce.
3. National and state governments are seen as complementary parts of a single governmental mechanism. All parts of that mechanism are designed to promote the well-being of all the nation's inhabitants. In addition to the separate spheres of power, there are also broad areas of shared powers.
4. Both intended to give the states an increased role in deciding how government revenues should be spent. Reagan, however, unlike Nixon, did not want the state and local governments to rely as heavily on the federal government's resources.
5. Governors and mayors are in favor of federal revenue sharing because they get to spend the money without having to ask their own citizens for higher taxes directly. Federal politicians, including members of Congress, might be against federal revenue sharing because they do not directly get to decide how the money is spent, but must nonetheless be responsible for raising the taxes to pay for it.

▲ By the time that Franklin Delano Roosevelt took office as president in 1933, over 5,000 banks had failed. In an effort to solve this and the other problems of the Depression, President Roosevelt pushed through Congress many new laws regulating agricultural prices, general wages, the banking industry, and the relationship between unions and businesses. FDR's New Deal programs brought about a new era of federalism. What term is used to describe this era of federalism?

asked Congress in 1972 to return a certain percentage of federal tax revenues each year to the state and local governments. Congress passed a general revenue-sharing law in which one-third of the designated funds went to the states and two-thirds were sent directly to local governments. Needless to say, revenue-sharing was quite popular and strongly supported by many governors, mayors, and other state and local officials. It was opposed by the Reagan administration (1980–1988), however, and was abolished due to the growing financial needs of the deficit-ridden federal government.

President Reagan did continue to carry out certain aspects of the new federalism. In 1981, in his first State of the Union Address, President Reagan said that he intended to restore those powers reserved to the states and to the people. His new federalism, similar to Nixon's, was a plan to give the states an increased role in deciding how government revenues should be spent. But Reagan, unlike Nixon, did not want the state and local governments to rely as heavily on the federal government's resources. Reagan wanted the state and local governments to spend as much as they raised themselves, but with less federal regulation on how they spent their own revenues. Reagan's attempt to dismantle forty domestic programs at the federal level, including social services, transportation, and community development, was strongly opposed by state governors. They saw Reagan's plan as a ploy to cut federal government expenditures on needed programs.

President George Bush continued where Reagan left off. The growing fiscal crisis at the federal level has forced the national government to continue to cut back on financial aid to the states and cities.

SECTION 5 REVIEW

1. How has the balance of political power between the state and the federal governments shifted throughout the years?
2. What is the federal government's role under a dual federalism system?
3. Briefly describe the doctrine of cooperative federalism.
4. How did President Reagan's new federalism differ from President Nixon's?
5. **For critical analysis:** Who might be in favor of federal government revenue sharing and why? Who would be against it and why?

TEACHING CHALLENGE TO THE AMERICAN DREAM

Read
To introduce this section, encourage the students to share and discuss their ideas: What is the Sunbelt? What is the Snowbelt? Do we live in either of these areas? Do you know people who do? What have you read or heard about these areas of the country? After a brief discussion, ask volunteers to read the section aloud to the rest of the class.

Discuss
Help the students discuss what they have read: What kinds of problems are being caused by shifts of population from the Snowbelt to the Sunbelt? What do you consider the best solutions to these problems? Would your thinking be different if you lived in the Sunbelt? In the Snowbelt? Why or why not?

Analyze and Apply
Have the students work in small groups to research the effects of reapportionment from the 1990 census. Ask the members of each group to select two states, one from the Snowbelt and the other from the Sunbelt: Were seats lost or gained by each of those states? If so, how many? Give the members of each group a chance to share their findings with the rest of the class.

Review
Use the following questions for review: What is the Snowbelt? How is the population there changing? What is the Sunbelt? How is the population there changing? Why do regional conflicts exist between these two areas?

This figure content is also featured on *West's American Government Videodisc* (see the index found in the *TRB).*

You Decide (Answers)
1. Answers will vary, e.g., the number of representatives in Congress is affected. Those states that lose representation will feel their interests are not being supported as well. States with increasing populations will receive more federal aid. This causes resentment. Also, more populated states with more representatives may obtain more federal government benefits, thereby creating resentment with less populated states.
2. The population is expected to continue to shift from the Snowbelt to the Sunbelt states.
3. A student would have to add up all federal benefits for the family, including veterans benefits if applicable, social security payments if applicable, subsidized federal government student loans, federal government scholarships, subsidized medical payments through Medicare, etc., and then compare all of these benefits with what the family pays in taxes.

Challenge to the American Dream

Snowbelt versus Sunbelt

In the past few decades, the population in the United States has shifted away from the Northeast, Midwest, and Northwest states, often referred to as the Snowbelt, to the South and the Southwest, often loosely called the Sunbelt. From 1950 to 1990 population in the Snowbelt increased 36.1 percent, whereas population in the Sunbelt increased 86.2 percent.

The shifting population has generally resulted in a greater amount of federal government benefits going to the Sunbelt than to the Snowbelt. Regional conflict has thereby been intensified. The Snowbelt states have tried to counter this changing power structure, and we can expect to see this battle continue for quite some time.

We continue to see defense and space program industries, funded by national revenues, growing in the Sunbelt states. Many federal anti-poverty programs have been concentrated in such Sunbelt cities as Houston, Atlanta, and Los Angeles. In addition, recent studies have shown that individuals and businesses in the eighteen Snowbelt states pay more in federal taxes than they receive in federal grants and government spending. Sunbelt states, by contrast, receive more from the federal government than they pay in taxes.

The 1982 change in the number of each state's members in the House of Representatives decreased the representation of the Snowbelt states by seventeen seats, giving the South and the West a congressional majority. As a result, the Snowbelt's coalition efforts to secure more federal funds will have to continue.

The power struggle should intensify even further after the effects of another reapportionment from the 1990 census. Nineteen seats have shifted from the East and Midwest to the South and West. Another nineteen will probably shift after the 2000 census. California, Texas, and Florida have been, and will continue to be, the biggest gainers. New York and Pennsylvania will be the biggest losers.

Not all is lost for the Snowbelt states. In recent years many Northeastern states have seen growth in high-technology industries. In contrast, many Sunbelt states suffered economic declines during downturns in the oil industry.

The challenge to the American dream is for Congress to distribute federal projects fairly throughout all of the country in spite of a shifting population.

Population Changes in Selected States, 1950–1990

States with largest population increases:*
1. Nevada (+653.45%)
2. Arizona (+390.7%)
3. Florida (+369.2%)
4. California (+181.9%)
5. Utah (+150.8%)

States with smallest population increases:
1. West Virginia (–10.2%)
2. North Dakota (+3.5%)
3. Iowa (+6.3%)
4. South Dakota (+7.2%)
5. Pennsylvania (+13.6%)

*Study does not consider Alaska or Hawaii.

You Decide

1. Why does a population movement from the colder Northern states to the warmer Southern and Western states necessarily result in a regional conflict within the national government?
2. Why will this regional conflict increase after the 2000 census?
3. How would you go about calculating whether your family receives more or less from the federal government than it pays in taxes?

Chapter Evaluation

To evaluate student mastery of chapter material, you might:

1. Use Chapter Test A from the *TRB.*

2. Use Chapter Test B from the *TRB.*

3. Construct your own test using items from the *West American Government Test Bank* found in the *TRB.*

4. Use the accompanying computerized test software to construct and print a customized chapter test.

Review Questions (Answers)

1. A unitary system is a centralized system in which state and/or local governments exercise only those powers given to them by the central government. A confederal system is a league of independent states. A federal system is a system in which authority is divided between a central government and several regional governments by an authority superior to both.

2. Authority is divided between the national and state governments. Both have the power to pass laws that directly affect the people.

3. The Articles of Confederation did not allow for a strong enough central government. The framers were, however, fearful of a too powerful central government. They compromised with a federal system.

4. Most are listed in Article I, Section 8. The implied powers are derived from Article I, Section 8, Clause 18, the necessary and proper clause.

5. This clause, as defined by the Supreme Court, allows the federal government to "all means which are appropriate" to carry out "the legitimate ends" of the Constitution.

6. By expressly denying powers and by not delegating powers.

7. In certain areas the Constitution gives both levels of government equal rights to pass legislation and to regulate specific activities. Concurrent powers are held separately but equally by both levels.

8. It prevents states from discriminating against citizens from other states.

9. It requires states to recognize one another's laws and court decisions.

10. Many bordering states have common problems and concerns and need interstate compacts in order to address them.

11. The federal government must guarantee a republican form of government, must protect each state against foreign invasion, must protect each state from domestic violence if the state is unable to do so, and must guarantee the territorial integrity of each state.

12. The supremacy clause establishes that national governmental power takes precedence over any conflicting state action.

13. The court ruled in favor of McCulloch who represented the national government. It ruled that the necessary and proper clause included "all means which are appropriate" to carry out "the legitimate ends" of the Constitution.

14. The balance of political power shifted from dual federalism to cooperative federalism during the depression where state and federal

CHAPTER 4 REVIEW

Key Terms

act of admission 88
alien 85
child custody 83
common-law marriage 82
concurrent majority 93
concurrent powers 83
confederal system 76
cooperative federalism 95
decentralization 90
Dennison rule 86
division of powers 78
dual federalism 94
elastic clause 80
enabling act 88
exports 80
expressed or enumerated powers 78
extradition 86
federal system 77
fugitive 86
full faith and credit clause 86
horizontal federalism 85
implied powers 80
inherent powers 80
interstate compacts 86
intrastate commerce 94
legal tender 80
loose constructionists 92
monopoly 92
necessary and proper clause 80
New Deal 95
new federalism 95
privileges and immunities clause 85
republican form of government 86
reserved powers 81
resulting powers 80
revenue-sharing program 95
secession 94
strict constructionists 92
supremacy clause 89
unitary system 76

Summary

1. The Constitution created a federal system—one based on the division of powers between the federal government and the states. Other forms of governmental systems are a unitary system, in which state and/or local governments exercise only those powers given to them by the central government, and a confederal system, which is a league of independent states.

2. Under the U.S. Constitution, the federal government has three types of powers: expressed or enumerated powers, implied powers, and inherent powers. Some powers are expressly denied to the federal government and some powers are reserved to the states. Local governments are created by their states and have no legal existence apart from them. Concurrent powers are those simultaneously held by both the federal and state governments.

3. Horizontal federalism defines relations among the states. Under this system, states may not discriminate against citizens of other states, and are obligated to give full faith and credit to the laws and activities of other states. They must also agree to extradite persons accused of crimes elsewhere. Many states have settled differences among themselves by entering into interstate compacts. The Constitution obligates the federal government to provide the state with a republican form of government, to protect each state against foreign invasion and domestic violence, and to respect each state's territorial integrity.

4. The supremacy clause of the Constitution makes the federal government the supreme governing body of the land. The Supreme Court's decision in *McCulloch* v. *Maryland* (1819) became the basis for strengthening the federal government's power. Since the Supreme Court decision in *Gibbons* v. *Ogden* (1824), the federal government has used the commerce clause to increase its authority over virtually all areas of economic activity.

5. The practice of federalism has changed throughout the years. Historically, we can view the changing model of federalism in the United States as having three eras: dual federalism, cooperative federalism, and new federalism.

Review Questions

1. Explain the differences between the three different types of governmental systems.
2. Explain how federalism creates a two-way system of government.
3. Why did the framers of our Constitution choose a federal framework?
4. What is the source of the national government's expressed powers? What is the source of its implied powers?
5. How has the necessary and proper clause enabled the national government to expand its powers?
6. On what basis does the Constitution deny certain powers to the national government?

governments cooperated in solving complex mutual problems.

Questions for Thought and Discussion (Answers)

1. Answers will vary, e.g., with no division of powers, governmental power would probably rest with a stronger central government.

2. Answers will vary, e.g., states should be given more power in their own affairs. For example, states should be able to set their own speed limits without losing federal highway funds.

3. Answers will vary, e.g., the nation must act as one in such matters as waging war and relating to foreign nations. Otherwise, we would not be taken seriously.

4. Answers will vary, e.g., the growth of the national government has been in response to such matters as the increased responsibility of the federal government for social programs, such as Social Security and Medicare, and the necessity for military readiness.

Social Studies Skills (Answers)

1. Federally owned land is identified by dark green shading.

2. According to the map, there are six states that contain no federally owned land.

3. The states that have 50 percent or more federally owned land are Alaska, Arizona, Colorado, Idaho, New Mexico, Nevada, Oregon, Utah, and Wyoming. California is very nearly 50 percent federally owned.

CHAPTER 4 REVIEW—Continued

7. Explain the concept of concurrent powers.
8. What does the privileges and immunities clause prevent?
9. Why is the concept of full faith and credit so important to interstate relationships?
10. What is the importance of the interstate compact?
11. What obligations does the Constitution impose upon the federal government with regard to the states?
12. What is the significance of the supremacy clause in our federal system?
13. What was the outcome of the case *McCulloch* v. *Maryland*?
14. Have there been any changes in the balance of political power between the state and national governments throughout the years?

Questions for Thought and Discussion

1. What do you think our government would be like if there were no division of powers between the national government and the states?
2. Should states be given greater power, less power, or do they currently have enough power?
3. Why do you think the powers to wage war and to relate to foreign nations belong to the national government?
4. What factors do you think have been responsible for the national government's growth of power?

Improving Your Skills

Communication Skills

Asking Effective Questions

Asking questions is one of the most important ways for us to learn facts, share ideas, and become informed. Asking effective questions will help you become a better-informed and more responsible citizen. Effective questions are designed to obtain specific information.

To ask effective questions requires preparation. When we don't obtain the information we seek from questions we ask, it is usually because we are asking the wrong source, asking the wrong questions, or asking them in the wrong way. Before you ask questions:

1. Determine the exact information you want to obtain.
2. Determine the best sources of that information.
3. Decide what questions will best draw out the information.
4. Decide how you should ask the questions. Remember that questions that can be answered with only a *yes* or a *no* will not give you much information.

Writing

Follow the four steps above to plan a class interview with a city or county official concerning a current issue in your community.

1. As a group, discuss the kinds of information you would like to obtain from the official. Write down ideas as they occur. Then narrow your ideas to a few specific issues.
2. Decide which city or county official would be the best source for that information.
3. Using the ideas you generated in Step 1, create a formal list of questions for the interview. Have your teacher approve your questions.

Social Studies Skills

Map Reading

Look at the map on page 91 (Federal Ownership of Land in the United States) to answer the following questions.

1. How is federally owned land identified?
2. Do any states have no federally owned land?
3. List the states in which the federal government owns 50 percent or more of the land.

Activities and Projects

1. Stage a debate on the following issue: Federal aid in the form of categorical grants gives the national government too much control over the states and should be abolished.
2. Call or write the district office of your local school district. Find out what kinds of state and federal aid your school district receives. Interview as many school officials as possible (principals, school board members, teachers, etc). Ask them to describe how they feel the aid (or lack of it) affects your school. Report your findings to the class.

Working with the Videodisc

The text below is from Professor Roger LeRoy Miller's introduction for the motion segment for Unit 2:

The Federalists who supported the ratification of the new Constitution promised some reluctant states that amendments would soon be passed to protect individual liberties against incursion by the national government. Nonetheless, James Madison, who drafted the Bill of Rights, had a hard time getting the House of Representatives to consider his amendments. Indeed, even as late as 1886 legal scholar Sir Henry Main referred to the American Bill of Rights as, and I quote, a "certain number of amendments on comparatively unimportant points." In spite of the public's lack of a pin-point understanding of what these amendments actually say, the Bill of Rights remains a cornerstone of our American political system that does indeed still guarantee freedom of speech, freedom of religion, freedom of the press, and rights of the accused, among others.

To access this segment, use the bar code below or the videodisc index found in the *TRB*.

Frame 16200

UNIT TWO

The Rights of All Citizens

Unit Contents

- *Chapter 5* Personal Freedoms
- *Chapter 6* Equality Under the Law

CHAPTER INTRODUCTION

Instructional Objectives

By the end of the chapter students should be able to:

- Discuss the origins of our system of personal freedoms and how they are guaranteed by the Bill of Rights.
- Describe how the First Amendment guarantees freedom of religion and how the Constitution affects the separation of church and state.
- Summarize the extent to which government protects as well as limits freedom of speech under the First Amendment.
- Identify the limits placed on freedom of the press. Specify what the right to assembly and petition means.

Using the Keynote

Ask one of the students to read the Voltaire quotation aloud. Then help the students discuss its meaning by posing questions such as these: Under what circumstances do you imagine Voltaire might have said this? What do you think he actually meant by saying this? Can you imagine any circumstances under which you would say—and mean—the same thing?

Introducing the Chapter

Begin by asking the students to consider the chapter title: What do you think personal freedoms are? Why are they important?

Then have the students read and discuss the chapter introduction: Why is defending the free expression of all persons the real test of democracy? Can any other forms of government pass this test? Why or why not? Why is the concept of limited government so important to this test of democracy?

Previewing the Sections

Section 1 Ask the students to glance through this section, noting especially the main headings. Then have them suggest at least five questions they expect to have answered as they study Section 1.
Section 2 Have volunteers find and read aloud the main headings and the subheadings, as well as the feature, in this section. Which issues referred to in these headings seem most interesting? Why?
Section 3 Let the students look through Section 3, noting the section title, the two main headings, and the Government in Action feature. How does the Government in Action Case Study relate to the section?
Section 4 Have the students glance through Section 4. Then ask: What is the press? What can you learn about freedom of the press from the main headings and the photographs within this section?
Section 5 Ask the students to look through Section 5 and briefly discuss it: How do you imagine these freedoms affect you? What questions do you hope to have answered as you study this section?

CHAPTER 5

Personal Freedoms

CHAPTER OBJECTIVES

To learn and understand

- The origins of our system of personal freedoms and how they are guaranteed under the Bill of Rights.
- The way the First Amendment guarantees freedom of religion and how the Constitution affects the separation of church and state.
- The extent to which the government protects as well as limits freedom of speech under the First Amendment.
- The limits placed on freedom of the press.
- What the right to assembly and petition means.

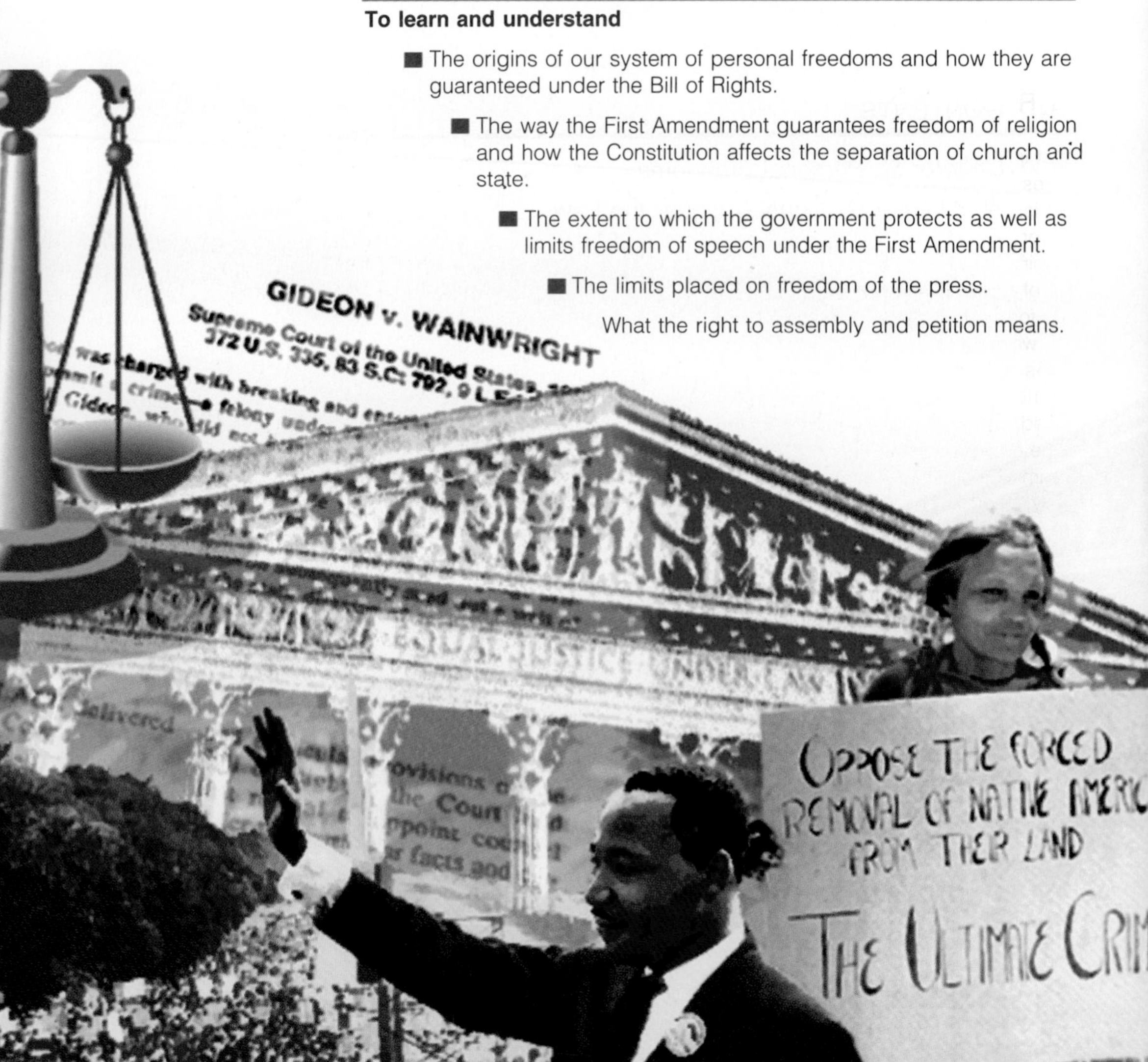

West's American Government Assignment Guide

Activity Sheets
Basic Concepts 5 *TRB* (Reteaching)
Enrichment Activity 5 *TRB*
Building Social Studies Skills 5 TRB

Quizzes
Chapter 5 Section 1 Quiz *TRB*
Chapter 5 Section 2 Quiz *TRB*
Chapter 5 Section 3 Quiz *TRB*
Chapter 5 Section 4 Quiz *TRB*
Chapter 5 Section 5 Quiz *TRB*

Tests
Chapter 5 Test A *TRB*
Chapter 5 Test B *TRB*
Chapter 5 Test Bank *TRB*
Chapter 5 WESTEST Computerized Testing

Social Studies Tool Kit Software
Chapter 5 Activity

Keynote

"I disagree profoundly with what you say, but I would defend with my life your right to say it."

—— **François Marie Voltaire (1694–1778) French philosopher**

INTRODUCTION

It is easy to say that all people in the United States should have the right to express themselves—that is, until they say or do something that offends you or someone else. Contrary to that concept, as the opening statement from Voltaire points out, the real test of a democracy is providing freedom of expression for *all* persons, regardless of whether you agree with what they say.

As you have learned, many early settlers came to America to escape religious persecution. Later, the United States was created out of a struggle to guarantee other personal freedoms. The founders dreamed of a country in which everyone could speak freely, write exactly what they felt, and openly practice any religion, all without penalty or interference.

As a result of this commitment, government in the United States has been firmly based on the concept of a *limited government,* which has *only* those powers the people have given to it. In a democracy it is essential that the people retain certain rights.

SECTION 1

Our System of Personal Freedoms

Preview Questions

- What guarantees of freedoms were included in the original Constitution?
- From what does the Bill of Rights protect us?
- Why is the due process clause of the Fourteenth Amendment so important?
- What does the Supreme Court have to do with the Bill of Rights?

Most of us agree that we must have basic freedoms; most of us even agree on what they should be. Most of us also recognize that to maintain order in our society, some lines must be drawn between individual rights and the rights of others or the community as a whole.

We begin to disagree, however, when we try to determine how, where, and when those lines are drawn. Sometimes people's rights seem to conflict with each other. For example, the right of the press to publish information about a crime might interfere with a defendant's right to have a fair trial. You may feel your rights are being invaded if you are forced to listen to music or to a speech that you find offensive.

Civil liberties are legal and constitutional rights that protect citizens *from* government actions. The First Amendment freedoms of religion, speech, press, **assembly** (to gather together for a common purpose), and **petition** (to address the government about its policies) are all civil liberties. Government cannot infringe upon these rights, nor can Congress pass laws **abridging** (diminishing or editing) them.

Constitutional Protections

The founders believed that the constitutions of the individual states had ample provisions to protect their citizens' rights. Most references to individual civil liberties, therefore, were not included in the Constitution until the Bill of Rights was created in 1791. Nonetheless, some safeguards in the original Constitution protected citizens against an overly powerful government.

For example, Article I, Section 9 of the Constitution provides that the writ of *habeas corpus* will be available to all citizens, except in times of rebellion or national invasion. A writ of ***habeas corpus*** (a Latin phrase that roughly means "you should hand over the body") is an order that an official must bring the prisoner into court, and the judge must be shown why the prisoner is being

SECTION 1

Points to Stress

- Guarantees of freedoms that were included in the original Constitution.
- The protections explicit in the Bill of Rights.
- The importance of the due process clause of the Fourteenth Amendment.
- The role of the Supreme Court relative to the Bill of Rights.

Kickoff Activity

Write this term on the chalkboard: *personal freedoms.* Ask the students to think about the term and its meaning, and have them list at least ten words or phrases that come to mind. After all the students have written their lists, encourage them to compare and discuss their ideas.

Working with the Preview Questions

Ask volunteers to read these study questions aloud. Remind the students to keep the questions in mind as they read the section, and explain that they will be asked to answer these questions later.

Teaching Strategies

Introduction

Ask the students to read the section introduction carefully. Then help the students discuss this introduction: How can the rights of one person or group interfere with the rights of another person or group? Whose rights are more important? How can conflicts like this be resolved?

Discussion Starter

Help the students discuss the significance of the *writ of habeas corpus:* Why is it so important? What do you think led the framers to include this safeguard in the Constitution?

Discussion Starter
Ask the students to explain and discuss bills of attainder: What are they? Why do you think they are prohibited by the Constitution (rather than the Bill of Rights)? What specific group do you imagine this provision was originally intended to protect?

Cooperative Learning
Have the students work in groups to discuss the prohibition of *ex post facto* laws: Why is this protection important? Whom does it serve? Why? After the group discussions, have representatives from each group share their ideas with the rest of the class.

Law Related Activity
The area of civil liberties is very important and it is crucial that students hear from those people who are involved in this arena on a regular basis. Arrange to have an outside resource person come in to address the class. The range of First Amendment topics to discuss is vast, and it would be prudent to allow students some input on the choice of speaker.

Possible speakers could be from the media to address press rights, a church official to address religious rights, or a special interest group to discuss the right to petition government. Speakers from a local law enforcement agency, the ACLU, a municipal official, or a judge would also be valuable.

Critical Thinking Skills
Guide the students in analyzing the importance of the Ninth Amendment: Does it make the previous eight amendments unnecessary? Why or why not? Would individuals be as well protected if the Ninth Amendment had not been included in the Bill of Rights? Why or why not?

Comprehension
Have the students review the complete Bill of Rights, found in the Resource Center.

Caption Answer Because of the dangers of second hand smoke, an individual who chooses to smoke is affecting not only him/herself but also many others who have to breathe his/her second hand smoke.

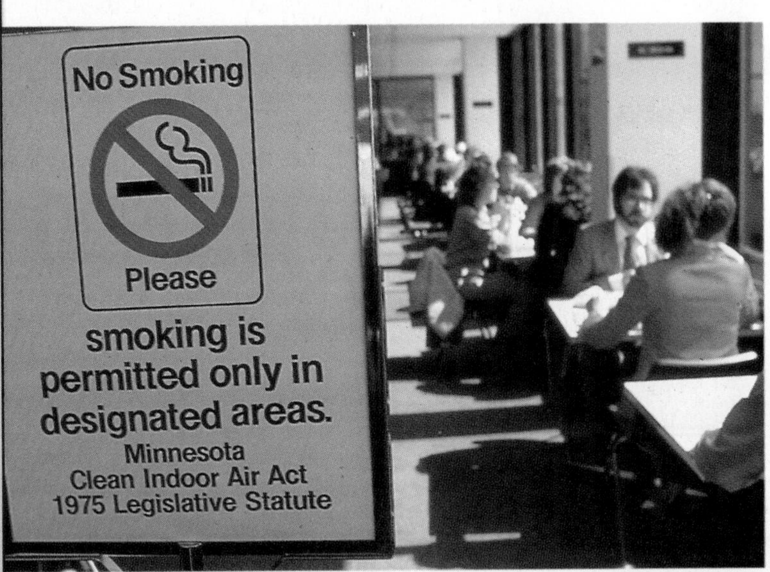

Many of our laws seek to strike a balance between individual rights and the rights of others and the community. In an effort to strike this balance on the issue of smoking, many communities have instituted laws banning smoking in certain areas and requiring certain businesses such as restaurants to establish smoke-free areas for their customers. How does the individual's right to smoke interfere with the rights of others?

kept in jail. If the court finds that the imprisonment is unlawful, it issues such a writ and the prisoner must be released. If our country did not have such a provision, political leaders could jail their opponents without giving them the opportunity to plead their case before a judge. Without this opportunity, many opponents could conveniently disappear, or be left to rot away in prison. The founders realized the importance of the writ of *habeas corpus.*

The Constitution also prohibits the Congress and state legislatures from passing *bills of attainder.* **Bills of attainder** are legislative acts that directly punish a specifically named individual (or a specifically named group or class of individuals) without a trial. A law cannot be passed by any legislature that identifies, convicts, or sentences a person or group of people for a real or imagined offense. For example, a law cannot be passed by your legislature that says students who attend your school and who drive over 35 miles per hour will automatically be sentenced to one night in jail.

The Constitution also prohibits Congress from passing *ex post facto* laws. ***Ex post facto*** roughly means "after the fact." An *ex post facto* law punishes individuals for committing an act that has become retroactively illegal. For example, say you went fishing in a nearby lake last week, when it was still legal to fish in that area. This week a law is passed saying that fishing in that area is illegal. You cannot be prosecuted for fishing there the previous week, because it was still legal to do so.

The *ex post facto* provision also prevents legislatures from increasing the penalty for a crime that was previously committed. You are subject only to the penalty that was in effect at the time.

The Bill of Rights

Even though these few individual protections against government were included in the original Constitution, as you learned in Chapters 2 and 3, there were no general listing of the rights of the people, or bill of rights. Public demand for the bill was strong, and several states ratified the Constitution only with the promise that such a listing would be added.

The first session of Congress in 1789 lived up to that promise with a series of proposed amendments. Ten of them, the Bill of Rights, were ratified by the states and became part of the Constitution on December 15, 1791. The first eight amendments grant the people rights. The Ninth Amendment states that the rights guaranteed in the Constitution are not the only rights the people have. The Tenth Amendment states that if the Constitution does not give a certain power to the federal government, nor denies it to the state governments, then the power belongs to the states or to the people. (This chapter deals mainly with the rights guaranteed under the First Amendment.)

The Bill of Rights protects individuals *against* abuses of power by the federal government. Consequently, the

Discussion Starter
Help the students discuss the quotation from Justice Hugo Black: In what sense is the Bill of Rights a collection of denials of the governments rights and powers? To whom does the Bill of Rights grant those rights and powers? What does this clarify about the form of our government?

Vocabulary
Ask the students to define the word *minority* as it is used in the term *minority rights.*

Discussion Starter
Encourage the students to discuss the protection of the rights of individuals or groups who do not side with the majority on any given issue: Why is it important that some rights cannot be submitted to a vote? What happens after a vote has been taken? Why should that kind of decision not be applied to personal freedoms?

The Bill of Rights

First Amendment	Guarantees freedom of religion, speech, press, assembly, and petition.
Second Amendment	Guarantees the right to keep and bear arms, since a state requires a well-equipped citizen army for its own security.
Third Amendment	Prohibits the lodging of soldiers in peacetime, without the dweller's consent.
Fourth Amendment	Prohibits unreasonable searches and seizures of persons or property.
Fifth Amendment	Guarantees the rights to trial by jury, due process of law, and fair payment when private property is taken for public use, such as in eminent domain; prohibits compulsory self-incrimination and double jeopardy (trial for the same crime twice).
Sixth Amendment	Guarantees the accused in a criminal case the right to a speedy and public trial by an impartial jury and with counsel; allows the accused to cross-examine witnesses against him or her, and to solicit testimony from witnesses in his or her favor.
Seventh Amendment	Guarantees a trial by jury for the accused in a civil case involving $20 or more.
Eighth Amendment	Prohibits excessive bail and fines, as well as cruel and unusual punishments.
Ninth Amendment	Establishes that the people have rights in addition to those specified in the Constitution.
Tenth Amendment	Establishes that those powers neither delegated to the national government nor denied to the states are reserved for the states.

▲ **FIGURE 5–1 The Bill of Rights.** On September 25, 1789, the Bill of Rights passed both houses of Congress and by December 15, 1791, had been ratified by three-fourths of the states. What does the Bill of Rights do that the original Constitution did not do?

Figure Answer While the original Constitution did list certain protections for the individual against government, it did not have a general listing of the rights of the people. By adding the Bill of Rights to the Constitution, these rights became a part of the Supreme Law of our land.

Bill of Rights begins with the words, "Congress shall make no law. . . ." According to Justice Hugo Black, who served on the United States Supreme Court from 1937 through 1971, the Bill of Rights is "a collection of 'Thou Shalt Nots'" directed at the government.

In a democracy, government policy tends to reflect the view of the majority. A major role of the Bill of Rights, however, is to protect minority rights against the will of the majority. Justice Robert Jackson, who sat on the Supreme Court from 1941 through 1954, said that "the very purpose of the Bill of Rights was to withdraw certain subjects from the vicissitudes [changes and variations] of political controversy, to place them beyond the reach of majorities." These rights "may not be submitted to a vote." In other words, certain rights should be protected for every citizen, whether the majority agrees on these rights or not.

Who then defines and applies these rights? Who stands guard over our civil liberties?

The Role of the Courts

When disagreements arise over how to interpret the Bill of Rights, it is the courts, especially the United States

Discussion Starter
Ask the students to consider the statement that each generation must learn to uphold its rights: How can people learn this? Who are the most important teachers? What experiences are most influential? Do you think it is as easy for your generation to learn this as it was for the generation 100 years ago? Why or why not?

Enrichment
Ask a small group of volunteers to research the life and work of Judge Learned Hand; have them summarize his accomplishments and influences in a short report for the rest of the class.

Enrichment
Ask groups of volunteers to research cases in which state governments have violated individual liberties; then let the volunteers share their findings with the rest of the class.

Caption Answer Student answers will vary but should reflect the understanding that Hand felt it is up to all Americans to work to protect liberty and personal freedoms.

Discussion Starter
Encourage the students to discuss the Due Process Clause: Why is it essential that the state not deprive persons of life, liberty, or property without due process of law? When does the state deprive persons of liberty, property, and even life?

Caption Answer Students' opinions on the issue of gun control and the Second Amendment will vary. You might want to point out to students that no federal court in history has ever overturned a gun law on Second Amendment grounds. As a follow-up to this discussion, you might wish to assign the Enrichment Activity for Chapter 5 that is found in the Teacher's Resource Binder.

TEACHING CITIZENSHIP SKILLS AND RESPONSIBILITIES

Read
Begin by having the students briefly discuss their responses to these questions: What responsibilities do citizens have? What specific responsibilities do *you* have as a citizen? Then ask volunteers to read the Citizenship Skills and Responsibilities section aloud to the rest of the class.

Discuss
Encourage the students to discuss the responsibilities presented here: Why is it important that all school-aged people attend school? Why is it important that *you* attend school? Why is obeying laws an important responsibility? Who relies on taxes? What happens when people do not pay their share of taxes?

Analyze and Apply
Ask the students to research your state's requirement for school attendance: At what age and under what circumstances may students leave school? How is school attendance enforced? You might also have the students research your school district's drop-out rate: How many students leave school before graduation? What do most of these students do? Then have the students meet in groups to compare

Supreme Court, that stand as the major guardians of individual liberties. All officers and agencies of the government are supposed to protect individual rights, but whenever a person claims that government has violated his or her civil liberties, he or she turns to the courts to interpret and apply constitutional guarantees.

Even though the courts stand guard over the rights and liberties of Americans, it is important to remember that ultimate responsibility to protect these rights lies with us, the American people. Each generation must learn anew to uphold its rights by voting, expressing opinions to elected representatives, and bringing cases to the attention of the courts when constitutional rights are threatened. Judge Learned Hand, an often-quoted United States Circuit Court judge, made the point this way:

> I often wonder whether we do not rest our hopes too much upon constitutions, upon laws and upon courts. These are false hopes; believe me, these are false hopes. Liberty lies in the hearts of men and women; when it dies there, no constitution, no law, no court can ever do much to help it.

▲ United States Circuit Court Judge Learned Hand questioned our reliance upon constitutional laws and courts to protect our individual liberties. What do you think Judge Hand meant when he said, "Liberty lies in the hearts of men and women . . . "?

Making the States Comply with the Bill of Rights

For many years the Bill of Rights was not applied to state or local governments. The founders believed that the states, being closer to the people, would be less likely to violate their own citizens' liberties.

State governments are bound to protect their citizens' rights through their state constitutions, most of which usually contain bills of rights. They are also bound to protect civil rights through a clause in the Fourteenth Amendment to the Constitution, known as the **due process clause.** It reads:

> No State shall . . . deprive any person of life, liberty, or property, without due process of law.

Due process is simply the right to be treated fairly under the legal system. That system and its officers are responsible to ensure that "rules of fair play" are

Since being injured by stray bullets from an assassination attempt on President Ronald Reagan by John W. Hinckley, Jr., James Brady and his wife, Sarah Brady, have led a campaign for the control of handguns in this country. Proponents of gun control maintain that the Second Amendment protects the right of the people to keep and bear arms, but only in connection with service in a "well-regulated militia" such as the National Guard. Opponents of gun control argue that the wording of the amendment clearly reflects the founders' desire to protect the right of gun ownership for individual citizens. How do you feel about gun control?

and discuss the information they have gathered.

Review

Ask the students these review questions: Why do citizens have responsibilities as well as rights? What are four important citizen responsibilities that are required by law?

Taking Action (Answers)

1. Answers will vary, e.g., taking care of the environment, volunteering for civic projects, learning about important issues that are on the ballot, reporting suspected criminal activity, etc.

2. Answers will vary, e.g., some students would drop out of school before age 16. If no laws had to be obeyed, there would be chaos. If no one had to pay taxes, government would be in serious difficulty and not be able to pay for needed activities, such as fire and police protection.

3. Answers will vary, e.g., yes, I think that women should serve the same as men in time of war. They may not necessarily be expected to fight on the battlefield, but there are numerous other jobs that they can do within the military. It is only by giving women the same responsibilities as men that they can take on their rightful roles in society.

Reteaching Strategies

1. Work with small groups of students to review civil liberties: What does the term *civil liberties* mean? Why are civil liberties protected by our Constitution?

2. Let the students work with partners or in small groups to outline this section. Check their work to be sure the main points are included, and no details are left out.

Evaluation Strategies

1. Have the students write their responses to the Preview Questions at the beginning of the section.

2. Have the students write their answers to the Section 1 Review questions.

3. Have the students take the Section 1 Quiz found in the *TRB*.

Section 1 Review (Answers)

1. Civil liberties are the legal and constitutional rights that protect citizens from government actions. The Bill of Rights guarantees freedom of religion, speech, press, assembly, and petition.

2. The Constitution provided that a writ of *habeas corpus* would be available to all citizens and prohibited bills of attainder. It also prohibited ex post facto laws. These are found in Article I, Sections 9 and 10. Article III guarantees a jury trial.

3. When there is disagreement over how to interpret the Bill of Rights, the courts, especially the Supreme Court, make the decisions.

4. States are bound to protect civil rights through the due process clause of the Fourteenth Amendment.

5. Answers will vary, e.g., no written law can force people to support a government. Protecting the rights of every person and upholding the values and interests of the country is the responsibility of all citizens.

CITIZENSHIP SKILLS AND RESPONSIBILITIES

Responsibilities of Citizens

You have begun to learn about your rights as a citizen. Along with those rights, you also share many responsibilities. These responsibilities help protect your rights and keep the country running smoothly and democratically. Certain responsibilities are required by law. Some of these include:

Attending School. Every state requires that young people attend school until they reach a certain age, which in most states is age 16. Attending school is vital to democracy, for it is through education that every American becomes an informed and effective citizen. An educated population is essential to our strength as a nation.

Obeying Laws. All citizens should know as much about the laws as they can. Obeying these laws is one of the most important responsibilities required of Americans. If a law seems unfair or unnecessary, citizens can work through government to change it.

Paying Taxes. All Americans must pay some amount of taxes. Although this is a duty about which we often complain, it is important to remember our tax dollars are used for services we rely on every day. These include fire and police protection, education, national defense, and protection of the environment.

Defending the Nation. American citizens have a responsibility to defend the nation. In peacetime, the military is made up of volunteers. Even in peacetime, however, 18-year-old males are required to register for the draft (even though there currently is no draft). **Draft registration** means giving your name, age, and address so that you can be contacted for military service in case the country suddenly needs to increase its armed forces.

TAKING ACTION

1. The list presented above is a list of *required* citizen responsibilities. Make a list of *voluntary* responsibilities that you have as an American citizen.
2. What do you think would happen if the above-listed four legally required responsibilities became voluntary? Write a paragraph explaining your answers.
3. Do you think women should be drafted for military service? If so, what roles do you think women should play in protecting the nation? Explain the reasons for your answer.

followed in making decisions, in determining guilt or innocence, and in punishing those who have been found guilty. Thus, "due process" means that the correct procedures have been followed and that everyone has been given an equal right to be heard.

The Supreme Court has interpreted the due process clause to mean that no state may deny any person any right that is "basic or essential to the American concept of ordered liberty." In a long series of cases, starting in 1925, the Supreme Court gradually began using the due process clause to say that states could not abridge a right that the national government could not abridge. Especially during the 1960s, the Supreme Court broadened its interpretations to limit state action in most areas in which federal action is banned. Many of these decisions, as you will see, have been controversial. For all practical purposes, however, the Bill of Rights guarantees individual rights against infringement by both state and national governments.

SECTION 1 REVIEW

1. What are civil liberties? List the civil liberties each American is guaranteed under the Bill of Rights.
2. What protections did the original Constitution provide against an overly intrusive government?
3. How are the courts one of the principal guardians of personal freedoms in this country?
4. How is the Bill of Rights applied to the states?
5. **For critical analysis:** Reread the quote from Judge Learned Hand on page 106. Explain what you think he means when he says we should not "rest our hopes for our personal liberties too much upon constitutions, laws, and courts."

SECTION 2

Points to Stress

- The importance of freedom of religion in a democracy.
- The definition of "separation of church and state."
- Distinctions between the right to believe and the right to practice religion as you wish.
- The intent of the establishment and free exercise clauses.
- Supreme Court decisions pertaining to freedom of religion.

Kickoff Activity
Write this question on the chalkboard: What does freedom of religion allow you to do? Have the students write several sentences in response to the question. Then let them share and discuss their ideas.

Working with the Preview Questions
Have the students read these study questions and discuss their responses, based on the knowledge they already have. Then ask them to keep these questions in mind as they read and take notes on Section 2.

Caption Answer The First Amendment to the Constitution both prohibits the establishment of official religion as well as guaranteeing the free exercise of religion when it states, "Congress shall make no law respecting an establishment of religion, or prohibiting the free exercise thereof. . . ."

Teaching Strategies

Introduction
Have a volunteer read aloud the first paragraph of the section introduction, and encourage the students to discuss the two situations presented there: Should the students be released from public school to attend religious classes? Why or why not? Should the school administrators be allowed to set aside 30 seconds for silent prayer? Why or why not? Encourage the students to express and defend differing points of view. Then ask: Why are these questions so difficult to answer? Are there right answers? If so, what makes those answers right? After the discussion, have the students finish reading the section introduction.

Discussion Starter
Encourage the students to discuss their responses to this relationship between government and religion in general: Do you think it is appropriate? Do you find it offensive? Do you think some individuals or groups find it offensive?

Enrichment
Have the students read about the history of the Pledge of Allegiance? How long has it been used? How has it been changed? When and under what circumstances was the reference to God added?

Comprehension
Ask the students to identify and discuss the essential difference between the situations in Champaign, Illinois and in New York City: Why is this difference important?

SECTION 2

Freedom of Religion

Preview Questions

- Why is freedom of religion important in a democracy?
- What does "separation of church and state" mean?
- What distinction is there between the right to believe and the right to practice your religion as you wish?

Imagine for a moment several possible problems that face students and administrators at public schools regarding the practice of religion. Joan, a sophomore at Blue High School, wants permission to leave school during class hours in order to attend religious classes at her church. Should she be allowed to leave? At Oak High School in a neighboring state, administrators have set aside thirty seconds during homeroom period to allow students to engage in silent prayer. Is this legal? Understanding the Constitution and how it has been interpreted by the Supreme Court can help you answer the questions just posed.

▼ The annual Hare Krishna Festival of Giant Chariots celebrated in Santa Monica, California is just one colorful example of religious freedom in the United States. What does the First Amendment say about religion?

The freedoms guaranteed by the First Amendment of the Constitution are essential for the survival of a democracy. Many nondemocratic governments in Eastern Europe that did not guarantee these rights found out how important they were when, as a result of mass demands for these rights, their governments began to collapse in 1989.

Its not surprising that our Bill of Rights provides for the protection of religious liberty first—many of the colonists came here to escape religious persecution. The First Amendment prohibits Congress from passing laws "respecting an establishment of religion." This is known as the **establishment clause.**

In 1802, President Thomas Jefferson referred to the First Amendment's establishment clause as "a wall of separation between church and state." This makes the United States different from many countries that are ruled by religious governments, such as the Islamic government of Iran. It also makes us different from nations that have in the past strongly discouraged the practice of any religion at all such as the People's Republic of China.

The establishment clause forbids the government to "establish" an official religion. What does this separation of church and state mean in practice?

Separation of Church and State

Church and government, while constitutionally separated by the establishment clause in the United States, have never been enemies or strangers. The establishment clause does not prohibit government from supporting religion *in general*, which remains a part of public life. Most government officials take an oath of office in the name of God, and our coins and paper currency carry the motto "In God We Trust." Clergy of different religions—rabbis, ministers, and others—serve with each branch of the armed forces. The Pledge of Allegiance contains a reference to God. Public meetings and even sessions of Congress open with prayers.

The "wall of separation" that Thomas Jefferson referred to, however, does exist and has been upheld by the Supreme Court on many occasions. The first ruling by the Supreme Court on the establishment clause came in *Everson* v. *Board of Education* (1947). The case involved a New Jersey law that allowed the state to pay

Discussion Starter
Guide the students in discussing the attempts of some schools to promote religion in general: How do you feel about such promotion of religion? Do you feel that it infringes on your freedom? On whose freedom does it infringe? What might be troubling or offensive about the prayer proposed by the State Board of Regents? Could this prayer be reworded so that it would not violate the Establishment Clause? If so, how? If not, why not?

Comprehension
Ask the students to identify and discuss the differences between the Kentucky law and the Alabama law. Why were both found unconstitutional?

Discussion Starter
Ask the students to describe how the Bible can be studied as literature and to explain why that study differs from religious activities. If any of the students have taken literature courses that included the Bible, encourage them to share their experiences.

Enrichment
Ask a group of volunteers to research this 1984 proposed amendment. What groups sponsored and supported the proposal? On what grounds? Who opposed the amendment? Why? Let the volunteers share their findings with the rest of the class.

Extension
Have the students identify and discuss the clubs that meet at their school: Which could be considered religious? Which could be considered political? What restrictions have been placed on them?

for bus transportation of students who attended parochial schools (schools run by churches or other religious groups). The Court upheld the New Jersey law because it did not aid the church *directly,* but provided for the safety and benefit of the students. The ruling both affirmed the importance of separating church and state, and set the precedent that not *all* forms of state and federal aid to church-related schools are forbidden under the Constitution.

The Issue of Released Time In some schools, students are allowed to leave regular classes to attend religious instruction sessions. Some concerned citizens have argued that this policy of **released time** violates the establishment clause. Two cases dealing with this issue have reached the Supreme Court. In *McCollum* v. *Board of Education* (1948), the Court said students could not be released from regular classes in order to attend a religious program in Champaign, Illinois, because public school classrooms and other facilities were being used for religious purposes. Four years later, however, in *Zorach* v. *Clauson,* New York City's released-time program was upheld, because the religious classes were conducted in a private location. The Court held that the schools were doing no more than accommodating the schedules of students to obtain religious instruction.

Education, Prayer, and the Bible On occasion, some schools have promoted a general sense of religion without proclaiming allegiance to any particular one. Whether the states have a right to allow this was the main question presented in *Engel* v. *Vitale* (1962), the "Regents' Prayer" case in New York. The State Board of Regents in New York had composed a nondenominational prayer (a prayer not associated with any particular religion) and urged school districts to use it in classrooms at the start of each day. It read:

> Almighty God, we acknowledge our dependence upon Thee, and we beg Thy blessings upon us, our parents, our teachers, and our country.

Some parents objected to the prayer, saying it was a violation of the establishment clause. The Supreme Court agreed and ruled that the Regents' prayer was unconstitutional. Speaking for the majority, Justice Hugo Black wrote that the First Amendment must at least mean "that in this country it is no part of the business of government to compose official prayers for any group of the American people to recite as part of a religious program carried on by government."

In 1980, a Kentucky law requiring that the Ten Commandments be posted in all public schools was found unconstitutional in *Stone* v. *Graham.* In 1985, the Supreme Court ruled that an Alabama law requiring a daily one-minute period of silence for meditation and voluntary prayer also violated the establishment clause.

In sum, the Supreme Court has ruled that the public schools, which are agencies of government, cannot sponsor religious activities. It has *not,* however, held that individuals cannot pray, when and as they choose, in schools or in any other place. Nor has it held that the Bible cannot be studied as a form of literature in the schools.

Religion is often a sensitive issue, and public reactions to the Court's rulings have been mixed. In 1984 one group proposed to amend the Constitution to allow Bible reading and recitation of the Christian prayer "The Lord's Prayer" in schools. The proposed amendment would have overruled the Supreme Court's decisions, but it did not produce the two-thirds vote in each house of Congress needed to send it to the states for ratification.

Religious Meetings in Schools Cases have arisen around the country in which students who want to pray or hold religious meetings or discussions on public school property have been barred from doing so by public officials. Congress sought to strike a reasonable balance when, in 1984, it passed the Equal Access Act. That law requires public high schools to allow students' religious and political clubs to meet on the same basis as do other extracurricular activity clubs. In 1990, the Supreme Court upheld the Equal Access Act on an 8-to-1 vote in *Board of Education of Westside Community Schools* v. *Mergens,* a case involving a high school in Omaha, Nebraska, in which students sought to form a Christian study group. "A high school need not permit any student activities not related to the curriculum," Justice Sandra Day O'Connor said in the opinion. "But if it does," she continued, "the school is bound by the Equal Access Act not to discriminate against any student group on the basis of its religious, philosophical, or political viewpoints."

Aid to Parochial Schools All property owners, except nonprofit institutions, must pay property taxes, of which a large part goes to support public schools. What about the students who attend private schools, which receive no public tax support?

Under certain circumstances parochial schools can constitutionally obtain state aid. Many states have provided aid to church-related schools in the form of

This case is excerpted in the *West's American Government Handbook of Selected Court Cases.*

Multidiscipline Strategies

World Religions/ Cultures
Begin with a brief class discussion: Which religions are practiced in the United States? Which of these religions do you consider most important? Why? Can any religions be considered unimportant? Why? After the discussion, let each student work with a partner to research a religion with which he or she is not already familiar: What are the central beliefs of the religion? What are the most important ceremonies and practices? Have the partners prepare oral or written reports of their findings.

Cooperative Learning
Have the students work in groups to learn about local parochial schools: What kind of state aid does each school receive? Has the school attempted to get other kinds of state aid? With what results?

Critical Thinking Skills
Have the students analyze and compare the arguments in favor of and against financial aid to parochial schools: Which arguments do you consider most persuasive? Why? Which do you consider most in keeping with the Constitution? Why? Encourage the students to express and defend differing points of view.

Vocabulary
Ask the students to discuss the key phrase, *excessive entanglement of government with religion.* What does each word in the phrase mean? How is the phrase open to interpretation?

Discussion Starter
Ask the students to consider the case of *Mueller* v. *Allen:* Why was the tax deduction considered fair? Why do you think such a deduction can be considered fair to taxpayers who do not have children attending schools (and therefore cannot take any such deductions)? Does this tax law mean that citizens without school-aged children are actually paying more taxes for schools than citizens with children in school? If so, can that be considered fair?

Discussion Starter
Ask the students to recall and discuss any publicly sponsored holiday displays (Christmas or Chanukah) in their communities: Where were the displays? What was included in them? Did they engender any controversy? If so, what were the issues and how were they resolved? If not, why not?

Caption Answer The Supreme Court has ruled that since public schools are agencies of the government, they cannot sponsor religious activities such as school prayer.

In 1962, it was customary for this San Antonio High School English class to open with a prayer. How did the Supreme Court rule on the issue of prayer in school?

textbooks, transportation, and equipment. Other forms of payment, such as providing for teacher's salaries and payment for field trips have been found unconstitutional.

Those who favor government financial aid to parochial schools argue that 12 percent of all American students attend private schools, 85 percent of which have religious affiliation. These students would otherwise be attending public schools at public expense. They argue that parents must be relieved of some of the double financial burden of paying to send their children to private schools while also paying local property taxes to support public schools.

Opponents argue that parents who send children to parochial schools make their own free choice, knowing full well that such schools are not supported with tax dollars. They should accept the consequences and not expect society to pay for their choice.

Since 1971, the Supreme Court has followed the **excessive entanglement** (involvement) **theory** when deciding cases that involve government aid to religious school groups. To be constitutional, a state's school aid must meet three requirements: (1) the purpose of the financial aid must be clearly secular (not religious); (2) its primary effect must neither advance nor inhibit religion; and (3) it must avoid an "excessive entanglement of government with religion."

The Court first used the test in *Lemon* v. *Kurtzman* (1971). The Court denied public aid to private and parochial schools for the salaries of teachers of secular courses, and for school-building maintenance and repairs. It held that the establishment clause is designed to prevent three main evils: "sponsorship, financial support, and active involvement of the sovereign [the government] in religious activity."

In *Mueller* v. *Allen* (1983), the Court upheld a Minnesota tax law that gave parents a state income tax deduction for costs of tuition, textbooks, and transportation for their elementary and secondary school children. Parents may claim the tax break no matter what schools, public or private, the children attend. Because the deduction was available to *all* parents, the Court found that the law meets the excessive entanglement standards.

The Court has also enforced the separation of church and state in other public places besides schools.

Christmas Displays Do publicly sponsored displays of religious holidays violate the wall of separation? The answer is not a simple yes or no. In 1984, by a bare majority of 5 to 4, the Supreme Court upheld a display of a Nativity scene depicting the birth of Christ in Pawtucket, Rhode Island, in *Lynch* v. *Donnelly.* It ruled that the display was acceptable because it also included symbols that are not necessarily religious, such as Santa, reindeer, and animals.

In 1989, the Court ruled against another Nativity scene in the Allegheny County Courthouse in Pennsylvania. This one was *not* surrounded by other decorations and *was* found to be in violation of the establishment clause. In the same case the Court ruled that an eighteen-foot modernistic menorah (a religious symbol used in the celebration of Chanukah, a Jewish holiday) at the nearby City-County building during Chanukah *did not*

TEACHING GOVERNMENT IN ACTION

Read
Begin by having the students discuss what they already know about the taxation of churches: Which kinds of taxes do churches pay? Why? Which kinds of taxes are churches not required to pay? Why? After a brief exchange of ideas, let volunteers read the Case Study aloud to the rest of the class.

Discuss
Help the students discuss the Case Study by posing questions such as these: Why is a "minimum and remote" involvement between church and state acceptable? How do you think the line between a "minimum and remote" involvement and an unconstitutional involvement can be defined? Do you agree that religious groups should be required to pay sales tax on the materials they sell, even when those materials are religious in nature? Why or why not?

Analyze and Apply
Have each student discuss the issues of taxation with a local religious leader (such as a minister, a rabbi, a priest, or an involved congregation member) or with a representative or active member of the ACLU. What opinion does each person express? What reasons does that person give to support his or her opinion? After the students have gathered this information, let them share and discuss what they have learned.

Review
Ask the students these review questions: Why are churches exempt from paying property taxes? Why are they not exempt from paying sales taxes?

This case is excerpted in the West's American Government Handbook of Selected Court Cases.

Think About It (Answers)
1. Answers will vary, e.g., government should maintain its neutrality toward all religious organizations. If one is tax-exempt, then they should all enjoy the same tax-exempt status.
2. Answers will vary, e.g., because religious organizations are not-for-profit organizations. Also, implicitly, states have encouraged more churches by not taxing church-owned property.

Discussion Starter
Encourage the students to discuss this statement: There is an important distinction between belief and practice. What is that distinction? Why is it important?

GOVERNMENT IN ACTION

CASE STUDY

Churches and Taxes

Traditionally, states and cities have not taxed churches and church-owned property used for religious purposes. In other words, such property is *tax exempt.* The Court upheld this practice in *Walz* v. *New York City Tax Commission* in 1970. Walz had challenged the exemption of churches from local property taxes. He argued that these exemptions raised everyone else's property tax bills, and that the exemptions amounted to a public support of religion.

The Court found that the tax exemptions only indicated a state's ''benevolent [charitable] neutrality'' toward religion, not active support of it. They stated the tax exemptions ''create only a minimal and remote [and therefore permissible] involvement between church and state.''

In 1990, the Court reached a different sort of decision on state tax and churches. In a defeat for the Jimmy Swaggart Ministries, the Court ruled unanimously that states may require religious groups to pay sales tax on religious materials they sell. It upheld California's tax on Swaggart Ministries' sales of a range of materials, from Bibles and song books to prerecorded audiocassettes.

In an opinion written by Justice Sandra Day O'Connor, the high court rejected arguments that a sales tax on religious materials violates the First Amendment's guarantee of religious freedom. ''The collection and payment of the generally applicable tax in this case imposes no constitutionally significant burden'' on the Swaggart organization's ''religious practices or beliefs,'' Justice O'Connor said.

Church groups reacted by saying it was the beginning of a disturbing trend that could mean taxing church property and income next. They feared it may be a trend away from treating religion as worthy of special protection under the Bill of Rights.

But a spokeswoman for the American Civil Liberties Union, an organization that fights abuses of constitutionally guaranteed personal freedoms, said the ruling affirms ''the neutrality with which government should treat all religions.''

THINK ABOUT IT

1. Should *all* types of religious organizations enjoy the same tax-exempt status?
2. Why do you think states have traditionally exempted churches and church-owned property from state and local taxes?

violate the First Amendment's establishment clause. The justices reasoned that it was accompanied by a forty-five-foot Christmas tree and a printed ''Salute to Liberty'' banner from the mayor linking the menorah and the Christmas tree, which made it acceptable. Justice Harry Blackmun, one of two justices who voted to approve the menorah display while disallowing the Nativity scene, said that unlike Christmas, Chanukah lacks a conventional nonreligious symbol such as a Christmas tree.

Free Exercise of Religion

Another aspect of religious freedom guaranteed by the First Amendment forbids the passage of laws ''prohibiting the free exercise of religion.'' The **free exercise clause** protects individuals' right to worship or believe as they wish, or to hold no religious beliefs at all. No law or act of government may violate this absolute constitutional right.

Belief and Practice are Distinct The free exercise clause does not necessarily mean that individuals can act any way they want on the basis of their religious beliefs. There is an important distinction between belief and practice. The Supreme Court has ruled consistently that the right to hold any *belief* is absolute. The government has no authority to compel you to accept or reject any

Discussion Starter
Encourage the students to consider and discuss *Reynolds* v. *United States:* Which did the Supreme Court value more highly—the duty to obey the law against polygamy or the right to follow religious beliefs? Why? Do you think the Supreme Court would reach the same decision today? Why or why not?

Enrichment
Ask a group of volunteers to research one or two cases in which parents—for religious reasons—have refused to accept traditional medical treatment for their children: How have the courts intervened? With what results? Let the volunteers share their findings with the class, and encourage the students to discuss these cases.

Discussion Starter
Ask the students about their experiences with saluting the flag: When and where have flag salutes been part of the routine or ceremony? Have you ever felt *obligated* to participate? Have you ever wanted to object to participating? Why or why not? Have you ever refused to participate? Why or why not? If you have refused, what were the consequences of your refusal?

Discussion Starter
Have the students compare and discuss the two flag-salute cases presented here: Why do you think the Court reversed its earlier decision? Do you agree with the statement of Justice Jackson? Why or why not?

Reteaching Strategies
1. Have the students work in small groups to compare and review their notes on this section. Encourage the students to refer to the text as they revise and reorganize their notes.
2. Working with small groups of students, review the two questions posed in the first paragraph of the section introduction: Should Joan be released from her public school during school hours to attend religious classes? Why or why not? Is it legal for Oak High School to set aside 30 seconds for silent prayer? Why or why not?

Caption Answer The practice was dangerous.

Evaluation Strategies
1. Have the students write their answers to the first four Section 2 Review questions.
2. Let the students discuss their ideas about the final Section 2 Review question in small groups. Then have each student work alone to write his or her own response.
3. Have the students take the Section 2 Quiz found in the *TRB.*

Section 2 Review (Answers)
1. The clause of the First Amendment that prohibits Congress from passing laws "respecting the establishment of religion."
2. In 1802, President Thomas Jefferson referred to the First Amendment's establishment clause as "a wall of separation between church and state," meaning that the two should remain firmly out of each other's affairs.
3. The clause of the First Amend-

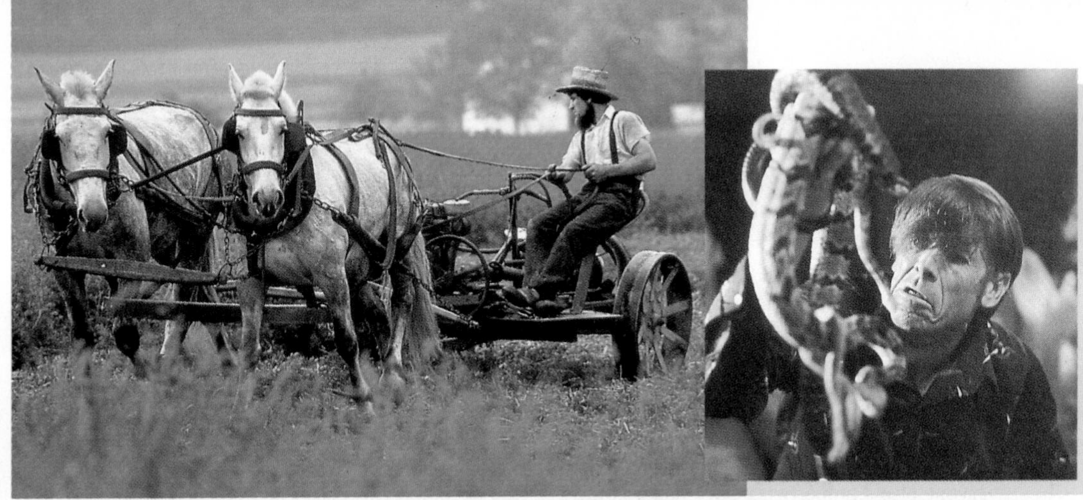

▲ The Supreme Court has generally accepted that people are free to believe and practice their religion so long as they don't jeopardize health, safety, or the morals of the community. For example, the Amish are free to follow their religious beliefs. Why then do you think the Supreme Court upheld a state law that forbids the use of poisonous snakes in religious rites (as shown here)?

particular religious belief. The right to *practice* one's beliefs may, however, have some limitations. As the Court itself once asked, ''Suppose one believed that human sacrifice were a necessary part of religious worship?''

The first time the Supreme Court dealt with the issue of belief versus practice was in *Reynolds* v. *United States* (1879). Reynolds was a Mormon who had two wives. Polygamy, or the practice of having more than one spouse at a time, was encouraged by the practice and teachings of his religion. It was also prohibited by federal law. Reynolds was convicted and appealed the case, arguing that the law violated his constitutional right to freely exercise his religious beliefs. The Court did not agree. It said that polygamy was a crime, and crimes are not protected by the First Amendment.

Through the years, the Supreme Court has followed the general principle that people are free to believe and to practice their religion as they wish, so long as their conduct does not threaten the health, safety, or morals of the community. For example, it has ruled that Christian Scientists cannot prevent their children from accepting medical treatment, such as blood transfusions, if the children's lives are in danger, even though accepting such treatment is against their religion. It has upheld laws forbidding the use of poisonous snakes in religious rites, as well as laws requiring religious groups to obtain permits before holding a parade.

The Flag-Salute Issue Can children be forced to salute the flag when this practice is against their religious beliefs? This question was raised when Lillian and William Gobitis, ages 10 and 12, were expelled from school for refusing to salute the American flag at the start of each day. The children and their parents were Jehovah's Witnesses, who believe that saluting a flag violates the Bible's command forbidding the worship of idols.

In this case, *Minersville School District* v. *Gobitis* (1940), the Court stated that the flag was a symbol of national unity, and ruled that the flag-salute requirement was not an infringement on the free exercise of religion.

Three years later, in a remarkable turnaround, the Court reversed that decision. In *West Virginia Board of Education* v. *Barnette* (1943), it ruled that a compulsory flag-salute law was unconstitutional. Justice Robert H. Jackson, writing for the majority, said:

> To believe that patriotism will not flourish if patriotic ceremonies are voluntary and spontaneous, instead of a compulsory routine, is to make an unflattering estimate of the appeal of our institutions to free minds.

SECTION 2 REVIEW

1. What is the establishment clause?
2. What is meant by separation of church and state?
3. What is the free exercise clause?
4. What are the key differences of opinion that lead some individuals to favor state aid to parochial schools and others to oppose it?
5. **For critical analysis:** In your opinion, where should the line be drawn between belief and practice? Use several examples to explain your answer.

ment that forbids the passage of laws "prohibiting the free exercise of religion."

4. Those in favor argue that students attending parochial schools would otherwise be attending public schools at public expense. Parents need to be relieved of the double burden of paying to send their children to private parochial schools and taxes. Those not in favor argue that parents who send their children to parochial schools make their own free choice, knowing those schools are not supported by tax dollars.

5. Answers will vary, e.g., the right to hold any religious belief should be absolute. The right to practice should also be respected unless it violates a law or brings harm to another person. For example, the practice of a religion which prevents a child from receiving medical attention he or she needs should not be allowed.

SECTION 3

Points to Stress

- The importance of freedom of expression in a democracy.
- Limits placed on free speech and freedom of the press.
- Supreme Court decisions relating to freedom of expression, speech, and freedom of the press.

Kickoff Activity

Ask the students this question: What is free speech? Give the students four or five minutes to write their responses; then encourage them to share and discuss their ideas.

Working with the Preview Questions

Let a volunteer read aloud the two study questions, and ask the students to suggest specific questions they expect to have answered as they read Section 3. Then have the students use the study questions as a guide for organizing note-taking sheets; have them use these sheets as they take notes on the section.

Teaching Strategies

Introduction

Have the students read and discuss the section introduction: Do you think it is still valid to say that the truth will survive in the free marketplace of ideas? How have the means of communication changed in recent decades, and how have those changes affected the "free marketplace of ideas"? Have you ever heard people making speeches that you found offensive? How did you respond? Encourage the students to share and discuss various experiences and ideas.

Comprehension

As the students read about pure speech, speech plus, and symbolic speech, ask volunteers to identify specific examples of each.

Caption Answer Student answers may vary but should mention that Justice Holmes was summing up the real challenge of free speech, and that is protecting the free speech and free exchange of ideas that are unpopular.

SECTION 3

Freedom of Speech

Preview Questions

- Why is freedom of expression important in a democracy?
- What are the limits placed on free speech and press?

How many times have you heard someone say, "I can say what I want. It's a free country"? This common expression reveals the underlying philosophy ingrained in our notion of what democracy in America means.

The right to free speech is the cornerstone upon which a democracy is built. Every person has the right to speak freely and to question its government's decisions. Citizens in a democracy also must have the chance to hear and judge for themselves what others have to say. Our system depends on people's ability to make sound, clear judgments on matters of public concern. In order to do this, people must be free to learn all the facts of an issue, so they can weigh the various interpretations and opinions. This allows people to help shape the decisions and policies of their government. It also makes it difficult for government to cover up any mistakes or injustices. As Supreme Court Justice Oliver Wendell Holmes put it: "The best test of truth is the power of the thought to get itself into the competition of the market." Holmes was simply saying that truth will survive in the free marketplace of ideas.

In many nondemocratic countries throughout the world, individuals do not have the right to free speech. For example, in the People's Republic of China, in Cuba, and in Iraq, most citizens rarely have been allowed publicly to oppose their government's policies. Many have even been executed for doing so. In other countries, such as South Africa, many individuals were jailed for criticizing that government. A government's desire to suppress the free speech of its citizens has resulted in violations of the citizens' basic **human rights**—fundamental rights, such as the right to speak freely, with which no government should interfere. Governments that violate these rights avoid being held accountable for these actions by imprisoning dissenters to silence them.

As we discussed earlier, no one in this country seems to have a problem protecting the free speech of those with whom they agree. The real challenge is protecting unpopular beliefs. The opinions of the majority, after all, need little constitutional protection. The protection needed is, in Justice Holmes' words: "not free thought for those who agree with us but freedom for the thought that we hate."

The First Amendment is designed to especially protect ideas that may be unpopular or different.

Types of Speech

What exactly is free speech? Speech is more than merely the spoken word; it means the broad freedom to communicate, which includes actions and nonverbal means. How far can this freedom go? To what degree are these forms of speech protected? To answer such questions the Supreme Court has distinguished three general categories of speech that are protected by the First Amendment.

Pure speech is the peaceful expression of thoughts, ideas, or opinions before a willing audience. This is the neighborly chat or the local candidate's campaign speech. It is your expression of ideas about a political issue or official. This type of speech is generally protected under the First Amendment.

Speech plus is verbal expression combined with some sort of action, such as marching or demonstrating. Because speech plus involves actions, it may be subject to government restrictions that do not apply to pure speech. The Supreme Court has ruled that while *speech plus* is protected by the First Amendment, it cannot obstruct traffic, block sidewalks, or endanger public safety.

▼ Supreme Court Justice Oliver Wendell Holmes said that we need to protect "not free thought for those who agree with us, but freedom for the thought that we hate." What do you think that Justice Holmes meant by these words?

TEACHING GOVERNMENT IN ACTION

Read
Introduce this feature by having the students discuss their own experiences with people who beg: How do you feel when people ask you for food or money? How do you usually respond? Why? After the discussion, ask the students to read the Case Study to themselves.

Discuss
Ask the students to recall the arguments presented in favor of begging and those opposed to it: Which do you find more persuasive? Why? Do you think people who are so poor that they need to beg should have the same rights as people who have enough money to live comfortably? Do they have the same rights? Why or why not? In your opinion, is panhandling one of the rights protected by the First Amendment? Encourage a lively exchange of ideas.

Analyze and Apply
Have the students research laws governing panhandling in their local community and in the state. What restrictions—if any—have been placed on the right to beg? What controversies—if any—have arisen around these restrictions? How have such controversies been resolved? Then let the students discuss their findings: Do you think local laws are fair? If so, why? If not, what should be done to improve them?

Review
Have the students respond to these review questions: What different court decisions have been made regarding the right to beg? What reasoning has been used to support those different decisions?

Think About It (Answers)
1. Answers will vary, e.g., yes, panhandling should be allowed because to restrict it would be a violation of freedom of speech; No, panhandling should not be allowed because it violates the right to privacy of others.
2. Answers will vary, e.g., panhandlers should be restricted from using violence or scare tactics.
3. Answers will vary, e.g., begging becomes harassment when the person approached feels threatened in any way.

Enrichment
Encourage the students to share what they may have read or heard about the Vietnam War protest movement. Then ask volunteers to read more about the protestors, their intentions, and their methods, and have the volunteers present their information in a bulletin board display.

Discussion Starter
Let a volunteer read aloud the quotation from Justice Oliver Wendell Holmes, and guide the students in

GOVERNMENT IN ACTION

CASE STUDY

The Right to Beg?

Do the poor have a constitutional right to beg? Is panhandling a form of speech protected under the First Amendment? In January, 1990, a federal judge ruled that people have a right to beg. ''The true test of one's commitment to constitutional principles,'' the judge wrote, ''is the extent to which recognition is given to the rights of those in our midst who are the least affluent, least powerful, and least welcome.'' He argued that begging is informative and persuasive speech.

In May of the same year, another federal court disagreed. It ruled that begging is not a constitutionally protected right, and upheld the power of the Metropolitan Transportation Authority of New York to bar panhandlers from the subways. The judge writing the majority opinion said, ''Whether intended as so or not, begging in the subway often amounts to nothing less than assault, creating in the passengers the apprehension of imminent danger.''

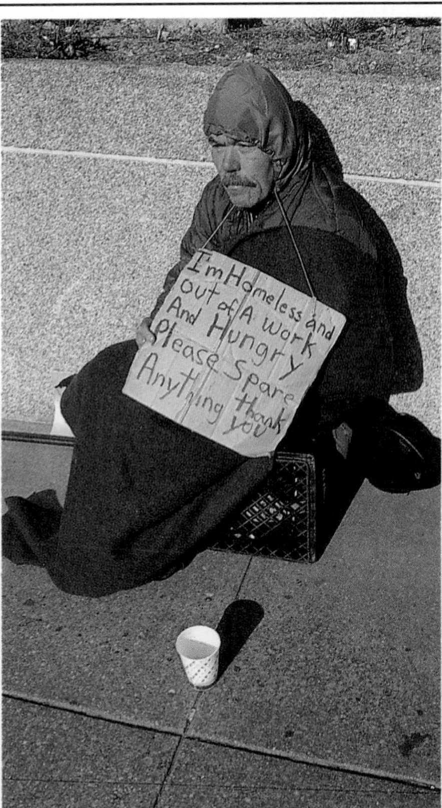

Opponents of begging argue that beggars have become bullies, that panhandlers are often frightening and aggressive. These opponents say that people who work hard for a living, often at low-paying, unpleasant jobs, have the right to be left alone by panhandlers. Beggars disrupt their lives, interfere with their right to privacy, and sometimes harass or scare them into giving money.

Advocates for the beggars say that by silencing the needy, the government would cut off their most effective means of communication. They argue that those frightened or frustrated by the panhandlers should be reminded that silencing a plea for help does nothing to satisfy or eliminate the desperate need for it. They argue that people beg when they are desperate. They have a right to speak and others have the duty to listen.

Panhandling has not historically been protected by the First Amendment, but rather has been regulated, monitored, and sometimes prohibited. Half of the states currently have statutes that limit or ban begging.

THINK ABOUT IT

1. Do you think people should have the right to beg?
2. What restrictions, if any, do you think should be placed on panhandlers?
3. At what point do you think begging becomes harassment?

discussing it: What do you think it means? What do you think may have prompted Holmes to make this statement? To what degree does this kind of restriction limit your right to free speech?

Cooperative Learning
Have a volunteer read aloud the quotation from Justice Hugo Black. Then divide the students into groups to discuss the quotation. Ask the members of each group to paraphrase the sentences, and then have the different groups compare and discuss their paraphrased sentences.

Comprehension
Let volunteers explain the differences between espionage, sabotage, and treason. Why is the government allowed to pass laws against these kinds of activities?

Vocabulary
Ask volunteers to look up and read aloud the definitions of *false, scandalous,* and *malicious.* How do these definitions help you understand what kind of criticism was illegal—and what kind was legal—under the Alien and Sedition Acts?

FYI

In their quest to define and defend free expression, the Supreme Court has dealt with a full spectrum of issues.

When it comes to obscenity, the Court ruled in *Young* v. *American Mini Theatres* that cities may regulate where adult theaters may be located without violating free speech. However, when a town tried to ban nude dancing in an adult book store, the Court said in *Schad* v. *Borough of Mt. Ephraim* that, "Entertainment . . . is protected by the Constitution," and "nude dancing is not without its First Amendment protections . . ." That was in 1981.

In June of 1991, the Supreme Court again waltzed with the constitutionality of nude dancing. Voting 5-4, the Court said laws requiring dancers to wear minimal clothing do not violate First Amendment protections. A South Bend, Indiana law required that dancers wear at least minimal covering. Chief Justice Rehnquist, writing for the Court, said the law "furthers a substantial government interest in protecting order and morality." Justice Souter, who joined the majority, said the ban on nudity was justified because it prevented "secondary effects" such as prostitution.

Symbolic speech involves nonverbal expressions using symbols. Picketing in a labor dispute, or wearing a black armband in protest of a government policy are fairly common examples. During the Vietnam War in the late 1960s and early 1970s, protesters often invoked symbolic speech by burning their draft cards (notices sent to them by the federal government confirming that they were available to be called for military service) to express their opposition to the war. The Supreme Court has given symbolic speech substantial protection. It has ruled, however, that some forms of symbolic speech are not protected under the First Amendment.

Limits Placed on Free Speech

Although Americans have the right to free speech, the Court has also ruled that there are instances when some speech goes too far. Public order must also be considered. Justice Oliver Wendell Holmes argued that "the most stringent protection of free speech would not protect a man in falsely shouting *fire* in a crowded theater."

Supreme Court justices have had different philosophies about what the Constitution means when it says, "Congress shall make no law. . . ." Some Justices have argued that the phrase should be taken literally. Supreme Court Justice Hugo Black observed in 1941 that:

> Freedom to speak and write about public questions is as important to the life of our government as is the heart of the human body. In fact, this privilege is the heart of our government! If that heart be weakened, the result is debilitation [lack of strength]; if it be stilled, the result is death.

Throughout our history, however, most justices of the Supreme Court have taken a more moderate position, arguing that the rights of free speech must be balanced against the need to keep order and preserve the government.

Early Restrictions on Expression At times in our nation's history, there have been individuals who have not supported our form of democratic government. Our government, however, has established a fine line between legitimate criticism and expression of ideas that may seriously harm society. Clearly, government may pass laws against violence, espionage, sabotage, and treason. **Espionage** is the practice of spying for a foreign power. **Sabotage** involves actions normally intended to hinder or damage the nation's defense or war effort. **Treason** is specifically defined in the Constitution as levying war against or adhering (remaining loyal) to enemies of the United States (Article III, Section 3).

But what about **seditious speech,** which urges resistance to lawful authority or advocates overthrowing the government?

Sedition Acts As early as 1798, Congress took steps to curb seditious speech when it passed the Alien and Sedition Acts, which made it a crime to utter "any false, scandalous, and malicious" criticism against the government. The acts were considered unconstitutional by

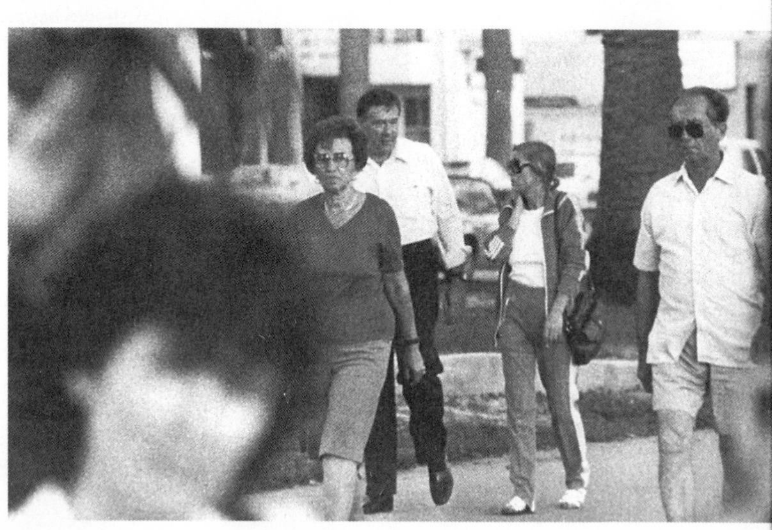

This FBI surveillance photo shows former FBI Agent Richard Miller (wearing white shirt with dark pants) walking with Svetlana Ogorodnikov (wearing jogging suit with sunglasses) in Santa Monica, California. In 1985, Miller was charged with conspiring to sell classified government information to Ogorodnikov, a suspected Soviet spy. What is the name of the crime Miller was accused of?

Caption Answer Miller was accused of espionage, the practice of spying for a foreign power.

Comprehension
Check the students' comprehension by asking these questions: What kind of activity does the Smith Act forbid? What legal means are available for facilitating the "overthrow" of the government?

This case is excerpted in the *West's American Government Handbook of Selected Court Cases.*

Enrichment
Ask two or three volunteers to work together in researching the investigations and hearings led by Senator Joseph McCarthy during this period: What motivated McCarthy? Why were so many people willing to accept his views? What effects did his investigations have? How and under what conditions was his work discredited? Ask the volunteers to present their findings in a short report to the rest of the class.

Cooperative Learning
Let the students divide into groups, and have the groups discuss the implications of *Brandenburg* v. *Ohio*. Ask the members of each group to list examples of specific actions and speeches that would be legal, and other examples that would be illegal. Encourage the groups to compare and discuss their lists.

Reteaching Strategies
1. Encourage the students to work with partners or in small groups to review the notes they have taken on Section 3. Have them refer to the text to clarify any misunderstandings; let individuals revise and rework their notes as necessary.
2. Have the students bring in newspaper clippings about speeches or about activities that can be considered speech: What kind of speech is involved in each example? How is that kind of speech protected?

Evaluation Strategies
1. Have the students write their answers to the Section 3 Review questions.
2. Have the students take the Section 3 Quiz found in the *TRB.*

Section 3 Review (Answers)
1. When the speech or press activities concern ideas that are unpopular or different.
2. Freedom of speech is a critical part of the underlying philosophy of what democracy means in America.
3. Pure speech is the peaceful expression of thoughts, ideas, or opinions before a willing audience, and is generally protected under the First Amendment. Speech plus is verbal expression combined with some sort of action, such as demonstrating, and may be subject to some government restrictions. Symbolic speech involves nonverbal expressions using symbols and has generally been protected under the First Amendment with some restrictions.
4. Answers will vary, e.g., the Alien and Sedition Acts would not be accepted today because the American public is very protective of their First Amendment rights.

many, but were never tested in the courts. Under these acts, several dozen individuals were prosecuted and some were actually convicted. In 1801, President Thomas Jefferson pardoned those sentenced under the acts, and Congress soon repealed them.

Congress passed another sedition law during World War I as part of the Espionage Act of 1917. The law made it a crime to "willfully utter, print, write, or publish any disloyal, profane, scurrilous [insulting], or abusive language" about the government. More than two thousand persons were tried and convicted under this act, which was terminated at the end of World War I.

In 1940, Congress passed the Smith Act, which forbade people from advocating the violent overthrow of the United States government. The Supreme Court first upheld the constitutionality of the Smith Act in *Dennis* v. *United States* (1951), in which eleven top leaders of the Communist Party had been accused and convicted of this activity. The Court found that their activities went beyond the permissible line of exercising individual rights of peaceful advocacy of change. According to the Smith Act, these activities threatened society's right to a certain national security. Two justices on the court, Justices Black and Douglas, dissented strongly from the majority opinion. Justice Black closed his dissenting opinion with the observation that:

> Public opinion being what it now is, few will protest the conviction of these Communist petitioners. There is hope, however, that in calmer times, when present pressures, passions and fears subside, this or some later Court will restore the First Amendment liberties to the high preferred place where they belong in a free society.

The statement proved to be correct as both an analysis and a prophecy. By 1957, federal authorities had obtained 145 indictments and 89 convictions under the Smith Act. But that same year the Court significantly modified its position. In *Yates* v. *United States* the Court established a legal distinction between the statement of a philosophical belief and the advocacy of an illegal action. It held that merely advocating the overthrow of the government cannot be made illegal. It would have to be shown that individuals actually intended, now or in the future, to overthrow the government by force and violence, or to persuade others to do so. In *Brandenburg* v. *Ohio* (1969), the Court ruled that advocating the use of force may *not* be forbidden "except where such advocacy is directed to inciting or producing *imminent* [immediate] lawless action and is likely to produce such action."

By the 1960s the court had so narrowed the interpretation of the Smith Act that it is no longer used to prosecute dissenters. The Court has since defined seditious speech to mean only the advocacy of immediate and concrete acts of violence against the government.

Section 3 Review

1. When do the rights of free speech and free press become especially challenging to apply?
2. Why is free speech important in a democracy?
3. What are the three types of speech and to what extent is each type protected by the First Amendment?
4. **For critical analysis:** Do you think the American public today would accept the Alien and Sedition Acts of 1798? Explain your answer.

Section 4

Freedom of Speech: The Press

Preview Questions

- Under what situations can speech be limited?
- What is meant by prior restraint?
- How does the First Amendment apply to films and other media?
- What speech is not protected?

The framers of the Constitution believed that the press should be free to publish a wide range of opinions and information. They believed that the liberties relating to freedom of speech should be extended to the press.

Guidelines Used in Free-Speech Cases

Over the years the court has developed guidelines or doctrines to use in deciding cases concerning freedom of speech and press. A **doctrine** is a theory or set of principles presented to support a belief.

Clear and Present Danger One guideline the Court has used resulted from a case in 1919, *Schenck* v. *United States.* Charles T. Schenck was convicted of printing and distributing leaflets urging men to resist the draft during World War I. The government claimed his actions violated the Espionage Act of 1917, which made it a crime to encourage disloyalty to the government or resistance to the draft.

SECTION 4

Points to Stress

- Situations under which speech can be limited.
- The definition of prior restraint.
- First Amendment rights as they apply to films and other media.
- Speech that is not protected.

Kickoff Activity

Ask the students to list at least five words or phrases that come to mind when people talk about the press. After all the students have completed their lists, encourage volunteers to read theirs aloud. What attitudes toward the press are indicated in these lists?

Working with the Preview Questions

Have volunteers read the study questions aloud, and encourage the students to discuss what they already know in response to these questions. Then explain that the students will be expected to answer these questions when they finish studying Section 4.

Teaching Strategies

Introduction

Ask a volunteer to read the brief section introduction aloud. Then encourage the students to discuss it: What was the press when the Constitution was framed? How has it changed since then? How do you think the Constitution affects the modern press?

Vocabulary

Ask the students to offer and discuss other examples of doctrines.

Discussion Starter

Encourage the students to identify and discuss specific examples of censorship.

Enrichment

Have all the students read about the uses of prior restraint during wartime. Each student should focus on the Gulf War in 1991, the invasion of Panama, or the invasion of Granada: Was prior restraint used? If so, how and with what intent? Then encourage the students to compare and discuss their findings.

Caption Answer Prior restraint is the stopping of an activity before it actually happens. In this case, prior restraint involves a form of censorship prior to publication.

This case is excerpted in the *West's American Government Handbook of Selected Court Cases.*

The Supreme Court upheld both the law and the convictions. Justice Holmes, speaking for the Court, stated:

> Words can be weapons . . . The question in every case is whether the words are used in such circumstances and are of such a nature as to create a *clear and present danger* that they will bring about the substantive evils that Congress has a right to prevent. It is a question of proximity [closeness] and degree.

Thus according to the **clear and present danger rule,** government should be allowed to restrain speech only when speech clearly presents an immediate threat to public order. It is often hard to say when speech crosses the line between being merely controversial and being a "clear and present danger," but the principle has been used in many cases since.

The clear and present danger principle seemed too permissive to some Supreme Court justices. Several years after the *Schenck* ruling, in the case of *Gitlow* v. *New York* (1925), the Court held that speech could be permissibly curtailed even if it had only a *tendency* to lead to illegal action. Since the 1920s, however, this guideline, known as the **bad-tendency rule,** has generally not been supported by the Supreme Court.

▲ Daniel Ellsberg (shown above) was one of thirty-six researchers to work on a Pentagon study of the War in Vietnam. In 1971, he released portions of this study to the *New York Times.* When the government tried to block publication of the study, saying that it threatened national security, the Supreme Court overruled the use of prior restraint in this case. What does prior restraint mean?

The Preferred-Position Doctrine Another guideline, called the **preferred-position doctrine,** states that freedom of speech is so essential to a democracy that it holds a preferred position. According to this doctrine, established by Justice Hugo Black in the 1940s, any law that limits this freedom should be presumed unconstitutional unless the government can show that the law is absolutely necessary. Freedom of speech should rarely, if ever, be diminished, because printed and spoken words are the prime tools of the democratic process.

Prior Restraint **Prior restraint** means stopping an activity before it actually happens. With respect to freedom of speech, prior restraint involves **censorship,** which occurs when an official removes objectionable material from an item before it is published or broadcast. An example of censorship and prior restraint would be a court ruling that two paragraphs in an upcoming article in the local newspaper had to be removed before the article could be published. The Supreme Court has generally ruled against prior restraint, arguing that governments cannot try to curb ideas *before* they are expressed.

A case involving this issue was *Near* v. *Minnesota* (1931). A newspaper in Minneapolis, Minnesota, had published charges of local corruption, calling officials "gangsters" and other ugly names. The State of Minnesota closed the paper down. The Supreme Court held that the constitutional guarantee of freedom of press does not allow this kind of prior restraint on a publication. Prior restraint can only be allowed in extreme cases, such as during wartime, or when a publication is obscene or incites readers to violence.

The ban against prior restraint was reaffirmed in *New York Times* v. *United States* (1971), also called the Pentagon Papers Case. The *Times* was about to publish the *Pentagon Papers,* an elaborate secret history of the United States government involvement in the Vietnam War, which had been obtained by a disillusioned former Pentagon official. The government wanted a court order to bar publication of this series, arguing that national security was being threatened and that the documents had been stolen. The *Times* argued that the public had the right to know about the information contained in the papers, and the press had the right to inform them. The Court rejected the government's plea to bar publication, holding that the government had not proven that printing the documents would in fact endanger national security.

Cooperative Learning
Let the students form groups in which to discuss the rights of students below college level: Do they have fewer rights than adults? What specific rights are denied to students? Why do you think these rights are denied? What specific rights are denied to students at your school? How do you feel about these restrictions? Encourage the members of each group to share and defend varying points of view.

Discussion Starter
Ask the students to recall and discuss recent cases in which reporters have tried to protect their confidential sources. (If no cases have been in the news recently, let several volunteers research interesting cases and present the facts of each to the class.) Whom did the reporter try to protect? Why? Was the reporter successful in protecting that source? Why or why not? What do you think of the reporter's stand? Is it legal? Whose interests does it serve?

Enrichment
Encourage students who are interested in the issue of reporters' confidentiality to read about the Woodward and Bernstein investigation of Watergate: What sources did they use? Who could have been their secret source, "Deep Throat"? Why do you think Woodward and Bernstein were never forced to reveal the identity of that source? Give the students who complete this research an opportunity to share and discuss their ideas with one another.

Critical Thinking Skills
Guide the students in analyzing the shield laws and their limitations: Should reporters enjoy rights not granted to other citizens? Why or why not? Whose interests are served by allowing reporters to keep their sources secret? Whose interests are served by insisting that reporters reveal their sources?

Discussion Starter
Ask several students to share their responses to the question posed at the beginning of Freedom of the Press and Fair Trial: Where should the line be drawn? Why is this such a difficult question to answer?

Critical Thinking Skills
Help the students analyze the issues in the reversal of Shepard's conviction: Who was responsible for the "circus"? What part did the press play in creating that circus atmosphere?

On some occasions, however, the Court has allowed prior restraints. In 1988, in *Hazelwood School District* v. *Kuhlmeier,* the Court, noting that students below college level have fewer rights than adults, ruled that high school administrators *can* censor school publications. It ruled that school newspapers are part of the school curriculum, not a public forum. Therefore, administrators have the right to censor speech that promotes "conduct inconsistent with the shared values of the civilized social order."

Confidentiality

Once in a while, a reporter has information that may provide essential evidence in a trial, but reporters want to protect the identities of the people and places the evidence came from. Many reporters argue that if they reveal their sources, their informants will no longer trust them and will not give them the information they need in order to keep the public informed. After all, they argue, much of what is said to them is said in the confidence that the people talking will not be named. State and federal courts have generally rejected this argument, and more than one reporter has gone to jail because she or he refused to reveal the sources of a story.

The Supreme Court held in *Branzburg* v. *Hayes* (1972) that reporters have no constitutional right to withhold information from a court. In the case, a reporter had been allowed to view individuals making hashish from marijuana if he promised to keep their names confidential. He kept his promise and refused to give the names to a grand jury.[1] The Court ruled that *anyone* would have to give such information in a case if called upon to do so. The same rule applies to the news media. If special exemptions are to be given, the Court said, they must come from Congress and the state legislatures.

In response, more than half of the states now have **shield laws** to protect reporters' notes and information from being revealed in court. For the most part, however, reporters have no more right to avoid presenting evidence than do other citizens.

Freedom of the Press and Fair Trial

Where is the line drawn between the right of a free press to comment about and criticize criminal cases, and the duty of the judiciary to ensure a fair trial? The Court has tried to balance suspects' rights with the rights of the press and the public to know.

Sidney Harris

This issue surfaced in 1954 when Dr. Samuel H. Sheppard was convicted of murdering his wife. He appealed his conviction to the Supreme Court, arguing that during pre-trial media coverage, so many lurid details about his life and behavior had circulated that it was impossible for him to have a fair trial. Finally, in 1966, the Supreme Court agreed, claiming that the press had created a virtual "circus," and reversed Sheppard's conviction.

In the 1970s, judges increasingly issued **gag orders,** which restrict publicity about a trial in progress or even a pre-trial hearing. (A pre-trial hearing is not a trial, but rather a preliminary examination by a judge to determine whether there is enough evidence to hold a person accused of a crime.) In 1976 a man was tried and charged with murdering six members of a neighboring family. A judge issued an order prohibiting the press from reporting information about the pre-trial hearing. The Supreme Court ruled against the judge's gag order, stating that it had violated the First Amendment and was unconstitutional prior restraint.

The Supreme Court ruled in *Gannet Company* v. *De Pasquale* (1979), that both the press and the public *can*

1. A grand jury consists of twelve to twenty-three persons who inquire into supposed violations of the law, in order to determine whether the evidence is sufficient to warrant a trial. (See Chapter 23.)

TEACHING BUILDING SOCIAL STUDIES SKILLS

Read
Introduce this section by letting the students discuss their own newspaper reading habits: How often do you read the paper? Which sections do you usually read? What questions—if any—do you ask yourself as you read? Do you consider reading news stories and editorials one of your responsibilities as a citizen? Why or why not? After the discussion, ask volunteers to read the Building Social Studies Skills text aloud to the rest of the class.

Discuss
Help the students discuss what has been read: How can you identify evidence? What are some examples of evidence supporting the statement that a certain textbook is harmful to students? What are some examples of generalizations? Should political cartoons be read as editorials or as news stories? Why? Why are news stories supposed to present "just the facts"—not opinions? Do you think it is possible to present only facts? Why or why not?

Analyze and Apply
Have the students work in groups to find news stories and editorials from several different newspapers, all on the same subject. Ask the group members to read all the articles critically, following the suggestions in the text: What differences can you identify between news stories and editorials? What are the differences between the news stories in different newspapers? What are the differences between the editorials in different papers?

Review
Have the students answer these review questions: What is a generalization? Why should you look for specific arguments rather than generalizations? What is the difference between an editorial and a news story?

Practicing Your Skills
In order to further reinforce students' understanding of this material you might ask them to complete the Practicing Your Skills activity as a written homework assignment.

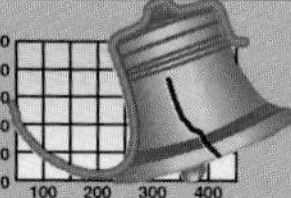

BUILDING SOCIAL STUDIES SKILLS

Reading a Newspaper Article Critically

Newspapers offer detailed information on what is happening all over the world, from Supreme Court cases to events in Eastern Europe to local baseball scores. Newspapers usually present more information about a story than do television or radio reports because they do not have the same constraints. But even newspapers do not have the space to report every detail of every story, nor can they represent all sides of every argument.

When you read newspaper articles, avoid jumping to conclusions. Remember that the article is usually an overview of a situation and may only contain one viewpoint or one aspect of the story. To avoid jumping to conclusions, think about the following as you read an article.

The Evidence A well-presented argument should always be accompanied and reinforced by some evidence. For example, suppose you were to read an article about the need to ban a certain textbook in your school district because the material in the book would be offensive or harmful to students. The article may thoroughly convince you of its viewpoint. But when you reviewed the article, no evidence was given of the actual contents of the book. It may have been that you were convinced only by a good writer's opinion and an emotional argument. Issues demand evidence, so look for it as you read.

Specificity of the Argument Is it possible that what seems like an argument is only a generalization? A **generalization** is an oversimplification that doesn't hold true in every specific case. Many political arguments are reduced to generalizations. For example, you may read an article quoting a politician who states, "Standard test scores continue to fall because of the poor attitudes of high-school-age students." Could it really be true that the attitudes of *all* high-school-age students are poor? Could there possibly be many other reasons for falling test scores that have little to do with students' attitudes?

Alternative Explanations To explain a certain event, an argument may be presented that sounds logically consistent and seems to have evidence to back it up. But other explanations may be equally valid. For example, you may read that stock prices fell yesterday because of a threat of another war in the Middle East. This may be followed by a good explanation with solid evidence that sounds perfectly logical. But there may be hundreds of other reasons why the stock market fell, some of which no one really understands. Just because an argument sounds logical doesn't mean it is wholly true.

Editorials versus News Stories You must always distinguish between an editorial article and a news story. Editorials are typically found in the editorial section of your newspaper, often toward the end of the first section. They present the opinions of the editorial staff of the newspaper. Regular news articles, in principle, report on actual events or on the opinions of the people interviewed. News stories are not supposed to present a point of view, although some do.

As you are aware, newspapers offer more details and substance than do television or radio news stories. By using the guidelines above, you can critically evaluate what you read in newspapers; thus you can make good political decisions based on the accuracy of the information presented. You might also try to adapt these guidelines for other media, so that you can also critically evaluate the news stories you see and hear on television.

PRACTICING YOUR SKILLS

Read one news story about politics and one political editorial. (You can find the latter in the editorial section of your newspaper.) Then compare and contrast the news story with the editorial, asking yourself the following questions:

1. How do the articles use evidence to support the story or issue?
2. If the articles are making arguments one way or another, how specific are the arguments? Where are there generalizations, if any?
3. Are there any alternative explanations for what's being presented?

Discussion Starter
Have the students discuss the Supreme Court's 1915 ruling about movies: Were movies then simply a business? Are they now simply a business? Should movies be treated differently from other forms of business? If so, how? If not, why not?

This case is excerpted in the *West's American Government Handbook of Selected Court Cases.*

Discussion Starter
To stimulate discussion, ask questions such as these: Why do you think Congress prohibited the advertising of cigarettes on radio and television? How effective do you think that advertising ban has been? Why do you think the tobacco industry has not challenged this ban on constitutional grounds?

Comprehension
Ask the students to explain why no person has completely unlimited rights of free speech and free press.

Discussion Starter
Encourage the students to discuss the three-part test for obscenity: How is each part open to interpretation? How helpful do you consider this test?

Enrichment
Let interested students research the details of the 2 Live Crew trials in 1990. Encourage them to present their findings in an original rap (or in a more conventional oral report).

Discussion Starter
Encourage the students to discuss fighting words: What specific phrases or sentences might be considered fighting words? To

Caption Answer Radio and television broadcasting makes use of the airwaves, which are considered public property. Therefore, their use of these airwaves is subject to greater control. As an extension activity, you might have the class debate this topic: Radio and television broadcasters should be no more regulated than print media press.

Cooperative Learning
Let the students form groups in which to read about and discuss the questions of government restrictions on cable television: What are the most recent decisions regarding such restrictions? What arguments can be made for restrictions? What arguments can be made against restrictions? Which arguments do you consider more persuasive? Why?

Discussion Starter
Ask a volunteer to read the quotation from Justice Harry Blackman aloud. Then ask: Do you agree that advertising is dissemination of information? Why or why not? Is there any kind of advertising that cannot—or should not—be considered information? If so, what? What assumptions about consumers are made when advertising is considered the dissemination of information? Do you think those assumptions are justified?

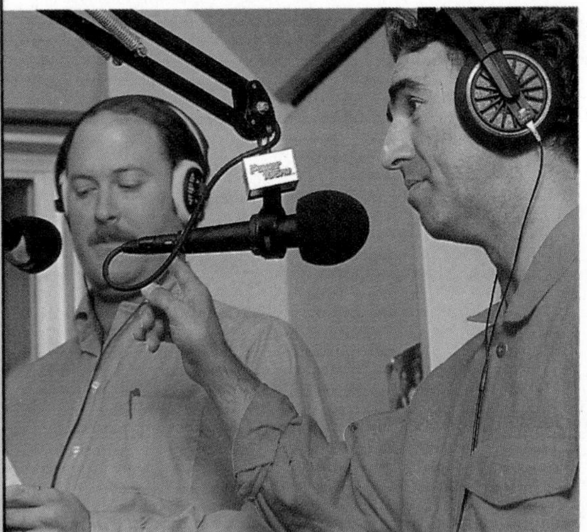

▲ Radio and television broadcasters such as popular Los Angeles disk jockey Jay Thomas (pictured here) are subject to many more restrictions than are newspaper reporters. Why are radio and television broadcasters more regulated than the print media press?

be excluded from hearings if it was likely that publicity would adversely affect the defendant. Then in *Richmond Newspapers, Inc.* v. *Virginia* (1980), the Supreme Court ruled that judges *cannot* close trials without some (*overriding* need).

Film and Other Media

Our founding fathers could not have imagined the many new ways in which information is disseminated (distributed and made public) today. Nevertheless, the Constitution has proved to be flexible enough to respond to these social and technological changes.

The Supreme Court took its first look at motion pictures in the early days of the movie industry. In 1915 a state law in Ohio barred the showing of any film that was not of "moral, educational, or harmless and amusing character." The Court upheld the Ohio law, ruling that movies were a business, "pure and simple," and *not* part of the press in this country. It said that freedom of press protections did not apply to the movies.

Almost forty years later, the Court reversed itself in *Burstyn* v. *Wilson* (1952). The city of New York had banned a movie from being shown because it was thought to be "sacrilegious." In this case the Supreme Court found that expression by means of motion pictures *is* included within the free speech and free press guarantees.

According to the Court, however, not all censorship of films is unconstitutional. *Teitel Film Corporation* v. *Cusack* (1968), established that a state or local government can ban a movie after proving at a judicial hearing that the film is obscene. Today, most audiences generally rely on the motion picture's own rating system to determine the appropriateness of each film. These are the ratings posted along with the movie such as G, PG, PG–13, etc.

Radio and television broadcasting are subject to many regulations because they use electromagnetic airways, which are considered public property. Access to these airways can be gained only through a license issued by the Federal Communications Commission (FCC), which also has the authority to regulate, penalize, and revoke such licenses. The Supreme Court has regularly rejected the argument that the First Amendment prohibits such regulation by the FCC.

The Supreme Court has given the growing cable television industry broader First Amendment freedoms than it has to traditional television. In *Wilkinson* v. *Jones* (1987), the Court ruled that the states cannot regulate "indecent" cable programming. It struck down a state law in Utah that prohibited cable broadcast of any sexually explicit or other "indecent material" between 7 A.M. and midnight each day. The Court's argument was in part that cable does not use public property (i.e., airwaves) to broadcast its material.

The transmission of TV broadcasts via satellite, however, continues to come under close scrutiny. In the early 1990s a number of small satellite broadcasting companies were sued by state governments because of the sexually explicit programs that were picked up in neighboring states. The constitutionality of the resulting restrictions on such companies has yet to be tested.

Advertising

Can advertisers use their First Amendment rights to prevent restrictions on the content of their advertising, otherwise known as **commercial speech**? Until the 1970s the Supreme Court said that advertising was not protected under the First Amendment. Then in *Bigelow* v. *Virginia* (1975), the Supreme Court said that a state law that prohibited the newspaper advertising of abortion services was unconstitutional. In 1976 it struck down another state law that forbade the advertising of prescription drug prices. According to Justice Harry Blackmun, "Advertising, however tasteless and excessive it sometimes may seem, is nonetheless dissemination of information as to who is producing and selling what product for what reason and at what price." Blackmun concluded that consumers are entitled to the "free flow of commercial information."

what extent does the definition of fighting words depend upon the circumstances in which they are uttered?

Reteaching Strategies

1. Work with small groups of students, guiding them in their responses to these questions: What is the press? What is freedom of the press? How can freedom of the press interfere with the right to a fair trial? What forms of speech are not protected? Why not?

2. Let students work with partners to write short paragraphs in response to this question: Do reporters usually have the right to protect their confidential sources? Why or why not?

Evaluation Strategies

1. Have the students write their responses to the Working with the Preview Questions at the beginning of the section.

2. Ask the students to write paragraphs in response to this question: Is censorship a violation of free speech? Why or why not?

3. Have the students write their answers to the Section 4 Review questions.

4. Have the students take the Section 4 Quiz found in the *TRB.*

This case is excerpted in the *West's American Government Handbook of Selected Court Cases.*

Section 4 Review (Answers)

1. According to the clear and present danger rule, government should be allowed to restrain speech only when speech clearly represents an immediate threat to public order. The preferred position doctrine states that freedom of speech is so essential to democracy that it holds a preferred position and limits on speech should be allowed only if it can be shown to be absolutely necessary.

2. Commercial speech is advertising and is protected unless it is false, misleading, or advertising illegal goods and services.

3. Libel, slander, obscenity, and "fighting words."

4. Libel is a published report of falsehoods that tend to injure a person's reputation. Slander is a public uttering.

5. Answers will vary. The entertainment industry will probably use the standards of communities with the largest number of people as standard measurements.

The government does, however, prohibit false and misleading advertisements as well as the advertising of illegal goods and services. The federal government has even forbidden the advertising of certain legally sold products. For example, in 1970 Congress prohibited the advertising of cigarettes on radio and television. The tobacco industry did not challenge the constitutionality of this action.

Unprotected Speech—Libel, Slander, Obscenity, and "Fighting Words"

Just because you have the right to free speech, does that mean you can say anything you want about anybody or anything at any time? Not exactly. *Not* all forms of expression are protected by the Constitution, and no person has unlimited rights to free speech and free press. Many reasonable restrictions have been placed upon these freedoms. For example, no person has the right to libel or slander another. **Libel** is a published report of falsehoods that tends to injure a person's reputation or character. **Slander** is the public utterance (speaking) of a statement that holds a person up for contempt, ridicule, or hatred. To prove libel and slander, however, certain criteria must be met. The statements made must be untrue, must include intent to do harm, and actual harm must have occurred. The Court has ruled, for example, that public officials cannot collect damages for remarks made against them unless they can prove the remarks were made with "reckless" disregard for accuracy.

Obscenity is another form of speech that is not protected under the First Amendment. Although the dictionary defines it as that which is offensive and indecent, what obscenity is exactly is hard to define. Supreme Court Justice Potter Stewart once said, "I know it when I see it." One problem in defining obscenity is that what is obscene to one person is realistic to another; what one reader considers indecent another reader sees as "colorful." Another problem is that even if a definition were agreed upon, it would change with the times. Major literary works of such great writers as D. H. Lawrence, Mark Twain, and James Joyce were once considered obscene in most of the United States.

After many unsuccessful attempts to define obscenity, the Supreme Court came up with a three-part test in *Miller* v. *California* (1973). It decided that a book, film, or other piece of material is legally obscene if:

1. The average person applying contemporary [present-day] standards finds that the work taken as a whole appeals to the prurient interest—that is, tends to excite unwholesome sexual desire.
2. The work depicts or describes, in a patently [obviously] offensive way, a form of sexual conduct specifically prohibited by an antiobscenity law.
3. The work taken as a whole lacks serious literary, artistic, political, or scientific value.

The very fact that the Supreme Court has had to set up such a complicated test shows how difficult it is to define obscenity. The Court went on to state, in effect, that local communities should be allowed to set their own standards for what is obscene. What is obscene to many people in one area of the country might be perfectly acceptable to those in another area.

One famous case in 1990 that illustrated this issue involved the group 2 Live Crew, a rap music group whose songs contained explicitly sexual lyrics. The group was arrested by sheriff's deputies when it made an appearance at a nightclub in Broward County, Florida. At the same time, a record store owner was arrested for selling 2 Live Crew's albums in violation of the obscenity law. A federal judge upheld the law that the local Broward County sheriff invoked in attempting to prevent the sale of the group's rap albums. Ironically, at two separate trials, 2 Live Crew was acquitted while the record store owner was found guilty.

Another form of speech that is not protected by the First Amendment is what the Supreme Court has called **"fighting words."** This is speech that is so inflammatory that it will provoke the average listener to violence. The Court has ruled that fighting words must go beyond merely insulting or controversial language. The words must be a clear invitation to immediate violence or breach of peace.

Section 4 Review

1. What are some of the guidelines the Supreme Court has developed to help it decide what is protected as free expression?
2. How does commercial speech differ from any other type of speech?
3. What kinds of speech are not protected by the First Amendment?
4. What is the difference between libel and slander?
5. **For critical analysis:** Allowing each community to decide what is and is not obscene leads to diversity in obscenity laws. How do you think this diversity affects the entertainment industry?

SECTION 5

Points to Stress

- The importance of the rights to petition and assemble in a democracy.
- The reason for limits that are placed on the rights to petition and assemble.
- The types of limits placed on these rights.

Kickoff Activity

Write these terms on the chalkboard: *freedom of assembly, freedom of petition.* Ask the students to write their own definitions of the two terms. Then let several volunteers read their definitions aloud.

Working with the Preview Questions

Let the students read these study questions to themselves and consider how the questions could be used in planning an outline of the section. Ask a volunteer to write the main headings of the outline on the chalkboard; have other students suggest revisions, if necessary. Then have the students outline Section 5 as they read it, using the main headings from the board.

Teaching Strategies

Introduction

Let volunteers read the section introduction aloud, and focus the students' attention on the influence a group of citizens, working together, can exert: What school groups or community groups have been organized around specific issues? What influence have those groups had over the pertinent decision-making process? How did working as a group increase the influence of concerned individuals?

Cooperative Learning

Let the students form groups in which to discuss the right to assembly. Have the members of each group define a specific situation in which a group of people is peaceably assembled. Then have group members suggest specific changes of time, place, and manner that would render that same assembly illegal. Encourage the groups to explore at least five different changes of circumstances.

This case is excerpted in the *West's American Government Handbook of Selected Court Cases.*

Comprehension

Guide the students in discussing the facts presented here about Irving Feiner: At what point did he violate the rights of others? Why do you think he was charged with disturbing the peace—rather than with some other offense? Why do you think the Court upheld his conviction?

Discussion Starter

Encourage the students to consider and discuss the precedent set by *Feiner* v. *New York:* Whose rights are given precedence by this decision? What power does this decision give to the police? What individuals or groups might object to the police's holding such power? Why?

SECTION 5

Freedom of Assembly and Petition

Preview Questions

- Why is freedom of assembly and petition important in a democracy?
- Why are there limits placed on the freedoms of assembly and petition?
- What are these limits?

It would be impossible to guarantee free speech in a democracy if people were not given the right to assembly and to publicly express their beliefs. An assembly is usually a group of people who gather together for a specific purpose. People, acting as a group, are often more successful in getting their ideas heard than they are acting individually. They are more likely to influence government policies and actions if they organize and collectively display their feelings. Consider, for example, twenty students who each thinks that the school library should have more books. If they act individually, they can talk to their friends, write letters to their principal, and tell their parents. But what if they join together and form "The Committee for School Library Improvement," and create a weekly newsletter, which they distribute to all the parents and school administrators? Certainly, acting as a group, the twenty students have a better chance of improving the library than if they had just acted as individuals.

The Constitution protects the right of people to assemble, or organize, to influence public policy. It also protects their right to petition, to express their views to public officials in the forms of petitions, letters, signs in a parade, or marches on a picketing line.

In 1937, the Supreme Court first ruled on the right to assembly in *De Jonge* v. *Oregon.* De Jonge had been convicted for conducting a public meeting sponsored by the Communist Party. The Supreme Court overturned his conviction, saying that under the First Amendment, "peaceable assembly for lawful discussion cannot be made a crime." The Supreme Court stated the rights of free speech, free press, and free assembly represent the "security of the republic." The case established that the right of assembly was of equal status as the rights of free speech and free press. It also established that the right of assembly was protected by the due process clause of the Fourteenth Amendment.

Limits Placed on Freedom of Assembly

To what extent can demonstrators be regulated? When, in the name of public peace, does the right to assembly end? The Constitution protects the right to assembly as long as it is *peaceable.* It does not give people the right to riot, to incite violence, to block public streets, or to endanger life, property, or public order. The Court has generally agreed that it is reasonable to make and enforce rules covering the time, place, and manner of assemblies. These rules can specify when and where assembly may take place.

Demonstrations are intended to bring issues to public attention. This means that they usually happen in highly visible public places. The more people who see and hear the demonstration, the better it is for the cause. Groups protesting the federal government's cleanup policies on nuclear waste do not demonstrate in someone's backyard. They choose public places, such as a park in New York City.

The need for public exposure also means there is a good chance that the demonstration will interfere with other citizens' rights to use the same places. There is also a good chance of conflict; because most demonstrations are held to protest something, there are usually plenty of people around who support the other side of the issue and may be upset by the demonstration. Therefore, the Supreme Court has often upheld state and local laws that require demonstrators to give advance notice and to obtain permits.

An early case for placing limits on assembly was *Cox* v. *New Hampshire* (1941). Cox was a member of a group that violated a law requiring a permit for a parade. The Supreme Court voted unanimously to uphold the permit law as constitutional, and rejected Cox's argument that the law violated his rights of free speech and assembly.

In 1950, a speaker named Irving Feiner was addressing an outdoor public meeting, inviting the audience to attend a meeting of the Progressive Party. During the speech, he criticized President Truman, the American Legion, and the mayor of Syracuse. He also urged African Americans to fight for civil rights. Feiner's remarks angered the crowd, almost to the point of rioting. He ignored police requests to stop and was arrested and convicted of disturbing the peace. In *Feiner* v. *New York* (1951) the Supreme Court upheld his conviction for unlawful assembly. It concluded that the police had not acted to suppress his speech, but rather had acted to preserve public order. The case set a precedent that police *may* break up assemblies to preserve peace.

Extension
Ask interested students to organize and present a debate on this question: Should members of the American Nazi Party be permitted to demonstrate in an area where their views will clearly be considered particularly offensive?

Discussion Starter
Ask the students to recall and discuss recent cases of picketing in or near their community: Who was picketing? What was the purpose of the picketing? What effects did it appear to have? What other issues—if any—did the picketing raise? How were those issues resolved?

Enrichment
Let a group of interested volunteers research the Taft-Hartly Act (more formally called the Labor-Management Relations Act). Have the volunteers work together to prepare and present a chart showing the regulations imposed by the act.

Reteaching Strategies
1. Have the students work with partners to review and revise their outlines of Section 5. Encourage them to refer to the text and to make any changes necessary.
2. Meet with small groups of students to discuss responses to these questions: Why is the difference between an individual citizen and a group of citizens important? How are the rights of individuals different from the rights of groups?

Evaluation Strategies
1. Have the students write their answers to the Section 5 Review questions.
2. Have the students take the Section 5 Quiz found in the *TRB*.

Limits on when and where an assembly may take place were tested in 1977 when the American Nazi Party decided to hold a rally and march through the Chicago suburb of Skokie, Illinois. Citizens and city officials objected because about one-half of the residents were Jewish and about 10 percent were survivors or relatives of people who died at the hands of Nazis in German death camps in World War II. They felt the march would cause pain to these people and could lead to violence and rioting.

Skokie's city government required the Nazis to post a $300,000 bond in order to obtain a parade permit. The Nazis claimed that the high-priced bond was set in order to prevent their march and infringed on their freedoms of speech and assembly. The American Civil Liberties Union (ACLU), an organization that negotiates many cases in which such freedoms are in question, defended the Nazis' claim and supported their right to march. The ACLU claimed that the Nazis had the right to hold their march and rally even though many disliked what they said and did.

Opponents said that allowing the group to march was not guaranteeing liberty, but license, or the irresponsible use of freedoms. They also quoted Justice Holmes when he said, "The most stringent protection of free speech would not protect a man falsely shouting *fire* in a theater and causing panic."

A federal district court ruled that the city of Skokie had violated the Nazis' First Amendment rights, and the Supreme Court let the lower court's ruling stand. As it turned out, the Nazis never did march in Skokie. Chicago loosened its parade requirements, and the Nazis settled for a couple of poorly attended demonstrations there.

Picketing

Picketing occurs when striking workers patrol a place of business, usually carrying signs protesting the business's policy, and asking workers and the public not to enter the place. The question of how much protection picketers should have under the First Amendment frequently has been debated. Because picketers gather and picketing conveys a message to the public, it is a form of both speech and assembly. Unlike other forms of demonstrations, however, it aims to persuade workers and customers not to deal with a business until the picketers' conditions are met. It can be a strong labor weapon that raises questions about its constitutionality.

In 1940, in *Thornhill* v. *Alabama*, the Supreme Court ruled that peaceful picketing is a form of free speech protected by the First Amendment. Since the *Thornhill* decision, however, the Court has ruled in a number of cases that labor picketing may be regulated under various national and state laws. The Taft-Hartley Act of 1947, for example, put some restrictions on the right to strike and the right to organize workers. It forbids picketing for such purposes as forcing employees to recognize a union other than the one already lawfully recognized. For example, if the Teamsters already represent the workers, the XYZ Union can't picket to convince employees they should switch unions.

▲ The Constitution guarantees the right of assembly to all groups regardless of whether or not their views are popular. In this photo, Chicago police (in the background) stand by to see that there is no violence at this rally held by members of the Ku Klux Klan. Have any limits been placed on freedom of assembly?

SECTION 5 REVIEW

1. Why is the right to assemble peaceably important in a democracy?
2. What limits may government place on the right to assemble?
3. **For critical analysis:** A 1990 Washington, D.C., rally of fewer than fifty Ku Klux Klansmen required that the D.C. police force spend almost a million dollars on security to prevent violence. Why do you think the government would be willing to spend such sums of money to protect an unpopular group's ability to assemble?

Caption Answer The Constitution protects the right to peaceable assembly. Any assembly that involves rioting, inciting violence, the unlawful blocking of public streets, or endangers life, property, or public order can be stopped. The Court has also agreed it is reasonable to make and enforce rules covering the time, place, and manner of assemblies.

Section 5 Review (Answers)
1. As a group, people are often more successful in getting their ideas heard and are more likely to influence government policies and actions.
2. The Constitution protects peaceable assembly, but does not give people the right to riot, to incite violence, to block public streets, or to endanger life, property, or public order.
3. Answers will vary, e.g., every person has the right to speak freely and assemble peaceably concerning their beliefs. Unpopular or different beliefs often require more protection.

TEACHING CHALLENGE TO THE AMERICAN DREAM

Read
Before the students read this feature, guide them in a short discussion of the American flag: What does it symbolize? What do you think it is intended to mean to citizens? How do you personally feel about the flag? After the discussion, have the students read Challenge to the American Dream to themselves.

Discuss
Encourage the students to discuss the issues raised in this feature: In the Dallas City Hall flag burning, how important is it that no one was physically injured or threatened? How important is it that witnesses were seriously offended? If you had been a witness to that event, how do you think you would have responded? Why? In the Supreme Court dissent, why do you think Chief Justice Rehnquist quoted Justice Holmes? What do you think Holmes' quotation means? How has the Supreme Court changed since 1990? Do you think today's Supreme Court would make the same decision about flag burning? Why or why not?

Analyze and Apply
Ask each student to interview at least five different people (from as many age groups as possible) about the issue of flag burning: Should it be a crime? Why or why not? Then have the students work together to collect their findings, organize them, and present them in a large chart.

Review
Have the students respond to these review questions: Why did the Supreme Court rule unconstitutional the Texas law that made flag burning a crime? What steps do some people want to take to make flag burning a crime?

You Decide (Answers)
1. Answers will vary, e.g., they dissented because they believed that the flag is unique and worthy of special treatment as a symol of the nation.
2. Answers will vary, e.g., no, the flag is the main symbol of the nation and should enjoy special status. No other symbol should be protected because it would become too complicated and too difficult to draw the lines.
3. Answers will vary, e.g., no, wearing a picture of an upside down flag would not be the same as burning. One is disrespect for the symbol while the other is destruction.

CHALLENGE TO THE AMERICAN DREAM

Burning an American Symbol

While the Republican National Convention was taking place in Dallas in 1984, a group of demonstrators dubbed the ''Republican War Chest Tour'' was protesting openly the policies of the president and a number of Dallas-based corporations. The demonstrators marched through the streets, chanting political slogans and stopping at several corporate locations to stage ''die-ins''—spray-painting buildings and potted plants to dramatize the consequences of nuclear war. During the march, one of the participants, Gregory Lee Johnson, accepted an American flag offered to him by a fellow protestor who had removed it from a flagpole outside one of the targeted buildings.

The demonstrations ended in front of Dallas City Hall, where Johnson unfurled the flag, doused it with kerosene, and set it on fire. While the flag burned, the protestors chanted, ''America, the red, white, and blue, we spit on you.'' After the demonstrators dispersed, one of the witnesses collected the flag's remains and buried them in his backyard. No one was physically injured or threatened, but some witnesses had been seriously offended.

Johnson was charged and convicted with desecration of a venerated object (destroying something that is highly respected), a violation of Texas law. The Texas Court of Criminal Appeals reversed the decision, holding that the state, consistent with the First Amendment, could not punish Johnson for burning the flag under these circumstances. The court found that Johnson's burning of the flag was expressive conduct protected by the First Amendment.

The Supreme Court affirmed this judgment. In a 1990 5 to 4 decision, the Court ruled that the defendant could not be convicted under a statute that was aimed at suppressing his free expression, and there was no evidence that his conduct disturbed the peace. The majority of justices found that flag burning is a form of political expression, and pure speech or expression cannot be punished.

Four justices dissented vigorously—Rehnquist, White, O'Connor, and Stevens. Chief Justice Rehnquist claimed that the Court was ignoring Justice Holmes' familiar saying that ''a page of history is worth a volume of logic.'' He wrote that, ''For more than 200 years, the American flag has occupied a unique position as the symbol of the nation, a uniqueness that justifies a governmental prohibition against flag burning. . . .'' He ended his opinion by saying, ''The government may conscript [draft] men into the Armed Forces where they must fight and perhaps die for the flag, but the government may not prohibit the public burning of the banner under which they fight.''

In June of 1990, the Supreme Court ruled that a new federal law making it a crime to burn or deface the American flag violated the free-speech guarantee of the First Amendment. The law was declared unconstitutional on the same grounds the Court used to invalidate the Texas statute.

The decisions provoked almost immediate calls for a constitutional amendment to override them and make it possible to prosecute flag burners. The challenge to the American dream here, according to some, is that the ''Stars and Stripes'' represents all that is good, democratic, and desirable in this country. Therefore, the ability to destroy such a symbol strikes at the very foundations of this nation's greatness.

You Decide

1. Why did the four Supreme Court justices dissent to the constitutional protection of burning the flag?
2. Should the destruction of any other American symbol, such as a replica of the Statue of Liberty, also be protected under the First Amendment? Explain why or why not.
3. Would wearing a picture of the American flag upside down on your tee-shirt be the same thing as burning the flag? Explain.

CHAPTER 5 REVIEW

Key Terms

abridging 103
assembly 103
bad-tendency rule 117
bills of attainder 104
censorship 117
civil liberties 103
clear and present danger rule 117
commercial speech 120
doctrine 116
draft registration 107
due process clause 106
espionage 115
establishment clause 108
ex post facto 104
excessive entanglement theory 110
fighting words 121
free exercise clause 111
gag orders 118
generalization 119
habeas corpus 103
human rights 113
libel 121
obscenity 121
petition 103
picketing 123
preferred-position doctrine 117
prior restraint 117
pure speech 113
released time 109
sabotage 115
seditious speech 115
shield laws 118
slander 121
speech plus 113
symbolic speech 115
treason 115

Summary

1. Although the original Constitution contains a few protections of personal freedoms, the most important ones are provided in the Bill of Rights. The Bill of Rights protects individuals from an overly intrusive government and protects the rights of the minority against the will of the majority. It is the courts, particularly the U.S. Supreme Court, that defines and applies these rights. The Fourteenth Amendment's due process clause ensures that the states carry out these protections.

2. The First Amendment guarantees freedom of religion. It provides for a separation of church and state in the establishment clause. The Supreme Court has drawn lines on the subject of religion in schools in a series of cases whose subjects range from releasing students for religious activities to prayer in public schools. It has generally ruled that public schools cannot sponsor religious activities. The free exercise clause of the First Amendment protects individuals' rights to worship or believe as they see fit, or to hold no religious beliefs at all. The free exercise of religion may be limited if religious activities are in violation of criminal laws. In contrast, the government may not demand that persons perform certain acts, such as saluting the flag, if these acts violate their religious beliefs.

3. The First Amendment also protects freedom of speech. The Supreme Court has distinguished three kinds of speech that are protected under this amendment: pure speech, speech plus, and symbolic speech. The right to free speech is not absolute and is balanced by the government's duty to maintain public order, preserve the government, and ensure fair trials.

4. The extent to which the government can limit free speech is judged on the basis of three principles: the clear and present danger rule, (rarely) the bad-tendency rule, and the preferred-position doctrine. The Supreme Court has generally ruled against prior restraint. Obscenity, libel, slander, and "fighting words" are forms of speech that are not normally protected under the First Amendment.

5. The Constitution protects the right to assembly as long as it is peaceable. The government may, however, impose reasonable restrictions on such activities in the name of public safety. The Court has generally agreed that it is reasonable for government to make and enforce rules regarding time, place, and manner of assemblies. Some forms of labor picketing have been subjected to restrictions, because they aim to persuade workers and customers not to deal with a business until the picketers' conditions are met.

Review Questions

1. What is meant by the concept of civil liberties?
2. What safeguards in the original Constitution protected citizens against an overly powerful government?
3. What is the Bill of Rights and why was it added to the Constitution?
4. What effect has the due process clause of the Fourteenth Amendment had on the Bill of Rights?

Chapter Evaluation

To evaluate student mastery of chapter material, your might:

1. Use Chapter Test A from the *TRB.*

2. Use Chapter Test B from the *TRB.*

3. Construct your own test using items from the *West American Government Test Bank* found in the *TRB.*

4. Use the accompanying computerized test software to construct and print a customized chapter test.

Review Questions (Answers)

1. Civil liberties are legal and constitutional protections protecting citizens from government actions.

2. The original Constitution provided that a writ of *habeas corpus* be available to all citizens. It prohibited Congress and state legislatures from passing bills of attainder and prohibited Congress from passing *ex post facto* laws.

3. The Bill of Rights is the first ten amendments to the Constitution and it was added to prevent an overly intrusive government at the insistence of several states who would otherwise refuse to ratify the Constitution.

4. The effect has been to expand the Bill of Rights' guarantee of individual rights to apply to state governments as well as the national government.

5. Freedom of speech, religion, press, assembly, and petition.
6. The establishment clause of the First Amendment prohibits Congress from passing laws "respecting an establishment of religion."
7. Thomas Jefferson was referring to the fact that the establishment clause draws a wall of separation between church and state which means it forbids the government to become involved in religion.
8. The government uses the excessive entanglement theory when deciding cases involving government aid to school groups. To be constitutional, a state's school aid must meet three requirements; (1) the purpose of the financial aid must be clearly secular; (2) its primary effect must neither advance nor inhibit religion; and (3) it must avoid an "excessive entanglement of government with religion."
9. The free exercise clause protects individuals' rights to worship or believe as they wish, or to hold no religious beliefs at all. The free exercise clause does not necessarily mean that individuals can act any way they want to on the basis of their religious beliefs.
10. Pure speech is the peaceful expression of thoughts, ideas, or opinions and is generally protected. Speech plus is verbal expression combined with action and is protected so long as it does not obstruct traffic, block sidewalks, or endanger public safety. Symbolic speech involves nonverbal expressions and most forms are protected.
11. Libel, slander, obscenity, and fighting words.
12. The clear and present danger rule, the preferred position doctrine, and prior restraint.
13. Prior restraint means stopping an activity before it actually happens. The Supreme Court has generally ruled against prior restraint, arguing that governments cannot try to curb ideas before they are expressed.
14. It has limited reporters' rights to withhold information from the courts. It has limited coverage of trials.
15. All types of speech except libel, slander, obscenity, and fighting words.
16. Freedom of assembly is limited when it threatens public order.
17. In a democracy, the supreme authority rests with the people and their rights must be protected to preserve a democracy.
18. Attending school, obeying laws, paying taxes, and defending the nation.
19. The Court found that flag burning is a form of political expression, and pure speech or expression cannot be punished.

Questions for Thought and Discussion (Answers)
1. Answers and discussion will vary, e.g., activities which infringe on the rights of others or threaten public safety should be considered illegal.
2. Answers and discussion will vary, e.g., freedom of speech and press should apply to new inventions to the same extent as they applied to speech and press in the past. New issues will have to be

CHAPTER 5 REVIEW—Continued

5. List the rights guaranteed under the First Amendment.
6. What is the establishment clause? What freedom does it provide for the American people?
7. What did Thomas Jefferson mean when he spoke of a "wall of separation between church and state"?
8. What is the excessive entanglement theory? How has it been used by the Supreme Court?
9. What does the free exercise clause protect? What doesn't it protect?
10. Describe the three general categories of free speech generally protected by the First Amendment.
11. What kinds of speech are not protected under the First Amendment?
12. What guidelines does the Supreme Court use when deciding what limits should be placed on free speech?
13. What is prior restraint? Is it constitutional?
14. In what ways has freedom of the press been limited?
15. What types of speech are protected?
16. What is the principal limit that the Constitution places on freedom of assembly?
17. Why are the rights guaranteed by the First Amendment essential in a democracy?
18. Name the four legally required responsibilities that you have as an American citizen.
19. What reasoning have the courts used to protect those who burn the American flag from prosecution?

Questions for Thought and Discussion

1. For many years the Communist Party was strictly outlawed in the United States. Today its candidates can compete openly in presidential and other elections. What activities of the Communist Party do you think should be considered illegal under current laws?
2. The founding fathers certainly could not have predicted the advent of mobile phones, communication satellites, cable television, and the like. At what point do you think that the First Amendment freedom of the press should apply to these and other new forms of communication?
3. Discuss the pros and cons of the constitutionality of regulating videotape rentals to prevent, for example, the spread of pornography to minors.
4. Many issues face the Supreme Court when civil liberties are on trial. The justices must balance the rights of individuals with the rights of society as a whole. Under what circumstances do you believe that the individual's rights must be restricted in order to benefit society? Be specific.
5. Facsimile transmission machines, or FAXs, are becoming increasingly popular in the United States and indeed in the world as their prices fall every month. As a result of this popularity, the glut of advertising via FAX transmission has become a problem. Advertisers send out notices via FAX machines to other businesses, thus occupying those businesses' machines and using up excess amounts of FAX paper. If you were a Supreme Court justice, how might you regulate FAX advertising?
6. How do you think the First Amendment's freedom of the press guarantee should be applied during wartime? Do you think that the government should be allowed to censor press coverage, or that the press should be allowed to report on what it sees? Give reasons to support your answers.

Improving Your Skills
Communication Skills

Summarizing

There was once an old television program called *Dragnet,* in which the star police officer, when trying to get key information from witnesses, would say, "Just the facts, ma'am." He was trying to get the main ideas of the case and did not want witnesses to go off on meaningless tangents. He did not want every detail and opinion; he wanted the witnesses to *summarize* what they knew.

Summarizing is condensing (cutting down) information, while focusing on the main ideas. A summary contains only the most relevant and interesting ideas. Being able to summarize enables you to communicate more effectively. It is also a useful study skill because it helps you keep your focus on the main ideas. Here are some guidelines to use when writing a summary:

1. Read the material carefully. If the material is lengthy, skim it first.
2. Determine the author's point of view as you review the material. (This may involve distinguishing be-

decided by the Supreme Court. The Constitution has proved flexible enough to respond to technological changes.

3. Answers and discussion will vary, e.g., pro: It is not constitutional to regulate videotape rentals in any way, shape, or form because what happens in the privacy of one's home is constitutionally protected privacy. Con: It is constitutional to regulate videotape rentals to the extent that minors must be prevented from being exposed to pornography. The government has a right to limit certain activities, even if such limitations infringe on privacy.

4. Answers and discussion will vary, e.g., freedom of the press should be curtailed when the right to a fair trial is threatened. Freedom of speech should not allow burning of the flag.

5. Answers and discussion will vary, e.g., as excessive as advertising may be, it should still be protected as free speech.

6. Answers and discussion will vary, e.g., the government should be allowed to censor press coverage during wartime in order to protect national security.

Social Studies Skills (Answers)

1. Five.

2. Sixth Amendment.

3. Tenth Amendment.

4. Yes, much more, because of inflation since 1789.

CHAPTER 5 REVIEW—Continued

tween evidence and opinion, or looking for generalizations, as you learned in the feature on reading the newspaper on page 119.)

3. Now rewrite the material in summary style, using your own words.
   a. Be sure to include only the main ideas.
   b. Eliminate all unimportant details.
4. Try to keep your summary to no more than 20 percent of the length of the original text.

Writing

Turn to page 121 under the section entitled "Unprotected Speech—Libel, Slander, Obscenity, and 'Fighting Words.'" Summarize the section. Then review your summary and ask yourself if you followed each of the four guidelines listed above.

Social Studies Skills

Reading an Information Table

Sometimes lists of information can be presented in a table form such as you see in Figure 5–1, The Bill of Rights on page 105. Use this figure to answer the following questions.

1. How many freedoms are listed for the First Amendment?
2. Which amendment guarantees the accused in a criminal case the right to a trial by jury?
3. Which amendment do you think could be named the "reserved powers" amendment?
4. The Seventh Amendment states that a jury trial is guaranteed in a civil case involving more than $20. Do you think $20 could buy more when the Bill of Rights was written than it can today?

Activities and Projects

1. Choose one of the Supreme Court cases mentioned in this chapter to do additional research on in your school or local library. Prepare a report that summarizes the arguments presented on both sides, then write a decision that you would make if you were a justice on the case.
2. Invite a newspaper or television reporter to your class to discuss the freedoms and limitations involved in the press and television. Ask the reporter to discuss how some of the issues mentioned in this chapter, such as libel and slander, are treated in these media.
3. Interview a member of the clergy to find out his or her opinion with respect to the separation of church and state. Prepare a summary of that person's opinion to present in class.
4. Write a letter to the editor of your local newspaper, expressing your views concerning the right to beg.
5. Stage a debate or class forum on this question: Should obscenity be protected as free speech?

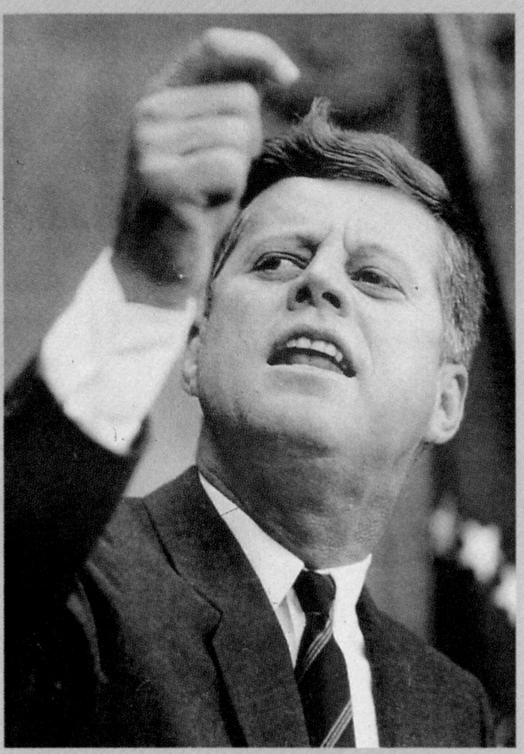

6. Give a written explanation of what you think John F. Kennedy meant when he said, "In giving rights to others which belong to them, we give rights to ourselves and to our country." In your explanation, provide three examples of cases in which this statement has proven true.

Observable Mastery

Divide the class into six groups and assign one of the following topics from the chapter to each: Establishment Clause, Free Exercise Clause, Freedom of the Press, Right to Assemble, Freedom to Petition. Each group should be responsible for the following aspects of the issue: What does the right mean? How has it been defined over time? What are important Supreme Court cases relating to this area? What is the outlook for the future on this issue? Each group should make a brief presentation to the rest of the class and allow for questions or discussion. This format can be adapted to cooperative learning lessons.

CHAPTER INTRODUCTION

Instruction Objectives
By the end of the chapter students should be able to:
- Discuss the concept of due process.
- Describe the importance of due process in the American system of civil liberties.
- State the rights of a person accused of a crime.
- Characterize the rights to equality under the law.
- Summarize the continuing struggle for equality.

Using the Keynote
Without identifying the source, read the introductory quotation aloud to the class.

Then let volunteers identify the speaker and discuss what they know about him and this speech. Explain to the class that King and his "I Have a Dream" speech will be discussed in more detail in a later part of this chapter.

West's American Government Assignment Guide

Activity Sheets
Basic Concepts 6 *TRB* (Reteaching)
Enrichment Activity 6 *TRB*
Building Social Studies Skills 6 *TRB*
Quizzes
Chapter 6 Section 1 Quiz *TRB*
Chapter 6 Section 2 Quiz *TRB*
Chapter 6 Section 3 Quiz *TRB*
Chapter 6 Section 4 Quiz *TRB*
Chapter 6 Section 5 Quiz *TRB*
Tests
Chapter 6 Test A *TRB*
Chapter 6 Test B *TRB*
Chapter 6 Test Bank *TRB*
Chapter 6 WESTEST Computerized Testing
Social Studies Tool Kit Software
Chapter 6 Activity

Previewing the Sections

Section 1 Ask a volunteer to read aloud the title and the three main headings in Section 1. Then ask the class: What do these headings indicate about the topics to be covered in Section 1? How do you think these topics relate to Equality Under the Law?
Section 2 Have the students glance through Section 2, noting the three main headings. Then ask: What do you already know about the topics covered in this section? What do you hope to learn about these topics?
Section 3 Let the students look through Section 3, paying particular attention to the nine main headings and the Government in Action feature. Ask the students: What do you expect to learn as you read this section? Why are the rights covered in this section important to all citizens?

CHAPTER 6

Equality Under the Law

CHAPTER OBJECTIVES

To learn and understand

- The concept of due process of law and its important place in the American system of civil rights.
- The rights of persons accused of a crime.
- The right to equality under the law.
- The continuing struggle for equality and the new challenges it brings.

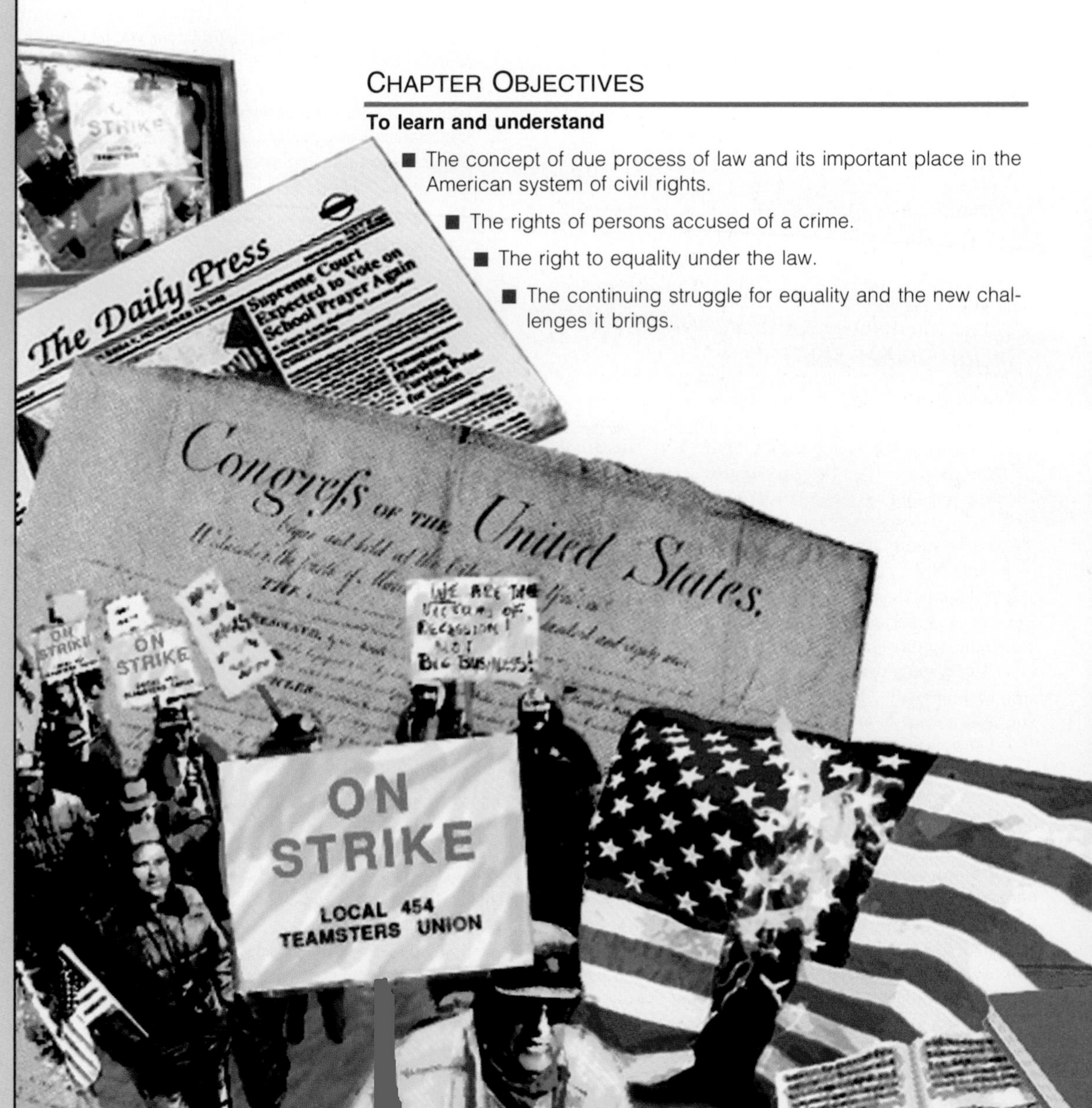

Section 4 Ask the students to page through this section together, pausing to note and discuss the photographs there: What do they indicate about the section content? What do you hope to learn as you study Section 4?

Section 5 Ask volunteers to read aloud the section title, the two main headings, and the Citizenship Skills and Responsibilities title. Based on this information, have the students note at least three questions they hope to have answered as they study Section 5.

Introducing the Chapter

Ask volunteers to read the Introduction aloud. Then open a class discussion by asking these questions: Why are fairness and equal treatment essential to the practice of democracy? What kinds of unfair and unequal treatment persist in the United States? Who suffers as a result of such treatment? Encourage all the students to contribute to this discussion.

Keynote

"I have a dream that one day this nation will rise up and live out the true meaning of the creed: 'We hold these truths to be self-evident: that all men are created equal.' "

—— **Martin Luther King, Jr.**
(1929–1968) Civil rights leader

INTRODUCTION

On August 28, 1963, Dr. Martin Luther King, Jr. delivered those powerful words before an audience of almost 250,000 in front of the Lincoln Memorial in Washington, D.C. His voice crossed the boundaries of color and religion that day, delivering the message that all Americans are entitled to fair and equal treatment under the law. Though the American democratic system has had many successes since then, it has not been entirely successful in extending those rights to all persons. Equal rights for all continues to be a significant issue in today's society.

In the previous chapter you read about the First Amendment rights that lie at the heart of democratic belief and practice. You may have realized that those rights would do you little good if government officials could judge you unfairly or make decisions about your well-being based on your race, religion, or gender. For example, if you were arrested for disturbing the peace during a demonstration, what good would those rights be if you were not allowed to tell your side of the story, to be treated fairly under the law, and to be judged by people of similar age and social status (otherwise known as your **peers**)? If you were trying to rent an apartment, would you not want to be treated with fairness, not on the basis that you are Hispanic or Jewish or Muslim or Asian or African American or female?

Dr. King looked forward to the day when all Americans would be treated with fairness. He said, "I have a dream that my four little children will one day live in a nation where they will not be judged by the color of their skin but by the content of their character."

In a democracy, there must be fairness and equal treatment afforded to all persons. This is especially critical in the courtroom, which is where the right to *due process* comes into play.

SECTION 1

Due Process of Law

Preview Questions

- What is the meaning of due process?
- What is the difference between procedural and substantive due process?

Our Declaration of Independence proclaims that "all men are created equal." As we all know, this does not mean that everyone is born with the same wealth, intelligence, strength, or ambition. Each one of us has a unique combination of qualities and characteristics. The words of the Declaration mean that all people should have equal *rights,* which is the cornerstone of the democratic ideal. All people, regardless of their physical, racial, ethical, sexual, financial, or religious makeup, should be treated equally before the law.

The Fifth Amendment declares that the federal government cannot deprive any person of "life, liberty, or property, without due process of law." The Fourteenth Amendment places the same restriction on state and local governments. The key words here are *due process,* which means that government must follow a set of **processes** (reasonable, fair, and standard procedures) that the citizen is due (entitled to) by virtue of being a citizen.

The concept of due process of law was originally derived from English common law, probably as early as Henry I (1100–1135), and from the Magna Carta, which was discussed in Chapter 2.

Due process of law has come to mean that government may not act unfairly or arbitrarily (based on individual judgment and impulse, not on reason or law). It may not act capriciously (unstably and undependably) or unreasonably. Of course, disagreements as to the meaning of these commands have plagued us from the

SECTION 1

Points to Stress

- Due process and its role in restricting arbitrary government action.
- Both the Fourteenth and Fifth Amendments which contain the due process clauses.
- The difference between procedural and substantive due process.
- The role the Supreme Court plays in defining and protecting due process.

Kickoff Activity

Write this statement on the chalkboard: *All men are created equal.* Ask the students to write short paragraphs describing their reactions to the statement. What do you think it means? How does it make you feel? When all the students have finished writing, let several volunteers read their paragraphs aloud.

Working with the Preview Questions

Let volunteers read the study questions aloud. Ask the students to share their ideas in response to these questions. Then ask: For what specific terms do you expect to find definitions in this section?

Teaching Strategies

Introduction

Let volunteers take turns reading aloud the paragraphs of the section introduction. Then encourage the students to discuss the content by posing questions such as these: When the Declaration of Independence was written, who was included in "all men"? As we understand the statement today, whom does it include? How can people's physical, racial, ethnic, financial, and religious make-up influence their experiences?

Discussion Starter
Guide the students in going over the examples included in the paragraph on Procedural Due Process. What is a stacked jury, a forced confession, denial of counsel, an unreasonable search? How and why might each of these occur? How does each violate procedural due process?

Discussion Starter
Ask several volunteers to make up and present to the class examples of unfair laws. As the class considers each suggestion, guide them in discussing whether the law is truly unfair and, if so, what makes that law unfair.

Caption Answer The right to a jury trial is an example of procedural due process which means that laws must be carried out in a method that is fair and orderly. Substantive due process requires that the laws themselves be fair.

Comprehension
Check the students' comprehension by asking them to distinguish between procedural due process and substantive due process.

Discussion Starter
Encourage the students to consider and discuss the fact that Supreme Court cases concerning procedural due process far outnumber those concerning substantive due process: Does this make sense to you?

Discussion Starter
Let the students consider the facts presented here about the *Rochin* v. *California* case: Was it relevant that Rochin had so often been in trouble with the police? Why or why not? Are there other details about Rochin's background that you think might be relevant to the case? If so, what details? At what point—or points—in the process do you think the police crossed the line and violated Rochin's right to procedural due process?

This case is excerpted in the *West's American Government Handbook of Selected Court Cases.*

Vocabulary
Ask the students to define "the rack and screw." In what sense do you think the procedures used were "too close to the rack and screw"?

Discussion Starter
Let the students consider and discuss the provisions of the Oklahoma law challenged in *Skinner* v. *Oklahoma:* Do you think it is right that a criminal who commits a series of crimes should face punishment for the series as well as for each individual crime? If all three of Skinner's felonies had been for robbery with firearms, do you think sterilization would have been an appropriate legal consequence? Why or why not? Why do you think Oklahoma excluded embezzlement and political offenses from the felonies that could result in forced sterilization? Do you think the state ever has the right to impose sterilization as a punishment for crime? If so, what kinds of crime? If not, why not? Encourage

▲ As a United States citizen, one is entitled to the right to a jury trial. The right to a trial by jury is an example of what type of due process?

time this nation was founded, and will undoubtedly continue to do so.

In order to understand due process, it is important to consider its two types: procedural and substantive.

Procedural Due Process

Procedural due process means that the law must be carried out by a *method* that is fair and orderly. It requires that certain procedures must be followed in administering and executing a law so that an individual's basic freedoms are never violated. As one political scientist suggested, at a minimum, "it denies governments the power to filch away private rights by hole-and-corner methods." Procedural due process prevents a host of unfair practices, such as forced confessions, denial of counsel (legal advice and representation) in criminal cases, and unreasonable searches.

Substantive Due Process—The Laws Themselves Must Be Fair

Fair procedures would obviously be of little use if they were used to administer unfair laws. For example, suppose you were arrested and properly advised of your rights and given every procedural due process right. You were convicted and sentenced to one year in prison. If the law that you were convicted of violating was unfair to begin with, it wouldn't much matter to you that all the proper procedures were used.

Thus, **substantive due process** requires that the *laws themselves* be reasonable. It is the idea that if a law is unfair or unreasonable, even if properly passed by the legislature, it must be declared unconstitutional.

Challenges to Due Process

The number of cases that reach the Supreme Court concerning procedural due process far outweighs the number of those concerned with substantive due process. An example of procedural due process being questioned was in *Rochin* v. *California* (1952). Rochin, often in trouble with the Los Angeles police because of his drug abuse problem, lived in a modest two-story house with his mother, his common-law wife, and an assortment of brothers and sisters. For some time the county had been trying to "get the goods" on Rochin—the authorities were looking for hard evidence to use in convicting him. After receiving what they thought was a reliable tip, deputy sheriffs went to his residence without search or arrest warrants. Finding the front door open, they entered with a soft "hello" and forced open the door of his room. They found Rochin sitting on his bed next to a night table where they saw two morphine capsules. One of the sheriffs asked, "Whose stuff is this?" Rochin quickly grabbed the capsules and attempted to swallow them. The officers jumped on him, tried to open his mouth, and administered a thorough beating, but Rochin succeeded in swallowing the pills. The deputies tied him up and took him to the hospital where Rochin was forced to vomit the two morphine capsules, which the agents then presented as evidence at his subsequent trial. Rochin was convicted of violating the state's narcotics laws.

When Rochin appealed to the Supreme Court, his conviction was overturned. The Court ruled that the deputies had violated the Fourteenth Amendment's guarantee of procedural due process. It ruled that the agents had used conduct that shocks the conscience, and that procedures used were unreasonable and "too close to the students to present and defend various points of view in this discussion.

Reteaching Strategies

1. Let the students work with partners to write brief definitions—in their own words—of these terms: *due process, procedural due process, substantive due process.*

2. Work with small groups of students to review the importance of due process: How does due process relate to the equality of all citizens?

Evaluation Strategies

1. Have the students write their responses to the Section 1 Review questions.

2. Have the students take the Section 1 Quiz found in the *TRB.*

Section 1 Review (Answers)

1. The Fifth Amendment and the Fourteenth Amendment.

2. Due process means that government must follow a set of processes (reasonable, standard, and fair procedures) that the citizen is entitled to by virtue of being a citizen.

3. Procedural due process means that the law must be carried out by a method that is fair and orderly. Substantive due process requires that the laws themselves must be reasonable.

4. Answers will vary. Other costs include additional administrative expenses that are necessary to protect procedural due process throughout the police system. Also, the judicial system suffers from additional costs and delay because of the necessity of ensuring procedural due process. The benefits of procedural due process are in upholding the Bill of Rights. Often this rests mainly with the limitation on the power of the police and the courts to step on individual rights.

"What's so great about due process? Due process got me ten years."

Handlesman, 1970, New Yorker Magazine, Inc.

the rack and screw.'' Justice Felix Frankfurter ended his opinion by stating that ''convictions cannot be brought about by methods that offend a sense of justice.''

An example of substantive due process being challenged is in *Skinner* v. *Oklahoma* (1942). Arthur Skinner had been convicted of three **felonies**, which are serious crimes punishable by one or more years in prison. Two of Skinner's felonies were robbery with firearms and one was stealing chickens. While serving his sentence in the penitentiary, the state of Oklahoma enacted a new statute, in 1935, the Habitual Criminal Sterilization Act. The statute defined a habitual criminal as a person who, already having been convicted two or more times for crimes ''amounting to felonies involving moral turpitude [shameful behavior]'' is then convicted of another such felony in Oklahoma and duly sentenced to a term of imprisonment. It also provided that the attorney general could institute ''a proceeding against such a person in the Oklahoma courts for a judgment that such person be rendered sexually sterile,'' meaning the person would no longer be able to produce children. Certain offenses, such as embezzlement and political offenses, were excluded from the statute, but Arthur Skinner's crimes were not. He had already committed his three felonies involving ''moral turpitude,'' and seemed a perfect candidate for sterilization. The attorney general began proceedings against him, properly following every prescribed aspect of procedural due process. The medical procedure was performed on Skinner.

When the case was appealed to the Supreme Court, it said the statute was unconstitutional. The Court warned that there are ''limits to the extent to which a legislatively represented majority may conduct biological experiments at the expense of the dignity and personality and natural powers of a minority.'' The Court also stated that when the law lays an unequal hand on those who have committed the same quality of offense (e.g., political criminals and thieves) and sterilizes one and not the other, the law is discriminatory.

One of the reasons behind the idea of due process is a basic democratic belief that any person suspected or accused of a crime must be presumed innocent until she or he is proven guilty. Therefore, *all* persons, including those accused of a crime, must be treated equally, following fair steps in the legal process.

Section 1 Review

1. Which two amendments in the Constitution contain due process clauses?
2. What does due process of law mean?
3. Explain the difference between procedural and substantive due process.
4. **For critical analysis:** Law enforcement officials sometimes argue that the overly ambitious application of procedural due process hinders their ability to successfully prosecute known criminals. This could be seen as one of the costs society bears of having procedural due process. What might be some other costs of procedural due process? What are the benefits?

Section 2

Rights of the Accused: Searching and Wiretapping

Preview Questions

- What constitutes an unreasonable search and seizure?
- How has the exclusionary rule developed?

President Abraham Lincoln asked in 1861, ''Must a government, of necessity, be too strong for the liberties of its own people, or too weak to maintain its own existence?'' Almost one hundred years before, the framers

SECTION 2

Points to Stress

- Actions that constitute unreasonable search and seizure.
- The development of the exclusionary rule.
- Those circumstances where lawful search and seizure can be made without a warrant.

Kickoff Activity

Ask the students to read the section title, and then have them list words and phrases that come to mind when they think of searching and wiretapping. When all the students have finished writing, read aloud and discuss several lists: How many of the ideas seem to have been suggested by TV shows and movies? How accurate do you imagine such depictions of criminal procedures are?

Working with the Preview Questions

Let a volunteer read the study questions aloud, and encourage students to discuss what they already know in response to these questions. Then have the students use the questions to prepare note-taking sheets that they can complete as they study Section 2.

Teaching Strategies

Introduction

Let a volunteer read aloud the Lincoln quotation at the beginning of the section introduction: What does the question mean? Why do you think Lincoln asked it? Does the question have a simple answer? Is it a question that should still concern us? Why or why not?

Have the students continue reading the section introduction to themselves; then let another volunteer read aloud the English judge's famous maxim: Do you agree with this maxim? Why or why not? Do you imagine that you would agree if you had just been robbed? Do you imagine you would agree if a family member had just been brutally murdered?

Discussion Starter

Allow the students to identify and discuss specific examples of probable cause, search and seizure, and search warrants. Students may draw their facts from personal experience, news reports, or films they consider accurate in their depiction of law enforcement.

Extension

Ask the students to consider and write a short essay discussing the second listed exception to the need for a warrant: How is this definition open to interpretation? Who makes that interpretation? What might be the consequences of a too-limited interpretation of the area within reach? What might be the consequences of a too-broad interpretation?

Caption Answer The reasonable suspicion that a crime has been committed is called probable cause. Police and the courts need probable cause to make an arrest.

Discussion Starter

Encourage the students to consider the fact that bags of trash left at the curb for regular collection can be searched without a warrant: Who do you think might object to this kind of search? Why? Would it be possible for the police to routinely search garbage in a given neighborhood before it was collected?

TEACHING GOVERNMENT IN ACTION

Read

To introduce this Case Study, ask the students to describe how the technology of communication has changed over the last two centuries—and even over the last two decades. What effect do these changes have on our ability to stay in touch with others? What effect do they have on our privacy? What effect do you think they have on the means by which police can gather evidence? After the introductory discussion, let the students read New Technology, New Questions to themselves.

of the Constitution had pondered this question. In fact, most of the words contained in the Bill of Rights are actually about the rights of persons accused of crimes. These rights were originally intended to protect the accused in *political* arrests and trials.[1] Today the protections of the Fourth, Fifth, Sixth, and Eighth Amendments are mostly applied to criminal cases.

The concern for criminals' rights stems from an old fear that in trying to make sure all criminals are apprehended and punished, the rights of innocent people may be abused. It goes back to an English judge's famous maxim: "I would much rather twenty guilty persons go free than one innocent be put to death." Much of the work of the Supreme Court has been involved in assuring that the evidence used against accused persons is constitutionally valid.

Collecting the Evidence

Police cannot arrest people on a whim; they need evidence to justify the arrest and courts need evidence to convict. Police and the courts need what is called **probable cause**, or reasonable grounds to believe a serious crime has been committed, before making an arrest. Yet the Fourth Amendment is quite specific in forbidding unreasonable **searches and seizures**, which refer to the methods that law enforcement personnel use to look for and collect the evidence they need to convict individuals suspected of crimes. To prevent unreasonable searches and seizures, police are usually required to have a **search warrant**—a court order that authorizes police to search the scene of a suspected crime. The warrant must describe the place to be searched and the person or objects to be seized.

Under certain circumstances, a lawful search and seizure can be made *without* a warrant:

- When police are in "hot pursuit" of a suspect.
- When a lawful arrest is made, officers do not need a warrant to search the area within reach of the person being arrested. This is defined as the area in which he or she might gain possession of a weapon or destroy evidence.
- When an arrest happens in a public place, provided the officer has probable cause to believe that that person has committed a crime, or is about to commit it.
- When a crime is committed in the presence of an officer.
- When searching an automobile, a boat, an airplane, or any other vehicle, if the police officer has good reason to believe the vehicle either contains evidence of a crime or is being used to commit one. This is because a "movable scene of crime" could disappear while the warrant is being sought.
- When searching bags of trash left at the curb for regular collection.
- When seizing evidence in plain view.

1. That is not to say that crime was not a major problem in the first one hundred years of this country. Some criminal historians have argued that the rate of crime in colonial America would equal present crime rates.

If a police officer has a reasonable suspicion of criminal activity, a suspect may be frisked or searched for weapons. What term is used to describe the reasonable suspicion that a crime has been committed?

Discuss
Encourage the students to discuss the information presented in the Case Study: Why are traditional telephone conversations protected? Why are conversations over cordless phones not protected? Does this mean that it is legal for others—besides the police—to eavesdrop on conversations over cordless phones? Why or why not?

Analyze and Apply
Let the students work in groups to research their state's laws governing the interception of cordless phone conversations. Also have them find out as much as possible about the attitudes and actions of local police departments. Does a trend seem to be developing? If so, what kind of trend?

Review
To review the Case Study, have the students answer these questions: What is the effect of the decision made in *Katz* v. *United States?* Why are conversations on cordless telephones not covered by that decision?

Think About It (Answers)
1. Answers will vary, e.g., police officials should have a warrant before intercepting cordless phone conversations because such communications should be within the Fourth Amendment's protection.
2. Answers will vary, e.g., FAX communications, computer networks, E-mail, CD-ROM diskettes, shortwave radios.

Discussion Starter
Help the students discuss the case of *Mapp* v. *Ohio:* What police actions make this a clear instance of violation of the exclusionary rule? How were Mapp's rights violated? What are some of the more subtle ways in which police actions may violate the exclusionary rule?

This case is excerpted in the *West's American Government Handbook of Selected Court Cases.*

Law Related Activity
Fourth Amendment search and seizure cases seem to interest students as much as anything. A recent and interesting case is *Greenwood* v. *California.* Allow students to debate the issue of searching and seizing trash at the curb. Begin with, Resolved: Garbage left at the curb to be picked up by a trash collector is constitutionally protected by the Fourth Amendment. Introduce the topic and specifics of the case to the students. A good starting point might be for them to make an anonymous mental list of things that they have thrown away in the past year or so that they do not want anyone to see. Ask students to relate this case to the exclusionary rule and the "plain view" doctrine. Allow students to research the particulars of the issue by reading the *Greenwood* and related cases.

CASE STUDY

GOVERNMENT IN ACTION

New Technology, New Questions

Living in the information age raises questions about searches and seizures that the framers of the Constitution could not have begun to imagine. They didn't know that we would enter an era of wiretapping, electronic eavesdropping devices, and videotaping, or that we would be communicating by facsimile transmission (FAX) machines, computer networks, and cordless telephones. Increasingly, our communications are transmitted, stored, and shared in ways that were unheard of only a few years ago.

In 1928, the Supreme Court first ruled on a case involving federal prohibition agents who had tapped the telephones of bootleggers (those who sold illegal beverages). The Court held that intercepting telephone conversations was not a search and seizure, so agents did not need a warrant. In *Katz* v. *United States* (1967), however, the Court ruled that police could not eavesdrop on telephone conversations without a court warrant, holding that such communications are within the Fourth Amendment's protection.

In 1989, when more than 9 million cordless phones were in use, the Court let an Iowa ruling stand that said police can intercept cordless phone conversations without a warrant. Lower courts have ruled that because the phones use a radio transmission, users can have no expectation of privacy. This makes cordless phone conversations fair game for police eavesdropping.

The Constitution does not mention privacy. The Supreme Court, however, has said the right to privacy is a constitutional right implied by several amendments, especially the Fourth. As technology makes it more and more possible for intrusions into private lives, there will be more complex cases for the courts to decide.

THINK ABOUT IT

1. Do you think police officials should be able to intercept cordless phone conversations without a warrant? Explain why or why not.
2. What other new forms of communication can you think of that might raise the same questions?

Exclusionary Rule

Since 1914, the federal courts have used the **exclusionary rule** to prevent the introduction of illegally seized evidence. According to the rule, all evidence obtained in an illegal search is excluded (inadmissible) in a federal criminal trial under the Fourth Amendment. No matter how incriminating—even a knife stained with the victim's blood—evidence usually cannot be introduced into a trial if it was not constitutionally obtained. The logic behind the exclusionary rule is that if police are forced to gather evidence properly, they will be rewarded with a conviction; if they are careless or abuse the rights of the suspect, they will not get a conviction. Those who criticize the exclusionary rule, however, argue that its strict application may permit guilty people to go free because of police carelessness or innocent errors.

For forty years after the exclusionary rule was established, the Court left the question of the use of such evidence for each state to decide. In 1960, Dollree Mapp, who lived in Cleveland, Ohio, was suspected of illegal gambling activities. The police broke into her home and, while searching the house from top to bottom, found a stash of obscene material. She was tried and convicted of possessing obscene material and appealed her case to the Supreme Court. In *Mapp* v. *Ohio* (1961), the Court ruled that the evidence was illegally seized and reversed her conviction. Since then, the exclusionary rule has been applied to both state and federal governments.

The exclusionary rule has been under considerable pressure from critics in recent years. Beginning in 1984, opponents of the rule won several important victories in the Supreme Court. The Court first found an "inevitable

Critical Thinking Skills
Guide the students in analyzing the inevitable discovery exception to the exclusionary rule: How does it affect the protection that the exclusionary rule is intended to offer citizens? Do you think this exception can and will be fairly used? Would you expect it to be challenged again? Why or why not?

Vocabulary
Ask the students to define the term *good faith.* Why is it sometimes difficult to determine whether people have acted in good faith?

Caption Answer The exclusionary rule, which states that illegally obtained evidence cannot be introduced in court.

Reteaching Strategies
1. Assign students partners with whom to review and discuss the notes they have taken while reading Section 2. Encourage the students to use the text to resolve any questions that arise and to revise their notes as necessary.
2. Have the students bring in news stories about local arrests. Work with small groups of students to discuss one or two of the news articles: How was evidence collected? From the facts given in the news story, do you believe all the evidence collected will be admissible in a criminal trial? Why or why not?

Evaluation Strategies
1. Have the students write their responses to the first three Section 2 Review questions.
2. Let the students work in groups to discuss their responses to the final Section 2 Review question. Then have each student work independently to write a one- or two-paragraph response to this question.
3. Have the students take the Section 2 Quiz found in the *TRB.*

Section 2 Review (Answers)
1. The Fourth Amendment prohibits unreasonable search and seizures.
2. When police are in "hot pursuit" of a suspect. When a lawful arrest is made, police may search the area within reach of the person being arrested. When an arrest happens in a public place, provided the officer has probable cause to believe that person has committed a crime, or is about to commit a crime.
3. According to the exclusionary rule, all evidence obtained in an illegal search is inadmissible in a federal criminal trial. Exceptions have been made with the "inevitable discovery rule," when honest mistakes have been made by officers, and when agents thought a warrant was valid and therefore acted in "good faith."
4. Answers will vary, e.g., when police officers get a search warrant they think is valid, and act in good faith, the evidence they collect should not be excluded if it later turns out that the warrant was defective for some "technical" reason.

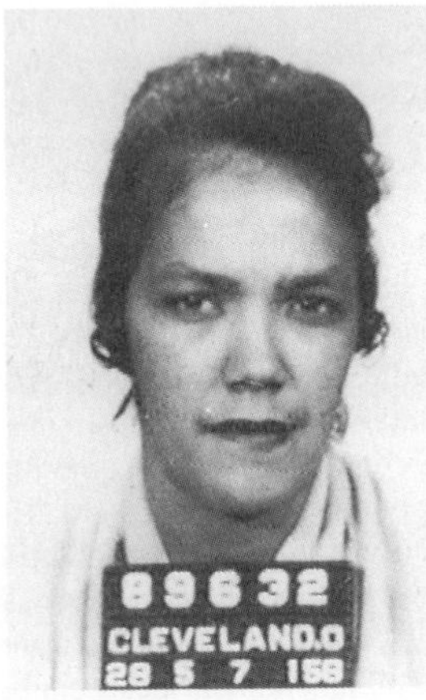

▲ Dollree Mapp, pictured above, was arrested for and convicted of possession of obscene material. The Supreme Court overturned her conviction because the evidence used against her was obtained through an illegal search and seizure. What rule was applied to the states as a result of this case?

discovery'' exception to the rule. In a case in which a murderer was tricked by Iowa police into leading them to the body of his victim, the Court ruled that the Iowa police could use the evidence. It said that tainted evidence (evidence obtained by unlawful search and seizure) could be used if it would have eventually been discovered by lawful means. The Court has also allowed room for honest mistakes by police officers. It allowed the use of evidence seized in a mistaken search of an apartment in Baltimore in a 1987 case.

The Court has also created an exception for ''good faith.'' This happened in a case in which federal agents in Los Angeles had used what they believed was a proper warrant to seize illegal drugs. Later, the warrant was found to be faulty. The Court upheld the agents' actions because they thought the warrant was valid and therefore acted in good faith.

The exclusionary rule was eroded further in 1991 in the case of *Arizona* v. *Fulminante.* Fulminante, while in prison, confessed to a fellow inmate (who later turned out to be a government informer) that he had abused and murdered his 11-year-old stepdaughter. The court ruled that because Fulminante voluntarily offered his confession, the evidence was not illegally obtained or coerced.

Wiretaps and Congress

When the Fourth Amendment was created, wiretapping was impossible. We can only speculate what the writers of this amendment would have said.

In 1968, Congress passed the Omnibus Crime Control and Safe Streets Act. It permits *court-approved* wiretapping by both federal and state law enforcement officials in the investigation of a large number of listed crimes. In 1978, Congress passed the Foreign Intelligence Surveillance Act, which requires officials to have warrants for wiretapping or other electronic bugging, even in national security cases.

Section 2 Review

1. What does the Fourth Amendment prohibit?
2. Under what circumstances has the Supreme Court ruled that a lawful search and seizure can be made without a warrant?
3. What is the exclusionary rule? What exceptions to the rule have been allowed by the Supreme Court?
4. **For critical analysis:** When, if ever, do you feel that it would be acceptable to use illegally obtained evidence in a criminal case?

Section 3

Rights of the Accused: A Fair Trial

Preview Questions:

- Why does the Constitution set out protections of persons arrested for a crime?
- How has the Supreme Court expanded Fifth-Amendment protections?
- What are the rights of persons arrested by the police?

Suppose that evidence against a criminal has been gathered, and the police are ready to make an arrest. In our system, the **burden of proof** rests on the prosecution. This means it is up to the prosecution to prove whether someone is guilty of a crime, and not the defense to prove innocence. The suspected criminal is not obliged to help the government prove that he or she indeed committed a crime. It is the prosecution that must show whether or not the criminal charges are true.

Self-Incrimination

The Fifth Amendment forbids forced **self-incrimination**. It says that no one shall be compelled in any criminal case to be a witness against himself or herself. This means you cannot be forced to blurt out a confession in the station house or at the trial. This ban on self-

SECTION 3

Points to Stress

- Reasons for constitutional protections of persons arrested for a crime.
- Supreme Court expansion of rights of the accused.
- The rights of those arrested by the police.
- Capital punishment and its constitutional basis.

Kickoff Activity

Let the students write short paragraphs in response to this question: What makes a trial fair? Have all the students complete their paragraphs before volunteers begin reading theirs aloud: What different ideas do the students include?

Working with the Preview Questions

Ask volunteers to read the study questions aloud, and encourage the students to discuss what they already know in response. Then explain that the students will find more complete answers as they study the section; they will be expected to answer these questions when they have completed Section 3.

Teaching Strategies

Introduction

Have one of the students read the section introduction aloud. Then encourage the students to respond to this question: Why aren't you obliged to help prove that you committed a crime?

Critical Thinking Skills

Guide the students in analyzing the right of an accused person to avoid self-incrimination: Why do you think this protection is provided? How effective do you imagine it really is? What effect do you think "taking the Fifth" probably has on most jury members? Do you think it has the same effect on most judges? Why or why not?

Extension

Ask the students to consider problems that might arise if a suspect does not speak or understand English: Do you imagine that the police are required to explain the Miranda Rules in the suspect's own language? What if the suspect can speak and understand some English but is more comfortable communicating in another language? *(Students should understand that the suspect must fully understand his or her rights before being questioned.)* What obligation should the police have to deal with each suspect in his or her own native language?

incrimination prevents the prosecution from shifting the burden of proof to the defendant.

A person may also claim his or her Fifth Amendment right in any number of noncriminal proceedings. Whether at a divorce proceeding, a Congressional hearing, or a disciplinary meeting before a local school board, a person need not provide evidence that is potentially self-incriminating. The Fifth Amendment also protects defendants against confessions obtained by force or violence. The Supreme Court has voided a number of state prosecutions because the methods used to obtain criminal confessions involved either the use or the threat of physical or psychological force.

This right can be **waived** (given up), but is not lost if the defendant takes the stand to testify on his or her own behalf. The accused may still claim the Fifth Amendment when on the witness stand. The Fifth Amendment does not protect a person from being fingerprinted or photographed, submitting a handwriting sample, appearing in a police lineup, or taking a blood test. The courts, not the individuals who claim it, decide when the Fifth Amendment applies. If pushed too far, the court can hold the person in **contempt**, which is disrespect for or disobedience of the court.

Expanding These Protections

In the mid-1960s, the Supreme Court decided two important cases that expanded protection against self-incrimination and forced confessions.

The first case was *Escobedo* v. *Illinois* (1964). Danny Escobedo had been picked up by Chicago police for questioning in the death of his brother-in-law. While he was being questioned, he asked to see his lawyer several times. The requests were refused, even though his lawyer was in the police station waiting to see him. Through a long night of questioning and without the help of his lawyer, Escobedo made several damaging statements, which were used later in court as part of the major evidence that led to his conviction for murder.

Four years later the Supreme Court freed him from prison. The Court said that a confession could not be used against a defendant if it was obtained by police who refused to allow him to see his attorney, and did not advise him of the right to refuse to answer their questions.

In an important decision two years later, *Miranda* v. *Arizona* (1966), the Court went further and established the need for the procedure that you might know today as "being read your rights." A man who suffered from mild mental retardation, Ernesto Miranda, had been convicted for the kidnapping and rape of an 18-year-old woman. Miranda was selected from a police lineup by the victim, questioned for two hours, and not advised of his rights. He confessed and was convicted. The Supreme Court struck down his conviction, ruling that the Fifth Amendment's protection against self-incrimination requires that suspects be clearly informed of their rights before they are questioned.

The guidelines set by the Court in the wake of this case have become known as the **Miranda Rules**. Under these rules, when police arrest someone suspected of a crime, the suspects must be:

- told of their right to remain silent.
- warned that anything they say can be used against them in court.
- informed of their right to have an attorney present during questioning.
- told that if they cannot afford to hire an attorney, one will be provided.
- told that they may bring any police questioning to an end at any time.

Police departments throughout the country were dissatisfied with the Miranda Rules. Officers felt that interrogation was crucial to any investigation, and warning suspects of their rights and letting them call a lawyer was almost certain to silence them. Most do take it seriously however, because the Supreme Court and lower courts have enforced it hundreds of times since 1967. Police usually read a "Miranda card" advising suspects

▲ The Fifth Amendment to the Constitution protects individuals from forced self-incrimination. This means that no one can be compelled to be a witness against himself or herself. Does the Fifth Amendment give an individual the right to refuse to be fingerprinted when arrested?

Caption Answer The Fifth Amendment does not protect a person from being fingerprinted or from having to submit to a number of other police procedures designed to gather evidence against a suspect. These procedures include submitting a handwriting sample, appearing in a police line-up, or taking a blood test or Breathalyzer test.

Discussion Starter
Encourage the students to discuss the attitude of the police toward the Miranda Rule: Why might police sometimes object to it? Do you consider these objections valid? Why or why not? In what respects can the Miranda Rule be considered a benefit to police officers?

This case is excerpted in the *West's American Government Handbook of Selected Court Cases.*

impression do you imagine the document itself created on members of the Supreme Court? What important legal points did Gideon make in this document? Do you think Gideon would have been better served by a trained lawyer? Why or why not?

This case is excerpted in the *West's American Government Handbook of Selected Court Cases.*

Comprehension
Ask several volunteers to restate Justice Black's explanation in their own words.

Vocabulary
Let volunteers define the words *partial* and *impartial.* Then ask: What is an impartial jury?

Enrichment
Have several interested volunteers read about the most current methods of selecting jury members: What kinds of consultants do lawyers sometimes hire to help them with selecting and persuading jury members? What kinds of advice are these consultants expected to give? What do statistics show about the success of such consultants? Have the volunteers use an interesting format—perhaps a short dialog or sketch—to share their findings with the rest of the class.

Caption Answer Suspects must be informed of their right to remain silent and that anything they say may be used against them in court. They must be informed of their right to have an attorney present during questioning, and that an attorney will be provided if they cannot afford an attorney. Finally, suspects must be informed that they have the right to bring police questioning to an end at any time.

Discussion Starter
Guide the students in considering defendants' rights to counsel: Is the right to a court-appointed lawyer intended to ensure that all defendants are treated equally? Do you think it succeeds in achieving this intention? Why or why not?

Comprehension
Check the students' understanding by asking: Why was it possible for state courts not to assure defendants the rights of the Sixth Amendment? *(Students should understand that this protection, like all the protections in the Bill of Rights, was not originally intended to be applied to the states.)*

Extension
Have volunteers research, read, and discuss Gideon's handwritten petition in an oral report to the class: What

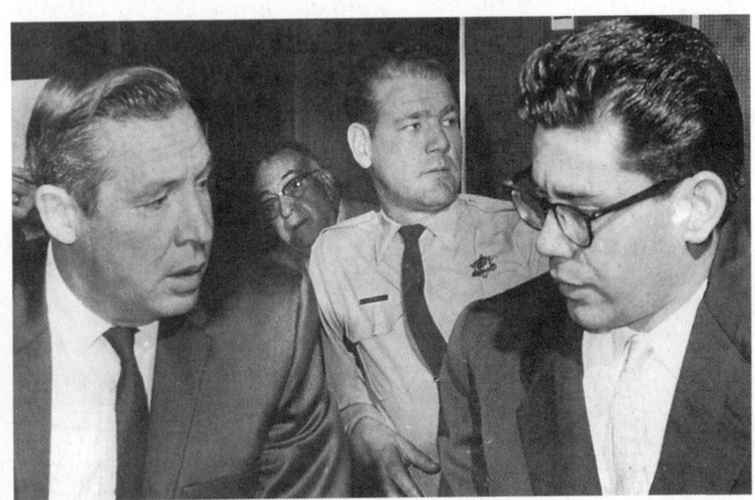

Ernesto Miranda (shown here with attorney John J. Flynn) confessed and was convicted of the kidnapping and rape of an 18-year-old woman. This conviction was overturned by the Supreme Court because police officers had not informed Miranda of his Fifth Amendment rights. This decision led to the institution of the Miranda Rules. What are the rights a suspect must be informed of under the Miranda Rules?

of their rights. Later, when Ernesto Miranda himself was murdered, the suspected murderer was read his rights from a Miranda card.

In several cases since *Miranda,* however, the Court has relaxed some of the restrictions of the Miranda Rules. For example, in 1984 the Court ruled that police do not have to read suspects their rights when "public safety" is at risk. In order to find a loaded gun, for example, the police could interrogate a suspect before advising him of his right to remain silent.

The Right to Counsel

The Sixth Amendment guarantees a defendant the right to have the assistance of counsel for his or her defense. This means that people accused of a crime have the right to hire a lawyer to represent their case in court. If they cannot afford to hire a lawyer, the Court will appoint one for them. Even lawyers taken to court hire other lawyers to represent them. (There is an old saying that lawyers who defend themselves have a fool for a client.)

The Sixth Amendment assures the right to counsel in federal courts, but until relatively recently, people who were tried in state courts did not have this right. In 1932, the Supreme Court ordered the states to provide an attorney for indigent (poor) defendants accused of a capital crime (those for which the death penalty could be imposed). Not until 1963, however, did the Supreme Court extend that right to everyone accused of a felony. The change occurred in the case of a penniless drifter from Florida named Clarence Earl Gideon.

Gideon was charged with robbing a pool hall in Florida by stealing change from a vending machine. He did not have any money to hire a lawyer so he asked the court to appoint one, but his request was denied. He was convicted of the crime and sentenced to a five-year jail term.

While in jail, Gideon studied law books and petitioned the Supreme Court himself for a retrial in a handwritten petition. The Court accepted his appeal and ruled unanimously that the due process clause of the Fourteenth Amendment required states to give defendants the Sixth Amendment right to counsel. Justice Black explained that "lawyers in criminal courts are necessities, not luxuries."

Gideon was released and retried with a lawyer. This time he was **acquitted** (released from the charge). More than a thousand other Florida prisoners and thousands more in other states who had been convicted without counsel were also released. As a result of *Gideon* v. *Wainwright* (1963), however poor you are, today you have a right to a lawyer.

The Court has extended the *Gideon* decision to apply not only in felony cases, but whenever there might be a jail sentence involved, even for a minor criminal offense.

The Right to Trial by Jury

The Sixth Amendment also provides defendants the right to be tried by an impartial jury in serious criminal cases. The Supreme Court has defined serious cases as

Discussion Starter
Ask the students to consider a defendant's decision to waive the right to a jury trial: Under what circumstances to you think a defendant might make that choice? What might a defendant hope to gain by having a bench trial? Also encourage the students to discuss any recent cases in the news involving bench trials rather than jury trials.

Discussion Starter
Encourage the students to discuss what they have read and heard about local grand juries. Do you know anyone who has served on a grand jury? What—if anything—has that person reported about grand jury duties? In what criminal cases have you heard mention of grand jury work?

Comprehension
Ask the students to contrast the work of grand juries with the work of trial juries: Why do grand juries work in secret? Why are trial proceedings public? Why are jury deliberations private? Whose rights are protected in each case?

Caption Answer Serious criminal cases are those cases for which the punishment can be six or more months imprisonment.

FYI

The Sixth Amendment guarantees a speedy and public trial by jury. As with all liberties, the general theme is met with unanimity and the specifics generate lawsuits. Can nameless jurors be impartial? Does a defendant have a constitutional right to know the names, addresses, and occupations of the jury?

Recently, federal prosecutors from the Northern District of Illinois requested that jurors' names be kept secret in order to thwart jury tampering or retaliation during a racketeering and narcotics trial. It is rare for judges to shield the identity of jurors, but it is on the rise. Defense lawyers insist that suspects are stigmatized and lose their presumption of innocence. Prosecutors contend that security outweighs any potential infringement on the rights of the accused. Defense lawyers further contend that withholding information limits their ability to question jurors about biases during jury selection. They also claim that the government has not established that jurors face a legitimate risk of harm. The United States Marshals Service publishes an annual report detailing threats, and only one case of a juror being threatened is on record.

Federal prosecutors also feel that potential jurors might rather face contempt charges than serve in a trial with a violent defendant.

those that could result in six or more months **incarceration** (imprisonment).

The jury is supposed to be impartial, which means those who have made up their mind before the trial should be excluded. It is also supposed to represent a fair cross section of the community, which means no group can be systematically excluded. No persons can be kept off a jury on the grounds of race, religion, color, national origin, or sex (even though the Court allowed the states to exclude women from jury duty until 1975).

The Constitution does not specify the size of a jury. Tradition in England and America has set jury size at twelve persons, and has required a **unanimous** (complete agreement by all) verdict in criminal trials. Some states have experimented with smaller juries and nonunanimous verdicts to save money. The Supreme Court has allowed states to have juries with a minimum of six people serving.

Defendants may waive (give up or relinquish) their right to a jury trial. The judge must be satisfied that the defendant is fully aware of his or her rights and understands what that action means. If the right is waived, a **bench trial**, one heard by a judge alone, is held. Of course a defendant may plead guilty or **no contest**, meaning he or she does not wish to contest the charge, and thereby avoids a trial.

The Grand Jury

The Fifth Amendment provides for a grand jury in federal **capital cases** (ones that might involve the death penalty). A federal grand jury proceeding is the formal process by which a person may be accused of a serious federal crime.

A **grand jury** is a body made up of twelve to twenty-three citizens that examines the evidence presented against a suspect. The purpose of the grand jury investigation is to see if enough evidence exists to hold a criminal trial. If the jury feels there is, an **indictment**, or formal charge of a crime against the accused, is handed down. If the grand jury does not find enough evidence, the charge is dropped.

A grand jury proceeding is not a trial. It does not determine guilt or innocence and is held in secret, unlike normal jury trials. Critics of the grand jury method say that it costs too much time and money for taxpayers.

Double Jeopardy

The Fifth Amendment says that no person shall be "twice put in jeopardy of life and limb." This means that once a defendant is acquitted of a crime, he or she is protected from being tried again for the same crime.

A person can be retried if the jury trial results in a **hung jury**, which means that it cannot reach a unanimous verdict. He or she can also be retried if there is a **mistrial**, an error in the proceedings. If the crime is in violation of both state and federal laws, the person can technically be tried by both a state and federal court.

Speedy and Public Trial

The Sixth Amendment provides that the accused shall enjoy the right to a speedy and public trial. The right to a speedy trial is meant to prevent prisoners

The Sixth Amendment to the United States Constitution grants defendants the right to be tried by an impartial jury in serious criminal cases. What constitutes a serious criminal case?

TEACHING GOVERNMENT IN ACTION

Read
Let the students begin by sharing what they already know about law in other countries and other cultures: Which countries have laws most similar to ours? What explains the similarities? Which cultures have laws quite different from the laws in this country? Why? After a brief discussion, let volunteers take turns reading the Case Study aloud to the rest of the class.

Discuss
Encourage the students to discuss the Case Study by asking questions such as these: Do you think that you, as a citizen of the United States, have a responsibility to learn about the laws—as well as the history and culture—of other countries? Why or why not?

Analyze and Apply
Let the students work in groups to research laws of other cultures. For example, one group might examine four or five crimes considered especially serious in the Islamic culture. Then ask the members of each group to find out how those same crimes are treated in our legal system.

Review
Ask the students these review questions: Why don't all countries have the same laws and the same legal system? How can understanding a country's history and culture help you understand that country's legal system?

Think About It (Answers)
1. Answers will vary, e.g., the Protestant religion probably influenced early laws.
2. A belief in a law of divine origin would be a belief that the law was made by God.

Comprehension
Let volunteers respond to these questions: What is the purpose of bail?

Discussion Starter
Let the students review and discuss the issue of capital punishment: Why is it such a difficult question to resolve? What do you consider the most persuasive arguments in favor of capital punishment? What do you consider the most persuasive arguments against it?

Reteaching Strategies
1. Let the students work with partners to write short paragraphs in response to the following questions: What is the burden of proof? Who bears that burden? Why?
2. Work with small groups of students to review and discuss the definitions of these terms: *self-incrimination, Miranda Rules, acquittal, grand jury, indictment.*

GOVERNMENT IN ACTION

CASE STUDY

Law in Other Cultures

Crime is defined very differently from culture to culture. The seriousness of crimes also varies greatly in different societies. For example, a crime such as public drunkenness, considered relatively minor in the United States, is a very serious crime in Egypt.

The laws and legal systems found in other countries can chiefly be explained by understanding a country's history and culture. The same can be said of our own country. This history can include its deeply held customs and religious beliefs, its theories about the origin of law, its values, and important developmental problems the country has experienced. For example, a country in which food shortages have always been a problem would probably consider stealing sheep or crops a very serious crime. Botswana, a country in the south of Africa that has suffered from famine, reserves its strongest legal penalty for cattle rustling.

In many Islamic countries the law is considered to be of divine origin. Disobeying the law is therefore seen as disobeying God, and brings with it very severe penalties. This view of divine law also means that laws cannot be easily changed by legislatures.

Almost all countries consider some acts legally and morally wrong. These universal crimes are the ones that threaten the survival of individuals or groups within a society, or the society itself. They include homicide (murder) under most circumstances, and treason, or betraying one's country.

THINK ABOUT IT

1. What particular religious beliefs in the United States may have influenced some of its laws?
2. What does it mean to say that law is of divine origin?

from sitting in jails for unreasonable amounts of time. Since 1980, the suggested time span has been one hundred days. If the criminal trial has not occurred by the end of that time period, the defendant should normally be set free.

The guarantee of a public trial is to prevent the courtroom from becoming a place of secret persecution. The Supreme Court has also ruled, however, that trials cannot be *too* public. It has reversed convictions when there was too much press coverage and other publicity that prevented the defendant from getting a fair trial.

Excessive Bail

The Eighth Amendment provides that excessive bail shall not be required. **Bail** is the amount of money or property a defendant is required to post (give to the court) as a guarantee that she or he will appear in court at the proper time. In determining the amount of bail, the judge considers the seriousness of the case, the criminal record of the accused, and the ability of the accused to post bail.

Under a 1984 law, **preventive detention** of some persons accused of committing federal crimes is permitted. Under that law, if federal judges have good reason to believe the person will commit another serious crime before the trial, they can order the holding of accused felons without bail. In 1987, the Supreme Court upheld that law. More than half the states also have adopted preventive detention laws.

Cruel and Unusual Punishment

The Eighth Amendment forbids cruel and unusual punishment. The authors of the Constitution were fearful of barbaric punishments such as boiling, tarring and feathering, crucifixion, burning at the stake, and whipping.

The Supreme Court has found relatively few punishments cruel and unusual. In *Louisiana* v. *Resweber* (1947), the court found that it was not unconstitutional to subject a convicted murderer to a second electrocution after the first attempt had failed. In *Rhodes* v. *Chapman*

Evaluation Strategies

1. Have the students write their responses to the Preview Questions at the beginning of the section.
2. Have the students write their answers to the Section 3 Review questions.
3. Have the students take the Section 3 Quiz found in the *TRB.*

Section 3 Review (Answers)

1. The Fifth Amendment requires indictment by a grand jury; protection against double jeopardy; the right against self-incrimination; the protection of due process of law; and the guarantee of just compensation for private property taken for public use.
2. A requirement that requires that suspects be clearly informed of their rights before being questioned.
3. Answers will vary, e.g., these rights are all meant to ensure that citizens are innocent until proven guilty, and will receive as much protection as is practical against the power of government.
4. The function of the grand jury is to see if enough evidence exists to indict the accused of having committed a crime.
5. Answers will vary, e.g., capital punishment is not cruel and unusual under the Eighth Amendment. It was not regarded as cruel and unusual by the founders who wrote the amendment, nor by those who ratified it.

SECTION 4

Points to Stress

- The difference between civil liberties and civil rights.
- The Equal Protection Clause of the Fourteenth Amendment.
- Guidelines used by the Supreme Court in deciding when a state law violates the equal protection clause.
- The significance of *Brown* v. *Topeka Board of Education.*
- Events that led to the passage of the Civil Rights Act of 1964.

Kickoff Activity

Write on the chalkboard *civil rights.* Ask the students to list at least eight words or phrases that they associate with civil rights. After the students have finished their lists, encourage them to share and discuss their lists informally.

Caption Answer Generally, the Court has maintained that capital punishment—if fairly applied—is Constitutional.

Working with the Preview Questions

Ask the students to read these study questions to themselves, and encourage volunteers to share their ideas about the answers.

Teaching Strategies

Introduction

Have one or two volunteers read the section introduction aloud to the rest of the class. Then open a class discussion by asking these questions: Why have some groups in this country not received equal rights and treatment? What forms of discrimination have you experienced or observed?

Criminals sentenced to punishment by execution in the state of Louisiana are strapped into this electric chair where, at midnight, they receive a charge of 2,000 volts for a full minute. What has the Supreme Court said about the constitutionality of capital punishment?

(1980), it found that putting two prisoners in a cell built for one is not cruel and unusual.

There are instances, however, when the Court has found some punishments to be cruel and unusual. It struck down **denaturalization** (loss of citizenship) as a legitimate punishment for leaving the United States in order to avoid military draft. It has also ruled that a prison inmate cannot be denied proper medical care.

Although most Americans feel that torture or other similar forms of punishment are cruel and unusual, there is no such agreement on capital punishment (punishment by execution). There has been much controversy over this issue throughout the years. In 1972 in *Furman* v. *Georgia,* the Court found that the death penalty was unconstitutional as it was then applied, which was mainly at judges' discretion. Thirty-five states enacted laws they thought would satisfy the Court's objections. Some made the death penalty mandatory for certain crimes and others set up a two-stage process with a separate hearing to decide on an appropriate sentence. The mandatory process was found to be unconstitutional, but the two-stage process was found to be constitutional. In 1976 in *Gregg* v. *Georgia* the Court ruled that the "punishment of death does not invariably violate the Constitution." It ruled that a well-designed two-stage process could eliminate the possibility that the death penalty would be inflicted in an arbitrary or capricious manner.

The Court ruled on various cases involving the death penalty during the 1980s and 1990s. In essence, it has maintained that if fairly applied, the death penalty is constitutional.

SECTION 3 REVIEW

1. What protection does the Fifth Amendment offer?
2. What are the Miranda Rules?
3. Why does the Constitution guarantee a right to counsel? A right to trial by jury? Protection against cruel and unusual punishment?
4. What is the function of a grand jury?
5. **For critical analysis:** In your opinion, is the death penalty cruel and unusual punishment? Give reasons for your argument.

SECTION 4

Equal Protection Under the Law

Preview Questions

- What is the difference between civil liberties and civil rights?
- What is the Fourteenth Amendment's equal protection clause? What are the Supreme Court's guidelines in deciding when a state law violates the equal protection clause?
- Why was *Brown* v. *Board of Education of Topeka* (1954) significant?
- What events led to the passage of the Civil Rights Act in 1964?

So far we have been discussing relationships between government and the individual. While civil liberties

TEACHING ARCHITECTS OF THE AMERICAN DREAM

Read

Let the students respond to these questions: Who was Dr. Martin Luther King, Jr.? What did he stand for? Whose interests did he promote? Why do we celebrate his birthday as a federal holiday? Encourage the students to share information about and personal responses to King and his work. Then let the students read the first part of this feature on their own. Have a volunteer prepare and then read aloud the excerpt from King's "I Have a Dream" speech, or play an audiotape or videotape of portions of this speech.

Discuss

Stimulate discussion by asking questions such as these: What was nonviolent confrontation with injustice? Why do you think people were able to use such tactics? Why do you think the Lincoln Memorial was chosen as the site for the speeches at the 1963 March on Washington? How do you feel when you hear King's words (and see the people gathered there, listening to him—if videotape is available)?

Analyze and Apply

Have each student interview at least one adult old enough to remember the 1963 March on Washington. Did that adult attend the march? Does he or she remember reading about it or watching it on TV? What reactions to the march does the adult now remember? What does the adult remember about King himself—his presence, his speeches, his influences? After the students have completed their interviews, let them meet in groups to compare and discuss what the adults remembered: What aspects of the memories are similar? Why are the memories different?

Review

Ask the students these review questions: When did Dr. Martin Luther King, Jr. live? What kind of

ARCHITECT OF The American Dream

Martin Luther King, Jr., was born in Atlanta Georgia in 1929. A Baptist minister who had inherited his father's and grandfather's deeply held religious beliefs, King became the chief architect of the civil rights movement.

Combining the teachings of his religious heritage with the philosophies of Henry David Thoreau and Mahatma Gandhi, King came to believe that real progress toward racial equality could only be achieved through nonviolent resistance to social injustice. He helped organize the Southern Christian Leadership Conference (SCLC) and, in 1957, began to speak in many parts of the South, always urging blacks to nonviolently oppose racial **segregation**—the separation of specific groups from the rest of society. King was jailed, beaten, and pelted with stones for his efforts to create peace.

In 1964, at age 35, Dr. King was awarded the Nobel Peace Prize. He was the youngest person to ever receive this distinction. Four years later, Dr. King was assassinated in Memphis, Tennessee.

One of the most powerful demonstrations led by Dr. King was a massive, nonviolent march to Washington, D.C., in 1963. The purpose of the march was to call the nation's attention to the need to end segregation, to create jobs, and to ensure freedom. The extraordinary impact of the event gave impetus to the passage of the Civil Rights Act of 1964. Standing before the Lincoln Memorial, he addressed the thousands of people present and the millions watching on television. In words that stirred all that heard them, Dr. King described his vision of the promise and future of America:

HIS WORDS

"In a sense we have come to our nation's Capital to cash a check. When the architects of our republic wrote the magnificent words of the Constitution and the Declaration of Independence, they were signing a promissory note to which every American was to fall heir. This note was a promise that all men would be guaranteed the unalienable rights of life, liberty, and the pursuit of happiness.

". . . So we have come to cash this check—a check that will give us upon demand the riches of freedom and the security of justice. We have also come to this hallowed spot to remind America of the fierce urgency of *now*. . . . *Now* is the time to open the doors of opportunity to all of God's children. *Now* is the time to lift our nation from the quicksand of racial injustice to the solid rock of brotherhood. . . .

"I say to you today, my friends, that in spite of the difficulties and frustrations of the moment I still have a dream. It is a dream deeply rooted in the American dream. I have a dream that one day this nation will rise up and live out the true meaning of its creed: 'We hold these truths to be self-evident—that all men are created equal.' . . . I have a dream that my four little children will one day live in a nation where they will not be judged by the color of their skin but by the content of their character.

rights did he champion? What method of confrontation did he promote?

Developing Critical Thinking Skills (Answers)

1. His values and beliefs are based on his religious training. He speaks with a religious fervor and frames his words as if giving a sermon. Much of his speech is interspersed with religious references, such as when he speaks of God's children.

2. When he spoke of his dream it was for the entire country. He realized that the equality he spoke of must be for all people to be meaningful.

3. The meaning of the statement "all men are created equal" is interpreted differently by different people. To some it meant only that all white men were created equal. The author of the Declaration of Independence, Thomas Jefferson, argued that the statement "all men are created equal" should apply to all men. Slavery, however, remained as an institution until the Civil War. The Civil Rights movement did not come until almost 100 years later, in response to slavery and its aftermath of discrimination.

Martin Luther King, Jr.

HIS WORDS–*continued*

"... So let freedom ring ... from every mountainside, let freedom ring ... to speed up that day when all of God's children, black men and white men, Jews and Gentiles, Protestants and Catholics, will be able to join hands and sing in the words of that old Negro spiritual, 'Free at last, free at last. Thank God Almighty, we are free at last!'"

DEVELOPING CRITICAL THINKING SKILLS

1. In what way does Dr. King's religious training show itself in his words?
2. What do you think is the meaning of the following comment, written by Dr. King while he was jailed in Birmingham, Alabama: "Injustice anywhere is a threat to justice everywhere"?
3. In his speech Dr. King invoked a sentence from the Declaration of Independence, concerning the self-evident nature of the truth that all men are created equal. Why, if such a truth is so self-evident, did there have to be a civil rights movement in the United States?

FOR FURTHER READING

Oates, Stephen. *Let the Trumpet Sound—The Life of Martin Luther King, Jr.* New York: Harper and Row, 1982.

Washington, James Melvin, ed. *A Testament of Hope—The Essential Writing of Martin Luther King, Jr.* San Francisco: Harper and Row, 1986.

Martin Luther King, Jr. and the Freedom Movement, by Lillie Patterson. New York: Facts On File, Inc., 1989.

Comprehension
Give several volunteers a chance to restate the quotation from the Fourteenth Amendment in their own words.

Discussion Starter
Encourage the students to consider the examples of reasonable and unreasonable laws that might be passed by a state. Why is each example either reasonable or unreasonable? Can you cite other examples of reasonable laws that apply to some citizens and not to others? Can you cite other examples of unreasonable laws?

Discussion Starter
Guide the students in considering and discussing the suspect classification guideline: Why is the burden of proof on the government to show that such laws are necessary? What kinds of laws made on the basis of race or national origin might be considered unreasonable?

Vocabulary
Have the students define the verb *segregate,* using a dictionary if necessary. What or who is segregated under segregation laws? You may also want to have the students check and compare the definition of *apartheid.*

Enrichment
Encourage interested students to research Jim Crow laws. When and where were they in effect? What did they regulate? How did people respond to them? Ask the researchers to write reports of their findings, and make these reports available to the rest of the class.

Enrichment
Help the students consider and discuss Homer Plessy's actions in the form of a one- or two-page essay. The essay should discuss the following: What do you think motivated Plessy to sit in the railway

protect citizens from government, civil rights protect people from people. **Civil rights** are the protections granted in the Constitution that recognize that *all citizens must be treated equally under the law.* Civil rights involve legislation that extends the rights protecting people from wrongs by other people. In this case the government becomes a potentially *positive* force for ensuring that the rights of minorities are protected against unjust actions by majorities and their elected representatives.

While it is true that the democratic ideal is for all people to have equal rights and treatment before the law, and while it is true that the Constitution guarantees those rights, this ideal has not always been reality. People put the ideals into practice and, as James Madison once pointed out, and as we all know, people are not angels. Even with the constitutional guarantees, there are some people who would try to deny those rights to others.

The Equal Protection Clause

Equal in importance to the due process clause of the Fourteenth Amendment is its final clause declaring that "no State shall . . . deny to any person within its jurisdiction the equal protection of the law." Known as the **equal protection clause**, it means that states must treat all their citizens in an equal manner, and may not draw *unreasonable* distinctions between different classes of people.

The government can, however, still pass reasonable laws applying to some citizens and not to others. For example, states may prohibit people under a certain age to marry or to purchase alcoholic beverages. States also tax certain groups of people differently than others. For example, putting a tax on luxury items such as yachts and private jets would only affect the wealthy and not others. These kinds of laws are considered reasonable. An unreasonable variation of these laws would be taxing only female purchasers of luxury items, or prohibiting marriages of all people of a certain religion.

Distinguishing between what is reasonable and what is unreasonable is not always as clear, and has been a difficult question for the courts. Over the years the Supreme Court has developed at least three guidelines for deciding when a state law violates the equal protection clause:

- **rational-basis test**—Whether the law reasonably relates to an accepted and proper goal of government.
- **suspect classification**—When classifications such as race or national origin form the basis of a law, the classifications are considered suspect and are subject to strict judicial scrutiny. The burden of proof is on the government to show that the law is necessary.
- **fundamental rights**—When a state law deals with fundamental rights, such as voting, freedom of speech, or freedom of religion, the rational-basis test is not enough. The state law must pass a much stricter test. Fundamental rights are those necessary for a concept of ordered liberty.

The equal protection clause was originally intended to protect the newly freed slaves after the Civil War. In the early years after the war, the United States government made an effort to protect the rights of blacks living in the former states of the Confederacy. The Thirteenth Amendment, which had granted the slaves' freedom, and the Fourteenth Amendment, which guaranteed equal protection under the law, were part of that effort. By the

"Jim Crow" laws were laws that segregated the black community from the white community. These laws affected nearly all public facilities including drinking fountains (as shown here). What other examples of Jim Crow laws can you think of?

Caption Answer Student answers will vary but might include mention of separate restrooms for blacks and whites, segregated public accommodations such as hotels, restaurants, bars, and transportation, and segregated schools. You might also point out to students that some "Jim Crow" laws went so far as to set curfews that required African Americans to be off the streets by 10 P.M. Ticket windows, and entrances and exits to sporting events and theaters were also segregated. Additionally, the races were segregated in prisons and hospitals, and even in death as morgues, funeral homes, and cemeteries were segregated.

car reserved for whites? How do you imagine he felt when he was told to move, when he was arrested, and when he was convicted? Can you imagine yourself taking a step as daring as the one Plessy took? If so, what do you imagine that step might be?

Extension
Have two or three volunteers research the career and accomplishments of Justice John Harlan. Ask the volunteers to prepare a bulletin board displaying important facts about his work and quotations from his Court opinions.

Discussion Starter
Let the students discuss the actions taken by the Brown family: Why do you think the Browns wanted their daughter to attend the all-white school? What factors do you think the parents considered before they decided to sue the Board of Education? How do you imagine each member of the Brown family felt when the suit was finally settled? Do you think the Browns imagined the consequences of their suit when they decided their child should attend a nearby school? Why or why not?

Cooperative Learning
Ask the students to work in groups to research the NAACP. Group members should learn when and how it was founded, what its aims and accomplishments have been, and how it functions today. Group members might also explore the use of the term *colored people* in the organization's name: What changes in preferred usage have occurred since the founding of the NAACP?

Critical Thinking Skills
Guide the students in analyzing the motivations of those who resisted school integration: How do people usually feel about change? What emotions do you think this kind of change aroused in people who opposed it? How did their actions reflect those emotions? Do you think that some people still oppose school integration? Explain your response.

late 1870s, however, Southern legislatures began to pass a series of segregation laws, which are laws that separate the white community from the black community. Such laws were commonly called ''Jim Crow'' laws (from a song used in the nineteenth century during blackface minstrel shows). Some of the most common Jim Crow laws involved the use of public facilities such as schools and buses. They also affected housing, restaurants, hotels, and many other facilities.

Separate-But-Equal Doctrine In 1892 a group of Louisiana citizens decided to challenge a state law that required railroads to provide separate railway cars for African Americans. A black man named Homer Plessy boarded a train in New Orleans and sat in the railway car reserved for whites. When he refused to move, he was arrested and convicted of breaking the law.

Four years later, in 1896, the Supreme Court upheld the conviction and provided a constitutional basis for these segregation laws. In *Plessy* v. *Ferguson,* the Court held that the law did not violate the equal protection clause because *separate* facilities for blacks were *equal* to those for whites. As the lone dissenter, Justice John Harlan insisted that ''our Constitution is color blind, and neither knows nor tolerates classes among citizens.'' The majority opinion, however, established the **separate-but-equal doctrine**, which was used to justify segregation in many areas of American life for the next fifty years.

In the late 1930s and 1940s, the Supreme Court gradually moved away from the separate-but-equal doctrine. The major breakthrough, however, did not come until 1954 in a case involving an African-American girl who lived in Topeka, Kansas.

End of the Separate-But-Equal Doctrine In the 1950s, Topeka's schools, like those in many cities, were segregated. Mr. and Mrs. Oliver Brown wanted their daughter, Linda Carol Brown, to attend a white school a few blocks from their home instead of an all-black school that was twenty-one blocks away. With the help of lawyers from the National Association for the Advancement of Colored People (NAACP), Linda's family sued the Board of Education.

In *Brown* v. *Board of Education of Topeka* (1954), the court reversed *Plessy* v. *Ferguson.* The Court unanimously held that segregation by race in public education is unconstitutional. Chief Justice Earl Warren wrote:

> Does segregation of children in public schools solely on the basis of race, even though the physical facilities and other tangible factors may be equal, deprive children of the minority groups of equal educational opportunities? We believe that it does. . . . [Segregation generates in children] a feeling of inferiority as to their status in the community that may affect their hearts and minds in a way unlikely ever to be undone. . . . In the field of education the doctrine of ''separate but equal'' has no place. Separate educational facilities are inherently unequal.

The Court ordered desegregation to begin ''with all deliberate speed,'' and the federal courts began to take an active role in supervising the process.

Reactions to School Integration The Supreme Court ruling did not go unchallenged. Bureaucratic loopholes were used to delay desegregation. Another reaction was ''white flight,'' white parents sending their children to newly established private schools while some public schools became 100 percent black. Arkansas's Governor Orval Faubus used the state's national guard to block the integration of Central High School in Little Rock, Arkansas, in 1957, which led to increasing violence in the area. The federal court demanded that the troops be withdrawn. President Eisenhower had to federalize the Arkansas National Guard to quell the violence, and Central High finally became integrated.

▼ Black student Elizabeth Eckford is subjected to the hate-filled epithets of white students as she passes through the lines of National Guardsmen during the first day of integration at Little Rock's Central High School in 1957. What Supreme Court decision led to desegregation?

Caption Answer *Brown* v. *Board of Education of Topeka* (1954) was the landmark case that led to the desegregation of public schools. This important case reversed the separate but equal doctrine that had been in place since the *Plessy* v. *Ferguson* decision in 1896.

Enrichment
Ask a group of volunteers to research the use of busing in your community's school district. Have students ever been bused? If so, what was the primary purpose of the busing? Which students were bused to what schools? How did community members react? Are some students in the district still being bused? If so, why? Have the volunteers summarize their findings in the form of a news story.

Discussion Starter
Encourage the students to discuss their own opinions of busing: What are the advantages and disadvantages of busing? What conditions have made busing necessary? Can those conditions be overcome without using methods such as busing? If so, how? Urge all the students to participate in the discussion, sharing and defending their own opinions.

Vocabulary
Let several volunteers define the word *boycott.* Then ask: What purpose is a boycott expected to serve? Whose participation was necessary to make the Montgomery bus boycott effective?

Extension
Have the students work with partners or in small groups to research the leading organizations and individuals of the civil rights movement. Choices for research topics include SCLC, CORE, SNCC, the Urban League, NAACP, Ralph Abernathy, Roy Wilkins, A. Philip Randolph, James Farmer, Jesse Jackson, Stokley Carmichael, Julian Bond. Ask the students to share their findings in reports, either oral or written.

FYI

De facto segregation results when racial groups are segregated by residential patterns. Since the 1971 Swann case, court remedies have not been limited to "walk-in schools." Integration by busing has been the most common and the most controversial method used. So-called magnate schools have also become a popular way of obtaining more racially mixed schools.

By 1970, school systems with ***de jure* segregation**—segregation that is legally sanctioned—had been abolished. That is not to say that segregation was eliminated. It meant only that no public school could legally identify itself as one reserved for all whites or all blacks.

The process of achieving complete desegregation, in fact, is still underway, and will continue wherever ***de facto* segregation** exists (when circumstances produce segregation even though no law requires it). Housing patterns are one of the major reasons for school segregation. In your community there may be concentrations of a single ethnic group in certain geographical areas. This creates school districts that are largely all black or all Hispanic or all white.

Attempts to eliminate such *de facto* segregation have included redrawing school district lines and reassigning pupils. **Busing**—the transporting of students by bus to schools physically outside their neighborhood—to achieve racially desegregated schools has also been tried. The Supreme Court first sanctioned busing in Charlotte, North Carolina, in 1971. Following this decision, the Court upheld busing in Northern cities—Columbus, Ohio; Dayton, Ohio; and Denver, Colorado. In 1974, however, the Supreme Court rejected the idea of busing black children from the city to the suburbs and white children from the suburbs to the city. In 1976, the Supreme Court allowed the Norfolk, Virginia, public school system to end fifteen years of court-ordered busing of elementary schoolchildren.

Busing is unpopular with many groups. It is criticized because parents and children lose the convenience of neighborhood schools, and is resented because of the courts telling local governments what to do. Some black parents have criticized busing because it disrupts their children's lives and because of the hostility of white students in the new schools. There is also resentment at the implication that minority children can learn only if they sit next to white children. Still others have favored busing as a way of improving minority children's education and career opportunities, and improving minority and majority children's ability to get along together.

The Civil Rights Movement

In 1955, one year after the *Brown* decision, an African-American woman named Rosa Parks in Montgomery, Alabama, boarded a public bus. When it became crowded, she refused to move to the "colored section" at the rear of the bus. She was arrested and fined for violating Alabama's segregation laws. Her refusal and arrest spurred the local African-American community to

Caption Answer Student answers will vary but should act as a catalyst for classroom discussion on this important topic. Students should be encouraged to support their opinions on either side of this issue.

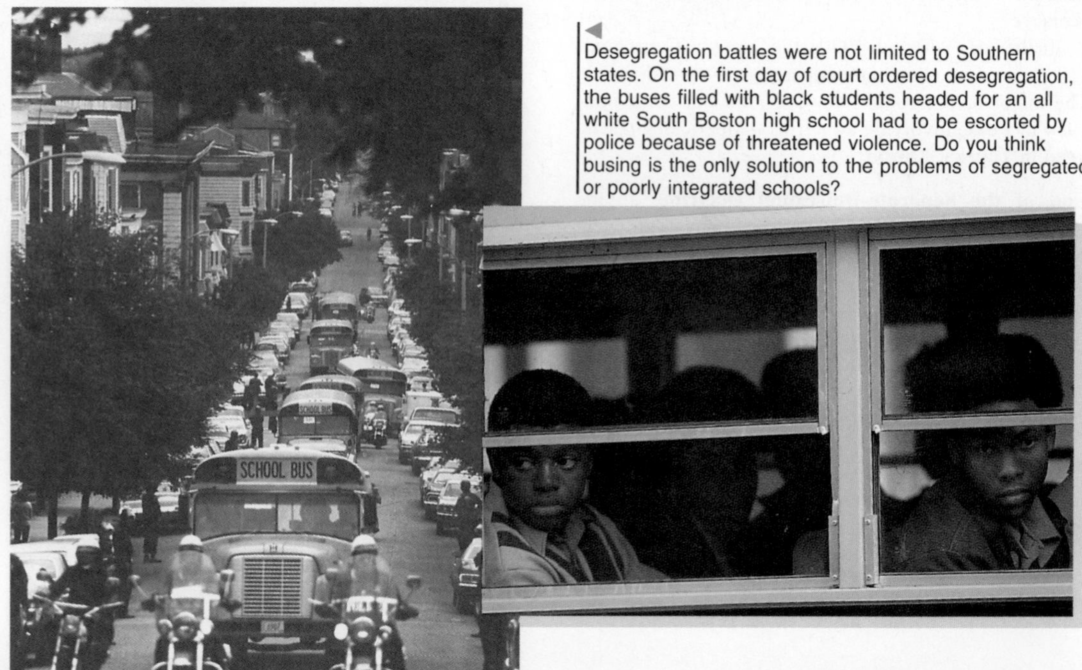

Desegregation battles were not limited to Southern states. On the first day of court ordered desegregation, the buses filled with black students headed for an all white South Boston high school had to be escorted by police because of threatened violence. Do you think busing is the only solution to the problems of segregated or poorly integrated schools?

TEACHING BUILDING SOCIAL STUDIES SKILLS

Read
Introduce this feature by letting the students discuss what they know about values: What is a value? Who has values? How do people develop values systems? How do they demonstrate their values? Then ask volunteers to read the feature aloud to the rest of the class.

Discuss
Encourage the students to discuss the information here: Although your values are strongly influenced by those around you, who makes the decisions about accepting and acting on specific values? What responsibilities do you take on when you begin to examine and evaluate your own values? Can you alter both your values and your biases? If so, how? If not, why not?

Analyze and Apply
Ask the students to start private journals in which they record thoughts about their own values and biases. Encourage the students to examine their values and biases and to work toward changes they consider appropriate. Remind the students to keep writing in these journals periodically.

Review
Have the students answer these review questions: What are values? What are biases? How can understanding your own biases help you when you examine political issues?

Practicing Your Skills (Answers)
As a follow-up activity, you might ask students to complete the Practicing Your Skills activity. Students can write their answers to each of the questions in the bulleted list. Students might wish to write these answers in their private journals mentioned in the Analyze and Apply activity for this Building Social Studies Skills feature. Explain to the students that this activity will help them to better understand their own values and biases. Remind students that their journals are private and will be read by no one else, including yourself.

BUILDING SOCIAL STUDIES SKILLS

Identifying Your Own Values and Biases

Each one of us has a set of values, that we may or may not consciously acknowledge. Out of those values arise value judgments about everything we consider. The influences of our parents, friends, schoolteachers, books we read, and so on all influence those values.

As a citizen, you must be able to examine issues, laws, court decisions, and other events. It is important to be aware of your values with respect to any given subject before you form an opinion. For example, if you are serving on a jury, your values may enter very strongly into your assessment of the testimony you hear. Be aware of how much your upbringing, such as your religion or a prejudice one of your parents might have, affects your views about what you hear and learn.

Biases and values are closely linked: Our biases are a result of our values, and affect the choices and judgments we make, such as when we analyze a political issue. If you have a bias against a particular group of people, you may resent a law favoring them even before you know what it means. If you have a bias against rich people or poor people, you may form an opinion about a court case concerning public welfare payments before you even know the particular facts. It is important that you try to conquer your biases when looking at political issues. If you succeed, you form a more objective picture of the arguments presented.

PRACTICING YOUR SKILLS

Read a magazine or newspaper article that concerns a civil rights issue such as immigration, housing for the poor, equal pay for women, or busing in public schools. After you read, ask yourself:

- To which groups of people mentioned in the article do I automatically react positively? To which ones do I react negatively? Why do I respond that way?
- How do my past experiences with a person or group of people from an ethnic or racial group make me feel about that group as a whole?
- What have my parents and teachers taught me about relating to different groups of people?
- Which groups of people have I not been exposed to and don't understand? How does this influence my opinion regarding their civil rights?

organize a year long **boycott** of the entire Montgomery bus system. (A boycott involves many people together not buying or using something.) The protest was led by a 27-year-old Baptist minister, Dr. Martin Luther King, Jr. During the protest period, he was jailed and his house was bombed. Despite the hostility and the overwhelming odds, the protesters were triumphant.

In 1956, a federal district court prohibited the segregation of buses in Montgomery, and the era of the **civil rights movement**, the movement by minorities and concerned whites to end problems of racial segregation, had begun. The movement was led by a number of diversified groups and individuals, including Dr. Martin Luther King, Jr. and his Southern Christian Leadership Council (SCLC). Other groups, such as the Congress for Racial Equality (CORE), and the National Association for the Advancement of Colored People (NAACP), also sought to secure equal rights for African Americans.

Civil disobedience, which is the deliberate and public disobedience of laws thought to be unjust, was one tactic used to gain civil rights. For example, in 1960 in Greensboro, North Carolina, four African-American students sat at the lunch counter at Woolworth's and ordered food. The waitress refused to serve them, but they stayed and were eventually arrested. Such nonviolent sit-ins, freedom marches, freedom rides, boycotts, lawsuits, and occasional violent confrontations were all tactics used by the civil rights movement to create awareness and bring about change.

The Civil Rights Act of 1964

As the civil rights movement demonstrated its strength, Congress began to pass civil rights laws. It became clear that while the Fourteenth Amendment prevented the government from discriminating, the private

Discussion Starter
Encourage the students to consider and discuss nonviolent civil disobedience: What is the intention of civil disobedience? What makes it so effective? Why can it be such a difficult tactic to use?

Comprehension
Check the students' comprehension by asking this question: Why was the Civil Rights Act—in addition to the Fourteenth Amendment—necessary?

TEACHING PROFILES

Read
Before the students read this Government in Action Profile of Rosa Parks, ask them the following questions: Can you name any heroes? (Students should be encouraged to name heroic people from politics, history, also possibly from entertainment or sports.) What makes someone a hero? Is it courage? Is it the willingness to accept personal risk for the greater good?, etc. Do you think heroes plan to be heroic? After the students have discussed these questions, ask a volunteer to read this profile of Rosa Parks.

Discuss
Encourage the students to discuss the information presented in this profile: Do you think Rosa Parks is a hero? Why or why not? Did she take a personal risk when she decided not to move to the back of the bus? Do you think she was frightened?

Analyze and Apply
Have class members read more about Rosa Parks. They should specifically find out about her job prior to December 1955, and about her life since her decision not to move to the back of the bus. Students should then work together to create a bulletin board display with information and photos of Rosa Parks and the Montgomery bus boycott.

Review
Have the students answer these review questions: Who was Rosa Parks? What did she do? What motivated her? Was her action planned or spontaneous? Why was her action such a stirring symbol to the African-American community in Montgomery, Alabama?

Think About It (Answers)
1. A boycott involves many people deciding together not to buy or use a product or service in order to force a change through economic pressure. The Montgomery bus boycott inspired confidence and pride in Alabama's African American community.
2. Students should understand that although Rosa Parks had not been overly involved with the Civil Rights movement prior to December 1955, her defiant stand for justice, which she took at personal risk, was recognized as heroic by all those connected with the Civil Rights movement.

GOVERNMENT IN ACTION

PROFILE

Rosa Parks

Early in December 1955 in Montgomery, Alabama, 40-year-old Rosa Parks boarded the bus to go home from work. The bus was filled, and when a white man boarded, the driver called on the four blacks to move to the back. Three got up and moved, but Parks, tired from a long day of working and the injustice of always having to move for white people, refused to move. She was promptly arrested.

The arrest of Parks ignited a protest that spread spontaneously through the African-American community. Several leaders, including the Reverend Martin Luther King, Jr., organized a boycott of the city's bus lines. The boycott inspired confidence and pride in the African-American community and a feeling spread that it was time for changes in race relations. Finally, in December 1956, as a result of the Supreme Court's intervention against segregation in public transportation, blacks and whites rode together on unsegregated buses for the first time in Alabama. The courage of Parks served as as catalyst to end segregation of buses, trains, lunch counters, and other public facilities in the South.

Rosa Parks was born on February 4, 1913, in Tuskegee, Alabama. Her childhood was marked by fears of the Ku Klux Klan and their persecution of African Americans. She studied at Alabama State College, worked briefly at clerical jobs, and finally became a tailor's assistant at a department store. Her husband, Raymond Parks, was a barber. The only indicator of her involvement in civil rights was her volunteer work for the NAACP, in which she helped campaign to register African-American voters.

Although Parks's action and arrest began civil rights activism in Alabama, she suffered for what she did. She was fired from her job within two months and her husband eventually lost his job as well. They were harassed and threatened. She went to work for the group that coordinated the boycott and began to speak for civil rights throughout the country. She and her husband eventually moved to Detroit, where she became involved in community work and continued to work for civil rights. She has been honored many times, and millions saw her appearance at the 1988 Democratic National Convention. She was hailed by Martin Luther King, Jr. just before his assassination as "the great fuse that led to the modern stride toward freedom."

▲ In December, 1955, Rosa Parks refused to obey a law requiring segregated seating on public buses. Parks' refusal and arrest helped to make her a hero of the civil rights movement.

THINK ABOUT IT

1. What is a boycott and what effect did the bus boycott have on Alabama's business community?
2. How do you think that an individual who was relatively uninvolved in the civil rights movement could become such an important figure in that movement?

Figure Answer The *Brown* case led the way to school integration; the *Gideon* decision insured legal counsel for all criminal defendants; the *Miranda* ruling demands that all accused persons be informed of their constitutional rights.

Cooperative Learning
Let the students work in groups to read and discuss the specifics of the Civil Rights Act of 1964. Then have each group member answer these questions: Which provision of the Civil Rights Act do you consider most important? Why?

Reteaching Strategies
1. Refer the students to the questions they posed as they began reading Section 4. Let the students work in groups to answer these questions, referring to the text as necessary.
2. Have the students work with partners to list the contributions of Dr. Martin Luther King, Jr. to the civil rights movement.

Evaluation Strategies
1. Have the students write their answers to the Section 4 Review questions.
2. Have the students take the Section 4 Quiz found in the *TRB*.

Section 4 Review (Answers)
1. The rational-basis test judges whether the law is reasonably related to an accepted and proper goal of government. Suspect classification tests whether classifications such as race or national origin form the basis of the law. If a state law deals with fundamental rights, such as voting, freedom of speech, or freedom of religion, it must pass a stricter test than the rational-basis test.
2. The separate-but-equal doctrine was established by *Plessy* v. *Ferguson* in 1896 when the Supreme court ruled that a law did not violate the equal protection clause because separate facilities provided for blacks were equal to those for whites.
3. The Court reversed *Plessy* v. *Ferguson* and held that segregation by race in public education is unconstitutional.
4. *De Jure* segregation is segregation that is legally sanctioned. *De facto* segregation is when circumstances, usually residential patterns, produce segregation even though no law requires it.
5. The Civil Rights Act of 1964 was the first and most comprehensive of all civil rights laws. It forbade discrimination in public accommodations on the basis of gender, color, race, religion, and national origin.
6. Between 1896 and 1954 there was a growing awareness in society that segregation between the races was patently unfair and not keeping with either the Bill of Rights, the Constitution, or the American Creed. Moreover, blacks were making their segregated plight a national issue by holding marches, rallies, and other public events. The press gave these events headlines and support. Separate can never truly be equal because separation in and of itself generates a sense of inequality.

In the Words of the Court

***Brown* v. *Board of Education* (1954)**
Chief Justice Warren: "In these days, it is doubtful that any child may reasonably be expected to succeed in life if he is denied the opportunity of an education. Such an opportunity, where the state has undertaken to provide it, is a right which must be made available to all on equal terms . . . We conclude that in the field of public education the doctrine of 'separate but equal' has no place. Separate educational facilities are inherently unequal."

***Gideon* v. *Wainwright* (1963)**
Justice Black: "That government hires lawyers to prosecute and defendants who have the money hire lawyers to defend are the strongest indications of the widespread belief that lawyers in criminal courts are necessities, not luxuries. The right of one charged with a crime to counsel may not be deemed fundamental and essential to fair trials in some countries, but it is in ours."

***Miranda* v. *Arizona* (1966)**
Chief Justice Warren: "As for the procedural safeguards to be employed,. . . the following measures are required. Prior to any questioning, the [accused] person must be warned that he has a right to remain silent, that any statement he does make may be used as evidence against him, and that he has a right to the presence of an attorney, either retained or appointed."

FIGURE 6–1 In the Words of the Court. This figure features excerpts from the written decisions from three of the important cases discussed in this chapter. How would you summarize the importance of each of these decisions?

sector—businesses, restaurants, and so on—could still freely refuse to employ and serve nonwhites.

The Civil Rights Act of 1964 was the first and most comprehensive of all the civil rights laws. It forbade specific forms of discrimination on the basis of gender, color, race, religion, and national origin:

- It outlawed discrimination in public places of accommodation, such as hotels, restaurants, snack bars, movie theaters, and public transportation.
- It cut off federal funds for any federal or state government project or facility that practiced any form of discrimination.
- It banned racial discrimination in employment.
- It outlawed arbitrary discrimination in voter registration.
- It authorized the federal government to sue to desegregate public schools and facilities.

SECTION 4 REVIEW

1. Explain the three types of guidelines the Supreme Court has used for deciding when a state violates the equal protection clause.
2. What was the separate-but-equal doctrine?
3. What was the Supreme Court decision in *Brown* v. *Board of Education of Topeka*?
4. What is the difference between *de jure* and *de facto* segregation?
5. What is the Civil Rights Act of 1964 and how does it protect minorities?
6. **For critical analysis:** How could the Supreme Court in *Plessy* v. *Ferguson* decide that separate-but-equal facilities for whites and blacks did not constitute discrimination? What changed between 1896, when the Court made that decision, and 1954, when the Court reversed itself? Why is separate never truly equal?

SECTION 5

Points to Stress

- The definition of affirmative action.
- Arguments in favor of and against affirmative action.
- Supreme Court interpretations that have allowed or prohibited different treatment of men and women.

Kickoff Activity

Write these questions on the chalkboard: In our country, who has the right to equality under the law? Which groups of people still feel excluded from that right? Give the students five minutes to write their responses. Then ask volunteers to share their ideas with the rest of the class.

Working with the Preview Questions

Read the study questions aloud to the class and ask: What note-taking headings do these questions suggest to you? Have the students agree upon certain headings and use them to prepare note-taking sheets. Remind the students to use these prepared sheets to take notes as they study Section 5.

Caption Answer Students should understand that discrimination in this country has traditionally been a problem that has plagued almost all racial groups other than whites. Therefore, when discrimination against whites is charged, it is often labeled reverse discrimination.

Teaching Strategies

Introduction

Let a volunteer read the section introduction aloud to the class. Then encourage the students to discuss their responses to these questions: Why should each group of people work on its own to seek equality in our country? What prevents all groups—majority and minority—from working together?

Enrichment

Ask several interested volunteers to research the Equal Employment Opportunity Commission: What are its powers and responsibilities? Who serves on it? How is it funded? How effective is it? Have the volunteers create a chart with relevant EEOC information to be displayed in the classroom.

Vocabulary

Ask volunteers to define the verb *remedy* as it is used here: to remedy past discrimination.

Discussion Starter

Encourage the students to share and discuss their own reactions to affirmative action programs: Do you think they are fair? Effective? Necessary?

Enrichment

Ask the students to research the question of quotas in hiring and school acceptances: What is the history of the quota system? Who now opposes any use of quotas? Who supports quotas? After the students have read about quotas, encourage them to discuss their own ideas about the uses of quotas in hiring and promoting employees and in accepting students.

SECTION 5

New Challenges

Preview Questions

- What are the arguments for and against affirmative action?
- How does the Constitution allow for laws that treat men and women differently?

The struggle for equality in America has persisted, and has extended to include many other groups. The civil rights movement served as an inspiration and model for the women's movement and the differently abled as well as for the efforts of Hispanics, Asian Americans, Native Americans, and other groups to seek social and economic equality. The rise of these new movements has brought even greater challenges for our society.

Beyond Equal Protection

A part of the Civil Rights Act of 1964 called for prohibiting discrimination in employment. The federal government began to legislate programs of **equal employment opportunity (EEO)**. Such programs require that employers' hiring and promotion practices guarantee the same opportunities to all individuals. Experience soon showed that because minorities often had less opportunity for education and relevant work experience than did whites, they were still excluded from many jobs. Consequently, a new strategy was developed.

Initiated by President Johnson, the new program came to be called **affirmative action**, which developed policies designed to overcome the results of past discrimination. The idea was that even though new laws make discrimination illegal, they cannot make up for the consequences of discriminatory practices of the past. For example, suppose an African-American male was unable to be promoted in his company because the company discriminated against him in the past. Even though those practices are suddenly illegal, the change in the present law does not make up for years of discrimination.

Affirmative action programs require employers to take positive steps to remedy *past* discrimination. This means that preference in jobs and college admissions might be given to members of groups that have been discriminated against in the past. All public and private employers who receive federal funds have been required to adopt and implement these programs. Thus, the policy of affirmative action was applied to all agencies of the federal, state, and local governments, and to all private employers who sell goods or services to any agency of the federal government. In short, it covers nearly all the nation's major employers and many of its smaller ones.

▲ When Alan Bakke was denied admission to the University of California's Medical School at Davis, he charged the University with reverse discrimination. What was the basis for his claim?

Affirmative Action Tested The Court's first major affirmative action case was *Regents of the University of California* v. *Bakke* (1978). Alan Bakke, a white male, had been denied admission to the University's medical school at Davis. The school had set aside 16 of the 100 seats in each year's entering class for nonwhite students, and it had filled that **quota** (specific number set aside) with several nonwhites less qualified than Bakke. He charged the University with **reverse discrimination**, discrimination against whites.

The Supreme Court was divided on the case. In a 5 to 4 decision it held that Bakke had been denied equal protection and should be admitted. The majority said that although the Constitution does not allow race to be used as the *only* factor in making affirmative action decisions, both the Constitution and the Civil Rights Act of 1964

TEACHING CITIZENSHIP SKILLS AND RESPONSIBILITIES

Read

Introduce this feature by asking students what they think is meant by the term *differently abled.* Students should understand that *differently abled* is one of many terms used to describe people with some form of physical disability. It is a term that has been chosen because it has fewer negative connotations than past terms, such as *handicapped, crippled, disabled,* etc. You might ask students if they know of any other nonderogatory terms that are currently being used. If you have a student in your class with a physical disability, he or she might wish to respond to this question. Additionally, you might wish to discuss the whole idea of labeling, whether it be the term *differently abled* or the term *disabled.* By using such labels, are these people dehumanized? Does this somehow make them seem to be less? It is important that students understand that people with physical disabilities, or the differently abled, are first and foremost, people. After this discussion is completed, have a volunteer read this feature to the class.

Discuss

Have the students discuss the information presented here. Do you know anyone who misuses parking spaces set aside for the differently abled? Why do you think these people do this? Why did Senator Harkin refer to the Americans with Disabilities Act of 1990 as an "Emancipation Proclamation" for disabled Americans? Do you think this is an accurate description of this act?

Analyze and Apply

Have a volunteer read aloud the list of steps that each citizen can take. Go over these with students to make sure they understand them. Then have each student, as a homework assignment, create their own access booklet for a public facility in your community. Students may choose a shopping mall, a fast food restaurant, public park, a school, etc. Each student should point out what steps this facility has taken to provide equal access, as well as any existing obstacles to access.

Review

Have the students answer these review questions: What is meant by the term *differently abled*? Why is equal access important? What does the Americans with Disabilities Act of 1990 do?

Taking Action (Answers)

Taking Action activities will vary. You might wish to make note of Activity 1, however, if you plan to tour a government building such as a courthouse, or county, state, or federal building as a part of your study of later chapters.

CITIZENSHIP SKILLS AND RESPONSIBILITIES

Equal Access for the Differently Abled

Most people have never had to cope with entering a building in a wheelchair only to find steps or a revolving door blocking the way. Most people have never known what it feels like to be prevented from entering an aisle or a fitting room or a restroom. Most people have never tried to enter a store without their sight. Most people have never been turned down for a job because of physical disability. Yet there are over 40 million Americans with some kind of disability which hinders their enjoyment of many of the privileges most of us take for granted everyday.

Whether you are differently abled in some way, have a friend or relative who is, or are just concerned about the problems of disability, there are steps you can take as a responsible citizen. This may mean many things, from respecting handicapped parking spaces, to being aware of laws passed for the differently abled, to taking action in your own community.

The most recent legislation passed to provide expanded access to public facilities is the Americans with Disabilities Act of 1990. This act prohibits job discrimination against Americans with physical and mental disabilities and requires access to public buildings and public services. "This is an emancipation proclamation for disabled Americans," proclaimed the bill's sponsor, Iowa Democrat Tom Harkin.

What you do as a concerned citizen in your community may make a big difference in quite a few lives. Here are some suggestions for taking action if you find that the differently abled are denied equal access to transportation, shopping, recreation, employment, or just plain living in your community.

- Write a letter or call the mayor's office detailing your complaint.
- Write a letter to the editor of your newspaper. Encourage friends to write letters.
- Go to meetings at which decisions are being made by public agencies and private companies that would affect the differently abled.
- Write a letter or make a personal visit to an inaccessible store's manager and discuss the problem. Encourage others to write letters.
- Some cities publish "Access" booklets listing information about the accessibility of buildings in the city. Find out if your hometown has one. If not, organize a group of volunteers to compile one.
- If you, or someone you know, has been discriminated against by a place of employment, file a written complaint. If you are not satisfied, write to:

  Office of Civil Rights
  Department of Health
  and Human Services
  300 Independence Avenue, S.W.
  Washington, DC 20201
- Ask family or friends to join in your campaign.
- Communicate your concerns to your state legislators.

TAKING ACTION

1. Take a tour of a government building and take notes regarding every feature designed to provide equal access for the differently abled. Report your findings to the class.
2. Make a list of five buildings in your community that would provide barriers for any differently abled group of people. Devise a plan of action to remedy the problems.

Discussion Starter
Ask the students to compare the two test cases, *Regents of the University of California* v. *Bakke* and *Kaiser Aluminum and Chemical Co.* v. *Weber.* What are the most important differences between the cases? Why do you think one case was decided in favor of affirmative action and the other against affirmative action? Would you have made the same decisions in the two cases? Why or why not?

Cooperative Learning
Have the students work in four groups to investigate the current status of women's rights in these four areas: administration of their children's estates, spousal benefits from the armed services, access to community service clubs, access to large private clubs.

Discussion Starter
Encourage the students to consider and discuss this statement: "Classification by sex is constitutional if the law is intended to serve an important governmental objective." What important governmental objectives can classification by sex serve? What kinds of laws do you think are legal under this consideration?

Reteaching Strategies
1. Ask the students to work in small groups to review and revise the notes they took on Section 5. Remind the students to refer to the text as they make any corrections or revisions in their notes.
2. Have the students work with partners to write their own definitions of these terms: *affirmative action, reverse discrimination, suffragist.*

Vocabulary
Ask volunteers to explain what a set-aside program is. If no one is familiar with the term, help the students use the context of the paragraph to define the term.

Discussion Starter
Guide the students in discussing the ruling in the case involving Alaskan cannery workers: According to this decision, who bears the burden of proving past discrimination? Why? Do you consider this fair? Why or why not?

Vocabulary
Ask the students to compare the two terms *suffragists* and *suffragettes:* How are they alike? How do they differ? To what period is the term *suffragette* more likely to be applied? Why? Can both still be used? Why or why not?

Discussion Starter
Have the students note the years in which women were still widely considered "the weaker sex" and thought to have their correct place "in the home." How many years have passed since those statements were generally accepted? What changes have taken place since then? What do you think may be the results of so many changes taking place so quickly?

do allow its use as *one among several* factors in such situations.

One year later, a major test of affirmative action programs in private employment came in *United Steelworkers of America* v. *Weber* (1979). The company had created training programs that had reserved half the positions for minorities. Brian Weber, a white worker, was not selected for the trainings on three occasions, even though he had more seniority than several of the African-American employees chosen.

The Supreme Court, in a 5 to 2 decision, upheld the company's affirmative action program. It ruled that the 1964 Civil Rights Act did not prohibit affirmative action in private industry.

Rejecting Some Affirmative Action In the late 1980s the Supreme Court issued a string of rulings that rejected some affirmative action programs. In *Richmond* v. *Crosin* (1989), the Court rejected a minority set-aside program for city government contracts in Richmond, Virginia. The city had provided that any company to which the city had awarded a construction contract had to subcontract, or set aside, at least 30 percent of the work for minority businesses. The Court ruled that the set-aside program denied white contractors their Fourteenth Amendment right to equal protection.

In another case in 1989, the Supreme Court ruled that white firefighters in Birmingham, Alabama, could challenge a minority-hiring plan after city officials and blacks had agreed to the plan. In response to this decision, courts across the country began reopening old civil rights cases and allowing white men to challenge the hiring and promotion of blacks under court decrees issued up to twenty years ago. Another ruling involved Alaskan cannery workers who charged their employers with employment bias. The Supreme Court ruled that statistical evidence was not enough proof to support the employees' claim of racial discrimination. The employees must also be able to show that the conditions they challenge are not the result of some legitimate business necessity.

Discrimination Based on Gender

Since the Constitution does not mention women, the Supreme Court ruled throughout most of U.S. history that laws discriminating against women did *not* violate the equal protection clause of the Fourteenth Amendment. Most often the laws that treated men and women differently were said to be necessary "to protect the weaker sex." Because of such discrimination, women have long sought to gain equal rights and responsibilities in American society.

In its early stage, the struggle for women's rights concerned the right to vote. In fact, **suffragists** (those advocating women's right to vote)[2], made sure that a proposed constitutional amendment to this effect was introduced at every congressional session from 1878 to 1919. This right was finally won with the passage of the Nineteenth Amendment in 1920.

Later came challenges to gender discrimination in other areas such as economic status, housing, and employment. In 1948, for example, a case came before the Supreme Court regarding a law forbidding any woman, other than the wife or daughter of a tavern owner, to work as a barmaid. The Court ruled in favor of the law on the grounds that it preserved the family unity and the morality of women. In 1961, in *Hoyt* v. *Florida,* the Court found no fault with a law that required men to serve on juries but gave women the choice of serving or not. It said, "It is still true that a woman's place is in the home."

The changing role of women—as evidenced by a larger percentage working outside the home—finally began to change the Court's position toward women in the 1970s. In *Reed* v. *Reed* (1971), the Court struck down an Idaho law that gave fathers automatic preference over mothers in the administration of their children's estate. In *Frontiero* v. *Richardson* (1973), the Court overturned a federal law that granted different benefits to male and female spouses of members of the armed services. In 1987, it upheld a California law that prohibits community service clubs from excluding women. In 1988, it upheld a New York City law that forbids gender discrimination by large private clubs.

The Court continued to allow gender-based distinctions in some cases. For example, in 1981 in *Rostker* v. *Goldberg,* it upheld Congress's power to require men, but not women, to register for the draft. The cases have said that classification by sex is constitutional *if* the law is intended to serve an important government objective.

Section 5 Review

1. What are affirmative action programs?
2. What is reverse discrimination?
3. **For critical analysis:** Why did it take until the 1950s for discrimination to become a major national issue?

2. The word *suffragists* comes from *suffrage,* which means the right to vote, especially in a political election. Universal suffrage gives everyone the right to vote. Women who advocated universal suffrage were called *suffragettes.*

Evaluation Strategies
1. Have the students write their answers to the Section 5 Review questions.
2. Have the students take the Section 5 Quiz found in the *TRB.*

Section 5 Review (Answers)
1. Affirmative action programs were developed to overcome the results of past discrimination.
2. Discrimination against white males caused by affirmative action programs.
3. Answers will vary, e.g., it took almost 100 years after the Civil War for African Americans to obtain a political strength sufficient to force discrimination onto the national agenda. Also, views about discrimination in general and particularly against African Americans changed dramatically. Further, there was much migration of African Americans to the North where they saw a less segregated society. Many of them returned to the South and decided to help southern African Americans fight discrimination.

TEACHING CHALLENGE TO THE AMERICAN DREAM

Read
Ask the students to review the meaning of these terms: *affirmative action* and *reverse discrimination.* How are the two related? Then let volunteers read the feature text aloud to the rest of the class.

Discuss
Help the students discuss the issues raised in this feature: Whose rights are served by affirmative action? Whose rights are served by the avoidance of reverse discrimination? Is either of those groups more important than the other? Is one kind of right a "higher good" than the other?

Analyze and Apply
Have the students investigate affirmative action policies and possible charges of reverse discrimination in local companies and schools. Let the students write up their findings in short reports, to be shared with the rest of the class.

Review
Ask the students these review questions: What is the central argument of those who support affirmative action? What is the central argument of those who oppose it?

You Decide (Answers)
1. Answers will vary, e.g., the first two would be advantageous for the company, the second two would be disadvantageous.
2. Answers will vary, e.g., they should give minorities equal opportunity without unfair advantage.
3. Answers will vary, e.g., no, real reverse discrimination cases are rare as, generally speaking, affirmative action programs have been designed with loopholes.

CHALLENGE TO THE AMERICAN DREAM

Does Affirmative Action Result in Reverse Discrimination?

In an attempt to compensate for discrimination against some, does affirmative action discriminate against others? When the number of jobs is limited and affirmative action provides more jobs for women and minorities, it leaves fewer jobs for white men. Is this reverse discrimination?

Supporters of affirmative action argue that preferential treatment in hiring minorities is needed to make up for discriminating against these groups in the past. Otherwise, they claim, members of these groups would be at a disadvantage when competing with white males, who have suffered no discrimination at all. Also, without a "break," some minority members may never have a chance to get into the mainstream.

Critics of affirmative action see it as reverse discrimination. Affirmative action demands that preference be given to nonwhites and females solely on the basis of their disadvantaged position, and without regard to individual merit. This might put white males under the same kind of discrimination that minorities and women were subjected to in the past. That, critics say, is wrong. White men should not be made to pay for the sins of their fathers and grandfathers.

Take a large automobile factory as an example. Suppose the owners of the company started a new affirmative action program whose goal was to have 30 percent of its management be minorities and women. The first position it wants to fill is a parts manager. Consider what might happen:

1. A woman or minority is hired who is more qualified than the white men who would have been considered. Result: The affirmative action program encouraged the employer to promote someone who should have been promoted before.
2. A minority or woman is chosen who is as equally qualified as any of the white males considered. Result: The chosen candidate was given extra consideration because of special status, but *is* just as qualified as any other applicant.
3. A woman or minority is chosen who is qualified for the job, but is less qualified than several of the applicants. Result: A woman or minority obtains a job for which she or he is *not as* qualified as other applicants.
4. A woman or minority is chosen who is not qualified for the job, even though qualified white males applied. Result: A woman or minority is given a job for which she or he is *not* qualified at all.

A company faced with the first two situations would in essence incur little, if any, cost in actively pursuing an affirmative action program. In contrast, a company faced with the latter two situations might incur costs, and better qualified applicants might believe they had been discriminated against.

In order to fulfill Martin Luther King, Jr.'s dream and have a nation that exemplifies the real meaning of the creed that "all men are created equal," discrimination both past and present must be dealt with.

The challenge to the American dream is to set up public policy in such a way as to overcome discrimination from the past while not furthering present or future discrimination. To the extent that Congress and the courts are unable to strike this balance, friction between various groups may grow.

You Decide

1. What do you think would be the advantages and disadvantages of each of the four situations described above?
2. How do you think current affirmative action policies could be improved?
3. Do you think that affirmative action often leads to reverse discrimination? Give reasons for your answer.

Observable Mastery

Divide students up into groups of three or four. Provide students with large sheets of paper or cardboard and markers. Have each group complete a "mapping" diagram for civil rights and civil liberties. For example, students could place "civil liberties" in the middle of the sheet and have the various amendments covered in the chapter radiating out like spokes. Under the amendments could come important Supreme Court cases, definitions, clauses, personalities, etc., until the material from the chapter was represented on the sheet.

Allow students to present their finished product to the class so they can explain why they emphasized what they did and so they might compare results. This could also be done individually, with the finished products displayed throughout the room.

Chapter Evaluation

To evaluate student mastery of chapter material, you might:

1. Use Chapter Test A from the *TRB.*

2. Use Chapter Test B from the *TRB.*

3. Construct your own test using items from the *West American Government Test Bank* found in the *TRB.*

4. Use the accompanying computerized test software to construct and print a customized chapter test.

Review Questions (Answers)

1. Due process means that government may not act unfairly or arbitrarily.

2. Procedural due process means that the laws must be carried out by a method that is fair. Substantive due process means that the laws themselves must be fair.

3. When police are in "hot pursuit" of a suspect. When a lawful arrest is made, and officers need to search the area within reach of the person being arrested. When an arrest happens in a public place, provided the officer has probable cause to believe that person has committed a crime or is about to commit it.

4. The exclusionary rule is important because it prevents the introduction of illegally seized evidence and prevents carelessness or abuse by officers. Some exceptions are when an officer acts in good faith, or if the evidence would inevitably have been discovered.

5. Self-incrimination is giving evidence or testimony that will implicate oneself in a crime.

6. The case brought about the requirements that police inform suspects of their rights before they are questioned and protects against self-incrimination.

7. Double jeopardy means that once a defendant is acquitted of a crime, he or she is protected from

CHAPTER 6 REVIEW

Key Terms

acquitted 136
affirmative action 148
bail 138
bench trial 137
boycott 145
burden of proof 134
busing 144
capital cases 137
civil disobedience 145
civil rights 142
civil rights movement 145
contempt 135
***de facto* segregation 144**
***de jure* segregation 144**
denaturalization 139
due process of law 129
equal employment opportunity 148
equal protection clause 142
exclusionary rule 133
felonies 131
fundamental rights 142
grand jury 137
hung jury 137
incarceration 137
indictment 137
Miranda Rules 135
mistrial 137
no contest 137
peers 129
preventive detention 138
probable cause 132
procedural due process 130
processes 129
quota 148
rational-basis test 142
reverse discrimination 148
search warrant 132
searches and seizures 132
segregation 140
self-incrimination 134
separate-but-equal doctrine 143
substantive due process 130
suffragists 150
suspect classification 142
unanimous 137
waive 135

Summary

1. There are two due process clauses in the Constitution. One in the Fifth Amendment restricts the national government. The second, in the Fourteenth Amendment, restricts state and local governments. These due process clauses require that the government act fairly (procedural due process) under fair laws (substantive due process).

2. The Constitution protects the rights of persons accused of crimes. They cannot be subjected to unreasonable searches and seizures, and evidence illegally acquired by police normally cannot be used against them in a trial. An accused person must be informed of his or her rights. He or she has the right to a fair trial, and the right to an attorney even if he or she cannot afford one. He or she also has the right to remain silent and to not give self-incriminating testimony; to be represented by an attorney before questioning; and to not be subject to cruel and unusual punishment.

3. Civil rights are the protections recognizing that all citizens must be treated equally under the law. The equal protection clause of the Fourteenth Amendment states that unreasonable distinctions cannot be drawn between different classes of people. In the early days of the United States there were widespread segregation laws. In *Plessy* v. *Ferguson* (1896) the Supreme Court ruled that separate-but-equal facilities were constitutional. In *Brown* v. *Board of Education of Topeka* (1954), it unanimously ruled for complete desegregation. Even though *de jure* segregation laws were illegal, *de facto* segregation continued. The civil rights movement facilitated the passage of the Civil Rights Act in 1964.

4. The struggle for equality continues and has expanded to include many other groups. Affirmative action programs, which grew out of equal employment opportunity programs, are designed to overcome the results of past discrimination. In the late 1980s the Supreme Court issued rulings that rejected some affirmative action policies.

Review Questions

1. What does "due process of law" mean?
2. What is procedural due process? What is substantive due process?
3. When may police conduct a lawful search without a warrant?
4. Why is the exclusionary rule important? Are there any exceptions to the rule? If so, when do they apply?
5. What is self-incrimination?
6. Explain the impact of *Miranda* v. *Arizona* (1966).
7. Explain the concept of double jeopardy.
8. How do the right to counsel, the right to trial by jury, and the right to a speedy and public trial help ensure a fair trial?
9. What is the equal protection clause?

being tried again for the same crime.

8. The rights ensure that the burden of proof will rest with the prosecution.

9. The equal protection clause is a clause in the Fourteenth Amendment declaring that "no state shall . . . deny to any person within its jurisdiction the equal protection of the law."

10. Affirmative action programs have been developed.

11. A movement led by Martin Luther King, Jr. and many others, which sought to create awareness of discrimination and bring about positive change for blacks.

12. To make up for past discriminatory practices.

13. Advocate equal access to entrepreneurs, community leaders, etc.

Questions for Thought and Discussion (Answers)

1. Answers will vary, e.g., such protections are appropriate in order to prevent the innocent from punishment. They are inappropriate when they become so stringent as to hinder the investigation and prosecution of criminals.

2. Answers will vary, e.g., segregation and discrimination had become a firmly entrenched part of society.

3. Answers will vary, e.g., many more women are in the workforce.

4. Answers will vary, e.g., discrimination in other areas would need to be eliminated, such as housing and employment discrimination so that all communities were desegregated.

Social Studies Skills (Answers)

1. Both cases involved the rights of the accused, or civil liberties.

2. *Gideon and Miranda* involved civil liberties, whereas *Brown* involved civil rights—the right to be free from discrimination.

CHAPTER 6 REVIEW—Continued

10. What efforts have been made to deal with *de facto* segregation?
11. What was the civil rights movement?
12. What is the purpose of affirmative action programs?
13. What are some of the ways you can help the differently abled in your community?

Questions for Thought and Discussion

1. Civil liberties for the accused have evolved over the years in various Supreme Court cases. In your opinion, when are such protections appropriate for persons accused of a crime? When are they inappropriate?
2. How do you account for the fact that even though the Fourteenth Amendment was ratified shortly after the Civil War, segregation continued to be widespread for many years?
3. What economic and social changes over the years have lead to the rise of political activism on the part of women?
4. In spite of attempts at desegregating public schools throughout the nation, many school districts continue to be predominantly white or black or Hispanic. What would it take for there to be truly desegregated schools throughout this country?

Improving Your Skills

Communication Skills

Forming an Opinion

Throughout your life you have been asked "What do you think?" or "What is your opinion?" If the question is simple, such as "What is your favorite food?" then your answer is simple. But sometimes the question is more complex, and an opinion is difficult to form. In this case, it is better to form your opinion carefully rather than make a quick "snap judgment" that you may regret later.

An opinion is a belief based on what seems to be true or probable. A good opinion is one made with *reasoned* judgment. Making a reasoned judgment involves investigating all of the available facts, carefully exploring your own feelings, and forming an opinion based on those facts and feelings. Remember these two guidelines:

1. ***Be sure that you use facts to form your opinion.*** Facts are evidence that can be proven and can support your opinion. Take the time to examine all the evidence.
2. ***Consider all sides of an issue with an open mind.*** Do not reject the opinions of others without listening to their reasons.

Writing

Re-read the "Challenge to the American Dream" feature in this chapter. Research and read one article on reverse discrimination in your library. Use the information obtained from your research and the guidelines listed above to form an opinion about whether, in the case you researched, reverse discrimination actually occurred. Write a formal opinion that explains your reasoned judgment. Cite the evidence you found, your feelings about the subject, and how you formed your opinion.

Social Studies Skills

Comparing and Contrasting

Reread the three excerpts from the three Supreme Court cases presented in Figure 6–1 on page 147.

1. What is similar about *Gideon* v. *Wainwright* and *Miranda* v. *Arizona*?
2. What is the difference between those two opinions and the first one, *Brown* v. *Board of Education of Topeka*?

Activities and Projects

1. Invite a local police officer to speak to your class. Some of the topics you might ask the officer to discuss could include: (1) the Miranda Rules; (2) procedures followed when dealing with criminal suspects; (3) rules the police follow when obtaining and handling evidence; and (4) how the police work to protect the rights of individuals and of society in general.
2. Research the women's rights movement and the goals it has sought to achieve. Research the philosophies and goals of several women's organizations in your area, then contact these organizations to find out about their current activities. Develop an oral report on your findings to present to the class.

Working with the Videodisc

The text below is from Professor Roger LeRoy Miller's introduction for the motion segment for Unit 3:

Politics—campaigning, getting voter approval, winning elections, getting legislation passed—may seem like a game, but it is a game that is deadly serious. For the people who win in the game of politics, the results mean political power and the ability to shape the political agenda of this nation, of our state governments, and of our local governments. It is not surprising that any potentially useful method to determine how well a politician is "doing" will be tried. In the first video clip in this segment you will see a speech-rating device that was a technological attempt at ascertaining the effectiveness of how a politician delivered his speeches and the effectiveness, of course, of the words that he delivered.
In the second half of this segment you will see some aspects of the much aligned, but often important, activity called lobbying. Some Americans think that if special interest groups weren't allowed to lobby so much, American politics would be better in some way and more responsive to the public in general. What you will view has to do with state lobbying efforts and issues, but the process is virtually identical in the hall of Congress in Washington, D.C.

To access this segment, use the bar code below or the videodisc index found in the *TRB.*

Frame 28800

UNIT THREE

The Politics of Democracy

UNIT CONTENTS

CHAPTER INTRODUCTION

Instructional Objectives

By the end of the chapter students should be able to:

- Discuss what it means to be a citizen.
- Describe America's policies concerning immigration.
- Specify the rights and responsibilities of citizens.
- Explain why tolerance and open-mindedness are important.

Using the Keynote

Ask one of the students to read aloud the Adlai Stevenson quotation, and encourage the class to discuss it by posing questions such as these: How are citizens both the rulers and the ruled? In what sense are citizens both the lawgivers and the law-abiding? Of what are citizens both the beginning and the end? Do you think Stevenson was speaking about the citizens of the United States during the twentieth century, or about citizens of an ideal democracy—or about some other citizens? Why?

Encourage interested students to research the career of Adlai E. Stevenson: What were his major achievements as a lawyer, as a governor, and as a candidate?

Introducing the Chapter

Let the students read the first part of the Introduction to themselves and then discuss their responses: What does your American citizenship mean to you? Why? What would you be willing to do to maintain your citizenship? What obligations do you believe your citizenship imposes on you?

Previewing the Sections

Section 1 Ask the students to find and read the four main headings within this section. Encourage the students to discuss their own citizenship.

Section 2 Have the students glance through Section 2, noting the main headings, the charts, and the Government in Action feature. Help the students anticipate the content of the section by asking: What questions do you hope to have answered as you study Section 2?

Section 3 Ask the students to look through Section 3, and have volunteers read aloud the section title and the three main headings. Ask the class: Why are rights associated with citizenship?

Section 4 Ask volunteers to find and read aloud the main headings and the photo captions in Section 4. Encourage the students to discuss what they hope to learn as they study this section: What information do you expect to find here? How do you think the information in this section pertains to your daily life?

CHAPTER 7

Citizenship: Privileges and Responsibilities

CHAPTER OBJECTIVES

To learn and understand

- What it means to be a citizen.
- The history of America's policies concerning immigration.
- The rights and responsibilities of citizens.
- Why tolerance and open-mindedness are important.

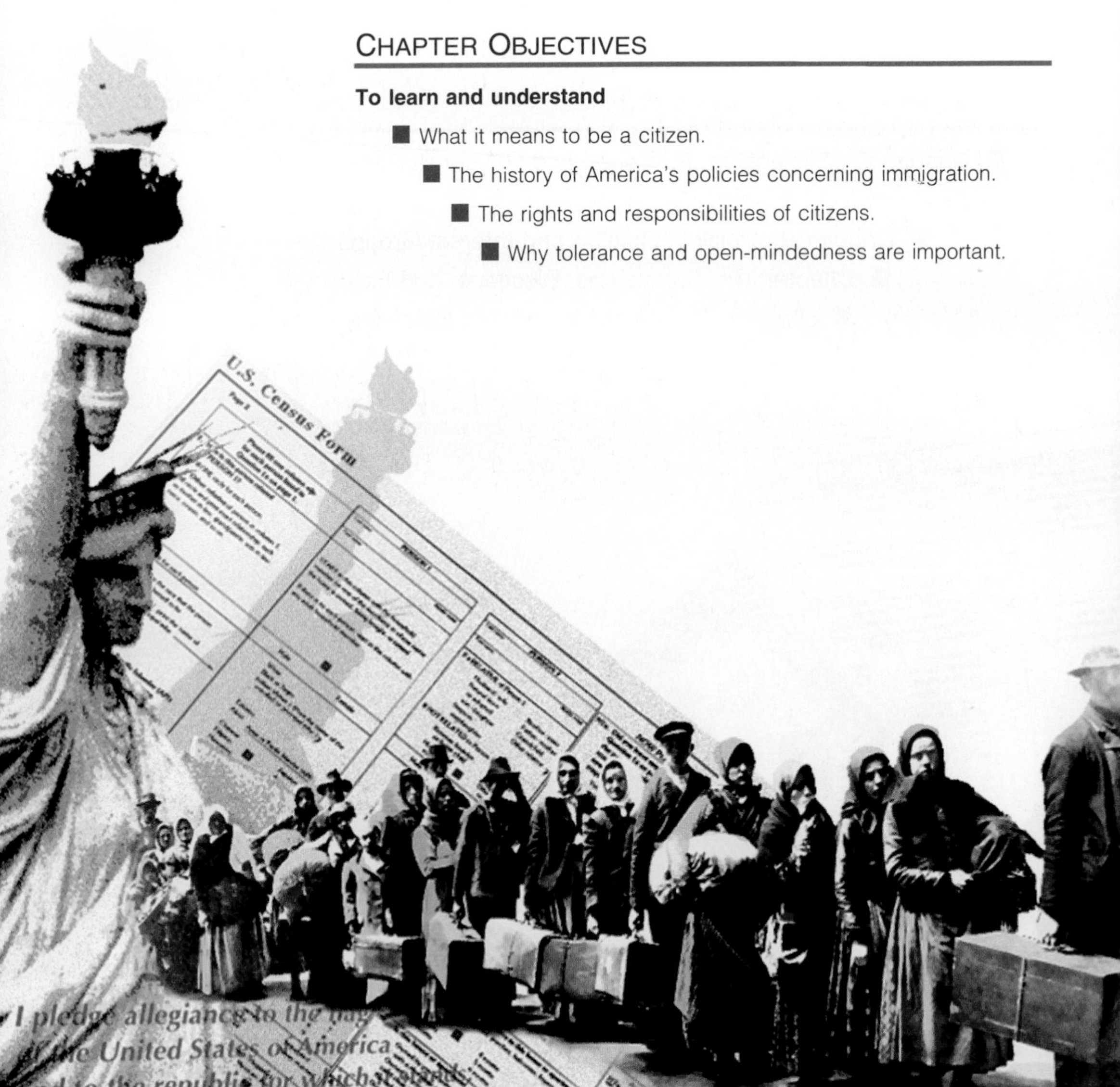

West's American Government Assignment Guide

Activity Sheets
Basic Concepts 7 *TRB* (Reteaching)
Enrichment Activity 7 *TRB*
Building Social Studies Skills 7 *TRB*

Quizzes
Chapter 7 Section 1 Quiz *TRB*
Chapter 7 Section 2 Quiz *TRB*
Chapter 7 Section 3 Quiz *TRB*
Chapter 7 Section 4 Quiz *TRB*

Tests
Chapter 7 Test A *TRB*
Chapter 7 Test B *TRB*
Chapter 7 Test Bank *TRB*
Chapter 7 WESTEST Computerized Testing

Social Studies Tool Kit Software
Chapter 7 Activity

Keynote

"As citizens of this democracy, you are the rulers and the ruled, the lawgivers and the law-abiding, the beginning and the end."

—— **Adlai E. Stevenson (1900–1965) U.S. Presidential Candidate**

INTRODUCTION

Many Americans born in the United States take their citizenship for granted. But to the millions of people around the world from South America to Southeast Asia who struggle to gain entry into the United States, it is a cherished dream. These people understand the precious value of American citizenship perhaps better than those who have always possessed it.

The United States is the first modern nation in which citizens deliberately took governmental power into their own hands. They created a governmental system in which the people, rather than a monarch or dictator or ruling party, have ultimate power. With the above words, Adlai E. Stevenson—who ran for president in 1952 against Dwight D. Eisenhower—summed up the meaning of American citizenship in our democracy.

SECTION 1

Who is a Citizen?

Preview Questions

- When did citizenship in the United States become a *national* issue?
- What is the significance of *Dred Scott* v. *Sandford* (1857)?
- What is the essence of the Fourteenth Amendment?
- What are three ways that American citizenship may be lost?

When the United States first became a nation, the concept of citizenship was not an issue of national concern. Indeed, the Constitution, including the first ten amendments, does not define citizenship. The framers of the Constitution left it up to state governments, rather than the federal government, to decide who was a citizen. Any citizen of a state was automatically assumed to be a citizen of the United States, at least in the minds of the framers. Today, citizenship is decided by the federal government, as you will learn about in this chapter.

The Dred Scott Case

The issue of state versus national citizenship became critical in a famous Supreme Court case, *Dred Scott* v. *Sandford* (1857). A slave named Dred Scott had been moved by his owner to Illinois, where slavery was illegal under state law. Dred Scott sued in court for his freedom. The Supreme Court, which at that time was dominated by Southern judges, ruled that Scott could not be a citizen of the United States because he was a slave and therefore he had no right to sue in court at all. The Supreme Court

▼ Prior to the ratification of the Thirteenth Amendment, which abolished slavery, African Americans, as enslaved persons, were not considered citizens of the United States. Why do you think the Supreme Court ruled this way?

SECTION 1

Points to Stress
- The period in the United States when citizenship became a national issue.
- The significance of *Dred Scott* v. *Sandford.*
- The essence of the Fourteenth Amendment.
- Ways in which American citizenship may be lost.

Kickoff Activity
Ask a volunteer to read the section title aloud. Then have the students write short paragraphs in response to the title question. You may want to ask some of the students to read their completed paragraphs aloud.

Working with the Preview Questions
Ask the students to read these study questions and then to use them to plan the main headings for a section outline. Let volunteers read their outline headings or write them on the board, and help the class members agree on an appropriate format. Then have the students fill in their outlines as they read Section 1.

Caption Answer Slaves were considered property. Their owners' property rights took legal precedence.

Teaching Strategies

Introduction
Let a volunteer read the section introduction aloud, and help the students discuss it: Why do you think the states—rather than the nation—initially decided who was or was not a citizen? Why do you think the Constitution did not define citizenship? If the Constitution were being written today, do you think it would include a definition of citizenship? Why or why not?

Critical Thinking Skills
Have the students work together to analyze the reasoning used by the Supreme Court in the Dred Scott case. How has the reasoning changed since that time? Why do you think it changed?

Comprehension
Ask the students to restate the quotation from the Fourteenth Amendment in their own words.

Cooperative Learning
Let the students work in groups to compare and discuss the personal implications of these sources of citizenship: Are you an American citizen? If so, what is the source of your citizenship? How many generations of your family have been American citizens? When and how did the first American in your family become a citizen?

Caption Answer In 1924, Congress passed a law naturalizing all Native Americans.

Comprehension
Have the students consider the implications of citizenship by *jus soli:* Does a child born here to noncitizens become a citizen? (Yes, unless they are diplomats, etc.)

Enrichment
Encourage interested students to research the citizenship of Native Americans: Why was it delayed? Why and how was it granted? How did Native Americans react to the delay and to the grant of citizenship? How did other, non-Native citizens react? Ask these students to share their findings with the rest of the class.

Comprehension
Ask volunteers to make up—or to cite actual—examples of *jus sanguinis.*

applied this ruling to Scott while he was in Illinois even though slavery was illegal there and African Americans had long been considered citizens in that state (as well as in most other Northern states). The reasoning of the Court was that when the Constitution was adopted, African Americans had not been recognized as citizens of the states. It did not matter whether they were slaves or free at that time. According to the logic of the Court, the only individuals who were United States citizens were those who were directly descended from state citizens in 1787, or immigrants who became citizens through legal means. Slaves, who fell into neither of these categories, were therefore not considered citizens.

The Thirteenth and Fourteenth Amendments Many individuals in most Northern states did not agree with the *Dred Scott* decision. Some historians believe that the ruling in that case was one of the major causes of the Civil War. As a result of this controversy, the Thirteenth Amendment, which abolished slavery, was passed at the close of the Civil War in 1865. But in passing this amendment, the nation was faced with the need to define who was a citizen. This question was finally answered in 1868 with the Fourteenth Amendment, which begins:

> All persons born or naturalized in the United States, and subject to the jurisdiction thereof, are citizens of the United States and of the State wherein they reside.

In essence, the Fourteenth Amendment reversed the *Dred Scott* decision by making state citizenship an automatic result of national citizenship. The Fourteenth Amendment created the two most common sources of American citizenship: (1) by birth anywhere on land considered American soil and (2) by the legal process called *naturalization.* There is yet a third source—by being born of a parent who is a U.S. citizen.

Citizenship by Birth

Most Americans are citizens simply because they were born in the United States.

Location of Birth—*Jus Soli* The Fourteenth Amendment states that all persons born in the United States are American citizens. This is called citizenship by location. In legal terms this is called citizenship by ***jus soli.*** *Jus soli* are two Latin words that translate as "the law of the soil."

Today, the United States comprises not only the fifty states, but also the District of Columbia, Guam, Puerto Rico, the Virgin Islands, the Northern Mariana Islands, and American Samoa. Additionally, American embassies in foreign countries and any ship or aircraft operated by agencies of the U.S. government are considered United States soil. Exceptions to the *jus soli* rule are those individuals born in the United States, but not subject to the jurisdiction, or control, of the United States government. These are usually children born to foreign diplomats stationed in the United States.

▲ Despite the fact that they were the first inhabitants of this land, Native Americans were not immediately recognized as citizens. When were all Native Americans naturalized?

Surprisingly, at the time the Fourteenth Amendment was passed, Native Americans, who were considered **wards**, or persons under the legal guardianship, of the U.S. government, were not granted citizenship under the Fourteenth Amendment. In 1924, Congress reversed this ruling by granting citizenship to all Native Americans who did not already possess it.

Law of the Blood—*Jus Sanguinis* Since 1790, Congress has included the so-called "law of the blood," or ***jus sanguinis***, as grounds for American citizenship. Under this law, a child born on foreign soil becomes an American citizen at birth if at least one of the parents is a U.S. citizen, and if that U.S. citizen lived in the U.S. (or in an American possession) for at least ten years, five of which occurred after the age of 14.

Discussion Starter
As the students discuss naturalization, ask: What do you think happens to the previous citizenship of a naturalized citizen? At what point in the process of naturalization do you think that happens? Why?

Enrichment
Divide the class into four groups, and have each group research the history of the Louisiana Purchase, of the acquisition of Florida or Alaska, or of the annexation of Texas. Ask the members of each group to write a short report to be shared with the rest of the class.

Extension
If possible, invite a person who has completed—or is going through—the naturalization process to visit your class. (The students may be able to suggest possible guests.) Ask this person to discuss the process and to answer the students' questions on the topic.

Cooperative Learning
Have the students work in small groups to read and discuss each of these qualifications: What is the importance of this qualification? Do you consider it an appropriate qualification for citizenship? Why or why not? Encourage all the members of each group to contribute to the discussion.

Citizenship by Choice—Naturalization

The U.S. Constitution in Article I, Section 8 declares that Congress shall have the power to "establish a uniform Rule of Naturalization." **Naturalization** is the process by which individuals who are not yet citizens become United States citizens. These individuals are called **naturalized citizens**, as opposed to native-born citizens described above. There are three ways for naturalization to occur: (1) by act of Congress; (2) by treaty; and (3) by individual action.

By Act of Congress On rare occasions, the U.S. Congress has passed laws naturalizing entire groups of people. As already mentioned, this was done in 1924 with respect to Native Americans who were not yet citizens. Prior to that, inhabitants of Hawaii and Puerto Rico were granted citizenship by Congress in 1900 and 1917 respectively. The same thing occurred for residents of the Virgin Islands (1927), Guam (1950), and the Northern Marianas (1977). We have already mentioned the collective naturalization of African Americans and others by the Fourteenth Amendment to the U.S. Constitution in 1868.

By Treaty The largest groups of people to become American citizens through collective naturalization have been naturalized when the United States has acquired new territory. Those living in the areas involved were naturalized by a treaty or a joint resolution of Congress. For example, when the Louisiana Purchase Treaty was signed in 1803, the United States purchased the Louisiana Territory from France. That treaty said that people living in the territory became U.S. citizens. The same occurred in the treaties in which the U.S. acquired Florida (1819) and Alaska (1867). Additionally, a joint resolution of Congress gave citizenship to all inhabitants of Texas in 1845.

By Individual Action Today naturalization most often occurs through individual action. Every year hundreds of thousands of people apply for citizenship in the United States. Each possible candidate for naturalization must have the following qualifications:

- They must be 18 years or older (except minors who normally become citizens when their parents are naturalized).

These individuals are at a ceremony to be sworn in as new United States citizens. What is the age requirement for individuals who wish to be naturalized?

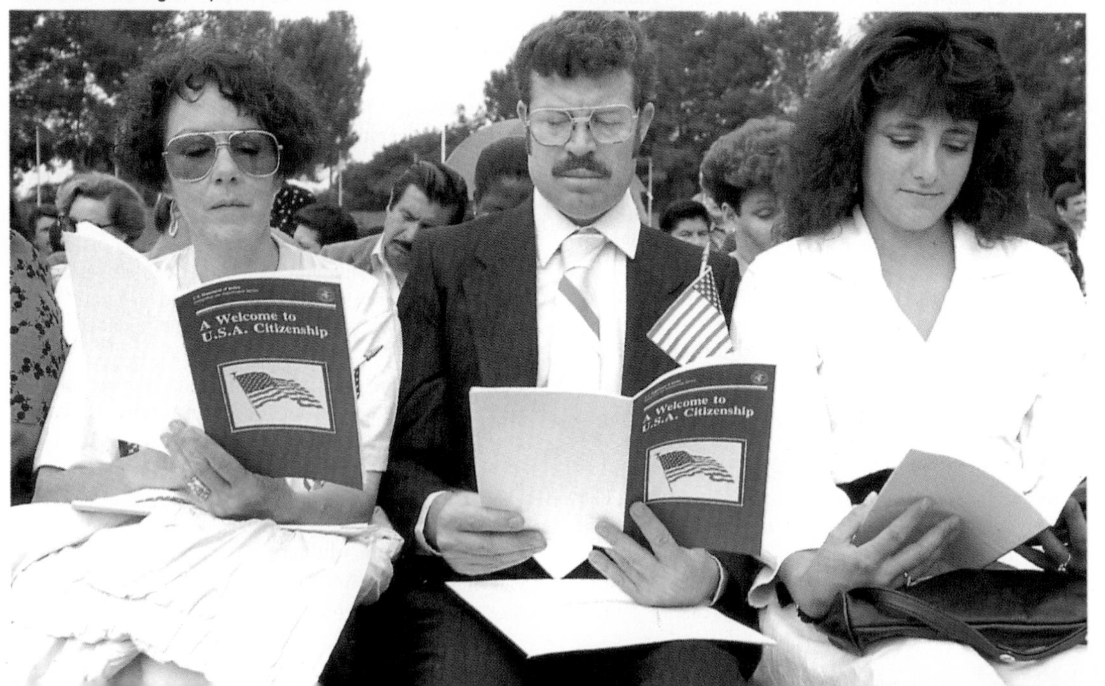

Caption Answer Individuals wishing to be naturalized must be eighteen years or older. Minors normally become citizens when their parents are naturalized.

FYI

Dual citizenship is possible for persons born abroad to American citizens, and for persons born in the United States of parents from a different country. Although a person enjoys all the rights of each nation, they are also subject to fulfilling responsibilities of each, such as military service and taxation.

Some people argue that native-born citizens ought to go through a citizenship ceremony just as naturalized citizens do, so that citizenship will be appreciated and not taken for granted. See Martin Edleman, *Democratic Theories and the Constitution,* State University of New York Press, 1984.

Enrichment
Ask two or three interested students to research the Mariel Boat Lift of 1980 and its results: How does this relate to the fourth listed qualification for citizenship (Be of high moral character and able to prove it)?

Vocabulary
Let volunteers define these terms: *draft evader, military deserter, anarchist, polygamist.*

Cooperative Learning
Let the students work with partners or in small groups to study and discuss the chart, How Non-Citizens Become Naturalized Citizens of the United States.

Extension
Ask a group of volunteers to research the process by which renounced citizenship can be regained: Is it possible to regain American citizenship? If so, under what conditions? How frequently is it done? Then have the volunteers make a chart or poster, summarizing their findings.

Figure Answer Answers will vary, e.g., because so many people seek U.S. citizenship.

This figure content is also featured on *West's American Government Videodisc* (see the index found in the TRB).

Vocabulary
Ask volunteers to define *treason*. Why is the commission of this crime grounds for revoking citizenship?

Discussion Starter
Let a small group of volunteers research the process of denaturalization. What examples do they find? What were the grounds for denaturalization in each case?

Reteaching Strategies
1. Help small groups of students review their outlines of Section 1. Encourage them to return to the text to resolve any disagreement about content revising their outlines accordingly.
2. Ask pairs of students to work together in writing one-paragraph responses to this question: What is the relationship between the Thirteenth Amendment and the Fourteenth Amendment?

Evaluation Strategies
1. Have the students write their answers to the Section 1 Review questions.
2. Have the students take the Section 1 Quiz found in the *TRB.*

Section 1 Review (Answers)
1. The court ruled that the only individuals who were United States citizens were those who were directly descended from state citizens in 1787 or immigrants who became citizens through legal means.
2. The Fourteenth Amendment created citizenship by birth anywhere on American soil, or by the legal process of naturalization.
3. Expatriation, by becoming a naturalized citizen of another country or renouncing American citizenship. Punishment for a person convicted of treason, inciting rebellion, or conspiring to violently overthrow the government. Denatu-

How Non-Citizens Become Naturalized Citizens of the United States

Application	Examination	Final Hearing
Candidates for citizenship must submit an application form, a card of fingerprints, and certain autobiographical data, such as where they were born, who their parents were, etc.	Each candidate appears before an officer at the closest Immigration and Naturalization Service office. The candidate must bring along two U.S. citizens to serve as witnesses. Every candidate must prove his or her qualifications, consistent with those presented previously. Candidates must also demonstrate a basic knowledge of American history and an understanding of our form of government.	The Immigration and Naturalization Service takes a minimum of 30 days to process an application, during which time it may seek additional information about the candidate. The information is presented to a judge in a citizenship court, with the recommendation that the candidate be granted citizenship. If the judge agrees, then the applicant appears before a judge, takes the oath of allegiance, and receives a certificate of citizenship. He or she has become a naturalized citizen of the United States.

FIGURE 7–1 How Non-Citizens Become Naturalized Citizens of the United States. As you can see, naturalization is a three-step process. The process appears simple, but usually is not. Why do you think the process usually takes a long time?

- They must have entered the U.S. legally and lived in the United States for at least five years.
- They must demonstrate an understanding of basic English words and phrases.
- They must be able to prove, if necessary, their high moral character.
- They must understand the basic concepts of American government and history.
- They must not have advocated the overthrow of the U.S. government by force or violence within the past ten years.
- They must not have belonged to any subversive organization within the past ten years.
- They must not be a draft evader, a military deserter, an anarchist, or a polygamist (a person with more than one spouse).

How Citizenship May Be Lost

While federal government is the *only* entity that can take away citizenship, state governments do have the right to deny certain privileges of citizenship, such as the right to vote, to their citizens who are convicted of crimes. The three basic ways Americans can lose citizenship are through *expatriation,* punishment for a crime, and *denaturalization.*

Expatriation The word **expatriation** comes from the prefix *ex-*, meaning ''from,'' and the Latin word *patria,* which means ''native country, or fatherland.'' To expatriate someone is to banish that person from his or her native country. Individuals can voluntarily become expatriates by becoming a naturalized citizen of another country or by renouncing their American citizenship to a representative of the United States government. Once renounced, citizenship cannot easily be regained.

Punishment for a Crime While states may not take away a person's citizenship for just any crime, the federal government can do so if a person is convicted of treason, of inciting rebellion, or of conspiring to violently overthrow the government.

Denaturalization In rare cases, a naturalized citizen may lose citizenship through a process called ralization, which occurs when the federal government learns that a naturalized citizen obtained his or her citizenship through fraudulent means.

4. Answers will vary, e.g., denaturalization is not "cruel and unusual" if the person is convicted of treason, which is essentially the same as renouncing one's citizenship.

SECTION 2

Points to Stress

- Differences between a refugee and an immigrant.
- Legal categories of aliens in the United States.
- The manner in which the nation's policy on immigration has changed.

Kickoff Activity
Write the word *immigrants* on the chalkboard, and ask the students to list at least eight words or phrases that come to mind in response to the word. Then encourage the students to share and discuss their lists: What responses are most common? Why? What differences are there among the responses? Why?

Working with the Preview Questions
Let volunteers read these study questions aloud, and ask the students to discuss what they already know in response to the questions. Then remind the students to keep these questions in mind as they study Section 2.

Teaching Strategies

Introduction
After the students have read the section introduction, ask: What is the difference between an immigrant and an alien? Why is the difference between the two important?

Comprehension
Ask volunteers to define the terms *resident alien* and *nonresident alien* in their own words and to explain the differences between the two.

Enrichment
Let a small group of volunteers research the "relocation" camps in which U.S. residents of Japanese descent were forced to live during World War II: Who was moved into these camps? Under what circumstances? What happened to the property of these families? How were they treated after the war was over? Then have the volunteers prepare an oral or visual presentation of their findings for the rest of the class.

Discussion Starter
Encourage the students to consider and discuss the situation of illegal aliens: Why do you think they come to the United States? What particular problems do they face here? How is their daily situation different from that of other aliens in this country? Why do you think illegal aliens put up with those differences in situation? If you were the citizen of another country, would you consider moving illegally to the United States? Why or why not?

denaturalization. Denaturalization occurs if the federal government learns that a naturalized citizen obtained his or her citizenship through fraudulent means.

Section 1 Review

1. What did the Supreme Court rule in the *Dred Scott* case?
2. According to the Fourteenth Amendment, who is a citizen of the United States?
3. In what three ways can American citizenship be lost?
4. **For critical analysis:** Former Justice Earl Warren believed that loss of citizenship as punishment for any crime, even for treason, was a "cruel and unusual" punishment, which you have learned is unconstitutional. Do you agree or disagree? Explain your answer. For what reasons, if any, do you think citizens should lose their citizenship? Explain your answer.

Section 2

Immigration and the Non-Citizen

Preview Questions

- What is the difference between a refugee and an immigrant?
- According to United States laws, what are the different types of aliens?
- How has the nation's policy on immigration changed over the years?

Not everybody living in the United States is a citizen of this country. Various words have been used to describe people who are not citizens, the two most common of which are *immigrants* and *aliens.* The difference between the two is important. **Immigrants** are individuals who live in the United States with the intention of becoming naturalized citizens and remaining here permanently. During the last decade, immigrants have made up more than one-third of the nation's population growth. **Aliens,** in contrast, are individuals living in this country who are not citizens and who might not have any intention of becoming citizens.

Types of Aliens

According to United States law, there are five different categories of aliens. Each category has important legal distinctions.

1. **Resident aliens** are individuals who have come to the United States to establish permanent residence. These are immigrants and are called resident aliens until they become naturalized citizens. Resident aliens may stay in the U.S. as long as they desire and are not required to seek American citizenship.
2. **Nonresident aliens** are individuals who expect to stay in the United States for a specified period of time. A journalist from Britain who has come to cover the presidential election is a nonresident alien. A Japanese tourist from Tokyo visiting San Francisco for the month of June is a nonresident alien. The head salesperson for a Swiss watch company who is in New York to promote a new line is a nonresident alien.
3. **Enemy aliens** are citizens of those nations with which America is at war. During World War I, when our nation was at war with Germany, German citizens who resided in the continental United States had to register with the U.S. government. During World War II, when Japan was one of our enemies, U.S. residents of Japanese descent living on the West Coast were considered, as a group, enemy aliens, even though more than half could not be technically classified as such. The U.S. government forced over one hundred thousand such individuals to live in "relocation camps" for most of the war.
4. **Refugees** are immigrants to the U.S. who are granted entry because they are politically unsafe or unwelcome in their own countries. In recent years, the U.S. has accepted refugees from Southeast Asia, Cuba, El Salvador, Nicaragua, Haiti, and Poland. Currently, fifty thousand refugees may enter the U.S. each year, but Congress can give the president power to waive this limit in emergencies. In 1978, for example, President Carter issued a special order that allowed 117,000 Cuban refugees to legally enter the United States. The Immigration Act of 1990 granted certain refugees from El Salvador temporary "asylum," or political protection, as well as permission to work.
5. **Illegal aliens** are individuals who enter the United States without a legal permit or who enter as tourists (nonresident aliens) and stay longer than their tourist status legally allows. Everyone entering the United

TEACHING GOVERNMENT IN ACTION

Read
Let the students begin by discussing what they already know about the census: What is the purpose of the census? How accurate does it seem to be? How do adults feel about completing census forms? Why? Then ask the students to work in groups to read the Government in Action feature.

Discuss
Encourage the students to discuss their responses to the information here: Why do you think so many people work for the Census Bureau?Why do you think so much money is spent on taking a census every ten years? Does this expenditure make sense to you? Why or why not? Why do you think everyone who deals with census information is sworn to secrecy? Given the fact that census data can be purchased for $100,000, who has access to the information? Who is denied access? Does this make sense to you? Why or why not?

Analyze and Apply
Ask the students to research the effects of the 1990 census on their state and city: What changes resulted from the census figures? Why? How did local politicians and activists react to the figures? Why? Encourage the students to share and discuss the findings of their research.

Review
Ask the students to answer these review questions: What document requires the national government to take a census? What is the primary reason for the census?

This figure content is also featured on *West's American Government Videodisc* (see the index found in the TRB).

GOVERNMENT IN ACTION

CASE STUDY

Taking the Census

The U.S. Constitution in Article I, Section 2 requires that the federal government take an "enumeration," or census, every ten years. The reason the Constitution requires this is because the number of representatives elected to the House of Representatives by each state depends on the number of its inhabitants. The census results are also used to determine where to build highways, schools, restaurants, and banks, as well as to decide how much money in federal grants should be allocated to local government institutions such as hospitals. In order to be as accurate as possible, the Bureau of the Census made a significant effort to include the homeless and undocumented aliens in the 1990 count.

The Bureau of the Census, which is part of the Department of Commerce, operates within the executive branch of the government. All the census forms sent in are processed by sophisticated optical scanners at lightning speeds. Actually the Census Bureau was the first major institution to use machine-readable punch cards in 1890. (Their inventor, Herman Hollerith, later started the company that became International Business Machines, otherwise known as IBM.)

To get this information for the latest census, almost a half a million part-time employees were hired in 1990, in addition to the Bureau's normal staff of almost ten thousand. Two hundred thousand of these part-time workers were used to survey their home neighborhoods, talking to people from door to door. Here are some of the questions that were asked:

- What is your age, date of birth, and marital status?
- How many years of schooling have you completed?
- How many years' active duty military service have you completed?
- What was your income last year?

U.S. Households by Type, 1990

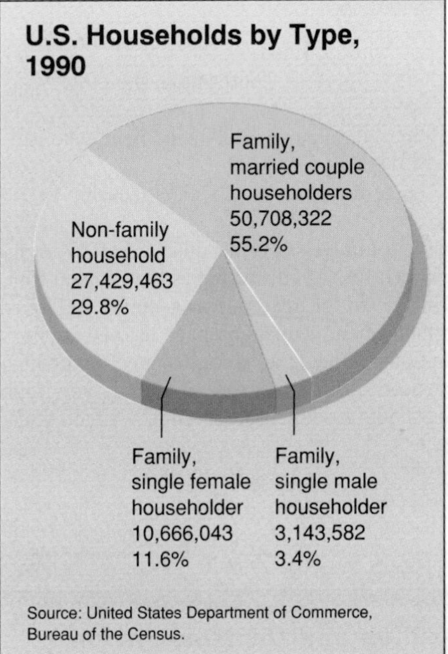

Source: United States Department of Commerce, Bureau of the Census.

- Are you of Spanish/Hispanic origin?
- Do you have complete plumbing facilities?
- Do you have complete kitchen facilities?
- Do you have a telephone?
- Which fuel is used most for heating your house or apartment?

All of the canvassers and people who handle census information are sworn to secrecy—they can only reveal the information they gather to authorized personnel. But if you are curious about these numbers, you can buy all of the data from the 1990 census in computer-readable form for only $100,000.* That may

* Census records do become public after seventy-two years, when they are sent to the federal achives.

Extension

Allow interested volunteers to research the steps that the Census Bureau took in 1990 in order to count the homeless population. Students should report on why these steps were taken, whether or not these steps were considered effective, etc. The students should then report their findings to the class in an oral report.

This figure content is also featured on *West's American Government Videodisc* (see the index found in the TRB).

U.S. Cities with Greatest Populations, 1990

Size Rank	City and State	1990 Population
1	New York, NY	7,322,564
2	Los Angeles, CA	3,485,398
3	Chicago, IL	2,783,726
4	Houston, TX	1,630,553
5	Philadelphia, PA	1,585,577
6	San Diego, CA	1,110,549
7	Detroit, MI	1,027,974
8	Dallas, TX	1,006,877
9	Phoenix, AZ	983,403
10	San Antonio, TX	935,933
11	San Jose, CA	782,248
12	Indianapolis, IN	741,952
13	Baltimore, MD	736,014
14	San Francisco, CA	723,959
15	Jacksonville, FL	672,971
16	Columbus, OH	632,910
17	Milwaukee, WI	628,088
18	Memphis, TN	610,337
19	Washington, D.C.	606,900
20	Boston, MA	574,283
21	Seattle, WA	516,259
22	El Paso, TX	515,342
23	Nashville–Davidson, TN	510,784
24	Cleveland, OH	505,616
25	New Orleans, LA	496,938

Source: United States Department of Commerce, Bureau of the Census.

seem expensive, but imagine how much it cost to obtain those numbers! The Census Bureau spent over $3 billion to produce the 1990 census, roughly half of which was spent in that year. The U.S. Postal Service had to deliver 20 million completed forms to the Census Bureau in the first two weeks of April, 1990, at a total cost of $70 million. It takes five thousand miles of microfilm to record all the forms.

THINK ABOUT IT

1. Do you think it is an invasion of privacy that Americans be asked so many questions about how they live, even though the Census Bureau keeps all files secret? Explain why or why not.
2. Some cities claim that the Census Bureau undercounted the number of city residents. Why would this be a concern?

Think About It (Answers)

1. Answers will vary. No, it is not an invasion of privacy because all the files are kept secret so it doesn't matter what the person tells about his or her private life. Yes, it is an invasion of privacy because no one really needs to know about how individuals lead their private lives.

2. Answers will vary, e.g., city governments might be concerned if the population of their city were undercounted because the city might receive less federal funding for social welfare and other programs.

Extension
Ask an interested volunteer to read about the INS: How and when was it established? What are its functions? Have the volunteer summarize his or her findings in a chart.

Discussion Starter
Guide the students in discussing the protection offered by the Constitution: How does the Constitution protect aliens in this country? Why do its protections extend to aliens?

Caption Answer Illegal aliens are individuals who come into the United States without a legal permit, or come in as tourists and stay longer than they are legally allowed.

Discussion Starter
Have the students discuss Hamilton's contention that immigrants should be treated as "first class citizens": What does this imply about the society in which he lived? Do you imagine he felt all newcomers should be treated as "first class"? Why or why not?

These United States Border Patrol Officers work along the United States/Mexico border near Laredo, Texas, to control the entry of illegal aliens into this country. What is meant by the term *illegal aliens*?

States is supposed to have a valid passport, visa, or entry permit. A **visa** is an authorization that allows an alien to enter this country legally, usually an official stamp placed on the inside of an individual's passport. Most visas for nonimmigrants are granted for a specific time period. A tourist, for example, may be allowed to travel legally in the United States for six months.

Illegal aliens can be **deported**, or forced to leave the United States. Over one million illegal aliens are deported each year. The problem of illegal aliens is a serious one that you will read more about at the end of this chapter.

The Rights of Aliens

American citizens have many rights given to them by their state constitutions and by the U.S. Constitution. In particular, the Bill of Rights guarantees the freedom of speech, assembly, and religion. These rights apply equally well to legal aliens whether they be resident or nonresident. In certain circumstances, many of these rights also apply to illegal aliens. In general, all legal aliens can legally own real estate and send their children to public schools; they cannot, however, vote in any election, be it local, state, or federal. Legal aliens normally are not required to serve in the military, nor are they called for jury duty. In exchange for their privileges, resident aliens must pay taxes and obey all laws.

All aliens are protected by the Constitution.

A Nation of Immigrants

According to the 1990 Census, Native Americans (American Indians, Eskimos, and Aleuts) make up less than one percent of the total United States population. This means that almost everyone in the United States can trace his or her roots to another country. The study of immigration in America is therefore a large part of the study of America itself.

Immigration Patterns

As you can see from the figure on page 168, immigration was greatest in absolute numbers from 1901 to 1910. The 1970s and the 1980s were also high periods of immigration, but relative to the percentage of the total population, immigration has been low in the last quarter century. Since 1821, a total of about 60 million people have immigrated to the United States.

Policies on Immigration

In the early days of our country, small numbers of people inhabited vast areas of land. It is not surprising, then, that most early Americans wanted to encourage immigration. During the constitutional debates in Philadelphia, Alexander Hamilton pointed out that immigrants could make an important contribution to the nation, and should be treated as "first-class citizens." Prior to 1800, there were virtually no constraints on immigration except for the Naturalization Act of 1798, which was basically an attempt to prevent members of the Anti-Federalist party from voting. The act had little to do with immigration policy, and was repealed four years after it was passed.

The states believed that there was strength in large numbers. They wanted more people to move to their states, and set up advertising campaigns to lure prospective citizens. By the time the Civil War broke out,

TEACHING GOVERNMENT IN ACTION

Read
Before allowing the students to read this profile, ask the following: Who is Cesar Chávez? Why do you think he has been included in this book? Why would he be included in this chapter? Allow students a few minutes to read this profile.

Discuss
Encourage the students to discuss their responses to the information presented in this profile. According to this feature, why did most Hispanic immigrants come to this country? What types of problems did they face? When did Cesar Chávez begin to work with farm workers? When did he achieve lasting success?

Analyze and Apply
Allow the students to work in groups to answer the following questions: How would the fact that most farm workers could not read or write English hinder their ability to lobby for needed social legislation? How would an organization such as the United Farm Workers help them in this area? Most of the successes discussed in this feature occurred during the 60s through the mid 70s. Do you think Chávez and the UFW would be as successful if they were beginning their efforts today? How do you think the efforts of the UFW affected the owners of large commercial farms? How do you think these efforts affected consumers? Do you think these groups made Chávez's job more difficult? Why or why not?

Review
Ask the students to answer these review questions: What organization was founded by Cesar Chávez? Who was this organization designed to help? Why did these people need help? What type of successes has the UFW achieved?

GOVERNMENT IN ACTION

PROFILE

Cesar Chávez

Hispanics number over 22 million, about 9 percent of the population, and are second only to African Americans in terms of numbers. It is estimated that they will overtake African Americans as the nation's largest minority in the coming decades.

Most of the Hispanic immigrants, including the undocumented or illegal migrants, came from poor rural areas to seek a better life in the United States by working on large commercial farms. Most could not read or write in English, and had very little or no security in their new jobs. As migrant workers, these men, women, and children labored for very low pay in poor working conditions. They moved, as the crops matured, to Oregon, Washington, Nebraska, and the Great Lakes states, living in substandard shacks or trailers. Social legislation passed to help them was weak and did little to help.

From the early 1900s on, some efforts were made to organize the workers but with little success. In the 1960's, however, Cesar Chávez, born in 1927, finally began making real headway in organizing the workers in the California vineyards and lettuce fields. In 1962 he organized farm workers into the organization called the United Farm Workers and started a five-year strike against California grape growers to force them to recognize the union. The UFW organized a nationwide boycott of table grapes. Sympathetic priests, civic groups, and students aided in Chávez's efforts. In 1965 he launched a strike that led to a nationwide boycott of produce not bearing the label of the United Farm Workers. In 1970, the strikers finally won and the strike ended in a pact with the growers. By 1975, Chávez and the strikers had convinced the California legislature to pass a bill that gave farm workers the same rights held by union members elsewhere.

THINK ABOUT IT

1. Do you think the fact that farm work is often migrant work made the task of organizing a union more difficult? Explain your answer.
2. Do you think this fact helps to explain why there was little effective social legislation enacted to help them? Explain your answer.

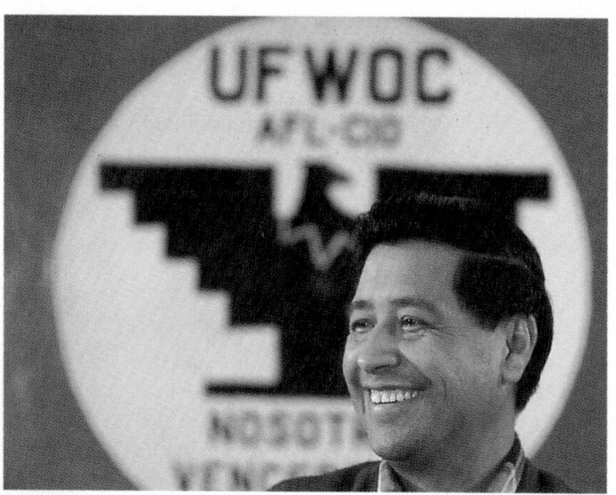

Cesar Chávez is shown here speaking in a meeting hall in Delano, California. In the background is the black Aztec eagle that is the emblem of the United Farm Workers Union.

Think About It (Answers)

1. Students should understand that the fact that farm work is often migrant work made the task of organizing the union more difficult, because it was hard to locate and enumerate the constituents, or future members, of the union. Furthermore, to some extent the problems that the workers faced varied from season to season and from farm to farm.

2. The migrant nature of farm work means that often the workers did not remain in one place long enough to develop any political power. Because they did not establish residency (and often because they were in this country illegally) they rarely registered to vote and could not use the power of block voting.

Enrichment
Ask interested volunteers to learn more about these two cases: How were the specifics of the cases different? Why were the two rulings different? What was the effect of each ruling?

Discussion Starter
Encourage the students to consider and discuss the attitude toward immigrants who "blended in" with the existing population: To what extent are similar attitudes evident in communities today? What are the effects of these attitudes? Why do you think such attitudes persist?

Critical Thinking Skills
Ask the students to analyze the government's right to restrict immigration based on nationalities: Do you think the Chinese Exclusion Act of 1882 was constitutional? Why or why not? Why do you think it was accepted as constitutional?

Discussion Starter
Encourage discussion by posing questions such as these: What do you think the expressed purposes of the Quota Act of 1921 were? Do you imagine the act had other, more subtle purposes? If so, what do you think they were? How did the National Origins Quota System affect the population growth of the United States?

Caption Answer The states believed that there was strength and prosperity in a large population.

Caption Answer Prior to the 1880s, most immigrants to this nation were from Northern and Western Europe.

Instruction

für

deutsche Auswanderer nach Texas,

nebst

der neuesten Karte dieses Staates,

nach dessen Grenzbestimmungen durch Congreß-Beschluß vom September 1850.

Sodann

einer Special-Karte über den vermessenen Theil des Grant-Gebiets des Texas-Vereines und einzelnen Plänen der von demselben gegründeten Städte Neu-Braunfels, Friedrichsburg und Indianola.

Herausgegeben

von dem Verein zum Schutze deutscher Einwanderer in Texas.

1851.

Im Selbst-Verlage des Vereins-Comite's zu Wiesbaden.

In Commission bei D. Reimer in Berlin.

Preis der Instruction sammt den drei oben erwähnten Kartenblättern und einem Exemplar des Comite-Berichts vom April 1850: 1 Thlr. 4 Sgr. Preuß. Cour. oder 1 fl 56 Kr.

Das Panorama von Neu-Braunfels wird separat verkauft.

Druck von W. Sträder in Neuwied.

▲ In the past, many states designed advertising campaigns to entice individuals to immigrate. Shown above is a cover for a guide book for immigrants to Texas from Germany that was published in 1851. This book promoted Texas as a great place for immigrants. Why would states want to encourage immigration?

over thirty states and territorial governments had immigration offices whose purpose was to attract immigrants. Some states passed laws requiring that new immigrants be inspected, particularly for diseases. In New York, for example, sick immigrants were not allowed to enter the state.

The legality of the states' regulation of immigration was upheld in *Mayor of New York* v. *Miln* (1837). In *Henderson* v. *Mayor of New York,* in 1875, however, the Supreme Court declared that state legislation on immigration was unconstitutional because state laws infringed on the exclusive power of Congress to regulate interstate and foreign commerce.

Restricting Immigration The 1880s saw the first true restrictions on immigration. Prior to that time, most immigrants, who were from Northern and Western Europe, blended in easily with the existing population in the United States. Most of these immigrants were Protestants, except for the Irish and a few Germans who were Catholic. The immigrants who arrived from the 1880s onward were, by contrast, from Eastern and Southern Europe. Their languages were different and their religions were either Jewish, Catholic, or Eastern Orthodox. Their customs seemed strange and foreign to the earlier immigrants.

At the same time as these new European arrivals, the Chinese started entering the Western states, particularly to help build the new railroads. Congress responded to this influx with the Chinese Exclusion Act of 1882, which halted entry of any Chinese immigrants to the U.S. for ten years. That act was the first one to establish the federal government's right to restrict immigration based on **nationalities**. More restrictive acts were passed in 1888 and 1891. They allowed the national government not only to exclude certain individuals—convicts, prostitutes, the insane, and so on—but also to deport aliens who entered the country in violation of these immigration laws.

Quotas The concept of limiting the rights of certain nationalities to immigrate resulted in the Quota Act of 1921. This act limited the annual number of immigrants from each nationality to 3 percent of the number of

▼ This photograph from 1900 shows immigrant women from Southern Europe leaving Ellis Island. These women represent the new immigrants, from Eastern and Southern Europe, who started to arrive in the 1880s. Where were most immigrants from prior to the 1880s?

Discussion Starter
Guide the students in considering the 1965 immigration law: What changes did it make? Why? How different were its effects from those of the earlier immigration laws?

Extension
Encourage the students to share and discuss any personal experiences with the Immigration Act of 1990: How has the act affected you? Your family members? Other people you know?

Cooperative Learning
Have the students work in groups to study and discuss the chart showing the Highlights of the 1990 Immigration Act: What is the significance of each fact here? Which special population—if any—does it seem to serve? Why?

Observable Mastery
Introduce the students to a fictitious immigrant from Central America. Instruct the students that they are to compile a written summary of information that the immigrant will need to know in order to understand citizenship in the United States. Students should be instructed to include ways citizenship is acquired and lost, the categories for aliens, as well as the rights of aliens. Finally, have students explain the Immigration Act of 1990. Students should be allowed to share their lists in order to help one another make improvements.

foreign-born persons of that nationality who were living in the United States in 1910. Most Asian groups were not included in the list of nationalities and, therefore could not legally emigrate to the United States for some time. The law did not apply to certain categories of educated people, such as professors, ministers, doctors, and lawyers. Immigration from the Western hemisphere was also unrestricted. The world responded, with seven hundred thousand immigrants entering the U.S. in 1924. The Immigration Act of 1924 and the National Origins Act of 1929 established a new quota system for each nationality, plus a limit on the total number of immigrants to be allowed entry at all (150,000 per year). The National Origins Quota System thus devised in the 1920s served as the basis for U.S. immigration policy for more than thirty-five years.

Current Immigration Policy Today's immigration policy is based largely on the Immigration Act of 1990, which revised several other acts including ones in 1965 and 1986.

The 1965 law had eliminated quotas based on national origin. As many as 270,000 immigrants could be admitted each year without regard to nationality, country of origin, or race, but not more than 20,000 persons could come from any one country. Close relatives of American citizens were given special status, as were aliens who have specialized occupational talents.

The maximum quota of 270,000 immigrants per year was always exceeded. The Refugee Act of 1980 allowed at least another 50,000 political refugees to legally enter the country each year. Congress and the president have since increased that number to about 100,000 per year. There are 150,000 special immigrants, mostly children and spouses of American citizens, who are also allowed entry. The Immigration Reform and Control Act of 1986 dealt mainly with illegal immigration. It also created a set of preferences for who could become a legal immigrant in the United States.

The big change in immigration law occurred in 1990 with the passage of the Immigration Act of 1990. This act raised the legal immigration levels by about 40 percent annually to 700,000. It stresses family reunification, provides amnesty for certain illegal immigrants (grants these immigrants legal status), and strikes down barriers blocking people with certain political beliefs. The new act's most significant feature was a tripling of the number of visas (to about 140,000 a year) granted to highly skilled professionals such as engineers, researchers, and scientists.

The chart below shows the highlights of the immigration act.

FIGURE 7–2 Highlights of the 1990 Immigration Act. The figure below outlines some of the important points from the 1990 Immigration Act. Does the 1990 Immigration Act set country-by-country quotas for immigrants?

Highlights of the 1990 Immigration Act

- Overall cap of 700,000 visas for legal immigrants. After three years, cap falls to 675,000.
- 40,000 visas for "priority workers," or aliens with "extraordinary ability" in arts, sciences, education, business, or athletics.
- 40,000 visas for aliens with advanced degrees or "exceptional ability."
- 40,000 visas for other skilled workers, such as professionals holding basic degrees.
- 10,000 visas for investors meeting certain economic criteria.
- 40,000 visas for three years for aliens from 35 countries with low immigration in recent decades. At least 40 percent of these must come from Ireland.
- 55,000 visas, in late 1995, for "diversity" immigrants from countries with low immigration in recent decades. Generally requires a high school education or two years of specific work experience.
- Salvadorans in the United States by September 19, 1990, receive temporary "asylum" and work authorization for 18 months.

Figure Answer No country-by-country quotas are included in the 1990 Immigration Act. Such quotas have been eliminated since the Immigration Act of 1965.

TEACHING BUILDING SOCIAL STUDIES SKILLS

Read
Let volunteers explain what a bar graph is and how it can be used. Then ask volunteers to read the Building Social Studies Skills feature aloud; guide the students in examining the sample graph.

Discuss
Encourage the students to discuss the information presented about bar graphs: How does a bar graph make information clearly accessible? What kinds of details are left out of bar graphs? What limits are there to the uses of bar graphs?

Analyze and Apply
Have each student find and bring to class a bar graph in a newspaper, magazine, or other publication. Let the students work in groups to examine the graphs and discuss the information presented there.

Review
Have the students answer these review questions: What are two of the most important uses of bar graphs? Why is it important to read the title of a bar graph?

Practicing Your Skills (Answers)
1. 1821–1830.
2. 1901–1910.
3. 18–64 years.
4. 17 years and younger.

Cooperative Learning
Let the students work in small groups to examine and discuss the chart on Immigration Patterns: What are the periods of largest immigration? Why do you think so many people immigrated during those times? What are the periods of smallest immigration? What do you think explains these lower levels of immigration?

Discussion Starter
Guide the students in discussing this flow of undocumented aliens: Why do you think most undocumented aliens come to the United States? What do you imagine they find here? How long do you think they usually stay in this country?

BUILDING SOCIAL STUDIES SKILLS

Reading Bar Graphs

A bar graph is a convenient way of showing large amounts of information at a glance. They are often used to show changes in trends that occur over time or to compare data.

When reading a bar graph, first read the title of the graph to find out what information is found there. Bars in a graph can run vertically, such as the one on page 169, or horizontally, such as the one on immigration on the right. One part of the information—ages, dates, percentages, and so on—is usually presented on the left vertical axis. Another part of the information is presented on the bottom horizontal axis. Sometimes, additional information, often indicated with different colors or shading, is presented within the bars themselves. To read graphs, simply note where the bars intersect with the vertical or horizontal axes.

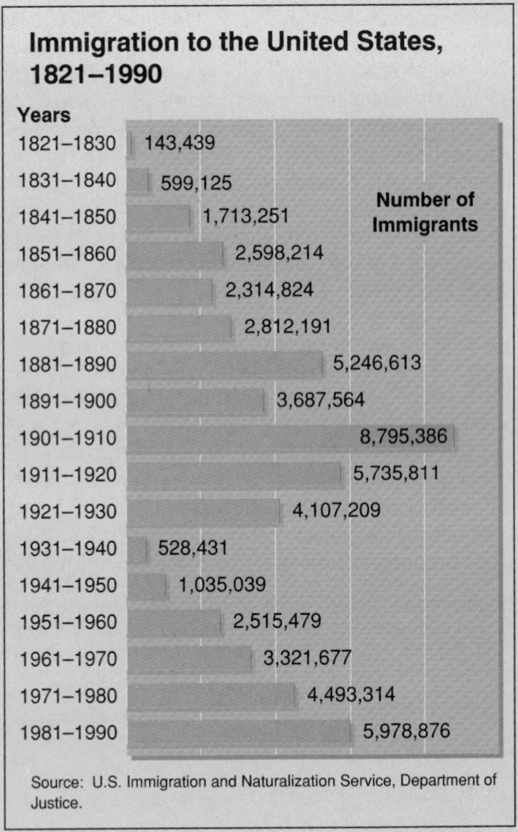

PRACTICING YOUR SKILLS

Use the bar graphs to the right and on page 169 to answer the following questions:

1. In which period did the lowest number of immigrants come to the United States?
2. In which period did the largest number of immigrants come to the United States?
3. Which population group grew the most from 1960 to 1990?
4. Which age group made up a smaller percentage of the total population in 1970 than in 1960?

Immigration to the United States, 1821–1990

Years	Number of Immigrants
1821–1830	143,439
1831–1840	599,125
1841–1850	1,713,251
1851–1860	2,598,214
1861–1870	2,314,824
1871–1880	2,812,191
1881–1890	5,246,613
1891–1900	3,687,564
1901–1910	8,795,386
1911–1920	5,735,811
1921–1930	4,107,209
1931–1940	528,431
1941–1950	1,035,039
1951–1960	2,515,479
1961–1970	3,321,677
1971–1980	4,493,314
1981–1990	5,978,876

Source: U.S. Immigration and Naturalization Service, Department of Justice.

The Immigration Controversy

The number of immigrants legally allowed into the United States does not necessarily represent the actual number of immigrants who come and stay here. This nation has a large flow of illegal aliens, also known as **undocumented aliens**. Many of these are tourists who overstay their visas and start working. Many are from Mexico and other Latin American countries. No one knows for sure how many illegal aliens arrive each year, but the estimate is at 2 million. The number of illegal aliens who permanently live in the United States is estimated to be between 5 and 12 million.

Periodically, the federal government has attempted to remedy the problem of illegal immigration. The latest attempt was in 1986, when the Immigration Reform and Control Act imposed severe penalties on employers who willfully hired illegal aliens (fines range from $250 to $10,000 for each offense). Employers who repeatedly violate this law can be jailed for up to six months.

Another aspect of the 1986 law was an **amnesty** program. (Amnesty means a general pardon for past

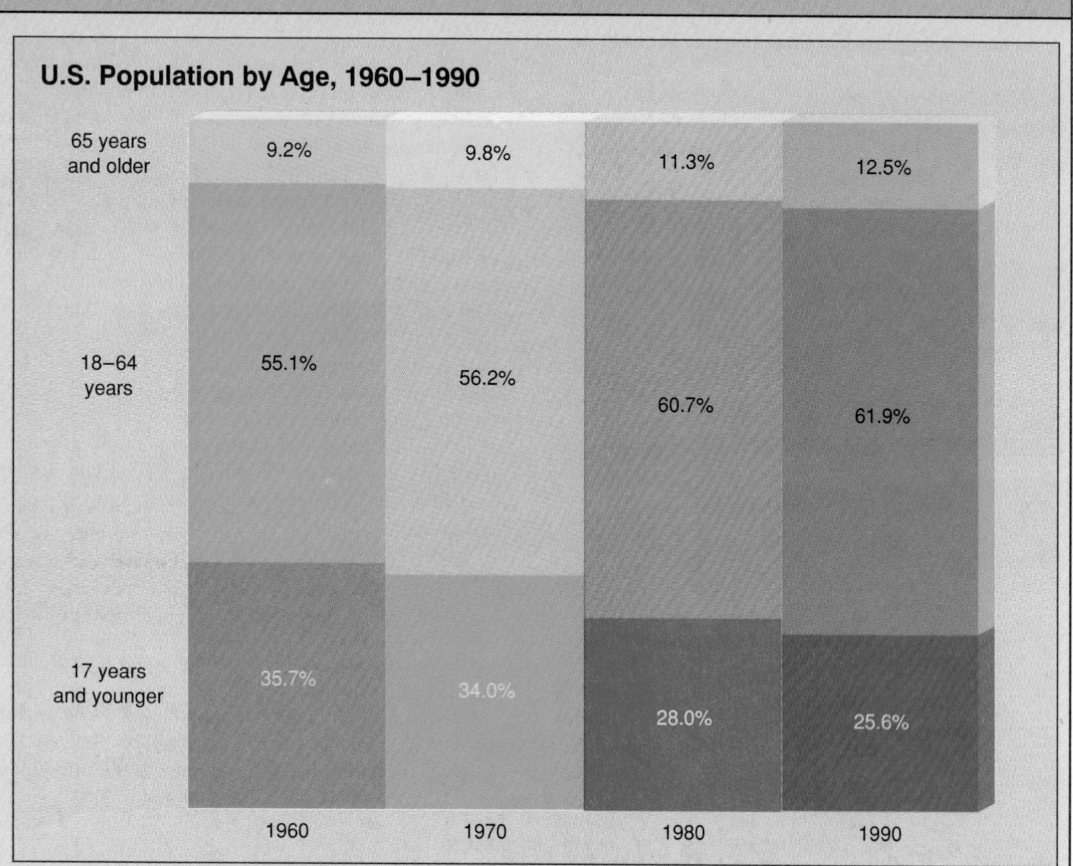

offenses, in this case illegally residing in the U.S.) From the summer of 1987 to the summer of 1988, illegal aliens who could prove that they had been in this country continuously for at least five years could apply to obtain temporary legal residency status. Eighteen months later they could then apply for permanent residency and eventually for citizenship. (See the Resource Center.)

Immigration policy is the focus of a continuing debate in the United States. Many Americans strongly believe that immigrants, especially illegal immigrants, prevent American citizens from being fully employed. These critics of liberal immigration policies further believe that increased immigration lowers American wages. Finally, such critics express the fear that new waves of immigrants will have difficulty fitting in with present-day American society.

Supporters of immigration point out the obvious—at one time or another all of us, except for Native Americans, were immigrants. Why should we arbitrarily decide that today immigration is ''bad'' for America? Additionally, many new immigrants to America take low-paying jobs that Americans leave unfilled anyway. In

This figure content is also featured on *West's American Government Videodisc* (see the index found in the TRB).

Discussion Starter
Ask the students to consider the fines levied against employers who willfully hire illegal aliens: Do you think fining the employers is a fair practice? Why or why not? Why do you imagine some employers might knowingly hire illegal aliens? Whom might employers be trying to help? Who might be hurt by such practices?

Discussion Starter
Encourage the students to discuss their responses to these questions: Why do you think the amnesty program was instituted? Whom was it intended to help? Was anyone hurt by the amnesty program? If so, who and how?

Extension
Ask interested students to prepare and present a debate on this question: Is immigration "bad" for America?

Reteaching Strategies

1. Let the students work in small groups to discuss their responses to the Preview Questions at the beginning of the section. Encourage the group members to refer to the text to resolve any uncertainties.
2. Ask the students to work with partners to write definitions—in their own words—of these terms: *immigrant, alien, visa, amnesty.*

Evaluation Strategies

1. Have the students write their answers to the Section 2 Review questions.
2. Have the students take the Section 2 Quiz found in the *TRB.*

Section 2 Review (Answers)

1. Resident aliens are individuals who have come to the United States to establish permanent residence. Nonresident aliens are individuals who expect to stay in the United States for a specified period of time. Enemy aliens are citizens of those nations at war with the United States. Refugees are immigrants to the United States who are granted entry because they are politically unsafe or unwelcome in their own countries. Illegal aliens are individuals who enter the United States without a legal permit or who enter as tourists and stay longer than tourist status allows.
2. Resident and nonresident aliens, like all citizens, have the rights given to them by the U.S. Constitution and state constitutions. In general, all legal aliens can legally own real estate and send their children to public schools. They must pay taxes and obey all laws.
3. The Chinese Exclusion Act of 1882 halted entry of any Chinese immigrants to the United States for ten years. More restrictive acts were passed in 1888 and 1890. The Quota Act of 1921 limited the annual number of immigrants from each nationality to 3 percent of the number of foreign-born persons of that nationality who were living in the United States in 1910.
4. Answers will vary, e.g., the program will encourage other foreigners to illegally immigrate to the United States because they might believe that such a program will be put into effect again.

SECTION 3

Points to Stress

- The meaning behind nationalization of the Bill of Rights.
- Rights and responsibilities of American citizenship.

Kickoff Activity

Give the students five minutes in which to write two lists: one of citizenship rights, the other of citizenship responsibilities. Encourage

addition, the majority of immigrants pay taxes and adjust rapidly to the requirements of life in their new country.

SECTION 2 REVIEW

1. List and briefly explain the five types of aliens under United States law.
2. What are the rights of aliens? What are their responsibilities?
3. What were the first restrictions placed on immigration in the United States?
4. **For critical analysis:** A 1986 amnesty program for illegal immigrants allowed many of them to obtain legal residency in this country. How do you think such a program would influence other foreigners wanting to illegally immigrate to the United States? Give reasons for your answer.

SECTION 3

Citizenship Rights and Responsibilities

Preview Questions

- What is meant by the nationalization of the Bill of Rights?
- What are some of the rights and responsibilities of American citizenship?

Citizenship involves both rights and responsibilities. A citizen owes **allegiance,** or loyalty, to her or his nation which, in turn, gives the citizen all the rights and protections of the law. Thus, American citizenship is an implied contract between the nation and the individual for mutual support and assistance.

Rights of Citizens

Citizens' rights are spelled out in the Constitution and in federal and state laws. One right all citizens have is simply to live on American soil. We also have the right to vote, to hold public office, and to travel freely throughout the United States. The federal government also tries to protect American citizens wherever they are in the world. Our major rights are guaranteed by the Bill of Rights as well as several additional amendments.

The Bill of Rights If you reread the First Amendment to the Bill of Rights, you will notice that it starts with the words "*Congress* shall make no law. . . ." Most citizens do not realize that, as originally presented, the Bill of Rights limited only the power of the federal government, not the power of the states. In other words, a citizen in the state of Virginia in 1795 could not successfully sue in federal court against a law passed in Virginia that violated one of the amendments in the Bill of Rights. Each state had (and still has) its own constitution, normally with its own bill of rights.

Whereas the states' bills of rights were similar to the federal one, there were some differences in content and, perhaps more importantly, differences in interpretation. A citizen in one state effectively had a different set of civil liberties than a citizen in another state. It was not until the Fourteenth Amendment was ratified in 1868 that our Constitution explicitly guaranteed due process

Most of our major rights are protected by the Bill of Rights, shown here as it was taken all over the nation for the public to view. Was the Bill of Rights originally intended to apply to state governments as well as the federal government?

Caption Answer The Bill of Rights was originally intended to apply solely to the federal government.

volunteers to read their lists to the rest of the class. Then point out that the students will learn more about these rights and responsibilities as they study Section 3.

Working with the Preview Questions
Ask the students to read and consider the section title and the two study questions. Then let the students suggest other questions they expect to have answered as they study Section 3. Record the questions on the board, and refer to them at the end of the section.

Teaching Strategies

Introduction
Let a volunteer read the section introduction aloud. Then ask: What is allegiance? Why do citizens owe allegiance to their nation? How do citizens show their allegiance?

Discussion Starter
Help the students discuss the rights spelled out in the Constitution and in federal and state laws: Which of these rights do you exercise? How and why? Which do you not exercise? Why? Do you expect to exercise those rights in the future?

Enrichment
Ask a group of interested students to research and report on your state's Bill of Rights.

Discussion Starter
Let a volunteer read the quotation from Section 1 of the Fourteenth Amendment aloud. Then ask: What is the purpose of this section? Why was it necessary? How can we see its effects today?

Comprehension
Ask volunteers to use their own words in answering these questions: What is the difference between citizens and persons (in the Fourteenth Amendment)? What is the difference between a civil right and a civil liberty?

Cooperative Learning
Let the students work in small groups to examine and discuss the chart, Incorporating the Bill of Rights into the Fourteenth Amendment.

Incorporating the Bill of Rights into the Fourteenth Amendment

Year	Issue	Amendment Involved	Court Case
1925	Freedom of speech	I	*Gitlow* v. *New York, 268 U.S. 652*
1931	Freedom of the press	I	*Near* v. *Minnesota, 283 U.S. 697*
1932	Right to a lawyer in capital punishment cases	VI	*Powell* v. *Alabama, 287 U.S. 45*
1934	Freedom of religion	I	*Hamilton* v. *Regents of the University of California, 293 U.S. 245*
1937	Freedom of and right to petition	I	*De Jonge* v. *Oregon, 299 U.S. 353*
1947	Separation of church and state	I	*Everson* v. *Board of Education, 330 U.S. 1*
1948	Right to a public trial	VI	*In re Oliver, 333 U.S. 257*
1961	No unreasonable searches and seizures	IV	*Mapp* v. *Ohio, 367 U.S. 643*
1962	No cruel and unusual punishment	VIII	*Robinson* v. *California, 370 U.S. 660*
1963	Right to a lawyer in all criminal cases	VI	*Gideon* v. *Wainwright, 372 U.S. 335*
1964	No compulsory self-incrimination	V	*Malloy* v. *Hogan, 378 U.S. 1*
1965	Right to privacy	I	*Griswold* v. *Connecticut, 381 U.S. 479*
1966	Right to an impartial jury	VI	*Parker* v. *Gladden, 385 U.S. 363*
1966	Right to counsel and no compulsory self-incrimination	V, VI	*Miranda* v. *Arizona, 384 U.S. 436*
1967	Right to a speedy trial	VI	*Klopfer* v. *North Carolina, 386 U.S. 213*
1973	No double jeopardy	V	*Colgrove* v. *Battin, 413 U.S. 149*

▲ **FIGURE 7–3 Incorporating the Bill of Rights into the Fourteenth Amendment.** The court cases listed above extended the protections of the Bill of Rights to apply to the citizens of states as well as the national government. Why do you think the Bill of Rights originally applied only to the national government?

This figure content is also featured on *West's American Government Videodisc* (see the index found in the TRB).

Figure Answer Students should understand that the framers of the Constitution were fearful of an overly powerful national government, but assumed that individual states would always protect the rights of their citizens.

of law to people in all states. Section 1 of the amendment provides that:

> No State shall make or enforce any law which shall abridge the privileges or immunities of citizens of the United States; nor shall any State deprive any person of life, liberty, or property, without due process of law; nor deny to any person within its jurisdiction the equal protection of the laws.

Section 5 of the amendment explicitly gives Congress the power to enforce these provisions by appropriate legislation.

Note the use of the terms *citizens* and *person. Citizens* have political rights, such as voting and running for office, but no *person,* citizen or alien, can be denied civil liberties (speech, press, and religion) nor have his or her property taken without equal recourse to the legal system. Note also that there is a distinction between the technical definitions of a civil *right* and a civil *liberty*: Civil rights are granted by the government; civil liberties are inherent.

The Nationalization, or Incorporation, of the Bill of Rights The Fourteenth Amendment (ratified in 1868)

Vocabulary
Ask the students to explain the meaning of this phrase: *fetter and degrade state government.*

Critical Thinking Skills
Ask the students to analyze the reasoning that led the Supreme Court to uphold the principle of dual citizenship. How might that reasoning have been altered to accept the incorporation theory?

Discussion Starter
Encourage the students to consider the implications of the Bill of Rights being uniformly applied by individual state governments: How does this affect citizens of various states? Why is it important?

Discussion Starter
Help the students discuss the legal duty of citizens to support the government: Why are these duties important? What would happen if citizens did not fulfill these duties? Is it all right for individual citizens to choose to ignore these duties? Why or why not?

Caption Answer
Students' answers will vary, but should express an appreciation of voting as not only a right, but also as a responsibility for citizens in our democracy. Students might also mention that some elections are decided by very small margins.

Discussion Starter
Ask the students to write short essays on the topic of the importance of each individual vote. The essays should answer the following: Do you think each vote makes a difference? If the outcome of an election has been predicted, does it still make sense to cast a vote? Why or why not? Encourage the students to express and defend differing points of view.

Extension
Have each student interview at least four adults about their voting habits: How many vote regularly in national elections? In state and local elections? What reasons do they give for voting—or for not voting.

Discussion Starter
Help the students discuss their duty to attend school: Why is this your duty as a citizen? What should you expect to contribute toward your education? What can and should you expect to get when you attend school? What can you—as students—do to help others fulfill this duty of citizenship?

was to be a national standard that would guarantee both due process and equal protection under the law for all persons throughout the nation. The courts did not agree with this process of making the amendment apply to all states. Many jurists still believed, as John Marshall stated in the *Barron* v. *Mayor of Baltimore* (1833) decision, that the states were "distinct governments framed by different persons and for different purposes." Marshall's statement in the *Barron* decision was plain: The Bill of Rights limits only the federal government and not the state governments. The *Barron* decision is still the general rule of law. It has been greatly modified in practice, though, through interpretations of the Fourteenth Amendment.

In 1873 in the *Slaughter-House* cases, the U.S. Supreme Court upheld the principle of **dual citizenship**—of a state and of the United States—arguing that to deprive states of their authority and their identity would "fetter and degrade state governments." In these cases Louisiana law prohibited livestock yards and slaughterhouses within New Orleans, except for the Crescent City Company's operation. Butchers and others adversely affected sought to have the law declared void, in part under the Fourteenth Amendment. The Supreme Court held that the Fourteenth Amendment creates two types of citizenship—federal and state—and that the amendment extends federal constitutional protection only to the privileges and immunities of national citizenship. The Court reasoned that the Louisiana statute did not infringe on any of the privileges and immunities of national citizenship, and was therefore not in conflict with the constitution.

Only gradually did the Supreme Court accept the **incorporation theory**, which declared that no state could act in violation of the U.S. Bill of Rights. Even to this day, the Court has not fully accepted this theory. The table on page 171 shows the rights that the Court has incorporated into the Fourteenth Amendment and in which case it first applied these rights. The practical implementation of the Fourteenth Amendment has taken place relatively slowly.

The last hundred years of Supreme Court decisions have bound the fifty states to accept most of the provisions that are contained in the U.S. Bill of Rights. The exceptions have usually involved the right to bear arms, the right to refuse to quarter soldiers (to provide them shelter), and the right to a grand jury hearing. Thus, for all intents and purposes, the Bill of Rights of the federal Constitution must be uniformly applied by all state governments.

Your Responsibilities as a Citizen

As American citizens, you have the legal duty to support the government by obeying the laws, paying taxes, serving on juries, and defending the nation whenever necessary. But good citizenship does not depend on each of you doing *only* what you are required by law to do. Rather, good citizenship means that you become a *participant* in this country's democratic system. Here are some ways in which you can participate:

Voting The common way in which Americans participate in their democracy is by voting. For most Americans, voting is the single most effective way they can affect the course of political events in their country. Votes for or against particular candidates ultimately determine who will represent the people's interests at the various levels of government.

Some people do not vote because they believe that their vote does not count. That is not always true. In 1948, Lyndon Johnson won the Texas Democratic primary for United States senator by 87 votes out of 940,000 cast. If those 87 people had not voted, Texas would have

▼ Voting is one way that most Americans participate. How would you respond to someone who argues that one vote makes no difference?

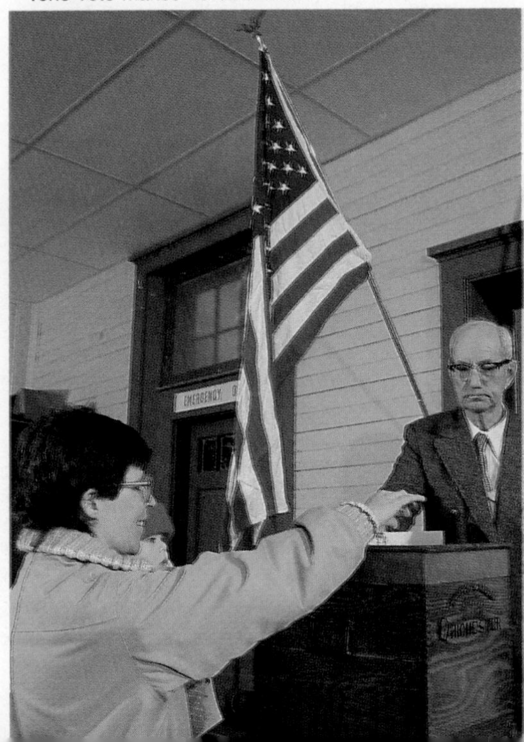

Discussion Starter
To help the students discuss the duty of defending the nation, pose questions such as these: Are there other, nonmilitary ways to help defend the nation? If so, what are they? Should those kinds of service also be counted as fulfilling the duty to register for military service? Why or why not?

Enrichment
Ask the students to find out how juries are selected. Also encourage them to discuss jury duty with adults who have served on juries.

Discussion Starter
Help the students consider and discuss the contributions they can make to the well-being of society: What contributions are you making now? What contributions do you plan to make in the future? Why are you waiting—is there something you can do now? What contributions do other members of your family make? Why?

Enrichment
Ask the students to work with you in identifying parents or other local adults with careers in public and community service. Have the students invite those adults to speak to the class, either individually or as members of a panel.

had a different senator. John F. Kennedy won the presidency in 1960 by a margin of only 120,000 votes in the popular election, less than one-fifth of 1 percent over Richard Nixon. In 1976, Jimmy Carter won over Gerald Ford for the presidency by a margin of only 2 percent. In local elections these types of close results occur all the time.

Voting trends in the United States are not encouraging. In the last few presidential elections, less than half of all eligible voters actually voted. Voter turnout is even less in state and local elections.

Defending Civil Rights As an American citizen you have a duty to not only understand your own civil liberties, but also those of your fellow Americans. That means that you have a responsibility to allow others the same liberties that you have been granted, even when their beliefs may be different from your own. This is especially true with respect to religion. You may not agree with the religious preferences of others, but you have a duty as an American citizen to accept each person's right to worship in her or his own way.

Good citizenship requires that each of us extends to others the rights guaranteed to all of us by the Constitution.

Paying Taxes Through federal, state, and local taxes government raises money to pay for the services that citizens demand. It is every citizen's responsibility to contribute by paying his or her share of taxes.

Attending School Our society depends on our schools to teach young citizens the skills and knowledge they need to become contributing members of society. A good education also prepares citizens to support themselves and to contribute to the economy.

A well-educated citizen can make more informed voting choices. Such individuals are often better equipped to face our diverse and rapidly changing society. Moreover, education fosters an understanding and appreciation of all peoples and cultures.

Defending the Nation It is also a citizen's responsibility to help defend the nation against threats to our peace and security. All young men must register for military service when they turn 18 years of age. This does not mean they will have to serve in the military but it does mean that they can be called in the event of a national emergency. Citizens may also volunteer to serve in the Army, Navy, Marines, Air Force, or Coast Guard.

Serving on a Jury or as a Witness All citizens have the right to a fair trial. To ensure this right, our Constitution guarantees that anyone accused of a crime has a right to a jury of peers. This means that you may be called upon to serve on a jury. During a trial, witnesses are often needed to prove guilt or innocence. At some time in your life you may see or hear events that may help determine the guilt or innocence of a person accused of a crime. If this is the case, you have the responsibility to serve as a witness in court if you are called to do so.

Contributing to the Well-Being of Society What would our country be like if everyone were willing to vote but not to participate in other ways? We would have no political parties, no help during election campaigns, no neighborhood-improvement projects, no community-service projects, and no political-action groups. No one would go to public meetings to express their opinions or to get more information. There would be no letters to the editor or to elected representatives. In fact, there would be no representatives because no one would ever run for public office. If this were the case, our representative government would not last very long. American democracy needs citizens to take interest and get involved in our democracy in order to survive.

Careers in Public and Community Services

Making sure that citizens' rights, privileges, and services are extended to all Americans is the job of the men and women who have chosen careers in public and community services. Over three million of those people are employed by the federal government in civilian positions ranging from letter carriers to judges. About two million more are employed by the nation's armed services. Nearly four million more are employed by state governments in positions that range from state trooper to fish and wildlife department employee. Another ten million people are employed at local levels in many positions such as school administrators, fire fighters, town clerks, and park maintenance employees. Public service employees ensure that children are educated, parks are maintained, garbage is disposed of, and that people are safe in their homes and on the street.

Jobs with the Federal Government Federal employees run the gamut from foreign service workers to agents of the Federal Bureau of Investigation and the Central Intelligence Agency. Federal workers may also be employed by the Immigration and Naturalization Service,

Multidiscipline Strategies

Career Investigation Have each student select one of the career fields mentioned here for further investigation. Encourage the students to select careers that interest them and for which they might be suited. Ask them to use resources such as the *Occupational Outlook Handbook* and the *Dictionary of Occupational Titles,* as well as pamphlets, magazines, newspapers, and other materials to learn about the required training, the working conditions, the employment outlcok, and the potential earnings for their chosen careers.

Vocabulary
Ask the students to consider these two terms: *political patronage* and *spoils system:* How are the two terms alike in denotative meaning? How are they different in connotative meaning?

Enrichment
Ask volunteers to find out how and why the Civil Service Commission was abolished. What agency now serves the function previously served by the commission? What effects has this change had? Have the volunteers write and post a short report on their findings.

Reteaching Strategies
1. Refer the students to the questions they posed at the beginning of this section. Let volunteers read those questions aloud, and encourage the students to share and discuss their responses. If the class feels that some of their questions have not been answered by the text, ask volunteers to research those questions and share the answers they find.
2. Ask the students to work in small groups, reviewing Section 3 as they write lists of citizens' responsibilities.

Evaluation Strategies
1. Have the students write their answers to the Section 3 Review questions.
2. Have the students take the Section 3 Quiz found in the *TRB.*

Section 3 Review (Answers)
1. It declared that no state could act in violation of the United States Bill of Rights.
2. Our major rights are guaranteed in the Bill of Rights. We also have the right to live on American soil, the right to vote, to hold public office, and to travel freely throughout the United States.
3. Voting, defending civil rights, paying taxes, attending school, defending the nation, serving on a jury or as a witness, and contributing to the well-being of society.
4. One must fill out an application and often take the Civil Service test.
5. Answers will vary, e.g., in order to have a democracy, people must vote and choose their representatives. Not voting is giving up an important right and responsibility.

SECTION 4

Points to Stress
- America's changing ethnic makeup, especially among school-age population.
- The characterization of tolerance.
- The ways in which Americans can be involved in cultural diversity.

Kickoff Activity
Write these questions on the chalkboard: What is *tolerance?* What is *open-mindedness?* How are the two related? Give the students five minutes in which to write their responses to the questions; then let volunteers read their responses aloud.

the Internal Revenue Service, the Department of Agriculture, the United States Postal Service, and the federal court system. Even men and women involved in space exploration are federal employees. The federal government also hires clerks, engineers, nurses, secretaries, public relations representatives, computer programmers, and people in many other positions.

Jobs with State and Local Governments While the number of federal employees has remained constant since 1950, the number of state and local civil servants has increased dramatically. The increase is partly due to cutbacks in federal programs and partly due to the continued growth of the nations' cities and suburbs. State services include tax collection, law enforcement, highway safety and maintenance, motor vehicle licensing and registration, and the administration of such assistance programs as unemployment insurance and workers' compensation.

Civil Service Until the 1880s, the federal government was staffed according to a system politely known as **political patronage**, but was more realistically called the **spoils system**. Under the spoils system, those elected to federal office would appoint their own friends and political allies to federal jobs after discharging the previous officeholder's appointees. This system failed to recognize the need for qualified, trained government employees and resulted in an entirely new group of federal employees every time a new party was elected to office. Obviously, this made it very difficult for the federal government to undertake any long-range programs.

The abuses of the spoils system became serious enough to merit congressional attention. In 1883 a bipartisan Civil Service Commission was established by Congress to prepare and administer competitive examinations given to applicants for government jobs. Several states also passed civil service laws and began to fill jobs through **civil service examinations**. These laws put into effect the idea that **merit**, or suitability, is the reason to hire someone for public service. Although the Civil Service Commission was abolished in 1978, merit remains the primary criterion for government employment, especially at the federal level.

Military Service Those who join a branch of military service may choose from many career options. Training is available in such areas as electronics, aviation, aircraft mechanics, computer programming, or ship navigation. Because the military must staff its ranks with volunteer enlistees, it finds that it is competing with civilian employers for workers. As a result, the military now offers benefits and training programs that encourage people to enlist and to stay in the service once their initial enlistment has expired. New recruits also receive good starting salaries, free room and board or a housing allowance, free medical care, paid vacations, and access to military commissaries.

SECTION 3 REVIEW

1. What is the incorporation theory?
2. What are your rights as a citizen?
3. Name your responsibilities as a United States citizen.
4. What is the procedure for getting a job with the government?
5. **For critical analysis:** Even though voting is the most common way a citizen participates in our democracy, not all of us vote. How does failing to vote reduce your effectiveness as a citizen?

SECTION 4

Tolerance and Open-mindedness

Preview Questions
- How is the ethnic makeup of America, especially its school-age population, changing?
- What does tolerance really mean?
- What are some ways in which Americans can expose themselves to our country's diverse cultures?

If there is one thing that the 1990 census made clear to all Americans, it is that America is truly a multicultural society. In 1980, for example, non-Hispanic whites represented a majority in six of the ten largest cities in America. In the 1990s, non-Hispanic whites are a majority in only three. The combined numbers of African Americans, Hispanics, Asians, and other minorities now constitute the majority population in Chicago, Dallas, Detroit, Houston, Los Angeles, New York, and San Antonio. Today, minorities account for one out of every four Americans. During the last decade the Asian population in America increased by 107 percent and the Hispanic population by 53 percent. In the past, African Americans were the majority among minorities. That is

Working with the Preview Questions

Have volunteers read these study questions aloud, and encourage the students to share what they think and know now: What do you think the ethnic makeup of America is now? How do you think that makeup is changing? Why? How can you be tolerant? Why should you be? How are you already involved in cultural diversity? What else can you do to become more involved? After the discussion, tell the students that they will return to these questions after they have read Section 4.

Teaching Strategies

Introduction

After the students have read the section introduction, let them share and discuss their reactions. Then ask: What does the word *minority* mean? How do you feel about phrases such as "African Americans, Hispanics, Asians, and other minorities"? In what sense are these groups "minorities"? In what sense are these groups not "minorities"? What does the use of the terms *minority* and *majority* imply to you? Why?

Citizenship Skills and Responsibilities

Applying for a Government Job

If you are interested in a job with the federal government, contact the nearest office of the U.S. Office of Personnel Management (OPM) or look in the *Yellow Pages* under ''Federal Information Center'' or ''U.S. Government.'' Call to ask for a pamphlet about the career area in which you are interested. The pamphlet will explain this three-step process.

1. **Obtaining a job announcement.** On request, the office will send you a document known as a job announcement. It will identify a job and tell you the salary, the location, and the job requirements. Read the announcement carefully to find out if you are qualified.
2. **Filling out the application.** If you are interested in the job, ask the job information center to send you an application form, or go to the center itself to obtain one. Read the form carefully and fill it out properly.
3. **Taking the Civil Service test.** A test is required for some government jobs. After the information center receives your application, it will notify you of the time and place at which to take the test. Sample tests can be sent to you to use as practice and preparation. Some time after taking the test, you will receive a score and be told whether you qualified for the job.

For more information see the OPM's *Federal Career Directory: A Guide for College Students* (available in libraries, or from the superintendent of Documents, Government Printing Office, Washington, DC 20402) You can also get a free pamphlet called *Working for the USA* from the Office of Personnel Management, (Washington, DC 20415), or from one of the federal job information centers it operates in major cities.

Taking Action

One of the best ways to find out if you would like to work for the government is by getting a summer job or an internship with a local, state, or federal agency. The federal government has summer staff positions available, such as congressional aide and legislative assistant. At the state level, jobs are available in state capitals as well as in regional offices. Summer jobs at the local government level may involve working at the county courthouse or town recreation center. Here are some places to contact:

- local and county government offices
- governors' offices and state agencies
- senators and members of Congress
- federal agencies

You can also write to the government offices listed below to obtain the following sources of information:

Summer Jobs: Opportunities in the Federal Government

Write:

Announcement 414
United States Office of Personnel Management
Superintendent of Documents
U.S. Government Printing Office
Washington, DC 20402

Washington Information Directory

Write:

Congressional Quarterly, Inc.
1414 Twenty-Second Street, NW
Washington, DC 20037

TEACHING CITIZENSHIP SKILLS AND RESPONSIBILITIES

Read

Introduce this feature by letting the students discuss what they know about government jobs: Who do you know who works for the government? How did that person get his or her job? What government jobs interest you? How do you think people apply for those jobs? Then ask volunteers to read Applying for a Government Job aloud to the rest of the class.

Discuss

Ask questions such as these, and encourage the students to discuss their responses: What information can you find in the *Yellow Pages?* How can this information be helpful when you are looking for a job? What summer jobs might be available locally with government agencies? Do you know anyone who has held this kind of summer job? What summer government jobs interest you? Why?

Analyze and Apply

Have the students work in groups to obtain career area pamphlets and job announcements, practice filling out application forms, and read about Civil Service tests.

Review

Help the students review by posing these questions: What office provides information about jobs with the federal government? What are the three main steps in applying for a job with the U.S. Government?

Critical Thinking Skills
Guide the students in analyzing the effects of the changing school-age population: What are the consequences of these diverse populations within single school districts—and within single schools? What obligations do schools have to educate students in their native language? What obligations do schools have to teach students English?

Reteaching Strategies
1. Pose again the Preview Questions. Let the students work in groups to share and discuss their responses to the questions. Have each group conclude its discussion by considering how their understanding of these issues has changed.
2. Let students work with partners to plan and write short essays on tolerance: What is tolerance? Why is it especially important in our country? How can it be achieved?

Evaluation Strategies
1. Have the students write their answers to the Section 4 Review questions.
2. Have the students take the Section 4 Quiz found in the *TRB.*

Section 4 Review (Answers)
1. African Americans, Hispanics, and Asians.
2. Texas and California.
3. Unable or unwilling to endure differences in opinions or beliefs.
4. Answers will vary, e.g., they have a lack of understanding and knowledge of other cultures, languages, and customs.

Discussion Starter
Let the students discuss their own reactions to the statement that "one of the enduring assets that the United States has developed is its ability to tolerate diversity": What specific examples of this ability can you cite? What other examples can you cite, showing that individual citizens sometimes fail to be tolerant?

Discussion Starter
Help the students discuss the extended definition of *tolerance:* Why does tolerance go beyond allowing others to coexist peacefully? Why is taking an interest in different ideas, practices, and ways of life essential for true tolerance?

Cooperative Learning
Ask the students to form small groups in which to consider and discuss the suggestions for becoming involved in the cultural diversity of the nation. Then have the members of each group select one of these suggestions and plan and carry out a group project based on the suggestion. Encourage the groups to share their projects and results with the rest of the class.

no longer true. While California may be the home of the nation's second largest concentration of African Americans, they are nonetheless outnumbered by Asians and Hispanics.

The School-Age Population is Changing

Public schools are finding themselves increasingly faced with the challenge of educating children with mixed backgrounds. In one high school in a Los Angeles suburb, students speak more than thirty languages.

This trend toward cultural diversity will continue into the future. In 1990 there were 45 million white children under the age of 18; by the year 2000 there will be 43 million and by the year 2010, there will be only 38 million. During the same twenty-year time span, immigration and other factors will increase the number of minority children from 19 to 23 million.

The Need for Tolerance and Open-mindedness

Many of our forebearers came to North America to escape religious, ethnic, and economic persecution. One of the enduring assets that the United States has developed from this history is its ability to tolerate diversity. Part of being a good citizen is being open-minded to the views, customs, appearances, actions, languages, and religions of others.

The *Random House Dictionary* defines **tolerance** as:

> A fair, objective, and permissive attitude toward those whose opinions, practices, race, religion, nationality, etc., differ from one's own.[1]

A further definition of *tolerance* includes "interest in and concern for the ideas, opinions, and practices that are foreign to one's own." Thus, tolerance can be taken to mean not only allowing others who are different to coexist peacefully, but actively taking an interest in their ideas, practices, and way of life. An American practicing good citizenship therefore is involved in the cultural diversity of her or his nation. Here are some ways in which this can be done:

- Learning one or more foreign languages.
- Seeing films in other languages.

OUR BERLIN WALL

Reprinted with permission. Clint C. Wilson, Sr.

- Maintaining friendships with people who are from different ethnic/cultural/national/religious backgrounds.
- Reading and studying about the origins of prejudice.
- Pointing out to others who are not open-minded that their lack of tolerance is inappropriate.
- Experimenting with cuisine and music from other cultures.
- Participating in multi-cultural conferences, forums, discussions, and so on.

While there is nothing in the Constitution or in any law that specifically requires Americans to be tolerant and open-minded, these qualities are part of the heritage of this nation. Our First Amendment rights form the *legal* basis of tolerance, but not the *psychological* basis. That comes from a conscientious effort to accept and explore the ideas and customs of others.

Section 4 Review

1. What minority groups are the most numerous in America?
2. In which states has immigration been an important factor in population growth?
3. What is the first dictionary definition of *intolerant*?
4. **For critical analysis:** How do you explain the attitudes of Americans who are intolerant and not open-minded with respect to members of minority and ethnic groups?

1. *The Random House Dictionary of the English Language,* 2nd ed., New York: Random House, 1987.

TEACHING CHALLENGE TO THE AMERICAN DREAM

Read

Begin by encouraging the students to review and discuss what they already know about immigration to the United States: How is the population of this country growing and changing? What effects do this growth and change seem to have on schools? On social welfare systems? On employment opportunities? After the discussion, ask volunteers to take turns reading Challenge to the American Dream aloud to the rest of the class.

Discuss

Encourage the students to discuss the content by posing questions such as these: Why do you think our country has an INS? What functions do you think the INS should serve? Why? Do American citizens who are unskilled workers have the same rights as American citizens who are skilled laborers? Is it fair that one group should face a greater financial threat as a result of illegal immigration? Why or why not? What role do you think fear plays in motivating individuals and groups who are determined to keep illegal aliens out of this country? What are those people afraid of? Why? What suggestions can you make for a fair and flexible immigration policy for the United States?

Analyze and Apply

Have the class form three groups, and ask each group to investigate the effects of immigration on local schools, local social welfare agencies, or local employment opportunities. Encourage the members of each group to work together: What questions do we want to answer? How can we find the answers to those questions? How can we organize the information we have collected? How should we present our organized information to other students?

Review

Ask the students these review questions: Why do illegal aliens come to the United States? Why does the INS spend time and money tracking illegal aliens and sending them back to their countries of origin? What do studies show about the effects of illegal aliens on employment opportunities for American citizens?

You Decide (Answers)

1. Answers will vary, e.g., the increased flow of educated and professional immigrants may not hurt any group of individuals, but will encourage competition in professional fields.

2. Answers will vary, e.g., no, not if the experience of Miami is indicative of the effect of immigrants on the unemployment rate.

CHALLENGE TO THE AMERICAN DREAM

Immigrants, American Jobs, and Wages

Almost a half a million individuals are legally allowed to immigrate to the United States every year, but during the same year another one to two million immigrate here illegally. These are the "undocumented aliens," otherwise known as illegal aliens, who come to this country mainly for better jobs. In the last few years, over a million illegal aliens per year were stopped by immigration officials, the majority of them at the Mexican border.

The amount of money and labor power devoted to tracking down illegal aliens and sending them back to their countries of origin continues to grow.

Why Prevent Illegal Aliens?

Why do Americans wish to prevent illegal aliens from coming to this country? The basic argument is that they displace American workers from their jobs. A question that arises from this argument, however, is why this wasn't always true. After all, we are a nation of immigrants. To understand the answer we must understand the impact illegal immigration has on American jobs and wages. The common notion is that when immigrants come to this country to look for jobs, they drive down the wages that Americans make. In principle, the result of this is more unemployment and lower wages for Americans. Also, given that illegal aliens usually will work at lower wages than U.S. citizens, immigration may cause unskilled workers in the United States to drop out of the labor force and seek welfare, which raises the cost of welfare payments.

Only recently have studies been done to find out whether immigration does in fact worsen conditions for American workers. To date there is little evidence that immigrants hurt employment opportunities for Americans. According to one researcher, a 10 percent increase in the number of immigrants decreases the average "native" wage by at most two-tenths of 1 percent. It has little effect on labor participation or on the unemployment rate.[2]

Consider some evidence. On April 20, 1980, President Fidel Castro declared that Cuban nationals wishing to emigrate to the United States could leave freely from the Port of Mariel. By September, 1980, about 125,000 Cubans undertook the journey in a flotilla of tour boats, fishing boats, and rafts. Miami's labor force grew by 7 percent almost overnight. What happened?

The economic conditions in Miami between 1980 and 1985 with respect to unemployment rates and wage levels were no different than those experienced in Houston, Atlanta, and Los Angeles. Yet those three cities did not experience a 7 percent increase in their labor forces. This one episode suggests that there is not much reason to worry that immigrants take away jobs from people who already live here.

The challenge to the American dream is to come up with a flexible immigration policy that satisfies many groups. That policy must recognize America's continuing need for skilled workers as well as our multi-cultural heritage and ability to accommodate peoples from diverse cultures. Immigration policy must also accommodate the need to provide public schooling and other social services to large numbers of immigrants who might arrive during a relatively short period of time.

You Decide

1. The Immigration Act of 1990 allows for an increased flow of educated and professional immigrants. Which groups of individuals working in the United States, if any, will be hurt by this increased flow? How?
2. Some argue that immigration should be reduced during periods of high unemployment in America. Do you think this is a reasonable approach to the "immigration problem"? Explain why or why not.

2. Borjas, George J. *Friends or Strangers: The Impact of Immigrants on the U.S. Economy.* New York: Basic Books, 1990.

Chapter Evaluation

To evaluate student mastery of the chapter material, you might:

1. Use Chapter Test A from the *TRB.*

2. Use Chapter Test B from the *TRB.*

3. Construct your own test using items from the *West American Government Test Bank* found in the *TRB.*

4. Use the accompanying computerized software to construct and print a customized chapter test.

Service Learning Activity

Students should have an opportunity to speak with individuals who are not United States citizens. Have students interview an alien, relating that individual's experience to the material in the chapter. It is vital that students address the topic of cultural tolerance along with the factual material. Encourage students to have questions prepared well in advance of the interview. As an option, students might wish to invite an exchange student to visit the class in order to discuss how citizenship differs in his or her country.

Review Questions (Answers)

1. It emphasized the importance of state citizenship.

2. By birth anywhere considered American soil and by the legal process called naturalization.

3. By an act of Congress, by treaty, and by individual action.

4. By expatriation, as punishment for treason, or by denaturalization which occurs if the federal government learns that a citizen has obtained citizenship through fraudulent means.

5. Resident aliens are individuals who have come to the United States to establish permanent residence. Nonresident aliens are individuals who expect to stay for a specified period of time. Enemy aliens are citizens of those nations with which America is at war. Refugees are immigrants granted entry because they are politically unsafe in their own countries. Illegal aliens are those who enter without a legal permit or who enter as tourists and stay longer than tourist status allows.

6. In the early days when our numbers were small, immigration was encouraged. In the 1880s, restrictions based on nationalities began. The concept of quotas began with the Quota Act of 1921.

7. It applied due process and equal protection under the law to all the states.

8. Often for economic reasons.

9. An interest in and concern for ideas, opinions, and practices that are foreign to one's own.

10. Voting, defending civil rights, paying taxes, attending school, defending the nation, serving on a jury or as a witness.

11. The system of political patronage was used until the 1880s. In 1883 a bipartisan Civil Service Commission was established by Congress to prepare and administer competitive examinations given to applicants for government jobs.

CHAPTER 7 REVIEW

Key Terms

Summary

1. The Fourteenth Amendment sets forth the two basic sources of American citizenship. The first, and most common, is by birth on American soil. The second is by a legal process called naturalization. There is also a third source—by being born of a parent who is a U.S. citizen. Citizenship may be lost by expatriation, punishment for a crime, or denaturalization.

2. Although the United States is a ''nation of immigrants,'' not everyone who lives here falls into that category. Those who reside here, but are neither citizens nor have the intention to become citizens, are considered to be aliens. According to the United States law, there are five different categories of aliens: (1) resident; (2) nonresident; (3) enemy; (4) refugee; and (5) illegal. American policies on immigration have gone through many changes. Immigration policy, and the numbers of people that should be allowed to immigrate each year, are a source of ongoing controversy.

3. Americans have both rights and responsibilities. The last hundred years of Supreme Court decisions have bound the fifty states to accept most of the guarantees for their respective citizens that are contained in the U.S. Bill of Rights. Responsible citizens should respect the laws, support the government, and participate in political life by voting and defending civil rights. Making sure that citizens' rights, privileges, and services are extended to all Americans is the job of the men and women who choose careers in public and community service.

4. The combined numbers of African Americans, Hispanics, Asians, and other minorities constitute a majority population in Chicago, Dallas, Detroit, Houston, Los Angeles, New York, and San Antonio. From 1990 to the year 2010 the number of white children under the age of 18 will drop from 45 million to 38 million, whereas the number of minority children will increase from 19 to 23 million. Tolerance is necessary in a multi-cultural society. Tolerance includes the interest in, and concern for, the ideas, opinions, and practices that are foreign to one's own. Tolerance and open-mindedness are part of the heritage of this nation.

Review Questions

1. What was the significance of *Dred Scott* v. *Sandford* (1857)?
2. What are the two basic sources of American citizenship according to the Fourteenth Amendment?
3. What are the three methods by which an individual can become a naturalized citizen?
4. How may a person lose his or her citizenship?
5. According to United States law, what are the five different categories of aliens and how are they defined?
6. How have U.S. policies concerning immigration changed over the years?
7. How did the Fourteenth Amendment lead to standardization of American citizens' rights?
8. Why did immigrants come to America in the late 1800s and early 1900s?
9. What does tolerance mean?
10. What are some of your responsibilities as a citizen?
11. Until the 1880s, how was the federal government staffed? How did civil service examinations change this system?

Questions for Thought and Discussion (Answers)

1. Answers will vary, e.g., the United States should encourage such people to immigrate here. Highly skilled people will contribute to society.

2. Answers will vary, e.g., those people with criminal records should not be allowed to immigrate.

3. Answers will vary, e.g., a system that forced people to vote would be more like a dictatorship. The freedom not to vote is as important in a democracy as the freedom of voting for the candidate of your choice.

4. Answers will vary, e.g., these homeowners are violating U.S. immigration laws and encouraging illegal immigrants to violate U.S. immigration laws. They should not be allowed to continue practices that bring down the wages and opportunities for legal aliens and citizens of the United States who also need employment.

CHAPTER 7 REVIEW—Continued

Questions For Thought and Discussion

1. Some countries are concerned with the fact that highly skilled people are emigrating from, or leaving, their countries to come to the United States, a situation often referred to as "brain drain." What do you think the United States government should do about the immigration of such people?
2. Which groups, if any, do you feel should *not* be allowed to immigrate to the United States? Explain your answer.
3. The United States gives its citizens the freedom to vote or not vote as they see fit. In some countries it is illegal to not vote, except for medical reasons. Those who are caught not voting must pay a fine. How do you think such a law would affect the system of government in the United States?
4. Many homeowners in California, Arizona, and Texas employ illegal Hispanic immigrants as housekeepers. On the one hand, these homeowners are helping the illegal immigrants violate U.S. immigration law. On the other hand, they are allowing them to live a better life than the one they left. What do you think are the pros and cons of homeowners hiring illegal aliens?

Improving Your Skills

Communication Skills

Expressing Your Opinion Effectively

When you express your opinion, you usually do it to inform or persuade others. Expressing your opinion effectively involves gathering convincing evidence and presenting it as clearly and forcefully as possible. Use the following guidelines to help you express your opinions to the best of your ability.

1. ***Define your audience.*** Knowing your audience is critical. Expressing your opinion to your friends calls for a different style of presentation than expressing your opinion to the city council. Knowing your audience helps you tailor your presentation accordingly. The audience can determine how serious or humorous you should be, whether spontaneous conversation would be more effective than a memorized speech, and other factors.
2. ***Define your goals.*** Decide what you wish to accomplish by expressing your opinion. Do you want to persuade your audience or just to inform them?
3. ***Gather convincing factual evidence and organize your ideas.*** Make sure you have the facts to back up your opinion and to answer any questions that might come up. Try to think of potential opposing arguments, and plan your responses to them. Organize your ideas according to which ones are most important.
4. ***Rehearse your presentation with family or friends.*** This will help you anticipate how an audience will respond.

Writing

Suppose your state legislature is considering raising the highway speed limit. You have the opportunity to express your opinion on the proposed measure. First, you must decide whether you are for or against the new limit. Then write an outline of the speech you will give to present your opinion.

Social Studies Skills

Reading a Pie Chart

Look at the pie chart on page 162.

1. Which type of household represents the smallest percentage of all households? The largest percentage?
2. What does the term "non-family household" mean?

Activities and Projects

1. Stage a debate on one of the following statements: (1) Immigrants are taking away the jobs of Americans. (2) Americans should be required by law to vote. (3) Any person or business caught hiring illegal immigrants should be fined $10,000.
2. Some people feel that for every right there is a responsibility. Make a chart listing all your rights as an American citizen down one side. For every right, list a corresponding responsibility down the other side.
3. Research and gather information on the 1986 and the 1990 immigration acts. Make a table showing how the 1990 act changed the 1986 act.
4. Research the requirements for naturalization in another country, and present your findings to the class.

Social Studies Skills (Answers)

1. A single male household or family; married-couple household or families.

2. Households that involve either a single person living alone or unrelated single persons living together, but not as a family.

CHAPTER INTRODUCTION

Instructional Objectives
By the end of the chapter students should be able to:
- Characterize the meaning and role of political parties.
- State the reasons for the two-party system in the United States.
- Describe the development of the two-party tradition in America.
- Characterize the nature and impact of third parties in American politics.
- Discuss the organization and structure of the two major parties.

Using the Keynote
Ask one of the students to read this quotation aloud, and then guide the students in discussing it: What kind of party was Jefferson referring to? How would you restate this sentence in your own words? What do you think Jefferson's intention was in making this statement? Why might Jefferson have held such negative views on political parties? What kinds of experiences and expectations might have led to those views?

Introducing the Chapter
Before the students begin reading the Introduction, ask: What guidelines does the Constitution give for forming and using political parties?

Then ask volunteers to take turns reading the Introduction aloud to the rest of the class. Encourage the students to discuss their reactions, especially to the fact that the Constitution does not deal with political parties at all. To stimulate further discussion, you might ask questions such as these: Why do you think the founders viewed political parties as a threat?

Previewing the Sections

Section 1 Ask the students to look through Section 1, noting especially the main headings, the figures, and the photographs. Ask: What do you anticipate learning about political parties from reading Section 1?

Section 2 Direct the students' attention to the title of Section 2: What does it indicate about the contents of the section? Then have the students page through the rest of the section, noting the time line, the cartoons, and the Building Social Studies Skills feature.

Section 3 Ask volunteers to read aloud the section title and the three main headings in Section 3. Let volunteers briefly explain what they already know about third parties, and remind the students that they will learn more as they study this section.

Section 4 Ask the students to find and read the two main headings in this section. Ask: What can you conclude from these headings about political party organization? What does the artwork here indicate about party structure?

CHAPTER 8

Political Parties

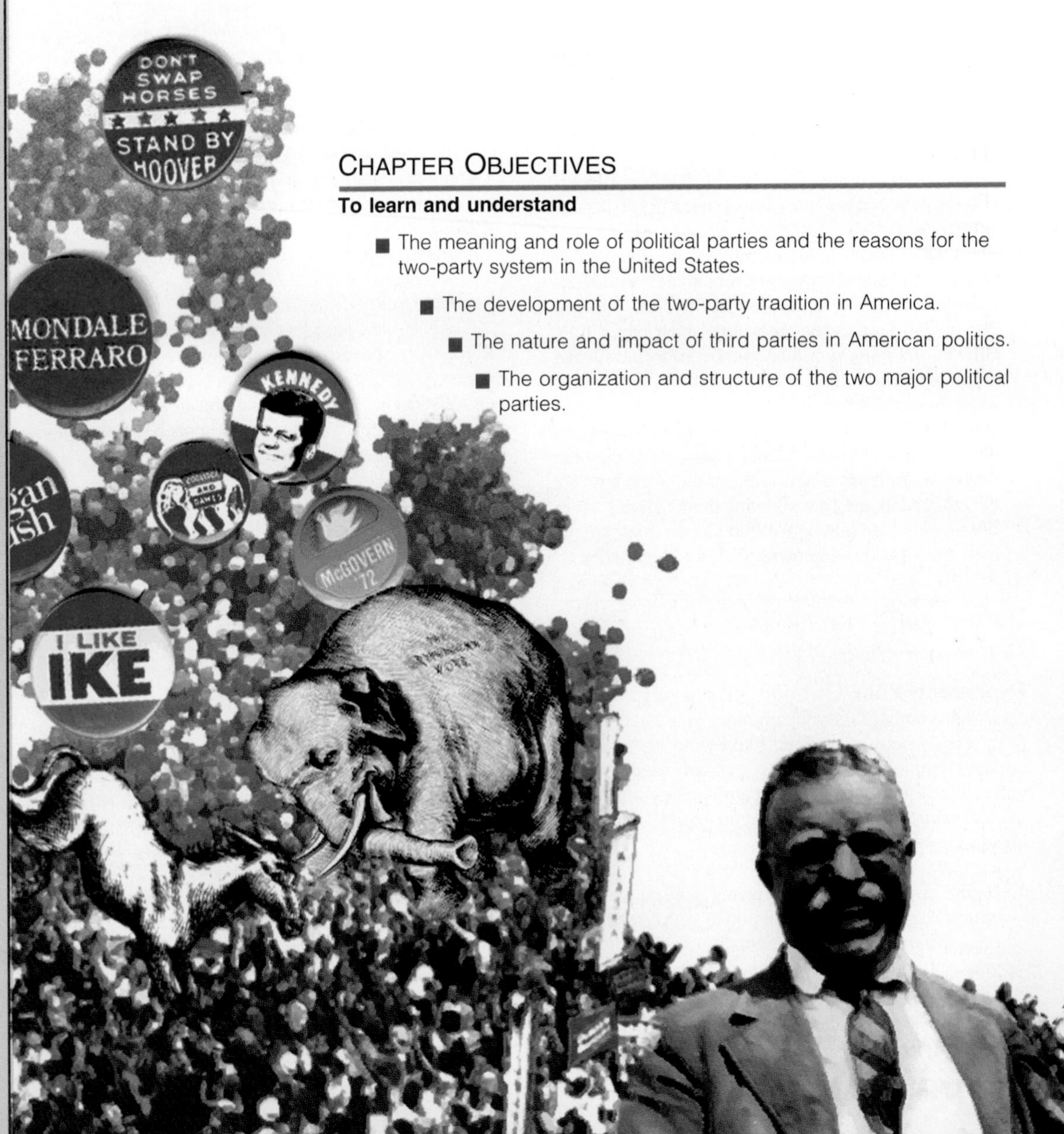

CHAPTER OBJECTIVES

To learn and understand

- The meaning and role of political parties and the reasons for the two-party system in the United States.
- The development of the two-party tradition in America.
- The nature and impact of third parties in American politics.
- The organization and structure of the two major political parties.

West's American Government Assignment Guide

Activity Sheets
Basic Concepts 8 *TRB* (Reteaching)
Enrichment Activity 8 *TRB*
Building Social Studies Skills 8 *TRB*
Quizzes
Chapter 8 Section 1 Quiz *TRB*
Chapter 8 Section 2 Quiz *TRB*
Chapter 8 Section 3 Quiz *TRB*
Chapter 8 Section 4 Quiz *TRB*

Tests
Chapter 8 Test A *TRB*
Chapter 8 Test B *TRB*
Chapter 8 Test Bank *TRB*
Chapter 8 WESTEST Computerized Testing
Social Studies Tool Kit Software
Chapter 8 Activity

Keynote

"If I could not go to heaven but with a party, I would not go there at all."

—— **Thomas Jefferson (1743–1826) Third President of the United States**

INTRODUCTION

Political parties were an unforeseen development in American political history. The founders defined many other important institutions, such as the presidency and Congress, and described their functions in the Constitution. Political parties, however, are not even mentioned.

In his farewell address, George Washington warned against the "baneful [very harmful] effects of the spirit of the party." Benjamin Franklin worried about the "infinite mutual abuse of parties, tearing to pieces the best of characters." John Adams, the second president, stated, "There is nothing I dread so much as the division of the Republic into two great parties, each under its own leader."

As you can see from Thomas Jefferson's quote above, he too started out with a critical view of political parties. In fact, most of the founders viewed parties as a threat to both the concept of popular government and the unity of the nation. Yet when popular elections were established, some method of organizing and mobilizing supporters of political candidates was needed. Thus, in spite of their anti-party feelings, several founders were active in establishing and organizing the first political parties to do just that. Thomas Jefferson also apparently changed his mind: He organized one of this nation's first political parties, first known as Republicans (not related to today's Republican Party).

Today political parties are firmly entrenched in American politics. They are one of the major vehicles of participation in our political system, and form an important link between citizens and the government. Some people even think that democracy is impossible without them. Remember from Chapter 1 that democracy was defined as a system in which the people rule and are the one and only source of any and all political authority. A democratic government is one in which the people can and do participate in national politics. By working together, citizens who share similar political views often have a greater impact on the government, which is why political parties came into existence. They provide a way for the public to choose who will serve in government and which policies will be carried out.

SECTION 1

The Meaning and Roles of Political Parties

Preview Questions

- What is a political party?
- What roles do political parties play?
- Why does America have a two-party system?
- Why do people join political parties?

Many citizens would like to be involved in helping government make decisions. Many of us, in fact, demand to have a say in the decisions that affect us. Political parties help meet this demand. A **political party** is a group of individuals outside of government who organize to win elections, to operate the government, and to determine policy. This definition applies to political parties in the United States as well as to political parties in most modern democratic nations. But the exact roles that parties play in politics differ with each nation's political system.

The Roles of American Political Parties

American political parties are sometimes described as three-dimensional, each party consisting of (1) a party-

SECTION 1

Points to Stress
- The definition of *political party.*
- Roles fulfilled by political parties.
- Reasons for the two-party system in America.
- Functions of political parties and reasons that people join them.
- Differences between the parties when platforms are compared.

Kickoff Activity
Write the following incomplete sentences on the chalkboard: A political party is. . . . The roles of a political party include. . . . Have the students write the two sentences, adding their own endings. Then encourage the students to compare and discuss their responses.

Working with the Preview Questions
Let volunteers read these study questions aloud to the rest of the class. Then ask the students to suggest main headings they might use in preparing note-taking sheets for use as they study Section 1.

Teaching Strategies

Introduction
After the students have read the section introduction, ask several volunteers to restate the definition of *political party* in their own words. Then have the students name as many political parties as they can: Which parties are active locally? Which parties function in other countries? Does your school have any political parties of its own? Why or why not?

Vocabulary
Let volunteers define the term *three dimensional* as it is used here. In what sense are political parties three dimensional?

Discussion Starter
As the students consider the party-in-the-electorate, ask: What role do voters who are registered as Independents play? Why would a voter choose to register without selecting a party affiliation? What role do citizens who are not registered to vote play? Why?

Enrichment
Ask volunteers to research the specific organization and officeholders for the Republican and Democratic parties. Have these volunteers prepare and present a chart summarizing their findings.

Comprehension
Ask the students to identify the specific people who form the party-in-government for both major political parties.

Caption Answer Party affiliation as declared in voter registration is not legally binding and can be changed at will.

Caption Answer The major goal of the party-in-government is to translate its campaign promises and party platform into public policy. They do this by helping to organize the government's agenda and by encouraging party members to vote for party policies.

Discussion Starter
Pose these questions to stimulate class discussion: Can a democracy function as a one-party system? Why or why not? Encourage the students to present and support various points of view.

Cooperative Learning
Have the students work in groups to review (or, if necessary, learn) what happened to the one-party systems of Eastern and Central Europe. What happened to the one-party system? How? Why do you think the people were so insistent on change?

Enrichment
Let a group of volunteers research the specific workings of the multiparty systems in selected European democracies: How many parties are active in each chosen country? How influential is each of those parties? How do the parties work together? On what major issues do they oppose one another? Have these volunteers make a short oral presentation of their findings.

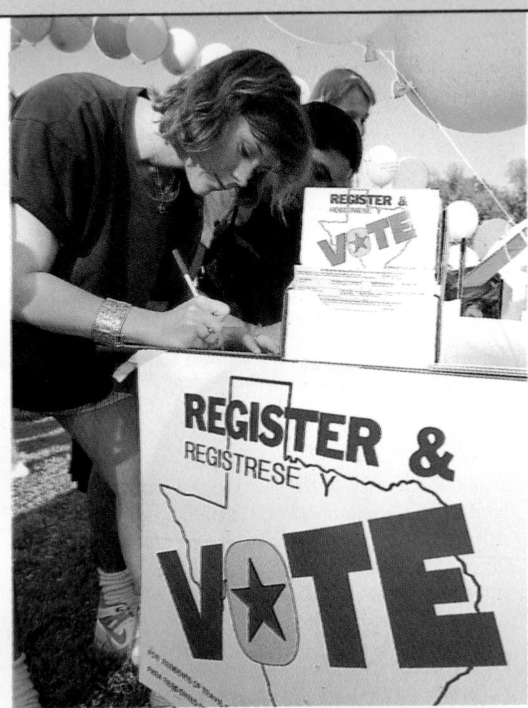

▲ When registering to vote, you have the right to declare your party affiliation. Once you have declared your party affiliation, can you change it?

in-the-electorate, (2) a party as organization, and (3) a party-in-government.

Party-in-the-Electorate The party-in-the-electorate is the largest component, consisting of all those people who describe themselves as Democrats or Republicans. There are no dues, no membership cards, and no obligatory duties. Members of the party-in-the-electorate need never work on a campaign or attend a party meeting. They may register as Democrats or Republicans, but registration is not legally binding and can be changed at will.

Party as Organization Each major party has a national organization with national, state, and local offices. The party organizations are made up of several levels of people who maintain the party's strength between elections, make its rules, raise money, organize conventions, help with elections, and seek candidates.

Party-in-Government The party-in-government consists of all the candidates who won the elections and are now in public office. Even though members of Congress, state legislators, presidents, and all other officeholders almost always run for office as either a Democrat or a Republican, they do not always agree on everything. The party-in-government helps to organize the government's agenda by coaxing and convincing its own party members to vote for its policies. If the party is to translate its promises into public policy, the job must be done by the party-in-government. (Elections normally requiring party affiliation are called **partisan elections**.)

Reasons for America's Two-Party System

In the United States, we have a **two-party system**, which means that two major parties dominate national politics—the Democrats and the Republicans. In a **one-party system**, a single party monopolizes the organization of governmental power and the positions of authority. The single party's functions are controlled by party leaders, and even if elections are held, party members, once on the ballot, have no competition. In most dictatorships, such as Iraq and The People's Republic of China, only one party is officially allowed to exist. Until recently, this was also true of many countries of Eastern and Central Europe, including the former Soviet Union.

Another alternative is a **multiparty system**, in which more than two political parties compete for power and electoral offices. This type of system exists in most European democracies such as France and Germany. In a multiparty system, parties are usually organized around

▲ As Senate Majority Leader, Democrat George Mitchell exemplifies the *party-in-government*. What is the goal of the party-in-government?

Vocabulary
Ask the students to explain what a consensus is and to identify other contexts in which consensus is a major consideration.

Discussion Starter
Encourage the students to discuss their responses to these questions: Do you believe in each of these basic principles as outlined in the Constitution? Why or why not? How do people who do not believe in these principles function within the United States?

Vocabulary
Ask the students to explain the meaning of this clause: American politics tends more toward the center. What is the center? How can we see this trend in our politics?

Discussion Starter
Guide the students in discussing their responses to these questions: How does the fact that both major parties are "middle-of-the-road" encourage the formation and activities of other, smaller parties? How does that same circumstance limit the possibilities for smaller parties?

different beliefs or interests such as religion, occupation, or political ideology. For example, Italy has nine national parties and several regional parties, including the Christian Democrats, the Socialists, the Radicals, the Liberals, and the Proletarian Unity Party. Israel has more than twenty parties. In the 1990 elections, Czechoslovakia had twenty-two political parties including the Communist Party, the Socialist Party, Public Against Violence, and the Alliance of Farmers and the Countryside.

Why has the two-party system become so firmly entrenched in America? A number of factors help to explain this phenomenon.

National Consensus and Moderate Views A **consensus** is a general agreement among citizens, sometimes defined as 75 percent or more of the people, on matters of public policy. In the United States, most citizens generally agree on certain broad social and economic issues. Most of us believe in the basic principles of government as outlined in the U.S. Constitution. For example, most of us believe that people have a right to own private property and the right to freedom of religion. We also believe that people should be free to choose where they live and work. Our differences usually lie more in *how* to attain the goals, rather than the goals themselves.

Because of this general political consensus, the United States does not have the conditions that would lead to numerous strong rival parties. Even though some Americans have disagreed during our history over many issues, we have not seen the prolonged and intense conflict that some countries have experienced. We have been deeply divided during such times as the Civil War in the 1860s, the Great Depression in the 1930s, and over such issues as civil rights and the war in Vietnam during the 1960s and 1970s. We have not, however, had long-lasting divisions based on religious beliefs as have occurred in the Middle East, nor on issues such as national origins, language, class, or social status, as have occurred in other places.

Unlike many European democracies, in which various radical political parties have strong support, American politics tend more toward center, or moderate, positions. There are no large, long-lasting groups that support radical governmental policies.

Political consensus and moderation in the United States has had another impact on our parties. It has given us two parties that look very much alike. Both tend to be moderate, middle-of-the-road parties built on compromise. For this they have often been criticized: their most stern critics think of them as ''tweedledum'' and ''tweedledee.''[1]

1. Two things that have different names, but are practically the same.

The lack of long-lasting divisions based on national origins, such as those that exist in South Africa, has helped the United States to develop national consensus on certain broad social and economic issues. How has this consensus affected our party system?

Caption Answer Because of the consensus, numerous strong parties have not developed in the United States. This consensus has also given us two parties that are very similar.

Enrichment
Have one or two interested students research the effect of "equal time" requirements on media coverage. What are these requirements? Have they been extended to third-party candidates? Why or why not?

Vocabulary
Let volunteers explain to the class the distinction between a plurality and a majority.

Extension
Encourage the students to discuss what they have read or heard about run-offs in local elections: Are they sometimes held? If so, why? If not, why not?

Caption Answer Students should understand that the national conventions are used to select the presidential and vice-presidential candidates.

Discussion Starter
Ask the students to share their responses to the idea that voting for a third-party candidate is "throwing away" a vote: Do you agree or disagree? Why? Do you really believe that every vote counts? What facts and reasons can you give to support your opinion?

Vocabulary
Ask the students to define the term *endorsement*. Then ask: In what sense is a nomination an endorsement?

Discussion Starter
Have the students discuss their reactions to this statement: "It is much easier for voters to choose between two candidates that have been selected by established political parties than to choose among many." What does this indicate about American voters? Are American voters really less politically sophisticated and concerned than voters in multiparty democracies? Why or why not?

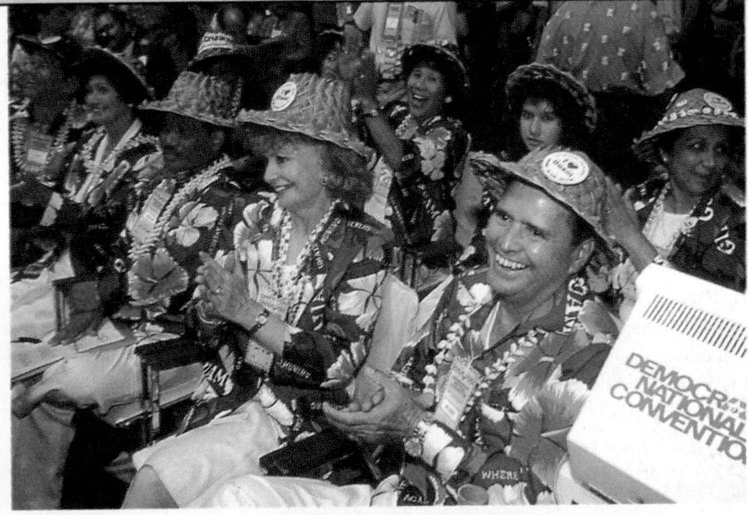

Recruiting and nominating candidates for political office is one of the most important functions of our two political parties. For what offices are candidates chosen in a party's national convention, as shown to the left?

Tradition The first major political division among Americans was between the Federalists and the Anti-Federalists over the ratification of the Constitution. Some people believe that this original two-sided political battle established the domination of the two-party system in this country. In addition, today's established institutions, such as the news media, do not encourage third parties. They do not typically spend much time covering third-party activities, but rather often focus exclusively on the Democrats and Republicans.

Our Elective Process Our elective process also lends itself to the two-party system. In most elections, only one candidate can win the election to each office, called the **single-member district system**. The candidate who gets the *most* votes obtains a **plurality** (the largest number), and wins the election, even if this means less than 50 percent of the total vote cast. For example, suppose you vote in a local election. There are a total of 1,000 votes available and three candidates are running for mayor: Gomez, Rosenfield, and Gladstone. Gomez receives 450 votes, Rosenfield receives 250 votes, and Gladstone receives 300. Gomez wins even though he received less than 50 percent of the total votes cast. (If a majority vote is required, then sometimes a **run-off election** must take place between the two candidates who got the highest number of votes.)

The single-member district system makes it very difficult for a third-party candidate to win. Most Americans think that voting for a third party candidate is throwing away their vote. They therefore usually vote for either a Democrat or Republican, which discourages third-party candidates from running. Our elective system makes it difficult for minor-party candidates to win elections, and without election victories parties tend to fade fast. Third parties have neither the numbers, recognition, nor money to endure or win most elections.

American election law also discourages third-party candidates. In most states, the established major parties need only a few signatures to place their candidate on the ballot, while a minor party must get many more signatures. The criterion is often based on the total party vote in the last election, which penalizes a new party that did not enter that election.

What Do Political Parties Do?

The Constitution does not provide for political parties, nor does it even mention them. Yet historically political parties have played a vital role in our democratic system. The main function that political parties perform in a large democracy is linking the people to the government. They link the people's policy preferences to actual government policies. Political parties also perform many other functions that no other body or institution of government performs.

Selecting Candidates One of the most important functions of the two political parties is to recruit and nominate (to select and approve of) candidates for political office. A party's endorsement for a candidate is called a **nomination**. This function provides a way to simplify voting choices for the **electorate** (voters). Political parties take the large number of people who want to run for office and narrow the field to one candidate. They accomplish this by the use of **primaries**, which is a preliminary election to choose a party's final candidate. In theory, the party chooses the best-qualified member to be the party candidate. It is much easier for voters to choose

TEACHING GOVERNMENT IN ACTION

Read
Begin by encouraging the students to discuss what they already know about the Reverend Jesse Jackson: Who is Jesse Jackson? Why do you think he is included in this chapter discussing political parties? After all the students have finished discussing what they know about Jackson, have a volunteer read the Profile aloud to the class.

Discuss
Help the students discuss the information presented here by asking questions such as these: What aspects of Jackson's childhood might have influenced his political and career choices as an adult? What important leaders has Jackson worked with? How might these leaders have influenced his values and decisions? Even though he did not win the Democratic nomination for president in 1988, many would argue that Jackson experienced amazing success. Do you agree with that statement? Why?

Analyze and Apply
Students should demonstrate their ability to analyze the information presented in this Profile and apply it to what they have learned, not only in this chapter, but also in Chapter 7 which dealt with civil rights, by writing a short essay on the following topic: Jesse Jackson's 1984 and 1988 bids for the Democratic presidential nomination reflect aspects of both the challenges and the successes of the American civil rights movement. After students have written their rough drafts, they should exchange essays with a partner for comments and criticisms. Students' final draft essays should reflect their work with a partner.

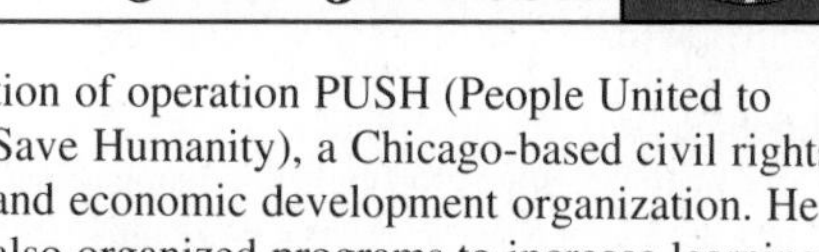

PROFILE

Jesse Jackson

Jesse Jackson was born on October 8, 1941, in Greenville, North Carolina. His childhood was one of deep poverty in which he secured his first job at age 6 delivering stove wood. Jackson attended public schools in Greenville and in 1959 enrolled at the University of Illinois where he had a football scholarship. After one year he returned to North Carolina and attended the Agricultural and Technical College of Greensboro. He was ordained as a Baptist minister in 1968 after attending a theological seminary in Chicago.

Jackson played an important role in the civil rights struggles of the 1960s, leading marches, picketings, and sit-ins. He joined Martin Luther King, Jr. in the Southern Christian Leadership Conference (SCLC) and became a close adviser and field organizer. In 1966, as head of the SCLC's Operation Breadbasket, the Conference began a systematic boycott of businesses that, it believed, exploited African Americans.

Soon after King's assassination, which Jackson witnessed, he announced the formation of operation PUSH (People United to Save Humanity), a Chicago-based civil rights and economic development organization. He also organized programs to increase learning skills among minority students.

Jesse Jackson became in 1983 the first African American to be a serious candidate for a major party's presidential nomination. Although Jackson was given little chance to win the nomination, he carried his campaign to the national convention in 1984. While campaigning, he won two primary elections outright and obtained more than ten percent of the vote in many others. He renewed his campaign to be selected as the Democratic Party's nominee for President in 1988 but was unsuccessful. He has argued that he had insufficient funding to use television advertising. Nonetheless, Jackson won more delegates in the Southern Democratic primaries than any other candidate. Jackson and his supporters, known as the Rainbow Coalition, had arrived as a national political force within the Democratic party.

Jackson, who is no stranger to controversy, has had a profound effect on the Democratic Party and American politics. Through the efforts of Jackson and his Rainbow Coalition, many Americans, who otherwise might have felt left out of the political process, have found a way to participate. These people are becoming able to work from within the system to pursue their American dream.

THINK ABOUT IT

1. How might Jesse Jackson's political success reflect the success of the civil rights movement?
2. Why do you think the name Rainbow Coalition was chosen by Jackson and his supporters?

Review
Review the material in this Profile with the students by again asking them the questions from the above activity under **Read.** Students' responses should demonstrate better understanding of Jesse Jackson and his importance.

Think About It (Answers)
1. Answers will vary, e.g., Jackson's ability to succeed within the system reflects how well African Americans have been able to gain access to the political system.
2. Answers will vary, e.g., Jackson's supporters chose this name because it represents people of all races and backgrounds.

Discussion Starter
Encourage the students to share and discuss their own experiences with canvassers and campaigns: Have you ever been a canvasser? Why or why not? If so, for what candidate or cause? Have you ever seen or spoken with canvassers at work? What was your response?

Extension
As they consider the roles parties play in coordinating policy making, ask the students: What happens to the exceptions—members of Congress who are not members of one of the major political parties? If the students are not sure, ask volunteers to research the question, focusing especially on recent examples.

Vocabulary
Let volunteers define the terms *watchdog* and *loyal opposition* for the rest of the class.

Comprehension
Have the students explain Rossiter's definition of political parties: What does this definition mean? Do you feel it trivializes the function of political parties in our democracy? Why or why not?

Discussion Starter
Focus the students' attention on the broad views that parties attempt to take on issues such as abortion: Can such broad views be effective in holding party members together? Are they more likely to be cohesive or divisive? Why? Would you make voting commitments based on a single issue? If not, why not? If so, what is that issue? Why is it so important to you?

between two candidates that have been selected by established political parties, than to choose among many.

Informing the Public Political parties help educate the public about important political issues. In recent years some of these issues have included defense and environmental policies, taxes, and inflation. Each party presents its view of these issues through television, newspapers, campaign speeches, rallies, debates, and pamphlets. These activities help citizens learn about the issues, consider proposed solutions, and form opinions.

Through these activities, political parties also help to stimulate citizens' interest and participation in public affairs. They ask people to work at party headquarters, or to help with door-to-door **canvasses**, in which they distribute campaign literature and ask people to vote for their candidate. They seek volunteers to work at polling places where people actually cast their votes, or to drive voters to the polling places. This provides important ways for citizens to participate in the political process and serve their community.

Coordinating Policymaking In our complex government, parties are essential for coordinating policy among the various branches. Each president, cabinet member, and member of Congress is also normally a member of one or the other party. The political party is usually the major institution through which the executive and legislative branches cooperate with each other. The president works through party leaders in Congress to promote the administration's legislative program. Parties also act as the glue of our federal structure by connecting the various levels of government with a common bond.

The party that does not control Congress or a state legislature, or has not elected a candidate to the presidency, also acts as a "watchdog" to keep an eye on the activities of the party in power. Such monitoring by the "loyal opposition" encourages the party in power to heed the public's wishes and to remain responsive. The party with fewer members in the legislature is the **minority party**. The party with the most members is the **majority party**.

Balancing Competing Interests Clinton Rossiter, a political scientist, described parties as "vast, gaudy, friendly umbrellas under which all Americans, whoever and wherever and however-minded they may be, are invited to stand for the sake of being counted in the next election." Political parties are **coalitions**—individuals and groups with a variety of interests and opinions that are drawn together. For example, in the Republican Party there are many groups with many different views on the issue of abortion. The role of party leaders in this situation is to adopt a broad enough view on the issue so that certain groups will not be alienated. In this way, different groups can hold their individual views and still come together under the umbrella of the Republican Party. The same process occurs within the Democratic

◀ President-elect Bill Clinton addresses the media following his first meeting with key members of Congress. Pictured here are, from left to right, Vice President-elect Al Gore, Senate Majority Leader George Mitchell, House Majority Leader Richard Gephardt, Senate Minority Leader Bob Dole, House Minority Leader Bob Michel, and House Speaker Tom Foley. Why would the president seek the support of these leaders?

Caption Answer These leaders wield a great deal of authority and influence within their parties and Congress.

Discussion Starter
Encourage the students to consider and discuss this statement: "Without parties, campaigns would effectively not exist." Do you think this is true? Why or why not? If we had no parties, what would we have in place of the campaigns we now know? Why?

Comprehension
To check their comprehension, ask the students: What is the difference between a party identifier and an active party member? Why is the difference important?

Extension
Have the students help you identify parents or other community members who are active as political party volunteers. Arrange for the students to invite these volunteers to speak to the class, either individually or as a panel. Help the students prepare relevant questions to ask the guests.

Caption Answer Parties also work at getting party members registered, conduct drives for new voters, and even provide workers for polling places.

Phoning voters and encouraging them to vote for party candidates is just one of the small, but important, tasks that party members perform to help coordinate campaigns. What are some other ways that parties are involved in campaigns?

Party. Both Democratic and Republican party leaders modify and compromise the contending views of different groups, and in so doing help to unify rather than divide their party members.

Running Campaigns Through their national, state, and local organizations, parties coordinate campaigns. Political parties take care of a large number of small and routine tasks that are essential to the smooth functioning of the electoral process. They work at getting party members registered and at conducting drives for new voters. They sometimes staff the polling places. Without parties, campaigns would effectively not exist.

Party Membership

What does it mean to belong to a political party? To be a member of a political party in the United States, you need only claim to be one. Generally, in the United States people belong to a political party because they agree with many of its main ideas and support some of its candidates. In other countries, such as the People's Republic of China, people belong to a political party because they are required to do so, whether they agree with the ideas and candidates or not.

What Do Party Members Do? In many European countries, being a party member means that you actually join a political party. You get a membership card to carry around in your wallet or purse, you pay dues, and you vote to select your local and national party leaders. In the United States, becoming a member of a political party is far less involved. American citizens have only to think of themselves as a Democrat, a Republican, or a member of a third party such the Libertarian Party or the American Independent Party. Members of parties do not have to pay dues, work for the party, attend party meetings, or support the party platform. In fact, they may do nothing more than occasionally vote for some of the party's candidates.[2] These people are sometimes known as party identifiers.

Other individuals—active members—choose to work for the party and even become candidates for office. Political parties need year-round support from these people to survive. During election campaigns in particular, candidates depend on party volunteers to mail literature, answer phones, conduct door-to-door canvasses, organize speeches and appearances, and, of course, donate money. Between elections, parties also need active members to plan the upcoming elections, organize fundraisers, and keep in touch with party leaders in other communities in order to keep the party strong.

Political party members in the United States have very different ideas about what it means to belong to a political party. There are diverse levels of interest and activity, but all of these members ''belong.'' Of course, both political parties welcome these various groups, and strive to attract as many members as possible.

2. In most states, a person must declare a preference for a particular party before voting in that state's primary election (discussed in Chapter 10). This declaration is usually part of the voter registration process.

FYI

There has been much speculation concerning the demise of political parties in America. To be sure, political parties do not hold the position or exercise the type of power that they did in the first half of the 20th century. It would be a mistake, however, to mourn political parties. On the contrary, parties are as or more vital than ever, and this is illustrated in the area of campaign money. Among the three major source categories of campaign funds, individuals, PACs, and parties, the parties gave out the most money. Their role is particularly crucial during the general election, when state organizations can contribute money provided by the national committee.

Specific dynamics including "bundling," where the party organization can take individual contributions to the party and give it all to one candidate, and the awarding of "party building funds" which is euphemistically referred to as "soft" money, will keep the parties in a position of power. If Congress passes legitimate campaign finance reforms then the role of political parties will be further enhanced.

TEACHING CITIZENSHIP SKILLS AND RESPONSIBILITIES

Read

Begin by encouraging the students to discuss their ideas about joining political parties: Have you already decided which party you want to join? If so, how did you reach your decision? If not, what do you plan to do as you make your decision? Do you think it is advisable to make this decision long before you register to vote? Why or why not? After this discussion, let volunteers take turns reading the Citizenship Skills and Responsibilities feature aloud to the rest of the class.

Discuss

Help the students discuss the information presented here by asking questions such as these: What do you think of the influences on party choice listed here? Which do you think is usually the strongest influence? Which do you think *should* be the most significant influence? Which form of party participation interests you most? Why? Are you interested in becoming a political leader? If not, why not? If so, do you think volunteering for a local party organization would be a good beginning for you?

Analyze and Apply

Have the students form small groups in which to gather and discuss information about various political parties. Ask the members of each group to select one or two parties and to collect as much information as possible about the aims, organization, and functioning of those parties.

Review

Ask the students these review questions: What are some of the reasons individuals are drawn to specific political parties? What can you do to become involved with the political party of your choice?

Taking Action

Student activities under Taking Action will vary. If you are conducting this class during an election year, you might allow students to visit local party campaign headquarters and write essays commenting on the similarities and differences between the party organizations.

CITIZENSHIP SKILLS AND RESPONSIBILITIES

Joining a Political Party

In the United States, the ideas and actions of each individual are important. One person can make a difference, even in a country as large and varied as ours. But there are also great advantages to working as part of a group. Taking part in political parties is one of the most important ways citizens can affect government decision making.

You may already think of yourself as a Democrat or a Republican. If not, you may soon find yourself drawn to one party or another. You may be drawn to a party because your family or friends support it, because you admire one of its leaders, or because you feel its candidates will act according to your views and beliefs. Your education, religion, ethnic background, and place of residence may also affect the way you view political parties.

If you are interested in becoming involved with a political party, local party organizations are often the easiest place to get started. You can volunteer to do different kinds of work for the local party: you may register new voters and distribute information; answer phones or conduct door-to-door canvases; provide transportation to voters on election day; become a member of the state party organization. Many national leaders gained valuable experience this way.

You can find the state and local offices of both major parties in the telephone directory or through newspapers. You can also contact the two major parties' national offices at these addresses:

Democratic Party
430 Capital St., SE
Washington, DC 20003

Republican Party
310 First Street, SE
Washington, DC 20003

You can contact minor parties at the following addresses:

- *American Independent Party* (P.O. Box 373, Simi Valley, CA 93063) This small party was founded in 1968 and has a national organization that sometimes runs conservative candidates for president and for certain state offices.
- *Citizens' Party* (2000 P Street, NW, Washington, DC 20036) This is a broad-based coalition founded in 1980 by an environmentalist named Barry Commoner.
- *Libertarian Party* (2300 Wisconsin Avenue, NW, Washington, DC 20007) This party was founded in 1971, with the goal of forming a voluntary society of free markets and free enterprise in which the role of government is severely limited. Its presidential candidate consistently gets on virtually every state ballot.
- *Prohibition National Committee* (P.O. Box 2635, Denver, CO 80201) This party was founded in 1869 and still occasionally runs presidential candidates. It advocates the repeal of all laws that legalize the manufacture and sale of alcoholic beverages.
- *Social Democrats, U.S.A.* (275 Seventh Avenue, New York, NY 10001) Founded at the turn of the century, this is a moderate socialist party. It was important during the Great Depression of the 1930s.
- *Socialist Labor Party* (P.O. Box 50210, Palo Alto, CA 94303) This party was established in 1891. It seeks the abolition of capitalism peacefully through the ballot box.
- *U.S.A. Green Party* (1710 Connecticut Avenue, Washington, DC 20036) Founded in 1972, this party emphasizes ecological issues. Its slogan is "We do not inherit the earth from our parents; we borrow it from our children."

TAKING ACTION

1. Do any minor parties have offices in your state or locality? Contact one and ask for information.
2. Locate the state and/or local offices of the two major political parties in your area. Contact one of them and ask for a copy of the party platform. Write a summary of that platform and present it to your class.

Vocabulary
Ask volunteers to use their own words in defining *solidarity.* Then ask: What else do people do to gain a sense of solidarity?

Comprehension
Ask volunteers to restate, in their own words, four reasons people join political parties.

Cooperative Learning
Have the students form groups in which to examine and discuss figure 8–1. What can you learn from studying this table? Which groups of people seem most attracted to the Democratic Party? Which to the Republican party? Does your personal experience confirm what the table shows? Explain.

Political Party Affiliation by Group, 1991

	Republican	Democrat	Independent	Other/Don't Know/Not Applicable
TOTAL SAMPLE	33%	32%	31%	4%
By Sex				
Men	35	28	33	4
Women	30	36	29	5
By Race				
White	35	28	33	4
Nonwhite	17	62	19	3
By Age				
18–29	34	24	35	7
30–49	32	30	35	3
50 and older	33	40	24	4
By Region				
East	33	32	30	5
Midwest	28	34	35	3
South	36	33	27	5
West	33	29	34	4
By Ideology				
Liberal	25	43	32	*
Moderate	25	34	41	1
Conservative	48	25	27	1
By Education				
Did not complete high school	25	39	30	6
High school graduate	32	35	29	4
Some college	34	29	34	2
College graduate	40	26	32	2
By Occupation				
Blue collar	29	33	33	5
Clerical/Sales	33	35	32	0
Professional/Business	35	25	36	3
White collar	35	28	35	2
By Annual Household Income				
Less than $20,000	29	39	28	4
$20–29,999	28	31	35	6
$30–49,999	32	33	32	3
$50,000 plus	46	22	31	1

Source: Survey by the Gallup Organization, July 25–28, 1991. Data provided by the Roper Center at the University of Connecticut.

▲ FIGURE 8–1 **Party Affiliation by Group—1991.** This table looks at political party affiliation among members of various groups. What can you determine about the relationship between household income and party affiliation?

This figure content is also featured on *West's American Government Videodisc* (see the index found in the *TRB*).

Figure Answer As the figure demonstrates, there seems to be a correlation between household income and party affiliation at the extreme ends of the scale.

People and Parties People join political parties for different reasons, according to political scientist James Q. Wilson. One reason is that people wish to express their **solidarity**, or mutual agreement with the views of friends, loved ones, and other like-minded people. They also join because they enjoy the excitement of politics. In addition, many believe they will benefit materially, by means of better employment or personal advancement, from joining a party. Finally, some join political parties because they wish to work for a set of ideas and

Discussion Starter
Let the students discuss generalizations they have heard about the Democratic Party and the Republican Party: What general comments have you heard people make? Why do you think people say—and think about—such general statements? How do you respond to such comments? Why?

Section 1 Review
1. Party-in-the-electorate, which consists of all the people who are members. Party as organization, which is the national, state, and local organization of each party. Party-in-government, which consists of all the candidates who won elections and are now in public office.
2. The consensus and moderate views of Americans, the tradition of a two party system, and our elective process.
3. Political parties link the people to government. They also recruit and nominate candidates, inform the public, coordinate policymaking, balance competing interests, and coordinate campaigns.
4. Some people join political parties to express their solidarity, or mutual agreement with other people. Some join to benefit materially by better employment or personal advancement. Others join because they wish to work for a set of ideas and principles they feel are important.
5. Answers will vary, e.g., even if the parties agree on certain issues, on other issues, there are significant policy differences and people often feel the need to identify with one party.

Discussion Starter
Focus the students' attention on this statement: "never have all members of any one group tied themselves *permanently* to either party." Why do you think this is the case? Do you think this is a good situation, or do you believe it would be better for groups to align themselves permanently with one major party or the other? Why? Can you think of any instances in which all the members of a group allied themselves temporarily with one of the parties?

Cooperative Learning
Let the students work in groups to select one of the major parties and then to gather and discuss information about specific planks in that party's platform.

Reteaching Strategies
1. Have the students work in small groups to review and improve the notes they have taken on Section 1. Encourage them to refer to the text.
2. Ask the students to work with partners in writing their own definitions of these terms: *two-party system, one-party system, multiparty system, plurality, consensus.*

Evaluation Strategies
1. Have the students write their answers to the Section 1 Review questions.
2. Have the students take the Section 1 Quiz found in the *TRB.*

principles that they feel are important in American politics and society.

Another political scientist, V.O. Key, believes that "people tend to have a broad image of parties. They see a party as generally dedicated to the interests of a particular set of groups within society." Thus when interviewed, people may make the following remarks when asked why they support the Democratic Party: "It seems like the economy is better when the Democrats are in control." "The Democrats are for the working people." Or people might say about the Republican Party: "The Republicans help the small business person more than the Democrats." "The Republicans deal better with foreign policy issues."

Regardless of how accurate these stereotypes are, individuals with similar characteristics—i.e., urban versus rural—do tend to align themselves more often with one or the other major party.

Family, age, occupation, place of residence, education, and economic status all influence party choice. (See Figure 8–1 on page 189.) Yet never have all members of any one group tied themselves *permanently* to either party. What causes a person to favor a certain party in one election may not hold true for the next.

Comparing Parties One way to compare today's Democratic and Republican parties is to study their **party platforms**, which are declarations of each party's beliefs and positions on major issues. The party's statement of its beliefs is called a platform because the candidates of the party "stand" on it. The platform is made of **planks**, which are the party's official positions on specific issues such as crime, drug abuse, or education. Each party's platform is adopted every four years at the party's national convention.

Section 1 Review

1. What are the three main roles of political parties?
2. What factors help to explain why we have a two-party system in the United States?
3. Describe the important functions performed by political parties.
4. Describe several reasons why people identify themselves with political parties.
5. **For critical analysis:** While debate among Republicans and Democrats is often times heated, critics of our two-party system claim that the two parties are essentially the same. If the critics are right, then why do some Americans become loyal members of one party or the other?

Section 2

The Beginning of the Two-Party Tradition

Preview Questions

- Why were the first political parties formed?
- Which was the first American political party to go out of existence?
- What great economic event brought the Democrats into power in this century?

The founders reacted negatively to the idea of strong political parties because they thought the power struggles that would occur between small economic and political groups would eventually topple the balanced democracy they wanted to create. Even though the founders viewed political parties as dangerous, as seen in Chapter 2, the first political *factions* in America were formed around the issue of supporting or opposing the Constitution. Once the Constitution was ratified, the two factions ceased to exist. George Washington ran for president without a party label and without opposition.

President Washington had barely taken office when factions once again arose in American politics. The first to emerge, led by Alexander Hamilton, was the Federalists. Its supporters believed that a democracy should be ruled by its wealthy and best-educated citizens. They supported a strong central government that would encourage the development of commerce and manufacturing. They favored vigorous executive leadership and a set of policies that were particularly beneficial to financial, manufacturing, and commercial interests.

Those who opposed the Federalists were the Republicans, led by Thomas Jefferson. They were more sympathetic to the "common man," and favored a more limited role for government. They believed the nation's welfare would be best served if the states had more power than the central government. In their view, Congress should dominate the government and its policies should help the nation's shopkeepers, farmers, and laborers. The party became known as the Jeffersonians, or the Democratic-Republicans. The name finally changed to the Democratic Party by the mid 1820s.

Once formed, political parties continued to be a part of American politics. Throughout the course of our history, some existing parties disappeared, some were transformed, and new ones appeared.

SECTION 2

Points to Stress

- Reasons for the formation of the first political parties.
- The first American political party to go out of existence.
- The great economic event that realigned the parties bringing the Democrats into power.

Kickoff Activity

Write the following question on the board: How do you imagine the founders would react to the two-party system as it functions in modern America? Give the students five minutes in which to write their responses. Then ask volunteers to read their answers aloud; encourage questions and comments.

Working with the Preview Questions

Let the students read and discuss their preliminary responses to these study questions. Explain to the students that they will learn more as they study Section 2 and that they will be expected to answer these questions more fully when they have completed the section study.

FIGHT IN CONGRESS BETWEEN LYON AND GRISWOLD, FEBRUARY 15, 1798.

▲ The rivalry between the Democratic-Republicans and the Federalists was at times very heated. This cartoon depicts a fight that took place in Congress on February 15, 1798, between Democratic-Republican Matthew Lyon and Federalist Roger Griswold. Which presidential election saw the first contest between the Democratic-Republicans and the Federalists?

From 1796 to 1860

The nation's first two parties clashed openly in the elections of 1796 in which John Adams, the Federalists' candidate to succeed Washington as president, defeated Thomas Jefferson. Over the next four years, Thomas Jefferson and James Madison worked to build the Democratic-Republican party, mentioned above. In the presidential elections of 1800 and 1804, Thomas Jefferson won the presidency under the Democratic-Republican banner. His party also won control of Congress. The Federalists never returned to power and became the first (but not the last) American party to go out of existence. (See the time line on the next page.)

The Democratic-Republicans dominated American politics for the next twenty years. Jefferson was succeeded in the White House by two more Democratic-Republicans—James Madison and James Monroe.

In the mid-1820s, the Democratic-Republicans had split into two groups. Andrew Jackson, who was elected president in 1828, aligned himself with the group that called themselves the Democrats. The Democrats were a group of mostly small farmers, debtors, frontiersmen, and slaveholders.

The other group, the National Republican (later the Whig Party), was led by the well-known Henry Clay and the great orator Daniel Webster. It was a coalition of bankers, businesspersons, and Southern planters. As the Whigs and Democrats competed for the White House throughout the 1840s and 1850s, the two-party system as we know it today emerged. Both parties were large, with supporters across the nation, and with well-known

Teaching Strategies

Introduction

Let the students read the section introduction independently. Then encourage discussion by posing questions such as these: What is the difference between a faction and a political party? At what point do you suppose a faction becomes a political party? Who was the "common man" favored by the Anti-Federalists? Is either modern major political party considered to be more sympathetic to the "common man"? Why do you think political parties, once established, continued as an essential part of American politics?

Vocabulary

Ask the students to define the two parts of the name *Democratic-Republican:* Does this improve your understanding of the names used by today's major political parties? How?

Caption Answer The presidential election of 1796 was a contest between Federalist candidate John Adams and Democratic-Republican candidate Thomas Jefferson.

Discussion Starter

Encourage the students to consider the two parties that developed from the Democratic-Republican party: What do you imagine the various members of the Democratic Party had in common? What do you think the members of the Whig Party had in common? What distinguished the two groups from one another? What significance do you find in the fact that both the Democrats and the Whigs remained vague on the issue of slavery?

Cooperative Learning
Have the students work in groups to study and discuss the time line, Political Parties in America Since 1789: Which facts stand out when you first look at this time line? How do the details of the time line affect your perception of those facts?

Figure Answer The Democratic party began in 1824 when Andrew Jackson ran against John Quincy Adams, presidential nominee of the National-Republican party.

Developing Skills for the Information Age

Political parties no longer communicate through a tightly controlled organization from party head to precinct worker. Elected officials today are more prone to use group phone hookups, satellite conferences, videotapes, computerized constituent "newsletters," and managed media events. The higher the office, the more sophisticated the techniques. For example, congressmen and senators have their own studios on Capitol Hill where tapes are made for distribution in district or state media markets. Have students contact local party officials with the task of discovering media techniques used by parties today. Students should compose a summary of their results.

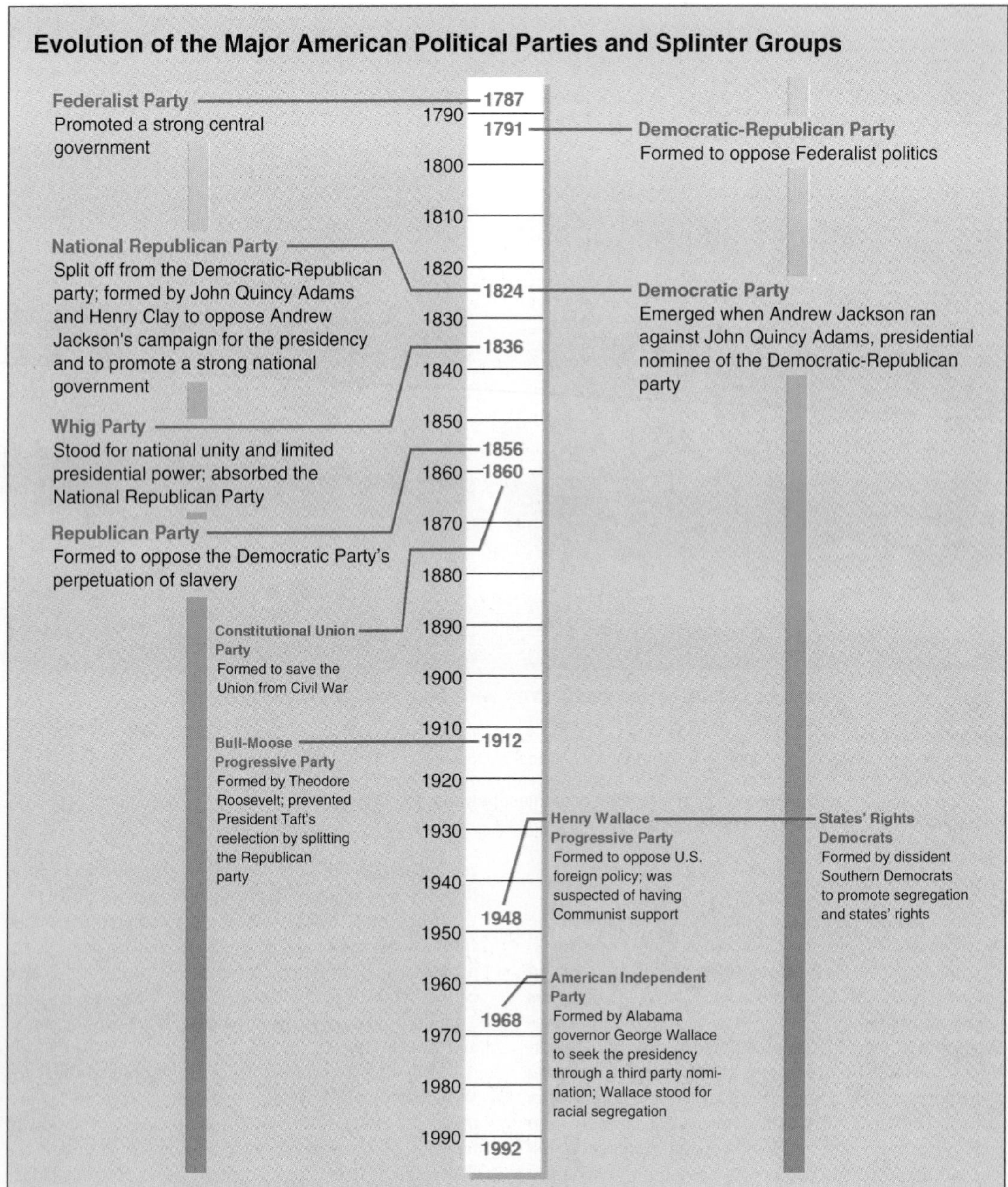
Evolution of the Major American Political Parties and Splinter Groups
Federalist Party
Promoted a strong central government
1787
1790
1791
Democratic-Republican Party
Formed to oppose Federalist politics
1800
1810
National Republican Party
Split off from the Democratic-Republican party; formed by John Quincy Adams and Henry Clay to oppose Andrew Jackson's campaign for the presidency and to promote a strong national government
1820
1824
Democratic Party
Emerged when Andrew Jackson ran against John Quincy Adams, presidential nominee of the Democratic-Republican party
1830
1836
1840
Whig Party
Stood for national unity and limited presidential power; absorbed the National Republican Party
1850
1856
1860
1860
Republican Party
Formed to oppose the Democratic Party's perpetuation of slavery
1870
1880
Constitutional Union Party
Formed to save the Union from Civil War
1890
1900
1910
Bull-Moose Progressive Party
Formed by Theodore Roosevelt; prevented President Taft's reelection by splitting the Republican party
1912
1920
1930
Henry Wallace Progressive Party
Formed to oppose U.S. foreign policy; was suspected of having Communist support
States' Rights Democrats
Formed by dissident Southern Democrats to promote segregation and states' rights
1940
1948
1950
1960
American Independent Party
Formed by Alabama governor George Wallace to seek the presidency through a third party nomination; Wallace stood for racial segregation
1968
1970
1980
1990
1992

▲ **FIGURE 8–2 Evolution of the Major American Political Parties and Splinter Groups.** The above figure shows the historical development that led to the Democratic and Republican parties as we know them today. When did the modern Democratic Party begin?

Critical Thinking Skills
Guide the students in analyzing the role played by the question of slavery in the formation of political parties: Did any party of the 1850s oppose slavery itself? Why or why not? What might have caused the Whig coalition to collapse?What aspect of slavery did the new Republican Party oppose? What particular appeal might that opposition have held for voters?

Extension
Encourage the students to discuss their responses to the Nast cartoons of the 1870s. Then have them bring in current cartoons featuring the Democratic donkey and the Republican elephant: How have the animal symbols changed? Why do you imagine these symbols have endured?

Comprehension
Ask volunteers to explain why the Great Depression destroyed the Republicans' majority support.

Caption Answer The Whig Party and the Democratic Party were formed when the Democratic-Republicans split into two groups in the mid-1820s.

Caption Answer The donkey and the elephant remain the symbols of the Democratic Party and the Republican Party today.

Multidiscipline Strategies

Art Political cartoons have been an important element of American politics for over 200 years. Have students bring in a collection of current political cartoons from a variety of sources. Have students write a brief summary that describes the purpose of the cartoon. Next, allow students to attempt their own political cartoon, along with an explanation of the cartoon's message. Post the political cartoons throughout the room.

▲ Henry Clay was one of the leaders of the Whig Party, which throughout the 1840s and 1850s competed with the Democratic Party. How did the Whig Party originate?

leaders. They both had grass-roots organizations of party workers committed to winning as many political offices (at all levels of government) for the party as possible. Both the Whigs and Democrats remained vague on the issue of slavery.

By the 1850s, both parties were split by the growing problem of slavery. The Democrats were divided into northern and southern camps; the Whig coalition fell apart and most Whigs were absorbed into the new Republican Party, which opposed the extension of slavery into new territories. Campaigning on this platform, they succeeded in electing Abraham Lincoln as the first Republican president in 1860.

Post–Civil War

By the end of the Civil War, the Republicans and the Democrats were the most prominent political parties. From the election of Abraham Lincoln in 1860 until the election of Franklin Roosevelt in 1932, the Republican Party, sometimes referred to as the Grand Old Party, or the GOP, remained the majority party in national politics, winning all but four presidential elections.

After the Great Depression

The social and economic impact of the Great Depression of the 1930s destroyed the majority support that Republicans had enjoyed for so long, and contributed to a realignment in the two-party system. A **realigning election** shows a lasting shift in fundamental party loyalties among a large portion of voters, so that what was the weaker party emerges as the dominant party. The landmark realigning election of 1932 brought Franklin Delano Roosevelt to the presidency and the Democrats back to power at the national level.

Roosevelt was reelected three times to a total of four terms. When he died, his vice-president, Harry S Truman,

The First Democratic Donkey

▲ In 1870, Thomas Nast drew a cartoon using the donkey as a symbol of the Democratic Party. In 1874, in another cartoon, the elephant was used as a symbol of the Republican Party. Although Nast didn't mean these cartoons as complimentary, both parties adopted these symbols. What symbols are used today?

TEACHING BUILDING SOCIAL STUDIES SKILLS

Read

Introduce this feature by encouraging the students to share and discuss what they already know about tables: What is a table? What kind of information can a table most effectively communicate? In what contexts have you recently read and used tables? After a brief discussion, have volunteers read the Building Social Studies Skills feature aloud to the rest of the class.

Discuss

Help the students discuss the information in the feature: In what circumstances are tables especially useful? Why is it important to follow all six listed steps in reading a table? What kinds of conclusions must you be careful not to draw from reading a table?

Analyze and Apply

Have the students find other tables in magazines, newspapers, or other books. Ask each student to bring at least one table to class. Then let the students work in small groups to study and interpret the tables brought by group members.

Review

To help the students review, ask: What are the six main steps in reading a table? What can you learn from reading a table? What kinds of information cannot be communicated in a table?

BUILDING SOCIAL STUDIES SKILLS

Interpreting Tables

What kinds of people are Democrats? What kinds of people are in the Republican Party? The answers to such questions are frequently presented in table form. Tables can effectively present a great deal of information in a limited space; they consolidate information so that it is easier to study. By examining a table, you can compare information and detect trends over time.

Follow these steps when reading a table:

- **Step 1.** *Read the title of the table.*
- **Step 2.** *Notice how the table presents its information by reading the vertical (↑) and horizontal (→) headings.*
- **Step 3.** *Note whether the numerical information presented is in whole numbers or percentages.* [If the data are percentages, of what are they a part?]
- **Step 4.** *Analyze the meaning of the percentages or numbers by comparing the various sets of figures.*
- **Step 5.** *See if the numbers are expressed in tens, hundreds, thousands, or larger.*
- **Step 6.** *Read the source for the data.*

Vote by Groups in Presidential Elections, 1960–1992

	1960		1964		1968			1972	
	JFK D	Nixon R	LBJ D	Goldwater R	Humphrey D	Nixon R	Wallace I	McGovern D	Nixon R
NATIONAL	50.1	49.9	61.3	38.7	43.0	43.4	13.6	38	62
SEX									
Male	52	48	60	40	41	43	16	37	63
Female	49	51	62	38	45	43	12	38	62
RACE									
White	49	51	59	41	38	47	15	32	68
Nonwhite	68	32	94	6	85	12	3	87	13
AGE									
Under 30 years	54	46	64	36	47	38	15	48	52
30–49 years	54	46	63	37	44	41	15	33	67
50 years and older	46	54	59	41	41	47	12	36	64
POLITICS									
Republican	5	95	20	80	9	86	5	5	95
Democrat	84	16	87	13	74	12	14	67	33
Independent	43	57	56	44	31	44	25	31	69
EDUCATION									
College	39	61	52	48	37	54	9	37	63
High school	52	48	62	38	42	43	15	34	66
Grade school	55	45	66	34	52	33	15	49	51

*Less than 1 percent

Practicing Your Skills (Answers)

1. 45 percent.
2. Yes, the table does support this statement.
3. The majority of under 30s have voted Democratic in five of the last eight elections.

PRACTICING YOUR SKILLS

Look at the table below and answer the following questions:

1. What percentage of women voted for the Democratic candidate in 1984?
2. Does the table support this statement: College graduates have supported Republican presidential candidates since 1968?
3. Do voters under thirty years of age always appear to support the Democrats?

When reading a table, remember that the statistics gathered from the table do not describe individuals. Rather, they describe behavior trends in various groups, or choices made over time. By looking at the tables on these pages, you can conclude that most people with college educations will probably vote for a Republican presidential candidate. You cannot conclude, however, that all people with college educations will vote for a Republican presidential candidate. You also cannot conclude that any one person with a college education will vote for a Republican presidential candidate.

Vote by Groups in Presidential Elections, 1960–1992 (continued)

1976			1980			1984		1988		1992		
Carter D	Ford R	McCarthy I	Carter D	Reagan R	Anderson I	Mondale D	Reagan R	Dukakis D	Bush R	Clinton D	Bush R	Perot I
50	48	1	41	51	7	41	59	45	53	43	38	19
53	45	1	38	53	7	36	64	41	57	41	38	21
48	51	*	44	49	6	45	55	49	50	46	37	17
46	52	1	36	56	7	34	66	40	59	39	41	20
85	15	*	86	10	2	87	13	86	12	NA	NA	NA
53	45	1	47	41	11	40	60	47	52	44	34	22
48	49	2	38	52	8	40	60	45	54	NA	NA	NA
52	48	*	41	54	4	41	59	49	50	NA	NA	NA
9	91	*	8	86	5	4	96	8	91	10	73	17
82	18	*	69	26	4	79	21	82	17	77	10	13
38	57	4	29	55	14	33	67	43	55	38	32	30
42	55	2	35	53	10	39	61	43	56	NA	NA	NA
54	46	*	43	51	5	43	57	49	50	43	36	20
58	41	1	54	42	3	51	49	56	43	NA	NA	NA

*Less than 1 percent
Note: 1976 and 1980 results do not include vote for minor party candidates.

Source: *The Gallup Report*, Novermber 1984, p. 32; *The New York Times*. November 5, 1992, p. B9.

Discussion Starter
Help the students consider the division that has so often existed between Congress and the president: Why do you think the nation's voters continue to elect a Republican president and a Democratic Congress? What do you think this indicates about the intentions of voters? Are there advantages in dividing the elected power?

Reteaching Strategies
1. Have the students work in pairs or small groups to write short outlines of Section 2.
2. Work with small groups of students to review the six steps in reading a table. Be sure group members understand each step.

Evaluation Strategies
1. Have the students write their responses to the Preview Questions at the beginning of the section.
2. Have the students write their answers to the Section 2 Review questions.
3. Have the students take the Section 2 Quiz found in the *TRB*.

Section 2 Review (Answers)
1. The Democratic-Republicans.
2. The problem of slavery.
3. The great Depression in the 1930s destroyed the majority support that the Republicans had enjoyed for so long and resulted in the realigning election of 1932.
4. Answers will vary, e.g., it probably doesn't mean much because it is Congress that passes legislation and budgets. If, though, there is an extremely strong Republican president and a relatively weak Democratically controlled Congress, then one might be able to talk about a Republican government.

SECTION 3

Points to Stress
- The different types of third parties and reasons for their formation.
- The impact of third parties on American politics.
- Reasons for the lack of electoral success of third parties.

Kickoff Activity
Give the students five minutes in which to list as many third, or independent, parties as they can think of. At the end of the allotted time, ask volunteers to read their lists aloud. When the lists are combined, how many different parties did the class list?

Working with the Preview Questions
Have the students read the study questions and discuss their responses, based on current knowledge. Remind the students that they can use these questions as a guide when studying Section 3.

Caption Answer The U.S.A. Green Party is an example of an issue oriented party.

assumed his office and also won the 1948 election. The Republicans under Dwight David Eisenhower won the 1952 and 1956 elections. From 1960 through 1968 the Democrats, headed by John F. Kennedy and Lyndon Baines Johnson, held power. The Republicans came back into power in 1968 and, except for President Jimmy Carter's one term in 1976, retained the presidency. On the other hand, the Democrats have generally dominated Congress since the Great Depression, no matter which party had a president in power.

SECTION 2 REVIEW

1. Which party dominated American politics at the beginning of the 1800s?
2. What national problem destroyed the Whig party in the 1850s?
3. When did the Democratic Party come into power? What was the reason for the change?
4. **For critical analysis:** It seems fairly clear that if both Congress and the presidency are dominated by the same party, that party controls the national government. What does it mean, then, to talk about a "Republican government" if the president is a Republican but Congress is controlled by the Democrats?

SECTION 3

Third Parties: Their Impact on American Politics

Preview Questions

- What are the different types of third parties and why are they formed?
- How do third parties influence American politics?
- Why do third parties have problems winning elections?

Throughout American history, smaller **minor parties,** sometimes called **third parties,** have competed for power in the nation's two-party system. Indeed, third parties have been represented in most of our national elections. Third parties have a difficult if not impossible time gaining credibility within the two-party-dominated American system; nonetheless, they have an important role in our political life.

Third Parties Come in Several Varieties

Third parties are as varied as the causes they represent, but all have one thing in common: Their members and leaders feel the need to challenge the major parties, because they believe that certain needs and values are not being properly addressed. Third parties name candidates who propose to remedy the situation.

Some third parties have tried to appeal to the entire nation; others have focused on particular regions, states, or locales. Most have been short-lived, but a few have lasted for a long time, such as the Socialist Labor Party, founded in 1891, and the Social Democrats, founded in 1901. The number and variety of third parties make them difficult to classify, but most fall into general categories.

Issue-Oriented Parties An issue-oriented third party is formed to promote a particularly timely issue. For example, the Free Soil Party was organized in the years before the Civil War in 1860 with the purpose of opposing the expansion of slavery into the Western territories. The Prohibition Party was formed in 1869 to advocate prohibiting the use and manufacturing of alcoholic beverages. The U.S.A. Green Party was founded in 1972 to raise awareness of environmental issues. Most issue-oriented parties fade into history as the issue that brought them into existence fades from

The U.S.A. Green Party was founded to promote environmental awareness and to combat pollution, such as this stream pollution. What type of party is the U.S.A. Green Party?

Teaching Strategies

Introduction
Let a volunteer read the section introduction aloud. Then encourage the students to speculate about the important place third parties have held in the political life of our nation: What is that place? What might explain the importance of third parties?

Discussion Starter
Guide the students in discussing the formation of third parties: What do you think motivates dissatisfied party members to continue working within one of the major parties? At what point do you imagine those people decide to leave their major party and form a new party? What factors probably influence that decision?

Extension
Encourage interested volunteers to research these issue-oriented parties: the Free Soil Party, the Prohibition Party, and the U.S.A. Green Party. Who founded each party? When? Why? How successful was the party? What happened to it? Let the volunteers work together to create a bulletin board or poster set summarizing their findings.

Comprehension
Let students respond to this question: Why are issue-oriented parties popular in multiparty systems?

Vocabulary
Let a volunteer define *ideology* in his or her own words. Then ask the students to suggest several examples of ideologies.

Caption Answer In the presidential election of 1912, Roosevelt's candidacy split the Republican vote and doomed the re-election hopes of Republican William Howard Taft, who was defeated by Democratic candidate Woodrow Wilson. You might refer students back to the table on page 192, where this information was provided. Students should also understand that Roosevelt had already served as president from 1901 to 1909 and only formed the Progressive, or Bull Moose, Party after failing to receive the nomination of the Republican party.

The Bull Moose Party of 1912 was a personality party that built up around the presidential campaign of Theodore Roosevelt. The photograph here shows Roosevelt campaigning in the summer of 1912. What effect did Roosevelt's candidacy have on the election?

public attention, is taken up by a major party, or is resolved.

Issue-oriented parties are popular in multiparty systems. For example, in Czechoslovakia there is the Romanies Party, defending Gypsy freedom; the Green Party, an environmental movement; the Coexistence, a movement emphasizing peace and ethnic tolerance; the Coalition of Special-Interest Unions, linking such groups as beekeepers, rabbit-raisers, anglers, and gardeners in pursuit of conservation of nature; and the Civic Freedom Movement, joining individuals who reject political parties.

Ideological Parties An **ideology** is a comprehensive set of beliefs about human nature and government institutions. Ideological parties are those that support a particular set of beliefs or political doctrine. For example, a party such as the Socialist Workers Party may believe that our free enterprise system should be replaced by one in which government or workers own all of the factories in the economy. They may feel that competition should be replaced by cooperation and social responsibility in order to secure an equitable distribution of income. In contrast, an ideological party such as the Libertarian Party may oppose government interference in private enterprise.

Splinter or Personality Parties A splinter party develops out of a split within a major party. Often this split involves the formation of a party to elect a specific person. Former president Theodore Roosevelt's Bull Moose Party of 1912 (also called the Progressive Party) is an example of a splinter party formed from the Republican Party. When Roosevelt did not receive the Republican Party's nomination, he created the Bull Moose Party to promote his platform. From the Democrats have come Henry Wallace's Progressive Party and the States' Rights (Dixiecrat) Party, both formed in 1948. In 1968 the American Independent Party was formed to support George Wallace's campaign for president.

Most splinter parties have been formed around a leader with a strong personality, which is why they are sometimes called personality parties. When that person steps aside, the parties usually collapse.

Third Parties' Impact on American Politics

While most Americans do not support third parties or vote for their candidates, third parties have influenced American politics in several important ways. First, third parties have brought many important political issues to the public's attention. They have exposed and focused on unpopular or highly debated issues that major parties have preferred to ignore. Third parties are in a position to take bold stands on issues avoided by major parties because they are not trying to be all things to all people. Progressive social reforms such as the **minimum wage** (the lowest legal wage), women's right to vote, railroad and banking legislation, and **old-age pensions** (retirement plans giving people money after they stop working) were first proposed by third parties. The Free Soilers of the 1850s, for example, were the first true antislavery party, and the Populists and Progressives put many social

Enrichment
Let a group of interested volunteers research the American Independent Party: Who was George Wallace, and what did he stand for? Why was a new party formed to support his candidacy? What was the party's goal in the 1968 election? How successful was the party's campaign? Ask these volunteers to write a short report of their findings, and make this report available to the rest of the class.

Discussion Starter
Encourage the students to consider the issues first brought forward by third parties: Why do you think the major parties avoided these issues at first? Why do you think the major parties were eventually forced to accept them? What current issues could possibly lead to the formation of new third parties?

Vocabulary
Let volunteers explain what the phrase *unsung heroes of American politics* means. In what sense are the third parties unsung heroes?

Vocabulary
Let volunteers explain what it means to take the *spoiler role.* How do third parties take that role?

Critical Thinking Skills
Help the students analyze the role played by third parties in giving frustrated Democrats and Republicans someplace else to go: How does this third-party role weaken the two major parties? How, on the other hand, does it strengthen them? Which do you think is the more important effect?

Discussion Starter
Encourage the students to discuss their responses to these questions: Would it make sense for a third-party presidential candidate to run in fewer than all 50 states? Why or why not?

Caption Answer Traditionally such candidates face obstacles in trying to raise enough money, in getting on the ballot in all states, and in persuading voters not to vote with one of the major parties.

Discussion Starter
Let the students discuss their reactions to the example of a fictional third-party that favored a national tax on businesses for air pollution clean-up: How widespread would the third-party support have to be before the issue would be adopted by one of the major parties? Based on what you have learned about the two major parties, which would be more likely to adopt this—admittedly hypothetical— proposal? Why?

Reteaching Strategies
1. Let the students work with partners to write one-paragraph responses to this question: Why are third parties important in American politics?
2. Work with small groups of students to review several answers to the question posed in the heading: Why do they (third parties) fail to win elections? Encourage the students to recall information, but allow them to refer to the text if necessary.

Evaluation Strategies
1. Have the students write their answers to the Section 3 Review questions.
2. Have the students take the Section 3 Quiz found in the *TRB.*

Section 3 Review (Answers)
1. Issue-oriented parties are formed to promote a particular timely issue. Ideological parties are formed to support a particular set of beliefs or political doctrine. Splinter or personality parties develop out of a split with a major party, often involving a specific person.
2. Third parties bring important issues to the public's attention. They can influence some election outcomes. They also provide a voice for voters who are frustrated with and alienated from the Republican and Democratic parties.
3. Third parties fail to win elections because of low membership, lack of money, and the public's

reforms on the political agenda. Some people have argued that third parties are often the unsung heroes of American politics, bringing new issues to the public forefront. Some of the ideas proposed by third parties were never accepted, while others were taken up by the major parties as they became more popular.

A second major sphere of third party influence has been in some election outcomes. They have taken victory from one major party and given it to another, thus playing the ''spoiler role.'' For example, in 1912, when the Progressive Party split off from the Republican Party, the presidential race consisted of Woodrow Wilson as the Democratic candidate, William Howard Taft as the regular Republican candidate, and Theodore Roosevelt as the Progressive candidate. The presence of the Progressive party ''spoiled'' the Republicans' chances for victory, which gave the election to Wilson, the Democrat. Without third-party action by Roosevelt, Taft could have won.

Third parties also provide a voice for voters who are frustrated with and alienated from the Republican and Democratic parties. In 1992, the candidacy of Ross Perot received a great deal of support from voters who expressed frustration with Republican and Democratic politics.

▲ Ross Perot, running as an independent, emerged as a major candidate during the 1992 presidential campaign. What obstacles do independent or third-party candidates face?

Why Do They Fail to Win Elections?

Third parties fail to win elections mainly because of low membership, lack of money, and the public's traditional habit of voting within the major parties. The American people have always had a two-party system and are accustomed to selecting only from the nominees of those parties.

One major problem for third parties is raising enough money for a modern campaign. Most Americans have come to believe that third-party candidates could never win, and are consequently unwilling to contribute to an underdog candidate's campaign. A 1974 law does, however, decrease the severity of this problem for third-party candidates in presidential elections. The law states that presidential candidates who receive over 5 percent of the votes will be partially repaid for their campaign expenses by the federal government. Third-party candidate John B. Anderson received enough votes to qualify for such reimbursement when he ran for president in 1980 (after losing the Republican nomination).

Another problem for third parties is getting candidates on the ballot in all fifty states. Before 1968, some state laws forced candidates to gather a considerable number of signatures in a short period of time before being listed on the state ballot. In 1968, third-party candidate George Wallace went to the Supreme Court to have such a law in Ohio ruled unconstitutional. States have since relaxed these requirements, but election laws in some states still favor two major parties and thereby work against minor parties.

Finally, any third party that succeeds in winning the support of a significant number of voters will soon fall victim to its own success. After all, the two major parties can easily adopt additional planks in their platforms to attract those individuals who are supporting the third party. In this way, the two major parties undermine any successful third-party campaign. Suppose, for example, that a third party is in favor of implementing a federal tax on all businesses, to be exclusively used for cleaning up air pollution. If that third party succeeds in gaining considerable voter support, then either or both of the major parties can simply support the tax as part of it or their own party platforms.

habit of voting within the major parties.

4. Answers will vary, e.g., Americans join third parties because the two major parties fail to address the issues about which they are concerned. They join third parties because they see the two major parties as essentially the same, and because these major parties fail to keep up with the changing times.

SECTION 4

Points to Stress

- The structure of the two major parties.
- State and local party organization.
- The four major components in the structure of national organizations for each party.

Kickoff Activity

Ask the students to write their responses to these questions: Why do political parties need structure? What kinds of structure do you think they have? After all the students have recorded their ideas, encourage them to share and discuss their responses.

Working with the Preview Questions

Let volunteers read the study questions aloud. Encourage the students to discuss their preliminary responses. Then ask them to prepare note-taking sheets with headings based on these study questions; have the students fill in their notes as they study Section 4.

Teaching Strategies

Introduction

Ask the students to read the section introduction. Then encourage discussion by posing these questions: Why are the theoretical structure and the actual structure of political parties not the same? Why do you think there is no single individual or group whom everyone in a party obeys? Do you think this situation is good for political parties? Why or why not?

Caption Answer Local party organizations are often quite independent from their state organizations.

Discussion Starter

Focus the students' attention on this statement from the text: In both the Democratic and Republican Parties, state and local organizations are separate from their national organizations. Why do you think this is the case? Could the parties be more effective if they were run by a single, nationwide organization? Why or why not?

Vocabulary

Ask volunteers to define the term *grass roots.* What does the phrase *the grass-roots level of politics* mean?

Discussion Starter

Guide the students in discussing the work of precinct captains or chairpersons: What do you imagine motivates people to undertake those jobs? Do you know anyone who is—or once was—a precinct captain or chairperson? Why did that person accept the responsibilities of the job? What results has that person had?

SECTION 3 REVIEW

1. Name the three different types of third parties and explain why they are formed.
2. What important influences do third parties have on the American political system?
3. What are some problems that third parties face?
4. **For critical analysis:** There is virtually no chance today that a third party's presidential candidate could ever win an election. What, then, do you think motivates millions of Americans to join third parties?

SECTION 4

The Structure of Political Parties

Preview Questions

- How are the two major parties structured?
- In general, how are state and local party organizations organized?
- What are the four major elements in the structures of both major national organizations?

In theory, both of the American political parties have a standard, pyramid-shaped organization much like a large company, with the bosses at the top and the employees at various lower levels.

Actually, neither major party is a closely knit or highly organized structure. They are both fragmented and are *decentralized,* which means there is no central power with a direct chain-of-command. If there were, the national chairperson of the Democratic or Republican Party, along with the national committee, could simply dictate how the organization was to be run, just as if it were General Motors or IBM. State party organizations are all very different and are only loosely tied to the party's national structure. Local party organizations are often quite independent from the state organization. There is no individual or group whom everyone in the party obeys. Rather, there are a number of personalities, frequently at odds with one another, who form a loosely identifiable leadership group.

State and Local Party Organizations

In both the Democratic and Republican Parties, state and local organizations are separate from their national organizations. Most state and local parties work closely with their national organization only during major elections.

▲ At the local level party volunteers handle many of the day-to-day tasks, such as canvassing neighborhoods to drum up support. To what degree are most local party organizations tied to the state organizations?

State Organizations The powers and duties of state party organizations differ from state to state. In general, the state party organization is built around a central committee and a chairperson. They work to raise funds, recruit new party members, maintain a strong party organization, and help members running for state offices.

The state chairperson is usually a powerful party member chosen by the committee. In some cases, however, the chairperson is selected by the governor or a senator from that state.

Local Organizations Local party organizations differ greatly, but generally have a party unit for each district in which elective offices are to be filled. These include congressional and legislative districts, counties, cities and towns, **wards**, and **precincts**.

A *ward* is a political division or district within a city designated for electing members of a city council. A *precinct* is the basic unit of party organization and of election polling districts. The grass-roots level, or local, foundations of politics are formed within voting precincts. These are where people vote on election day, and where individual polling places are located. Political parties elect or appoint precinct captains or chairpersons who organize the precinct, assist new members, register voters, and take care of party business.

TEACHING GOVERNMENT IN ACTION

Read
Introduce this feature by writing the following term on the chalkboard: *the political machine.* Encourage discussion: What does this term mean? What does it make you think of? Why? Do you think the days of the political machine are over? What examples can you cite to support your opinion? After this introductory discussion, let the students read Government in Action independently.

Discuss
Ask questions such as these to guide the students in discussing the case study: Do immigrants and the poor seem to need the same kind of help they needed when the machine provided so many services? Why or why not? Do you think the current situation might make the machine an important force again? Explain your ideas. What do you know about Tweed and Tammany Hall? What do you know about Mayor Richard J. Daley? (If necessary, ask volunteers to read about Tweed and Daley and share their findings with the rest of the class.)

Analyze and Apply
Let the students work in groups to investigate the government of their local city or town—or, if group members prefer, of a nearby large city. Encourage the students to use various research techniques, including interviewing, to discover whether and in what forms machine politics affected the local government.

Review
To help the students review, ask these questions: What is "the machine"? When and why did it flourish? Why did big city machines die?

Think About It (Answers)
1. Answers will vary, e.g., they could help immigrants and the poor with social services and jobs.
2. Answers will vary, e.g., public outcry about the corruption. Competition from those who were not a part of the machine, but wanted to be a part of the political process in the city nonetheless.

Comprehension
Ask the students to identity several well-known members of Congress who are considered national party leaders.

Discussion Starter
Encourage the students to share and discuss the facts or images they most vividly remember from the last national convention. From your own memories and those of your classmates, what can you conclude about how the national convention was conducted? What can you conclude about how it was covered in the media? How do you think the convention and the convention coverage are related?

GOVERNMENT IN ACTION

CASE STUDY

Machine Politics

Today urban party organization is fairly quiet and sleepy, except in a few places. This was not always the case. At one time in history, urban political parties were *the* party organizations in America. From the last years of the nineteenth century through the 1930s, many cities were operated by what was known as the ''machine,'' a system within a party by which each city block had its organizer, each neighborhood had its political club, each district or ward had its leader, and the whole machine had its ''boss.'' **Patronage**, or rewarding party faithfuls with jobs or contracts, held the machine together. The machine was especially helpful to immigrants and the poor, who often needed help with language barriers, social services, and jobs. These people, in exchange for this assistance, gave the machine their loyalty. Politically, machines linked together fragmented neighborhoods and ethnic groups into a strong political power base that could elect and reelect a mayor—or boss.

However helpful at times, some machines turned out to be quite corrupt. The Tammany Society, for example, which dominated New York City politics for more than a century, was especially notorious. One of its most infamous leaders was William ''Boss'' Tweed, whose scandalous behavior was exposed by the *New York Times* in 1871. Readers were entertained and shocked by stories of millions of dollars in kickbacks that politicians received from businesses that sought government contracts. The stories also detailed overlooked civil and criminal violations, as well as phony leases and padded bills that were paid to members of the Tweed machine. Tweed was imprisoned, but many other members fled the country with their wealth intact.

The years of the great machines, in places such as New York City, Jersey City, Kansas City, and Philadelphia, are over now. When Mayor Richard Daley of Chicago died in 1976, he was widely called the last of the big-city bosses. Big-city machines died mostly because their function of providing social services (and reaping the rewards of votes) has been taken over by state and national agencies. Reformers claimed that local government should involve administration rather than politics, and that human services and jobs should be provided in an efficient and honest manner, without the payoffs, kickbacks, and graft that had long characterized machine politics. They sought to break up the centralized machine power and have been largely successful.

THINK ABOUT IT

1. What advantages, if any, can you see to machine politics in a big city?
2. What other reasons can you think of for the breakup of machine politics?

National Party Organization

On the national level, presidents are considered to be the official leaders of their party. In some cases, well-known members of Congress are viewed as national party leaders. Beyond the leaders, there are four major elements in the structure of both major parties: the national convention, the national committee, the national chairperson, and the congressional campaign committees.

The National Convention Most of the public attention that the party receives comes at the **national convention** held every four years during the summer before the presidential election. These conventions are extensively covered by the news media and as a result have become quite extravagant. They are often described as the party's national voice and are usually held in major cities such as New York, Chicago, Miami, or San Francisco.

Caption Answer Students should understand that the parties use the attention garnered by the elaborately staged conventions to promote themselves and their candidates.

Discussion Starter
Encourage the students to discuss the responsibility of the national party committees for seeing that their party wins the presidency: What do the national committees do to fulfill this responsibility? What other individuals or groups should view this goal as their responsibility as well? Why?

Extension
Ask the class: Who is the national chairperson of the Republican Party? Of the Democratic Party? Have these people been in the news recently? What have you read and heard about them? (If the students cannot identify these chairs, assign volunteers to find out about them.)

Caption Answer Each party's presidential candidate chooses a chairperson, who is then elected by the National Committee.

Reteaching Strategies
1. Have groups of students compare and discuss the notes they took while reading Section 4. Encourage the students to revise or correct their notes, referring to the text if necessary.
2. Ask the students to work with partners in writing their own definitions of these terms: *ward, precinct, patronage, party ticket.*

Evaluation Strategies
1. Have the students write their answers to the Section 4 Review questions.
2. Have the students take the Section 4 Quiz found in the *TRB.*

Section 4 Review (Answers)
1. Generally, the state party organization is built around a state central committee and chairperson. Local party organizations differ greatly, but generally have a party unit for each district in which elective offices are to be filled. These include congressional and legislative districts, counties, cities and towns, wards and precincts.
2. The main elements of the national party organization are the national convention, the national committee, the national chairperson, and the congressional campaign committees.
3. The purpose of the national party convention is to choose the party's presidential and vice-presidential candidates and to write the party platform.
4. While a diagram of the structure of the political parties may look like that of a typical business, there are no true direct lines of authority. The party national chairperson, for example, cannot easily hire and fire those in the state party organizations nor can that chairperson actually dictate specifically what the state party organizations are to do.

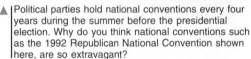

▲ Political parties hold national conventions every four years during the summer before the presidential election. Why do you think national conventions such as the 1992 Republican National Convention shown here, are so extravagant?

▲ Each party has a national party chairperson, such as former Democratic National Party Chairperson Ron Brown, shown here. Brown became secretary of commerce in the Clinton administration. The chairperson serves as the head of the national party. How is the national party chairperson selected?

The national conventions are attended by delegates chosen by the states in various ways. The delegates' most important job is to choose the party's presidential and vice presidential candidates, which together make up the **party ticket**. They also write the party platform, which sets forth the party's positions on national issues and makes promises to initiate certain policies if the party wins the presidency.

The National Committee Each state elects a number of delegates to the **national party committee**. The Republican National Committee and the Democratic National Committee each directs party business during the four years between national conventions. Their most important duty, however, is to plan the next national convention, and to plan how to obtain a party victory in the next presidential election.

The National Chairperson Each party's national committee elects a **national party chairperson** to serve as head of the national party. The chairperson is chosen by the party presidential candidate at a meeting of the national committee right after the national convention. The duties of the national chairperson are to direct the work of the national committee from party headquarters in Washington, D.C. This leader is involved in fund-raising, publicity, promoting party unity, recruiting new voters, and other activities. During the presidential election years, the committee's attention is focused on the national convention and the presidential campaign.

The Congressional Campaign Committees Each party has a campaign committee, made up of senators and representatives, in each house of Congress. Members are chosen by their colleagues and serve for a two-year term. The committees work to help reelect party members to Congress.

As you have seen, though the founding fathers did not plan for political parties, our two-party system developed even before the Constitution was ratified. The two parties that dominate the American political scene perform many functions, such as selecting candidates, providing public information, and running campaigns. While alternative parties continue to exist, there is no reason to believe that the two-party system, as it exists today, will not continue well into the coming century.

SECTION 4 REVIEW

1. What is the structure of most state and local party organizations?
2. What are the main elements of the national party organization?
3. What are the purposes of a national party convention?
4. **For critical analysis:** How does the structure of the Democratic and the Republican parties differ from that of a typical big business?

TEACHING CHALLENGE TO THE AMERICAN DREAM

Read
Ask a volunteer to read aloud the feature title, and encourage the students to discuss their responses to the title question. Then have the students read the feature independently.

Discuss
Stimulate class discussion of Challenge to the American Dream by posing questions such as these: Do you think voters who register as independents show a lack of commitment? Why or why not? Does split-ticket voting show commitment? If so, to what? What are media consultant and public relations specialists? What kinds of work do they usually undertake? What do they do for political candidates? Do you consider candidates who rely heavily on media consultants and public relations specialists any less trustworthy than candidates who present themselves more straight-forwardly to the public? Why or why not? What advantages can you see in a lack of guaranteed rewards for those who work loyally for one of the major parties? What disadvantages can you see? Which do you consider more significant—the advantages or the disadvantages?

Analyze and Apply
Have the class work together to plan a survey about party affiliation and voting habits. Remind the students to include answers to these questions in their plan: Whom will we survey? What information do we want to collect? What questions should we ask to gather that information? Whom will each student interview? How will we tabulate and summarize our findings? Then have the students carry out the survey they have planned. What conclusions can be drawn from the results of the survey?

Review
Ask the students these review questions: What is party identification? What is straight-ticket voting?

Service Learning Activity

Students need to understand what Tip O'Neil meant when he said, "All politics is local." Have students work with a local party organization, be it at the township, county, or perhaps state level. Students will witness how few party activists there are and also how parties go about fulfilling their functions. Students might need some help in determining which party they have the most in common with and which party they want to support. The phone numbers and addresses of local party organizations will be in the local phone directory. Students should be encouraged to keep a journal of their experiences.

This figure content is also featured on *West's American Government Videodisc* (see the index found in the *TRB*).

CHALLENGE TO THE AMERICAN DREAM

Is the Party Over?

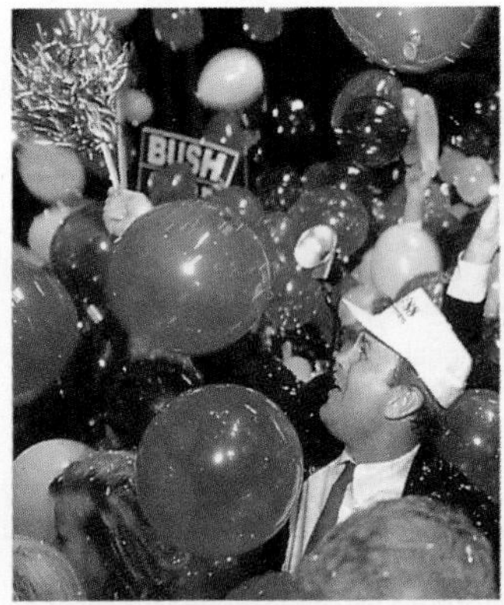

Political parties have been important in governing America in the past, and they are likely to continue to be important in the future. There is no doubt, however, that they are not as powerful and influential as they once were. In fact, as the chart on this page indicates, the percentage of individuals identifying themselves as independents has increased over the last fifty years.

Party identification is linking oneself to a particular party. Since 1960 there has been a sharp drop in the number of voters willing to identify themselves as Republicans or Democrats, and a growing number who regard themselves as **independents**, people who are not committed to any political party. In the 1940s, only about 20 percent of voters classified themselves as independents. By the beginning of the 1990s, this percentage had increased to over one-third, and more recent polls show it holding steady at about that level.

Not only have ties to the two major parties weakened, but voters are less willing to vote a **straight ticket**—voting for all the candidates from one party. There has been a big increase in **split-ticket voting**, which is voting for candidates of both parties for the different offices at the same election. For example, you would be splitting the ticket if you voted for both a Republican presidential candidate and a Democratic congressional candidate.

Another reason why some people have become less attached to political parties is because they feel that the parties today cannot keep up with changing times. This

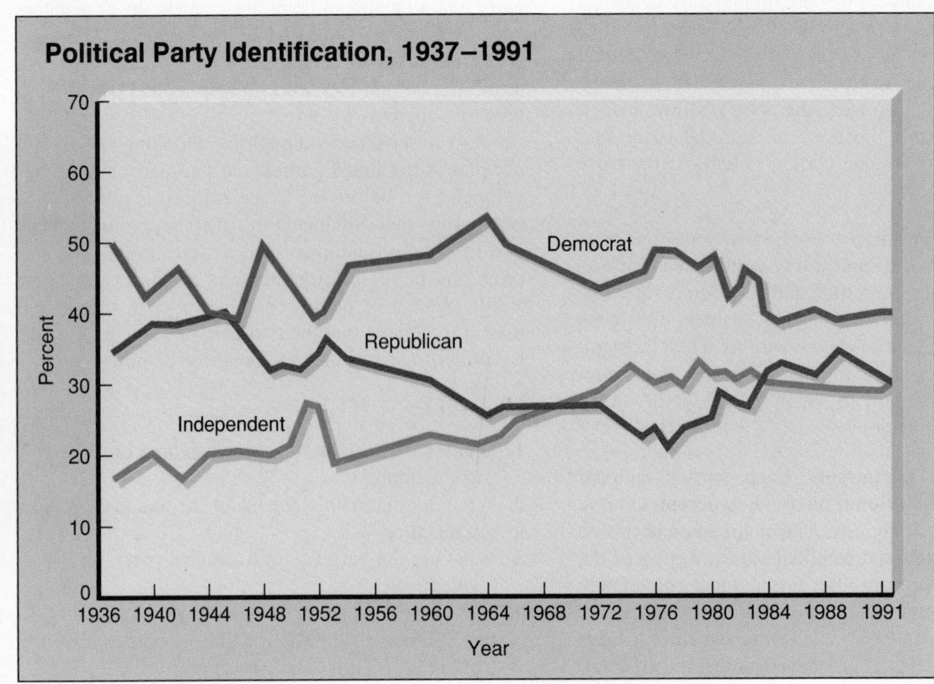

What is split-ticket voting? Which is becoming more common?

You Decide (Answers)

1. Answers will vary, e.g., the increase is having little affect; the two major parties are still firmly in power.

2. Answers will vary, e.g., those in government are less committed to their party because they no longer need the same amount of assistance from the party as they did in the past. They must now rely more on the assistance of special interest groups.

3. Answers will vary, e.g., political parties could recruit members more actively. They could relax their stance on certain issues to draw more people.

4. Answers will vary, e.g., the United States will not have anything other than a two-party system because the system is a firmly entrenched tradition.

CHALLENGE TO THE AMERICAN DREAM

Is the Party Over?—*Continued*

factor, combined with the growing power of special interest groups, leads many to feel that being a party member is insignificant.

Another factor that weakens political parties is that candidates are much less dependent on party organizations than they used to be. A number of factors are responsible for this change. For example, candidates raise more of their own campaign funds. Media consultants and public relations specialists have taken over many of the functions traditionally performed by the party. Changes in the technology of campaigning—especially the heavy use of television, direct-mail advertising, and professional campaign managers—have also made candidates much less dependent on party organizations.

This trend, along with the increase in the number of voters who call themselves independents, and the practice of ticket-splitting suggest that parties have lost much of their hold on the loyalty of voters. Some would argue that those who serve in government are therefore less committed than officeholders were years ago.

Is the party over? If indeed more and more Americans become political independents, then the two-party system that has dominated American politics for so many years may still exist, but the parties themselves may become weaker. This may be a challenge to the American dream in the sense that working for one of the major political parties may not guarantee the rewards that existed in the past.

You Decide

1. How do you think the increasing number of independents affects the two major political parties?
2. Why do you think this trend causes those in government to be less committed to their party than officeholders were years ago?
3. What do you think political parties can do to regain their importance in elections? Is it worth it for the parties to do this? Give reasons for your answer.
4. What possibilities do you think there are for the United States to have anything other than a two-party system?

Multidiscipline Strategies

Research Each political party is responsible for determining rules for the national nominating convention. This includes the number and method of selection for convention delegates. Have students find out how many delegates each party allows, how the delegates are selected, and how many are needed for nomination. Students will also be able to see what percentage is selected by primaries and caucuses, and in the case of the Democrats, the percentage of super-delegates. Related to this is the relative power of each state based on the number of delegates they can garner at the convention. There are many sources that have this material, including popular publications like *U.S News and World Report* and the *Washington Post,* particularly during the primary period. A place to start is *The Elections of 1988,* Michael Nelson (ed.), Congressional Quarterly.

CHAPTER 8 REVIEW

Key Terms

canvasses 186
coalitions 186
consensus 183
electorate 184
ideology 197
independents 202
majority party 186
minimum wage 197
minor parties 196
minority party 186
multiparty system 182
national convention 200
national party chairperson 201
national party committee 201
nomination 184
old-age pensions 197
one-party system 182
partisan elections 182
party identification 202
party platform 190
party ticket 201
patronage 200
planks 190
plurality 184
political party 181
precincts 199
primaries 184
realigning election 193
run-off election 184
single-member district system 184
solidarity 189
split-ticket voting 202
straight ticket 202
third parties 196
two-party system 182
wards 199

Chapter Evaluation
To evaluate student mastery of chapter material, you might:
1. Use Chapter Test A from the *TRB*.
2. Use Chapter Test B from the *TRB*.
3. Construct your own test using items from the *West American Government Test Bank* found in the *TRB*.
4. Use the accompanying computerized test software to construct and print a customized chapter test.

Review Questions (Answers)
1. A political party is a group of individuals outside government who organize to win elections, to operate the government, and to determine public policy. Party-in-the-electorate consists of all those people who are members. Party as organization is the local, state, and national organizations. Party-in-government consists of all the candidates who won the elections and are now in public office.
2. Some nations have a one-party system in which a single party monopolizes the organization of governmental power. Other nations have a multiparty system in which more than two parties compete for power and electoral offices. The two-party system has become firmly entrenched in America because of the general consensus of most Americans, tradition, and our elective process.
3. Political parties link the American public to the government, which is important in a democracy. They recruit and nominate candidates for political office. They inform the public about important political issues. They coordinate policymaking, balance competing interests, and run campaigns.
4. Some members identify with a party and may do nothing more than occasionally vote for some of the party's candidates. Others are active members and work for the party. Some even become candidates for office. People join because they wish to express their solidarity or because they wish to work for a set of ideas or principles.
5. American Independent Party, Citizens Party, and the Libertarian Party.
6. Family, age, occupation, place of residence, education, and economic status all influence party choice.
7. The founders thought that strong political parties would cause power struggles between small economic and political groups that would eventually topple the balanced democracy.
8. The Federalists supported a strong central government and the Anti-Federalists favored a more limited role for government.
9. The Republicans followed by the Democrats were the most dominant by the end of the Civil War.
10. Issue-oriented parties, splinter or personality parties, and ideological parties.
11. Third parties bring important issues to the public's attention. They have influenced some election outcomes. They have provided a voice for voters who are frustrated with or alienated from the Republican and Democratic parties.

CHAPTER 8 REVIEW—Continued

Summary

1. Political parties are groups of individuals who are organized to win elections, operate the government, and determine public policy. American political parties are sometimes described as three-dimensional, each one consisting of the party-in-the-electorate, the party as organization, and the party-in-government. The United States has a two-party system. Alternatives to this system are the multiparty system, such as in many countries of Europe, which have several major and many lesser parties, or the one-party system, in which only the party of the ruling group is allowed. Our two-party system is the result of our general consensus and moderate views, our political tradition, and our elective process. Political parties select candidates, inform the public, coordinate policymaking, balance competing interests, and run campaigns. Party members have joined parties for material and ideological reasons, and to express solidarity with fellow party members. Taking part in political parties is an important way for citizens to affect government decision making.

2. The founders reacted negatively to the idea of strong political parties, but the first political factions in America—the Federalists and the Anti-Federalists—were formed to support or oppose the Constitution. The Anti-Federalists became the Democratic-Republicans and dominated American politics for the next twenty years and then split into two parties—the Democrats and the Whigs. The Whig Party was absorbed into the new Republican Party in the 1850s. By the end of the Civil War, the Republicans and the Democrats were the most prominent political parties, and continue to be so.

3. Smaller third parties have also competed for power in the nation's two-party system. They are formed because they believe that certain needs and values are not being properly addressed by the major parties. There are three general types of third parties: (1) issue-oriented parties formed to promote particular issues; (2) ideological parties to support a particular set of beliefs or political doctrines; and (3) splinter or personality parties formed from a split with a major party. Many important issues of American politics have been brought to the public's attention by third parties. These parties have also influenced some election outcomes. Third parties fail to win elections because Americans are accustomed to selecting only nominees of the two major parties. They also have difficulty raising enough money to compete in expensive campaigns.

4. In theory, the two major political parties in the United States have standard, pyramid-shaped organizations. In actuality, each major party is fragmented and decentralized. In both the Democratic and Republican parties, state and local organizations are separate from their national organizations. There are four major elements in the structure of both major party national organizations: the national convention, the national committee, the national chairperson, and the congressional campaign committee. Since 1960 there has been a sharp drop in the number of people identifying themselves as Republicans or Democrats; more people are calling themselves Independents.

Review Questions

1. Define what a political party is and explain the roles that parties play in American politics.
2. What factors help to explain America's two-party system? How is this system different from those of other nations?
3. What are the main activities that political parties perform and why are they important?
4. What do party members do and why do people join political parties?
5. Name three minor parties in the United States.
6. What are reasons that individuals identify with political parties?
7. Why did the founders react negatively to the idea of political parties?
8. What were the first political parties in the United States and why were they formed?
9. By the end of the Civil War, what were the dominant parties in the United States?
10. Name the three different types of third parties.
11. What effects have third parties had on American politics?
12. Describe the structure of the national party organization.
13. How can you find the state and local offices of both major parties in your area?
14. Describe the trend over the past thirty years regarding people identifying themselves with the two major parties.

12. There are four major elements in the structure of both parties: the national convention, the national committee, the national chairperson, and the congressional campaign committees.
13. In the telephone directory or newspapers or by contacting the national offices.
14. There has been a drop in the number of voters willing to identify themselves as Republicans or Democrats.

Questions for Thought and Discussion (Answers)
1. Answers will vary, e.g., the media have taken over the role of informing the public about important issues. Issues are debated in newspapers and on television and political parties may or may not be involved.
2. Answers will vary, e.g., local parties have their own agenda and set of issues. Some of these issues might be remote from the national party structure.
3. Answers will vary, e.g., the Republican platform generally supports strengthening the power and responsibilities of the states while limiting the national government's role in the economy. The Democratic platform, on the other hand, generally pushes for a strong national government and often supports government regulation of the economy and social programs for the poor.
4. Answers will vary, e.g., because each party is striving to appeal to a wide range of people, they have a tendency to choose a moderate candidate. Each party has an ideology broad enough to allow many variations and there are moderate candidates who could be placed within both parties' wide boundaries.

CHAPTER 8 REVIEW—Continued

Questions for Thought and Discussion

1. Some commentators believe that the media have taken over some of the functions of political parties. Discuss what these functions might be and why the media are able to take them over.
2. Although there is a national party structure for both the Democrats and the Republicans, most of the power of political parties lies primarily at the county and state levels. Discuss why the national party apparatus cannot control local politics.
3. Discuss what you believe to be the major differences between the platforms of the Republicans and the Democrats.
4. On at least several occasions, both the Democrats and Republicans have asked the same individual to run as their presidential candidate. This occurred, for example, with Dwight D. Eisenhower. Explain how such a phenomenon could exist.

Improving Your Skills

Communication Skills

Skimming for Information

You have learned the SQ3R reading strategy on page 73, which will help you to thoroughly understand and remember details as you read a textbook. There are certain times when you must read material quickly, such as when deciding which newspaper articles to use in a research project. **Skimming** is a technique that allows you to assess the key concepts of an article or chapter without reading the entire selection. When skimming for information, look at headings, topic sentences, (usually the first or second sentence in a paragraph) and conclusions. Know what information you are looking for ahead of time.

Writing

Practice your skimming techniques by going to the library and researching one of the following religions: Islam, Judaism, Christianity, Hinduism, Buddhism, or any other. Find three books on religion in general and skim them quickly until you find the main facts about the subject. Then write down five facts you learned about the religion you selected.

Social Studies Skills

Reading a Time Line

Information and data are often organized according to when different events occurred. The battles of the Civil War, World War I and World War II can be organized in this fashion. Indeed much of information of an historical nature throughout the field of social studies can be presented in this way. When information is put together in a chart in chronological order (ordered by dates), the chart is called a time line. Look at the time line on the formation of political parties on page 192 and answer the following questions:

1. Over a what year period does the time line extend?
2. The distance between horizontal lines on the time line represent how many years?
3. Which started earlier, the Republican Party or the Democratic Party?
4. If you were reading an updated time line in the year 2010, what might have changed?

Activities and Projects

1. Research a party organization in your state or city. Visit the party headquarters if possible, and find out about its structure, its activities, and how it works with the national party organization. Ask about the main problems it faces in your area, and in which activities you and your classmates could become involved. Write a short report and present your findings to your class.
2. Stage a class debate on the following topic: Resolved—The two-party system in the United States shall be centered around one party called the Conservatives and the other called the Liberals.
3. Determine through research whether your state is predominantly controlled by Democrats or by Republicans. Do this by finding out how many years out of the last twenty-five each party has controlled the state legislature and how many years each party has controlled the governorship. Write a short report.
4. Try to determine whether the city (or county) in which you live is controlled by Democrats or Republicans. List the reasons for your conclusion.
5. Invite an election official to discuss political party participation in your county or plan a panel discussion of local party leaders focusing on community issues.

Social Studies Skills (Answers)
1. The time line covers a 205 year period (1787–1992).
2. The distance between the horizontal lines represents ten years.
3. The Democratic Party formed earlier, in 1824. (Some students may confuse the National Republican Party with the Republican Party, which formed later.)
4. Answers will vary. The Democratic and Republican parties will most likely dominate the time line, although new third parties, based on environmental or social issues, may arise.

CHAPTER INTRODUCTION

Instructional Objectives
By the end of the chapter students should be able to:
- Characterize the nature of public opinion.
- Describe how public opinion is measured.
- Discuss the factors that affect public opinion.
- Identify the purposes and goals of interest groups.
- Describe the types of interest groups.
- Explain the various strategies used by interest groups to affect public policy.

Using the Keynote
Begin by having a volunteer read aloud the quotation from Franklin D. Roosevelt. Then encourage discussion by posing questions such as these: What is public opinion? How is it expressed? In what sense does public opinion sustain a government? Do you believe a government truly cannot be better than the public opinion that sustains it? Why or why not?

Introducing the Chapter
Let another volunteer read the brief Introduction to the rest of the class. Encourage the students to discuss and comment on the content: Does this Introduction change in any way your understanding of the Roosevelt quotation? If so, how? What are the responsibilities of individual citizens toward their government? How does the failure of citizens to accept these responsibilities affect the government? What are the responsibilities of the government toward citizens, both as groups and as individuals? What can happen if the government fails to fulfill those responsibilities? Encourage the students to present and support various responses to these questions.

Previewing the Sections

Section 1 Have the students page through Section 1 and discuss what they hope to learn from it: What subject is covered in this section?
Section 2 Let volunteers read aloud the section title and the headings in Section 2. Encourage the students to share their ideas about public opinion—what it is and how it is formed.
Section 3 Ask the students to page through Section 3, paying particular attention to the section headings, the figure, and the photographs. Then ask: What do they indicate about this section?
Section 4 Have volunteers read aloud the title, the main headings, and the Government in Action title in Section 4. Encourage the students to discuss what they anticipate learning from this section.
Section 5 Let the students glance through Section 5, noting especially the section title, the headings, and the photographs. Then have each student complete this statement: I anticipate that studying Section 5 will change my ideas about. . . .

CHAPTER 9

Public Opinion and Interest Groups

CHAPTER OBJECTIVES

To learn and understand
- The nature of public opinion and how it is measured.
- The many factors that affect public opinion.
- The purposes and goals of interest groups and their many different types.
- The various strategies used by interest groups to affect public policy.

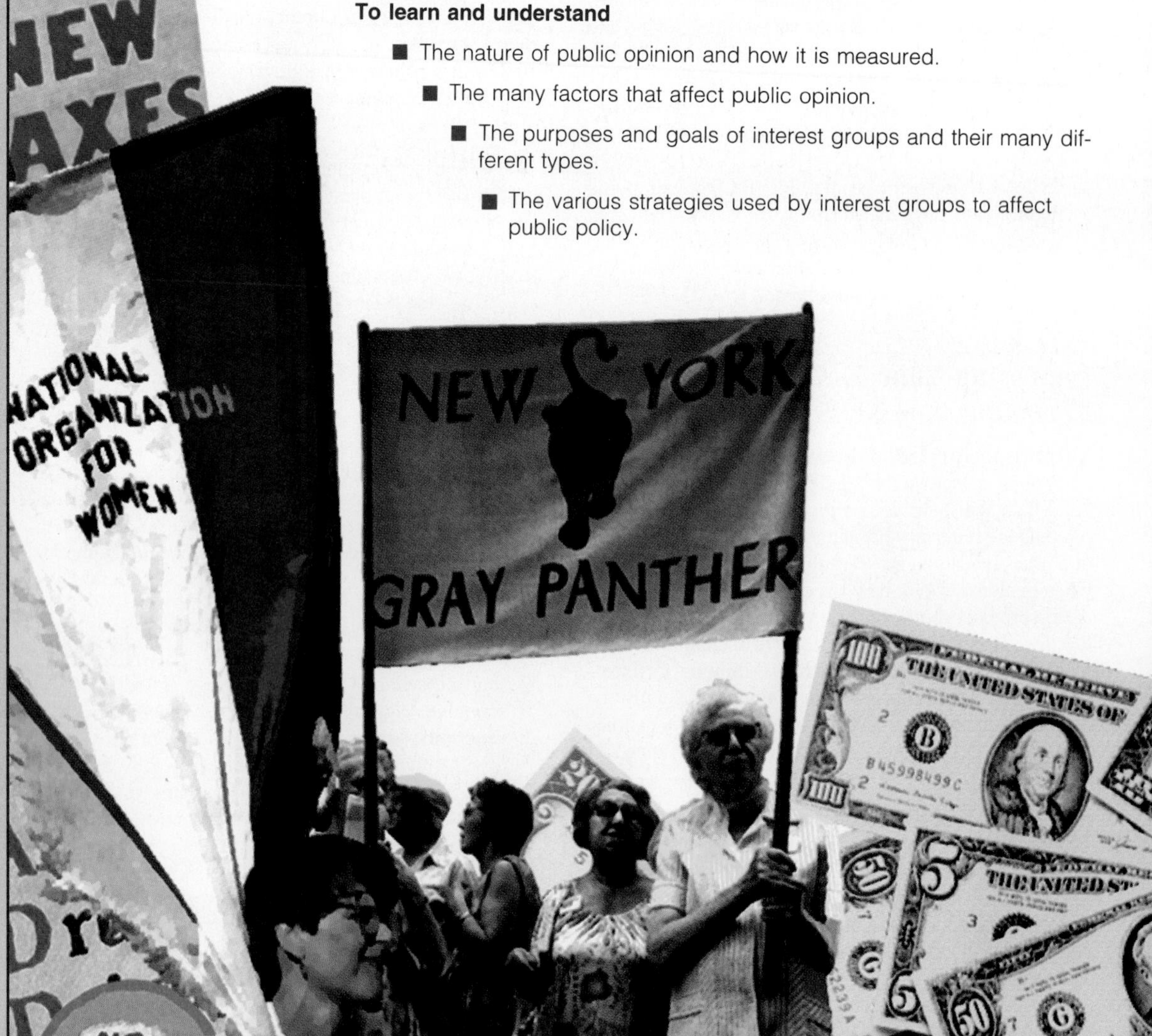

West's American Government Assignment Guide

Activity Sheets
Basic Concepts 9 *TRB* (Reteaching)
Enrichment Activity 9 *TRB*
Building Social Studies Skills 9 *TRB*

Quizzes
Chapter 9 Section 1 Quiz *TRB*
Chapter 9 Section 2 Quiz *TRB*
Chapter 9 Section 3 Quiz *TRB*
Chapter 9 Section 4 Quiz *TRB*
Chapter 9 Section 5 Quiz *TRB*

Tests
Chapter 9 Test A *TRB*
Chapter 9 Test B *TRB*
Chapter 9 Test Bank *TRB*
Chapter 9 WESTEST Computerized Testing

Social Studies Tool Kit Software
Chapter 9 Activity

Keynote

"A government can be no better than the public opinion that sustains it."

—— **Franklin D. Roosevelt (1882–1945) Thirty-second President of the United States**

INTRODUCTION

Above all else, the aim of a democratic government is to convert the will of the people into public policy. When President Roosevelt spoke the words in the quotation above, he was reminding both the people and the government of this. He was reminding them of their responsibilities to make our democratic system work. In order to translate the will of the people into public policy, citizens must form opinions and openly express them to their elected public officials. Unless Americans make clear to their senators, representatives, and state and local officials where they stand on important issues, these officials will never know what the people want. Only when the people's *opinions* are communicated effectively can they be translated into public policy.

SECTION 1

Definition and Measurement of Public Opinion

Preview Questions

- What is public opinion and why is it important in American politics?
- What is a public opinion poll and how does it work?

The public holds opinions—sometimes very strong ones—about a range of issues, from the ethics of capital punishment to the appearance of the latest fashion. In this chapter, however, we are concerned with **public opinion:** the individual attitudes or beliefs shared by a significant portion of adults about politics, public issues, and public policy. Notice that the definition implies that there is rarely a *single* public opinion. If everyone were of one mind about some question, it would not be much of an issue.

Public opinion is important in American politics because opinions can determine how government handles such issues as gun control, abortion, and the death penalty. Public opinion is the sum total of a complex collection of opinions held by many people. When you hear a news report or read a magazine article stating that "a significant number of Americans" feels a certain way about an issue, you are probably hearing that a particular opinion is held by a large enough number of people to make government officials turn their heads and listen. For example, in the 1990s, as polls began showing that Americans were concerned about environmental problems, many politicians began voicing strong public stances on environmental issues. Public opinion is most often cast in terms of percentages: 62 percent feel this way, 27 percent do not, and 11 percent have no opinion.

Remember that public opinion is limited to only those issues that are in the public arena, such as taxes, health care, social security, clean-air legislation, unemployment, and so on. The issue must be of interest to a significant number of people, and must be cause for some kind of political action, social action, or media coverage.

Measuring Public Opinion

If public opinion is to affect public policy, then public officials must be made aware of it. They must know how strongly people feel about the issues. They must also know when public opinion changes. Of course, the most common ways public officials learn about public opinion are through election results, personal contacts, interest groups, and media reports. The only *relatively* precise way to measure public opinion, however, is through the use of public opinion polls.

A **public opinion poll** is a numerical survey of the public's opinion on a particular topic at a particular moment. Because a poll cannot, of course, survey the entire population, polls are based on scientific polling tech-

SECTION 1

Points to Stress
- The definition of public opinion.
- Public opinion's importance to the American political system.
- The definition of public opinion poll.
- The method of conducting a public opinion poll.

Kickoff Activity
Have the students read the section title; then ask them to write their own definitions of the term *public opinion*. After everyone has finished writing, ask several volunteers to share their definitions with the rest of the class.

Working with the Preview Questions
Let volunteers read these study questions aloud, and encourage the students to discuss what they already know in response. Then ask the students to suggest other specific questions they hope to have answered as they study Section 1; record these questions on the chalkboard, and return to them at the conclusion of the section.

Teaching Strategies

Introduction
Assign the students to read the section introduction independently. Then encourage them to discuss the introduction by posing questions such as these: When—and how—does an idea or attitude become public opinion? Do you think there are two versions of public opinion—official and unofficial? If so, whose opinions are not included in the official version? If not, how are the opinions of people from every group included in the official version?

Discussion Starter
Encourage the students to discuss the means by which public opinion poll samples are formed: How do you imagine the people included in a sample are chosen? Do you think you—or any of your family members—could ever be included in a sample? Why or why not?

Discussion Starter
Guide the students in discussing the problems with straw polls: What general segment of the population are you most likely to find in shopping centers? How would their responses differ from those of other citizens? Who is most likely to respond to mail-in polls? Are people who are uninterested in an issue or who have not yet formed an opinion likely to respond? How does this lack affect the results of the poll?

Discussion Starter
Ask questions such as these to stimulate discussion of biased samples: What other approaches—in addition to that used by the *Literary Digest*—might produce biased samples? Why do you think some polls draw upon biased samples? Is the selection of a biased sample ever intentional? Why?

Enrichment
Ask two small groups of volunteers to research Gallup and Roper. Researchers should gather information about the individual, the establishment of his polling organization, and the development and current status of that organization. Have the members of each group share their findings in brief oral reports to the rest of the class.

Caption Answer *Public opinion* is the individual attitudes or beliefs shared by a significant portion of adults about politics, public issues, and public policy,

Multidiscipline Strategies

Math Have students conduct a public opinion poll. Students first should brainstorm potential topics, and after that should develop questions. Records need to be kept on the demographics of each respondent so that the poll results can be evaluated. A good place to start is within the school; students can break down the respondents by class (freshman, sophomore, etc.) and faculty, and gender. This is a good opportunity to incorporate basic math skills. The percentages of each who answered should be tabulated and represented in graph, table, or chart form. Students need to review the results and consider various reasons for the answers given.

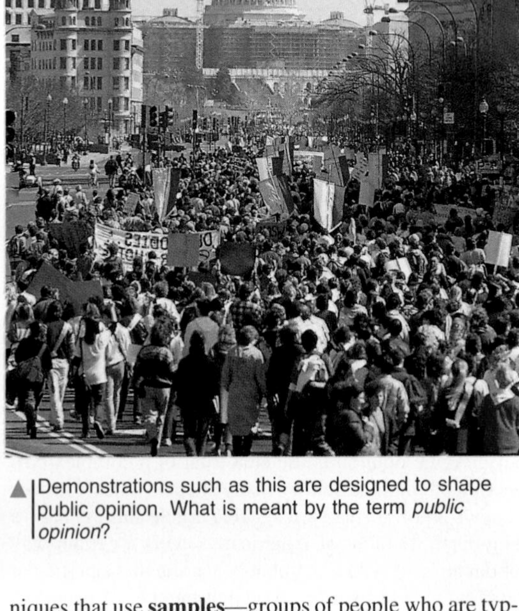

▲ Demonstrations such as this are designed to shape public opinion. What is meant by the term *public opinion*?

niques that use **samples**—groups of people who are typical of the general population.

Early Polling Efforts During the 1800s, one way to spice up a magazine or newspaper article was by doing a **straw poll,** or mail survey, of readers' opinions. Straw polls try to read the public's collective mind simply by asking a large number of people the same question. Straw polls are still used today: Some newspapers have interviewers who ask adults in shopping centers and other central locations to "cast ballots" on certain issues. Many newspapers and magazines still run "mail-in" polls but more and more of this type of polling makes use of telephone technology and "900" telephone numbers.

The major problem with straw polls is that there is no way to ensure that the opinions expressed are representative of the larger population. Generally speaking, such opinions usually represent only a small portion of the population. For example, opinions gathered at a yacht club might differ from opinions gathered at a thrift store. A survey of readers of the *Wall Street Journal* will likely differ from a *Reader's Digest* survey.

The most famous of all straw-polling errors took place in the *Literary Digest* in 1936. The magazine sent out millions of postcard ballots for the purpose of predicting the presidential election outcome. The *Digest* predicted that Alfred Landon would easily defeat incumbent Franklin D. Roosevelt. Instead, Roosevelt won by a landslide.

How did the magazine go so wrong? The *Digest* had drawn a **biased sample**, one which did not accurately represent the population. Its editors had sent mail-in cards to citizens whose names appeared in telephone directories, to its own subscribers, and to automobile owners—in all a staggering 2,376,000 people. In this mid-Depression year of 1936, however, people who owned a car or a telephone or who subscribed to the *Digest* were certainly not representative of the majority of Americans. The vast majority of Americans were on the opposite end of the socioeconomic ladder. Despite the enormous number of people surveyed, the sample was unrepresentative and consequently inaccurate.

Several newcomers to the public opinion poll industry, however, did predict the Roosevelt landslide victory. These organizations are still at the forefront of the poll-taking industry: the Gallup poll of George Gallup and Roper Associates, founded by Elmo Roper.

Sampling How can interviewing a small sample of 1,500 to 2,000 voters possibly indicate what *millions* of voters think? Clearly, the sample must be representative of all the voters in the population. A sample must consist of a group of people who are *typical* of the general population, so that, if the sample is properly selected, the opinions of those in the sample will be representative of the opinions held by the population as a whole. If the

TEACHING CITIZENSHIP SKILLS AND RESPONSIBILITIES

Read

Introduce this feature by encouraging the students to discuss their own experiences with the opinion and editorial pages of newspapers and magazines: Do you read the letters on these pages? Why or why not? If so, what kinds of opinions have you seen expressed there? Have you ever written a letter of opinion to a newspaper or magazine? If so, what prompted your letter? If not, why not? After this introductory discussion, let volunteers take turns reading Citizenship Skills and Responsibilities to the rest of the class.

Discuss

You may want to stimulate discussion by posing questions such as these: How is writing a letter to the editor similar to writing an essay for your English class? How is it different? Why is knowing the purpose of your letter an essential first step? What kinds of mistakes can you avoid by doing research—even if you are already reasonably certain of your facts? Does it really matter if your letter isn't neat or if it contains one or two errors in grammar or spelling? Why or why not?

Analyze and Apply

Ask all the students to bring to class letters to the editor printed in newspapers and magazines. Then let the students work in small groups to analyze the content of the letters. Encourage the group members to work together in revising any letters they consider unclear, inaccurate, or failing in a sense of fair play and justice. (You may want to have the students work in these same groups to write and revise their own letters as directed in Taking Action.)

Review

To help the students review Citizenship Skills and Responsibilities, ask these questions: What do letters to the editor express? What are three important points to remember in planning and writing a letter to the editor?

CITIZENSHIP SKILLS AND RESPONSIBILITIES

Writing a Letter to the Editor

Too often, we think that the only way to participate in politics is by voting, but there are many forms of political participation. One of the many ways in which public opinion is expressed in this country is by writing a letter to the editor of a newspaper or magazine. Letters to the editor are usually printed on the opinion and editorial (op-ed) page of the newspaper, and on the pages immediately following the table of contents in a magazine. Usually, newspapers and magazines print letters that best represent a variety of their reader's opinions. Use the following guidelines to help you compose your letter:

- **Know your purpose for writing.** Before you begin writing, be sure to know whether you are trying to inform, persuade, inquire, or complain.
- **Know your subject.** Research your subject before you write your letter so you can back up your opinions with facts.
- **Make sure your letter is neat and well-organized.**
- **Use precise language.** Don't try to impress anybody with your vocabulary. Avoid harsh, sarcastic language. The important thing is to convey your message.
- **Get to the point.** There is not enough space available for long-winded introductions or explanations. Plan your opening sentence carefully for the best initial impact. Deal with only one topic.
- **Use correct grammar and spelling.**
- **Appeal to your readers' sense of fair play and justice.** Challenge them to think about and respond to the issue.
- **Try to be optimistic and practical.** If your letter is in response to a problem, offer potential solutions.

For the final draft, type your letter on one side of the paper using double spacing. Sign your name and give your address and telephone number. You can use a pen name or initials if you wish.

TAKING ACTION

1. Select an issue affecting your school that you would like to write about for a local newspaper. Write a draft of your letter and read it to the class. Ask for constructive criticism from students and teachers.
2. Locate the address of the local newspaper and send it a neatly typed copy of your finished letter.

sample is not properly chosen, then the results of the poll may not reflect the ideas of the general population.

The most important principle in sampling is randomness. A **random sample** means that each person within the entire population being polled has an equal chance of being chosen. For example, if a poll is trying to measure how women feel about an issue, the sample should include respondents in proportion to the entire female population. That is, if 10 percent of all women in the United States are Hispanics, then 10 percent of the respondents should be Hispanic women. If 25 percent of the female population is between the ages of 25 and 40, then 25 percent of the sample must be in this age group.

Polls can be surprisingly accurate when they are conducted properly. Politicians, the news media, and the public place a great deal of faith in the accuracy of poll results. Policymakers use polls to determine how the majority feels on issues. Supporters of polling argue that it is a tool for democracy. In contrast, critics of polling think that it makes politicians reactors rather than leaders. Others argue that polls can discourage voters from voting if the numbers predict that their candidates will lose.

Problems with Polls The methods used by public-opinion pollsters have improved dramatically since the days of *Literary Digest,* but they are not entirely without limitations or faults. For example, the wording of questions can slant answers toward a certain bias. Consider a question about whether a new library should be built in town. One way to poll opinions about this issue is simply to ask, "Do you believe the town should have a new library?" Another way to ask the same question is, "Are you willing to pay higher property taxes so that the town can build a new library?" Undoubtedly,

Critical Thinking Skills
As the students evaluate the arguments for and against polling, encourage them to consider and discuss other means by which members of the public might express their opinions. For example, some have suggested Congressional mailings as a method of gathering opinions. What advantages and disadvantages might be associated with this method?

misused, creating public opinion instead of measuring it.
5. Sampling error is the difference between what the sample results show and what the result would be if the entire population were interviewed.
6. Answers will vary, e.g., supporters of polling argue that polls serve democracy by providing a link between the people's opinions and those who represent them. Those who criticize polls believe that politicians find out what people believe, and then make up a political campaign based on those opinions.

SECTION 2

Points to Stress
- The definition of *political socialization.*
- Political socialization agents.
- The difference between formal and informal socialization.
- The process of political socialization and the influences involved.

Kickoff Activity
Have the students work independently to list at least five factors that have affected their own political opinions. Then encourage the students to share, compare, and discuss their written lists.

Reteaching Strategies
1. Work with groups of students to discuss answers to the questions they posed at the beginning of the section in Working with the Preview Questions.
2. Have pairs of student work together to write their own definitions of these terms: *public opinion, straw poll, biased sample, random sample.*

Evaluation Strategies
1. Have the students write their answers to the Section 1 Review questions.
2. Have the students take the Section 1 Quiz found in the *TRB.*

Section 1 Review (Answers)
1. Public opinion is the individual attitudes or beliefs shared by a significant portion of people about politics, public issues, and public policy.
2. The major problem with early efforts is that the samples were not representative of the entire population.
3. A sample must consist of a group of people who are typical of the general population. Samples must be random, which means that each person within the entire population being polled has an equal chance of being chosen.
4. The questions can be biased or reduce complex issues to simple yes or no answers. They can also be

depending on how the question is phrased, the poll results will differ.

Another criticism is that polls often reduce complex issues to simple "yes" or "no" questions. For example, if asked whether or not they favor aid to foreign countries, the answer might need more explanation than a "yes" or "no." Responses could vary according to the recipient country, or the purpose or type of aid. The poll would nonetheless force respondents into a "yes" or "no" answer that does not necessarily reflect their true feelings. Quite simply, opinion polls can be biased and must be interpreted with care.

Public opinion polls can also be misused. Instead of measuring public opinion, they can end up creating it. For example, in order to gain popularity, a candidate might claim that all the polls show he or she is ahead. People who want to support the winning candidate (rather than the candidate they believe in) may support this person despite their true feelings.

Some people also question polls' reliability. After all, drawing accurate random samples is a difficult process. The answers given to pollsters may not be reliable. Those interviewed may be influenced by the interviewer's personality or tone of voice. They may answer without having any information on the issue. They may give the answer that they think will please the interviewer. Any opinion poll contains a **sampling error**, which is the difference between what the sample results show and what the true result would be if everybody in the country had been interviewed.

Another problem with opinion polls of voter preferences is that they cannot reflect rapid shifts in public opinion, unless they are taken frequently.

Section 1 Review

1. What is public opinion?
2. What were some problems with the early polling efforts?
3. How does sampling work? How does random sampling relate to that process?
4. What are some of the problems with public opinion polls?
5. What does the sampling error of a poll represent?
6. **For critical analysis:** Explain why supporters of polling argue that it is a tool for democracy, and why critics of polling think that it makes politicians reactors rather than leaders. Then explain which opinion you agree with and why.

Section 2

Factors that Affect Public Opinion

Preview Questions

- What is political socialization and what are agents of socialization?
- What is the difference between informal and formal political socialization?
- How does the process of political socialization take place and what influences are involved?

When asked, most Americans are willing to express an opinion on political issues. Not one of us, however, was born with these opinions. Most views that are expressed as political opinions are acquired through a learning process called **political socialization**. This is a complex process that begins in early childhood and continues on through a person's life during which one acquires and develops political attitudes and beliefs.

Political Socialization

Most political socialization is informal, almost accidental, and other political socialization is formal. Informal political socialization usually begins with the family. Although parents do not normally sit down and say "Let us explain to you the virtues of becoming a Republican," children nevertheless come to know their parents' feelings, beliefs, and attitudes. Words such as *acquire, absorb,* and *pick up* perhaps best describe the informal process of political socialization.

Formal political socialization involves activities such as taking a government class in high school. Studies have shown, however, that most political socialization is informal. There is little evidence that formally learning about political views has lasting impact on people's political opinions. Rather, the strong early influence of the family later gives way to the multiple influences of school, peers, television, co-workers, and other influences. The groups of people who influence the political views of others are called the **agents of political socialization**.

The Importance of Family Most parents or caregivers do not deliberately set out to form their children's political ideas and beliefs. They are usually more concerned with the moral, religious, and ethical values of their offspring. Yet children first see the political world

Working with the Preview Questions
Let volunteers read these study questions aloud, and encourage the students to discuss what they already know in response. Then ask the students to use these questions as guides when they take notes on Section 2.

Teaching Strategies

Introduction
After the students have read the section introduction, ask a specific question about a current political problem in your city or state such as "What do you think should be done about the litter problem in our parks?" Let several volunteers share their opinions about the problem and its solution: How are the opinions of various students different? Why are they different? What has influenced the opinion of each student?

Critical Thinking Skills
Guide the students in analyzing this statement: Most political socialization is learned informally. Why is this the case? What are the implications of this fact?

Extension
Ask each student to write several paragraphs in response to these questions: Under what circumstances do you hear your family members discuss political issues? Are you usually directly included in these discussions? How do you feel you have been influenced by these discussions?

Discussion Starter
Poll the class to see how many students consider themselves affiliated with their parent's political parties. Encourage the students to discuss their reasons for accepting—or rejecting—their parents' political choices.

Discussion Starter
Encourage the students to recall events and activities from their earlier school experiences that have influenced their political attitudes.

Caption Answer Student answers will vary, but might include such influences as family, peers, school, celebrities, television, films, books, and so on.

Extension
Allow interested volunteers to interview your school's principal. Volunteers should ask her or him questions about the role of educators as it relates to political socialization. Does she or he feel it is the responsibility of the school to develop citizenship skills? Which citizenship skills would he like to see students acquire while attending your school? How well does he think the school accomplishes this task? Students should work together to summarize their findings in the form of a news story. This can be either in the form of a written news story as would appear in a newspaper, or they might wish to use audio or video tape recorders and produce a radio or television news story.

Political socialization begins in early childhood and continues through a person's life. What influences do you think help to shape a person's political viewpoint?

through the eyes of their families—the most important force in political socialization. Children do not "learn" political attitudes the same way they learn to ride a bike. Rather, they learn by absorbing their parents' everyday conversations and stories about politicians and issues, and by watching their parents' actions. They also learn by what their brothers and sisters say and do, and the kinds of situations in which their parents place them. Families play such a crucial role in political socialization because they dominate a child's early years in terms of time and emotional commitment. The powerful influence of family is not easily broken.

The family's influence is strongest when children clearly perceive their parents' attitudes. For example, in one study, more high school students could identify their parents' political party affiliation than they could identify any other of their parents' attitudes or beliefs. In most cases, the political party of the parents becomes the political party of the child.

Educational Influence Education is a powerful influence on an individual's political attitudes. From their earliest days in school, children learn about the American political system. They say the Pledge of Allegiance and sing patriotic songs. They celebrate national holidays such as President's Day and Veteran's Day, and learn the history and symbols associated with them. In the upper grades, children learn more about government and democratic procedures through civic education classes, and through student government and other clubs. They also learn citizenship skills through school rules and regulations.

The level of education a person has also influences his or her political values. For example, more educated men and women tend to vote and participate more often in politics, support civil rights and civil liberties, think that the United States should be active in international affairs, and show more knowledge about politics and policy.

The Mass Media The **mass media**—newspapers, magazines, television, and radio—also have an impact on political socialization.[1] The most influential of these media is of course television. Grade school children spend an average of thirty-two hours per week watching television, more time than they spend in academic classes. Television does not necessarily decrease the level of information about politics. It is the leading source of political and public affairs information for most people.

The media can also determine what issues, events, and personalities are in the public eye. When people hear the evening's top stories, they usually automatically assume that these stories concern the most important issues facing the nation. But by publicizing some issues and ignoring others, and by giving some stories high priority

1. The term *media* is the plural for the word *medium*. Thus *media* will always be used as a plural noun in this book.

Discussion Starter
Stimulate discussion of the impact of mass media on political socialization by asking questions such as these: Which mass media are most important in your home? Why? How do you feel you are influenced by these media? Do you think you are usually aware of their influence? Why or why not?

Enrichment
Divide the class into three groups. Ask each group to research the effects of media coverage on one of the following: the famine in Ethiopia, the Vietnam War, and the 1991 Persian Gulf war. Have the members of each group summarize their findings in a short written report, to be made available to other class members.

Cooperative Learning
Divide the class into four or five groups. Have the members of each group work together to list at least six specific steps citizens can—and should—take to make themselves careful and critical consumers of media information.

Discussion Starter
Encourage the students to discuss opinion leaders. You may want to pose these questions: Whom do you consider important opinion leaders in your state and community? Why? In your school community? Why? Do all the class members name the same individuals as opinion leaders? If not, why not?

Discussion Starter
Focus the students' attention on the fact that media coverage helps determine what people will talk and think about, and thus focuses the attention of politicians on specific issues. Ask the students: In what sense is this a cycle? To what extent do the media control the cycle? What can individual citizens do to control the cycle?

Caption Answer Student answers will vary. You might wish to encourage class discussion by asking the students to describe how public opinion was shaped by the media or entertainers on this issue and whether or not the media or the entertainers who brought the issue to the public's attention seemed to take a stand on the particular side of the issue.

▲ During the 1980s, a group of very prominent entertainers recorded "We are the World." This event, which was designed to raise money for famine relief efforts, also went a long way toward shaping public opinion on the issue. Can you think of a recent issue that has been brought to the public's attention by entertainers?

and others low priority, the media decide the relative importance of issues. They help determine what people will talk and think about, and which issues politicians will therefore act upon.

For example, due in part to a prolonged famine in Africa, millions of people, particularly Ethiopians, have died of starvation since 1982. The famine got little media coverage at first, and for several years little was done by the U.S. government to help. When the television networks finally broadcast dramatic film footage of corpses and suffering, they called attention to the tragedy. The United States and other Western countries began contributing food and money. The publicity led rock singers to collaborate on a record—''We Are the World''—which brought further public attention and more donations.

Likewise, television played a significant role in shaping public opinion about the Vietnam War, which has been called the first ''television war.'' Part of the public opposition to the war in the late 1960s came from the daily scenes and narrative accounts of destruction, death, and suffering. The war to free Kuwait from Iraqi occupation in 1991 also had extensive media coverage, though some critics feel that this coverage may have shown only the better side of the United States' efforts.

Clearly, the media play an important role in shaping public opinion. The *extent* of that role, however, is often debated. Some studies have shown that the media may not have as much power to influence the opinions of people as has been thought. Generally, people watch television and read articles with preconceived ideas (already established beliefs) about the issues. These ideas act as a screen to block out any information that does not fit with them. For example, if you are already firmly convinced that being a vegetarian is beneficial to your health, you probably will not change your mind if you watch a TV show that asserts that vegetarians live no longer on average than people who eat meat. Apparently, the media are most influential with those persons who have not yet formed an opinion about certain issues or political candidates.

Opinion Leaders Every state and community has well-known citizens who are able to influence the opinions of their fellow citizens. These people might be public officials, religious leaders, teachers, or celebrities. They

TEACHING BUILDING SOCIAL STUDIES SKILLS

Read
Begin by letting several volunteers share what they know or learned in section one about public opinion polls: What topics were the subjects of recent polls? Who takes public opinion polls? Who responds to them? After the introductory discussion, have a volunteer read How to Read a Public Opinion Poll aloud to the rest of the class.

Discuss
Encourage a discussion of the content by posing questions such as these: How can you find out who paid for a poll? Why is this information important? What is the significance of the sample? Why are the methods by which the interviews were obtained and conducted important to your evaluation of a poll? What examples can you suggest to support the idea presented in the quotation from Elmo Roper?

Analyze and Apply
Have the students work in groups to conduct their own polls. The members of each group should select a topic of interest to the school community and then design and conduct their own poll to identify public opinion on that topic. Ask each group to present its results to the rest of the class.

Review
Ask these questions to help the students review Building Social Studies Skills: Why are all poll results not equally reliable? What are at least three important questions you should ask yourself in evaluating any public opinion poll?

Practicing Your Skills
Student activities will vary. Skills 1 and 2 can be combined and presented as an oral report to the class. You might also wish to assign 3 as an essay assignment.

BUILDING SOCIAL STUDIES SKILLS

How to Read a Public Opinion Poll

We are flooded with information from public opinion polls reported to us by television, newspapers, and magazines. They claim to tell us a variety of things: whether the president's popularity is up or down; how people feel about government regulation; whether people feel more strongly about environmentalism than they did a few years ago; and who is ahead in the next presidential nomination.

As you are bombarded with this information, keep in mind that not all poll results are equally reliable. Before you believe what the poll is leading you to conclude, ask the following questions:

1. **Who paid for the poll?** If a poll is known to be sponsored by a particular candidate, interest group, or party, the results may be presented in a misleading way. Take this into account and look carefully at how the poll results are worded.
2. **Who was interviewed?** A poll should reveal something about the population sampled. The best samples are scientifically random samples in which everyone has an equal chance of being interviewed. As a rule, you should be skeptical of person-in-the-shopping-mall interviews that you might hear about on local television news. Almost certainly, the people in the mall are not an accurate cross section of all the people in the community. Shopping malls tend to attract younger, middle-class, and female shoppers.
3. **How were the interviews obtained?** By telephone? By mail? In person? Many pollsters think that people are less honest over the telephone than in person, but because telephone surveys cost less than person-to-person interviews, they are often used. Also be wary of mail questionnaires because only a small percentage of people, those who tend to have higher incomes, better jobs, and more education, complete and return them. They are therefore not representative of the general population.
4. **When were the interviews conducted?** If they were conducted a year ago, the results may be outdated. This is particularly true if a change has taken place that would cause people to feel differently.
5. **How were the questions worded?** Elmo Roper, a famous pollster, once said:

   > If you ask people about any subject that they've got very strong opinions on, how you word the question really doesn't matter. When they don't have convictions, how you ask the questions and in what sequence you ask them are critical. You can flip-flop the answers ten points one way or the other just because of a relatively subtle phraseology difference or the context in which you ask the questions.

6. **Be skeptical of raw statistics.** It is possible to use raw statistics to slant a story. Raw statistics don't take account of any biases built into the way the data were collected. For example, if only men were interviewed about their opinions on increased taxes to pay for a new stadium, the raw statistics would be suspect.

PRACTICING YOUR SKILLS

1. Look through at least three news or business magazines such as *Time, Newsweek, U.S. News and World Report,* and *Business Week.* Make photocopies of all of the opinion polls, then analyze them in terms of the following questions:
   a. How many individuals were polled each time?
   b. What percentage of the adult population does this represent?
2. Determine whether any of these opinion polls were done over the phone or by person-to-person interviews. Decide which of the polling techniques has the most credibility.
3. Watch the TV news for seven consecutive days. Write down the number of times the newscasters refer to the results of opinion polls. Can you tell by the statements concerning the polls whether the number of individuals polled was small or large? Can you determine whether the polls were done over the phone or in person? After answering these questions, decide how much credibility you wish to give to each poll result.

Cooperative Learning
Let the students form small groups in which to discuss the influence of peer groups on their political socialization.

Discussion Starter
Pose questions such as these to encourage a discussion of the influence of economic status on political socialization: In your experience, are Republicans generally wealthier than Democrats? If so, why do you think this is the case? If not, why do you think the association between wealth and Republicans is so generally made?

Extension
Ask the students to interview citizens in various age groups about their political preferences. Then have the students consolidate the results of their interviews and examine their findings for any correlations between chronological age and political preference.

Reteaching Strategies
1. Ask the students to work in small groups to review and compare their notes on Section 2. Encourage the students to make corrections or revisions in their own notes as necessary.
2. Ask each student to list, in order of importance, the four most significant influences on his or her political socialization.

Evaluation Strategies
1. Have the students write their answers to the Section 2 Review questions.
2. Have the students take the Section 2 Quiz found in the *TRB*.

Section 2 Review (Answers)
1. Political socialization is a complex process that begins in early childhood and continues through a person's life during which one acquires and develops political attitudes and beliefs.
2. Family, schools, the mass media, and peer groups.
3. The strongest influence is one's family.
4. Peer groups consist of friends, co-workers, and club or church members. Peer group pressure is any influence these people exert to get one another to conform to their beliefs.
5. Answers will vary, e.g., the political leaders control, to a certain degree, which events will receive media coverage. Also, the political tendencies of newspaper editors and reporters determine what gets reported. Further, if one major event is occurring in the world and another occurs a few days later, the press will typically not give equal billing to both simultaneously.

SECTION 3

Points to Stress
- The definition of *liberal.*
- The definition of *conservative.*
- The characterization of an ideologue and why they are rare in American politics.
- The role of self interest in motivating public opinion.

are those to whom others listen and from whom they draw ideas and convictions about various issues of public concern. These opinion leaders play a significant role in the formation of public opinion. Martin Luther King, Jr. was an example of a powerful opinion leader during the civil rights movement.

Peer Groups Once a child enters school, the child's friends become a major influence on his or her attitudes and beliefs. A **peer group**, which consists of a person's close friends, co-workers, club members, or church group members, is another factor in political socialization. Most of this socialization occurs when the peer group is actively involved in political activities. For example, your political beliefs might be influenced by a peer group with which you are working on a common political cause such as pollution control in your neighborhood or saving an endangered species. Your political beliefs probably would not be as highly influenced by a peer group with which you collect stamps or make pottery, though.

Economic Status and Occupation A person's economic status may influence his or her political views. For example, poorer people are more likely to favor government assistance programs than are more wealthy people. On an issue such as abortion, lower-income people are likely to be more conservative—i.e., be against abortion—than are upper-middle-class people (of course there are many exceptions). But in general, people in lower economic classes tend to identify with and vote for the Democratic Party.

Where a person works will also affect her or his opinion. Individuals who spend a great deal of time working together tend to be influenced by that group of co-workers. For example, labor union members working together for a company will tend to have similar political opinions, certainly on the issues of government involvement in labor. Individuals working for a nonprofit corporation that depends on government funds will tend to support governmental spending in that area. Business managers are more likely to favor tax shelters and aid to businesses than are people who work in factories. People who work in factories are more likely to favor a national health care program.

Age While it might appear at first that a person's chronological age should determine political preferences, apparently age does not seem to matter. There are, however, some differences: Young adults are a bit more liberal than more elderly Americans on most issues. Young adults tend to be more progressive on such issues as racial and sexual equality.

What little increased conservativism there may be on the part of older Americans may be explained simply by the fact that individuals maintain the values they learn when they first became politically aware. Forty years later those values may be considered relatively conservative. Additionally, people's attitudes are sometimes shaped by the events that unfold as they grow up. Individuals who grew up during an era of Democratic Party dominance will likely remain Democrats throughout their lives. The same will hold true for those who grew up during an era of Republican Party dominance.

SECTION 2 REVIEW

1. What is the process of political socialization?
2. Name four groups that act as agents of political socialization.
3. What is the strongest influence on a person's political socialization?
4. What does peer group pressure mean?
5. **For critical analysis:** Every year events occur in other countries that, if widely publicized, would shock deeply the American public. Yet only a small percentage of these events ever get publicized. What do you think determines which world events receive widespread media coverage?

SECTION 3

Categorizing Political Attitudes

Preview Questions
- What is a liberal?
- What is a conservative?
- What is an ideologue?

Most political attitudes are often labeled as either conservative or liberal. Indeed, political office holders and candidates frequently identify themselves as either liberal or conservative, or they are identified as such by the media. In the 1990s, some commentators have referred to certain politicians as ''post–cold war liberals'' and as ''neoconservatives,'' where the prefix *neo-* means ''new.'' While these terms may be hard to define, we know that they refer to parts of a political spectrum that go from the left (extremely liberal) to the right (extremely

Kickoff Activity
Ask each student to list at least six words or phrases describing his or her own political attitude. After all the students have completed their lists, encourage volunteers to share their ideas with the rest of the class.

Working with the Preview Questions
Have the students read and share their responses to these study questions. Remind the students they will learn more about these topics as they study Section 3; ask the students to be prepared to write their answers to these questions at the conclusion of the section.

Teaching Strategies

Introduction
Let the students read the section introduction independently. Then ask: Do you consider yourself a political liberal or a political conservative? Why? Encourage all the students to respond briefly; help the students examine the differences in their responses.

Discussion Starter
Ask the students to name at least three political leaders who are known as liberals and three who are known as conservatives. Then guide the students in discussing the policies and approaches each is known to support. (Assign students to research these issues, if necessary.) Why has each been labeled a liberal or a conservative? Does the label appear to be accurate? Why or why not?

Vocabulary
Ask volunteers to recall the non-political definitions of *moderate* and *radical*. How do these general definitions help clarify the use of these terms in a political context?

Enrichment
Allow several students to work together in researching noteworthy radicals and reactionaries. Who are they? Within what organization—if any—did they work or are they working? What policies and actions do they support? Then have the students summarize their findings in one or two large posters to be displayed in the classroom.

Caption Answer Liberals are generally in favor of increased spending for social programs, while conservatists generally favor increased spending for defense programs.

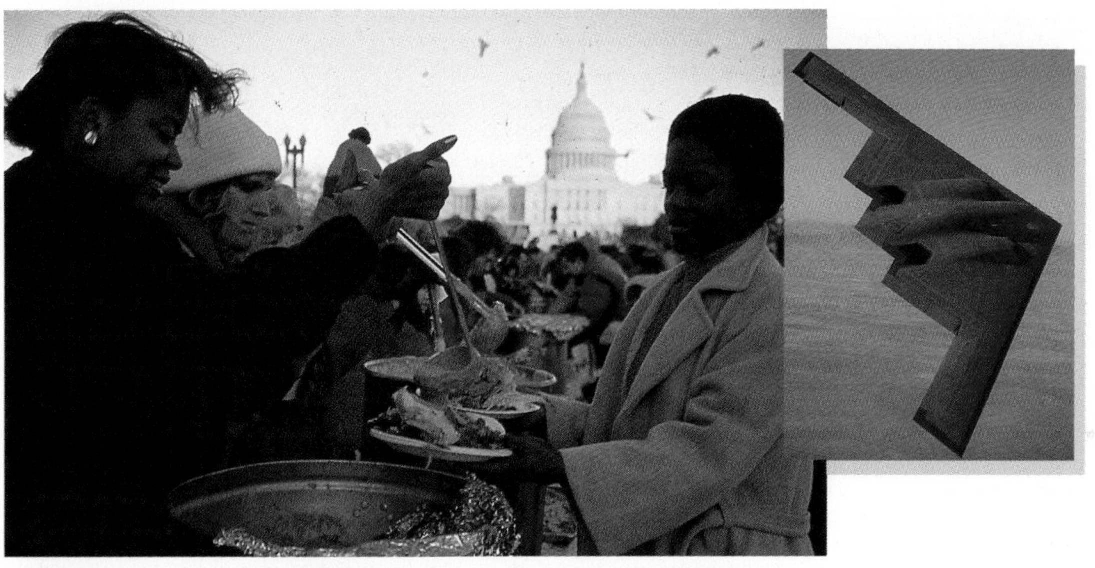

▲ The American political arena features a persistent conflict between the goals of liberals and those of conservatives. Which group would be more likely to support increased spending for social programs such as providing food for the homeless? Which group would be more likely to support increased defense spending for such programs as the construction of Stealth bombers?

conservative). The terms liberal and conservative have changed their meaning over the years, and will continue to change as political attitudes and ideologies evolve.

Liberals versus Conservatives

As was previously mentioned, the two most commonly used labels with respect to political and social ideals are liberal and conservative. **Liberals** have a viewpoint toward public policy that almost always values change. **Liberalism** generally supports the ideal that the national government should take an *active* role in solving the nation's domestic problems. Further, liberals believe that the federal government must look out for the interests of the individual against the majority.

Conservatives have a viewpoint toward public policy in which the goal is to *conserve* tradition and the ways of the past. Conservatives believe that the federal government is already too big and should not be expanded further. They think that the non-governmental sector of society—businesses and consumers—should be left more alone than has been the case in the past few years.

While it can be said that liberals generally support social welfare programs that assist the poor and the disadvantaged, conservatives are more in favor of limiting such programs. Liberals generally accept the notion of expanding the federal government, whereas conservatives favor giving state and local governments more control over their own citizens and finances. Liberals generally favor decreased defense spending; conservatives generally favor maintaining or increasing it.

The Left, the Center, and the Right

People who find their political views between the liberal and conservative camps are generally called **moderates**. Moderates rarely classify themselves as either liberal or conservative. On the extreme left is the **radical left**, radicals whose followers are willing to work against the established political agencies to reach their goals. They may even accept or advocate the use of violence or overthrowing the government in order to obtain those goals.

On the extreme right are the **reactionaries**, who resist change much more strongly than do either moderates or conservatives. Reactionaries not only do not want society to change, they are willing to actively fight against social change in order to return to the values and social systems they believe existed in the past. Like the radical left, reactionaries may even resort to violence to achieve their goals.

Extension
Have three or four students draw a large political spectrum chart on a sheet of butcher paper. Then allow each student to write his or her name on the chart, choosing a location to indicate his or her own political attitude.

Discussion Starter
Encourage the students to compare the political attitudes of the class with those of Americans in general, according to the current Gallop poll results. (The students may refer to the political spectrum chart on which they wrote their names.) How do you explain the similarities or differences between the attitudes of your class and those of the population in general?

Figure Answer Most Democrats and Republicans tend toward the center of the spectrum.

This figure content is also featured on *West's American Government Videodisc* (see the index found in the *TRB*) and is available in the transparency package.

Discussion Starter
Guide the students in discussing ideologues: Are you an ideologue? Why or why not?

Vocabulary
Ask the class: What is self-interest? Why is self-interest such a powerful motivator?

Reteaching Strategies
1. Work with small groups of students to review the meanings of these terms: *liberal, conservative, moderate.* Be sure each group member can define those terms in his or her own words.
2. Ask each student to write a short paragraph describing his or her own political attitudes.

Evaluation Strategies
1. Have the students write their responses to the Preview Questions at the beginning of the section.
2. Have the students write their answers to the Section 3 Review questions.
3. Have the students take the Section 3 Quiz found in the *TRB.*

Section 3 Review (Answers)
1. Liberalism is a belief that the national government should take an active role in solving the nation's domestic problems. Liberals feel that the federal government must look out for individual interests against the majority. Conservatives believe that the federal government is already too big and should not be expanded further. They think businesses and consumers should be left alone by government.
2. People who hold very strong political opinions.
3. Answers will vary, e.g., the labels provide us with a means of comparison. They provide us with a way to look at and measure various points of view. If, however, no mutually agreed-upon definition of these two terms is used, their application loses any comparative value.

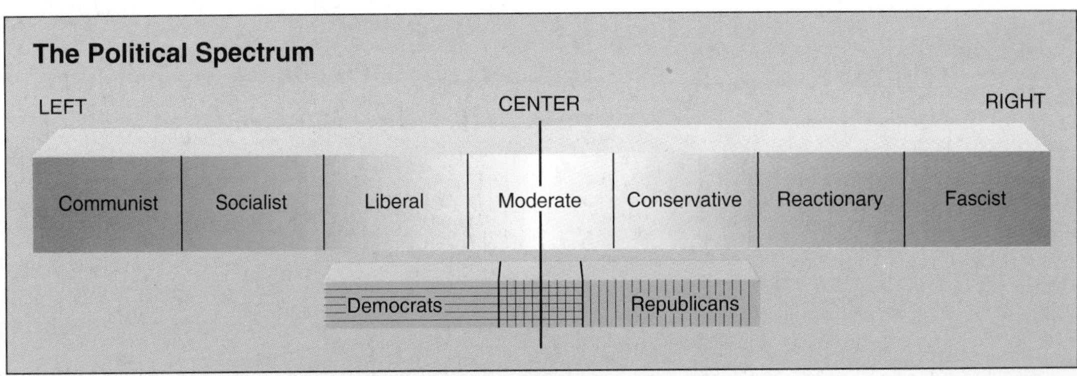

▲ FIGURE 9–1 **The Political Spectrum.** The figure above shows the political spectrum from the left to the right. Where do most Democrats and Republicans fall on this scale?

Look at the diagram of the political spectrum shown in Figure 9–1.

Democrats and Republicans fit somewhere in between liberals and conservatives, although generally Democrats tend to be liberal and Republicans conservative. There are, however, Democrats who are more conservative than certain liberal Republicans. Both radicals (extreme left) and reactionaries (extreme right) favor extreme and immediate change and may be willing to use violence.

The Average American versus the Ideologues

Most Americans, when asked, can typically identify themselves as liberal, conservative, or somewhere in between. Surprisingly enough, however, more people identify themselves as moderates than either liberals or conservatives. The Gallup polling organization, along with the *New York Times* and CBS News, routinely ask individuals what their ideological self-identification is. During the last two decades, between 35 to 50 percent of those polled have considered themselves moderate, between 17 and 21 percent have considered themselves liberal, and between 26 and 33 percent have considered themselves conservative. (The remainder held no opinion.)

Many Americans consider individuals who are extremely liberal or extremely conservative to be **ideologues**, people who hold very strong political opinions. Most Americans, however, are not interested in *all* political issues, and have a mixed set of opinions that do not fit under a conservative or liberal label. Research shows that only about 10 percent of Americans could conceivably be identified as ideologues. The rest of the population looks at politics more in terms of party lines—Democratic or Republican—or from the viewpoint of their own economic well-being.

Ideology versus Self-Interest

Public opinion polls do certainly show that political issues are not as important to people as the problems that impose themselves on their daily lives. In other words, it is one thing to support more aid to the poor if you in fact are poor; it is quite another if you are extremely well off. It is one thing to support increased government funding for long-term medical care if you are a bedridden elderly person. It is quite another to support such a political program if you are young, healthy, and making a high income.

Some researchers have determined that self-interest is a great motivator of public opinion. Individuals who have suffered at the hands of a criminal often express harsh opinions about issues such as capital punishment or building more prisons. People who have been suddenly laid off will often express negative opinions about the current president's ability to manage the economy.

In any event, the evidence suggests that the majority of Americans hold the strongest political convictions about issues which have a direct effect on their own lives.

SECTION 3 REVIEW

1. How do liberals differ from conservatives?
2. What kinds of people are considered ideologues?
3. **For critical analysis:** Of what use are the labels *conservative* and *liberal*?

SECTION 4

Points to Stress

- The definition of *interest group.*
- The purposes of interest groups in American politics.
- Differences between political parties and interest groups.
- The various types of interest groups.

Kickoff Activity

Write these questions on the chalkboard: What is an interest group? What examples of interest groups can you list? Give the students four or five minutes to write their responses to the questions. Let volunteers read their responses aloud, and remind the students that they will learn more about interest groups as they study Section 4.

Working with the Preview Questions

Ask volunteers to read these study questions to the rest of the class. Then have the students look through the section text, noting the headings that indicate answers to these questions. Remind the students to keep these questions in mind as they read Section 4.

Teaching Strategies

Introduction

Let a volunteer read the section introduction aloud. Then encourage discussion by posing these questions: What are your own particular interests? What are the interests of your parents or other family members? What formal associations do you and your family members have? What are your informal associations?

SECTION 4

Interest Groups

Preview Questions

- What is an interest group? What purposes do interest groups serve in American politics?
- How do interest groups differ from political parties?
- What are the various types of interest groups?

Every single one of us has interests we want represented in government: Farmers want higher prices for their products; young people want good educational opportunities; environmentalists want clean air and water; the homeless want programs for food and shelter; and criminals want fair trials. Throughout our nation's history, organizing to protect these interests has been a natural part of democracy. As the French political observer Alexis de Tocqueville wrote in his often-cited book *Democracy in America* (1835), Americans have a tendency to form "associations," and have perfected "the art of pursuing in common the object of their common desires." The old adage "there is strength in numbers" is true in American politics. The right to organize groups is even protected by the Constitution, which guarantees people the right "peaceably to assemble, and to petition the Government for redress of grievances." The Supreme Court has defended this important right over the years.

Defining Interest Groups

To define an interest group seems simple enough. *Interest* refers to objectives and policy goals that people have in common; a *group* is an accumulation of people. An **interest group** is therefore an organization of people sharing common objectives who actively attempt to influence government policymakers through direct and indirect methods. They are also called **pressure groups**, which refers to their attempts at putting pressure on government to act in their interests.

Whatever their goals—more or fewer social services, higher or lower prices—interest groups pursue them on every level and in every branch of government. On any given day in Washington, you could catch national interest groups in action. If you breakfasted in the Senate dining room, you might see congressional committee staffers reviewing testimony with representatives from women's groups. Later that morning you might visit the Supreme Court and watch a civil rights lawyer arguing over a discrimination suit. Lunch in a popular Washington restaurant might find you listening in on a conversation between an agricultural lobbyist and a

▲ In his book *Democracy in America,* Alexis de Tocqueville, wrote that Americans tend to form "associations" for "pursuing in common the object of the common desires". What did he mean?

▲ Molly Yard, shown here, is the former president of the National Organization for Women, one of many interest groups that can be found in our nation's capital. What is meant by the term *interest group?*

Vocabulary

Ask the students to consider the terms *interest group* and *pressure group.* Are there any differences in denotation? What are the differences in connotation? Who is likely to use each term? Why?

Enrichment

Ask the students to consider the description of national interest groups in action: What does this tell you about how interest-group representatives work to achieve their goals?

Caption Answer Student answers will vary. You might wish to encourage class discussion by asking students whether or not the American tendency to form associations is a result of our democratic system, which requires plurality to affect change.

Caption Answer An interest group is an organization of people who share common objectives and actively attempt to influence government policy relating to those objects.

Discussion Starter
Guide the students in considering and discussing each of the listed purposes served by interest groups: Do you think interest groups should be serving this purpose? Why or why not?

Discussion Starter
Help the students consider the differences between political parties and interest groups: Can you suggest some interest groups that might attract members of both major political parties? How do you imagine active party members function within that interest group? How do you imagine members of that interest group function within their separate political parties?

Critical Thinking Skills
Guide the students in analyzing the relationship between extremist interest groups and mainstream politicians: How can the two serve one another's needs? How might they come into conflict?

Enrichment
Ask a group of volunteers to locate a copy of the current *Encyclopedia of Associations* and to browse through it; then have them report to the class on the organization and the contents of the work.

Discussion Starter
Encourage the students to discuss what they know about the Chamber of Commerce and the National Association of Manufacturers: What evidence of their activities can you recall? What kinds of functions do they sponsor? Are any of your family members or acquaintances members of either group? If so, why do those people belong? How do they feel the groups benefit them?

representative. That afternoon you might visit an executive department, such as the Department of Labor, and watch bureaucrats working out rules and regulations with representatives from a labor interest group. Then you might stroll past the headquarters of the National Rifle Association (NRA), the American Association of Retired Persons (AARP), or the National Wildlife Federation (NWF).

Despite the bad press that interest groups tend to get in the United States, they do serve several purposes in American politics:

- Interest groups help bridge the gap between citizens and government and enable citizens to explain their views on policies to public officials.
- Interest groups help raise public awareness and inspire action on various issues.
- Interest groups often give specialized and detailed information to public officials that might be difficult to obtain otherwise. This information may be useful in making public policy choices.
- Interest groups serve as another check on public officials to make sure they are carrying out their duties responsibly.

How Do Interest Groups Differ from Parties?

It is important to remember that although interest groups and political parties are both groups of people joined together for political purposes, they differ in several important ways:

- Interest groups are often policy *specialists,* whereas political parties are policy *generalists.* Political parties are broad-based organizations that must attract the support of many opposing groups and consider a large number of issues. Interest groups, in contrast, have only a handful of key policies to push. An environmental group will not be as concerned about the economic status of Hispanics as it is about polluters. An agricultural group is more involved with pushing farm programs than it is with unemployment in the cities.
- Interest groups are usually more tightly organized than political parties. They are often financed through contributions or dues-paying memberships. Organizers communicate through conferences, mailings, newsletters, and other regular correspondences.
- A political party's main sphere of influence is the electoral system; parties run candidates for political office. Interest groups try to influence the outcome of elections, but unlike parties they do not compete for public office. Although a candidate for office may be sympathetic to or even be a member of a certain group, he or she does not run for election as a candidate of that group.
- Interest groups can hold extremist views, but can still serve to help politicians and the government choose policies and actions.

The Interest-Group Explosion

American democracy embraces almost every conceivable type of interest group, and the number is increasing rapidly. A look at your telephone directory, or even better, the Washington, D.C., directory, will give you an idea of the number and variety of groups. No one has ever compiled a *Who's Who* of interest groups, but you can get an idea of the number and variety by looking through the annual *Encyclopedia of Associations.*

Some interest groups have large memberships such as the AARP, with 32 million members. Others, such as the Tulip Growers Association, have as few as fourteen members. Some are household names that have been in existence for many years, such as the NRA, while others crop up overnight. Some are highly structured and run by a professional full-time staff, while others are loosely structured and informal.

The most common interest groups are private interest groups, which seek public policies that benefit the economic interests of their members and work against policies that threaten those interests. Other groups, sometimes called **public interest groups**, are formed with the broader goal of working for the "public good."

Business Business has long been well organized for effective action. There are hundreds of business groups now operating in Washington, in the fifty state capitals, and at the local level across the country. Two umbrella organizations that include most corporations and businesses are the Chamber of Commerce and the National Association of Manufacturers (NAM). In addition to over two hundred thousand individual businesses, the Chamber has four thousand local, state, and regional affiliates. It has become a major voice for the nation's thousands of small businesses. The NAM chiefly represents big business and has thirteen thousand members.

The hundreds of **trade and product organizations** are far less visible than the Chamber of Commerce and

Enrichment
Ask each student to identify and read about a specific trade or product organization: What is the purpose of the group? Who belongs? What are its major activities? Have each student write a one-paragraph summary to be shared with the rest of the class.

Extension
Go over figure 9–2 with the class. Allow volunteers to read the entries for each interest group profiled here. Then have students select and research an interest group of their own. Students should prepare a summary, such as those in this figure, for the interest group they choose. Student group summaries should include the name of the interest group, when the interest group was founded, a profile of its membership, a description of its activities, a budget if possible, and an address and phone number for the interest group. Allow volunteers to collect these profiles and to create a bulletin board similar to this figure for your classroom.

Profiles of Selected Interest Groups

AARP

Name: American Association of Retired Persons (AARP)
Founded: 1958
Membership: 32,000,000 working or retired persons 50 years of age or older.
Description: The AARP strives to better the lives of older people, especially in the areas of health care, worker equity, and minority affairs. The AARP sponsors community crime prevention programs, research on the problems associated with aging, and a mail-order pharmacy.
Budget: $322,000,000
Address: 601 E St. NW; Washington, D.C. 20049
Phone: (202) 434-2277

LWVUS

Name: League of Women Voters of the United States (LWVUS)
Founded: 1920
Membership: 110,000 volunteer women and men 18 years of age or older.
Description: The LWVUS promotes active and informed political participation. It distributes candidate information, encourages voter registration and voting, and takes action on issues of public policy. The group's national interests include international relations, natural resources, and social policy.
Budget: $3,550,000
Address: 1730 M St. NW; Washington, D.C. 20036
Phone: (202) 429-1965

NEA

Name: National Education Association (NEA)
Founded: 1857
Membership: 2,000,800 elementary and secondary school teachers, college and university professors, academic administrators, and others concerned with education.
Description: The NEA's committees investigate and take action in the areas of benefits, civil rights, educational support, personnel, higher education, human relations, legislation, minority affairs, and women's concerns.
Budget: $147,500,000
Address: 1201 16th St. NW; Washington, D.C. 20036
Phone: (202) 833-4000

NRA

Name: National Rifle Association of America (NRA)
Founded: 1871
Membership: 3,000,000 persons interested in firearms.
Description: The NRA promotes rifle, pistol, and shotgun shooting, as well as hunting, gun collecting, and home firearm safety. It educates police firearm instructors and sponsors teams to participate in international competitions.
Budget: $56,000,000
Address: 1600 Rhode Island Ave. NW; Washington, D.C. 20036
Phone: (202) 828-6000

SC

Name: Sierra Club (SC)
Founded: 1892
Membership: 565,000 persons concerned with the interrelationship between nature and man.
Description: The Sierra Club endeavors to protect and conserve natural resources, save endangered areas, and resolve problems associated with wilderness, clean air, energy conservation, and land use. Its committees are concerned with agriculture, economics, environmental education, hazardous materials, the international environment, Native American sites, political education, and water resources.
Budget: $35,000,000
Address: 730 Polk St.; San Francisco, CA 94109
Phone: (415) 776-2211

▲ **FIGURE 9–2 Profiles of Selected Interest Groups.** The above figure examines five interest groups and provides information about their membership, activities, and budgets. Which of the interest groups profiled has the largest budget? Which has the smallest budget?

Multidiscipline Strategies

Health There are numerous political issues relevant to the medical science profession today. Students should set out to see what the opinions of members of this profession are concerning issues like: AIDS testing, including doctors and nurses; euthanasia and living wills; parental consent abortion laws. The people in the medical profession are organized into groups in order to deal with issues such as those listed. Students should research the interest groups that serve the medical profession. Students might also look at interest groups other than medical interest groups that focus on health issues. As with all sensitive and controversial issues, teachers need to provide guidance during all stages of the exercise.

Figure Answer The American Association of Retired Persons has the largest budget of $322,000,000 yearly. The LWVUS has a budget of only $3,550,000.

Enrichment
Let a group of volunteers research the founding and development of the AFL-CIO. Ask these students to prepare a chart or time line showing the highlights of the AFL-CIO's history; display the chart or time line in the classroom.

Extension
Invite several union members or organizers to speak to the class. (If possible, have the students select the individuals who will speak, and have volunteers write invitations to them.) Ask the speakers to discuss their experiences with union membership, and encourage the students to ask questions.

Discussion Starter
Help the students consider the variety of agricultural interest groups: Why do you think so many different interest groups have been organized? What different purposes do you think the different groups serve? Do you imagine agricultural interests could be better served by a single interest group? Why or why not?

Discussion Starter
Encourage the students to share and discuss their own experiences with unions: Are family members or friends union members? If so, why do they belong? What benefits does union membership offer them? What attitudes toward unions have you heard expressed within your family or among adult acquaintances? What do you think explains these attitudes?

Caption Answer Organized labor currently makes up approximately 16 percent of the United States labor force. You might, however, wish to point out to students that the gains that labor unions make for their members often translate into gains for nonorganized labor.

NAM, but they are also important in seeking policy goals for their members. Trade associations run the political and alphabetical gamut from aerospace to angora goats, through builders and pickle producers, to trucking and theater owners. Trade and product organizations usually support policies that benefit business in general, although they may not agree on specific issues. For example, people in the oil industry work for policies that favor the development of oil as an energy resource. Other business groups have worked for policies that favor the development of coal, solar power, and nuclear power. Trucking companies would work for policies that would result in more highways being built. Railroad companies would, of course, not want more highways built because that would hurt their business.

Labor Interest groups representing labor have been some of the most influential groups in the country. They date back to at least 1886 with the formation of the American Federation of Labor (AFL). The largest and most powerful one today is the AFL-CIO (the American Federation of Labor-Congress of Industrial Organizations), an organization consisting of eighty-eight unions representing approximately 13 million workers. Several million others are members of non–AFL-CIO unions such as the International Brotherhood of Teamsters, the United Mine Workers, the International Longshoremen's Union, and the Warehousemen's Union.

▼ Labor unions have been some of the most influential groups in our nation's history. Here, the New York Health Care Worker's Union stages a protest against proposed pay cuts. What percentage of the United States labor force is made up of union members?

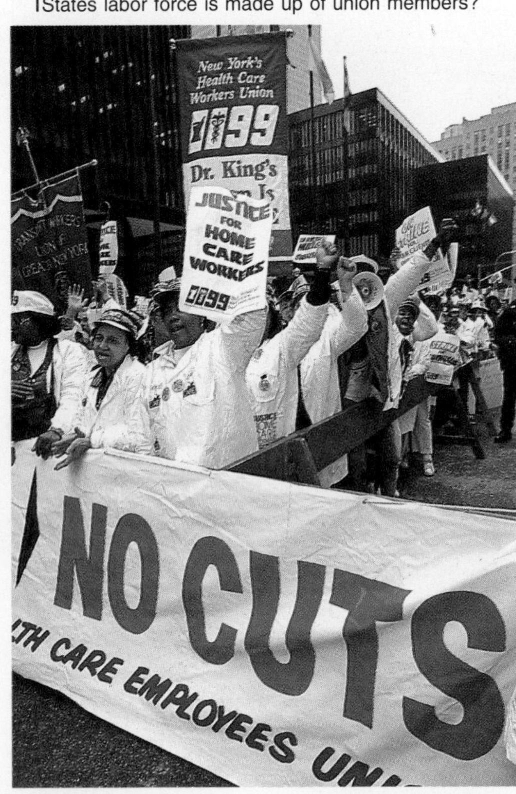

Like labor unions everywhere, American unions press for policies to ensure improved working conditions and better pay for their members, but there are also issues on which they compete with or oppose each other. For example, separate unions of bricklayers and carpenters may try to change building codes to benefit their own members even though such changes may hurt the other union. Labor groups also differ over such matters as laws restricting racketeering in unions and controls over union finances. They may also compete for new members. For example, in California, the Teamsters, the AFL-CIO, and the United Mine Workers have competed to organize farm workers. Today, these unions are competing to organize farm workers in Texas, Florida, and other states. Also, organized labor does not represent all of America's workers. It represents only 16 percent of the **labor force**—the total of those over 16 who are working or who are actively looking for a job. Workers who do not belong to labor unions sometimes have different interests.

Although unions had great strength and power in the late 1800s and the early 1900s, their strength and political power have waned in the last two decades. They are still a powerful lobbying force, however, and do work for their members.

Agricultural Groups Many groups work for general agricultural interests at all levels of government. Several broad-based agricultural groups represent nearly 4 million American farmers, from peanut farmers to dairy producers to tobacco growers. They are the American Farm Bureau Federation, the National Grange, and the National Farmers' Union. The Farm Bureau, with about 3 million members, is the largest and generally the most effective of the three mentioned. The Grange, founded in 1867, is the oldest and has a membership of about 450,000 farm families. The National Farmers Union comprises nearly 250,000 smaller farmers. Specialized groups, such as the Associated Milk Producers, Inc. (AMPI), also have a strong influence on farm legislation.

Enrichment
Have two or three volunteers research the founding and growth of Consumers Union: Why was it started? How did it grow? What are its major activities today? Let the volunteers give a short report to the rest of the class, using visual aids if possible.

Cooperative Learning
Divide the class into five or six groups, and have each group select and investigate a local consumer group. Then let each group select a representative who can present the group's findings to the rest of the class.

Extension
Help the students plan and conduct a survey of people 65 years and older: How many of the people belong to groups that promote the interests of the elderly? To which groups do they belong? Why do they belong—or why do they choose not to belong?

Enrichment
Invite a representative from the AARP to speak to your class. He or he should point out the benefits the AARP offers to seniors. You might also ask him or her to speak on those issues which the AARP is currently pursuing in Congress. Students should be told to prepare questions in advance for the speaker.

Discussion Starter
Encourage the students to discuss the various environmental interest groups: With which of the organizations listed here are you familiar? What other environmental interest groups can you name?

Enrichment
If any of your students, or if you yourself, are a member of any of the environmental groups listed here or of another environmental group, this person should speak to your class about the aims and activities of the group, the financial commitment he or she makes (if any), and why he or she chose to join this group.

Caption Answer The Farm Bureau is the largest agricultural group, with 3.3 million members.

Caption Answer Students should understand that the high cost of health care is a key issue for older citizens, as they are more likely than younger people to need health services.

▲ There are many groups that work to make government better meet the needs of agricultural interests. Here, tractors are parked on the Mall near the United States Capitol as farmers demonstrate in an attempt to bring their problems to the nation's attention. What is the name of the largest, most broad-based agricultural group?

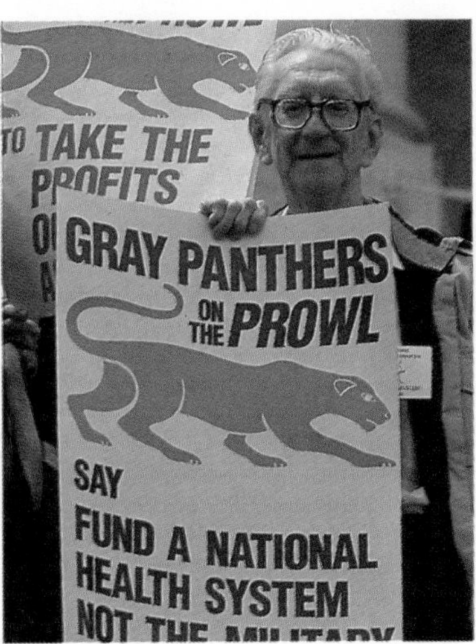

▲ The Gray Panthers is a group dedicated to promoting the interests of older Americans. Why would members of this organization be in favor of a national health system?

Like special interest labor groups, many product areas of agriculture have formed their own organizations. These include specific farm commodities such as dairy products, soybeans, grain, fruit, corn, cotton, beef, sugar beets, and so on. Like business and labor groups, farm organizations sometimes find themselves in competition. In some Western states, for example, barley farmers, cattle ranchers, and orchard owners may compete to influence laws concerning water rights. Different groups also often disagree over the extent to which the government should regulate farmers.

Consumer Groups Groups organized for the purpose of consumer rights were very active in the 1960s and 1970s. Some are active today. The most well-known and perhaps the most effective are those public interest consumer groups organized under the leadership of consumer activist Ralph Nader. (See the *Government in Action* feature on page 222.) Another well-known consumer group is Consumers Union, a nonprofit organization started in 1936. In addition to publishing *Consumer Reports,* Consumers Union has been influential in pushing for the removal of phosphates in detergents, lead in gasoline, and pesticides in food. Consumers Union strongly criticizes government agencies when they act against consumer interests.

In each city there are consumer groups that have been organized to deal with such problems as poor housing, discrimination against minorities and women, granting credit, and business inaction on consumer complaints.

Elderly While the population of the nation as a whole has tripled since 1900, the number of elderly has increased eightfold. Persons over 65 account for 13 percent of the population, and many of these people have united to call attention to their special needs and concerns. Interest groups formed to promote the interests of the elderly have been very outspoken and persuasive. As pointed out before, the AARP has over 30 million members. With 1,300 employees and eighteen lobbyists, it has become a potent political force. The Gray Panthers is another organization formed to promote the interests of the elderly.

Environmental Groups The current concern for the environment has led to the blossoming membership of established environmental groups and the formation of many new groups. They are becoming some of the fastest growing and most powerful interest groups in Washington. The National Wildlife Federation grew from four and a half million members to almost six million members in the last five years. Some of the other major environmental groups include the Sierra Club, the National Audubon Society, and the Environmental Defense Fund.

These groups have organized to support pollution reduction and control, wilderness protection, and natural

TEACHING GOVERNMENT IN ACTION

Read
Write the name *Ralph Nader* on the chalkboard and ask the students: Who is this? What attitudes and activities does his name bring to mind? After several volunteers have shared their responses, ask the students to read the Government in Action profile independently.

Discuss
Encourage a discussion of the Profile by asking questions such as these: What do you think motivates Nader? Do you think there are any potential dangers in a large network of public interest groups such as those of the "Naderite" organizations? Why or why not?

Analyze and Apply
All of the following are "Naderite" organizations and a part of Public Citizen, Inc.: Congress Watch; Critical Mass; the Health Research Group; the Freedom of Information Clearinghouse; the Tax Reform Research Group; Public Citizens Litigation Group; the Capitol Hill News Service; and the Fight to Advance the Nation's Sports (FANS). Have the students work in small groups to select and research one of these groups. What is the specific purpose of the group? Where and how does it function? Who belongs? How can one join? Have each group of students prepare a small chart summarizing this information.

Review
Ask the students these review questions: What is Public Citizen, Inc.? What industries and organizations have Nader and his Raiders challenged? Why?

Think About It (Answers)
1. Answers will vary, e.g., someone trying to make changes would likely face opposition from those who were benefiting from the way things already are. In order to overcome this obstacle, a person would need to enlist community support.
2. Answers will vary, e.g., helping the plight of the homeless—organizing food campaigns and petitioning the mayor to provide shelters; litter on the highways—organizing clean-up campaigns.

Enrichment
You may want to discuss—or invite other teachers to discuss—NEA and AFT membership among teachers at your school; encourage the students to ask questions.

Discussion Starter
Ask the students to identify and describe local church-related organizations and ethnic-related organizations with which they are familiar. What purpose does each intend to serve?

Reteaching Strategies
1. Let the students work with partners to write brief outlines of Section 4.
2. Working with small groups, encourage all the students to explain and discuss the importance of interest groups: How would the national government function without interest groups? Would the needs of in-

GOVERNMENT IN ACTION

PROFILE

Ralph Nader: Consumer Activist

Some of the most well-known and perhaps the most effective public interest groups were organized under the leadership of consumer activist Ralph Nader. Nader's rise to the top began when, as a young attorney, he wrote *Unsafe at Any Speed,* a critique of General Motor's purported attempt to prevent the public from learning detrimental information that linked its Corvair car to highway deaths. When General Motors hired a detective to spy on Nader, he sued and won a $280,000 settlement. Partly as a result of Nader's book, Congress began to consider testimony in favor of an automobile safety bill.

Nader became a recognized champion of consumer interests and used the settlement money to help start Public Citizen, Inc., a consumer advocacy group, as well as numerous other organizations protecting consumers' rights.

Nader and Public Citizen's staff, commonly referred to as ''Nader's Raiders,'' challenged not only the automobile industry but many other industries, as well as the Federal Trade Commission and Congress itself. The actions of Nader and his raiders have brought about changes in many industrial practices and a number of consumer protection laws.

Since the time when Public Citizen, Inc. was formed, Nader has turned over much of his income to other public interest groups he has formed or sponsored. In all, there are more than fifteen national ''Naderite'' organizations promoting consumer interests.

THINK ABOUT IT

1. What problems might someone trying to make changes in the community face? How could these problems be overcome?
2. Think of two consumer-related problems or issues you would like to change. How could you go about changing them?

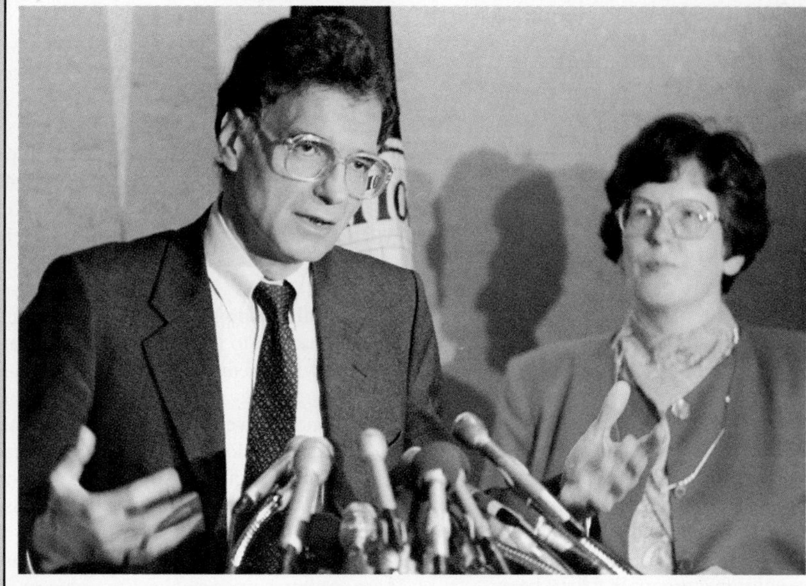

dividual citizens be met as well as they are now? Why or why not?

Evaluation Strategies

1. Have the students write their answers to the Section 4 Review questions.

2. Have the students take the Section 4 Quiz found in the *TRB*.

Section 4 Review (Answers)

1. Interest groups help bridge the gap between citizens and government and enable citizens to express their views on policies to public officials. They help raise public awareness.

2. Interest groups are often policy specialists, while parties are policy generalists. Interest groups are more tightly organized than political parties. The party works mainly through the elective process.

3. Any four groups mentioned in this section such as business, labor, consumer, and agricultural groups.

4. Answers will vary, e.g., it is possible that the goals of one group will conflict with those of another. For example, a person might be a member of the NRA, which *opposes* gun control, and also be a member of a local citizens crime control interest group, which, among many other things with which the person agrees, *supports* gun control.

resource and wildlife conservation. They have organized to oppose strip-mining, nuclear power plants, logging activities, chemical waste dumps, and many other environmental hazards.

Professional Groups Most professions that require advanced education or specialized training have organizations to protect and promote their interests. These groups are concerned mainly with the standards of their professions, but they also work to influence government policy.

Four major groups are the American Medical Association (AMA), representing physicians; the American Bar Association (ABA), representing lawyers; and the National Education Association (NEA) and the American Federation of Teachers (AFT), both representing teachers. Each has an impact on public policy in their areas. In addition there are dozens of less well-known and less politically active professional groups such as the Screen Actors Guild and the National Association of Social Workers.

Women's Groups Groups advocating women's equality have swelled with the women's rights movement. The National Organization for Women (NOW) is the largest women's group with almost three hundred thousand members. With a national board made up of national salaried officers as well as regional representatives, NOW is well organized. NOW has established the Legal Defense and Education Fund, which focuses on education and public information concerning women's rights.

Church-Related Organizations Many church-related organizations try to influence public policy in several important areas. The National Council of Churches, for example, has spoken out on civil rights, human rights, and other social issues.

Ethnic Organizations A number of ethnic groups in the United States have formed organizations to influence public policy at all levels of government. The National Association for the Advancement of Colored People (NAACP) lobbies for improvement in the political, social, and economic status of African Americans. Hispanics have a number of organizations to do the same. They include the Mexican-American Legal Defense and Education Fund and the League of United Latin American Citizens. Asian Americans have the Organization of Chinese Americans and the National Asian Pacific American Legal Consortium.

As America becomes more culturally diverse and economically complex, we will most likely see an even greater array of interest groups.

Section 4 Review

1. How do interest groups fit into American politics?
2. How does an interest group differ from a political party?
3. Name four different types of interest groups.
4. **For critical analysis:** One individual may belong to several different interest groups at one time. Is it possible that the goals of one group may conflict with those of another to which this same individual belongs? Explain.

Section 5

How Groups Try to Shape Policy

Preview Questions

- At which level or levels of government do interest groups operate?
- What are some of the methods used by lobbyists to influence public policymakers?
- What is the difference between the direct and the indirect techniques used by lobbyists?
- What are some of the indirect techniques that interest groups employ?
- How have government regulations affected lobbyists?

Interest groups operate at all levels of government and use a variety of strategies to steer policies their way. They sometimes attempt to directly influence the policymakers themselves, while at other times they try to shape public opinion, which indirectly influences policymakers. The extent and nature of their activities depend on their goals and their resources.

Direct Techniques

Lobbying, providing election support, and rating legislative behavior are some of the direct techniques used by interest groups.

Lobbying The term *lobbying* comes from the foyer or lobby of the legislature itself, where petitioners used to

SECTION 5

Points to Stress

- The levels of government at which interest groups operate.
- Methods used by lobbyists to influence public policy.
- Differences between direct and indirect techniques used by lobbyists.
- The indirect techniques that lobbyists employ.
- Reasons for negative perceptions of lobbyists.
- The relationship between government regulations and lobbyists.

Kickoff Activity

Write the following question on the chalkboard: Based on what you already know, what techniques do you think interest groups use to shape government policy? Give the students five minutes in which to write their responses; then ask several volunteers to share their ideas with the rest of the class.

Working with the Preview Questions

Let volunteers read these study questions aloud. Then have the students work together to write main outline headings, based on these questions. Have the students fill in their outlines as they study Section 5.

Teaching Strategies

Introduction

Let the students read the section introduction independently. Then let one or two volunteers respond to this question: Based on what you have just read, what do you expect to learn from reading the rest of this section?

Cooperative Learning Divide the class into five or six groups. Ask the members of each group to select a specific major interest group (such as the AARP or the NRA) and to research that group's recent lobbying activities. If possible, group members should identify a specific lobbyist and read about that person's background and current work. You may want to have the groups report their findings to the rest of the class.

Discussion Starter Encourage the students to discuss what they know about the NRA: What is the purpose of this organization? Who supports it? Why? How has this group become so powerful? Do you support the aims of the NRA? Why or why not?

Enrichment Ask one or two interested volunteers to research the status of the most recent drugs being tested—or made available—for the treatment of AIDS: How are interested citizens attempting to change the availability of these drugs? What methods are those citizens using? How effective do they seem to be? Let the volunteers report their findings to the rest of the class.

Discussion Starter Help the students consider the information lobbyists use: Why is the accuracy of the information they provide so important? What might happen if a lobbyist's information were inaccurate? How do you think lobbyists gather information?

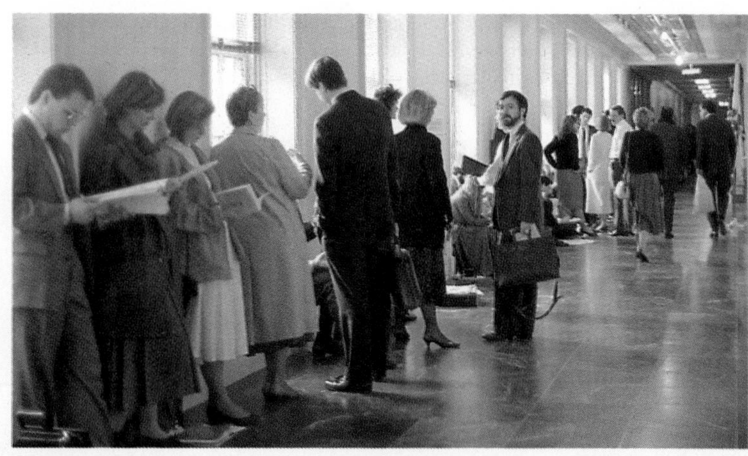

This part of our nation's capital is often referred to as Gucci Gulch because of the well-dressed lobbyists who wait here to meet and talk with legislators. What do lobbyists do?

Caption Answer Lobbyists work for organized interest groups and seek to convince legislators to enact legislation which promotes the interests of their particular interest group.

corner legislators to speak about their concerns. Today, **lobbying** means all the attempts by organizations or individuals to influence the passage, defeat, or contents of legislation and of the administrative decisions of government. A **lobbyist** is a representative of an organized lobby who handles the group's lobbying efforts. Most of the larger interest groups have lobbyists in Washington, D.C. These staffs often include former members of Congress or former employees of executive bureaucracies who are experienced in the methods of political influence and who ''know people.'' Many lobbyists also work at state and local levels. In fact, lobbying at the state level has increased in recent years as states play a bigger role in policy-making.

Lobbying is one of the most widely used and effective ways to influence legislative activity. For example, Mothers Against Drunk Driving (MADD) has had many lobbying successes at both the state and federal levels. (See ''Government in Action'' on page 226.) The NRA has successfully blocked most gun control laws, in spite of majority opinions in favor of them. An NRA brochure describes its lobby operation as ''the strongest, most formidable grass-roots lobby in the nation.'' The NRA, however, has been defeated in a few lobbying efforts by police and other gun-control interest groups.

While lobbying can be directed at the legislative branch of government, it is also directed at administrative agencies and even at the courts. For example, individuals stricken with Acquired Immune Deficiency Syndrome (AIDS) formed a strong lobby in the early 1990s to force the Food and Drug Administration to allow patients to use experimental anti-AIDS drugs before the drugs were fully tested. Lobbying can also be directed at changing international policies. For example, after the political changes that opened up Eastern Europe to business in the late 1980s and early 1990s, intense lobbying by Western business groups helped persuade the United States and other industrial powers to reduce controls on the sale of high-technology products, such as personal computers, to Eastern European countries.

Lobbyists use several methods to achieve their goals:

1. *Making personal contact with key legislators to make known the lobbyist's interests.* This is one of the more effective direct lobbying techniques. A competent lobbyist must be persuasive, have a good understanding of human nature, and present a strong case with accurate information. It is to the lobbyist's advantage to provide accurate information so the legislator will rely on the individual or interest group in the future.

For example, a lobbyist from the Sierra Club lobbying for clean-air legislation would need to be familiar with all aspects of the problem before contacting a congressional staff member. He or she must present accurate information, otherwise the Club's credibility and effectiveness would be damaged, if not destroyed.

Lobbyists also invite legislators to social occasions such as golf outings, cocktail parties, boating expeditions, dinners, and other events. They feel that communicating in a relaxed atmosphere is more effective. The extent to which the legislators would then feel obligated to help the lobbyists is difficult to gauge.

Critical Thinking Skills
Have the students evaluate lobbyists' practice of inviting legislators to social occasions: Who benefits from this practice? How? Are there groups or individuals who suffer as a result of this practice? If so, who and how? Do you think this is an appropriate method for lobbyists to use? Why or why not?

Discussion Starter
Ask the students to consider the information interest groups provide to legislators and other government officials: How can it be biased? Do you believe the biases are always unintentional? Why might intentional biases be introduced into the information? How can such biases be identified? Whose responsibility is it to identify biases in information?

Cooperative Learning
Let the students work together in groups of four or five; have each group write a profile of an effective lobbyist, noting specifically the personality traits and training that would be needed. Then let the groups share and compare their profiles.

Enrichment
You may want to have one or two interested volunteers research James Watt's service as Secretary of the Interior: Why did environmental groups oppose his appointment? What did he accomplish as Secretary of the Interior? Why did he leave, and who replaced him? Let the volunteers present their findings in a brief oral report.

Comprehension
Ask the students this comprehension question: How do PACs differ from interest groups?

2. *Providing expertise to legislators or other government officials.* Lobbyists often have knowledge and expertise that is useful in drafting legislation, which is a major strength for an interest group. Because many harried members of Congress cannot possibly be experts on everything they vote on, and therefore eagerly seek information to help them make up their minds, some lobbying groups do research and present their findings to those officials. For example, one of the major strengths of Ralph Nader's public interest organizations is their ability to provide accurate and normally reliable information about consumer issues.
3. *Offering "expert" testimony before congressional committees for or against proposed legislation.* A bill to regulate firearms, for example, might concern several interest groups. The NRA would probably oppose the bill and representatives from that interest group might be asked to testify. Groups that would probably support the bill, such as police or wildlife conservationists, might also be asked to testify. Each side would offer as much evidence as possible to support its position.
4. *Assisting legislators or bureaucrats in drafting legislation or prospective legislation.* Lobbyists are a source of ideas and sometimes offer legal advice on specific details.
5. *Following up.* Even after a lobbying group wins a legislative victory, the battle is not over. Executive agencies responsible for carrying out legislation can often increase or decrease the power of the new law. Lobbyists also often try to influence the bureaucrats who implement the policy. For example, beginning in the early 1960's, regulations outlawing sex discrimination were broadly outlined by Congress. Both women's rights' groups favoring the regulations and interest groups opposing the regulations lobbied for years to influence how those regulations were carried out.

Interest groups also try to influence who gets appointed to bureaucratic positions. For example, environmental groups lobbied unsuccessfully in 1981 to oppose the appointment of James Watt as President Ronald Reagan's first secretary of the interior, because they believed he was unsympathetic to the environmental movement and was not qualified for the job.

Providing Election Support Interest groups often become directly involved in the election process. Many interest group members join and work within political parties in order to influence party platforms and the nomination of candidates. They provide campaign support for legislators who favor their policies and sometimes urge their own members to try to win posts in party organizations. Most importantly, interest groups urge their members to vote for the candidates that support the views of the group. They can also threaten legislators with the withdrawal of votes. No candidate can expect to have support from *all* interest groups, but if the candidate expects to win, he or she must have support (or little opposition) from powerful interest groups.

The modern-day effort to get dollars into campaigns is through **political action committees (PACs)**, which are groups organized to collect money and provide financial support for political candidates. Interest groups funnel money through PACs to candidates whom they

Interested lobbyists look on as Congress conducts budget hearings. What particular types of skills do you think an effective, successful lobbyist must have?

Caption Answer Answers will vary, but students should understand that lobbyists should be personable, knowledgeable in their particular subject area, and assertive.

Developing Skills for the Information Age

Special interest groups are constantly presenting their views to the public. Have students scan electronic and print media for stories on special interest groups. Students should match the technique(s) used by the groups with those mentioned in the chapter. This activity will reveal how interest groups rely on the media to mobilize public opinion. Students should be encouraged to see how treatment and techniques differ based on different media sources. Summaries of the results should be shared with the class.

TEACHING GOVERNMENT IN ACTION

Read
Introduce this Government in Action feature by asking the students to discuss what they already know about MADD: Why was the organization founded? Who supports it? Are there local chapters? Who—if anyone—opposes the activities of MADD? Why? After this introductory discussion, ask volunteers to read the Case Study aloud to the rest of the class.

Discuss
Use these questions to help the students discuss the Case Study: After her daughter's death, what choices might Candy Lightner have made? Why do you think she made the choice she did make—and took such strong action? Why do you think so many parents were eager to support MADD? Why is MADD such a powerful force? What legal changes has MADD supported? Do you believe MADD has affected the attitudes of people across the country? If so, how? If not, why not?

Analyze and Apply
Ask the students to gather information about membership in MADD. Encourage the students to attend a MADD meeting or send away for MADD literature to learn more about the organization. Students should summarize what they learn in an oral report to the class.

Review
Ask the students these review questions: What is the purpose of MADD? Who formed the group? Why?

Think About It (Answers)
1. Even though the problem was even worse at times prior to 1980, it required a single individual to get mad enough about the problem to want to do something about it.
2. Obviously those who drink and drive might be against harsher legislation against drunk drivers because they might be dealt with more harshly by the police and the court system.

GOVERNMENT IN ACTION

CASE STUDY

Mothers Against Drunk Driving (MADD)

The formation of this interest group began with a tragedy. On May 3, 1980, Cari Lightner, age 13, was walking in a bicycle lane near her home in Fair Oaks, California. She was on her way to a church carnival when she was struck from behind by a swerving car. She was hit so hard that she was hurled 120 feet down the road. The driver of the car never stopped, but was arrested four days later.

The driver was drunk at the time of the accident. In fact, when he killed Cari, he had been out of jail on bail for only two days because of another hit-and-run drunk driving accident. Although he had been convicted of drunk driving and related offenses three times in four years, he had served only forty-eight hours in jail. The police told Candy Lightner, Cari's mother, that the driver would probably never go to jail because drunk driving was not considered a serious crime in California. The driver, in fact, never did go to prison, but served eleven months in a work camp and halfway house.

Candy Lightner was shocked and angry. After extensive research she found out that nothing effective was being done to keep drunk drivers off the road and that drunk drivers could literally ''get away with murder'' without fear of being punished. ''Death caused by drunk driving is the only socially acceptable form of homicide,'' she concluded.

Candy Lightner decided to do all she could to help other victims and to prevent such tragedies from happening again. She quit her job to form an interest group called Mothers Against Drunk Driving, or MADD. She began her campaign by convincing the California governor and legislature that stiffer penalties were needed for drunk driving offenses. She quickly gained the support of other parents who had experienced similar tragedies.

Once launched, MADD proved to be a powerful force. Members wrote letters, gave speeches, and issued press releases. MADD sponsored community-awareness meetings and educational seminars. They circulated petitions calling for state and federal action. They applied for corporate and foundation grants. They took their fight to Washington, D.C., where they held press conferences, lobbied, and urged stronger legislative action on drunk driving.

Now headquartered near Dallas, the organization has 383 chapters and 600,000 members. Since the founding of MADD, all fifty states have tightened their drunk driving laws. Media coverage, stiffer penalties and laws, and commissions and task forces to study the problem are all accomplishments of which MADD can be proud.

THINK ABOUT IT

1. Drunk driving has been a problem for many years in the United States. Why do you think organizations such as MADD hadn't been formed prior to 1980?
2. Who might be in favor of *not* passing harsher legislation against drunk drivers? Why?

Enrichment
Let interested volunteers identify the legislators included on the current Dirty Dozen list and the CWA's current "heroes" and "zeroes" lists. Ask the volunteers to present posters showing these lists; encourage the students to discuss why each legislator was included.

Discussion Starter
What do you usually think of when you hear or use the term *grass roots*? How is this image altered when you know that the grass-roots movement is being engineered by special interest groups? Do you think this is an appropriate activity for lobbyists and interest groups? Why or why not?

Discussion Starter
Help the students discuss the reactions of policymakers to opinions initiated by interest groups: How do you think the knowledge that a specific interest group generated a barrage of letters and phone calls might affect a legislator's response to the opinion expressed?

Enrichment
Ask several volunteers to research specific lawsuits brought by environmental groups in the last decade: What was the issue raised in each suit? How was the suit resolved? What was the effect of that resolution? Let the volunteers summarize their findings for the rest of the class.

Enrichment
Have two groups of volunteers research the successful opposition to the Bork nomination. Who opposed the nomination? Why? Why was the effort successful? Let the volunteers report their findings to the rest of the class; encourage the other students to ask questions and discuss their responses to the information.

think will benefit them the most. (PACs are discussed in greater depth in Chapter 10.) The number of PACs has grown astronomically, along with the amounts of money they spend on elections. Although campaign contributions do not guarantee that officials will vote the way the groups wish, it usually does ensure that they will have the ear of the public officials they have helped to elect. PACs have also succeeded in bypassing campaign-contribution limits, which has created the same type of "vote-buying" privileges that wealthy individual contributors enjoyed in the past.

The Ratings System Some interest groups try to directly influence legislators through their **ratings system**. They select legislative issues that they feel are important to their groups' goals and rate legislators on the percentage of times they vote favorably on that legislation. For example, one environmental group identifies twelve members of Congress whose voting record on environmental issues is unacceptable and labels them the "Dirty Dozen." The Communication Workers of America (CWA) label policymakers who take a position consistent with their own as "heroes," and those who take the opposite position as "zeroes." Needless to say, legislators do not want to earn membership on the "zeroes" lists of these groups.

Indirect Techniques

Interest groups also try to influence public policy indirectly through third parties or the general public. Such indirect techniques may appear to be spontaneous, but are equally well planned. Public officials also are often more impressed by contacts from voters than from lobbyists.

Shaping Public Opinion Public opinion ultimately trickles back to policymakers, so interest groups cultivate their public image carefully. If public opinion favors a certain group's interests, then public officials will be more obligated to listen and more willing to pass legislation favoring that group. This is often referred to as bringing grass-roots pressure to bear on officials, or mounting campaigns for the people back home. Such efforts may include television publicity, newspaper and magazine advertisements, mass mailings, and public relations techniques to improve the group or industry's public image. For example, environmental groups run television ads to dramatize threats to the environment. Oil companies respond to criticism about increased gas prices with advertising showing their concern about public welfare. The goal of all these activities is to convince both the public and the policymakers that the public overwhelmingly supports the interest group's position.

Mobilizing Constituents Interest groups sometimes urge members and other constituents to write letters or call government officials to show their support for or opposition to a certain policy. Large interest groups can generate hundreds of thousands of letters and calls. They often provide letter forms or postcards for constituents to fill out and mail. The NRA has successfully used this tactic to fight strict federal gun-control legislation by delivering a half a million letters to Congress within a few weeks. Policymakers recognize that such opinions were initiated by interest groups, but they are still made aware of an issue that is important to that group.

The Court System Achieving policy goals through the legal system offers another avenue for influencing the political process. Civil rights groups paved the way for litigation in the 1950s and 1960s with major victories in cases concerning equal housing, school desegregation, and labor market equality. Litigation is also used by environmental groups such as the Sierra Club. For example, an environmental group might challenge in court developers who threatens to pollute the environment. The legal challenge will force the developers to bear the costs of defending themselves and possibly delay the project. The next time, developers might be more willing to make concessions and avoid lengthy and costly legal battles. In fact, much of the success of environmental groups has been linked to their use of lawsuits.

Groups also try to influence courts indirectly by lobbying the Senate to support or oppose judicial nominees. For example, in 1987 nearly two hundred groups mobilized to support or oppose President Reagan's Supreme Court nominee, Robert Bork. Their actions resulted in the Senate rejecting Bork's nomination.

Demonstration Techniques Some interest groups stage protests to make a statement in a dramatic way. The Boston Tea Party of 1773, in which American colonists dressed as Native Americans and threw tea into the Boston Harbor to protest British taxes, is testimony to the fact that the tactic has been around for a long time.

In recent years, many groups have generated protest marches and rallies to support or oppose issues such as legalized abortion, busing, American support for the *contras* in Nicaragua, nuclear weapons, and government

Service Learning Activity

Students should be encouraged to visit a lobbyist or special interest group member and observe their activities. Lobbyists can be found at all levels of government, so even lobbyists or group members who try to affect policy at the local level would be sufficient. Students should be encouraged to select interest groups that they personally agree with so they can volunteer time and service.

If it is not possible for students to see a lobbyist work in his own environment, then a lobbyist should be invited in as a guest speaker. Any discussion or activity concerning lobbyists should include lobbying as a prospective profession.

Discussion Starter
Let several students respond to this general question: What is your opinion of interest groups and lobbyists? Then ask the same kind of questions about specific interest groups—the NRA and the Sierra Club, for example. Again, let several students respond. Help the students recognize how reactions altered when specific groups (with which they might strongly agree or disagree) were considered: Is it possible to condone some special interest groups while condemning others? Why or why not?

Enrichment
Ask volunteers to find a current or recent *Congressional Quarterly* and to read several lobbyists' reports. Let these students share their findings and reactions with the rest of the class.

Discussion Starter
Pose questions such as these to stimulate discussion: What is the relationship between First Amendment rights and indirect lobbying?

Reteaching Strategies
1. Have the students work in small groups to compare and discuss the notes they took while reading Section 5. Encourage the students to correct or add to their notes as necessary.
2. Work with small groups of students to discuss direct and indirect techniques used by lobbyists: How are they different? What are examples of each?

Evaluation Strategies
1. Have the students write their answers to the Section 5 Review questions.
2. Have the students take the Section 5 Quiz found in the *TRB.*

Section 5 Review (Answers)
1. Lobbying, providing election support, and rating candidates.
2. Interest groups often become directly involved in the election process. They offer campaign support, contributions, and urge their members to vote for candidates that support the views of the group.
3. Shaping public opinion, mobilizing constituents, litigation, and demonstration techniques.
4. The Federal Regulation of Lobbying Act of 1946 states that groups register with the clerk of the House and the secretary of the Senate. Groups must register information and give quarterly reports on their activities.
5. Answers will vary, e.g., no further restrictions should be placed on interest groups because they would violate First Amendment rights. Or, yes, many more restrictions should be placed on special interest groups because they have too much influence on public policy. Such restrictions might include a financial accounting that is made public every three months to show Americans how much they are spending and how, a registration of all lobbyists at both state and federal levels no matter how little they lobby, etc.

assistance to farmers, and many other interests. Greenpeace, an environmental and peace activist group, has staged many creative protest activities to generate publicity for their causes such as protests against whaling operations.

Why Do Interest Groups Get Bad Press?

Despite their importance to democratic government, interest groups, like political parties, are sometimes criticized by both the public and the press. Our image of interest groups and their special interests is not very favorable. You may have run across political cartoons depicting lobbyists prowling the hallways of Congress, briefcases stuffed with money, waiting to lure representatives into a waiting limousine.

These cartoons are not entirely factual, nor are they entirely fictitious. President Richard Nixon was revealed to have yielded to the campaign contributions of milk producers by later authorizing a windfall increase in milk subsidies. In 1977, ''Koreagate,'' a scandal in which a South Korean businessman was accused of offering lavish ''gifts'' to several members of Congress, added to the view that politicians were too easily susceptible to the snares of special interests. In the early 1990s, it was revealed that a number of senators who received generous contributions from one particular savings and loan association turned around and supported a ''hands off'' policy by savings and loan regulators. The savings and loan association in question later got into financial trouble, costing the federal government billions of dollars to bail it out.

Despite these incidents, a few bad apples do not spoil the whole interest group barrel. For every dishonest action, there are hundreds of honest transactions between interest group leaders and public officials. For every lobbyist who attempts to bribe a public official, there are hundreds who try only to provide public officials with solid facts that support the goals of their groups.

Regulation of Interest Groups

Interest groups are not free to do whatever they choose. In principle, they are regulated. In 1946 Congress passed the Federal Regulation of Lobbying Act in an attempt to control lobbying. It is the only major law regulating interest groups, and it applies only to those that lobby Congress. The act states:

1. That any person or organization that receives money to be used principally to influence legislation before Congress must register with the clerk of the House and the secretary of the Senate.
2. That any group or person registering must identify their employer, salary, amount and purpose of expenses, and duration of employment.
3. That every registered lobbyist must give quarterly reports on his or her activities, which are published in the *Congressional Quarterly.*
4. That anyone failing to satisfy the specific provisions of this act can be fined up to $10,000 and receive a five-year prison term.

The act is very limited and has not regulated lobbying to any great degree. First, the Supreme Court has restricted the application of the law to only those lobbyists who *directly* seek to influence federal legislation. Any lobbyist indirectly seeking to influence legislation through efforts to shape public opinion does not fall within the scope of the law. Second, the act requires only that persons or organizations whose principal purpose is to influence legislation need register. Any interest group or individual claiming that their principal function is something else need not register. Many groups can avoid registration in this way. Third, the act does not cover lobbying directed at agencies in the executive branch or those that testify before congressional committees. Fourth, the public is almost totally unaware of the information in the quarterly reports and no agency that oversees interest-group activities has been created by Congress.

The problem, of course, is that any stricter regulation of lobbying may run into constitutional problems because of the potential abridgment of First Amendment rights. As long as the Supreme Court does not view indirect lobbying as falling within the scope of the law, lobbying will be difficult to control.

Section 5 Review

1. Name three methods used by special interest groups to directly influence policymakers.
2. How do lobbyists attempt to influence policymakers throughout the electoral process?
3. Describe four techniques by which lobbyists indirectly influence legislators.
4. What federal regulation of interest groups exists?
5. **For critical analysis:** What additional restrictions, if any, do you think should be placed on interest groups? Explain whether you think any further restrictions would violate the First Amendment rights of these groups.

TEACHING CHALLENGE TO THE AMERICAN DREAM

Read

Before the students read this Challenge to the American Dream feature, encourage them to summarize and respond to what they have learned about interest groups and lobbying: What are interest groups? What functions are they intended to serve? Are they the most appropriate organizations for serving those purposes?

Discuss

Help the students discuss the Challenge to the American Dream feature: What idea was Madison expressing in his definition of a faction? How would you use your own words to restate Madison's explanation of the relationship between liberty and factions? Do you consider interest groups effective watchdogs? Are they the organizations best suited and most appropriate to this function? Why or why not? Do the size and power of interest groups pose a threat to democracy? Why or why not?

Analyze and Apply

Have each student work individually or with a partner to plan and write a persuasive essay on interest groups. Each essay should respond to this question: Do interest groups serve democracy, or do they threaten it? Remind the students that their essays should present a clear opinion and should include details and examples to support that point of view. Give the students an opportunity to read their completed essays aloud, or post them in the classroom so the students can read one another's work.

Review

Ask these questions to help the students review: What was James Madison's attitude toward factions? What are the major arguments of those who defend interest groups? Of those who oppose interest groups?

You Decide (Answers)

1. Answers will vary, e.g., interest groups allow Americans to organize and communicate their wishes to their representatives. They can offer expert testimony about areas of concern. Interest groups have power that is out of proportion with the number of people they represent.

2. Answers will vary, e.g., James Madison meant that the more freedom that is given to groups, the larger and more powerful they will become.

3. Answers will vary, e.g., yes, it is impossible to have a democracy without interest groups because interest groups are the only way that democratic actions can be influenced in a nation with 250 million people. If interest groups were eliminated, then there would be little, if any, input into the political decision-making process and therefore legislation would only reflect what legislatures wanted themselves.

CHALLENGE TO THE AMERICAN DREAM

Can Lobbying Endanger Democracy?

One of this nation's founding fathers, James Madison, seemed to be referring to interest groups when he wrote about the danger of factions. Madison defined a faction as a group "united and actuated [activated] by some common impulse of passion, or of interest, adverse to the rights of other citizens, or the permanent and aggregate [total] interest of the community."

If this is true of factions, or interest groups, then what is to be done about them? James Madison considered this question and came up with a mixed answer. "Liberty is to faction," he said, as "air is to fire." Air may feed fire, but it is also "essential to animal life." Madison believed that the formation of these factions is inevitable in a democracy, but he also believed that the cure—eliminating them—is worse than the disease.

Today there are both those who defend interest groups and those who condemn them. Those who defend them say that interest groups make government more responsive. They provide necessary and important services by communicating the people's wishes to their representatives. They allow certain groups of Americans to be represented according to their economic, social, or occupational interests. They also enable Americans to organize and participate in the American political system, and are a means through which citizens can pressure the government to follow policies they want. Interest groups act as "watchdogs" and protest government policies that are harmful to their members. Proponents also argue that since there are many interest groups competing for power, lawmakers are kept from being controlled by one interest group. Competition among interest groups prevents any one group or combination of groups from dominating American politics.

Critics of interest groups argue that some interest groups are too large and too powerful. They feel that some have vast amounts of resources that enable them to directly influence the decisions of public officials. Some have an influence on government far beyond their proportionate size or their relative influence on the public. Opponents of interest groups argue that the groups represent only a small portion of Americans. Moreover, the minority who are represented by these groups are generally more affluent, better educated citizens. Critics maintain that less advantaged members of our society do not have the resources to organize and advance their interests. As a result, interest groups do not adequately represent the public interest.

Critics also argue that these groups do not in fact represent the views of all the people for whom they claim to speak, and are often dominated by a limited group of leaders. Critics further claim that some groups use tactics that, if they were to become widespread, would undermine the whole political process. These practices—bribery, threats, and other illegal or unethical means—are not common, but the danger is there.

The potential challenge to the American dream that interest groups pose cannot be taken lightly. As long as the costs of interest-group–sponsored legislation is spread out over a large number of Americans but the benefits are concentrated in a small number of individuals or companies, interest groups will always have the upper hand. They will always be the ones who can raise money to influence legislation. While interest groups are clearly part of the democratic process, they may also potentially threaten its long-term viability.

You Decide

1. Give two arguments in favor of and against interest groups.
2. What did James Madison mean by the statement, "liberty is to faction as air is to fire"?
3. Given what you have learned about interest groups, do you agree with Madison's claim that they are inevitable in American society? Why would the cure be worse than the disease?

Chapter Evaluation
To evaluate student mastery of chapter material, you might:
1. Use Chapter Test A from the *TRB.*
2. Use Chapter Test B from the *TRB.*
3. Construct your own test using items from the *West American Government Test Bank* found in the *TRB.*
4. Use the accompanying computerized test software to construct and print a customized chapter test.

Review Questions (Answers)
1. Attitudes and beliefs shared by a significant number of persons on matters of government and politics.
2. Through election results, personal contacts, interest groups, and media reports.
3. Early polling efforts were generally not representative of the entire population.
4. The factors involved in political socialization including family, education, mass media, opinion leaders, and peer groups.
5. Families play a crucial role in political socialization because they dominate a child's early years. Education is a powerful influence because children begin to learn about the American political system in school. The mass media plays an important role because it is the leading source of political information for most people. Opinion leaders in communities influence other citizens because people seek their advice.
6. Liberals have a viewpoint toward public policy that almost always involves change. They believe that the national government should take an active role in solving the nation's domestic problems. Conservatives have a viewpoint toward public policy in which the goal is tradition. They believe that the federal government is already too big and should not be expanded.
7. Interest groups help bridge the gap between citizens and government and enable citizens to express their views. They raise awareness on public issues and inspire action. They give specialized and detailed information to public officials and serve as a check on public officials to make sure they are carrying out their duties responsibly.
8. Answers will vary, e.g., business interest groups represent many types of businesses. Labor interest groups represent groups of workers interested in improved working conditions and better pay. Agricultural groups consist of broadbased groups such as The American Farm Bureau Federation and of product areas such as dairy products or fruit. Consumer groups have organized for the purposes of consumer rights.
9. Lobbyists make personal contacts with key legislators. They provide expertise to legislators. They testify before congressional committees. They assist legislators or bureaucrats in drafting legislation.
10. They try to shape public opinion through television and newspaper advertisements and through mass mailings. They urge members to write letters or make calls to government officials. They also

Chapter 9 Review

Key Terms

agents of political socialization 210
biased sample 208
conservatives 215
ideologues 216
interest group 217
labor force 220
liberals 215
liberalism 215
lobbying 224
lobbyist 224
mass media 211
moderates 215
peer group 214
political action committee (PAC) 225
political socialization 210
pressure groups 217
public interest groups 218
public opinion 207
public opinion poll 207
radical left 215
random sample 209
ratings system 227
reactionaries 215
samples 208
sampling error 210
straw poll 208
trade and product organizations 218

Summary

1. Public opinion is the beliefs and attitudes about politics and public policy shared by a large portion of the population. The most common ways that public officials learn about public opinion is through election results, personal contacts, interest groups, and media reports. One way to measure public opinion is through the use of scientific public opinion polls which, in order to be useful, must use a random sample.

2. Many factors affect public opinion. Most views that are expressed as political opinions are acquired through a learning process called political socialization, which is a complex, lifelong learning process. Some of the agents of political socialization include the family, the educational establishment, the mass media, opinion leaders, and peer groups. Economic status and age can also influence one's political socialization process.

3. Liberals have a viewpoint toward public policy that tends to involve change, and believe in expanding the federal government. Conservatives believe that public policy should maintain tradition, and that state and local governments should rely less on the federal government. Most Americans consider themselves moderates, neither liberal nor conservative.

4. Interest groups are organizations of people sharing common objectives who actively attempt to influence government policymakers through direct and indirect methods. Although both interest groups and political parties are banded together for political purposes, they are very different. Most interest groups seek change based on specific issues, whereas political parties must support a wider range of causes. Private interest groups primarily seek economic benefit for their own members, but public interest groups are formed with the broader goal of working for the "public good." Both public and private groups represent a wide range of interests.

5. Interest groups operate at all levels of government and use a variety of strategies to affect public policy. Some of the direct techniques used by these groups include lobbying, providing election support, and rating legislative behavior. Interest groups also try to influence public policy through indirect methods such as shaping public opinion, mobilizing constituents, litigation, and demonstrations. In principle, lobbying has been regulated by the Federal Regulation of Lobbying Act of 1946, but this act is very limited.

Review Questions

1. What is meant by public opinion?
2. What are the most common ways by which public officials learn about public opinion?
3. Explain what went wrong with early polling efforts.
4. What are the factors that help explain how public opinion is formed?
5. Explain how four of the agents of political socialization influence our political opinions.
6. What distinguishes a conservative from a liberal?
7. What purposes do interest groups serve in American politics and how do they operate?
8. Briefly describe three types of private interest groups.

try to achieve policy goals through the court system.

11. The act requires that any person or organization that receives money to be used principally to influence legislation must register and identify their employer, salary, expenses, purposes, and duration of employment. The act requires that every registered lobbyist must give quarterly reports, which are published in the Congressional Quarterly. If anyone fails to satisfy the provisions, they can be fined up to $10,000 and receive a five-year prison term.

12. Know your purpose and subject. Make sure the letter is neat and well-organized. Get to the point and use correct grammar and spelling. Appeal to the reader's sense of fair play and justice. Try to be optimistic and practical. Type the letter using double spacing and sign your name.

Questions for Thought and Discussion (Answers)

1. Answers will vary, e.g., my parents, because they discussed politics at the dinner table since I was very young. Or, my best friend's father who is a newspaper reporter and discusses politics every time I visit their house.

2. Answers will vary, e.g., environmental groups could be classified as public interest groups because they are working to better the environment shared by all.

3. Answers will vary, e.g., stricter regulation of lobbying would restrict individuals and groups from expressing their opinions. It would endanger freedom of speech.

Social Studies Skills (Answers)

1. In order to place different types of political ideologies; yes, both fascists and communists are extremists and use the state to crush opposition.

Observable Mastery

Write the term *Public Opinion* on the board. Have students define the term and compile a list of the factors that affect public opinion. After they have listed the agents of political socialization have them enumerate the positive and negative features of opinion polls.

Then, have students draw the political spectrum on the board. Give them a list of groups and individuals to place on the spectrum, such as Democrats and Republicans, the Sierra Club, the NRA, George Bush, Jesse Jackson, etc. Finally, have students list the direct and indirect methods employed by lobbyists in order to affect public policy.

CHAPTER 9 REVIEW—Continued

9. In what ways do interest groups try to directly influence policymakers?
10. Describe four methods of influencing legislation used by lobbyists.
11. What are the requirements of the Federal Regulation of Lobbying Act of 1946?
12. Briefly describe the guidelines for writing a letter to a newspaper or magazine editor.

Questions for Thought and Discussion

1. What individuals in your life do you think have had the most influence on your political perspectives? In what ways have they influenced you?
2. What kinds of interest groups, if any, do you think could be seen as either public interest or private interest groups? What arguments could you present for them to be classified either way?
3. Why might stricter regulation of lobbying endanger First Amendment rights?

Improving Your Skills

Communication Skills

Formulating a Thesis Statement

Many times throughout your studies, you will be asked to write about your ideas or what you have learned. Before writing an essay, and even before researching a topic, you should write a thesis statement, which should explain the reason for your essay. Here is a sample thesis statement from Section 3 of this chapter:

> Most political attitudes are often labeled as either conservative or liberal.

Just as this statement expresses the main idea of that section, writing a thesis statement for your essay will help you clarify your topic and thus focus your research.

The following steps will help you formulate a thesis statement:

1. ***Choose a general topic that interests you.*** Begin to gather and list facts and information about the general topic.
2. ***Gradually narrow the topic in stages.*** As you gather more information and facts, look for related facts and make choices about which are really important.
3. ***Organize the facts.*** Discard the information that has no bearing on your topic, keeping only those that are directly related.
4. ***Decide what you believe the facts mean.***
5. ***Formulate a thesis statement that can be fully proven by the collected facts.***

Writing

Using your own words, rewrite each of the following thesis statements taken out of the chapter:

1. Above all else, the aim of a democratic government is to convert the will of the people into public policy.
2. Public opinion is important in American politics because opinions can determine how government handles such issues as gun control, abortion, and the death penalty.
3. Most political socialization is informal, almost accidental, and other political socialization is formal.
4. Education is a powerful influence on an individual's political attitudes.
5. The media can also determine what issues, events, and personalities are in the public eye.

Social Studies Skills

Understanding a Pictogram

Look at the pictogram on page 216, Figure 9–1. Why does it have a right side, a left side, and a center? Are there any elements of those on the extreme right—fascists—which also apply to those on the extreme left—communists?

Activities and Projects

1. Develop your own schoolwide "straw poll" on three issues facing high school students in the United States today. Report to the class on your findings and describe the techniques you used.
2. Identify an important national issue that is currently under debate. Research two interest groups that are involved with the issue. Write a summary page on each.

CHAPTER INTRODUCTION

Instructional Objectives

By the end of the chapter students should be able to:

- Summarize the nominating process used throughout the United States.
- Describe the various nominating methods.
- Characterize the organization of campaigns and how they are financed.
- Describe the structure of elections.
- Summarize the role of the media in campaigns and elections.

Using the Keynote

Introduce Chapter 10 by having a volunteer read aloud the quotation from Theodore H. White. Guide the students in discussing the quotation by posing questions such as these: Who are the tyrants, priests, parties, and mandarins who, in other nations, determine what people will think and talk about? (You might ask a volunteer to look up the word *mandarin* in the dictionary and read the definition to the class.) Why do they exert such power in other nations? Why do they lack that power in the United States? Do you believe the press really does have that authority in the United States? Why or why not?

Introducing the Chapter

After the students have read the Introduction independently, ask these questions to stimulate discussion and assess student knowledge: Why do we hold popular elections? How has the election process changed over the history of our nation?

Previewing the Sections

Section 1 Ask volunteers to read aloud the headings and the photo captions in Section 1. Then encourage the students to discuss briefly what they know about nominations and to suggest questions they hope to have answered as they study this section.

Section 2 Have the students look through Section 2, and ask volunteers to read aloud the section title and the four main headings. Then encourage the students to begin considering the section content by asking these questions: Who participates in campaigns? Who is affected by campaigns? How?

Section 3 Let the students look through Section 3, noting and commenting on its content. Then ask volunteers to suggest questions they hope to have answered as they study the section.

Section 4 Ask the students to page through Section 4, noting the section heads, the artwork, and the special features. Then ask: What topics are covered in this section?

CHAPTER 10

Campaigns, Elections, and the Media

CHAPTER OBJECTIVES

To learn and understand

- The nominating process and the various methods of nomination used throughout the United States.
- How campaigns are organized and financed.
- How elections are organized and carried out.
- The role of the media in campaigns and elections.

West's American Government Assignment Guide

Activity Sheets
Basic Concepts 10 *TRB* (Reteaching)
Enrichment Activity 10 *TRB*
Building Social Studies Skills 10 *TRB*
Quizzes
Chapter 10 Section 1 Quiz *TRB*
Chapter 10 Section 2 Quiz *TRB*
Chapter 10 Section 3 Quiz *TRB*
Chapter 10 Section 4 Quiz *TRB*

Tests
Chapter 10 Test A *TRB*
Chapter 10 Test B *TRB*
Chapter 10 Test Bank *TRB*
Chapter 10 WESTEST Computerized Testing

Keynote

"The press in America . . . determines what people will think and talk about—an authority that in other nations is reserved for tyrants, priests, parties, and mandarins."

—— **Theodore H. White (1915–1986) Political Commentator**

INTRODUCTION

The very nature of our government is representative democracy, a system in which the people elect officials to represent them in making laws and running the government. Because over 250 million Americans cannot all gather in one place to make laws and run the government, we need a means by which we can choose representatives who will govern with our consent and truly act on our behalf. We also need a method for holding chosen officials responsible to the people. Popular election is the method we use to accomplish these democratic goals.

Participating in elections today involves more than spending a few minutes voting for someone to represent us. Voters elect over five hundred thousand people each year to a multitude of federal, state, and local offices.

At the turn of the century, a presidential candidate and his entourage piled into a train to carry information to voters at railroad stops across the country. Today the media, not the railroad, carry the candidate and the issues to us. As illustrated by the above quote by Theodore H. White, a political commentator who has written many books on recent presidential campaigns, the media in the United States have a power equivalent to that held by kings and tyrants in other countries. The media are extremely influential in the United States and must be reckoned with by every political candidate. After all, the name recognition given by the media can determine whether the candidate wins or loses.

In this chapter we will look at three very important parts of our representative democracy. These parts are campaigns, elections, and the media. From the day the first candidate announces his or her intention to run for an office, through the endless photo opportunities and the overwhelming media blitz, to the day of the election, campaigns, elections, and the media are irrevocably tied to one another in modern America.

SECTION 1

Step One: The Nomination

Preview Questions

- What are the methods by which candidates are nominated in the United States?
- What are direct primaries and what different forms do they take?
- How are presidential candidates nominated?

American political campaigns are usually long, complicated, and expensive events, producing hours of film, volumes of newsprint, thousands of posters and buttons, and finally a winning candidate who becomes a public official for the next few years. The first step in this long process is the **nomination**, the choosing of the candidates within each party who will then seek office by running against the candidates chosen by the other party.

Nominations are a critical step in the election process because they narrow the field of possible candidates and limit a party's choice to one person. The methods by which candidates are nominated have varied from time to time and from state to state. They can be grouped in general categories.

Self-Nomination and Petition

Until the early 1800's, **self-nomination**, or simply announcing one's own desire to run for public office, was the most common way of becoming a candidate. This method is still used at the small-town and rural political levels in many parts of the country.

Self-nomination does not mean that a person's name will automatically appear on the **ballot**—the card or other object on which voters indicate their choices in the election. The candidate must first file a **petition**, a formal request to be listed on the ballot with a certain number

SECTION 1

Points to Stress
- Methods by which candidates are nominated in the United States.
- The definition and forms of direct primaries.
- The nominating process for presidential candidates.

Kickoff Activity
Have the students write their responses to these questions: How many different nominating processes do you think there are? Why might we use more than one method? After all the students have written their responses, ask volunteers to share their ideas with the rest of the class.

Working with the Preview Questions
Read these three study questions to the class. Then ask the students to keep these questions in mind as they read and take notes on Section 1.

Teaching Strategies

Introduction
Before the students read the section introduction, encourage them to discuss their responses to this question: What purposes do nominations serve? What problems would develop if we attempted to hold elections without first having organized nominations? After a brief discussion, let the students read the introduction independently; then encourage them to continue the discussion, revising their responses as appropriate.

Discussion Starter
Encourage the students to discuss their own experiences with petitions: Where have you seen people gathering signatures on petitions? What specific petition concerns can you recall?

Enrichment
Let a group of volunteers research write-in candidates in state or local elections: Who has run as a write-in candidate? Why? With what success? Ask the volunteers to summarize their findings in a brief report to the rest of the class.

Vocabulary
Ask the students to consider the term *smoke-filled room:* What origin of the term is explained here? How do people use the term today? Who is excluded from smoke-filled rooms?

Discussion Starter
Guide the students in considering opposition to the caucus system: Why would candidates oppose it? What obstacles would they face in opposing the caucus system? Which kinds of candidates—if any—might not oppose the system? Why?

Comprehension
Have volunteers explain the most important differences between the caucus system that faded away during the nineteenth century and the modern caucus system still used in some local nominations.

Extension
Ask two sets of volunteers to research the nominating conventions held by the Republican and Democratic parties: Who served as delegates at the most recent local party convention? Who was selected to represent the area at the next state convention? Let the volunteers prepare and display charts showing what they have learned.

Discussion Starter
Encourage the students to consider the problems that developed in party conventions. Have volunteers restate, in their own words, the ideas expressed by Charles

Caption Answer Jackson felt it was undemocratic and wielded too much power.

▲ This 1824 cartoon shows Andrew Jackson being attacked by dogs, who represent supporters of the caucus system. Why did Jackson protest the caucus system?

of signatures determined by the state to show that the candidate has some public support.

A self-nominated candidate might not be able to gather enough signatures to win a place on the ballot. In this case, she or he may decide to run as a **write-in candidate**, someone who will campaign without being listed on the ballot, and will ask voters to write his or her name on the ballot on election day. For these votes to count, most states require the write-in candidate to register with the local board of elections. Write-in candidates have rarely been successful at winning public office.

Party Caucus

The Constitution gives no instructions for nominating candidates for the presidency and vice presidency. Thus, in 1797 the leaders of the two parties decided to keep political power in their hands by holding congressional conferences later called **caucuses**.[1] In these early meetings the party leaders, who were wealthy and influential members of the community, would choose the candidates in secret. The voters at large would have no part in choosing those who were nominated. The caucus was frequently referred to as "the smoke-filled room," because meetings were often held in small rooms that soon filled up with smoke because the windows were closed to guarantee secrecy.

By the presidential race of 1820, the caucus method of nomination had become a controversial issue. The system was called "King Caucus" by Andrew Jackson and other presidential candidates who felt it was undemocratic and too powerful. Party leaders were faced with rising opposition and were forced to find other methods of nominating candidates. As it faded away in presidential politics, the caucus system soon diminished at the state and local levels as well.

The caucus is still used for some local nominations, especially in New England. These modern caucuses, however, are open to the general public and bear little resemblance to the original caucus.

Party Nominating Convention

As the caucus method diminished around the country, it was replaced in many states by party conventions. A **nominating convention** is an official meeting of a political party to choose its candidates and to select **delegates**, persons sent to a higher level convention to represent the people of one geographical area. For example, delegates at a local party convention would nominate candidates for local office, and would also choose delegates to represent the party at the state convention. By 1840, the convention system had become the most common way of nominating candidates for government offices at every level.

A party convention was intended to be more democratic than a party caucus because more people were allowed to take part. Yet, like the party caucus, the convention method was abused. Historian Charles Beard described the corruption of party leaders in the late 1840s:

> They packed [conventions] with their henchmen, who drove out or overwhelmed dangerous opponents. They padded the rolls of party members with the names of dead men. . . . They stuffed the ballot boxes, and they prepared the slates which were forced through the nominating convention in the face of opposition.

These practices soon came to the attention of the public. Amidst mounting criticism, state legislatures turned away from conventions as a means of nominating local and state party candidates. The convention is still used, however, in some states such as Connecticut, Delaware, Michigan, and Utah. At the national level, the

1. This word apparently was first used in the name of a men's club called the *Caucus Club* of colonial Boston sometime between 1755 and 1765. It comes from a Latin word meaning "drinking vessel." Many early political and government meetings took place in a pub.

Beard. Then ask other volunteers to identify the most important differences—and the most important similarities—between the caucus system and the nominating convention system.

Enrichment
Let a few volunteers gather information on primary elections in your state: When was the most recent primary election held? For what offices were candidates chosen? When will the next primary election be held? What offices will be the subject of those primaries? Let the volunteers prepare and distribute an information sheet for their classmates.

Enrichment
Select two or three volunteers to gather information on registering to vote in your state: Where can you register to vote? What are the requirements for registration? What is involved in the registration process? Ask these volunteers to prepare a bulletin board with the information they have gathered; encourage the other students to study the bulletin board and to ask any questions they may have.

Discussion Starter
Help the students consider the position of voters who wish to register as independents: Do you imagine that some such voters register as members of major parties just so they can vote in closed primaries? Why or why not? Why do you think some independent voters object to affiliating themselves with a party? Do you believe that closed primaries restrict the rights of independent voters? Why or why not?

◀ This illustration depicts the first Republican convention, which was held under the oak trees at Jackson, Michigan on July 6, 1854. What system of nominating candidates was replaced by the party conventions?

Caption Answer The party conventions replaced the caucus system of nominating candidates. You might want to point out to students that the convention depicted here was not the first nominating convention in our country, but the first for the Republican Party.

party convention is used to select the presidential candidates of the two major parties from the winners of the state primaries and conventions.

The Direct Primary

In most states the convention method was gradually replaced by the **direct primary**—an election held *within* each party to pick its candidates for the general election. This is the method most commonly used today to nominate candidates for office.

Although the primaries are *party* nominating elections, they are now closely regulated by the states. The states usually set the dates and conduct the primaries. They also provide polling places, election officials, registration lists, and ballots, in addition to counting the votes.

Most state laws require that the major parties use the primary to choose their candidates for the Senate and the House, for the governorship and all other state offices, and for most local offices, as well. In a few states, however, different combinations of nominating conventions and primaries are used to pick candidates for the top offices.

Because state laws vary, there are several different kinds of primaries used throughout the country.

Closed Primaries In a **closed primary**, only party members can vote to choose that party's candidates, and they may vote only in the primary of their own party. Thus, only Democrats can vote in the Democratic primary to pick candidates of the Democratic party. Only Republicans can vote for the Republican candidates. A person usually establishes party membership when he or she registers to vote. In some states such as Illinois, a person may register right at the polling place.

Regular party workers favor the closed method because it promotes party loyalty; independent voters oppose it because it excludes them from the nominating process.

Open Primaries An **open primary** is a direct primary in which voters can vote for a party's candidates whether or not they belong to the party. In most open primaries, all voters receive both a Republican and Democratic ballot. Voters then choose either the Democratic or the Republican ballot in the privacy of the voting booth.

Discussion Starter
Stimulate class discussion by asking these questions: How do you imagine the major political parties react to wide-open elections? Why? What is your reaction to these elections? Why?

Comprehension
Check the students' comprehension by asking these questions: How are open and closed primaries different? How are they alike?

Extension
Ask the students: Does our state have run-off primaries? How do you know? If no one can answer the question, let a volunteer find out and report back to the class.

Vocabulary
Let volunteers define the words *partisan* and *nonpartisan.*

Discussion Starter
Guide the students in considering the importance of a good showing in early primaries: What do you think a good showing is? Do you think it is measured in absolute or relative terms? Why does a good showing produce the results mentioned in the text? What positive—and negative—effects might these results have for the candidate? What other results do you think a good showing might produce? How do you think a "bad showing" in early primaries might be defined? What negative results would it probably have?

Caption Answer Students should understand that since no Republicans were listed on this ballot, it was used for a closed primary.

FYI

Primaries are supposed to be intra-party struggles, and for that reason party leaders do not like the open primary system. Open primaries allow independents and members from the other party to vote in the primary, thus reducing the influence of regular party members. This crossing over does not always result in the loss of power to regular party members, but it does add uncertainty. Open primaries also allow for raiding, a process where one party crosses over with the intent of voting for the other party's weakest candidate, thus making victory possible in the general election.

Closed primaries were established in an attempt to stop all of this. However, The Supreme Court in *Tashjian* v. *Republican Party of Connecticut,* 1986, held that closed primary laws cannot forbid independents from participating if the *party* chooses to allow it, hence making even closed primaries subject to the influence of party outsiders. To date, 12 states have open primaries of some form, and 38 have closed primaries.

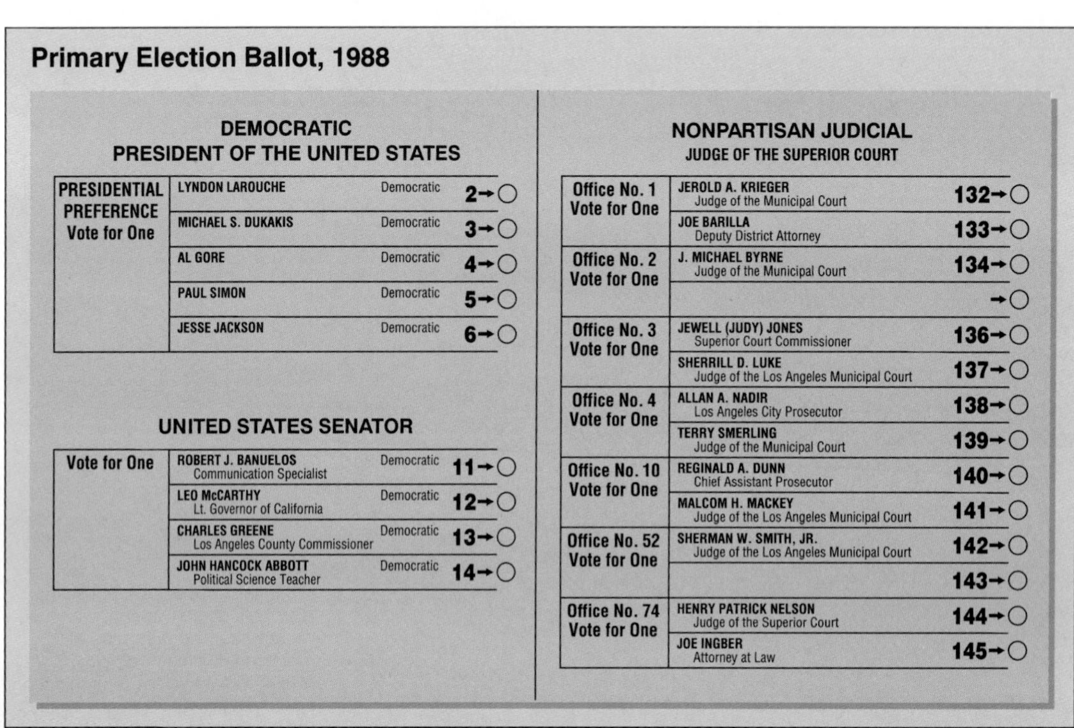

Primary Election Ballot, 1988

DEMOCRATIC
PRESIDENT OF THE UNITED STATES

PRESIDENTIAL PREFERENCE Vote for One	LYNDON LAROUCHE	Democratic	2→○
	MICHAEL S. DUKAKIS	Democratic	3→○
	AL GORE	Democratic	4→○
	PAUL SIMON	Democratic	5→○
	JESSE JACKSON	Democratic	6→○

UNITED STATES SENATOR

Vote for One	ROBERT J. BANUELOS Communication Specialist	Democratic	11→○
	LEO McCARTHY Lt. Governor of California	Democratic	12→○
	CHARLES GREENE Los Angeles County Commissioner	Democratic	13→○
	JOHN HANCOCK ABBOTT Political Science Teacher	Democratic	14→○

NONPARTISAN JUDICIAL
JUDGE OF THE SUPERIOR COURT

Office No. 1 Vote for One	JEROLD A. KRIEGER Judge of the Municipal Court	132→○
	JOE BARILLA Deputy District Attorney	133→○
Office No. 2 Vote for One	J. MICHAEL BYRNE Judge of the Municipal Court	134→○
		→○
Office No. 3 Vote for One	JEWELL (JUDY) JONES Superior Court Commissioner	136→○
	SHERRILL D. LUKE Judge of the Los Angeles Municipal Court	137→○
Office No. 4 Vote for One	ALLAN A. NADIR Los Angeles City Prosecutor	138→○
	TERRY SMERLING Judge of the Municipal Court	139→○
Office No. 10 Vote for One	REGINALD A. DUNN Chief Assistant Prosecutor	140→○
	MALCOM H. MACKEY Judge of the Los Angeles Municipal Court	141→○
Office No. 52 Vote for One	SHERMAN W. SMITH, JR. Judge of the Los Angeles Municipal Court	142→○
		143→○
Office No. 74 Vote for One	HENRY PATRICK NELSON Judge of the Superior Court	144→○
	JOE INGBER Attorney at Law	145→○

▲ **FIGURE 10–1 Primary Election Ballot, 1988.** The figure above is an excerpt from a primary election ballot. In what type of primary was this ballot used?

A different version of the open primary is used in Alaska, Louisiana, and Washington, where it is known as the ''wide open'' primary, or **blanket primary**. In each of these states, the voters receive a single large ballot listing each party's candidates for each nomination. Voters may choose candidates from different parties. This means that a voter may help choose a Democratic candidate for one office, and a Republican candidate for another office.

Runoff Primaries Candidates for most offices must win only a **plurality** of votes—more votes than any other candidate—to be declared the winner. They do not need to win a majority of the votes. In some states, however, candidates are required to win by a majority. If none of the candidates receives a majority in the primary election, a **runoff election** is held, in which the two candidates who won the most votes in the first primary election run against each other. The person who wins the runoff election becomes the party's candidate in the general election.

Nonpartisan Elections In most states, some offices are filled in **nonpartisan elections**—elections in which candidates do not run under party labels. Nonpartisan elections are most often used at the local level to choose, for example, candidates for the school board, hospital board, city council, and other local offices. Nonpartisan ballots are also used to elect about half of all state judges.

Nominating Presidential Candidates

In some respects, being nominated for president is tougher than being elected. The nominating process narrows a very large number of hopefuls down to a single candidate from each party. Choosing presidential candidates is unlike nominating candidates for any other office. One reason for this is that the nomination process combines several different methods.

State Primaries About three-fifths of the states hold presidential primaries, held between February and June of a presidential year, to select delegates to attend the national convention. For a candidate, a good showing in

Discussion Starter
Help the students focus on the importance of the timing of state primaries: Who cares most about a state's position in the primaries lineup? Why? Whose interests are served by holding a state primary early? Are those interests the ones most important to the election of candidates? Why or why not?

Comprehension
Let volunteers answer these comprehension questions: How are preference polls and mandatory preference polls different? How are they alike?

Enrichment
Ask volunteers to find answers to these questions: How are delegates to the presidential nominating conventions chosen in your state? When are the delegates chosen? Who were the delegates to the most recent conventions? Which candidates did those delegates support?

Critical Thinking Skills
Guide the students in analyzing and judging the various systems of selecting delegates to presidential nominating conventions: What are the advantages and disadvantages of each system? Which system do you think is most efficient? Which do you consider most democratic? Do you think all the states should adopt a single system? Why or why not?

early primaries means plenty of media attention as television networks and newspaper reporters play up the results. The other state primaries that follow shortly after the big primaries tend to serve as contests to eliminate unlikely candidates.

Because the results of early primaries tend to influence later primaries, some large states that have late primaries have tried to hold them earlier. For example, California, the state with the most electoral votes, holds its primary in June, well after the nominating process has begun in most other states. By then, the identities of the presidential nominees have virtually been assured. In 1990, Democratic lawmakers tried to move the California primary date to March, but failed to win legislative approval. In 1991, California Democrats devised a plan calling for nearly one-third of the Democratic delegates to be selected at caucuses three months before the primary election. That number is about the same as the combined total chosen in February in the Maine and Iowa caucuses and in the New Hampshire primary.

Attempts at moving the primary to March continue. By the time you read this, California may have one of the earliest primaries.

The array of laws that determine how the primaries are set up, who may enter them, and who may vote in them are made up by state legislatures and state parties. For example, several different methods of voting are used in presidential primaries. In some states, primary voters only select delegates to a party's national convention and do not know which candidates the delegates intend to vote for at the convention. In other states, the delegates' names, along with the names of the candidates they support, appear on the ballot. In still other states, the names of the candidates for the nomination and the delegates appear separately. Voters may then cast separate votes for candidates and for delegates. This is known as a **preference poll**.

Some states, Texas among them, use a form of the preference poll in which delegates are selected at a state convention. The voters then cast ballots for candidates, and the delegates must vote for the winning candidate at the national convention. This method is called the **mandatory preference poll**.

In some states, instead of presidential primaries, delegates to the convention are chosen by caucuses or conventions. Iowa, for example, holds caucuses to choose delegates to local conventions. These delegates, in turn, choose those who will attend the state and national conventions. Other states use a combination of conventions and primaries.

National Party Conventions Presidential nominating conventions have been described as giant pep rallies, or "the Fourth of July of American politics." Despite the hats, conga lines, and blaring horns and sirens, each convention's task is a serious one—to adopt the official party platform and to decide who will be the party's presidential candidate.

National party conventions have been described as giant pep rallies. Despite this outward appearance, national party conventions do manage to complete some important tasks. What tasks are accomplished at the national party conventions?

Caption Answer At the convention, the party adopts its official platform and selects its presidential and vice presidential candidates.

Enrichment
Let several volunteers research the keynote speakers at recent presidential nominating conventions: Who was chosen to make the keynote address at each convention? Why was that person chosen? What—if anything—was remarkable about that person's speech? What impact does that speech appear to have had? Ask the volunteers to summarize their findings in an oral report to the rest of the class.

Discussion Starter
Encourage the students to discuss the presidential nominating conventions they have read about or seen on TV: At what point in the convention did people know who would be nominated as the presidential candidate? What suspense—if any—was involved in the convention? Was there suspense in nominating conventions several decades ago? What has happened to change that situation? Are there any conditions under which a nominating convention might still be suspenseful? Do you think the loss of suspense affects the importance of the presidential nominating conventions? Why or why not?

Critical Thinking Skills
Ask the students to consider these questions: Are presidential nominating conventions necessary? Are they worth having? Encourage the students to share and defend various points of view.

Reteaching Strategies
1. Let the students work with partners to compare and discuss the notes they have taken on Section 1. Encourage the students to refer to the text as necessary, and to make additions or corrections to their notes.

2. Work with groups of students; guide the group members in making a small flow-chart that shows the steps in the nominating process for a presidential candidate in your state.

Evaluation Strategies
1. Have the students write their answers to the Section 1 Review questions.
2. Have the students take the Section 1 Quiz found in the *TRB.*

Section 1 Review (Answers)
1. Nominations narrow the field of possible candidates.
2. Self-nomination means announcing one's own desire to run for public office. The candidate must first file a petition—a formal request to be listed on the ballot with a certain number of signatures. Party caucuses were meetings of certain party leaders to choose candidates. Nominating conventions are official meetings of a political party to choose its candidates. The direct primary is an election held within each party to pick its candidates for the general election.
3. The direct primary is the most commonly used method today. It is an election held within each party in which voters choose candidates to run for office in the general election.

For four days in late July or August, the two or three thousand delegates at the convention theoretically represent the wishes of the voters and political leaders of their home states. On the first day of the convention, delegates hear the reports of the **Credentials Committee**, which inspects each prospective delegate's claim to be seated as a legitimate representative of his or her state. (This does not mean physically seated, but rather accepted as a legitimate delegate.) When the eligibility of delegates is in question, the committee decides who shall be seated. In the evening there is usually a **keynote speaker**—someone of national importance—to whip up enthusiasm among the delegates. The second day includes committee reports and debates on the party platform. Of course, other things are happening on an unofficial agenda: Backers of certain candidates are seeking to influence uncommitted delegates and change the minds of those pledged to other candidates. Delegates from state caucuses also are meeting to discuss strategies and how they will vote.

The third day is devoted to nominations and voting. Balloting begins with an alphabetical roll call in which states and territories announce their votes. By midnight, the convention's real work is over and the presidential candidate has been selected. The vice presidential nominations and the acceptance speeches occupy the fourth day.

Conventions today are not as important in the nominating process as they once were. There is the same hoopla, extravagance, long speeches, and demonstrations, but because so many delegates are selected by primaries, we usually know who will be nominated before the convention begins. There are only a few delegates who are actually uncommitted when they arrive at the convention. Even though conventions may be less important in determining nominations, they are important in developing the party platform and in promoting political representation.

Section 1 Review

1. Why are nominations an important part of the electoral process?
2. Briefly explain the different methods of nomination used throughout the country.
3. What is the nominating method most commonly used today and how does it work?
4. What is the process by which a candidate for president is nominated?
5. **For critical analysis:** Which nomination method do you think is most appropriate for a representative government? Explain your answer.

Section 2

The Campaign

Preview Questions

- How are campaigns typically organized and planned?
- What are the basic provisions of the Federal Election Campaign Act?
- What is the purpose of PACs and how do they function?

Once nominated, candidates concentrate on campaigning. The term *campaign* was not always a part of Americans' political vocabulary. It was originally a military word: Generals mounted campaigns, using their scarce resources (soldiers and materials) to achieve military objectives. In political campaigns, resources are also scarce, and have to be timed and targeted carefully.

There are many different ways to campaign. Which method a candidate uses often depends on the particular office sought and the amount of competition for that office. A candidate running for the school board may put up posters, talk to voters door-to-door, and speak at several luncheons. In contrast, for a candidate running for a higher office, a campaign becomes much more complicated, much more time consuming, and many times more expensive.

The goal of any campaign is to win the election. To accomplish this, a campaign must be organized and carefully planned, and must have sufficient funds.

Campaign Organization

The success of any campaign depends on the people who organize it. In a small local election, a campaign may be handled by a few friends, while in a national race thousands of individuals are involved. A presidential campaign, for example, may have as many as five hundred paid staff and one million volunteers.

Candidates for major offices set up campaign organizations similar to the one in Figure 10–2 on page 239. As you can see, the **campaign manager** coordinates and plans the campaign strategy, while other staff members provide leadership in specific areas such as print publicity or weekly polling. Critical to any major campaign are the volunteers, who make up the great majority of campaign workers. Volunteers handle the bulk of day-to-day work such as putting up posters, handing out pamphlets, answering phone calls, helping register voters, and seeing that voters get out on election day.

4. About three-fifths of the states hold presidential primaries to select delegates to attend a national convention. In some states, delegates are chosen by caucuses or conventions. Candidates are officially chosen at the national convention.
5. Answers will vary, e.g., open primaries are most appropriate for a representative government because voters may choose candidates from different parties. They are not limited to their registered party.

SECTION 2

Points to Stress
- The organization and planning of a typical campaign.
- Basic provisions of the Federal Election Campaign Act.
- The purpose of PACs and how they function.

Kickoff Activity
Write the term *political campaign* on the chalkboard; ask the students to list at least eight different words or phrases that the term brings to mind. After all the students have written their lists, encourage volunteers to share and compare their responses.

Working with the Preview Questions
Let volunteers read these three study questions to the rest of the class. Then help the students work together to use these questions in composing an outline format. Ask all the students to follow this format in taking notes on Section 2.

Teaching Strategies

Introduction
Have the students read the section introduction independently. Then ask them to respond to these questions: How are political campaigns like military campaigns? How does the comparison to military campaigns help you understand political campaigns? Do you think the comparison obscures the meaning or importance of political campaigns in any way? If so, how?

Discussion Starter
Let the students share their ideas about volunteering for presidential campaigns: Have you ever volunteered to help a presidential candidate? If so, who and why? If not, why not? Do you know people who have volunteered to work for presidential candidates? What do you imagine motivates these volunteers?

Figure Answer The campaign manager develops overall campaign strategy, manages the campaign finances, and oversees campaign staff.

This figure content is also featured on *West's American Government Videodisc* (see the index found in the *TRB*) and is available in the transparency package.

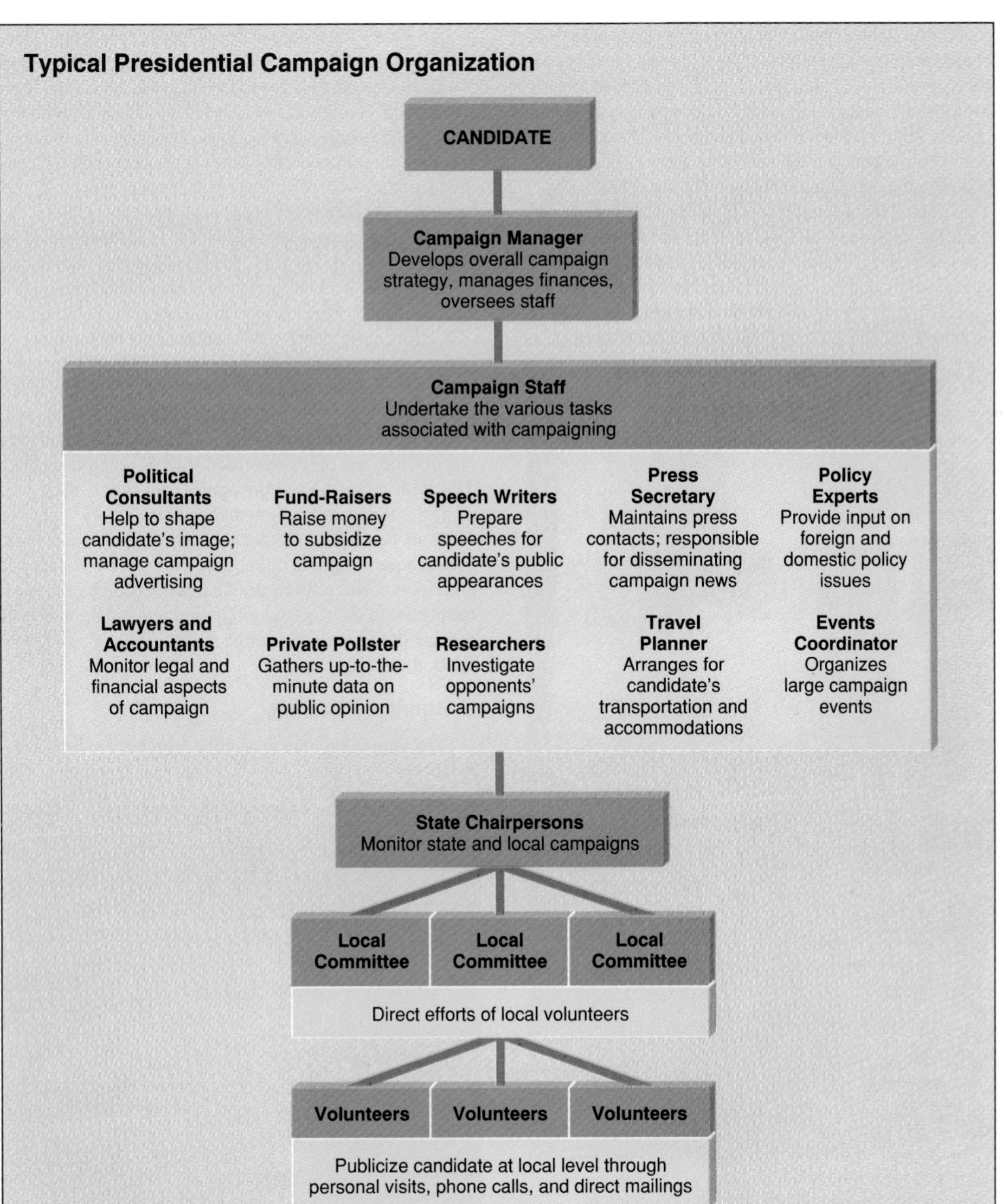

Typical Presidential Campaign Organization
CANDIDATE
Campaign Manager
Develops overall campaign strategy, manages finances, oversees staff
Campaign Staff
Undertake the various tasks associated with campaigning
Political Consultants
Help to shape candidate's image; manage campaign advertising
Fund-Raisers
Raise money to subsidize campaign
Speech Writers
Prepare speeches for candidate's public appearances
Press Secretary
Maintains press contacts; responsible for disseminating campaign news
Policy Experts
Provide input on foreign and domestic policy issues
Lawyers and Accountants
Monitor legal and financial aspects of campaign
Private Pollster
Gathers up-to-the-minute data on public opinion
Researchers
Investigate opponents' campaigns
Travel Planner
Arranges for candidate's transportation and accommodations
Events Coordinator
Organizes large campaign events
State Chairpersons
Monitor state and local campaigns
Local Committee
Local Committee
Local Committee
Direct efforts of local volunteers
Volunteers
Volunteers
Volunteers
Publicize candidate at local level through personal visits, phone calls, and direct mailings

▲ **FIGURE 10–2 Typical Presidential Campaign Organization.** The figure above presents a look at how people involved in a presidential campaign are organized for action. What is the role of the campaign manager?

Discussion Starter
Help the students discuss the role of political consultants in campaigns: Is it significant that paid professionals usually take over the jobs previously handled by volunteers or by amateur politicians? If not, why? If so, what is the significance? What effect do you imagine this change has on candidates? On the people who do volunteer to support the candidate? On voters?

Discussion Starter
Encourage the students to discuss what they have heard or read about the political consultants and consulting firms named in the text: With which candidates have these firms and individuals been associated most recently? What have you read or heard about their attitudes and activities? Do you expect that political consultants and consulting firms will always deal exclusively with a single political party? Why or why not?

Extension
Ask a group of volunteers to prepare for and then present a debate on this issue: Professional campaign managers distract politicians and voters from the most important issues of a campaign.

Enrichment
Guide the students in discussing image building: What is an image? What does the term *image building* imply? Do you consider it significant that candidates now employ consultants to manage their image building? Then have each student write a two-page essay discussing image-building in today's campaign. Students should use one of the following thesis statements for their essays: *In modern political campaigns, image is everything,* or *in modern political campaigns, image is not everything.*

To run a successful campaign today, the candidate's organization must be able to raise funds, get media coverage, produce commercials, convey the candidate's position, hire pollsters, research the opposing candidate, schedule the candidate's time effectively, make sure the candidate's name is well known by the public, and get the voters to the polls. What is different about today's campaigns is that often these tasks are put into the hands of paid professionals called **political consultants**, rather than volunteers, political parties, or amateur politicians. Political consultants are paid large fees to devise a campaign strategy, create a campaign theme, and manage the **image building** of the candidate. Image building is using public and private polls to mold the candidate's image to meet the particular needs of the campaign.

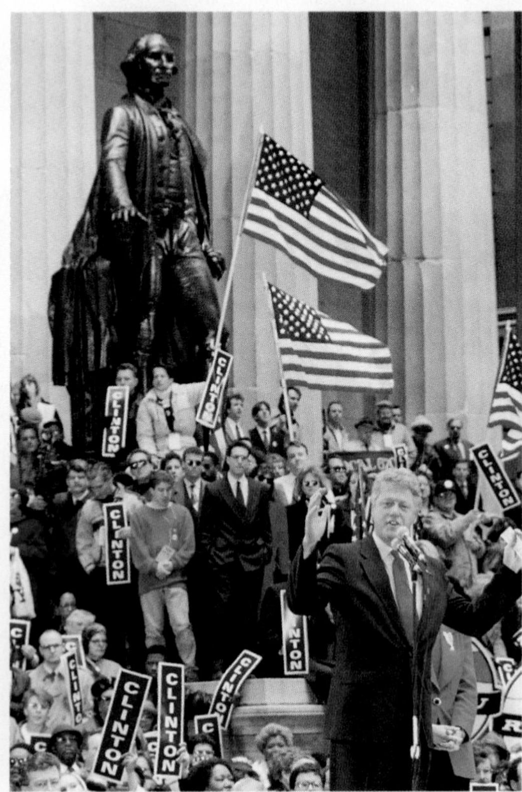

Bill Clinton made effective use of public appearances during the 1992 campaign. Who do you think is generally responsible for planning the candidate's public appearances?

Any serious candidate running for governor, state legislator, U.S. Congress or the presidency has a paid political consultant who daily suggests new campaign ideas to the candidate and decides what new advertising spots are needed. Most of these campaign consultants are not politically neutral—they will only work for candidates from one particular party. Some political consultants have become so popular that they choose the candidates they wish to handle. Two California firms—Whitaker and Baker and Spencer-Roberts—have had great success in handling only Republican candidates, such as Ronald Reagan, who decided to run for governor of California in 1965 and won against the incumbent Governor Edmond G. ''Pat'' Brown. At the national level, Democratic political consultants include Patrick Caddell, Peter Heart, and Joseph Napolitan Associates.

Some critics of professional campaign managers argue that they are only concerned with personalities rather than with issues and philosophies, but this is their job. A professional campaign manager is simply a public relations person who looks at each election as a contest between personalities rather than between two opposing principles. Critics also argue that professional campaign managers, in their quest to help their candidate win, will reshape the candidate's public image so that it bears little relation to reality.

Campaign Planning

The campaign plan is usually centered on the voters. A strategy is needed to decide many matters. For

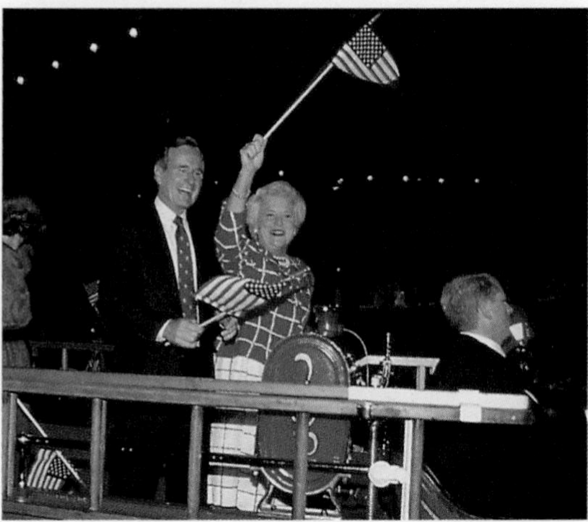

In some cases, paid political consultants plan nearly every move the candidate makes. How do you think this affects the choices available to voters?

Caption Answer Planning campaign appearances is normally the responsibility of the campaign manager and the paid political consultants.

Caption Answer Answers will vary, e.g., it is misleading because voters only see how well the candidate can be managed and not how well he can manage himself.

TEACHING GOVERNMENT IN ACTION

Read
Introduce this Government in Action feature by having the students read the title, "Criticisms of the Mass Media in Campaigns," and discuss their own reactions to it: What criticism have you read or heard aimed at the use of mass media in political campaigns? Based on what you have already learned, do you think these criticisms are valid? Why or why not? After this discussion, let volunteers take turns reading the feature aloud to the rest of the class.

Discuss
Help the students discuss this "Criticism of the Mass Media in Campaigns" by posing questions such as these: Who bears the responsibility for the voters' becoming informed about the issues? If voters demanded more information, would the mass media provide it? Why or why not? What dangers do you see in the production of "cookie cutter" commercials? How do you react to this practice? What do you think accounts for the trend toward negativity in media coverage of candidates?

Analyze and Apply
Let the students work in groups to select and research recent political campaigns. Have the group members gather and discuss examples of mass media advertising and coverage of that campaign.

Review
Have the students respond to these review questions: Why were television and radio originally seen as a democratizing force? What are three major criticisms now leveled at mass-media campaigns?

Think About It (Answers)
1. Answers will vary, e.g., reforming mass-media campaigns would require restrictions on the media. This would violate First Amendment freedoms.
2. Answers will vary, e.g., yes, mass media campaigns have reduced political campaigning to a series of slogans and meaningless "sound bytes." No, because mass media campaigns allow more people to get involved in the political process simply by watching television.

Discussion Starter
Let the students share and discuss their own experiences with door-to-door campaigning: Have you ever met candidates or their volunteers under these circumstances? How did you react? Do you consider this an effective way to campaign today?

Discussion Starter
Ask the students to consider the three major media—television, radio, and newspapers: Do the media reach different audiences? If so, how would you characterize each audience? How do you imagine campaigns tailor advertising and exposure of the candidate to suit these different audiences?

GOVERNMENT IN ACTION

CASE STUDY

Criticisms of the Mass Media in Campaigns

Originally, television and radio were seen as a democratizing force. They helped break down party machines and let candidates speak directly to the electorate.

But now another effect of television is becoming clear. "The rise of electronic media has had an effect of draining content out of campaigns," according to Arthur Schlesinger, Jr., a prominent American historian.

One of the main criticisms of current mass-media campaigns is that they reduce the personal element in American politics. Because TV and radio media allow only 30-second spots to cover most issues, the issues are often presented in shortened or oversimplified form. Complex issues such as environmental policy or military spending are reduced to mere slogans that fit the designated time frame. As a result, in-depth discussions about issues are avoided and voters may consequently not be properly informed.

Another criticism of mass-media campaigns is that they are run by campaign consultants normally located in cities not very close to where the campaigns are targeted. These consultant-run campaigns are sometimes called "cookie-cutter" campaigns in which the candidates simply use computerized preformed commercials and fill in the blanks with their particular information. The problem with these campaigns is that they are removed from the lives of the people who have a stake in the community in which the candidate is running for office.

Another criticism is that the mass media have dramatically darkened the tone and content of political campaigns. Thomas Patterson, professor of political science at the Maxwell School of Government, said that in the 1960 presidential campaign, 60 percent of the coverage of the presidential candidates in *Time* and *Newsweek* was favorable. In 1988, only 30 percent was favorable. The same trend is found in newspapers and television.

THINK ABOUT IT

1. Do you think it is difficult for critics of mass-media campaigns to propose reforms? Explain your answer.
2. Do you agree or disagree with these criticisms? Explain your answer.

example, should the candidate wage an aggressive or a low-key campaign? What stand should the candidate take on issues such as the environment, schools, water, highways, and a variety of other problems? What theme or campaign slogan should be adopted? How much money should be spent on television, radio, or newspaper advertising?

Door-to-Door Techniques Over the years, a variety of standard campaign techniques have been developed and are included in most campaigns. Door-to-door campaigning requires that the candidate knock on voters' doors and talk with them briefly. Campaign workers also use these techniques to talk with voters. Candidates also go to factory gates or shopping centers to seek out voters and talk with them.

Mass Media and Computerized Techniques Although the traditional campaign techniques mentioned above are still widely used, one of the major developments in contemporary American politics is the rise of a new style of campaigning based mainly on reaching the voter through the use of mass media—television, radio, and newspapers. Modern campaigns also use computers and polls to constantly keep track of and use campaign information. Experts estimate that some three hundred companies currently specialize in computer services and software for political campaigns.

In order to find out what is most important to the voters, information based on opinion polls—both public and private—becomes a major part of campaign strategy. Often presidential hopefuls will have private polls taken. In the 1980 presidential campaign, for example, Jimmy

Discussion Starter
Encourage the students to share their responses to politicians' use of polls during campaigns: How can polling help both the candidate and the voters? What negative effects might polling have? Do you think these negative effects could outweigh the benefits of polling? Why or why not?

Enrichment
Have the students work with partners to select specific recent campaigns and research the expenditures of both candidates. Ask each pair of students to prepare an information card detailing these expenditures; post all the cards on a classroom bulletin board.

Discussion Starter
Ask questions such as these to stimulate discussion: What specific problems do you see in the connection between money and campaigns? Which of these do you consider most dangerous? Why? Do you consider any of these problems unimportant? Why or why not?

Extension
Ask interested volunteers to learn more about the FEC: Who serves on the commission? Why do these individuals appear to have been selected for the FEC? Is service on the FEC a full-time job? How effective is the commission considered to be? Why? Let these volunteers summarize their findings for the rest of the class.

This figure content is also featured on *West's American Government Videodisc* (see the index found in the *TRB*).

Figure Answer Students should understand that, unlike Congressional candidates, presidential candidates must mount a national campaign, thus incurring much greater expenditures. You might explain to students that since the provision of public funds for presidential elections began, all major candidates have chosen to take advantage of this funding method and have been bound by the expenditure limitations of the law.

Congressional Campaign Spending, 1983–1990

	House of Representatives (amount in millions of dollars)				Senate (amount in millions of dollars)			
	1983–1984	1985–1986	1987–1988	1989–1990	1983–1984	1985–1986	1987–1988	1989–1990
Total Disbursements	203.5	239.3	256.5	265.1	170.5	211.6	201.1	180.1
Disbursements by Party:								
Democrats	111.0	128.7	145.1	150.8	82.0	89.0	107.6	87.6
Republicans	91.8	110.5	110.5	113.2	88.3	122.6	93.2	92.5
Others	.7	.1	.9	1.1	.2	(z)	.3	(z)
Disbursements by Position:								
Incumbents	114.9	132.5	156.5	163.0	72.1	89.3	101.3	113.5
Challengers	54.7	48.8	51.0	46.7	38.3	66.2	55.9	54.6
Open Seats	33.9	58.0	49.0	55.4	60.1	56.1	44.0	11.9

(z) = Less than $50,000, or .05 percent.
Source: Federal Election Commission

▲ **FIGURE 10–3 Congressional Campaign Spending 1983–1990.** As you can see from the figure above, campaigning for a congressional seat has become very expensive in this country. Do you think it would be more expensive to run a presidential campaign? Why?

Multidiscipline Strategies

Language Arts Have students assume the role of political reporter. They should "cover" a local political story, such as a meeting of the school board or the city council, or perhaps a campaign appearance. Students should share their stories with the rest of the class. If possible, students should include photographs of the event. An alternative would be to create a news video of the same type of event listed above. Students should compare their stories to actual media coverage of the event.

Carter relied on polls conducted by his personal pollster, Patrick Caddell. Ronald Reagan relied on private pollster Richard Wirthlin in 1980 and 1984. By polling the potential voters in the state or nation, the candidate can find out his or her strengths and weaknesses and try to fix problem areas in his or her public image through advertising. As the election approaches, many candidates use **tracking polls**, which are polls taken almost every day, to find out how well they are competing for votes. They enable the campaign organization to fine tune the candidate's speeches and advertising in the last critical days.

Campaign Financing and Regulation

The sophisticated vote-getting techniques that candidates employ have made campaigning very expensive. Huge sums are spent for television and radio time, printing costs, advertising, travel, and office rent, to list only a few expenses. The more important the office sought, the more money is likely to be spent. It is estimated that over $2 billion was spent at all levels of government campaigning in 1988 (a presidential election year) and over $1 billion in 1990. Some candidates are able to use part of their own money to run for office, but most rely on contributions from individuals and organizations.

The connection between money and campaigns gives rise to some of the most difficult problems in American politics. The biggest fear is that contributors might be able to influence people running for office by giving large gifts or loans. There is also the possibility that some special interest groups will try to buy favored treatment from those who are elected to office. To prevent these abuses, laws have been passed to regulate campaign finances.

In the wake of the scandals uncovered by the Watergate break-in in 1972, Congress and the Supreme Court restructured campaign financing rules. Although not related to the Watergate scandal, President Richard Nixon's questionable campaign financing brought about calls for campaign reform, notably from such public interest lobbies as Common Cause and the National Committee for Effective Congress. In 1974, the House and Senate passed the Federal Election Campaign Act, which in essence did the following:

- **Established an independent agency known as the Federal Election Commission (FEC) set up by Congress in 1974 to carry out this act.** The Commission has six members, appointed by the president, subject to the approval of the Senate.

Enrichment
Have one of the students do research on the rate at which presidential candidates accept federally supported funding and spending limits: Since 1974, have any presidential candidates refused this funding? If so, which candidates? Why? Ask the students to report this information to the rest of the class.

Discussion Starter
Guide the students in considering the limitations on contributions: How does the limit for individuals compare to the limit for groups? How could this difference be manipulated to allow groups to contribute more than $5,000 to a single candidate? Have any groups tried this tactic? If so, which groups and with what results? (You may want to have volunteers research answers to the final two questions.)

Cooperative Learning
Divide the class into six or seven groups; ask the members of each group to select and read about a specific PAC: From whom did the PAC collect money last year? To which candidates did the PAC contribute? Why? With what success? Then let the groups share their information with the rest of the class.

Discussion Starter
Focus the students' attention on the distribution of PAC funds to congressional candidates: What are the implications of this distribution? Do you think this split represents—or helps to cause—a general tendency to support incumbents? Why?

- **Provided public financing for presidential primaries and general elections.** Presidential candidates who raise some money on their own in at least twenty states can get a check from the U.S. Treasury to help pay for primary campaigns. For the general election campaign, presidential candidates get federal funding for almost all expenses *if* they are willing to accept campaign spending limits.
- **Limited presidential campaign spending.** Any candidate accepting federal support must agree to limit expenditures to amounts set by federal law.
- **Required disclosure.** Candidates must file periodic reports with the FEC that list who contributed to the campaign and how the money was spent.
- **Limited contributions.** Citizens can contribute up to $1,000 to each candidate in each federal election or primary. The total limit for any individual in one year is $25,000. Groups can contribute a maximum of $5,000 to a candidate in any election.

The Growth of PACs

The 1974 reforms and their subsequent amendments encouraged a new way of contributing to campaigns by allowing corporations, labor unions, and special interest groups to set up political action committees (PACs) to raise money for candidates.

Top 15 PAC Contributions to Congressional Candidates (January 1, 1989–June 30, 1990)

Group	Amount in millions
Democratic-Republican Independent Voter Education Committee (International Brotherhood of Teamsters)	$6.4
American Medical Association	3.0
National Association of Realtors	2.7
National Congressional Club (Senator Jesse Helms' political organization)	2.6
American Federation of State, County, and Municipal Employees	2.4
Voter Guide (bipartisan California group)	2.3
American Telephone and Telegraph Company, Inc.	2.3
Association of Trial Lawyers of America	2.3
United Automobile Workers	2.0
Committee on Letter Carriers Political Education	1.9
National Rifle Association Political Victory Fund	1.8
American Citizens for Political Action (a conservative fund-raising committee)	1.7
National Education Association	1.7
Machinists Nonpartisan Political League	1.6
C.W.A.-COPE Political Contributions Committee (Communications Workers of America)	1.5

Source: Federal Election Commission

▲ **FIGURE 10–4 Top 15 PAC Contributions to Congressional Candidates (January 1, 1989–June 30, 1990).** The above figure lists the 15 political action committees that made the largest contributions to congressional campaigns over an 18-month period ending in 1990. What was the total contribution of all 15 of these PACs during that period?

This figure content is also featured on *West's American Government Videodisc* (see the index found in the *TRB*).

Figure Answer During the specified period these PACs contributed $36.2 million to Congressional campaigns.

Discussion Starter
Encourage the students to share their reactions to the option of contributing $1 of tax payment to the Presidential Election Campaign Fund: Do you think this option is a good idea? Why or why not? If you have already filed your own tax form, did you check the contribution box? Do your family members check the contribution box? Why or why not?

2. Have the students take the Section 2 Quiz found in the *TRB*.

Section 2 Review (Answers)
1. Typically, the campaign manager coordinates and plans the campaign strategy. Most campaign workers are volunteers.
2. Door-to-door campaigning, advertising, and using computers and polls to keep track of campaign information.
3. The act provided public financing for presidential primaries and general elections. It limits campaign spending and requires candidates to file periodic reports with the FEC that list who contributes to the campaign and how money was spent. It limits contributions to campaigns.
4. A PAC is an organization designed to collect money and provide financial support for a political candidate.
5. Answers will vary, e.g., individuals might not fully understand the option or might be further expressing a sense of voter apathy.

SECTION 3

Points to Stress
• The types of elections in the United States and their differences.
• The different types of ballots.
• How the electoral college works.

Discussion Starter
Guide the students in discussing the money spent on national conventions: Do you consider this level of spending appropriate? If so, what do you feel the parties and the voters gain from the conventions? If not, how do you feel the parties might more wisely spend some of that money?

Discussion Starter
Ask the students whether they feel public funding and spending limitations should be introduced for the campaigns of candidates for the Senate and House of Representatives. Encourage the students to explain their ideas.

Reteaching Strategies
1. Have the students work in groups to compare and discuss their outlines of Section 2. Encourage the students to make any revisions or additions that will improve their understanding of the section content.
2. Let the students work with partners to write, in their own words, definitions of these terms: *campaign manager, political consultant, image building, FEC, PAC.*

Evaluation Strategies
1. Have the students write their responses to the Section 2 Review questions.

This is how a PAC works. A union, corporation, or interest group decides to channel some of its money into the political campaign of a candidate who supports their goals. They create a PAC by registering with the FEC. The PAC can then collect money from executives, employees, stockholders, or members to donate to the campaign of their choosing. No PAC may give more than $5,000 to each candidate for each election, but there is no overall limit on PAC giving. Each may contribute up to $5,000 to as many different candidates as it chooses. There are over 4,600 PACs and they are estimated to have put more than $380 million into the presidential and congressional campaigns of 1992. They also spend money to defeat candidates whose positions they oppose.

PACs are not limited to making campaign contributions. They may conduct their own campaigns for presidential and congressional candidates. They also spend hundreds of thousands of dollars for television commercials and other independent efforts to praise or attack candidates they support or oppose. They may spend as much money as they choose, providing the candidates themselves don't control how the money is spent. A sample of what PACs spent in a recent year is shown in Figure 10–4 on page 243.

Campaign Spending Most of the spending limits imposed by the current laws apply only to presidential campaigns. Presidential candidates campaigning for office can choose whether or not to accept federal funding. If they do not accept, they must then raise all campaign monies on their own, and can spend as much as they choose. If they do accept, they are limited in the amount they may spend. In 1988, for example, no candidate could spend more than $23.05 million in the preconvention period. After the conventions, presidential candidates Dukakis and Bush could spend $46.1 million each on their campaigns.

Public funding of presidential campaigns was provided for in the Revenue Act of 1971, which set up the Presidential Election Campaign Fund. Under this act, persons who file a federal income tax return may request that $1 of their tax payment go to the fund. The monies in the fund are to be used to pay for preconvention campaigns, national conventions, and presidential election campaigns. Presidential hopefuls must raise at least $100,000 in contributions from individuals in order to receive money from the fund. It must be gathered in $5,000 lots, from each of at least twenty states, with each lot built from individual donations of not more than $250. The FEC will then match qualifying contenders the first $250 of each individual's donation up to a total of half of the overall limit. This requirement is meant to discourage candidates who are not seriously committed to campaigning.

Upon applying, both major parties automatically receive a grant to pay for their national convention. This has been true for every convention since 1976. In 1988, both parties received $9.22 million each from the FEC. Every presidential nominee from a major party automatically qualifies for a public subsidy to cover some of the costs of the general election campaign. In 1988, the Bush and Dukakis campaigns each received $46.1 million from the FEC. A third-party candidate qualifies only if he or she received more than 5 percent of the popular vote in the previous presidential election or 5 percent in the current election.

Candidates for the Senate and House of Representatives receive no public funding for their campaigns. They must raise money from private individuals and organizations. There are no ceilings on how much they may spend.

Section 2 Review

1. Describe how a typical campaign is structured.
2. What are some techniques used in campaigning?
3. What are the provisions of the Federal Election Campaign Act?
4. How do PACs function and what is their purpose?
5. **For critical analysis:** The Revenue Act of 1971 allows individuals to earmark $1 of their tax payment for presidential election campaigning. This doesn't seem like much, so why would a person choose not to check the $1 box on his or her income tax returns?

Section 3

The Structure of American Elections

Preview Questions
- What are the various types of elections in the United States and how do they differ?
- What is a ballot and what forms does it take?
- How does the electoral college system work?

There finally comes the time when the last debate is debated, the last poll is reported, and the last television reporter has commented: It is time for the elections. Dem-

Kickoff Activity
Write the following question on the chalkboard: What are your most vivid memories from the last election? Ask the students to write short paragraphs (or, if they prefer, lists of images) in response to the question. After everyone has finished writing, give the students time to compare and discuss their impressions.

Working with the Preview Questions
Let volunteers read these study questions aloud. Encourage volunteers to share their responses, and remind the students that they will learn more about these topics as they study Section 3.

Teaching Strategies

Introduction
Ask one of the students to read the section introduction aloud. Then encourage the students to discuss their responses to these questions: Why is it so important that our elections be free, honest, and accurate? What would happen if even a few elections were not? Who is responsible for ensuring that American elections remain free, honest, and accurate? Is that responsibility being taken seriously?

Comprehension
Ask the students to identify the dates on which the last general election was held and on which the next general election will be held.

Discussion Starter
Have the students recall and discuss recent news of elections being called in other democratic countries: In which country were elections most recently held? Why were they called? What were the results? How do you think the system of elections used in that country differs from the American system?

Discussion Starter
Help the students discuss recall elections: Does our state allow recall elections? If so, have any recall elections been held during the past five years? For what reasons? With what results? Do you think recall elections should be allowed? Why or why not?

Enrichment
For this activity, you will need a voting precinct map for your community. Have the students identify the voting precincts in which they live: What are the boundaries of that precinct? Where is the precinct's polling place? Ask each student to write a paragraph reporting this information.

Caption Answer Student answers will vary. You might wish to extend the class discussion by bringing in a precinct map of your community to show the class.

ocratic government cannot succeed unless elections are free, honest, and accurate. Because most of the elective offices in the United States are at the state and local level, most of the election law in the United States is state law. The Constitution grants the power to fix "the times, places, and manner of holding elections" to the state legislatures, but the Constitution gives Congress the power to alter such regulations. Congress has required the use of secret ballots and has passed several laws to protect the right to vote for certain groups of people. Congress also has the power to regulate certain aspects of the presidential election process, to forbid certain corrupt practices, and to regulate campaign finances.

Kinds of Elections

Two important kinds of elections in the United States are general elections and special elections.

General Election The most familiar kind of election is the **general election**, a regularly scheduled election at which voters cast their final votes for selection of public officeholders. General elections are held in even-numbered years on the first Tuesday after the first Monday in November for the president, the vice president, and senators and representatives of Congress. The president and vice president are elected every four years, senators every six years, and representatives every two years. General elections are also held to choose state and local government leaders, often at the same time as those for national offices. The fact that American elections are held at these fixed intervals—every two or four years, for example—may seem too obvious to mention, but it is not that way in most democracies. In parliamentary systems, elections may be called irregularly. In Great Britain, for example, elections must be called every five years, but may be called earlier if the majority party thinks it can boost its control of Parliament or if the government loses the support of its parliamentary coalition.

Special Elections A **special election** is held whenever an issue must be decided before the next general election. For example, an important city official might resign or die before the end of his or her term. The city may decide to hold a special election to fill the vacancy.

In each of these kinds of elections, voters elect both federal and state office holders. In many states voters also participate in direct lawmaking through the initiative, referendum, and recall processes described on page 540.

Polling Places

State law divides local units of government into smaller voting districts, or precincts. State law usually restricts the size of precincts and local officials set the boundaries. Within each precinct, voters cast their ballots at one *polling place*.

A precinct election board supervises the polling place and the voting process in each precinct. It sets hours for the polls to be open according to the laws of the state and sees that ballots or voting machines are available. In most states it provides the list of registered voters and makes certain that only qualified voters cast ballots in that precinct. When the polls close, the board counts the votes and reports the results, usually to the county clerk or board of elections.

Representatives from each party, called poll watchers, are allowed at each polling place to make sure the election is run fairly.

▼ Voters in Santa Cruz, California can cast their votes in this bakery that serves as a polling place for each election. Name some other possible polling places.

Extension
Ask volunteers to bring copies of ballots or actual old ballots to class for all the students to examine and discuss.

Discussion Starter
Focus the students' attention on each of the four main features of the Australian ballot: Why is this feature important?

Discussion Starter
Ask the students to share their responses to "straight party" voting: Who do you imagine votes this way? Why? Do you consider straight party voting responsible? Why or why not?

Enrichment
Guide the students in sharing their responses to lengthy ballots: Should voters be asked to make so many decisions? Why or why not? Then have students conduct an informal poll on this subject. Each student should interview at least five people of voting age and ask them the following questions: 1. Do you think that election ballots are too long? 2. Did you vote in the last election? 3. How did the length of the ballot affect your decision to (not) vote? Have students share their polls with the rest of the class.

Discussion Starter
Let the students consider Edison's invention: What were some of Edison's other important inventions? What do you imagine motivated Edison to invent a voting machine? What impact has this invention had? What advantages do modern voting machines offer voters? How important are these advantages? What disadvantages, if any, do they pose for voters? How might those disadvantages be overcome?

Discussion Starter
Encourage the students to discuss computerized voting: Can this method be abused? If so, how? If not, why not? How do you feel about computerized voting ma-

Ballots

In the early days of our country, voters gathered in a central place and called out their vote. They could be applauded or booed as they voiced their preferences. Of course, with this method of voting, people were unduly influenced by others and many people wanted the system changed. By the mid-1800s, political parties passed out paper ballots to voters. The ballots were different colors to symbolize different parties, and the ballot box was in public view; thus, anyone watching still knew who voted for whom.

Because voters were still subject to vote-buying and political pressure, many local and state governments came under the control of **political machines**, highly organized party organizations that were very powerful in many large cities in the nineteenth and early twentieth centuries. These political machines won elections by giving government favors—well-paying public jobs or public construction contracts—instead of competing fairly. They put their own interests before the interests of the public.

Australian Ballot The balloting system was improved in 1888 when a new method of voting was introduced from Australia. The **Australian ballot** had four main features: (1) it was printed by election officials at public expense; (2) it listed the names of all candidates in an election; (3) it was distributed only at the polling places to qualified voters; and (4) the actual voting was done in secret. There are two variations of the Australian ballot used in the United States today.

- **Office-group ballot.** With the **office-group ballot**, all candidates for each office are listed together. For example, all candidates for state senator are listed under that heading along with their party affiliation. Initially it was common for the names to appear in alphabetical order. Today, in most states, the names are now rotated, so that each candidate has a chance to be listed first. Sometimes this ballot is called the *Massachusetts ballot,* because that state first used it in general elections in 1888.
- **Party-column ballot.** The **party-column ballot** lists candidates under their party label. For example, the Republican candidates for senator, representative, governor, state legislator, and local office are listed under the Republican column. There is often a place at the top of the ballot where a voter, with one mark, can vote for all of one party's candidates. This encourages "straight-party" voting, especially if the party has a strong candidate at the head of the ticket. This style is losing favor because differences between the two parties seem to be less apparent, and voters' identification with party labels appears to be weakening.

Length of Ballots Besides selecting many public officials, voters must often vote on a number of local and statewide issues as well. Because all of these choices must be listed on the ballot, the ballot is typically lengthy, and has been called the "bedsheet ballot." Many people criticize such ballots today because they believe they are too long. In 1990, for example, the California ballot had over eight pages. Critics feel it is almost impossible to make intelligent and informed decisions on so many candidates and issues and complain of "ballot fatigue." They argue that the smaller the number of elected officials on a ballot, the better chance there is that voters will know the candidates' qualifications.

Others argue that the greater the number of officials elected to office, the more democratic the system. They argue that the public has the right to get as involved as it can in government decision making.

Voting Machines

Thomas Edison took out the first patent for a voting machine in 1868, and his invention was initially used in an election in Lockport, New York, in 1892. Now, over half of all voters in the United States cast ballots on voting machines, which have steadily replaced paper ballots.

Voting machines differ in some details, but all work in much the same way. By pulling a large lever, the voter encloses himself or herself within a curtain. The ballot appears on the face of a machine and voters make choices by pulling down the small levers over the names of the candidates they choose. The machine is programmed so that voters can cast only one vote per contest. Once all the levers are in the desired positions, the voter opens the curtain. This action records the votes and clears the machine for the next voter.

Many election districts use computerized voting machines. The voter marks a square or punches a hole on a card and the computer reads the card, then totals the votes for each candidate and prints out the results. Voting machines speed up the voting process by doing away with the need for manual counting. They reduce the number of persons needed to administer elections and increase the amount of voters that can be handled per precinct. They can also minimize fraud and counting errors.

chines? How do you imagine older voters feel?

Critical Thinking Skills
Help the students analyze the continued use of the electoral college: Which of the conditions that motivated the establishment of the electoral college still exist? Do the changes in these motivating conditions imply that the electoral college is no longer necessary? No longer useful? Why or why not?

Caption Answer Voting machines make handling the ballots and tallying the votes much easier for election officials. Additionally, most voting machines are engineered so that voters can only cast one vote per contest.

Enrichment
Have a volunteer research and report the answer to this question: What laws—if any—does your state have regulating the votes cast by electors?

Comprehension
Use these questions to check the students' comprehension: How many electors does your state have? How is that number determined?

Discussion Starter
Ask the students to consider the fact that the District of Columbia has electors in the electoral college: Why is this significant? What does this signify about the unusual status of the District?

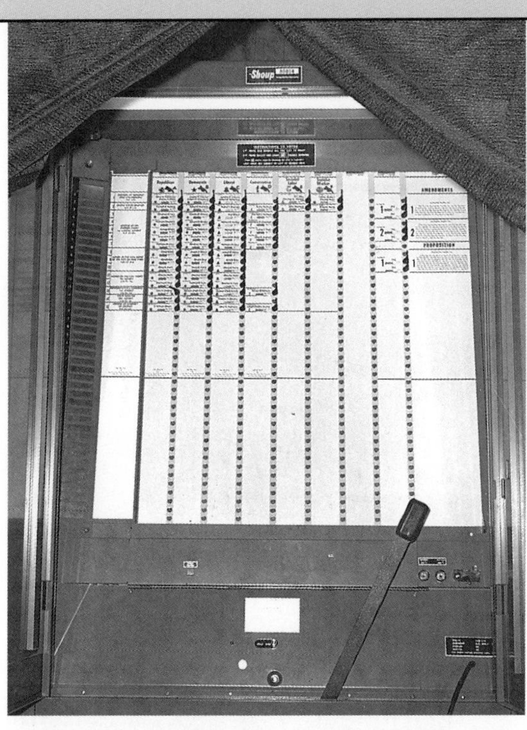

▲ This voting machine was first used in the 1964 presidential elections in New York City. What do you think are the advantages of using voting machines in elections?

Electing the President

It is true that *nominating* the presidential and vice presidential candidates is different from nominating officials for any other office. The same is true of *electing* the president and vice president: It is a complex system with its own set of rules.

The Electoral College System The writers of the Constitution argued long and hard about the method of electing the president. Many did not want the president to be directly elected by the people because they did not trust the average person's judgment, and feared that citizens scattered all across the new country would have a hard time learning enough about the candidates to make a wise choice. At that time there were, after all, problems with time lapses in communication and transportation. They wanted the president to be elected by the nation's elite (a small group of wealthy, powerful, and hopefully reasonable leaders), and not by the people directly, so they provided for presidential *electors.* The result was the **electoral college system**, in which direct votes by the citizens do not actually elect the president.

Fortunately, over time, political practice has made the electoral vote more responsive to popular majorities. In the early days electors could vote any way they chose, but today virtually all electors vote for the candidate who got the most votes in their state; some states have even made it illegal for electors not to vote this way. These changes have helped democratize the electoral system. (The electoral vote could, however, be won by the candidate receiving fewer popular votes but the majority of electoral votes.)

The Electoral College System Today The first step in the electoral college process is the general election in which all registered voters may vote for the president and vice president. This is called a **popular vote**, or the vote of the people.

Most voters today believe that they actually vote directly for a president or vice president, when in fact they are choosing a slate of **electors**, people who will cast the official votes for them. These electors are chosen by the states' political parties, subject to the laws of the state. Each state has as many electoral votes as it has United States senators and representatives. In addition, there are three electors from the District of Columbia.

The electoral college system is a **winner-take-all system**, in which the candidate who receives the largest

▼ The popular vote, which is open to all registered voters, is only one step in electing a president and vice president. Who actually casts the votes that decide presidential elections?

Caption Answer The electoral college casts the deciding votes in a presidential election. The president is chosen by receiving a majority (at least 270) of the votes cast by the 538 electors.

Multidiscipline Strategies

Research Students need to understand just how few Americans get involved in the candidate selection process. Have students get totals of the following for the 1988 Presidential election: Population, people of voting age, people registered to vote, people who voted in the general election, and people who voted in the primaries. Students will learn, for example, that even though more than 90 million people voted in the general election, that figure was only 50.1 percent. During the primaries, only 23 million people cast ballots in the Democratic primaries, while only 12 million cast ballots in the Republican primaries. Have students summarize the data, providing implications for the current system.

Congressional Quarterly's Guide to U.S. Elections, U.S. Bureau of the Census, and *The World Almanac and Book of Facts* are sources that will help with this exercise.

Enrichment
Let students volunteer to research the elections in which no candidate received an electoral college majority (1800 and 1824) and the elections in which the winner of the electoral vote lost the popular vote (1876 and 1888). Ask the volunteers to work together in planning and presenting a short oral report of their findings.

Discussion Starter
Focus the students' attention on the fact that more than 500 amendments proposing changes in the electoral system have been defeated: What does this fact imply about the electoral system?

Reteaching Strategies
1. Let the students work in small groups to review and discuss Section 3. Have each group member ask at least one question about the section content; if necessary, help the group members answer one another's questions.
2. Have the students work with partners to draw simple flow-charts summarizing the effects of one individual's vote for a presidential candidate, through the electoral college, to the final election of the president.

Evaluation Strategies
1. Have the students write their responses to the Section 3 Review questions.
2. Have the students take the Section 3 Quiz found in the *TRB*.

Section 3 Review (Answers)
1. General elections are regularly scheduled elections at which voters make their final selection of public officeholders. Special elections are held when an issue must be decided before the next general elections.
2. State law divides local units of government into precincts. Within each precinct, voters cast their ballots at one polling place.

This figure content is also featured on *West's American Government Videodisc* (see the index found in the *TRB*) and is available in the transparency package.

Figure Answer The founders feared that average citizens would not be adequately informed to make wise decisions in this area; they wanted the president to be elected by the elite of the nation.

FYI

Not everyone loves to hate the Electoral College. Many political observers feel that, although not perfect, the current system is better than anything that could replace it. Specifically, the current system magnifies majorities, hence giving winners a clear mandate even in races that have close popular votes. The current system also reduces the effects of voter fraud. Third party candidates have little chance to succeed under the current system, which some feel strengthens our two-party system.

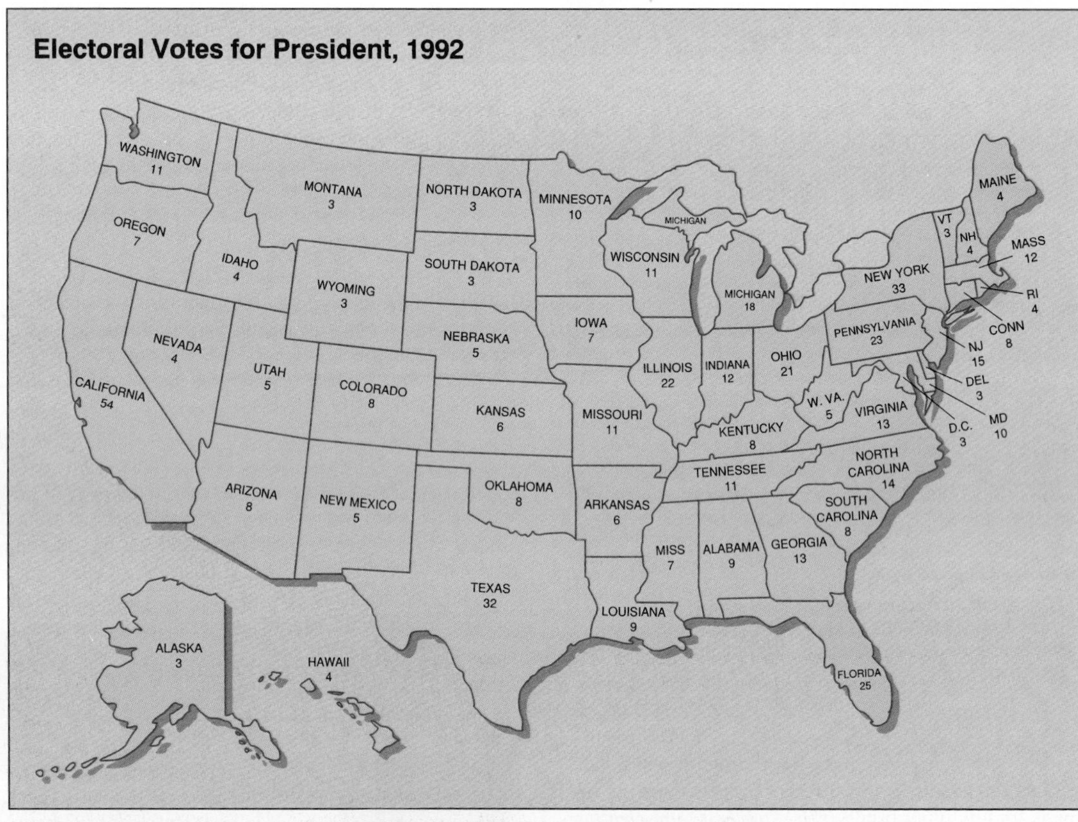

▲ **FIGURE 10–5 Electoral Votes for President, 1992.** Each state has the same number of electors as it has United States senators and representatives. Why did the founders of our country choose to use the electoral college system for electing the president?

popular vote in a state is credited with *all* that state's electoral votes—one vote per elector. This is true no matter what the margin of victory.

In December, after the general election, members of the electoral college meet in their state capitals to cast their votes for president and vice president. Although they are not legally bound to do so by Article 1, Section 2 of the Constitution, the electors usually vote for the candidate who won popular support in their state. In 1976, an elector from Seattle, Washington, voted for Ronald Reagan even though Gerald Ford had won the majority of popular votes in that state. It has only been on rare occasions that an elector breaks a pledge to vote for the party's nominee. It has never affected the outcome of an election.

The votes are sealed and then sent to the Senate. The ballots are counted and certified before a joint session of Congress early in January. The candidates who receive a majority of the electoral votes are officially declared president and vice president.

To be elected, a candidate must receive more than half of the 538 electoral votes available.[2] This means that a candidate needs 270 votes to win. If no candidate gets an electoral college majority, the House of Representatives votes on the candidates, with each state delegation casting only a single vote. (This has happened twice—in 1800 and in 1824.)

The winner-take-all system makes it possible for a candidate to be elected who lost the total popular vote

2. The number of electoral votes equals the total number of senators and representatives (535) plus three votes for the residents of Washington, D.C. Please see Amendment XXIII on page 671.

3. The Australian ballot is printed at public expense and lists the names of all candidates. It is distributed only at the polling places to qualified voters and the actual voting is done in secret. The office-group ballot lists all candidates together. The party-column ballot lists candidates under their party label.
4. Through the popular vote, voters are choosing which parties' slate of electors will be chosen. These electors, in turn, cast the official votes for president.
5. Answers will vary, e.g., yes, the electoral vote should be replaced by a direct popular vote because there is no reason that a vote in California should be any different than a vote in Wyoming. Every vote should count toward electing the president equally. No, let's not change a system that works just fine.

SECTION 4

Points to Stress

- Types of television coverage used by candidates during campaigns.
- Negative advertising.
- The various propaganda techniques.

Kickoff Activity

Ask the students this question: How important do you think the media are in political campaigns and elections? Have the students write short paragraphs in response; then encourage volunteers to read their responses aloud. Remind the students that they will learn more about the media-campaign-election relationship as they read Section 4.

Working with the Preview Questions

Read each of these study questions aloud, and encourage the students to share and discuss what they already know in response to the questions. Then ask the students to keep these questions in mind as they work through Section 4.

but won the electoral vote. This has happened twice—in the elections of Rutherford B. Hayes in 1876 and Benjamin Harrison in 1888. Critics of the electoral college point out that this could happen again. In 1960, John F. Kennedy, a Democrat, defeated Richard Nixon, a Republican. If only nine thousand people in Illinois and Missouri had voted for Nixon instead of Kennedy, Nixon would have won the electoral college votes in those two states. As a result, Nixon would have won the election while still losing the popular vote by a narrow margin.

The electoral system has been criticized by many as being out of date and undemocratic. Over the years, more than five hundred amendments calling for changes in the electoral system have been brought before Congress. Proposals have ranged from modifying it to throwing it out completely and electing the president by direct popular vote. All amendments on the subject have failed.

SECTION 3 REVIEW

1. How would you classify the various types of elections in the United States?
2. How does state law divide local government for election purposes?
3. What is an Australian ballot? What are the different types of Australian ballots?
4. How does the electoral college system work to elect the president?
5. **For critical analysis:** Should the electoral vote for president be replaced by a direct popular vote? Explain why or why not.

SECTION 4

The Role of the Media in Campaigns and Elections

Preview Questions

- What types of television coverage are used by candidates during campaigns?
- What is negative campaign advertising?
- What is propaganda and what are some propaganda techniques?

The media, especially television, have had a wide-ranging effect on politics in general. Their most immediate and obvious impact, however, is during campaigns and elections. Years ago, the biggest expense in a campaign budget might have been the campaign train rental. Today, the biggest expense is unquestionably television advertising, which consumes about half of the total budget for a major campaign.

The Candidates and Television

Candidates use several types of television coverage in campaigns: debates, political advertising and news coverage.

Debates The first great television debate was in 1960 between Republican presidential candidate Richard M. Nixon and the youthful Democratic Senator John F. Kennedy from Massachusetts. Too rushed to shave before the debates, Nixon used a cosmetic product called "Lazy Shave" to hide his five o'clock shadow. As a result he looked unshaven and drawn in contrast to Kennedy's fresh appearance. In the debate itself, Nixon answered questions like the college debater he once was, while Kennedy aimed his remarks directly at the television audience. Many believe the debate turned the tide in Kennedy's favor and established the importance of good television appearance for a presidential candidate.

Since that first debate, many others have helped influence the outcome of elections. Television debates are a unique opportunity for voters to find out how candidates differ on issues, but they are also a way for candidates to capitalize on the power of television to project a positive image. They view television debates as a chance to

▼ The presidential debate between candidates Richard Nixon and John F. Kennedy, which was held in 1960, was the first great television debate. Why was this debate so important?

Teaching Strategies

Introduction

Ask a volunteer to read the section introduction to the rest of the class. Then let the students discuss their responses to the idea of spending nearly half of a campaign's budget on television advertising: How do you imagine this concentration of funds affects the candidate? Why? How do you think it affects voters? Why?

Caption Answer Students should understand that Kennedy's appearance and ease before the cameras helped turn the tide in that election and ushered in an era where candidates had to include television in their thinking.

Enrichment

Suggest that interested volunteers research contemporary news coverage and editorials related to the Kennedy-Nixon debates. Let them present their findings to the rest of the class in an oral report.

TEACHING BUILDING SOCIAL STUDIES SKILLS

Read

Introduce this feature by letting the students recall and discuss specific political commercials they have seen on television: How did the commercials treat their subject? What attitudes toward voters did the commercials convey? How did you respond to the commercials? After this introductory discussion, ask volunteers to read the Building Social Studies Skills feature aloud to the rest of the class.

Discuss

Focus the students' attention on the table of advertising spending: What does this chart indicate? How do you react to this trend? Why?

Stimulate further discussion of the feature by asking questions such as these: Who bears the responsibility for voters' being persuaded by emotional appeals in advertising, rather than by facts? Who should accept the responsibility of reversing this situation? What is the importance of each of the evaluation questions viewers can ask about television ads? Do you think most viewers use such evaluation techniques? If not, why don't viewers and voters evaluate television ads more carefully?

Analyze and Apply

Let the students work in groups to plan and write an effective ad for a political candidate. (They may choose candidates in a school or local campaign, or they may create imaginary candidates.) Have each group present its ad to the rest of the class; ask the students in the "audience" to evaluate the ad.

Review

Use these questions to help the students review the Building Social Studies Skills feature: What trend is evident in campaign spending on television advertising? What major objections do critics raise against the use of television advertising in political campaigns?

BUILDING SOCIAL STUDIES SKILLS

Evaluating Political Commercials

Most candidates now spend large amounts of money on television commercials. In fact, as the figure on the next page illustrates, the amount spent on political advertising rises significantly with every election year.

Television commercials do provide exposure for and information about candidates and their issues. They also provide an opportunity for candidates to speak directly to the electorate.

Many people, however, feel that the growing use of television advertising is also draining out the content of campaigns. The issues are often presented in a shortened or overstated form. As with printed ads, TV ads reduce complex issues such as balancing the federal budget, military policy, or cleaning up the environment to mere slogans. Commercials use emotional appeal, rather than facts, to persuade voters. There is also a trend toward more negative advertising, which may involve blaming other candidates for current social problems or attacking their personal lives.

Remember that political commercials, like any other commercial, are trying to sell you a product or service. In this case the ''product'' is a political candidate. Knowing how to evaluate television ads during an election campaign will help you learn to evaluate political candidates and issues. Start by asking yourself:

- **Which individual or group paid for the commercial?** All political advertising is required by law to identify who paid for it. Think about why the ad's sponsor is interested in electing the candidate.
- **What forms of communication are used?** Is the message conveyed through urgent music, shocking pictures, soft images, popular symbols? What is the narrator's tone of voice? What's the story line? Recognizing these elements of an ad will tell you how it is trying to make you feel.
- **Does the ad present facts or does it appeal directly to your emotions?**
- **Is the ad about the candidate being advertised, or does it only attack her or his opponent?** Does it blame another candidate for current problems? Is it negative or positive advertising?
- **Does the ad deal with issues that are appropriate to the office?** For example, a candidate for governor might take a stand on military spending. (Military spending is normally a question for the federal level and not the state level, and therefore has no real bearing on that race.)
- **Does the ad tell you anything substantial about the candidate or does it only seek to boost her or his image?** Look at the propaganda techniques listed on page 255 and 256 to find out if any are used.

Regardless of their strengths or weaknesses, it seems that political candidates, like laundry detergent and soft drinks, are destined to be sold through television commercials. As voters, it is up to each of us to sift through the advertising hype and make sound judgments regarding each candidate's qualifications and abilities.

improve their own image, or a chance to point out the failings of their opponent. The post-debate commentaries by news analysts also play a crucial role in what the public thinks, even when the commentaries are biased.

Political Advertising The first political commercials appeared on television in the 1952 presidential campaign, along with the first televising of party conventions. In the United States there were only about 15 million television sets at that time, a total that climbed to about 54 million in 1960, 93 million in 1970, and well over 100 million today.

Making a political commercial is just like any other type of advertising. The ad writers have thirty or sixty seconds to communicate a message that viewers will remember. Usually she or he will center the ad around the most positive personality traits of a candidate.

The phenomenon of **negative campaign advertising**, however, has somewhat changed these methods. One of the most negative campaign announcements

Discussion Starter
Help the students consider advertising's emphasis on candidates' personality traits: What are some positive personality traits for political candidates? How important are such traits for a candidate? Are those traits also important for a president? Why or why not?

Extension
Ask the students to talk with friends and relatives who might have voted in the 1964 Johnson-Goldwater campaign. What do those people recall about the campaign? Do they remember the TV ad described here? If so, how did they react to it? Give the students an opportunity to share and discuss what they found out from their talks.

Discussion Starter
Encourage the students to discuss their own responses to negative advertising: What examples can you cite? What did you think of those negative ads? Do you think negative advertising can backfire? If so, how and why?

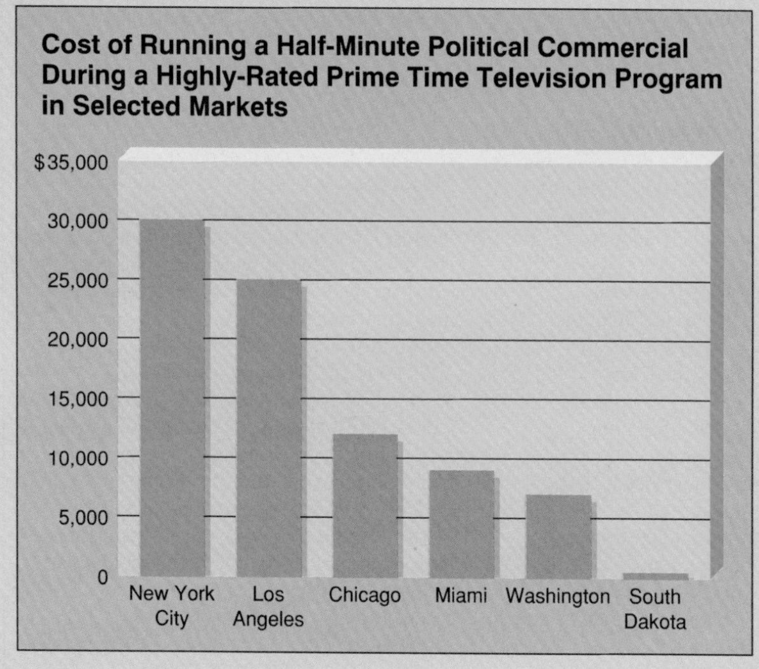

This figure content is also featured on *West's American Government Videodisc* (see the index found in the *TRB*).

PRACTICING YOUR SKILLS

1. Use the questions on page 250 to evaluate a political commercial on local television. If there is no current election, see if you can view footage of previous campaign ads at a local television station. If this is not possible, look at campaign ads in old editions of your local or national newspapers. Then evaluate the ads according to the guidelines presented.
2. Do you think negative advertising about a political opponent is fair? Find examples of what you feel is negative advertising to support your position. Present the ad and your opinions to the class.

Developing Skills for the Information Age

Record national, state, and local campaign commercials. Show the commercials to the class and have them list the following: Propaganda techniques, if any, that were employed; the sponsor of the commercial; the theme or message of the commercial. This can also be done with printed campaign materials like brochures, billboards, and posters. Students should complete a reaction paper which summarizes the results and either supports or rejects the types of campaign commercials they evaluated. If students think that certain commercials are particularly effective or offensive then they should write to the sponsors or candidates to let them know.

appeared in President Lyndon Johnson's campaign against Barry Goldwater in 1964. In this ad, a little girl stood quietly in a field of daisies. She held a daisy and pulled off the petals, counting to herself. Suddenly, when she reached the last petal, a deep voice was heard counting, "10, 9, 8, 7, 6 . . ." When it hit zero, the unmistakable mushroom cloud of an atom bomb filled the screen. Then President Johnson's voice was heard saying, "These are the stakes: To make a world in which all of God's children can live, or to go into the dark. We must either love each other or we must die." A message then read: "Vote for President Johnson on November 3." The implication, of course, was that Goldwater would lead the country into a nuclear war. Even though the ad was removed within a few days, it remains a classic example of negative advertising.

Every election year since then has been marked by some amount of negative advertising. In 1988 a negative ad produced for the Bush campaign mentioned Michael Dukakis' support for granting Massachusetts prisoners

TEACHING CITIZENSHIP SKILLS AND RESPONSIBILITIES

Read
Ask the students to read the title, Talking Back to Your Television, and to share their responses to it: How can you talk back to your TV? Why would you want to? How effective can this kind of talking back be? Why? After this introductory discussion, have the students read the Citizenship Skills and Responsibilities feature independently.

Discuss
Encourage the students to discuss each of the organizations listed here: With which are you already familiar? What do you know about those organizations and their activities? Which of the organizations interests you? Why?

Analyze and Apply
Have the students work in small groups to discuss their own concerns about television programming. The members of each group should agree on a specific problem they want to address; then they should learn more about that problem and plan actions they—and other students—can take to help solve that problem.

Review
Ask the students these review questions: How can you find out about the policies of a local TV station? What is one example of a citizen-action organization that attempts to influence the media? What is the central interest of the organization?

Taking Action
You might wish to assign these activities as extra credit work. Students could share their work with the class in oral reports.

CITIZENSHIP SKILLS AND RESPONSIBILITIES

Talking Back to Your Television

Several groups have been successful in influencing local TV programming when they believed their local television station was not living up to its public service obligations as a free user of public air waves. Concerned citizens have objected to various problems, such as a station's hiring practices, its programming, and the percentage of time given to news and public affairs. If you want to find out about your local station's policies, go to the station's headquarters and ask to see its public file.

The public file that stations must keep available to citizens includes applications filed with the FCC, data on station ownership, employment practices, an FCC manual entitled "The Public and Broadcasting—a Procedure Manual" (if the station is commercial), letters from the audience, and a list of the ten problems needing service in that community and how the station's programming meets those needs.

There are a number of citizen-action organizations that attempt to monitor or influence television programming in various ways. If you are concerned or interested in the quality or content of what is being broadcast today, some of the following organizations might be helpful to you:

- **Accuracy in Media (AIM)** (1275 K St. NW, Washington, DC 20005) is a nonprofit educational organization dedicated to fighting what it considers distorted news reporting by the major media.
- **Action for Children's Television (ACT)** (46 Austin St., Newtonville, MA 02160) is an organization dedicated to making networks more responsive to the views of teachers and parents who are concerned with the quality of children's television programming.
- **Media Access Project** (1609 Connecticut Ave. NW, Washington, DC 20009) is a public interest law firm that represents individuals and groups trying to increase public access to the mass media. They have represented minorities, environmentalists, and consumers.
- **National Black Media Coalition** (38 New York Ave. NE, Washington, DC 20002) is made up of over seventy African-American organizations that are dedicated to eliminating racism from broadcasting.
- **National Organization for Women (NOW)** (1776 K St. NW, Washington, DC 20006). NOW's *Media Project* gives assistance to those working to promote both employment and positive images of women in broadcasting.

TAKING ACTION

1. Contact one of the above organizations and find out more about their activities. Report back to the class on what you discover.
2. Think of one way in which you could influence a local media source. Write out the steps you would use to do so.

brief working leaves from prison, or furloughs, while he was governor of that state. It showed a picture of a revolving door with men in striped uniforms leaving a prison gate and then cut to a picture of Willie Horton, a convicted murderer who was released on furlough and committed yet another killing while he was on official leave from the penitentiary. The ad was meant to give the impression that Dukakis was soft on crime.

The practice of negative advertising became widespread in recent campaigns, and is expected to continue. Its effectiveness is the main reason for its continued growth. Research seems to indicate that negative commercials can at least temporarily create large swings in public opinion.

Critics, many of whom are politicians themselves, have stepped forth with suggestions to curtail such methods. At least five bills have been introduced in the Senate, the most far reaching of which would outlaw political commercials that refer to a candidate's opponent unless the sponsoring candidate appears personally in the ad. The measure would also require radio and television stations to offer free time for candidates to respond to ads sponsored by independent political committees—groups not affiliated with a particular candidate but that

Enrichment
Let interested volunteers research efforts made to curtail negative advertising: What restrictions have been proposed? Which have been accepted? Why? Why have other restrictions been rejected? Who supports restrictions on advertising? Who opposes restrictions?

Vocabulary
Ask the students to define *defamation.* What are the laws against defamation?

Discussion Starter
Help the students discuss the candidates' interest in "events that appear photogenic and interesting on the evening news." Why do campaigns focus on such events? How do the voters respond to those events? Do these events represent the real interests of voters? If not, what could voters do to express their interests? Are any groups of voters taking such actions? Why or why not?

Extension
Have the students conduct an informal poll of five adults asking how they—and their family members—gather information about politics: How much do you rely on television news? Do you use other media sources as well? If so, which sources and why? If not, do you feel you get as much information as you want or need from TV news broadcasts?

Discussion Starter
Encourage the students to respond to critics' arguments that TV election stories give little or no relevant information about candidates and issues: Do you agree? If so, who is responsible for this problem? What can viewers and voters do to help resolve this problem?

Campaigns and candidates are natural targets for media attention. How do candidates and their campaign staffs work to make the most of this attention?

Caption Answer Candidates and their campaign staffs learn to be aware of camera angles and timing; additionally, they attempt to make what the candidate is doing visually appealing and interesting for television news. You might point out that being featured "in the news" is often viewed by campaign staffs as free advertising.

try to influence the outcome of elections. (No political advertisement may contain false material, however. Laws against defamation preclude this.)

News Coverage Candidates try to manipulate their images though advertising, but they have less control over the other face of media—the news. To take advantage of the media's interest in campaigns, whether at the presidential or congressional levels, the campaign staff tries to influence the quantity and type of coverage. Besides becoming aware of how camera angles and timing affect a candidate's appearance, the staff learns to plan its political events to accommodate the press. The staff attempts to make what its candidate is doing appear photogenic and interesting. It also knows that journalists and political reporters compete for stories, and that they can be manipulated through granting favors such as an exclusive personal interview with a candidate.

The Impact of Television

Many voters receive much of their information about politics by watching the TV news. For this reason, television has had an impact on the way people see the candidates, understand the issues, and cast their votes. Research indicates that, in general, roughly one-third of all voters decide whom to vote for before the conventions, another third during the conventions, and a final third during the fall campaign. Because television is the major information source on both conventions and campaigns, it probably plays an important role in these voting decisions, even though voters rarely attribute such influence to television itself.

Critics argue that television has made the issues seem unimportant because it focuses on the candidates' personalities and their exciting activities. They argue that in order to capture viewers, television tries to reduce campaign and election stories to thirty-second ''soundbytes'' that catch viewers' attention, but give little or no relevant information.

As a former actor, Ronald Reagan was especially at home in front of the camera and has been called the television president. Why are some observers critical of television's role in modern campaigns?

Caption Answer Critics argue that television minimizes the role of issues and qualifications while maximizing the role of the candidate's appearance and personality.

TEACHING GOVERNMENT IN ACTION

Read
Introduce this feature by asking: Who is Connie Chung? Why do you think a profile of a noted television journalist was included in this chapter? Then allow a volunteer to read this Government in Action feature aloud to the class.

Discuss
How have the media in America changed in terms of ethnic, racial, and sexual make-up over the last century? How do you think this change effects what we see on television news, hear on radio news, or read in newspapers? How does Connie Chung represent an example of these changes? What type of experience does Chung bring to her role as a television journalist?

Analyze and Apply
In order for students to gain an insight into the importance of media in America, have them conduct a survey of students at your school. For this survey, respondents should be asked to look at a list of ten names, five of which should be television journalists and five of which should be cabinet members. Respondents should be asked to identify each person by what he or she does for a living. Students should work together as a class to compile their results.

Review
Use these questions to help the students review the Building Social Studies Skills feature: Where was Connie Chung born? Where did she grow up? How would you describe her professional background?

Think About It (Answers)
1. Answers will vary, e.g., television journalists switch networks in order to receive a higher salary and greater exposure.
2. Student answers will vary, but should include mention of her college degree and her early professional experiences.

Discussion Starter
Help the students consider Mondale's comment: How would you restate Mondale's comments in your own words? How important is it for a presidential candidate to be "warmed up to television"? Why? Is it also important for the president to be "warmed up to television"? Why or why not?

GOVERNMENT IN ACTION

PROFILE

Connie Chung

The media in America have changed dramatically in terms of the ethnic, racial, and gender makeup of their participants over the last century. Connie Chung represents a prime example of this change.

Connie Chung was born on August 20, 1946 in Washington, D.C. She was the youngest child of William Ling and Margaret Chung. Of the nine other children born to her parents, five died in China during World War II. In 1944 the Ling-Chungs moved to America. Connie grew up around Washington, D.C. While in college she was a copy clerk with a television station in Washington, D.C. When she graduated in 1969 she worked as a secretary at the same television station (WTTG).

She quickly became an on-the-air reporter covering everything from anti-war demonstrations to congressional activity on Capitol Hill, to murders and airplane disasters. She went on to work at CBS's Washington bureau, continuing to take on just about any assignment.

By 1976 Ms. Chung was living in Los Angeles and working as anchorperson for the local CBS station. She appeared three times a day and boosted that station's ratings so much that in less than seven years her salary jumped from $27,000 a year to $600,000.

Her next job was with NBC where she did everything from early morning news broadcasts to co-writing and hosting prime-time documentaries. She won a host of honors and awards from her peers and from outside of the industry.

Chung has kept her interest in politics keen through all of these years. In 1988, for example, she covered the presidential elections from their primaries on. She did exit-poll analysis of many primary elections and she acted as a floor correspondent during the national nominating conventions.

In 1989 she left NBC to go back to CBS where she frequently substitutes as news anchor for Dan Rather.

Think About It

1. What motivates a television journalist to switch networks?
2. How do you think Connie Chung prepared for becoming a television journalist?

Television also dictates how a campaign is run. Almost every decision that consultants make about a candidate's activities—where to eat dinner, what to wear, and what to say about the Middle East—is calculated according to its potential media impact. Many observers see this as a new era of politics in which the slick slogan and smooth image will dominate.

Overall, television has created a new kind of political candidate—one who must be at ease with the camera. These days, no candidate can ignore this important part of campaigning. As Democratic candidate Walter Mondale commented after he lost the 1984 presidential election, "I never warmed up to television and television never warmed up to me."

Discussion Starter
Let the students share and discuss their ideas about propaganda: What images does the word *propaganda* bring to mind? Why? How accurate are those images? What examples of propaganda can you cite? Which of those examples—if any—are intended to benefit the public? How successful do you think they are?

Cooperative Learning
Have the students work in groups to list at least five glittering generalities that candidates might use. Then have the group members list at least two different specific statements candidates could use in place of each glittering generality.

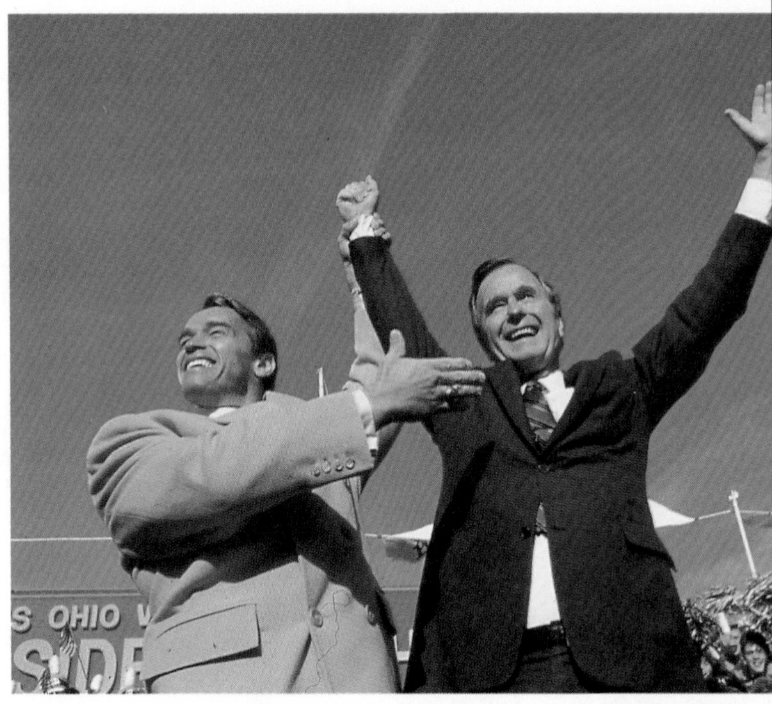

There are many forms of propaganda used by candidates. One form of propaganda involves getting well-known people to publicly support the candidate. Here film star Arnold Schwartzenegger lends his support to George Bush. Why might this technique be effective with some voters?

Caption Answer Students should understand that some voters might be swayed by seeing or hearing that a popular entertainer or sports figure supports a particular candidate. Often these voters begin to transfer their good feelings toward the celebrity to the candidate.

News organizations, according to the critics, believe that policy issues are of less interest to voters than the campaign game itself. The result is that news coverage is disproportionately devoted to campaign strategies, guesses about who is ahead, and poll results, rather than substantive information about the issues.

Remember that even if the evening news is not the best source of facts, good sources do exist. Public television, special network programs, magazines, and newspapers all provide more complete, in-depth coverage, so one should supplement one's television watching with these other sources. It may take more work to seek out good information, but if being an informed citizen is important, it is worth the effort.

Recognizing Propaganda Techniques

A message that is meant to influence people's ideas, opinions, or actions in a certain way is called **propaganda**. The word *propaganda* usually has a negative meaning and is associated with using lies or false information. But propaganda itself can be either positive or negative: Although it can include lies, it can also contain truthful (or mostly truthful) information. A message is called propaganda when it tells only one side of the story, distorts the truth, or appeals mostly to people's emotions. Even commercial advertising is a type of propaganda.

Sometimes political candidates and PACs make use of different kinds of propaganda. Seven of the most common propaganda techniques are discussed below. When you read or listen to political messages, ask yourself if these techniques are being used.

1. **Glittering generalities** **Glittering generalities** is the technique of using vague words or ideas that sound exciting but do not really say much. The words or ideas usually stand for something that everyone believes, but have no specific meaning. For example, a candidate might say, "I stand for freedom and a strong America." Almost every American agrees with such a statement, but it says nothing about the candidate or what he or she will do if elected.
2. **Card stacking** **Card stacking** is using only those facts that support a candidate's argument, while ignoring any other aspects. For example, a candidate may state that her opponent voted against raising

Multidiscipline Strategies

Language Arts Propaganda techniques are often included in the language arts curriculum; encourage the students to bring in English textbooks that include information on propaganda. After the students have shared and discussed this further information, have them write short persuasive essays in which they intentionally use at least two different techniques of propaganda. Let the students read their essays in small groups; ask the group members to identify the propaganda techniques—intentional and unintentional—in each essay.

Enrichment
Encourage the students to suggest terms candidates or campaigners might use in name-calling. Remind the students, if necessary, to include terms that might be rejected as distasteful by both the right and the left. Have the students identify the intentions of candidates who might employ the name-calling technique.

Evaluation Strategies
1. Have the students write their answers to the Section 4 Review questions.
2. Have the students take the Section 4 Quiz found in the *TRB*.

Section 4 Review (Answers)
1. Candidates use televised debates, political advertising, and news coverage.
2. Negative campaign advertising is advertising by candidates which is meant to be detrimental to the opponent's campaign.
3. Answers will vary, e.g., glittering generalities is a method of using vague words that sound exciting but actually say little. Card stacking is using only those facts that support a candidate's argument, while ignoring any other aspects. Testimonials involve getting famous people to support a candidate. The bandwagon method is convincing people that everyone else is joining the movement, so they should, too.
4. Answers will vary, e.g., plain-folks, testimonials, and bandwagon techniques are acceptable when truthful.

Cooperative Learning
Let the students work in groups to list at least ten individuals, groups, or symbols with which political candidates might want to be associated. Then have the groups compare their lists.

Reteaching Strategies
1. Let the students work in small groups to review Section 4, writing an informal outline of its content.
2. Have pairs of students work together to list at least two different specific examples of each of the seven propaganda techniques presented in the text.

Caption Answer Students should understand that, by donning a t-shirt and cap for jogging, Bill Clinton was trying to show himself as "just one of the folks."

▲ Another propaganda technique is called the "plain folks" technique. How does this photograph illustrate this technique in action?

Social Security benefits without mentioning that he did so because the proposed increase was too small.

3. **Testimonials** Using **testimonials** involves getting a well-known person, such as a prominent government official or famous entertainer, to endorse (publicly support) a candidate or issue. People admire the endorser and therefore accept his or her judgment about the person or issue being endorsed.
4. **Name calling** **Name calling** refers to giving people or things a bad label so that they will be rejected or disliked. For example, a candidate might call his opponent a "radical," "un-American," or "liberal."
5. **Plain folks** **Plain folks** is a technique involving a candidate going out of her or his way to convince voters that she or he is an average American citizen just like them. For example, candidates might have their picture taken eating a hot dog, or playing softball with children, or meeting with working citizens outside a factory or supermarket. She or he might stress her or his modest beginnings, growing up in a poor family, and so on.
6. **Bandwagon effect** The **bandwagon effect** is a method of convincing people that everyone else is joining the movement, so they should too. This method plays on the voters' fears that they are being left out of something. Thus announcing a public opinion poll that shows a candidate is ahead may be enough to convince undecided voters that this candidate will be a winner, and that they should "hop on the bandwagon."
7. **Transfer** **Transfer** is associating a person with a respected person, group, or symbol. For example, a candidate might say, "I have always said, just as Abraham Lincoln always believed, that . . ." A candidate might make a commercial of himself or herself standing before a plane with troops returning from the Persian Gulf War in 1991 and greeting the soldiers' families. The events in the background probably have nothing to do with the candidate but the setting gives the impression that they do.

Recognizing these seven propaganda techniques is just one of the tasks you must accomplish to make wise voter decisions. You must also recognize the strategies behind political advertising and the limitations of television news coverage. Wading through the flood of information both from the media and from candidates can be a tiresome chore. It is the responsibility of each of us to vote and make the best possible choices when we vote.

SECTION 4 REVIEW

1. What types of television coverage do candidates use during campaigns?
2. What is negative campaign advertising?
3. Define three of the seven propaganda techniques and explain how each is used.
4. **For critical analysis:** In your opinion, which propaganda techniques, if any, are more acceptable than others in political campaigns? Give reasons for your answer.

TEACHING CHALLENGE TO THE AMERICAN DREAM

Read

Begin by letting the students discuss their ideas about the relationship between money and political campaigns: What is the current relationship? Should it be changed? If so, how? If not, why not? After a brief discussion, ask several students to participate in reading the Challenge to the American Dream feature aloud to the rest of the class.

Discuss

Stimulate discussion of the feature by asking questions such as these: What do you think the quotation from Tip O'Neil means? Do you think he was correct? Why or why not? Do you consider buying media time a form of protected free speech? If so, why? If not, how is it different from other forms of protected speech? Is it possible to be a well-funded office-holder and still provide equal access to rich and poor constituents? Why do you think each of these reforms has been proposed? What effect would each have?

Analyze and Apply

Have the students investigate the stance their political representatives take toward reforming the campaign finance system. Ask the students to read news accounts, magazine articles, brochures, and press releases related to the topic. Then encourage the students to write to their senators and representatives—on either the state or the federal level—to request clarification of the officeholder's position or to express their own opinions to their representatives.

Review

To help the students review this feature, ask them these questions: Why is campaign money necessary to keep new ideas and options available? In what sense is money a corrupting influence on politics?

You Decide (Answers)

1. Answers will vary, e.g., individuals should be free to contribute as much as they want in a democracy. Limiting their contributions is limiting their rights.
2. Answers will vary, e.g., our political system deters good candidates who do not have the resources to raise the money needed.

CHALLENGE TO THE AMERICAN DREAM

The Overwhelming Importance of Campaign Money

THE VOTE THAT REALLY COUNTS

By permission of Bill Mauldin and Wil-Jo Associates.

The former Speaker of the House of Representatives, Thomas P. (Tip) O'Neill once said, "There are four parts to any campaign: The candidate, the issues, . . . the campaign organization, and the money. Without money you can forget the other three."

Money leads to a dilemma in politics. Many people feel that individuals and groups should be allowed to buy as much media time as they want and can afford in order to express their points of view. They argue that buying media time is just another form of constitutionally protected freedom of speech. Many people also believe that individuals and groups should be allowed to provide as much money as they want to their favorite candidates.

Other people are very uneasy when they see those with great wealth buying political media time. They believe money threatens our democratic ideal of political equality, which tells us that government should represent us all, poor and rich. Thus everyone should have equal access to government.

The public, members of Congress, and presidents have all expressed concern with the campaign finance system and the rising costs of campaigns. Several proposals for reforming the system have been offered, including complete government funding for campaigns and allowing each candidate a fixed amount of free media time.

The challenge to the American dream is finding a way to allow candidates their constitutionally guaranteed freedom of speech while preventing our representative government from representing only monied interests that can contribute heavily to election campaigns.

You Decide

1. Do you think that groups and individuals should be allowed to contribute as much money as they want to whichever candidates they choose? Explain why or why not.
2. Do you feel that our political system might deter good candidates from running for office? Explain.

CHAPTER 10 REVIEW

Key Terms

Australian ballot 246
ballot 233
bandwagon effect 256
blanket primary 236
campaign manager 238
card stacking 255
caucuses 234
closed primary 235
Credentials Committee 238
delegates 234
direct primary 235
electoral college 247
electors 247
general election 245
glittering generalities 255
image building 240
keynote speaker 238
mandatory preference poll 237
name calling 256
negative campaign advertising 250
nominating convention 234
nomination 233
nonpartisan elections 236
office-group ballot 246
open primary 235
party-column ballot 246
petition 233
plain folks 256
plurality 236
political consultants 240
political machines 246
popular vote 247
preference poll 237
propaganda 255
runoff election 236
self-nomination 233
special election 245
testimonials 256
tracking polls 242
transfer 256
winner-take-all-system 247
write-in candidate 234

Service Learning Activity

Students should be encouraged to work on a campaign, and if possible it should be for a candidate from the Democratic or Republican parties. Students should keep a journal of their experiences, recording those things learned first-hand about a campaign. Students should answer as many questions as possible about the campaign, including: How was the candidate nominated? What role do special interest groups play in the campaign? What is the role of the media? What form does the campaign organization take? What type of ballot will be used on election day?

Chapter Evaluation

To evaluate student mastery of chapter material, you might:

1. Use Chapter Test A from the *TRB.*

2. Use Chapter Test B from the *TRB.*

3. Construct your own test using items from the *West American Government Test Bank* found in the *TRB.*

4. Use the accompanying computerized test software to construct and print a customized chapter test.

Review Questions (Answers)

1. The purpose of the nominating process is to choose candidates within each party who will then seek office by running against the candidates chosen by the other party.

2. Self-nomination is announcing one's own desire to run. A party caucus is a meeting of certain party leaders to choose candidates. A party nominating convention is an official party meeting to choose candidates. Direct primaries are elections within parties to choose candidates.

3. A direct primary is an election within a party to pick a candidate for the general election. In a closed primary, only party members can vote to choose that party's candidates. In an open primary, voters can vote for a party's candidates whether or not they belong to the party.

4. Run-off primaries are those in states which require candidates to win by a majority. If no candidate receives a majority in the primary, a runoff election is held.

5. A national party convention is used to nominate presidential candidates.

6. In order to win an election, a campaign strategy must be planned and coordinated. In today's campaigns, these tasks are often put in the hands of paid professionals called political consultants.

7. Through the passage of regulation, such as the Federal Election Campaign Act of 1974, which limited and regulated campaign spending.

8. The purpose of PACs is to collect money and provide financial support for political candidates.

9. A general election is a regularly scheduled election at which voters make their final selection of public officeholders.

10. Special elections are held whenever an issue must be decided before the next general election. A recall election is an election that gives citizens the power to remove an elected official from office before the end of his or her term.

CHAPTER 10 REVIEW—Continued

Summary

1. The first step in the election process is the nomination, that is the naming or choosing of the candidates from each party who will seek office. The methods of nomination used in American politics are (1) self-nomination and petition, (2) party caucus, (3) nominating convention, and (4) direct primary. In a closed direct primary, only party members can vote to choose that party's candidates, and they may vote only in the primary of their own party. In an open direct primary voters can vote in either party primary without disclosing their party affiliation. Runoff primaries are used in states in which a candidate must receive a majority of votes. Nonpartisan primaries are used to nominate candidates for nonpartisan offices. About three-fifths of the states hold presidential primaries to choose delegates to attend the national convention, where presidential candidates are actually nominated.

2. Election campaigns must be well organized and well planned. The campaign manager coordinates and plans the campaign strategy. Some candidates hire political consultants, who are paid professionals, to devise campaign strategies and work on the candidate's public image. Campaigns have become very expensive and the connection between money and campaigns has created difficult problems in American politics. The Federal Election Campaign Act of 1974 established the Federal Election Commission (F.E.C.), provided for public financing for presidential primaries and general elections, limited presidential campaign spending, required disclosure of finances, and limited contributions. Political Action Committees (PACs) may be organized to help finance political campaigns.

3. Because most elective offices in the United States are on the state and local levels, most election laws are state laws. A general election is a regularly scheduled election at which voters cast their final votes for public officeholders. General elections are held in the even-numbered years on the first Tuesday after the first Monday in November. State law divides local units of government into precincts, within each of which voters cast their ballots at one polling place. In 1888 the Australian ballot was introduced in the United States, which had four main features: (1) it was printed by election officials at public expense; (2) it listed the names of all candidates in an election; (3) it was passed out only at the polling places to qualified voters; and (4) the actual voting was done in secret. In an office-group ballot, all candidates are listed together, regardless of party affiliation. In a party-column ballot, candidates are listed under their party label. Over half of all voters cast ballots on voting machines. In the United States, the electoral college, not the popular vote, determines our next president.

4. The media, especially television, have had a wide-ranging effect on politics in general, especially on campaigns and elections. Candidates use several types of television coverage during campaigns: debates, political advertising, and news coverage. The use of negative advertising is becoming more widespread. Television has had an impact on the way people see the candidates, understand the issues, and cast their votes. Propaganda is a message meant to influence people's ideas, opinions, or actions in certain ways.

Review Questions

1. What is the purpose of the nominating process?
2. Describe the methods by which candidates can be nominated.
3. What is a direct primary? How does a closed primary differ from an open primary?
4. What other types of primaries are there?
5. What is the purpose of national party conventions?
6. Why is the organization and planning of a campaign important?
7. How has Congress tried to regulate campaign finances?
8. Explain the purpose of PACs.
9. What is a general election?
10. What are the other types of elections in the United States and what are they called?
11. What is an Australian ballot and what forms does it take?
12. How did the electoral college system develop and how does it work today?
13. Name the three ways that candidates use television coverage in their campaigns.
14. What is propaganda? What are four commonly used techniques?
15. What is one way in which you can "talk back to your television"?

11. An Australian ballot is printed at public expense and lists all candidates. It is distributed only at polling places to qualified voters and the actual voting is done in secret. An office-group ballot lists all candidates together. A party-column ballot lists candidates under their party label.
12. The electoral college developed because the founders did not want the president to be elected directly by the people. Today it is a group of persons chosen in each state and the District of Columbia every four years who make a formal selection of the president and vice president.
13. Candidates use televised debates, political advertising, and news coverage.
14. Propaganda is a message meant to influence people's ideas, opinions, or actions. Some techniques are glittering generalities, card stacking, testimonials, and name calling.
15. By contacting Accuracy In Media and finding out about their activities.

Questions for Thought and Discussion (Answers)

1. Answers will vary, e.g., open primaries give voters the most choices. They are not restricted by party lines.
2. Answers will vary, e.g., if voting were not secret, elections would not be free because people could be unduly influenced and intimidated.
3. Answers will vary, e.g., limits on individual and group contributions have led to the growth of PACs. They should not be further regulated because it would further limit freedom of expression.
4. Answers will vary, e.g., by using the direct popular election instead of the electoral college system we would eliminate the possibility that a candidate may be elected who lost the total popular vote but won the electoral vote. The system would be more democratic because the people would make their choice directly.
5. Answers will vary, e.g., the media depends on the candidates to provide news for coverage and relies on the candidates to pay for advertising. The candidates depend on the media to provide publicity and coverage of debates and other activities.
6. Answers will vary, e.g., the two major political parties deserve greater amounts of coverage because they represent a greater percentage of the population.

Social Studies Skills (Answers)

1. To show how many electoral votes each state has for president.
2. Each state has a number of electors equal to the number of its United States senators plus representatives.
3. California.
4. Three.
5. Seven plus the District of Columbia (Alaska, Delaware, Montana, North Dakota, South Dakota, Vermont, Wyoming, and Washington, D.C.).
6. No.
7. Eleven states (CA-54, NY-33, TX-32, FL-25, PA-23, IL-22, OH-21, MI-18, NJ-15, NC-14, GA-13).

CHAPTER 10 REVIEW—Continued

Questions for Thought and Discussion

1. If you could choose a primary system for your state, which would you choose? Give reasons for your answer.
2. Why are secret ballots critical to free elections?
3. What factors do you think have led to the growth in the number of PACs? Do you think they should be further regulated? Explain.
4. How would our presidential elections change if we abolished the electoral college and used the direct popular vote instead?
5. Explain why the media and candidates are dependent on each other.
6. Should the media be required to provide equal coverage for all candidates and for all political parties? Is is fair that the two major political parties can buy or otherwise obtain greater coverage in the news than the minor parties? Explain why or why not.

Improving Your Skills
Communication Skills

Comparing and Contrasting

Comparing and contrasting is a skill you will need to fully understand and evaluate information, write and deliver oral reports, and express your opinion. To compare and contrast items means putting them side by side and looking for the similarities and differences. It may be helpful to look for the similarities first and then go on to search for differences.

Check carefully that the categories you are using to make the comparison/contrast apply to both items. For example, if you are comparing and contrasting two mayoral candidates you should be sure that your list of categories, such as experience in government, leadership abilities, voting records, positions on environmental issues, knowledge of community, and so forth, can be applied equally to both candidates.

Writing

Choose two candidates for any level of political office from a past or current election. Write a list of ten categories by which to compare and contrast the candidates. List the similarities between the candidates with respect to your categories. Then list the differences between the candidates. Write a summary statement of similarities and of differences.

Social Studies Skills

Reading Maps

Look at the map of the United States on page 248. Answer the following questions:

1. What is the reason for showing the map?
2. How is the number of electoral votes determined for each state?
3. Which state has the most electoral votes for president?
4. What are the fewest possible electoral votes that a state can have?
5. How many states have the minimum electoral votes?
6. Will it ever be possible for a state to have fewer than 3 electoral votes?
7. A president can be elected with 270 electoral votes. Determine the minimum number of states that the candidate must win in order to obtain 270 votes and list those states.

Activities and Projects

1. Interview a candidate or a candidate's aide who has campaigned in a recent election. Ask the candidate about how the campaign was organized, planned, and financed. Report your results to the class.
2. Prepare a campaign plan for an imaginary candidate. Invent a campaign theme and decide on how the campaign should be organized. Then think of how your staff can make the best use of the media. Present your plan to the class.
3. Prepare a bulletin board display that lists all the propaganda techniques and gives examples of each one.
4. Stage a debate on the following statement: Candidates for president shall not be allowed to spend more than $25 million for their campaign, candidates for senator $5 million, and for representative no more than $3 million.

CHAPTER INTRODUCTION

Instructional Objectives

By the end of the chapter students should be able to:
- Summarize the history and expansion of the right to vote in the United States.
- Describe the factors involved with voting and nonvoting.
- Identify those factors affecting the behavior of voters.

Using the Keynote

Ask a volunteer to read aloud the quotation from Franklin D. Roosevelt, and encourage the students to discuss their responses to Roosevelt's statement: How could the American people deprive themselves of the right to vote? Do you believe we are depriving ourselves of that right? If so, what are we doing to cause that deprivation? Why are the American people themselves the only ones with that power? Do you think measures should be taken now to ensure that Americans do not deprive themselves of the right to vote? Help the students express and support various points of view in response to these discussion questions.

Introducing the Chapter

Ask volunteers to read the chapter Introduction aloud to the rest of the class. Pose questions such as these to stimulate discussion: Why do you think the United States has such a low rate of voter participation? What do you think this low rate of participation indicates? Why? Do you think it is a cause for concern? Should this rate be changed? Do you believe it can be changed? If so, how?

Previewing the Sections

Section 1 Let the students page through Section 1, noting the main headings and figures. Encourage a brief discussion of the contents: What do you expect to learn as you study this section?

Section 2 Ask volunteers to read aloud the section title, the main headings, and the titles of the graphs and special features in Section 2. Then ask the students: What trends are discussed in this section? To whom are these trends important? Why?

Section 3 Have the students find and read the four main headings and the special feature titles in Section 3. Then help the students anticipate the section content by asking these questions: Which kinds of reasons for voting will be covered in this section? Which of those reasons are relevant to your own experiences?

CHAPTER 11

Voters and Voting Behavior

CHAPTER OBJECTIVES

To learn and understand

- The history and expansion of the right to vote in the United States.
- What factors affect voting and nonvoting.
- The factors affecting the behavior of voters.

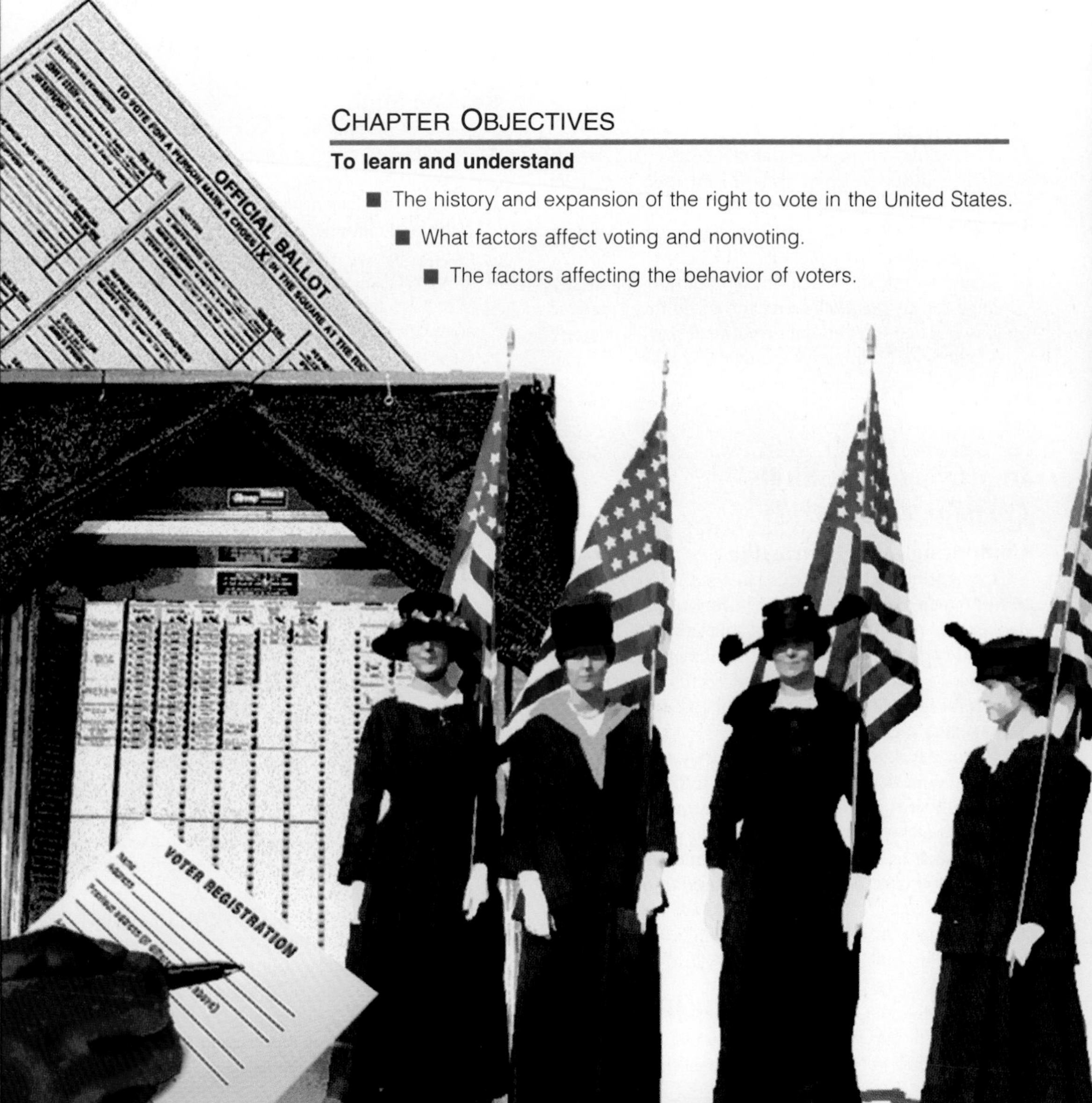

West's American Government Assignment Guide

Activity Sheets
Basic Concepts 11 *TRB* (Reteaching)
Enrichment Activity 11 *TRB*
Building Social Studies Skills 11 *TRB*
Quizzes
Chapter 11 Section 1 Quiz *TRB*
Chapter 11 Section 2 Quiz *TRB*
Chapter 11 Section 3 Quiz *TRB*

Tests
Chapter 11 Test A *TRB*
Chapter 11 Test B *TRB*
Chapter 11 Test Bank *TRB*
Chapter 11 WESTEST Computerized Testing
Social Studies Tool Kit Software
Chapter 11 Activity

Keynote

Nobody will ever deprive the American people of the right to vote except the American people themselves.

—— **Franklin D. Roosevelt (1882–1945) Thirty-Second President of the United States**

INTRODUCTION

The right to vote—the **franchise**—is vital to the success of a representative democracy. After all, democracy means "rule by the people." In order to rule, the people must elect representatives to act on their behalf. Voting in elections is a method by which we as citizens can directly participate in the governing process in this country.

The struggles that many groups have waged in this country have resulted in the right to vote for all American citizens ages 18 and over. There are over 185 million people in the **electorate** (the potential voting population), yet less than 50 percent of these citizens actually vote, while turnout in several other nations often exceeds 85 percent. In fact, the United States has one of the lowest rates of voter participation of any democracy in the world.

Are Americans becoming more apathetic toward politics, more hostile toward candidates, less trustful of government, or less confident of their own abilities to make a difference in an election? If any or all of these are true, then American democracy may be in trouble, as Franklin D. Roosevelt pointed out in the opening quote of this chapter. If, in contrast, many people do not vote simply because they are content with the way things are, then there might be less reason for concern.

Many of you will have the opportunity to vote yourselves for the first time in the very near future. By looking at the history and the expansion of the right to vote in the United States, perhaps you will begin to understand why so many people have sacrificed so much to secure for themselves, and for us, the right to vote.

In this chapter we will survey the history of voting in America, as well as current patterns of voter behavior and voter turnout.

SECTION 1

History of Voting and Current Requirements

Preview Questions

- What were the early restrictions placed on voting in America?
- How were African Americans denied the vote? What events changed this?
- How did women gain the right to vote?
- What are current voting eligibility requirements?

In America today, all citizens at least 18 years of age have the right to vote. This was not always true, however: restrictions on **suffrage**, the legal right to vote, have existed since the founding of our nation. Expanding the right to vote has been an important part of the gradual democratization of the American electoral process.

Several of the founding fathers felt that because many of the government's functions were economic in nature, it was fair and reasonable that only those people who had an interest in property should be allowed to vote. No one even thought about extending the vote to African Americans (most of whom were slaves) or to women. The notion of allowing all citizens to vote was, according to South Carolina delegate Charles Pinckney, merely "theoretical nonsense." Consistent with the first Chief Justice of the Supreme Court John Jay's statement that "the people who own the country ought to govern it," most states limited suffrage to adult white males who owned property. The logic behind this type of reasoning was challenged by Thomas Paine in his pamphlet *Common Sense:*

> Here is a man who today owns a jackass, and the jackass is worth $60. Today the man is a voter and goes to the

SECTION 1

Points to Stress
- Early restrictions placed on voting in America.
- The ways in which African Americans were denied the right to vote.
- Events that led to African-American suffrage.
- The manner in which women won suffrage.
- Current voting eligibility requirements.

Kickoff Activity
Ask the students these questions: If an election were held tomorrow, would you be eligible to vote? Why or why not? Let all the students write their responses; then encourage volunteers to share and discuss what they have written.

Working with the Preview Questions
Have volunteers read the study questions to the rest of the class. Encourage the students to share and discuss what they already know in response to these questions. Then ask the students to suggest further questions they hope to have answered as they study Section 1.

Teaching Strategies

Introduction
After the students have read the section introduction, focus their attention on the quotation from Supreme Court Chief Justice John Jay: What attitude was he expressing? Who probably shared this attitude? How do people regard such an attitude today? In spite of such regard, do you think some people still hold the attitude expressed by Jay?

Enrichment
Ask interested volunteers to research the religious restrictions on voting: What religious groups were not permitted to vote? Why? Under what circumstances were those restrictions lifted? Let the volunteers share their findings in a brief oral report to the rest of the class.

Discussion Starter
Guide the students in considering universal white male suffrage: Why do you imagine men without property first won the right to vote in the western states? How and why do you think the acceptance of these voting rights moved east? Who is included in universal white male suffrage? Who is excluded?

◀ George Caleb Bingham's painting *The County Election,* shown here, depicts rural voters lining up to vote in the nineteenth century. What common traits do all of the voters shown in this painting share?

Caption Answer Students should recognize that all of the voters depicted Bingham's painting are white males.

polls and deposits his votes. Tomorrow the jackass dies. The next day the man comes to vote without his jackass and cannot vote at all. Now tell me, which was the voter, the man or the jackass?

Early Restrictions

The Constitution left the power to set suffrage qualifications to the individual states. Some states placed so many restrictions on the right to vote that only five to six percent of the adult population was eligible. There were numerous restrictions based on property ownership, race, sex, religious beliefs, and payment of taxes.

Religious restrictions were the first to be removed, and by 1810 they were abolished in all states. Next, with the growth of democratic sentiment and the expansion of the western frontier, property ownership and tax-payment requirements gradually began to disappear. Men without property were first given the right to vote in the Western states, and by 1850 an era of universal white male suffrage had arrived.

Women and the Right to Vote

During the era when the Constitution was written, some women argued for women's rights but were largely ignored. Beginning in the 1820s in Tennessee school board elections, women had the right to vote in some places on the local level. The first time a woman voted on the national level occurred in 1807, when the New Jersey constitution failed to explicitly prevent women from voting. The state legislature acted quickly to amend the constitution, making it clear that women were not allowed to vote.

After the Civil War in 1869, Susan B. Anthony and Elizabeth Cady Stanton organized the National Women Suffrage Association, which adopted as its goal a

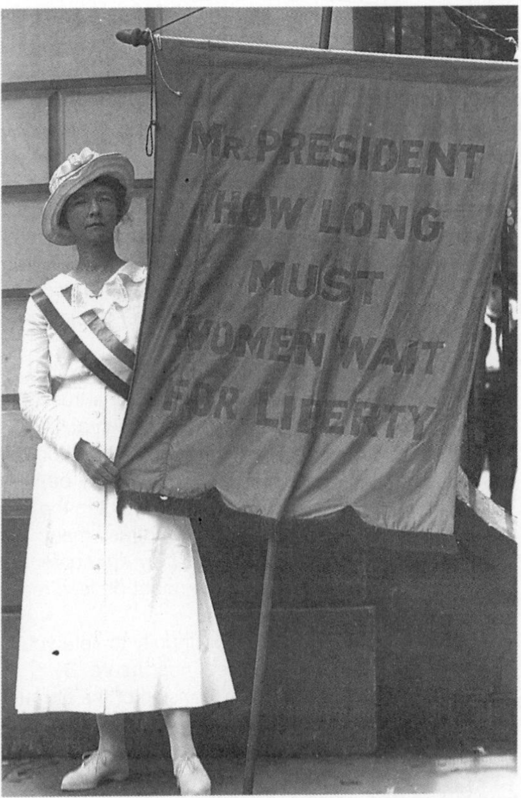

▲ The woman shown above was one of a group of suffragettes that picketed the White House in 1917 to call the nation's attention to their cause. Was this effort effective?

Caption Answer Students should understand that the around the clock picketing of the White House and other demonstrations were effective in gaining some support for the movement. The Women's Suffrage Movement was also aided by a change in public opinion engendered by the contributions of women to the war effort during World War I.

Discussion Starter
Encourage the students to discuss the attitude toward women's suffrage held by most members of Congress and compare it to that expressed by the Wyoming territorial legislature: What do you think accounts for this extreme difference? Do you think such differences in attitudes toward the rights of women continue to exist today? Why or why not?

Discussion Starter
Help the students consider and discuss the tactics used during the early 1900s to achieve a constitutional amendment granting women the vote: What is your reaction to these tactics? Do you think they were necessary? Appropriate? How effective do they appear to have been? Do you think women's rights groups continue to employ similar tactics? Encourage the students to share and explain various ideas in response to these discussion questions.

Cooperative Learning
Divide the class into small groups; let group members work together to read and study the chart, The Extension of the Right to Vote: What is the significance of each action? How does it continue to affect people today?

Extension of the Right to Vote

Year	Action	Impact
1870	Fifteenth Amendment	Discrimination based on race outlawed.
1920	Nineteenth Amendment	Discrimination based on sex outlawed.
1924	Congressional Act	All Native American Indians given citizenship.
1944	*Smith* v. *Allwright*	Supreme Court prohibits white primary.
1957	Civil Rights Act of 1957	Justice Department can sue to protect voting rights in various states.
1960	Civil Rights Act of 1960	Courts authorized to appoint referees to assist voter registration procedures.
1961	Twenty-third Amendment	Residents of District of Columbia given right to vote.
1964	Twenty-fourth Amendment	Poll tax in national elections outlawed.
1965	Voting Rights Act of 1965	Literacy test prohibited; federal voter registrars authorized in seven southern states.
1970	Voting Rights Act Amendments of 1970	Voting age for federal elections reduced to 18 years; maximum 30-day residency requirement for presidential elections; state literacy test abolished.
1971	Twenty-sixth Amendment	Minimum voting age reduced to 18 for all elections.
1975	Voting Rights Act Amendments of 1975	Federal voter registrars authorized in ten more states; bilingual ballots to be printed if 5 percent or more of state population does not speak English.
1982	Voting Rights Act Amendment of 1982	Extended provisions of two previous voting rights act amendments; allows private parties to sue for violations.

▲ **FIGURE 11–1 Extension of the Right To Vote.** The table above shows the major landmarks in the effort to grant all Americans the right to vote. Which of the above landmarks reduced the minimum voting age to 18 for all elections?

This figure content is also featured on *West's American Government Videodisc* (see the index found in the *TRB*) and is available in the transparency package.

Figure Answer The Twenty-sixth Amendment (1971) lowered the minimum voting age to 18.

women's suffrage amendment to the Constitution. They lobbied Congress and the state legislatures for women's voting rights. The first suffrage bill was introduced in Congress in 1868, and each year thereafter until 1893.

When Wyoming applied to join the union in 1889, it had already granted women the right to vote. At first, Congress tried to bar Wyoming for that reason, but surrendered when the Wyoming territorial legislature declared, "We will remain out of the Union 100 years rather than come in without the women."

Vigorous campaigns by women suffragists between 1910 and 1914 led seven other states, all west of the Mississippi, to give women the right to vote. Throughout the early 1900s, however, strong opposition existed, even within progressive circles, to a constitutional amendment granting women the vote. On President Wilson's inauguration day in 1913, a group of militant suffragists organized a demonstration that ended in a near riot. Other demonstrations bordered on violence and leaders were jailed and fined. In 1917, the National Women's Party organized an around-the-clock picket line at the White House. They were arrested and subsequently force fed during hunger strikes, which embarrassed the Woodrow Wilson administration and won some support for the movement. These efforts, along with women's contributions to the war effort during World War I, led Congress in 1919 to pass the Nineteenth Amendment, which granted the vote to women.

TEACHING ARCHITECTS OF THE AMERICAN DREAM

Read

For this activity, you will need a Susan B. Anthony dollar coin. These can be obtained at almost any bank. Pass the coin around to the class, then ask volunteers to explain who Susan B. Anthony was. Why would her likeness be on a U.S. coin? Why do you think she was included as an Architect of the American Dream in this text? After the discussion, allow volunteers to take turns reading aloud this feature to the class.

Discuss

Use the following questions to stimulate a class discussion regarding this material. How were women discriminated against in the early days of our country? Why do you think this occurred? How do you think Susan B. Anthony's religious convictions affected her political convictions? What political cause did Anthony first devote her political efforts to? Why was Anthony arrested in 1872? What other American political leaders can you think of have been arrested for acting on their political convictions?

Analyze and Apply

Have students turn to the Table of Features found at the front of this book. Ask a volunteer to list the political figures who are included in the Architect of the American Dream features. Then have each student volunteer the name of someone else they feel qualifies as an "Architect of the American Dream." Students should then create their own Architect of the American Dream feature for that

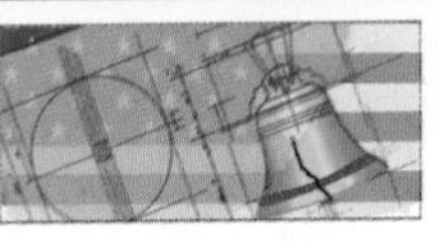

ARCHITECT OF The American Dream

In the early days of our country, women had none of the rights that are taken for granted today. They could not own property unless their husbands controlled it, could not sue anyone in the courts, could not be legal guardians of their own children if they divorced, and could not become involved in politics. It was believed that women did not need a formal education, and should not be treated as equals of men. Women were also not allowed to vote, which meant that over 50 percent of adult citizens in the nation had no voice in electing those who governed. As women became more educated, a few became more outspoken about their lack of legal rights. One such leader among these women was Susan B. Anthony.

Susan B. Anthony was born February 15, 1820, in Adams, Massachusetts. She was raised in a Quaker household, and from her religious upbringing developed a belief in the equality of all men and women before God. She became a teacher in her father's school and served as the head of the female department of the Canajoharie Academy in New York. Abandoning education for reform activities, she devoted her first efforts to temperence (discouraging the use of alcoholic beverages) and the abolitionist cause, being among the first to advocate black suffrage after the Civil War.

Gradually, she shifted her energies to the women's suffrage movement. She quickly became a key organizer in a series of state and national women's rights conventions. In 1869, she and Elizabeth Cady Stanton formed the National Woman Suffrage Association to fight for a women's suffrage amendment to the United States Constitution. Ridiculed by men and ignored by many women, the movement's leaders faced a long uphill fight. In 1872, Anthony was arrested when she challenged the law by voting in that year's presidential election. She was tried by a judge who refused to let her speak in her own defense.

Anthony spent the rest of her life traveling and lecturing on women's rights. She was president of the National Woman Suffrage Association between 1892 and 1900 as they continued their struggle. Although many states began to give women more rights, full equality was still years away. Anthony died on March 13, 1906, fourteen years before her dream was realized. But her seventy-plus years of effort and dedication finally met with success in 1920, when the necessary number of states ratified the Nineteenth Amendment, which declared that "The right of citizens of the United States to vote shall not be denied or abridged by the United States or by any State on account of sex."

HER WORDS

It may be delayed longer than we think; it may be here sooner than we expect; but the day will come when man will recognize woman as his peer, not only at the fireside but in the councils of the nation. Then, and not until then, will there be the perfect comradeship, the ideal union between the sexes that shall result in the highest development of the race. What this shall be we may not attempt to define, but this we know, that only good can come to the individual or to the nation through the rendering of exact justice.

individual. Each Architect of the American Dream feature created by students should include a short biographical sketch, an excerpt of his or her words, and a bibliography. Have students share their completed projects with the class in the form of an oral report. You might extend this activity by allowing the students to illustrate their projects and by displaying the illustrations in your classroom.

Review
Use the following questions to review the content of this Architect of the American Dream feature. Who was Susan B. Anthony? When did she begin to work for women's suffrage? Why was she arrested in 1872? How did she explain her actions?

Developing Critical Thinking Skills

1. Answers will vary, but students should realize that Anthony was referring to women assuming leadership roles not only in homes, but in business and politics, as well.

2. In Anthony's view, the "highest development of the race" would be the attainment of personal and political liberty for all members of the human race, male and female.

3. The Fifteenth Amendment, ratified in 1870, guarantees citizens the right to vote. Rights derived from the Constitution cannot be abridged by the states. The problem was in the definition of "citizen" which had been narrowly interpreted as strictly white, property-owning males.

Susan B. Anthony

▲ The suffragettes shown above are celebrating the ratification of the Nineteenth Amendment giving women the right to vote.

Upon voting illegally in 1872:

Friends and fellow citizens: I stand before you under indictment for the alleged crime of having voted in the last presidential election, without having a lawful right to vote. . . . I not only committed no crime, but instead simply exercised my citizen's right, guaranteed to me and all United States citizens by the National Constitution beyond the power of any state to deny.

Developing Critical Thinking Skills

1. What did Anthony mean when she argued that women should be recognized as peers to men "not only at the fireside but in the councils of the nation"?
2. What do you think Anthony meant when she spoke of "the highest development of the race"?
3. Where in the Constitution did Anthony find support for her statement that every citizen has the right to vote, and that that power cannot be denied by any state?

For Further Reading

Dorr, Rheta C. *Susan B. Anthony, the Woman who Changed the Mind of a Nation.* New York: AMS Press Inc., 1980

Flexner, Eleanor. *Century of Struggle.* New York: Atheneum, 1974.

Hahn, Emily. *Once Upon a Pedestal.* New York: Thomas Y. Cromwell, 1974.

Comprehension
Ask the students to recall the content of the Fifteenth Amendment and to comment on the significance of the year in which it was adopted.

Discussion Starter
You may want to help the students discuss the efforts made by some groups to obstruct African Americans from voting: In the face of such obstacles, why do you think African Americans persisted in pursuing their right to vote? How do you imagine you would feel if people used such tactics to prevent you from voting? How do you think you would respond?

Vocabulary
Let volunteers explain, in their own words, the meaning of *grandfather clause* as it is used here. Then have other students explain (or, if necessary, research) the more general definition of this term.

Enrichment
Encourage volunteers to research some of the cases that helped to expand African-American suffrage, as well as the specific provisions of the Civil Rights Act of 1957. Ask these volunteers to write a report of their findings, to be shared with the rest of the class.

African Americans and the Right to Vote

The Fifteenth Amendment guaranteed suffrage to African-American males in 1870. It said, "The right of citizens to vote shall not be abridged by the United States or by any state on account of race, color, or previous condition of servitude." Yet for the next century the gap remained wide between these words and their true implementation as states tried to outdo each other in imaginative ways to prevent African Americans from voting. Certain groups of white Southerners began to obstruct black Americans from voting through methods ranging from mob violence to economic restrictions. For example, registrars often closed their offices when blacks tried to register, or whites threatened blacks with loss of housing or jobs if they tried to vote. Other tactics included locating polling places far from African-American neighborhoods, or moving the polling places at the last minute without notifying potential voters.

Legal means were also used to **disenfranchise** blacks—effectively remove their ability to vote—and often poor whites as well. States sometimes used **literacy tests** as a criterion for voting, supposedly to ensure that voters could read and write and thus evaluate political information. Such tests required those who wished to register to vote to interpret sometimes complicated written passages. Most African Americans, many of whom had been denied an education, were functionally illiterate and so were not allowed to vote. Although many whites were also illiterate, fewer were barred from voting because local election registrars exercised their own discretion in deciding who had to take the test, how to administer it, and how to evaluate it. A **grandfather clause** exempted those whose grandfathers had the right to vote before 1867 from taking these literacy tests. This was, of course, before African Americans could legally vote in the South. Obviously, literacy tests were used primarily to take away African-American voting rights.

The **poll tax**, a fee of several dollars, was another device used to deny African-American voting rights. At the time this tax was often a sizeable chunk of a working person's monthly income. It was a burden not only on most blacks, but on immigrants, small farmers, many working-class citizens, and many poor whites in general.

▲ In this 1867 election in the nation's capital, African Americans showed that they were eager to participate in the election process by serving as polling place judges and by lining up as early as 2:00 A.M. for the opportunity to vote. When were all African-American males given the Constitutional right to vote?

Caption Answer The Fifteenth Amendment, which guaranteed suffrage to African-American males was ratified in 1870.

Early Legislation The civil rights movement of the 1950s and policy changes of the 1960s helped end both formal and informal barriers to African-American suffrage. Led by decisions of the Supreme Court, the lower federal courts had begun to strike down many of these discriminatory practices in the 1940s and 1950s. Because the courts can only act case by case, this process was slow. Finally, in response to the civil rights movement led by Martin Luther King, Jr., Congress passed several civil rights laws beginning in the late 1950s, including the Civil Rights Act of 1957, which set up the United States Civil Rights Commission and gave the federal attorney general the power to legally prevent interference with any person's right to vote in federal elections. The Civil Rights Act of 1964 was a much broader measure that forbade the use of any registration requirement in an unfair or discriminatory manner.

As progressive as the legislation was, it relied too much on judicial action, as the dramatic events in Selma, Alabama, in 1964 illustrated. Dr. Martin Luther King had begun a voter registration drive in that city, hoping to focus national attention on the issue of African-American voting rights. Dr. King and his followers were met with abuse and violence by local whites, city and county police, and state troopers. Witnessing the violence on national television, the nation was horrified and many demanded action. President Lyndon Johnson urged

Extension
Ask a group of volunteers to research the background of the situation in Selma, Alabama, in 1964, the actions led by Dr. King, and the reactions of the white population, including police and troopers. When the volunteers have completed their research, encourage them to plan an interesting presentation of the material for the rest of the class.

Discussion Starter
Guide the students in discussing their responses to these questions: How do you think television coverage affected the events in Selma? Do you imagine the outcome might have been different if the violence there had been covered only by the print media? If it had not been covered by the media at all? Encourage the students to present and support various points of view.

Discussion Starter
Focus the students' attention on the use of federal voter registrars: What questions about states' rights does this action raise? How do you imagine the affected states responded? Why? Why did the federal government have the authority to send its own registrars?

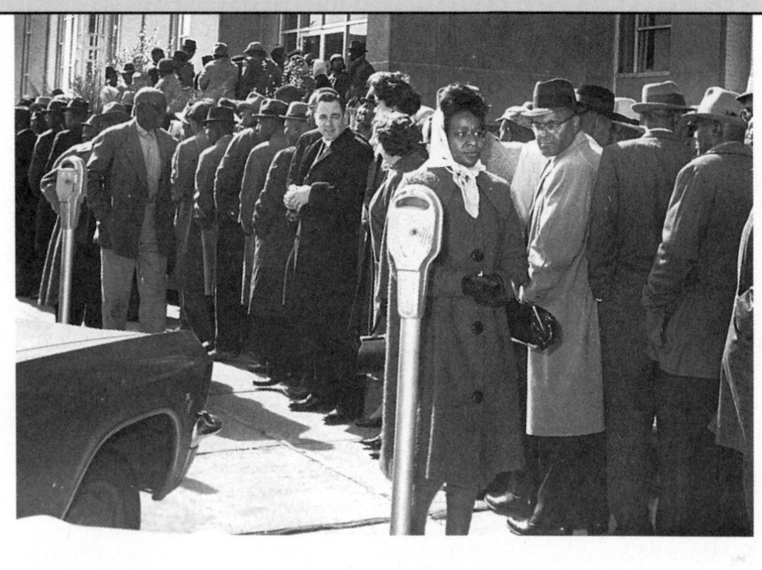

In this photo, African Americans led by the Reverend Martin Luther King, Jr., lined the sidewalk leading to the Dallas County Courthouse in Selma, Alabama, as they waited to register to vote. What was the purpose of King's voter-registration drive?

Congress to pass new and stronger legislation to ensure African-American voting rights. Congress acted quickly.

Voting Rights Act of 1965 The Voting Rights Act of 1965 finally made the Fifteenth Amendment an effective part of the Constitution. The act made it illegal to interfere with anyone's right to vote in any election held in this country, whether federal, state, or local. It suspended the use of literacy tests and sent federal voter registrars into states and counties where less than 50 percent of the voting population was registered. All of Mississippi, Alabama, Louisiana, South Carolina, large

Caption Answer The 1964 voter-registration drive was part of an effort by King and other African-American leaders to focus attention on the issue of African American voting rights. This attention soon led to the Voting Rights Act of 1965.

African-American Voter Registration Before and After the Voting Rights Act of 1965

State	1960	1966	Percent Increase
Alabama	66,000	250,000	278.8
Arkansas	73,000	115,000	57.5
Florida	183,000	303,000	65.6
Georgia	180,000	300,000	66.7
Louisiana	159,000	243,000	52.8
Mississippi	22,000	175,000	695.5
North Carolina	210,000	282,000	34.3
South Carolina	58,000	191,000	229.3
Tennessee	185,000	225,000	21.6
Texas	227,000	400,000	76.2
Virginia	100,000	205,000	105.0

Source: U.S. Bureau of the Census, *Statistical Abstract of the United States 1982-83* (Washington, D.C.: Government Printing Office, 1982).

FIGURE 11–2 African-American Voter Registration Before and After the Voting Rights Act of 1965. This table illustrates the change in African-American voter registration after passage of the Voting Rights Act of 1965. What states showed the most dramatic increase of African-American voter registration as illustrated here?

This figure content is also featured on *West's American Government Videodisc* (see the index found in the *TRB*) and is available in the transparency package.

Figure Answer Mississippi, with a 695.5 percent increase, led all states, while Alabama, South Carolina, and Virginia also had increases in excess of 100 percent.

Discussion Starter
Help the students discuss bilingual ballots: Are bilingual ballots available in your community? Why or why not? If so, in what languages are ballots printed? Why is it important to provide bilingual ballots? What objections to bilingual ballots have been raised?

Enrichment
Ask two or three volunteers to research the movement for the 18-year-old vote in your state: Who supported the movement? What opposition was raised? When and under what conditions were 18-year-olds granted the vote in your state? Then have the volunteers prepare a chart or bulletin board summarizing the findings of their research.

Reteaching Strategies
1. Have the students work with partners to write their own definitions of these terms: *suffrage, disenfranchise, registration, residency.*
2. Have the students write paragraphs explaining the voting requirements in your state. Then let the students work in small groups to compare and discuss—and, if necessary, revise—their paragraphs.

Evaluation Strategies
1. Have the students write their answers to the Section 1 Review questions.
2. Have the students take the Section 1 Quiz found in the *TRB.*

Section 1 Review (Answers)
1. Several of our nation's founders felt that since many of the government's functions were in the economic sphere, it was fair and reasonable that only those people who had an interest in property should be allowed to vote.
2. Although the Fifteenth Amendment guaranteed suffrage to African Americans in 1870, many barriers remained. African Americans were prevented from voting through methods ranging from mob violence to economic restrictions. The civil rights movement of the 1950s and policy changes of the 1960s helped end both formal and informal barriers.
3. The women's suffrage movement was active after the Civil War. The first suffrage bill was introduced in Congress in 1868 and each year thereafter until 1893. The women's suffrage movement became more active between 1910 and 1914. In 1920, the Nineteenth Amendment was ratified, granting women the right to vote.
4. An individual must be 18 years of age or older. In every state except North Dakota, he or she must register. Another state requirement is residency, which requires that a person live within a state for a specified period of time.
5. Answers will vary, e.g., if the requirements were uniform throughout the states there would be more voters participating in elections. Voters would not be confused and discouraged by various differences between states.

parts of North Carolina, and some counties in five northern states were covered by registrars. The Voting Rights Act stipulated that new election laws could not go into effect without approval by the U.S. Department of Justice.

The constitutionality of the Voting Rights Act was upheld in *South Carolina* v. *Katzenback* (1966), and it has been renewed and expanded several times. Just before Independence Day in 1982, Congress passed and President Reagan signed into law a twenty-five year extension of the Voting Rights Act. It now covers more states and other minorities, including Hispanics, Asians, Native Americans,[1] and Native Alaskans, and thus serves as a basic protection for minority voting rights. For example, states must provide bilingual ballots in counties in which 5 percent or more of the population speaks a language other than English.

Current Eligibility Requirements

In 1961, the Twenty-third Amendment included the voters of the District of Columbia in the presidential electorate. In 1964, the Twenty-fourth Amendment eliminated the poll tax (and any other tax) as a condition for voting in any federal election. This left young people as the remaining disenfranchised group of citizens. Many thought it strange that men could be sent to war at age 18 but could not vote until they were 21 in most states.

During World War II, Georgia had lowered its minimum voting age. By the time the Vietnam War in the 1960s was at its peak and the argument for the 18-year-old vote was at its strongest, Kentucky and Alaska had lowered the minimum age as well. In the 1970 elections, voters in Maine, Massachusetts, Montana, and Nebraska approved the 18-year-old vote. In 1971 Congress adopted the Twenty-sixth Amendment giving 18-year-olds the right to vote.

Legal restraints on the right to vote are now largely a thing of the past for all citizens over 18. The table on page 263 summarizes the major amendments, Supreme Court decisions, and laws that have brought this about. There are still, however, legal *requirements* for voting. One requirement, in every state except North Dakota, is **registration**, which is the act of telling voting officials your name, address, and other important information. In general, a person must register well in advance of an election, but in some states people are allowed to register up to and on election day. Registration provides officials with lists of eligible voters and is intended to prevent fraudulent voting.

Another state requirement is **residency**, which requires that a person live within a state for a specified period of time in order to qualify to vote. The length of time a person must reside in the state or district varies widely from state to state. In 1972, the Supreme Court declared lengthy residency requirements unconstitutional for voting in state and local elections and suggested that thirty days was an ample residency period. Most states have changed or eliminated their residency requirements to comply with that ruling.

Another requirement is citizenship. Aliens may not vote in any public election held anywhere in the United States.

The right to vote is now widely held. Most states do, however, disqualify prison inmates, mentally ill people, convicted felons, and election-law violators.

SECTION 1 REVIEW

1. How did several of our founding fathers feel about who should and should not be allowed to vote?
2. How have the voting rights of African Americans evolved since 1870?
3. How did women gain the right to vote?
4. What are the current eligibility requirements?
5. **For critical analysis:** Although voting restrictions have for the most part been eliminated, there are still differences in how easy it is to register in the various states. If these differences were eliminated would there be more voters participating in our elections?

SECTION 2

More Suffrage, Less Participation

Preview Questions

- What are the reasons citizens do not vote in the United States?
- What types of people are most likely to vote in the United States?

Historian William Bennet Munro once commented:

> It all goes to prove what a strangely perverse creature the American citizen is. Refuse him the right to vote, and he

1. All Native Americans were granted the right to vote in 1924 when they were granted full U.S. citizenship.

SECTION 2

Points to Stress

- Reasons citizens do not vote in the United States.
- The types of people most likely to vote in the United States.
- The effects of low voter turnout.
- Proposed reforms that might increase voter turnout.

Kickoff Activity

Ask the students these questions: Do you think voter participation is declining? Why or why not? Let the students write their responses before they share and discuss their ideas.

Working with the Preview Questions

Let the students read these study questions, and encourage them to share their responses, based on what they already know. Then ask the students to keep these questions in mind as they take notes on Section 2.

Teaching Strategies

Introduction

Let volunteers read the section introduction aloud and encourage them to discuss their reactions to the information presented there: What does it mean that so few Americans choose to vote? Why do you think the percentage of participating voters is so much lower in the United States than in other countries? How does the low voter participation affect elected officials in the United States? How does it affect political parties and individual voters? Do you expect the decline in voter participation to be a continuing trend? Why or why not?

Discussion Starter

Let the students discuss their own ideas about why people do not vote: What reasons have you heard people offer for not voting? Which of those reasons make sense to you? What arguments would you offer in response to each reason for not voting?

Discussion Starter

Focus the students' attention on absentee ballots: Who is intended to benefit from absentee ballots? Do those groups actually benefit? What other groups might benefit from absentee voting? How could they benefit? What groups might suffer as a result?

Extension

Ask the students about Americans' sense of political ineffectiveness: What causes this attitude? Ask the students to write a paragraph detailing what should be done to help Americans feel politically effective.

Discussion Starter

Guide the students in considering the quotation from the woman interviewed by CBS News: Whom does she mean when she says voting only encourages "them"? Why do some citizens want to avoid encouraging "them"? How do you respond to this woman's attitude? Do you know others who express—or who hold without expressing—this kind of attitude?

would take up arms to wrest it from his rulers. But give this right to him freely, and he tucks it away in moth balls.

One by one, the barriers to voting have fallen away as the struggles over the extension of suffrage have given more Americans the right to vote than ever before. Yet there are millions of Americans who, for one reason or another, do not vote. **Voter turnout** is the percentage of eligible citizens who take part in the election process—the percentage that actually "turn out" to cast a ballot on election day. Compared with other countries, the level of voter turnout in the United States is in the bottom 20 percent. Only in Switzerland is the turnout lower than in the U.S.

In 1988, little more than 50 percent of persons of voting age voted in the presidential election. Only 44.7 percent voted in the congressional elections that year. Statistics show that voter turnout has been declining steadily over time.

Low voter turnout is even more pronounced at the state and local levels. Even though it seems as if people would vote more often in elections that directly affected them, the figures do not confirm this assumption. In local elections for such offices as mayor, city council and county attorney, it is fairly common for only 25 percent or less of the electorate to vote.

Voters are more likely to vote for lower offices when higher-office elections are being held, especially in national elections when the presidency is involved. For example, the average voter turnout for congressional seats is higher when a presidential election is also held. When an election for governor is held, more participation occurs in the election for state representatives.

Why Some People Do Not Vote

Why are there so many nonvoters when Americans have strived so hard for the right to vote? Why, even in a presidential election, do nearly half of all those who could vote stay away from the polls? There are a number of possible reasons why more Americans do not vote.

Unable to Vote A certain percentage of voters simply cannot vote on any given election day. In each of the past few presidential elections, 5 to 6 million citizens were too ill or are physically handicapped, and thus could not go out and vote. Another 2 to 3 million were away from their home precincts at the time of the elections. (It should be noted that absentee ballots are generally available for those who know in advance that they will be unable to vote at their polling place.)

Residency and Registration Requirements Some people do not vote because they do not meet the residency or registration requirements of their states. In the past, one could register only at an official building and only during normal working hours. In recent years, more and more states have added mobile registrars, who open booths in shopping centers, schools, and neighborhoods that are open evenings and weekends. Almost half the states now allow registration by mail. Nonetheless, the very fact that Americans must register—often well in advance—is thought by some experts to be one reason for low voter turnout.

One problem with the residency requirements is that American society is highly mobile. When a citizen moves to a new state, he or she must wait out the required period before becoming eligible to vote in that state. Absentee ballots remedy this problem somewhat, but for many Americans this still remains an inconvenience.

No Sense of Political Effectiveness More and more Americans seem to believe that political participation is not worthwhile because they will have no influence on changing the course of events. They simply do not believe that they or their votes can have an impact on how government is run. They do not vote because they believe it "won't make any difference."

Being "Turned Off" by Political Campaigns Some people are affected by negative advertising, the superficial treatment of issues, the constant input on how to vote, and dissatisfaction with the candidates. A woman once interviewed by *CBS News* expressed it this way: "I never vote. It only encourages 'them.'"

TEACHING GOVERNMENT IN ACTION

Read
Before the students read this Government in Action Case Study, let them share and discuss their own experiences with voting by mail: Do you know people who have ever voted by mail? Why did they choose this method? Do you know people who regularly vote by mail? Why do they do this? What do you think of voting by mail? Why? After the discussion, ask two or three students to read the Case Study aloud to the rest of the class.

Discuss
Help the students discuss the Case Study by posing questions such as these: How do you react to the information here about the 1982 California gubernatorial race? Do you think the Republicans' use of absentee ballots was appropriate? Why or why not? Can citizens vote by mail in your state? Do you think they should be allowed to? Why or why not? Is early voting available in your state? Do you think it should be? Why or why not? Is making voting more convenient for people who already vote anyway actually an advantage? Why or why not?

Analyze and Apply
Let the students work in groups to gather statistics on voter turnout in your state's most recent gubernatorial election: What percentage of registered voters cast ballots? What percentage of the voters—if any—used absentee ballots? What percentage—if any—voted early? Ask the group members to report these statistics in a chart or graph.

Review
To help the students review this Case Study, ask these questions: What procedures are being used to encourage people to vote? Why are such measures necessary? How effective do they seem to be?

Think About It (Answers)
1. Answers will vary, e.g., absentee ballots should be available in all states to anyone eligible to vote. Because voter turnout is so low in the United States, any method to make the process easier should be utilized.

GOVERNMENT IN ACTION

CASE STUDY

Voting by Mail

Absentee voting has become a significant factor in numerous political races. A case in point involves the 1982 California gubernatorial race between Democratic Los Angeles Mayor Tom Bradley and Republican Attorney General George Deukmejian. The polls taken right outside the polling booths showed that Bradley had won by a landslide. And the polls were right—until the **absentee ballots** were counted. (Such ballots are filled in and mailed.) Deukmejian won only 48.6 percent of the vote at the polls. But he won 60 percent of the absentee vote, which gave him a 113,000-vote margin to win the election.

Why did the Republicans do so well with absentee ballots? The California Republican Party took advantage of the state's liberal voting requirements to mass mail absentee ballot applications to over 2 million Republican households.

Because voter turnout is lower in the United States than in any democracy in the world, anything to get more people to vote, including emphasis on voting by mail, may be appropriate. Polls show that one of the most common reasons Americans give for not voting is that they are "too busy." By the 1990s, almost one in five votes in California were voted by mail. In Texas the number is almost one in four.

Currently, voting by mail works well in a limited number of states, in particular Alaska, California, Kansas, Oregon, and Washington. The reason is that only in those states can "all registered voters" vote by mail. In other states the process requires voters to first submit an application for an absentee ballot to the county clerk. Then the clerk has to mail out the ballots. The voter must return the ballot before election day, although some states accept ballots postmarked with the election date. In any event, in most states voting by mail currently takes effort and planning.

One thing is certain: The easier it is to vote by mail the more people do it. In 1990 less than 8 percent of all voters nationwide cast absentee ballots. In contrast, in California twice that percentage voted that way. In one special election for the California State Assembly held in 1990, the majority of votes was cast by mail.

Early Voting

Early voting is an alternative to absentee voting. In Texas a law passed in 1987 allows people to vote in person at special locations for sixteen days, ending four days before the election. In the following year one in four Texans voted early.

But Do More People Vote?

It would seem that voting by mail and early voting would stop the decline of voter participation. The facts, however, do not necessarily indicate this. In Texas and in California there continues to be a decline in overall turnout in spite of the increasing number of ballots cast before election day. It may be that absentee balloting and voting before the election simply make voting more convenient for people who would vote anyway.

THINK ABOUT IT

1. Should absentee ballots be available in all states to anyone who is registered for any election? Explain why or why not.
2. What are the disadvantages of allowing early voting?
3. If making it easier for people to vote does not increase voter participation levels, what do you think will?
4. Do you think that you would be more likely to vote if allowed to use an absentee ballot?

2. Answers will vary, e.g., early voting might make the process more complicated for election officials.

3. Answers will vary, e.g., increased interest in political affairs by the people. Political campaigns that were more positive and less offensive would encourage more people to vote. A national campaign to encourage voter participation could also encourage people to vote.

4. Answers will vary, e.g., yes, because I could vote when convenient.

Discussion Starter

Help the students consider citizens who feel they cannot afford the time and effort involved in voting: What are the results of voters refusing to invest that time and effort? What are the "costs" of those results?

Enrichment

Let several interested students research the religious beliefs that prevent some citizens from voting: What are those beliefs? What percentage of the voting-age population holds such beliefs? How does their not voting affect elections, elected officials, and other voters? Ask these students to share their findings with the rest of the class in a brief oral report.

Discussion Starter

Focus the students' attention on education as a factor affecting turnout of voters: Why do you think education is such an important factor in voting? What are the implications of this importance? Does this situation contribute to a sense (for at least some voters) that our country is run by an elite group of wealthy, highly educated leaders? If so, what can be done about this sense? If not, why not?

People are also put off by the excessively long campaigns and the large number of officeholders they are expected to elect, from members of Congress to local county assessors or even dog catchers. The problem is compounded because elections for different offices are held at different times, which can cause "ballot fatigue."

Time-Consuming Election Procedures Some people are discouraged not only by long ballots, but also by long lines at the polls and inconvenient registration requirements. Given these inconveniences, some people do not want to bother. To some, voting is too costly in time and effort, especially if they attempt to be well-informed of the issues before voting.

Lack of Interest Some people lack sufficient interest to vote. They are indifferent or apathetic.

Satisfaction with the Status Quo Others are not interested in voting because they approve of the way the nation's business is being handled. They believe that no matter who is elected, things will continue to go well for themselves and for the country.

Disenfranchised Citizens In any given election, some people cannot vote because they are resident aliens. Others are confined to mental institutions or prisons. Still others do not or cannot vote because of personal religious beliefs.

Undecided Citizens There are those people who fail to vote because they cannot make up their minds. They are undecided about which candidate to support. Sometimes this is not caused by lack of information, but by *too much* information from dozens of candidates, which then confuses voters.

Why Some People Do Vote

Having looked at why some people do not vote, let's examine what types of people do vote.

Education The more education a person has, the more likely it is that she or he will be a regular voter. People who graduated from high school vote more regularly than those who finished only grade school, and college graduates vote more often than high-school graduates. Among factors affecting turnout, this one is the most important.

Age Voter turnout increases as the age groups become older until age 65, at which point there is a slight decline. Greater participation with age is likely due to the fact

Developing Skills for the Information Age

The impact of television is felt at all stages of an election. News networks, in their quest to be "first," have added to the problem of nonvoting by declaring projected winners before polls close. This could cause a person to change their vote, in order to support a "winner," or keep a person from voting at all. Some news stations have voluntarily agreed not to announce data from key precincts or exit polls until polls close; others reserve the right to announce voting trends.

Have students write a letter to local television executives asking their policy on providing election results. Students should be encouraged to impress upon the networks that the actual final results reflecting the will of the voters is what they wish to hear! Students should monitor the manner in which networks handle election results during the next election.

TEACHING CITIZENSHIP SKILLS AND RESPONSIBILITIES

Read
Introduce this feature by letting the students discuss their own responses to voting: Have you ever voted? If so, when? How did you feel about voting? If you are not yet qualified to vote, do you expect to vote regularly when you are old enough? Why or why not? After this introductory discussion, let volunteers read the Citizenship Skills and Responsibilities feature aloud to the rest of the class.

Discuss
Encourage the students to discuss the feature by asking questions such as these: Why do you think registration laws vary from state to state? What have you heard or read about absentee voting? What objections might be raised to absentee voting? What arguments might be presented in favor of absentee voting?

Analyze and Apply
Have the students work in small groups to plan and make posters that explain the voter registration process and that encourage citizens to vote. If languages other than English are spoken in parts of your community, encourage at least some of the groups to make posters in appropriate languages.

Review
Ask these questions to help the students review the Citizenship Skills and Responsibilities feature: What is the purpose of voter registration? What is an absentee ballot? How do you use a standard voting machine?

Comprehension
Have the students recall (or review) the organizations that are encouraging voter participation and influence among members of racial and ethnic minorities.

Critical Thinking Skills
Guide the students in evaluating the two points of view about low voter turnout: Do you believe low voter turnout actually endangers our representative democratic government? Do you believe that low voter turnout merely means that people are satisfied?

Reteaching Strategies
1. Let the students work in small groups to compare and discuss the notes they took while reading Section 2. Encourage the students to refer to the text to resolve any questions.
2. Ask each student to write a paragraph describing his or her own point of view about the low voter turnout in the United States.

Evaluating Strategies
1. Have the students write their answers to the Section 2 Review questions.
2. Have the students take the Section 2 Quiz found in the *TRB*.

CITIZENSHIP SKILLS AND RESPONSIBILITIES
Voting

In most democratic countries, people are automatically registered to vote when they reach voting age. In every state in the U.S. but North Dakota, you must register to vote before you are allowed to cast a ballot in an election. This means you must go to a local election board or temporary registration office set up at a school, a shopping center, or some other public place several weeks or even several months before the election. Specific registration laws vary considerably from state to state. When you register, you will need to fill out a form with information such as your birth date, current address, and signature. From these registration forms, election officials draw up a list of eligible voters. Registration is used as a means of preventing voters from voting more than once.

Most states require that you meet minimum residency requirements. You must have lived in the state in which you plan to register for a certain period of time, which can vary from a few days to as long as fifty days. Some states have no residency requirement. If you move to a new state that has a residency requirement that you do not meet or if you will be unable to go to your poll, you can use an absentee ballot. This is a ballot that you fill out and send to your place of voting. You can also use an absentee ballot when you go away to college. Be sure to contact voting officials, usually at the local board of elections, within a certain number of days before the election to get your absentee ballot.

Check the laws in your state to find out if there is a closing date on voter registration. The closing date varies from the day of the election itself to fifty days prior to the election.

On election day, as a registered voter, you will enter the polling place and check with an election official who will look up your name to see that you are registered. In some places the official will give you a printed ballot or punch card that lists the candidates and measures on which you will vote. Many polling places have voting machines. To use them you simply enter t!.. booth and pull the lever to close the curtain behind you. A ballot will be posted for you to mark. You will find the names of the candidates, their political parties, and the offices for which they are running.

If your state uses a standard voting machine, you will see a series of small levers over the names of the various candidates. To vote, you simply push down the levers over the name of the candidates you choose. If you push down the wrong lever, put it back up and pull down the correct one. Check over your ballot before leaving. When you open the curtain, the machine registers your votes.

TAKING ACTION

1. Find out about the voting requirements in your state and compare them to the requirements in two other states.
2. Write a letter to a state legislator indicating why you believe your state voting requirements are too restrictive, too lenient, or appropriate.

that older people are more settled, are already registered, and have had more experience with voting.

Marital Status Married people vote more frequently than single people.

Income The higher a person's income, the greater likelihood that she or he will vote.

Minority Status Racial and ethnic minorities are underrepresented among the ranks of voters. However, in several recent elections, participation by these groups has increased.

Government Employees Those who depend on government and government programs tend to vote more than other groups. These people also tend to know more about how government operates.

These factors are all cumulative: The greater the number of these traits in a person, the higher the

Section 2 Review (Answers)
1. Voter turnout is the percentage of eligible citizens who take part in the election process. Compared with other countries, voter turnout in the United States is in the bottom 20 percent.
2. Some people are unable to vote because they are ill, handicapped, or away from their home precincts at the time of elections. Strict residency and registration requirements prevent others from voting. Some people feel that voting is not worthwhile because they will have no influence on changing the course of events and others are offended by political campaigns. Others are discouraged by time-consuming election procedures.
3. The more education a person has, the more likely he or she will be a regular voter. Voter turnout increases as age groups become older. Married people vote more frequently than single people. The higher the person's income, the more regularly the person votes.
4. Answers will vary, e.g., the more education a person has, the more he or she has been exposed to political issues. Being exposed to political issues causes more concern about society and the person is more likely to want to vote on these issues.

SECTION 3

Points to Stress
- The affect of party identification on voting.
- Candidate image as an influence on voters' choices.
- Policy voting.
- The socioeconomic factors affecting voters' choices.

Caption Answer Answers may vary, but students should understand that older people are more settled, often already registered, and probably have more experience voting. Additionally, these people may be better aware of the effect that government can have on their lives.

Kickoff Activity
To introduce Section 3, ask the students to read the section title and then to write lists of at least five factors they believe influence people's voting choices. After all the students have completed their lists, let volunteers share and compare their responses.

Working with the Preview Questions
Ask volunteers to read these study questions aloud to the class. Then help the students work together to use these questions in planning an outline format for the section.

Teaching Strategies

Introduction
Let one of the students read the brief section introduction aloud. Then encourage the students to share their own attitudes about voting.

As you've learned, the likelihood that one will vote increases as one gets older. Why do you think this link between participation and age exists?

likelihood of voting. For example, a well-educated, married, well-to-do person would be more likely to vote than a less-educated, lower-income, single 20-year-old.

The Effect of Low Voter Turnout

There are two points of view about low voter turnout. To some people, low voter turnout endangers our representative democracy because fewer individuals are actually participating in the decisions of government and public policy. It is a sign of apathy about our system, or that people feel alienated from or angry with the way government is run. It may also be a sign that people are not concerned about the issues.

To others, low voter turnout is nothing about which to be concerned. They believe the decline in voter participation is simply a sign that people are satisfied with the status quo. Nonvoters are obtaining the type of government they want without voting. They believe that representative democracy is a reality even if small numbers of eligible voters take part in elections.

Ideas for Reform

Whatever the reason may be, voter turnout might be increased by a number of techniques. One is increased voting by mail, a subject discussed in the "Government in Action" feature on page 270. Another is voter registration as a requirement of being an American citizen. This concept has been included in a proposed bill called The National Voter Registration Act. Additionally, some observers believe that if ballots were shorter, there would be higher voter turnout. Another possibility is to allow people to vote via television. The technology to do so is available, but it is still too costly for widespread use. In the future, though, when the cost is lower, it may become possible. Because so many Americans spend so much time in front of their television sets, perhaps these "viewer elections" will reverse the low voting record of this nation's citizens.

Section 2 Review

1. What is voter turnout? How high has the voter turnout level been in the United States?
2. Explain five causes for low voter turnout in the United States.
3. What are the characteristics of those persons most likely to vote?
4. **For critical analysis:** Explain why you think the more education a person has the more likely he or she will be a regular voter.

Section 3

Why People Vote as They Do

Preview Questions
- How does party identification affect voters' choices?
- How does the image of the candidate affect voters' choices?
- What is policy voting?
- What are the socioeconomic factors affecting voters' choices?

How do people develop attitudes about voting? What prompts some to vote Republican and others to vote Democratic? What persuades voters to choose certain kinds of candidates? Clearly, there is more involved than

Enrichment
Ask several interested students to gather information on the strength of party identification: How is it measured? How is it changing? Can any trends be identified? Let the researchers prepare and present a chart summarizing their findings.

Discussion Starter
Help the students consider the images projected by various presidential candidates: What kind of image do you think attracts American voters? Why? What is the relationship—if any—between that kind of image and the ability of a president to lead the country effectively? Should voters be led to want a different kind of image in presidential candidates? If so, how could that kind of change be effected?

Discussion Starter
Have the students consider and discuss the major issues that stimulate policy voting: What are those issues? Why do they evoke such firm responses? What examples can you cite of voters who have ignored their usual party allegiance in order support a particular policy point-of-view?

Cooperative Learning
Have the students work in groups to add to the list of issues that create heated debates in campaigns. Then have each group member rank the issues in the group's expanded list according to his or her level of interest; encourage the group members to compare and discuss the rankings they have given each issue.

Enrichment
Let several volunteers work together to research the issue of American hostages held in Iran during Carter's presidency: Who was held? For how long? What attempts were made to free the hostages? When and how were the hostages released? What are the current theories on the background of that release? Have these volunteers present their findings to the rest of the class in a brief oral report.

measuring one's own position against the candidates' positions and then voting accordingly. Voters choose candidates for many reasons, some of which are explored here. These questions cannot be answered with absolute certainty, but particularly because of the technology of opinion polling, researchers have collected more information on voting than any other form of political participation in the United States. The information sheds some light on why people decide to vote for particular candidates.

Party Identification

Although the proportion is shrinking, many voters have a standing allegiance to a political party, or a **party identification**. These identifications can be a general guide to voters' choices. People choose the party with which they generally agree, so they do not have to concern themselves with every issue that comes along. They can generally rely on their party identification to guide them. Of course, party identification is influenced by family, age, peer groups, and other factors, but regardless of how it is developed, it is one of the most prominent and lasting predictors of how a person will vote.

There are indications, however, that party identification has lost some of its impact. As we saw in Chapter 8, there has been an increase in split-ticket voting—voting for candidates of both parties at the same election. There are also a large number of voters who now call themselves independents. Despite this label, many independents actually do support one or the other party quite regularly.

Candidates' Images

All candidates try to portray an image of honesty, decisiveness, leadership, and integrity, but they all have very different backgrounds, personalities, appearances, and levels of knowledge and experience. Voters often base their decisions more on their *impression* of candidates than on the candidates' *actual* qualifications.

Democratic presidential candidate Adlai Stevenson, who lost to Republican Dwight D. Eisenhower in 1952 and 1956, was perceived as being too intellectual and sophisticated for many people to be comfortable with as president. Republican Barry Goldwater, who lost to Lyndon Johnson in 1964, was viewed as more willing than Johnson to lead the nation into war. Republican Richard Nixon's positive image in 1968 and 1972 allowed him to win over negatively evaluated opponents. Many voters turned against President Carter in 1980 because they felt he was weak in the face of events that confronted his administration. One of the keys to George Bush's victory in 1988 was his ability to raise his image during the campaign while Dukakis's ratings fell. A candidate's image remains one of the keys to voter support.

Policy Choices

Policy voting occurs when people vote for candidates who share their stand on the issues. If a candidate for Senate in your state supports a strong defense program and opposes gun-control laws, and you agree and vote for her for those reasons, you have engaged in policy voting. If a presidential candidate believes in lowering the federal deficit by raising taxes and you agree and vote for her for that reason, then this is also policy voting. In order to actually engage in real policy voting, persons must have a clear view of their own policy positions, and must know where the candidates stand on important policies.

Historically, different issues have had different impact. Usually economic issues have had the greatest influence on voters' choices. When the economy is doing well, it is very difficult for a challenger, particularly at the presidential level, to defeat the **incumbent**—the person already in office. When the economy is doing poorly—inflation is increasing or unemployment is rising—the incumbent is at a disadvantage.

Foreign-policy issues become important during election time. Public protests over the war in Vietnam had an effect on the elections of 1968 and 1972. President Carter's inability to bring American hostages home from Iran in 1980 may have cost him his reelection. (The hostages were not released until after Ronald Reagan was already elected.[2]) President Bush's decisive actions after Iraq's invasion of Kuwait in August 1990, and the resulting successful rout of the Iraqi army by the United States, improved the president's public image, which did not carry over into the 1992 elections.

In accordance with the level of public concern, protecting the environment has recently emerged as an important campaign issue. Once dismissed as a fringe cause by many politicians, environmentalism has reached the forefront of American politics. Many candidates are

2. Actually, the hostages were released during Ronald Reagan's inauguration ceremonies in January 1981. Some believed that Iran did not want Carter to be president when the hostages were released. Others alleged that Reagan, or at least his advisors, "made a deal" with Iran *not* to release the hostages prior to the November 1980 election. These allegations were not discussed in public until the spring of 1991.

TEACHING BUILDING SOCIAL STUDIES SKILLS

Read
Let the students begin by reading the Building Social Studies Skills title and discussing why they might want to analyze a photograph: What can you learn from looking at a photograph superficially? What other kinds of information might you discover by studying the same photograph? What kinds of photographs do you think you should take the time to analyze? Why? After this introductory discussion, have the students read the Building Social Studies Skills feature independently.

Discuss
Stimulate discussion by posing questions such as these: How do you think a photograph can be intentionally misleading? Unintentionally misleading? How can reading the caption or title help you analyze a photograph? What can you do to determine the photographer's viewpoint? Why is understanding that viewpoint important?

Analyze and Apply
Have each student bring in at least one photograph, preferably from a newspaper, news magazine, or history book. Then have the students work in groups to analyze the photographs supplied by the group members.

Review
Ask the students these review questions: How can a photograph be misleading? What four tips can help you analyze a photograph?

Practicing Your Skills (Answers)
1. The subject is voter turnout. The location is a polling place.
2. The voting booths help you to recognize it as a polling place. The most telling detail is the lack of voters. The lone voter makes it clear that it is the day of an election.
3. Answers will vary, e.g., there is greater opportunity for voting than there are people willing to vote.
4. Answers will vary, e.g., the photographer is trying to make a point about poor voter turnout.

Enrichment
Encourage interested students to research the Green Parties of Europe: Around what issues are they organized? What is the relationship between the European Greens and the green vote in this country? Ask these students to write a short report, to be made available to the rest of the class.

BUILDING SOCIAL STUDIES SKILLS

Analyzing a Photograph

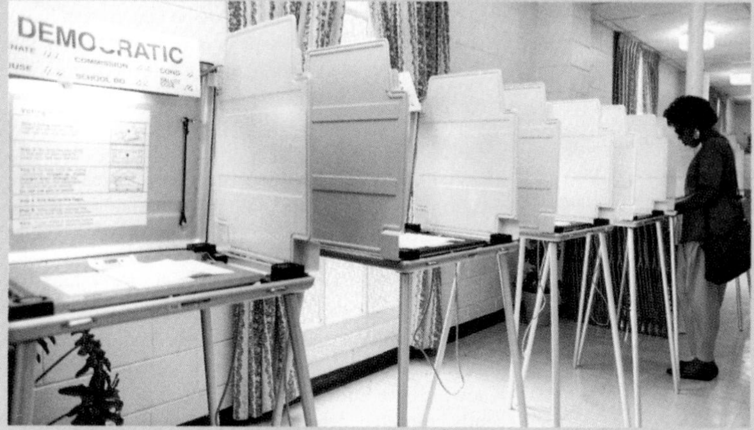

Photographers have documented much of the nation's political history and their work has become an important part of the American historical record. Government textbooks, newspapers, and magazines are all filled with photographs of political events. Pictures can often help you visualize events much more vividly than the written word. They can tell a story, give important details, or express a certain mood.

Remember, however, that a photograph can also be misleading. It captures only one moment, and the events that precede or follow that event are not shown. Sometimes a photographer poses or frames a subject, which can create a certain viewpoint or leave out important details. If the photograph is taken out of context, it can also be misleading, and present only what the photographer wishes to record.

To analyze a picture, use these tips:

- **Determine the subject of the photograph.** Read the caption or title if there is one.
- **Study the details of the photograph.** Look beyond the main subject to the background. Ask yourself what these details tell you about the context of the photo.
- **Try to decide what the photographer's viewpoint is.** Is he or she trying to present the subject in a positive or negative light?
- **Try to determine whether the photograph is an accurate depiction of the event.** Read about the event and look at other pictures to help you decide.

PRACTICING YOUR SKILLS

1. What is the subject of the photograph above? Where is the location?
2. What details in the photograph give you information?
3. What generalizations can you draw from this photograph about voter participation?
4. What is the photographer's point of view?

suddenly proclaiming themselves as environmentalists, in an attempt to capture the **green vote**—the vote from those who favor stronger laws to protect and preserve the environment.

Some of the most heated debates in campaigns take place over social issues such as women's rights, the death penalty, and religion in schools. Political corruption and crime in the streets have also become important campaign issues.

All candidates try to distinguish their stand from their opponents' stands on the issues, in order to attract as many voters as they can.

Discussion Starter
Help the students consider and discuss the reversal of the trend for younger voters to support Democratic candidates: What do you think accounts for this reversal? Do you see a new trend among younger voters? If so, what is that trend and how do you believe it will develop?

Critical Thinking Skills
Guide the students in analyzing the theory that a gender gap exists: Based on your own personal experiences, do you believe there is a difference between the way men vote and the way women vote? Why or why not? Does the theory itself make sense to you? Why or why not? What statistics can you cite to support—or oppose—the theory of a gender gap? Encourage a lively exchange of ideas.

Discussion Starter
Help the students discus the relationship between education and voting: Does this relationship hold true among the voters you know? In your opinion, should this kind of relationship exist? Why or why not? If so, what makes it a positive relationship? If not, what might be done to change the situation?

Comprehension
Ask the students to recall the fundamental beliefs of the Republican and Democratic parties: How do those beliefs explain the information about which occupational groups tend to support each party?

Enrichment
Let one or two volunteers research the issues, interests, and influences of the Southern Democrats: How do they differ from other Democrats? How powerful have Southern Democrats been in the past within the larger Democratic Party? What is their status today? Why? Ask the volunteers to prepare a chart summarizing what they have learned.

Reteaching Strategies
1. Have the students work in small groups to read and compare their outlines of Section 3. Remind the students to refer to the text and to revise their outlines as necessary.
2. Let the students work with partners to write, in their own words, definitions of these terms: *party identification, incumbent, socioeconomic factors, gender gap.*

Evaluation Strategies
1. Have the students write their answers to the Section 3 Review questions.
2. Have the students take the Section 3 Quiz found in the *TRB.*

Section 3 Review (Answers)
1. People choose a party with which they generally agree, so they can rely on party identification to guide their votes.
2. Voters often base their decisions on their impression of candidates rather than issues.
3. Socioeconomic factors include a person's age, gender, education, income level, religion, occupation, and geographic location.
4. Answers will vary, e.g., socioeconomic factors influence, to an extent, the ideas and beliefs to which a person will be exposed during the ongoing process of political socialization.

Socioeconomic Factors

Many things determine how a person votes. Some are related to what are called **socioeconomic factors**, which are all of the social and economic circumstances of a person's life. These factors include a person's age, education, income level, religion, occupation, and geographic location. Some have to do with the family and circumstances into which an individual is born, and others have to do with choices made throughout an individual's lifetime. The difficulty in searching for socioeconomic factors in voting behavior is that voters may not be aware of these factors or the ways they influence their political views.

Age A voter's age affects how he or she votes. Younger voters have been more likely to be Democrats, and older voters are more likely to vote Republican. In elections from 1952 through 1980, voters under 30 clearly favored the Democratic presidential candidates. This trend reversed itself in 1984 when voters under 30 voted heavily for Ronald Reagan. George Bush maintained that support in 1988.

Gender The level of voter participation is about equal for both sexes, as are attitudes on almost all issues. A number of studies have indicated, however, that men and women do vote differently when issues of force, both in foreign affairs and in dealing with human rights or domestic unrest, are prominent in an election. Until recently there seems to have been no fixed relationship between voter preference and gender in presidential elections. Some analysts now argue, however, that there is in fact a **gender gap**—a difference between the way females voted compared to males—which became a determinant in the 1980 presidential election of Ronald Reagan. Reagan obtained 15 percentage points more than Carter among male voters, whereas women gave about an equal number of votes to each candidate. In 1988, the gender gap had lessened to a difference of 4 percentage points.

Education There is a relationship between the level of a voter's education and how she or he votes. As a general rule, people with more formal education are more likely to vote Republican while those who stopped going to school earlier are more likely to vote Democratic.

Occupation and Income Because we spend so many of our waking hours working, it is not surprising that occupation can influence voting decisions. Professionals, business people, and white-collar workers tend to vote Republican. Factory workers, laborers, and especially union members are more likely to vote Democratic. Voters in the middle- to upper-income brackets are more likely to be Republicans, while those with lower incomes tend to be Democrats.

Religion and Ethnic Background Traditionally, the majority of Protestants have voted Republican, while Catholics and Jews have tended to be Democrats. Italian, Irish, Polish, Eastern European, and Slavic voters have generally supported Democrats, while northern European and Anglo-Saxon voters have voted Republican.

African Americans voted principally for Republicans until Roosevelt's New Deal. Since then they have identified with the Democratic party and have given the Democratic presidential candidate a clear majority of their votes in every election since 1952, although this majority began to weaken in the 1980s.

Geographic Region For more than one hundred years after the Civil War, most Southerners, regardless of background or socioeconomic status, have been Democrats. Known as the **Solid South**, this strong coalition has recently crumbled in the presidential elections, but the rural vote in the South still tends to be Democratic. The Democrats also draw much of their strength from large Northern and Eastern cities. Rural areas, except in the South, tend to be Republican. They also receive strong support from the West, parts of the Midwest, and from Maine and New Hampshire in the Northeast.

Over the years, the right to vote has been extended to include nearly all American citizens eighteen years of age or older. The Fifteenth, Nineteenth, Twenty-third, Twenty-fourth, and Twenty-sixth Amendments to the Constitution deal with extending the right to vote. Despite this broadened opportunity, voter turnout has declined. Various socioeconomic factors affect voting behavior.

Voting remains an essential component of our representative democracy. As Grover Cleveland pointed out to the nation in his inaugural address, "Your every voter, as surely as your chief magistrate [the president], exercises a public trust."

Section 3 Review

1. What influence does party identification have on how a person will vote?
2. How do candidates' images and policies affect voter's choices?
3. What are the socioeconomic factors that can influence voter's choices?
4. **For critical analysis:** Why do you think socioeconomic factors would influence a person's voting choices?

TEACHING CHALLENGE TO THE AMERICAN DREAM

Read

Read aloud the title of this Challenge to the American Dream feature: An Indifferent Electorate. Encourage the students to share and discuss their responses to this title: Is the electorate truly indifferent? If so, what are the implications of that indifference? What are its effects? If not, why is the electorate so widely perceived as indifferent? Should that perception be changed? How? After a brief discussion, let volunteers take turns reading the feature aloud to the rest of the class.

Discuss

Help the students discuss the feature by asking questions such as these: What is your response to the statistic quoted by Buchanan? How do you respond to the idea expressed by O'Neil? Whose responsibility is it to see that this trend is reversed? What do you think of the suggestions made by the Markle Commission? How effective do you expect they could be? What other suggestions would you put forward?

Analyze and Apply

Ask the students to write letters to the editors of local newspapers, expressing their views of voter attitudes and their ideas about reversing the trend toward increasing indifference. Let the student's work with partners to review and edit their letters; then encourage the students to send their letters.

Review

Use these questions to help the students review this Challenge to the American Dream feature: What statistics show that the American electorate is indifferent? What changes have been suggested to reverse the trend of indifference?

You Decide (Answers)

1. Answers will vary, e.g., the fourth suggestion to call on candidates to shun distorted manipulative advertising would improve voter participation.

2. Answers will vary, e.g., those people who are unaware of the issues or disinterested should not participate.

3. Answers will vary, e.g., many people believe that one vote doesn't matter. Others are against politics in general. Others want to leave the political process to politicians.

Observable Mastery

1. Have students compile profiles on "typical" American voters, those people most likely to vote. Then have students develop a list that includes reasons for nonvoting in the United States.

2. Students should list all of the constitutional foundations for voting, from the 1870s to the 1980s.

CHALLENGE TO THE AMERICAN DREAM

An Indifferent Electorate

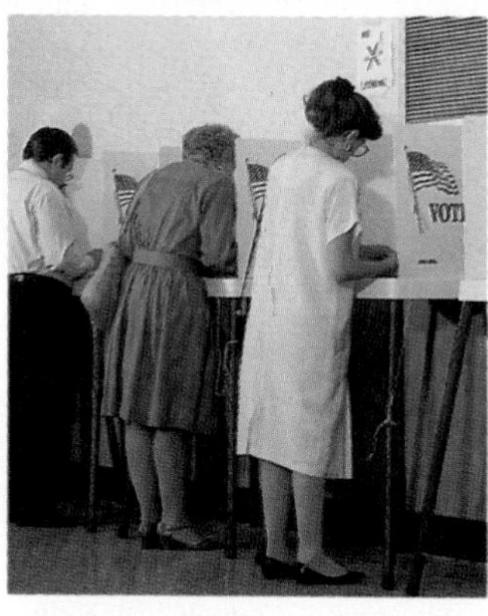

In the beginning of this chapter, Franklin D. Roosevelt was quoted as saying, "Nobody will ever deprive the American people of the right to vote except the American people themselves." If a commission set up in 1988 to do a two-year study of presidential politics is correct, the American people may be doing just that. The commission found an "astonishing" indifference to elections in America. They found that half of the population didn't even know who the candidates for vice president were in 1988. Bruce Buchanan, executive director of the Markle Commission on the Media and Electorate, said: "It is astonishing that 49 percent of the public did not know that Lloyd Bentsen was the Democratic nominee for vice president. . . ."

Robert M. O'Neil, head of the commission, stated: "American voters today do not seem to understand their rightful place in the operation of democracy."

The group suggested a series of steps to reverse this trend, which include the following: (1) a national campaign to encourage voter participation; (2) congressional requests to the television networks to give more broadcast time for political programming (although they did not all agree that broadcasters should be required to provide free time to presidential candidates); (3) a requirement for four presidential debates as a condition for a candidate's receiving federal campaign money; and (4) a call on candidates to shun distorted manipulative advertising.

Voting patterns may not be changed significantly, even if such reforms are undertaken. Some observers link the decline in voting with a variety of other factors: a decline in party identification, a decline in newspaper reading, and an increase in TV viewing.

The challenge to the American dream is to keep the average American interested enough in politics to prevent ill-meaning and wrong-headed politicians from being elected and thereafter leading this nation down the wrong path. Certainly a renewed spirit of participatory democracy would be a welcome step in the right direction.

You Decide

1. Given what you have learned about why people don't vote, what effect, if any, do you think the panel's suggestions would have on participation in the electoral process?
2. Do you think it's important for all people to be involved in the political process? Why or why not?
3. What do you think are some other reasons why people do not concern themselves with the political process?

CHAPTER 11 REVIEW

Key Terms

absentee ballot 270
disenfranchise 266
electorate 261
franchise 261
gender gap 276
grandfather clause 266
green vote 275
incumbent 274
literacy tests 266
party identification 274
policy voting 274
poll tax 266
registration 268
residency 268
socioeconomic factors 276
Solid South 276
suffrage 261
voter turnout 269

Chapter Evaluation

To evaluate student mastery of chapter material, you might:

1. Use Chapter Test A from the *TRB*.
2. Use Chapter Test B from the *TRB*.
3. Construct your own test using items from the *West American Government Test Bank* found in the *TRB*.
4. Use the accompanying computerized test software to construct and print a customized chapter test.

Review Questions (Answers)

1. There were numerous restrictions based on property ownership, race, sex, religious beliefs, and payment of taxes.
2. The Fifteenth Amendment guaranteed suffrage to African Americans, but many states continued to prevent African Americans from voting by formal and informal means.
3. Literacy tests, used as a criterion for voting, were used because many African Americans were also denied an education. Grandfather clauses exempted those whose grandfathers had the right to vote before 1867 from taking literacy tests.
4. The civil rights movement of the 1950s and 1960s.
5. The Nineteenth Amendment prohibits denying or abridging a citizen's right to vote on account of gender. The women's suffrage movement led to the passage of the Nineteenth Amendment.
6. Inability to vote because of illness, handicap, or being away from home precincts at the time of elections. Strict residency and registration requirements. No sense of political effectiveness. Discouragement by negative advertising and superficial treatment of important issues. Satisfaction with the status quo.
7. Higher levels of education, older age, being married, higher income, and those who depend on government.
8. One view is that low voter turnout endangers our representative democratic government. The other view is that low voter turnout is nothing to be concerned about because it is simply a sign that people are satisfied with the status quo.
9. Party identification serves as a general guide to voter's choices. Voters often base their decisions on candidates' images. Policy voting is significant but not as much so as voting along party lines or voting for a candidate's image.
10. Socioeconomic factors include a person's age, education, income level, religion, occupation,

CHAPTER 11 REVIEW—Continued

Summary

1. In the United States today, all citizens of at least 18 years of age have the right to vote. In our nation's past, there have been many restrictions on suffrage, but today almost all legal barriers to voting have been eliminated. The Fifteenth Amendment guaranteed suffrage to African-American males in 1870, but various methods were used for the next century to restrict their ability to vote. The civil rights movement, the Civil Rights Act of 1964, and the Voting Rights Act of 1965 finally made the Fifteenth Amendment an effective part of the Constitution. The passage of the Nineteenth Amendment in 1920 prohibited voter discrimination on the basis of sex. The passage of the Twenty-sixth Amendment in 1971 gave 18-year-olds the right to vote.

2. Even though these barriers to voting have been abolished, only about half of those citizens eligible to vote practice this right. Some of the reasons include inability to vote due to illness or physical handicap, not meeting residency and registration requirements, not having a sense of political effectiveness, being "turned off" by political campaigns, the time-consuming election procedures, lack of interest, and satisfaction with the status quo. There are also a certain number who cannot vote because they are confined to mental institutions or prisons. The characteristics that influence whether or not a person votes include education, age, marital status, income and minority status, and government employment. Some people view low voter turnout as a threat to representative democracy, while others view it as a sign that people are satisfied with the way things are.

3. Several factors influence voters' choices. Party identification is the most prominent indicator of how a person will vote. Voters are also influenced by the image they have of a candidate. Policy voting occurs when people vote for candidates who reflect their own views on the issues. Voters are also influenced by socioeconomic factors such as age, sex, education, occupation and income, religion and ethnic background, and geographic region.

Review Questions

1. What were some of the early restrictions placed on the right to vote in the United States?
2. What did the passage of the Fifteenth Amendment guarantee? How did many states respond to this amendment?
3. Explain some of the early tactics used to prevent African Americans from voting.
4. What events led to the passage of the Voting Rights Act of 1965?
5. What does the Nineteenth Amendment prohibit? What events led to its passage?
6. List and explain five possible reasons for not voting.
7. What are the characteristics that make people most likely to vote?
8. What are two views about the effects of low voter turnout?
9. Do party identification, candidates' images, and policy choices affect voters' choices?
10. How do socioeconomic factors influence whether or not a person votes?
11. What are the typical voting requirements?
12. What ideas did the "Challenge to the American Dream" feature present as suggestions for getting people more involved in elections?

Questions for Thought and Discussion

1. How do you think people would respond to a compulsory voting law in the United States? How would it affect the way the electoral system works?
2. Historical struggles over the extension of suffrage have given more Americans the right to vote than ever before, yet only about half of those eligible vote. How would you explain this phenomenon? Do you think it is a problem? Why or why not?
3. Absentee ballots account for almost 8 percent of all votes cast throughout the United States in any one election year. Some commentators believe, nonetheless, that election results would not be any different even if absentee ballots were not allowed. Do you agree or disagree? Why or why not?
4. Some argue that low voter turnout is not a problem provided that those who do not go to the polls believe the government is being run correctly. Do you agree or disagree with this statement? Give reasons for your answer.

and geographic location which all influence whether or not a person votes and how a person votes.
11. They will require a minimum age of 18 and a requirement that the voter be registered. There may often be a minimum length of residency requirement as well.
12. (1) A national campaign to encourage voter participation; (2) Congressional requests to the television networks to give more broadcast time for political programming; (3) a requirement for four presidential debates as a condition for a candidate's receiving federal campaign money; and (4) a call on candidates to stop negative advertising.

Questions for Thought and Discussion (Answers)

1. Answers will vary, e.g., those who stay away from the polls tend to be the least educated, the poor, the young, the elderly, minorities, and the unemployed. If these people were compelled to vote, the population would be better represented. However, it is unhealthful for a democracy to force people to vote.
2. Answers will vary, e.g., even though more people are eligible to vote, they cannot be forced to vote. This is not a problem because it means they are satisfied with the status quo.
3. Answers will vary, e.g., election results would not be affected if absentee ballots were not allowed because most of those who take the trouble to vote absentee would find a way to vote on election day.
4. Answers will vary, e.g., those who believe the government is being run correctly should still vote to ensure that the situation is not changed.

CHAPTER 11 REVIEW—Continued

Improving Your Skills

Communication Skills

Using Library Resources

Before writing a report or giving an oral report, you will need to do research in the library. Before you begin, there are several basic resources with which you should be familiar.

Card Catalog: Use the card catalog when trying to find a specific book. Every book in the library is listed on separate cards in the card catalog, which is arranged alphabetically. Books are usually listed in several ways: by author, by title, and by subject. On the front of each drawer of the card catalog is a label that will tell you what parts of the alphabet the drawer covers. Each card usually tells you the title, author, Dewey Decimal number, publisher, date, and number of pages of the book.

Library Scanner: Many libraries use a computer scanner instead of a card catalog. Just like the card catalog, every book in the library is listed on a scanning screen by title, author, and subject.

Reader's Guide to Periodical Literature: If you are not looking for a specific book, but for articles on a general subject, a good place to start is with the *Reader's Guide to Periodical Literature.* The *Reader's Guide* lists all the articles published in almost two hundred magazines, and is itself published ten times a year. Articles are listed under a general subject and the listing contains the author, the magazine, the volume of the magazine, the page number, the date it was published, and whether or not it is illustrated.

News Banks: Many libraries have a computerized system called a news bank or something similar. You choose a specific topic and the computer tells you where to look in newspapers throughout the United States. Then you have to go to the newspaper room of the library in which you will find newspapers from many major cities on microfiche machines. You can read the appropriate articles and have copies made of the ones you want. These systems are located in university libraries and major libraries throughout the country. (Remember, many university libraries allow anybody to use them, but only students and faculty can check out books.)

Writing

Think about a major topic related to politics that you would like to learn more about, such as the latest presidential campaign, the life of an important political figure, a congressional ethics scandal, or restrictions on congressional terms in office. Using the resources listed in this feature, develop a list of at least four references related to that topic that you find in your library. Write a one-paragraph summary about what is included in each reference. You can obtain a summary of the information included in each reference by reading the preface and the table of contents if it is a book, or by reading the first few paragraphs if it is a newspaper article.

Social Studies Skills

Reading Political Cartoons

Study the cartoon on page 271 and answer the following questions.

1. Who is the man slumped in the chair supposed to represent?
2. Why is wanting a king the logical progression from voter apathy?
3. What does candidate apathy mean?
4. Do you think the cartoonist is sympathetic to the feelings of the man in the chair?

Activities and Projects

1. Use library resources to gather information about voter turnout in European nations and in the United States. Compare and contrast the information you find, and prepare a report that explains the similarities and differences. Present the report to the class.
2. Interview an election official in your state to find out about registration and residency requirements. Prepare a bulletin board display that shows what the procedures are in your area.
3. Develop and produce a voter's brochure that could be used for new residents in your state. Include voter requirements and procedures for your state, and a brief write-up that tries to persuade citizens to vote.
4. Stage a debate on one of these statements: (1) The United States should enact a compulsory voting law; (2) There should be no registration or residency requirements placed on voting.

Social Studies Skills (Answers)

1. The typical, or average, voter.
2. That way there doesn't have to be any voting or worrying about candidates.
3. Candidates themselves show no interest in what they are doing or in the election process.
4. Answers will vary, but probably no.

Working with the Videodisc

The text below is from Professor Roger LeRoy Miller's introduction for the motion segment for Unit 4:

The Constitution describes the duties and functions of the Congress first. There are numerous expressed powers of the Congress listed one by one. Over the years, these powers have expanded as the nation has become more complex. The Constitution did not, however, spell out in detail how the Congress was to carry on its day-to-day activities. Over the last 200 years, the two houses have developed very definite ways to govern themselves as they carry out the governing of this nation.

In the following video segment, some of the details of the way Congress does, and can, act are presented.

To access this segment, use the bar code below or the videodisc index found in the *TRB*.

Frame 41400

UNIT FOUR

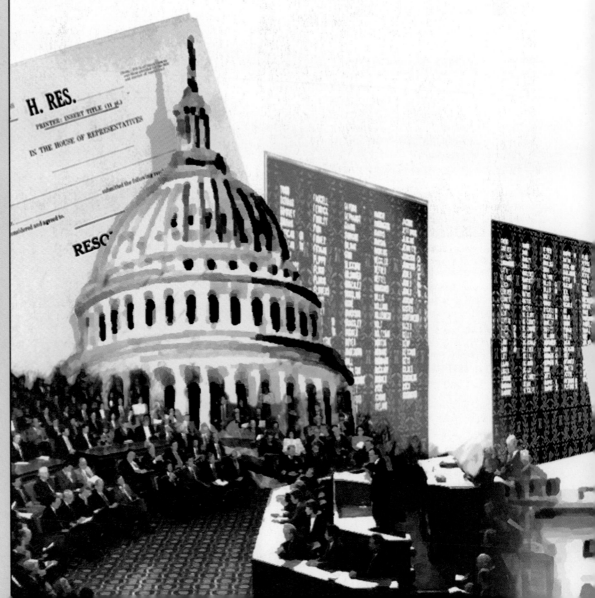

The Federal Legislative Branch

UNIT CONTENTS

CHAPTER INTRODUCTION

Instructional Objectives

By the end of the chapter students should be able to:

- Summarize the creation and evolution of the American Congress.
- Describe the profile of the members of Congress and their responsibilities.
- Characterize the structure and organization of Congress.

Using the Keynote

Have a volunteer read the quotation from William O. Douglas aloud and let the students share their initial responses to the statement. Then, to encourage a closer examination of the statement, ask questions such as these: What does Douglas mean when he says the language of the Constitution "is not ambiguous or qualified"? How would it be different if the language of Article I, Section 1 was qualified? Or ambiguous?

Introducing the Chapter

Ask the students to read the chapter Introduction independently. Then encourage discussion by posing questions such as these: How do you respond to the notion that Congress is the national branch of government closest to the people? Do you believe that Congress truly is "the voice of the people"? Why or why not? Do other voters regard their Congressional representatives as their voice in the government? Why or why not? How do you think an understanding of the structure and function of Congress might affect voters' attitudes toward Congress? Encourage the students to present and support various points of view in response to these questions.

Previewing the Sections

Section 1 Let the students page through Section 1. Then ask: What familiar information is presented in this section? What further aspects of the topic do you expect to find covered here?

Section 2 Ask volunteers to read aloud the title of Section 2, the main heading, the subheadings, and the figure titles. Then have the students suggest questions they expect to have answered as they study this section.

Section 3 Have the students glance through Section 3, paying particular attention to the headings, the figure titles, and the special feature titles. Then ask: What kinds of information are presented in this section?

Section 4 Let the students glance through Section 4, and ask volunteers to identify the topics covered in this section. Then ask the students: Why is understanding the structure of Congress important? How will the information in this section help you?

CHAPTER 12

The Organization of Congress

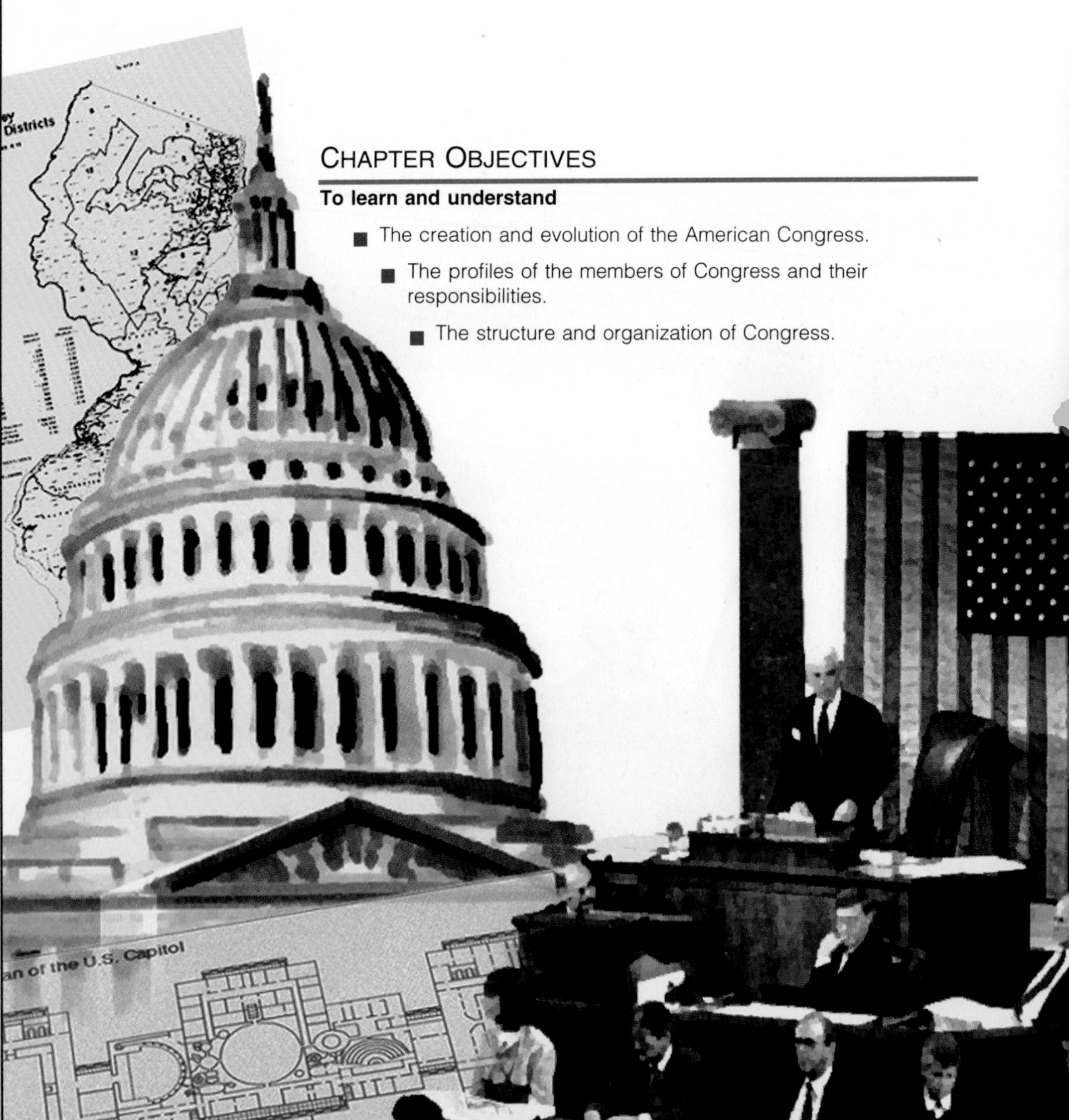

CHAPTER OBJECTIVES

To learn and understand

- The creation and evolution of the American Congress.
- The profiles of the members of Congress and their responsibilities.
- The structure and organization of Congress.

West's American Government Assignment Guide

Activity Sheets
Basic Concepts 12 *TRB* (Reteaching)
Enrichment Activity 12 *TRB*
Building Social Studies Skills 12 *TRB*
Quizzes
Chapter 12 Section 1 Quiz *TRB*
Chapter 12 Section 2 Quiz *TRB*
Chapter 12 Section 3 Quiz *TRB*
Chapter 12 Section 4 Quiz *TRB*

Tests
Chapter 12 Test A *TRB*
Chapter 12 Test B *TRB*
Chapter 12 Test Bank *TRB*
Chapter 12 WESTEST Computerized Testing
Social Studies Tool Kit Software
Chapter 12 Activity

Keynote

"The language of the Constitution is not ambiguous or qualified. It places not some legislative powers in Congress; Article I, Section 1 says, "All legislative powers herein granted . . . ."

—— **William O. Douglas (1898–1980) Associate Justice United States Supreme Court**

INTRODUCTION

Congress was established as the first branch of government and is often called the federal branch closest to the people. This is because members of Congress are elected directly by the people, whereas the president and vice president are elected through the electoral college and Supreme Court members are appointed by the president with the approval of the Senate. Thus, among this nation's leaders, members of Congress are most directly accountable to its citizens. Because of this, Congress is sometimes called "the voice of the people."

The founders granted Congress the most critical function of a democracy: translating the public will into public policy. As the opening quote from William O. Douglas points out, they devoted the First Article of the Constitution to Congress, which reads:

> *All legislative powers herein granted shall be vested in a Congress of the United States, which shall consist of a Senate and House of Representatives.*

Despite the fact that Congress makes the policies that shape our lives, many Americans do not understand its myriad committees, complicated procedures, and endless debates.

Each American is represented by a congressperson and two senators. These members of Congress are elected to serve the public. As American citizens, it is important that we understand Congress and its responsibilities to ensure that this powerful institution remains the voice of the people. In this chapter, you will read about the creation and development of the United States Congress. You will also look at the men and women who make up Congress and the structure and organization of its two houses.

SECTION 1

Creation and Evolution of Congress

Preview Questions

- What is a bicameral legislature? Why did the founders create a bicameral legislature in this country?
- How is the total number of seats apportioned in the House of Representatives? How is it reapportioned every ten years?
- What are congressional districts? What methods have been used over the years to unfairly draw them?

The founders of the American republic believed that a central legislature should be responsible for the bulk of the power exercised by a national government. Their experience with King George III of England and his often dictatorial or incompetent royal governors had left them with a deep suspicion of strong executive authority. They were also aware of how ineffective the Congress had been during its brief existence under the Articles of Confederation.

As a result of these concerns, Congress is charged under the Constitution with the **legislative power**—the power to make laws. The founders intended Congress to be the central institution of American government and therefore gave it more powers than any other branch. As James Madison said, Congress is "the first branch of the government."

Bicameral Legislature

The founders of this nation did not, however, agree about the organization of Congress. In fact, one of the most serious conflicts of the Constitutional Convention

SECTION 1

Points to Stress
- The meaning of a bicameral legislature and the reasons for the creation of one in this country.
- The description of Congressional terms.
- The manner of apportionment for seats in the House and the process reapportionment.
- Characteristics of Congressional districts and methods used over the years to draw them.

Kickoff Activity
Write the following question on the chalkboard: When and how was Congress created? Give the students five minutes in which to write their responses; then ask volunteers to share and discuss their ideas.

Working with the Preview Questions
Let the students read these study questions, and encourage volunteers to share their responses based on what they already know. Then remind the students to keep these questions in mind as they study Section 1.

Teaching Strategies

Introduction
Let one of the students read the section introduction aloud to the rest of the class. Then pose discussion questions such as these: What is legislative power? Why is it so important? Whom does it affect? How? How different do you imagine our country would be today if the founders had vested a single individual with legislative power? What do you think Madison meant by calling Congress "the first Branch of the Government"? Do you believe it still is? Why or why not?

Comprehension
Ask the students to recall (or review) the basis of the debate and the process by which the Great Compromise was finally adopted.

Enrichment
As the students consider the bicameral legislature adopted by the Convention, you might ask them also to explore a unicameral legislature: What is it? Which countries have a unicameral legislature? How does it function? In what important respects is it different from a bicameral legislature?

Discussion Starter
Help the students consider the Senate as a safeguard against the passage of "emotional" legislation: What attitudes does this concern reveal? Do you believe those attitudes have changed completely? Why or why not? What evidence can you cite to support your belief? What ideas and attitudes are expressed in the quotation from Washington?

Extension
Ask the students to identify the number of the current Congress. When did this term begin? When will the next Congress convene?

was a long and heated debate between the large and small states over congressional representation. After a month of struggle, the delegates finally adopted the Great Compromise, which you read about in Chapter 2.

By a narrow margin, the Convention voted for a **bicameral legislature**, a Congress of two houses—a Senate and a House of Representatives. The British Parliament, which the framers and most other Americans knew quite well, had consisted of two houses since the 1300s. Each American state, large or small, would be represented by two senators, thereby giving each state equal power in the Senate. In the House, however, representatives would be distributed according to population, so that the larger the state's population, the more representatives it would have. The Constitution requires that each state, no matter how small, have at least one representative.

Besides the needed compromise, the founders favored a bicameral legislature so that the two houses might serve as checks on each other's power and activity. The House was to represent the people as a whole—the will of the majority—by having its members apportioned by population. The Senate was to represent the states, and would protect the interests of the small states by giving them the same representation as the larger states. Because the House was to be elected directly by the people, it was to be the ''common person's'' chamber. The Senate, originally to be chosen by the elected representatives sitting in state legislatures, was to protect the elite interests against the tendencies of the House to protect the masses (similar to the division between the House of Commons and the House of Lords in England). The Senate was to be a safeguard against the passage of ''emotional'' legislation. As George Washington was said to have remarked, ''We shall pour House legislation into the Senatorial saucer to cool it.''

Congressional Meetings

Each Congress lasts for a meeting period, or a **term**, of two years. Each term is numbered consecutively beginning from March 4, 1789. The date for the **convening** (formal opening) of each term was reset by the Twentieth Amendment in 1933 and now begins on January 3 of an odd-numbered year unless Congress sets another date.

Each term of Congress is divided into two regular **sessions**, or meetings—one for each year. Until about 1940, Congress remained in session for only four or five months, but the complicated rush of legislation and increased demand for services from the public in recent

The Congress of the United States has been called the federal branch of government closest to the people. Why is this description used?

Caption Answer Congress is often called the federal branch closest to the people because members of Congress are elected directly by the people at the district and state levels, whereas the president and vice president are elected by the electoral college and the Supreme Court members are appointed.

Discussion Starter
Help the students discuss Congressional recesses: What is the stated purpose of these recesses? What do citizens expect of their Congress members during recesses? What do you think most Congress members actually do during this time? Do you believe Congress members continue to serve their constituents during recesses? Why or why not?

Enrichment
Let interested students volunteer to research the special sessions of Congress called by the president: What was the purpose of each special session? What was its outcome? Ask the volunteers to work together to prepare a chart or a written report summarizing their findings.

Extension
Have the students recall (or find out) how many representatives your state has. Did your state gain or lose seats as a result of the 1990 census?

Enrichment
Ask five volunteers to research the nonvoting members sent to the House of Representatives by the District of Columbia, American Samoa, Guam, the American Virgin Islands, and Puerto Rico: What authority do these members have? What are their responsibilities? How are they regarded in Congress? At home? Which are trying to gain voting status? Why and how? With what success? Let the volunteers prepare and present short oral reports of their findings.

Discussion Starter
Encourage the students to consider the concern in 1920 that the House might be growing too big for effective action: Do you think a legislative body of any size can be organized to function effectively? Why or why not? If not, what size is too large? Is some size too small for effective action? If so, what?

Caption Answer The population figures from the census are used for reapportionment of House seats among the states.

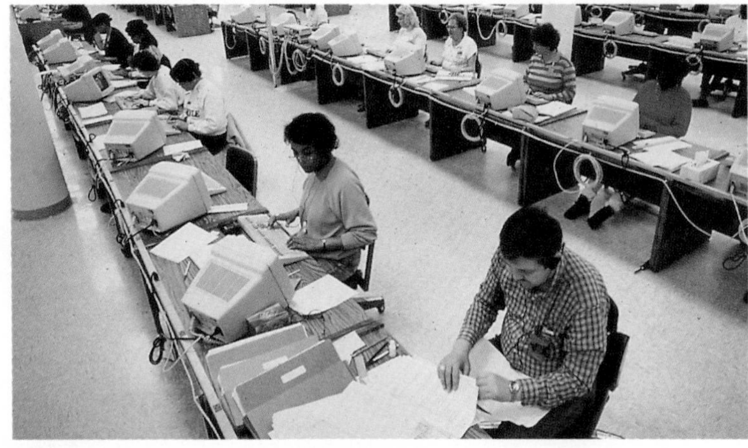

Every ten years, the Census Bureau takes an official count of our population. How does this census affect Congress?

years have forced Congress to remain in session through most of each year.[1] Both houses, however, schedule short **recesses**, or breaks for holidays and vacations.

Congress remains in session until its members vote to adjourn. Neither house may adjourn a session without the consent of the other. Only the president may call Congress to meet during a scheduled recess. Such meetings are called **special sessions** and only twenty-six such sessions have ever been held. The fact that Congress is now so busy and meets nearly year-round makes the need for a special session unlikely.

Apportionment of the House of Representatives

The Constitution provides that the total number of House seats shall be **apportioned** (distributed) among the states on the basis of their respective populations. Because representation in the House is based on population, the more people a state has, the more representatives it will send to the House. California, for example, with a 1990 population of almost 30 million, has fifty-two representatives. North Carolina, with a population of 6.7 million, has twelve representatives. Wyoming, with a population of 460,000, has one representative. Each state is guaranteed at least one seat, no matter what its population. Today seven states have only one representative. The District of Columbia, American Samoa, Guam, and the American Virgin Islands each send nonvoting delegates to the House. Puerto Rico, a self-governing possession of the United States, is represented by a nonvoting resident commissioner.

Reapportionment The Constitution directs Congress to take a **census**, or official count of the population, every ten years. This allows Congress to increase the number of House seats according to changes in the population. The census results are then used to apportion the seats among the states.

With each census year, the number of representatives in the House has grown. By 1910, it had reached 435. In the census year of 1920, as our population swelled, House leaders and many Americans were concerned that an even larger House would get out of hand. Many thought it was growing too big for effective action. When the official census figures were revealed in 1921, the House stalled for eight years before taking any action to increase its membership.

In 1929, President Hoover called a special session of Congress to address the situation and urged it to provide apportionment guidelines for the upcoming 1930 census. As a result, Congress passed the Reapportionment Act of 1929, which established a permanent system of **reapportionment**, or redistribution, of the 435 House seats following each census. The law provides that:

1. The size of the House remains stable at 435.
2. After each census, the Census Bureau determines the number of seats each state should receive according to the census results.

1. Some observers maintain that another reason Congress *can* stay in session longer is because of the invention of air conditioning. Prior to that, none of its members wanted to stay in session during the hot and sticky spring, summer, and fall months.

Cooperative Learning
Let the students work in groups to study and discuss the map on this page: In which states were the largest changes made? What trends can you identify in various parts of the nation? What significance do you attach to those trends? How do your state and your section of the country appear to be affected?

Extension
Let the students respond to these questions: In which Congressional district do you live? Which member of the House represents the voters of that district? Where are the local offices of that representative located?

Discussion Starter
Guide the students in discussing representatives of single-member districts and at-large representatives: What distinct advantages can you identify in each system? What are the disadvantages of each? Why do you think Congress passed the law requiring single-member districts?

This figure content is also featured on *West's American Government Videodisc* (see the index found in the *TRB*).

Figure Answer The Northeast region was hardest hit, as Massachusetts, New Jersey, New York, Pennsylvania, Michigan, Ohio, West Virginia, and Kentucky all lost seats. You might wish to extend this activity by referring students back to the Snowbelt/Sunbelt feature found in Chapter 4.

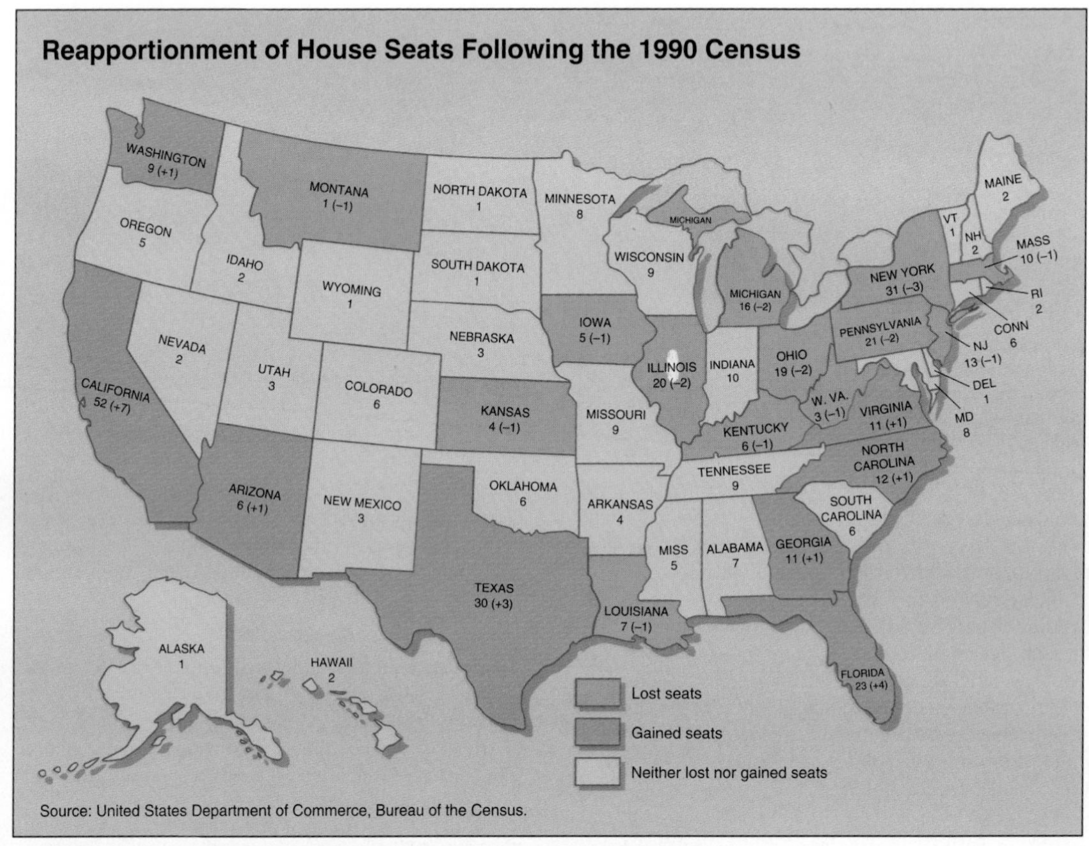

▲ **FIGURE 12–1 Reapportionment of House Seats Following the 1990 Census.** The map above shows the apportionment of House seats for each state based on the population figures from the 1990 census. Based on this map, what region of the country lost the most seats?

3. The Census Bureau presents a plan to the president that shows the distribution of seats.
4. The president submits this information in a message to Congress. If Congress does not voice its opposition within sixty days, the plan goes into effect.

Thus, shifts in our nation's population greatly affect the distribution of House seats. In the last few decades, increasing numbers of Americans have moved from northeastern and midwestern states to the sunbelt states of the South and the West. The map in Figure 12–1 illustrates this trend by showing the changes made in each state's House seats after the 1990 census was taken.

Congressional Districting Senators are elected to represent all of the people in the state, while representatives are elected by the voters of a particular area known as a **congressional district**. The 435 members of the House are chosen by the voters in 435 separate congressional districts across the country. If a state's population allows it to have only one representative, such as in the case of Wyoming and Vermont, the entire state is one congressional district. Texas, by contrast, has thirty congressional districts and hence thirty representatives. The lines of the congressional districts are chosen by state legislatures. This often means that the party with the majority in the legislature will attempt to redraw districts so as to improve that party's power.

This system was not always used. The Constitution makes no provisions for congressional districts, and in the early 1800s each state was given the right to decide

Discussion Starter
Have the students discuss the states' reaction to the 1842 Act: Why do you think states tried to ignore the 1842 Act? What advantages were they trying to gain? Why? What situations might have enabled states to effectively ignore this legislation?

Vocabulary
Have volunteers identify and define the prefix that helps clarify the meaning of *malapportionment*.

Critical Thinking Skills
Help the students analyze the significance of the "one person, one vote" rule: What makes this concept so important to our form of democracy? Do you think our country could function successfully as a democracy without adhering to this rule? Why or why not?

This case is excerpted in the *West's American Government Handbook of Selected Court Cases.*

Comprehension
Ask the students to explain (in their own words) the differences between packing and cracking (p. 291).

Discussion Starter
Encourage the students to respond to the cartoonist's depiction of 1812 gerrymandering: What facts does the drawing show? What attitudes does it communicate? How do you imagine voters responded to this drawing? Why?

whether or not to have districts at all. Most states set up **single-member districts** in which voters in each district elected one of the state's representatives. In states that chose not to have districts, representatives were chosen **at large**, from the state as a whole.

Over the years, many people became dissatisfied with this system, claiming it was unfair for a political party whose candidates won the congressional election by a slight margin to win all of the House seats for the state. In 1842 Congress responded by passing an act that required all states to send representatives to Congress from single-member districts. It gave each state legislature the responsibility of drawing its own district lines, but required that each district be made up of **contiguous** (adjoining) boundaries. Later revisions of the law required that districts contain, as nearly as possible, an equal number of people. This requirement is important because each House member would then represent approximately the same number of people, and the people would be equally represented in the House. Districts were also required to be of compact territory, which meant that states could not draw boundaries that spread one district into parts throughout the state.

The requirements of the 1842 act, however, were largely ignored by states as many state legislatures continued to seek advantages for their own political parties. They did so in two ways, which are discussed below.

- **Congressional districts of unequal population** If congressional districts are not made up of equal populations, the value of people's votes is not the same. One way that legislatures used this fact to ensure their power was to create districts with unequal populations. For example, many state legislatures traditionally were controlled by rural areas. By creating districts that were not equal in population, rural leaders hoped to block the transfer of representatives to growing urban areas. There was a point during the 1960s, for example, when there were many states in which the largest district had twice the population of the smallest district. This meant that in these states a person's vote in the largest congressional districts had only half the value of a person's vote in the smallest districts.

The Supreme Court finally addressed this issue. In *Baker* v. *Carr* (1962), the Court ruled that the Tennessee state legislature's **malapportionment** violated the constitutional requirement of equal protection under the law. Finally, in 1964 it ruled in *Wesberry* v. *Sanders* that congressional districts must have equal population. This principle has come to be known as the "one person–one vote" rule; that is, one person's vote has to count as much as another's vote. The long-standing tendency of state legislatures to apportion in the ways that overrepresented rural voters began to be corrected.

- **Gerrymandering** Since the early 1800s, the practice of drawing district boundaries to benefit a certain party, group, or candidate has been called **gerrymandering**. Gerrymandering often results in very oddly shaped election districts. This practice took its name in "honor" of Elbridge Gerry, governor of Massachusetts. In 1812, the state legislature carved up Essex County in a way that favored his party, making the district look like a salamander. A cartoonist, observing a map that detailed the strange shape of the districts, penciled in a head, wings, and claws and commented that the map now resembled a salamander. A news editor replied, "Better say a *gerrymander*!"

Two different methods of gerrymandering have been used. One way, called "packing" by

▲ This cartoon depicts the original "gerrymander." When Elbridge Gerry had this Massachusetts district drawn to ensure the election of a Republican in 1812, a cartoonist added a head, wings, and claws so that it resembled a salamander. Thus, the gerrymander was born.

TEACHING BUILDING SOCIAL STUDIES SKILLS

Read
Let the students read the feature title, Using a Political Map, and discuss their ideas about the feature content: What is a political map? How does it differ from other kinds of maps? After this introductory discussion, ask several students to read the feature aloud to the rest of the class.

Discuss
Help the students discuss what they have just read by posing questions such as these: Why is it important to begin reading a map by studying the map's title? How does studying a map's legend help you understand the map? Why is it important to understand the map's directions and distance scales?

Analyze and Apply
Ask each student to bring a political map to class; encourage the students to search out unusual or particularly interesting maps. Then have the students work in small groups and discuss all the group members' maps.

Review
Ask the students these review questions: What is a map? What are the four basic guidelines for using a political map?

This figure content is also featured on *West's American Government Videodisc* (see the index found in the *TRB*).

Building Social Studies Skills (Answers)
1. Four states, plus the District of Columbia, lost population.
2. The average population gain in the 46 states was 11.05 percent.
3. No, only the relative loss or gain of population.

Discussion Starter
Let the students share their reactions to gerrymandering: Why is it used? By whom? Whom does it help, and whom does it hurt? Why do you think gerrymandering is so much more infrequently used today than it was during the nineteenth century?

Reteaching Strategies
1. Let the students work with partners to write short answers to the Preview Questions from the beginning of the section.
2. Work with small groups of students to review gerrymandering: What is it? When and how can it be used? Then let the group members describe how gerrymandering could be used to benefit various groups within your state.

Evaluation Strategies
1. Have the students write their answers to the Section 1 Review questions.
2. Have the students take the Section 1 Quiz found in the *TRB*.

Section 1 Review (Answers)
1. Congress is charged with legislative power, which is the power to make laws.
2. The founders created a bicameral legislature so that each house might serve as a check on the other. (Note that you might remind

BUILDING SOCIAL STUDIES SKILLS

Using a Political Map

A good source for finding political information is a political map. A map is an illustration, drawn to scale, of an area under study. To effectively gather information from a map, follow these guidelines:

1. **Study the map's title.** The title will tell you the subject and purpose of the map, and may also give information about the time period and area that the map represents.
2. **Study the map legend, or key.** The legend, or key, contains information that explains special symbols used on the map. Before trying to interpret the map, study the legend to make sure that you know what all the colors, shadings, and lines represent.
3. **Check the map's directions.** Some maps have a compass rose or direction indicator. If not, it is always assumed that north is at the top of the map.
4. **Study the distance scales.** Maps present their scales in miles or kilometers. A scale must be used to determine the distance between two places.

Special-Purpose Maps Many types of special-purpose maps are also used to study government and politics. These maps relate specific data to a geographic area.

Study the map below and answer the following questions:

1. How many states lost population between 1980 and 1990? What was the average population loss among these states?
2. What was the average population gain in the states that gained population?
3. Is it possible to tell from this map what the population size is in any state?

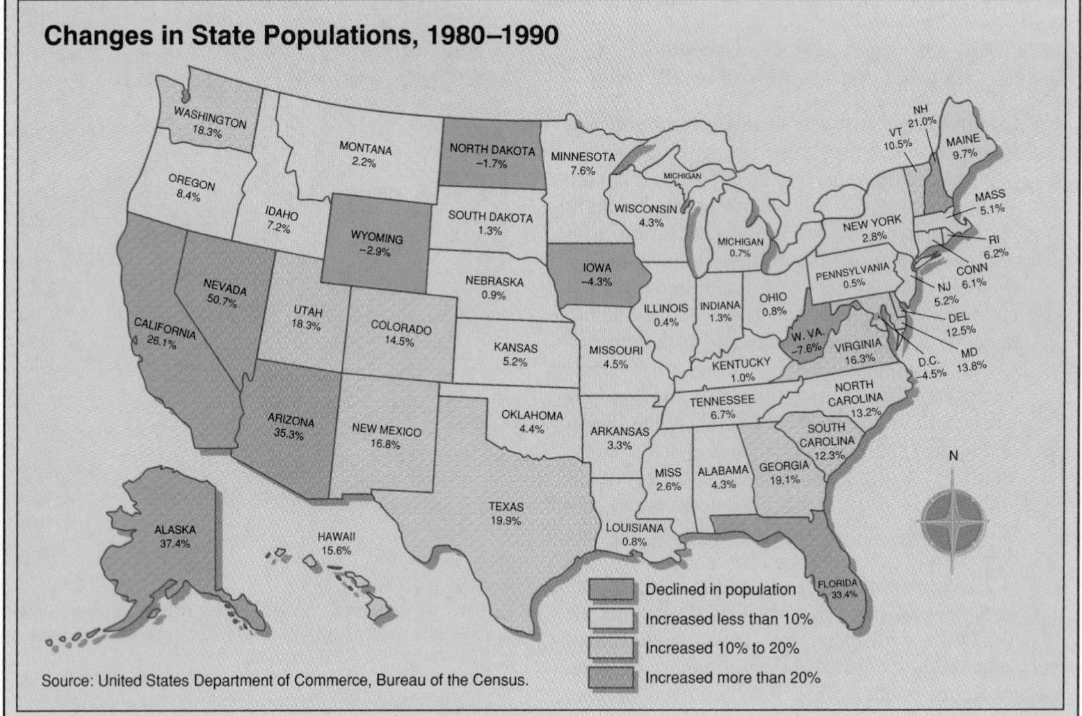

Source: United States Department of Commerce, Bureau of the Census.

students the composition of the two houses was a compromise between the large and small states, i.e., the House with representation based on population and the Senate providing equal representation of two senators from each state.)

3. Apportionment is the distribution of seats in a legislative body among electoral districts based on population. The Reapportionment Act of 1929 provides that the size of the House remains fixed at 435. It provides that after each census, the proportionate number of seats each state should receive will be determined.

4. The lines of congressional districts are chosen by state legislatures. Two cases, *Baker* v. *Carr* and *Wesberry* v. *Sanders,* led all states to follow the principle of "one person, one vote" in drawing Congressional districts.

5. Answers will vary, e.g., yes, ten years is too long; a five-year census would more adequately represent the changing populations of the states. The cost of the census, however, makes a five-year census impractical.

SECTION 2

Points to Stress

- Terms of office and the constitutional qualifications for members of the House of Representatives.
- Terms of office and constitutional qualifications for members of the Senate.
- Methods mentioned in the Constitution that allow the House and Senate to judge the conduct of their members.

Kickoff Activity

Write this question on the chalkboard: What are the most important differences between the House and the Senate? Give the students time to write their responses; then encourage them to share and discuss their ideas.

Working with the Preview Questions

Let volunteers read these study questions aloud, and have the students discuss what they already know about these topics. Then ask the students to use these questions as guidelines for note-taking as they study Section 2.

Teaching Strategies

Vocabulary

Let volunteers explain the meaning of the term *lower house.*

Discussion Starter

Guide the students in discussing the term of office for members of the House: do you believe this short term makes representatives more responsive to the people? Why or why not? Do representatives spend more time than senators and other elected officials campaigning for reelection? If so, do you think a shorter term would reduce the time they spend campaigning?

Caption Answer The framers felt that the shorter term for the House would make the representatives more responsive to the people.

politicians, is drawing the congressional district lines so they include as many of the political party's voters as possible. The other method, called "cracking" by politicians, involves drawing the lines so that the opponent's strength is divided among two or more districts. In this way the opponent has a more difficult time getting enough votes to win an election.

Because gerrymandering has not been specifically outlawed, there are still instances of its use today, although with much less frequency. The Court ruled in *Wesberry* that congressional districts must be "compact and contiguous." These requirements combined with the one person–one vote ruling usually have prevented the worst forms of gerrymandering.

Section 1 Review

1. With what basic governmental power is Congress charged?
2. Why did the founders create a bicameral legislature?
3. What is apportionment? What was the significance of the Reapportionment Act of 1929?
4. How have congressional districts been determined in the past? How are they determined today?
5. **For critical analysis:** Does the fact that a census is only taken every ten years cause problems of unfair representation for those states whose population is growing rapidly? Explain.

Section 2

House and Senate Organization

Preview Questions

- What are the terms of office and constitutional qualifications set forth for members of the
- House of Representatives? For members of the Senate?
- How does the Constitution allow the House and Senate to judge the conduct of their members?

House of Representatives

With its 435 members, the House of Representatives is over four times larger than the Senate, but is still referred to as the lower house of Congress.

Terms of Office Members of the House of Representatives are elected for two-year terms. The framers believed that such a short term of office would make representatives more responsive to the people. Many people still believe this today; others argue that a two-year term is impractical because representatives spend too much time during the second year campaigning for the next election. A constitutional amendment to lengthen the term for House membership has been proposed several times, but has never been successful.

Elections are held in November of even-numbered years, and representatives begin their term of office January 3 following the November election. This means that all 435 members must run for reelection at the same time and the House begins anew following each election.

Despite the short terms of office, there is still a great deal of continuity among members of the House. In the past decade well over 90 percent of all House incumbents have been reelected. In 1990, 96 percent of the incumbents who ran were reelected. Some representatives have been reelected over a dozen times.

There are several possible explanations for the repeated successes of incumbents. One explanation, although the least likely one, is that voters know how their representatives vote on important policy issues, agree with their positions, and want to send them back to Washington. The more likely factor for their success, however, is visibility. Incumbents work very hard at making themselves known throughout their districts so that at the

▼ Members of the House of Representatives such as John Lewis (R., Georgia), who was elected in 1990, serve two-year terms. Why are House terms so short?

TEACHING GOVERNMENT IN ACTION

Read
Prepare students for this feature by reviewing the role of the senate minority leader. Ask the students to read the feature silently, paying particular attention to the appointments in the daily schedule.

Discuss
Guide the students in discussing this profile by asking these questions: Other Republican senators have been in Congress longer than Bob Dole. Why do you think Dole holds the important post of Senate minority leader? How have his two bids for the Republican presidential nomination helped his public recognition? Do you see any advantages to seeking the party's nomination for office even if there is a good chance you would fail? Why? Should the Republican party win a majority of seats in the next election, what possible role could Senator Dole fill?

Analyze and Apply
Have students study the schedule in the profile feature. Which appointments are directly concerned with issues that involve Kansas? Which appointments might indirectly be of benefit to the voters of Kansas? Which appointments involve issues of national interest? Why would Dole be involved in presenting an award to President Havel of Czechoslovakia? Ask students to decide whether, on this particular day, Dole operated more in his role as the representative of Kansas or as a national leader.

Review
Ask students the following questions to check their understanding of this feature: What state does Bob Dole represent? What are the responsibilities of the Senate minority leader? What positions did Dole hold that helped prepare him for his senator's role? How many of Dole's appointments involve his Kansas constituency?

Think About It (Answers)
1. By organizing other senators of the same party to work to support the president's legislation, by serving on key Senate committees, and by persuading opposing senators to reconsider their stances.
2. Dole would be able to use his position to encourage other senators to support legislation, such as agricultural farm subsidies, that would benefit a midwestern state. His position also gives him greater access to the president.

GOVERNMENT IN ACTION

A DAY IN THE LIFE

Senator Bob Dole

Bob Dole, Republican Senator from Kansas, is recognized as one of the most influential political leaders in the United States. Since 1984, he has been senate minority leader.

Senator Dole grew up in rural Kansas and entered the military soon after graduating from high school. While fighting in Italy during World War II, he was seriously wounded and spent more than four years recovering in hospital wards. After studying at the University of Kansas and Washburn University, he began a long and varied political career that included service as a Kansas State Representative, County Attorney, U.S. Congressman, and U.S. Senator.

Dole has twice declared himself a candidate for the presidency and was the Republican party's nominee for vice president in 1976. The following schedule is representative of Dole's busy day:

Wednesday

9:30	Agriculture Committee
10:00	Meeting with Natan Sharansky
11:00	Meeting with Burton Eller, CEO National Cattlemen's Association
11:30	Meeting with Drew Jennings, Chairman and CEO of Kansas City Power & Light
12:00	Photo with young Japanese government employees; and with Elizabeth Taylor, Executive Director, Kansas National Water Well Association
2:30	Joint Congressional Leadership and award presentation to President Havel of Czechoslovakia
3:30	Photo with Japanese food agency team
4:00	Meeting with Stephen Roy, President of Intercontinental Energy Group
4:30	Meeting with Dick Krecker, President and CEO of Blue Cross/Blue Shield of Kansas City; and Jeannie Brocato, Vice President of Congressional Relations
4:45	Meeting with John Macomber, Chairman, Export-Import Bank, and Frederick Ruth, Vice President, Congressional Affairs
6:00	Accept "Yes, I Can" award from the Foundation for Exceptional Children

THINK ABOUT IT

1. How can a Senate leader help the President pass legislation on Capitol Hill?
2. How might Dole's position as Senate minority leader benefit his home state of Kansas?

Discussion Starter
Ask the students to share their responses to franking privileges: Do you believe this is an appropriate privilege? Can it be misused? Is it misused? Should it be more closely regulated? Could it become an effective tool for gathering public opinion? Why or why not?

Extension
Encourage the students to notice and share mail that their families receive from representatives and senators: How can you identify the use of the franking privilege? For what purposes do your members of Congress use their franking privileges? Do you approve of these uses? Why or why not?

Enrichment
Let interested students gather information about local casework and porkbarrel efforts made by representatives; have these students prepare and present an oral report summarizing the information they gather.

Vocabulary
Let the students speculate about the origin of the term *porkbarrel.* Then ask a volunteer to research its development and use.

Discussion Starter
As the students read about each of the qualifications for members of the House, pose questions such as these: Why is this qualification significant? Whom does it disqualify? Do you think this is an appropriate qualification? Why or why not?

Discussion Starter
Ask the students whether they think representatives should be required to live in the districts they represent. Why or why not? Do you think voters would support a candidate who did not live in the district? A candidate who had just moved into the district? An incumbent who had moved out of the district? Encourage the students to present and support various ideas on this subject.

Enrichment
Let volunteers research specific cases in which representatives have been expelled or formally censured for misconduct: What actions led up to those forms of punishment? How were the decisions about punishment reached? What reactions were there? Have these volunteers share their findings in brief written reports.

Comprehension
Ask the students what crime can lead to the reprimand of a representative. Be sure the students understand that no legal offenses are involved; this is a means of punishing misconduct or unbecoming behavior.

Discussion Starter
Ask the students to identify the senators from their state. Then encourage discussion by posing questions such as these: What do you know about the efforts and interests of your senators? How influential do they seem to be? How effective do you consider them? Do you support your senators? Why or why not?

voting booth, voters will at least recognize their names on the ballot. Incumbents frequently travel back to their home district (the average member will visit about thirty-five times a year). They also enjoy the **franking privilege**, which is a free mail service designed to keep voters informed about current issues and the representative's voting record. Instead of postage, they use their printed signatures, called franks, on official correspondence. In one recent five-year study, incumbents seeking reelection in the Senate sent over $15 million worth of free mailings during the election year. Incumbent representatives sent over $75 million worth of free mailings each reelection year.

Additionally, incumbents win friends and votes by servicing "the folks back home." They do this in two ways: through **casework**, which is helping individual constituents cut through bureaucratic red tape to get what they want, and through **porkbarrel**, which is bringing federal funds to their districts in the form of federal projects, contracts, or grants available to cities, colleges, and businesses and other organizations.

Another explanation for an incumbent's success is that a current member of the House (or Senate) is usually in a better position to raise campaign funds than an opponent. Incumbent representatives raise on average six times more for their reelection than do challengers.

There is no limit on the number of terms a representative may be reelected to the same office. Many people believe, however, that the number of terms a representative can serve should be limited. (This issue will be discussed further in the "Challenge to the American Dream" feature at the end of this chapter.)

Qualifications The Constitution sets forth the qualifications for election to the House of Representatives. Members of the House must be at least 25 years of age, citizens of the United States for at least seven years prior to the election, and legal residents of the state from which they are elected.

Although not required by the Constitution, representatives traditionally live in the district they represent. This practice is rooted in the belief that representatives should be familiar with the needs of the people in the area they represent.

The Constitution also gives the House the power to judge the qualifications of its members and to refuse a seat to an elected member. From 1823 to 1967, the House refused to recognize nine members as legitimate lawmakers and denied them their seats. This power, however, was limited by the Supreme Court in 1969 in *Powell v. McCormack.* In that decision, the Court ruled that Congress could not exclude any member-elect who meets the Constitution's standards of age, citizenship, and residence.[2]

Conduct of Members The Constitution gives the House the power to punish the misconduct of its members, through **censure** (condemnation) or **expulsion** (forcing the member from office). In its two-hundred-year history the House has expelled four members: three for treason during the Civil War and one for corruption in 1980. Twenty-three representatives have been formally censured for misconduct. In a censure proceeding, the member must stand in the well (lowest part) of the chamber and face his or her colleagues as the misconduct charges are read.

Since the 1970s, both the House and Senate have been faced with frequent cases of misconduct by members that they have not wanted to punish by expulsion or censure. For this reason Congress devised a less severe form of censure called **reprimand**. The member need not be present when the House votes on the action. After the House or Senate has voted to reprimand one of its members for misconduct, no additional action is taken against the member. Seven members of the House were reprimanded from 1976 through 1992.

In 1989, Speaker of the House Jim Wright resigned his seat under charges of unethical behavior. The House Ethics Committee charged him with a number of violations of House rules, most of which centered around Mr. Wright's financial dealings with individuals and companies that had an interest in legislation before the House.

The Senate

The Senate is the smaller house of the two, but is known as the upper house of Congress. The Constitution

2. Before the *Powell* case, the House in 1900 refused to seat Brigham H. Roberts of Utah because he was a practicing polygamist. In 1919 and 1920 it excluded Victor L. Berger of Wisconsin because he had been convicted of sedition during World War I. His conviction was later overturned and he was seated in 1921. Adam Clayton Powell of New York was barred in 1967 because the House found he had misused public funds, defied the courts of his state, and been "contemptuous" in refusing to cooperate with its investigation of him. The Supreme Court ruled in this case that Powell had been "duly elected . . . and was not ineligible to serve under any provision of the Constitution, the House was without power to exclude him from membership."

Comprehension
Check the students' comprehension by asking these questions: What are the differences between the terms of office for representatives and for senators? What is the significance of those differences?

Cooperative Learning
Let the students form groups in which to discuss the qualifications for senators: What is the significance of each qualification? How does it differ from the related qualification for representatives? Why do you think the qualifications are different? Do you think they should be? Why or why not?

Reteaching Strategies
1. Let the students work with partners to compare and discuss the notes they took while reading Section 2. Encourage the students to refer to the text and to revise their notes as necessary.
2. Have each student write a paragraph about his or her representative in the House and one of the senators from your state. These paragraphs should include basic biographical information and brief summaries of Congressional activities.

Figure Answer Most politicians would prefer to be a member of the Senate because it offers a longer term, more prestige, and a greater chance for national leadership. You might also point out to the students that senators earn slightly more.

This figure content is also featured on *West's American Government Videodisc* (see the index found in the *TRB*) and is available in the transparency package.

Evaluation Strategies
1. Have the students write their answers to the Section 2 Review questions.
2. Have the students take the Section 2 Quiz found in the *TRB.*

Section 2 Review (Answers)
1. Members of the House of Representatives are elected for two-year terms. Senators are elected for six-year terms.
2. One reason incumbents are relected is their high visibility. Another reason is that incumbents win votes by doing favors that are possible because they are in office.
3. Members of the House must be at least 25 years of age, must be citizens of the United States for at least seven years prior to the election, and must be legal residents of the state from which he or she is elected. Senators must be at least 30 years of age, must be citizens of the United States for at least nine years, and must be legal residents of the state from which they are elected.
4. The Constitution gives the House the power to censure or expel any member for misconduct. The Constitution allows the Senate to judge the qualifications of its members and to exclude a member-elect by majority vote. It can also censure another member for misconduct.

Differences Between the House and the Senate

House*	Senate*
Members chosen from local districts	Members chosen from an entire state
Two-year term	Six-year term
Originally elected by voters	Originally (until 1913) elected by state legislatures
May impeach (indict) federal officials	May convict federal officials of impeachable offenses
Larger (435 voting members)	Smaller (100 members)
More formal rules	Fewer rules and restrictions
Debate limited	Debate extended
Floor action controlled	Unanimous consent rules
Less prestige and less individual notice	More prestige and media attention
Originates bills for raising revenues	Power of "advice and consent" on presidential appointments and treaties
Local or narrow leadership	National leadership

*Some of these differences, such as term of office, are provided for in the Constitution, while others, such as debate rules, are not.

FIGURE 12–2 Differences Between the House and the Senate. This table lists the differences between the United States House of Representatives and the Senate. In which of these two houses of Congress would most politicians prefer to be a member? Why?

calls for each state to have two senators, regardless of the state's size or population. Article V of the Constitution specifies that "no state without its consent shall be deprived of its equal suffrage in the Senate," which guarantees that the states' equal representation in the Senate cannot be changed by amendment. Thus, as long as the original Constitution is in effect, each state will always have two senators to represent it.

Before the adoption of the Seventeenth Amendment in 1913, senators were chosen by state legislatures. Since that time, senators have been chosen by the people at large in the November general elections of even-numbered years.

Terms of Office Senators are elected for six-year terms. The two senators from each state never run for election in the same year unless a vacancy occurs because of death, retirement, or resignation. If this happens, the governor of the state may call a special election to choose a replacement, or in some cases the state legislature allows the governor to appoint a replacement until an election is held. In addition, the terms of all senators are staggered so that every two years the terms of only one-third of the senators end. This ensures that all the seats are never up for election at the same time. Because of this, the Senate is considered a "continuous body."

The founders designed the Senate this way to give stability to the legislative branch. Senators have more time than representatives to understand and deal with issues before they must think about the next election. The six-year term is supposed to make senators less subject to the pressures of public opinion and the pleas of special interests than members of the House of Representatives. The longer term in office gives senators more time to act as national leaders before facing the electorate again.

5. Answers will vary, e.g., no other constitutional requirements should be mandated. In a democracy, all citizens should be allowed to run for office.

SECTION 3

Points to Stress

• Characteristics of the members of Congress.
• Compensation, special benefits, and privileges of members of Congress.
• The various roles fulfilled by a Congress member.

Kickoff Activity

Ask the class this question: What do members of Congress actually do? Let the students list at least six words or phrases in response to the question; then encourage the students to compare and discuss their ideas.

Working with the Preview Questions

Ask one of the students to read these study questions aloud. Then have the students work together to write main outline headings based on these questions. Have all the students follow this outline format as they take notes on Section 3.

Teaching Strategies

Introduction

Let one of the students read this brief section introduction aloud. Then encourage discussion by posing questions such as these: Why are members of Congress not a representative cross section of the American people? Which groups are excluded? Which groups are represented, but not in proportion to their numbers? Why? Do you believe Congress should be a representative cross section of the American people? Why or why not? If so, how could this change be achieved?

Enrichment

Let a group of volunteers gather information on Congressional membership 40 years ago. Ask these volunteers to prepare a chart that compares the profile then to the profile shown in the text chart. After the volunteers have presented their chart to the rest of the class, encourage the students to identify and discuss the changes that have taken place: Can a trend be discerned?

Figure Answer Students should note that there is a disproportionately large number of white, college educated males in Congress.

This figure content is also featured on *West's American Government Videodisc* (see the index found in the *TRB*) and is available in the transparency package.

Qualifications A senator must meet a somewhat different set of qualifications than a representative. Members of the Senate must be at least 30 years of age, citizens of the United States for at least nine years, and legal residents of the states from which they are elected.

Conduct of Members The Constitution allows the Senate to judge the qualifications of its members and to exclude a member-elect by a majority vote. The Senate can also censure or express disapproval of another member for misconduct while in office. Misusing public funds, for example, would be grounds for censure. When being censured, the senator involved must stand on the Senate floor and publicly hear the misconduct charges made against him or her. In the history of the Senate only nine members have been censured by their fellow senators.

SECTION 2 REVIEW

1. What is the length of office for representatives? For senators?
2. What are two possible reasons why incumbents are frequently reelected?
3. What are the constitutional requirements for a representative? For a senator?
4. How do members of Congress punish the misconduct of their members?
5. **For critical analysis:** Do you feel the constitutional requirements for a representative should be changed? For a senator? Why or why not?

SECTION 3

Members of Congress and Their Responsibilities

Preview Questions

- What are the general characteristics of members of Congress?
- Who sets the salary for members of Congress? What are some of the special benefits and privileges they receive?
- What are the different roles a congressperson plays?

Although members of Congress act as the people's representatives, by no stretch of the imagination are they a representative cross section of the American people. The whole process of recruiting, nominating, and selecting congressional candidates ensures that only certain types of individuals serve in Congress.

Profile of Members

If we look at a collective portrait of Congress, it is quickly evident what an atypical collection of Americans they are. Members tend to have very high levels of income, education, and occupational status compared to the rest of the population. Nearly all have college degrees, and a majority have graduate or professional degrees. Law is the dominant occupation, with other

Profile of the 103rd Congress (1993–1995)

Characteristic	House	Senate	U.S. Population, 1990
Age (Median)	51.7	58.0	33.0
Male	89.0%	94.0%	49.1%
Female	11.0%	6.0%	51.9%
Nonwhite	15.0%	4.0%	28.0%
College Educated	98.0%	99.0%	21.4%
Not College Educated	2.0%	1.0%	78.6%

◀ FIGURE 12–3 **Profile of the 103rd Congress.** This table looks at the make-up of the 103rd Congress in terms of ethnicity, gender, and educational background as compared with the general population. What conclusions can you draw about the differences between the 103rd Congress and the general population from this table?

Discussion Starter
Guide the students in discussing the professional backgrounds of Congress members: Why do you think law is the dominant occupation? How do the study and practice of law prepare a person for participation in Congress? Why are "elite" occupations well represented in Congress? Do you think this is appropriate? Fair? Do you think it should be changed? Why or why not? If so, what would be necessary to effect this kind of change?

Discussion Starter
Encourage the students to discuss the fact that Congress is predominantly white, Anglo, and male: Do you believe these people can effectively represent the best interests of people from other backgrounds? Why or why not?

Discussion Starter
Guide the students in discussing the fact that Congress sets its own pay and compensation: How do you respond to this information? Who else might be in a position to set the pay and compensation of Congress? Do you think this responsibility should be transferred to another group—or even to an individual? If so, why and how? If not, why not?

Enrichment
Let interested students research the payment of speakers' fees for members of Congress: How and why has this form of compensation changed? Ask the volunteers to present their findings in a brief oral report.

Cooperative Learning
Let the students work in groups to research the movement to cut Congressional perks during 1991: What caused this movement? How did the public respond? How did members of Congress respond?

Occupations of the Members of the 103rd Congress

Occupation	House	Senate	Congress, Total
Actor/Entertainer	1	0	1
Aeronautics	2	1	3
Agriculture	19	9	28
Business or Banking	129	27	156
Clergy	2	1	3
Education	65	12	77
Engineering	5	0	5
Homemaking	1	0	1
Journalism	24	8	32
Labor Officials	2	0	2
Law	179	58	237
Law Enforcement	10	0	10
Medicine	6	0	6
Military	0	1	1
Professional Sports	1	1	2
Public Service/Politics	86	12	98
Real Estate	27	4	31

*Because some members have more than one occupation, totals are higher than total membership.

▲ FIGURE 12–4 **Occupations of the Members of the 103rd Congress.** The above table shows the former occupations of the members of the 103rd Congress. What was the most common former occupation for members of the 103rd Congress?

Figure Answer Law was the number one former occupation of the members of the 103rd Congress with business or banking coming in a strong second.

This figure content is also featured on *West's American Government Videodisc* (see the index found in the *TRB*).

''elite'' occupations, such as business and banking, also well represented.

An overwhelming number of those elected to Congress have been white, Protestant males of Western European descent.

Compensation and Benefits

Congress sets its own pay and compensation. The members of both houses are now paid an annual salary of $125,100. The Speaker of the House receives the same pay as the vice president, $160,600 a year. The Senate's **president *pro tempore*** (president for a given term) and the majority and minority floor leaders in each house make $138,900 a year.

In addition to their salaries, members of Congress enjoy a number of other benefits and special privileges. Each member is allowed a tax deduction to help keep up two residences, one in Washington and the other at home. They receive allowances to pay for their office staff and assistants, for trips home, telephones, telegrams, newsletters, and so on.

Each member pays small amounts for generous life and health insurance policies. A medical staff offers free outpatient care at the Capitol, and full care can be had at low rates in military hospitals. Also, each member has a generous pension plan. Based on the number of years they served in Congress, they can receive up to $60,000 a year in retirement benefits. Each member has free parking, plants for the office, subsidized meals in the Senate

TEACHING GOVERNMENT IN ACTION

Read
Begin by asking the students about Patricia Schroeder: Who is she? In what capacity does she serve the country? What do you know about her ideas and activities? After the students have shared what they already know, let volunteers read the Government in Action Profile aloud to the rest of the class.

Discuss
Help the students discuss the Profile by asking questions such as these: In what respects does Schroeder fit the typical profile of a member of Congress? How does she differ from that profile? What are the family issues that Schroeder supports? What makes these *family* issues? Do you believe these issues are of greater concern to women than to men? Why or why not? What is the significance of Schroeder's place among the most respected women in this country? Which other women do you think—or know—were named to that list?

Analyze and Apply
Let the students work in groups to explore one of Schroeder's particular issues or groups. Then have the group members report to the rest of the class on the particular problems involved, the other supporters, and the people who oppose that issue or group.

Review
Ask the students these review questions: What sets Patricia Schroeder apart from other members of Congress? What particular interests and issues does Schroeder support?

GOVERNMENT IN ACTION

PROFILE

Patricia Schroeder

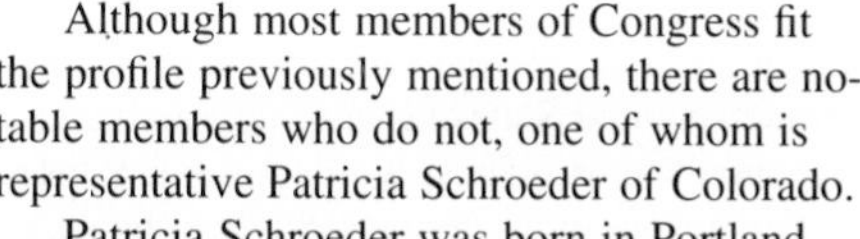

Although most members of Congress fit the profile previously mentioned, there are notable members who do not, one of whom is representative Patricia Schroeder of Colorado.

Patricia Schroeder was born in Portland, Oregon, in 1940. She attended the University of Minnesota and Harvard Law School where she received her law degree. She was elected as a Democrat to Congress in 1972 and has won reelections ever since. In 1988 she received 68 percent of the vote and in 1990 she received 64 percent. She is the most senior of the women in the House and serves as the deputy majority whip. She was the first woman to serve on the House Armed Services Committee and is a member of several other congressional committees, such as the House Select Committee on Children, Youth, and Families, the House Judiciary Committee, and the House Committee on the Post Office and Civil Service.

Patricia Schroeder is co-chair of the Congressional Caucus for Women's Issues, and has been a leading supporter of family issues such as daycare for children of working mothers, unpaid leave for new parents, and special programs for latchkey children (those who spend part of each day alone and unsupervised). Schroeder is firm in her belief that the U.S. government has failed in its responsibilities to the American family. She has commented that "There's no capital city in the world that talks more about family and does less." Schroeder is also a proponent of women's and environmental issues. She has supported the Equal Rights Amendment and the removal of restrictions for women in the military. Schroeder has also drafted legislation that would create an experimental army unit in which women could voluntarily assume combat roles. Additionally, she has led efforts against wasteful defense spending, and has supported nuclear weapon test bans.

Patricia Schroeder has become known for her outspokenness, courage, intelligence, and keen sense of humor. In a 1991 Gallup Poll, she was ranked as one of the six most respected women in America.

THINK ABOUT IT

1. Because members of Congress are not representative of the general population in terms of age, income, sex, race, and so on, does that mean they do not represent the public interest?
2. What do you think the main obstacles a woman, African American, or other minority member might run into while seeking election to Congress? How could these obstacles be overcome?
3. Why do you think the number of minorities in Congress in proportion to their representation in the population is still so low?

Think About It (Answers)

1. Answers will vary, e.g., Congress does not represent the public interest because it does not reflect the socioeconomic background of the population at large. It is therefore not sensitive enough to the needs of the poor, the uneducated, and ethnic minorities. **Or,** Congress does represent the public interest. One's values, interests, and beliefs are not exclusively determined by socioeconomic background. Civil Rights laws, for example, were passed by this "unrepresentative" group.
2. Answers will vary, e.g., women and minority members run into barriers in acquiring the education and employment that could give them the background needed to be elected. Equality in other areas would give them a better chance of being elected.
3. Answers will vary, e.g., discrimination in other areas limits the opportunities to run for Congress.

Discussion Starter
Encourage the students to share and discuss their reactions to the fact that top interest-group officials are more highly paid than the Congress members whom they lobby.

Vocabulary
Let volunteers define the terms *libel* and *slander* for the rest of the class.

Discussion Starter
Encourage the students to compare the information presented about the efforts and compensation of Congress members with what they know about the efforts and compensation of business executives and other professionals: Do you think that, like members of Congress, executives and other professionals—doctors, for example—often work 60 hours or more a week? How do you think the pay of Congress members compares to the pay of those in the private sector? What probably accounts for this difference? Do you think it is appropriate—or should this situation be changed?

Enrichment
Have all the students read about the current or most recent policymaking activities of Congress. Then give the students an opportunity to compare and discuss what they have read.

Discussion Starter
Guide the students in discussing the advantages and the disadvantages of the two different concepts of representatives: that of instructed delegate and that of trustee.

and House dining rooms, free recreational facilities, and research help from the Library of Congress.

Salaries of congresspeople are high in comparison to the average American family income of about $40,000, but they are low in comparison to people in the upper ranks of business, professional sports, and other professions. The presidents of some large corporations make millions of dollars per year, as do some professional athletes and entertainers. The annual salaries of many lawyers and doctors are in the hundreds of thousands. Congressional salaries are even quite low in comparison with the salaries of top officials of the interest groups that lobby Congress.

Privileges of Members

Members of Congress also have certain special constitutional privileges to protect them while carrying out their legislative duties. Article I, Section 6, commands that senators and representatives

> shall in all Cases, except Treason, Felony and Breach of the Peace, be privileged from Arrest during their Attendance at the Session of their respective Houses, and in going to, and returning from the same; . . .

Originally, this arrest immunity clause was designed to protect the legislative branch against interference by the executive branch. Before the colonies became independent, British officials often harassed colonial legislators and kept them from performing their duties. American leaders wanted to prevent this from reoccurring. The arrest immunity provision applies to arrests in civil cases, but does not protect members from criminal arrests. The provision has been of little importance in our national history.

A more important privilege set out in the Constitution is the speech and debate clause, which guarantees freedom of speech to members while they are conducting congressional business. This provision allows members to address their colleagues in open debate without fear of lawsuits for making harmful or false statements. A member may make any allegations or other statements he or she wishes in connection with official duties and not normally be sued for libel or slander, or be otherwise subject to legal action. This privilege does not cover speeches, articles, or conversations made in public apart from legislative business. This form of protection is called **congressional immunity**. The goal of this provision of the Constitution is to protect the freedom of legislative debate.

The Roles

In 1899, one senator said, ''God made a day twenty-four hours long for the ordinary man. After a man becomes a United States senator, he requires a day forty-eight hours long.'' These words still ring true for senators as well as for representatives. Studies show that national legislators work almost sixty-hour weeks while Congress is in session. They must spend a great deal of time learning about the issues on which they will vote, reviewing bills introduced by other legislators, and getting support for their own bills. Committee and subcommittee work occupy a great deal of time. They also try to be present on the floor of the House or Senate chambers as much as possible where they listen to speeches, give speeches, and vote on bills. Every day there are dozens of people wanting to see them: a fellow member with questions about a bill, a lobbyist with arguments against a bill, a constituent visiting the Capitol. Between meetings, members prepare bills, study reports, attend party functions, and write speeches and articles.

Most hearings are held midweek, with Wednesday being the crest of the midweek wave. This phenomenon is known colloquially as ''the Tuesday–Thursday Club,'' bespeaking Congress's desire to arrange long weekends to stay in touch with their home states and constituencies.

The 535 members of Congress have several different but closely related roles.

Policymaker The Constitution requires that policymaking be the primary role of Congress and its members. Congress is the highest elected body in the country charged with making the legal rules that govern our society. Policymaking includes conducting investigations to identify problems, researching and deciding upon bills, and voting intelligently for policies in the national interest. Policymakers decide many important matters such as establishing the rate of federal taxes and the size of the federal budget.

Representative A congressperson is also a representative, expected by ''the folks back home'' to represent their views in Washington. They are supposed to reflect and translate into action the interests and concerns of constituents. Some political philosophers argue that representatives should vote exactly as their constituents

Enrichment
Have two or three volunteers research the specific casework activities of local representatives and/or senators. Ask these volunteers to prepare and present a brief oral report on their findings.

Discussion Starter
Encourage the students to discuss the importance of casework: Why do members of Congress consider it so important? How do you think constituents view casework? Why? Do you believe it is overemphasized? Why or why not?

Cooperative Learning
Let the students work in groups to identify the committees and subcommittees on which their representatives and senators serve.

Discussion Starter
Help the students discuss members of Congress as politicians and party members: Why do Congress members need to play these roles? Whom do they serve in playing these roles? What are the likely results if Congress members neglect their roles as politicians and party members?

Caption Answer Answers will vary, but should reflect an understanding of the roles discussed on these pages.

Members of Congress, such as Representative Dan Rostenkowski of Illinois and Senator Lloyd Bentsen of Texas shown here, have several different roles. Which of these roles do you feel is the most important?

would have them vote. They should vote the preference of the constituents as if the constituents themselves were present and voting. This is the concept of representative as *instructed delegate,* in which delegate means the agent of the people. Others argue that representatives should vote according to their own best judgment and evaluation of the issue, which is the concept of representative as *trustee*, someone who administers the affairs of another.

Constituent Servant Representatives and senators not only represent the voting decisions of their constituents but also act as constituent servants. In this way they work as intermediaries between their constituents and the imposing and complicated federal bureaucracy. Helping constituents with problems is part of a congressperson's casework.

The average member of Congress is swamped with thousands of constituents' requests from the moment he or she takes office. These requests range from appearing in a local parade with the mayor of a city, to helping to secure an appointment to a service academy such as West Point, to helping with Social Security benefits, to helping with an immigration or passport problem. These small but time-consuming tasks take up hours of a congressperson's day, even though the routine tasks are delegated to the staff. This is time spent away from the main responsibility of policymaking, but a constituency well served is a constituency well satisfied, especially at the next election. So important is constituency service to legislators that it has been suggested (somewhat mischievously) that they prefer to maintain the complexity of the federal bureaucracy in order to maximize the number of occasions to perform good deeds for their constituents.

Committee Members The typical senator is a member of eleven committees and subcommittees; the average representative is a member of six. If a member is on a committee long enough, he or she will become a policy expert whose advice is sought by other members. As you will learn in the upcoming "Government in Action" feature on page 304, if members are able to sit on committees whose subject matter especially concerns their constituencies, they can potentially be more effective as constituent representatives.

Politician and Party Member All of the roles members of Congress play are somehow related to their role as politician and party member. In order to continue as policymakers, constituent servants, and representatives, they must get reelected, and reelection campaigns take

Developing Skills for the Information Age

After the President, the Congress is the most media-covered government institution. Given the structure and size of the Congress and the nature of its work, it is more difficult for the press to comprehensively cover the Congress. Have students watch various television sources to see how the Congress is covered by the media. *Meet the Press, Face the Nation, This Week with David Brinkley, Washington Week in Review,* and *The MacNeil - Lehrer News Hour* are good places to start. Nightly news, as well as C-SPAN, could also be used if possible.

Students should look for the type of member who is covered in terms of leadership, state, and committee assignments and chairs. Students should write an evaluation of what they discovered.

TEACHING CITIZENSHIP SKILLS AND RESPONSIBILITIES

Read

Let the students read the title of this feature and briefly discuss what they expect to find here: What methods do you already know for finding out about the activities of Congress? Then let volunteers read the feature aloud to the rest of the class.

Discuss

Encourage the students to discuss this Citizenship Skills and Responsibilities feature by posing questions such as these: How else could you find out who your representative or senators are? How could you find the local telephone numbers for your representative and senators? How much might calls to these Washington phone numbers cost citizens in your state? What can you learn about the activities of Congress by watching C-SPAN?

Analyze and Apply

Let the students work in groups to locate and investigate all the resources named within this feature.

Review

Ask the students these review questions: What information can you find in the *Congressional Directory?* What information can you find in the *Weekly Report?*

Taking Action (Answers)

1. You might want to ask students to create a flow chart showing the progress of the bill they are following.
2. Students should present their findings to the class in the form of an oral report or as a poster.

Reteaching Strategies

1. Let the students work in groups to compare and discuss their outlines of Section 3. Remind the students to make any necessary changes in their own outlines.
2. Work with small groups of students; guide them in discussing the specific ways in which Congress fails to reflect a cross section of the American people.

Evaluation Strategies

1. Have the students write their answers to the Section 3 Review questions.
2. Have the students take the Section 3 Quiz found in the *TRB.*

Section 3 Review (Answers)

1. The "average" member of Congress is a white, male lawyer, with a high level of income, education, and occupational status.
2. Each member is allowed a tax deduction to keep up two residences. They receive allowances for pay for their staff and assistants, for trips home, telephones, and newsletters. They receive insurance, pensions, free parking, subsidized meals and free recreational facilities.
3. A clause in the Constitution which guarantees freedom of speech to members while they are conducting congressional business.
4. Policymaker includes identify-

CITIZENSHIP SKILLS AND RESPONSIBILITIES
How to Find Out What's Going On in Congress

Who is in Congress? If you want to find out who is in Congress or who your representatives or senators are, you can look in the *Congressional Directory,* published each year by the federal government and available in most libraries or from the U.S. Government Printing Office, Washington, DC 20402. It includes biographies of lawmakers, lists of committees and staff members, and maps of districts. The *Almanac of American Politics,* edited by Michael Barone and others and published every two years by *National Journal*, can help you learn more about your members' views. Another resource that summarizes and evaluates each member's performance and describes each district is *Politics in America: Members of Congress in Washington and at Home* (Washington, D.C.: Congressional Quarterly Press).

Your representative and senators have telephone numbers in both Washington, D.C., and in your state.

What Is Happening in Congress? If you want to know whether or not a bill has been introduced in the current session, or what the current status is of a bill in Congress, you can call the Legislative Status Office, 202-225-1772. Its computer can produce a free printout overnight. To find out whether a bill has been passed, call 202-456-2226. To learn what the current legislative program is, call 202-225-7400 for the House, or 202-224-8601 for the Senate. You can also obtain a copy of a bill from the House or Senate Document Room. Both the Democratic and Republican parties prepare tapes to provide running accounts of proceedings on the floors of both houses. To listen to these tapes call:

Senate Democratic: 202-224-8541
Senate Republican: 202-224-8601
House Democratic: 202-225-7400
House Republican: 202-225-7430

If you want to follow what happens in Congress, you can subscribe to the *Weekly Report,* published by a private Washington research organization called Congressional Quarterly (CQ). Many libraries have this publication or you can subscribe as a student for $90 a year, from CQ, 1414 22nd Street NW, Washington, DC 20037.

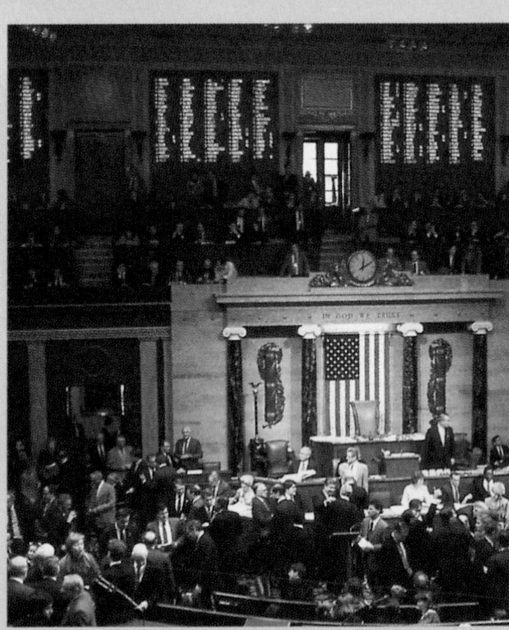

TAKING ACTION

1. Read through a local or national newspaper or a national news magazine. Find an article that mentions a proposed bill in Congress. With the information presented in the feature, determine the status of the bill in Congress. Contact the office of your senator or representative to find out his or her views on the bill. Follow the progress of the bill over the next few weeks as it passes through the houses.
2. Use one of the references listed above to help you make a profile of the representative for your district or one of the senators for your state. In the profile include what committees the member is on, how many staff members he or she has, what bills he or she has introduced recently, and what political action committees (PACs) support him or her.

ing problems, researching bills, and voting; representative includes the task of speaking and acting for his or her constituents; constituent servant includes helping constituents to deal with bureaucracy; committee member includes duties on committees and subcommittees; politician and party member includes tasks involved with re-election and dealing with the party. **5.** Answers will vary, e.g., senators should vote according to their own best judgment. They were elected by the people of their state because of their views and sound judgment and are in a better position to know the circumstances surrounding issues.

SECTION 4

Points to Stress

- The way in which the Speaker of the House is chosen and the powers of the position.
- Other House leadership positions and their functions.
- The role of the president of the Senate.
- The evolution and importance of the committee and subcommittee system.
- Different types of committees in Congress.
- The various types of congressional support available to members of Congress.

Kickoff Activity

Ask each student to write at least four questions he or she still has about the structure and the activities of Congress. After all the students have finished writing, ask volunteers to read their questions aloud; encourage the students to suggest answers to one another's questions.

Working with the Preview Questions

Have volunteers read these study questions aloud to the rest of the class; let the students briefly discuss what they already know in response to these questions. Then ask the students to keep these questions in mind as they study and take notes on Section 4.

Caption Answer The Speaker of the House is elected by a majority vote of the members of the House of Representatives at the beginning of each Congressional term. Students should understand, however, that the Speaker is really selected by the majority party, which then normally will vote as a block for its choice.

Teaching Strategies

Introduction

Ask one of the students to read the section introduction aloud. Then ask the class questions such as these: Which is the majority party in the Senate? In the House?

Enrichment

Have two interested volunteers research the representatives who have served as Speaker of the House during the past 40 years. Let these students present their findings in a chart, identifying the name, party affiliation, and years of service for each Speaker.

time and energy. Every action they take as policymakers, representatives, and constituent servants affects votes in the next election. Even if they dislike politics, without being a politician they will not be around long enough to shape policy.

SECTION 3 REVIEW

1. How would you describe the average congressperson?
2. What are some of the benefits received by members of Congress?
3. What is the speech and debate clause?
4. Briefly describe each of the different roles that a congressperson plays.
5. **For critical analysis:** Should senators always vote the way their constituents want, or should they vote according to their own best judgment? Give reasons for your answer.

Speaker of the House Thomas Foley, shown here, is the presiding officer of the House and the leader of the majority party in the House. How is the Speaker of the House selected?

SECTION 4

The Structure of Congress

Preview Questions

- How is the Speaker of the House chosen and what are his or her powers?
- Who are the other House leaders and what are their functions?
- Who presides over the Senate and what is his or her role?
- Why has the committee and subcommittee system evolved in Congress?
- What are the different types of committees?
- What are the various types of congressional support?

The organization of Congress is based on political party lines. The **majority party** in each house is the one with the greatest number of members. Being the majority party is quite important because that party chooses the major officers of each house of Congress, controls debate on the floor, selects all committee chairpersons, and has a majority on all committees.

House Leadership

Both the House and the Senate have a system of leadership. Before Congress begins work, members of each party in each house meet to choose their leaders. The Constitution provides for the presiding officers of the House and Senate; Congress may choose what other leaders it feels it needs.

Speaker of the House Chief among those leaders in the House of Representatives is the **Speaker of the House**. This office is mandated by the Constitution, to be filled by majority vote at the beginning of each congressional term. The speaker has traditionally been a long-time member of the majority party who has risen in rank and influence through years of service in the House. The candidate for Speaker is selected by the majority party caucus; all the rest of the House must do is approve the selection.

As the presiding officer of the House and the leader of the majority party, the Speaker has a great deal of power. In the early nineteenth century the Speaker had even more power and was known as the "king of the congressional mountain." Speakers known by such names as "Uncle Joe Cannon" and "Czar Reed" ruled the House with almost exclusive power. A revolt in 1910 reduced the Speaker's powers and gave them to some of the committees. Today, the Speaker still has many important powers, which include:

- Controlling substantially which bills get assigned to which committees.
- Presiding over the sessions of the House, recognizing or ignoring members who wish to speak.

Enrichment
Ask a pair of interested volunteers to research the process by which the most recent Speaker was selected. Let these volunteers share their findings with the rest of the class in a short oral report.

Cooperative Learning
Let the students work in groups to discuss the listed powers of the Speaker: Why is each of these powers significant? How does it allow the Speaker to influence the activities of others? What responsibilities do you imagine are associated with each of these powers?

Enrichment
Ask a small group of volunteers to research instances in which the Speaker has defeated a proposal by refraining from voting. Let these students prepare a bulletin board summarizing the examples they have researched.

Vocabulary
To check the students' comprehension, ask them to define the noun *caucus* as it is used here.

Discussion Starter
Encourage the students to discuss the role of the minority leader: Why is it a less powerful position than that of majority leader? Why is this role nonetheless significant in the structure and functioning of Congress? How is its importance of the minority leader affected when the president is a member of the minority party?

Extension
Who are the majority and minority whips? If the students do not know, ask one of them to find out and report to the rest of the class.

Caption Answer The primary duty of the minority leader is to maintain and support party cohesion among the minority party members of the House.

- Voting in the event of a tie, interpreting and applying the rules, ruling on points of order (questions about procedures asked by members), putting questions to a vote, and determining the outcome of most of the votes taken.
- Playing a major role in making important committee assignments, which all members desire.
- Scheduling bills for action.

The Speaker may choose whether to vote on any measure. If he or she chooses to vote, the Speaker appoints a temporary presiding officer (called the Speaker *pro tempore*) who then occupies the Speaker's chair. The House rules say that the only time the Speaker *must* vote is to break a tie, because a tie automatically defeats a measure. The Speaker does not often vote, but by choosing not to vote in some cases the Speaker can actually cause a tie and defeat a proposal that is unpopular with the majority party.

The Speaker of the House is second in the line of **presidential succession**. That is, in the event that the president and vice president cannot serve, the Speaker would become president of the United States.

The Speaker also has a good deal of political clout inside and outside Congress. If the Speaker belongs to the same party as the president, he or she often acts as the administration's spokesperson in the House. When the Speaker's party is different from the president, he or she is often a national spokesperson for his or her party. The Speaker also derives power from the fact that he or she has a good deal of control over the information and communications channels in the House.

Majority Leader The **majority leader** of the House is elected by the caucus of party members to act as spokesperson for the party and to keep the party together. The majority leader's job is to help plan the party's legislative program, to organize other party members to support legislation favored by their party, and to make sure the chairpersons on the many committees finish work on bills important to the party. He or she makes speeches on important bills, stating the majority party position.

Minority Leader The **minority leader**, as the name suggests, is the leader of the minority party. Although not as powerful as the majority leader, the minority leader has similar responsibilities. The primary duty of minority leaders is to maintain cohesion within the party. They persuade influential minority party leaders to follow the party's position and organize fellow party members in constructive criticism of the majority party's policies and programs.

▲ Congressman Robert Michel of Illinois is the minority leader of the House of Representatives. What is the primary duty of the minority leader?

Whips The leadership of each party includes assistants to the majority and minority leaders known as **whips**. Whips originated in the British House of Commons, where they were named after the "whipper in," the rider who keeps the hounds together in a fox hunt. The term originated from the pressure these assistant floor leaders place on party members to follow the party's positions. Whips try to determine how each member is going to vote on certain issues and advise the floor leaders on the strength of party support. Whips also try to see that members are present when important votes are to be taken and that they vote with the party leadership. For example, if the Democratic Party strongly supported a child care bill, the Democratic Party whip might meet with other Democratic members to try to persuade them to vote with the party.

Discussion Starter
Help the students consider and discuss the position of the current vice president: In which areas does the vice president appear to be most active? What vice presidential involvements in Senate activities—if any—have been recently reported by the media? What kind of relationship does the current vice president seem to have with the Senate?

Discussion Starter
Encourage the students to discuss and compare the influence of the president pro tempore and the Speaker: Which seems to be the more powerful position? Why?

Discussion Starter
Encourage a discussion of the committee system by asking questions such as these: Why do you think the committee system became necessary in Congress? Do you think the workings of Congress might change—as by technological innovations—to make another such revision in systems necessary? If not, why not? If so, what kinds of changes do you anticipate?

The United States Constitution mandates that the vice president of the United States serve as president of the Senate. Does the vice president have a powerful role in the Senate? Why or why not?

Caption Answer Students should understand that the vice president has little influence in the Senate, and since the vice president is not an elected member of the Senate, he may not take part in Senate debates and only vote in event of a tie.

Senate Leadership

The Constitution makes the vice president of the United States the **president of the Senate**. As presiding officer, the vice president may call on members to speak and put questions to a vote. The vice president, however, is not an elected member of the Senate and may not take part in Senate debates. He or she may cast a vote in the Senate only in the event of a tie. In practice, the vice president has little influence in the Senate and is rarely even present.

Although their role in the Senate is limited, a few vice presidents have been able to influence legislative matters, largely because of their personal abilities. The most successful have been those who were once senators themselves and thus had close personal relationships with their former colleagues.

Because vice presidents are rarely available to preside over the Senate, senators also elect another presiding officer, the president *pro tempore* (usually called just "*pro tem*"), who serves in the absence of the vice president. The president *pro tem* is elected by the whole Senate and is ordinarily the member of the majority party with the longest continuous term of service in the Senate. In the absence of both the president *pro tem* and the vice president, a temporary presiding officer is selected from the ranks of the Senate, usually a junior member of the majority party.

The real power in the Senate is held by the majority floor leader, the minority floor leader, and their whips. The **majority floor leader** is the most powerful officer and chief spokesperson of the major party. He or she directs the legislative program and party strategy. The **minority floor leader** commands the minority party's opposition to the policies of the majority party and directs the legislative strategy of his or her party.

Committees and Subcommittees

South Carolina's Senator Ernest Hollings once remarked that a senator could run naked through the chamber and no one would notice because senators would be handling committee business. Members of Congress do indeed spend much of their time on committee work because most of the actual work of legislating is performed by committees and subcommittees within Congress.

Congress was not always made up of committees. Both houses got along fine without permanent committees in the early years of the republic. The committee system was not created by the Constitution, but the House began to slowly establish it from 1795 on, and the Senate began to follow suit in 1816. Members of Congress are so busy, and the congressional agendas are so long, that through the years committees and subcommittees have gained more and more responsibility and power.

Multidiscipline Strategies

Language Have students select a fictional source that directly or indirectly deals with Congress and/or congressional personalities. Students should evaluate the manner in which Congress is depicted in the story, recording both accurate and inaccurate portrayals. What effect might such coverage have on the public, if any? This activity would be a good extra-credit assignment, and when students are done, they should be allowed to share their findings with the class. Examples of Congress in fiction include *Mr. Smith Goes to Washington* and *The Candidate.*

Discussion Starter
Help the students discuss the ways in which Congress uses committees: How is this structure similar to that of business organizations? How is it different? What do you think accounts for these differences? Do you believe Congress might be made more efficient if it were structured just like a major business firm? Do you think that kind of efficiency would benefit voters? Why or why not?

Discussion Starter
Have the students consider and discuss the advantages—and the disadvantages—of having committees that serve as filters.

Cooperative Learning
Let the students form groups in which to explore the specific issues now being considered by standing committees in the Senate or the House.

Discussion Starter
Ask the students to consider the possible effects of term limits on the structure and functioning of committees in the Senate and the House: What changes would be necessitated by term limits? Why? What role do these changes seem to take in the public's consideration of term limits?

Cooperative Learning
Ask the students to work in groups to figure the current percentages for Democrats and Republicans in both the House and the Senate. Then have the group members select several standing committees and check the Democratic and Republican membership of each committee: Do the percentages match those of the larger body?

Caption Answer The system provides for a rational division of the work of Congress. It also allows members to develop expertise in particular areas.

FYI

As stated in the chapter, there was a proliferation of subcommittees in the middle 1970s. Many young Democrats were elected during the post-Watergate era with notions of breaking the *good-old-boy* seniority system of the Congress. These "young Turks" were partially successful, gaining subcommittee chairs and changing the way committee assignments and leadership positions were granted, in exchange for agreeing to restore some power to the Speaker of the House. There were so many new representatives wanting new subcommittee positions that Speaker of the House Tip O'Neil joked that since he did not know their names it was safe to address them as "Mr. Chairman"! Not surprisingly, these same members of Congress now feel that the seniority system is a pretty good thing!

▲ Lawmakers, such as Senator Barbara Mikulski (D., Maryland), shown here, spend a great deal of their time in committees. What are the advantages of the committee system?

This evolution has taken place for several reasons. First, Congress receives as many as twenty thousand bills a year. If the entire Congress considered each one of these bills, the process would be endless. It is obviously impossible for senators and representatives to study and research the specific content of each one. Breaking up into committees allows members to split up the bills among smaller groups of representatives and senators who can specialize in the few issues considered by the committees on which they serve. Committee members often become experts on the kinds of bills that come before their committees and can therefore make informed judgments about them.

Second, the committee system allows committees to screen the thousands of bills that are introduced into Congress during every term. Committees decide which bills are ready to go through the system and which deserve further examination. Members of the committees listen to experts, lobbyists, and citizens who support and oppose the bills, and decide which bills have a chance to become law. Committees are supposed to serve as filters to ensure that only the most important and responsible legislation is permitted to reach the House and Senate floor for a vote.

Standing Committees The permanent and most powerful committees of Congress are called **standing committees**. Before any bill can be considered by the entire House or Senate, it must be approved by a majority vote in the standing committee to which it was assigned. Each standing committee deals with a certain policy area such as agriculture or foreign affairs, and approves the bills related to those areas.

The number of these committees has varied over the years: Today, there are twenty-two standing committees in the House and sixteen in the Senate listed in the table on page 303. The size of these committees has varied from twelve to fifty-seven members in the House and from ten to twenty-eight members in the Senate.

Standing committees are controlled by the majority party in each house. The committee chairperson is chosen by the majority-party caucus and is almost always the majority member who has served for the longest period of time on that particular committee. This is known as the seniority rule, discussed in the "Government in Action" feature on page 304.

The majority of members of the standing committee are also members of the majority party, but committee membership is generally divided between the parties according to the number of members in each house. For example, if the Democrats hold 60 percent of the seats in the House and the Republicans hold 40 percent, a ten-member committee will have six Democrats and four Republicans.

Most House and Senate committees are also divided into **subcommittees**—smaller groups of committee members with special limited areas of jurisdiction that study one aspect of the subject handled by the standing committee.

The number and power of subcommittees has grown in recent years. Today, there are about 250 subcommittees in Congress. Since the early 1970s, the role of subcommittees in the lawmaking process has increased and there is evidence that subcommittees are sometimes more powerful than the standing committees themselves.

Select Committees In addition to standing committees, there are a number of special committees, called

Enrichment
Ask interested volunteers to work in small groups to research the formation and functioning of specific select committees. Have each group make a brief oral report, summarizing its findings for the rest of the class.

Enrichment
Let several volunteers work together to read more about the permanent joint committees: What are their titles? What purposes do they serve? Who serves on each? Ask these volunteers to prepare and present a chart summarizing their information.

Discussion Starter
Help the students consider and discuss the importance of conference committees: Why do the two houses often pass different versions of the same bill? What approach to this situation might be used instead of a conference committee? Which approach do you consider most useful? Why?

Standing Committees in Congress

House Committees	Senate Committees
Agriculture	Agriculture, Nutrition, and Forestry
Appropriations	Appropriations
Armed Forces	Armed Services
Banking, Finance, and Urban Affairs	Banking, Housing, and Urban Affairs
Budget	Budget
District of Columbia	Commerce, Science, and Transportation
Education and Labor	Energy and Natural Resources
Energy and Commerce	Environment and Public Works
Foreign Affairs	Finance
Government Operations	Foreign Relations
House Administration	Governmental Affairs
Interior and Insular Affairs	Judiciary
Judiciary	Labor and Human Resources
Merchant Marine and Fisheries	Rules and Administration
Post Office and Civil Service	Small Business
Public Works and Transportation	Veterans Affairs
Rules	
Science and Technology	
Small Business	
Standards of Official Conduct	
Veterans' Affairs	
Ways and Means	

▲ FIGURE 12–5 **Standing Committees in Congress.** Before any bill can be considered by the entire House or Senate, it must be approved by a majority vote in the standing committee to which it was assigned. Why do you think these committees are called standing committees?

This figure content is also featured on *West's American Government Videodisc* (see the index found in the *TRB*).

Figure Answer Students should understand that standing committees got this name because these are permanent committees that continue from Congress to Congress.

select committees, which are set up to do specific, usually temporary jobs. They investigate special problems that are not covered by the standing committees, and make recommendations to their house in Congress. For example, there is a select committee on hunger and a select committee on narcotics abuse and control.

Sometimes select committees are created to investigate sensitive matters. One example was the Select Committee to Study Government Operations with Respect to Intelligence Activities, established in 1975 to review the Central Intelligence Agency (CIA) and other intelligence agencies. The Senate's Select Committee on Presidential Campaign Activities, known as the Senate Watergate Committee, was set up in 1973 to investigate "the extent, if any, to which illegal, improper, or unethical activities were engaged in by any persons . . . in the presidential election of 1972." Other examples include the House Assassinations committees to investigate the deaths of President John F. Kennedy; his brother, Senator Robert Kennedy; and Dr. Martin Luther King, Jr. In 1987 the Senate Select Committee on Secret Military Assistance to Iran and the House Select Committee to Investigate Covert Arms Transactions with Iran were established to investigate issues surrounding the Iran-*contra* scandal. In 1991 a House committee started to investigate allegations that in 1980 Reagan made a deal with Iran about the fate of U.S. hostages in order to make President Carter look bad.

Joint Committees There are also **joint committees** whose membership is drawn from both the Senate and the House. When they are appointed for a specific purpose, for example to investigate alleged wrongdoing, they are usually referred to as "select" or "special" committees. A few of these joint committees are permanent. They are created to give a full congressional

TEACHING GOVERNMENT IN ACTION

Read

Begin by letting the students review and briefly discuss what they know about the importance of committees in Congress. Then explain to the students that they will learn more about these committees and their leaders in this Case Study; have volunteers read the Case Study aloud to the rest of the class.

Discuss

Encourage the students to discuss the Case Study by posing questions such as these: Why do you think the committees named here are considered "key committees"? What are the purposes and powers of each? Which individuals and groups might be especially interested in these committees? What committees do you think are of particular interest to Congress members from your state? Why? Why are political parties important in committee functioning? Why are the committee chairpersons so important? Do you think committees could function successfully without powerful chairpersons? Why or why not? What are the advantages of the seniority system? What are its disadvantages? Do you consider the advantages of the system more important—or the disadvantages? Why?

Analyze and Apply

Let the students work in groups to learn more about the most important committees in the Senate and the House. The group members should work together to chart the membership of a chosen committee and to identify the major issues with which that committee has dealt during the past decade. Give each group an opportunity to share its findings with the rest of the class.

Review

Ask the students these review questions: Why are committee assignments so important to members of Congress? How are committee chairpersons selected?

Think About It (Answers)

1. Answers will vary, but should reflect an understanding of the issues that are important to your state and of the committees that are most important.

2. Answers will vary, e.g., the seniority system is not fair because it overlooks ability and discourages new members. Seniority should be used as only one criterion among many.

GOVERNMENT IN ACTION

CASE STUDY

The Politics of Congressional Committees

One of the first worries of new members coming into Congress is getting on the right committee. Committees assignments are extremely important to a congressperson's career. Some committees are more prominent and significant than others. For example, in the Senate the key committees are Finance, Foreign Relations, and Appropriations. Key committees in the House are Rules, Ways and Means, Appropriations, and International Relations.

Assignment to the right committee can help strengthen a member's career in several ways. First, it can increase a lawmaker's chance for reelection if he or she is assigned to a committee that deals with bills that can benefit his or her district or state. Membership on an agriculture committee, for example, might be sought if the member is from a farming region. Second, membership on certain committees, such as Appropriations, means that a member will be able to exert influence over other congressional members not on the committee, because the issues the committee handles are important to all members of Congress. Third, membership on some committees means the opportunity to determine national policy in areas he or she thinks are important. For example, a member might want to help formulate policies in education, health, or foreign affairs.

Just after the elections, new members request assignment to committees on which they want to serve. They also try to line up party leaders and senior lawmakers to support their requests. The average representative serves on six committees and subcommittees, while the average senator serves on eleven committees and subcommittees. Each party in each house has a slightly different way of selecting its committee members, but party leaders almost always play a key role in this process.

Committee chairpersons are the most influential members of the committee. They play dominant roles in scheduling hearings, hiring staff, appointing subcommittees, and managing committee bills when they are brought before the full house. Chairpersons can give a bill top priority if they favor a bill or delay it if they do not.

Traditionally, chairpersons have been selected by the unwritten rule of **seniority**, which means that the chair goes to the member of the majority party who has served longest on the particular committee. Critics of the seniority system argue that it ignores ability, puts a high value on length of service, and discourages new members. Critics also note that the rule means that committee heads always come from ''safe'' districts, and are least likely to be challenged for reelection. With no fresh leadership, critics claim a committee is often out of touch with current public opinion. Those who favor the system say that it means that powerful and experienced lawmakers will head the committees. They claim the rule is easy to apply, and nearly eliminates the possibility of disputes within a party.

With recent modifications, the seniority system is still used today. The House Republican Conference now selects several members of House committees by secret ballot. House Democrats use secret ballots to choose a committee chair whenever 20 percent of their caucus requests that procedure.

THINK ABOUT IT

1. On which committees do you think congressional members from your state and district would want to serve? Why would they want to serve on those committees?
2. Do you agree or disagree with the seniority system? Give reasons for your answer.

Discussion Starter
Encourage the students to consider the changes in the workload of Congress: How have the increases in population affected Congress? How have the increases in constituents' demands affected Congress? Do you imagine that these trends will continue, or do you foresee a change in this trend? Why? How might technological advances affect the workload of Congress? Do you consider changes in this area likely? Why or why not?

Discussion Starter
Let the students discuss their reactions to the allowances for senators' personal staffs: Do you think the basis of allocation is reasonable? Fair? Do the sums involved seem appropriate to you? Why or why not? What changes—if any—would you suggest for the allocation of funds for senators' personal staffs?

Cooperative Learning
Divide the class into groups, and have the members of each group learn about the important personal staff members of selected representatives and senators. Specifically, the group members should work together to try to learn the identity and professional background of the Congress member's AA, LD, LA, and, if possible, caseworkers and LCs.

Caption Answer The Senate Select Committee on Secret Military Assistance to Iran and the House Select Committee to Investigate Covert Arms Transactions with Iran were both select committees.

In 1987, both the House and the Senate created committees to investigate secret military assistance to Iran and other issues surrounding the Iran-*contra* scandal. What type of committees were these?

overview to a complex subject. For example, the Joint Economic Committee (JEC) studies the complex questions relating to the American economy as a whole and issues its findings to Congress and to the public. Other joint committees have been set up to study matters of atomic energy and defense.

Conference Committees The Constitution requires that in order for a bill to become a law it must be passed in identical form by each chamber of Congress. In many instances, however, the two houses pass different versions. A **conference committee** is a temporary joint body created solely to iron out the differences between the House and Senate versions of the bill. The committee must work out a final bill that is written in language agreeable to both houses before the bill can be sent to the president. The strategic role of conference committees will be discussed in Chapter 14.

Congressional Support

From the time when the first Congress met until today, the United States population has grown from 4 million to over 250 million. This dramatic increase in population has brought an equally dramatic increase in the workload of congressional members. Furthermore, constituents are demanding more service and members of Congress are providing it, because senators and representatives know its value when election time rolls around. As more citizens turn to Congress for help, Congress hires more staff to take care of them.

Along with the increase in workload has come an increase in the technicality and complexity of legislation. No members could possibly have the specialized background to understand all the details of every piece of legislation, so they must rely on help from staff. Congress now employs over 32,000 people for assistance.

Personal Staff Personal staff includes people working directly for the individual senators and representatives in their Washington and district offices. The average House member has about twenty personal staff members and the average senator has about twice that number. Allowances to pay for a senator's personal staff are scaled according to the population of that senator's state. These allowances range from $780,000 per year to about $1.5 million.

Staff titles and positions vary from staff to staff, but Figure 12–6 on the following page provides an overview of the typical positions in each senator's and representative's office.

Lawmakers have several types of personal staff members in their offices. The **administrative assistant**, called the AA, runs the lawmaker's office, supervises the lawmaker's schedule, and gives advice on political matters. She or he is responsible for directing and supervising the member's staff. The AA is typically a close, personal, and political friend or advisor of the member of Congress.

The **legislative director**, called the LD, will often decide who among the staff should do what. The legislative director has one or more **legislative assistants**,

Multidiscipline Strategies

Math The workload of Congress has increased to the point that the calendar is full and issues are put off until the next session. Between 10,000 and 15,000 bills are introduced each year! Have students get recent copies of *Congressional Quarterly Weekly Reports.* Students should compare the number of votes taken by the House with those taken by the Senate. Which house has more on its agenda and why? Students should also be encouraged to scrutinize the roll call on specific bills that interest them the most in order to see the numerical voting results. What percentage of bills do they feel are frivolous or unnecessary? What percentage of the vote was Republican? Democrat? What was the numerical breakdown for their own state's delegation and senators? What percentage of the House or Senate abstained? If a bill passed, are there enough votes to override a Presidential veto?

Discussion Starter
Have the students discuss the work done by different kinds of staff members: Who do you think is attracted to working on a Congress member's personal staff? Why? Who do you think is attracted to working on the staff of a Congressional committee or subcommittee? Why? How do you think the two groups are similar? Different?

Discussion Starter
Help the students consider the responsibilities of caseworkers: Why do caseworkers usually work in their Congress member's home district rather than in Washington? How do caseworkers help their Congress member fulfill his or her responsibilities? What effects can they have on the Congress member's image among his or her constituents?

Extension
Ask the students to find out who the current comptroller general is and what particular attitudes and interests he or she has.

Enrichment
Ask several interested students to learn more about the Library of Congress: What other functions does it serve? Who can have access to the materials there? Under what conditions? Let these students report their findings to the rest of the class.

Enrichment
Have a volunteer find out more about the GPO: What kinds of publications are available? How can members of the public find out about and receive those publications? Ask the student to write a brief fact-sheet with this information to be distributed to the rest of the class.

This figure content is also featured on *West's American Government Videodisc* (see the index found in the *TRB*).

Figure Answer The Administrative Assistant is the most powerful member of the lawmaker's staff. This is depicted in the chart by the AA's placement directly beneath the lawmaker and above all other staff members.

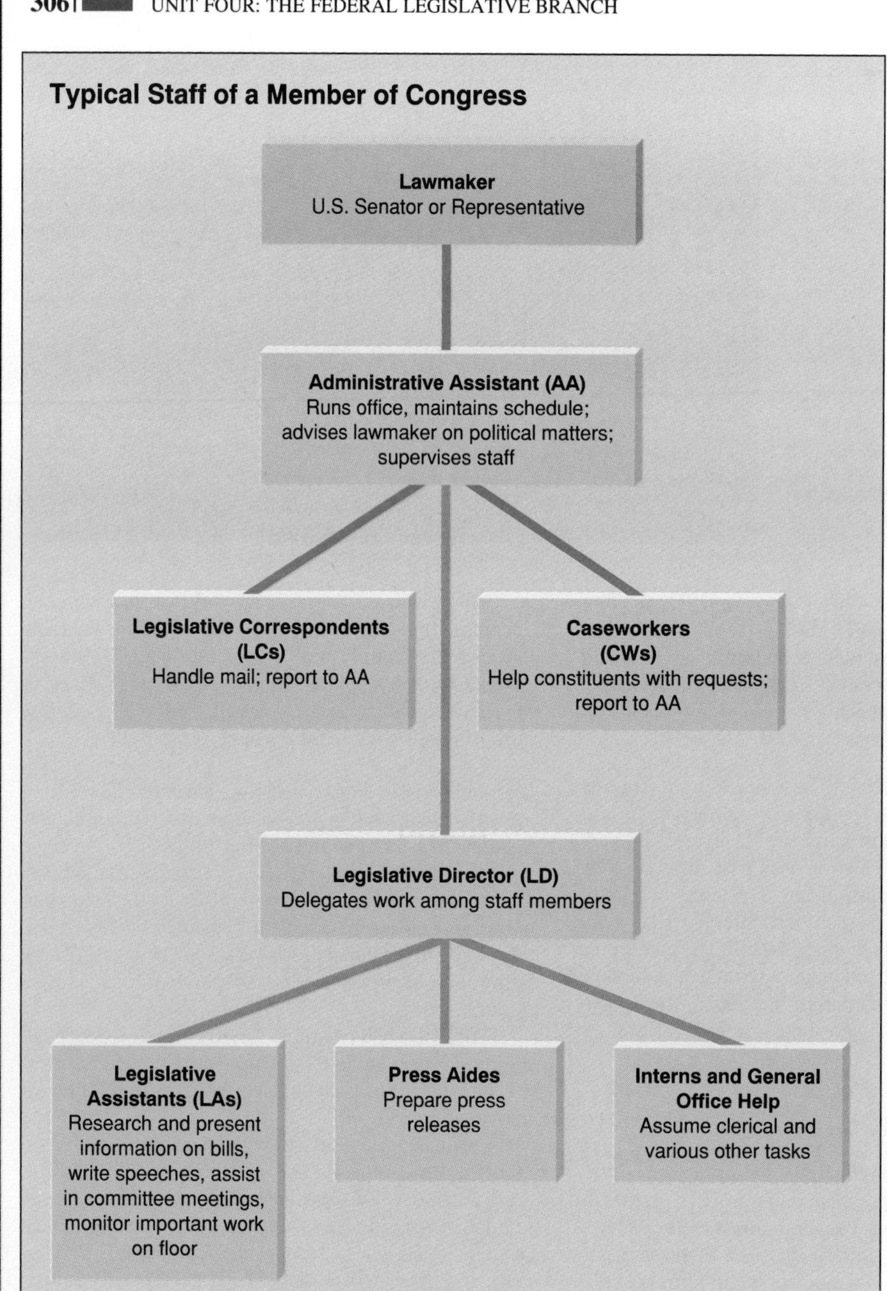
Typical Staff of a Member of Congress
Lawmaker
U.S. Senator or Representative
Administrative Assistant (AA)
Runs office, maintains schedule; advises lawmaker on political matters; supervises staff
Legislative Correspondents (LCs)
Handle mail; report to AA
Caseworkers (CWs)
Help constituents with requests; report to AA
Legislative Director (LD)
Delegates work among staff members
Legislative Assistants (LAs)
Research and present information on bills, write speeches, assist in committee meetings, monitor important work on floor
Press Aides
Prepare press releases
Interns and General Office Help
Assume clerical and various other tasks

▲ **FIGURE 12–6 Typical Staff of a Member of Congress.** The chart above represents the organization of a typical lawmaker's staff. Who is the most powerful member of the lawmaker's staff? How do you know?

Reteaching Strategies

1. Help the students work in groups to recall and answer the questions they posed during the Kickoff Activity.

2. Let the students work in pairs to write, in their own words, definitions of these terms: *presidential succession, Speaker of the House, president pro tempore, whip, standing committee, select committee.*

Evaluation Strategies

1. Have the students write their answers to the Section 4 Review questions.

2. Have the students take the Section 4 Quiz found in the *TRB.*

Section 4 Review (Answers)

1. The Speaker of the House is the head of the House of Representatives and presides over sessions of the House.

2. The majority leader is elected by the caucus of party members to act as spokesperson for the party and to keep the party together. The minority leader is the leader of the minority party. Whips are assistants to the majority and minority leaders and try to determine how each member is going to vote on certain issues and advise the floor leaders on the strength of party support.

3. The vice president is president of the Senate. Because vice presidents are rarely available, another presiding officer, the president *pro tempore* serves in his or her absence. The majority floor leader is the most powerful officer and chief spokesperson of the majority party. The minority floor leader directs the legislative strategy of his or her party.

4. Committees allow members to split up the many bills they receive among smaller groups of representatives and senators who can specialize in the few issues considered by the committees on which they serve. Committees also allow for a screening of the thousands of bills that are introduced each term.

5. Standing committees are permanent, and before any bill can be considered by the entire House or Senate, it must pass through the standing committee to which it was assigned. Select committees are set up to do specific, usually temporary jobs. Joint committees are made up of members of both the House and Senate and are created to give full congressional overview to a complex subject. Conference committees are temporary joint bodies created solely to iron out differences between House and Senate versions of a bill.

6. Each member of Congress has a personal staff for assistance. Further support is provided by several agencies, such as the GAO, the Library of Congress, the CBO, and the GPO.

7. Answers will vary, e.g., the increase in the number of staff has made it easier for incumbents to get elected. Incumbents are better able to keep in touch with constituents and do favors which win votes.

called LAs, who make sure that the lawmaker has all the information he or she needs about bills for which the member is responsible. An LA studies and does background research on bills in Congress, drafts bills, and writes speeches and articles for the lawmaker. LAs also assist in committee meetings and keep track of the work taking place on the floor of Congress.

Caseworkers manage the numerous requests for help from constituents. For example, a caseworker might help a major university through the steps involved in obtaining a federal grant. Or, a caseworker might simply arrange for a citizen to take a tour of Capitol Hill. Lawmakers usually have offices in key cities in their state or district. Many caseworkers work in these offices.

Lawmakers also have **legislative correspondents** (LCs) to handle mail, press aides to prepare press releases, general office help, and interns.

Committee Staff Besides the personal staff of lawmakers, every committee and subcommittee in Congress has staff members who serve the needs of that committee. The larger and more important the committee, the larger the staff working for it. A committee staff collects and analyzes information on issues, identifies and researches problems, suggests policies, schedules committee hearings, and prepares reports. Because the essential work of Congress depends on the committee system, committee staffs have grown even faster than personal staffs.

Support Agencies Several agencies provide services that help Congress and are a part of the legislative branch of the government.

1. *General Accounting Office.* The largest of these support agencies is the General Accounting Office (GAO). It reviews the financial management of government programs created by Congress to see that spending is proper and reasonable and to assure that federal funds are spent for the purposes that Congress intended. The GAO is headed by the *comptroller general,* a person appointed by the president, with the Senate's approval, to a fifteen-year term.
2. *The Library of Congress.* The Library of Congress was established in 1800 by Congress to "purchase such books as may be necessary for the use of Congress." It now contains over 20 million items, and is an information and fact-finding center for legislators and their assistants. The library has a Congressional Research Service (CRS), which every year answers some 250,000 requests for information from lawmakers, congressional staff, and committees. CRS workers will research anything from the crime rate in Bulgaria to the number of spotted owls in Oregon.
3. *The Congressional Budget Office.* The Congressional Budget Office (CBO) serves Congress by providing technical and computer services and coordinating the budget-making work. It also studies the budget proposals put forward by the president each year, and predicts the economic consequences of proposed and actual legislation. The CBO prepares a report on the budget each April.
4. *The Government Printing Office.* The Government Printing Office (GPO) prints the *Congressional Record,* which is a daily record of all the bills introduced in both chambers and of the speeches and testimony presented in Congress. Voters can write asking about a particular lawmaker's position on an issue, such as prayer in schools or gun control, and the GPO staff will send a copy of the *Record* containing a speech by a lawmaker on the issue. The GPO also does all the national government's printing and provides copies of many government publications to the public free or at a low cost.

As you have learned, Congress was established as the first branch of the federal government and was meant to be the branch closest to the people. Through the years, however, the growth of Congress and its ever increasing workload have forced upon this branch of government many changes that the framers of the Constitution could not have predicted. Today, Congress is larger, it's busier, and its membership has begun to reflect the ethnic and cultural diversity of our nation. Additionally, its work is increasingly done in the meeting rooms of its committees and subcommittees. Despite these changes, however, Congress remains the "Voice of the People."

SECTION 4 REVIEW

1. What is the role of the Speaker of the House?
2. Who are the other leaders in the House and what are their functions?
3. How is Senate leadership organized?
4. What purposes do committees serve?
5. Describe the functions of the different types of committees in Congress.
6. What types of support do members of Congress receive?
7. **For critical analysis:** How do you think the increase in the number of staff personnel for each member of Congress has made it easier for incumbents to be reelected?

TEACHING CHALLENGE TO THE AMERICAN DREAM

Read
Let the students begin by discussing what they already know about term limits: Who is interested in limiting the number of terms served by members of Congress? Why? What are the most convincing arguments you have heard in favor of term limitations? In opposition to term limitations? Do you have a strong opinion about term limitations? If so, what is your opinion? Then have several students read the Challenge to the American Dream feature aloud to the rest of the class.

Discuss
Use questions such as these to encourage discussion of the feature: Why do you think twelve years has been suggested as a limit for members of Congress? Do you think a shorter limit—or a longer one—might be better? Do the survey results given here seem to match the general opinion of your classmates? Which of the arguments in favor of term limitations do you find most persuasive? Why? Which of the arguments against term limitations do you find most persuasive? Why? Who is responsible for the high rate of incumbent re-elections? Why? What can the public do to limit the terms of some Congress members without passing a Constitutional amendment? Do voters seem unwilling to accept this responsibility? Why or why not?

Analyze and Apply
Let each student assume the role either of a long-term member of Congress running for re-election or of a new candidate running against an established incumbent. Have the students, in their chosen roles, plan and present short campaign speeches that deal with the issue of term limits.

Review
Use these questions to help the students review the Challenge to the American Dream feature: Approximately what percentage of the public backs the idea of term limits for members of Congress? What are two important arguments in favor of term limits? What are two important arguments against term limits?

You Decide (Answers)
1. Answers will vary, e.g., limiting terms would not make members of Congress more responsive to the people. Members who feel they have a chance of a long-term career in Congress would be more interested in their constituent's problems and concerns. The more terms a representative serves, the more experience he or she has and the better able he or she is to help the people.

CHALLENGE TO THE AMERICAN DREAM

Limiting Terms Served in Congress

In the past several elections, 96 percent or more of House incumbents who ran were reelected. Does the public think that incumbent members of Congress get reelected too easily and serve too long? Supporters of a constitutional amendment or state initiatives that would restrict representatives and senators to twelve years of service argue that they do. After the 1992 elections, 15 states had some form of congressional term limits in effect.

The idea of limiting the time that members can serve in Congress is not new. Some members of the 1st Congress suggested term limitation, but in 1789 a resolution to restrict members to six years was rejected. Self-imposed limits on officeholders were previously a part of this country's public-service ethic. Members would voluntarily return to private life after a couple of terms. As late as 1860, the average length of House service was four years. The number of new members in the House never dipped below 30 percent. After the 1992 elections, over 20 percent of House members were new.

People who support limiting congressional terms say that lengthy terms have produced a class of career officeholders who have become protected by the advantages of incumbency, lost touch with the people they serve, and in some cases have sunk to corruption. They say that limiting terms would put Congress on equal footing with the president, who is barred from serving more than two four-year terms. They argue that the current system gives unfair advantage to the Democrats who control the House and have therefore extraordinary advantages over others who run for election. Thomas Hartnett, a South Carolina Republican who retired from the House in 1987, calls today's Congress ''a ruling class,'' which is insulated from accountability to the people. He believes limiting terms is the answer: ''It's time we told members that after a limited number of terms, we give you a gold watch and send you home to live under the laws you passed while you were in Congress.''

Opponents of limiting terms in Congress challenge the notion that there is a ''permanent'' Congress. Despite the high reelection rate of incumbents who choose to run, about half of the current Congress have only been in office since 1980. Opponents of limiting terms argue that limits might place even more legislative power in the hands of unelected committee staffs, who would often keep their positions much longer than elected members of Congress. ''Power would flow from elected to unelected officials,'' says Thomas Mann of the Brookings Institution in Washington, D.C.

Opponents also argue that limiting terms would enhance the power of interest groups. Members who knew they had to seek a new line of work in twelve years would want to cultivate the possibility of jobs after their terms and would cater to special interest groups who might provide those jobs. Term limitation also limits the rights of voters to continue to choose whom they elect. Limiting terms infringes on democracy, say the opponents. Some Democrats argue that the limitation of terms is just a way for Republicans to try to gain control of Congress because the present system of Democratic majority is maintained by not limiting terms.

The challenge to the American dream is to find ways to control the undesirable effects of having senators and representatives stay in Congress year after year, if in fact no term-limitation legislation ever becomes a reality.

You Decide

1. Do you think that limiting terms would make members of Congress more responsive to the people? Why or why not?
2. Why would limiting terms to twelve years limit the rights of voters to choose whom they elect? Is this an infringement on democracy?
3. What have you learned about the advantages of incumbency? How do you think limiting terms would affect these advantages?

2. Answers will vary, e.g., limiting terms would disallow voters from voting for the incumbent. This is an infringement on their freedom to vote as they wish.
3. Answers will vary, e.g., the advantages of incumbency would be severely eroded because term limitation would limit the amount of time that a representative would have his or her name in the limelight. Also, those in Congress for fewer terms build up fewer ties with special interest groups.

Chapter Evaluation

To evaluate student mastery of chapter material, you might:
1. Use Chapter Test A from the *TRB*.
2. Use Chapter Test B from the *TRB*.
3. Construct your own test using items from the *West American Government Test Bank* found in the *TRB*.
4. Use the accompanying computerized test software to construct and print a customized chapter test.

Observable Mastery

As a review of Chapter 12 and an introduction to the rest of the treatment of Congress, have students create large wall charts on the following aspects of Congress: Characteristics of each house (i.e., numbers, qualifications, terms, methods of disciplinary action); Profile on membership of the House and Senate; Roles that could be fulfilled by congressmen; Structure of Congress (i.e., committees, and positions of leadership); and Compensation, benefits, and privileges of congressmen. This can be done individually or in cooperative groups.

Review Questions (Answers)

1. The founders created a bicameral legislature partly because they were already familiar with the British Parliament. They also favored a bicameral legislature so that the two houses could serve as checks on each other. They also saw it as a politically necessary compromise between the large and the small states.
2. Each Congress lasts for a meeting period, or term, of two years. Each term begins on January 3 of an odd-numbered year.

CHAPTER 12 REVIEW

Key Terms

Summary

1. Congress is the legislative (lawmaking) branch of government. The founders created a bicameral legislature because they were familiar with the British bicameral system, and because they wanted the two branches to serve as checks on each other. A term of Congress lasts for two years and there are two regular sessions per term. Only the president may call a special session of Congress. The Constitution provides that the total number of seats in the House shall be apportioned among the states on the basis of their populations by taking a census every ten years. The Reapportionment Act of 1929 established a permanent system of reapportionment without increasing the number of House members past 435.

2. The House is made up of congressional districts drawn by state legislatures. Members of the House are elected for two-year terms, while Senators are elected for six-year terms. The Constitution sets forth basic qualifications for both senators and representatives. Both the House and Senate have constitutional power to punish the misconduct of their members.

3. Congress is not a cross section of the American public. Members tend to have a higher level of income, education, and occupational status than the rest of the population. Congress has always been predominantly white, Anglo, and male. Congress sets its own pay and compensation, and enjoys many privileges and benefits. The roles congressional members play include policymaker, representative, constituent servant, committee member, and politician.

4. Congress is organized along political party lines. Chief among the leaders in the House is the Speaker of the House. Other leaders in the House include the majority leader, minority leader, and whips. The Constitution makes the vice president of the United States the president of the Senate. The president *pro tempore* serves in the absence of the vice president. There are four kinds of committees, which do the basic work of Congress: standing committees, which are permanent and the most powerful; select committees, which are temporary and set up to do specific jobs; joint committees, which are made up of members from both houses; and conference committees, which are temporary joint committees created to iron out differences between House and Senate versions of the same bill. Congressional staff and support agencies assist lawmakers in carrying out the work of Congress.

Review Questions

1. Why did the founders create a bicameral legislature?
2. On what date does a new term of Congress begin? How long does a term last?

3. The Constitution provides that the total number of House seats shall be apportioned among the states on the basis of population.
4. Gerrymandering is the practice of drawing district boundaries to benefit a certain party, group, or candidate. The Court ruled that congressional districts must be compact and contiguous, and that congressional districts must have equal population.
5. There is a great deal of continuity in the House because well over 90 percent of all House incumbents are reelected.
6. The terms of senators are staggered in six-year terms so that every two years the terms of only one-third of senators end.
7. By censure or expulsion.
8. Members tend to be white males, with high levels of income, education, and occupational status. Nearly all have college degrees, and a majority have graduate or professional degrees. Law is the dominant occupation.
9. The speech and debate clause guarantees freedom of speech to members while they are conducting congressional business.
10. Policymaker—includes conducting investigations to identify problems, researching bills, and voting intelligently. Representative—representing and translating into action the interests and concerns of constituents. Constituent servant—helping constituents with problems concerning the federal bureaucracy. Committee members—being a member of committees and subcommittees. Politician and party member—concerning themselves with reelection.
11. The Speaker of the House presides over the House.
12. The majority leader of the House and the majority floor leader of the Senate are the chief spokespersons for their party. They direct the legislative programs and party strategies. The minority leader of the House and minority floor leader of the Senate are the leaders of the minority party. Whips are assistants to the majority and minority leaders.
13. Committees screen the thousands of bills that are introduced in Congress. They allow members to specialize in certain areas.
14. Standing committees are permanent and before any bill can be considered by the entire House or Senate, it must pass through the standing committee to which it was assigned. Select committees are set up to do specific jobs. Joint committees are made up of both House and Senate members to give a full congressional overview to a complex subject. Conference committees are temporary joint committees created to iron out the differences between the House and Senate versions of a bill.
15. The administrative assistant runs the lawmaker's office, supervises his or her schedule, and gives advice on political matters. The legislative director often decides who among the staff should do what. Legislative assistants make sure that the lawmaker has all the information he or she needs about bills for which the member is responsible.

CHAPTER 12 REVIEW—Continued

3. How are House seats divided among the states?
4. What is gerrymandering? What events have reduced its use?
5. Despite the fact that representatives serve short terms, why is there a great deal of continuity in the House?
6. How did the Constitution ensure that the Senate would be a continuous body?
7. How does Congress punish the misconduct of its members?
8. What are the typical characteristics of members of Congress?
9. What special privileges do members of Congress have to protect themselves while carrying out their duties?
10. List and briefly explain the five roles of a member of Congress.
11. What is the role of the Speaker of the House?
12. Who are the leaders in each political party in both Houses and what are some of their duties?
13. What purposes do committees serve in Congress?
14. Briefly describe the four types of committees and their purposes in Congress.
15. What kinds of activities are performed by a congressperson's personal staff?
16. What agencies perform support services for Congress?
17. Describe two ways to find out what is going on in Congress.
18. What are the arguments for and against limiting terms of members of Congress?

Questions for Thought and Discussion

1. Can you think of situations in which the different roles of a congressperson might come into conflict with one another? Describe three such instances and present possible ways to resolve them.
2. How would Congress be different if it were an exact cross section of the American public?
3. Do you think members of Congress are ever offered bribes or other inducements for favors? Do you think this practice is common? Give evidence to support your answer.
4. Should members of Congress vote the way they think is best for the country or should they vote the way their constituents want them to? Give reasons for your answer.
5. Describe the ways that a member of Congress can be placed on important committees and subcommittees. What do you think is the single most important requirement for getting an important committee assignment in Congress?

Improving Your Skills
Communication Skills

Continuity in Writing: Transitional Phrases

Before writing an essay or report, it is important to know how to connect your ideas to make them more readable and clear to the reader. Continuity in writing is strengthened by using transitional phrases—bridges that carry the reader from one sentence to the next.

Compare these two paragraphs:

1.

Incumbent representatives are more visible than opponents. They are better able to keep constituents informed. They win friends by servicing constituents. They are in a better position to raise campaign funds. They get reelected over 90 percent of the time.

2.

Incumbent representatives are more visible than opponents. They are better able to keep constituents informed. They win friends by servicing constituents. They are in a better position to raise campaign funds. Consequently, they get reelected over 90 percent of the time.

The difference between the two paragraphs is the word *consequently*. Without this transitional word, the relationship of the last sentence to the preceding sentences is unclear. The transitional word or phrase links the last sentence to the list of statements supporting it.

Use the following tips to strengthen the continuity of your writing.

- ***Use logic***. Organize your sentences so that ideas progress naturally and logically.
- ***Use transitional words and phrases to show relationships between ideas***. Study the list below for ideas:

16. The General Accounting Office reviews the financial management of government programs created by Congress to see that spending is proper and reasonable. The Library of Congress is the information and fact-finding center for legislators and their assistants. The Congressional Budget Office provides technical and computer services and coordinates budget-making work. The Government Printing Office prints the *Congressional Record* which is a daily record of all the bills introduced in both chambers and of the speeches and testimony presented in Congress.
17. Two ways of finding out what is going on in Congress are to look in the appropriate publication, such as the *Congressional Directory,* and to call the Legislative Status Office to query particular bills or actions.
18. Those in favor of the proposition believe limiting terms in Congress would bring the representatives in closer touch with their constituencies, would do away with unfair seniority advantages, and would make members more accountable to the people. Those opposed say too much power would be shifted from elected officials to appointed committee members, and that it would undemocratically restrict the rights of the people to elect the best person for the job.

Questions for Thought and Discussion (Answers)

1. Answers will vary, e.g., the role of politician may come into conflict with that of policymaker when the member votes on a bill in the national interest which is unpopular in his or her state.
2. Answers will vary, e.g., if Congress were an exact cross section of the American public, it would be more responsive and sensitive to the needs of all people.
3. Answers will vary, but students should understand that instances of bribery have occurred.
4. Answers will vary, e.g., members should vote the way their constituents want them to because they were elected by these people to represent their interests. They were not elected to act on their own opinions, but on those of the people they represent.
5. Answers will vary, e.g., each party in each house has a slightly different way of selecting its committee members, but party leaders almost always play a key role. Just after elections, new members request assignment to committees on which they want to serve. They try to line up party leaders and senior lawmakers to support their requests. This type of backing might be the single most important requirement for getting an important committee assignment.

Social Studies Skills (Answers)

1. Color helps us distinguish clearly between the states that lost seats, gained seats, or had no change in the number of house seats after the 1990 census.
2. 1990.
3. 29.
4. 13.
5. 2.375.

Chapter 12 Review—Continued

Result: consequently, thus, as a result, therefore
Summary: in conclusion, in summary, in short
Sequence: first, second, then, finally, meanwhile
Emphasis: most importantly, especially
Addition: also, furthermore, further, moreover, including

Writing

Pick two topics from this chapter. On each topic write two separate short paragraphs. In the first one do not use any transitional words or phrases. In the second one use at least one or more of the transitional words listed above. After you have completed this assignment, write down how the transitional words and phrases make a difference in the two paragraphs for each of the topics.

Social Studies Skills

Reading Political Maps

Look at the map on page 286. It shows the reapportionment of seats in the House of Representatives for the year 1992 through 2001.

1. How is color used in this map?
2. When was the data collected to make this map?
3. How many states saw no change in their number of representatives?
4. How many states suffered a reduction in their number of representatives?
5. Of those states that gained seats, what was the size of the average gain in seats?

Activities and Projects

1. Prepare a biography of your representative or one of your senators using the resources list on page 298, your library, and information you can obtain from the congressperson's office. Present your report to the class.
2. Make a list of the committees and subcommittees that your senators have been on for the last decade. Establish whether the committees and subcommittees they have been on have been particularly important for your state or region. For example, if you live in an area where there is aerospace manufacturing, has your senator been named to a committee or subcommittee that determines spending in the area of national defense? Write a short report that summarizes your research results.
3. Describe the job of a member of the House or Senate by creating a want ad for a congressperson. In the ad include qualifications, benefits and salary, and skills needed. Also include facts that demonstrate the typical responsibilities of members.
4. Find out which select committees are currently active. Keep track of the action of one of these committees for one month. Present the results of what you learn in a two-page report, a short speech, or a bulletin board.

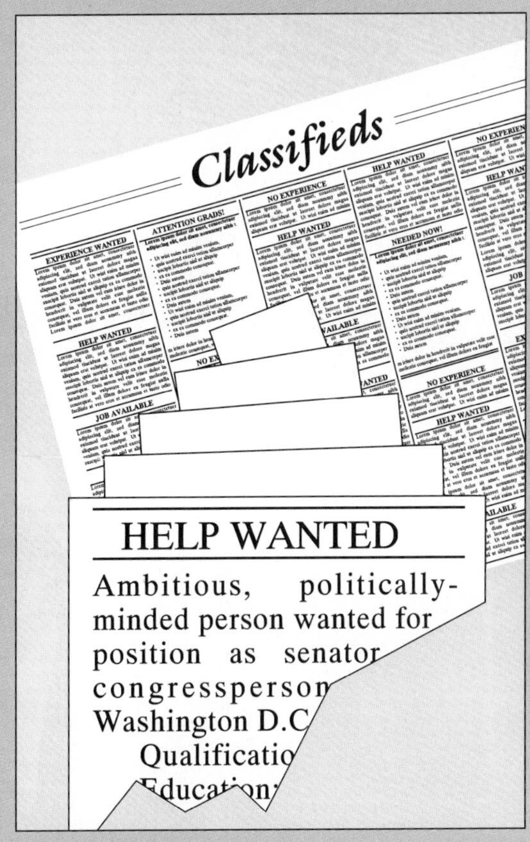

CHAPTER INTRODUCTION

Instructional Objectives

By the end of the chapter students should be able to:

- List the legislative powers of Congress.
- Describe the concepts of expressed and implied powers.
- Identify the nonlegislative powers of Congress.

Using the Keynote

Begin by asking the students to define the term *tyranny:* What is it? Under what conditions does it exist? What happens to citizens who live under tyranny? How do they respond? Then let a volunteer read aloud the quotation from James Madison. Encourage discussion by asking: How did Madison define *tyranny?* How is his definition different from the definitions we have already discussed? Why do you think Madison named these conditions "the very definition of tyranny"? How would you restate this quotation in your own words? In concluding this discussion, you may want to have the students recall the time during which Madison served as president: What were the conditions in this country during his presidency? Do you think Madison's idea still holds true?

Introducing the Chapter

Before the students read the Introduction, you may want to write the word *power* on the chalkboard. Ask the students questions such as these: What is power? How can it be used?

Then focus the discussion on the power to make laws: Who holds the power to make laws in this country? Why is that such an important power? What responsibilities are associated with that power?

Previewing the Sections

Section 1 Have the students look through Section 1, noting the main headings, the subheadings, and the special features. Then have the students list at least five questions they expect to have answered as they study this section.

Section 2 Have volunteers read aloud the main headings, the table titles, the special feature titles, and the photo captions in Section 2. Then help the students anticipate the section content by asking questions such as these: What does nonlegislative mean? What do you already know about the nonlegislative powers of the Congress? Why is understanding these powers important to every citizen?

CHAPTER 13

The Powers of Congress

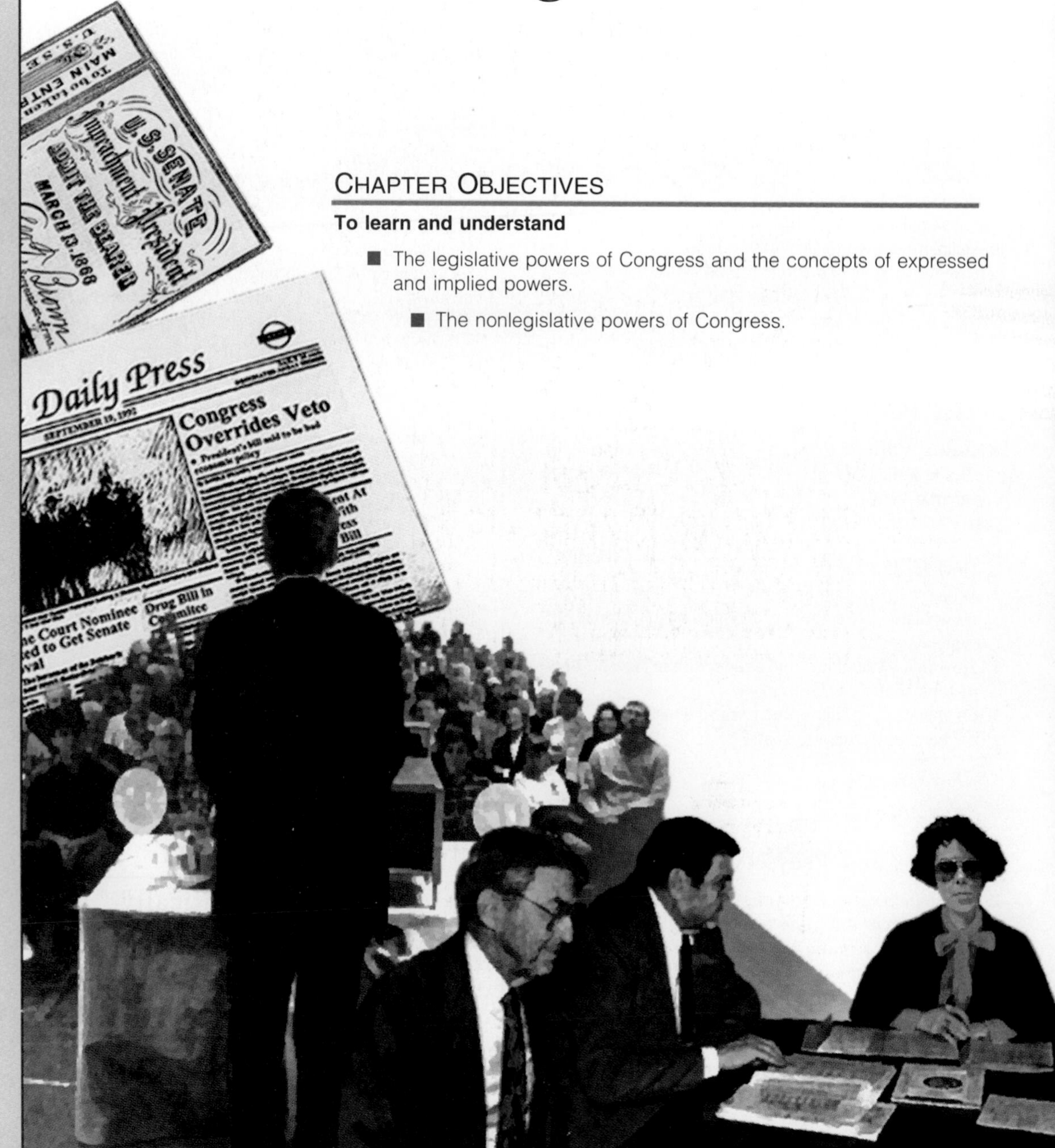

CHAPTER OBJECTIVES

To learn and understand

- The legislative powers of Congress and the concepts of expressed and implied powers.
- The nonlegislative powers of Congress.

West's American Government Assignment Guide

Activity Sheets
Basic Concepts 13 *TRB* (Reteaching)
Enrichment Activity 13 *TRB*
Building Social Studies Skills 13 *TRB*

Quizzes
Chapter 13 Section 1 Quiz *TRB*
Chapter 13 Section 2 Quiz *TRB*

Tests
Chapter 13 Test A *TRB*
Chapter 13 Test B *TRB*
Chapter 13 Test Bank *TRB*
Chapter 13 WESTEST Computerized Testing

Social Studies Tool Kit Software
Chapter 13 Activity

SECTION 1

Points to Stress
- The expressed powers.
- Powers of Congress regarding the budget and economy.
- Powers Congress has relative to foreign affairs.
- The extent of the expressed powers possessed by Congress.
- The necessary and proper clause and its applications.

Kickoff Activity
Ask the students to think about the term *tax:* What does this term bring to mind? Explain to the students that the power to tax is only one of Congress's legislative powers.

Working with the Preview Questions
Let volunteers read these study questions aloud, and encourage the students to discuss what they already know in response to each question.

Teaching Strategies

Introduction
After the students have read the brief section introduction, let several volunteers restate Article I, Section 1 in their own words. Then guide the students in defining and comparing the meanings of *delegated, expressed,* and *enumerated.* Encourage the students to create their own sentences demonstrating the specific meanings of these words.

Discussion Starter
Focus the students' attention on the phrase *power of the purse:* What is this power? Why is it so important? Is this an important power only within the government—or is it significant in businesses, and even families?

Keynote

"The accumulation of all powers, legislative, executive, and judiciary, in the same hands, whether one, a few, or many . . . may justly be pronounced the very definition of tyranny."

—— **James Madison**
(1751–1836) Fourth President of the United States

INTRODUCTION

The power to make laws for an entire nation is a tremendous responsibility. The founders recognized this, which is perhaps why they devoted the first and lengthiest article of the Constitution to carefully spelling out the powers of Congress. It is also why they reserved certain powers to the states, denied large areas of power to Congress, and gave other powers to the judicial and executive branches. They also stipulated that some powers would be shared. They felt, as illustrated by James Madison's statement above, that powers must be divided among the three branches of government. This sharing and division of powers is part of the system of checks and balances they created to avoid what James Madison called "the very definition of tyranny." For example, the president can veto an act of Congress and the Supreme Court has the power to declare acts of Congress unconstitutional. Although the powers of Congress are great, they are also limited.

SECTION 1

Legislative Powers

Preview Questions

- What is the concept of expressed powers?
- What powers does Congress have concerning the nation's budget and economy?
- What powers does Congress have concerning foreign affairs?
- What other expressed powers does Congress possess?
- What is the necessary and proper clause and how has it been applied?

Article I, Section 1 of the Constitution provides that all powers to make laws for the United States government shall be given to Congress. It reads:

> All legislative Powers herein granted shall be vested in a Congress of the United States, which shall consist of a Senate and House of Representatives.

That is, Congress is the only one of the three branches of the federal government that has the power to make laws. Because legislative powers are directly listed, they are referred to as the **expressed powers**. Sometimes they are also called the **delegated** or **enumerated powers**.

Expressed Powers

Although the powers of Congress are spelled out in the Constitution, the actual scope of these powers is not. The wording is brief and very general. The scope and content of these powers has been defined by how Congress has used its powers over the years, and by the interpretations handed down by the Supreme Court.

The Power to Tax and Spend The first power listed in Article 1, Section 8, gives Congress the power to:

> [levy] and collect taxes, duties, imports, and excises, to pay the debts, and provide for the common defense and general welfare of the United States.

This clause gives Congress the power to collect and to spend money. This "power of the purse" is among the most important powers of Congress. The main purpose of the power to tax is to raise the money needed to finance the operations of government. Under the Articles of Confederation, Congress had no power of taxation; as a result the government never had enough money to function well. To remedy this, the Constitution granted Congress such power.

Discussion Starter
Help the students discuss Congress's power to collect income taxes: How and why did Congress secure this power for itself? What other groups have the power to collect income taxes? Does your state exercise that power? Why or why not? How do most people respond to the requirement of paying income taxes? How do you think income taxes affect the relationships between members of Congress and their constituents?

Enrichment
Let a group of volunteers research Congress's use of tariffs on imported goods: On what specific goods are tariffs charged? Why? Whom are these tariffs intended to protect? How have businesses and consumers responded to these tariffs? What international concerns have the tariffs raised? Have these volunteers report their findings to the rest of the class.

Cooperative Learning
Let the students work in small groups to identify and learn about specific departments and agencies (such as the Department of Defense and the Environmental Protection Agency named in the text). The group members should work together to find out about the responsibilities and the power of their chosen department or agency; then they should gather information about its current budget. Have the members of each group share their findings with the rest of the class.

Critical Thinking Skills
Guide the students in analyzing the importance of Congress's power to raise and spend money: What other powers are associated with Congress's power to raise and spend money? How does this affect the attitudes and deportment

Originally, Congress was not allowed by the Constitution to impose a direct tax except in proportion to each state's population. A **direct tax** is any tax that must be paid directly to the government by the taxpayer (as opposed to an **indirect tax**, such as a sales tax, which is paid to a merchant, who in turn remits it to the government). This prevented the federal government from levying taxes on personal or corporate income. In 1913, Congress ratified the Sixteenth Amendment to change this. According to this amendment,

> The Congress shall have the power to lay and collect taxes on incomes, from whatever source derived, without apportionment among several States, and without regard to any census or enumeration.

The Sixteenth Amendment provided for the collection of income taxes without regard to a state's population. Income taxes have since become a major source of federal taxes.

Congress also has the power to levy taxes to regulate the growth and strength of our economy. For example, tariffs on imported goods raise the price of foreign goods and are sometimes used to protect American companies from foreign competition. Congress also uses its taxation power to regulate the economy by decreasing or increasing tax rates. For example, Congress may try to stimulate the economy by lowering individual income taxes, thus giving taxpayers more income to spend.

All **revenue bills**—bills proposed to raise money—must start in the House of Representatives, and almost all important work on tax laws occurs within the House Ways and Means Committee. The Senate, however, must vote in favor of a revenue bill in order for it to become law.

After the money is raised through taxes, Congress's role does not stop. Congress also has power of **appropriation**, which means it has the power to authorize government spending. Article 1, Section 9 of the Constitution states, "No money shall be drawn from the Treasury, but in consequence of [except by] appropriations made by law." Thus, before the federal government can spend money, Congress must pass a law authorizing that a certain amount of money can be spent on a particular program. For example, Congress must approve spending before the Department of Defense or the Environmental Protection Agency can carry out their programs.

The powers to raise and spend money are more important than they seem. They allow Congress to determine national policy in many different areas because policy does not take place without money. Government agencies could not operate without money to carry out their many programs and services, such as national defense, highway construction, maintenance of national parks, and public assistance.

The Power to Borrow The powers to tax and spend are not enough because the government often spends more than it collects in taxes and other revenues. The Constitution also gives Congress the power to borrow

Federal money raised through taxes is used for many projects, such as this road construction project on Interstate 95 in North Carolina. Is this an example of a revenue or an appropriation?

Caption Answer Students should understand that revenue is money raised, while appropriations represent money spent.

of other groups and of individuals toward the Congress?

Enrichment
Ask one of the students to learn more about government bonds and to share answers to these questions with the rest of the class: Who can buy government bonds? Who buys most bonds? How and where can bonds be purchased? How does the buyer make money on a government bond? How does the government make money on a bond?

Comprehension
To help the students understand the size of the national debt, you might ask these questions: How many millions of dollars is the national debt? How many thousands of dollars? You may also want to have the student write out the figure for 3 trillion.

Enrichment
Ask all the students to research the most recently approved federal budget: What important changes were made from the previous budget? What compromises were made between the interests of the executive branch and those of Congress? How were those compromises achieved?

Extension
Let several interested students research bankruptcy: How does an individual declare bankruptcy? What are the results of declaring bankruptcy? What different kinds of bankruptcy are available to companies? What are the requirements and the results of each? Have the students summarize this information in a chart to be posted in the classroom.

Discussion Starter
Help the students discuss Congress's regulation in interstate commerce: Why is the power to regulate this commerce important? To whom is it important? Why?

money to help pay for the cost of government. One method of borrowing is by authorizing the sale of **government bonds**, which are government "IOU's" bought by individuals or companies. In exchange for borrowing the money, the government promises to repay the buyer of the bond at a later time plus interest.

Of course the debt incurred does not just disappear. The borrowed money makes up the **national debt**—the amount of money the government owes at any given time period. In 1992, the nation's debt to the public was about $3 trillion. The Constitution does not state how much this debt can be, so Congress has tried to do so by setting a ceiling, or limit, on it. The ceiling, however, has been raised year after year as the government continues to borrow more money.

Ultimate control of spending is not entirely up to Congress. It is directly related to the national economy and the **federal budget**, which is the federal government's financial plan for how it operates. The federal budget lays out in detail how much money the government will spend, how it will be divided among agencies and programs, and from what sources the money will come. Since 1921 the executive branch has prepared a federal budget proposal every year and submitted it to Congress every January. The House and Senate budget committees and the Congressional Budget Office can then adjust the budget by adding or eliminating programs. The final budget agreement is usually a compromise between what the executive branch wants and what Congress wants.

"BROTHER, CAN YOU SPARE A HUNDRED BILLION OR SO TOWARD THE INTEREST ON THE LAST TRILLION OR TWO?"
©1984 HERBLOCK

from Herblock Through The Looking Glass (W.W. Norton, 1984)

Coining Money and Setting Bankruptcy Laws The Constitution gives Congress the power "to coin money [and] regulate the value thereof." This **currency power** was given to Congress to prevent the problems and confusion caused by each state issuing its own brand of money under the Articles of Confederation. The uniform value of coins and paper money is fixed by Congress and is the same in any state or territory. All the currency issued by the federal government is considered legal tender and must be accepted as payment for all debts. In relation to its currency power, Congress has the power to punish *counterfeiters*—people who print false paper money or other government notes or who make coins illegally.

Congress also has the power to set uniform laws for dealing with bankruptcy throughout the United States. **Bankruptcy** is being legally declared unable to pay one's debts. Congress can establish the legal proceedings by which the person filing for bankruptcy has the things he or she owns distributed among those to whom the debt is owed.

Commerce Power Article 1, Section 8 of the Constitution gives Congress the power to "regulate Commerce with foreign Nations, and among the several States, and with the Indian Tribes." Commerce means the buying and selling of goods on a large scale. Trade between states is known as **interstate commerce**. Under the Articles of Confederation, Congress had no power to regulate interstate commerce and very little authority over foreign trade. This lack of control led to intense rivalries and economic wars among the states. They began taxing each other's goods and restricting the flow of products across their borders. The result was chaos.

In order to give the nation a stable economy, the writers of the Constitution gave Congress a broad grant of power to regulate both foreign and interstate commerce. What "commerce" has meant, however, has not always been clear. In the first case to reach the Supreme

Cooperative Learning
Divide the class into five or six groups, and ask the members of each group to discuss the broad definition of commerce established by the Supreme Court. Then have group members work together to list at least 12 specific transactions that fall under this broad definition of commerce.

Discussion Starter
Help the students use this broadening definition of commerce to review the concept of the Constitution as a living document: Why were the framers unable to interpret commerce as it is now interpreted? How did the framers avoid restricting the Constitution to their understanding of commerce?

Discussion Starter
Encourage the students to consider the powers Congress holds over foreign relations: What relationship between the president and the Congress is facilitated by this distribution of powers? How do the current president and the current Congress seem to handle these relationships?

Enrichment
Ask three groups of students to research the three wars that Congress never declared—the Korean War, the Vietnam War, and the Persian Gulf War: Why was each war entered into? Why did Congress never declare that war? What results has that lack of a formal declaration of war had? Why? Let each group present its findings to the rest of the class in an oral report.

Caption Answer Article I, Section VIII of the Constitution gives Congress the power to "regulate commerce with foreign nations and among the several states, and with the Indian tribes."

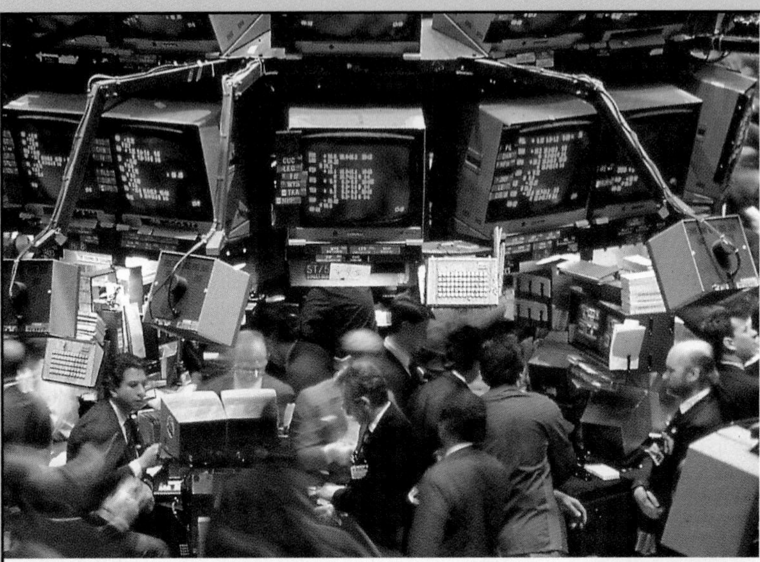

◀ Commerce can take many forms, from a small transaction at a local convenience store to the hustle and bustle of the New York Stock Exchange, shown here. From where does Congress derive its power to regulate commerce?

Caption Answer
Congress's authority in foreign relations comes from such powers as treaty approval, the declaration of war, the approval of appointments for diplomatic officers, and its control over funding for national defense.

Court involving the commerce clause (*Gibbons* v. *Ogden* in 1824), Chief Justice John Marshall interpreted "commerce" to mean not only the buying and selling of goods and services, but nearly all forms of commercial and business activity. Today, this includes banking and finance, radio and television broadcasting, labor management relations, and railroad and airline transportation.

Marshall's broad interpretation of commerce has given Congress the power to regulate these and other areas of life far beyond what the framers originally envisioned. For example, Congress used the commerce clause to pass the Civil Rights Act of 1964, which prohibits discrimination because of race, religion, or national origin in places of public accommodation such as restaurants, motels, and hotels. It also prohibits discrimination in employment. The commerce clause has also been used as a basis for minimum wage laws and for laws protecting workers' rights. It has been used to pass laws prohibiting the transportation across state borders of explosives, diseased livestock, narcotics, and falsely labeled drugs.

Power in Foreign Relations Congress shares powers concerning foreign relations with the president, who is primarily responsible for American foreign policy. Congress's authority in foreign relations comes from many of its other powers, which include the power to approve treaties, to declare war, to approve the appointments of diplomatic officers made by the president, and to regulate foreign commerce. Through its spending power, Congress also has control over funding for national defense and foreign aid.

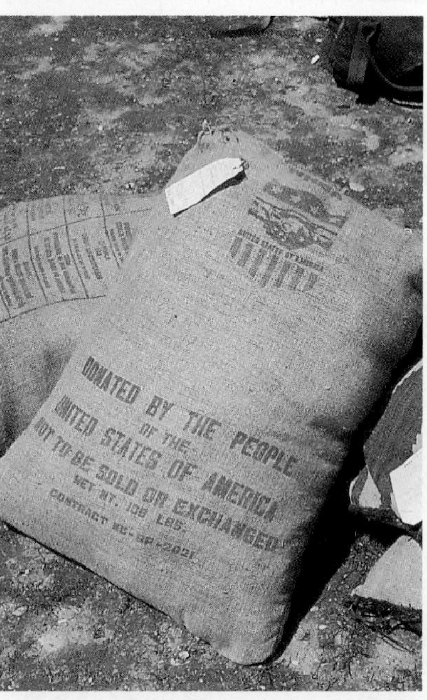

▲ One way Congress has power in foreign relations is through its control over funding for foreign aid, such as this wheat bound for Afghanistan. What are other ways in which Congress has power in foreign relations?

The War Powers The Constitution grants war powers to both the legislative and executive branches. Only Congress has the power to declare war and is responsible for raising and maintaining the armed forces of the United States. The president, however, is commander in chief.

Vocabulary
Ask volunteers to define the noun *resolution* as it is used here, the *War Powers Resolution:* How is a resolution different from a law? From a proclamation?

Enrichment
Have two volunteers research the 60-day and 90-day limits: Have they ever been invoked? If so, when and where? Let these volunteers tell the rest of the class about their findings.

Enrichment
Ask another volunteer to investigate regulation of the post office: What body oversees its functioning? How can postal rates be changed? When was the last postal rate change approved? Why? Have this volunteer prepare a short written report, to be posted in the classroom.

Discussion Starter
Encourage the students to discuss copyrights and patents: Why are these rights important? Who makes use of them? When and how can they be used? How are copyrights and patents different? What specific examples of each can you cite?

Comprehension
Have the students recall and review the process of naturalization.

The framers almost overwhelmingly rejected the proposal to give the president the power to initiate war because they believed that Congress would not rush into war as quickly as a president would.

Congress has declared war only five times in our history. American forces have, however, been involved in combat on foreign soil many times without a declaration of war by Congress. Most of the military actions were ordered by presidents who claimed military force was needed to protect American lives, interests, or property abroad. The Korean War (1950–1953), the Vietnam War (1964–1973) and the Persian Gulf War (1991) were fought without a formal declaration of war by Congress.

During the Vietnam War, many members of Congress felt the president's power to involve the nation in undeclared wars must be checked. In an effort to regain its constitutional war-making power and to limit the president's power, Congress passed the War Powers Resolution in 1973. This law requires the president to inform Congress of the circumstances and scope of the proposed military action within forty-eight hours of sending American troops abroad. If Congress does not approve the action within sixty days, the president must withdraw the troops. The deadline may be extended to ninety days if the president states that additional time is needed for a safe withdrawal.

Judicial Powers Congress has the power to create federal courts below the level of the Supreme Court. In addition, the Senate must approve the appointment of judges to these courts and to the Supreme Court. Congress also has the power to impeach any civil officer of the United States. The power of impeachment is a nonlegislative power that we will discuss shortly.

Powers to Establish Post Offices, Copyrights, and Patents The Constitution gives Congress the power ''to establish post offices and post roads,'' which means Congress may pass laws concerning the carrying and protection of the mails. This includes the power to prevent the use of mails for fraud (deception or trickery usually used to cheat someone out of money) or for the carrying of outlawed materials.

Granting copyrights and patents is also a congressional power. A **copyright** is the exclusive right of a person to publish, print, or sell his or her literary, musical, or artistic work for a definite period of time. Copyrights cover a wide variety of creative works such as books, plays, paintings, sculptures, musical compositions, song lyrics, motion pictures, and photographs. Under the present law, a copyright is in effect for the lifetime of the person who created the work plus fifty years. A **patent** is the exclusive right of an inventor to use or sell his or her invention for a definite number of years. Presently, a patent is in force for seventeen years.

Powers of Naturalization and Dominion Over Territories The exclusive power ''to establish an uniform rule of naturalization'' belongs to Congress. This is the process by which people from foreign countries may become American citizens. Naturalization was discussed in Chapter 7.

Spectators to the impeachment trial of President Andrew Johnson were admitted by ticket only. Impeachment is only one of Congress' powers related to the judiciary. What other judicial powers does Congress have?

Caption Answer Congress has the power to create federal courts below the level of the Supreme Court, and the Senate has the power to approve the appointment of judges to these courts and to the Supreme Court. It might also be noted that Congress makes *all* the laws that are adjudicated by federal courts.

TEACHING BUILDING SOCIAL STUDIES SKILLS

Read

Introduce this feature by asking the students to give their own definitions of these terms: *cause, effect, correlation.* Then ask several students to read the feature aloud to the rest of the class.

Discuss

Help the students discuss the content of this Building Social Studies Skills feature by asking questions such as these: Why is there a correlation between being young and not voting? What do you think causes young people not to vote? What caused the deaths of the presidents elected in years ending with zero? What is a spurious correlation? What other spurious correlations can you cite?

Analyze and Apply

Let the students work in small groups to discuss what they know of local politics—within the town or county, within the state, or even within the school. Ask the members of each group to write five cause-and-effect statements about local politics and five statements of correlation.

Review

Present these review questions: What is the difference between a cause-and-effect relationship and a correlation? Why is understanding that difference important?

BUILDING SOCIAL STUDIES SKILLS

Cause and Effect versus Correlation

The world is full of correlations, or relationships. There seems to be a correlation, for example, between exercising and good health. But it is important to remember that correlation is not the same as causation. Causation occurs when a change in one variable *causes* a change in another. There are scientific ways to prove such causation.

There are numerous correlations that can be discovered in American politics. During election time, analysts might expect to find correlations between being African American and voting Democratic, being wealthy and voting Republican, and being young and not voting at all. Although certain demographic traits are correlated or associated with voting patterns, these are not *causal* explanations. Being under thirty does not cause people not to vote. Rather, the transient lifestyles of younger Americans and their lack of attachment to a community and family tend to keep them away from the polls.

Consider another example. Every president elected in a year ending with the number zero, from William H. Harrison in 1840 to John F. Kennedy in 1960, died in office. The correlation is between years ending in zero and presidential death. It seems quite obvious, however, that presidential death was not *caused* by the years ending in zero. Instead, this is one of those strange coincidences (called *spurious correlations* by social scientists) in American politics.

These and other correlations have nothing to do with causation. In reading and hearing about American politics it is important not to read causation into information that is simply correlational.

PRACTICING YOUR SKILLS

1. Write a brief essay describing a cause and effect relationship with which you are familiar. Explain why this is a cause and effect relationship and not merely a correlation.
2. Read an article concerning the stock market. This can be found in the business section of your local newspaper, or in a national newspaper such as the *Wall Street Journal*. Try to determine whether the writer's assessment of why the stock market went up or down involves a correlation between two events or a true cause-and-effect relationship.

Congress also has the power to acquire, manage, and dispose of various federal territories. Thus Congress has passed laws to govern territories such as the Virgin Islands, Guam, Puerto Rico, and other areas that are not states. The power also covers hundreds of military installations, national parks, dockyards, prison facilities, and other federal holdings throughout the United States.

Implied Powers

Not all of the powers of Congress are specifically listed in the Constitution. There are other powers known as **implied powers**, which are based on the last clause in Article 1, Section 8. This clause gives Congress the power:

> To make all laws which shall be necessary and proper for carrying into execution the foregoing powers, and all other powers vested by this Constitution in the Government of the United States, or in any department or office thereof.

This clause, called the **necessary and proper clause**, is also referred to as the **elastic clause** because it has allowed Congress to stretch and greatly expand its powers. Much of the adaptability of the Constitution can be traced to this provision.

Strict or Loose Interpretation? What do the words of the necessary and proper clause mean? How far can Congress stretch its powers? Almost from the time the words were written, their meaning has been under debate. The first dispute erupted in 1789 when Alexander Hamilton, as secretary of the Treasury, urged Congress to set up a federal bank.

A group opposing the idea, led by Secretary of State Thomas Jefferson, argued that the Constitution gave Congress no such power. This group was known as the **strict constructionists**, those that maintained that Congress could do only the things absolutely necessary to carry out its expressed powers.

Comprehension
Ask the students to identify areas and factualities in their state that are federal holdings.

Discussion Starter
Ask the students about the importance of implied powers for Congress: Why is it important that congress not be limited to powers specifically defined within the Constitution? What problems might arise from the use of implied powers? Why?

Discussion Starter
Guide the students in discussing the elastic clause of the Constitution: How would you define the phrase *necessary and proper?* Are both words—*necessary* and *proper*—essential to this phrase? Why or why not? What attitudes are implied by the views of the strict constructionists? By those of the loose constructionists? Would you have sided with the strict constructionists or the loose constructionists? Why? Encourage the students to express and support varying points of view.

Powers Granted to Congress by Article I, Section 8, of the Constitution

Expressed Powers

Taxation of goods Congress can set and collect taxes on goods as they are manufactured, sold, used, or imported [Clause 1].

Borrowing money Congress can borrow money on the credit of the United States [Clause 2].

Regulation of commerce Congress can regulate interstate and foreign trade [Clause 3].

Bankruptcy Congress can make laws with respect to bankruptcy [Clause 4].

Naturalization Congress can determine how aliens can become U.S. citizens [Clause 4].

Money Congress can mint coins and can print and circulate paper money [Clause 5].

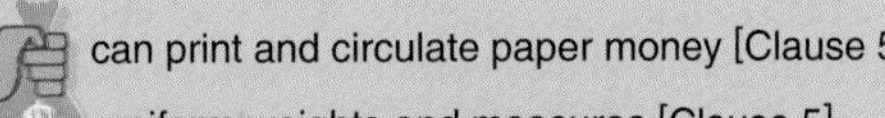

Standards Congress can establish uniform weights and measures [Clause 5].

Punishment of counterfeiters Congress can punish counterfeiters of American currency [Clause 6].

Post offices and roads Congress can establish post offices and all routes over which mail is carried [Clause 7].

Copyrights and patents Congress can grant copyrights to authors and composers, and patents to inventors [Clause 8].

Lower courts Congress can set up all federal courts except the Supreme Court [Clause 9].

Punishment for certain acts in international waters Congress can prohibit acts of piracy outside U.S. territory and can punish certain other acts that all nations prohibit [Clause 10].

Declaration of war Congress can declare war and, until international law banned such action in the mid-nineteenth century, could authorize private parties to capture and destroy enemy ships in wartime [Clause 11].

The army Congress can raise and maintain an army [Clause 12].

The navy Congress can create and maintain a navy [Clause 13].

Regulation of the armed forces Congress can set rules for military forces [Clause 14].

The militia Congress can call into service the militia (known today as the National Guard) [Clause 15].

Regulation of the militia Congress can organize, arm, and discipline the militia, and can govern it when it is in the service of the United States [Clause 16].

Creation of Washington, D.C. Congress can govern Washington, D.C., and can erect such buildings there that would seem necessary for the seat of the U.S. government [Clause 17].

Implied Powers

The Elastic Clause Congress can make all laws necessary and proper for executing the foregoing expressed powers [Clause 18].

▲ FIGURE 13–1 **Powers Granted to Congress by Article I, Section 8, of the Constitution.** The table above lists both the expressed and the implied powers granted to Congress by the Constitution. How would you describe the difference between the expressed powers and the implied powers?

This figure content is also featured on *West's American Government Videodisc* (see the index found in the *TRB*) and is available in the transparency package.

Figure Answer Students should understand that the expressed powers are very specifically stated, while the implied powers are derived from the elasticity of the "necessary and proper clause."

TEACHING GOVERNMENT IN ACTION

Read

Before the students begin reading this Case Study, let volunteers define the verb *impound* and the noun *impoundment*. Then let the students read the Case Study independently.

Discuss

Encourage the students to discuss the Case Study by posing questions such as these: What do you think happened to "excess" funds before Congress authorized impoundment? Why is there a built-in conflict between the Congress and the president?

Analyze and Apply

Have the students work in small groups to apply the concept of impoundment to another organization with a budget, such as the school, a family, or a small business: Should impoundment be used within that organization? Why or why not? Have the group members reach an agreement and then work together to write a persuasive essay expressing that point of view.

Review

To help the students review the Case Study, ask these questions: What is impoundment? When and why was it established? When and why was it revoked?

Think About It (Answers)

1. Answers will vary, e.g., the president should have the power of impoundment. Members of Congress are reluctant to cut programs that benefit their district or state. The president has a better overall view of what the entire nation is spending.

2. Answers will vary, e.g., members of Congress do not want programs cut that benefit their district or state.

3. Answers will vary, e.g., Congress would be more likely to spend more for domestic programs because they are directly accountable to constituents for programs.

4. Answers will vary, e.g., although partisan conflicts will arise, the differing priorities of the offices are a more significant factor. The president's broad cuts often have very specific negative consequences for a lawmaker's constituents.

Reteaching Strategies

1. Have the students work in groups to review the information in the section. As they review, have them list the lessons that the framers learned from the Articles of Confederation—specific powers granted to Congress that had not been included in the Articles.

2. Let partners work together to write their own definitions of these terms: *power of the purse, direct tax, indirect tax, appropriation, national debt.*

Evaluation Strategies

1. Have the students write their responses to the Section 1 Review questions.

GOVERNMENT IN ACTION

CASE STUDY

Who Controls the Federal Budget?

For more than a century after the creation of the American republic, Congress, with few exceptions, controlled the nation's purse strings. The increasing complexity of the American economy, however, has led to fragmented congressional control over the budget and an expanded role for the president. In 1921, when Congress created the Bureau of the Budget, it authorized the president to withhold funds from being spent in order to save money if "excess" funds had been authorized by Congress. This process in which the president either defers or refuses to spend money appropriated by Congress is known as **impoundment**.

During the next half-century, monies appropriated by Congress for various purposes were withheld by presidents, but no major confrontations between Congress and any president erupted. Then Richard Nixon arrived in the White House. President Nixon believed Congress was spending too much, so he extended impoundment power to new levels, impounding by some estimates as much as $2.5 billion that had been appropriated by Congress for various purposes. In 1974 Congress acted to restore its "power of the purse" by passing the Budget and Impoundment Control Act, which established a permanent budget committee for each house of Congress and put severe limits on the president's ability to impound funds. It also created the Congressional Budget Office (CBO) to provide financial experts to help members of Congress plan the budget. The act requires that appropriated funds be spent unless both houses vote in favor of a presidential request that they not be spent.

Analyses of the Budget and Impoundment Control Act indicate that it has had limited success in changing the budget process. It did equip Congress with more staff resources for evaluating the budget, but has done little or nothing to control the level of federal government spending. The new House and Senate Budget Committees have provided additional access points for members of Congress and special interests to win appropriations. The outcome was higher spending in the 1970s, 1980s, and 1990s.

The endless debate over the size and content of the federal budget between Congress and the president may reflect a built-in conflict between the two branches. Congress has always been more locally focused and responds to local constituencies and pressures. Congresspersons hesitate to make difficult decisions about cutting programs that benefit their district or state. The presidency, in contrast, is seen as a forum for national interests. As long as this is the case, the two branches will probably disagree over taxing and spending.

Additionally, for much of the post World War II period, the political parties of the president and that of the majority of Congress have been different. Necessarily, conflicts over the budget will arise with a Republican president and a Democratic Congress or a Democratic president and a Republican Congress.

THINK ABOUT IT

1. Should the president have the power of impoundment? Explain.
2. Why would members of Congress want to control the president's power of impoundment?
3. Who would be likely to spend more for domestic programs, Congress or the president? Explain.
4. Which do you think is more likely to cause a budget conflict: The differing priorities of the Office of the President and membership in Congress, or the fact that the president is not a member of the same party that a majority of the members of Congress belong to? Give reasons for your answer.

2. Have the students take the Section 1 Quiz found in the *TRB*.

Section 1 Review (Answers)

1. Article I, Section I of the Constitution.
2. These powers allow Congress to determine national policy in many different areas because policy does not take place without money.
3. The power to borrow, the power to coin money and to make laws with respect to bankruptcy, commerce power, power in foreign relations, war powers, judicial powers, powers to establish post offices and copyrights and patents, and powers of naturalization and dominion over territories.
4. Because it has allowed Congress to stretch and greatly expand its powers. It enables Congress to act beyond the specific listing of expressed (or delegated) powers of Article I, Section 8.
5. The Supreme Court ruled that the necessary and proper clause gave Congress the right to make any laws necessary to carry out its other powers.
6. Answers will vary, e.g., the necessary and proper clause does not allow Congress to involve itself in every aspect of American life. It only gives Congress the right to make laws necessary to carry out its other powers that are set out in the Constitution. In contrast, it is true that the federal government has increasingly become involved in more and more aspects of everyone's life.

Alexander Hamilton and his followers looked at the Constitution a little differently. These people were known as the **loose constructionists**, those that believed that the necessary and proper clause gave Congress the power to do anything that might be reasonably "implied" in any of the expressly delegated powers. They argued that the federal bank was the necessary and proper way to carry out the express powers of making currency, taxing, regulating commerce, and borrowing money.

President Washington was persuaded by Hamilton's argument and signed the federal bank bill into law. For the next twenty years, its existence went unchallenged in the courts.

McCulloch* v. *Maryland In 1816, however, with the chartering of the Second Bank of the United States, the debate was reopened. This time the question of strict or loose construction of the Constitution was ruled upon by the Supreme Court in *McCulloch* v. *Maryland* (1819). The Court found the creation of the Second Bank to be necessary and proper in order to carry out the federal government's monetary powers. Far more importantly, the Court thereby supported the loose constructionists' idea that the necessary and proper clause gave Congress the right to make any laws necessary to carry out its other powers.

Over the years, however, the Supreme Court has required that the necessary and proper clause be linked with one or more of the expressed powers before Congress invokes it to take action. The basis for any implied power must always be found among the expressed powers. The doctrine of implied powers has been used, for example, to improve rivers, canals, and other waterways, to create the United States Air Force, to define and provide punishment for federal crimes, and to fix minimum wages.

Section 1 Review

1. Where are the expressed powers set out in the Constitution?
2. Why are commerce and money powers important?
3. What are the other expressed powers of Congress?
4. Why is the necessary and proper clause also called the elastic clause?
5. What is the significance of *McCulloch* v. *Maryland*?
6. **For critical analysis:** Does the necessary and proper clause, when liberally interpreted, allow the federal government to involve itself in virtually any aspect of American life? Explain.

Section 2

Nonlegislative Powers

Preview Questions:

- What role does Congress play in the impeachment process?
- What role has Congress played in the constitutional amendment process?
- What advice and consent must Congress give to the president as part of its nonlegislative powers?
- What powers of investigation does Congress have?
- What is the oversight function and what are the methods of oversight?

As the legislative branch, Congress' most important duty is to make laws; but the Constitution also gives Congress a number of duties besides lawmaking. It requires some nonlegislative functions to be carried out by both houses of Congress, and others to be carried out by only the House or the Senate. Some of these powers involve Congress with the other two branches of government.

Power of Impeachment

One of the most important but least used judicial powers of Congress is the power of impeachment. Article 1, Section 2 of the Constitution grants Congress the power to **impeach**, or to bring formal charges against, any member of the executive or judicial branches of government accused of misconduct or wrongdoing. *Impeachment is not, however, a determination of guilt.*

The House of Representatives has the exclusive power to bring charges of impeachment by a majority vote. Then the case goes before the Senate for trial to determine the person's guilt or innocence. Conviction requires approval of two-thirds of the senators. If the impeachment involves the president, the Chief Justice of the Supreme Court presides over the trial. If convicted, the official may be removed from office and prohibited from ever holding public office again. Once the proceedings are over, the person can be indicted, tried, convicted, and punished in regular courts.

Only thirteen officials have ever been impeached by the House—one president, one senator, one Supreme Court justice, and ten federal judges. Of these, the Senate has convicted five of them, all of whom were federal

SECTION 2

Point to Stress

- Congress's role in the impeachment process.
- The role of Congress in the Constitutional amendment process.
- The advice and consent role Congress plays.
- The powers of investigation possessed by Congress.
- The oversight function and the methods of oversight.

Kickoff Activity

Write the following term on the chalkboard: *advice and consent.* Have the students list at least five words or phrases that the term brings to mind.

Working with the Preview Questions

Ask a volunteer to read these study questions aloud to the rest of the class. Encourage the students to share and discuss the ideas they have now in response to the questions; remind the students that these questions serve as a guide to the content of the section.

Teaching Strategies

Introduction

Have one of the students read the section introduction aloud. Encourage the students to discuss how and why governmental powers are distributed among the House, the Senate, and the other branches of the federal government.

Comprehension

Focus the students' attention on this statement in the text: Impeachment is not a determination of guilt. Why is this distinction important? What term in criminal law is comparable to *impeachment?*

Discussion Starter
Help the students consider and discuss the numbers necessary for conviction in an impeachment: Why do you think a simple majority was not considered sufficient? Why do you think a unanimous vote for conviction is not required? Do you think a two-third vote is fair? Why or why not?

Enrichment
Let a small group of interested students research the background for the recommendation made by the House Judiciary Committee to impeach President Nixon: What events led up to this recommendation? What happened when Nixon resigned the presidency? Ask these students to plan and present a summary of their findings.

A figure on the nonlegislative powers of Congress is featured on *West's American Government Videodisc* (see the index found in the *TRB*) and is available in the transparency package.

Comprehension
Have the students recall what they know about recent amendment proposals: What were the proposals? What outcome did each have?

Vocabulary
Ask the students to explain the meaning of *ceremonial*. Then have them identify other ceremonial roles and discuss the importance of ceremonial roles: Do they still matter to the members of government? To the voters? Why or why not?

Discussion Starter
Ask the students to consider the power of Congress to choose the president and the vice president: Is it likely that Congress will have another opportunity to exercise that power? Why or why not?

Enrichment
Let volunteers research the circumstances under which Gerald Ford and Nelson Rockefeller were confirmed to the vice presidency; have the volunteers report their findings to the rest of the class.

"Hey guys, do you really think we need that clause about impeachment in there?"

judges. The one president to be impeached, Andrew Johnson, was acquitted by the Senate. In 1974, the House Judiciary Committee recommended impeaching President Nixon, but Nixon resigned from office before the case came to a vote in the full House.

Power to Propose Constitutional Amendments

Congress shares with the states the power to propose constitutional amendments. (See Chapter 3). The Constitution provides that amendments may be proposed by a two-thirds vote of both houses of Congress, or at the request of two-thirds of the state legislatures Congress can call for a national convention to propose amendments.

So far, all constitutional amendments have been initiated by Congress. The states have approved twenty-six of the proposed amendments and have failed to ratify only six. To be adopted, an amendment must be ratified by three-quarters of all state legislatures (thirty-eight states) or by a majority vote of conventions in three-quarters of all states. Congress decides which of these procedures is used.

Power to Choose a President

Congress has two responsibilities related to the election of a president. First, in a joint session of Congress, the president of the Senate is authorized to count the electoral votes and declare the winner. This process has become largely ceremonial. Second, if no person has a majority of the electoral votes, the House of Representatives chooses the president, and the Senate chooses the vice president. The House has used this electoral power only twice: to choose Thomas Jefferson in 1801 and John Quincy Adams in 1825.

Under the Twenty-fifth Amendment, both the Senate and the House must confirm the president's choice for vice president whenever that post is vacant due to illness, death, or resignation. That process has been used twice: Gerald Ford was confirmed vice president in 1973 and Nelson Rockefeller in 1974.

Giving Advice and Consent

According to the Constitution, the Senate must approve presidential appointments to many important positions in the executive and judicial branches. Most such appointments involve the promotions of military officers, and Senate action is only a formality. Each year,

TEACHING GOVERNMENT IN ACTION

Read

Before reading this Government in Action profile on Bill Archer, ask the students to name as many individuals from the House of Representatives as they can think of. Ask them why the members of the House of Representatives do not receive the same media attention that the president and important members of his administration do. Is the work that congressmembers do likely to make them as visible as other Washington politicians? Ask whether they feel it would be relatively easy or difficult for a junior member of the House of Representatives to receive much national publicity. Then have volunteers read aloud this Government in Action feature.

Discuss

Help the students to discuss the contents of this feature by asking the following questions: Do you think Texas would be an important state to represent in the Congress? Why or why not? Do you think Houston would be an important city to represent? Why do you think Archer switched parties at the beginning of his political career? How do you think the voters who elected him under one party felt when he switched? Do you think it is more important to consider the individual or the party he is representing when voting in an election?

Analyze and Apply

Have the students work in small groups to analyze Archer's typical daily schedule as provided in the feature. Have each group create a pie chart that would graph the total hours according to categories, such as committee work, "informal work" such as would be done during social events, and any other categories that the students may decide upon. The students should answer the following questions to help them in preparing the graphs: Approximately what percentage of the time is spent in actual meetings? What percentage in "socializing"? What activities, if any, were not mentioned in the daily schedule?

Review

To check their understanding of this feature ask them the following questions: What district does Congressman Archer represent? What committee does Archer serve on? Why do you suppose he is limited to serving on this one committee?

Think About It (Answers)

1. Answers will vary, e.g., a politician may find that on key issues he or she supports the stand taken by the other party, or that the political philosophy of most of the constituency has gradually grown closer to that of the other party.

2. Most bills involving programs needing new tax revenue originate in the Ways and Means Committee. Archer could help block or pass these bills, depending upon their affect on the Seventh District.

GOVERNMENT IN ACTION

A DAY IN THE LIFE

Congressman Bill Archer

Congressman Bill Archer is a Republican congressman from the Seventh District of Texas representing the west side of Houston. A prominent figure on Capitol Hill, Archer is the ranking Republican on the powerful Ways and Means Committee in the House of Representatives. While most members of the House serve on two standing committees, the demands of the Ways and Means Committee are so great that members of this committee are forbidden by House rules from sitting on any other standing committee.

Congressman Archer served as a Texas state representative for two terms beginning in 1966. Originally elected as a Democrat, Archer switched parties during his tenure as a Texas state representative. In 1970, when George Bush decided to resign his Seventh District House Seat to run for the U.S. Senate (Bush lost to Lloyd Bentsen in the election), Bill Archer ran for the vacant seat and has held it since. Archer is extremely popular in his home district and has routinely won reelection by huge margins.

Like all members of Congress, Archer's day is filled by the demands of his position. Many of these demands center around the important business of the Ways and Means Committee and his particular duties as the representative of the Seventh District of Texas. Congressman Archer describes his normal day as follows:

> My normal day begins with a breakfast meeting at 8:00 a.m. or so, followed by appointments with constituents in the office until 10:00 a.m. or 10:30 a.m.
>
> The Ways and Means committee generally meets at 10:00 a.m. and continues meeting throughout the day. The House begins its session usually at noon. The remainder of the day is spent shuttling back and forth between the House floor and the Committee hearing room, with additional time spent in my office in appointments or handling correspondence, phone calls, etc. In addition, there are usually receptions in the evening hosted by visiting groups from Texas—and I go to as many of those as I can to visit with constituents who are there. Usually, I do not get home until 8:00 p.m. or later in the evening.

THINK ABOUT IT

1. What reasons can you think of for a politician to switch parties?
2. How might the Seventh Congressional District of Texas benefit from Archer's position on the Ways and Means Committee?

Discussion Starter
Encourage the students to examine the recent trend toward a closer examination of appointees: What do you think explains this trend? What specific examples of close examination can you cite? Do you consider this trend healthy? Why or why not?

Discussion Starter
Let the students discuss the Senate's role in giving "advice and consent" for the ratification of treaties: How has this role changed? What caused the changes? Do you imagine that further changes will take place? If so, what kinds of changes?

Enrichment
Have one or two students research the results of the Senate's rejection of the Treaty of Versailles: How were the United States' relationships with other countries affected? How was the League of Nations affected? Let these students report their findings to the rest of the class.

Discussion Starter
Help the students discuss the first Congressional investigation: Why do you think Congress undertook this investigation? On what do you think Congress based its assumption of power to investigate? Who—if anyone—do you think probably objected to Congress's assuming this power? Why?

Caption Answer The Senate has proven to be uncommonly selective in its approval of Supreme Court nominations, rejecting approximately 20 percent of the names submitted.

Discussion Starter
Ask the students why the Senate is so selective in approving Supreme Court nominations: How long do justices serve on the Supreme Court? What kinds of influence can they exert there? How do presidents usually use nominations to the Supreme Court? Do you think this use of the power to nominate is appropriate? Why or why not?

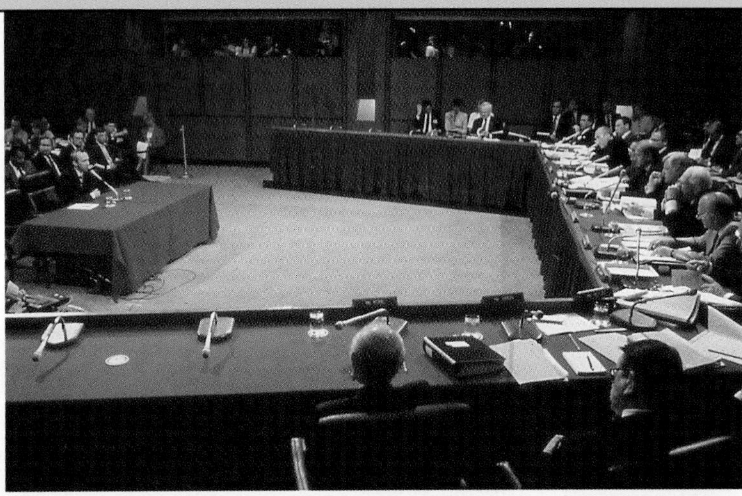

Confirmation hearings, such as the one shown here for then Supreme Court nominee David Souter, are conducted by the Senate prior to voting for or against the approval of Supreme Court appointments. Has the Senate rejected many Supreme Court nominees?

however, the Senate looks more closely at several hundred nominations to major posts, which include appointments to the Cabinet (see Chapter 15), independent boards and agencies, major foreign service posts, and all federal judicial posts including Supreme Court nominees.

Over the years, the Senate has approved most presidential choices of Cabinet officers.[1] In the last twenty years, however, senators have examined the appointees more closely, and have tended to raise more questions about the candidates' finances, personal background, and private lives. For example, when President Bush nominated former Texas senator John Tower to be his secretary of defense, lengthy hearings were held, particularly concerning his private life. The Senate finally voted to reject the Tower appointment. Bush also lost his first judicial nomination (the first of more than 70) in 1991 when a Senate committee rejected Kenneth Ryskamp for a federal appeals court seat.

Presidential choices of federal officials who serve in the various states as federal judges, United States attorneys, or regional directors of federal agencies are also often debated. By the long-standing practice of **senatorial courtesy**, the Senate usually will reject a nominee for a state appointment to federal office if senators from the state concerned are opposed to the nomination.

The Senate is most selective in the approval of Supreme Court nominations. About 20 percent of the names submitted for Court membership have been rejected by the Senate.

In major foreign policy affairs, the Senate also has the responsibility to give its "advice and consent" to treaties made by the president. This is done by a process of ratification, in which two-thirds of the members present must vote in favor of the treaty. During the years following the adoption of the Constitution, the Senate as a whole advised the president before the treaty was signed. Today, the president usually consults with the Senate Foreign Relations Committee and certain influential senators. When a treaty comes up for vote, the Senate can approve, reject, or amend it.

The most controversial battle in the twentieth century over Senate ratification of a treaty was in 1919, when the Senate rejected the Treaty of Versailles, the general peace agreement to end World War I. The treaty included provisions for the League of Nations. Forty-nine senators voted for the pact and thirty-five against, but the vote was seven short of the necessary two-thirds. More recently, in 1980, Senate opposition to the second Strategic Arms Limitations Treaty (SALT II) between the United States and the former Soviet Union was so strong that the treaty was never submitted for ratification.

Even though the House does not have the right under the Constitution to ratify treaties, it does control the purse strings for funding needed to put some treaties into effect. For this reason, the president usually finds it politically beneficial to consult with influential House members on most treaty matters.

In recent years, presidents have often bypassed the Senate by entering into executive agreements with other countries. (See Chapter 16.)

Investigative Powers

Through its investigative committees, Congress determines where new laws are needed, reviews the effectiveness of existing laws, and sees whether the executive branch is administering programs as they were intended

1. Of the more than six hundred Cabinet appointments made, only twelve have been rejected. The first rejection was in 1834 when the Senate rejected Roger B. Taney, President Andrew Jackson's nominee for secretary of treasury.

TEACHING CITIZENSHIP SKILLS AND RESPONSIBILITIES

Read

Let the students begin by reading and reacting to the title of this feature, How to Communicate with Members of Congress: Why do voters—and others—want to communicate with members of Congress? What particular interests do you have in communicating with your representative or senators? What do you already know about communicating with your Congress members? After a brief discussion, let several volunteers read the feature aloud to the rest of the class.

Discuss

Ask questions such as these to stimulate discussion of the feature: Why is each of these guidelines for letters important? What might happen to your letter if you disregard these guidelines? Where and how might you be able to visit one of your legislators? What plans should you make before you call a legislator's office? Why? Why are legislators interested in speaking to student groups?

Analyze and Apply

Have the students work together to plan an appropriate invitation for one of their legislators to speak at a school function. Help them work together to plan, write, and send a letter issuing that invitation.

Review

Ask the students these review questions: What are three of the guidelines you should follow in writing to a member of Congress? Where and how can citizens visit their legislators?

Enrichment

Ask one of the students to research and report to the rest of the class on the Supreme Court's 1927 decision upholding the constitutionality of Congressional investigations.

Discussion Starter

Encourage the students to consider and discuss fact-finding trips made by members of Congress: What purpose do such trips have? Do you believe the purpose of most trips could be more effectively or efficiently served by other means? If so, by what means? If not, why not? What attitude do constituents often have toward their Congress members' fact-finding trips? Why? Do you support these negative attitudes? Why or why not?

CITIZENSHIP SKILLS AND RESPONSIBILITIES

How to Communicate With Members of Congress

Members of Congress get hundreds of letters, calls, and visits weekly, and cannot possibly handle every request personally. If you want your views heard, you need to know what to do. There are certain steps you can take to make your communication with congressional representatives more effective.

Write Follow these guidelines for effective written communication:

- Address the person properly, using his or her full title.
- Make your letter as brief as possible. Get straight to the point.
- If the subject of the letter is a bill or issue, mention it in the first paragraph.
- Write as soon as possible. Make sure the issue is current.
- Give reasons for supporting your position. Be specific and constructive.
- Be sure your letter is well thought out. Such a letter is more likely to be considered.
- Refer to any personal contact you or your family have had with the member, his or her family, friends, or staff.
- Avoid signing a form letter. Compose one in your own words.
- Compliment the member for a job well done if you feel he or she is serving your district or state well.

Visit If you go to Washington, D.C., you may be able to visit your legislator there. A few weeks before your trip, call or write for an appointment. If you do not or cannot go to Washington, you can visit your legislator when he or she is in your home district: during holidays, congressional recess, and some weekends. Call the local or district office and arrange an appointment with the member's assistants. In your visit, use the same guidelines presented for writing a letter: Be brief, give reasons for your position, be specific and constructive, and give credit where it is due.

Call Phone calls can be made by dialing 202-224-3121, the number for both the House and Senate. Then ask for the member's office. Identify yourself and explain the reason for your call. You will be given the opportunity to speak with a staff member who handles the subjects about which you are concerned.

Invite One of the best ways to see your legislator is to invite him or her to speak to a group. Legislators are sometimes interested in speaking to student groups. Remember your legislators are more likely to listen to you in the future if their contacts are positive.

TAKING ACTION

1. Compose a letter to one of your legislators voicing a concern you have about a current issue.
2. Arrange a visit to a legislator's office when he or she is in your district. Carefully prepare what you will say ahead of time. Report to the class after your visit.

to be carried out. Subjects may range from foreign policy or the influence of organized crime to the collapse of the savings and loan industry.

The power to conduct investigations is not specifically granted in the Constitution. Nevertheless, the first congressional investigation was held in 1792 to look into the slaughter of six hundred American soldiers led by General Arthur St. Clair on the Ohio frontier. In 1927, the Supreme Court upheld the constitutionality of congressional investigations, and Congress has conducted investigations ever since.

Most congressional investigations are conducted by standing committees or their subcommittees. Occasionally investigations are conducted by select committees. Investigations may last for a few days or go on for months. Committee staff members may travel around the country collecting evidence and finding witnesses. For example, in 1985 members of the House Appropriations Committee visited United States embassies in Europe and the Mideast to investigate their security systems, and to see for themselves what was needed to deal with terrorist attacks on United States embassies. Fact-finding

Enrichment
Let volunteers research specific examples of persons who have been held in contempt of Congress: Under what circumstances were these people charged? What were the results of each charge? Ask the volunteers to prepare a bulletin board with information about the individuals they researched.

Enrichment
Have one or two volunteers investigate the immunity granted to the witnesses in the Iran-Contra hearings: What were the immediate results of those grants of immunity? What longer-term results have the grants of immunity had? Why? Ask the volunteers to report their findings to the rest of the class.

Vocabulary
As the students consider the meaning of *oversight,* have them read the footnote about this term. Then ask volunteers to give example sentences demonstrating the two different meanings of *oversight.*

Discussion Starter
Guide the students in discussing Congress's reviews of the agency budgets: What do you think Congress considers in these reviews? Why? Do you think Congress has the time or the resources to carry out effective reviews? If not, do you think that Congress should relinquish this oversight function? Why or why not?

Caption Answer Although Congressional committees have the power to issue subpoenas, to find persons in contempt of Congress, and to grant immunity, these committees are not a court of law.

Witnesses such as Secretary of State James Baker, shown here, are often called to testify before congressional committees. Do congressional committees have the same powers and authority as a court of law?

Service Learning Activity

Congressional representatives often have one or more offices in their district. Have students determine where the offices are for their congressperson. Most of these offices are willing to take on student volunteers who are serious and responsible. Have students, who wish to do so, volunteer to work for an extended period in one of the district offices. If that is not possible, have students arrange to interview one of the congressional support staff members. This could be an administrative assistant, legislative director, constituent case worker, or media advisor.

trips have also helped Congress make laws concerning other issues such as crime prevention, farm-price supports, and aid to African famine victims.

Congressional committees have the power to issue a **subpoena**, which is a legal order requiring a person to appear before a congressional committee (or a court of law). Sometimes dozens of witnesses are called to testify. Committees can also require witnesses to testify under oath, and prosecute witnesses for perjury (lying under oath). If a person refuses to testify or cooperate, he or she can be held in **contempt of Congress** and may be arrested and jailed.

Committees can also grant witnesses **immunity**, which is freedom from prosecution, if the witness provides certain information that helps to solve a crime. Witnesses granted immunity can give testimony about activities in which they may have been involved without fear of prosecution. The Watergate Committee for example, granted immunity to twenty-seven witnesses.

Despite these powers, a congressional committee is not a court of law. A congressional investigation, however, may result in a criminal indictment of individuals in state or federal court. It could also mean changes in a government program, loss of government contracts for businesses, or passage of new laws and regulations.

Oversight Function

The power to examine how effectively the executive branch and its officials carry out the laws passed by Congress is part of Congress' **oversight function**, sometimes referred to as the "watchdog function."[2]

Congress has defined its oversight functions in several laws. The Legislative Reorganization Act of 1946 calls for Congress to exercise "continuous watchfulness" over executive agencies. In the Reorganization Act of 1970, Congress states that "Each standing committee shall review and study, on a continuing basis, the application, administration, and execution" of laws relating to its interests.

Methods of Oversight Congress exercises its oversight function in several ways. One method, as you have just seen, is by holding committee hearings and investigations. A second oversight technique is to require agencies to submit reports to Congress on their activities. During one term, Congress may receive more than 1,000 such reports from various agencies.

Congress also exercises oversight by controlling the budget. The House and Senate review the budgets of all executive agencies every year. If it evaluates the agency positively, Congress may reward the agency by increasing the budget, while others may receive cuts or status quo budgets (budgets at the present level).

Lawmakers often dispatch one of the congressional support agencies such as the Government Accounting Office (GAO) to undertake a study of an executive agency's work. In fact, nearly every important piece of

2. The term *oversight* can have two opposing meanings. In casual conversation, one talks about an oversight, meaning something that was inadvertently missed or ignored. In the context of this chapter, *oversight* means "carefully watched over."

TEACHING GOVERNMENT IN ACTION

Read

To introduce this feature on Daniel Inouye, review with students some of the history of Hawaii. Remind students of Hawaii's unique position as the latest of the 50 states to enter the union and of the multicultural diversity of the state. Ask if any students have visited the state and to give their impressions of the differing life styles they observed. Then ask volunteers to read the feature aloud.

Discuss

Ask students the following questions to help stimulate class discussion of this feature: What was Senator Inouye's ethnic and family background? Where did Inouye serve during World War II? What does his war record tell you about how much combat action he saw? Do you think his ethnic background made it more difficult or less difficult for him during the war? Why do you think Inouye was appointed to serve on the CIA, the Iran-*contra,* and the Watergate investigatory committees? What does that indicate about his personal and professional integrity?

Analyze and Apply

In the time directly following World War II, it was almost a necessity that a politician needed to have seen active military duty to win an election. Have students break into small groups to discuss whether the voting public today still considers military service to one's country an important requirement of their leaders. Can students recall cases where a person's military service (or lack of) played part in a campaign? Ask one student from each group to present its views to the rest of the class.

Review

Check students' understanding of the feature by asking the following questions: When did Hawaii become a state? Where was Senator Inouye born? How long has he served in the United States Senate? What are some of the qualities for which the senator is valued?

Think About It (Answers)

1. Many American citizens of Japanese descent were placed in internment camps, an action for which the American government has since apologized.

2. The chairperson of standing committees is usually the senior member of the majority party. There are other Democrats on his committees who have more seniority.

GOVERNMENT IN ACTION

PROFILE

Daniel Ken Inouye

▶ Senator Daniel Inouye (seated center) has held many important positions in the Senate, including chairman of the special Senate committee that investigated the Iran–*contra* affair in 1986.

Senator Daniel Inouye first became a congressman in Hawaii when it became a state in 1959. He was elected to the Senate in 1962 and has remained there, receiving 73 percent of the vote in the last election. Inouye was born in Honolulu on September 7, 1924. His paternal grandparents left Japan to work in the sugar plantations in Hawaii when his father, Hyotaro, was 4 years old. In March 1943, Inouye enlisted in the Army and served in Europe with a group of Japanese Americans led by white officers. Just weeks before the war ended, he lost his right arm in an attack against a German bunker in northern Italy. He received the Distinguished Service Cross, Bronze Star, Purple Heart with Cluster, Good Conduct Medal, five unit citations, and five battle stars. As he worked to graduate from the University of Hawaii and the George Washington School of Law in 1952, he took an interest in politics.

Daniel Inouye's name is not often heard outside the Senate corridors, but when it is heard, the occasion tends to be important. As senior Democratic senator, he was appointed chairman of the special Senate committee to look into the Iran-*contra* affair in 1986. He had already served on the special Senate committee that investigated the Watergate scandal. In 1976, when Congress was seeking to curb abuses by the CIA, he became the first chairman of the Senate Select Committee on Intelligence. Although he has never served as the chairman of a standing Senate committee, he has risen to the number three position among Senate Democrats, and was recommended to Walter Mondale as vice-presidential candidate in 1984.

Inouye is often cited for his loyalty to the Senate and to his friends, and he has a record of making difficult decisions. Even though some would say he lacks the political clout of some of his junior senators, when a job opens up that calls for honesty and courage, senators seem to turn to their colleague from Hawaii.

THINK ABOUT IT

1. While Inouye was serving in the Army during World War II, something else was happening to many Japanese Americans living on the West Coast of the United States. What was it?
2. What are some reasons that Inouye has never been a chairman of a standing Senate committee? (HINT: Could it have to do with the size of the state he represents?)

Enrichment

Ask volunteers to gather further information on the initial North investigation that was dropped to avoid presenting a public challenge to a popular president: What committees were involved? What facts had their investigations uncovered? How was major media coverage of these initial investigations avoided? Let the volunteers share their findings with the rest of the class.

Evaluation Strategies

1. Have the students write their answers to the Section 2 Review questions.
2. Have the students take the Section 2 Quiz found in the *TRB.*

Section 2 (Answers)

1. The House of Representatives has the exclusive power to bring charges of impeachment and the Senate tries all impeachment cases.
2. Amendments may be proposed by a two-thirds vote of both houses of Congress or by a convention called by Congress at the request of the legislatures of two-thirds of the states.
3. In a joint session of Congress, the president of the Senate is authorized to count the electoral votes and declare the winner. If no person has a majority of the electoral votes, the House of Representatives chooses the president and the Senate chooses the vice president.
4. The Senate must approve presidential appointments to many important positions in the executive and judicial branches including appointments to the Cabinet, independent boards and agencies, major foreign service posts, and all federal judicial posts including Supreme Court nominees.

Extension

Ask all the students to read about a recent presidential veto: What legislation was vetoed? Why did the president veto it? How did the Congress respond to the veto? Then help the students share and discuss what they have learned: What trend does the current president seem to have established regarding the power to veto legislation?

Discussion Starter

Help the students discuss the examples given in the text of actions that Congress may not take: Why is Congress's restriction from these activities important? Whom are these restrictions intended to serve? How? Do you think members of Congress might attempt to use implied powers to gain the right to undertake these activities? If so, do you think Congress could be successful? Why or why not?

Reteaching Strategies

1. Let the students work with partners to compare and revise the notes they took while reading Section 2. Ask the students to refer to the text as necessary, and to make additions or corrections to improve their own notes.
2. Have the students write paragraphs explaining their new understanding of the term *advice and consent.*

legislation passed by Congress directs the GAO to study its effects. The GAO issued 880 reports and 3,800 legal rulings in 1991, for example, and began 1,500 audits and investigations. Three-fourths of the agency's recommendations are adopted.

Limits of Oversight For several reasons, Congress is limited in its ability to effectively perform the oversight function. The actions of the executive branch are not reviewed on a regular basis and sometimes the review hearings are not effective. Federal agency representatives often spend too much time on minor details and neglect broader problems. Members are often under a great deal of pressure because of other issues, and meetings are sometimes poorly attended.

The complexity, size, and number of federal programs also makes oversight difficult. There are dozens of executive agencies, many of which have large numbers of employees.

Political considerations also influence how seriously oversight functions will be carried out. In the 1980s, for example, it became known that some of President Reagan's staff had allowed arms to be sold to Iran in exchange for Iran's help in releasing American hostages held in the Middle East. The profits from those arms sales were then funneled to the *contra* rebels in Nicaragua. Both of these actions were in violation of U.S. law. A year before this scandal became publicized, two congressional committees had begun investigating fund-raising efforts for the Nicaraguan *contras* that had been undertaken by a member of the president's staff, Colonel Oliver North. The previous investigations were dropped, however, because some key members on the congressional committees did not wish to challenge a popular president.

Limits on the Powers

There are important limits to the seemingly sweeping powers of Congress. One way Congress is limited is by the system of checks and balances. The president, as head of the executive branch, can veto proposed legislation passed by Congress. The judicial branch can declare laws passed by Congress unconstitutional.

The Constitution also explicitly places certain prohibitions on Congress. The purpose of the Bill of Rights was to limit or deny certain powers to the federal government such as prohibiting it from restricting freedom of speech. Congress is also limited by the fact that the Constitution does not delegate certain powers to Congress. Thus, Congress may not create a national school system, establish units of local government, require that all eligible persons vote on election day, or pass a national divorce law. Congress cannot do these and a great many other things because it has not been given the power to do them.

Article I, Section 9 of the Constitution lists specific limits placed on Congress. The most important of these limits protect the rights of citizens. The Constitution says that Congress shall not take away a citizen's right to a writ of habeas corpus, except in times of invasion or civil war. (As you learned in Chapter 5, a writ of habeas corpus is the paper that orders the police to bring a citizen charged with a crime before a judge. The court then decides if there is enough evidence to hold the citizen. If not, the citizen must be released.)

The Constitution also prevents Congress from passing bills of attainder. (As you learned in Chapter 5, a bill of attainder is a law that convicts a person of a crime without a trial.) In addition, Congress shall not pass ex post facto laws—laws that make a particular act a crime and then punish people who committed the act *before* the law was passed.

The Constitution also does not allow Congress to grant titles of nobility to any person, or to pass commerce laws more favorable to one state than to another.

These limits on the powers of Congress are in place so that the legislative branch does not come to exemplify James Madison's "very definition of tyranny." As you have learned, Congress still possesses the powers needed to perform its immense job. Through those powers expressed in the Constitution and those implied by the necessary and proper clause, Congress is able to act as an effective legislative body. Congress also wields nonlegislative powers in such areas as impeachment, the constitutional amendment process, investigation, and oversight.

Section 2 Review

1. Which house of Congress has the exclusive power to impeach?
2. How may a constitutional amendment be proposed?
3. What are Congress' responsibilities concerning the election of the president?
4. Which appointments must the Senate approve?
5. What are the major methods of oversight that Congress may use?
6. **For critical analysis:** Are Congress' current powers to oversee the president's actions sufficient to prevent the president from becoming too powerful? Explain your answer.

5. By holding committee hearings and investigations, requiring agencies to submit reports to Congress, and by controlling the budget.
6. Answers will vary, e.g., the complexity, size, and number of executive agencies makes it difficult for Congress to oversee adequately the executive branch.

TEACHING CHALLENGE TO THE AMERICAN DREAM

Read
Introduce this Challenge to the American Dream feature by having the students discuss their own ideas about limits on Congressional power to investigate: Should the investigative power of Congress be limited? If so, why and how? If not, why not? Encourage the students to present and support various points of view in this introductory discussion. Then have the students read the feature independently.

Discuss
After the students have read the feature, ask them to reconsider the ideas they expressed in the introductory discussion: Have you revised your opinion about limits on the Congressional power to investigate? If so, what facts influenced you? If not, why not? To stimulate further discussion, ask questions such as these: How would you restate Wilson's quotation in your own words? How would you restate Lippmann's quotation in your own words? How do you react to Lippmann's choice of words? What do you think of the HUAC investigations? Do you think Congress could ever conduct that kind of investigation again? Why or why not?

Analyze and Apply
Have each student select a specific individual who was called to testify before the House Committee on Un-American Activities: Why was that person called? What testimony—if any—did that person give? How was that person's professional life affected? How was his or her personal life affected? Instruct the students to write short reports, and circulate all the reports among the class members.

Review
Ask the students these review questions: What arguments are made in favor of Congress's power to investigate? What arguments are made in opposition to that power?

You Decide (Answers)
1. Answers will vary, e.g., the same rules applied in court trials should be applied to congressional investigations to avoid violation of individuals' constitutional rights.
2. Answers will vary, e.g., the public must be the judge of whether or not the investigation is valid or a publicity effort.

Challenge to the American Dream

Limits on the Congressional Power to Investigate

One of the more controversial powers of Congress has been its power to conduct investigations while fulfilling its legislative function. Part of the controversy stems from the fact that these investigative powers are not explicitly stated in the Constitution. Over the decades, however, the authority to conduct investigations has been viewed as essential to Congress' main functions of passing and administering legislation, informing the people of various public affairs, and protecting the integrity of the federal government.

It has been argued that without the authority to obtain factual information upon which to base its legislative decisions, Congress could not effectively exercise any of the powers bestowed upon it. In 1885 Woodrow Wilson said that, "the informing function of Congress should be preferred even to its legislative function." Just prior to his appointment to the Supreme Court in 1937, Senator Hugo Black referred to congressional investigations as a "useful and fruitful" function of Congress. Others, however, have disagreed. National columnist Walter Lippmann once characterized the congressional investigation as "that legalized atrocity in which congressmen, starved of their legitimate food for thought, go on a wild and feverish manhunt and do not stop at cannibalism."

One of the most controversial modern-day investigations by Congress occurred after World War II in the climate of growing concern about the spread of communism. During the late 1940s and into the 1950s, committees in both chambers of Congress used their investigative powers against individuals suspected of being Communist sympathizers or members of subversive organizations. The House Un-American Activities Committee (HUAC) called over three thousand witnesses during this period and questioned many of them on their political beliefs, affiliations, and actions deemed potentially dangerous to the United States government. Many suspects and witnesses invoked the Fifth Amendment protection against self-incrimination and others refused to testify, insisting that the committee's interrogation went beyond Congress's legislative function. Nearly 150 people were cited for contempt of Congress.

Senator Joseph McCarthy headed one of these investigating committees in the Senate in the 1950s. He repeatedly made unsubstantiated (unprovable) charges against public officials and private individuals suspected of political subversion. His allegations, along with those of the HUAC, resulted in a series of security investigations into the backgrounds and activities of public employees, scientists, screenwriters, movie directors, and academics. Additionally, loyalty oaths were imposed on public employees, and anti-Communist legislation was passed. Although he never had any evidence to prove or support his accusations, it was not until December of 1954 that McCarthy was censured by the Senate. This, however, did little to help the ruined reputations and lives of those whom he had destroyed. Later, there were many calls for reforming the congressional investigation process to prevent the recurrence of such abuses.

The challenge to the American dream is to allow Congress to carry out its lawful job of oversight without allowing it to violate the constitutional rights of those being investigated.

You Decide

1. In a court of law, the accused has many more rights and guarantees than individuals who come under the investigation of congressional committees. Do you think that the same rules that apply to court trials should be applied to congressional investigations? Why or why not?
2. Some have argued that many senators and representatives have started congressional investigations in order to put themselves in the public limelight. Is there any way to determine a valid congressional investigation as opposed to a publicity effort? Explain.

Chapter Evaluation

To evaluate student mastery of chapter material, you might:

1. Use Chapter Test A from the *TRB.*

2. Use Chapter Test B from the *TRB.*

3. Construct your own test using items from the *West American Government Test Bank* found in the *TRB.*

4. Use the accompanying computerized test software to construct and print a customized chapter test.

Review Questions (Answers)

1. Expressed powers are those directly listed in the Constitution.

2. The powers to tax and spend are important because they allow Congress to determine national policy in many different areas because policy does not take place without money.

3. Because the government is allowed to borrow money.

4. Commerce power is the power to regulate both foreign and interstate commerce. The definition of commerce has expanded over the years to include nearly all forms of commercial and business activity.

5. Only Congress has the power to declare war and is responsible for raising and maintaining the armed forces. The president is commander-in-chief of the armed forces.

6. The necessary and proper clause is also called the elastic clause because it has allowed Congress to greatly expand its powers.

7. The Court found that the creation of the Second Bank to be necessary and proper in order to carry out the federal government's monetary powers. It supported the idea that the necessary and proper clause gave Congress the right to make any laws necessary to carry out its other powers.

8. Some examples of nonlegislative powers are the power of impeachment, the power to propose constitutional amendments, the power to choose the president if the electoral college fails to do so, giving advice and consent, and investigative powers.

9. Congress uses its investigative powers to see where new laws are needed, to review the effectiveness of those laws, and to see whether the executive branch is ad-

Chapter 13 Review

Key Terms

appropriation 314
bankruptcy 315
contempt of Congress 326
copyright 317
currency power 315
delegated, expressed, or enumerated powers 313
direct tax 314
elastic clause 318
federal budget 315
government bonds 315
immunity 326
impeach 321
implied powers 318
impoundment 320
indirect tax 314
interstate commerce 315
loose constructionists 321
national debt 315
necessary and proper clause 318
oversight function 326
patent 317
revenue bills 314
senatorial courtesy 324
strict constructionists 318
subpoena 326

Summary

1. Article I Section 1 of the Constitution requires that all power to make laws shall be given to Congress. The powers that are specifically provided for—the expressed powers—include the power to tax and spend; the power to borrow and coin money and set bankruptcy laws; the commerce power; the power to approve treaties, to declare war, to create federal courts below the level of the Supreme Court; to establish post offices, copyrights, and patents; and powers of naturalization and dominion over territories. The powers known as implied powers are based on the necessary and proper clause. Early in our history the issue of whether to interpret the clause strictly or loosely was debated. In *McCulloch* v. *Maryland* (1819) the Court ruled that the necessary and proper clause gave Congress the right to make any laws necessary to carry out its other powers.

2. The Constitution also gives Congress a number of nonlegislative duties, which include the power to impeach government officials and to propose constitutional amendments. The Senate must approve presidential appointments to many important positions in the executive and judicial branches. The Senate must also give its advice and consent to ratifying treaties made by the president. Through its investigative committees, Congress also has the power to hold hearings during which it investigates important problems, such as fraud by government contractors. The power to oversee and scrutinize how effectively the executive branch and its officials carry out the laws passed by Congress is called the oversight function. Congress exercises this function by holding committee hearings and investigations, requiring agencies to submit reports, reviewing the budgets of agencies, and dispatching one of the congressional support agencies such as the GAO to study an executive agency's work.

Review Questions

1. What are expressed powers?
2. Why is the congressional power to tax and spend important?
3. Why does the nation have a national debt?
4. Explain the commerce power of Congress and how the definition of commerce has expanded.
5. How does Congress share war powers with the president?
6. Why is the necessary and proper clause also called the elastic clause? How has this clause been used?
7. How was the main issue in *McCulloch* v. *Maryland* resolved? Why is it an important precedent?
8. What are Congress' nonlegislative powers?
9. How has Congress used its investigative powers?
10. Name four guidelines for writing a letter to a member of Congress.
11. How has the congressional power to investigate evolved and how is it limited?

Questions For Thought and Discussion

1. Do you agree with the War Powers Resolution of 1973, which limits the president's power to send troops into combat without congressional approval? Why or why not?

ministering programs as they were intended to be carried out.

10. Address the person properly, be as brief as possible, make sure the issue is current, and give reasons for taking your stand.

11. The congressional power to investigate has evolved from the view that it is essential to Congress's main functions of passing and administering legislation. It is limited by the complexity, size, and number of federal programs.

Questions for Thought and Discussion

1. Answers will vary, e.g., the president must have the power to send troops without congressional approval in times of emergency. There are situations that require quick action.

2. Answers will vary, e.g., leadership positions in Congress depend on leadership positions in both parties.

3. Answers will vary, e.g., Congress should have less control over economic activities carried on within each state's borders. Each state is better able to handle its own economic affairs.

Observable Mastery

Allow the students to create a bulletin board reflecting the expressed, implied, and nonlegislative powers of Congress. Students should divide the board up into the three appropriate but not necessarily equal divisions. It would be a good basis for discussion to decide what proportion of the board ought to go to which powers. Have students bring in photos, headlines, cartoons, and anything else that manifests an example of the powers. Encourage students to be creative. The materials could reflect people, institutions, events, symbols, and words.

Social Studies Skills (Answers)

1. To show the powers granted to Congress by the U.S. Constitution.

2. A. Clothes
B. The Statue of Liberty
C. A hand holding money
D. An envelope
E. A book
F. A gavel
G. A ship sinking
H. A soldier
I. A sailor
J. Soldiers
K. The Capitol

3. The clothes represent goods that can be taxed by Congress.

4. The power of Congress to determine how aliens can become U.S. citizens because the Statue of Liberty is what immigrants first saw from their ships in former times in the United States.

5. A book.

CHAPTER 13 REVIEW—Continued

2. How do the leadership positions in the Democratic and Republican parties affect leadership positions within Congress?
3. Originally, the framers of the Constitution wanted to ensure that Congress could not involve itself in the states' internal affairs. Nonetheless, the necessary and proper clause has been expanded so that Congress now has control over virtually all economic activities, even when they are strictly carried out within each state's borders. Do you think this is a fair exercise of congressional power? Give reasons for your answer.

Improving Your Skills

Communication Skills

Common Considerations in Writing:

Whether you are writing a letter, a report, or an essay, you must consider three common considerations: the reader, the purpose, and the subject matter.

Know Your Reader: Before you write anything, think about who the reader is. You would write a letter to your friend very differently than one to your congressperson. When you understand the needs of your reader, you will be able to write a more meaningful message.

Know Your Purpose: Before you begin writing, think about what the purpose of your writing is. Most writing is done for one of the following reasons:

- to inform
- to request
- to inquire
- to confirm
- to persuade
- to entertain

Know Your Subject: Know as much as possible about the subject of your writing. Use the research guidelines on page 279 and the interview techniques on page 97, if necessary. Think of innovative ways to learn about your subject.

Writing

1. Think of an issue about which you are concerned. Compose one letter to a friend and one letter to a congressional representative expressing your views. Compare the two letters. Describe your purpose in writing the letter. Make a list of any other information you could obtain that would improve your letters. Identify where the information could be located.

Social Studies Skills

Understanding Symbols

Many charts and graphs in your textbook have symbols to help illustrate key points and to make such diagrams easier to read and understand. Look at Figure 13-1 on page 319.

1. What is the focus of this figure?
2. Make a list of all of the symbols that are used.
3. How does the top-most symbol relate to the first power of Congress?
4. To which power does the symbol of the Statue of Liberty refer and why?
5. What is the symbol used that relates to Congress' copyright powers?

Activities and Projects

1. Divide into groups of five or six. Ask each member to collect articles from newspapers and magazines that describe congressional actions. Create a bulletin board display, grouping each article according to which type of congressional power—expressed, implied, or nonlegislative—the action falls under. Discuss how each article illustrates those powers.
2. Debate the following—Resolved: No member of Congress shall serve on any committee for more than six years.
3. Research how often the War Powers Act of 1973 has been effectively used. Write a short report detailing your findings.

CHAPTER INTRODUCTION

Instructional Objectives

By the end of the chapter students should know how to:

- Describe the ways in which the House and Senate organize to begin a new term.
- List the various steps involved in the lawmaking process, from introduction of a bill to voting on the bill.
- Explain the final stages before a bill actually becomes law.

Using the Keynote

Before the students begin reading, ask them to discuss their ideas about Congress at work: Imagine that you are visiting Congress in session—what do you see? (If appropriate, ask the students to describe actual visits they have made to Congress.) Who is doing what? How is the work of Congress being conducted? Encourage the students to use details in describing the scenes they imagine.

Then let a volunteer read aloud the keynote quotation from Woodrow Wilson: How does Wilson's statement alter your ideas about the workings of Congress? What are the implications of this statement?

You may also want to ask the students to recall (or research) Wilson's background: What was his own experience with Congress? How did he learn about the functioning of Congress?

Introducing the Chapter

Ask a volunteer to read the Introduction aloud to the rest of the class. You might ask questions such as these to stimulate discussion: Why is the making of laws such an important responsibility? Whom do these laws affect? Why and how? To whom is it important to understand how laws are made? Why?

Previewing the Sections

Section 1 Ask the students to look through Section 1: What main headings do you find? What do the photographs show? What do you expect to learn from studying this section?

Section 2 Have the students glance through Section 2. Ask volunteers to read aloud the headings, the photo captions, the figure title, and the special feature titles. Encourage the students to share and discuss what they already know about the topics covered in this section.

Section 3 Have the students look through Section 3, and ask volunteers to read aloud the section title and the headings. Then encourage the students to begin considering the section content by asking these questions: How do the two houses of Congress agree on the exact wording of a bill? What actions are required before a bill that has been passed by Congress can become law? Remind the students that they will learn more about the answers to these questions when they read Section 3.

CHAPTER 14

How Congress Makes Laws

CHAPTER OBJECTIVES

To learn and understand

- The ways in which the House and Senate organize to begin a new term.
- The various steps involved in the lawmaking process, from the introduction of a bill to voting on the bill.
- The final stages before a bill actually becomes law.

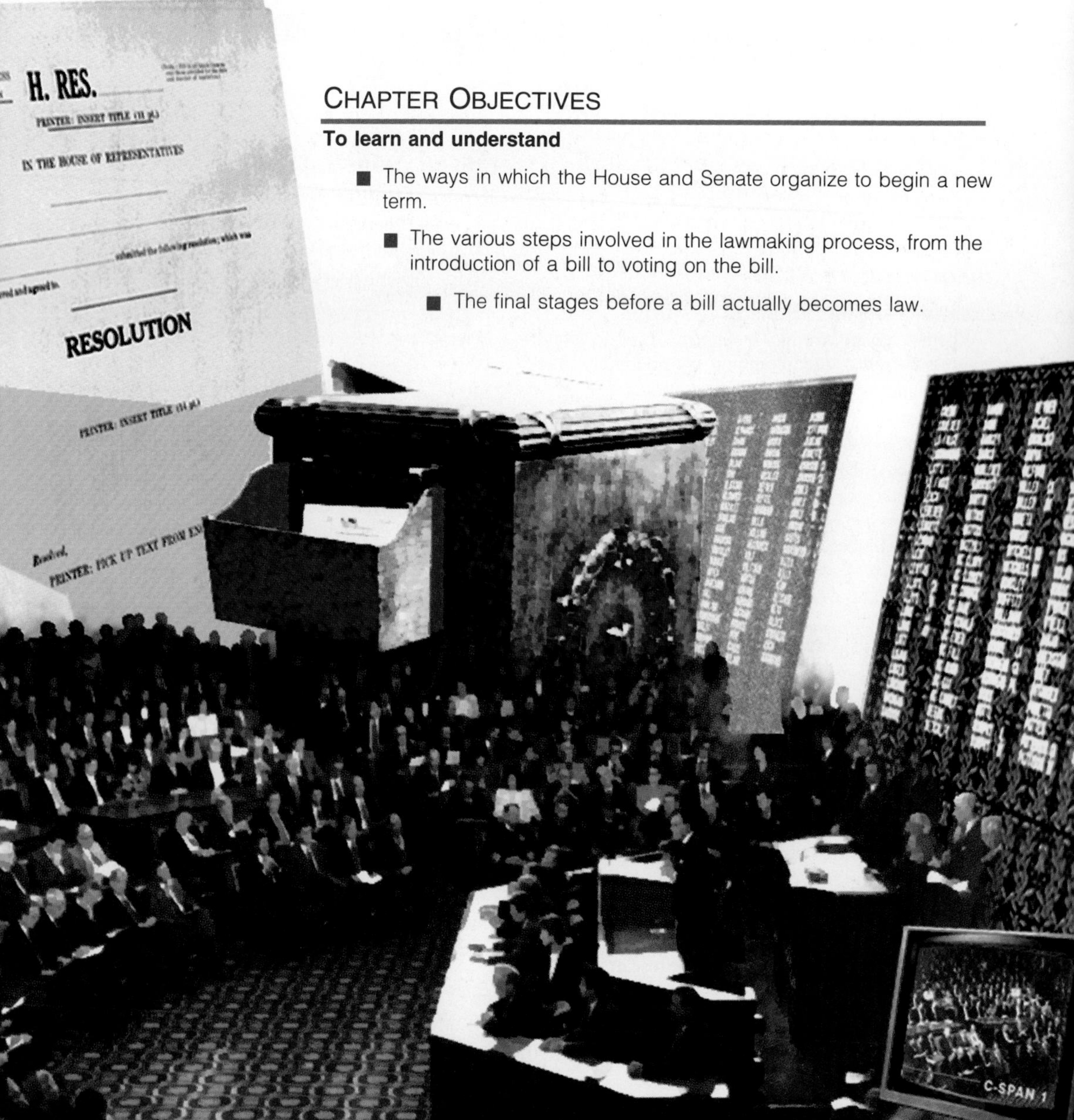

West's American Government Assignment Guide

Activity Sheets
Basic Concepts 14 *TRB* (Reteaching)
Enrichment Activity 14 *TRB*
Building Social Studies Skills 14 *TRB*

Quizzes
Chapter 14 Section 1 Quiz *TRB*
Chapter 14 Section 2 Quiz *TRB*
Chapter 14 Section 3 Quiz *TRB*

Tests
Chapter 14 Test A *TRB*
Chapter 14 Test B *TRB*
Chapter 14 Test Bank *TRB*
Chapter 14 WESTEST Computerized Testing

Social Studies Tool Kit Software
Chapter 14 Activity

Keynote

"Congress in its committee rooms is Congress at work".

—— **Woodrow Wilson**
(1856–1924) Twenty-Eighth President of the United States

INTRODUCTION

You have seen how Congress is organized to carry out its functions and you have learned about the powers of Congress. You will now take a look at how Congress performs its most important function: lawmaking. The laws of Congress have helped shape this country into the nation we have today, and those laws will continue to guide the nation in the future.

This chapter will explore how the lawmaking process actually works. First you will look at the opening of a congressional session and the different forms new legislation may take. Then you will read about the steps that a bill must go through in order to become a law. As reflected in Woodrow Wilson's quote above, while some congressional work takes place on the floor of the House and Senate, much of it takes place in committees. Still other work by Congress is done informally in political conferences. This has caused some writers to compare the operation of Congress to a great stage play in which much of the action takes place offstage.

SECTION 1

Congress Begins Its Work

Preview Questions:

- What roles do political caucuses play during the congressional term?
- How are the opening days of the House and Senate different?
- What are the different types of legislation considered each year?

As you learned already, a new term of Congress begins every two years on January 3 of every odd-numbered year. During each term, out of the thousands of bills that are introduced, few become law. The legislative process that each of these bills passes through is complicated. Consequently, Congress must organize itself so that congressional members can consider all of these bills.

This process of organization begins with the political parties with which members of Congress identify. After all, those political parties are largely responsible for getting members elected to the offices they now must fill. It is not surprising, then, that the houses of Congress are also made up of political groups that begin work even before each term begins.

Political Caucuses

Before a new term begins, Democratic and Republican members of the House and Senate meet in separate private party conferences called **caucuses**. Both the Senate and House hold two party caucuses—one for Republicans and one for Democrats. These caucuses meet in order to reach agreement among themselves about key issues so they can act as a unified force, and to plan the party's strategy for the upcoming term. They also choose the party leaders who will organize and direct party activities during the congressional term. These choices are often made on the basis of seniority.

The number of caucuses has grown in recent years. Caucuses have generally been organized on the basis of regions and special interests. Examples are the Congressional Sunbelt Council and the Congressional Steel Caucus. They have also been organized on the basis of gender and ethnicity: The Black Caucus, the Congressional Women's Caucus, and the Hispanic Caucus are other examples of such groups. The activities of these caucuses are directed toward their fellow members of Congress and toward administrative agencies such as the Federal Trade Commission (FTC) and the Federal Aviation Administration (FAA). Within Congress, they press for

SECTION 1

Point to Stress
• The role of political caucuses during the Congressional term.
• Differences between the opening day of the House and Senate.
• The various types of legislation considered each year.

Kickoff Activity
Ask the students to think about what probably happens at the beginning of each new term of Congress. Have each student list at least three different things that they think take place during that time. After all the students have finished their lists, encourage volunteers to share and compare their ideas.

Working with the Preview Questions
Have one of the students read these study questions aloud. Encourage volunteers to discuss what they already know in response to the questions. Then ask the students to use these questions as a guide for taking notes on Section 1.

Teaching Strategies

Introduction
Assign the students to read the section introduction independently. Then ask: Why is affiliation with a political party so important for members of Congress? What responsibilities do you think members of Congress have toward their parties? How do those responsibilities relate to the members' responsibilities toward their constituents?

Comprehension
Ask the students to recall (or review) the specific titles and roles of the party leaders chosen at this time.

Cooperative Learning
Let the students form groups in which to learn more about specific nonparty caucuses. Have the group members select a caucus and find answers to these questions: When and why was the caucus formed? Who belongs? To which political parties do the members belong? What are the current activities of that caucus? Ask the members of each group to prepare and present a short report for the rest of the class.

Extension
If the timing is appropriate, encourage the students to watch C-SPAN's coverage of the opening day of the House. Otherwise, ask the students to read newspaper and news magazine reports of recent opening days.

Enrichment
Ask a volunteer to gather the names of Congressional representatives who have, over the past 20 years, served as Clerk of the House. Have the volunteer present the information in a chart or in a bulletin board display.

Discussion Starter
Guide the students in discussing the formalities involved in the appointments made at the beginning of the term: Since these officers have already been chosen, why do the members of the House follow these procedures? What purposes are served in carrying out such formalities? To whom are these formalities important? Why? Do you think these formalities should interest voters? Why or why not?

Caption Answer Answers will vary, e.g., the environment and the economy are two of the more pressing issues today.

Opening day in the Congress focuses attention on the pressing issues to be discussed in the coming congressional term. What issues do you think the current Congress should be addressing?

committees to hold hearings, push particular legislation, and lobby for votes on bills they favor. Thus, even before the term begins, members of Congress have set the legislative process in motion.

Opening Day of Congress

On the opening day of Congress, members of each chamber meet in their own wing of the Capitol building, shown in Figure 14–1 on the next page.

Every House member is up for election every two years, so each term begins anew. All members have to be sworn in, whether it is their first term or their tenth; rules have to be made; and organization has to be decided upon. The **clerk of the House** from the previous session presides at the beginning of the first day's session. The chamber is called to order and a roll call is taken. The members then *officially* elect a Speaker of the House. This election is only a formality because the Speaker has already been chosen by the majority party caucus. The Speaker of the House is sworn in by the member of the House who has served the longest. The Speaker then swears in the rest of the representatives.

Next the House *officially* elects its nonmember, or staff, officers such as the clerk, sergeant at arms, and postmaster. Again these choices have previously been decided by the majority party caucus. Then the rules that will govern how the House proceeds throughout the term are adopted. The rules of the House have been evolving for over two hundred years and they are usually readopted with little or no change. Finally, members are appointed to permanent committees, and committee chairpersons, also determined previously by majority party caucus, are formally selected. The opening day of the House ends with the House telling the Senate that it is ready for the president's annual message to Congress.

Opening Day in the Senate

On opening day in the Senate, only one-third of the Senate's members are beginning new terms, which makes the Senate a continuous body. This means its members have less organizational business to attend to than do members of the House. The Senate swears in its recently elected members and fills vacancies in its organizations and committees. The Senate then informs the House that it is ready for the president's annual address.

State of the Union Address

After both houses have organized, a joint committee of the two officially notifies the president that Congress is in session and ready to begin work. Within a few days, the president delivers his annual **State of the Union Address**. Members of both houses, together with the members of the Cabinet, the Supreme Court, the foreign service corps, and other dignitaries, assemble in the large chamber of the House of Representatives to hear the annual address.

The State of the Union Address was originally a long and often boring speech. Our third president, Thomas

Extension

Again, if the timing permits, have the students watch television coverage of the State of the Union message; otherwise, show a videotape of a recent message or ask the students to recall media coverage of the last message. Encourage the students to discuss both the formalities involved in the presentation and the content of the speech itself.

Discussion Starter

Encourage the students to share their reactions to the diagram of the Capitol Building: What can you learn from studying this diagram? What sense does it give you about the purposes and the functioning of Congress?

Floor Plan of the U.S. Capitol

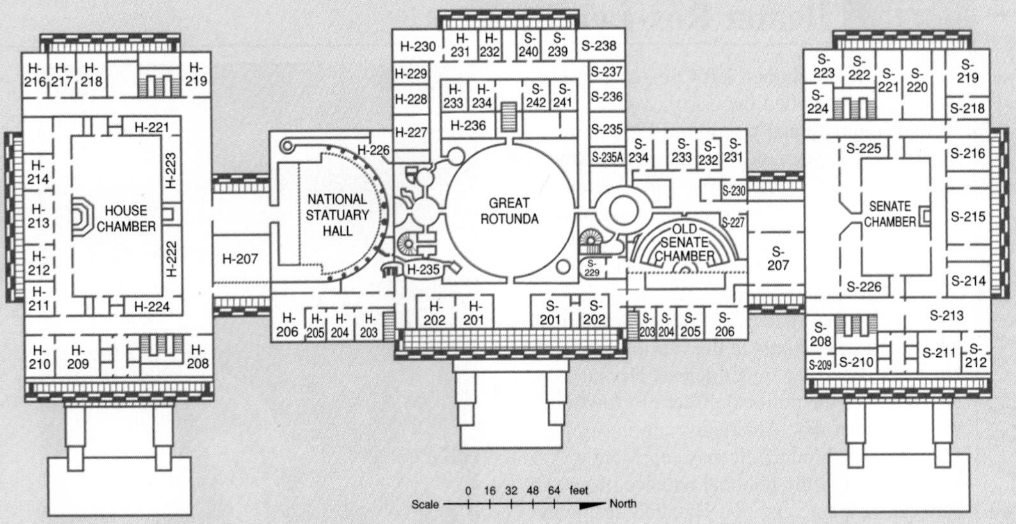

Rooms on Second Floor of the Capitol

House Side

H-201, 202, 203, 204, 205, 206. Speaker.
H-207. House reception room (Sam Rayburn Room).
H-208. Committee on Ways and Means.
H-209, 210. Speaker's Rooms.
H-211. Parliamentarian.
H-212, 213, 214. Representatives' retiring rooms.
H-216, 217, 218. Committee on Appropriations.
H-219. Minority Whip.
H-221, 223. Republican cloakrooms.
H-222, 224. Democratic cloakrooms.
H-226. House document room.
H-227, 228, 229, 230, 231, 232, 233, 236. Minority Leader.
H-234. Prayer room.
H-235. Congresswomen's Suite.

Senate Side

S-201, 202, 203, 204, 205, 237, 238, 239, 240, 241, 242. Senators' offices.
S-206. President *Pro Tempore.*
S-207. Senator's conference room (Mike Mansfield Room).
S-208, 209. Secretary of the Senate.
S-210. Secretary of the Senate (John F. Kennedy Room).
S-211. Secretary of the Senate (Lyndon B. Johnson Room).
S-212. Vice President.
S-213. Senators' reception room.
S-214. Ceremonial Office of the Vice President.
S-215. Senators' retiring room (Marble Room).
S-216. President's Room.
S-218, 219. Official Reporters of Debates.
S-220. Bill Clerk and Journal Clerk.
S-221, 222, 223, 224. Majority Leader (Robert C. Byrd Rooms).
S-225. Democratic cloakroom.
S-226. Republican cloakroom.
S-227. Executive clerk.
S-229, 243. Assistant Republican Leader.
S-230, 231, 232, 233, 234, 235, 235A, 236. Republican Leader (Howard H. Baker, Jr. Rooms).

FIGURE 14–1 Floor Plan of the U.S. Capitol. The above floor plan is for the second floor of the U.S. Capitol where both the Senate and House of Representatives meet. According to this floor plan, which of the congressional leaders is given the most space? Why do you think this is?

Figure Answer The Speaker of the House, with H-210 and H-209, is given the most space in the Capitol. Students should understand that this is commensurate with the enormous power wielded by the Speaker of the House of Representatives.

TEACHING GOVERNMENT IN ACTION

Read

Introduce this feature by asking the students to recall as many famous naturalized Americans as possible (Alexander Hamilton, John Paul Jones, Henry Kissinger, Helena Rubenstein, etc.) and list these names on the board. Remind students of the many contributions made to this country by non-native born individuals. Then ask volunteers to read aloud the feature profile.

Discuss

In order to discuss this feature, students should be aware of the "negative campaign tactics" that were used in this election. Ask the students the following questions to stimulate a discussion of this feature: Why was this congressional seat so hotly contested? Do you think the Democrats felt they "owned" this seat? What do you think Ros-Lehtinen's opponent meant by the term "an American seat"? What is meant here by the phrase "an ethnic war"? How did Ros-Lehtinen's ethnic heritage work to her advantage in this election?

Analyze and Apply

If the timing is appropriate, ask the students to follow a local or national election campaign. Have them listen to speeches or read articles in the media and note any comments that appear to appeal to a bias or prejudice in the voters. Have them write these comments down and bring them to class to share with the other students. In small groups discuss how these comments contribute to a negative campaign.

Review

Help students review the contents of this feature by asking the following questions: What political situation were Ros-Lehtinen's parents escaping when they came to the United States? How did Ros-Lehtinen prepare for her role as a U.S. Representative? What other bias, besides her ethnicity, might Ros-Lehtinen have faced in her election campaign?

Think About It (Answers)

1. Article II of the Constitution states that the president must be a "natural-born citizen," which would deny naturalized citizens the opportunity to become president.

2. Answers will vary. Her own background as a member of a minority group would give her special insights that could be useful in dealing with other minority groups.

GOVERNMENT IN ACTION

PROFILE

Ileana Ros-Lehtinen

Ileana Ros-Lehtinen left Cuba as a child when her parents fled the Castro regime. In a special congressional election in Florida in 1989, Ros-Lehtinen, now a naturalized American citizen, defeated a native-born American for the seat. As a Republican, she took over a seat that had been Democratic for the past forty years and was held much of that time by one person, Claude Pepper.

Ros-Lehtinen is a conservative Republican who spent seven years in the Florida legislature before running for Congress. Her election demonstrates the political effect of growth in the number of new Americans coming from Hispanic backgrounds. It may represent a turning point in the political balance of power between Hispanic and non-Hispanic residents in Florida. A major challenge facing her in Congress will be the job of smoothing relations between the Hispanic community and other ethnic groups.

Ros-Lehtinen's Latin American heritage overshadowed most other issues during the campaign. Her opponent urged voters to keep the congressional seat "an American seat." Voting was described as "an ethnic war," sharply divided along racial and ethnic lines. The issue of Ros-Lehtinen's ethnic heritage was used by both sides in the campaign. As it turned out, her background worked to her advantage.

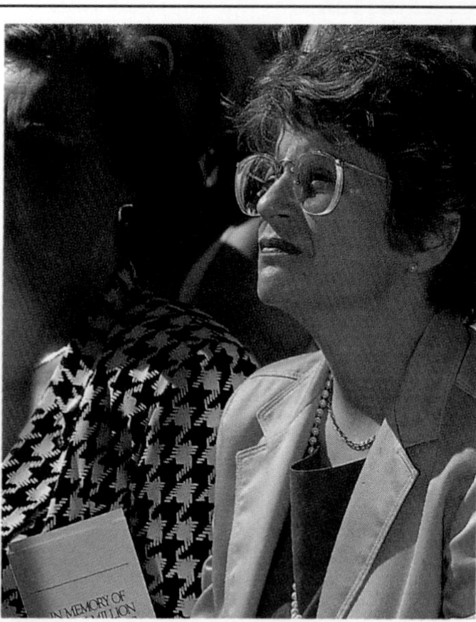

THINK ABOUT IT

1. Does the Constitution allow naturalized American citizens to hold all federal offices?
2. How might Ros-Lehtinen go about "smoothing relations between the Hispanic community and other ethnic groups"?

Jefferson, started a precedent when he submitted the speech in writing, claiming that speaking before Congress was too much like a British monarch's opening speech to Parliament. In 1913, Woodrow Wilson broke the precedent by personally delivering his first State of the Union Address. He used the speech as a chance to outline his administration's overall agenda and to urge the passage of certain programs.

The media, especially television, have added to the importance of the speech over the years, and today presidents use it as a ceremonial way of reporting on the "health" of the nation and its concerns, both domestic and foreign. It is also a speech in which the president lays out the administration's broad policies and makes legislative recommendations.

Bills and Resolutions

Congress considers several different kinds of legislation each year. Most pieces of legislation are in the form of bills. **Bills** are drafts of laws presented to the House and Senate for enactment.

Critical Thinking Skills
Guide the students in analyzing the modern use of the State of the Union Address: To whom is the president speaking when he delivers this message? Why does the president try to reach more than one group in this speech? How does he attempt to reach those various audiences? Which of those audiences do you consider most important? Which audience do the president and his speech writers consider most important?

Discussion Starter
Ask the students to consider the importance of understanding the various types of bills and resolutions: Do you expect that you will ever be directly involved in introducing or acting upon legislation in the United States Congress? Why or why not? If your answer is no, do you still need to understand the process by which legislation is introduced and acted upon in Congress? Why or why not?

Extension
Ask the students to identify (or read about) specific bills that have been before Congress for more than a year.

Discussion Starter
Let the students discuss their ideas in response to these questions: What kind of media coverage do private bills usually get? Why? Do you consider this discrepancy in coverage between public bills and private bills appropriate? Why or why not?

Vocabulary
Be sure the students are familiar with the definition of the adjective *concurrent.* You may also want to have them identify and define the prefix in the adjective.

Enrichment
Ask small groups of volunteers to research and report on recent concurrent resolutions.

One of the first official functions of any new Congress is to listen to the president deliver his annual State of the Union Address. How have the media changed the State of the Union Address?

Caption Answer The media, especially television, have made this speech more important and have prompted presidents to use the speech as an opportunity to outline their policies and legislative recommendations. Additionally, presidents also use this speech as a way of campaigning for their policies.

Public Bills There are two kinds of bills: public and private. **Public bills** involve matters of national interest. For example, a federal tax increase, a proposal for health-care guidelines, a proposed ban on assault-style automatic weapons, a clean air bill, or an appropriation of funds for a military program would all be public bills. Public bills are often controversial, such as a civil rights bill or a gun-control bill, and may be debated for months or possibly years before they ever become law.

Private Bills **Private bills** are those bills that apply to certain persons or places rather than to the nation as a whole. For example, a private bill might pay a settlement to a woman whose car was demolished by a U.S. Postal Service truck, or a private bill might grant the right to enter the United States to a certain group of refugees.

Joint Resolutions **Joint Resolutions** (a formal declaration of opinion by vote of both houses of Congress and sent to the president for his approval) are very similar to bills: They must go through the same steps as a bill to become law, and when they are passed they have the same force of law. Joint resolutions often deal with temporary or unusual matters or correct an error in an earlier law. For example, money for a special military action overseas might be authorized by joint resolution. Joint resolutions are also used to propose constitutional amendments.

Concurrent Resolutions **Concurrent resolutions** deal with matters requiring the action of the House and Senate, but for which a law is not needed. They are measures intended to express an opinion or an official policy. For example, a concurrent resolution might express an opinion of Congress commemorating the anniversary of a successful space exploration or the welcoming of an important visitor, such as the Queen of England. A concurrent resolution may set the date for the adjournment of Congress. Concurrent resolutions must be passed by both chambers of Congress, but do not require the president's signature and do not have the force of law.

Simple Resolutions A **simple resolution** deals with matters affecting only one house of Congress and is

Senators such as Howard Metzenbaum (D., Ohio), shown above, consider several kinds of legislation each year. What is the most common form of legislation considered by members of Congress?

Caption Answer Bills, both public and private, are the most common form of legislation considered by Congress.

TEACHING GOVERNMENT IN ACTION

Read

Have the students begin by reading and speculating about the Case Study title: How many laws do you image are proposed during a single term of Congress? Of those, how many do you think are passed? After several students have shared their ideas, let volunteers read the Case Study aloud.

Discuss

Use questions such as these to help the students discuss the Case Study: Why is Congress "*in principle* for all Americans who want government to pass legislation in their favor"? What kinds of legislation do people want? Which individuals and groups have greater access to Congress for achieving those things? Why? Since so many bills fail to become law, why do you think so many are introduced? Does this process make sense? Is it fair? Why or why not? How do you react to the situation in Congress regarding the restructuring of the financial industry? What—if anything—should be done to change that situation? How do most members of the voting public react to the decision many Congress members have made to "duck hard issues"? How do you think voters *should* respond to such decisions? Why? Why do you think such a small group of elderly voters was able to defeat a bill that had bipartisan support? Should such a small group be able to exert so much influence? Why or why not? How might the process of introducing bills that clearly have no chance of passing sometimes "backfire" on Congressional members?

Analyze and Apply

Have the students work in small groups to study the process through which proposed laws must pass. Ask each group to select a specific bill introduced into the House or the Senate during the past term of Congress. Then have group members work together to track all the steps through which the bill passed and to determine what finally happened to the bill—and why that was the result. Let the members of each group draw a chart or create another kind of display to summarize their findings.

Review

Ask the students these review questions: What percentage of bills introduced into Congress become public laws? What are three reasons that so few of the introduced bills become law?

Think About It (Answers)

1. Answers will vary, e.g., there are numerous steps required in passing legislation, giving opponents many chances to defeat it.
2. Answers will vary, e.g., lawmakers should not introduce legislation they know will never be passed because it takes time away from important issues that need their attention. It would be difficult, however, to prevent lawmakers from doing so.

GOVERNMENT IN ACTION

CASE STUDY

Many Laws Proposed, Few Passed

In principle, Congress is for all Americans who want government to pass legislation in their favor. Business groups, farmers, labor unions, various interest groups, federal agencies, the president, and many others all look to Congress to pass laws favorable to their interests. As many as twenty thousand bills are introduced in the House and Senate during a congressional term, yet fewer than 10 percent of these bills become public laws. As President Kennedy once noted, "It is very easy to defeat a bill in Congress. It is much more difficult to pass one." Why do so few of the bills introduced become law?

One reason is that the lawmaking process is long and complex. The steps involved in passing a new law leave many opportunities for members of Congress to delay, alter, or kill a bill. These legislative hurdles give opponents of the bill numerous advantages: If their efforts to stop the bill fall short at one step along the way, they can always try again further down the line.

Bills that are opposed by important interest groups are not likely to be passed. Because members of Congress depend on interest-group money to get reelected, they are reluctant to antagonize these groups. For example, in every Congress since 1978, the House and Senate Banking Committees have tried to restructure the financial industry by attempting to overhaul a 1933 law. But reform has been hopelessly deadlocked because of the conflicting interests of big banks, small banks, insurance companies, and securities firms.

With the rise of negative campaigning, many members have concluded that it is safer to duck hard issues than to make any choices at all and risk losing favor with one side or the other. They increasingly appoint outside commissions and task forces to study any truly controversial problem, a process that often takes many months and does not produce a solution. For example, the Bipartisan Commission on Comprehensive Health Care devoted nine months and $1.5 million to propose an annual $66 billion "solution" to the health needs of the uninsured elderly. The report was immediately abandoned because feuding panelists omitted any reference to how the program was to be funded.

A plan designed to shield the elderly from the high costs of health care for major illnesses had strong bipartisan support, but was dropped when a small but vocal group of well-off seniors spoke in revolt over the plan's required tax-rate increases. "Five percent of the elderly swung us around like a dead cat," said Senator Alan Simpson, a Republican from Wyoming.

Another reason so few bills become law is that lawmakers sometimes introduce laws knowing they have no chance of passing. They may introduce such bills because they want to draw public attention to legislation in such areas as crime control or education or because they want to go on record in support of the idea. They may introduce such a bill to satisfy a group of voters from their district or an important special interest group. This can help them avoid criticism during election time because they can report they have taken "action" on the issue. They can blame committees and other lawmakers for the bill's failure to become law.

THINK ABOUT IT

1. Why do opponents of a bill have an advantage over supporters?
2. Should lawmakers be able to introduce bills that they know have no chance of becoming law? Why or why not?
3. Should lawmakers be able to introduce bills for the benefit of interest groups? Why or why not?

3. Answers will vary, e.g., lawmakers should be able to introduce any bill, but should be ruled by their consciences and their desire to represent their constituencies.

Discussion Starter

Encourage the students to discuss their reactions to the use of riders: What is the purpose of riders? Do you think this purpose is one that should be served by members of the Congress? Why or why not? What do you consider the most convincing arguments in favor of the use of riders? Against the use of riders?

Enrichment

Have a pair of volunteers research controversial riders. Ask the volunteers to select at least five specific riders and prepare a bulletin board display about them.

Reteaching Strategies

1. Let the students work in small groups to compare and revise the notes they have taken on Section 1. Encourage the students to make any necessary changes to ensure that their own notes are complete and correct.

2. Let the students work in groups to write short news reports about the activities of Congress on a fictional, but typical, opening day.

Evaluation Strategies

1. Have the students write their answers to the Section 1 Review questions.

2. Have the students take the Section 1 Quiz found in the *TRB*.

Section 1 Review (Answers)

1. Caucuses meet in order to reach agreement on key issues so parties can act as a unified force. They also plan the party's upcoming strategy and choose party leaders.

2. Since only one-third of the Senate's members are beginning a new term, the Senate has much less organizational business to attend to.

3. The State of the Union Address reports on the domestic and foreign concerns of the nation. It also lays out the administration's broad policies and makes legislative recommendations.

4. Public bills involve matters of national interest. Private bills are those that apply to certain persons or places.

5. Answers will vary, e.g., there has to be an official selection process made when all members are present in the House in order to publicize the selection of House officers. Also, ceremony plays an important part in our traditions.

Figure Answer Students should understand that this figure lists public bills.

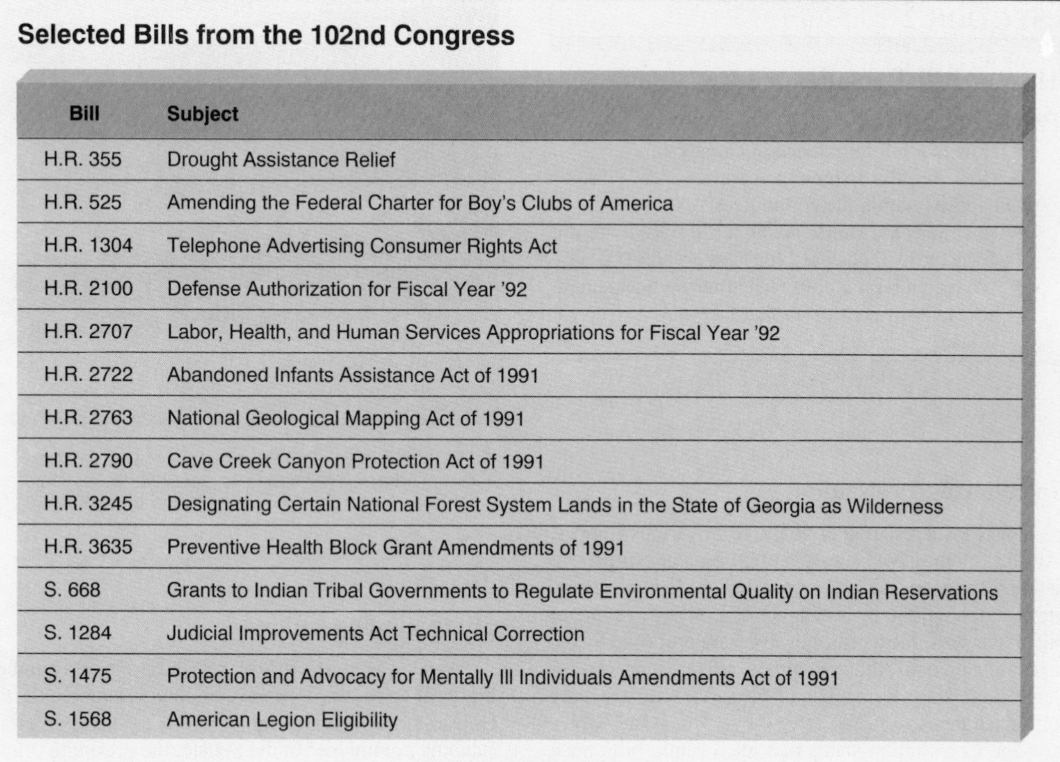

Selected Bills from the 102nd Congress

Bill	Subject
H.R. 355	Drought Assistance Relief
H.R. 525	Amending the Federal Charter for Boy's Clubs of America
H.R. 1304	Telephone Advertising Consumer Rights Act
H.R. 2100	Defense Authorization for Fiscal Year '92
H.R. 2707	Labor, Health, and Human Services Appropriations for Fiscal Year '92
H.R. 2722	Abandoned Infants Assistance Act of 1991
H.R. 2763	National Geological Mapping Act of 1991
H.R. 2790	Cave Creek Canyon Protection Act of 1991
H.R. 3245	Designating Certain National Forest System Lands in the State of Georgia as Wilderness
H.R. 3635	Preventive Health Block Grant Amendments of 1991
S. 668	Grants to Indian Tribal Governments to Regulate Environmental Quality on Indian Reservations
S. 1284	Judicial Improvements Act Technical Correction
S. 1475	Protection and Advocacy for Mentally Ill Individuals Amendments Act of 1991
S. 1568	American Legion Eligibility

▲ **FIGURE 14–2 Selected Bills from the 102nd Congress.** As you have learned, Congress considers different types of bills. What type of bills are listed above?

passed by that house alone. Simple resolutions are regularly used to adopt a new rule or procedure or to amend an existing one. Resolutions may also be used to express an opinion. For example, the Senate may pass a resolution in support of an action taken by the president toward The People's Republic of China. Like concurrent resolutions, they are not sent to the president for approval, and they do not have the force of law.

Riders A bill or resolution usually deals with only one subject. Sometimes, however, a rider is attached to the bill. A **rider** is a provision that is unlikely to pass on its own so it is attached to an important measure that is likely to pass into law. The rider's sponsors hope it will "ride" through the legislative process on the strength of the measure in the bill. Riders become law if the bill to which they are attached is passed. Riders often deal with controversial issues and sometimes have led to the defeat of the bill to which they are attached.

Section 1 Review

1. What is the purpose of party caucuses prior to the convening of Congress?
2. How do the opening days of the House and Senate differ?
3. What does the president discuss in the State of the Union Address in modern times?
4. What types of bills are proposed in Congress? How do they differ?
5. **For critical analysis:** If the Speaker of the House, the clerk, the sergeant at arms, and other officials have already been chosen by the majority party caucus, why do you think the House continues to *officially* elect its officers on opening day?

SECTION 2

Points to Stress

- The manner in which a bill is introduced in Congress.
- The way that bills are assigned to committees and the operation within committees.
- Action on a bill taken in the House and the methods for taking votes.
- Action on a bill taken in the Senate and the way it differs from that taken in the House.

Kickoff Activity
Have the students list at least three different sources from which they think bills in Congress might originate. Then have the students rank their sources according to the frequency of use. After all the students have completed their lists, let volunteers share their ideas.

Working with the Preview Questions
Read each of these study questions aloud, and encourage the students to share and discuss their responses. Remind the students to keep these questions in mind, looking for more complete answers, as they study Section 2.

Teaching Strategies

Discussion Starter
You may want to let the students recall their own ideas about the sources of bills introduced in Congress. (See the Kickoff Activity.) How do your ideas compare with the information given here? How do you explain the differences?

Vocabulary
As the students consider the definitions here for *hopper* and *sponsors,* ask volunteers to explain other uses of these nouns.

Caption Answer Bills are then printed, distributed, and numbered according to when they were introduced.

Multidiscipline Strategies

Math The topic of compensation for House of Representative members is polarizing. Some feel that Congress members are too prone to vote themselves pay hikes, while others feel that we get a good value for our money, especially if we want to attract qualified and competent individuals. Have students contact their Congress member's local or Washington office to get an average workday or use the Day in the Life feature found in this unit. Students should compute an "hourly wage" for their Congress member based on the average workday they discover and the $124,400 salary of representatives. With certain benefits, the compensation of a representative could also safely be calculated at $150,000. Let students discuss whether this is an adequate amount of money, adding variables such as time away from families and campaigning for reelection.

SECTION 2

How a Bill Becomes a Law

Preview Questions

- How is a bill introduced in Congress?
- How are bills assigned to committees? What happens within the committees?
- How does the House act on a bill? What are the different methods used for taking votes?
- What action on a bill is taken in the Senate and how is it different from that taken in the House?

▲ To introduce a bill in the House, a representative simply drops the written proposal into the hopper, shown above. What happens to the bill next?

Introducing Legislation

Ideas for legislation originate from various sources. An idea might have been suggested by a constituent or a lobbyist, or it might have originated in a federal agency or been thought up by a member of Congress or one of his or her staff. Most bills, however, are proposed by the executive branch. Although almost anyone may suggest legislation, only a member of Congress can formally introduce it.

The Constitution states that all revenue bills must first be introduced in the House of Representatives, but any other type may begin in either house. A representative introduces a bill by simply dropping the written proposal into the **hopper**, a box near the clerk's desk. A senator introduces a bill by presenting it to the clerk at the presiding officer's desk, or formally presents the bill from the floor of the Senate. Those who draft and propose bills are called **sponsors**. Bills are then printed, distributed, and numbered according to when they are introduced. For example, H.R. 288 would be the 288th measure introduced in the House during the congressional term. Having received a number, the bill is entered in the House *Journal* and in the *Congressional Record* for the day. The House *Journal* and the *Congressional Record* are official publications of Congress.

When the number of the bill is printed in the *Congressional Record,* then the bill has been placed at *first reading.* For a bill to become law, it must have *three* readings at different stages of its progress through either house. The second reading usually occurs when floor debate begins. The third takes place after any amendments have been added to the bill and the House is ready to take a final vote.

Study by the Committee

As soon as a bill is introduced and assigned a number, it is sent to the appropriate standing committee. In the House, the Speaker assigns the bill to the appropriate standing committee. In the Senate, the presiding officer assigns bills to the proper committees. For example, a farm bill would be sent to the Agriculture Committee; a gun-control bill would be sent to the Judiciary Committee. Committee chairpersons may, in turn, send the bill on to a subcommittee. For example, a bill concerning conventional military weapons in Europe would be sent to the Senate Foreign Relations Subcommittee on European Affairs. Each committee sorts the bills it receives and considers only those it feels are important. The chairperson may decide to **pigeonhole** a bill, that is, put it aside and ignore it. Most bills that are pigeonholed die in committee.

If a bill is not pigeonholed, it is placed on the committee agenda or assigned to a subcommittee. The committee staff members go to work researching the bill and sometimes hold public hearings, during which people who support or oppose the bill may express their views. Committees also have the power to order witnesses to testify at public hearings. Witnesses may be executive agency officials, experts on the subject, or representatives of interest groups concerned about the bill. Depending on the interest in the subject, the hearings may be attended by only a few people or by a large group. For

Comprehension
Let the students define the term *reading* as it is used here: How many formal readings does a bill have? How many times do you guess members of Congress and their aides actually read a specific bill?

TEACHING GOVERNMENT IN ACTION

Read
Introduce this feature by asking the students to recall the 1988 presidential election. Which two individuals represented the Democratic ticket in this election? Explain to the students that these two men, Michael Dukakis, former Governor of Massachusetts, and Lloyd Bentsen, Senator from Texas, have political careers that have continued despite their defeat in the 1988 election. Then ask students to read this Government in Action feature.

Discuss
Stimulate a class discussion of this feature by asking the following questions: What Senate committee does Lloyd Bentsen chair? How would you describe Senator Bentsen's schedule? How might Bentsen's experiences in the business world help shape his current stands as a senator?

Analyze and Apply
Go over the senator's schedule with the class, noting especially the length of his workday. You might also note that Senator Bentsen has several things scheduled at the same time. Students should understand that Bentsen's schedule includes all those things he feels are important that he attend. In many cases, his attendance, however, must be brief. After the students have discussed the schedule, ask them to write a short essay detailing whether or not they feel the demands of the job of a U.S. senator are equal to the rewards of the job.

Review
Review the content of this feature by asking the following questions: When was Lloyd Bentsen first elected to Congress? When did he leave Congress? When did he return? What Senate committee does Bentsen chair? In what policy areas does he have the most influence? Why?

Think About It (Answers)
1. Answers will vary. Senator Bentsen balanced the ticket geographically, being from a large, populous, southern state.
2. Although based in Washington, D.C., a senator is completely dependent upon his local constituency for reelection. He must also keep in close touch with his electorate to best represent their interests.

GOVERNMENT IN ACTION

A DAY IN THE LIFE

Senator Lloyd Bentsen

Senator Lloyd Bentsen, Democrat from Texas, was first elected to Congress in 1948 at age 27. After six years, he left Congress to begin an insurance business. In 1970, he decided to run for office again. This time he ran for the U.S. Senate, and defeated a Republican congressman from Houston named George Bush.

As chairman of the Senate Finance Committee, Bentsen was extremely influential in policy areas, such as taxes and international trade. He ran as the vice-presidential candidate of Michael Dukakis in the 1988 election. Upon taking office in 1993, President Bill Clinton named him his secretary of the Treasury. No doubt his schedule as a member of the Cabinet is different from the sample listed here, but it is certainly just as full.

Wednesday

9:45	Senate Convenes
10:30	Meeting with Lt. Governor Brereton Jones and Wendell Ford of Kentucky
11:15	Finance Committee Executive Session, Re: Honda Audit
12:00	Meeting with John Mobley
12:30	Texas Congressional delegation—Closed luncheon
12:30	Democratic Caucus
12:30	Meeting with Senator Robert Byrd, W. Virginia
2:00	Meeting with Texas cardiologists
2:00	Finance Medicare Subcommittee
2:30	Meeting with Fruit of the Loom executives
3:00	Meeting on Pensions
3:30	Meeting with the National Governor's Association on Medicare funding
4:00	Texas Academy of Family Physicians
4:00	Reception for Leonid Kravchuk, leader of Ukraine
4:30	Meeting with Texas letter carriers
7:00	CNN's Moneyline, live interview on economic policy
8:00	Dinner honoring the president of the World Bank

THINK ABOUT IT

1. Aside from being an able and experienced legislator, what other attributes made Bentsen an attractive running mate for Massachusetts Governor Michael Dukakis?
2. During this day Senator Bentsen has met several times with his Texas constituents. Why do you think this is important?

Discussion Starter
Help the students consider the example of the two hearings held on March 20, 1991: What accounts for the difference between the coverage given to the Senate Foreign Relations Committee hearing and that given to the House Banking Committee hearing? What are the probable effects of such differences in coverage? Should all Congressional hearings be given equal news coverage? Why or why not?

Enrichment
Have two or three volunteers research the content of the two example hearings: What testimony did Glaspie present? What information about overcharging in mortgage accounts was made public in the House Banking Committee hearing? Ask the volunteers to share their findings with the rest of the class; then encourage the students to discuss again the appropriateness of the different coverage given these two hearings by the media.

Vocabulary
Let volunteers explain the connotations of the noun *junkets:* What do these connotations tell about public attitudes toward many of the trips made by Congress members?

Discussion Starter
Ask the students to share and discuss their own attitudes toward junkets: How necessary do you consider such trips? How helpful to understanding the basic issues of a bill might such trips be? Do you believe junkets should be encouraged or limited? Why? How?

Discussion Starter
Guide the students in discussing the importance of the actions a committee might take on a bill: What do you imagine usually happens to a bill that is reported favorably? Why? How can changes made by the committee affect the possibility of a bill's becoming law? How might such changes alter the purpose the bill was originally introduced to serve? What is the difference between reporting a bill unfavorably and pigeonholing a bill?

Extension
Help the students discuss the importance of the House Rules Committee: How does this committee influence the work of all the other committees? Then ask the students to find and list the names of all the current members of the House Rules Committee.

Comprehension
Let volunteers list the specific differences between the methods for scheduling used in the House and in the Senate.

example, on March 20, 1991, April Glaspie, the former U.S. Ambassador to Iraq, was called to testify before the Senate Foreign Relations Committee concerning the United States diplomatic action with Iraq prior to the Persian Gulf War. The hearing was attended by a large group of senators, twenty-five photographers, a network camera pool, and three full tables of reporters. It was covered live by Cable News Network (CNN) and the Senate cable system. On the other side of Capitol Hill, a House Banking Committee hearing about overcharging in certain types of mortgage accounts was attended by only a few people.

Sometimes a subcommittee will make a trip to gather information on the bill. These trips, called **junkets**, are made to locations affected by the proposed measure. For example, if proposed legislation concerns an urban housing project, a member of the Senate Committee on Banking, Housing, and Urban Affairs may visit an inner-city area. If proposed legislation concerns wolves in a national park, the National Parks and Public Lands Subcommittee of the House Committee on Interior and Insular Affairs may visit the national park in question.

The subcommittee then meets to approve the bill as is, add new amendments, or draft a new bill. This meeting is known as the **markup session**. If members cannot agree on changes, a vote is taken. When a subcommittee completes its work on a bill it goes to full committee, which then meets for its own markup session. It may hold its own hearings, amend the subcommittee's version, or simply approve the subcommittee's recommendations.

Finally the committee will report the bill back to the full House. It can report the bill favorably, report the bill with amendments, or report a newly written bill. It can also report it unfavorably, but usually it will have been pigeonholed earlier instead. Along with the bill, the committee will send to the House or Senate a written report that explains the committee's actions, describes the bill, lists the major changes made by committee, and gives opinions on the bill.

Scheduling Legislation

Next, the bill is placed on a calendar and scheduled for debate. A **calendar** is a schedule of the order in which bills will be taken up on the floor. There are five calendars in the House, depending on the nature and subject matter of the bill. These calendars are:

1. **The Union Calendar.** Formally called The Calendar of the Committee of the Whole House on the State of the Union, all government property, revenue, and appropriations bills go on this calendar.
2. **The House Calendar.** All other public bills go on this calendar.
3. **The Private Calendar.** Formally known as The Calendar of the Committee of the Whole House, almost all private bills go on this calendar.
4. **The Consent Calendar.** This is for all bills removed from the first-two-mentioned calendars and agreed to by unanimous consent. These are typically minor bills.
5. **The Discharge Calendar.** All petitions designed to discharge bills from committees are placed on this calendar.

There is an elaborate schedule for House consideration of certain bills, but these arrangements are not always followed closely. The **House Rules Committee** plays a major role in the scheduling process. This committee, along with the House leaders, regulates the flow of the bills through the House. The Rules Committee can move bills ahead quickly, hold them back, or stop them completely. It can also set up special rules that limit the time set for debate and the number of amendments that can be suggested for the bill.

The Senate is much smaller and only a few leading members control the flow of bills to committees and to the floor. The Senate has only one calendar, the **Calendar of General Orders**, which lists all bills to be considered by the Senate. The Senate brings bills to the floor by "unanimous consent," a motion by which all members present on the floor set aside the Senate's formal rules and consider a bill from the calendar. In contrast to the procedure in the House, individual senators have the power to disrupt work on legislation.

The Constitution requires that before any action can take place on the floor, a certain number of members must be present. This number, known as a **quorum**, is a majority of the full House (218 members) or a majority of the Senate (51 members).

Action in the House

When a bill reaches the House floor, it receives its second reading as the clerk reads the bill through. After each paragraph, amendments may be offered and debate can take place. Many bills are minor and pass with little or no opposition. Because of its large size and the number of bills introduced, the House has developed several procedures to speed up the legislative process for some of the more important matters.

Discussion Starter
Encourage the students to discuss their responses to these questions: How do you think representatives decide which bills are "minor"? What is the difference between a minor bill and an important bill? How many representatives need to consider a bill important in order for that bill to be treated as a major bill on the House floor?

Discussion Starter
Help the students consider the uses of the House acting as a Committee of the Whole: What are the advantages of using this system? Which groups are most likely to benefit? What are the disadvantages of using this system? Which groups are most likely to suffer? Under what circumstances do you think the Committee of the Whole is most likely to sit? Why?

Extension
If possible, have all the students watch a specific debate on C-SPAN; then encourage them to discuss their responses to both the content and the form of the debate.

Cooperative Learning
Have the students work in groups to read about and discuss the four methods used in the House for taking floor votes: Why and under what circumstances is each form of voting used? What advantages—and disadvantages—do you think may be associated with each form of voting?

Caption Answer The electronic voting system, which makes use of the 48 electronic voting stations, is used for roll call, or record, votes.

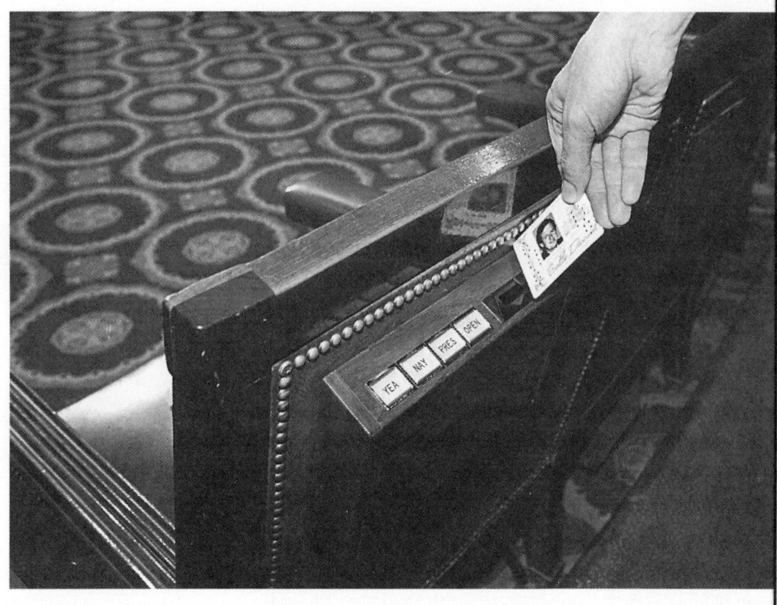

In 1973, the House of Representatives installed 48 electronic voting stations, such as the one shown here. For what type of vote are these stations used?

Committee of the Whole To speed along the passage of an important bill, the entire House may sit as a **committee of the whole**. In this committee, a temporary chairperson is appointed by the Speaker of the House and the usual formal House rules do not apply. At least 100 members must be present in order to conduct business, instead of the official quorum of 218. The measure is debated or amended, with votes on amendments as needed. The committee of the whole can approve or reject bills by a majority vote. The committee adjourns when it completes its action, and the House returns to its normal session and procedures. The Speaker presides once again, the full House hears the chairperson report the committee's recommendations, and it formally adopts them.

Debate Because of its large size, the House has severe limitations on floor debate. The Speaker recognizes those who may speak and can force any member who does not "stick to the subject" to give up the floor. Normally, the chairperson of the standing committee reporting the bill will take charge of the session during which it is debated. You can often watch such debates on C-SPAN (a cable television service that covers congressional activities, among other things).

Any member may propose an amendment to a bill during floor debate. At any time, any member may "move the previous question," which is a demand for a vote on the issue before the House. If that motion passes, only forty minutes of further debate is allowed before a vote is taken.

Vote After a House bill has been fully debated and amended, it is ready for a vote. The bill now has its third reading and a vote on the entire floor is taken. The House uses four different methods for taking floor votes:

1. Voice votes are the most common method of taking a floor vote. In a **voice vote**, the presiding officer asks those members in favor to say "Aye," and those opposed to say "No." The Speaker determines which side has the most voice votes.
2. If a member questions the results of the voice vote, a **standing vote** may be demanded. First, those in favor of the bill stand and are counted, then those opposed stand and are counted.
3. A **teller vote** may be demanded at the request of one-fifth of a quorum. The Speaker appoints two tellers, one member from each party. The members pass between them and are counted, for and against. Teller votes are rare today and have been replaced by electronic voting.
4. A **roll-call vote,** also known as a **record vote**, is recorded electronically. In 1973, the House installed a computerized voting system in which members insert a plastic card and press a button in one of forty-

TEACHING CITIZENSHIP SKILLS AND RESPONSIBILITIES

Read
Ask one of the students to read the feature title aloud, and encourage the students to discuss their ideas about it: Who should be able to locate and interpret Congressional voting records? Why? How often and how regularly do those people actually examine Congressional voting records? Why? What—if anything—can or should be done to change this situation? After this introductory discussion, have volunteers read the feature aloud to the rest of the class.

Discuss
Pose questions such as these to stimulate discussion of the Citizenship Skills and Responsibilities feature: How do you feel about the various reasons Congress members have for changing their votes? Which of these reasons—if any—do you consider unethical? Why? What—if anything—can or should be done to change these patterns of vote-changing? What can you do to discover and understand the set of standards used by various groups to rate Congress members? Why is it important to understand each group's standards?

Analyze and Apply
Have the students work in small groups to write their own set of standards for evaluating the work of members of Congress. Then let the groups use their standards to rank at least two well-known senators and at least two well-known representatives. Allow the members of each group to share their standards and ratings with the rest of the call.

Review
Use these questions to help the students review the Citizenship Skills and Responsibilities feature: Where can you find information about the specific results of record votes in the House and the Senate? How can you use studies prepared by interest groups as an aid

Developing Skills for the Information Age

The vast majority of people who want to be informed about the laws under consideration by Congress get their news from newspapers or television news. This is not always an adequate way to be informed. Have students watch the news and read newspapers for at least one week to see what actions of Congress are covered. Be sure students bring in a record of what they found.

Then have students bring in the same week's Congressional Quarterly Weekly Report, and have them watch the PBS program Washington Week in Review. Students should look for vital bills that were considered by Congress but not covered by the media, and should also judge how well the papers and news programs did compared with the other two sources.

CITIZENSHIP SKILLS AND RESPONSIBILITIES

Locating and Interpreting Congressional Voting Records

If you want to be an informed citizen concerning the voting records of your representatives and senators, you can obtain this information. All record or roll-call votes are printed in the *Congressional Record,* or Congressional Quarterly's *Weekly Report,* both of which are found in most large libraries. Some large newspapers such as the *Washington Post* and the *New York Times,* as well as some local papers, usually print weekly summaries of how local members voted on key issues.

Reading these final votes, however, does not give you the full picture. A member of Congress may have voted one way during committee and the other way in the final process. He or she may have wanted to go on record as voting according to public opinion in the final stage of passage. Members may also have changed their votes after the voting was completed. For example, they might have voted against the interests of their district, but when they discovered their vote was not crucial to its passage, they may have changed it to look good in the eyes of their constituents.

One way of examining a member's voting behavior throughout the process is by reading studies prepared by interest groups. Dozens of groups prepare studies and rate congressional members' voting records. (Remember, though, that these groups have their own set of standards—find out what they are.) Some of these groups include:

Consumer Federation of America
1012 14th St. NW
Washington, DC 20005

Environmental Action
1346 Connecticut Ave. NW
Washington, DC 20036

Women's Lobby, Inc.
1345 G St. SE
Washington, DC 20003

American Farm Bureau Federation
425 13th St. NW
Washington, DC 20004

TAKING ACTION

1. Write to one of the groups listed above to obtain information about its organization and its ratings of the senators and representatives in your state. Decide whether you think the group would be considered liberal, middle-of-the-road, or conservative. Then determine whether your members of Congress are considered liberal, middle-of-the-road, or conservative by the group. You might want to extend this activity by presenting your findings to your senators and representatives in the form of a letter. Ask them to respond to the group's assessment of their performance.
2. Obtain a record of one of your state's senator's voting record over the last year. Determine where on the political spectrum that senator's views lie. Compare your determination with one of the rating systems that you have already obtained from one of the groups listed above. How would you explain the differences, if there are any, between their evaluation and yours?

eight voting stations around the floor. Their votes are flashed on large display panels above the Speaker's desk, on other walls of the House, and on consoles located on the leadership tables. The board shows which members have voted as well as how they voted.

If a bill is approved by a majority, it is signed by the Speaker. A page then carries it to the Senate and places it on the vice president's (Senate president's) desk. (Congressional pages are juniors in high school who normally spend one school year living in Washington, D.C., and working for a senator or representative. There are normally about 100 of them who run errands between offices, work on the floor of the two houses, and answer phones in the cloak room.)

Action in the Senate

Although the steps in the lawmaking process are similar in both chambers, there are differences in floor to your own understanding of Congressional voting records?

Vocabulary
You may want to have a volunteer recall the definition of the noun *page* as it is used here.

Discussion Starter
Guide the students in discussing the differences in debate rules in the House and the Senate: What are the reasons for these differences? What is their significance?

Enrichment
Ask the students to research recent uses of the filibuster—or of the threat of a filibuster—in Senate debates: What was the issue of debate? Who filibustered or threatened to filibuster? Why? With what results? Give the students an opportunity to compare and discuss their findings.

Vocabulary
Ask the students to look up the derivation of *cloture* and to identify other words that are related in both derivation and meaning.

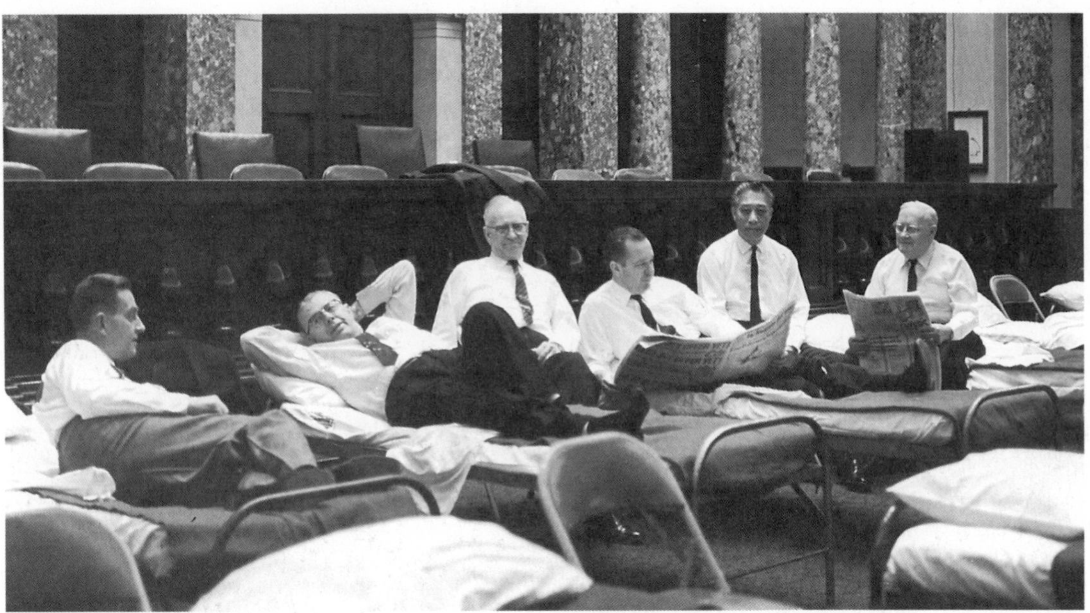

▲ During a filibuster over the passage of the Civil Rights Act in 1957, cots were set up in the old Supreme Court Chamber so that senators could rest. This filibuster by Senator Strom Thurmond of South Carolina was a record-setting 24 hours and 18 minutes long. What is the point of a filibuster?

debates. While floor debates are strictly limited in the House, debates are usually unlimited in the Senate. Generally, senators may speak on the floor for as long as they wish and there is no rule that they speak only about the measure under consideration. There is no routine motion to call for a vote. The Senate's dedication to freedom of debate is intended to encourage the fullest possible discussion of matters on the floor.

The Filibuster One way for a single senator or a group of senators to defeat a bill they oppose is to filibuster against it. To **filibuster** means to keep talking until a majority of the Senate either abandons the bill or agrees to modify its most controversial provisions. Essentially, filibustering is a tactic to delay or block action by "talking a bill to death."

All that senators need do to filibuster is stay on their feet and keep talking. After three hours, they may talk about any topic they want or even read a book aloud. In 1935, for example, Senator Huey Long (Democrat from Louisiana) spoke for more than fifteen hours and shared his recipes for southern-style cooking. Senator Strom Thurmond of South Carolina set the record for a filibuster when he spoke against the Civil Rights Act of 1957 for twenty-four hours and eighteen minutes. Although later efforts have not equalled these, the practice on a less dramatic scale is still often used. Even the threat of a filibuster has resulted in the Senate's failure to consider a number of bills and the amending of many more.

Cloture Rule **Cloture** is a parliamentary rule by which debate is ended and an immediate vote is taken on the matter under discussion. The Senate can end filibusters by using the **cloture rule**, a procedure that limits debate by allowing a minimum of sixteen senators to move that debate be limited. If three-fifths of the entire Senate (sixty senators) approves, no senator may speak for more than one hour on the bill being considered. After that time, the bill under consideration must be brought to a vote. Obtaining a vote in favor of cloture, however, is usually difficult. Many senators hesitate to support most cloture motions because of the Senate tradition of open debate and because they themselves may want to filibuster a bill in the future.

Voting in the Senate

Voting in the Senate is very similar to voting in the House. However, there are no teller votes in the Senate.

Caption Answer Filibusters are designed to kill a bill by "talking it to death."

Multidiscipline Strategies

Speech Have each student listen to a recording of a notable speech given during a Congressional debate. (Or have the students watch speeches on C-SPAN.) Ask the students to analyze the speeches, answering questions such as these: What main idea did the speaker present? What specific facts did the speaker use to support that idea? What other details did the speaker use to clarify his or her main idea? How did the organization of the speech contribute to its effectiveness? How did the speaker's presentation influence your response to the speech?

Enrichment
Let students study and discuss figure 14–3, How a Bill Becomes a Law. You might then wish to take this opportunity to run a mock Senate or mock House of Representatives. In a mock Senate, students should choose states that they will represent. You can then select someone to act as president of the Senate.

Explain to students that they will be asked to submit and decide on a number of bills. Allow four or five volunteers to write their own bills to be submitted. You might wish to instruct students as to the subject matter of these bills so that you will need no more than three committees to discuss the bills.

Allow students at least one full class period to act as the Senate and have them work through the steps shown in this figure. You might wish to construct your own House version of any bills that are approved so that you can act as the conference committee representative for the House.

Figure Answer Members from both chambers work together to create a compromise version of the two bills at the conference committee stage of the process.

This figure content is also featured on *West's American Government Videodisc* (see the index found in the *TRB*) and is available in the transparency package.

Reteaching Strategies
1. Have students work in pairs to list the most important differences between the House and the Senate in dealing with proposed legislation.
2. Ask the students to use the *Congressional Record*, the *Weekly Report*, or a local newspaper; have them record votes cast by their representative during a given one-month period.

Evaluation Strategies
1. Have the students write their answers to the Section 2 Review questions.
2. Have the students take the Section 2 Quiz found in the *TRB*.

Section 2 Review (Answers)
1. A representative introduces a bill by dropping the written proposal into the hopper, a box near the clerk's desk. A senator introduces a bill by presenting it to the clerk at the presiding officer's desk.
2. If the bill is not pigeonholed, it is placed on the committee agenda for consideration or assigned to a subcommittee.
3. Bills are placed on a calendar and scheduled for debate.
4. A procedure that allows the House to consider, as a committee, certain important bills under less formal rules in order to speed the passage of these bills.
5. Because of its large size, the House has severe limitations on floor debate. Debates are usually unlimited in the Senate.
6. Answers will vary, e.g., senators allow it because they believe there will come a time when they can use it to stop or delay action on a bill which they oppose. Senators allow it because it is part of the tradition of the Senate that makes the Senate different from the House.

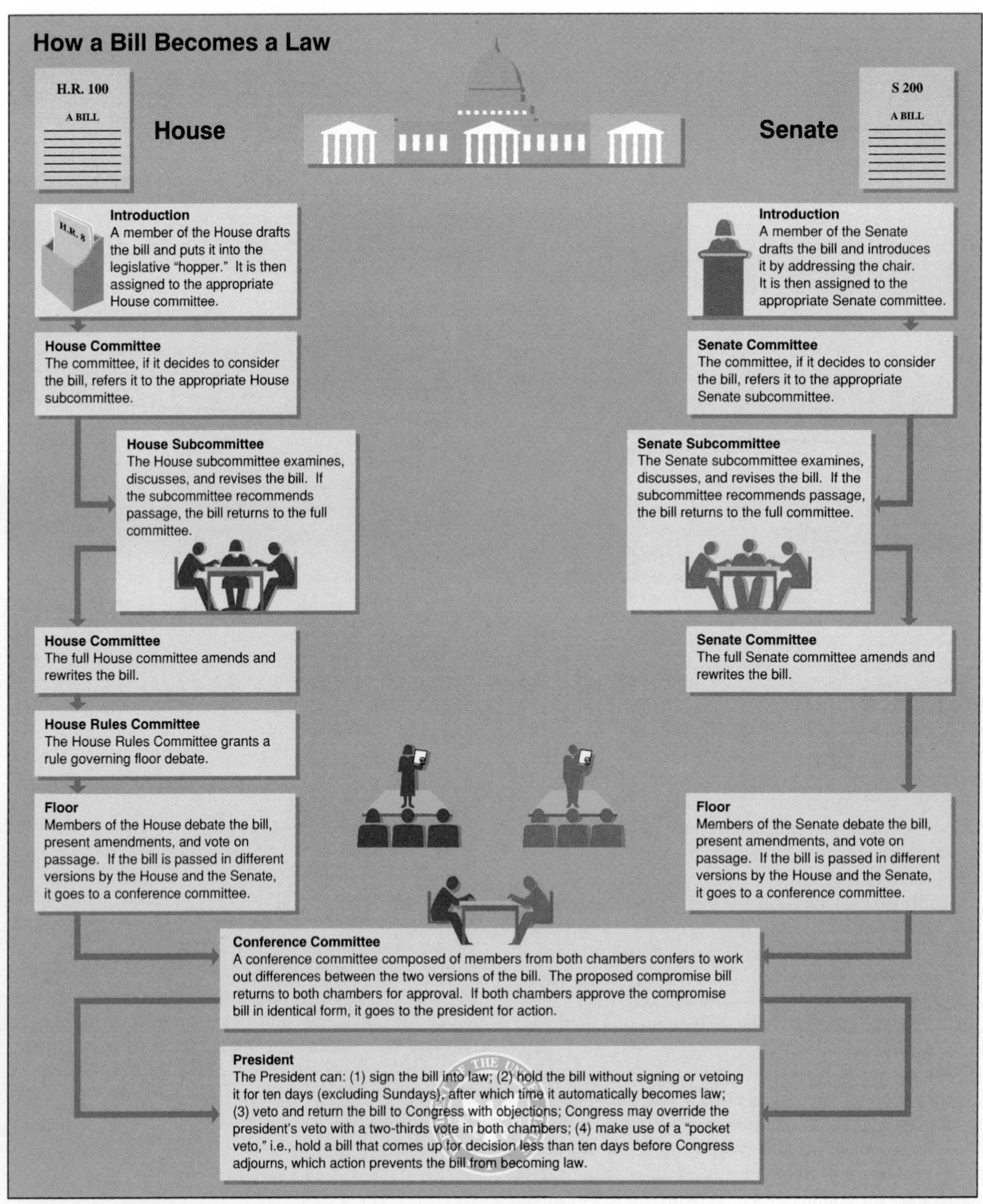

How a Bill Becomes a Law
H.R. 100
A BILL
House
S 200
A BILL
Senate
Introduction
A member of the House drafts the bill and puts it into the legislative "hopper." It is then assigned to the appropriate House committee.
Introduction
A member of the Senate drafts the bill and introduces it by addressing the chair. It is then assigned to the appropriate Senate committee.
House Committee
The committee, if it decides to consider the bill, refers it to the appropriate House subcommittee.
Senate Committee
The committee, if it decides to consider the bill, refers it to the appropriate Senate subcommittee.
House Subcommittee
The House subcommittee examines, discusses, and revises the bill. If the subcommittee recommends passage, the bill returns to the full committee.
Senate Subcommittee
The Senate subcommittee examines, discusses, and revises the bill. If the subcommittee recommends passage, the bill returns to the full committee.
House Committee
The full House committee amends and rewrites the bill.
Senate Committee
The full Senate committee amends and rewrites the bill.
House Rules Committee
The House Rules Committee grants a rule governing floor debate.
Floor
Members of the House debate the bill, present amendments, and vote on passage. If the bill is passed in different versions by the House and the Senate, it goes to a conference committee.
Floor
Members of the Senate debate the bill, present amendments, and vote on passage. If the bill is passed in different versions by the House and the Senate, it goes to a conference committee.
Conference Committee
A conference committee composed of members from both chambers confers to work out differences between the two versions of the bill. The proposed compromise bill returns to both chambers for approval. If both chambers approve the compromise bill in identical form, it goes to the president for action.
President
The President can: (1) sign the bill into law; (2) hold the bill without signing or vetoing it for ten days (excluding Sundays), after which time it automatically becomes law; (3) veto and return the bill to Congress with objections; Congress may override the president's veto with a two-thirds vote in both chambers; (4) make use of a "pocket veto," i.e., hold a bill that comes up for decision less than ten days before Congress adjourns, which action prevents the bill from becoming law.

▲ FIGURE 14–3 **How a Bill Becomes a Law.** The above figure maps out the steps involved in the process for enacting laws. At what stage in the process do members from both chambers work together to create a compromise bill?

SECTION 3

Points to Stress

- The reason and purpose for forming conference committees.
- Options available to the president on receiving a bill passed by Congress.

Kickoff Activity

Remind the students that they have probably read and heard news coverage of the final steps in passing bills into law; ask them to list what they already know about those steps. After all the students have finished writing, encourage them to compare and discuss their lists.

Working with the Preview Questions

Have the students read and discuss their responses to the two study questions. Then remind the students to look for more complete answers to these questions as they study Section 3.

Teaching Strategies

Introduction

Ask one of the students to read this brief section introduction aloud. Then help the students discuss it by asking questions such as these: How often do you think a bill is passed in identical form by both chambers of Congress? What probably distinguishes the bills that are passed in identical form? Why do so many bills pass in two different versions?

You may also want to ask several volunteers to research what happened to the two versions of the environmental law passed in 1990; have these volunteers present their findings to the rest of the class.

Comprehension

Have the students recall or review (in Chapter 13) the formation and functions of conference committees.

Discussion Starter

Guide the students in discussing the changes that might be made to a bill by a conference committee: Why are new proposals not supposed to be considered? Why do you think that, in reality, they often are? What do you imagine would happen if the rules governing a conference committee were more closely followed? Why?

Cooperative Learning

Let the students work in groups to read about and discuss the four choices a president has in handing a bill passed by Congress: What would motivate the president to choose each form of action? How might Congress—and the voting public—be expected to react to each choice? Why?

Section 2 Review

1. How are bills introduced in the House? How are they introduced in the Senate?
2. What happens during permanent committee meetings?
3. How are bills scheduled for debate?
4. What is the committee of the whole?
5. How does debate differ in the House and in the Senate?
6. **For critical analysis:** Why do you think the Senate allows unlimited debate in the form of a filibuster?

Section 3

The Final Stages

Preview Questions:

- When is a conference committee formed and what is its purpose?
- What options does a president have on receiving a bill passed by Congress?

Bills passed in one chamber are then sent to the other chamber where the legislative process begins again. To become law, a bill must be passed in *identical* form by both chambers of Congress. For example, in 1990 both chambers passed legislation that would revise and expand environmental laws for the first time in thirteen years. The two bills varied significantly in their prescriptions for acid rain, toxic pollutants, automobile emissions, and urban smog. What happens when the two houses pass separate versions of the same bill?

Conference Committees

When the House or the Senate will not accept the other's version of a bill, the measure is turned over to a **conference committee**—a temporary joint committee of the two houses. The conference committee members try to work out the differences between the two bills and come up with an acceptable compromise bill.

Members of the committee, called **conferees** or managers, are made up mostly of members of the standing committees that handled the bill in each house. In theory, the conference committee can only consider those points in a bill on which the two houses disagree; no proposals are allowed to be added. In reality, however, the conference committee sometimes makes important changes in the bill or adds new provisions.

Once conferees agree on the final compromise bill, a **conference report** is submitted to each house. The bill must be accepted or rejected by both houses as it was written by the committee, with no further amendments made. If the bill is approved by both houses, it is ready for action by the president.

Presidential Action

The Constitution requires that all bills passed by Congress must be submitted to the president for approval. The president has four choices in handling the bill:

1. The president may approve the legislation by signing it, at which point the bill becomes law.
2. A president who is not strongly in favor of the bill can refuse to act on it for ten days, excluding Sundays. If the president does not sign the bill while Congress is in session, the bill becomes law after the ten-day lapse. A president may use this procedure if he mostly approves of the bill but objects to some of its provisions. By letting the bill become law without his signature, the president indicates his dissatisfaction with these provisions. This procedure is rarely used.

▲ When the president signs a bill passed by Congress, it becomes law. What are the three other ways a president may deal with a bill passed by Congress?

Caption Answer The president may allow the bill to become law without signing it; the president may veto the bill at which point it is returned to the House in which it originated; or if a bill is passed during the last ten days of Congress, the president may kill the bill by refusing to sign it. This is called the pocket veto.

TEACHING BUILDING SOCIAL STUDIES SKILLS

Read
Begin by letting the students discuss their own ideas about analyzing information: Who needs to analyze information? When and why? What skills are involved in analyzing information? What experiences—both successful and unsuccessful—have you had with analyzing information? After this introductory discussion, let several students take turns reading the Building Social Studies Skills feature aloud to the rest of the class.

Discuss
Help the students discuss the feature by asking questions such as these: What is the difference between a primary source and a secondary source? Which primary source documents have you used in social studies research? What kinds of secondary sources have you used? Why is it important to reach your own conclusions rather than accepting the conclusions presented by others?

Analyze and Apply
Have the students work with partners or in small groups to select a specific research topic in government or political science. Ask the students to gather and list with their sources at least ten facts and ten opinions related to the chosen topic. Post the lists of facts and opinions; encourage the students to read and discuss one anothers' lists.

Review
Ask these questions to help the students review the Building Social Studies Skills feature: Why is it important to be able to analyze information? What four steps should you follow in analyzing any information in social studies?

Comprehension
Ask volunteers to explain the differences between letting a bill become law without the president's signature (choice 2) and a pocket veto (choice 4): How do the outcomes of these actions differ? Why is the timing of these two actions important?

Extension
Ask the students to read about recent uses of the four different kinds of action a president can take in response to a bill submitted for approval.

Reteaching Strategies
1. Let the students work with partners to write outlines of the information presented in Section 3.
2. Work with small groups of students to discuss responses to these questions: What role does the president play in passing bills? How can the Congress pass a bill that the president does not approve?

Evaluation Strategies
1. Have the students write their answers to the Section 3 Review questions.
2. Have the students take the Section 3 Quiz found in the *TRB*.

BUILDING SOCIAL STUDIES SKILLS
Analyzing Information

A reader in any social studies subject must be able to analyze information. When you do research about any topic in government and political science, as well as in any other social studies subject, you will read books, articles, biographies, and primary source documents such as laws or constitutions.

When you analyze information, you have to break it apart and decide how much of what you are reading is cause and effect, how much is fact and opinion. After you take the information apart you have to put it back together and draw your own conclusions. Here are the steps you should follow when you analyze any information in social studies.

1. **Carefully read the material.** If you don't understand what you are reading, you cannot analyze it correctly. When you read the material, look for the main ideas and supporting details.
2. **Keep asking yourself questions.** While you read, ask yourself who is involved and why, when the main events actually occurred, and other key questions. The main question you want to keep asking yourself is "Why?"
3. **Determine whether there is bias.** If you are reading a speech by a political candidate, the bias may be easy to find. If you are reading an analysis written by a researcher, identifying bias may be more difficult.

   In your examination of bias, you need to separate fact from opinion. A fact is something that can be proven or verified; an opinion is a subjective viewpoint that cannot be confirmed.
4. **Reach a conclusion.** After you have analyzed the information in the manner presented above, you need to reach a conclusion. For example, after reading an article on your senator you might conclude that he or she supports gun control.

PRACTICING YOUR SKILLS

Look in your local daily newspaper and select an article from the first page to analyze. For the article you choose, write down a list of the facts presented in one column and a list of the opinions in another column. Then determine whether you can detect any bias in what you have read.

3. The President may **veto**, or refuse to sign the bill. (*Veto* is Latin for "I forbid.") The bill must then be returned to the house in which it originated, together with the president's objections to the bill. Congress may try to amend the bill to suit the president and repass it, or it may try to override the president's veto by a two-thirds vote of the members present in each house. Although it seldom happens, an override would pass the bill over the president's veto. The president who holds the record for the greatest number of vetoes is Franklin D. Roosevelt, who vetoed 631 bills during his thirteen years in office. Congress overrode only nine of those vetoes.
4. The president may kill a bill passed during the last ten days Congress is in session by simply refusing to act on it. This is called a **pocket veto**. The president simply does not sign the bill and because Congress in no longer in session, it does not have the opportunity to override the veto.

Each time a bill makes it through all these stages and becomes law it stands as an example of the legislative process in action. This process has continued for over two hundred years but also begins anew with each congressional term, when both the House and Senate organize for action. As the nation has evolved and become more complex, so too has this process, with committees and subcommittees playing an ever increasing role. Regardless of these changes, the legislative process remains a vital part of our representative democracy.

SECTION 3 REVIEW

1. What happens when the two chambers of Congress pass two different versions of the same bill?
2. What is the purpose of a conference committee?
3. **For critical analysis:** Do you think it is necessary for a bill to go through so many steps to become a law? Why or why not?

Section 3 Review (Answers)

1. A conference committee is formed to try to work out the differences between the two bills and come up with a compromise.

2. The purpose of a conference committee is to agree on a compromise.

3. Answers will vary, e.g., each step is necessary to prevent hastily passed legislation.

TEACHING CHALLENGE TO THE AMERICAN DREAM

Read

Let the students read the feature title. Then ask them: In what way can the signals or messages received by members of Congress present a challenge to the American dream? Encourage the students to express and support various ideas. After a brief discussion, have the students read the feature independently.

Discuss

Use questions such as these to stimulate discussion of the Challenge to the American Dream feature: Do you think members of Congress sometimes have a better understanding than their constituents of what is right for their home state or district? Why or why not? Whose interests are served when members of Congress follow the lead of other legislators or of their staff members? Are these the interests that Congress is intended to serve? How strong a loyalty do you think members of Congress owe to their political parties? Who benefits when legislators vote according to the party line? On what issues has the current president tried to influence Congress or specific members of Congress? What methods has the president used? With what success? Do the members of the voting public benefit from the activities of interest groups? If so, how? If not, why not?

Analyze and Apply

After the students have discussed their ideas in response to the "You Decide" questions, have them work in small groups to formulate a list of guidelines that members of Congress should follow when voting. Encourage the groups to compare and discuss their completed lists of guidelines.

Review

Ask the students these review questions: What are three of the most important factors influencing the way legislators vote? How does each work to influence the decisions made by members of Congress?

You Decide (Answers)

1. Answers will vary, e.g., members should make decisions mainly based on the needs and wishes of their constituents. Probably the needs of their most needy constituents should be considered first.

2. Answers will vary, e.g., lobbyists and interest groups have too much influence on members of Congress.

CHALLENGE TO THE AMERICAN DREAM

Do Members of Congress Get the Wrong Signals?

As representatives of the people, shouldn't lawmakers always base their decisions on what their constituents want? It doesn't always work this way. Many factors may influence a legislator's decision-making process.

Voters The political career of all lawmakers depends on how the voters back home feel about their decisions. Thus, a major influence on lawmakers' decisions is what they believe the voters want.

Other Lawmakers and Staff Legislators sometimes take cues from other trusted or more senior members of Congress. Because members do not have the time to study the details of all the pieces of legislation they handle, they turn to key colleagues for advice on how to vote. In addition, a legislator's personal staff can have a great deal of influence. While many staffers do routine work, others help draft legislation, meet with lobbyists, and decide what should take priority in the legislator's day. The way the staff member filters information may very well determine how that member of Congress votes.

Party Influence Both major parties generally take stands on major issues and come out in favor of or in opposition to specific legislation. In the House of Representatives, members vote with their party about two-thirds of the time. Senators are a little less likely to follow their party's position. On some issues, members of the party tend to vote together more often. When voting on labor issues, for example, Democrats tend to lean toward the side of the unions and Republicans lean toward business interests.

The President Presidents try to influence congressional members by giving or withholding favors and support. For example, in the 1960s, Senator Frank Church of Idaho was critical of President Johnson's policies regarding the Vietnam War. When he showed the president a newspaper column written by journalist Walter Lippmann to support his view, President Johnson said, "All right, the next time you need a dam for Idaho, you go ask Walter Lippmann."

Recent presidents have actively lobbied members of Congress who seem undecided on an issue by inviting them for a visit at the Oval Office, by calling them, and by having key aides and cabinet officers testify at hearings. Presidents can also appear on national television to try to gain support from voters who will in turn influence lawmakers.

Lobbyists and Interest Groups The main purpose of the many lobbyist and interest groups is to persuade members of Congress to vote for legislation in their interests. Lobbyists, some of them former members of Congress, can provide current legislators with crucial information and often with assurances of financial aid in the next campaign. They visit lawmakers and try to persuade them to support their positions.

The challenge to the American dream is whether members of Congress can vote on proposed legislation in a manner that is consistent with their role as representatives and trustees of the people. In particular, if they allow interest groups to overwhelmingly influence their voting decisions, then the best interest of the public may not be served. If they let an overly strong president influence their voting decisions, then only when the president's views represent the best interests of the nation will the public be best served.

You Decide

1. How do you think members of Congress should make decisions? Which factor should have the greatest influence on their decision making?
2. Which groups or individuals, if any, do you feel have too much influence on members of Congress?

Chapter Evaluation

To evaluate student mastery of chapter material, you might:

1. Use Chapter Test A from the *TRB.*

2. Use Chapter Test B from the *TRB.*

3. Construct your own test using items from the *West American Government Test Bank* found in the *TRB.*

4. Use the accompanying computerized test software to construct and print a customized chapter test.

Review Questions (Answers)

1. Caucuses meet in order to reach agreement among party leaders about key issues. They also meet to plan the party's strategy and to choose party leaders.

2. All members (or new members in Senate) have to be sworn in, rules have to be made (in House), and organization has to be decided upon.

3. Public bills involve matters of national interest. Private bills are those that involve certain persons or places. Joint resolutions often deal with temporary or unusual matters or correct an error in earlier law. Concurrent resolutions deal with matters requiring the action of the House and Senate, but for which a law is not needed. They express an opinion or an official policy. Simple resolutions deal with matters affecting only one house of Congress and are passed by that house alone.

4. Ideas for legislation can come from constituents, lobbyists, federal agencies or a member of Congress. Most are proposed by the executive branch. A representative introduces a bill by dropping the written proposal into the hopper. A senator introduces a bill by presenting it to the clerk at the presiding officer's desk.

5. Committee staff researches the bill and sometimes holds public hearings during which people who support or oppose the bill may express their views. The committee then meets to approve the bill, add new amendments, or draft a new bill in a markup session. The committee then reports the bill back to the full house.

6. Bills are placed on a calendar.

CHAPTER 14 REVIEW

Key Terms

bills 336
calendar 342
Calendar of General Orders 342
caucuses 333
clerk of the House 334
cloture 345
cloture rule 345
committee of the whole 343
concurrent resolutions 337
conferees 347
conference committee 347
conference report 347
filibuster 345
hopper 340
House Rules Committee 342
joint resolutions 337
junkets 342
markup session 342
pigeonhole 340
pocket veto 348
private bills 337
public bills 337
quorum 342
record vote 343
rider 339
roll-call vote 343
simple resolution 337
sponsors 340
standing vote 343
State of the Union Address 334
teller vote 343
veto 348
voice vote 343

Summary

1. Before a new term begins, Democratic and Republican members of the House and Senate meet in separate party caucuses to reach agreement among themselves on key issues and to plan the party's strategy for the upcoming term. They also choose party leaders to organize and direct party activities during the congressional term. The House of Representatives is reorganized and begins anew every two years, while the Senate is a continuous body. After both houses are organized, the president delivers the State of the Union Address, which outlines the administration's broad policies and makes legislative recommendations. Bills are proposed laws and are either public (concerning matters of national interest) or private (concerning specific persons or places). Joint resolutions deal with temporary or unusual matters and when passed have the force of law. Concurrent resolutions are measures intended to express an opinion or a public policy and do not have the force of law. Simple resolutions deal with matters affecting only one house of Congress and are passed by that house alone. They do not have the force of law.

2. Although almost anyone may suggest legislation, only a member of Congress can formally introduce it. Bills introduced in either house are referred to standing committees. Bills that are reported out of committee may then be debated and voted on by members on the floor of the House and Senate. Debate is severely limited in the House, but is unlimited in the Senate. Filibustering is a common technique to kill a bill in the Senate.

3. To become a law, a bill must be passed in identical form by both chambers of Congress. When the two chambers do not agree, a conference committee attempts to iron out differences and produce a compromise version acceptable to both houses. The bill is then sent to the president, who has the choice of signing it, letting it become law without signing it, or vetoing it.

Review Questions

1. What are the purposes of private party caucuses?
2. What happens in the House and Senate on the opening day of Congress?
3. Briefly describe the two types of bills that may be introduced and the three types of resolutions that may be passed in Congress.
4. Who may propose legislation for Congress to consider? How is a bill formally introduced?
5. Describe what happens when a committee considers a bill.
6. What procedure has the House developed to speed up the legislative process?
7. How does debate in the Senate differ from debate in the House?
8. What is a filibuster and what is the cloture rule?
9. When is a conference committee formed and what is its purpose?
10. What options does the president have upon receiving a bill passed by both houses?

7. Debate in the House is severely limited, while debate in the Senate is virtually unlimited.

8. To filibuster means to keep talking until a majority of the Senate either abandons the bill or agrees to modify some of its most controversial provisions. Cloture is a rule by which debate is ended and an immediate vote is taken on the matter under discussion if three-fifths of the entire Senate approves.

9. A conference committee, a joint temporary committee, is formed when the House or the Senate will not accept the other's version of a bill.

10. The president may approve the legislation by signing it, may allow the bill to pass without his signature, may veto the bill, or may kill a bill passed during the last ten days of Congress by refusing to act on it.

Questions for Thought and Discussion (Answers)

1. Answers will vary, e.g., individual congresspersons may be affected by news coverage, knowing their constituents may be watching. This knowledge may cause them to speak for unnecessarily long periods of time to gain publicity. It may, however, cause them to be more sensitive to the needs and wishes of their constituents.

2. Answers will vary, e.g., the process is complicated, providing many points at which special interest groups can influence or block legislation. Even if the process were more streamlined, however, special interest groups would only act more quickly with different methods to block legislation.

3. Answers will vary, e.g., debate should be limited to a certain time period in both the House and Senate.

Social Studies Skills (Answers)

1. The main difference is that a bill has to also go through the House Rules Committee prior to floor debate, whereas a bill in the Senate goes straight from the full Senate Committee to the floor.

CHAPTER 14 REVIEW—Continued

Questions for Thought and Discussion

1. The sessions of the House and Senate are now broadcast on cable stations around the country. How, if at all, do you think this affects the operation of Congress and the behavior of individual congresspersons? Do you think committee sessions should be broadcast?
2. Is the process of lawmaking too complicated? Does it give too many opportunities for special interest groups to block needed legislation? Explain.
3. What, if any, reforms do you think should be made in congressional legislation-producing procedures?

Improving Your Skills

Communication Skills

Composing an Essay

An essay is a short report written on a specific topic. When writing an essay, follow these guidelines:

1. ***Read the directions carefully.*** Look for terms that will help you identify what information is asked for. Words such as *purpose, reasons, details* or *objectives* are examples of such terms. Look also for performance terms that will tell you what to write. Some performance clues include:

   - **Discuss:** tell in some detail.
   - **Describe or show:** create a picture with actions and examples.
   - **State:** Make a complete formal statement.

2. ***Make a short outline.*** In order to know where you are going with your essay, you need to create an outline. The more detailed your outline, the smoother the writing of your essay will be.
3. ***Write the first draft.*** Using the logical flow of information you have written down in your outline, start your first draft. The more detailed your outline, the simpler this task will be. Make sure that in your first paragraph your topic, or thesis, statement appears. Be precise in your writing and stay with your topic. Include examples to support your statements.
4. ***Edit your first draft.*** When you edit your first draft you should ask yourself the following questions:

   - Does my essay stay on the topic?
   - Does it contain any unnecessary information?
   - Is it missing any information?
   - Is it interesting and informative?
   - Do I support my thesis statement?

   Keep these questions in mind as you edit your draft. Make sure that you have used correct grammar and spelling. If you are writing with a word processor, you may be able to run your essay through a spelling checker and even a grammar checker.
5. ***Make a polished draft.*** The final draft of your essay should look like a final draft. It should not contain spelling or grammatical errors, nor should it wander from the central topic.

Writing

Following the five steps given above, write an essay on one of the following topics:

- Filibustering
- How a bill becomes law
- The difference between the opening days of the House and of the Senate

Social Studies Skills

Understanding Flow Charts

Examine the flow chart on page 346.

1. What differences are there, if any, between the flow on the right-hand side and the flow on the left-hand side.

Activities and Projects

1. Gather information on a problem related to a current issue. Use the guidelines presented in the previous ''Improving Your Communication Skills'' feature to write a bill that proposes a solution.
2. Stage a class debate on the following: ''Resolved—Filibustering should be eliminated from the Senate.''
3. Stage a mock committee hearing on an issue currently being debated in Congress.

Working with the Videodisc

The text below is from Professor Roger LeRoy Miller's introduction for the motion segment for Unit 5:

In the game of American politics, if often seems that the president holds all the cards. He is this country's head of state, chief executive, chief legislator, commander in chief of its armed forces, chief diplomat, and of course, chief media *persona*. Each president has had a different view of his role. In the following segment, noted broadcaster David Frost interviews presidents Ford, Carter, Reagan, and Nixon.

In the second part of this segment you will be introduced to the office of the presidential press secretary and some of the ideas of those who have held this office. The presidential press secretary is not mentioned in the Constitution or indeed in any legislation, but he or she is vital to the operation of the modern executive branch.

To access this segment, use the bar code below or the videodisc index found in the *TRB*.

Frame 600

UNIT FIVE

The Federal Executive Branch

Unit Contents

CHAPTER INTRODUCTION

Instructional Objectives

By the end of the chapter students should be able to:

- Describe how the office of president was created and its constitutional structure.
- Characterize the role of the vice president and how it has changed.
- Discuss the role of the cabinet in the executive branch of government.
- Outline the agencies within the Executive Office of the President and their functions.

Using the Keynote

Before the students begin reading the chapter, ask them to share their ideas about the presidency: What do you think it would be like to be the president? What makes the president's job different from any other job in the country? In what respects would the job be exciting? In what respects might it be daunting? If you were given the opportunity to become president, would you accept it? Why or why not?

After this introductory discussion, have the students read and discuss the Truman quotation: What did Truman find most difficult about being president?

Introducing the Chapter

Let a volunteer read the Introduction aloud to the class. Then encourage the students to discuss their responses to questions such as these: Why do you think Americans have come to expect more and more from our presidents? How would you define the current expectations of the population? Do you believe that members of your generation expect more—or less—of the president than do members of older generations? Why?

Previewing the Sections

Section 1 Ask volunteers to find and read aloud the section title, the main headings, the feature title, and the figure titles in Section 1. Then give the students an opportunity to discuss what they expect to learn as they study this section.

Section 2 Have the students look through Section 2, noting especially the main headings, the feature title, and the photographs. Ask the students to list at least three questions they hope to have answered as they study this section.

Section 3 Let the students page through Section 3, paying particular attention to the section title, the main headings, and the special feature title. Ask: What is the cabinet? To whom are members of the cabinet responsible?

Section 4 Let volunteers read aloud the section title, the main headings, the figure title, and the photo captions in Section 4. Then ask: What kinds of information do you expect to find presented in this section? To whom is this kind of information important?

CHAPTER 15

The Presidency

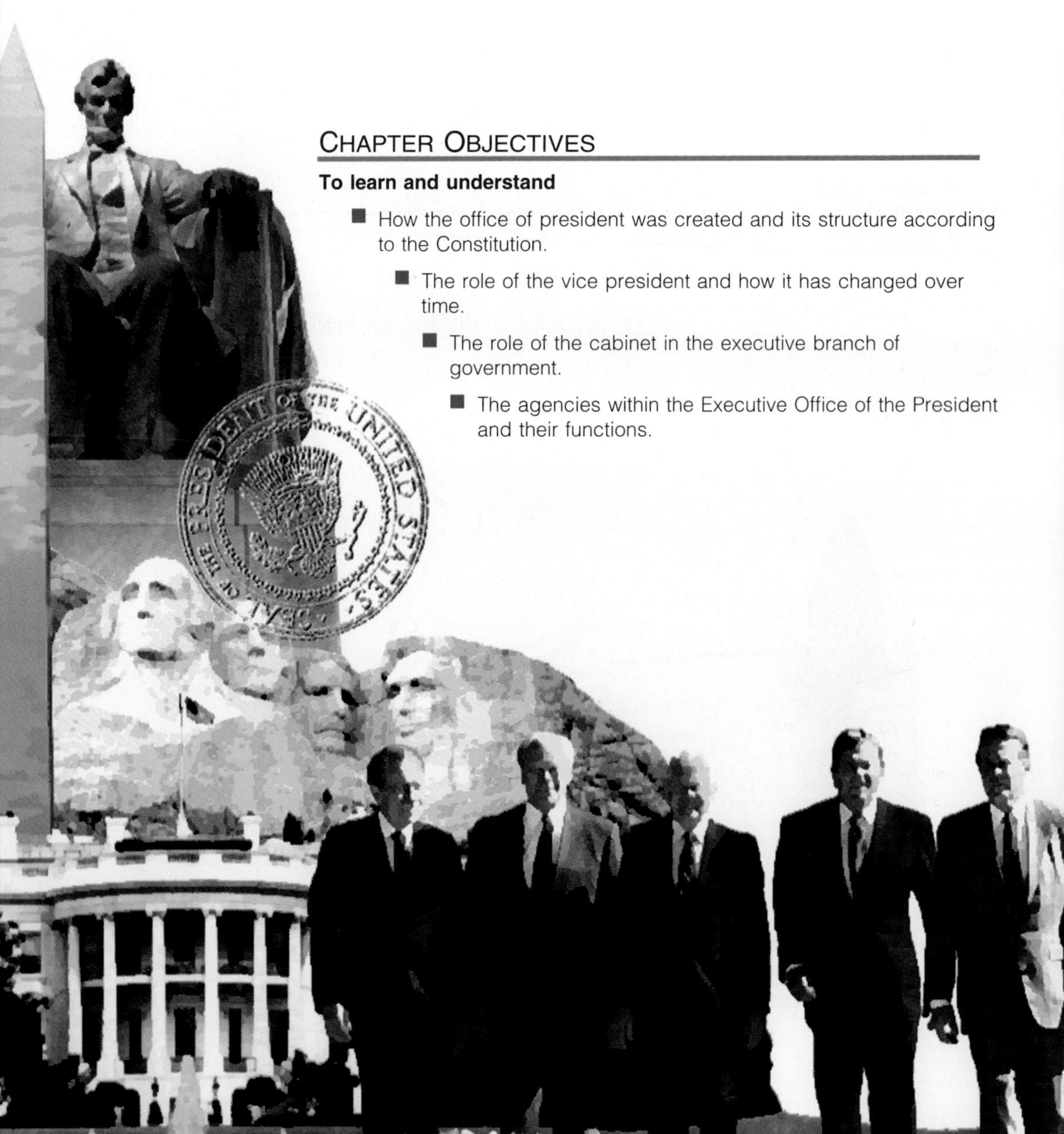

CHAPTER OBJECTIVES

To learn and understand

- How the office of president was created and its structure according to the Constitution.
- The role of the vice president and how it has changed over time.
- The role of the cabinet in the executive branch of government.
- The agencies within the Executive Office of the President and their functions.

West's American Government Assignment Guide

Activity Sheets
Basic Concepts 15 *TRB* (Reteaching)
Enrichment Activity 15 *TRB*
Building Social Studies Skills 15 *TRB*

Quizzes
Chapter 15 Section 1 Quiz *TRB*
Chapter 15 Section 2 Quiz *TRB*
Chapter 15 Section 3 Quiz *TRB*
Chapter 15 Section 4 Quiz *TRB*

Tests
Chapter 15 Test A *TRB*
Chapter 15 Test B *TRB*
Chapter 15 Test Bank *TRB*
Chapter 15 WESTEST Computerized Testing

SECTION 1

Points to Stress

- The manner in which the office of the president was created.
- The formal and informal qualifications for becoming president.
- The term and compensation of the president.
- The Constitutional provisions for presidential succession.

Kickoff Activity

Write the following question on the chalkboard: Who can become president of the United States? Give the students four or five minutes in which to write detailed responses to the question. After the students have finished writing, encourage them to share and compare their answers.

Working with the Preview Questions

Let volunteers read the study questions aloud, and encourage the students to discuss what they already know in response to each question. Then have the students work together to write an outline format based on these questions. Ask the students to use that format to outline Section 1.

Teaching Strategies

Introduction

After the students have read the brief section introduction, ask them these questions: What does the adjective *executive* mean? To what verb is it related? Why is the president also called the chief executive? Why is the presidency considered one of the most powerful offices in the world?

Comprehension

Ask the students to recall (or review) the central ideas expounded by Locke and Montesquieu (see Chapter 4).

Keynote

"No one who has not had the responsibility can really understand what it is like to be president. . . . There is no end to the chain of responsibility that binds him, and he is never allowed to forget that he is president."

—— Harry S Truman
(1884–1972) Thirty-Third President of the United States

INTRODUCTION

Our governmental system, like all others, demands a strong executive authority. Over the years, Americans have come to expect more and more from our presidents. Besides their numerous constitutional responsibilities, we now make our presidents responsible for our economy, our environment, our energy supplies, and our international relations. Public expectations, strong presidential personalities, technology, and history have combined to make the office of the presidency a powerful one.

Although the president is the head of just one of the three branches of government, he, with the exception of the vice president, is the only official elected by the entire nation. As a result, the president stands as a symbol not only of the federal government but of the entire country as well. As Harry S Truman pointed out in the opening quote, no one, except the president himself, understands what it really means to be president.[1] The responsibility of leading one of the greatest military and economic powers in the world can never be understated. And as Truman pointed out, the president never forgets for a moment that he is indeed in this position of responsibility.

Truman further pointed out that the president must constantly remain in control of many situations, both at home and abroad. He explained, "A president either is constantly on top of events, or, if he hesitates, events will soon be on top of him. I never felt that I could let up for a single moment." On Truman's desk in the Oval Office rested a sign that symbolized his understanding of the fact that often the president is held ultimately responsible for the success or failure of the government. The sign read, "The buck stops here."

1. The lack of a period after the S is not a typographical error. S was Harry Truman's middle name. The initial S represents the names of his grandfathers, but has no other significance.

SECTION 1

The Office of President

Preview Questions

- How was the office of the presidency created?
- What are the formal and informal qualifications for becoming president?
- What are the conditions of a presidential term?
- What kinds of compensation does the president receive?
- What is presidential succession?

As the head of the executive branch of our federal government, the president holds one of the most powerful and important elective offices in the world. When the founders of this country created the presidency in 1787, the United States was a new nation of only 4 million people. They had no idea that the president would become such a powerful figure.

Creating the Presidency

Creating the executive branch of the federal government was one of the most important tasks faced by the delegates to the Constitutional Convention of 1787. Given their previous experience with kings and royal governors, most delegates did not want a monarchy—not even an elected monarchy, which Alexander Hamilton once argued for in a two-hour-long speech. The delegates wanted the ultimate source of power to rest with the people. They also recognized, from watching the Articles of Confederation in action, the need for an executive branch. In addition to analyzing the British monarchy and the roles of governors in American colonial and state governments, as we learned in Chapter 2, the founders also studied the writings of European thinkers such as Locke and Montesquieu.

Discussion Starter
Guide the students in comparing a committee executive with an individual executive: How do the two differ as concepts? What advantages—and disadvantages—would you expect to find associated with each? Do you consider the two forms equally practical? Why or why not? How do you imagine the choice of a committee executive might have changed the development of our nation?

Critical Thinking Skills
Help the students analyze and evaluate the definition given by the Constitution to the office of the president: What limits were placed on the president's responsibilities? On the president's powers? Why do you image the founders chose to define the presidency in this way?

Caption Answer There was much debate over how much power should be vested in the chief executive. However, the experience of the government under the Articles of Confederation convinced the founders that a certain amount of executive authority was necessary.

Caption Answer Students should understand that the office of president had evolved and changed to meet the changing needs and circumstances of our government as the world has similarly evolved and changed.

Multidiscipline Strategies

Language Arts Have each student work alone or with a partner to select a president of particular interest. Ask the students to gather biographical information about the presidents they have selected, trying to form a clear image of the individual's main interests, concerns, and attitudes. Then have the students write fictional vignettes about those presidents, illustrating an important facet of the president's character or work. Let the students read their vignettes to the rest of the class, or compile them in a booklet made available to the whole class.

▲ Today, the president of the United States holds one of the most important and powerful elective offices in the world. Did all of the founders of our government agree that a powerful chief executive was needed?

For weeks delegates quarreled over how much power the executive branch should have and what the relationship of the executive to the legislative branch should be. Some delegates, such as James Madison and Gouverneur Morris, argued for a strong, independent executive that would be a "check" on an overly ambitious legislature. Others wanted a weak executive appointed by Congress and subject to its will. Everyone was seeking a proper balance of power. Morris said, "Make him too weak: the legislature will usurp [take for itself] his power. Make him too strong: he will usurp on the legislature." Some liked the idea of a *committee executive,* several persons each holding executive power in different areas. In the end, they rejected such a committee arrangement and opted for a single official who, according to one political scientist, James Q. Wilson, could act with "energy, dispatch, and responsibility."

The delegates' debates resulted in the creation of the office of the president—a uniquely American institution. Nowhere else in the world at that time was there a democratically elected chief executive. On April 30, 1789, George Washington, with his left hand on the Bible, raised his right hand and swore to "preserve, protect, and defend the Constitution of the United States." Since that time over forty Americans have repeated these same words and have held the office of president.

The source for the president's authority is Article II of the Constitution, which says that "the executive power shall be vested in the president of the United States of America." This makes the president of the United States the nation's **chief executive**, or head of the executive branch of the federal government. The Constitution then sets out the president's relatively limited constitutional responsibilities. Because the Constitution defined presidential powers in broad general statements, the founders were uncertain as to just how the president would perform the various roles. Only experience would tell.

The past two centuries have seen the office formed and expanded by the personalities and policies of the various occupants, and by custom and tradition. Over the years, the office has evolved to meet changing needs and circumstances.

▲ Strong presidents such as Theodore Roosevelt, shown here operating a steam shovel during the construction of the Panama Canal in 1906, have helped the office of president evolve. Why is it important that the office of president evolve and change?

Discussion Starter
Ask the students to consider the formal qualifications for the presidency: Who is excluded by these qualifications? Why do you think the founders chose to exclude members of those groups? Do you consider it reasonable—or fair—to exclude them? Why or why not?

Discussion Starter
Ask the students how they feel about the background shared by most presidents: Why do you think the background described here is typical of most presidents? Do you believe people who fit this description can fully and fairly represent the people of the United States? Why or why not?

Comprehension
Let volunteers define *political acceptability:* Why is this a reasonable qualification for the presidency?

Dwight David Eisenhower is shown here talking to paratroopers preparing to invade continental Europe in June of 1944. Eisenhower's success as a general helped him to be elected president in 1952. What informal qualification for the presidency did Eisenhower lack?

Caption Answer Eisenhower lacked experience in an elective office.

Qualifications

The Constitution lists only three formal qualifications for becoming president. Other informal qualifications have grown over the years out of personal qualities that Americans have come to expect their presidents to have.

Formal Qualifications The Constitution says that the president must (1) be a ''natural-born citizen,''[2] (2) be at least thirty-five years old, and (3) be a resident of the United States at least fourteen years before taking office.

One of the symbols of the American dream is the thought that ''anybody can become president of this country.'' Indeed, there are millions of Americans who meet the above three constitutional requirements, yet very few people will ever actually become president. Like members of Congress, most presidents thus far in history have had similar backgrounds. They have all been white and male. Most have been descendants of immigrants from northern Europe. Most have been lawyers, members of Congress, or state governors. In reality, then, there seems to be important *informal* requirements for becoming president of the United States.

Informal Qualifications *Political experience* has become an unwritten but important qualification for the presidency. One of only two presidents in this century without electoral experience was Dwight D. Eisenhower, whose success as a general in the United States Army during World War II led to his election as president. The most common nominees for presidential candidates have been U.S. senators or state governors. Experience in government and politics allows these individuals not only to form the political alliances necessary to obtain the nomination, but to become known to the public. Current public officials have the resources to build a political following and to campaign.

Another informal qualification is *political acceptability.* Candidates with a *moderate* position reflect the views of the majority of Americans and are more likely to be nominated and elected. Usually, candidates with

2. Martin Van Buren, the eighth president, was the first president actually born in the United States. The Constitution made an allowance for presidential candidates who were born before the Republic was formed.

Enrichment
Have a volunteer research the 1980 election in which Reagan defeated Carter: How can the defeat of the moderate candidate in this election be explained? Ask the volunteer to write a short report, to be shared with the rest of the class.

Vocabulary
Ask the students to define the term *self-made men:* Who qualifies as a self-made man? Why?

Discussion Starter
Guide the students in discussing the four-year term: Do you agree that four years is enough time in which to establish stable policies? Should the president also spend that time gaining experience and demonstrating abilities? Why or why not? Why do you think the framers selected four years—rather than three, or five, or six? Do you think a different period of time would be better? If so, what period? Why?

Enrichment
Ask a small group of volunteers to research the background of the Twenty-second Amendment: Why was it passed? Who supported it? Why? Who opposed it? Why? Was it directed at a specific individual or party? Have the volunteers report their findings to the rest of the class.

Discussion Starter
Encourage the students to share their reactions to the president's salary and expense allowance: Does the president's income seem high to you—or low? What other jobs in the United States pay about $200,000 per year? Which positions pay more? What percentage of the population probably earns less than $200,000 per year? Do you believe the president's salary should be raised or lowered? Why?

Caption Answer
Kennedy came from a very wealthy, Roman Catholic family. Additionally, students might be aware of the fact that Kennedy was younger than most presidents at the time of his election.

▲ Most U.S. presidents have been married, Protestant, and financially successful men from financially modest families. In what ways did President John F. Kennedy differ from this profile of the average president?

extremely liberal or extremely conservative political views have little chance of winning a nomination, much less an election. There are exceptions, however, such as the election of conservative Republican Ronald Reagan over the moderate incumbent president Jimmy Carter in 1980.

Historians and political scientists have also pointed out common characteristics shared by many presidents. Traditionally, candidates have been married, Protestant, and financially successful.[3] A few, such as Harry S Truman, have come from poor families; others have come from wealthy families such as Theodore and Franklin Roosevelt and John F. Kennedy. Most, however, have come from more modest circumstances and have been self-made men. All modern presidents except Harry Truman have had college educations.

Term

The Constitution states that a president "shall hold his office during the term of four years." The framers of the Constitution agreed, as Alexander Hamilton wrote in *The Federalist Papers,* that four years was long enough for a president to gain experience, demonstrate abilities, and establish stable policies.

The Constitution placed no limit on the number of terms a president might serve. George Washington served two terms as president but declined to seek a third one. He established a tradition followed by all presidents well into the twentieth century. Franklin D. Roosevelt, however, broke this tradition in 1940, when he ran for a third term and won, and in 1944, when he ran for a fourth term and won again. In 1951, the Twenty-second Amendment, which provides that no person may serve more than two terms as president, was added to the Constitution.

Compensation

A president receives a salary, determined by Congress, which cannot be increased or decreased during the term of office. Currently, the president receives $200,000 a year in salary and $50,000 a year for travel, entertainment, and other official expenses.

Of course, the president receives many other special benefits, one of which is the White House, a luxurious 132-room mansion on 18.3 acres of land in the heart of the nation's capital. The White House is equipped with a staff of over eighty persons, including chefs, gardeners, maids, butlers, and a personal tailor. There is a tennis court, a swimming pool, a bowling alley, and a private movie theater. The president is also provided with a special fleet of automobiles, jetliners, and helicopters, including the presidential jet, Air Force One. In addition there is Camp David, the resort hideaway in the Catoctin Mountains of Maryland; medical and dental care; a large suite of offices, including the Oval Office; a large staff; and Secret Service protection for his family. The president does, of course, pay taxes, just like other citizens of the United States.

Presidential Succession

Eight presidents have died in office: four died of natural causes and another four died from assassins'

3. James Buchanan was the only unmarried president. John F. Kennedy was a Roman Catholic. No woman, African American, or Hispanic American has held the office of president or vice president. Until 1984, when the Democrats nominated Representative Geraldine Ferraro for vice president, no person from these groups had ever been chosen to run for high office by a major party. It seems likely, however, that in the future candidates will be selected from a broader spectrum of Americans.

Enrichment
Ask a group of volunteers to explore the tax returns of recent presidents: Are the president's tax returns always made public? Why or why not? What do the public tax returns of the current president and the two previous presidents tell you about these individuals? Have the volunteers prepare a chart or other display summarizing their findings.

Enrichment
Let interested volunteers research the circumstances of the four assassinations; then have the volunteers present oral reports to the rest of the class.

Enrichment
Ask for volunteers to research the circumstances and the significance of the resignations of Vice President Agnew and President Nixon. Let these volunteers summarize their findings for the rest of the class.

Discussion Starter
As the students consider the line of succession to the presidency, ask them questions such as these: Why is this list so long? Under what circumstances might the secretary of energy, for example, succeed to the presidency? Why do you imagine the Succession Act was passed in 1947? What were the general conditions in the country and the world at that time? How might those conditions have affected the act?

Figure Answer Students should understand that the assassination of John F. Kennedy in 1963 led lawmakers to worry about the need for clear lines of succession to the presidency.

This figure content is also featured on *West's American Government Videodisc* (see the index found in the *TRB*) and is available in the transparency package.

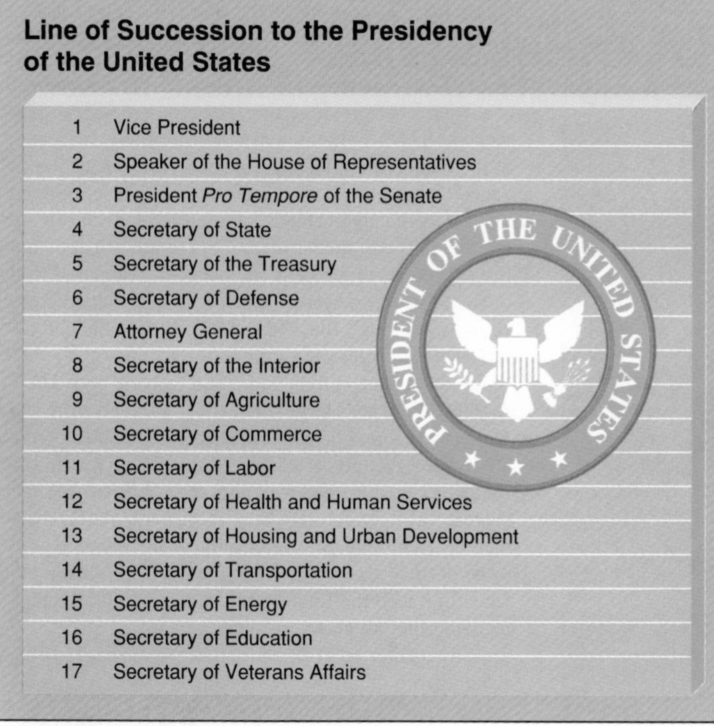

Line of Succession to the Presidency of the United States

1	Vice President
2	Speaker of the House of Representatives
3	President *Pro Tempore* of the Senate
4	Secretary of State
5	Secretary of the Treasury
6	Secretary of Defense
7	Attorney General
8	Secretary of the Interior
9	Secretary of Agriculture
10	Secretary of Commerce
11	Secretary of Labor
12	Secretary of Health and Human Services
13	Secretary of Housing and Urban Development
14	Secretary of Transportation
15	Secretary of Energy
16	Secretary of Education
17	Secretary of Veterans Affairs

▲ **FIGURE 15–1 Line of Succession to the Presidency of the United States.** The table above shows the lines of succession as established by the Presidential Succession Act of 1947 and the Twenty-fifth Amendment in 1967. In 1974, Gerald Ford became the first president to take office under the provisions of this amendment. What event led to the passage of this amendment?

bullets. One president has been forced to resign.[4] Because of this possibility, it is very important that the office of president have an established order of **succession**, a legal procedure by which government leaders will succeed to the presidency should the president die, become disabled, or be removed from office.

Order of Succession The Constitution originally said that if the president died or could no longer serve in office, the "powers and duties" of the office were to be carried out by the vice president. It did not indicate that the vice president would actually become president. In 1841, however, this is exactly what happened when President William Henry Harrison died: Vice President John Tyler not only took over Harrison's duties, but became president. Thus began a tradition of vice presidents assuming the presidency.

In 1967, a few years after the assassination of President John F. Kennedy, the Twenty-fifth Amendment was passed, which officially settled the question of presidential succession. The amendment says that the vice president does indeed become president when the office is vacant. Because the vice presidency is then vacant, the new president chooses a new vice president, subject to majority vote of both houses of Congress.

The Twenty-fifth Amendment was used for the first time in 1973 when Vice President Spiro Agnew resigned from office. President Nixon named Gerald Ford as his

4. Henry Harrison (pneumonia) April 4, 1841; Zachary Taylor (gastroenteritis) July 9, 1850; Abraham Lincoln (assassination) April 14, 1865; James A. Garfield (assassination) September 19, 1881; William McKinley (assassination) September 14, 1901; Warren Harding (illness) August 2, 1923; Franklin D. Roosevelt (cerebral hemorrhage) April 12, 1945; John F. Kennedy (assassination) November 22, 1963. Richard Nixon resigned August 9, 1974.

FYI

James Barber offers an in-depth examination of the importance of a president's personality in his book *The Presidential Character.* Based upon their childhood and other experiences, he classifies presidents into four types according to their assertiveness in office and how "positive" or "negative" their feelings are about the office. The four character types are "active-passive," "active-negative," "passive-positive," and "passive-negative." According to Barber, FDR, Truman, Kennedy, Ford, and Carter were "active-positive," enjoying the exercise of power and striving to achieve results. Wilson, Hoover, Johnson, and Nixon are identified as "active-negative," who strive for significant achievements but get little enjoyment from effort.

TEACHING ARCHITECT OF THE AMERICAN DREAM

Read

Before the students study this Architect of the American Dream feature, introduce the topic by going around the room, calling on each student and asking him or her to name at least one word that he or she feels describes Abraham Lincoln. After all the students have had an opportunity to respond, allow volunteers to take turns reading aloud this Architect of the American Dream feature to the class.

Discuss

Stimulate a class discussion of this material by asking the following questions: How would you describe Lincoln's childhood? How do you think his childhood affected his decisions as president? What type of occupational experiences did Lincoln have prior to the start of his political career? In this feature, it is said, "Lincoln became well known for his ready wit, down-home logic, and seemingly endless supply of clever anecdotes." How do you think these attributes helped Lincoln in his political career? Do you think these are attributes that would be helpful to a modern politician? Why or why not? What did Lincoln mean by his phrase "a house divided against itself cannot stand"? Why do you think political scientists and historians often rank Lincoln as one of our greatest presidents? How long is four score and seven years? (87) What type of government does Lincoln describe in the Gettysburg Address when he uses the words "government of the people, by the people, for the people"?

ARCHITECT OF The American Dream

The man who preserved the American Union during the Civil War and who proved to the world that democracy could be a lasting form of government was born on February 12, 1809 in Hardin, Kentucky, in a one-room, dirt-floor, log cabin. Whenever the young Abraham and his sister, Sarah, didn't have to help their parents, they attended school in a log schoolhouse. From the age of seven to twenty-one, however, the future president only had about a year of formal schooling. He said in his autobiography that "Of course when I came of age I did not know much. Still somehow, I could read, write, and cipher . . . ; but that was all."

In 1830, Lincoln settled in southern Illinois, where he operated a store, practiced surveying, and served as postmaster at New Salem while he studied law. In 1836, after he was admitted to the bar, he moved to Springfield where he opened a law office and quickly obtained a reputation as an outstanding jury lawyer. He also became well known for his ready wit, down-home logic, and seemingly endless supply of clever anecdotes. Lincoln was a member of the Illinois legislature from 1834 to 1842. He was nominated to run for the U.S. Senate at the Illinois Republican Convention. His acceptance speech popularized the phrase, "A house divided against itself cannot stand," a reference to the growing conflict between the North and the South. Lincoln and his opponent, incumbent Stephen A. Douglas, faced one another in a series of seven famous debates across Illinois. Although Lincoln lost the election, he had established himself as a national figure.

Lincoln was nominated for and won the presidency in 1860. By 1861, seven states had seceded from the Union, and Lincoln was thrust into the center of the Civil War. As late as August 1862, he expressed his reluctance to turn the war into a crusade to free the slaves. "My paramount object in the struggle," he declared, "is to save the Union, and it is not either to save or to destroy slavery." In September 1862, however, Lincoln issued the Emancipation Proclamation, which declared that all slaves in states or parts of states still fighting against the United States on January 1, 1863, would, from that time on, be forever free.

Lincoln was a diplomat in handling both his cabinet and generals, and after numerous military victories, easily won reelection in 1864. On April 14, 1865, in Ford's Theater in Washington D.C., John Wilkes Booth, a deranged actor sympathetic to the Southern cause, shot the president in the back of the head with a .44 single-shot derringer. He was the first chief executive to die at the hands of an assassin.

Lincoln has been called a keen and profound politician, a shrewd diplomat, a great storyteller, and a skillful judge of men. Historians and political scientists who rank presidents often rank him with the greatest.

The Battle of Gettysburg, which took place over three days in July of 1863, was the bloodiest engagement of the Civil War. The combined casualties of the Union and Confederate Armies numbered over 50,000 men. It was a decisive battle for the Union Army and marked the last time that the Confederate Army would have the strength to carry the War into Union territory. In November of that same year, President Lincoln wrote the following speech as he traveled by train to Gettysburg to dedicate a national memorial cemetery. The Gettysburg Address, which was delivered before a large crowd, is one of the most famous American political speeches.

Analyze and Apply
Divide the class into four groups. Assign each group one of the following topics on which they should work together to prepare an oral presentation:
1. Abraham Lincoln's childhood.
2. The Lincoln/Douglas debates.
3. Lincoln as Commander-in-Chief.
4. How Lincoln's assassination affected the nation and reconstruction.

Each group's report should be no less than five minutes in length and should include some original source material. For example, the group preparing a report on the Lincoln/Douglas debates should include passages from the debates in their presentation.

Review
Use the following questions to review this Architect of the American Dream feature on Abraham Lincoln: Where did Lincoln first get political experience? Who won the election between Abraham Lincoln and Stephen Douglas? Specifically, who was freed by the Emancipation Proclamation? Why is the Battle of Gettysburg significant?

Developing Critical Thinking Skills (Answers)
1. Lincoln meant that the sacrifices made by the soldiers had already sanctified the ground, more than any ceremony could.
2. Lincoln had predicted that the world would "little note nor long remember" his Gettysburg Address, whereas the words of this speech have inspired generations of Americans.
3. The unfinished work referred to in the speech is that of preserving the nation as one.

Abraham Lincoln

Shown here is the first reading of the Emancipation Proclamation before Abraham Lincoln's cabinet in 1862; standing left to right: Chase, Smith, Blair; seated left to right: Stanton, Lincoln, Welles, Seward, Bates.

His Words

"Four score and seven years ago our fathers brought forth on this continent, a new nation, conceived in Liberty, and dedicated to the proposition that all men are created equal.

Now we are engaged in a great civil war, testing whether that nation or any nation so conceived and so dedicated, can long endure. We are met on a great battle-field of that war. We have come to dedicate a portion of that field, as a final resting place for those who here gave their lives that that nation might live. It is altogether fitting and proper that we should do this.

But, in a larger sense, we can not dedicate—we can not consecrate—we can not hallow—this ground. The brave men, living and dead, who struggled here, have consecrated it, far above our poor power to add or detract. The world will little note, nor long remember what we say here, but it can never forget what they did here. It is for us the living, rather, to be dedicated here to the unfinished work which they who fought here have thus far so nobly advanced. It is rather for us to be here dedicated to the great task remaining before us—that from these honored dead we take increased devotion to that cause for which they gave the last full measure of devotion—that we here highly resolve that these dead shall not have died in vain—that this nation, under God, shall have a new birth of freedom—and that government of the people, by the people, for the people, shall not perish from the earth."

Developing Critical Thinking Skills

1. What did Lincoln mean when he said, "We can not consecrate . . . this ground"?
2. Lincoln made a prediction in this speech that turned out to be completely inaccurate. What was that prediction and why was it inaccurate?
3. What was the "unfinished work" that Lincoln mentioned in this speech?

For Further Reading

Sandberg, Carl. *Abraham Lincoln: The Prairie Years and the War Years.* (Six volumes.) New York: Harcourt, Brace, and World, 1926–1939.
Oates, Stephen B. *Abraham Lincoln: The Man Behind the Myths.* New York: Harper, 1984.
Charnwook, Lord. *Abraham Lincoln.* Garden City, New York: Garden City Publishing, 1917.

TEACHING BUILDING SOCIAL STUDY SKILLS

Read

Before students read this Building Social Studies Skills feature, use the following questions to assess students' current knowledge of political debates. How many of you have ever seen a political debate on television? What was the topic? Why do candidates participate in political debates? How are these debates structured? After the students have answered these questions, ask them to read this Building Social Studies Skills feature.

Discuss

Use the following questions to stimulate a class discussion of this Building Social Studies Skills feature. What was special about the presidential debate in 1960? How did this change the way candidates look at debates? In what ways might candidates seek to use the setting to their advantage? How might a candidate play up his or her strengths in a debate? How might he or she downplay his weaknesses? How do the candidates treat the important issues during a debate? Why?

Analyze and Apply

To help students further understand the role of debates in the American political process, you might wish to hold a mock presidential debate in your classroom. Students should choose two or more candidates for the debate. Three or four other students should act as the debate panel and write questions for the candidates to answer. Each candidate should use the information in this feature to seek to make the best possible impression on the debate audience. Those students who act as the audience should grade each candidate on his ability to manipulate the setting, to point out his opponent's strengths and his opponent's weaknesses, and his or her ability to score points in response to the panel's questions.

Review

Use the following questions to review this Building Social Studies Skills feature: How was the setting important in political debates? What type of image is a candidate most likely to attempt to convey during a political debate? Do you think watching a debate is the best way to find out the candidate's stand on the important issues? What can you learn about candidates from watching them debate?

Comprehension

Let the students explain, in their own words, the conditions under which the vice president becomes acting president; then have them suggest specific examples of each condition.

Reteaching Strategies

1. Have the students work in groups to compare and discuss their outlines of Section 1. Then encourage the students to add to or revise their own outlines as necessary.

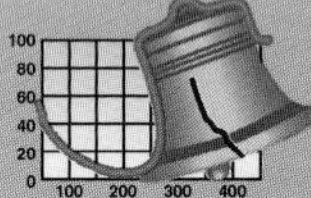

BUILDING SOCIAL STUDIES SKILLS

Analyzing a Political Debate

Political debates have long been a part of American campaigning. Ever since the famous Lincoln-Douglas debates in the late 1850s, American voters have enjoyed seeing their candidates face off in a one-to-one battle of words.

The presidential debate between John F. Kennedy and Richard Nixon in 1960 was the first televised presidential debate. Since that historic debate, there have been many presidential debates shown on television. Political debates also occur among congressional candidates at the state and local levels.

When you watch a political debate, there are a number of points you should keep in mind.

1. **The setting.** Kennedy's victory in the 1960 debate showed the world the importance of looking good on television. This lesson has not been lost on today's politicians. Candidates and their advisors go to great lengths to look good during televised debates. For example, in the 1976 debate between incumbent President Gerald Ford and the challenger, Jimmy Carter, campaign staff workers for both candidates engaged in heated negotiations regarding the size of the podium to be used during the debate. The handlers of Ford, who was tall, wanted both candidates to use tall podiums so that Carter would appear even shorter than he was. Carter's people, on the other hand, wanted short podiums, so that he would appear taller than he was. After much discussion, medium-sized podiums were chosen in a compromise decision.
2. **The candidates' strengths and weaknesses.** Going into a debate, each candidate will seek to highlight his or her perceived strengths and the opponent's perceived weaknesses. Likewise, each candidate will also seek to minimize his or her weaknesses and the opponent's strengths. For example, in 1984 Ronald Reagan's age began to be perceived as a weakness for the incumbent president. Most political commentators agreed that after a poor showing in the first of two presidential debates, it was important that Reagan appear forceful and energetic in the next debate. The president's campaign staff coached him to look relaxed and robust for the second debate. Reagan's success in doing so helped push him toward a landslide victory in the election.
3. **The issues.** Although debates are supposed to center on the important political issues of the day, it is important to understand that the candidates themselves do everything they can to avoid any specific discussion of issues. Rather, candidates prepare short, catchy speeches about various topics to be delivered in response to issue questions. These speeches are generally superficial. Given these points, it is easy to see why some commentators believe that political debates are not really useful. Much, however, can be learned from political debates. These debates are highly charged with risk for the candidates. When watching a political debate, one can get a glimpse of the candidate's ability to deal with pressure situations. Voters get a better opportunity to see the candidates in a less controlled environment than at any other time during the campaign.

When analyzing a political debate, you should remember to assess the setting, the candidates' strengths and weaknesses, and the issues. Remember to ask yourself what you know about each candidate and what he or she will most want to convey to voters during the debate. What issues is he or she most likely to want to address?

PRACTICING YOUR SKILLS

Obtain either a transcript or a videotape of an important political debate. After reading or viewing the debate, answer the following questions:

1. What aspects of the setting might have favored one of the two candidates? Why?
2. How specific were candidates in responding to issue-related questions?
3. In your opinion, which candidate won the debate?
4. Did either of the candidates hold news conferences after the debate to claim victory?

2. Let pairs of students work together to write brief descriptions of two fictional presidents: one who fits the typical presidential profile, the other who meets the formal qualifications but is unusual in some respects.

Evaluation Strategies

1. Have the students write their answers to the Section 1 Review questions.

2. Have the students take the Section 1 Quiz found in the *TRB.*

Section 1 Review (Answers)

1. The president must be a natural-born citizen, at least 35 years old, and a resident of the United States at least 14 years before taking office.
2. Political experience and political acceptability have come to be informal qualifications.
3. Two terms.
4. The legal procedure by which the vice president will succeed to the presidency should the president die, become disabled, or be removed from office. This amendment further specifies the procedure for filling the vice presidency and for declaring the president incapacitated, allowing the vice president to become acting president.
5. Answers will vary, e.g., individuals with the ability to raise large amounts of money for political campaigns have a better chance of becoming president. Also, it is probably true that anybody from a minority group would have a difficult time getting a national party to nominate him or her.

new vice president, and Ford's nomination was approved by Congress. A year later, when President Nixon resigned from office, Vice President Ford became president and Ford nominated Nelson Rockefeller to be vice president. Congress again approved the nomination. Gerald Ford thereby became the first person in the history of the republic to become president without ever having been elected as either vice president or president.

The order of succession following the vice president was fixed by Congress according to the Presidential Succession Act of 1947. (See page 359).

Presidential Disability The Twenty-fifth Amendment also describes the steps to be followed should a president become disabled while in office. The amendment provides that the vice president shall become acting president under one of two conditions: If the president informs Congress of an inability to perform in office; or if the vice president and a majority of the cabinet inform Congress, in writing, that the president is disabled. In either case, the president may resume the powers and duties of the office by informing Congress that no disability exists. If, however, the vice president and a majority of the cabinet contend that the president has not recovered, Congress has twenty-one days to decide the issue by a two-thirds vote in the House and Senate.

There have been a few times in history when presidents have become disabled. James Garfield lingered for eighty days before he died from an assassin's bullet in 1881. Woodrow Wilson suffered a paralytic stroke in 1919 and was an invalid for the rest of his second term. President Eisenhower suffered several temporary but serious illnesses while in office, including a heart attack in 1955, ileitis in 1956, and a mild stroke in 1957.

When President Ronald Reagan underwent surgery for removal of a cancerous growth on July 13, 1985, he informally followed the provisions of the Twenty-fifth Amendment when he temporarily transferred power to Vice President George Bush. Just before the operation began, Reagan signed letters to the Speaker of the House and the president pro tem of the Senate indicating that the vice president "shall discharge those powers and duties in my stead commencing with the administration of anesthesia to me. . . ." When he recovered from surgery later in the day, Reagan transmitted another letter to both officials announcing that he was again in charge. Although officials in his administration at the time claimed that Reagan's actions set no precedent, most legal experts saw his acts as the first *official* use of this provision of the Twenty-fifth Amendment.

Section 1 Review

1. What are the three qualifications for being president that are required by the Constitution?
2. What informal qualifications have Americans come to expect in presidents?
3. How many terms can a president serve?
4. What is defined by the Twenty-fifth Amendment?
5. **For critical analysis:** The formal qualifications for the office of the president are few and therefore many Americans could become president; yet the informal qualifications have much more significance than the formal qualifications. What do you think really determines who can and cannot become president?

Section 2

The Office of Vice President

Preview Questions:

- What are the duties of the vice president?
- What are the qualifications and compensation for the vice president?
- How is the vice president selected to run for office?

John Adams, the nation's first vice president, described his post as "the most insignificant office that ever the invention of man contrived or his imagination conceived." Thomas Jefferson, who was next in the position, found the office "honorable and easy" and "tranquil and unoffending." During most of American history, the office of vice president has been seen as a fairly insignificant position, and has been avoided by some ambitious politicians. In 1848, Daniel Webster declined the Whig Party's nomination as vice presidential candidate by saying, "I do not propose to be buried until I am dead."

The vice presidency has been the subject of many jokes. Alben Barkley, vice president under Harry Truman, often told the story of a woman who had two sons. One of them, Barkley said, joined the United States Navy and went to sea. The other one became vice president of the United States, "and neither of them was ever heard of again."

But as John Adams also said, "I am vice president. In this I am nothing, but I may be everything." Despite

SECTION 2

Points to Stress

- Duties of the vice president.
- The qualifications and compensation for the vice president.
- The manner in which the vice president is selected to run for office.

Kickoff Activity

Write the following title on the chalkboard: vice president of the United States. Ask the students to list at least eight words or phrases that come to mind when they read the title. After all the students have finished writing, let volunteers read their lists aloud; encourage the students to discuss the reasons for each listed word or phrase.

Working with the Preview Questions

Ask the students to read and consider these study questions. Then have them page through Section 2, noting the headings that indicate where information related to each question will be presented. Remind the students to keep the study questions in mind as they read the section.

Teaching Strategies

Introduction

After the students have read the section introduction, give them an opportunity to identify and discuss their favorite quotations regarding the vice presidency.

TEACHING CITIZENSHIP SKILLS AND RESPONSIBILITIES

Read

As an introduction to this Citizenship Skills and Responsibilities feature, ask the students to recall what they already know about ideology: What is an ideology? Who has an ideology? Why do those individuals have ideologies? How did they acquire or develop their ideologies? After a brief discussion, let volunteers read the feature aloud.

Discuss

Guide the students in discussing the feature: Which do you consider the most important influences on the development of your own political ideology? How have they influenced you? What expressions of your political ideology have you already undertaken? Which do you expect to undertake in the future? Why? Which do you intend to avoid? Why?

Analyze and Apply

Ask the students to consider their own involvement in school, community, and local political organizations. Then have them prepare and present short speeches on this topic: Why I Am (Am Not) a Political Person.

Review

Use these questions to help the students review the feature: What is an ideology? What are at least three activities that express a person's political ideology?

Discussion Starter

Help the students discuss the duties of the vice president: Why do you think the Constitution grants the vice president only two duties? What do you think the intentions of the framers might have been? Do you think today's vice president would meet the expectations that the framer's held for an individual in this position? Why or why not?

Enrichment

Have a small group of volunteers read about the vice president's residence on the grounds of the Naval Observatory. Ask these volunteers to present interesting facts about the history of the residence and about the observatory itself on a classroom bulletin board display.

Cooperative Learning

Let the students work in groups to read about the vice presidential candidates in recent elections: In what respects did each candidate balance the ticket for his or her running mate? Which pairs of candidates were elected? In which cases might a lack of balance have contributed to the defeat of the presidential and vice presidential candidates?

Extension

Ask the students to find out how a vice president can be removed from office. You may also want to have the students research the resignation of Vice President Agnew: Who decided that he should resign? Why? Could he have been removed from office if he had refused to resign? Why or why not?

CITIZENSHIP SKILLS AND RESPONSIBILITIES

Discovering the Political You

An *ideology* is a collection of political, economic and social beliefs and opinions. In Chapter 9 you learned about political socialization and the many influences that affect your political ideology. Among these were family, school, friends, and co-workers. The process begins early in your childhood and continues throughout adulthood.

Throughout your life as a citizen you will be called upon to express your political ideology in many ways: voting, joining special interest groups, participating in community projects, and possibly running for public office. Even your actions in day-to-day life reflect your political ideology. Try to gain a good understanding of what you believe in and why: You will be more confident of your beliefs when confronted with questions and decisions. Start by exploring the roots of the political you.

TAKING ACTION

Write an autobiographical account of your political roots. Begin by asking yourself the following questions:

- Who is the first president I remember? What do I remember about him?
- What characteristics and qualifications do I feel the president should have? Why?
- How do I feel about the current president's policies and actions?
- How would I describe my parents' political beliefs? Who did they vote for in the last presidential election? Do they belong to a political party? Are they active in public affairs and politics? Do I agree or disagree with their views?
- How would I describe the political beliefs of my best friends? Which political issues do I discuss with them? How do my beliefs differ from theirs?
- How would I describe the political attitude of most people in my community?
- What impact have school and teachers had on my political views?
- How have the media—television, newspapers, magazines, or radio—influenced my views? Which publications do I enjoy reading?
- What influences have other groups or individuals had on my political views?
- What personal experiences have affected my feelings about social issues?

the slighting of the vice presidency, the office is important. Remember that if the president should die, become disabled, or be removed from office, the vice president becomes our new national leader.

Duties

The vice president is given only two duties by the Constitution. The first duty is to preside over the Senate. Aside from casting a tie-breaking vote, however, this responsibility is mainly ceremonial. Recent vice presidents have usually turned much of this job over to the president *pro tempore* of the Senate.

As you have learned, another vice-presidential duty under the Twenty-fifth Amendment is to help decide whether the president is disabled and to assume the duties of the presidency if necessary.

Qualifications and Compensation

The official qualifications for vice president are the same as those for the president. A vice president must be a natural-born citizen, at least thirty-five years of age, and a resident of the United States for at least fourteen years. The vice president receives a salary of $160,000 a year, plus a yearly expense allowance. The official residence of the vice president is a mansion on the grounds of the Washington Naval Observatory. The vice president has an office in the White House and in the capitol with a large staff, special transportation, including the official vice-presidential plane, Air Force Two, and protection by the Secret Service.

Selection

The selection process normally begins at each party's national convention when the presidential nominee

Reteaching Strategies

1. Work with small groups of students to review Section 2. Help them discuss their responses to the Preview Questions, referring to the appropriate parts of the text.

2. Let the students work in pairs or small groups to compose paragraph-long explanations of the term *balance the ticket.*

Evaluation Strategies

1. Have the students write their answers to the Section 2 Review questions.

2. Have the students take the Section 2 Quiz found in the *TRB.*

Section 2 Review (Answers)

1. Historically, the office of vice president has been viewed as unimportant, but more involvement of the vice president over the years has changed this view slightly.

2. To preside over the Senate, to vote in ties, and to help decide whether the president is disabled and to assume the duties of the presidency if necessary.

3. The presidential nominee names his own running mate. He or she must be a natural-born citizen, at least 35 years of age, and a resident of the United States for at least 14 years.

4. Answers will vary, e.g., the vice president should receive all information that the president receives in order to provide assistance in presidential decision making and to ensure thorough personal knowledge if he or she suddenly becomes president.

SECTION 3

Points to Stress

- The development of the cabinet and its current role.
- Factors the president takes into account when choosing cabinet members.

Caption Answer The Constitution sets forth three duties for the vice president. These are to preside over the Senate, to vote in ties, and to help determine whether the president is disabled and to assume the duties of the presidency, if necessary.

Kickoff Activity

Give the students five minutes in which to list as many current members of the cabinet—with their titles—as possible. At the end of the time period, encourage the students to compare and discuss their lists.

Working with the Preview Questions

Encourage the students to discuss their responses to these study questions. Then ask the students to use these questions as a basis for taking notes as they study Section 3.

Vice presidents such as Dan Quayle, shown here, often represent the president and the people of the United States at the funerals of foreign leaders. Is this one of the duties of the vice president as set forth in the Constitution?

names his own running mate. Often, this choice is influenced by the need to pick someone to **balance the ticket**, improve the presidential candidate's prospects of winning. Thus, the vice-presidential candidate often comes from a region of the country or a wing of the party that is different from that of the presidential candidate. If the presidential nominee is from the South, the vice-presidential nominee may be from the North or West. If the presidential nominee is from an urban background, it is not a bad idea to have a vice-presidential nominee from a rural background.

Like the president, the vice president is officially elected by the electoral college (see Chapter 10), and serves a four-year term. Unlike the president, however, there is no limit to the number of terms a vice president may serve. The vice president is not subject to removal from office by the president.

More Involvement?

The assassination of President John F. Kennedy in 1963, and attempts on the lives of Presidents Gerald Ford and Ronald Reagan have focused more public attention on the office of vice president. Since the time of President Eisenhower, presidents have begun to take their vice presidents more seriously, involving them in some policy discussions and diplomacy. Vice presidents often represent the president overseas, take part in cabinet meetings, and serve on the National Security Council and on various commissions. By becoming more involved, the vice president assumes a slightly more influential role in the administration, and is more qualified to take over the presidency if necessary.

Section 2 Review

1. What has the historical attitude been toward the vice presidency? How has this attitude changed?
2. What are the constitutional duties of the vice president?
3. How is the vice president selected? What are the constitutional qualifications for becoming vice president?
4. **For critical analysis:** Do you think the vice president should automatically be a member of the National Security Council, attend all cabinet meetings, and receive all intelligence information that crosses the president's desk? Why or why not?

Section 3

The Cabinet

Preview Questions:

- How was the cabinet developed? What is its role today?
- What factors does the president take into account when choosing cabinet members?

The **cabinet** is an advisory group chosen by the president to help accomplish the work of the executive

Teaching Strategies

Introduction

Before the students read the section introduction, ask them to check the definitions of *cabinet* given in a dictionary: Which is the definition of the noun as it is used here? Which other definitions are closely related? How are they related?

After the students have read the introduction, help them consider the cabinet members named here. Ask the students to recall (or read about) the other accomplishments of each: How does a position in the cabinet seem to have affected the career of each individual named here? How do you imagine a cabinet post usually affects the lives and careers of individuals who serve today?

Extension

Have the students find and record the name of the secretary who heads each of these departments.

Enrichment

Let interested volunteers research the 12 cabinet appointments rejected by the Senate: Who was the appointee in each case? What reasons did the Senate give for rejecting the president's candidates? What other motivations—if any—lay behind the rejection? Have each volunteer report his or her findings to the rest of the class.

Discussion Starter

Guide the students in considering the choices presidents make for cabinet posts: Why do presidents usually choose members of their own political party? Might there be good reasons for selecting a member of the other political party for a particular cabinet post? If so, what would those reasons be? If not, why not?

Caption Answer The presidential cabinet, by tradition established by Washington, is made up of the heads of all 14 executive departments.

This portrait depicts President Washington with the members of the first presidential cabinet. Shown here are Secretary of War Henry Knox, Secretary of Treasury Alexander Hamilton, Secretary of State Thomas Jefferson, and Attorney General Edmund Randolph. Who forms the presidential cabinet today?

branch. Although the cabinet is not mentioned in the Constitution, every president has had one.[5] The cabinet has evolved out of tradition since 1789 when Congress set up four executive departments, and President George Washington met regularly on policy matters with the department heads. At the time, these were Secretary of State Thomas Jefferson; Secretary of War Henry Knox; Secretary of Treasury Alexander Hamilton; and Edmond Randolph, the attorney general. Newspaper writers of the day called this group Washington's ''cabinet.'' Every president since Washington has relied to some degree on the advice and work of the cabinet.

By long-established tradition, the heads of the executive departments form the cabinet. Today, the cabinet is made up of the secretaries of the fourteen executive departments, the vice president, and other key officials chosen by the president. The fourteen departments of the executive branch are:

- State
- Treasury
- Defense
- Justice
- Interior
- Agriculture
- Commerce
- Labor
- Health and Human Services
- Housing and Urban Development
- Education
- Energy
- Transportation
- Veterans' Affairs

Who Are the Cabinet Members?

The president appoints the heads of the executive departments, thereby appointing the cabinet members. Each of these appointments is subject to confirmation by the Senate. The cabinet is viewed as part of the president's official ''family,'' and the Senate gives the president considerable freedom in selecting cabinet members. Rejections have been rare. Out of 500 such appointments, only 12 have been turned down.

Presidents choose cabinet members for several reasons. Political party affiliation plays an obvious role. Republican presidents usually choose Republicans, and Democrats usually choose Democrats. Usually, presidents award a few cabinet posts to important party members who supported their presidential campaign.

Presidents also try to appoint individuals with broad experience in the given areas, such as transportation or labor. Because each department has thousands of employees and programs and spends billions of dollars each

5. The Constitution in Article II, Section 2 does state, however, that the president may require ''the Opinion, in writing, of the principal Officer in each of the executive Departments upon any Subject relating to the Duties of their respective Offices.''

Extension
Ask the students whether the current secretaries of interior, housing and urban development, and agriculture have the "typical" backgrounds suggested in the text.

Discussion Starter
Let the students share and discuss their ideas about the resignation of cabinet members: Why do you think they resign after a new president is elected? Under what circumstances might a cabinet member—or several cabinet members—refuse to resign? Do you imagine that their resignations could be forced? If so, how? If not, why not?

Enrichment
Ask three small groups of students to investigate the cabinets of Washington, Buchanan, and Eisenhower: Who served in each cabinet? How did each president rely on his cabinet members? What kind of relationship existed between the president and the cabinet members? How has this relationship been explained? Have the members of each group present their findings to the rest of the class.

Discussion Starter
Encourage the students to share and discuss their reactions to Lincoln's attitude.

▲ Although many presidents have held regularly scheduled meetings with the cabinets, the cabinet itself has no power as a body. What then, is the role of the presidential cabinet?

Caption Answer Students should understand that the cabinet acts solely as an advisory body and has no more power or influence than each president allows.

year, the secretaries must also be good managers and coordinators. If they do not handle their jobs well, the president will be criticized.

The president also tries to balance the nominees geographically according to their background. For example, the secretary of the interior is usually someone from a Western state who has experience dealing with land policy and conservation issues. This is because of the large store of natural resources in the West and federal ownership of large portions of Western land. The secretary of housing and urban development is usually someone with an urban background. The secretary of agriculture is usually from one of the farming states.

Presidents sometimes take into account the desires of interest groups that are affected by the cabinet department's policies. For example, the secretary of labor is generally someone acceptable to labor unions. The secretary of treasury could be a well-known banker or someone with close ties to the financial community.

Recent presidents have also considered gender, race, ethnic backgrounds, and other personal characteristics when choosing department heads. Public pressure has forced presidents to try to create a cabinet that reflects the ethnic and cultural diversity of the nation.

By custom, cabinet members resign after a new president is elected. In this way, the new president can create a new cabinet.

The Role and Influence of the Cabinet

The cabinet has no power as a body; the president alone determines the extent of the cabinet's power and influence. Presidents are not required by law to even form a cabinet or to hold regular meetings; therefore, meetings may be held frequently or infrequently, depending on the individual president. Meetings are held in the Cabinet Room of the White House and are usually closed to the public and the media. Frequently, they are attended by other government officials such as the director of the Office of Management and Budget.

Changing Roles Presidents have never been obliged to follow the advice of their cabinets; how much presidents use the cabinet as a whole is strictly up to them. Some presidents, such as George Washington, James Buchanan, and Dwight Eisenhower, relied on their cabinets often for advice and assistance. Other presidents relied on their cabinets very little. On one famous occasion when President Abraham Lincoln convened his cabinet to read them the draft of the Emancipation Proclamation, he started off by saying; "I have gotten you together to hear what I have written down. I do not wish your advice about the matter, for that I have determined myself." On another occasion, Lincoln is reported to have rejected a unanimous negative vote of his cabinet,

TEACHING GOVERNMENT IN ACTION

Read
Begin by having the students read and discuss the feature title, "The Conflicting Roles of Cabinet Heads": What different roles do you think cabinet heads have? How might these roles conflict? What effects could such conflicts have? After a few minutes discussion, ask the students to read the feature independently.

Discuss
Help the students discuss the content of the feature: When and under what circumstances might cabinet members feel a conflict between their roles as representatives of the president's policies and their roles as heads of their own departments? Why do you think disputes sometimes arise between individual cabinet members and the White House staff? What can the effects of such disputes be?

Analyze and Apply
Have the students work with partners to select an individual who has held at least one cabinet post for two or more years. Ask the partners to work together in researching this person's cabinet work; they might read interviews, newspaper articles, stories in news magazines, and so on. Then ask the partners to write a short essay about the cabinet member.

Review
Use these questions to help students review the feature: To whom are cabinet members expected to be responsive? How can conflicts between the various roles of cabinet members affect the members' effectiveness?

Think About It (answers)
1. Answers will vary, e.g., presidents might turn to others, such as White House advisors and staff members, because cabinet members might have interests that conflict with presidential needs. Also, presidents may have close trusted personal friends to whom they may wish to turn for advice.
2. Answers will vary, e.g., they must be approved by Congress and so must answer questions. They are also dependent on Congress for funding for their department.
3. Answers will vary, e.g., cabinet members' first loyalties should be to the president because the nation's well-being as a whole is more important than the well-being of their particular departments.

Extension
Have each student select a post-World War II president and then research and write a short report on that president's use of his cabinet.

Reteaching Strategies
1. Work with small groups of students, helping them to review and discuss their notes on Section 3. Encourage each student to make any additions or changes that will improve his or her notes.

GOVERNMENT IN ACTION

CASE STUDY

The Conflicting Roles of Cabinet Heads

Cabinet members have two major, and sometimes conflicting, roles to play. First, as cabinet members, they serve as advisors to the president. As you have seen, the extent to which a president uses the cabinet for advice depends strictly on each president's view of the cabinet. As cabinet members, nevertheless, they represent the president's policies to the rest of the executive branch, to Congress, and to the employees in their department.

The second role that cabinet members play is as the administrative heads of their executive departments. They must push for their departments' programs, and ensure that the departments' goals and activities respond to the needs of the citizens that the departments serve. Even though secretaries of departments hold their office at the discretion of the president, they have large bureaucracies to manage. They must listen to the needs of interest groups affected by their departments and sometimes become a spokesperson for those groups. Pressure from their staff and interest groups may cause secretaries to act more like lobbyists for their departments than as presidential advisors, sometimes to the point of undermining a president's policies.

Even though the president appoints them, cabinet members must be responsive to other groups. They must rely on the career officials in their departments who remain on the job from one administration to the next, and who run the departments on a day-to-day basis. These career officials are usually dedicated to the interests that the departments have developed over the years, and they may push secretaries in directions that are not always in accord with the president's own plans and policies.

Secretaries must also answer to members of Congress. Powerful legislators with interests in the departments' activities and policies may try to influence cabinet members. Their ideas may differ from those of the president. Because these legislators have the power to approve the programs within their department and to appropriate money to run the department, secretaries cannot ignore these members of Congress.

Cabinet members must be responsive to interest groups. Departments such as the Department of Labor and the Department of Health and Human Services deliver services to various organized interest groups, which expect the department and the secretaries to respond to their requests. Secretaries cannot ignore these special interests because these groups have supporters in Congress.

THINK ABOUT IT

1. Why would a president turn to others besides cabinet members for advice?
2. In what way do cabinet members have to answer to Congress?
3. In the event of a conflict, should a cabinet member's first loyalties be to the president or to the department that he or she heads? Give reasons for your answer.

saying, ''seven nays, one aye—the ayes have it.'' Lincoln's vote was, of course, the one aye. Woodrow Wilson went even further—he held no cabinet meetings at all during World War I.

Other presidents have bypassed their official cabinet altogether, and have relied on informal groups of political friends for advice. Andrew Jackson, for example, began meeting with a small group of friends and minor government officials to discuss important matters. Because they often met in the White House kitchen, they came to be called the **Kitchen Cabinet**. Franklin Roosevelt created his famous ''brain trust''—a group of business executives, professors, research specialists, and other special advisors, including the chief justice of the Supreme Court, who helped him construct many of the New Deal programs of the 1930s.

2. Let the students work with partners to write paragraphs explaining the importance of the cabinet within the executive branch of government.

Caption Answer Some presidents have relied on the cabinets very little, others have completely bypassed their cabinets. More recently, presidents have increasingly ignored their cabinets to rely on White House aides.

Evaluation Strategies

1. Have the students write their answers to the Section 3 Review questions.

2. Have the students take the Section 3 Quiz found in the *TRB.*

Section 3 Review (Answers)

1. The cabinet evolved out of tradition since 1789.

2. The cabinet is made up of the secretaries of 14 executive departments.

3. Political party affiliation and broad experience in the given area are considered by the president. Presidents also try to balance nominees geographically according to their background and sometimes take into account the desires of interest groups that are affected by the cabinet departments' policies.

4. Answers will vary, e.g., the president must please the constituencies of the particular executive department.

During the Persian Gulf conflict in 1990 and 1991, President Bush made effective use of certain cabinet members, such as Secretary of Defense Richard Cheney, shown here. Do all presidents strongly rely on their cabinets?

Several recent presidents have tried to make greater use of the cabinet. Most, however, end up turning elsewhere for advice. They generally begin working closely with cabinet members and gradually drift away to depend more on a few top White House staff members. For example, in the beginning of his term, President Carter wanted to make greater use of his cabinet members. After two years in office, there was general disunity in the cabinet and during one week, he fired or accepted the resignations of five cabinet members. To compensate for this chaos, he expanded the authority of his personal White House staff. Similarly, President Reagan pledged to make his cabinet an important part of his administration. He said that the cabinet would be his ''inner circle of advisors.'' After a year in office, however, Reagan was depending on his White House aides rather than the cabinet for advice. President Bush effectively used his secretary of state, James Baker, and his secretary of defense, Richard Cheney, for advice during the Persian Gulf conflict in 1990 and 1991.

SECTION 3 REVIEW

1. How was the cabinet created?
2. Who serves on the cabinet?
3. What factors does the president consider when choosing cabinet members?
4. **For critical analysis:** Although the president picks his department heads, they are not always in agreement with his policies. Why do you think this is so? (*Hint*: The president's constituency is the entire American public. Who is the constituency of a particular executive department?)

SECTION 4

The Executive Office of the President

Preview Questions

- What are the agencies of the Executive Office of the President?
- What are the duties of these agencies?

Around 1900 the White House Office consisted of a few presidential assistants, secretaries, bookkeepers, and household staff. By 1932, it included only thirty-seven people. Starting in 1939, when President Franklin D. Roosevelt first set up the **Executive Office of the President (EOP)** to cope with the increased responsibilities brought on by the Great Depression, the EOP has grown rapidly with the rest of government.

The EOP is made up of the top advisors and assistants who help the president carry out major duties. Over the years, the executive office has changed, according to the needs and leadership style of each president. It has become an increasingly influential and important part of presidential government. Figure 15–2 on page 370 shows the staffing of the Executive Office of President.

White House Office

Of all the executive staff agencies, the White House Office has the most direct contact with the president. The White House Office consists of the president's key aides whom the president sees daily, and several hundred professional and clerical staff. The most important advisors occupy the West Wing, where the president's Oval Office and the Cabinet Room are located. (Some of the staff do work in the East Wing.)

The Staff The White House Office is led by the **chief of staff**, who advises the president on important matters and directs the operations of the presidential staff. The chief of staff, who is often a close, personal friend of the president, has been one of the most influential of the presidential aides in recent years. A number of other top officials, assistants, and special assistants to the president also aid him in areas such as national security, the economy, and political affairs. A **press secretary** meets with reporters and makes public statements for the president. The counsel to the president serves as the White House lawyer and handles the president's legal matters. The White House staff also includes speechwriters, researchers, the president's physician, the director of the staff for

SECTION 4

Points to Stress

- The agencies of the Executive Office of the President.
- Duties of the agencies of the Executive Office of the President.

Kickoff Activity

Ask the students to list at least six different White House duties that are probably assumed by staff members, rather than being directly undertaken by the president. Encourage the students to compare and discuss their completed lists.

Working with the Preview Questions

Let the students read these study questions and briefly discuss what they already know in response to them. Remind the students to keep these questions in mind as they study Section 4.

Teaching Strategies

Introduction

Ask one of the students to read the section introduction aloud; then help the students study and discuss figure 15–2 on page 370. Encourage discussion by asking questions such as these: Why do you think the White House Office has grown so remarkably since the beginning of this century? Do you think it would be possible for the White House Office to become *too* big? Why or why not? How important can the EOP be? Who determines its importance? Its effectiveness?

Enrichment

Ask volunteers to read about, and report on, notable press secretaries. (Examples include Pierre Salinger and James Brady.)

Extension
Ask the students to identify the individuals who now serve as counsel to the president, the president's physician, the director of staff for the first lady, and the correspondence secretary.

Discussion Starter
Help the students discuss the duties of the White House staff in guiding the president's attention: How can the staff help the president by screening out the less important issues? Could this kind of screening weaken the president's effectiveness? If so, how? Who should be considered responsible?

Extension
If the timing is appropriate, ask the students to watch a television broadcast of a complete presidential press conference. Then have them read news stories about the press conference and notice how the conference is covered in television news shows: What is included in the media coverage? What is left out? What attitude toward the president is implied by this kind of coverage of the press conference?

Discussion Starter
As the students read about the OMB, ask them to consider why this has become such an influential unit of the executive office: What changes within our government and our society are reflected in the rise of the OMB?

Enrichment
Have the students recall (or read about) recent budget-related negotiations between the Congress and the administration: What powers are held by each group? How do they attempt to use their power?

Figure Answer The White House Office has the most direct contact with the president.

This figure content is also featured on *West's American Government Videodisc* (see the index found in the TRB) and is available in the transparency package.

Executive Office of the President

Department	Year Established
White House Office	1939
Council of Economic Advisers	1946
National Security Council	1947
Office of the United States Trade Representative	1963
Council on Environmental Quality	1969
Office of Management and Budget	1970
Office of Science and Technology Policy	1976
Office of Administration	1977
Office of Policy Development	1977
Office of National Drug Control Policy	1989

FIGURE 15–2 Executive Office of the President. This table shows the various departments for the Executive Office of the President, and the year each department was established. Which of these departments has the most direct contact with the president?

the first lady, and a correspondence secretary. Altogether, there are over four hundred men and women who work in the White House Office.

Duties of White House Staff The White House staff has several duties. First, the staff investigates and analyzes problems that require the president's attention. Staff members who are specialists in specific areas, such as diplomatic relations or foreign trade, gather information for the president and suggest solutions. White House staff members also screen the questions, issues, and problems that people present to the president, so matters that can be handled by other officials do not reach the president's desk. The staff also provides public relations support. For example, the press staff handles the president's relations with the White House press corps and sets up **press conferences**. Finally, the White House staff makes sure the president's decisions are carried out. Several staff people are usually assigned to work directly with members of Congress for this purpose.

Setting up press conferences and releasing information to the White House Press Corps is one of the important duties of White House staff members such as White House spokeswoman Dee Dee Myers. What are some of the other duties of White House staff?

Caption Answer White House staff members handle a wide variety of duties, including researching areas that require the president's attention, screening the people, questions, issues, and problems that are presented to the president, and working with Congress to see that the president's policies are enacted and that the president's decisions are carried out.

Office of Management and Budget

The **Office of Management and Budget (OMB)** was originally the Bureau of the Budget. Under recent presidents, the OMB has become an important and influential unit of the executive office. The main function of the OMB is to assist the president in preparing the proposed annual **budget**, which the president must submit to Congress in January of each year. The **fiscal year** (official accounting period) for the federal government runs from October 1 to September 30. The budget for the federal government lists the revenues and expenditures expected for the coming year. It indicates which programs the federal government will pay for and how much they will cost. Thus, the budget is an annual statement of the public policies of the United States translated into dollars and cents. Making changes in the budget is a key way for presidents to try to influence the direction and policies of the federal government.

Extension
Ask an interested volunteer to read about the current director of the OMB: What background did the director bring to this position? When did he assume this office? What do the director's particular policies and interests appear to be? How effective is the current director considered to be? Why? Let this volunteer present a brief oral report to the rest of the class.

Cooperative Learning
Assign the students to work in small groups to read about the current national security advisor, the current director of the CIA, and the current chairman of the Joint Chiefs of Staff: What background does each bring to the position? Why does each seem to have been chosen for that position? What kind of relationship does each seem to have with the president? With the media?

Discussion Starter
Encourage the students to consider the function of the domestic policy staff: Which cabinet departments are directly concerned with issues treated by the domestic policy staff? How do you think those departments interact with the domestic policy staff? What kinds of conflicts might arise between the groups?

Enrichment
Let two interested volunteers read the most recent *Economic Report of the President:* What analysis is presented there? What recommendations are made? Ask the volunteers to write a short summary of the report, to be shared with the rest of the class.

Preparing the federal budget is a long, complicated process similar to that of preparing a business firm or municipal government budget. First, each government agency estimates the amount of money it needs for the coming year. Then, the OMB sets objectives for each federal program. It then reviews all estimates at a series of budget hearings, at which agencies must defend their dollar requests. The figures of each department are then revised and fitted into the president's overall program. They become part of the budget document the chief executive submits to Congress. After the budgets of the various agencies are resolved, the next step is to get the administration budget passed by Congress, which has budget proposals of its own.

The president appoints the director of the OMB with the consent of the Senate. The director of the OMB has become at least as important as cabinet members and is often included in cabinet meetings. He or she oversees the OMB's work and argues the administration's position before Congress. The director also lobbies members of Congress to support the president's budget or to accept key features of it. Once the budget is approved by Congress, the OMB has the responsibility of putting it into practice. It oversees the execution of the budget, checking the federal agencies to ensure that they use funds efficiently.

Beyond its budget duties, the OMB also reviews new bills prepared by the executive branch. It checks all legislative matters to be certain that they agree with the president's own positions.

National Security Council

The **National Security Council (NSC)** was created in 1947 to provide advice and managerial assistance with matters concerning American military and foreign policy, as well as national security. The NSC members are the president, the vice president, and the secretaries of state and defense. A national security advisor appointed by the president directs the staff of the NSC. The director of the Central Intelligence Agency (CIA) and the chairman of the Joint Chiefs of Staff have also become members. The Joint Chiefs of Staff is made up of the commanding officers of each of the four branches of armed services plus a chairperson.

When serious world crises have developed, most presidents have immediately called the NSC into session. Many have used the council as a regular working group to discuss foreign policy. The role of the NSC is largely decided by each president, and each president uses it differently. President Bush relied heavily on some members of his National Security Council, especially General Colin Powell, the chairman of the Joint Chiefs of Staff, during the Persian Gulf War in 1991.

Office of Policy Development

Originally set up as the domestic policy staff, the Office of Policy Development advises the president on domestic policy matters such as trade, energy, housing, and farming. The office studies the nation's needs and makes domestic policy suggestions to the president. Once domestic policies are formed, this office helps the president put the government's programs into effect.

Council of Economic Advisors

The **Council of Economic Advisors (CEA)** was created by Congress in 1946 to advise the president on economic matters. It analyzes the national economy, advises the president on how the economy is doing, and recommends measures to maintain economic stability in the nation. The council helps the president prepare his annual *Economic Report of the President.* The council usually includes three leading economists, appointed by the president with the consent of the Senate, and a small staff of persons who prepare statistics.

Other Units in the Executive Office

Several other agencies in the executive office assist the president with the many other responsibilities of the executive branch.

Council on Environmental Quality The Council on Environmental Quality (CEQ) was created in 1969 to

"First of all, let me explain exactly what advice the president wants to hear."
Dunagin's People by Ralph Dunagin. Reprinted with special permission of NAS, Inc.

Cooperative Learning Divide the class into six groups, and have each group research the membership and the functioning of one of these agencies: the Council on Environmental Quality, the Office of Science and Technology, the National Space Council, the Office of United States Trade Representative, the Office of National Drug Control Policy, and the Office of Administration. Then ask the members of each group to share what they have learned with the rest of the class.

2. Have the students work in groups to discuss possible answers to the fourth Section 4 Review question.

3. Have the students take the Section 4 quiz found in the *TRB*.

Section 4 Review (Answers)

1. The White House Office consists of the president's key aides, including a number of senior advisors and other top aides, and several hundred professional and clerical staff. The staff conducts preliminary investigations and analysis of problems that require the president's attention, screening issues and problems. The staff also provides public relations support and makes sure the president's decisions are carried out.

2. The OMB assists the president in preparing the annual budget, in managing the executive departments, and in maintaining coordinated efforts with Congress.

3. The NSC provides the president with advice and managerial assistance with matters concerning the American military, foreign policy, and national security.

4. Answers will vary, e.g., the responsibilities of the executive office have grown tremendously. Disadvantages include more expense to the public and more bureaucracy.

Caption Answer The office is responsible for planning and coordinating the efforts of the more than 50 federal agencies involved with drug control.

Reteaching Strategies

1. Have the students work with partners to review and write topic outlines of Section 4.

2. Let the students work in small groups to write, in their own words, explanatory sentences about these terms: *EOP, chief of staff, press secretary, press conference, OMB, fiscal year, NSC,* and *CEA.*

Evaluation Strategies

1. Have the students write their answers to the first three Section 4 Review questions.

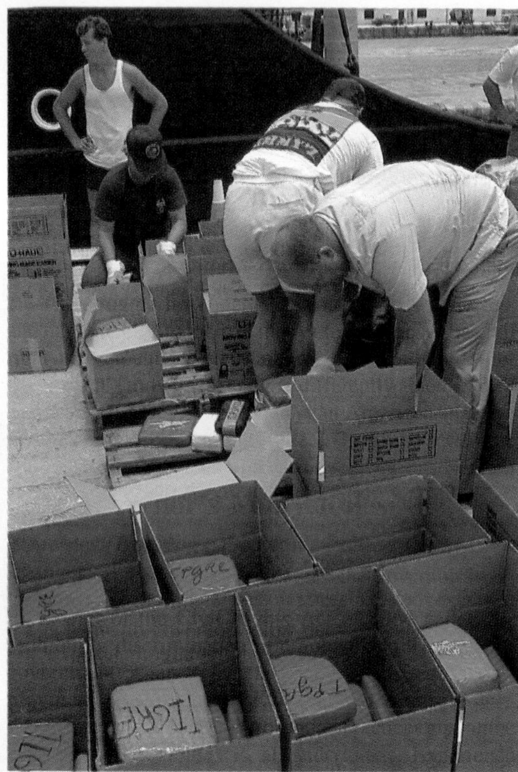

▲ Federal agents, such as these shown tagging two tons of cocaine seized in a drug bust, are in the middle of a war on drugs. What is the role of the Office of National Drug Control in the war on drugs?

assist the president on matters of environmental policy. It studies government programs designed to protect the environment and assists the president in preparing a yearly report on the environment to Congress. The council is made up of three members appointed by the president with Senate approval.

Office of Science and Technology The Office of Science and Technology advises the president on all scientific, engineering, and other technological matters that have a bearing on national policies and programs. It reviews the federal government's contributions to science and technology. The director, chosen by the president with Senate approval, is drawn from the nation's scientific community.

National Space Council The National Space Council advises the president on the nation's civil and military efforts in outer space. The vice president chairs the council, and its other members include the secretaries of state, defense, commerce, and transportation, the administrator of the National Aeronautics and Space Administration (NASA), and the directors of the CIA and OMB.

Office of United States Trade Representative This office establishes and carries out United States trade policy. The trade representative, appointed by the president and approved by the Senate, speaks for the United States at international trade meetings and directs negotiations and trade agreements with foreign governments.

Office of National Drug Control Policy The Office of National Drug Control Policy was established in 1989. The director is appointed by the president with Senate approval and is regularly identified by the press as the nation's "drug czar." The office is responsible for drafting continuing plans to wage the federal government's war on drugs, and for coordinating the efforts of the more than fifty federal agencies that deal with drug control.

Office of Administration The Office of Administration is the general housekeeping agency for all the other units of the executive office. It provides them with support services such as information gathering, financial management, data processing, library services, record keeping, and general office help.

All of the offices and agencies covered in this section form just a part of the "chain of responsibility" that Truman said "bind" the president. From the time that George Washington took the oath of office and stepped into the newly created executive branch, each person to hold the position has helped to define the office of president in our government.

SECTION 4 REVIEW

1. What is the White House Office and what are its functions?
2. What are the duties of the Office of Management and Budget?
3. What is the function of the National Security Council?
4. **For critical analysis:** Seventy years ago, the White House staff consisted of fewer than forty people. Today, it numbers in the hundreds. Why do you think it has grown so much over the years? What advantages and disadvantages can you see to having a larger White House staff?

TEACHING CHALLENGE TO THE AMERICAN DREAM

Read

Before the students begin reading the Challenge to the American Dream feature, encourage them to discuss their responses to these questions: Why is the role of the vice president so important? Why is it, at the same time, relatively unimportant? How important is the competence of the vice president? Whose responsibility is it to ensure that competence? Why? After the discussion, ask the students to read the feature independently.

Discuss

Pose questions such as these to help the students discuss the feature: Assuming that the vice president should be assigned a broader scope of duties, do you consider a constitutional amendment necessary for defining those duties? Why or why not? Why do most presidents prefer to keep their vice presidents in the background? What do you think a president might gain by having a vice president who serves as an active policy-making member of the administration? Why do you imagine presidents are so often willing to forgo those benefits?

Analyze and Apply

Have the students work in small groups to write detailed "help wanted" ads for individuals to fill the office of vice president. The ads should include a complete job description and a list of qualifications.

Review

Help the students review by asking these questions: What are the formal qualifications for the position of vice president? What are the dangers of having a vice president who does little or nothing while in office?

You Decide (Answers)

1. Answers will vary, e.g., it should remain as it is. The vice president should have the same formal qualifications as the president.
2. Answers will vary, e.g., most presidents wish the publicity to remain with them. They want to receive credit and popularity for their decisions and actions.
3. Answers will vary, e.g., the vice president should become president only temporarily, until another special popular election can be held for president.

Observable Mastery

Conduct a classroom brainstorming exercise. Alternate quickly among students allowing each to present one aspect that was covered in the chapter. Get as much information from the chapter on the board as possible, offering hints to those students that might need help.

Then have the students organize the information in a logical form. For example, all information concerning the vice president should be grouped together, as would all information about the Executive Office of the President.

CHALLENGE TO THE AMERICAN DREAM

Can the Vice President Handle the Job?

In terms of formal standards, the vice president has the same qualifications as the president. The actual duties of the vice president, however, are much more limited. Indeed, it is possible for the vice president to do almost nothing during his or her entire term in office. This means that if the president dies, or is otherwise incapacitated, the nation may end up with a leader who has not spent much time learning about what the president does. For this reason, some have proposed a constitutional amendment that would give a much broader scope of duties to the vice president. These could include formally making the vice president part of the budget-making process, requiring that the vice president always be part of the National Security Council and attend its meetings, and other similarly important duties.

To be sure, most presidents would not particularly favor such a change. Most prefer to have their vice presidents stay in the background, leaving the limelight to the presidents themselves. Some even argue that the president, while a candidate, typically will pick a vice-presidential candidate who agrees to "keep a low profile." Certainly Vice President Bush did not make many headlines when he served with Ronald Reagan from 1981 to 1988. It is hard to imagine that any modern president would want to have a new set of rules requiring that the vice president be an active policy-making member of the administration.

Other political commentators believe that too much fuss is made about the lack of vice-presidential qualifications. After all, they say, how many presidents had enough experience in national politics prior to being elected? Jimmy Carter was a peanut farmer and governor of Georgia before being elected president. Ronald Reagan came to the White House after serving as governor of California and a career as an actor. Neither of these men had extensive experience in national politics. Indeed, it would be difficult to prove some correlation between our presidents' previous backgrounds and how well they actually performed while in office.

▲ The vice president is "a heartbeat away" from having to step in as president. Here, Lyndon Johnson, en route to Washington, D.C., takes the oath as president following the assassination of John F. Kennedy in 1963.

However convincing this last argument might be, most Americans still feel uneasy about the thought of the president leaving office for whatever reason and having an untested, inexperienced vice president take over. The challenge to the American dream is first to consider the qualifications of vice-presidential candidates just as seriously as those of presidential candidates, and second to let the president know that he should not allow his vice president to remain strictly "in the wings."

You Decide

1. What other formal qualifications, if any, should be applied to the position of vice president?
2. Why do you think presidents allow their vice presidents to remain in the background?
3. Gerald Ford became president after having been appointed vice president, thereby becoming our only unelected president. Do you think there should be a change in the Constitution to prevent this? If so, why?

Chapter Evaluation

To evaluate student mastery of chapter material, you might:

1. Use Chapter Test A from the *TRB.*

2. Use Chapter Test B from the *TRB.*

3. Construct your own test using items from the *West American Government Test Bank* found in the *TRB.*

4. Use the accompanying computerized test software to construct and print a customized chapter test.

Review Questions (Answers)

1. The president must be a natural-born citizen, at least 35 years of age, and a resident of the United States at least 14 years before taking office.

2. The president may serve two terms.

3. The Twenty-fifth Amendment settles the issue of presidential succession and describes the steps to be followed should the president become disabled during office. It provides that the vice president should become acting president if the president informs Congress of an inability to perform in office or if the vice president and a majority of cabinet members inform Congress in writing, that the president is disabled.

4. To preside over the Senate, to vote in the event of a tie, and to help decide whether the president is disabled and to assume the duties of the presidency if necessary.

5. The presidential nominee names his own running mate.

6. The president appoints cabinet members, subject to Senate confirmation.

7. Each president determines the extent of the cabinet's power and influence.

8. The Office is led by the chief of staff. A number of other top officials, assistants, and special assistants to the president aid him in areas such as national security and the economy.

9. The OMB assists the president in preparing the annual budget, which the president must submit to Congress in January of each year.

10. NSC members include the president, the vice president, the secretaries of state and defense. A

CHAPTER 15 REVIEW

Key Terms

balance the ticket 365
budget 370
cabinet 365
chief of staff 369
chief executive 356
Council of Economic Advisors (CEA) 371
Executive Office of the President (EOP) 369
fiscal year 370
Kitchen Cabinet 368
National Security Council (NSC) 371
Office of Management and Budget (OMB) 370
press conferences 370
press secretary 369
succession 359

Summary

1. The president of the United States holds one of the most powerful elective offices in the world. Article II of the Constitution states that the president shall hold the nation's executive power. The past two centuries have seen the office expand. The president must satisfy three constitutional qualifications: (1) being a natural-born citizen, (2) being at least thirty-five years old, (3) being a resident of the United States at least fourteen years before taking office. Other informal qualifications have also developed such as political experience and political acceptability. The president is chosen to serve a four-year term and may serve only twice. He is paid $200,000 a year and receives many other benefits. The vice president assumes the presidency should the office become vacant. The order of succession following the vice president was fixed by Congress according to the Presidential Succession Act of 1947.

2. The vice presidency has historically been seen as an insignificant position, but has become increasingly important in recent years. The vice president's constitutional duties are to preside over the Senate, to help decide whether a president is disabled, and to assume the duties of the presidency if necessary. The official qualifications for vice president are the same as those for president. The person chosen by a party to run for president usually names his own running mate. Often his choice is influenced by the need to pick someone to balance the ticket.

3. The cabinet is an advisory group chosen by the president to help accomplish the work of the executive branch. The cabinet is not mentioned in the Constitution but has evolved out of tradition. The president appoints the heads of executive departments, thereby appointing the cabinet members. In choosing cabinet members, the president takes several factors into consideration such as political party affiliation, experience in the given area, geographic background, and the desires of interest groups. The cabinet has no official power as a body, and the extent of the power and influence of the cabinet is strictly up to the individual president.

4. The Executive Office of the President (EOP) is made up of the top advisors and assistants who help the president carry out major duties. The White House Office is led by the chief of staff, who in recent years has been one of the most influential of presidential aides. Other EOP agencies include the Office of Management and Budget, the National Security Council, the Office of Policy Development, and the Council of Economic Advisors.

Review Questions

1. What qualifications must a president have, according to the Constitution?
2. According to the Twenty-second Amendment, how many terms may a president serve?
3. What did the Twenty-fifth Amendment establish?
4. What are the constitutional duties of the vice president?
5. How is the vice president selected?
6. How is the cabinet chosen?
7. How are the role and influence of the cabinet determined?
8. How is the White House Office organized?
9. What is the function of the Office of Management and Budget?
10. Who are the members of the National Security Council?
11. Why is it important to gain an understanding of your political ideology?
12. What are the arguments in favor of and what are the arguments against giving the vice president greater political responsibility during his term?

national security advisor, appointed by the president, directs the staff. The director of the CIA and the Joint Chiefs of Staff also regularly attend the meetings.

11. It is important to understand your political ideology because you must express it in many ways such as voting, joining special interest groups, participating in community projects, and possibly running for public office.

12. One argument in favor is that if the vice president becomes president, he or she needs to know more about the office. One argument against is that presidents themselves often don't have much political experience when they begin office.

Questions for Thought and Discussion (Answers)

1. Answers will vary, e.g., there should be no other formal qualifications because no one should be excluded based on any other formal qualifications.

2. Answers will vary, e.g., the role of vice president will expand as the responsibilities of the executive office increase. Presidents will come to rely more on their vice presidents to perform many of the duties they now perform themselves.

3. Answers will vary, e.g., the secretary of defense and the secretary of state had great influence over President Bush during the Persian Gulf War in 1990 and 1991.

4. Answers will vary, e.g., the office has grown because presidents have added people and new agencies in response to crises over the years. It has grown because problems facing our industrial society are complex.

CHAPTER 15 REVIEW—Continued

Questions for Thought and Discussion

1. What qualifications or characteristics do you think a president should have? Which of the recent presidents, if any, have had these qualifications or characteristics?
2. Do you think the role of the vice president will expand or diminish in the future? What factors do you think will have a bearing on his or her role and influence?
3. Which cabinet members currently have the most influence on the president? Give evidence to support your answer.
4. Why do you think the Executive Office of the President has grown so dramatically? Do the numerous agencies and staff really assist the president in his job?

Improving Your Skills

Communication Skills

Paraphrasing

In doing homework, answering questions, and writing reports, you will sometimes be asked to **paraphrase**. Paraphrasing is restating someone else's writing or ideas in your own words. Paraphrasing will help you recognize the main idea, condense information, and organize material. Paraphrasing might be useful when answering questions such as, "What were the president's views on the new budget?" or "What were the instructions for completing this assignment?"

Follow these guidelines when paraphrasing:

- Read or listen to the material carefully.
- Review the information, and while retaining the author or speaker's point or view, rewrite it in your own words. Do not include any ideas of your own.
- Include all the ideas of the original material, but reword them using your own writing style, tone, and vocabulary.

Writing

Turn to the "Architect of the American Dream" feature on page 360. Write an account of Lincoln's speech as if you were a newspaper reporter covering the event. You might wish to add to your story by reporting facts about the battle and the day. Use a history book to find any additional facts you may need.

Social Studies Skills

Comparing Similarities and Differences

One key social studies skill that you should master is the ability to compare similarities and differences between and among political systems, political parties, interest groups, political documents, and, of course, politicians and world leaders. In order to make such comparisons accurately you must specifically choose issues on which to base your analysis. For example, when you compare the two major political parties, decide in advance on which points you will focus, such as each party's stand on abortion, expanded health care, research funds for AIDS, and so on. The same system should be used for comparing leaders, such as current and past presidents, or political candidates.

Use the above ideas to compare the similarities and differences between one or more of the following:

1. The Republican party and the Libertarian party.
2. Direct democracy and representative democracy.
3. The two senators from your state.
4. The last two major presidential candidates.
5. President Herbert Hoover and President Franklin D. Roosevelt.
6. The National Rifle Association and the American Medical Association.
7. *The Federalist Papers* Numbers 10 and 51.

Activities and Projects

1. Choose a cabinet member and research his or her background, experience, and influence on the president. Write a biographical account of the cabinet member that includes your opinion on whether this person is qualified to head his or her particular department.
2. Conduct a class debate on the following: Resolved—The president shall hold a single term of office for six years only.

CHAPTER INTRODUCTION

Instructional Objectives

By the end of the chapter students should be able to:

- Outline the powers of the president mentioned in the Constitution and the additional powers that have developed with the office.
- Discuss the many interrelated roles of the president.
- Summarize the limits placed on presidential powers.

Using the Keynote

Begin by asking the students to recall Franklin Roosevelt: When was he president? Under what conditions did he serve in this position? For what is he best remembered?

Then let a volunteer read aloud Roosevelt's quotation, and guide the students in discussing it: What is the tone of this statement? How can you tell? How might the same idea be expressed in a statement with a different tone? How do you imagine Roosevelt felt about the presidency? Why? Encourage the students to express and defend various responses to these questions.

Introducing the Chapter

Let a volunteer read the Introduction aloud to the rest of the class. Then encourage the students to discuss their responses to these questions: Do you agree that being president is the "biggest job in the world"? Why or why not? What particular aspects of the job make it unusually demanding? What benefits of the job might help offset the pressures of those demands? What kind of individual do you consider best suited—in terms of temperament and intelligence—for the job? Why?

Previewing the Sections

Section 1 Ask the students to look through Section 1: What special features are included in this section? What photographs and figures are included? What do you expect to learn as you study Section 1?

Section 2 Ask volunteers to read aloud the section title and the main headings in Section 2; let other volunteers read aloud the titles of the special features and figures. Then have the students list at five familiar facts they expect to find in this section and at least three questions they hope to have answered.

Section 3 Let the students page through Section 3, noting especially the main headings and the photo captions. Then ask the students to suggest what they expect to learn in this section and to explain why the topic is important to all citizens.

CHAPTER 16

The President at Work

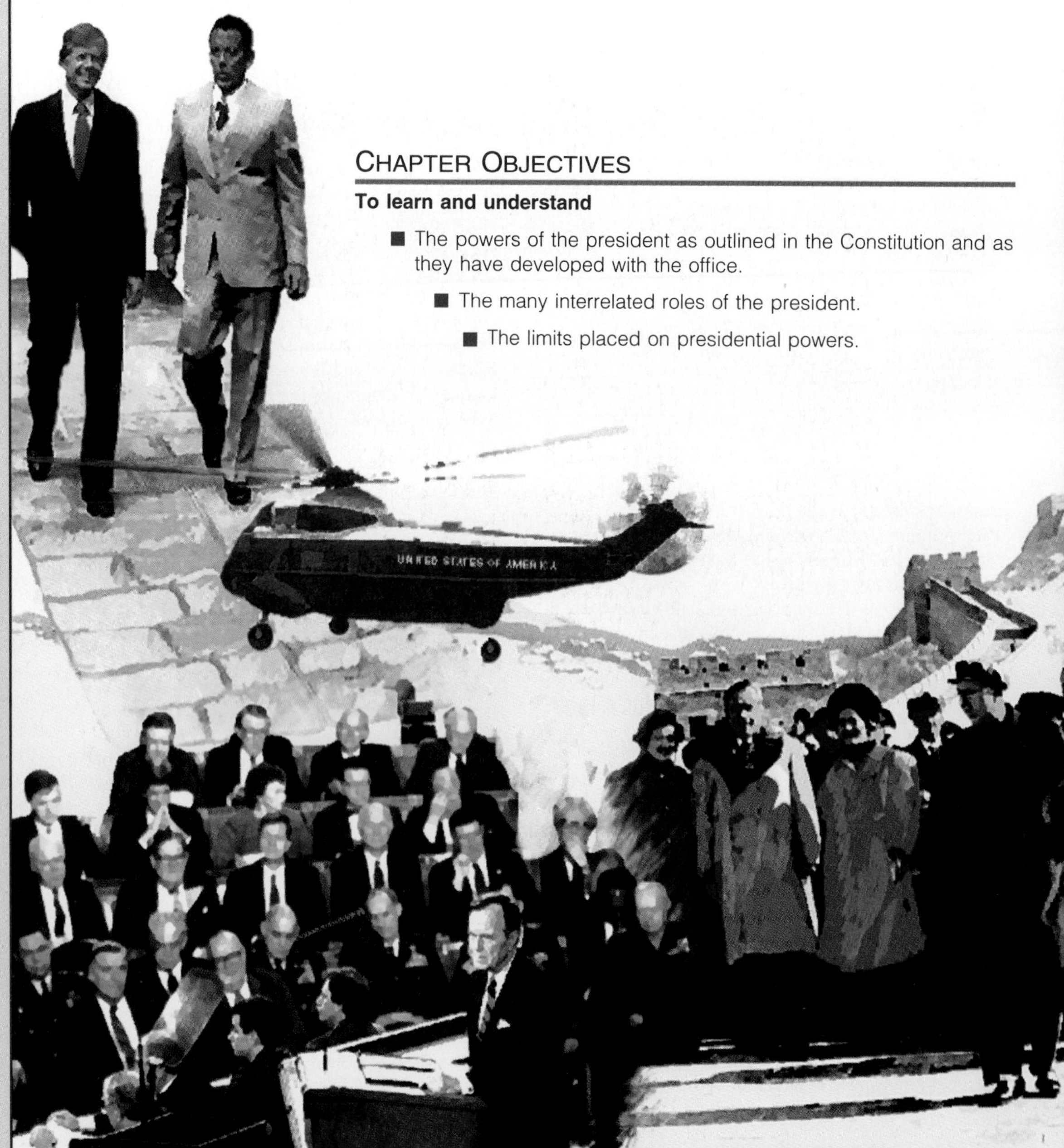

CHAPTER OBJECTIVES

To learn and understand

- The powers of the president as outlined in the Constitution and as they have developed with the office.
- The many interrelated roles of the president.
- The limits placed on presidential powers.

West's American Government Assignment Guide

Activity Sheets
Basic Concepts 16 *TRB* (Reteaching)
Enrichment Activity 16 *TRB*
Building Social Studies Skills 16 *TRB*
Quizzes
Chapter 16 Section 1 Quiz *TRB*
Chapter 16 Section 2 Quiz *TRB*
Chapter 16 Section 3 Quiz *TRB*

Tests
Chapter 16 Test A *TRB*
Chapter 16 Test B *TRB*
Chapter 16 Test Bank *TRB*
Chapter 16 WESTEST Computerized Testing

SECTION 1

Points to Stress
- Powers of the president listed in the Constitution.
- Sources that have built upon presidential powers.
- The manner in which strong presidents have contributed to the growth of presidential powers.
- The way that the media has enhanced the power of the presidency.

Kickoff Activity
Ask the students to read the section title and then to list at least eight things that they know presidents do. When all the students have completed their lists, encourage them to compare and discuss their ideas.

Working with the Preview Questions
Ask the students to read and briefly discuss their responses to these study questions. Then instruct the students to keep these questions in mind as they read and take notes on Section 1.

Teaching Strategies

Discussion Starter
Help the students consider the vagueness of the presidential powers granted in Article II of the Constitution: What dangers were there in describing the powers vaguely, rather than listing specific powers to be granted to the president? What advantages were there in keeping the description vague?

Discussion Starter
Help the students consider and discuss their reactions to each of the presidential powers listed here: Does this list in any way change your evaluation of the job the president undertakes? If so, how?

Keynote

"The first twelve years are the hardest."

—— **Franklin D. Roosevelt (1882–1945) Thirty-Second President of the United States**

INTRODUCTION

As Franklin D. Roosevelt's statement reveals, serving in the nation's highest public office is never easy, even after many years. The president heads the largest organization in the nation, a government that has about 3 million civilian and 1½ million military employees. Entrusted with carrying out the laws of the land, the president is also chief architect of American foreign policy, an increasingly difficult task in our rapidly changing world. The president is head of the world's most powerful military arsenal, negotiator of treaties with other nations, chief collector of taxes, and chief persuader of public opinion. With a multitude of powers and duties that have increased greatly over time, the office of the presidency has grown to become more powerful and more complex. As President Harry S Truman once said, "The pressures and complexities of the presidency have grown to a state where they are almost too much for one man to endure."

SECTION 1

Presidential Powers

Preview Questions

- What are the constitutional powers of the president?
- What other sources are presidential powers built upon?
- How have strong presidents contributed to the growth of presidential powers?
- How have the media enhanced the power of the presidency?

The Constitution is the first place to look to find out what our presidents are supposed to do and how they are supposed to do it. Article II of the Constitution outlines the powers of the president, as shown in the list below.

The president's powers are, of course, limited by the checks and balances of the other two branches of government. But the president can use these limited powers in a variety of ways.

Constitutional Powers

Article II begins by simply stating that "the Executive Power shall be vested in the President of the United States of America."

As you have learned, the founders wanted a strong president, but had difficulty agreeing on the amount of strength and level of power the president should have. As a result, Article II grants the president broad but vaguely described powers. From the very beginning there were differing views as to what exactly the "executive power" clause enabled the president to do. Because this power is not precisely defined, its meaning can change with differing circumstances.

Sections 2 and 3 of Article II go on to list specific presidential powers. You will see what these powers mean in practice later in the chapter when the president's many roles are discussed. According to Sections 2 and 3, the president has the power:

1. to serve as commander in chief of the armed forces and the state militias;
2. to appoint heads of executive departments with Senate approval;
3. to grant reprieves and pardons, except in cases of impeachment;
4. to make treaties, with the advice and consent of the Senate;
5. to appoint ambassadors, federal court judges, justices of the Supreme Court; and other top officials, with Senate consent;

Enrichment
Assign interested volunteers to research Richard Nixon's abuse of this presidential access to information; then have the students plan and present a short skit (or an oral report) summarizing their findings.

Discussion Starter
Encourage the students to discuss their understanding of and reaction to Truman's remark: How can the president persuade people with persuasion? Who should be responsible for understanding what people "ought to do"? Why?

Cooperative Learning
Divide the class into seven groups, and assign each group one of the "strong presidents" identified here: Washington, Jefferson, Jackson, Lincoln, Theodore Roosevelt, Wilson, Franklin Roosevelt. Have the members of each group work together to gather evidence of their assigned president's strengths—particular powers he assumed in office. Then let the groups share their findings with the rest of the class.

Discussion Starter
Encourage the students to discuss the particular importance of Washington as a strong president: Why was his example so important? What attitude toward the presidency did he seem to have? How has his attitude affected other presidents?

Comprehension
Ask volunteers to recall for the class the attitude Lincoln displayed toward his cabinet: What relationship do you see between that

Caption Answer Specific presidential powers are listed in Sections 2 and 3 of Article II of the Constitution.

Receiving ambassadors and other representatives from foreign countries, such as Chief Buthelezi of South Africa's Zulu Tribe, is one of the president's constitutional powers. Where in the Constitution are specific presidential powers listed?

6. to deliver the annual State of the Union Address to Congress and to send other messages to Congress from time to time;
7. to call either or both houses of Congress into special sessions;
8. to receive ambassadors and other representatives from foreign countries;
9. to commission all military officers of the United States;
10. to ensure that all laws passed by Congress are carried out.

Other Sources of Power

Today the president has much more power than the Constitution alone suggests, and it comes from many sources. For example, a call from the president to a head of state, a senator, a military commander, or a television producer, rarely goes unanswered. The president can summon up a report on a foreign ruler or a recommended appointee by using intelligence sources and law enforcement agencies. For example, the president can find out just about anything he wants to know about the current head of the government in Germany. If the president wants to know anything about the current leader of an American environmentalist group, he can find it out. Such power comes from the fact that he has access to various kinds of classified information. The president has access to whomever he wishes to see; he can determine who gets certain jobs; and he can guide how federal money is spent. All these factors make people highly responsive to the president's demands.

After three years on the job, Harry Truman made this remark about the powers of the president:

> The president may have a great many powers given to him in the Constitution and may have certain powers under certain laws which are given to him by the Congress of the United States; but the principal power that the president has is to bring people in and try to persuade them to do what they ought to do without persuasion. That's what the powers of the president amount to.

Besides this "persuasive" power of the office, presidents have developed other powers, derived from many sources. One important source of these powers is the actions of strong past presidents that have evolved into customs.

Strong Presidents Certain presidential powers that are today considered part of the rights of the office were simply assumed by strong presidents and then carried on by their successors. In this way, the greatest growth in presidential powers has been through what is often called inherent powers—powers that seem to be attached to the office itself. Since the birth of the republic in 1787, many presidents have strengthened the executive branch by their actions. Most experts agree that the strongest presidents have been George Washington, Thomas Jefferson, Andrew Jackson, Abraham Lincoln, Theodore Roosevelt, Woodrow Wilson, and Franklin D. Roosevelt. Each one ruled in difficult times and acted decisively, and each set a precedent for a certain activity.

For example, George Washington took the liberty of removing officials from office even though he was not given this authority in the Constitution. He also established the practice of meeting regularly with the heads of the three departments that then existed. He began the attitude and Lincoln's attitude toward Congress?

Discussion Starter
Guide the students in discussing Theodore Roosevelt's statement about his stewardship theory: Do you think the president has the responsibility—or the right—to determine which actions serve the common well-being of all people? If so, why does he have that responsibility and right? If not, who has that responsibility and right?

Enrichment
Let a group of interested volunteers read about some of the activities involving the armed services identified in the text: Where and when did each begin? What specific orders did the president give? Did the Congress debate and vote on the activity? If so, with what outcome? How did the American public respond to the situation? Ask the volunteers to summarize their findings in a bulletin board display.

Comprehension
Ask the students to recall and explain the practice of impoundment.

Enrichment
Encourage several students to work together in researching racial segregation in the American armed forces: When were racially segregated forces first used? How was the segregation justified? When and under what circumstances was it ended? What legacies of racial segregation remain in today's armed forces? Let these students share their findings in a brief oral report.

practice of submitting proposed legislation to Congress, which set a precedent of the president as chief legislator. He began the practice of vetoing legislation. As commander in chief, he used troops to put down a rebellion in Pennsylvania, and as chief diplomat, he made foreign policy without consulting Congress. This latter action took Congress by surprise and laid the groundwork for our long history of active foreign-policy making by the president.

President Lincoln, confronting the problems of the Civil War, took important actions while Congress was not in session. He suspended certain constitutional liberties, spent funds that Congress had not appropriated, blockaded Southern ports, and banned "treasonable correspondence" from the United States mails. All of these acts were done in the name of his powers as commander in chief and his responsibility to "take care that the laws be faithfully executed."

Theodore Roosevelt defined his position for a strong presidency in what he called the "stewardship theory." He said:

> My belief was that it was not only his [the president's] right but his duty to do anything that the needs of the Nation demanded unless such action was forbidden by the Constitution or by the laws. . . . I did not usurp power [seize power without legal authority], but I did greatly broaden the use of executive power. In other words, I acted for the public welfare, I acted for the common well-being of all our people, whenever and in whatever manner was necessary, unless prevented by direct constitutional or legislative prohibition.

Franklin D. Roosevelt expanded the presidential power over the economy during the Great Depression in the 1930s, and since that time Americans expect the president to be actively involved in economic matters and social programs.

Military Powers Many presidents have exercised military powers that Congress often argues are outside the president's authority. The United States has been involved in over two hundred activities involving the armed services, while Congress has declared war only five times. In 1846, President James K. Polk provoked Mexico into a war. Before the United States entered World War II, Franklin D. Roosevelt ordered the Navy to "shoot on sight" any German submarine that appeared in the Western Hemisphere security zone. Truman ordered, without congressional approval, American armed forces into the Korean conflict between North and South

▲ As commander in chief of the nation's military forces, presidents often send troops into combat situations. Here, U.S. forces are shown during the military invasion of Panama in 1989. Why does Congress often argue with this use of presidential power?

Korea. The United States entry into the Vietnam War was done without congressional approval. No congressional vote was taken prior to President Bush sending troops into Panama in 1989 or before sending hundreds of thousands of American troops into the Middle East in 1990. (He did, however, obtain congressional approval to use American troops to expel, with the use of force, Iraq from Kuwait on January 16, 1991.)

Powers through Custom and Executive Orders Another example of how presidential power is derived through custom is the practice of impoundment, which you learned about in Chapter 14. Also, the president has the power to issue an **executive order**, which is an order issued by the president to carry out policies described in laws that have been passed by Congress. Executive orders have the force of law. In 1941 President Franklin D. Roosevelt issued an executive order that denied defense contracts to companies that discriminated against workers because of their "race, creed, color, or national origin." In the late 1940s President Harry Truman used an executive order to end racial segregation in the nation's armed forces.

The powers that are derived from customs can be lost if they are not exercised. President Eisenhower assumed the presidency after Roosevelt and Truman, both of whom were activists—they sought much new

Caption Answer Students should understand that Congress often argues with this use of presidential power because presidents are committing troops and initiating military action while circumventing Congress' constitutional authority to declare war.

Enrichment
Ask the students to identify the presidents who followed Eisenhower and to investigate the approaches and activities of each president: Which of these presidents do you think did, in spite of the precedents set by Eisenhower, become an activist president? Why?

Discussion Starter
Encourage the students to compare and discuss their responses to these questions: Do you think it was inevitable that the presidency—rather than the larger congressional branch—was the first institution of American government to realize and use the power of the media? Why or why not?

Extension
Encourage the students to interview family members, acquaintances, or neighbors who remember hearing Roosevelt's fireside chats: What impression did these radio broadcasts make? How did people respond? Encourage the students to share and discuss what they learned from these interviews.

Discussion Starter
Guide the students in discussing Bush's attempts to manage the media's coverage of his presidency: Why do you think Bush chose to lower his television profile? Why do you think the majority of network news stories about Bush were, nonetheless, negative? Do you believe Bush made a wise decision in attempting to attract less TV news coverage than his predecessor? Why or why not?

Figure Answer President Bush's diplomatic performance received the greatest percentage of positive evaluations. On the other hand, the administration's efforts in dealing with the savings and loan crisis received no positive evaluations.

This figure content is also featured on *West's American Government Videodisc* (see the index found in the *TRB*).

Developing Skills for the Information Age

The chief executive has been called a "Prime-Time Minister" who sits on an electronic throne. No factor has increased the power of the president more than television. Unlike Congress, with the president there is only one man to focus on, and it is easier to cover the deceptively placid White House than contentious Capitol Hill.

Have students follow the television coverage of the president. What types of functions attract television coverage? What is the impact on the president? Should there be any changes in the way the president is covered by television? Students should summarize their results and discuss their attitudes in a brief essay.

Media Evaluations of the Bush Administration During 1990

Subject	Good Press (Positive Evaluations)	Total News Stories Aired on ABC, CBS, and NBC
George Bush	36%	455
Total Administration	32%	1,791
Presidential Performance		
Dealing with Congress	23%	30
Diplomatic Performance	57%	96
Political Status	43%	56
Policy Issues		
Domestic Policy	17%	381
Drugs	35%	48
Taxes	19%	26
Budget	14%	64
Environment	10%	41
Civil Rights	7%	27
Savings & Loan	0%	19
Foreign Policy	39%	447
Panama	52%	29
Defense	45%	44
Persian Gulf	40%	197
Soviet Union	33%	48
China	33%	39

Source: Center for Media and Public Affairs

▲ **FIGURE 16–1 Media Evaluations of the Bush Administration During 1990.** Listed above are the number of news stories regarding the Bush administration during 1990. In which area did the Bush administration receive the greatest percentage of positive evaluations?

legislation. But Eisenhower's temperament and political philosophy led him to believe that strict limits should be placed on the exercise of presidential power. He was particularly hesitant to send in federal troops to enforce racial integration in the public schools after the 1954 Supreme Court decision declaring segregation unconstitutional.[1] His less forceful use of presidential power made it more difficult for those who came afterward to be activist presidents.

1. He eventually did send in the troops, however, to carry out the decision.

The Media and the Presidency

The presidency was the first institution of American government to use the vast power of the media to enhance its own power. Franklin D. Roosevelt first used the power of the media in his series of "fireside chats," during which he talked informally on the radio of the nation's problems and his ideas for solving them. Roosevelt was a skillful communicator and listeners felt he was speaking to them personally. He consequently had a powerful influence upon millions of people. Among recent presidents, Ronald Reagan, called "the great communicator," was successful in using the media to his great

TEACHING BUILDING SOCIAL STUDIES SKILLS

Read
Introduce this feature by letting the students discuss their own experiences with reading biographies. You might ask questions such as these: What is a biography? What is the difference between a biography and an autobiography? What biographies have you read as part of school assignments? What biographies have you read on your own? What did you learn from the biographies you read? What did you enjoy about those biographies? After this discussion, ask one of the students to read the Building Social Studies Skills feature aloud to the rest of the class.

Discuss
Pose questions such as these to stimulate discussion of the feature: What is the difference between a biography and a work of historical fiction? What can you learn from each? What can you expect from biography that you cannot expect from historical fiction? What are some of the most important reasons for reading a biography? How can following each of these guidelines help you achieve your purposes in reading a biography?

Analyze and Apply
Have the students work in groups to gather information from biographies. Ask the members of each group to select a specific period of American history; have each member read (or at least skim) a biography of a different American who lived during that period. Then have the group members compare and discuss what they learned about their individual subjects and about their chosen period in American history.

Review
Use these questions to help the students review the Building Social Studies Skills feature: What is at least one important reason for reading biographies? What are three guidelines to follow while reading a biography?

Comprehension
Ask the students to recall (or, if necessary, ask them to have older family members recall) the TV coverage of Bush's announcement in 1991 that he had ordered troops to bomb Iraq.

Critical Thinking Skills
Help the students analyze Friendly's statement regarding the president's ability to command national attention via the media: Who benefits by this presidential power? Who might be threatened by it? Does the media also have power over the president? If so, what advantages and disadvantages may be associated with that media power?

Extension
Have the students collect and discuss articles (from both newspapers and news magazines) about the president. Students should then decide whether each article is positive or negative regarding the president.

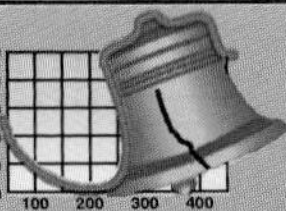

BUILDING SOCIAL STUDIES SKILLS

Reading Biographies

As you study American government you will often find yourself studying people and the roles they played in shaping and influencing our nation's history. One way to learn about people who helped shape our government is through biographical accounts. A biography is the story of a person's life; information for biographies is usually derived from both primary and secondary sources. A biography usually presents the details of the person's life as well as conveys his or her beliefs, ideals, and personality. It tells of the person's accomplishments and how he or she helped to shape our country.

Use the following guidelines when reading an historical or political biography:

- Determine and track the major events in the person's life.
- Identify the personality traits, ideals, motivations, attitudes, and values that the person held. Try to determine how these traits influenced historical events surrounding the person's life.
- Try to determine what effects the person's upbringing had on his or her personal development.
- Track the person's accomplishments and assess their impact and significance on American history and government.
- Determine any author bias. Does the author or the biography generally agree or disagree with the philosophies and actions of the person he or she is writing about?

PRACTICING YOUR SKILLS

1. At your school or local library, skim through three separate biographies on one American president. Make a list of how those biographies differ. For example, one may be anecdotal, relating minor events in the president's life. Another might emphasize the president's early years. Yet another might examine only the political factors that influenced that president.
2. Read the concluding chapter in two of the biographies. Can you get a sense from your reading whether the author of the biography liked or disliked the president about whom he or she was writing? Write a short analysis of your reasoning.

advantage. Listeners also felt that he was talking to them personally.

President Bush, in contrast, chose to lower his television profile while increasing his access to reporters. During his first year in office, Bush attracted only a third as much coverage as Reagan had in 1981. Even excluding the surge of coverage after the assassination attempt on Reagan in 1981, Bush made less than half as much TV news coverage as his predecessor. In contrast, by April 1991, Bush had already held 76 press conferences, compared to Reagan's 48 while in office. This media-management style of lowering television visibility while increasing access to reporters was designed to minimize the extent of media criticism. Yet, as Figure 16–1 on page 380 shows, about three out of five stories on network news about President Bush were negative.

Despite the sometimes negative coverage, television gives presidents the opportunity to communicate directly to the people whenever they wish to do so. Unlike other politicians, the president can get air time whenever he wants, reaching over 70 million people. When President George Bush went on TV for the first time after he ordered American troops to bomb Iraq on January 16th, more than 100 million Americans were watching. This was the largest United States TV audience for a single program in history. Fred W. Friendly, an influential television producer, once observed that "no mighty king, no ambitious emperor, no pope or prophet, even dreamt of such awesome a pulpit, so potent a magic wand. . . . The president, in his ability to command the national attention, has diminished the power of all other politicians."

Newspapers and magazines are other powerful media sources that provide ways for presidents to bring their ideas to the public's attention. One two-year study of *Time* and *Newsweek* magazine coverage found that more

Reteaching Strategies
1. Let the students work with partners to compare and review the notes they have taken while reading Section 1. Encourage the students to revise or add to their notes if necessary.
2. Work with small groups of students, helping them discuss their responses to these questions: Is the current president a strong president? Why or why not?

4. The media gives the president the opportunity to directly communicate with the people and command national attention.
5. Answers will vary, e.g., to some extent the president does have an unfair advantage because he or she gets free publicity all the time. No one can compete with the president in this sense.

SECTION 2

Points to Stress
- The president's function as chief of state.
- The president's powers as chief executive.
- The president's powers as commander in chief and the ways they have been disputed.
- The manner in which treaties are made and the role of the Senate.
- The manner in which the president plays chief legislator.

Kickoff Activity
Give the students five minutes in which to list the most important roles played by the president. At the end of the allotted time, encourage the students to compare and discuss their lists.

Evaluation Strategies
1. Use the Section 1 Review questions for an oral quiz.
2. Have the students take the Section 1 Quiz found in the *TRB.*

Caption Answer The White House press corps is made up of reporters from many different news organizations and media who are assigned to cover the president full time.

Section 1 Review (Answers)
1. Article II states that the executive power shall be vested in the president. Sections 2 and 3 of Article II list the specific presidential powers including serving as commander-in-chief. The president also appoints federal judges, members of the Supreme Court, and executive officials, and makes treaties, all with the advice and consent of the Senate.
2. The president gains power from having access to classified information and whomever he wishes to see. Presidents have also gained power from past actions of strong presidents that have evolved into customs.
3. Certain presidential powers that are today considered part of the rights of the office were simply assumed by strong presidents and then carried on by their successors.

▲ Presidential news conferences, such as the one shown here, are one way in which the president communicates with the White House press corps. Who makes up the White House press corps?

than half of the lead stories dealt with the American president and his activities. President-watching, one of our favorite American pastimes, actually gives the president more power.

The prominence of the president in the media is fostered by the **White House Press Corps**, which is a group of reporters from different news organizations assigned to cover the presidency full time. They spend most of their time waiting (often in a White House lounge reserved especially for them) for a story to break and for their twice-daily briefing by the president's press secretary. Consequently, the president can do very little without it becoming news. No other nation allows the press such access to its highest government official.

Section 1 Review

1. What are the powers of the president as expressed in the Constitution?
2. What other factors have enhanced presidential power?
3. Explain the role strong presidents have had in the historical growth of presidential power.
4. How does the media's role contribute to presidential power?
5. **For critical analysis:** Do you think the fact that the president has immediate access to the media gives him an unfair advantage over other policy and opinion makers in the United States? Why or why not?

Section 2

The Many Presidential Roles

Preview Questions

- What is the president's function as chief of state?
- What are the president's powers as chief executive?
- What is the president's role as commander in chief? How has this role been disputed?
- By whom are treaties made? What part does the Senate play in making treaties?
- How does the president play the role of chief legislator?

We have only one president in office at any given time. The individual in that office, however, must play a number of different roles simultaneously. Each of these roles is closely interrelated with each of the others.

The framers did not describe exactly how the president should fulfill these many roles. Expecting that George Washington would be the nation's first leader, they trusted that he would serve as a model for future presidents. As Washington himself stated, "My station is new . . . I walk on untrodden ground. There is scarcely any part of my conduct that may not hereafter be drawn into precedent."

Through George Washington's examples, and the examples of the presidents that have followed, presidential roles have become more clearly defined over the years. The way in which presidents carry out their roles depends on many factors such as domestic and international issues of the time, personality, and the people the president has working in the executive branch.

Chief of State

Every nation has at least one person who is the ceremonial head of state. In most democratic countries, the jobs of chief of state and head of government are occupied by different people. In Britain, for example, the queen acts as the ceremonial leader and chief of state, while the real head of government is the prime minister. In the United States, those roles are fused into the presidency. As Theodore Roosevelt put it, the president is both "a king and a prime minister."

As chief of state, the president represents the nation to the rest of the world, and engages in a number of

Working with the Preview Questions
Have volunteers read these study questions aloud, and encourage the students to discuss what they already know in response to each. Then remind the students to keep these questions in mind as they study Section 2, looking for more complete answers to each question.

Teaching Strategies

Introduction
Let the students read the section introduction independently. Then guide them in discussing the introduction by asking questions such as these: How would you recast Washington's statement in your own words? What might have happened if, in the early years of the United States, the citizens had elected a president who refused to follow Washington's example? What difference might that president have made in our form of government? In the history of our country?

Enrichment
Encourage interested volunteers to research the role of the Queen in today's British government: What functions does she fulfill? What is her relationship to the Prime Minister? How has the role of the British monarch evolved? What changes in the monarchy have been suggested? Have these volunteers prepare a written report, to be shared with the rest of the class.

Comprehension
Let several volunteers restate, in their own words, Roosevelt's explanation of the president's role.

Discussion Starter
Ask questions such as these to help the students discuss the president's ceremonial role: What media coverage of these events have you seen? How do you react when you see or read about such activities? How do other people seem to regard these activities? Do you consider these ceremonial activities important? Why or why not?

Comprehension
Give several volunteers an opportunity to explain their understanding of the presidential oath of office.

Enrichment
Have a small group of volunteers research the appointments—including the one that Congress refused to approve—that Nixon made to the Supreme Court. What appears to have motivated each selection? What kinds of records have Nixon's appointees developed on the Court? Let the volunteers share their findings in a brief oral report.

Caption Answer Students should understand that in performing the role of chief of state the president acts as a personal symbol of the nation and, therefore, many of his activities are largely symbolic or ceremonial in nature.

activities that are largely symbolic or ceremonial in nature, such as:

- throwing out the first baseball to open the baseball season;
- turning on the lights on the national Christmas tree;
- dedicating parks and post offices;
- launching charity drives;
- making personal phone calls to congratulate the country's heroines and heroes.

In performing the role of chief of state, the president becomes the personal symbol of the nation. The president and the president's family are in the public eye almost every day. Some have argued that by having the president perform these ceremonial functions, less time is available to do ''real work.'' Others feel this role is uniquely American and is important in conveying that presidents are more than just politicians.

Chief Executive

Executive power is the ability to carry out and enforce the laws. The president is the nation's chief executive, constitutionally bound to enforce the acts of Congress, the decisions of the federal courts, and treaties to which the United States is a signatory.

Two constitutional provisions refer to this power. The first is the oath of office the president must take:

> I do solemnly swear (or affirm) that I will faithfully execute the office of President of the United States, and will, to the best of my ability, preserve, protect, and defend the Constitution of the United States.

The other provision is the Constitution's command that ''he shall take care that the laws be faithfully executed.'' These laws apply to many areas of public concern such as taxes, civil rights, Social Security, housing, environmental welfare, and public health. To assist the president in the various tasks of the chief executive, the president has a federal bureaucracy, which you will read about in the next chapter.

The Powers of Appointment and Removal With Senate consent, the president names most of the top-ranking officers of the federal government. Among them are ambassadors and other diplomats, cabinet members and their top aides, the heads of independent agencies, and all federal judges, attorneys, and marshalls. The president also appoints, with Senate approval, the justices of the Supreme Court. This is a formidable power that can shape the course of government. For example, during the Nixon Administration, the seats of four Supreme Court justices became vacant. Nixon appointed four

▼ A president's ceremonial duties do not necessarily end with his term in office. Here, President Bush, with former presidents Reagan, Carter, Ford and Nixon, join together to celebrate the opening of the Reagan Library in Simi Valley, California. What characteristic is common to most of those activities that are performed by the president as a part of his role as chief of state?

TEACHING GOVERNMENT IN ACTION

Read

Introduce this feature to the class by asking them to recall the text's three previous Day in the Life features (Bill Archer, Bob Dole, Lloyd Bentsen). How do you suppose the typical schedules of these three lawmakers are similar to a typical schedule for the president? How do you suppose they might differ? Allow all the students a chance to share their responses, then ask volunteers to take turns reading this Government in Action feature to the class.

Discuss

Use the following questions to stimulate a class discussion of this Government in Action feature: How would you describe George Bush's childhood? How might his childhood have affected the political decisions he makes today? What role did George Bush play in World War II? How do you think this role affected his political career? What did Bush do following World War II? What do his college experiences tell you about Bush? How would you describe Bush's early political career? How would you describe his political career during the 1970s? Why do you think Ronald Reagan selected George Bush to be his running mate? Why do you think Geroge Bush selected Dan Quayle to be his running mate? How would you describe the president's schedule shown here?

Analyze and Apply

Divide the class into small groups and ask each group to go over the president's schedule, printed here. For each item on the schedule, the group should identify the specific

GOVERNMENT IN ACTION

A DAY IN THE LIFE OF

President George Bush

On January 20, 1989 George Herbert Walker Bush was sworn in as the 41st president of the United States. This was the culmination of a political career that began in 1964 and that included a wide variety of both elective and appointed positions.

George Bush was born on June 12, 1924 in Milton, Massachusetts, to Dorothy Walker Bush and Prescott Bush, who served as a Republican senator from Connecticut from 1952 to 1962. Following his graduation from Phillips Academy, Andover, Massachusetts, in June, 1942, Bush enlisted in the United States Navy. He received his wings and commission while only eighteen years old, making him the youngest pilot in the Navy at that time.

On active duty from August, 1942, to September, 1945, Bush flew torpedo bombers during World War II. In 1944, while making a bombing run over an island 600 miles south of Japan, Bush's plane was hit by anti-aircraft fire. Although the plane was severely damaged and on fire, he completed his mission before flying towards sea where he bailed out and was rescued by a Navy submarine. For his courageous service in the Pacific theater, Bush was awarded the Distinguished Flying Cross and three Air Medals.

In January of 1945, Bush married Barbara Pierce. Following World War II, Bush entered Yale University where he studied economics and served as captain of the varsity baseball team, graduating Phi Beta Kappa in 1948. After his graduation from Yale, George and Barbara Bush moved to Texas where he worked as an oil field supply salesman. In 1951, he co-founded a small oil field development company. Two years later, he co-founded the Zapata Petroleum Corporation and in 1954, at the age of thirty, he became co-founder and president of a third firm, Zapata Offshore, which pioneered experimental offshore drilling equipment.

In 1964, George Bush made his first attempt at elective office, losing a bid for a Senate seat. In 1966, Bush was elected to the United States House of Representatives, serving the Seventh Congressional District of Texas.

During his two terms in the House of Representatives, Bush served on the Ways and Means Committee. In 1970, Bush again unsuccessfully ran for the Senate. During the 1970s, Bush held a number of important government positions. In 1971, he was named U.S. Ambassador to the United Nations. He served in this capacity until 1973 when he left to become Chairman of the Republican National Committee. In October, 1974, Bush traveled to Beijing where he served as chief of the U.S. Liaison Office during the critical period when the United States was establishing ties with the People's Republic of China. In 1976, Bush was appointed Director of the Central Intelligence Agency.

role, or roles, the president is playing. Allow the groups sufficient time to complete this activity, then have each group assign a leader who will share their responses with the rest of the class. Work as a class to settle any differences among the responses.

Review

Use the following questions to review the contents of this feature. What type of educational background does George Bush have? In what branch of the armed services did George Bush serve? What line of work did George Bush first enter following college? What was George Bush's first elected position? To what other political positions was Bush appointed?

Think About It (Answers)

1. Answers will vary, e.g., Bush's wartime experiences probably helped him as a politician. The public is, generally speaking, more receptive to politicians who have distinguished themselves while serving in the armed forces.
2. Answers will vary, e.g., Bush's political positions in the 1970s have probably helped to give him an increased level of expertise in foreign affairs.

In July, 1980, Republican presidential candidate Ronald Reagan selected George Bush to be his running mate. Four months later, Bush was elected vice president. He was sworn into office on January 20, 1981. Reagan and Bush were reelected in 1984. After eight years as vice president, George Bush ran for and received the 1988 Republican nomination for the presidency. Selecting Indiana Senator Dan Quayle as his running mate, George Bush hit the general election campaign trail in a contest against Democratic challenger Michael Dukakis. Soon, George Bush moved from the vice president's office to the Oval Office. Today, President and Mrs. Bush are the parents of five children and have twelve grandchildren.

The following is a representative day at the White House for President Bush.

8:00	Intelligence briefing. Oval Office.
8:15	National Security briefing. Oval Office.
8:45	Meeting with the Chief of Staff. Oval Office.
10:30	Presentation of National Medal of Science and Technology. Rose Garden.
11:00	Meeting with President Fujimori of Peru. Oval Office/Cabinet Room.
12:15	Luncheon with President Fujimori. Old Family Dining Room.
1:15	Departure statements with President Fujimori. South Lawn.
2:40	Teleconference with NASA students. NASA Headquarters.
3:30	Meeting with Secretary Brady. Oval Office.
4:30	Meeting with the Chief of Staff. Oval Office

THINK ABOUT IT

1. What effect do you think George Bush's wartime experiences have had on his political life?
2. How do you think Bush's political posts during the 1970s affect his foreign policy decisions as president? Explain.

Enrichment
Have an interested student research the case of *Myers* v. *United States* and then summarize the central issue and the decision for the rest of the class.

This case is excerpted in the *West's American Government Handbook of Selected Court Cases.*

Enrichment
Assign a small group of students to research the amnesty Carter granted to draft evaders: Who supported the amnesty? Why? Who opposed it? Why? In what ways was the amnesty limited? What were the effects of the amnesty? Ask the students to plan and give a skit—or other form of presentation—summarizing their findings.

Caption Answer A pardon is a release from legal punishment, while a reprieve is a postponement of a legal punishment.

Discussion Starter
Help the students consider and discuss some of the reasons underlying the difference between Washington's military involvement and that of modern presidents: How has military force changed in the past 200 years? How were wars and conflicts conducted then? How are they conducted now? Would it be considered reasonable for a modern president to lead American troops in battle? Why?

Discussion Starter
Guide the students in discussing Truman's remark about the decision to use the atomic bomb: Why was this such an important decision? Why do you think Truman was so insistent on clarifying his own responsibility for the decision? Do you think he could have attributed the responsibility to his military advisors or to scientists who developed the bomb? What personal advantages—and disadvantages—might be associated with accepting such an awesome responsibility?

Enrichment
Let two or three volunteers research the "black box" or "football" the president always has: How can the device be used? Why must the president always have it? Under what specific circumstances has a president approached using the device? Why has it not been used?

justices to the Court who had more conservative views than their predecessors. President Reagan appointed three more and President Bush two during his first term. Because Supreme Court Justices are appointed for life, this represents lasting power for any president.

The Constitution does not comment on the president's power to remove appointed officials from office. This power has been assumed by presidents since George Washington and contested by Congress only on occasion. In *Myers* v. *United States* (1926), the Supreme Court ruled that the president had the right to fire executive branch officials, including those who had been appointed with Senate approval. In addition, the president can remove all heads of cabinet departments and all individuals in the Executive Office of the President.

Reprieves, Pardons, and Amnesty The president has the power to grant reprieves and pardons for offenses against the United States except in cases of impeachment. A **reprieve** is a postponement of a legal punishment. A **pardon** is a release from legal punishment that is granted in order to remedy a mistake made in a conviction or given to an offender who presumably has been rehabilitated (able to "go straight"). In 1925, the Supreme Court upheld this power, stating that the president could reprieve or pardon all offenses "either before trial, during trial, or after trial, by individuals, or by classes, conditionally or absolutely, and this without modification or regulation by Congress." In one controversial case, for example, President Ford granted "a full, free, and absolute pardon" to Richard Nixon for any crimes the former president might have committed in connection with the Watergate scandal that occurred in 1972 during Nixon's presidential reelection campaign.

The president also has the power to grant **amnesty**, which is a special pardon given to a group of people who have committed an offense against the government. In 1977, for instance, President Carter granted limited amnesty to the young men who had evaded the draft of the armed forces during the Vietnam War.

Commander in Chief

Partly because the presidency was tailored for George Washington, the Constitution made the president commander in chief of the nation's armed forces. Alexander Hamilton wrote in *The Federalist Papers* that "of all the cares and concerns of government, the direction of war most peculiarly demands those qualities which distinguish the use of power by a single hand." As president, George Washington actually led troops to crush the

▲ On September 8, 1974, President Gerald Ford signed one of the most controversial pardons in American history when he granted a "full, free and absolute pardon" to former President Richard Nixon. What is the difference between a pardon and a reprieve?

Whisky Rebellion in 1794. Although more recent presidents do not take the power quite so literally, their military decisions have changed the course of history. Although he shares war powers with Congress, the president's position in military affairs is dominant.

War Powers Under the Constitution, war powers are divided between Congress and the president. As you know, Congress is given the power to declare war, and the power to raise and maintain the country's armed forces. The president is given the power to lead the armed forces as commander in chief.

Over the years, the president has gathered an enormous amount of power as commander in chief. For example, Harry Truman made the decision to drop the atomic bomb on the Japanese cities of Hiroshima and Nagasaki. "The final decision," he said, "on where and when to use the atomic bomb was up to me. Let there be no mistake about it." Numerous times in our history presidents have sent American soldiers to troublesome spots on the globe, even though Congress did not declare war. President Lyndon Johnson personally selected targets and ordered bombing missions during the Vietnam War. President Nixon personally made the decision to invade Cambodia in 1970. President Reagan sent troops to Lebanon and Grenada in 1983, and ordered American fighter planes to attack Libya in 1986 in retaliation for terrorist attacks on American citizens.

What might be expected to happen if the president did use the device? Have the volunteers make a classroom bulletin board displaying the facts they have gathered.

Vocabulary
Let volunteers define the nouns *armistice* and *cease-fire:* What is the difference between the two terms?

Enrichment
Have a group of volunteers read about the background and the effects of the rationing and the controls instituted during World War II: What necessitated these measures? How did people react to them? Ask the volunteers to discuss their findings with the rest of the class.

Discussion Starter
Encourage the students to discuss Johnson's use of federal troops to control rioting: Do you think the use of federal troops was necessary? Should the states have been required to control their own citizens? Could the president have sent federal troops to a state in which the governor had not requested assistance? Guide the students in explaining and defending their responses.

Vocabulary
Ask volunteers to define the noun *diplomacy:* What is the relationship between *diplomacy* and *diplomat?* Why is this an important relationship to keep in mind when considering the president as the nation's chief diplomat?

Extension
Ask one of the students to gather information about the Panama Canal Treaty: What did the treaty involve? Who opposed the treaty? Why? Have this student summarize the answers for the rest of the class.

As commander in chief, the president must also take responsibility for the most difficult of all military decisions—if and when to use nuclear weapons. Wherever the president goes, an aide is always nearby carrying the computer-coded device that contains all the codes necessary to order a nuclear attack. This device, also known as the "black box" or the "football," is an ever-present reminder of the world-threatening consequences of nuclear war and the awesome responsibilities of the president.

The War Powers Act As commander in chief, the president can respond to a military threat quickly without waiting for congressional action. This power to commit troops and involve the nation in a war upset more and more members of Congress as the undeclared war in Vietnam dragged on for many years into the early 1970s. Criticism of the president's role in Vietnam led to the War Powers Act of 1973, which limited the president's war-making powers. The law, passed over Nixon's veto, limited the president's committing of troops abroad to a period of sixty days, or ninety if needed for a successful withdrawal. If Congress does not authorize a longer period, the troops must be removed.

Other War Powers Presidents also have other war powers. They can make secret agreements with other countries. They may set up military governments in conquered lands. They may also end fighting by calling an **armistice**, or a **cease-fire**, which is a truce, or temporary end to battle. They also have a good deal of control over domestic affairs during times of war. During World War II, for example, President Roosevelt introduced gasoline and food rationing, wage and price controls, and government control of industries producing products needed for the war. During military buildup before the war in the Middle East in 1991 President Bush commandeered the temporary use of numerous jets owned by private American airline companies to transport troops and supplies.

Enforcement Powers The president's powers as commander in chief go beyond war powers. The president has the power to deal with national emergencies during peacetime. For example, after the assassination of Dr. Martin Luther King, Jr., in 1968, riots broke out in many cities. At the request of several state governors, President Lyndon Johnson dispatched the National Guard to control the rioting. Also, if there is a natural disaster, such as a flood or hurricane, the president can respond by sending needed supplies or troops to help keep order.

Chief Diplomat

A **diplomat** is a person who represents one country in dealing with representatives of another country. According to the Constitution, the president is the nation's **chief diplomat**. As such, the president directs the foreign policy of the United States and is the most important representative of the United States in relations with other nations.

Proposal and Ratification of Treaties A **treaty** is a formal agreement between two or more sovereign states. The president has the sole power to negotiate and sign treaties with other countries. The Senate, however, must approve the treaty by a two-thirds vote of the members present before it becomes effective. If the treaty is approved by the Senate and signed by the president, it then becomes law.

Woodrow Wilson lost his effort to persuade the Senate to approve the Treaty of Versailles,[2] the general peace agreement to end World War I. The treaty would have also made the United States a member of the League of

2. Versailles, located about twenty miles from Paris, is the name of the palace built by the King of France, Louis XIV. It served as the royal palace until 1793 and was then converted into a national historical museum, which it remains today. The preliminary treaty ending the American Revolution was signed between the U.S. and Great Britain at Versailles in 1783.

▲ President Jimmy Carter is shown here signing the Panama Canal treaty in 1978. What was the purpose of this treaty?

Caption Answer The Panama Canal Treaty was a formal agreement between the United States and Panama to return the Panama Canal to Panamanian control.

Discussion Starter
Help the students discuss the importance of executive agreements: How do they affect the power of the president? Does the president have complete power in reaching and executing such agreements? Why or why not?

Enrichment
Let an interested volunteer read about the 1969 discovery that specific executive agreements had been kept secret: Which presidents were involved? What agreements had never been made public? How were these secret agreements discovered? What was the reaction in Congress and among voters? Have these volunteers present a short report, summarizing the information they have gathered.

Enrichment
Assign a pair of students to research and report on the recognition of the People's Republic of China: Why was recognition withheld for so long? Which president first recognized the Chinese government? Why? What was the significance of establishing this relationship? How did the public respond to this change?

Discussion Starter
Guide the students in considering and discussing the president's power to recall ambassadors: Under what circumstances does this power seem to be used? What purpose do you believe this kind of recall serves? How effective do you imagine it is? What problems could arise as a result of recalling ambassadors? Why?

Caption Answer As chief diplomat, the president directs the foreign policy of the nation, and is its most important representative in relations with other nations.

Multidiscipline Strategies

Art Assign each student to collect at least five political cartoons dealing with the president, if possible all by different cartoonists. Then have the students work with partners to identify and describe the use of these elements of art within the cartoons: lines, shapes, and space. How do these elements of art contribute to the effectiveness of each political cartoon? Finally, have the partners work together to write an analysis of the use of those art elements in the cartoon they consider most effective.

Nations. In contrast, President Carter convinced the Senate to approve of a treaty returning the Panama Canal to Panama by the year 2000 (over such objections as that of Senator Hayakawa, Republican of California, who said, ''We stole it fair and square.'') The treaty was approved by a single vote.

The Power to Make Executive Agreements Presidential power in foreign affairs is enhanced by the ability to make **executive agreements**, which are pacts between the president and other heads of state. Such agreements do not require Senate approval (even though Congress may refuse to appropriate the necessary funds to carry out such an agreement), but have the same legal status as treaties.

Executive agreements may have a wide range of purposes. Some are routine matters, such as promises of trade or assistance to other countries, but others concern matters of great importance. In 1940, for example, President Franklin D. Roosevelt established an important executive agreement with Prime Minister Winston Churchill of Great Britain, which provided for the United States to loan American destroyers to Great Britain to help protect its land and shipping during World War II. In return, the British allowed the United States to use military and naval bases on British territories in the Western Hemisphere.

Some have charged that presidents have kept executive agreements secret that involve matters of importance. Congress passed a law in 1950 requiring that all executive agreements signed each year be made public. Some executive agreements were still kept secret, however, by presidents who believed the secrecy of such agreements was important to our national security. For example, in 1969, Congress discovered that several presidents had never made public a number of executive agreements that involved giving American military support to South Vietnam, Thailand, and Laos. To prevent abuse of this power, Congress passed a law in 1972 that requires the president to inform Congress within sixty days of making any executive agreement.

Power of Recognition The president has the power to accept the legal existence of another country's government. This is called the **power of recognition**. In modern times, the simple act of receiving a foreign diplomat has been the equivalent of recognizing the diplomat's government. It means a recognition of the legitimacy of another country's government and is a prerequisite for diplomatic relations or negotiations between that country and the United States.

▲ In 1972, acting as chief diplomat, President Nixon made an historic trip to the People's Republic of China. What are the basic diplomatic duties of the president?

Withholding recognition can be a way of showing disapproval for a national government. Presidents have not, for example, given diplomatic recognition to the communist government of Cuba as a way of expressing disapproval of the policies of the Cuban government. The government of the People's Republic of China was not recognized until 1979, thirty years after it was established. President Bush withheld recognition of the Baltics when they declared their independence in 1991. He gave it only after the European community had already recognized them. Recognition can also be withdrawn as a way of expressing disapproval of a government's actions or policies. In 1979, for example, President Carter formally broke diplomatic ties with the revolutionary Khomeni government in Iran after American citizens were taken and held as hostages in that country.

The president can recognize a foreign government by receiving a foreign diplomat from that country, or by sending an **ambassador**—an official government representative—to that country. If the United States disapproves of the conduct of a nation that has already been recognized, the president may recall the American ambassador to that country or may ask the country to recall its ambassador from the United States. In 1980, President Carter called back the American ambassador to the former Soviet Union to protest that nation's invasion of Afghanistan.

Comprehension
Ask the students these questions: What is the difference between *chief executive* and *chief legislator?* Which is the president? Why?

Discussion Starter
Help the students discuss the State of the Union message and the changes it has undergone: To whom were the first State of the Union messages addressed? Whom does the president consider his audience for this speech now? Why?

Extension
Ask the students to gather information about recent examples of the president's efforts to influence members of Congress: What are the issues involved? Which members of Congress is the president trying to influence? How? Why? With what success?

Caption Answer While the Constitution does not use the words *chief legislator*, it does state that the president should "from time to time, give to the Congress information of the State of the Union, and recommend to their consideration such measures as he shall judge necessary and expedient." It also gives him what is probably his greatest influence over the Congress, the power to veto Acts of Congress.

Chief Legislator

Nowhere does the Constitution use the words *chief legislator,* but it does instruct the president to "from time to time, give to the Congress information of the state of the Union, and recommend to their consideration such measures as he shall judge necessary and expedient." The president has in fact become a major shaper of the congressional agenda.

Legislative Programs Congress has come to expect the president as chief legislator to develop a legislative program. Woodrow Wilson began the tradition of using the State of the Union Address as a chance to outline the administration's legislative programs and to urge their passage. Each year since then, the president uses the address to present a legislative program to Congress. Especially since the advent of radio and television, the State of the Union Address is as much a message to the American people and to the world as it is to Congress. Its impact on public opinion can determine the way Congress responds to the president's agenda.

Congress also receives from the president a suggested budget, and the annual *Economic Report of the President.* The budget message suggests what amounts of money the government will need for its programs. The *Economic Report of the President* talks about the state of the nation's economy and recommends ways to improve it. From time to time, the president also submits special messages on certain subjects. These messages all call on Congress to enact the laws the president thinks are necessary.

Besides these formal avenues, the president also works closely with members of Congress to influence them to support particular programs. The president writes, telephones, and meets with various congressional leaders to discuss pending bills. He also sends aides to lobby on Capitol Hill. The president uses press conferences, public appearances, and televised events to persuade the public who will in turn persuade legislators to support the administration's legislative programs.

One study of the Washington **agenda**—the set of actions that actually get discussed and acted on—found that "no other single actor in the political system has quite the capability of the president to set agendas in given policy areas." As one lobbyist told a researcher, "Obviously, when a president sends up a bill [to Congress], it takes first place in the queue. All other bills take second place."

Veto Power The Constitution gives the president another, more direct, power over legislation—the **veto power**. As you learned in Chapter 14, each bill passed

The president acts as chief legislator by developing a legislative program and by meeting with and lobbying members of Congress, as shown here, to support that program. What does the Constitution say about the president's role as a legislator?

Multidiscipline Strategies

Math Presidential effectiveness as chief legislator is hampered in the latter part of the presidential term. Modern presidents realize that their legislative agenda is more likely to succeed in the first half of the term, and as a consequence that is when there is a flurry of legislative activity. When this does not happen, as with President Bush's first term, political observers suspect that there is no important legislative agenda.

Have students discover what happens to the success rate of presidents in the last half of their terms, particularly if that president is a lame-duck, as was the case with Reagan. For example, in 1981, 81 percent of the bills on which he took a position passed consistent with his stance. In 1987, only 48 percent of the bills on which he took a stance passed consistent with his position. Students should calculate the differences in percentages among presidents since Eisenhower, and should speculate as to why the differences exist. The *Congressional Quarterly* has been keeping track of this since 1953.

Cooperative Learning
Let the students work in small groups to research and discuss recent examples in which the threat of a presidential veto has motivated Congress to stop or change a bill.

Enrichment
Encourage interested students to research interest in granting the president the power of a line-item veto: Which individuals and groups have supported granting the president that power? Why? Who has opposed the line-item veto for the president? Why? Ask these students to prepare and display a chart of their findings.

Extension
Ask the students to find out (or recall) whether the governor of your state has the power of line-item veto. Encourage interested students to research the states that grant this power to their governors.

Figure Answer Franklin Roosevelt, who served more than three terms and who was very aggressive about pursuing his own legislative program in order to enact his New Deal policies, had the most total vetoes, with 635. Andrew Johnson, who battled with radical Republicans over Reconstruction following the Civil War and who was impeached by the House and fell one vote short of the required two-thirds majority for conviction in the Senate, had the most vetoes overridden, with 15.

This figure content is also featured on *West's American Government Videodisc* (see the index found in the *TRB*).

Presidential Vetoes

Years	President	Regular Vetoes	Vetoes Overridden	Pocket Vetoes	Total Vetoes
1789-1797	Washington	2	0	0	2
1797-1801	J. Adams	0	0	0	0
1801-1809	Jefferson	0	0	0	0
1809-1817	Madison	5	0	2	7
1817-1825	Monroe	1	0	0	1
1825-1829	J.Q. Adams	0	0	0	0
1829-1837	Jackson	5	0	7	12
1837-1841	Van Buren	0	0	1	1
1841-1841	Harrison	0	0	0	0
1841-1845	Tyler	6	1	4	10
1845-1849	Polk	2	0	1	3
1849-1850	Taylor	0	0	0	0
1850-1853	Fillmore	0	0	0	0
1853-1857	Pierce	9	5	0	9
1857-1861	Buchanan	4	0	3	7
1861-1865	Lincoln	2	0	5	7
1865-1869	A. Johnson	21	15	8	29
1869-1877	Grant	45	4	48	93
1877-1881	Hayes	12	1	1	13
1881-1881	Garfield	0	0	0	0
1881-1885	Arthur	4	1	8	12

FIGURE 16–2 **Presidential Vetoes.** The tables on these pages demonstrate the use of presidential vetoes by each president through 1990. Which president exercised the most vetoes? What do you know about this president that helps to explain these numbers?

by both houses of Congress is sent to the president for approval. The president's options upon receiving the bill are (1) to sign it and make it law; (2) to veto it and return it to Congress; (3) to take no action, permitting the bill to become law without signing it; or (4) if Congress is due to adjourn within ten working days, kill the bill by simply not acting on it (the so-called "pocket veto").

Veto power allows the president to act as a check on Congress. Congress has overridden a very small percentage of presidential vetoes, as can be seen in Figure 16–2 on these two pages. Sometimes just the threat of a veto will force Congress to stop a bill or to change it to fit the president's wishes.

A presidential veto is a rejection of an entire bill. The president does not have the power to do a **line-item veto**, which is the power to veto only part of a piece of legislation, as some state governors can do. At the federal level, an entire bill must be accepted or rejected.

Special Sessions As you have learned, only the president has the power to call special sessions of Congress. Should an important issue arise while Congress is not in

Discussion Starter
Encourage the students to consider the president's role as party leader: Do you imagine that the president's activities in this role ever conflict with his other roles? Why or why not? How important do you consider the presidential role as head of a political party? Why?

Presidential Vetoes (continued)

Years	President	Regular Vetoes	Vetoes Overridden	Pocket Vetoes	Total Vetoes
1885-1889	Cleveland	304	2	110	414
1889-1893	Harrison	19	1	25	44
1893-1897	Cleveland	42	5	128	170
1897-1901	McKinley	6	0	36	42
1901-1909	T. Roosevelt	42	1	40	82
1909-1913	Taft	30	1	9	39
1913-1921	Wilson	33	6	11	44
1921-1923	Harding	5	0	1	6
1923-1929	Coolidge	20	4	30	50
1929-1933	Hoover	21	3	16	37
1933-1945	F. Roosevelt	372	9	263	635
1945-1953	Truman	180	12	70	250
1953-1961	Eisenhower	73	2	108	181
1961-1963	Kennedy	12	0	9	21
1963-1969	L. Johnson	16	0	14	30
1969-1974	Nixon	26*	7	17	43
1974-1977	Ford	48	12	18	66
1977-1981	Carter	13	2	18	31
1981-1989	Reagan	39	9	28	67
1989-1990	Bush	12	0	1	13
Total		1,431	103	952	2,383

*Two pocket vetoes, overruled in the courts, are counted here as regular vetoes.
Source: Louis Fisher, *The Politics of Shared Power; Congress and the Executive,* 2nd ed. (Washington, D.C.: Congressional Quarterly Press, 1987), p. 30; *Congressional Quarterly Weekly Report,* June 23, 1990, p. 1934.

session, the president may call a special session to deal with it. Today, such sessions are almost never needed because Congress meets throughout most of the year.

Political Party Leader and Politician

The president is also head of his political party—not by any authority of the Constitution, whose authors abhorred parties, but by tradition and practical necessity. George Washington was the only president elected without the backing of a political party. All other presidents have been elected with the help of a party, and have become the national leaders of the parties that nominated them.

As party leader the president has a number of major duties: to choose a vice president after his own nomination; to make several thousand high-government appointments, mainly to party faithfuls, (a system known as **patronage**); and to demonstrate that he is trying to fulfill the party platform. The successes of the president in these areas are recalled in the party's election campaigns, and any failures haunt the party at the polls.

Multidiscipline Strategies

Language Arts Ask the students to form small groups, and have the members of each group select one recent president. Then have the group members work together to identify memoirs written by that president, by members of that president's cabinet, and by presidential aides or other members of the administration. Instruct the members to read (or at least skim) the various memoirs; then help them discuss and analyze the different perceptions of the presidency presented by the various authors.

TEACHING GOVERNMENT IN ACTION

Read
Introduce this feature with a short class discussion of the line-item veto: What is it? Who has the power of the line-item veto? What are the advantages—and disadvantages—of granting the president a line-item veto? Then have the students read the Government in Action feature independently.

Discuss
Guide the students in discussing the feature by posing questions such as these: Why do you think so many governors have the line-item veto, but the president does not? If the president were granted a line-item veto, would Congress still have control over federal spending? Why or why not? How would the granting of a line-item veto affect the work of Congress on other (nonfinancial) bills? Why? Do you think it is reasonable to argue that granting the president a line-item veto would take up too much Congressional time? Should decisions about what is right be made on the basis of how much time or effort is involved? Why or why not?

Analyze and Apply
Let the students form teams in which they plan and present debates on this issue: Resolved—The president should be granted the power of the line-item veto.

Review
Pose these questions to help the students review the Government in Action feature: What are two arguments presented in favor of the line-item veto? What are two arguments presented against it?

GOVERNMENT IN ACTION

CASE STUDY

The Line-Item Veto

In forty-three states, governors have the power of the line-item veto—the power to reject certain items of a bill without killing the entire bill. Generally, line-item vetoes have been used with appropriations bills. U.S. presidents do not have this power. If they object to a part of the bill, they must reject the whole bill. Every president since Woodrow Wilson has favored a constitutional amendment to add the line-item veto to the president's powers. In 1984, President Ronald Reagan said that as governor of California he found the line-item veto a ''powerful tool against wasteful and extravagant spending. It works in forty-three states—let's put it to work in Washington, D.C., for all the people.''

Proponents of the line-item veto argue that it is needed to give the president greater control over the budget process by controlling overall congressional spending. For example, suppose an appropriations bill comes before the president to increase spending for the Department of Education. The president agrees with the major part of the bill and Congress knows that the president will not want to veto the bill even though there are several specific expenditures with which he disagrees. Without the line-item veto, the president must either accept or reject the entire bill. If he had the line-item veto power, he could veto the particular items that he felt were objectionable or wasteful. He would not have to make the painful decision to kill the entire bill. Proponents also argue that the line-item veto would make members of Congress more reluctant to approve special projects for interest groups unless the projects could be shown to contribute to broader national goals. If such was not true, the special projects would be specifically vetoed.

Opponents of the line-item veto argue that it would grant too much power to the president and upset the delicate balance so wisely crafted by the founding fathers. They argue that it could be used as a weapon to punish or pressure the president's opponents in Congress. They also argue that it would throw the congressional schedule into chaos. Since the Congress could override the line-item vetoes, each vetoed line would have to be considered individually. This would add more debates and votes to an already overcrowded calendar.

THINK ABOUT IT

1. How might the line-item veto help the president control spending?
2. In what way might the line-item veto limit special-interest legislation?
3. Would the line-item veto upset the balance of power that the founders set up in the Constitution? Explain.

Presidents may support the party by attending party fund-raisers or by sending assistants to help elect or re-elect party members running for office as mayors, governors, or members of Congress.

As we learned in the chapters on Congress, congresspersons are politicians as well as lawmakers, always concerned about their constituencies and the next election. The president is in the same position. Like all politicians, the president wants to win elections and battles in Congress, and wants to maintain a high level of public approval.

Other Roles

In recent years, the president has also taken on the role of being the nation's economic leader. A president's popularity, measured in the polls, often rises and falls with the nation's economic well-being. The public,

Think About It (Answers)

1. Answers will vary, e.g., the president would be able to veto specific expenditures that he deemed unnecessary without vetoing the entire bill.

2. Answers will vary, e.g., it would make Congress more reluctant to approve special projects for interest groups because the president could specifically veto these items within a bill.

3. Answers will vary, e.g., it might upset the balance because it would give the president more power than Congress.

Extension

Ask the students to read about (or recall) how the president or presidential assistants have worked on behalf of local candidates for mayor, governor, and member of Congress.

Enrichment

Let a group of volunteers research recent examples of the rise and fall of presidential popularity, as it is associated with the nation's economic state. Have these volunteers plan and prepare a chart or graph that shows what they have learned.

Figure Answer Students should understand that the roles often overlap. For example, the role of chief legislator might overlap with that of political party leader when the president proposes legislation to Congress through the State of the Union Address which is consistent with his party's platform.

This figure content is also featured on *West's American Government Videodisc* (see the index found in the TRB) and is available in the transparency package.

Roles of the President

Role	Description	Specific Functions
Chief of State	Performs certain ceremonial functions, as personal symbol of the nation	• Throws out first baseball of baseball season • Lights national Christmas tree • Decorates war heroes • Dedicates parks and post offices
Chief Executive	Enforces laws and federal court decisions, along with treaties signed by the United States	• Can appoint, with Senate approval, high-ranking officers of the federal government. Does not require Senate approval to dismiss presidential appointees from the executive branch. • Can grant reprieves, pardons, and amnesty
Commander in Chief	Leads the nation's armed forces	• Can commit troops for up to 90 days in response to a military threat (War Powers Act) • Can make secret agreements with other countries • Can set up military governments in conquered lands • Can end fighting by calling a cease-fire (armistice) • Can handle national emergencies during peacetime, such as riots or natural disasters
Chief Diplomat	Directs U.S. foreign policy and is the nation's most important representative in dealing with foreign countries	• Can negotiate and sign treaties with other nations, with Senate approval • Can make pacts (executive agreements) with other heads of state, without Senate approval • Can accept the legal existence of another country's government (power of recognition) • Receives foreign chiefs of state
Chief Legislator	Informs Congress about the condition of the country and recommends legislative measures	• Proposes legislative program to Congress in traditional State of Union Address • Suggests budget to Congress and submits annual economic report • Can veto a bill passed by Congress • Can call special sessions of Congress
Political Party Leader	Heads political party	• Chooses a vice president • Makes several thousand top-government appointments, often to party faithfuls (patronage) • Tries to execute the party's platform • May attend party fund-raisers • May help reelect party members running for office as mayors, governors, or members of Congress

▲ **FIGURE 16–3 Roles of the President.** The table above lists the roles of the president and cites examples of the actions and functions of each role. Can you think of any instances in which these roles might overlap?

Developing Skills for the Information Age

The chapter enumerates the many roles of the president: chief of state, chief executive, commander-in-chief, chief diplomat, chief legislator, political party leader-politician and, under "Other Roles," economic leader, and chief citizen. Have students scrutinize the print and electronic media for stories about the president. Students should do two things with each feature. First, they should categorize the story according to the role(s) represented. Next, they should record if the feature was positive, negative, or neutral toward the president. A summary of the results should be handed in that shows which roles are covered most often and evaluates the nature of media coverage.

Reteaching Strategies

1. Let the students work with partners or in small groups to review Section 2. Encourage them to take notes on the section content as they participate in this review.

2. Have the students write their own definitions of these terms: *reprieve, pardon, amnesty, armistice, treaty, veto, line-item veto.*

tends party fund-raisers and sends assistants to help elect or reelect party members running for offices.

6. Answers will vary, e.g., as party leader, the president could be in conflict with other roles. The interests of the president's political party may not be the interests of the entire nation.

SECTION 3

Points to Stress

- The ways that Congress can check presidential powers.
- The ways that the judiciary can check presidential powers.
- The ways that politics can restrain presidential powers.

Kickoff Activity

Let the students read the section title, and then ask them to write short paragraphs explaining why checks on the president's powers are necessary. After everyone has finished writing, let several volunteers read their paragraphs to the rest of the class.

Caption Answer Students should understand that the presidents are aware of their debt to the party for their own election. Presidents also understand that the election of others from their parties will help them in implementing their policies.

Evaluation Strategies

1. Have the students write their answers to the Section 2 Review questions.

2. Have the Students take the Section 2 Quiz found in the *TRB.*

Section 2 Review (Answers)

1. As chief of state, the president is the ceremonial head of the nation. As chief executive, the president is in charge of administering the entire executive branch of government and must carry out and enforce the laws.

2. As commander-in-chief, the president is given the power to lead the armed forces.

3. As chief diplomat, the president directs the foreign policy of the United States and is the most important representative of the United States in relations with other nations.

4. The president presents legislative programs to Congress, vetoes legislation, and has the power to call special sessions of Congress.

5. As party leader, the president chooses a vice president and makes several thousand high government appointments. He also at-

◄ Presidents often lend their support to others from their party who are running for office. Why do you think most presidents are willing to do this?

Congress, and business and labor communities increasingly look to the president to lower unemployment, to fight inflation, to keep taxes down, and to promote economic growth. We give our presidents numerous tools with which to manage the economy, including the duty of preparing the budget, which gives the president the opportunity to determine the government's spending priorities for the coming year. The Employment Act of 1946 directed the president to submit an annual economic report to Congress and declared for the first time that the federal government had the responsibility to promote productivity, high employment, and stable purchasing power. The law created the Council of Economic Advisors (CEA) to give the president economic advice.

The office of the presidency also automatically makes its occupant the nation's chief citizen. The president is expected to be representative of all the people and to work for the public interest. "The presidency," said Franklin Roosevelt, "is not merely an administrative office. That is the least of it. It is preeminently a place of moral leadership."

Section 2 Review

1. What are the functions of the president as chief of state and chief executive?
2. As commander in chief, what are the president's powers?
3. What are the president's powers as chief diplomat?
4. How does the president practice the role of chief legislator?
5. Explain why the president is the leader of his political party.
6. **For critical analysis:** Do you feel the president's role as political party leader is in conflict with any of the other roles? Explain why or why not.

Section 3

Checks on the President's Powers

Preview Questions

- How can the Congress check presidential powers?
- How can the judiciary check presidential powers?

The framers of the Constitution were well aware of the possible abuses of an overly strong chief executive. To avoid these abuses, they built in a system of checks and balances. Both Congress and the judiciary have powers that restrict the president. The president is also checked to some degree by certain unwritten limitations.

Congressional Limitations

As you have learned, the president has the power to veto legislation, but Congress may override a president's veto. Even though it is not often done, the override remains as a powerful check by Congress on presidential

Working with the Preview Questions
Have the students read these study questions and then look through Section 3: Where do you expect to find the answers to each question? What other information will be presented in this section? Then remind the students to keep the study questions in mind as they read Section 3.

Teaching Strategies

Introduction
After the students have read the brief section introduction, encourage discussion by asking questions such as these: What are the possible abuses of a too-strong chief executive? What problems do you think the framers foresaw and tried to avoid? What made them sensitive to such potential problems?

Vocabulary
Let volunteers explain the meaning of the phrase *the power of the purse.*

Extension
Ask a group of students to research the events leading up to the vote to impeach Andrew Johnson. Then have them prepare and display a time-line showing these events.

TEACHING CITIZENSHIP SKILLS AND RESPONSIBILITIES

Read
Begin by having the students read the feature title and share their ideas about contacting the president: Why might you want to get in touch with the president? How would you go about it? Then let volunteers read the feature aloud to the rest of the class.

Discuss
Encourage the students to discuss the feature by asking questions such as these: How seriously do you think the president takes the letters and calls that come into the White House? Which are most likely to receive serious attention? If you decide to write to the president, what guidelines should you follow in composing and preparing your letter? How should you word a telegram to the president? What preparations should you make before telephoning the White House? Why?

Analyze and Apply
Have the students work in small groups to collect letters to the editor from local newspapers and, if possible, from major city newspapers. Then have the group members imagine themselves as presidential aides and decide which letters should be saved for the president's attention. Ask the students to write a memo or cover letter that they would leave, with the selected letters to the editor, on the president's desk.

Review
Ask the students this review question: What are four different ways in which you can communicate your ideas to the president?

CITIZENSHIP SKILLS AND RESPONSIBILITIES

How to Contact the President

You, as an American citizen, have a right and sometimes a duty to let the president know directly about your opinion on an important public policy matter. Each president receives thousands of letters and numerous phone calls a day. Of course no president actually reads all of these letters, but many of them are read by his assistants. They tally up public opinion for and against a particular issue. When President Reagan started sending advisors and military aid to the Central American country of El Salvador in 1981, he immediately began to receive a flood of letters, which ran ten-to-one against his policy. His decisions thereafter were partly molded by such strong public opposition to militarizing that country. The opposite occurred when President Bush sent troops to the Middle East after Iraq invaded Kuwait in 1990.

Your views can, and should, be brought to the president's attention. Whenever you strongly agree with or oppose the actions taken by the president, you can contact the White House directly. Address your letter to the following:

The President of the United States
The White House
1600 Pennsylvania Ave. NW
Washington, DC 20500

You can also send a telegram to that address, or you can telephone the White House at 202-456-1414.

A less well-known, but perhaps equally effective, way to express your views to the president is by writing a letter to the editor of a major newspaper. The president's aides in the White House clip letters from newspapers across the country. These letters provide a digest of public opinion for the president and his staff to review on a regular basis.

Whether you choose to write the president directly, or to write a letter to the editor of a major newspaper, it is important to remember that your views are more likely to be given serious consideration (your letter is more likely to be printed) if your letter is well written, clearly organized, and neatly prepared. A letter that is well thought out and neatly typed can be a very effective tool for communicating your feelings to the president.

TAKING ACTION

1. As a class, choose a policy issue that concerns you today. Have each student compose a letter to the president. Send them directly to the White House.
2. Write a letter to a major newspaper editor about the same issue, remembering that it might be made part of a digest of letters given to the president by his aides.

powers. Since George Washington's presidency, only about 4 percent of all presidential vetoes have been overridden by Congress. The most occurred under the administration of Andrew Johnson (1865–1869) during which time there were fifteen. Both Harry Truman and Gerald Ford saw twelve of their presidential vetoes overridden.[3]

Congress also has "the power of the purse" over the president. For example, President Nixon tried to restrict government spending because of a worsening economy by cutting domestic programs while at the same time increasing some areas of military spending. Congress undermined these plans by appropriating funds for welfare programs that the president did not want and cutting appropriations for the weapons programs he favored.

The power of impeachment is considered the ultimate congressional check on the presidency. The Constitution says that Congress may impeach the president for "treason, bribery, or other high crimes or misdemeanors." Congress has only used this power once. In 1868 the House of Representatives voted to impeach President Andrew Johnson, charging that he violated the Tenure Office Act, which prohibited him from removing executive officials without consent of the Senate. The Senate, which tries cases of impeachment, found Johnson not guilty. In 1974, a House committee voted to recommend impeachment of President Nixon because of his part in

3. Gerald Ford wins the prize in this century, though, with the largest percentage of vetoes overridden—25 percent, or more than six times the average for all presidents.

Extension
Have the students read about the make-up of the current Supreme Court: How many of the justices were appointed by the current president? How many were appointed by a previous president with whom the current president had a close alliance? Then help the students discuss how these justices might feel about opposing the president's decisions.

Discussion Starter
Help the students discuss their ideas about executive privilege: Do you believe the president should have the right to withhold information? Why or why not? Should there be limits on that right? If so, what kinds of limits, and who should impose them? If you were the president, would you expect to have—and use—executive privilege?

Enrichment
Have a volunteer research and report on *United States* v. *Nixon:* What was the central issue? How was it presented by both sides? What were the effects of the Court's decision in the case?

Discussion Starter
Encourage the students to discuss what they know about recent Supreme Court nominations: Why does the president seem to have made each nomination? What questions—if any—were raised by each appointment? How has the Senate responded to each recent appointment? Why?

Discussion Starter
As the students consider political limitations on the president, guide them in discussing their responses to these questions: What is the relationship between public opinion and media attention? What is the relationship between public opinion and the power of the president? How does media attention influence that relationship?

Reteaching Strategies
1. Work with small groups of students. Help them review the means Congress has of limiting presidential power, and help them cite recent examples of each.
2. Have the students work with partners to write paragraphs explaining executive privilege and its uses.

Evaluation Strategies
1. Have the students write their answers to the Section 3 Review questions.
2. Have the students take the Section 3 Quiz found in the *TRB*.

Section 3 Review (Answers)
1. Congress may override a president's veto. Congress also has "the power of the purse" over the president. The power of impeachment is the ultimate check on the presidency.
2. The Supreme Court has the power to review the president's actions in cases that come before them.
3. Answers will vary, e.g., the president's power is not unlimited because Congress retains the power to override vetoes.

the 1972 Watergate break-in scandal, but he resigned from the presidency before the affair reached the full House.

During the 1970s several laws limiting presidential power were passed by Congress. American involvement in Vietnam and the Watergate scandal led in 1972 to a limitation on the president's use of secret executive agreements. The 1973 War Powers Act required the president to consult with Congress before committing American troops to war. As you learned in the Government in Action case study on the budget in Chapter 13, the 1974 Budget Impoundment Control Act restrained presidential power to impound funds from executive agencies.

Other congressional checks include the Senate's approval (or lack of approval) of major appointments and treaties from the president.

Judicial Limitations

As you learned in Chapter 13 the Supreme Court case *Marbury* v. *Madison* affirmed the Supreme Court's right to review a president's actions. The president and the Supreme Court, however, are not as closely involved in the day-to-day operations of each other's affairs as are the president and Congress. In most instances, Supreme Court justices are inclined to respect the president's decisions and viewpoints.

The Supreme Court has, however, imposed some limits on the president's domestic power. In 1936, the Court declared several laws unconstitutional that had been passed by Congress as part of President Franklin Roosevelt's New Deal Program. In 1952, for example, the Court said that President Truman could not issue an executive order unless it was provided for by the Constitution or by an act of Congress. In 1975, the Court limited the power of the president to impound (withhold) money appropriated by Congress.

The Court has also set limits on a president's claim to **executive privilege**—the special right to withhold information. Presidents usually claim executive privilege based on the need for secrecy in carrying out foreign affairs or in matters of national security. George Washington first invoked the right of executive privilege when he refused to supply the House of Representatives with his own papers and documents on a matter of diplomacy on the grounds that Congress was not constitutionally entitled to them. In 1974, in the Watergate scandal, President Nixon claimed that executive privilege entitled him to keep his White House tapes and other materials from Congress, and even to prevent his officials from testifying before Congress. In *United States* v. *Nixon* that same year, the Court ruled that the president could not use such a claim to withhold evidence in a criminal trial.

The fact that the Senate must approve judicial appointments made by the president limits the actions that the president may take toward shaping the Supreme Court. Usually, presidents nominate justices who are acceptable to congressional leaders and to their supporters. Also, the justices chosen for the Court are not bound to follow the president who appointed them. Because the Supreme Court is an independent body, the justices may follow their own interpretations of the law. In fact, sometimes the persons appointed to the Supreme Court disappoint the presidents who chose them by taking opposing views. For example, President Dwight D. Eisenhower appointed Earl Warren as chief justice in 1953. Warren soon moved away from Eisenhower's conservative stand on social issues, and led the Court to many liberal decisions that were disliked by the Eisenhower administration.

Political Limitations

One of the most severe restraints on the president is not legal, but political. Public opinion and media attention put pressure on the president and can greatly influence how power is exercised. Without favorable public opinion, a president cannot succeed in carrying out a political program, especially if the president would like to run for a second term of office.

Despite the congressional, judicial, and political limitations, the office of president of the United States remains one of the most powerful in all the world. This power is derived from the Constitution, from institutional sources, and from the actions of strong presidents in the past. The president uses this power to perform his many functions and fulfill his many roles. As you can see, along with these powers comes the burden of enormous responsibility.

SECTION 3 REVIEW

1. How may Congress limit the president's powers?
2. How may the Supreme Court limit the president's powers?
3. **For critical analysis:** If the Congress only overrides presidential vetoes 4 percent of the time, does this mean that the president has unlimited power to reject bills passed by the Congress? Why or why not?

TEACHING CHALLENGE TO THE AMERICAN DREAM

Read

Introduce the topic of this Challenge to the American dream feature, and encourage the students to share and discuss what they already know about the Watergate break-in and its repercussions. Then let volunteers take turns reading the feature aloud to the rest of the class.

Discuss

Guide the students in discussing the information in the feature and their reactions to that information: Why was the break-in originally dismissed as a "third-rate burglary"? Why do you think the FBI investigated? How—if at all—do you think a president might justify spying on candidates of the other party and sabotaging their campaigns? How did Nixon abuse the right of executive privilege? What do you think would have happened if Nixon had not resigned?

Analyze and Apply

Have the students interview family members or friends who remember the Watergate investigations: How did they react to the situation at the time? In what light do they consider the Watergate scandal now? Then give the students an opportunity to share and discuss the results of their interviews.

Review

Use questions such as these to help the students review the Challenge to the American Dream feature: What are three ways in which Nixon abused his presidential power? How did Congress respond to this abuse of power?

CHALLENGE TO THE AMERICAN DREAM

The Abuse of Presidential Power

On June 17, 1972, the police caught five intruders inside the offices of the Democratic National Committee at the Watergate, a complex of business offices and apartment buildings in Washington, D.C. The break-in was quickly dismissed as a "third-rate burglary," and seemed destined to be forgotten. But it soon became clear that there was more to the story. First the FBI began investigating the incident, and later the Senate formed a special committee to investigate the Watergate case. The press, especially the *Washington Post,* followed up on clues. These investigations turned up the following:

- Crisp, consecutive $100 bills found on the burglars were traced to CREEP, the Committee for the Reelection of the President, a pro-Nixon campaign group. About $420,000 (taken mainly from Nixon campaign contributions), was used as "hush money" to keep the burglars quiet about who had hired them and what they were doing.
- CREEP solicited big contributions from people being investigated by government agencies, and sought illegal contributions from corporations.
- CREEP collected money from the dairy industry about the same time the president approved an increase in the federal price supports for milk.
- The president approved the formation of a Special Investigations, or "Plumbers Unit," in the White House to stop security leaks. The "Plumbers" tapped the phones of administration officials, poked through private files, and broke into private offices.
- The acting director of the FBI destroyed vital Watergate evidence at the instigation of two of the president's top assistants.
- An "enemies list" of people who opposed Nixon was compiled by the president's staff. The income-tax forms of people on the enemies list were singled out for investigation by the Internal Revenue Service.

President Nixon blocked many of the efforts by Congress and the courts to find out if the White House had ordered the Watergate break-in. He did so by invoking the doctrine of executive privilege—the special right to withhold information, usually in affairs dealing with national security and foreign affairs. The Supreme Court finally ruled that neither the president nor members of the executive branch could use executive privilege to withhold information about a crime.

Thus, the president was forced to surrender information in the form of tape recordings that had been made by concealed microphones in various White House offices and in the Executive Office Building. On the tape for June 23, 1972, Nixon was heard approving a plan to use the CIA to block the FBI investigation of the break-in.

In July 1974, the House Judiciary Committee recommended that the House of Representatives impeach President Richard Nixon on the grounds of obstructing justice, abusing presidential powers, and obstructing the impeachment process. It appeared likely that, for the first time since 1868, the president of the United States would be impeached. President Nixon resigned before the impeachment hearings and was later pardoned by his successor, President Gerald Ford.

The challenge to the American dream is to ensure that the president is never above the law. The American form of democracy is one in which laws rule rather than men and women.

You Decide

1. Do you think that President Nixon should have gone to trial for any criminal activities for which he had been responsible? Why or why not?
2. What, if anything, can Congress do to ensure that no future Watergate scandals occur?

You Decide (Answers)

1. Answers will vary, e.g., President Nixon should have been held responsible for any criminal activities for which he was responsible and therefore gone to trial. After all, no person, even a president, is above the law.
2. Answers will vary, e.g., Congress cannot eliminate future scandals such as occurred at Watergate, but Congress can minimize the probability of their occurring by making sure that every president knows he or she will be held criminally responsible for any similar type actions.

Law Related Activity

The chapter listed the various checks and constraints on the president. One of these is judicial limitation. *United States* v. *Nixon* is an excellent illustration of this judicial check. Have students research the particulars of the case, citing the major legal positions of each side. Students should state what the Court's decision was and if they agree with it or not. Different cases may also be used, such as *New York Times* v. *United States.* Excerpts from the case are included in *WEST'S AMERICAN GOVERNMENT HANDBOOK OF SELECTED COURT CASES.*

Chapter Evaluation
To evaluate student mastery of chapter material, you might:
1. Use Chapter Test A from the *TRB.*
2. Use Chapter Test B from the *TRB.*
3. Construct you own test using items from the *West American Government Test Bank* found in the *TRB.*
4. Use the accompanying computerized test software to construct and print a customized chapter test.

Review Questions (Answers)
1. Executive power.
2. Access to classified information and to people. The ability to guide how federal money is spent. The actions of past strong presidents which have evolved into tradition.
3. Strong presidents, such as Washington, Jefferson, Lincoln, and the Roosevelts, assumed certain powers that later became tradition.
4. The media have enabled the president to communicate directly to the people and command national attention. It has enhanced the power of the presidency.
5. As chief of state, the president is the ceremonial head of the nation.
6. As chief executive, the president has the responsibility to administer the executive branch of the government and to carry out and enforce laws.
7. Congress is given the power to declare war, and the power to raise and maintain the country's armed forces. The president is given the power to lead the armed forces as commander-in-chief. The War Powers Act limited the president's committing of troops abroad to a period of 60 days, or 90 if needed for a successful withdrawal. If Congress does not authorize a longer period, the troops must be removed within 90 days of their commitment.
8. As chief diplomat, the president directs the foreign policy of the nation and is the most important representative of the United States in relations with other nations.
9. A treaty is a formal agreement between two or more sovereign states. The president negotiates the treaty, but it must be approved by the Senate. An executive agreement is a pact between the president and another head of state which does not require Senate approval.

Chapter 16 Review

Key Terms

agenda 389
ambassador 388
amnesty 386
armistice 387
cease-fire 387
chief diplomat 387
diplomat 387
executive agreements 388
executive order 379
executive privilege 396
line-item veto 390
pardon 386
patronage 391
power of recognition 388
reprieve 386
treaty 387
veto power 389
White House Press Corps 382

Summary

1. There are several sources of presidential power. The Constitution grants broad powers to the president. The presidency has derived additional powers from the fact that the president has access to powerful resources, such as information on important people. Certain presidential powers that are today considered part of the rights of the office were simply assumed by strong presidents and then carried on by their successors. The media, especially television, have also enhanced the power of the president.

2. The president has many different but interrelated roles. The president serves the dual roles of chief of state and chief executive. The president is commander in chief of the armed services and, as such, has certain war powers. As chief diplomat, the president has the power to negotiate and sign treaties with other countries, but the Senate must approve the treaties by a two-thirds vote. The president also has the power to recognize other countries. As chief legislator, the president has become a major shaper of the congressional agenda. The president is also a political party leader and politician.

3. To avoid any misuse of power, the framers of the Constitution built in a system of checks and balances. Congress has the power to override the president's veto. Congress also has the "power of the purse," and the ultimate power of impeachment. Finally, the Supreme Court has the right to review the president's actions.

Review Questions

1. What basic power is granted to the president in the Constitution?
2. What other sources contribute to presidential power?
3. How have strong presidents contributed to the powers of the presidency?
4. What effect have the media had on the presidency?
5. What is the president's role as chief of state?
6. What are the powers of the president as chief executive?
7. How are the war powers divided between the president and Congress? How does the War Powers Act attempt to limit the president's war powers?
8. As chief diplomat, what are the powers and duties of the president?
9. How does a treaty differ from an executive agreement?
10. How does the president recognize the legal existence of another country's government? Can the president repeal that recognition?
11. Explain the president's role as chief legislator.
12. Why is the president a political party leader?
13. How can Congress check the powers of the president?
14. How can the Supreme Court restrain the president's powers?
15. What is one way to contact the White House?
16. Briefly describe how President Nixon's actions in the Watergate scandal were abuses of presidential power.

Questions for Thought and Discussion

1. In your opinion, what is the most important role that the president plays? Why do you think that role is so important?
2. Do you think the power of the presidency has increased or decreased in recent years? What do you think accounts for this?
3. What do you think the president should do if Congress passed a law that violated his party platform?

10. The president can recognize a foreign government by receiving a foreign diplomat from that country or by sending an ambassador to that country. The president may recall the American ambassador to that country or may ask the country to recall its ambassador from the United States.
11. Each year, the president presents a legislative program to Congress. He has the power to veto legislation and the power to call a special session of Congress. He also has the power to focus national attention on the Congress' response to his suggested programs.
12. The president is the political party leader by practical necessity and tradition.
13. Congress may override a president's veto. Congress has "the power of the purse" over the president, and the ultimate power of impeachment.
14. The Supreme Court can review the president's actions in cases that come before the Court.
15. You may contact the White House by writing a letter.
16. The president was involved in the cover-up of a crime, obstructing justice, and using a government agency in a way forbidden by law.

CHAPTER 16 REVIEW—Continued

4. The roles of the president are sometimes in conflict. Name some instances when the political needs of the president may not be consistent with the needs of the nation.
5. How has television changed the relationship between the president and the American people? How has it affected his power?

Improving Your Skills

Communication Skills

Synthesizing

Synthesizing means combining two or more sources of information into a single unified whole. Learning to synthesize information will help you answer questions, make decisions, take notes, do research, and write reports. Synthesizing is necessary whenever you have to take two or more sources of information and blend the ideas in a coherent way that reflects your own writing or speaking style. When synthesizing, follow these guidelines:

- Read the materials carefully and decide on your point of view, opinion, and approach.
- Select the ideas or examples that support your ideas. Think about how your ideas and the ideas in the sources relate to each other.
- Combine these ideas into a synthesized whole.

Writing

Find three articles about a recent presidential decision or issue. Write a synthesis of the articles based on your view of how the ideas presented are interrelated.

Social Studies Skills

Evaluating a Policy Decision

As a student of American government, you must also be able to evaluate policy decisions. The following guidelines will help you evaluate decisions made by government officials at every level.

- Determine the nature of the decision and the surrounding circumstances at the time the decision had to be made.
- List what other choices and alternatives were available at the time. Remember that some alternatives that are apparent now may not have been apparent at the time.
- Determine the risks and benefits of each alternative. Each one will probably have several short- and long-term effects. Remember that some long-range effects may not be immediately evident.
- Make a decision, based on your considerations.
- Analyze the results of the decision. Determine whether or not a good decision was made, all things considered.

1. Choose a recent policy decision made in your school or community. Evaluate the policy decision by using the steps above. Report your evaluation to the class.
2. As a group, discuss and evaluate a national policy decision using the steps above.

Activities and Projects

1. Collect cartoons that refer to a current issue that the president is addressing. Paste the cartoons on a posterboard or in a booklet and write a summary of each one. In your summary, discuss whether the messages the cartoonists are trying to convey are positive or negative, and whether or not you agree with the cartoonists' depictions of the president's actions. Then try to determine the president's actual stand on the issue, and draw your own editorial cartoon in which you express your views on his stand.
2. Keep close track of the president's activities for three weeks by watching news programs and reading newspapers and magazines. Notice how closely you can or cannot keep track of his daily life. Keep track of what you learn in a president's log. Report your results to the class and explain why you think the media are so interested in what the president does.
3. Have the class debate the following statement: Resolved—The president shall be given the power to exercise a line-item veto.
4. Make a list of ten executive orders that one president made during his administration.
5. Make a list of ten executive agreements that one president made during his administration.

Questions for Thought and Discussion (Answers)

1. Answers will vary, e.g., the most important role is that of chief executive. This role is not shared by other branches. Alternatively, the most important role is that of commander-in-chief because in this role the president ensures the national defense.
2. Answers will vary, e.g., the power has increased because strong presidents continue to set new precedents. The power of Congress has become more fragmented.
3. Answers will vary, e.g., the president should view the law objectively, without preference for his party.
4. Answers will vary, e.g., the time the president spends on party matters and elections is not consistent with the needs of the nation which needs the president's attention focused on important national matters.
5. Answers will vary, e.g., television has caused the American public to be more concerned with the actions of the president. It has also caused the American public to be more curious about the president and his family's personal lives. This widespread coverage has made the president more powerful.

CHAPTER INTRODUCTION

Instructional Objectives

By the end of the chapter students should be able to:

- Characterize the nature, size, and growth of the federal bureaucracy.
- Describe the makeup of the various departments.
- Summarize the purposes and functions of federal independent agencies and government corporations.
- Discuss how civil service works.
- Explain how bureaucrats make policy.

Using the Keynote

Begin by reading the Keynote Quotation aloud. Encourage the students to discuss the quotation and their reaction to it: Why do citizens expect their government to be—or provide—solutions to their problems? In what sense can government be considered a problem to its citizens? Which individuals and groups express sentiments similar to that voiced in the quotation? Why? How do you feel about the fact that the Keynote Quotation is from a president? Can you think of other presidents who might have expressed similar feelings?

Introducing the Chapter

Ask one of the students to read the Introduction aloud to the rest of the class. Then focus the students' attention on the word *bureaucrat:* What is the definition of this noun? What connotations does it have? What images does the chapter title, The Bureaucracy in Action, raise in your mind? Why? What daily benefits do you think you receive from the government bureaucracy? How do you imagine life would be different without that bureaucracy?

Previewing the Sections

Section 1 Have the students page through Section 1. Let volunteers explain what they expect the central themes of this section to be.
Section 2 Ask volunteers to read aloud the section title, the main headings, the figure titles, and the photo captions here. Then let the students suggest at least three specific questions they expect to have answered as they study Section 2.
Section 3 Let the students look through Section 3, noting especially the figures: What do these figures indicate about the section content?
Section 4 Ask the students to scan Section 4. Have the students list at least three facts relating to this topic with which they are already familiar.
Section 5 Have volunteers read aloud the Section 5 title and the main headings. Then encourage the students to discuss what information they expect to find in this section.

CHAPTER 17

The Bureaucracy in Action

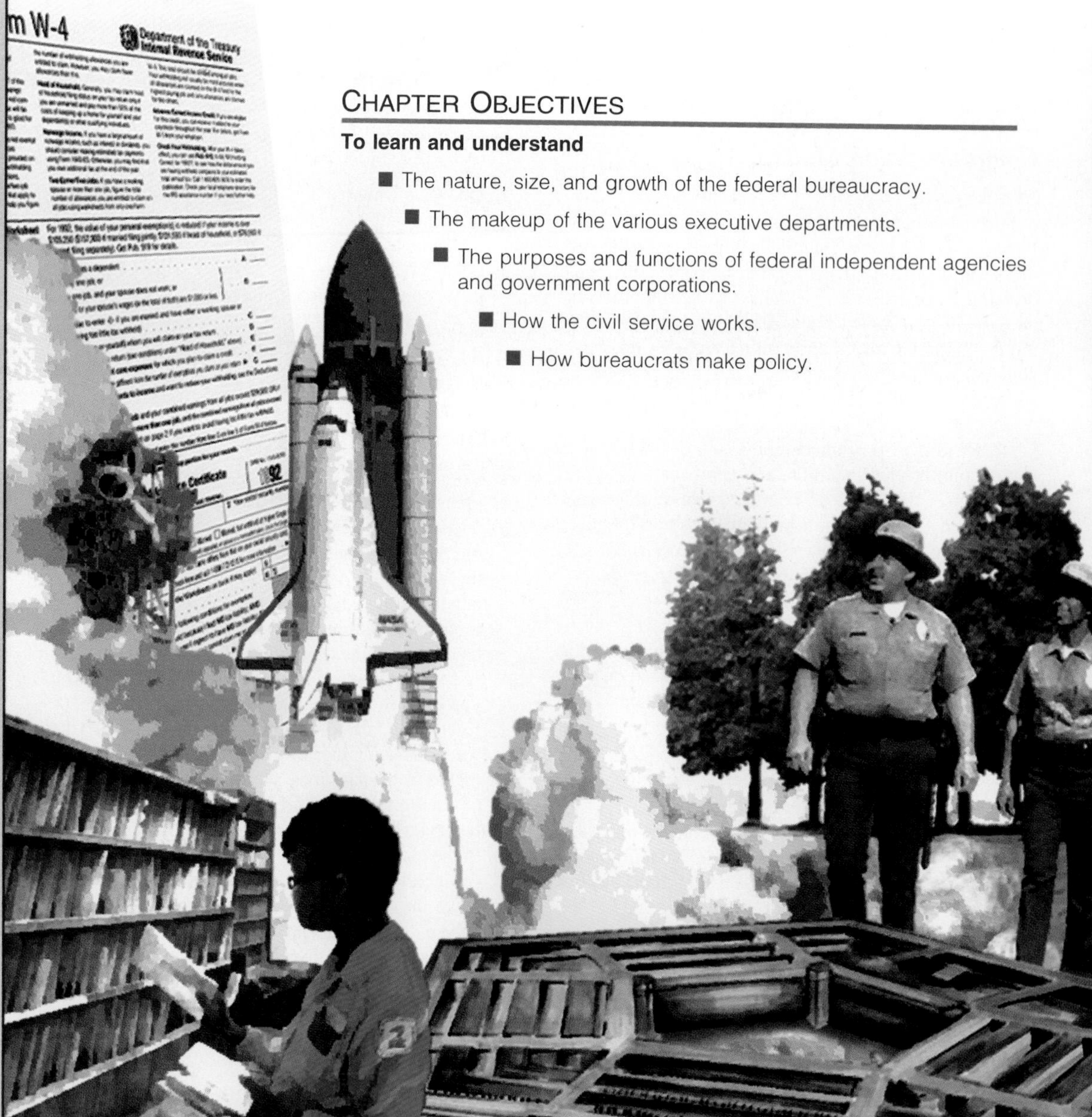

CHAPTER OBJECTIVES

To learn and understand

- The nature, size, and growth of the federal bureaucracy.
- The makeup of the various executive departments.
- The purposes and functions of federal independent agencies and government corporations.
- How the civil service works.
- How bureaucrats make policy.

West's American Government Assignment Guide

Activity Sheets
Basic Concepts 17 *TRB* (Reteaching)
Enrichment Activity 17 *TRB*
Building Social Studies Skills 17 *TRB*

Quizzes
Chapter 17 Section 1 Quiz *TRB*
Chapter 17 Section 2 Quiz *TRB*
Chapter 17 Section 3 Quiz *TRB*
Chapter 17 Section 4 Quiz *TRB*
Chapter 17 Section 5 Quiz *TRB*

Tests
Chapter 17 Test A *TRB*
Chapter 17 Test B *TRB*
Chapter 17 Test Bank *TRB*
Chapter 17 WESTEST Computerized Testing

Social Studies Tool Kit Software
Chapter 17 Activity

SECTION 1

Points to Stress
- The definition and organization of bureaucracy.
- The manner in which the U.S. bureaucracy has grown.

Kickoff Activity
Write the word *bureaucracy* on the chalkboard. Have the students read the word and then list at least six words or phrases that come to mind in response to it. When all the students have completed their lists, have volunteers read their lists aloud and encourage the students to discuss their responses.

Working with the Preview Questions
Let a volunteer read these study questions aloud to the class. Have the students briefly discuss what they already know in response to these questions. Then remind the students that they will find more complete answers as they study Section 1; ask them to keep the questions in mind as they read.

Teaching Strategies

Introduction
Ask volunteers to read the section introduction aloud. Then guide the students in discussing its content: What does the statement, *power to act resides in the position rather than in the person,* mean? What examples can you cite to illustrate that statement?

Vocabulary
Have volunteers explain the definition—and the connotations—of the term *red tape* used in the cartoon caption.

Keynote

"Government is not the solution to our problem; government is the problem".

—— **Ronald Reagan**
(1911–) Fortieth President of the United States

INTRODUCTION

Did you eat breakfast this morning? If you did, **bureaucrats—**individuals who work in the offices of government—had a lot to do with your breakfast. If you had bacon, the meat was inspected by federal agents. If you drank milk, the price was affected by rules and regulations of the Department of Agriculture. If you looked at a cereal box, you saw fine print about minerals and vitamins, which was the result of regulations made by several other federal agencies.

Despite the negative implications of the word, a bureaucrat is simply a member of a large administrative organization—a **bureaucracy**—that carries out the policies of elected government officials. Bureaucrats deliver our mail, clean our streets, and run our national parks. Life without the government bureaucracy would be quite different.

Some critics think that the bureaucracy has grown too big, as President Ronald Reagan expressed in the opening quote above. But before we can examine the growth of the bureaucracy, we need first to look at its nature.

SECTION 1

Bureaucracy: Its Nature and Size

Preview Questions

- What is a bureaucracy and how is it organized?
- How much has the bureaucracy in our country grown?

The concept of a bureaucracy is not confined to the federal government. Any large-scale organization has to have a bureaucracy. Even small businesses operate as bureaucracies, for bureaucracy simply means an organization that is structured in a pyramid-like fashion. In each bureaucracy, everybody (except the head of the bureaucracy) reports to at least one other person. For the federal government, the head of the bureaucracy is the president of the United States.

A bureaucratic form of organization allows each person to concentrate on his or her area of knowledge and expertise. In your school, for example you do not expect the school nurse to solve the problems of the principal. You do not expect the football coach to solve the problems of the finance department.

Another key aspect of any bureaucracy is that the power to act resides in the *position* rather than in the *person.* In your school, the person who is currently vice

'Frankly, trimming the bureaucracy has me worried. . . . It just means fewer people to handle all the red tape."

Reprinted with special permission of NAS, Inc.

Discussion Starter
Guide the students in considering Reagan's campaign promises to reduce the size of the federal bureaucracy: Why is this promise so appealing to voters? Why is it so difficult to implement? How do you imagine voters would respond to a candidate who admitted that fulfilling his or her other campaign promises would involve increasing the size of the government bureaucracy?

Extension
Let interested volunteers research the methods by which the sum of 500 1798-dollars is converted to 5,000 modern-dollars. What information is required to make such a conversion? How can that information be gathered? Ask the volunteers to prepare a bulletin board display with the answers to these questions, including several examples if possible.

Discussion Starter
Help the students consider the significance of the fact that 15 percent of the entire labor force is employed by the government: According to this figure, how many of you will be working for the government ten years from now? How many of your adult family members, friends, and acquaintances now work for the government? In addition to those people, how many government employees do you come into contact with during daily life?

Caption Answer Student answers will vary, but might mention that collecting and disbursing revenue have become major tasks for the government. You might wish to use this caption question as a discussion starter. Follow this up by asking those students who do feel the government has gotten too big, where they would make cuts. What about services? Which services would be affected?

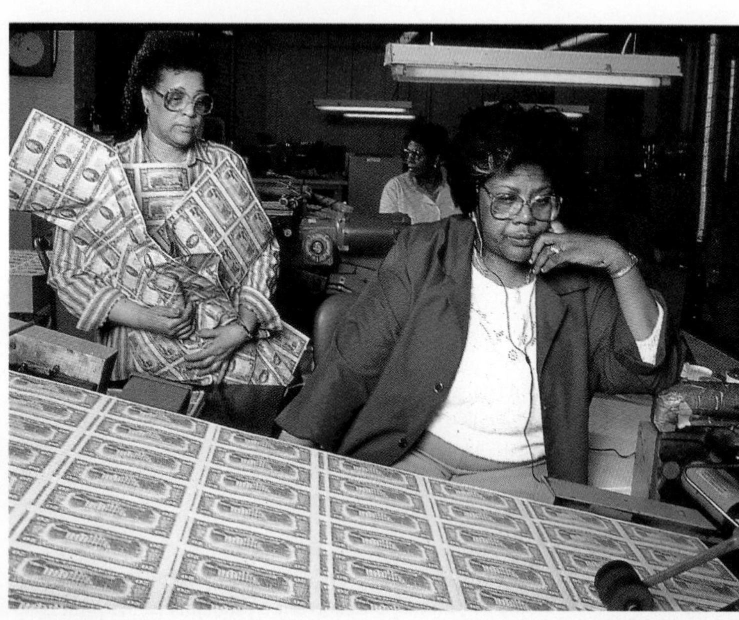

The Department of the Treasury, like all government departments, has grown dramatically throughout the history of our nation. In 1789, there were only 39 employees in the Department of the Treasury. By 1992, this number had grown to 165,000. Why did this department grow so much?

principal has more or less the same authority as any other previous vice principal.

The Growth of Bureaucracy

Today the word *bureaucracy* automatically evokes a negative reaction. During election time throughout the nation there are calls from politicians to "cut big government and red tape," and "get rid of overlapping and wasteful bureaucracies." President Ronald Reagan campaigned on a platform of reducing the size of the federal bureaucracy in 1980, but it actually grew larger during his eight years as president.

No one campaigns for office on a platform calling for a bigger bureaucracy, but candidates promise to establish programs that would require many new employees—which means the bureaucracy would have to grow. Americans constantly demand more services, and with each new service comes a new group of bureaucrats.

The federal bureaucracy that was created in 1789 was small. There were only three departments with a few employees in each: (1) The Department of State (nine employees); (2) The Department of War (two employees); and (3) The Department of the Treasury (thirty-nine employees).

By 1798 the federal bureaucracy was still tiny. The secretary of state had seven clerks. His total expenditures on stationery and printing amounted to $500, or about $5,000 by today's standards. The Department of War spent a grand total of $1.4 million each year, or about $13 million in today's terms.

The times have changed. The federal bureaucracy has grown to about three million employees and spends over $1.5 trillion each year. The Executive Office of the President alone has over 1,500 employees. State governments employ another 3.5 million civilians and local governments employ nearly 10 million. (You'll find out more about state and local governments in Chapters 21 to 25.) In total, about 15 percent of the entire labor force is employed directly by federal, state, and local governments, including those in the military.

Throughout the 1980s, expenditures by all levels of government were about 35 percent of the total value of the goods and services produced in a year. Some part of this was financed by fees and borrowing. The greatest single source of goverment revenue comes from the taxes paid by the average citizen.

TEACHING BUILDING SOCIAL STUDIES SKILLS

Read
Introduce this special feature by asking the students to recall what they already know about organization charts: What purposes do organization charts serve? Who should understand how to read organization charts? Why? After a brief discussion, let volunteers read the Building Social Studies Skills feature aloud.

Discuss
Help the students discuss the information in this feature: What does each box in this chart show? Where are vertical lines used? What do they indicate? Where are horizontal lines used? What do they indicate?

Analyze and Apply
Let the students work in small groups to draw their own organization charts. The members of each group might choose a familiar organization—such as their school government or a local business—or they might make up an organization. Then have the group members work together to plan, draw, and display a clear chart of that organization.

Review
Use these questions to help the students review the Building Social Studies Skills feature: What is the difference between a vertical line and a horizontal line on an organization chart? Which position is usually shown at the top of an organization chart?

Practicing Your Skills (Answers)
1. The regional analyst answers to the deputy director for planning, who answers to the executive director.
2. Decisions are made by the board of directors, who are at the top of the chart, and implemented by the executive director and the staff.
3. None.

BUILDING SOCIAL STUDIES SKILLS

Reading an Organization Chart

Organization charts are used to illustrate the parts of both private and government organizations and how they operate. Each person, department, or segment is illustrated with a symbol or box which is usually labeled with the title of the office or its administrator. (Vertical lines between the boxes or symbols show levels of responsibility and horizontal lines show lines of authority.) In most organization charts, the person or department with the most power and authority is shown at the top.

In any formal organization chart there is a chain of command which shows how the company, club, agency, or department organizes its activities. That is what is shown in an organization chart.

Every chart will show lines of authority typically going from the person or group with the most authority down to lower and lower levels of authority. Typically, an organization has departments. For example, in the chart shown for the Santa Barbara County Association of Governments, there is someone who is head of the planning department and someone who is head of the program development department.

Typically, each lower level must report to a higher level. Therefore, in the Santa Barbara County Association of Governments, both the deputy director of planning and the deputy director of program development would report to the executive director, who in turn reports to the board of directors.

PRACTICING YOUR SKILLS

1. Describe the flow of power and authority from the regional analyst to the executive director.
2. How are decisions arrived at in this agency? How can you tell?
3. Which positions have the same authority as executive director?

Santa Barbara County Association of Governments

Board of Directors
5 County Supervisors
3 City Councilpersons
3 City Mayors

Executive Director
Oversees planning and program development

Deputy Director (Planning)
Oversees comprehensive regional planning

Deputy Director (Program Development)
Oversees and develops regional programs such as long-range transportation and rideshare programs

Planning Division
3 Transportation Planners
1 Regional Analyst

Clerical Support
1 Executive Secretary
1 Clerk Typist
1 Administrative Services Officer

Program Development Division
1 Transportation Planner
1 Ridesharing Program Coordinator
1 Clerk Typist

Discussion Starter
Guide the students in studying and discussing the Organization Chart of the Federal Government: Which of these organizations do you feel most affect your daily life? How?

Extension
Encourage the students to find and share organization charts of other groups, such as businesses or state or local governments.

Figure Answer The federal government employs approximately 3 million people, administering programs funded by Congress each year with over $1.5 trillion.

Reteaching Strategies
1. Have the students work with partners to write short paragraphs describing the functions of a bureaucrat.
2. Work with small groups of students. Help them calculate the percentage of growth (in terms of the number of employees) in the federal bureaucracy from 1787 until today.

Developing Skills for the Information Age

The federal bureaucracy is the family dog of American politics, constantly getting kicked. And like the family dog, it often does not deserve it and can't fight back. Students should be encouraged to see how the bureaucracy is treated by the media. There are several sources that can be scrutinized. *National Journal* is printed weekly and has a published index to its articles. *The Washington Monthly* takes an irreverent view of clumsy bureaucracy with each issue. The *Wall Street Journal* and *Fortune* magazine periodically feature stories on the bureaucracy. *Taylor's Encyclopedia of Government Officials: Federal and State* features the bureaucracy in its issues, publishing a cumulative index in March, June, September, and December. Less frequent yet germane are the features done by electronic media such as *60 Minutes* or *20/20*. Students should submit a summary of their findings.

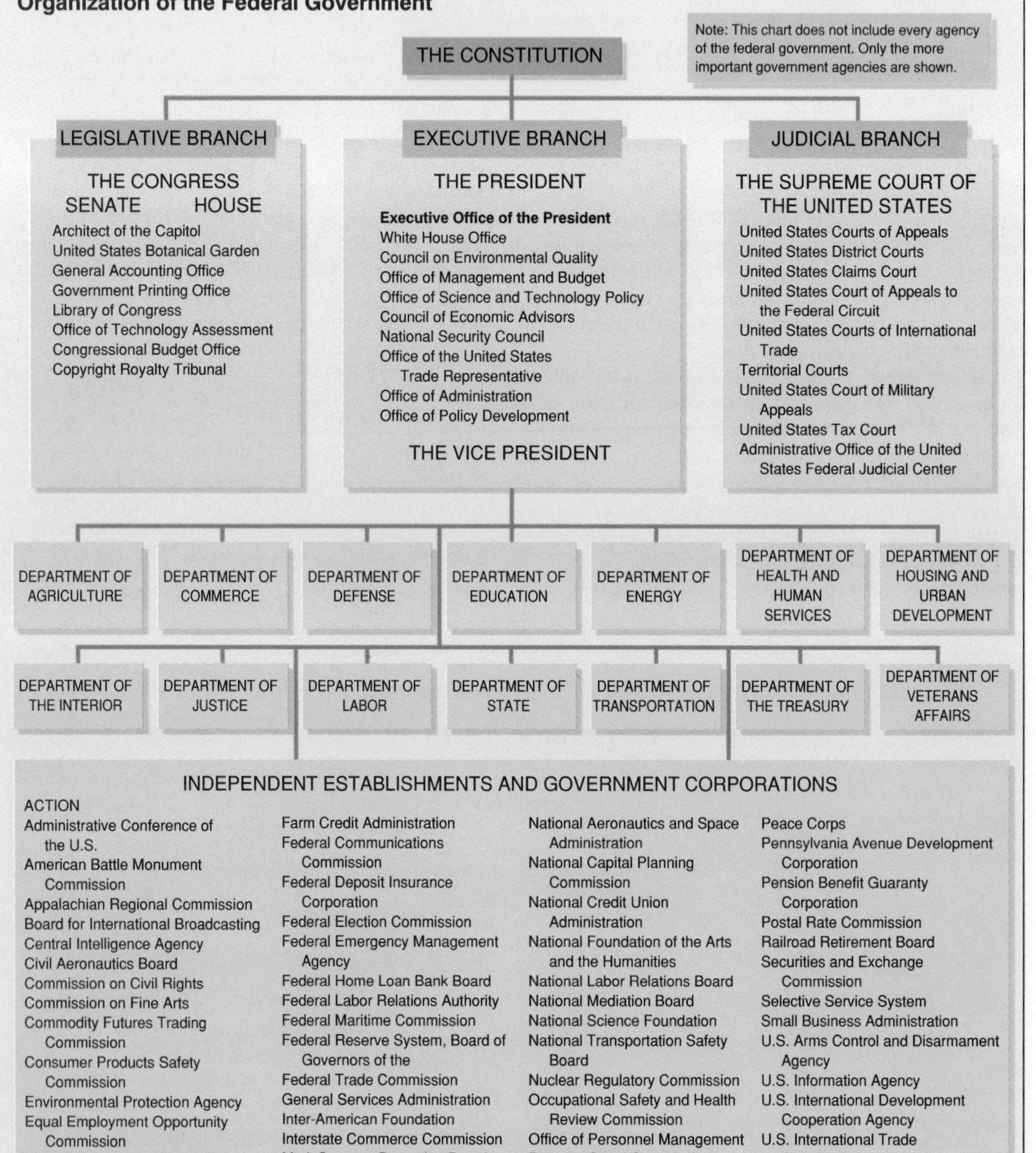

FIGURE 17–1 Organization of the Federal Government. The table above details the organization of the federal government including the more important executive departments, independent executive agencies, independent regulatory agencies, and government corporations. Approximately how many people are employed by the federal government?

Evaluation Strategies

1. Have the students write their answers to the Section 1 Review questions.

2. Have the students take the Section 1 Quiz found in the *TRB*.

Section 1 Review (Answers)

1. A large administrative organization with clear lines of authority normally hierarchically structured.

2. The federal government that was created in 1787 had only three departments. In response to an enormous growth in government responsibilities, particularly during the "New Deal" era, the federal bureaucracy has grown to over three million employees.

3. Answers will vary, e.g., there are 50 state governments and thousands of local governments, all of which carry out a vast number of government programs.

SECTION 2

Points to Stress

- The major executive departments and their duties.
- Departments that primarily serve the president.
- The organization of executive departments.

Kickoff Activity

Remind the students that executive departments are headed by the secretaries who serve in the president's cabinet. Then give the students five minutes in which to list as many of the executive departments as they can. Encourage the students to compare—and revise—their completed lists.

Working with the Preview Questions

Read these study questions to the class, and ask the students to identify the part of Section 2 in which they expect to find the answer to each question. Then remind the students to keep the questions in mind as they read the section.

How the Federal Bureaucracy Is Organized

A complete organization chart of the federal government would be large enough to cover an entire wall. A simplified version is provided in Figure 17–1 on page 404. The executive branch consists of a number of bureaucracies that provide services to Congress, the federal courts, and to the president directly.

There are four major types of bureaucratic structures within the executive branch of the federal government:

- Executive Departments
- Independent Executive Agencies
- Independent Regulatory Agencies
- Government Corporations

Each type of bureaucratic structure has its own relationship to the president and its own internal workings.

Section 1 Review

1. What is a bureaucracy?
2. Describe the growth of government bureaucracy in historical terms.
3. **For critical analysis:** Why do you think state and local bureaucracies (in total) are so much larger than the federal bureaucracy?

Section 2

The Executive Departments

Preview Questions:

- What are some of the major executive departments and their duties?
- Which departments primarily serve the president?
- How are the departments organized?

You have already been introduced to the various executive departments in Chapter 15 when you read about the president at work with his cabinet and other close advisors. The fourteen executive departments, called line organizations, are the major service organizations of the federal government. They are directly accountable to the president and are responsible for performing government functions, such as training troops (Department of Defense), printing money (Department of the Treasury), and enforcing federal laws setting minimum safety and health standards for workers (Department of Labor).

Each department was created by Congress as the need arose, and each manages a specific policy area. The head of each department is known as the secretary. For the Department of Justice the head is called the attorney general. Each department head is appointed by the president, and confirmed by the Senate.

Figure 17–2 on the next two pages provides an overview of each of the departments in the executive branch and their main duties.

Organization within Departments

While there are organizational differences among the departments, each generally follows a typical bureaucratic structure. For example, the organization of the Department of Agriculture provides a model for how an executive department is organized.

One aspect of the secretary of agriculture's job is to carry out the president's agricultural policies. Another aspect, however, is to promote and protect the department. The secretary will spend time ensuring that Congress allocates enough money for the department to work effectively. The secretary also makes sure that **constituents**—the people the department serves, usually owners of major farming corporations—are happy. In general, the secretary tries to maintain or improve the status of the department with respect to all the other departments and units of the federal bureaucracy.

The secretary of agriculture is assisted by a deputy secretary and several assistant secretaries, all of whom are nominated by the president and put into office with

The activities of the secretary of agriculture can have a major impact on American farmers everywhere. What are the basic duties of the secretary of agriculture?

Teaching Strategies

Introduction

Ask one of the students to read this section introduction aloud. Then help the students consider its content by asking questions such as these: How would you define the term *line organization?* What is the primary function of the executive departments? Whom does the president typically select as the secretaries to head these departments? What role does Congress play in the functioning of the departments?

Caption Answer The secretary of agriculture's basic duties include carrying out the president's agricultural policies, promoting and protecting the department, seeing to the need of constituents, and protecting the position of the department within the federal hierarchy.

Discussion Starter

Help the students discuss the possible conflicts among roles that a secretary may face. Why do such conflicts arise? How do you think they should be resolved?

Cooperative Learning
Divide the class into 14 pairs or small groups, and assign each one of the executive departments. Ask the members of each group to learn more about the assigned department and to contribute to a bulletin board about the accomplishments and responsibilities of the executive departments.

Figure Answer The Department of Interior is responsible for federally owned lands and parks.

This figure content is also featured on *West's American Government Videodisc* (see the index found in the *TRB*).

Executive Departments

Department (Year Established)	Principal Duties	Most Important Sub-Agencies
State (1789)	Negotiates treaties; develops our foreign policy; protects citizens abroad.	Passport Agency; Bureau of Diplomatic Security; Foreign Service; Bureau of Human Rights and Humanitarian Affairs; Bureau of Consular Affairs; Bureau of Intelligence and Research
Treasury (1789)	Pays all federal bills; borrows money; collects federal taxes; mints coins and prints paper currency; operates the Secret Service; supervises national banks.	Internal Revenue Service (IRS); Bureau of Alcohol, Tobacco, and Firearms; United States Secret Service; U.S. Mint; Customs Service
Interior (1849)	Supervises federally owned lands and parks; operates federal hydroelectric power facilities; supervises Native-American affairs.	United States Fish and Wildlife Service; National Park Service; Bureau of Indian Affairs; Bureau of Mines; Bureau of Land Management
Justice (1870)	Furnishes legal advice to the president; enforces federal criminal laws; supervises the federal corrections system (prisons).	Federal Bureau of Investigation (FBI); Drug Enforcement Administration (DEA); Bureau of Prisons (BOP); United States Marshals Service; Immigration and Naturalization Service (INS)
Agriculture (1889)	Provides assistance to farmers and ranchers; conducts research to improve agricultural activity and to prevent plant disease; works to protect forests from fires and disease.	Oil Conservation Service; Agricultural Research Service; Food and Safety Inspection Service; Federal Crop Insurance Corporation; Farmers Home Administration; Forest Service
Commerce (1903)	Grants patents and trademarks; conducts the national census; monitors the weather; protects the interests of businesses.	Bureau of the Census; Bureau of Economic Analysis; Minority Business Development Agency; Patent and Trademark Office; National Oceanic and Atmospheric Administration; United States Travel and Tourism Administration
Labor (1913)	Administers federal labor laws; promotes the interests of workers.	Occupational Safety and Health Administration (OSHA); Bureau of Labor Statistics; Employment Standards Administration; Office of Labor-Management Standards; Employment and Training Administration

▲ **FIGURE 17–2 Executive Departments.** The figure on this page and the next lists and describes each of the 14 executive departments, their principal duties, and most important sub-agencies. Which of these departments is responsible for the maintenance and care of federally owned lands and parks?

Executive Departments (continued)

Department (Year Established)	Principal Duties	Most Important Sub-Agencies
Defense (1947)[1]	Manages the armed forces (Army, Navy, Air Force, Marines); operates military bases; responsible for civil defense.	National Guard; Defense Investigation Service; National Security Agency; Joint Chiefs of Staff; Departments of the Air Force, Navy, Army
Health and Human Services (1953)	Administers the Social Security and Medicare programs; promotes public health; enforces pure food and drug laws; is involved in health-related research.	Social Security Administration; Family Support Administration; Office of Human Development Services; Public Health Service
Housing and Urban Development (1965)	Concerned with the nation's housing needs; develops and rehabilitates urban communities; promotes improvements in city streets and parks.	Office of Block Grant Assistance; Emergency Shelter Grants Program; Office of Urban Development Action Grants; Assistant Secretary for Fair Housing and Equal Opportunity
Transportation (1967)	Finances improvements in mass transit; develops and administers programs for highways, railroads, and aviation; involved with offshore maritime safety.	Federal Aviation Administration (FAA); Federal Highway Administration; National Highway Traffic Administration; United States Coast Guard; Urban Mass-Transit Administration
Energy (1977)	Involved in conservation of energy and resources; analyzes energy data; conducts research and development.	Energy Information Administration; Economics Regulatory Administration; Bonneville Power Administration; Office of Nuclear Energy; Energy Information Administration; Office of Conservation and Renewable Energy
Education (1979)[2]	Coordinates federal programs and policies for education; administers aid to education; promotes educational research.	Office of Special Education and Rehabilitation Services; Office of Elementary and Secondary Education; Office of Postsecondary Education; Office of Vocational and Adult Education
Veterans Affairs (1989)	Promotes the welfare of veterans of the U.S. armed forces	Health Care Service Benefit Programs; Memorial Affairs; Medical Training

[1] Formed from the Department of War (1789) and the Department of the Navy (1798).
[2] Formed from the Department of Health, Education, and Welfare (1953).

FYI

History has seen many cries for bureaucratic reform. President Reagan appointed a commission to study the bureaucracy and recommend reforms. The Grace Commission, named after chairperson J. Pete Grace, reported many findings. Among them were that the federal government is the largest borrower, lender, employer, and insurer. Further, it is responsible for the medical care of over 40 million people, provides over 90 million subsidized meals each day, and spends twice as much per day on hospitalization as the private sector. The Grace Commission recommended that presidential veto power be expanded, military commissaries end, user fees for national park services be increased, and fringe benefits to government employees be reduced. The Grace Commission made over 4,000 recommendations, most of which were ignored by Reagan.

Detractors felt that the Grace Commission exaggerated the problems and misled the public, making them believe managing waste could cure the deficit. Others felt that it was biased for members of the private sector to call for privatization of bureaucratic services when the private sector would benefit. Finally, the Grace Commission did not emphasize the services government must provide.

Ironically, as a consequence of the report, new rules and regulations were added by Congress, adding to the red tape that the Grace Commission argued against.

TEACHING GOVERNMENT IN ACTION

Read

Introduce this feature to your students by reminding them that in America, we have, as John Adams coined the phrase, "a government of laws, and not of men." Ask a volunteer to explain to the class what it means to have a government of laws, and not of men. Then explain to students that, as they enter the workforce, they will find that many of these laws are designed to protect them as employees. Ask them why they think employees need protecting. Allow the students to share their responses to this question, then have volunteers take turns reading this Government in Action feature aloud to the class.

Discuss

Stimulate a class discussion of this content by asking: How has the composition of the American workforce changed over the last two hundred years? How many people comprise the civilian labor force? What types of laws are listed here that deal with compensation? What does the Federal Occupational Safety and Health Act of 1970 specify about the workplace? What are fringe benefits? What is discrimination? Why do you think so much modern legislation is designed to protect workers from discrimination? Does such discrimination still take place in the workplace? Why or why not? How do you feel about the laws against wrongful discharge? Should an employer have the right to fire anyone he or she wants regardless of the reasons? Why or why not?

Analyze and Apply

To further expand your students' understanding of this content, you might wish to invite a representative from the personnel department of a major local employer to speak to your class. He or she should discuss the laws that govern employment policies within his or her firm.

GOVERNMENT IN ACTION

PERSONAL LAW

Your Rights as an Employee

The composition of the American workforce has changed dramatically. When our nation's government was established over 200 years ago, 90 percent of American workers could be classified as farmers. Today, only a very small percentage of Americans work in agriculture. Most work in offices (32 percent), factories (15 percent), restaurants, stores, or retail outlets (13 percent), or schools or medical facilities (15 percent). As you have learned in this chapter, close to 15 percent of the American workforce is employed by the government.

To protect the rights of a civilian labor force of more than 122 million workers, government regulations and laws have been established.

Your Basic Employee Rights

Every employee is entitled to be compensated (paid) by their employer for the work which they have done. Many salespeople are paid a commission, that is, a percentage of the sales made. The federal government sets legal minimum wages that you have to be paid, typically called the *minimum wage.* There are also laws about how much you have to be paid extra if you work over a specified number of hours a week, such as 37½ hours. If you do not receive such overtime pay, you can sue for the money owed.

Every employee is entitled to safe working conditions. According to the Federal Occupational Safety and Health Act of 1970, employers must furnish a place of employment that is free from recognized hazards that may cause serious physical harm or death. Most states have similar regulations.

While you as an employee have no legal right to fringe benefits, virtually all jobs offer them to you. Fringe benefits include medical insurance, retirement plans, vacations and holidays with pay, legal-aid plans, maternity and paternity leave, and many others.

Fighting Discrimination

A major part of modern legislation protecting workers involves preventing and punishing discrimination. For example, the federal Equal Pay Act of 1963 prohibits employers from offering different wages solely on the basis of gender for jobs that require equal skill, effort, and responsibility. The Civil Rights Act of 1964 makes it unlawful for employers to "refuse to hire or discharge any individual, or otherwise discriminate against any individual, with respect to compensation, terms, conditions, or privileges of employment because of such individual's race, color, religion, sex, or national origin." In 1967, Congress passed the Age Discrimination and Employment Act which makes it unlawful for employers to discriminate against persons because of their age. In 1990, Congress passed the Americans with Disabilities Act which prohibits discrimination in employment against persons with disabilities and demands that employers make reasonable accommodations for disabled persons in the workplace, if at all possible.

Wrongful Discharge

In many states, if you think you have been fired improperly, you can sue your employer for wrongful discharge. Your employer has to prove that he or she had good cause (for example, insubordination, lack of business, bankruptcy) to let you go.

In most states, at a minimum, the following three rules have emerged:

1. Your employer cannot fire you because you refuse to follow a company order to lie or engage in an illegal action.
2. If you have a contract with your employer, even if it is only *implied,* and you have been carrying on your duties in good faith and honestly, your employer may be held

He or she should also discuss how workforce supply and demand also shape employment policies within his or her firm. After you have made arrangements for the speaker to visit your class, you might have each student prepare at least three questions for the speaker. Student questions should reflect an understanding not only of this personal law feature, but also of the product or service that is offered by the employer.

Review

Use the following questions to review the content of this Government in Action feature. What is compensation? What do minimum wage laws do? What types of fringe benefits must employers provide to their employees according to the law? What are four acts designed to fight discrimination in the workforce? What is wrongful discharge?

Think About It (Answers)

1. Answers will vary, but should reflect the realization that employers must, by law, be able to justify their hiring or firing according to the three guidelines in the feature.

2. As of this writing, there is no legal obligation on the part of the employer to provide benefits such as health insurance, although many companies do provide such benefits. Many legislators feel, however, that such a basic need as health care should be provided and are introducing bills that would make such coverage by employers mandatory.

3. Answers will vary. Although it is true that overall, women do not spend as many consecutive years in the workforce as men, and that they frequently occupy lower positions with the same qualifications, employers do tend to violate the Act because it is difficult to prove this discrimination.

4. Answers will vary. Students might feel that it would be better to concentrate on enforcing the existing legislation, or that no matter what the letter of the law specifies employers will be able to find ways around it if they can.

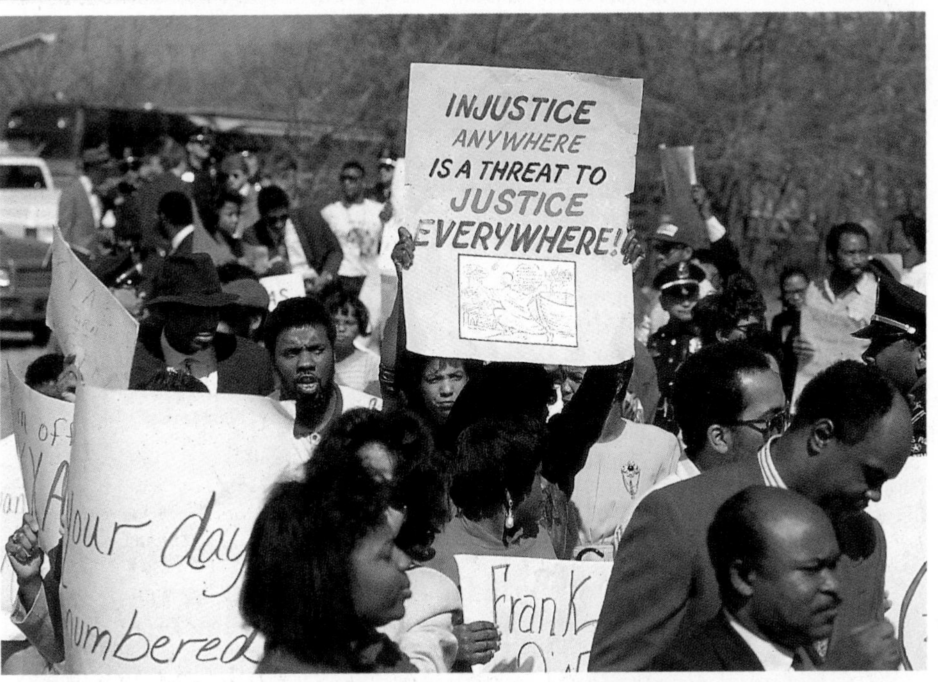

Discrimination based on race or gender is still a problem in many areas of American life. The Equal Pay Act of 1963, the Civil Rights Act of 1964, and the Civil Rights Act of 1991 are all designed to eliminate such discrimination in the workplace.

liable if you are fired in violation of that contract.

3. If you have received favorable job evaluations for a long period of time, especially when accompanied by salary increases, then your employer will be held in violation of an implied *agreement of continued employment* if he or she fires you.

THINK ABOUT IT

1. Under what circumstances, if any, would it be appropriate to allow employers to hire and fire employees at will? Explain.
2. Does everyone who works have a right to a minimum amount of fringe benefits, such as health insurance? Explain.
3. The Equal Pay Act outlaws different pay based solely on gender. Nonetheless, women in America, on average, make less than men. Does this necessarily mean the Equal Pay Act continues to be violated by employers? Explain.
4. There has been a great deal of legislation designed to eliminate discrimination in the workplace. Do you think that more legislation is needed? If so, what type of legislation would you recommend?

Discussion Starter
Encourage the students to consider how far a secretary can go in opposing the interests of the president: What power does the president have over the secretary? How likely is the president to exert that power? Under what kinds of circumstances? Given the power of the president, what choices might a secretary have to make? Why?

Vocabulary
Let volunteers define the term *holding companies:* What attitudes toward these large departments are conveyed in this term?

Reteaching Strategies
1. Have the students work with partners to review Section 2, writing a brief outline of the most important points.
2. Work with small groups of students, helping them discuss the problems associated with the departments that are considered "holding companies."

Evaluation Strategies
1. Have the students write their answers to the Section 2 Review questions.
2. Have the students take the Section 2 Quiz found in the *TRB.*

Caption Answer Students should understand that the Secretary of Agriculture also might lobby to see that a portion of the defense budget be transferred to his department.

Section 2 Review (Answers)
1. Answers will vary, e.g., the Department of State negotiates treaties, develops foreign policy, and protects citizens abroad; the Department of Labor administers labor laws and promotes the interest of workers.
2. The secretary heads the department and is assisted by a deputy secretary and several assistant secretaries.
3. Answers will vary, e.g., the Department of Interior could have goals regarding environmental concerns while the president has conflicting goals concerning economic development in wilderness areas. Such a conflict would most likely find resolution by congressional action.

SECTION 3

Points to Stress
- Reasons for the creation of independent executive agencies.
- The purposes and functions of independent regulatory agencies.
- The definition of government corporations.

Kickoff Activity
Ask the students the following questions: What do you think are the most important differences between executive agencies and regulatory agencies? Give the students five minutes in which to write their responses. Then encourage them to compare and discuss their ideas.

Working with the Preview Questions
Have the students read and discuss these study questions. Let them work together to write an out-

Senate approval. The secretary and assistants have staff who help with all sorts of jobs, such as hiring new people and generating positive public relations for the Department of Agriculture.

Closeness to the Chief Executive

Some observers of the executive departments like to group them according to their closeness to the chief executive. The so-called ''inner'' departments—State, Defense, Justice, and Treasury—are there primarily to serve the president. The secretaries (and attorney general) of these departments are typically those who are closest politically and personally to the Oval Office. The rest of the departments—known as the ''outer'' departments—are so called because their functions deal more with their own constituencies. The goals of the outer departments often differ markedly from the president's. For example, the president may want to reduce the federal budget deficit by reducing federal spending. He may ask the secretary of agriculture to cut back on programs that help certain wealthy farmers. The secretary of agriculture, who probably wants to please his constituents, may resist the president's suggestion to cut back.

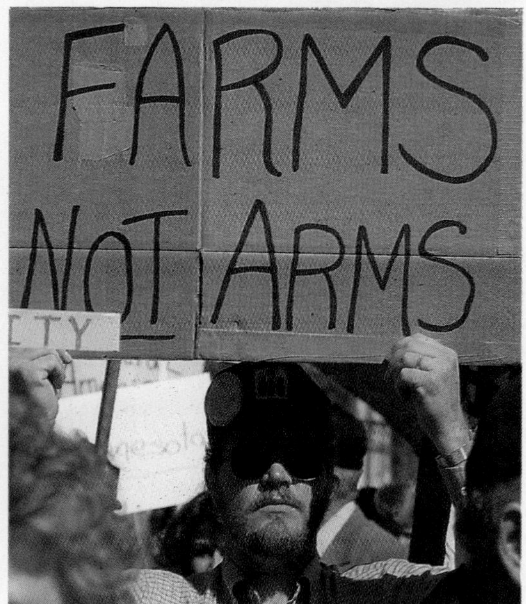

▲ This American is demonstrating in support of his belief that government dollars should be spent on agriculture rather than on weapons and defense. Which secretary might also argue this point of view?

A couple of departments are so large and have so many agencies and interests combined into one organization that they have been called ''holding companies.'' These include the departments of Health and Human Services (HHS), Housing and Urban Development (HUD), and Defense. Those three departments tend to suffer from internal conflicts as each subunit tries to expand its functions or budget at the expense of other subunits.

Section 2 Review

1. Name some of the major executive departments and their duties.
2. Briefly describe the organization within an executive department.
3. **For critical analysis:** Describe a situation in which an executive department would have goals markedly different from those of the president. How could this situation be resolved?

Section 3

Independent Agencies and Government Corporations

Preview Questions
- Why were independent executive agencies created?
- What are the purposes and functions of independent regulatory agencies?
- What are government corporations?

The three remaining major parts of the federal bureaucracy consist of independent executive agencies, independent regulatory agencies, and government corporations. In this section you will learn about the most important aspects of each of these three parts of the bureaucracy.

Independent Executive Agencies

Independent executive agencies are federal bureaucratic organizations that have a single function. They are independent in the sense that they are not located within a department; rather, independent executive agency heads report directly to the president who has appointed them. It is only through joint cooperation between the president and Congress that a new federal line format based on these questions. Record their format on the chalkboard, and have the students follow it to take notes on Section 3.

Teaching Strategies

Introduction
Let the students read the section introduction independently. Then encourage them to share their ideas about the three remaining parts of the federal bureaucracy: What do you think each does? What groups might be examples of each?

TEACHING GOVERNMENT IN ACTION

Read
Introduce this feature by asking students to recall or refer to the information about the Department of Agriculture from the figure on page 406. Ask a volunteer to list the principal duties of the Department of Agriculture. (Provides assistance to farmers and ranchers; conducts research to improve agricultural activity and to prevent plant disease; works to protect forests from fires and disease.) Then have a volunteer read this Day in the Life feature to the class.

Discuss
Stimulate a class discussion of this feature by asking the following questions: Who is Edward Madigan? Who appointed Madigan? What aspects of Madigan's background make him an appropriate choice for the position of secretary of agriculture? How would you describe Madigan's schedule as shown here?

Analyze and Apply
This feature discusses the many constituencies that Madigan, as secretary of Agriculture, must serve. Break the class into groups and have each group choose a different cabinet secretary to research. Each group should then find out the constituencies, including the public and private interest groups, that their particular secretary must serve. Groups should present their findings to the class in the form of an oral report.

Review
Review this feature content with the students by asking the following questions: What are Edward Madigan's responsibilities as secretary of agriculture? What type of political experience did Madigan have before he was appointed to this position? What particular constituencies must the secretary of agriculture serve?

Think About It (Answers)
1. Madigan's appointment was agreed to by all members of the Senate. This was not the case for Supreme Court Justice Clarence Thomas.
2. There is no legal or constitutional reason why an urban congressperson could not become secretary of agriculture, but it would not be a popular choice from a political standpoint, since the individual would most likely lack the experience, contacts, and constituency needed for the position.

GOVERNMENT IN ACTION

A DAY IN THE LIFE

Secretary of Agriculture Edward Madigan

Edward Madigan became the 24th United States secretary of agriculture in March of 1991, after he was nominated by George Bush and unanimously confirmed by the Senate. As secretary of agriculture, Madigan guided the implementation of federal laws that make up our national agricultural policy.

Madigan began his political career in the Illinois House of Representatives, where he served for six years. In 1972, Madigan, a Republican, was elected to the House of Representatives, serving Illinois' 15th Congressional District, an area that contains some of the nation's richest farmland. For eight of his eighteen years in Congress, he was the ranking Republican on the House Agricultural Committee, where he helped formulate American farm policy. Madigan resigned his post when the Clinton administration took over in 1993.

His schedule, shown below, reflects the need for the secretary to satisfy a number of constituencies, including farmers, the president, the Department of Agriculture, and others.

Thursday

7:45	Weather and Economic briefing
8:00	Senior staff meeting
9:00	Meeting with the Chief of Staff
10:00	Cabinet meeting
11:30	Telephone interview with the *Des Moines Register*
12:00	Lunch with the American Farm Bureau Federation Board
1:00	Nutrition Education Taskforce Meeting
2:00	Personal time (signing mail, phone calls, etc.)
3:15	Meeting with members of the House Agricultural Committee
4:30	Meeting with agency administrators
5:00	Commodity Club reception
5:30	Speech to Commodity Club

THINK ABOUT IT

1. Madigan's nomination to be secretary of agriculture was unanimously confirmed by the Senate. What does this mean? Can you think of a presidential nomination that was not unanimously confirmed by the Senate?
2. Madigan spent many years representing an area of Illinois that is primarily agricultural. Could a Congressperson representing an urban area ever become secretary of agriculture?

TEACHING CITIZENSHIP SKILLS AND RESPONSIBILITIES

Read
Introduce this feature by letting the students discuss what they already know about the Freedom of Information Act: What is the Freedom of Information Act? Who can make use of it? How? After a brief discussion, let volunteers take turns reading the Citizenship Skills and Responsibilities feature aloud.

Discuss
Pose questions such as these to help the students discuss the feature: What information might you be interested in obtaining from the federal government? What information might interest your family members and friends? Why? Do you agree that the Freedom of Information Act "gives real meaning to each citizen's right to know"? Why or why not? Why might people be curious about whether or not the FBI has a file on them? Before the Freedom of Information Act was passed, how could people find out whether or not the FBI had opened a file on them? Why do you think Congress exempted itself from the Freedom of Information Act? Do you believe that Congress is thus abridging your right to know? Why or why not?

Analyze and Apply
Have the students work in small groups to research news stories that have been made possible by the Freedom of Information Act. Then have the groups share their findings in written or oral reports.

Review
Ask the students these review questions: When was the Freedom of Information act passed? What does it allow citizens to do?

CITIZENSHIP SKILLS AND RESPONSIBILITIES

Using the Freedom of Information Act

Sample Letter for Requesting Information from an Executive Department or Agency

Agency Head or FOIA Officer
Title
Name of Agency
Address of Agency
City, State, zip

Re: Freedom of Information Act Request.

Dear __________ :

Under the provisions of the Freedom of Information Act, 5 U.S.C. 552, I am requesting access to (identify the records as clearly and specifically as possible).

If there are any fees for searching for, or copying, the records I have requested, please inform me before you fill the request. (Or: . . . please supply the records without informing me if the fees do not exceed $_________.)

(Optional) I am requesting this information (state the reason for your request if you think it will assist you in obtaining the information.)

(Optional) As you know, the act permits you to reduce or waive fees when the release of the information is considered as "primarily benefiting the public." I believe that this request fits that category and I therefore ask that you waive any fees.

If all or any part of this request is denied, please cite the specific exemption(s) that you think justifies your refusal to release the information, and inform me of the appeal procedures available to me under the law.

I would appreciate your handling this request as quickly as possible, and I look forward to hearing from you within 10 days, as the law stipulates.

Sincerely,

Signature
Name
Address
City, State, zip

Source: U.S. Congress. House Committee on Government Operations. *A Citizen's Guide on How to Use the Freedom of Information Act and the Privacy Act Requesting Government Documents,* 95th Congress, 1st session (1977).

Comprehension
Ask questions such as these to help the students understand independent agencies: How does forming an independent agency help the president focus public attention on a specific issue? How might that attention be lost if the issue were dealt with in an existing executive department?

Extension
Have the students read about the Civil Rights Commission: What is its purpose? Who serves on the Commission now? On what issues is the Commission currently focused? How successfully does the current Commission seem to be fulfilling the original purpose of the Civil Rights Commission? Give the students an opportunity to discuss what they have learned from this research.

Enrichment
Let two groups of volunteers research and report on the CIA and the GSA; ask them to explain the structure and function of each agency to the rest of the class.

Discussion Starter
Encourage the students to consider and discuss the small agencies in the bulleted list. Why do you imagine each exists? What function does each probably serve? How important do you consider these small agencies? Do you think that taxpayers should continue to fund these minor agencies? Why or why not?

CITIZENSHIP SKILLS AND RESPONSIBILITIES

Using the Freedom of Information Act (Continued)

The Freedom of Information Act was passed in 1966 and amended in 1974. It allows people like yourself to obtain information from federal government agencies provided that the information is not classified or concerned with sensitive issues. You cannot, for example, obtain criminal investigation files or information on anyone's private financial transactions. Nor can you obtain interoffice memoranda or letters used in internal decision making within any government agency. If an agency does not comply promptly with your request for information, however, you can sue that agency and expect a speedy judicial hearing. The agency must then explain why it has refused to supply the requested information. If the judge decides against the government, the government has to pay your legal fees. Currently, federal agencies receive about five hundred thousand requests for information every year, of which over 90 percent are completely filled. The Freedom of Information Act gives real meaning to each citizen's right to know.

Why do people make requests for information? Many times individuals are simply curious to know whether the Federal Bureau of Investigations (FBI) has a file on them. Reporters often use this act to obtain background information in order to write stories about federal actions and policies.

If you wish to obtain information from an executive department or agency, use the formula letter on the previous page.

Because Congress has exempted itself from the Freedom of Information Act, it is not obligated to provide you with the information you request.

TAKING ACTION

Make a request to a specific agency, such as the FBI, about information related to yourself, or have one of your parents use the form letter presented to make such a request. Ask, for example, what files the agency has on you (or your parents), if any.

independent executive agency can be created. The decision is jointly made by the president and Congress about where in the executive department the agency will be located.

The Reasons for Independent Agencies Prior to the twentieth century, the federal government did almost all of its work through the executive departments. In the 20th century, by contrast, presidents have asked for executive agencies to be kept separate, or independent, from existing departments. In doing so, a president can focus public attention on the new agency. Today there are more than 200 independent executive agencies.

Sometimes agencies are kept independent because of the sensitive nature of their functions; other times Congress has created independent agencies in order to protect them from **partisan politics**—politics in support of a particular party's ideology. The Civil Rights Commission is a case in point. Congress wanted to protect the work of the Civil Rights Commission from the influences of not only its own political pressure groups, but also from the president. The Central Intelligence Agency (CIA) is another good example. Both Congress and the president know that the intelligence activities of the CIA could be abused if it were not independent. Finally, the General Services Administration (GSA) was created as an independent executive agency in 1949 in order to monitor federal government spending. It needed to be independent of the Congress, whose spending it is supposed to oversee.

The Most Important Independent Executive Agencies Among the over 200 independent executive agencies a few stand out in importance either because of the mission they were established to accomplish or because of their large size. The table in Figure 17–3 on the following page lists some of the major independent executive agencies.

While the independent executive agencies listed in Figure 17–3 are often in the news, the majority of these agencies, which have few employees and very small budgets, are relatively unknown. Among them are:

- The Migratory Bird Conservation Commission
- The American Battle Monuments Commission

Discussion Starter
Guide the students in discussing the agencies covered in the chart, Major Independent Executive Agencies: Why does each of these agencies stand out? What else do you know about each agency? Which of the agency's current activities or projects have been in the news recently?

Vocabulary
Let volunteers explain the use of the term *the alphabet soup of the government* as applied to the independent regulatory agencies.

Enrichment
Ask volunteers to research the CAB: When and why was it founded? What were its major accomplishments? When and why was it disbanded? Have these volunteers summarize their findings in a time-line or other visual display.

Figure Answer Some agencies are independent because of the sensitive nature of the functions (CIA), others are independent in order to protect them from partisan politics (Federal Election Commission, Commission on Civil Rights, etc.).

This figure content is also featured on *West's American Government Videodisc* (see the index found in the *TRB*).

Selected Independent Executive Agencies

Name	Date Formed	Principal Duties
Central Intelligence Agency (CIA)	1947	Gathers and analyzes political and military information about foreign countries so that the United States can improve its own political and military status; conducts activities outside the United States, with the goal of countering the work of intelligence services operated by other nations whose political philosophies are inconsistent with our own.
General Services Administration (GSA)	1949	Purchases and manages all property of the federal government; acts as the business arm of the federal government, overseeing federal government spending projects; discovers overcharges in government programs.
National Science Foundation (NSF)	1950	Promotes scientific research; provides grants to all levels of schools for instructional programs in the sciences.
Small Business Administration (SBA)	1953	Protects the interests of small businesses; provides low-cost loans and management information to small businesses.
Commission on Civil Rights	1957	Evaluates information on discrimination that is based on sex, race, national origin, religion, or physical handicap.
National Aeronautics and Space Administration (NASA)	1958	Responsible for U.S. space program, including building, testing, and operating space vehicles.
Federal Election Commission	1974	Ensures that candidates and states follow the rules established by the Federal Election Campaign Act.

▲ **FIGURE 17–3 Selected Independent Executive Agencies.** The table above lists the major independent executive agencies, the date each was formed, and the principal duties of each agency. Why are these agencies independent?

- The Citizens' Stamp Advisory Committee
- The East-West Foreign Trade Board
- The Susquehanna River Basing Commission

Independent Regulatory Agencies

Independent regulatory agencies are responsible for a specific type of public policy. Their function is to create and implement rules that regulate private activity and protect the public interest in a particular sector of the economy. They are sometimes called the "alphabet soup" of government, because most such agencies are known in Washington by their initials.

One of the earliest agencies was the Interstate Commerce Commission (ICC), established in 1887. At the time the ICC was founded, Americans were beginning to seek some form of government control over businesses and industries. The goal of the ICC was to make

Discussion Starter
Help the students discuss the purpose of the FTC's "cooling-off" regulation: Whom is the regulation intended to benefit? Why? Who should know about the regulation?

Extension
Ask the students to find out who does have authority over members of independent regulatory commissions: To whom are they responsible? Why?

The U.S. space program, which includes the missions of the U.S. Space Shuttle Atlantis and its crew shown here, is the responsibility of the National Aeronautics and Space Administration (NASA). What type of agency is NASA?

Caption Answer NASA is an Independent Executive Agency.

technical, non-political decisions about allowable rates and profits for different transportation and shipping businesses. These rates were to be for the benefit of the entire public. Changing these rates would not require congressional legislation every time a new rule was proposed because the agency had the power to make such changes.

After the ICC was formed, other agencies were created to regulate aviation (the Civil Aeronautics Board, or CAB, no longer in existence), communication (the Federal Communication Commission, or FCC), the stock market (the Securities and Exchange Commission, or SEC), and many other areas of business.

Figure 17–4 on the next page lists the major independent regulatory agencies.

Administration of Regulatory Agencies All regulatory agencies are administered independently of the executive, judicial, and executive branches of government. The regulatory agencies therefore combine some functions of all three branches of government.

They are legislative in that they make rules that have the force of law. For example, the Federal Trade Commission (FTC) enacted a three-day ''cooling-off'' rule with respect to door-to-door sales. Anytime you sign a

Multidiscipline Strategies

Science Federal regulatory agencies and independent executive agencies perform a variety of technical and scientific services for the American public. Although it is difficult to separate politics from any government job, the focus of this activity is for students to contact an agency by letter with the intent to discover the technical nature of the agency's task. Some suggested agencies to contact are NSF, NASA, EPA, and the NRC. Information on how to acquire addresses may be found in *United States Government Manual,* published annually. Students should share their findings with the class.

The Interstate Commerce Commission (ICC) was established in 1887 to help regulate transportation and shipping businesses. What type of agency is the ICC?

Caption Answer The ICC is an independent regulatory agency.

Cooperative Learning Divide the class into nine groups, and assign each group one of the agencies from the chart, Major Independent Regulatory Agencies. Ask the group members to work together in researching that agency's local activities—within your state or community. Then have each group report back to the rest of the class.

Figure Answer All of the independent regulatory agencies are administered independently of the executive, judicial, and legislative branches of government.

This figure content is also featured on *West's American Government Videodisc* (see the index found in the *TRB*).

Multidiscipline Strategies

Consumer Education Ask the students to gather practical information about the FTC's cooling-off rule: If you have changed your mind about a contract or purchase from a door-to-door salesperson, what step should you take? If you have any problems, whom should you contact? How? Once the students have collected the appropriate information, have them select effective methods of spreading that information to consumers in their community. Let the students work in groups to prepare flyers, posters, public service announcements, or other communiqués.

Selected Independent Regulatory Agencies

Name	Date Formed	Principal Duties
Interstate Commerce Commission (ICC)	1887	Responsible for regulating interstate surface transportation via trucks, buses, trains, and inland waterways.
Federal Reserve System Board of Governors (Fed)	1913	Responsible for determining policy with respect to interest rates, credit availability, and the money supply.
Federal Trade Commission (FTC)	1914	Responsible for preventing businesses from engaging in unfair trade practices, for stopping the formation of monopolies in the business sector, and for protecting consumer rights.
Securities and Exchange Commission (SEC)	1934	Responsible for regulating the nation's stock exchanges, in which shares of stocks are bought and sold; requires full disclosure of the financial profiles of companies that wish to sell stocks and bonds to the public.
Federal Communications Commission (FCC)	1934	Responsible for regulating all communications by telegraph, cable, telephone, radio, and television.
National Labor Relations Board (NLRB)	1935	Responsible for protecting employees' rights to join unions and to bargain collectively with employers; attempts to prevent unfair labor practices by both employers and unions.
Equal Employment Opportunity Commission (EEOC)	1964	Responsible for working to eliminate discrimination that is based on religion, sex, race, national origin, or age; examines all claims of discrimination.
Environmental Protection Agency (EPA)	1970	Responsible for undertaking programs aimed at reducing air and water pollution; works with state and local agencies to help fight environmental hazards (has been suggested recently that status be elevated to a department).
Nuclear Regulatory Commission (NRC)	1974	Responsible for ensuring that electricity-generating nuclear reactors in the United States are built and operated safely; regularly inspects operations of such reactors.

▲ FIGURE 17–4 **Selected Independent Regulatory Agencies.** The table above lists the major independent regulatory agencies, the date each was formed, and the principal duties of each. Which branch of the federal government is responsible for administering these agencies?

TEACHING GOVERNMENT IN ACTION

Read

Let the students read the Case Study title, and ask them to define these terms: *regulation, deregulation,* and *reregulation.* How are the three related? After a brief discussion, have the students read the feature independently.

Discuss

Guide the students in discussing this Government in Action feature: Why do you think the focus of regulation has changed over the years? Is it reasonable to expect government agencies to provide a "better quality of life for all"? Why or why not? How would you define the term *over-regulation?* Do you believe deregulation actually brings benefits to all consumers? Why or why not? What happened within the savings and loan industry in the late 1980s? Who was held responsible? Why? Who do you think the critics of deregulation are? Why do you think they call for reregulation?

Analyze and Apply

Have the students form small groups in which to discuss the issues of deregulation and reregulation. Ask the group members to work together to write a persuasive essay or prepare a persuasive speech, favoring either deregulation or reregulation. Remind the students that their essays or speeches should present clear main ideas, supported by persuasive facts and details.

Review

Use questions such as these to help the students review the Government in Action feature: What is over-regulation? What is deregulation? What is reregulation?

Think About It (Answers)

1. Answers will vary, e.g., even though the number of passengers killed each year has increased since deregulation, the number of passengers killed per passenger mile flown has dropped dramatically, actually by more than 80 percent in the last 20 years. Therefore, airline safety is much greater today than it was prior to deregulation.

2. Answers will vary, e.g., often the consumer ends up paying for government regulation through higher product prices and reduced choice. This has to be the case in a competitive society because corporations must pass on their higher costs to consumers in order to survive.

GOVERNMENT IN ACTION

CASE STUDY

Deregulation and Re-regulation

Since the first independent regulatory agency (the Interstate Commerce Commission) was formed in 1887, the regulation of American business has increased almost every year. Indeed, business regulation has become a major function of the federal bureaucracy as well as of many state and local bureaucracies. In the beginning, most regulation was economic—regulating the prices that companies could charge. Then social regulation became increasingly important. Its aim has been a better quality of life for all through a less polluted environment, better working conditions, and safer and better products. For example, the Food and Drug Administration (FDA) helps protect the public against impure and unsafe foods, drugs, cosmetics, and other potentially hazardous products. The Consumer Product Safety Commission (CPSC) has created minimum standards for the safety of consumer products.

In the 1970s, the mood of the country and of decision makers in Washington began to turn against what they called ''overregulation.'' In 1978 the Airline Deregulation Act was passed, which reduced route restrictions and decontrolled the prices for all passengers of domestic airlines. Two years later, an act was passed that phased out the regulation of interest rates that banks and savings-and-loans institutions could pay their depositors. In the same year the railroads were partially deregulated as was the trucking industry. In 1982, interstate transportation by bus was deregulated.

Those who support deregulation claim that its benefits have far outweighed its costs. The benefits have clearly been lower prices to most consumers who use trucking, airline, and long-distance telephone services. Small savers have been able to obtain higher yields on their savings accounts.

But deregulation also has its costs. In the airline industry, for example, business travelers taking short trips on less heavily traveled routes are paying more today than they did prior to airline deregulation. Also, the increased competition in the airline industry brought about by deregulation has forced numerous airlines to go out of business, as Eastern Airlines and Pan American did in 1991. The workers in those companies certainly lost out as did the people who invested in them. Additionally, deregulation and increased competition has left many small towns across the country without passenger air service. The deregulation of the savings-and-loan industry created huge problems, which caused a crisis in the 1980s that will end up costing American taxpayers $500 billion to repair.

Not surprisingly, critics of deregulation are now arguing for a change, which they call *re-regulation.* They want more regulations put back into the banking and airline industries, and into industry in general. The mood in Washington certainly has changed from the late 1970s and 1980s. Since the election of George Bush in 1988, both Congress and the president showed receptiveness to increasing the regulation of American businesses.

THINK ABOUT IT

1. Since the deregulation of airlines, there are more airline passengers killed each year than there were prior to deregulation. Nonetheless, airline officials claim that it is safer to fly now then ever before. How could they make such a claim? (Hint: What has happened to the number of passengers flying each year since deregulation?)
2. Who ends up ultimately paying the increased cost for improved product safety and quality brought about through government regulation? Why is this true?

Discussion Starter
Guide the students in discussing the Postal Service as a government corporation: What are the advantages—and disadvantages—of maintaining the service as a part of the government? What could be expected to happen if the Postal Service became a private corporation? Who would most likely benefit? Why? Who would probably suffer? Why?

Discussion Starter
Have the students study and discuss the chart, Major Government Corporations: What is the purpose of each corporation named here? Why do you think it is a government corporation—rather than an independent agency, for example? To whom do you think the work of each corporation is most important? Why?

Service Learning Activity

It is a myth that most bureaucrats live and work in the Washington, D.C. area. The truth is that only 12 percent of bureaucrats work in Washington, with the rest working in regional and field offices around the country fulfilling services. California alone has close to 4,000. With this in mind it will not be difficult for students to contact and talk to a federal employee. This will help students dispel the stereotype toward the lazy, incompetent federal worker. A *Washington Post* poll indicated that 71 percent of people who had dealings with the federal government were satisfied with the individual service they received. Students should ask the employees about how they got their position, what it is like to be a government versus private employee, how they feel about the Hatch Act, and other issues prepared in advance by the students.

contract or buy something from a door-to-door salesperson, you have three days in which to decide whether or not you like the deal. If you decide against the purchase, you must be refunded all your money.

Regulatory agencies are executive in that they provide for the enforcement of those rules. If, for example, a door-to-door sales company does not abide by the three-day cooling-off rule, the FTC can shut down its business.

Regulatory agencies are also judicial in that they decide disputes involving the rules that they have made. For example, many of the initial rules decided by the Department of Labor (DOL) in 1991 for application of the Americans with Disabilities Act of 1990 were disputed by businesses. These disputes will be handled by the DOL for many years. (And many will end up in federal court.)

Commission Members Members of the regulatory agencies are appointed by the president with the consent of the Senate. They do not, however, report to the president, which is why these agencies are called independent. By law, all members of a regulatory agency cannot be from the same political party.

Government Corporations

The newest form of federal bureaucracy is the **government corporation**, a business that is owned by the government. Government corporations are not exactly like corporations in which you buy stock, become a shareholder, and collect dividends. The U.S. Postal Service is a government corporation, but it sells no shares. If a government corporation loses money in the course of doing business, it is not shareholders but taxpayers who foot the bill.

Government corporations are like private corporations in that they provide a service that could be handled by the private sector. They are also like private corporations in that they charge for their services, though sometimes they charge less than what a consumer would pay through a private-sector corporation.

Look at some of the major government corporations in Figure 17–5 on the next page.

Although government corporations are independent, they are all attached to some executive department and are therefore subject to the control of the secretary of that department. For example, the Commodity Credit Corporation (CCC)—a lending bank for farmers—is

Reteaching Strategies
1. Let the students work with partners to review and revise their outlines of Section 3.
2. Work with small groups of students, helping them discuss the distinctions between independent executive agencies, independent regulatory agencies, and government corporations.

Evaluation Strategies
1. Have the students write their answers to the Section 3 Review questions.
2. Have the students take the Section 3 Quiz found in the *TRB.*

Section 3 Review (Answers)
1. Answers will vary, e.g., the CIA gathers and analyzes political and military information about foreign countries. The Small Business Administration protects the interests of small manufacturers and other small businesses.
2. They are formed to create and implement rules that regulate private activity and protect public interest in particular sectors of the economy. They are administered independently of the executive, judicial, and legislative branches.
3. A business that is owned and operated by the government.
4. Answers will vary, e.g., the government corporation would be more concerned with making a profit and would perhaps be more efficient. Alternatively, there will be little if any difference because a government corporation does not have to make a profit and has no shareholders. Indeed, the U.S. Postal Service has operated at a loss for many years.

Selected Government Corporations

Name	Date Formed	Principal Duties
Tennessee Valley Authority (TVA)	1933	Operates a Tennessee River control system and generates power for a seven-state region and for U.S. aeronautics and space programs; promotes the economic development of the Tennessee Valley region; controls floods and promotes the navigability of the Tennessee River.
Federal Deposit Insurance Corporation (FDIC)	1933	Insures individuals' bank deposits up to $100,000; oversees the business activities of banks.
Commodity Credit Corporation (CCC)	1933	Attempts to stabilize farm prices and protect farmers' incomes by purchasing designated farm products at prices above what they would get in the marketplace.
Export/Import Bank of the United States (Ex/Im Bank)	1933	Promotes American-made goods abroad; grants loans to foreign purchasers of American products.
National Railway Passenger Corporation (AMTRAK)	1970	Provides an integrated balanced national and intercity rail passenger service network; controls 23,000 miles of track with 505 stations.
U.S. Postal Service (formed from the Postmaster General of the Treasury Department [1789])	1971	Delivers mail throughout the United States and its territories; is the largest government corporation, with almost 800,000 employees.

▲ **FIGURE 17–5 Selected Government Corporations.** This table lists some of the major government corporations, the date each was formed, and the principal duties of each corporation. Four of these corporations were formed in 1933. What do you know about the year 1933 that helps to explain this fact?

This figure content is also featured on *West's American Government Videodisc* (see the index found in the *TRB*).

Figure Answer Students should understand that the country was in the middle of the Great Depression in 1933, and that these corporations were all formed as a part of Franklin Delano Roosevelt's New Deal policies, designed to alleviate some of the effects of the depression.

located within the Department of Agriculture. The secretary of agriculture chairs its seven-member board. It is as if the CCC were a **line organization** in the U.S. Department of Agriculture.

A line organization is one whose head has direct responsibility for all of the actions of the employees within that particular group. Moreover, there is someone above the head of that group who has definite authority over its head. All line organizations are characterized by the fact that the management at one level has authority over employees at the next lower level; thus the line of authority between supervisor and subordinate is well defined.

SECTION 3 REVIEW

1. Briefly describe two independent executive agencies and their functions.
2. Why were independent regulatory agencies created? What powers do they have?
3. What are government corporations?
4. **For critical analysis:** If an independent executive agency is changed into a government corporation, as occurred in 1971, when the U.S. Post Office was transformed into the U.S. Postal Service, what difference, if any, will there be in the way the service will operate?

SECTION 4

Points to Stress

- The manner in which civil service has changed from our early history.
- Ways that Congress has attempted to reform the civil service.
- Civil service reforms enacted by President Carter.

Kickoff Activity

Ask the students to list at least eight words and phrases that express their ideas about and their reactions to the term *civil service.* When all the students have completed their lists, encourage them to share and discuss their ideas.

Working with the Preview Questions

Give the students an opportunity to read these study questions and discuss their current responses. Then remind the students to keep the study questions in mind, looking for more complete answers, as they read Section 4.

Teaching Strategies

Introduction

Let the students read the section introduction independently, and then ask about *Policy and Supporting Position:* Who would want a copy of this book? Why? Do you think that you might want to read and use this book? Why or why not?

Vocabulary

Have volunteers define the term *natural aristocracy:* Who probably considered Jeffersonian Republicans members of a natural aristocracy? Why? Who might have disagreed with this perception? Why?

Discussion Starter

Ask the students to consider the importance of keeping administrators on, regardless of presidential changes: What advantages does this consistency provide? What would happen if every president started with an entirely new group of bureaucrats?

Vocabulary

Let several students define the terms *spoils* and *spoils system.*

Vocabulary

Ask volunteers to explain the word *stalwart.*

SECTION 4

How the Civil Service Works

Preview Questions

- How has the civil service changed from our early history?
- In what ways has Congress attempted to reform the civil service?
- What were the reforms of the civil service enacted by President Carter?

Every bureaucratic institution has two groups: political appointees and civil servants. It is usually the president who makes political appointments to most of the top jobs in the federal bureaucracy. These jobs are considered "political plums." Descriptions of 2,800 of these positions can be found in a book called *Policy and Supporting Positions,* also known as the "plum book," published by the U.S. Government Printing Office in Washington, D.C. The remaining three million individuals who work for the federal government belong to the **civil service**, meaning that they are not appointed, but go through a formal application process.

A Short History of the Federal Civil Service

When the federal government was formed in 1789, it had no career public servants, but rather consisted of nonprofessional bureaucrats who were almost all Federalists. When Jefferson took over as president, he found that few in his Democratic-Republican party were holding federal administrative jobs, so he fired more than one hundred officials and replaced them with members of the so-called **natural aristocracy**—that is, with his own Jeffersonians (which became today's Democrats). For the next twenty-five years, a growing body of federal administrators gained experience and expertise, becoming in the process professional public servants. These administrators stayed in office regardless of who was elected president. The bureaucracy had become a self-maintaining, long-lived element within government.

To the Victor Belongs the Spoils When Andrew Jackson took over the White House in 1828, he could not believe how many appointed officials (appointed before he took office, that is) were overtly hostile toward him and his Democratic party. The bureaucracy—indeed an aristocracy—considered itself the only group fit to rule. But Jackson was a man of the people, and his policies were populist in nature. Because the bureaucracy was reluctant to carry out his programs, Jackson did the obvious: He fired more federal officials than any other president before him. The **spoils system**—an application of the principle that to the victor belongs the spoils—reigned. In the new Jackson administration, the Northeastern aristocrats were out and the common folks were in.

In addition to putting his own people on the federal payroll, Jackson decided to reorganize the bureaucracy in order to ensure that his policies were carried out. During his eight years in office, almost every department and bureau was restructured.

The Civil Service Reform Act of 1883 Jackson's spoils system survived for a number of years, but over time it became increasingly corrupt. In addition, the size of the bureaucracy increased by 300 percent between 1851 and 1881. Reformers began to examine the professional civil service that was established in several European countries, which operated under a **merit system** in which job appointments were based on competitive examinations. The cry for civil service reform began to be heard more loudly.

The ruling Republican Party was divided in its attitude toward reform. A faction of the party, called the "stalwarts," opposed reform of any sort. When Charles J. Guiteau was denied a bureaucratic position and assassinated President James A. Garfield, a moderate reformer, in 1881, he was heard to shout "I am a stalwart, and Arthur is president now!" After Garfield's assassination Chester A. Arthur, a stalwart vice president, became president. Ironically, it was under the stalwart Arthur administration that civil service reform actually occurred, partly as a result of public outrage over Garfield's assassination. The movement to replace the spoils system with a permanent career civil service found the cause that would carry it to victory.

Finally, in 1883, the Pendleton Act (also known as the Civil Service Reform Act) was passed, which brought to an end the period of Jacksonian spoils. The act established the principle of employment on the basis of open competitive examinations and created the Civil Service Commission to administer the personnel service. Only 10 percent of federal employees, however, were covered by the merit system. Later laws, amendments, and executive orders increased the coverage to more than 90 percent of the federal civil service.

Enrichment
Assign one of the students to research and report on the assassination of Garfield: Where, when, and how did the assassination take place? What were the reactions to it? What were its most important effects? What were Garfield's most important accomplishments? To what extent did Arthur follow through on Garfield's programs?

Enrichment
Ask a small group of volunteers to research the agencies created as part of Roosevelt's New Deal: What were the titles of these agencies? What were their functions? How effective were they? What happened to each new agency? Have the volunteers present their findings in a chart or other visual display.

Discussion Starter
Encourage the students to discuss the fact that civil service employees are prohibited from taking part in the management of campaigns: What purpose does this prohibition serve? Whom is it intended to protect? Do those groups need protection? Why or why not? Do you think this prohibition infringes on the rights of civil service employees? Why or why not?

Enrichment
Encourage volunteers to research and report on this division of the Civil Service Commission into the OPM and the MSPB: What was the purpose of dividing the commission? How effective does the division appear to have been? Why? What other reforms—if any—have been suggested?

Caption Answer The Civil Service Reform Act was passed in 1883. Ironically, this was done during the presidency of stalwart Chester A. Arthur, who became president with the death of Garfield.

▲ The art above depicts the assassination of President Garfield, who was shot by Charles J. Guiteau in 1881. Guiteau was angry after being denied a civil service position under Garfield. When was the United States' system of civil service reformed?

The Hatch Act of 1939 In principle, a civil servant is politically neutral. But in reality civil servants know that politicians are the ones who appropriate funds and determine the growth of their agencies. In 1933, when Franklin D. Roosevelt established the New Deal, a virtual army of civil servants was hired to staff the numerous new agencies that were created to cope with the problems of the Great Depression. Because the Democratic Party provided jobs for these individuals, it seemed natural for them to campaign for Democratic party candidates. The Democrats controlling Congress in the mid-1930s did not object to this campaigning. But in 1938 a coalition of conservative Democrats and Republicans took control of the Congress and forced the Hatch Act of 1939 (also known as the Political Activities Act) into law.

The main provision of this act is that civil service employees cannot take an active part in the political management of campaigns. The act also prohibits the use of federal authority to influence nominations and elections, and outlaws the use of bureaucratic rank to pressure federal employees to make political contributions.

More Current Reforms of Civil Service

The Civil Service Commission worked well, according to those who observed the bureaucracy. But a persistent group of reformers felt that the commission had taken on too many tasks. President Jimmy Carter, a particularly concerned critic, worked out a series of reforms that were adopted by Congress on October 13, 1978. One of the reforms was to split the Civil Service Commission into the Office of Personnel Management (OPM) and the Merit Systems Protection Board (MSPB).

Extension
Ask the students to learn more about the competitive exams given for civil service jobs: How does one prepare for these exams? When and where are the exams given? How does one apply to take the exam? What other steps must be completed first? Then give the students an opportunity to share and discuss what they have learned.

Section 4 Review (Answers)
1. The spoils system became more and more corrupt.
2. Civil service employees cannot take an active part in the political management of campaigns. It also prohibits use of federal authority to influence nominations and elections.
3. One reform split the Civil Service Commission into the Office of Personnel Management and the Merit Systems Protection Board. The OPM hires most federal employees and the goal of the MSPB is to protect the integrity of the federal merit system.
4. Answers will vary, e.g., many bureaucrats who remain in office have set goals and agendas that may not coincide with the new president's; the president will have a difficult time changing these goals and agendas. These bureaucrats also have power derived from long relationships with important members of Congress.

SECTION 5

Points to Stress
- Techniques used by departments and agencies to gain support from Congress.
- Definition of iron triangle.
- Steps taken in recent years to reform the bureaucracy.

Figure Answer Within the civil service, each individual hired is assigned a GS rating.

Enrichment
Have several students research the particular kinds of jobs represented by each GS rating. Ask these volunteers to present the results of their research in a chart or a bulletin board display.

Discussion Starter
Help the students discuss their responses to the salaries offered for civil service jobs: How do they compare to earnings offered in private sector jobs? What benefits are associated with civil service jobs that are often not provided by private companies?

Reteaching Strategies
1. Ask the students to write up a chronological list, with dates, of the major events in the development of the modern civil service.
2. Let the students work in groups to discuss the merit system. Have the members of each group work together to list the advantages of this system.

Evaluation Strategies
1. Have the students write their answers to the Section 4 Review questions.
2. Have the students take the Section 4 Quiz found in the *TRB.*

General Schedule (GS) Ratings and Their Respective Minimum Salaries, 1992

Rating	1992 Salary
GS-1	$ 9,619
GS-2	10,816
GS-3	11,802
GS-4	13,248
GS-5	14,822
GS-6	16,521
GS-7	18,358
GS-8	20,333
GS-9	22,458
GS-10	24,732
GS-11	27,172
GS-12	32,567
GS-13	38,727
GS-14	45,763
GS-15	53,830
GS-16	63,135

Source: *Current Salary Schedules of Federal Officers and Employees* (U.S. Government Printing Office: Washington, D.C., 1992).

FIGURE 17–6 General Schedule (GS) Ratings and Their Respective Minimum Salaries, 1992. This table shows each of the GS ratings and their respective minimum salaries for the year 1992. Which civil service employees are assigned GS ratings?

The Office of Personnel Management (OPM) The OPM is in charge of hiring most of the employees of federal agencies. Members of the OPM are appointed by the president and confirmed by the Senate. Among the OPM's elaborate rules for hiring, promoting, and firing is one that requires potential employees to take competitive examinations for most civil service jobs. If an applicant passes the examination, she or he is sent to an agency that has a job opening that requires skills that fit the applicant's own. For each federal agency job that is open, the OPM sends three names to the agency for consideration (this is called the "rule of three"). In general, the agency has to hire someone on the list.

Within the civil service, each individual hired is assigned a general schedule or GS rating. As the table in Figure 17–6 shows, in 1992 the salary range extended from modest to relatively high-paying status.

The Merit Systems Protection Board (MSPB) The MSPB was created as an independent agency with an independent staff. Its goal is to protect the integrity of the federal merit system, which it accomplishes by undertaking studies of the merit system, and by hearing charges of wrongdoing and appeals of adverse agency actions against civil servants. The MSPB can order corrective and disciplinary action against executive agencies, and in rare cases against employees. The MSPB also has an independent legal staff, which investigates illegal personnel practices and can prosecute officials who violate civil service rules and regulations.

Kickoff Activity
Instruct the students to read the section title; then have them write short paragraphs explaining the kinds of policies they think bureaucrats make. After all the students have written their paragraphs, ask several volunteers to share their ideas with the rest of the class.

Working with the Preview Questions
Have the students work together to use these study questions in developing an outline format. Then assign all the students to fill in their own copies of the class outline, taking complete notes on Section 5.

Teaching Strategies

Introduction
Let a volunteer read the section introduction aloud. Then encourage the students to discuss their responses to these questions: How would you define *neutral competency?* Do you consider it a meaningful goal? An achievable goal? Why or why not?

Discussion Starter
Guide the students in discussing the fact that federal bureaucrats are prohibited from directly lobbying Congress: Do you consider this a reasonable restriction? Why or why not? What purpose is it intended to serve? How significant do you consider that purpose? Why is this restriction so hard to follow? So hard to enforce?

Critical Thinking Skills
Ask the students to analyze the activities of Pentagon bureaucrats in presenting the specialized spy planes to members of Congress and their staff members: Are the bureaucrats' activities an example of lobbying? Why or why not? If these activities should not be considered lobbying, what should they be considered?

Vocabulary
Let volunteers share their responses to these questions: Why do you think the term *iron triangle* has been used to describe this alliance? What does this imply about the relations among legislators, bureaucrats, and interest groups?

SECTION 4 REVIEW

1. What events led to the Civil Service Reform Act of 1883?
2. What are the main provisions of the Hatch Act of 1939?
3. What changes did President Carter make in the civil service?
4. **For critical analysis:** Out of the three million federal government jobs, a new president can only appoint fewer than three thousand individuals. Does this mean that the president can be held "hostage" to an established government bureaucracy whose goals may differ from the president's? Explain.

SECTION 5

Bureaucrats as Policymakers

Preview Questions

- How do departments and agencies act as politicians?
- What is the iron triangle?
- What steps have been taken in recent years to reform the bureaucracy?

Federal bureaucrats are expected to exhibit **neutral competency**, which means that they are supposed to apply their technical skills to their jobs without regard to political issues. They should not be swayed by the thought of personal or political gain. For example, a bureaucrat in the Department of Defense is not supposed to look the other way if she sees a company doing shoddy work on building a fighter jet. Even if this bureaucrat is hoping that the same company might offer her a job after she retires, she is supposed to apply her skills to solve the problem without letting that hope interfere.

In reality, each independent agency and each executive department is interested in its own survival and expansion. Each is constantly battling the others for a larger share of the budget. All agencies and departments wish to retain or expand their functions and staff; in order to do this, they must gain the goodwill of the White House and of Congress.

How Bureaucrats Act as Politicians

Bureaucratic agencies of the federal government are prohibited from directly lobbying Congress. Departments and agencies, nonetheless, have developed techniques to help them gain congressional support. Each organization maintains a congressional information office, which specializes in helping members of Congress by supplying any requested information and solving casework problems. For example, if a member of the House of Representatives gets a complaint from a constituent that her Social Security checks are not arriving on time, that member of Congress may go to the Social Security Administration within the Department of Health and Human Services and ask that something be done. Typically, requests from members of Congress are acted upon quickly.

The Department of Defense is an example of an organization that has earned a reputation for being able to create publicity for itself to win support from Congress on many occasions. When President Ronald Reagan wanted Congress to approve the sale of specialized spy planes to Saudi Arabia, the Department of Defense arranged for such a plane to be stationed near Washington, and invited members of Congress as well as staff members to take guided tours that explained the plane's complex technology. In this way, both the Defense Department and President Reagan got what they wanted from Congress.

Bureaucrats as Policymakers—The Iron Triangle

Analysts have determined that one way to understand the bureaucracy's role in policymaking is to examine something called the **iron triangle**, which is defined as the three-way alliance among legislators (members of Congress), bureaucrats, and interest groups. Presumably, the laws that are passed and the policies that are established benefit the interests of all three sides of the iron triangle.

Consider the bureaucracy within the Department of Agriculture. It consists of 127,500 individuals working directly for the federal government and thousands of other individuals who work indirectly for the department as contractors, subcontractors, or consultants. Now consider that there are various interest groups or client groups that are concerned with what the federal government does for farmers. Some of these are the American Farm Bureau Federation, the National Cattleman's Association, the National Milk Producers Association, the Corn Growers Association, and the Citrus Growers Association. Finally, take a close look at Congress and you will see that there are two major committees concerned with agriculture in the House and in the Senate: the House

Vocabulary

Let volunteers explain the term *whistle-blower* and suggest several examples.

Discussion Starter

Help the students consider the whistle-blowing action undertaken by Fitzgerald: How do you imagine he decided to undertake such an action? What risks did he assume? What benefits might he have hoped to gain? If you had been in his position, do you think you would have acted in the same way? Why or why not?

Discussion Starter

Help the students consider the reactions of Spanton's boss: Why do you think he tried to get Spanton fired? What do his actions imply about his own attitudes and actions?

Discussion Starter

Encourage the students to share their reactions to the fact that 35 percent of all calls to federal agencies' hot lines are followed up: Does this figure seem high or low to you? How do you think agencies account for the figure?

Critical Thinking Skills

Guide the students in evaluating the advantages and disadvantages of "blowing the whistle" within the federal bureaucracy: What problems can a whistle blower expect to face? What other disadvantages might a whistle blower have to deal with? What personal benefits can a whistle blower expect? Under what conditions do you imagine the benefits outweigh the risks? Why?

Reteaching Strategies

1. Let the students work with partners to review and, if necessary, revise their outlines of Section 5.
2. Have the students write short paragraphs explaining these two terms: *neutral competency* and *iron triangle*.

Evaluation Strategies

1. Have the students write their answers to the Section 5 Review questions.
2. Have the students take the Section 5 Quiz found in the *TRB.*

Section 5 Review (Answers)

1. Each department maintains a congressional information office that specializes in helping members of Congress by supplying information and solving casework.
2. They are allied for mutual benefit.
3. Congress includes protection for whistle-blowers in the 1978 Civil Service Reform Act.
4. Answers will vary, e.g., prohibiting individuals from lobbying would interfere with their constitutional rights.

TEACHING CHALLENGE TO THE AMERICAN DREAM

Read

Begin by asking the students to read and respond to the title of the Challenge to the American Dream feature: Why is the issue covered here important? To whom should it be important? Who should assume

Committee on Agriculture and the Senate Committee on Agriculture, Nutrition, and Forestry, each of which has seven subcommittees. This triangle is an alliance of mutual benefit. The workings of the iron triangle are complicated but well established in almost every part of the bureaucracy.

The secretary of agriculture is nominated by the president (and confirmed by the Senate) and is head of the Department of Agriculture. But that secretary cannot even buy a desk lamp if Congress does not approve the appropriations for the department's budget. Within Congress, the responsibility for considering the Department of Agriculture's request for funding belongs first to the House and Senate appropriations committees and then to the agriculture subcommittees under them. The members of those committees, most of whom represent agricultural states, have been around a long time and have their own ideas about what is appropriate for the Agriculture Department's budget. They carefully scrutinize the ideas of the president and the secretary of agriculture.

Finally, the various interest groups—including producers of farm chemicals and farm machinery, agricultural cooperatives, grain dealers, and exporters—have vested interests in whatever the Department of Agriculture does and in whatever Congress lets the Department of Agriculture do. Those interests are well represented by the lobbyists who crowd the halls of Congress. Many lobbyists have been working for agricultural interest groups for decades. They know the congressional committee members and Agriculture Department staff extremely well and routinely meet with them.

Helping Out the Whistle-Blowers

The term **whistle-blower**, as applied to the federal bureaucracy, has a special meaning: it is someone who blows the whistle, or reports, on gross governmental inefficiency or illegal action. One of the most famous whistle-blowers is A. Ernest Fitzgerald, who worked for the Defense Department as a cost analyst. In 1968 Fitzgerald went before a congressional committee and stated that the Lockheed C-5A transport plane had cost more than Congress had appropriated for it. He also pointed out that the plane was not worth the money. Upon close scrutiny, his accusations proved to be accurate, but Mr. Fitzgerald was fired from his job. A court ordered the Defense Department to give him back his job, and a later decision awarded him $350,000 in back pay and damages.

In 1982 another whistle-blower, George Spanton, working as a $50,000-a-year Pentagon auditor, accused Pratt-Whitney Aircraft of overcharging the federal government $150 million. His reward for whistle-blowing was a bitter struggle with his own superiors at the Pentagon's Defense Contract Audit Agency. Spanton's boss tried to get him transferred to another job within the agency, but Spanton filed an appeal with the Merit Systems Protection Board, charging that the transfer was in retaliation for his "candid audits." The special counsel to the board supported Spanton and even filed disciplinary charges against Spanton's superiors.

Congress included some protection for whistle-blowers in the 1978 Civil Service Reform Act. Specifically, that act prohibits reprisals against whistle-blowers by their superiors, and it set up the Merit Systems Protection Board as part of this protection. There is little evidence, however, that potential whistle-blowers have truly received much improved protection. An attempt by Congress to increase that protection was vetoed by President Reagan in 1988.

Many federal agencies also have toll-free hotlines that employees can use to anonymously report bureaucratic waste and inappropriate behavior. About 35 percent of all calls are followed up on, and some have resulted in dramatic savings for the government. The General Accounting Office hotline alone generates millions of dollars of savings every year.

Government whistle-blowers are helping to change the situation summed up in the quote from President Reagan that appeared at the beginning of this chapter. As you have learned, the bureaucracy is an important and complex part of our government. Within our bureaucracy are executive departments, independent agencies, and government corporations, each relying on the work of both political appointees and civil servants. It is these individuals, who run our national parks, deliver our mail, and protect our food supply, that make up the bureaucracy and provide many of our nation's vital services.

SECTION 5 REVIEW

1. How do bureaucrats act as politicians?
2. How do the three sides of the iron triangle relate to each other?
3. What recent attempts have been made to reform the bureaucracy?
4. **For critical analysis:** The effectiveness of the iron triangle could presumably be reduced if interest groups were not allowed to lobby in Congress. What problems would this proposed reform pose?

responsibility for involving more minorities and women in public service? After the introductory discussion, ask several students to participate in reading the feature aloud.

Discuss
Guide the students in discussing this feature: What do you think of Jackson's idea about the federal bureaucracy? Is his idea still relevant today? Why or why not? Why should we expect that 51 percent of public servants would be women and 12 percent of public servants would be African Americans? Do you believe that women have a better chance of rising to executive positions in the private sector than in the federal bureaucracy? Why or why not? Do you believe the same is true for African Americans and Hispanics? Why or why not? Do you believe that reverse discrimination exists? Why or why not? Why do you imagine Bush (in spite of his campaign promises) has done so little to improve the status of women and minorities with the federal bureaucracy? What might motivate a president to make such changes?

Analyze and Apply
Have the students work in groups to investigate various state and local bureaucracies: How closely do the numbers of women, African Americans, and Hispanics at various levels of the bureaucracy represent the percentage of those groups within the population? Let each group share its results with the rest of the class, and encourage the students to discuss the implications of their findings.

Review
Ask questions such as these to help the students review the Challenge to the American Dream feature: At which levels of the federal bureaucracy are women and African Americans most likely to hold jobs? During which recent decade did women and minorities make the most gains?

You Decide (Answers)
1. Answers will vary, e.g., the make-up of the federal bureaucracy should represent a higher-than-average level of education.
2. Answers will vary, e.g., professional competence through testing and evaluation of performance should come before ethnic, racial, and age factors. The most qualified and competent should be hired if we want the government run as competently and efficiently as possible.

Chapter Evaluation
To evaluate student mastery of chapter material, you might:
1. Use Chapter Test A from the *TRB*.
2. Use Chapter Test B from the *TRB*.
3. Construct your own test using items from the *West American Government Test Bank* found in the *TRB*.
4. Use the accompanying computerized test software to construct and print a customized chapter test.

CHALLENGE TO THE AMERICAN DREAM

Minorities and Women in Civil Service

Americans expect the federal bureaucracy to be open and responsive to all people. That means that not just the most well-educated individuals as well as the well-connected should be chosen for public service jobs. Andrew Jackson recognized this when he installed a large number of "common folk" in bureaucratic positions. His idea was that the federal bureaucracy would be more responsive if more people who were in office resembled those whom they were supposed to help.

If we apply the idea that the civil service workforce should be representative of today's American population, we should expect 51 percent of all civil servants to be women and 12 percent to be African Americans. The actual federal bureaucracy today however, does not reflect the diversity of the American population. Women, for example, account for less than 10 percent of the top-level jobs in the federal government. Most women work in the lowest ranks of civil service jobs, doing mostly service and clerical work. The situation of African Americans is not much better. In the lowest four grades of the federal civil service almost 30 percent are held by African Americans. At the executive level, this percentage drops to less than 4 percent. Hispanics have faired even worse, accounting for only 2 percent of the top-level jobs.

The main gains by women and minorities in the federal bureaucracy, which occurred during the 1970s, started to slow down or even disappear in the 1980s and early 1990s. White males have started to resort to the courts to fight against what they see as reverse discrimination in the federal government. Reverse discrimination purportedly occurs when white males are discriminated against in favor of females and minorities.

The Reagan and Bush administrations appointed fewer African Americans than the previous three administrations. While President George Bush promised to appoint more minorities and women to civil service positions, he did not significantly change the overall status of women and minorities within the federal bureaucracy.

The challenge to the American dream is for the federal bureaucracy to be more reflective of the gender and cultural diversity of American society. Without adequate representation of all groups in America, the federal bureaucracy might never truly reflect the will of the people.

You Decide

1. Should the makeup of the federal bureaucracy represent the educational level of the general population of the United States? Why or why not?
2. Should federal agencies that deal with specific minorities, such as the Bureau of Indian Affairs, be staffed by members of those minorities?

CHAPTER 17 REVIEW

Key Terms

Review Questions (Answers)

1. The system of administrative agencies of the executive branch of government.
2. As Americans have demanded more services over the years, and Congress has responded with new and expanded government programs, the federal bureaucracy has grown.
3. Answers will vary, e.g., the Departments of State, Treasury, and Defense.
4. The Departments of State, Defense, Justice, and Treasury.
5. Because of the sensitive nature of their functions and to protect them from partisan politics.
6. Independent regulatory agencies are responsible for a specific type of public policy and they are administered independently of the executive, judicial, and legislative branches.
7. A government corporation is a business owned by the government.
8. It established the principle of employment on the basis of open competitive examinations and created the Civil Service Commission to administer the personnel service.
9. The Hatch Act prohibited civil service employees from taking an active part in the political management of campaigns.
10. The OPM is in charge of hiring most federal employees. The MSPB was created to protect the integrity of the federal merit system and hear charges of wrong-doing and appeals of adverse agency actions against civil servants.
11. Bureaucrats gain congressional support through information offices set up to provide information to members of Congress. They also help shape public policy through a three-way alliance known as the iron triangle.
12. Legislators, bureaucrats, and the interest groups that those bureaucrats influence form an alliance for mutual benefit.

CHAPTER 17 REVIEW—Continued

Summary

1. A bureaucracy is an organization that is structured in a pyramid-like fashion. The federal bureaucracy is headed by the president. The government at all levels spends more than 40 percent of the nation's annual income.

2. The fourteen executive departments, called line organizations, are the major service organizations of the federal government and are directly accountable to the president. Each department was created by Congress as the need arose and each manages a specific policy area. The head of each department is known as the secretary, except for the head of the Department of Justice, who is known as the attorney general. Each department head is appointed by the president and must be confirmed by the Senate. The so-called ''inner'' departments—State, Defense, Justice, and Treasury—exist primarily to serve the president.

3. Independent executive agencies report directly to the president. They have a single function and were created to be independent because of the sensitive nature of their functions or to protect them from partisan politics. Independent regulatory agencies are responsible for a specific type of public policy. They implement rules to protect the public interest in their particular sector. A government corporation is a business that is owned by the government. The United States Postal Service is an example of a government corporation.

4. Most federal workers belong to the civil service. In our nation's early history, federal workers were appointed on the basis of the president's political party preferences. But because of inefficiency and corruption, many Americans called for reform. In 1883, the Civil Service Reform Act was passed, which created the Civil Service Commission and established the principle of federal employment on the basis of open competitive examinations. In 1978, the Civil Service Commission was divided into the Office of Personnel Management, in charge of hiring federal employees, and the Merit Systems Protection Board, to protect the integrity of the federal merit system.

5. Even though bureaucratic agencies are prohibited from lobbying Congress, they have developed techniques to help them gain congressional support. The so-called iron triangle is a three-way alliance among legislators, bureaucrats, and the interest groups that those bureaucrats influence. Presumably, each group helps satisfy the other groups' needs and in turn receives what it needs. An important reform in the last few years involves more protection for so-called whistle-blowers.

Review Questions

1. What is the federal bureaucracy?
2. Describe the way the federal bureaucracy has grown.
3. Name three executive agencies.
4. Which departments make up the ''inner'' departments?
5. Identify two reasons Congress has set up independent agencies.
6. What are independent regulatory agencies responsible for and how are they administered?
7. What is a government corporation?
8. How did the Pendleton Act change the way federal employees are chosen?
9. What rule did the Hatch Act establish?
10. What is the main function of the Office of Personnel Management and of the Merit Systems Protection Board?
11. How does the federal bureaucracy help to shape public policy?
12. How does the iron triangle work?
13. What does the Freedom of Information Act allow citizens to do?
14. Is the federal bureaucracy representative of the population in terms of race and gender? Why or why not?

Questions for Thought and Discussion

1. The bureaucracy has often been called the ''fourth branch of government.'' Do you agree with this assessment? Why or why not?
2. What steps, if any, do you think should be taken to make the bureaucracy more open, efficient, and responsive?
3. Many administrations have sought to reduce the confusion, size, and complexity of the federal bureau-

13. It allows people to obtain information from federal government agencies provided the information is not classified or concerned with sensitive issues.
14. The federal bureaucracy does not represent the population in terms of race and gender because women and minorities are underrepresented at the top levels of management.

Questions for Thought and Discussion (Answers)
1. Answers will vary, e.g., the bureaucracy serves as a fourth branch of government because of the influence it exerts on public policy.
2. Answers will vary, e.g., there should be more incentives for bureaucrats to excel and more protection and encouragement for whistle-blowers. There should be less job security for bureaucrats.
3. Answers will vary, e.g., once established, agencies are difficult to get rid of. They have developed friends in Congress and supporters in powerful interest groups. They have created a need for the agency even if there wasn't one to begin with.
4. Answers will vary, e.g., the cap on salaries could be removed and the opportunities for advancement increased.
5. Answers will vary, e.g., the Secretary of Defense should be held ultimately responsible.

Social Studies Skills (Answers)
1. No, only selected agencies.
2. No, it is not. It is an independent agency, but part of the executive branch.
3. No, the 14 executive departments are of equal importance in the organization chart.

CHAPTER 17 REVIEW—Continued

cracy. Why do you think their attempts have generally not succeeded?
4. How might the federal government make civil service a more appealing career to you and your friends?
5. You may have heard news stories of $5,000 screwdrivers and $500 nails being purchased by the Department of Defense. Who do you think is responsible for such waste and inefficiency?

Improving Your Skills

Communication Skills

Giving an Oral Report

Oral reports are a way of sharing information with your classmates. If you are well prepared and know the information, you will most likely feel more confident, because you will know what you are presenting.

Begin with a written report that you have researched and created according to earlier exercises in this text. Having researched the topic yourself, you will be prepared to elaborate on the subject or answer questions that might come up. The more you have researched the topic, the more sure of yourself you will be. Follow these suggestions:

- Reread your written report several times. Review some of your most significant sources of information.
- Write an outline from your report that covers the most important points. Include examples and details you think are particularly important and illustrative.
- Transfer your outline to index cards, which you can use while giving your oral report. Use abbreviations that will help trigger your memory. Put some type of mark, a star, or check, for instance, in places at which you want to give examples or details.
- Practice delivering your oral report as often as you can to friends and family. Ask them for criticism and helpful tips. Practice maintaining eye contact with them, which will help make your speech more interesting. Also practice in front of the mirror so you can improve your presentation. Pay close attention to your tone of voice, how loud you are speaking, how fast you are speaking, and how convincing you sound.

Writing

Create a written report and then transform it into an oral report.

Social Studies Skills

Working with Organization Charts

Look at Figure 17–1 on page 404. Answer the following questions:

1. Does the chart show all of the federal agencies that exist today?
2. Is the U.S. Information Agency part of the judicial branch? If it is not, to what branch of government does it belong?
3. In this chart, does the fact that location of the Department of State is below that of the Department of Education mean that one has a higher ranking within the executive branch than the other?

Activities and Projects

1. Learn the details of the federal hiring process and find out how to apply for a federal job by contacting the federal job center in your state. Look under Federal Information Center in your telephone directory, or contact the Office of Public Affairs, OPM, 1900 E Street NW, Washington, DC 20415. You can also look up the OPM's regional office in your area in the *Government Annual* found in most libraries.
2. Do a research project on the Freedom of Information Act. How many of the over five hundred thousand requests received each year actually come from private citizens like yourself, as opposed to individuals making requests for businesses or attorneys?
3. Do a research project on either the U.S. Postal Service or AMTRAK. In particular, determine to what extent over the years those government corporations have been funded by the fees collected and to what extent they have been subsidized by American taxpayers.
4. Stage a class debate on the following statement: Resolved—The size of the federal bureaucracy shall be frozen at three million individuals.

Working with the Videodisc

The text below is from Professor Roger LeRoy Miller's introduction for the motion segment for Unit 6:

Alexander Hamilton, writing in *The Federalist Papers, No. 78,* maintained that the Supreme Court would be the "least dangerous branch of the federal government" because it had no enforcement powers nor could it raise money. The first Supreme Court chief justice, John Jay, resigned to become governor of New York because he thought the Court would never play an important role in American society. The next chief justice, Oliver Ellsworth, quit to become envoy to France.

Nonetheless, in 1803 something happened that was to change the role of the Supreme Court from that year ever after. It was the landmark case of *Marbury* v. *Madison,* decided by the Supreme Court under Chief Justice John Marshall. *Marbury* v. *Madison* resulted in the establishment of the Court's ability to wield the power of *judicial review.* As the Court said, "a law repugnant to the Constitution is void." The following reenactment of this famous case gives you a flavor of the issues and the players.

To access this segment, use the bar code below or the videodisc index found in the *TRB.*

Frame 11400

UNIT SIX

The Federal Judicial Branch

Unit Contents

CHAPTER INTRODUCTION

Instructional Objectives

By the end of the chapter students should be able to:

- Discuss the types of law in the United States and their origins.
- Describe the organization of the federal court system.
- Summarize the process by which cases reach the Supreme Court.
- Differentiate between judicial activism and judicial restraint.

Using the Keynote

Introduce this chapter by reading aloud the Keynote Quotation. Encourage the students to discuss the de Tocqueville quotation: How would you state de Tocqueville's idea in your own words? How do you respond to his statement? Do you agree or disagree? Why?

In addition, you may want to have the students recall who de Tocqueville was and what he wrote; or you might have volunteers read about de Tocqueville's life and accomplishment and report their findings to the rest of the class.

Introducing the Chapter

Ask a volunteer to read the Introduction aloud, and encourage the students to discuss it: How did Frazee's refusal of the job offer relate to his application for unemployment benefits? What are the usual requirements for receiving such benefits? How would you explain the decision of the Supreme Court in Frazee's case? How does this case demonstrate the truth of the de Tocqueville quotation?

Previewing the Sections

Section 1 Ask the students to page through Section 1, noting especially the main headings and the two special features: What do you expect to learn about in studying Section 1?
Section 2 Let volunteers look through Section 2 and read aloud the main headings and the figure titles. Then ask: What do you expect to learn about the organization of the federal court system?
Section 3 Instruct the students to glance through Section 3. Ask: What new concepts do you expect to understand after studying Section 3?
Section 4 Let the students look through Section 4. Then ask the students to list at least three questions they expect to have answered in Section 4.
Section 5 Have the students scan Section 5. Ask: How do the topics covered in Section 5 seem to relate to the information in previous sections of Chapter 18?

CHAPTER 18

The Federal Courts

CHAPTER OBJECTIVES

To learn and understand

- The law in the United States and its origins.
- The organization of the federal court system.
- The process by which cases reach the Supreme Court.
- The concepts of judicial activism and judicial restraint.

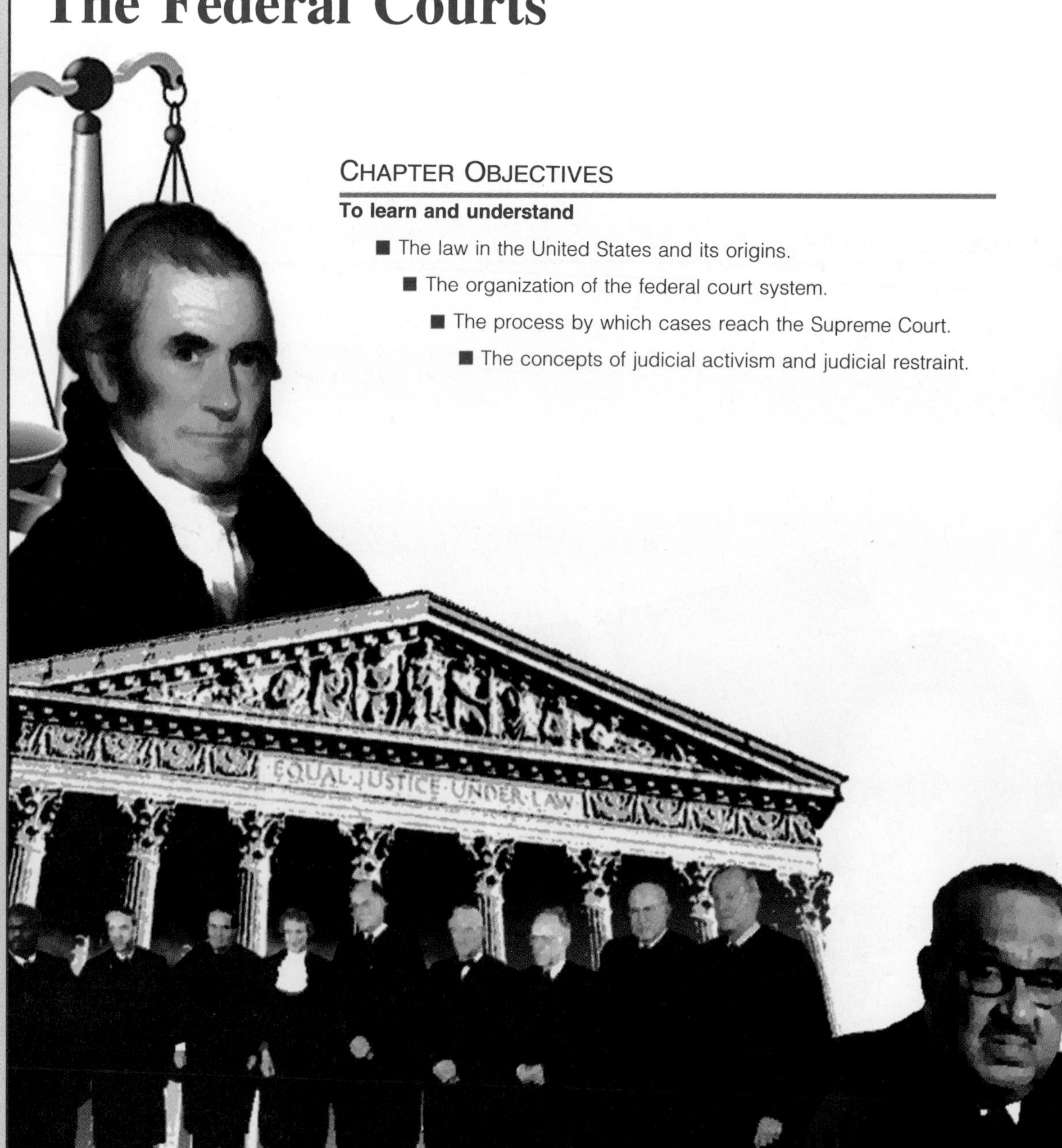

West's American Government Assignment Guide

Activity Sheets
Basic Concepts 18 *TRB* (Reteaching)
Enrichment Activity 18 *TRB*
Building Social Studies Skills 18 *TRB*

Quizzes
Chapter 18 Section 1 Quiz *TRB*
Chapter 18 Section 2 Quiz *TRB*
Chapter 18 Section 3 Quiz *TRB*
Chapter 18 Section 4 Quiz *TRB*
Chapter 18 Section 5 Quiz *TRB*

Tests
Chapter 18 Test A *TRB*
Chapter 18 Test B *TRB*
Chapter 18 Test Bank *TRB*
Chapter 18 WESTEST Computerized Testing

SECTION 1

Points to Stress
- The difference between common law and statutory law.
- Characteristics of constitutional law.
- Differences between civil and criminal law.
- The meaning of court jurisdiction.

Kickoff Activity
Let the students read the Section 1 title. Then give them five minutes in which to write their answers to this question: Where do you think our law comes from? At the end of the allotted time, encourage the students to compare and discuss their responses.

Working with the Preview Questions
Have volunteers read aloud the study questions here, and give the students an opportunity to discuss what they already know in response to each question. Then ask the students to take notes in response to these study questions as they read Section 1.

Teaching Strategies

Introduction
After the students have read the section introduction independently, encourage discussion by asking questions such as these: Who were the Normans? Why was their conquering England such an important occurrence? How do you think a system of settling disputes by local customs might function? How effective do you think it might be? What is the meaning of the word *common* in the term *common law?*

Comprehension
Ask several volunteers to give examples demonstrating their understanding of the term *case law.*

Keynote

"The peace, the prosperity, and the very existence of the Union are nestled in the hands of . . . federal judges. Without them the Constitution would be a dead letter."

—— **Alexis de Tocqueville**
(1805–1859) French Political Writer

INTRODUCTION

A few years ago, William Frazee, who was unemployed, applied to Kelly Services for temporary work. When Kelly Services offered him a temporary retail position that would require him to work on Sunday, however, Frazee refused the job. He told the temporary employment company that, as a Christian, he could not work on "the Lord's day." Then Frazee applied to the Illinois Department of Employment Security for unemployment benefits. He claimed that there was good cause for his refusal to work on Sunday. But the Illinois government denied his application. Frazee appealed his case by maintaining that the denial of unemployment benefits violated his First Amendment right to the free practice of his religion. His case eventually went to several different courts in Illinois and finally reached the Supreme Court of the United States. In *Frazee* v. *Illinois Department of Employment Security* (1989) the court declared that, indeed, by denying Frazee unemployment benefits, the state of Illinois had violated the freedom of religion clause of the First Amendment.

For Mr. Frazee and countless other Americans, French political commentator Alexis de Tocqueville's opening quote could not ring any truer. It is indeed the federal judges who make certain that the Constitution is not a "dead letter."

The judges in the federal courts continue to examine and re-examine the Constitution and their own decisions so that justice and the Constitution are well served. As Supreme Court Justice Louis Brandeis pointed out, "The Court bows to the lessons of experience and the force of better reasoning, recognizing that the process of trial and error, so fruitful in the physical sciences, is appropriate also in the judicial function." Thus, through "trial and error," the Supreme Court may overrule its earlier decisions as it protects what Alexis de Tocqueville described as "the peace, the prosperity, and the very existence of the Union".

SECTION 1

Law and Where It Comes From

Preview Questions
- What is the difference between common law and statutory law?
- What is constitutional law?
- What is the difference between civil and criminal law?
- What does it mean for a court to have jurisdiction?

In 1066 the Normans conquered England, and William the Conqueror and his successors began the process of unifying the country under Norman rule. One of the means they used to do this was the establishment of the king's court, or *curia regis.* Before the Norman conquest, disputes had been settled according to local customs. The king's court sought to establish a common, or uniform, set of customs for the whole country. As the number of courts and cases increased, the most important decisions of each year were gathered together and recorded in *Year Books.*

Judges, settling disputes similar to ones that had been decided before, used the *Year Books* as the basis for their decisions. If a case was unique, judges had to create new laws, but whenever possible they based their decisions on the general principles suggested by earlier cases. The body of judicial law that developed under this system is still used today and is known as **common law**—the body of law that developed from custom and court decisions in England and the United States.

Common Law

Common law began as the ancient unwritten law of England. The **case law** of the United States since the

Discussion Starter
Guide the students in considering the fact that some laws will not be enforced: Why might a law be declared unconstitutional? How might that happen? What real examples can you cite of laws that were passed by Congress—and perhaps even enforced for a while—and then were declared unconstitutional? How does the possibility of laws' being declared unconstitutional contribute to our government's system of checks and balances?

Vocabulary
Let volunteers define the adjective *statutory* as used in the term *statutory law.* To what noun is the adjective related?

Discussion Starter
Help the students discuss their responses to the modern courts' task of interpreting what the rulemakers meant: How do you think this is done? Do you consider it a reasonable or achievable goal? Why or why not? What are the implications of this task for those who are writing laws and decisions today? Why?

Comprehension
Ask several students to identify specific issues that are covered by civil law. What kinds of cases and legal concerns might arise around these civil issues?

TEACHING GOVERNMENT IN ACTION

Read
As an introduction to this feature, let the students discuss their own ideas about lawyers in criminal cases: Are all accused persons defended by lawyers? Is it their right to be represented by a lawyer? Under what circumstances might a

Caption Answer Civil law spells out the duties that individual citizens have to one another and that the government has to citizens, such as contracts, etc. Criminal law has to do with wrongs committed against the public as a whole.

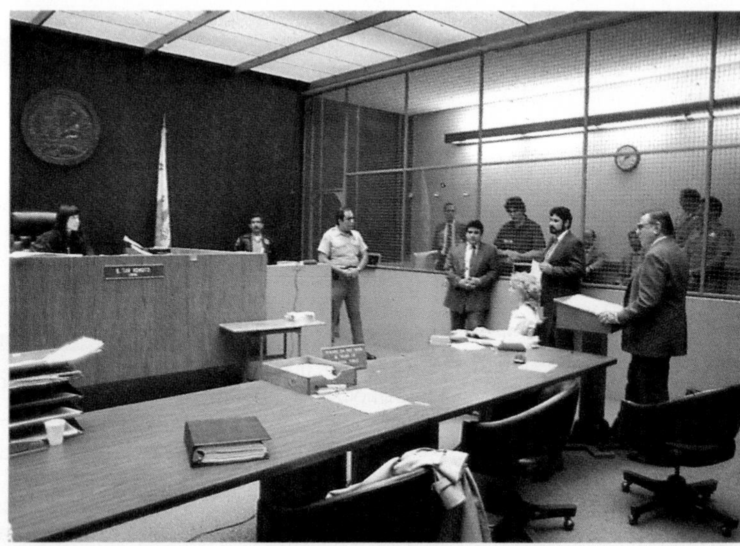

In this criminal courtroom, the suspected criminals are kept encaged behind a barrier. What is the difference between criminal law and civil law?

American Revolution is a predominant part of our common law, consisting of rules of law announced in separate court decisions. Case law includes all reported court cases that interpret statutes, regulations, and the Constitution. Such interpretations become part of the authoritative law on the subject and further serve as a **precedent**, or an example for future cases. The case involving Mr. Frazee was a precedent-setting case decided by the Supreme Court of the United States.

Constitutional Law

The federal government and the states have separate constitutions that set forth the general organization, powers, and limits of their respective governments. The U.S. Constitution is the supreme law of the land. A law in violation of the Constitution, no matter what its source, will be declared unconstitutional and will not be enforced. Similarly, unless they conflict with the U.S. Constitution, state constitutions are supreme within their respective borders. The U.S. Constitution defines the powers and limitations of the federal government. All powers not granted to the federal government are retained by the states or by the people.

Statutory Law

Statutes enacted by the U.S. Congress and the various state legislative bodies make up another source of law, which is generally referred to as **statutory law**. The statutory law of the United States also includes laws passed by cities and counties, none of which can violate the U.S. Constitution or the relevant state constitutions. Today, legislative bodies and regulatory agencies assume an ever-increasing share of lawmaking. Much of the work of modern courts consists of interpreting what the legislators meant when the law was passed and applying it to a present set of circumstances.

Civil versus Criminal Law

Civil law spells out the duties that exist between persons or between citizens and their governments. Law concerning contracts for business transactions, for example, is part of civil law. If you sign a contract to purchase a car on credit, the law governing that transaction is civil law.

Criminal law, by contrast, has to do with wrongs committed against the public as a whole. Criminal acts are prohibited by local, state, or federal government statutes. In a criminal case, the government seeks to impose a penalty (fines and/or imprisonment) upon a person suspected of having violated a criminal law. When someone robs a convenience store, that person has committed a crime and if caught and proven guilty, will normally be in prison for some period of time.

defendant appear without a lawyer? What is a lawyer expected to do for a defendant in a criminal case? Why? After this introductory discussion, ask volunteers to read the Case Study aloud to the rest of the class.

Discuss

Encourage a class discussion of this Government in Action feature by posing questions such as these: Is there a difference between the right to have a lawyer and the right to be provided with a lawyer? Do you think the implication of the Sixth Amendment is that the government is obligated to provide counsel for a defendant? Why or why not? What reasoning do you imagine lay behind the decision in *Betts* v. *Brady?* What is the due process clause of the Fourteenth Amendment? How did Gideon feel that he had been denied his due process rights? What is the ACLU? Whom is it intended to serve? How effective do you believe it has been?

Analyze and Apply

Let the students work in groups to find out more about the lawyers who are appointed to represent criminal defendants who cannot afford to hire their own lawyers. The members of each group may decide whether to learn about public defenders or about private practice lawyers doing *pro bono* work; the students can gather their information by reading reference works, biographies and other nonfiction books, or magazine articles, and/or by interviewing lawyers. Then lead a class discussion in which the members of all the groups share and compare their findings.

Review

Use the following questions to help the students review the Case Study: On what grounds did Gideon ask that his conviction be overturned? What is the continuing effect of the Supreme Court's decision in Gideon's case?

Think About It (Answers)

1. Persons accused of felonies who can show that they are unable to afford a lawyer must be given one at government expense.
2. State governments must allot money to pay for attorneys' fees for those who cannot afford one.

Comprehension

Let several volunteers give examples of the kinds of legal cases that could not be heard in local courts.

Enrichment

Assign one of the students to research summonses: What are they? How are they served? When and why are they served? What response do they require? Then ask this student to summarize his or her findings for the rest of the class.

GOVERNMENT IN ACTION

CASE STUDY

Gideon v. *Wainwright*

The Sixth Amendment to the U.S. Constitution provides that "in all criminal prosecutions, the accused shall enjoy the right . . . to have the assistance of counsel for his defense." By the passage of the Fourteenth Amendment in 1868, following the Civil War, this and other rights and privileges contained in the Bill of Rights were to be secured for all U.S. citizens, and no state could "deprive any person of life, liberty, or property without due process of law." Nearly a century passed, however, before the right to counsel was made available to accused persons in state criminal proceedings. As late as 1942 the Supreme Court held in *Betts* v. *Bradey* that, except in capital cases, criminal defendants were not automatically guaranteed the right to have a lawyer present when they were tried in court.

In 1963, however, the *Betts* v. *Brady* precedent was overturned by the decision in *Gideon* v. *Wainwright,* which became a landmark case in securing the right to counsel for criminal defendants.[a] The case began in 1962 when Clarence Earl Gideon sent a petition to the Supreme Court to review his most recent conviction—breaking into a pool hall and stealing money in Panama City, Florida. In his petition, Gideon claimed he could not afford to pay a lawyer to file the petition for him. He also claimed that his conviction and sentencing to a five-year prison term violated the due process clause of the Fourteenth Amendment. Gideon reported that when he asked for the assistance of a lawyer at the time of his trial, the court refused. The heart of Gideon's petition was his claim that "to try a poor man for a felony without giving him a lawyer was to deprive him of due process of law."

Gideon was successful. He had the help of the American Civil Liberties Union (ACLU) and its appointed lawyer, Abe Fortas, whom President Johnson later appointed to the Supreme Court. The Court decided in Gideon's favor, stating that persons accused of **felonies** (serious crimes) who can show they are unable to afford a lawyer must be given one at the government's expense. Represented by a court-appointed attorney, Gideon was retried and found to be innocent of the charges.

THINK ABOUT IT

1. What change in criminal procedure resulted from Clarence Earl Gideon's petition?
2. How does the Supreme Court's decision in favor of Gideon change the way state governments must spend their money?

a. A biography of Clarence Earl Gideon and the significance of this case is presented in Anthony Lewis, *Gideon's Trumpet* (New York: Vintage Books, 1964).

Jurisdiction

In Latin, *juris* means "law," and *diction* means "to speak." Thus, **jurisdiction** literally refers to the power "to speak the law." Jurisdiction applies either to the geographical area within which a court has the right and power to decide cases, or to the right and power of a court to decide matters concerning certain persons, property, or subject matter. Before any court can hear a case, it must have jurisdiction over the person against whom the suit is brought, the property involved in the suit, and the subject matter.

Jurisdiction over Persons and Property Generally, a court's power is limited to the geographical boundaries of the state in which it is located. Thus, a court has jurisdiction over anyone who can be served a **summons** (an order to appear in court) within those boundaries. A court normally will also have jurisdiction over residents

TEACHING CITIZENSHIP SKILLS AND RESPONSIBILITIES

Read

Introduce this Citizenship Skills and Responsibilities feature by letting the students share their own ideas about and experiences with jury service: Which of your family members or friends has served on a jury? What did that person tell you about the jury work and about the case? How did serving on a jury seem to affect the person? What attitude toward jury service do you hear expressed by adults in your community? By your peers? What is your own attitude toward jury service? Why? After the discussion, ask the students to read the Citizenship Skills and Responsibilities feature independently.

Caption Answer The term *jury duty* comes from the assumption that serving on a jury is one of the duties of American citizenship.

Discuss

Help the students discuss the content of this feature by asking questions such as these: What are the reasons for being excused from jury duty in your state? Why are those reasons considered valid excuses? What compensation do most workers get from their employers while they are away from work on jury duty? What does *biased* mean? Why is it important to discover whether a juror might be biased? What is the purpose of the oath jurors take in court? Why is it important for jurors to disregard everything they see or hear outside the courtroom? Do you believe jurors can completely put aside their personal prejudices when making decisions? Why or why not? What is sequestering? Why are juries sometimes sequestered? What is the meaning of *settling out of court?* When and why is a hung jury possible? What is the significance of a hung jury?

Analyze and Apply

Ask the students to work on their own or with partners to interview adults who have served on juries. Encourage the students to gather as much information and as many personal responses from their interviewees as possible. Then have

CITIZENSHIP SKILLS AND RESPONSIBILITIES

Serving on a Jury

▲ These jurors listen attentively while the lawyer makes her point. Why do you think serving on a jury is often referred to as jury *duty*?

If you are an American citizen of sound mind and have never committed a serious crime, you may one day be summoned by a state or federal court for **jury duty**. Names of jurors are usually chosen from tax assessor's polls, lists of registered voters, and driver's license registrations.

If your name is chosen, in most states the clerk of the court will send you a jury qualification form, which you must fill out and return. You will then receive a summons requiring you to appear in court at a particular time and place. If for some reason you cannot be there, you must explain this to the court. There are few valid reasons for being excused. The court will respond by either excusing you from jury duty or ordering you to appear. If you don't appear when so ordered, the court has the power to send a sheriff's deputy to bring you to court.

Being employed is not a valid excuse to be exempted from jury duty. The law protects you from being fired from your job or penalized in any way the students write either news stories or short stories that relate what they have learned about jury experience.

Review
Ask the students review questions such as these: Who can be summoned for jury duty? Why are potential jurors interviewed by lawyers on both sides before they can be qualified to serve in a particular case?

for the time you spend serving on a jury. (Be sure to notify your employer as soon as you have been called for jury duty.)

When you appear in court, you may be asked to wait in a room with other prospective jurors until you are called. Then you will be escorted to the courtroom. You will be asked to take an oath that you will answer questions truthfully. Lawyers on both sides will ask you questions to determine whether or not you are likely to be biased. They will ask you questions about your background, beliefs, your relationship to the people involved in the trial, and whether you have already formed an opinion about the case. If one or the other lawyers finds a reason why you may be biased in the case, you will be disqualified by the judge.

If you are accepted to serve on the jury, you will take another oath in court along with the other jurors, and will be told when you are to reappear.

Before the trial begins you will be instructed by the judge on court procedures, which include:

- Nothing you see or hear outside the courtroom can be considered in reaching your verdict.
- It is your sworn duty to decide the case by considering only the testimony and evidence you hear and see in the courtroom proceedings. Your personal prejudices or sympathies should have no bearing.
- You may not speak to anyone outside the courtroom—not even your family—about the trial.

When the trial begins, you must listen carefully to all the testimony. You may not be permitted to take notes, so you must try to remember the details of what you hear. In some cases, you might be told that the case has been settled out of court. If this happens you will be dismissed. If the case continues, both sides will be presented. Cases can last anywhere from one day to several weeks. When both sides have presented their cases, the judge will instruct you about the law to be applied. Then you and the other jurors will be asked to decide the facts of the case.

You and the other jurors will be taken to a private room. You will have the opportunity to share your views about the evidence you have heard. You must listen to the other jurors' views, and may try to persuade the others to take your position. A fellow citizen's future and your community are at stake, so you should take the responsibility seriously.

Sometimes juries take a considerable amount of time to discuss and evaluate all the evidence. If the jury cannot agree on a verdict (a situation which is called a **hung jury**), either another trial is held with a different jury or the matter is dropped.

Most juries are able to come to a unanimous decision. When all of the jurors agree on their verdict, the jury members will be ushered back into the courtroom. They will pronounce their decision. This decision is final and the trial is ended. Generally, the judge thanks the jury and dismisses it.

Serving on a jury can be interesting and educational. It is also an opportunity for you to participate in our system of equal justice under the law.

Taking Action

1. Stage a mock trial in your class. Choose a prosecuting attorney, a defense attorney, a defendant, a judge, and a jury. Perhaps you can use the case of William Frazee presented in the introduction of this chapter as the fact pattern for your mock jury trial.
2. Arrange to be an observer in a jury trial in the court nearest to your house. Listen to the evidence presented and determine what your verdict would be if you were on the jury.
3. You may be excused from jury duty under special circumstances. Make a list of the reasons that you think might be serious enough to prevent you from serving on a jury.

Comprehension
Let several students explain, in their own words, the distinction between original jurisdiction and appellate jurisdiction. Be sure all the students can answer this question: What must happen before a case appears before a court having appellate jurisdiction?

Reteaching Strategies
1. Have the students work in small groups to compare and review the notes they have taken on Section 1. Remind the students to make any necessary corrections or additions to their own notes.
2. Let the students work with partners to write, in their own words, definitions of these terms introduced in Section 1: *common law, case law, precedent, jurisdiction.*

Evaluation Strategies
1. Have the students write their answers to the Section 1 Review questions.
2. Have the students take the Section 1 Quiz found in the *TRB.*

Section 1 Review (Answers)
1. Common law is law that has developed from case law and precedent. Statutory law is made up of the laws passed by Congress and the various state legislatures.
2. The U.S. Constitution, the laws of Congress, and the treaties made under the authority of the United States "shall be the supreme law of the land." (Article VI, Section 2)
3. Civil law spells out the duties that exist between persons or between citizens and their governments. Criminal law has to do with wrongs committed against the public as a whole.
4. Courts having original jurisdiction are those courts in which the case is being heard for the first time. Courts having appellate jurisdiction act as reviewing courts.
5. Answers will vary, e.g., individuals have the right to a jury of peers. In order to get a fairly representative group, persons must be chosen in some random manner. Only certain types of people would volunteer to serve on a jury if it weren't required.

SECTION 2

Points to Stress
- Origins of the federal court system.
- The three tiers that make up the federal court system.
- The manner in which cases reach the Court of Appeals.
- The boundaries of federal judicial power.
- The difference between concurrent and exclusive jurisdiction.
- The situations in which a federal question arises.
- The meaning of judicial review.

Kickoff Activity
Write the following term on the chalkboard: *going to court.* Then give the students five minutes in which to list all the words and phrases that the term brings to mind. At the end of the five minutes, encourage the students to share and discuss their lists.

of the state and people who do business within the state. In some cases, if an individual has committed an offense such as causing an automobile injury or selling defective goods within the state, the court can exercise jurisdiction even if the individual is a resident of another state. A court can further exercise jurisdiction over a corporation in the state where it is incorporated (legally formed), in the state where the company has its main plant or office, and in any other state where it does business.

Original and Appellate Jurisdiction Courts having **original jurisdiction** are courts in which the case is being heard for the first time. In other words, these courts are where the trial of a case begins. In contrast, courts having **appellate jurisdiction** act as reviewing courts. In general, cases can be brought to them only on appeal from an order or a judgment of a lower court.

SECTION 1 REVIEW

1. How does common law differ from statutory law?
2. What is the supreme law of the land?
3. Explain the difference between civil law and criminal law.
4. What is the difference between original and appellate jurisdiction?
5. **For critical analysis:** Why do you think it is necessary for the government to require citizens to serve on juries rather than just using those who volunteer for jury duty?

SECTION 2

The Federal Court System

Preview Questions
- How did the federal courts develop?
- What three tiers make up the federal court system?
- What kinds of cases reach the court of appeals?
- What are the boundaries of federal judicial power?
- What is the difference between concurrent and exclusive jurisdiction?
- When does a federal question arise?
- What is judicial review?

How the Federal Courts Developed

It is probably true that the framers expected the Supreme Court to reign supreme and be important. But they probably did not expect the other federal courts to play such a large role in public policy-making. Alexander Hamilton, for example, wrote in *The Federalist Papers,* Number 78, that the courts would play a relatively neutral role in public affairs. He and the other founders did not want federal judges to make public policy. Clearly times have changed since then, particularly with respect to the federal judiciary. Federal courts today go so far as to dictate policy on such issues as the number of prisoners per cell in a state prison, or whether state-financed public schools are spending enough money.

The evolution of the federal court system can be divided into three specific periods of American history:

- From 1787 to 1865, when the states challenged the federal government's supremacy and the issue of slavery was predominant.
- From 1866 to 1937, when the relationship between government and the economy was established.
- From 1938 to the present, when the great issues have been social equality and personal liberty.

National Supremacy and the Issue of Slavery Under the leadership of Chief Justice John Marshall, who served from 1801 to 1835, the Supreme Court dealt with the great question of the relationship between the states and the federal government. In one landmark case, Marshall and his Supreme Court declared a certain congressional act as unconstitutional, thereby creating the doctrine of judicial review discussed in Chapter 3. In an equally important case, the Court held that the federal government could make all laws that were necessary and proper to attain constitutional goals. Marshall established that federal law was indeed supreme over state law. These accomplishments may seem obvious today, but in the early nineteenth century they were almost revolutionary decisions.

Roger B. Taney succeeded Marshall as chief justice. In 1857 Taney wrote the decision in the *Dred Scott* case in which he held that African Americans were not citizens of the United States. The Court had made a mistake. Some have argued that this mistake created the climate that led to the Civil War.

Allowing Segregation While the Civil War reestablished the supremacy of the federal government, the scope of powers of the federal and state governments

Caption Answer During Earl Warren's tenure as Chief Justice, the Court was especially concerned with protecting the liberties and rights of citizens from government interference.

Working with the Preview Questions
Have the students read and consider these study questions; encourage volunteers to share their ideas about the answers—or the kinds of answers—they expect to find. Then instruct the students to keep the questions in mind as they read Section 2 and to be prepared to answer the questions later.

Teaching Strategies

Discussion Starter
Help the students discuss their responses to these questions about the development of the federal courts: Why and how has the role of the courts evolved? How is this evolution related to the Constitution and to the intentions of the framers? What does it indicate about the interests and intentions of American leaders throughout our history?

Enrichment
Ask several volunteers to work together in researching the life and accomplishments of John Marshall. Have them present their findings in a bulletin board display. (If possible, have the students complete this display in time to coordinate with the class consideration of Architect of the American Dream: John Marshall [pages 440–441].)

Enrichment
Have one of the students research and report on Roger B. Tanney: Why and by whom was he appointed? How widespread a reaction against Marshall did Tanney's appointment represent? Why is he so much less familiar than his predecessor?

Comprehension
Let volunteers explain how the Civil War called the supremacy of the federal government into question and how the end of the war reestablished that supremacy.

Enrichment
Ask an interested student to research Earl Warren's training, political background, and activities on the Court: Who appointed Warren to the Supreme Court? Why? What was the trend of the Court while Warren served? Why? Have this volunteer present a short oral report to the rest of the class.

▲ Earl Warren, shown here, was chief justice of the United States Supreme Court from 1953 to 1969. What issues were of special concern to the Court during Warren's tenure?

was not yet fully defined. The dominant issue facing the Supreme Court from the Civil War to the New Deal in the 1930s was to what extent the federal or state governments could regulate economic activities. During this period the Court supported private property, but also allowed for reasonable regulation of business activities.

At the same time, the Court was narrowly interpreting the Fourteenth and Fifteenth Amendments so that they did not fully include the rights of African Americans and other groups. During this period the Supreme Court upheld segregation in schools and on railroad cars, and allowed African Americans to be excluded from voting in many states.

The Modern Era From 1937 to 1974 the Supreme Court failed to overturn even one federal law that regulated business. It did, however, find unconstitutional thirty-six laws passed by Congress that violated individual political liberties. When Chief Justice Earl Warren took his seat in 1953, the Supreme Court began its most activist period. The Court was especially concerned with protecting the liberties and rights of citizens from government interference. It continues to do so even today, but with less fervor than it did under Earl Warren.

The Federal Court System

The federal court system is a three-tiered structure that consists of trial courts, intermediate courts of appeals, and the Supreme Court. Figure 18–1 shows how the federal court system is organized.

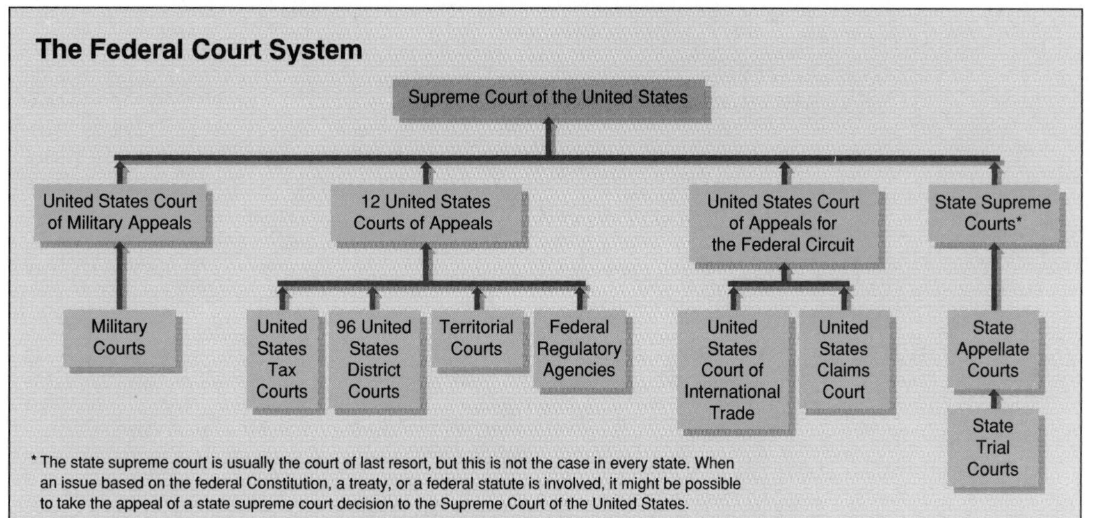

▲ **FIGURE 18–1 The Federal Court System.** The table above shows the organization of the federal court system. From looking at the table, what do you know about the relationship of the United States Claims Court to the United States Court of Appeals for the Federal Circuit?

This figure content is also featured on *West's American Government Videodisc* (see the index found in the *TRB*) and is available in the transparency package.

Caption Answer Students should understand that the United States Court of Appeals for the Federal Circuit is a higher court than the United States Claims Courts and, therefore, hears appeals from the United States Claims Court.

Enrichment
Ask the students to identify the federal district court or courts in your state.

Discussion Starter
Encourage the students to consider why appeals are maintained as a possibility in many cases: Whom does the provision of appeal serve? Why? What could happen in a court system that did not provide for appeals? How?

Figure Answer There are 12 judicial circuits that make up the U.S. Courts of Appeals, or Circuit Courts.

This figure content is also featured on *West's American Government Videodisc* (see the index found in the *TRB*) and is available in the transparency package.

Multidiscipline Strategies

Literature Henrik Ibsen wrote a play entitled "An Enemy of the People." This play is an excellent representation of individual belief versus community order. Our judicial branch is responsible for protecting individual rights against the tyranny of the majority. Majorities very seldom need protection. You might wish to have students read Ibsen's play, "An Enemy of the People." It will act as an excellent basis for discussion on the topic of justice for the minority.

U.S. District Courts

At the federal level, the trial court of general jurisdiction is the district court. There is at least one federal district court in every state. The number of districts can vary over time, according to population changes and the size of caseloads.

In the Federal Judgeship Act of 1984, Congress increased the total number of district court judgeships in the United States. The law now provides for 563 district court judgeships within the 96 judicial districts.

U.S. Courts of Appeals

Congress has established twelve **judicial circuits** that hear appeals from the district courts located within their respective circuits. The decisions of the courts of appeals are final in most cases, but appeal to the U.S. Supreme Court is possible. Appeals from federal administrative agencies, such as the Federal Trade Commission (FTC), are also made to the U.S. courts of appeals. See Figure 18–2 below for the geographical boundaries of U.S. district courts and U.S. courts of appeals.

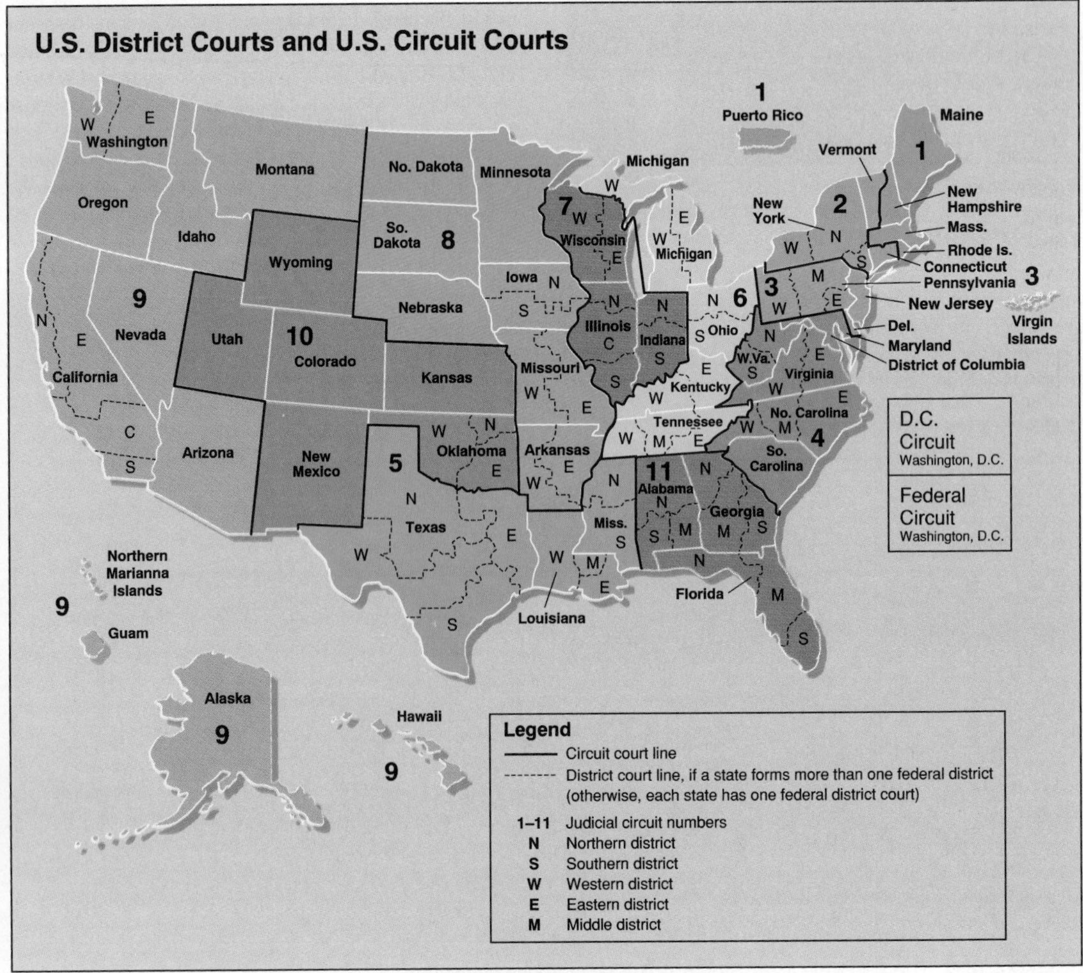

▲ FIGURE 18–2 **U.S. District Courts and U.S. Circuit Courts.** The map above shows the U.S. District Courts and the U.S. Courts of Appeals, or Circuit Courts. How many judicial circuits make up the U.S. Circuit Courts?

Discussion Starter
Guide the students in discussing the map, U.S. Courts of Appeals and U.S. District Courts, noting especially its relevance to their own area.

Vocabulary
Be sure the students understand the definition of *inferior* as it is used here.

Extension
Have one of the students check and report on the instances in which the Supreme Court has original jurisdiction, as explained in Article III, Section 2.

Comprehension
Let volunteers explain how the provision of Congressional control over the number and kind of courts contributes to our government's system of checks and balances.

Under the Federal Judgeship Act of 1984, there are now 168 circuit court judgeships with 13 circuits (including the federal circuit).

The Supreme Court

The Supreme Court is the highest level of the three-tiered federal court system. According to the language of Article III of the Constitution, there is only one national Supreme Court. All other courts in the federal system are considered inferior. Congress is empowered to create other inferior courts as it deems necessary, which include the U.S. courts of appeals, the district courts, and any other courts of limited jurisdiction.

The Supreme Court consists of nine justices, all of whom are nominated by the president and confirmed by the Senate. As with all federal district and appeals judges, Supreme Court justices receive lifetime appointments (since under Article III they "hold their offices during Good Behavior"). Although the Supreme Court has original jurisdiction in rare instances such as those involving ambassadors (set forth in Article III, Section 2), most of its work is as an appeals court. The Supreme Court can review any case decided by any of the federal courts of appeals, and it also has authority to review some cases decided in the state courts.

Jurisdiction of the Federal Courts and Judicial Review

Because the federal government is a government of limited powers, the jurisdiction of the federal courts is also limited. Article III of the U.S. Constitution established the boundaries of federal judicial power.

The Constitutional Boundaries of Federal Judicial Power In line with the checks-and-balances system of the federal government, Congress has the power to control the number and kind of inferior courts in the federal system. Except in those cases in which the Constitution gives the Supreme Court original jurisdiction, Congress can regulate the jurisdiction of the Supreme Court. Although the Constitution sets the outer limits of federal judicial power, Congress can set other limits on federal jurisdiction. Furthermore, the courts themselves

Caption Answer The court is supreme among U.S. Courts. As the language of Article III of the Constitution points out, there is only one national supreme court, and all other courts within the United States are considered inferior.

The nine justices of the Supreme Court, all of whom are nominated by the president and confirmed by the Senate, are pictured here. Why do you think the framers of the Constitution chose to call this court the *Supreme Court*?

TEACHING ARCHITECT OF THE AMERICAN DREAM

Read

Introduce this feature by asking a volunteer to recall the landmark case of *Marbury* v. *Madison*. What were the issues of this case? How did this case change the Supreme Court's role in our system of checks and balances? Who was Chief Justice of the Supreme Court at the time of this case? Then tell the students that they are about to read a feature about this chief justice, John Marshall. Point out to students that just as the actions of George Washington helped to define the presidency, the actions and decisions of John Marshall and the Marshall court helped to define the role of the Supreme Court. Then allow volunteers to take turns reading this feature aloud to the class.

Discuss

Was John Marshall the first Chief Justice of the Supreme Court? How would you describe Marshall's background? What role did he play during the War for Independence? How long did Marshall study law prior to practicing? How does that compare with the educational requirements for today's lawyers? How would you describe Marshall's political career? How long was Marshall on the Court? What did Marshall feel was the appropriate role for the Court within our system? How did Marshall feel about the Constitution?

Analyze and Apply

In order to further enrich student understanding of John Marshall and the decisions of the Marshall court, have the students choose

ARCHITECT OF The American Dream

John Marshall has been called the architect of the American constitutional system, even though his true genius wasn't appreciated until after his death in 1835. Until John Marshall became the fourth chief justice of the Supreme Court, the Court was seen as having little power, with almost no influence over the other two branches of government. John Marshall changed all that. After he had been chief justice for a few years, the Court began to assume its place as the third equal branch of government, and in a series of brilliant decisions from 1810 to 1835, Marshall almost single-handedly gave new power to the Constitution.

John Marshall was born in a log cabin in Germantown, on the Virginia frontier, on September 24, 1755. He was the first of fifteen children born to Thomas Marshall, a descendant of Welsh immigrants, and his wife, Mary Keith Marshall, who was the daughter of a Scottish clergyman. He grew up on a farm and had only two years of formal schooling. As a young man he fought in the colonial army during the American Revolution as lieutenant and captain. Later he attended six weeks of law lectures at William and Mary College, and began to practice law in 1781. His legal library at the time consisted solely of notes he had taken while reading a borrowed copy of Francis Bacon's *Abridgement of English Law*.

Early in his legal career, Marshall was recognized as an excellent attorney and was elected to the first of four terms in the Virginia Assembly. When the Constitution was submitted to the Virginia legislature to be ratified, Marshall played a leading role in the fight to adopt it. He turned down the position of attorney general offered to him by George Washington, and also declined the post of minister to France. He won a seat in Congress in 1799, and in 1800 became secretary of state to John Adams. A year later, he was appointed chief justice of the Supreme Court.

John Marshall's thirty-four years on the bench established the prestige of the Court. In his talks and writings he argued that the nation needed an effective judiciary with the power to review the acts of the states and to decide whether the actions of the other two national branches were consistent with the principles of the Constitution. His opinion in *Marbury* v. *Madison* (1803) is regarded as the classic justification of judicial review and the fundamental premise on which the United States constitutional doctrine rests. In *McCulloch* v. *Maryland* (1819), he ruled that when state and federal powers conflict, the federal powers are stronger.

In these and other cases, Marshall established three basic principles that became the foundation of the federal union: (1) the principle of judicial review—that the Supreme Court had the power to determine when a law of Congress was unconstitutional. This idea was debated and denied, but was eventually accepted; (2) the Supreme Court had the power to set aside laws of state legislatures when these laws were contrary to the federal Constitution; (3) the Supreme Court had the power to reverse the decisions of state courts. Other significant rulings by the Marshall court in essence refused to bind the federal government to the literal limits of its expressed powers. Rather, he argued that it is necessary for those interpreting and living under the Constitution to treat it as a ''living'' document that can be accommodated to the changing needs of the American people.

one of the three cases excerpted in the His Words section of this feature and write a two- to three-page paper about that decision. Student papers should include background information about the issue in question, details of the case, and a thorough examination of the decision and its impact.

Students should be allowed to share their papers with the class. As a means of comparing the Marshall Court with the current Court, you might allow some students to research a current case and prepare similar papers about these cases.

Review

Use the following questions to review this Architect of the American Dream feature. Who was John Marshall? When was he appointed to the Supreme Court? How long did he serve as Chief Justice of the Supreme Court? Why are *Marbury* v. *Madison, Gibbons* v. *Ogden,* and *McCullogh* v. *Maryland* important cases? What did each of these cases establish?

Developing Critical Thinking Skills (Answers)

1. Answers will vary, e.g., it is the judicial branch of government, and no other, that must decide when a law of Congress or a state legislature is unconstitutional. There must be a final authority on such matters and the final authority is the Supreme Court.

2. Article VI, Section 2, which includes the supremacy clause.

3. Answers will vary, e.g., *Marbury* v. *Madison* established the principle of federal judicial review and *McCulloch* v. *Maryland* established that the federal government was supreme and that the Constitution gave Congress the right to do whatever was "necessary and proper" to carry out any of its specific powers.

John Marshall

"THIS, SIR, IS MY CASE! IT IS THE CASE NOT MERELY OF THAT HUMBLE INSTITUTION, IT IS THE CASE OF EVERY COLLEGE IN OUR LAND!...IT IS, SIR, AS I HAVE SAID, A SMALL COLLEGE. AND YET..."

◀ Daniel Webster, *standing,* argues before the Supreme Court in a twentieth-century painting by Robert Burns. Chief Justice John Marshall, *fourth from the left,* presides over the Court.

His Words

From *Marbury* v. *Madison* (1803):
"To what purpose are (congressional) powers limited, and to what purpose is that limitation committed to writing, if these limits may, at any time, be passed by those intended to be restrained? . . . It is a proposition too plain to be contested that the Constitution controls any legislative act repugnant to it. . . . A legislative act contrary to the Constitution is not law . . . it is emphatically the province and duty of the judicial department to say what the law is. . . ."

From *Gibbons* v. *Ogden* (1824):
"We are now arrived at the inquiry, What is this power? It is the power to regulate; that is, to prescribe the rule by which commerce is to be governed. This power, like all others vested in Congress, is complete in itself, may be exercised to its utmost extent, and acknowledges no limitations other than are prescribed in the Constitution."

From *McCulloch* v. *Maryland* (1819):
"Let the end be legitimate, let it be within the scope of the constitution, and all means which are appropriate, which are plainly adapted to that end, which are not prohibited, but consist with the letter and spirit of the constitution, are constitutional."

Developing Your Critical Thinking Skills

1. What did Marshall mean when he said that it is the "duty of the judicial department to say what the law is"?
2. What clause in the Constitution was Marshall referring to when he said that "the Constitution controls . . ."?
3. Study *Marbury* v. *Madison* on page 60 and *McCulloch* v. *Maryland* on page 89. How did each of these decisions establish basic principles that have helped to strengthen the federal government?

For Further Reading

Leonard Baker, *John Marhsall: A Life in Law,* MacMillan, New York, (1974).
Albert Beveridge, *The Life of John Marshall,* Houghton Mifflin, Boston, (1916–1919).

Discussion Starter
Encourage the students to make up and discuss sample cases that involve diversity of citizenship: Why would each example case be heard in federal district court? Also help the students consider the significance of the $50,000 base: Why do you think a base amount was imposed? Why do you think this amount was selected?

Vocabulary
Let volunteers define the adjectives *concurrent* and *exclusive* as they are used here.

Cooperative Learning
Have the students form small groups. Then ask the members of each group to work together to restate, in their own words, the quotation from the Supreme Court's decision in *Marbury* v. *Madison.*

Reteaching Strategies
1. Have the students form groups in which to discuss their answers to the Preview Questions.
2. Work with small groups of students; guide them in reviewing and discussing figure 18–1, The Federal Court System. Be sure each student understands the three tiers and the relationships among the various courts.

Evaluation Strategies
1. Have the students write their answers to the Section 2 Review questions.
2. Have the students take the Section 2 Quiz found in the *TRB.*

Section 2 Review (Answers)
1. From 1787 to 1865, when the nation was building, during which period the states challenged the federal government's supremacy and the issue of slavery was predominant. From 1866 to 1937, when the relationship between government and the economy was established. From 1938 to the present, when the great issues have been social equality and personal liberty.
2. The federal court system is a three-tiered structure that consists of trial courts, intermediate courts of appeal, and the Supreme Court.
3. The Constitution sets the outer limits of federal judicial power, but Congress can set other limits on federal jurisdiction. Congress has the power to control the number and kind of inferior courts in the federal system. Congress can regulate the jurisdiction of the Supreme Court except in those cases in which the Constitution gives the Supreme Court original jurisdiction.
4. When the plaintiff's cause of action is based on the United States Constitution, a treaty, or a federal law.
5. The power of the Supreme Court to declare laws and actions of national, state, or local governments invalid if they violate the Constitution.
6. Answers will vary, e.g., no, the system is not fair because many auto accidents involve less than $50,000 in damages. If you are involved in one in another state, you may not get a fair trial because the judge and/or jury may be partial to the person who lives in that state with whom you had the auto accident.

can make rules that further limit the types of cases they will hear.

Diversity Jurisdiction Federal district court jurisdiction extends to cases involving **diversity of citizenship**. Diversity of citizenship cases are those arising between citizens of different states; between a foreign government and citizens of a state or of different states; or between citizens of a state and citizens or subjects of a foreign country. The amount in the dispute must be more than $50,000 before a federal court can take jurisdiction. For example, if you reside in California and have an automobile accident while driving in Texas with another driver who resides in New York, you could sue in federal court if you claim damages greater than $50,000 (otherwise the suit must normally be brought in a state court).

Federal Questions Whenever the cause of action of a **plaintiff** (the one suing) is based at least in part on the United States Constitution, a treaty, or a federal law, then a **federal question** arises. The case comes under the judicial power of federal courts. Any lawsuit involving a federal question can originate in a federal court. People who claim that their constitutional rights have been violated can begin their legal procedures in a federal court.

When both federal and state courts have the power to hear a case, as is true in suits involving diversity of citizenship, **concurrent jurisdiction** exists. Cases that can be tried only in federal courts or only in state courts are cases of **exclusive jurisdiction**. Federal courts have exclusive jurisdiction in cases involving federal crimes, bankruptcy, patents, and copyrights. They also have exclusive jurisdiction in suits against the United States, and in some areas of maritime law. States have exclusive jurisdiction in such areas as divorce and adoptions.

Judicial Review The problem often arises as to whether or not a law is contrary to the mandates of the Constitution. **Judicial review** is the process for making such a determination. The federal judiciary alone has the authority and power to determine whether a particular law violates the Constitution.

The power of judicial review was first established in *Marbury* v. *Madison* in 1803. In determining that the Supreme Court had the power to decide that a law passed by Congress violated the Constitution, the Court stated:

> It is emphatically the province and duty of the Judicial Department to say what the law is. . . . If two laws conflict with each other, the courts must decide on the operation of each. . . . So if the law be in opposition to the Constitution . . . [t]he Court must determine which of these conflicting rules governs the case. This is the very essence of judicial duty.

Section 2 Review

1. Identify and describe the three historical periods in the evolution of the federal court system.
2. Briefly describe the organization of the federal court system.
3. What are the constitutional boundaries of federal judicial power?
4. When does a federal question arise?
5. What is judicial review?
6. **For critical analysis:** If you are involved in an auto accident in another state, you may have to undergo a trial in that state. You might feel that you would get a fairer hearing in a federal court. But unless the amount at issue is over $50,000 you cannot ask for a federal trial. Do you think this is a fair system? Why or why not?

Section 3

How Cases Reach the Supreme Court

Preview Questions

- What is a writ of *certiorari* and in what situations may the Supreme Court issue one?
- What are the four types of opinions issued by the Supreme Court?
- What procedures are followed by the Supreme Court when deciding a case?

Many people are surprised to learn that there is no absolute right of appeal to the United States Supreme Court. The Supreme Court is given original jurisdiction in a small number of situations. In all other cases, it acts as an appeals court. Thousands of cases are filed with the Supreme Court each year; yet on average, it hears only about two hundred. To bring a case before the Supreme Court, a party must request the Court to issue a **writ of *certiorari***, which is an order that the Supreme Court issues to a lower court, requesting the latter to send

SECTION 3

Points to Stress

- The definition of writ of *certiorari* and the situations under which it may be issued.
- The four opinions issued by the Supreme Court.
- Procedures followed by the Supreme Court when deciding a case.

Kickoff Activity

Ask the students to write short paragraphs in response to this question: What makes the Supreme Court supreme? When everyone has finished writing, let volunteers read their paragraphs aloud; encourage the students to compare and discuss their ideas.

Working with the Preview Questions

Have volunteers read these study questions aloud. Then guide the students in preparing an outline format, based on the questions, to be used in taking notes on Section 3.

Teaching Strategies

Introduction

Assign several students to read this section introduction aloud to the rest of the class. You may then want to divide the class into eight groups, and assign each situation to one of the groups. Have the members of each group work together to find specific cases to illustrate their assigned situation; let the groups share and discuss their cases.

Comprehension

Have one or more students explain the meaning of the statement that the Supreme Court "does not hear any evidence": Do witnesses testify? How does the Court gather the information it uses to reach a decision?

Vocabulary

Be sure all the students can define *opinion* as the word is used here.

Enrichment

Let interested volunteers research and report on dissenting opinions that have been as significant—or more significant—than the majority opinions in their cases: What ideas were expressed in these dissenting opinions? How and why did those ideas prove influential?

Comprehension

Give several of the students an opportunity to restate, in their own words, the idea expressed by Jackson.

Discussion Starter

Focus the students' attention on the statement that "the process of judicial implementation may take a long time, or it may never occur at all." What does this mean? How significant is the time involved in implementation? How does it affect citizens? How does it affect the court system?

it the record of the case in question. Parties can petition the Supreme Court to issue a writ of *certiorari*, but whether the Court will do so is entirely within its discretion. In no instance is the Court required to issue a writ of *certiorari*.[1]

Below are some of the situations in which the Supreme Court may issue a writ of *certiorari*.

1. When a state court has decided a substantial federal question that has not been determined by the Supreme Court or when a state court has decided such a question in a way that is probably in disagreement with the trend of the Supreme Court's decisions.
2. When two or more federal courts of appeals disagree with each other.
3. When a federal court of appeals has decided that an important state question is in conflict with state law.
4. When a federal court has decided that an important federal question is in conflict with the relevant decisions of the Supreme Court.
5. When a federal court has departed from the accepted and usual course of judicial proceedings.
6. When a federal court of appeals holds that a state statute violates federal law.
7. When the highest state court of appeals holds a federal law invalid or upholds a state law that has been challenged as violating federal law.
8. When a federal court holds an act of Congress unconstitutional and the federal government or one of its employees is a party to the lawsuit.

Most petitions for writs of *certiorari* are denied. A denial is not a decision on the merits of a case, nor is it an indication of agreement with a lower court's opinion. Denial of a writ also has no value as a precedent. The Court will not issue a writ unless at least four justices approve of it. This is called the "rule of four." Typically, writs are granted only to petitions that raise the possibility of resolving important questions about the Constitution.

Decisions and Opinions

The United States Supreme Court normally does not hear any evidence, as is true with all appeals courts. The Court's decision is based upon the written records of a case. The attorneys can present **oral arguments**—those presented only in person rather than on paper—after which the case is privately examined by the justices.

When the Court has reached a decision, the decision is written. It contains the **opinion** (the Court's reasons for its decision), the rules of law that apply, and the judgment.

There are four types of written opinions for any particular case decided by the Supreme Court. When all justices unanimously agree on an opinion, the opinion is written for all the justices of the entire Court, and can be deemed a **unanimous opinion**. When there is not a unanimous opinion, a **majority opinion** is written, which outlines the views of the majority of the justices involved in the particular case. Often one or more justices who feel strongly about making or emphasizing a particular point that was not made or emphasized in the unanimous or majority written opinion will write a **concurring opinion**. That means the justice writing the concurring opinion concurs (agrees) with the conclusion given in the unanimous or majority written opinion but agrees for reasons that are different from the rest of the judges. Finally, in other than unanimous opinions, one or more dissenting opinions are usually written by those justices who did not agree with the majority. The **dissenting opinion** is important because it often forms the basis of the arguments used years later that cause the Court to reverse the previous decision and establish a new precedent.

After a Decision Is Reached

President Andrew Jackson was once supposed to have said after Chief Justice John Marshall made an unpopular decision that "John Marshall has made his decision; now let him enforce it." This quote goes to the heart of **judicial implementation**, the procedure by which Court decisions are actually translated into law and thereby affect the behavior of the individuals who live under those laws. The Court does not have the executive power to implement its decisions, nor does it have control of the budget to pay for such implementation when government funds are required. There is no Supreme Court police force, nor is there a Supreme Court keeper of the purse strings. Other units of government have to carry out the Court's decisions.

That means the process of judicial implementation may take a long time, or it may never occur at all. School-sponsored prayers were banned in public schools in 1962, yet it was widely known that the ban was ignored in many

1. Between 1790 and 1891, Congress allowed the Supreme Court almost no discretion over which cases to decide. After 1925, the Court could choose in almost 95 percent of appealed cases to decide whether to hear arguments and issue an opinion. Beginning with the term in October 1988, mandatory review was eliminated altogether.

TEACHING GOVERNMENT IN ACTION

Read

Let the students read the title of this Case Study, and encourage them to respond to the question: What are your First Amendment rights? How can they be abridged? Are individuals' rights different under different circumstances? Why or why not? After a brief introductory discussion, have the students read this Government in Action feature independently.

Discuss

Guide the students in discussing the feature: Why do you think the principal ordered these two articles deleted from the school newspaper? Why do you think the students objected to the principal's action? Why do you imagine these three students chose to pursue their objections with a lawsuit? What would you consider "reasonable" restraint of a student's speech? What do you imagine the administrators of your school or school district might consider "reasonable" restraint? What kind of article in a school newspaper might result in a lawsuit against the school? In what specific ways do you think school officials might have the right to restrict the speech of teachers? Why? What does *coextensive* mean? Why are students' rights not automatically coextensive with adults' rights? What did Brennan mean by the term *enclaves of totalitarianism?* How real do you consider the danger Brennan cited?

Analyze and Apply

Let the students form several groups in which to explore different aspects of this question as it relates to your community. For example, members of one group might talk with the school's principal and vice principals; members of another group might interview

GOVERNMENT IN ACTION

CASE STUDY

Students and the First Amendment

In May 1983 Robert Reynolds, the principal of Hazelwood East High School near St. Louis, Missouri, ordered that two articles scheduled to appear in the school-sponsored student newspaper be deleted. One article dealt with student pregnancy, the other with the effects of parents' divorces on Hazelwood High students. The principal argued that the articles didn't properly protect student identities and dealt with subjects not suitable for younger students. He also asserted his right to censor the paper.

Three students working on the paper, the *Spectrum,* sued the school district, arguing that their First Amendment right to freedom of expression had been violated. After a **bench trial**—heard only in front of the judge—the U.S. District Court of the Eastern District of Missouri held that the students' First Amendment rights had not been violated. The court argued that school officials may restrain students' speech when this seems ''reasonable'' and when it is related directly to a school activity.

The case was appealed, and the U.S. Court of Appeals for the Eighth Circuit disagreed with the district court judge's decision. The court held that the newspaper was a public forum because it was intended as a ''conduit for student viewpoint'' and that school officials were entitled to censor only if the publication could have resulted in a lawsuit.

On a writ of *certiorari,* the United States Supreme Court, in *Hazelwood School District* v. *Cathy Kuhlmeier,* on January 13, 1988, reversed the court of appeals' ruling by a vote of 5 to 3. Justice Byron White, writing for the majority, argued that ''school officials may impose reasonable restrictions on the speech of students, teachers, and other members of the school community.'' The majority also noted that students' rights ''are not automatically coextensive with the rights of adults in other settings.''

In his dissent, Justice William Brennan (joined by Justices Thurgood Marshall and Harry Blackmun) said the decision might make public schools into ''enclaves of totalitarianism. . . .''

This Supreme Court decision prompted several state legislatures to consider writing specific state laws that spell out students' rights and, in some cases, that grant student publications specific privileges against such censorship.

THINK ABOUT IT

1. Do you think the principal's action violated the student-editors' rights?
2. To what extent does a school principal have the obligation to prevent students from publishing material that may be offensive to other students or to the school?

school districts. After the Court ordered schools to desegregate ''with all deliberate speed'' in 1955,[2] the governor and state legislators in Little Rock, Arkansas, violently opposed the Court's decision, which forced citizens to take the law into their own hands. A riot broke out in 1957, which caused President Eisenhower to federalize the state's national guard in order to quell the riot.

The Supreme Court at Work

The Supreme Court by law begins its regular annual term on the first Monday in October and usually adjourns in late June or early July of the following year. Special sessions may be held after the regular term is over, but only a few cases are decided in this way. More commonly, cases not heard in one session are carried into the next regular session. Cases that are brought to petition or appeal to the Court are scheduled for an oral argument

2. *Brown* v. *Board of Education* (1954).

members of the school board or other governing body; members of a third group might investigate policies at local elementary schools for younger children. Give the members of all groups an opportunity to share and discuss what they have learned.

Review
To help the students review this case study, ask these questions: Why did three students at Hazelwood East High School sue their school district? In how many courts was their case heard? How was their case finally resolved?

Think About It (Answers)
1. Answers will vary, e.g., the principal's actions were a violation of the students' First Amendment rights because students' personal expressions should be a protected right.

2. Answers will vary, e.g., the students should be the judge of whether or not they are offended. If so, they are free to discontinue reading the newspaper, write a letter to the editor, or otherwise let their opinions be known.

Extension
Have the students recall television news coverage of the first day of the current (or most recent) Supreme Court term.

Enrichment
Ask one of the students to research and report on the qualifications for lawyers presenting cases before the Supreme Court.

Extension
If possible, help the students invite to class a local lawyer who has presented at least one case before the Supreme Court or your state's supreme court. Arrange for the lawyer to discuss his or her experience and then to answer the students' questions.

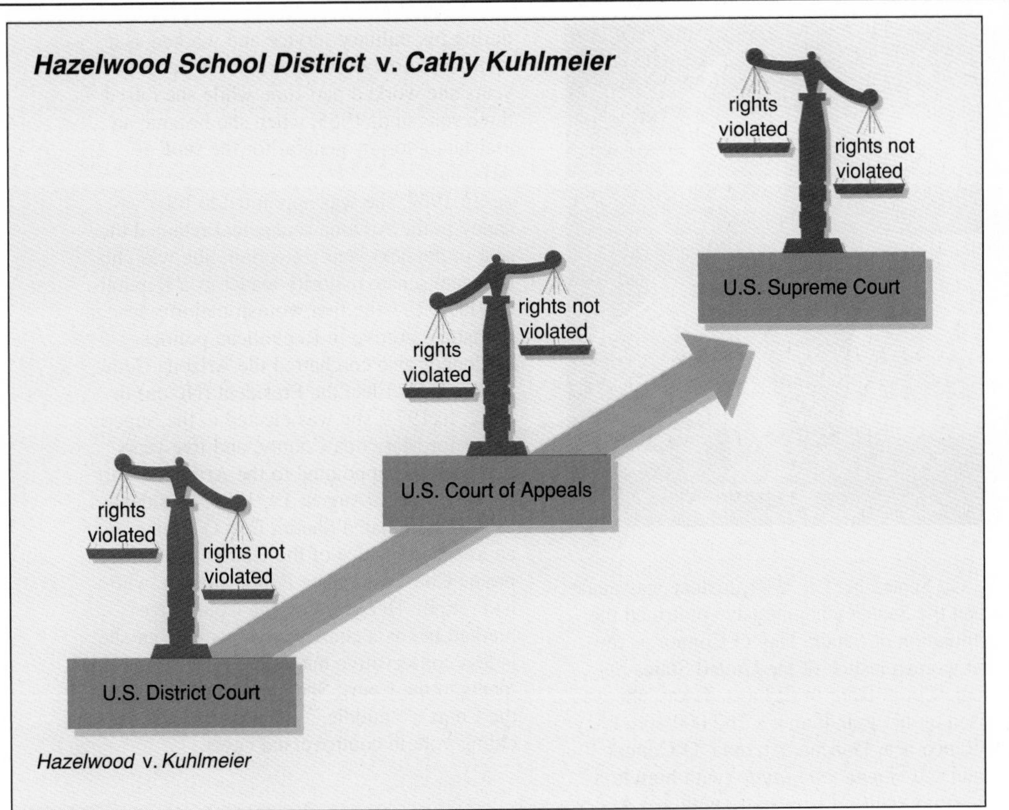

▲ ***Hazelwood School District* v. *Cathy Kuhlmeier*.** The figure above details the decisions of each court that heard *Hazelwood School District v. Cathy Kuhlmeier*. With which court do you agree? Why?

This figure content is also featured on *West's American Government Videodisc* (see the index found in the *TRB*) and is available in the transparency package.

or denied a hearing in a written "orders list" released on Mondays.

The Court hears oral arguments on Monday, Tuesday, Wednesday, and sometimes Thursday, usually for seven two-week sessions scattered from the first week in October to the end of April or the first week in May. Recesses are held between periods of oral arguments to allow the justices to consider the cases and handle other Court business. Oral arguments run from 10 A.M. to noon and again from 1 to 3 P.M., with thirty minutes granted for each side's argument, unless special exceptions are granted. All statements and the justices' questions are tape recorded during these sessions. Unlike most courts, lawyers addressing the Supreme Court can be questioned by the justices at any time during oral argument.

Deciding a Case: Private Research All of the crucial work on cases is done through private research and

TEACHING GOVERNMENT IN ACTION

Read
Introduce this feature about Sandra Day O'Connor by reading the first sentence of the feature aloud to the class. Explain to students that O'Connor will always be a very important historical figure, if for no other reason than her position as the first woman on the Supreme Court. Have a volunteer read the rest of this feature aloud to the class.

Discuss
Stimulate a class discussion of this material by asking the following questions: Do you think there is additional pressure on O'Connor because she is the only woman on the Supreme Court? Now that the Supreme Court is comprised of eight men and one woman, does it fairly represent the population of the United States?

Analyze and Apply
To further the students' understanding of the makeup of the current court, ask them to choose one of the eight remaining justices and write a profile of that man. The profile should be similar to this profile of Sandra Day O'Connor.

Review
Use the following questions to review the content of this feature: From what university did O'Connor receive her law degree? What experiences with discrimination has O'Connor had?

Think About It (Answers)
1. Her experiences as a deputy county attorney, a civilian attorney for the army, assistant attorney general for the State of Arizona, a superior court judge, and a judge for the Arizona Court of Appeals have all helped to prepare O'Connor for her job.
2. Women have begun to earn recognition and acceptance in the highest levels of government only recently.
3. Answers will vary, but might reflect the belief that O'Connor should be personally aware of many of the discrimination issues.
4. Answers will vary. Different reasons include the relative scarcity of opportunities for women at the lower courts to prepare them for a Supreme Court position.

Reteaching Strategies
1. Let the students work with partners to review and, if necessary, revise their outlines of Section 3.
2. Work with small groups of students. Guide the group members in writing a chronological list of the steps through which a case passes from its beginning to its final decision by the Supreme Court.

Evaluation Strategies
1. Have the students write their answers to the Section 3 Review questions.

GOVERNMENT IN ACTION

PROFILE

Sandra Day O'Connor

On September 21, 1981, history was made when the Senate unanimously confirmed the nomination of Sandra Day O'Connor as the first woman justice of the United States Supreme Court. Born in El Paso, Texas, she was raised on her grandfather's 162,000-acre Lazy B Ranch near Duncan, Arizona. O'Connor graduated *magna cum laude* (with high honors) from Stanford University with a B.A. degree in economics in 1950. Two years later, she earned her LL.B. (law degree) from Stanford University Law School where she was an editor of the *Stanford Law Review* and a member of the Order of the Coif, an honorary society. In law school, she was a classmate of one of her future colleagues on the U.S. Supreme Court, William H. Rehnquist.

As was common for women professionals in the early 1950s, O'Connor had some difficulty in finding employment in which she could use her legal training. After serving briefly as deputy county attorney for San Mateo County, California, from 1952 to 1953, she accompanied her husband to Germany during his military service and worked as a civilian attorney for the army. For several years she worked part time while she raised three sons until 1965, when she became an assistant attorney general for the state of Arizona.

In 1969, she was appointed to fill a vacancy in the Arizona senate and retained the seat in the next year's election. She was chosen state senate majority leader as a Republican in 1972—the first woman majority leader in history. Active in Republican politics, O'Connor also co-chaired the Arizona Committee to Re-Elect the President (Nixon) in 1972. In 1974, she was elected to the Superior Court for Maricopa County, and five years later she was appointed to the Arizona Court of Appeals. On August 19, 1981, President Reagan nominated Sandra Day O'Connor as an associate justice of the United States Supreme Court to replace Potter Stewart, who had retired. Her years on the Court have marked her as a conservative justice, but she is less conservative than more recent appointments to the Court. She has come to occupy the Court's "middle," often casting the deciding vote in controversial cases.

THINK ABOUT IT

1. What experience qualified Sandra Day O'Connor for her job?
2. Why did it take until 1981 for a woman to be placed on the Supreme Court?
3. Do you think O'Connor's experience in looking for a job as a female lawyer in the early 1950s helped her when she became the first woman justice to be placed on the Supreme Court?
4. It's been over ten years since President Reagan nominated Sandra Day O'Connor. In that time, there have been no other females nominated. Why do you think this is?

2. Have the students take the Section 3 Quiz found in the *TRB.*

Section 3 Review (Answers)

1. Answers will vary, e.g., when two or more federal courts of appeals have decided that an important state question is in conflict with state law. When a federal court of appeals has decided that an important question is in conflict with state law. When a federal court has decided that an important federal question is in conflict with the relevant decisions of the Supreme Court. When a federal court has departed from the accepted and usual course of judicial proceedings. (See list on page 443.)
2. The written decision of the Court containing the reasons for its decision, the rules of law that apply, and the judgment. A unanimous opinion is when all the judges agree. A majority opinion outlines the views of the majority of justices. A concurring opinion is written when a justice agrees with the final decision but wants to emphasize particular points. A dissenting opinion is written by justices who disagree with the majority decision.
3. Each justice does private research and consideration of the case's issues with the assistance of law clerks. Each Friday, the justices meet to discuss the cases. When the conference is over, the chief justice, if in the majority, will assign the writing of opinions. Decisions are announced orally by the author of the opinion.
4. Answers will vary, e.g., this does not mean the system is flawed. Each person still has their case heard in a court of law and has the right to appeal.

consideration of the case's issues. Each justice on the Supreme Court is entitled to four **law clerks**, recent graduates of law schools who undertake much of the research and preliminary drafting necessary for the justices to form an opinion. It is sometimes suspected that because of their extensive assistance, the law clerks form a kind of junior court in themselves, deciding the fate of the appeals and petitions. Some unhappy lawyers have even suggested that the Senate should no longer confirm the appointment of justices, but rather the appointment of law clerks. Despite such criticism, while clerks do help in screening the large volume of petitions and in the preliminary research work for cases under review, the justices themselves are the ones who decide the cases.

Deciding a Case: The Friday Conference Each Friday during the annual Court term, the justices meet in conference to discuss cases under consideration and to decide which new appeals and petitions the Court will accept. These conferences take place in an oak-paneled chamber and are strictly private—no law clerks, secretaries, tape recorders, or video cameras are allowed.

In the justices' conference, certain procedures are traditionally observed. Upon entering the room, each justice shakes hands with all present. The justices then sit by order of seniority around a large, rectangular table. Each case is discussed by each justice in that order, with the chief justice starting the discussion. The chief justice determines the order in which the cases are called, guides the discussion, and in most cases sets the tone for a case.

In the Court of Chief Justice John Marshall, after each discussion a vote was taken in reverse order of seniority. Today, justices seldom vote formally; instead, the chief justice gets a sense of what the majority wants by listening to the justices' individual arguments. When each conference is over, the chief justice, if in the majority, will assign the writing of opinions. When the chief justice is not in the majority, the most senior justice in the majority assigns the writing. Since 1965, decisions have been announced on whichever day they are ready to be released. They are usually presented orally, in summary form, in open session by the author of the opinion. Concurring or dissenting opinions may also be presented by other justices.

After the necessary editing and the publication of preliminary prints, the official Court decision is placed in the *United States Reports,* the official record of the Court's decisions, which is available in many libraries. These decisions are also printed in West Publishing Company's *Supreme Court Reporter,* which is available about a year sooner.

Section 3 Review

1. Name four situations in which the Supreme Court may issue a writ of *certiorari.*
2. What is an opinion of the Court? What four types of opinions may the court issue?
3. Briefly describe the process by which the Supreme Court makes its decisions.
4. **For critical analysis:** Do you think the fact that no one unconditionally has the right to have his or her case heard before the Supreme Court means that our judicial system is flawed? Why or why not?

Section 4

Supreme Court Appointments and Ideology

Preview Questions

- How are Supreme Court justices nominated? Are they always confirmed?
- What are the characteristics of most Supreme Court justices?

The power to nominate Supreme Court justices belongs solely to the president. This is not to say, however, that the president's nominations are always confirmed. In fact, almost 20 percent of the presidential nominations for the Supreme Court have been either rejected or not acted upon by the Senate. Many bitter battles over Supreme Court appointments have ensued when the Senate and the president have not seen eye to eye about political matters.

From the beginning of Andrew Jackson's presidency in 1829 to the end of Ulysses S. Grant's presidency in 1877, the U.S. Senate had a long record of refusing to confirm the president's judicial nominations. This trend changed from 1893 until 1968, during which time the Senate rejected only three Court nominees. From 1968 through 1983, however, there were two rejections of presidential nominees to the highest court, both of whom were appointed by president Richard Nixon—G. Harold Carswell and Clement Haynsworth. Both were from the South because Nixon wanted to increase his Southern support. Both were rejected because of questions about their racial attitudes. In addition, one of President Lyndon Johnson's nominations was not acted on, and his choice for chief justice in 1968—Abe Fortas, a then-current

SECTION 4

Points to Stress

- The nomination process for Supreme Court justices.
- Characteristics of most Supreme Court justices.

Kickoff Activity

Ask the students to list the names of as many of the current Supreme Court justices as they can recall. Once all the students have completed their lists, read the names aloud and have the students check and correct their own lists with the list found in the Resource Center at the back of this book.

Working with the Preview Questions

Guide the students in reading and considering these study questions. Remind the students to keep the questions in mind as they study Section 4.

Teaching Strategies

Introduction

Ask two or three students to read the section introduction aloud to the rest of the class. Then stimulate discussion with questions such as these: What do you think leads to the relatively high rate of rejection of presidential nominations for the Supreme Court? What does this rate indicate about the relationship between the president and the Senate?

Discussion Starter
Guide the students in discussing Taft's unique career, in which he served first as president and then as a justice: What advantages do you imagine Taft brought to his work on the Supreme Court? In what respects—if any—do you think his background might have been a disadvantage?

Critical Thinking Skills
Ask the students to analyze and compare the powers held by the president and the powers held by the chief justice of the Supreme Court: Which position is likely to have the stronger immediate influence? Which position is likely to have the stronger long-term influence? In which position can an individual exert a stronger personal influence? Which position would you prefer to hold? Why?

Discussion Starter
Encourage the students to consider the lack of minority representation on the Supreme Court: Do you believe the justices can fairly deal with issues with which they have no personal experience? What kinds of understanding and insight can minority justices bring to the Court? How important do you consider the contributions they might make?

Caption Answer Bitter battles often ensue during the confirmation process, and the Senate has either rejected or refused to act on almost 20 percent of all nominations to date.

In 1987, Ronald Reagan had two Supreme Court nominees, Robert Bork and Douglas Ginsberg, fail to get past the Senate and onto the Court. Here he is shown with his third choice, Anthony Kennedy, who was approved by the Senate. Are many nominees rejected by the Senate?

member of the Court—was withdrawn after a question arose during confirmation hearings involving Fortas's association with an industrialist convicted of violating laws dealing with the trading of stocks. That problem resulted in Fortas's eventual resignation from the Court.

President Ronald Reagan found two of his nominees for a Supreme Court vacancy rejected by the Senate. Both were then current judges in the courts of appeals. In 1987, he first nominated Robert Bork, who sometimes faced hostile questioning by the Senate on his views of the Constitution. Next Reagan nominated Douglas Ginsburg, who ultimately withdrew his nomination when the press leaked information about his alleged use of marijuana during the 1970s. Finally, the Senate approved Reagan's third choice, Anthony Kennedy.

Ideology plays an important role in the president's choices for the Supreme Court. It also plays a large role in whether or not the Senate confirms that choice. There has been an extremely partisan distribution of presidential appointments to the federal judiciary. In the two hundred year history of the U.S. Supreme Court, fewer than 14 percent of the justices nominated by a president have been from an opposing political party.

Who Becomes a Supreme Court Justice?

Although the Constitution sets no specific qualifications for those who serve on the Supreme Court, all who have served share certain characteristics. The makeup of the federal judiciary is far from typical of the American public. Figure 18–3 summarizes the backgrounds of all of the 106 Supreme Court justices to 1992.

In general, the justices' partisan attachments have been mostly the same as those of the presidents who appointed them.

As you can see in the table, the most common occupational background of the justices has been private legal practice or state or federal judgeships at the time of their appointment. Those ten justices who were in federal executive posts at the time of their appointment held the high offices of secretary of state, comptroller of the treasury, secretary of the Navy, postmaster general, secretary of the interior, chairman of the Securities and Exchange Commission, and secretary of labor. In the "other" category in the table are two justices who were professors of law (including William Howard Taft, a former president), and one justice who was a North Carolina state employee responsible for organizing and revising the state's statutes.

Most justices were in their fifties when they assumed office, although two were as young as thirty-two and one as old as sixty-six. The average age of newly sworn justices is about fifty-three.

Note also that the great majority of justices have had a college education. By and large, those who did not attend college or receive a degree lived in the late eighteenth and early nineteenth centuries when a college education was much less common than it is today. In recent years, justices have typically had degrees from such pres-

Discussion Starter
Help the students discuss and respond to figure 18–3, Profile of Supreme Court Justices to 1992: What portrait of the "typical justice" emerges from this table? In what respects is that typical justice different from you? From the general population? What do you consider the significance of those differences?

Profile of Supreme Court Justices to 1992

	Number of Justices (106 = Total)
Occupational Position Before Appointment	
Private legal practice	25
State judgeship	21
Federal judgeship	26
U.S. Attorney General	7
Deputy or Assistant U.S. Attorney General	2
U.S. Solicitor General	2
U.S. Senator	6
U.S. Representative	2
State governor	3
Federal executive post	9
Other	3
Religious Background	
Protestant	83
Roman Catholic	10
Jewish	5
Unitarian	7
No religious affiliation	1
Age on Appointment	
Under 40	5
41–50	31
51–60	56
61–70	14
Political Party Affiliation	
Federalist (to 1835)	13
Democratic-Republican (to 1828)	7
Whig (to 1861)	1
Democrat	42
Republican	42
Independent	1
Educational Background	
College graduate	90
Not college graduate	16
Sex	
Male	105
Female	1
Race	
Caucasian	104
Other	2

FIGURE 18–3 Profile of Supreme Court Justices to 1992. This table summarizes the backgrounds of all 106 Supreme Court Justices to 1992. Note that all but 16 of these individuals were college graduates. During what period of our country's history did these 16 justices serve on the Court?

This figure content is also featured on *West's American Government Videodisc* (see the index found in the *TRB*).

Figure Answer The Justices who did not attend college or receive a degree lived in the late 18th and early 19th centuries when a college education was not as common or as important as it is today.

tigious institutions as Yale, Harvard, or Columbia. It is interesting that many of the earlier college-educated justices did not hold their degrees in law. In fact, it was not until 1957 that all the then-current members of the Court were law school graduates.

The religious background of Supreme Court justices is strikingly atypical of that of the American population as a whole, even making allowances for changes over time in the religious composition of the nation. Catholics (and certain Protestant denominations, notably Baptists

Figure Answer The minimum salary for District Court or other special federal court judges is $89,500 per year. The maximum salary for a federal judge is $115,000 for the Chief Justice of the Supreme Court.

This figure content is also featured on *West's American Government Videodisc* (see the index found in the *TRB*).

Enrichment
Let interested students research and report on the "Jewish seat" on the Court: When and why was Cardoza appointed to the Court? What were the reactions to his appointment? Who else has held this "Jewish seat"? By whom was it regarded as important?

Discussion Starter
Help the students consider and discuss figure 18–4 on the salaries for justices and judges: What is your reaction to these levels of compensation? How do these salaries compare to the salaries earned by private-practice lawyers?

Reteaching Strategies
1. Ask each student to write a brief topic outline, summarizing the information presented in Section 4.
2. Have the students work in pairs to write paragraphs describing the "typical justice" of the Supreme Court.

Evaluation Strategies
1. Have the students write their answers to the Section 4 Review questions.
2. Have the students take the Section 4 Quiz found in the *TRB.*

Section 4 Review (Answers)
1. They have been rejected for various reasons including questions about their racial attitudes and questions involving association with criminals.
2. The most common occupational background has been private legal practice or state or federal judgeships. Most were in their fifties when they assumed office and most have had a college education.
3. Answers will vary, e.g., the position is an important one and senators from each party want appointees who represent that party's interests.

SECTION 5

Points to Stress
- Arguments against judicial activism and judicial restraint.
- Checks that the legislative branch has on the judicial branch.
- Checks that the executive branch has on the judicial branch.

Kickoff Activity
Give the students five minutes in which to write their own definitions of the terms *activism* and *restraint.* Then ask volunteers to read their definitions aloud, and encourage the students to compare and discuss their responses.

Working with the Preview Questions
Have the students read these study questions, and let volunteers identify the paragraphs or parts of Section 5 in which they expect to find the answers. Then ask the stu-

Pay Scale for Federal Judges

Court	Salary
Supreme Court	$100,000 (except for the chief justice, who receives $115,000)
Court of Appeals	$95,000
District Court	$89,500
Other Special Federal Courts	From $89,500 to $95,000

FIGURE 18–4 Pay Scale for Federal Judges. This table shows the pay scale for federal judges at each federal judiciary level. What is the minimum a federal judge can make? What is the maximum a federal judge can make?

and Lutherans) have been underrepresented, whereas Protestants in general (Episcopalians, Presbyterians, Methodists, and others), as well as Unitarians, have been overrepresented among the justices. Typically, there has been a "Catholic seat" on the Court, with interruptions, and a "Jewish seat" existed without a break from 1916 until 1969, when Fortas resigned.

Payment

The Constitution in Article III, Section 1 states that federal judges "shall, at stated times, receive for their services a compensation which shall not be diminished during their continuance in office." This means that while in office, justices cannot have their salaries lowered. Congress determines the salaries for the justices of the Supreme Court and the judges of all other federal courts as well.

In addition, federal judges receive advantageous retirement benefits. If, for example, justices have been on the bench for at least ten years and retire at age 70, they receive full salary for the rest of their lives. If they have been on the bench for fifteen years, they may retire at full salary at age 65.

SECTION 4 REVIEW

1. For what reasons has the Senate rejected presidential nominations for the Supreme Court?
2. Name the most common characteristics of the people who have historically served on the Supreme Court.
3. **For critical analysis:** If Supreme Court justices are supposed to make decisions that are free from political bias, why has the Senate confirmation of justices become such an ideological battle?

SECTION 5

Judicial Activism and Judicial Restraint

Preview Questions

- What are some of the arguments that support judicial activism? What are the ones that support judicial restraint?
- What checks does the legislative branch place on the judicial system?
- What checks does the executive branch place on the judiciary?

Judicial scholars like to characterize different Supreme Courts and Supreme Court justices as being either activist or restraintist. Those advocating the practice of **judicial activism** believe the Court should use its power to alter the direction of the activities of Congress, state legislatures, and administrative agencies such as the Federal Trade Commission and the Federal Aviation Administration. Those advocating the practice of **judicial restraint** believe the Court should only rarely use its powers of judicial review. In other words, whatever popularly elected legislatures decide should not be thwarted by the Supreme Court, as long as such decisions are not unconstitutional.

During the early years of the nation, the Supreme Court certainly was in no position to exercise judicial activism. Indeed, in *The Federalist Papers,* Alexander Hamilton stated that "the judiciary is beyond comparison the weakest of the three departments of power." The Supreme Court during its first decade proved that remark, as it handled few matters and decided only one important case.

dents to take notes as they read the section, using the study questions as a guide.

Teaching Strategies

Introduction
Have volunteers read this section introduction aloud, and guide the students in discussing it: How is the distinction between activism and restraint different from the distinction between liberalism and conservatism? What would you expect from an activist conservative judge? A restrained conservative judge? An activist liberal judge? A restrained liberal judge?

Discussion Starter
Help the students discuss the independence of our judicial system: What makes our system so independent? Whom does this independence benefit? Why? What other systems can you cite that function with less independence? On whom are those judicial systems dependent? Who usually suffers as a result?

TEACHING BUILDING SOCIAL STUDIES SKILLS

Read
Before the students read this Building Social Studies Skills feature, give them an opportunity to discuss their own ideas about fact and opinion: How do they differ? Why is understanding the difference important? Then let the students read the feature independently.

Discuss
Guide a discussion of the feature by asking questions such as these: If the State Endowment for Humanities no longer provides funds to writers, is the example statement still a fact? Why or why not? If you agree that the art funded by the State Endowment for Humanities is ugly, is the example statement still an opinion? Why or why not? What other statements of fact can you make about the State Endowment for Humanities? What makes each a statement of fact? What other statements of opinion can you make about the State Endowment for Humanities? What makes each a statement of opinion?

Analyze and Apply
Have the students work in groups to find and analyze newspaper articles relating to a single topic. Assign group members to select at least one news story and one editorial: Which is intended to present facts? Which is intended to present opinion? What facts and opinions can you identify in both articles?

Review
To help the students review this feature, ask them to define *fact* and *opinion.*

BUILDING SOCIAL STUDIES SKILLS

Distinguishing Between Fact and Opinion

When investigating issues, it is important that one distinguish between statements of fact and statements of opinion. It is also important to recognize that, while statements of fact may appear to be true, they may be based on inaccurate or false information. A *fact* is a statement that can be proven by evidence such as records, documents, or unbiased historical sources. An *opinion* is a statement that may contain some truth, but also contains personal opinions or value-based statements.

Consider the following statement: "The State Endowment for Humanities provides state funds to artists and writers." This statement would be a fact because it could be easily verified by state government records. Consider this statement: "The State Endowment for Humanities funds ugly art." Whether or not the art is ugly is an opinion. It is a statement based on personal values. It cannot be proven with facts and leaves room for disagreement.

Use these guidelines when distinguishing between fact and opinion:

- Ask yourself what idea the writer or speaker wants you to accept.
- Pinpoint the statements being used to communicate or support the idea.
- Ask yourself if and how these statements can be verified or proven.

PRACTICING YOUR SKILLS

Find a copy of a politician's speech. (Look in *Vital Speeches of the Day,* which you can find in your school or local library, or you can find excerpts from speeches in the *New York Times.*) Read at least two pages of the speech. Make a list of statements of fact and the statements of opinion, and tell why you think each statement is what it is. Finally, explain why you agree or disagree with the view presented.

The difference between activist judges and those who exercise restraint is not always the same as the difference between political liberals and conservatives. In the early 1930s, for example, the Supreme Court was activist and conservative, ruling that extensive regulation of business was unconstitutional. In the later 1930s, however, the Court became restrained and liberal, ruling that regulation was in fact constitutional.

In the 1950s and 1960s, the Court was activist and liberal. Many of the Court's critics believed it should have exercised more restraint. They criticized the first *Brown* v. *Board of Education* decision in 1954 (see Chapter 6) on the grounds that the highest court settled a problem of school racial segregation that should have been resolved by Congress or have been left to the states.

Critics of the current courts call them "mini-legislatures." They argue, for example, that in *Baker* v. *Carr* (1962) the federal courts wrongly exercised jurisdiction over the issue of state legislative districting plans and that the U.S. Supreme Court has no right to intervene in such state matters.

Another activist decision in the 1970s was *Roe* v. *Wade,* (1973), in which the U.S. Supreme Court gave women the right to an abortion during the first and second trimesters of pregnancy. This decision struck down state statutes that only permitted abortions in special cases. In the late 1980s and early 1990s, Supreme Court decisions indicated an unmistakable change in the Court's attitude toward civil rights (see Chapter 6). Some critics fear that the current Court, with its conservative majority, will become increasingly activist in this and other areas in the 1990s and beyond.

The question of judicial activism is closely linked to the actual constraints on our judicial system.

What Checks Our Courts?

Our judicial system is probably the most independent in the world. But the courts do not have absolute independence, for they are part of the political process. Political checks limit the extent to which courts can exercise judicial review and still make activist changes. These checks are exercised by the legislature, the executive branch, other courts, and the public.

Legislative Checks Courts may make rulings, but often the legislatures at the local, state, and federal levels are required to appropriate funds to carry out those rul-

Enrichment
Ask a group of volunteers to find specific examples of all three means by which legislatures can check the influence of the courts. Have these volunteers prepare and present a chart of their findings.

Discussion Starter
Encourage the students to discuss the fact that lower courts sometimes ignore decisions made by the Supreme Court: How do you think this can be allowed to happen? What—if anything—should be done when a lower court ignores or goes against a Supreme Court decision? Why? Do you think a lower court might ever be correct in ignoring rulings of the higher court? Why or why not?

Enrichment
Ask the students to do further reading on the *Dred Scott* case and then to discuss their findings: Who was involved? How did the case reach the Supreme Court? How did the Court justify its decision? To what extent did public opinion support the Court's decision? How did the decision stir public attitudes against the Court and its ruling? How did the *Dred Scott* case contribute to the onset of the Civil War?

Reteaching Strategies
1. Ask the students to work with partners, comparing and discussing their notes on Section 5. Encourage the students to refer to the text and to revise their notes if necessary.
2. Let the students work in small groups to write original paragraphs explaining the differences between judicial activism and judicial restraint and discussing the significance of those differences.

Evaluation Strategies
1. Have the students write their answers to the Section 5 Review questions.
2. Have the students take the Section 5 Quiz found in the *TRB*.

Section 5 Review (Answers)
1. Judicial activism is the belief that the Supreme Court should play an active role in shaping American life. Judicial restraint is the belief that the Supreme Court should rarely use its powers of judicial review.
2. Legislatures can pass new laws that overturn court rulings. Legislatures might not appropriate funds to carry out the Court's decisions. Court rulings can be overturned by constitutional amendments proposed by Congress.
3. Presidents can appoint new justices and judges with views in line with their administration. A president, governor, or mayor can refuse to enforce court rulings.
4. Higher courts can reverse the decisions of lower courts. If the court's decisions are at odds with the national consensus, it will lose its support and some of its power.
5. Answers will vary, e.g., a more conservative president would be more likely to nominate a justice who believed in judicial restraint.

ings. When such funds are not appropriated, the court in effect has been checked. A court, for example, may decide that prison conditions must be improved, but if a legislature does not find the funds to carry out such a ruling, the decision is basically nullified.

Court rulings can also be overturned by constitutional amendments at both the federal and state levels. Many amendments to the U.S. Constitution check the state courts' ability to allow discrimination, for example. Recently, however, proposals to amend the Constitution in order to reverse the courts' decisions on school prayer, flag burning, and abortion have failed.

Finally, legislatures can pass new laws that overturn court rulings. This may happen particularly when a court interprets a statute in a way that Congress disapproves of, or when a court finds no relevant statute to apply in certain cases. The legislature can then pass a new statute to counter the court's ruling.

Executive Checks Presidents have the power to change the direction of the Supreme Court and the federal judiciary by appointing new justices and judges whose ideologies are more in line with the current administration. Also, a president, governor, or mayor can refuse to enforce a court's rulings. As quoted earlier, President Andrew Jackson, in response to Chief Justice Marshall's ruling that a state could not pass laws governing Native Americans on their own territory within that state, said, "John Marshall has made his decision. Now let him enforce it."

'It's nothing personal, Prescott. It's just that a higher court gets a kick out of overruling a lower court."

The Rest of the Judiciary Higher courts can reverse the decisions of lower courts, but lower courts can also put a check on higher courts. The Supreme Court, for example, cannot possibly hear all of the cases that go through the lower courts. Lower courts can and have directly or indirectly ignored Supreme Court decisions by deciding in the other direction in particular cases. Only if a case goes to the Supreme Court can the Court correct such a situation.

Public Checks History has shown members of the Supreme Court that if their decisions are noticeably further ahead of or at odds with a national consensus, it will lose its support and some of its power. Perhaps the best example was the *Dred Scott* decision of 1857, in which the Supreme Court held that slaves were not citizens of the United States, nor were they entitled to the rights and privileges of citizenship. The Court ruled, in addition, that the Missouri Compromise banning slavery in the territories was unconstitutional. Most observers contend that the *Dred Scott* ruling contributed to making the Civil War inevitable.

Observers of the court system believe that the judges' sense of self-preservation forces them to develop a sense of self-restraint. Some observers even argue that this sense of self-restraint is more important than the other checks previously discussed.

After studying this chapter you should be able to see why Alexis de Tocqueville contended that federal judges keep the Constitution from becoming a "dead letter."

Section 5 Review

1. Briefly describe the practices of judicial activism and judicial restraint.
2. What legislative checks are placed on the courts?
3. What executive checks are placed on the courts?
4. What other checks are placed on the courts?
5. **For critical analysis:** What type of president normally wants to nominate a Supreme Court justice who believes in judicial restraint?

TEACHING CHALLENGE TO THE AMERICAN DREAM

Read

As an introduction to this Challenge to the American Dream feature, encourage the students to discuss their own ideas about the current Supreme Court: Do you consider the current Court liberal or conservative? Why? Do the general views of the justices conform to your views? If not, do you feel you are unfairly served by the Supreme Court? Why or why not? After a brief discussion, ask for volunteers to read the feature aloud to the rest of the class.

Discuss

Pose questions such as these to help the students discuss the Challenge to the American Dream feature: What are the meaning and the significance of the quotation from the *Wall Street Journal.* How does the source of the quotation affect your evaluation of its significance? Do you believe voters can validly object to Supreme Court nominees because those individuals are not sympathetic to the voters' views? Why or why not? How and why could a biased court bring about civil unrest?

Analyze and Apply

Have the students work in small groups to discuss the background and qualifications they consider most important in a Supreme Court justice. Then ask the group members to work together to write a one-page advertisement for a new justice, including a brief description of job responsibilities and a more detailed explanation of the requirements the students have chosen to set forth. Provide an opportunity for all the students to read and discuss the other groups' advertisements.

Review

Ask the students to review questions such as these: Why does the Supreme Court seem to be "firmly headed in a conservative direction"? Why is it important for the Supreme Court to act neutrally on major issues?

You Decide (Answers)

1. Answers will vary, e.g., affirmative action programs might be severely restricted. The rights of the accused might be limited.

2. Answers will vary, e.g., yes, the Court would better represent the "will of the People" if the justices were elected. Note that students should also understand that popularly elected justices might not be as apt to protect minority rights.

CHALLENGE TO THE AMERICAN DREAM

Has the Federal Judiciary Become Too Conservative?

Justice Thurgood Marshall

Presidents often attempt to pick justices who share their beliefs. Although it is not possible to predict with certainty how a judge will vote on any particular case, a judge's record, including written opinions and/or public statements, offers the best guide.

In the beginning of the 1990s, there were few remaining liberal justices. By 1990, the liberal justices left were William Brennan (age 84), Thurgood Marshall (age 81), Harry Blackmun (age 81), and John Stevens (age 70). The remaining five justices were more conservative and younger. On June 28 of that year, the *Wall Street Journal* summarized the latest Supreme Court session by saying that the Court is "now firmly headed in a conservative direction."

When Justice Brennan retired in 1990, President Bush nominated New Hampshire Judge David Souter. Civil rights leaders and women's groups argued that Souter was not sympathetic to their views. He was nonetheless confirmed in Senate nomination hearings.

In 1991, liberal Justice Thurgood Marshall retired. President Bush nominated a conservative, Clarence Thomas, to replace him. Thomas was confirmed only after one of the most politicized confirmation hearings in history. Thomas clearly holds much more conservative views than Thurgood Marshall. Only two liberals remain on the Court as of 1992. The conservative direction of the Court is guaranteed for some time.

The challenge to the American dream is for Supreme Court justices, whatever their philosophical beliefs, to make decisions that provide justice not only for the individuals involved in the court cases, but also for our society as a whole.

You Decide

1. What aspects of American social, political, and economic life might change if the Court becomes 100 percent conservative?
2. Would the composition of the court more nearly represent the "will of the people" if the justices were elected rather than appointed?

CHAPTER 18 REVIEW

Key Terms

appellate jurisdiction 436
bench trial 444
case law 431
civil law 432
common law 431
concurrent jurisdiction 442
concurring opinion 443
criminal law 432
dissenting opinion 443
diversity of citizenship 442
exclusive jurisdiction 442
federal question 442
felonies 433
hung jury 435
judicial activism 450
judicial circuits 438
judicial implementation 443
judicial restraint 450
judicial review 442
jurisdiction 433
jury duty 434
law clerks 447
majority opinion 443
opinion 443
oral arguments 443
original jurisdiction 436
plaintiff 442
precedent 432
statutory law 432
summons 433
unanimous opinion 443
writ of *certiorari* 442

Chapter Evaluation

To evaluate student mastery of chapter material, you might:

1. Use Chapter Test A from the *TRB.*
2. Use Chapter Test B from the *TRB.*
3. Construct your own test using items from the *West American Government Test Bank* found in the *TRB.*
4. Use the accompanying computerized test software to construct and print a customized chapter test.

Review Questions (Answers)

1. Laws based on judicial decisions that are based on accepted traditions and customs.
2. Civil law spells out the duties that exist between persons or between citizens and their governments. Criminal law has to do with wrongs committed against the public as a whole.
3. Jurisdiction refers either to the geographical area within which a court has the right to decide cases, or to the right of a court to decide matters concerning certain persons, property, or subject matter.
4. The three tiers are made up of trial courts, intermediate courts of appeals, and the Supreme Court.
5. Courts of appeals hear appeals from the district courts.
6. It established the power of judicial review.
7. A party must request the Court to issue a writ of *certiorari* and the Court then decides whether or not to grant the writ.
8. When the federal court of appeals has decided that an important state question is in conflict with state law or when the court of appeals holds that a state statute violates federal law. (See complete list, page 443.)
9. A unanimous opinion when all justices agree. A majority opinion outlining the views of the majority. A concurring opinion when a justice agrees with the conclusion but agrees for different reasons. A dissenting opinion when a justice does not agree with the majority.
10. Research and consideration of the issues is done by each justice and his or her four law clerks. Each Friday the justices meet to discuss the cases and certain procedures are observed. Decisions are announced orally by the author of the opinion.
11. Justices are nominated by the president but must be confirmed by the Senate.
12. College educated, usually lawyers, in their fifties when nominated, and Protestants.
13. Judicial activism is the Supreme Court playing an active role in altering the direction of Congress, state legislatures, and administrative agencies. Judicial restraint is the Supreme Court rarely using its powers of judicial review.
14. Legislatures can pass new laws that overturn court rulings.

CHAPTER 18 REVIEW—Continued

Summary

1. Common law began as the ancient unwritten law of England but today includes the laws made by legislatures and the case law background of England and of the American colonies prior to the American revolution. Statutory law is law enacted by state legislatures and the U.S. Congress. A law in violation of the Constitution, no matter what its source, will be declared unconstitutional and will not be enforced. Civil law spells out the duties that exist between persons or between citizens and their governments. Criminal law, in contrast, has to do with wrongs committed against the public as a whole. Jurisdiction refers to the geographical area within which a court has the power to decide cases.

2. The federal court system is a three-tiered structure that consists of trial courts, intermediate courts of appeals, and the Supreme Court. Congress has established twelve judicial circuits (plus the federal circuit) that hear appeals from the district courts located within their respective circuits. Article III of the Constitution established the boundaries of federal judicial power. Among the cases in which federal courts have jurisdiction are cases involving federal law and cases involving diversity of citizenship, bankruptcy, patents, and copyrights.

3. Thousands of cases are filed with the Supreme Court each year, yet on average, it hears only about two hundred. To bring a case before the Supreme Court, a party requests the Court to issue a writ of *certiorari,* which is an order issued to a lower court requiring it to send the record of the case in question. Whether the Court will issue the writ is entirely within its discretion. The Court's decisions are written in an opinion. When all justices unanimously agree on an opinion, it is written for the entire court in a unanimous opinion. When there is not a unanimous opinion, a majority opinion is written, outlining the views of the majority of justices involved in the particular case. In other than unanimous opinions, one or more dissenting opinions are usually written by those justices who did not agree with the majority. Law clerks undertake much of the research and preliminary drafting necessary for the justices to form an opinion. Each Friday during the annual term, the justices meet in conference to discuss cases under consideration and to decide which new appeals and petitions the Court will accept.

4. The power to nominate Supreme Court justices belongs solely to the president, but the nominee must be confirmed by the Senate. Ideology plays an important role in the president's choices and in the Senate's confirmation. The makeup of the federal judiciary is not typical of the American public.

5. Those advocating the practice of judicial activism believe the Court should use its power to alter the direction of the activities of Congress, state legislatures, and administrative agencies. Those advocating the practice of judicial restraint believe the Court should only rarely use its powers of judicial review. Political checks limit the extent to which courts can exercise judicial review. The legislature, the executive branch, other courts, and the public all place checks on the courts.

Review Questions

1. What is common law?
2. What is the difference between civil law and criminal law?
3. What is meant by jurisdiction?
4. Briefly describe the three-tiered structure of the federal court system.
5. What is the role of the court of appeals in the federal court system?
6. What was the significance of *Marbury* v. *Madison*?
7. How do cases reach the Supreme Court?
8. Name several situations in which the Supreme Court may issue a writ of *certiorari.*
9. Describe the four types of written opinions that can be presented by the Supreme Court.
10. Briefly describe the procedures the Supreme Court justices follow when deciding a case.
11. How are Supreme Court justices nominated? What role does the Senate play in the nomination process?
12. Name the most common characteristics of the Supreme Court justices.
13. Define the practices of judicial activism and judicial restraint.
14. What political checks limit the extent to which the courts can exercise judicial review and make activist changes?
15. What does it mean to be summoned for jury duty?

Legislatures can fail to appropriate funds to carry out decisions. Court rulings can be overturned by constitutional amendments. Presidents can appoint judges and justices with their beliefs. Higher courts can reverse lower courts. The public withdraws support if decisions are noticeably at odds with the national consensus.

15. The court has called you to serve. It is your duty to appear at the time and place specified or submit a valid excuse.

Questions for Thought and Discussion (Answers)

1. Answers will vary, e.g., life terms are advantageous because the justices gain knowledge and experience over the years. The judges are able to decide cases based on their interpretations of the Court and law instead of election results. They are disadvantageous because the justice cannot be made to reflect the will of the people.

2. Answers will vary, e.g., no, judges should not be popularly elected because they would become too involved in partisan politics. Judges should be knowledgeable in the law, experienced on the bench, fair, and honest.

3. Answers will vary, e.g., when the Supreme Court decides on an issue, it often changes laws pertaining to that issue. In effect, it is making the law.

4. Answers will vary, e.g., judges should use the evidence presented and their best judgment.

Social Studies Skills (Answers)

1. The judicial districts in the East are much smaller than those in the West. This is probably because when they were created, the West was (and still is) relatively less densely populated than the East.

CHAPTER 18 REVIEW—Continued

Questions for Thoughts and Discussion

1. Do you think it is a good idea that Supreme Court justices are appointed for life? What are the advantages and disadvantages of such an arrangement?
2. Do you think federal judges should be popularly elected? What qualifications would you like to see in a federal judge?
3. Some analysts argue that the Supreme Court often makes the law instead of interpreting it. Do you agree or disagree with this statement? Give reasons for your answer.
4. Sometimes cases arise in which there is no precedent. How do you think a judge should decide such a case?

Improving Your Skills

Communication Skills

Conducting an Interview

Interviewing people who have worked in and around government is an excellent way of learning more about how our government works. These people can often offer insights and firsthand information that is difficult to obtain by reading newspapers and watching the news. To conduct a successful interview you will need to be well prepared and organized. Follow these guidelines:

- **Arrange the details, in person or by telephone, with the person to be interviewed.** Politely and clearly identify yourself, your school, and your teacher. Tell the person why you would like the interview. If the person agrees, suggest a few different times and dates that might be convenient for the person.
- **Decide in advance what information you want to obtain from the interview.** Decide ahead of time which questions will most likely lead to that information. Prioritize the questions, taking into consideration the amount of time you have with that person. Avoid questions that require only yes or no answers. Try to ask questions that will encourage the person to go into detail about the subject matter. Encourage the person to use examples and stories to illustrate the point.
- **Write down a formal list of questions.** If you are working in a group, decide who will ask which questions and in what order. Check the questions with your teacher.
- **Practice asking the questions to classmates.**
- **During the interview, try to make the person feel welcome and comfortable.** Do not become argumentative.
- **After the interview, thank the person.** Send a thank-you note as a final follow-up.

Writing

Suppose that you have the opportunity to interview a Supreme Court justice. Decide what information you would most like to know from this person. Create a formal list of ten questions, written down in order of priority, that you would most likely ask. Give a brief explanation of why you think each of these questions is important.

Social Studies Skills

Map Reading

Carefully examine again Figure 18–2 on page 438. What can be said about the size of the judicial districts in the East relative to the size of those in the West? How would you explain this difference?

Activities and Projects

1. Research a presidential appointee to the Supreme Court who has been rejected by the Senate. In your research, try to find out why the Senate opposed the nominee. Then decide whether you think the Senate's decision was correct. Report your findings to the class.
2. Go to the nearest courthouse in which you would be allowed to sit in on a jury trial. Sit in on a trial, taking note of what the issue is, who the accused is, and the arguments of the two different sides. Write a summary of what happened during the time you spent in the trial.
3. Stage a debate in class on the following: Resolved—The makeup of the federal judiciary should better represent the makeup of the nation in terms of gender, ethnicity, and race.

Working with the Videodisc

The text below is from Professor Roger LeRoy Miller's introduction for the motion segment for Unit 7:

Foreign and defense policies constitute a major aspect of what the federal government does. The state department is only one of the several major executive agencies that involves itself with how we deal with other nations and how we protect ourselves. In recent years the state department has undertaken a controversial policy initiative—that of drug interdiction at the source in Latin American countries. In the video clip you are about to see, a state department foreign service officer has organized a group of Peruvians to eradicate the source of cocaine—the coca bush—before it has been harvested. Since this film was taken, the U.S. defense establishment has also participated in such coca plant eradication programs in Latin America. There is little doubt among observers that such programs are effective on the spot—many coca bushes are destroyed.

Several larger questions do remain unanswered though. Should the U.S. government be involved in the internal policies of Latin American countries? And what are the long-term prospects for such drug-eradication programs?

To access this segment, use the bar code below or the videodisc index found in the *TRB.*

Frame 22200

UNIT SEVEN

American Policy in a Changing World

UNIT CONTENTS

CHAPTER INTRODUCTION

Instructional Objectives
By the end of the chapter students should be able to:
• Discuss how the government regulates the economy through monetary and fiscal policy.
• Summarize the different ways to solve the drug problem.
• Outline the methods used by the government to fight poverty.
• Characterize the government's policies in dealing with the environment.

Using the Keynote
Before the students begin reading Chapter 19, give them an opportunity to discuss their own ideas and feelings about taxes: Who pays taxes? Why? How are our taxes used? With what attitudes toward taxation are you familiar? What is your own attitude toward taxes? Why?

After a brief discussion, have one of the students read aloud the Holmes quotation aloud, and help the students discuss it: What did Holmes mean by *civilization?* In what sense do taxes pay for civilization? What audience do you imagine Holmes had in mind when making this statement? Is the statement still relevant today? Why or why not?

Introducing the Chapter
Have one of the students read the Introduction aloud to the rest of the class. Then encourage the students to discuss the content by asking questions such as these: How does the government create public policy? How do you—and other citizens—participate in that process? Which public policies do you consider most important? Why?

Previewing the Sections

Section 1 Ask the students to look through Section 1, noting especially the section title, the main headings, and the figures. Ask: What specific topics are covered in Section 1? What questions do you expect to have answered in the section?
Section 2 Let volunteers find and read aloud the main headings in Section 2; let others read aloud the titles of the figures. Then ask: What aspects of taxation will be presented in this section? Who needs to understand taxation?
Section 3 Have the students page through Section 3; ask them to pay particular attention to the main headings and the photographs presented here. Then guide the students in a brief discussion of the problem of poverty: Whose problem is it?
Section 4 Ask the students to browse through Section 4 and then discuss their responses to these questions: What central issue is presented in this section? What do you anticipate learning about that issue?

CHAPTER 19

Economic Policy, Poverty, and the Environment

CHAPTER OBJECTIVES

To learn and understand

- How the government exercises its power to regulate the economy through monetary and fiscal policies.
- The different kinds of taxes and systems of taxation.
- Some of the methods the government has used to fight poverty.
- The government's policies in dealing with the environment.

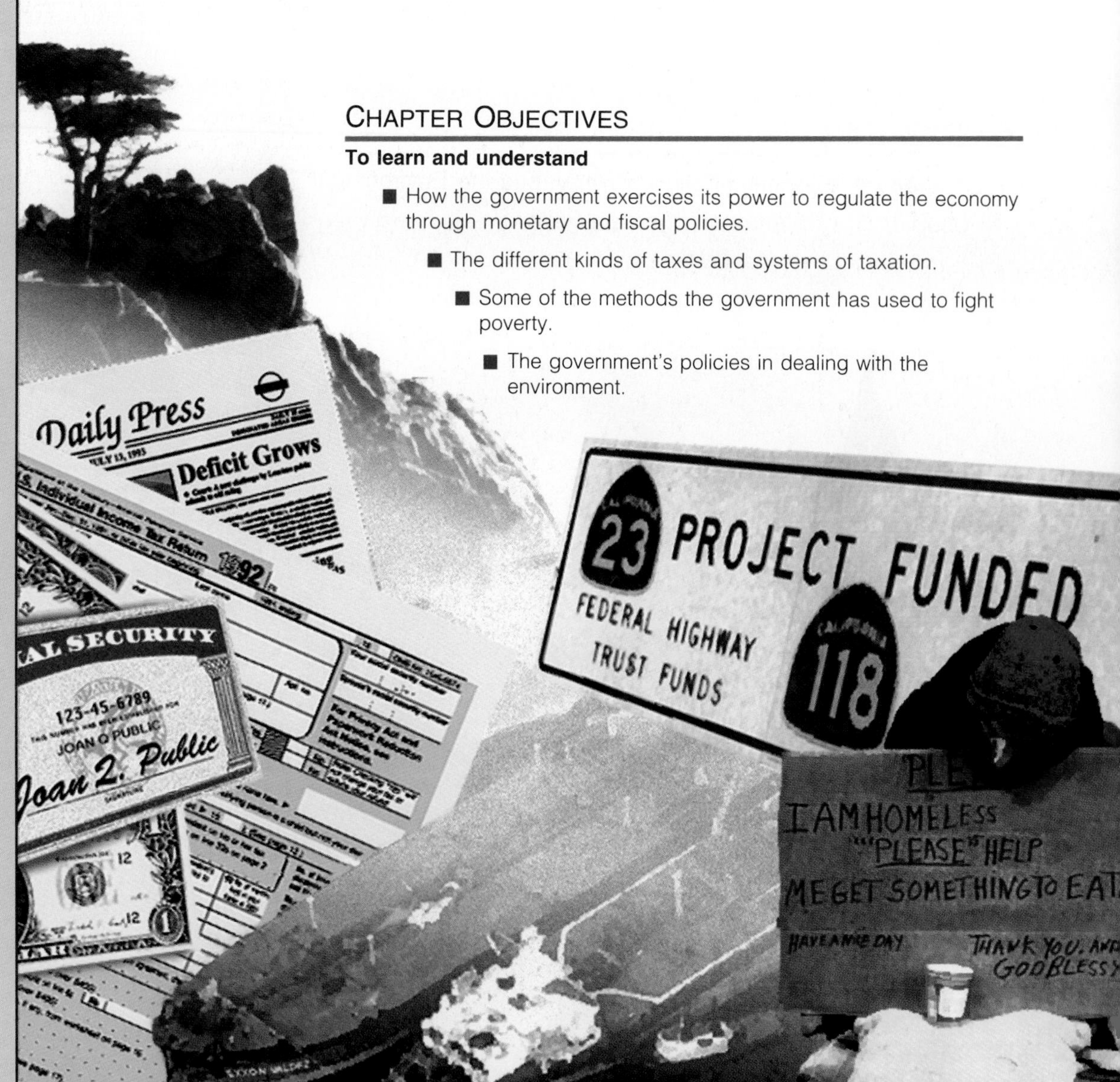

West's American Government Assignment Guide

Activity Sheets
Basic Concepts 19 *TRB* (Reteaching)
Enrichment Activity 19 *TRB*
Building Social Studies Skills 19 *TRB*

Quizzes
Chapter 19 Section 1 Quiz *TRB*
Chapter 19 Section 2 Quiz *TRB*
Chapter 19 Section 3 Quiz *TRB*
Chapter 19 Section 4 Quiz *TRB*

Tests
Chapter 19 Test A *TRB*
Chapter 19 Test B *TRB*
Chapter 19 Test Bank *TRB*
Chapter 19 WESTEST Computerized Testing

Social Studies Tool Kit Software
Chapter 19 Activity

Keynote

"Taxes are what we pay for civilization."

—— Oliver Wendell Holmes (1841–1935) United States Supreme Court Justice

INTRODUCTION

The basic function of government is to create and carry out public policies, of which there are hundreds. There are national economic policies, such as controlling unemployment and inflation, creating jobs, and implementing systems of taxation. (As Oliver Wendell Holmes points out in the opening quote, without taxes society cannot function.) There are national social policies that strive to clean up the environment and provide needed services for the poor and elderly. And there are policies to maintain a strong national defense. In this chapter you will read about national economic policies and selected social programs. In Chapter 20, you will read about defense and foreign policy.

SECTION 1

Monetary and Fiscal Policy

Preview Questions

- What are the tools used by the government to regulate and promote the economy?
- How does monetary policy affect the economy?
- What role does the Federal Reserve System play in the nation's economy?
- What is fiscal policy and who determines it?
- What is deficit spending? How does the public debt affect the economy?

The basic tools that the federal government uses to manage the national economy are monetary policy and fiscal policy. **Monetary policy** includes regulating the amount of money in circulation. This is the responsibility of an independent agency called the **Federal Reserve System**. **Fiscal policy**, which is the responsibility of the president and Congress, involves adjusting federal taxes and spending in an attempt to improve the nation's economy.

Monetary Policy

You may have read or heard a news report in which a business executive or public official complained that money is "too tight." Or you may have run across a story about an economist warning that money is "too loose." In these cases, the terms *tight* and *loose* refer to the monetary policy of the Federal Reserve System, also known as "the Fed." Monetary policy involves monitoring and adjusting how much money is in circulation, which affects the amount of credit (money available to buy goods and services sold with promise of payment later), which consequently affects business activity in the economy.

Like any other good or service, credit has a cost. For people who want to buy items on credit, the cost is interest (the amount the creditor charges for using the loaned money). As interest rates (the cost of credit) increase, the extent to which businesses and consumers want to use it decreases. In contrast, when the cost of credit drops, the amount of credit businesses and consumers want to use rises.

If the country has a **loose monetary policy**, credit is abundant and inexpensive to use. Under such a policy, people are usually willing to borrow more. Consumers will take out loans to buy new cars, new homes, and other desired items. Businesses will borrow to expand or to start new plants and hire more workers. These workers will have more income to spend, which, in turn, will stimulate further production. If, in contrast, a country has a **tight monetary policy**, credit is expensive and in

SECTION 1

Points to Stress
- Tools used by the government to regulate and promote the economy.
- Effects of monetary policy on the economy.
- The Federal Reserve System's role in the economy.
- Fiscal policy and those who determine it.
- Deficit spending, public debt, and the manner in which public debt affects the economy.

Kickoff Activity
Write this phrase on the chalkboard: *the economy.* Ask the students to list at least eight different words and phrases that come to mind when they think about the economy. When all the students have completed their lists, encourage them to share and discuss their ideas.

Working with the Preview Questions
Have volunteers read these five study questions aloud. Let volunteers point out the paragraphs or headings within Section 1 that indicate answers to the questions. Then remind the students to keep these questions in mind as they read the section.

TEACHING STRATEGIES

Introduction
Let one of the students read the section introduction aloud to the rest of the class. Focus the students' attention on the terms *monetary policy* and *fiscal policy:* What do *monetary* and *fiscal* mean? What is the distinction between these two kinds of policy? Why are both important?

Cooperative Learning Divide the class into groups, and guide each group in studying and discussing figure 19–1, Brief History of Our National Banking and Monetary Policies: Why is each event significant? What is the importance of backing bank notes with gold (1791)? What do you think were the central arguments in support of—and in opposition to—a strong national bank (1816)? What happened during the depression of 1839–43? How do you imagine this depression compared to the more familiar Great Depression? What effects can you see today of the first issuing of Federal Reserve Notes in 1914? How did the Great Depression change people's lives? What were the effects of bank collapses? Of Roosevelt's policy regarding banks? What was the intent of laws passed in the late 1960s and 1970s regarding consumers and banks? What were the effects of those laws? What were the intended effects of allowing savings and loans to compete more directly with commercial banks (1980s)? What were the actual effects? How did the public react to the Thrift Bailout Act? Why?

Brief History of Our Nation's Banking and Monetary Policies

Year	Development in U.S. Banking and Monetary Policies
1791	In response to Alexander Hamilton's proposal, Congress established in Philadelphia the First Bank of the United States, and gave it a twenty-year charter. The bank—the largest corporation in the country—was a private business, though the government supplied one-fifth of its starting capital. It served as a depository for government funds, loaned money to the government and to private individuals and businesses, and regulated the activities of banks with state charters. It also issued bank notes backed by gold, which provided reliable currency.
1816	Following the financial confusion caused by the War of 1812, Congress established the Second Bank of the United States. Like the First Bank, it brought order to the banking system. Opposition remained, however, to a strong national bank. In 1832, President Andrew Jackson vetoed legislation to extend the Second Bank's charter; the following year he withdrew federal funds. The bank closed in 1836.
1835	Inflation increased and continued until 1837, leading to a depression from 1839 to 1843. Between 1836 and 1863, two sets of banks—private unincorporated banks and incorporated banks with charters from state governments—were allowed to co-exist. Passed in 1863, the National Banking Act required all federal banks to invest a portion of their capital in U.S. government bonds, prohibited them from making real estate loans, and required them to hold reserves in the form of gold, cash, or deposits in larger banks.
1913	To control the amount of money in circulation, Congress established the Federal Reserve System. It served as the nation's central bank and could regulate reserves in state and national banks, loan money to member banks, and control the growth of the money supply. In 1914, the system began issuing Federal Reserve Notes, which soon became the predominant form of money in circulation.
1929–1933	Stocks and other investments owned by banks lost much of their value. Bankrupt businesses and individuals were unable to repay their loans. A nationwide financial panic caused thousands of banks to collapse. When President Franklin Roosevelt took office on March 4, 1933, four-fifths of the states had stopped all banking operations. The following day, Roosevelt declared a "bank holiday," closing all banks. Each bank was allowed to reopen only after it had proven itself to be financially sound. Congress passed the Glass-Steagall Banking Act in June, establishing the Federal Deposit Insurance Corporation (FDIC). The new agency helped restore public confidence in banks by insuring funds of individual depositors against bank failure.
1960s–1970s	Congress passed a series of laws protecting consumers in dealing with banks and other depository institutions. The Truth in Lending Act of 1968, the Equal Credit Opportunity Act of 1974, and the Community Reinvestment Act of 1977 established the rights and responsibilities of banks and consumers. They also provided individuals with procedures to file complaints if treated unfairly.
1980s	As part of the general move toward deregulation of business, Congress passed the Depository Institutions Deregulation and Monetary Control Act of 1980. It gradually removed ceilings on the interest that financial institutions could pay on savings, and permitted interest payments on checking accounts. It also allowed savings and loan associations and savings banks to compete more directly with commercial banks. In addition, it gave the Federal Reserve System the power to set reserve requirements on *all* financial institutions, not just member banks in the Federal Reserve System. Savings and loans got into serious trouble. Congress passed the Thrift Bailout Act of 1989, which will cost taxpayers at least $500 billion.
1990s	Savings and loans continue to go out of business. Commercial banks also start getting into trouble.

FIGURE 19–1 Brief History of our Nation's Banking and Monetary Policies. The figure above presents a look at our nation's banking and monetary policies over the last 200 years. Which aspect of banking and monetary policy do you think will lead to additional legislation in the coming years?

Figure Answer Students should understand that as thrifts continue to go out of business and as commercial banks also begin to experience major financial difficulty, Congress will be forced to step in to somehow mitigate this situation.

Discussion Starter
Encourage the students to share and discuss their responses to these questions: What is credit? How do individuals use credit? How do businesses use it? What are the advantages of using credit? What are the possible dangers of using credit? How can individuals and businesses protect themselves against those dangers?

Comprehension
Help the students consider conditions under a loose money policy and under a tight money policy: What are consumers likely to do in each situation? How can consumers' actions affect the policy?

Extension
Have the students read and discuss news reports about inflation in the United States.

Comprehension
Be sure the students can identify their own Federal Reserve district on the map, and let volunteers point out the closest bank city and/or branch city.

short supply. Consumers may not buy as many new cars and homes. Business executives may postpone or cancel plans for expansion. Workers who become unemployed because of the business slowdown will have less income to spend. As a result, businesses may cut back even more. A weakening of the economy and possibly a serious decline may follow.

If this is the case, why would any nation want a tight money policy? If money becomes too plentiful too quickly under a loose monetary policy, the result could be **inflation**, when all prices increase and the purchasing power of the dollar decreases. For example, during the Revolutionary War the supply of Continental currency grew so rapidly that the notes became almost worthless. An expression that came out of the era was, ''Not worth a Continental.''

The goal of monetary policy is to strike a balance between tight and loose money. It is the Federal Reserve's responsibility to ensure that money and credit are plentiful enough to allow the economy to expand. The Fed cannot, however, let the money supply become so plentiful that rapid inflation results. The time line in Figure 19–1 on page 460 gives a brief history of our nation's banking and monetary policies.

The Monetary Authority: The Federal Reserve System

Congress established our current central bank, the Federal Reserve, in 1913. It is led by a board of governors that consists of seven individuals, including the powerful chair. The Federal Reserve System is divided into geographic areas. The map below shows the twelve Federal Reserve districts and their main offices. The Fed is an

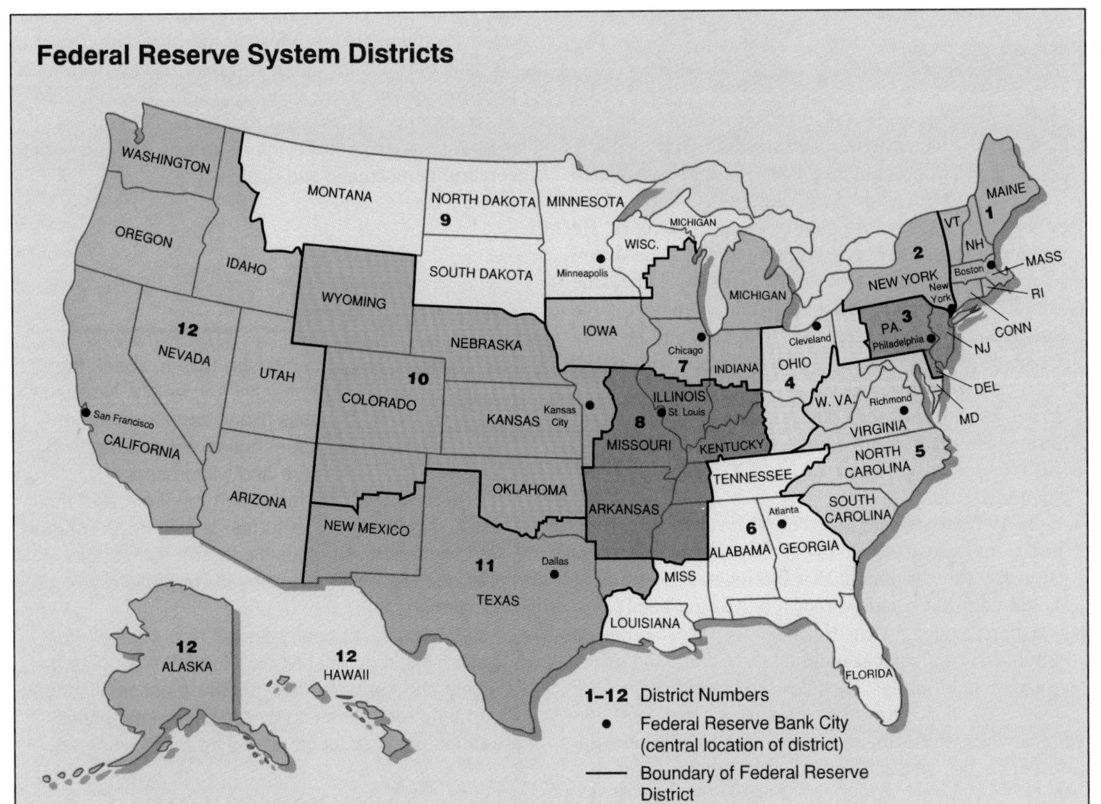

FIGURE 19–2 Federal Reserve System Districts. This map shows the 12 Federal Reserve districts and their main offices. Under what principle is the Federal Reserve's monetary policy supposed to operate?

This figure content is also featured on *West's American Government Videodisc* (see the index found in the *TRB*) and is available in the transparency package.

Figure Answer The Fed's monetary policy is supposed to be counter-cyclical. However, students should understand that often, this is not the case.

TEACHING ARCHITECT OF THE AMERICAN DREAM

Read

Before the students begin reading this feature, encourage them to share and discuss what they already know about Franklin Roosevelt: Who was he? For what accomplishments is he best remembered? After this introductory discussion, let the students read the feature independently. Then have one of the students (if possible, one who has practiced) read aloud the excerpt from Roosevelt's speech.

Discuss

Ask questions such as these to guide the students in discussing this Architect of the American Dream feature: How did each aspect of Roosevelt's background help prepare him for the presidency? In what respects did he fit the typical profile of a president? How did he differ from that typical profile? What was the Great Depression? What kinds of problems did people face during that period? How does the situation of the United States during Roosevelt's presidency compare to the situation in our country today? Why do you think Roosevelt chose to break the no-third-term tradition? Why do you think voters reelected him again? Imagine that you were an unemployed worker, listening to Roosevelt's speech on the radio—how would you have responded? Why?

Analyze and Apply

Ask the students to consider the situation in the United States today. Then have them write their own speeches to the nation, beginning with the same opening line Roosevelt used. What truth needs to be frankly and boldly spoken today? If time permits, let the students present their speeches to the rest of the class.

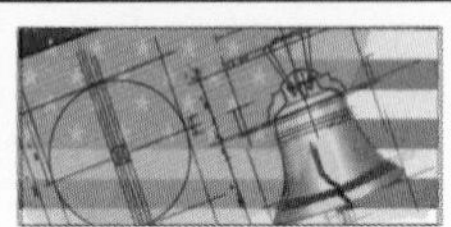

ARCHITECT OF The American Dream

Franklin Delano Roosevelt was born in Hyde Park, New York, on January 30, 1882. He graduated from Harvard and studied at Columbia University Law School, and went on to practice law in New York. He became state senator in 1911 and served as assistant secretary of the Navy from 1913 to 1920. He became James Cox's vice-presidential running mate on the Democratic ticket in 1920, but both Cox and he were defeated. In 1921 Roosevelt was stricken with polio. Paralyzed from the waist down, he fought to regain partial use of his legs and established the Warm Springs Foundation in Georgia for others so afflicted. He was elected governor of New York in 1928 and again in 1930.

In 1932 he defeated Herbert Hoover for president during the midst of the Great Depression. He campaigned on the argument that the federal government should help to provide direct relief to the needy and give direct aid to farmers. He called for a broad program of public works, such as building large dams and major government buildings. He proposed laws to protect the small-bank depositor, the stock purchaser, and the homeowner. Referring to the unemployed workers, the desperate farmers, and others, Roosevelt stated that these "forgotten" Americans "at the bottom of the economic pyramid" had to have a "new deal." He began his administration with a ringing call to the American people to face the future with courage and faith. "The only thing we have to fear is fear itself," he confidently stated. His calm words helped to lift the American people from their despair and to rally them behind his new administration. The New Deal was interrupted by the United States' entry into World War II, but for five years a steady stream of New Deal measures poured out of Washington, each of which was an attempt to restore the nation's social, economic, and political health.

Roosevelt was largely responsible for U.S. aid to Great Britain after France surrendered to Hitler. He contributed notably to achieving unity among the Allies during World War II and conducted his own foreign relations rather than relying on the State Department. He was the first president to break the no-third-term tradition and he was elected to a fourth term in 1944. Three months after his fourth term had begun, and on the verge of the Allies' victory he was stricken with a cerebral hemorrhage and died.

HIS WORDS*

"This is pre-eminently the time to speak the truth, the whole truth, frankly and boldly. Nor need we shrink from honestly facing conditions in our country today. This great nation will endure as it has endured, will revive and will prosper.

So, first of all, let me assert my firm belief that the only thing we have to fear is fear itself—nameless, unreasoning, unjustified terror which paralyzes needed efforts to convert retreat into advance. . . .

Our greatest primary task is to put people to work. This is no unsolvable problem if we face it wisely and courageously. It can be accomplished in part by direct recruiting by the government itself, treating the task as we would treat the emergency

*Excerpted from the First Inaugural Address, March 4, 1933.

Review
Let the students respond to these review questions: What political experience did Roosevelt have before he was elected president? What are at least three programs Roosevelt introduced to help people deal with the problems of the Great Depression?

Developing Critical Thinking Skills (Answers)
1. Answers will vary, e.g., most were probably encouraged that the man who was elected to lead them out of the crisis spoke with such conviction about the chances of recovery; some may have felt that Roosevelt had never really experienced the fear of not having enough to eat or being able to feed one's family.
2. Answers will vary, e.g., he probably meant that the government would enter into areas and programs previously reserved to the states and also engage in deficit spending in order to put people back to work.
3. To the Congress of the United States.

Franklin Delano Roosevelt

This December 1943 conference in Teheran, Iran attended by Josef Stalin of the Soviet Union, President Roosevelt, and Winston Churchill of the United Kingdom, was one of five historic conferences among the Allied leaders. During the three-day conference pictured here, Roosevelt, Stalin, and Churchill devised definite plans for the defeat of Germany and Japan and the end of the Second World War.

of a war, but at the same time, through this employment, accomplishing greatly needed projects to stimulate and reorganize the use of our natural resources.

. . . Our Constitution is so simple and practical that it is possible always to meet extraordinary needs by changes in emphasis and arrangement without loss of essential form.

That is why our constitutional system has proved itself the most superbly enduring political mechanism the modern world has produced. It has met every stress of vast expansion of territory, of foreign wars, of bitter internal strife, of world relations.

It is to be hoped that the normal balance of executive and legislative authority may be wholly adequate to meet the unprecedented task before us. But it may be that an unprecedented demand and need for undelayed action may call for temporary departure from that normal balance of public procedure.

I am prepared under my constitutional duty to recommend the measures that a stricken nation in the midst of a stricken world may require."

Developing Critical Thinking Skills

1. When Roosevelt spoke these words, the nation was in the greatest economic depression it had ever seen. How do you think people who were unemployed at the time might have reacted to his statement, "The only thing we have to fear is fear itself"?
2. What did Roosevelt mean when he called for a "temporary departure from that normal balance of public procedure"?
3. To whom was Roosevelt going "to recommend the measures" required?

For Further Reading

Gies, Joseph, *Franklin D. Roosevelt*. Garden City, New York Doubleday, 1971
Alsop, Joseph, *FDR* 1882–1945: *A Centenary Remembrance*. New York, Viking, 1982
Burns, James MacGregor, *Roosevelt: The Soldier of Freedom*. New York, Harcourt Brace Jovanovich, 1972

Discussion Starter
Guide the students in discussing membership on the Board of Governors of the Federal Reserve: How do the president and the Senate exert some control over the members? What kinds of members do you imagine they select? How independent do you think the Board of Governors can be? Why?

Vocabulary
Ask one of the students to define the term *countercyclical.* What is the significance of the intention of the Federal Reserve to maintain a counter-cyclical monetary policy?

Discussion Starter
Guide the students in discussing the fact that evidence shows the Fed usually does the opposite of what is required: What should be learned from this evidence? Why? Do you think the lesson will be accepted? Why or why not?

Comprehension
Let volunteers explain the purpose of lowering taxes during times of recession and raising taxes during times of inflation.

Enrichment
Ask three small groups of volunteers to research the CCC, the WPA, and the CETA: Who established each program? Why? What purpose was it intended to serve? What were its major accomplishments? How long did it last? Then have all three groups work together to prepare a bulletin board displaying their findings.

Cooperative Learning
Let the students work in groups to consider and discuss the Employment Act of 1946: How would you recast this act in your own words? What are the implications of this act? Whom is it intended to benefit? How?

independent commission, which means it is free from the direct political control of either Congress or the president. It has the vital responsibility for determining the nation's monetary and credit policies. All members of the Board of Governors are appointed by the president, with the appointments being approved by the Senate. Each member can serve up to fourteen years on the board.

The Fed's Record

In principle, the Federal Reserve's monetary policy is supposed to be countercyclical (acting in the opposite direction the economy is going). The economy goes through so-called **business cycles**, the extremes of which are **recessions** (and sometimes **depressions** which are very bad recessions) when unemployment is high and businesses are not working at full capacity, and boom times when unemployment is low and businesses are operating at peak capacity. Such booms often result in inflation.

In order for its policy to be countercyclical, the Federal Reserve must take actions that act counter to the trend of national business activity. Researchers who have watched the Fed since 1914 have concluded that often its policy has not been countercyclical because of the time it has taken the Fed to act. By the time the Fed started pumping money into the economy, for example, it was time to withdraw it; by the time it started reducing the rate of growth of the money supply, it was time to start increasing it.

Fiscal Policy and Employment

While monetary policy is carried out by the independent Federal Reserve System, fiscal policy is determined by Congress and the president. Traditionally, fiscal policy has involved lowering taxes during times of recession and raising them during times of inflation. Alternatively, fiscal policy can include increasing government spending during times of recession (which is generally done by borrowing money to increase the total demand in the economy) and decreasing government spending during times of inflation. But fiscal policy can also include targeting specific aspects of society that are malfunctioning. For example, public works programs such as the Civilian Conservation Corps (CCC) and the Works Progress Administration (WPA) during the Great Depression in the 1930s, and the Comprehensive Employment and Training Act (CETA) in the 1970s, were designed to use federal tax dollars directly to employ unemployed individuals.

The government formally took on the responsibility of reducing unemployment when it passed the Employment Act of 1946, which reads as follows:

> The Congress hereby declares that it is the continuing policy and responsibility of the federal government to use all practicable means consistent with its needs and obligations and other essential considerations of national policy, with assistance and cooperation of industry, agriculture, labor and state and local governments to coordinate and utilize all its plans, functions, and resources for the purpose of creating and maintaining, in a manner calculated to foster and promote free competitive enterprise and the general welfare, conditions under which there will be afforded useful employment opportunities, including self-employment, for those able, willing, and seeking to work and to promote maximum employment, production, and purchasing power.

The effect of this legislation was to require the federal government to monitor the unemployment rate and the overall state of the national economy and adjust fiscal policy as needed.

Fiscal Policy and the Federal Budgeting Process

The preceding discussion of fiscal policy might give the impression that there is some overriding policy that a single agency puts into effect for the benefit of the nation as a whole.

It is important to realize that no single governmental body designs and implements fiscal policy. The president, with the aid of the director of the Office of Management and Budget (OMB), the secretary of the treasury, and the Council of Economic Advisors, only recommends the desired mix of taxes and government expenditures. It is Congress, with the aid of its many committees (the House Ways and Means Committee, the Senate Finance Committee, and the Senate Budget Committee, to name a few), that enacts fiscal policy. The president, however, does have veto power over congressional fiscal policy. Disagreement as to proper fiscal policy might—and usually does—emerge among members of Congress or between Congress and the president. Although the procedure required for an ultimate solution is clearly spelled out in the U.S. Constitution, in practice resolving these conflicts is often a tedious and time-consuming process, during which numerous hearings may be called, and many experts may give testimonies.

In sum, our government's regulation of monetary and fiscal policies can be compared to driving a car with only an accelerator and a brake, but no steering wheel. All

Discussion Starter
Encourage the students to discuss the fact that no single governmental body designs and implements fiscal policy: Why is this fact significant? Why doesn't our country have a single individual or organization to serve that function? In what kinds of countries is the fiscal policy designed and implemented by a single governmental body? What are the effects of that control?

TEACHING GOVERNMENT IN ACTION

Read
Introduce this Case Study by asking the following questions: What purposes might be served if pennies and dollar bills were eliminated? What problems might arise? What do you think the government should do? After a short discussion, let volunteers read the feature aloud to the rest of the class.

Discuss
Help the students discuss the Case Study by posing questions such as these: What do you do with your pennies? How often do you lose them? Does anyone in your family save pennies? If so, what happens to those coins? Whose argument—Benfield's or Brown's—do you find more persuasive? Why? Why does each group support the issue of one-dollar coins? Why do you think the Susan B. Anthony coin met with such public resistance? Do you think a new one-dollar coin would be accepted today? Why or why not?

Analyze and Apply
Let the students work with partners to write letters to the editor, expressing and supporting an opinion on a change in U.S. currency. Remind the students that a letter to the editor should be clear and concise; it should state an opinion and present facts to support that opinion. The letter should also be neat and correct. Display all the completed letters in the classroom, and encourage the students to read and comment on each other's work.

Review
Ask the students these review questions about the Case Study: What are the major arguments in favor of getting rid of the penny? In favor of keeping it? Why do some people want to replace one-dollar bills with one-dollar coins?

Think About It (Answers)
1. Answers will vary, e.g., the copper and zinc industries would lose. The American public would gain by ridding itself of a nuisance.
2. Answers will vary, e.g., the metal industry that produces the coin's materials would gain as well as vending and video machines. The public would lose because it might be heavier in purses and wallets to carry one-dollar coins than paper.

CASE STUDY

Making Sense of Dollars and Cents

GOVERNMENT IN ACTION

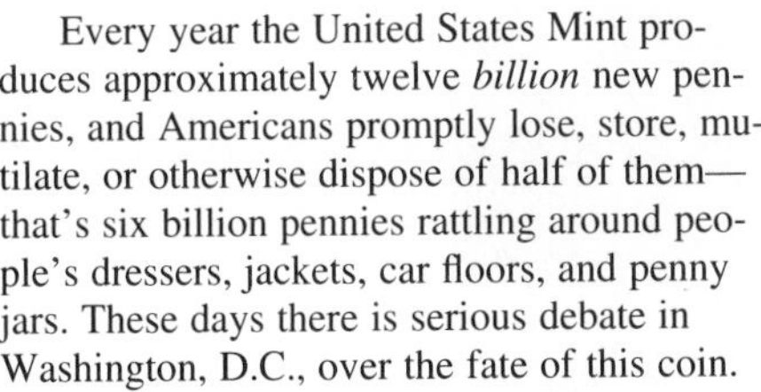

Every year the United States Mint produces approximately twelve *billion* new pennies, and Americans promptly lose, store, mutilate, or otherwise dispose of half of them—that's six billion pennies rattling around people's dressers, jackets, car floors, and penny jars. These days there is serious debate in Washington, D.C., over the fate of this coin.

The penny has its supporters and opponents. James Benfield, the founder and only paid employee of the Coin Coalition, an organization intent on getting rid of the penny, claims that "the penny's a nuisance." Michael Brown, in contrast, opposes abolition of the smallest U.S. currency unit, arguing that rounding off prices ($4.00 instead of $3.98) would cost U.S. consumers over half a billion dollars each year. Brown is a spokesman for Americans for Common Cents, an organization backed by the zinc industry (the penny is 97 percent zinc), the manufacturers of the blanks (which are stamped out as pennies), and U.S. coin collectors.

The controversy about pennies was stimulated by the Senate Banking Committee's "coinage reform," an effort to pinpoint needed changes in U.S. currency. This reform also brought about the movement to create a one-dollar coin and to do away with the one-dollar bill. This idea is supported by the U.S. vending machine industry (including video machine manufacturers), the American Council for the Blind, the copper industry, the convenience store industry, and mass-transit business. It is opposed by the ink and paper producers that supply these ingredients for the printing of paper currency.

Opponents of the paper dollar bill claim that handling such bills manually, including straightening and unfolding them, arranging them right side up, and counting them, is a very expensive and time-consuming process. Also, the U.S. Treasury spends over $300

million each year shredding and replacing worn-out dollar bills. The paper dollar bill is difficult for visually impaired people to identify. Dollar coins in vending machines and mass-transit turnstiles, in contrast, would be convenient and reduce both the handling of smaller coins and the need to make change. The copper industry supports a proposed copper dollar for obvious reasons.

In 1979, a one-dollar coin, called the Susan B. Anthony dollar, was introduced but failed to gain public acceptance. In response to this failure, the new strategy would involve introducing a new coin dollar and phasing out entirely the paper dollar, which would force Americans to use the coin. This was successfully done in Canada in 1987 with the Loon dollar coin. A 1991 Gallup poll, however, showed that while 62 percent of the American population opposes abolishing the penny, 85 percent opposes abolishing the dollar bill in favor of a dollar coin.

THINK ABOUT IT

1. Who do you think would lose if the penny were eliminated? Who would gain?
2. Who would lose and who would gain if the one-dollar bill were replaced with the one-dollar coin?

Discussion Starter
Help the students discuss the comparison of our monetary and fiscal policy to the accelerator and brake on a car: Is anyone steering the car (which represents our economy)? If so, who and how? If not, why not? Encourage the students to present and support various responses.

Comprehension
Let volunteers explain, in their own words, what the national debt is: Who owes this debt? To whom? Why?

Vocabulary
Let volunteers define the term *rolled over:* In what other contexts can this meaning of the term be used?

Enrichment
Ask two or three students to research and then chart the answer to this question: To whom is the national debt owed? Let the students present and explain their chart to the rest of the class.

Caption Answer There is no single governmental body that designs and implements fiscal policy. The president, the director of the OMB, the Secretary of the Treasury, and the Counsel of Economic Advisors work together to recommend a fiscal policy through the budget. It is Congress with its committees that enacts fiscal policy.

Multidiscipline Strategies

Economics As with political systems, economic systems are predicated on certain philosophical beliefs. An excellent source of major economic ideology is *The Worldly Philosophers: The Lives, Times, and Ideas of the Great Economic Thinkers,* Simon & Schuster, 6th ed., 1986. Students can explore the beliefs of Adam Smith, Malthus, Ricardo, Robert Owen, Marx, Veblen, Keynes, and Schumpeter, among others. Divide students up into groups of two or three and assign one philosopher to each. Allow them to present the basic economic tenets of their "thinker" to the class.

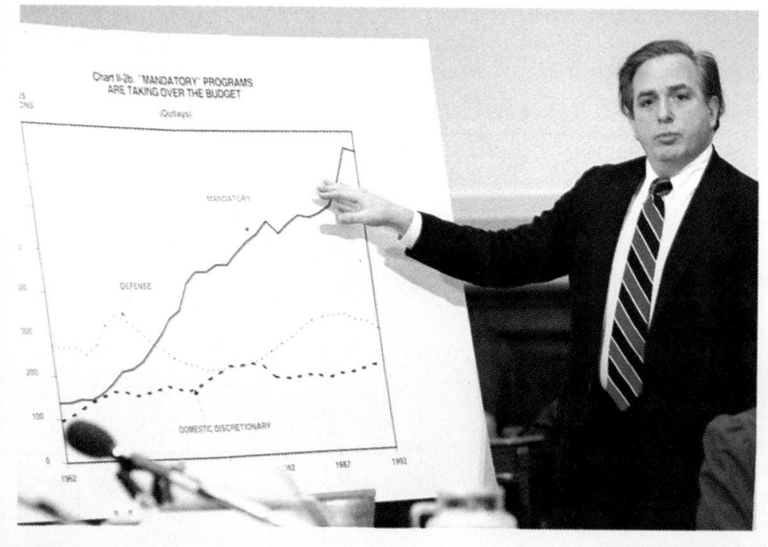

Richard Darman, the Director of the Office of Management and Budget, is shown here as he discusses the president's 1992 budget proposal with the House Appropriations Committee. Which governmental body is responsible for designing and implementing fiscal policy?

the government can do is speed the economy up or slow it down. It seldom is successful at keeping it steady.

Government Spending and the Public Debt

Whenever the federal government spends more than it receives in tax revenues, it runs a **budget deficit**. The federal government has run a deficit in every year except two since 1960. As you learned in Chapter 13, the Constitution gives Congress the power to borrow money. Every time a budget deficit occurs, the federal government borrows money by issuing **U.S. Treasury bonds**. The sale of these bonds to corporations, private individuals, pension plans, foreign governments, foreign businesses, and foreign individuals adds to the **public debt** (also called the **national debt**), defined as the total amount the federal government owes to these parties. Each year there is a federal government budget deficit. The amount of that deficit is *added* to the public debt. Figure 19–3 on page 467 shows what has happened to the public debt over time. Politicians and the public alike are concerned about this problem.

Is the Public Debt a Burden to the Public?

We often hear about the burden of the public debt. Some argue that the government is eventually going to go bankrupt, but as long as the government can collect taxes to pay for interest on its public debt, that will never happen. What does happen is that when Treasury Bonds come due, they are simply "rolled over," or refinanced. That is, if a $1 million Treasury Bond comes due (gets cashed in) today, the U.S. Treasury pays it off with the money it gets from selling another $1 million bond.

As for the interest payments on these bonds, they are paid by federal taxes. Not all of the interest payments are paid to Americans. Corporations, governments, and private citizens in other countries can and do legally purchase U.S. Treasury Bonds in the open market. About 16 percent, or one in six dollars, of our national debt is owed to foreigners. Some fear that if foreigners own too large of a percentage of our national debt, they may have too much influence over our federal government.

Discussion Starter
Help the students study and discuss figure 19–3, Public Debt of the Federal Government: What can you learn from studying this graph? What trend does it indicate? Do you expect this trend to continue? Why or why not?

Discussion Starter
Guide the students in discussing the revisions made to the Gramm-Rudman-Hollings Deficit Reduction Act: What are the implications of all these revisions? Do you think it makes sense to pass such a deficit reduction act if its terms are impossible to meet? Why or why not?

Public Debt of the Federal Government, 1940–1993 (est.)

Year	Net Public Debt*
1940	42.7
1945	235.2
1950	219.0
1955	226.6
1960	237.2
1965	261.6
1970	284.9
1975	396.9
1980	709.3
1983	1,141.8
1986	1,736.2
1989	2,190.3
1990	2,410.3
1991	2,717.6
1992 (est.)	2,995.4
1993 (est.)	3,301.2

* In billions of current dollars.

FIGURE 19–3 Public Debt of the Federal Government 1940–1993. By looking at this table, you can see the alarming increase in public debt. From what source does the money used to pay the interest payments on this debt come?

Figure Answer Interest payments on this debt are paid by federal taxes.

There is another factor to consider in this dilemma. Even though most interest payments are being paid to American citizens, the more the federal government borrows to meet these payments, the greater the percentage of its budget is committed to making these payments. This reduces the government's ability to supply money for needed community services, such as transportation, education, and housing programs. Indeed, a simple projection of the government's current spending trends would show that some time in the twenty-first century, the federal government will be spending almost 100 percent of its budget on interest payments! While this is unlikely to occur, it highlights the problem of running larger and larger deficits and borrowing more and more money to cover them.

The Difficulty of Reducing the Deficit—The Gramm-Rudman Act

In 1985 Congress passed the Gramm-Rudman-Hollings Deficit Reduction Act in an effort to require that Congress reduce the size of its budget deficits. Gramm and Rudman are the members of Congress who originally sponsored the bill (the act is often simply referred to as "Gramm-Rudman"). According to the act,

Senator Phil Gramm

TEACHING BUILDING SOCIAL STUDIES SKILLS

Read
As an introduction to this Building Social Studies Skills feature, let the students share and discuss their own experiences with line graphs: What kinds of information have you learned from line graphs? For what purposes have you drawn line graphs? Then have the students read the feature independently.

Discuss
Ask questions such as these to help the students discuss the feature: What are the possible periods of time that might be shown in a line graph? Why is each step—reading the title, reading the horizontal axis, and reading the vertical axis—important?

Analyze and Apply
Let the students form groups in which to plan and draw their own line graphs. Instruct the group members to work together in selecting an appropriate topic, in gathering information on that topic, and in drawing a line graph to show the gathered information.

Review
Ask questions such as these to help the students review this Building Social Studies Skills feature: What is usually shown on the horizontal axis of a line graph? What is usually shown on the vertical axis?

This figure content is also featured on *West's American Government Videodisc* (see the index found in the *TRB*).

Practicing Your Skills (Answers)
1. Approximately 2 percent.
2. More than 20 percent.
3. Approximately 1979.

Critical Thinking Skills
Help the students analyze the statement that, at least according to some observers, our governing body can no longer be fiscally responsible: What are the implications of this statement? Who *is* expected to be fiscally responsible? Why? Do we have the right—or the obligation—to expect fiscal responsibility from Congress? Why or why not?

Reteaching Strategies
1. Work with small groups of students; help them discuss the answers to the Preview Questions at the beginning of Section 1.
2. Ask the students to use their own words in writing definitions of these terms: *loose money policy, tight money policy, budget deficit, national debt, off-budget items.*

Evaluation Strategies
1. Have the students write their answers to the Section 1 Review questions.
2. Have the students take the Section 1 Quiz found in the *TRB*.

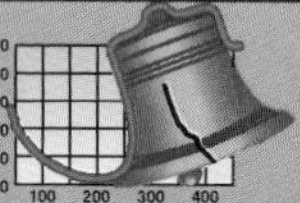

BUILDING SOCIAL STUDIES SKILLS
Reading Line Graphs

Line graphs are used to show changes in trends over a period of time. The federal deficit, a president's popularity, or a student's grades over a period of years could all easily be shown on a line graph.

To read a line graph, begin by reading the title, then read the axes. The horizontal axis usually shows time on a scale of days, months, or years. The vertical axis usually gives a scale for measuring quantities.

The graph below shows the percentage of U.S. debt that has been owned by foreigners over a thirty-five-year timespan. Study the graph and answer the questions that follow.

PRACTICING YOUR SKILLS

1. What was the lowest percentage of U.S. public debt held by foreigners?
2. What was the highest percentage of U.S. public debt held by foreigners?
3. In approximately which year was the percentage of U.S. public debt held by foreigners the highest?

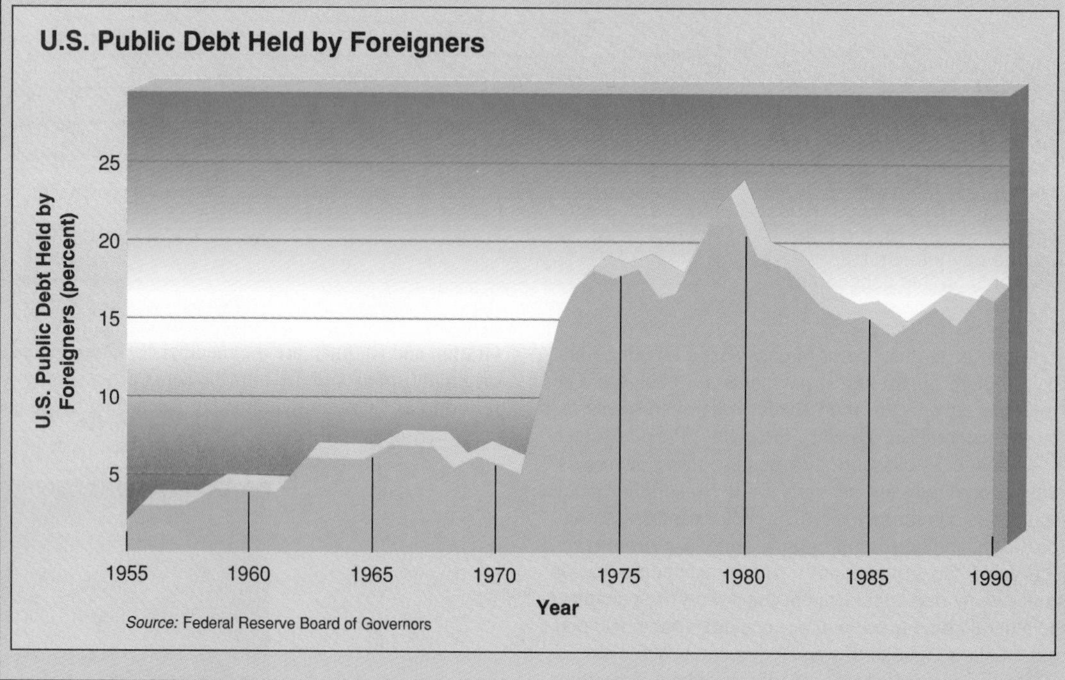

the deficit was required to drop from $171.9 billion in 1986 to zero in 1991. After the first two years of failure to comply with the target deficit reductions, Congress passed a revised act requiring that the 1988 deficit be $144 billion and that it drop to zero by 1993. The first three years of the Revised Deficit Reduction Act saw Congress again fail to meet deficit reductions. In 1990, another revised of set Gramm-Rudman targets was proposed, allowing for a 1991 deficit of over $200 billion, excluding the cost of the savings and loan bailout. In fact, the true deficit in 1991 turned out to be closer to $300 billion and an estimated $350 billion in 1992.

Some observers believe that Congress's inability to comply with its own law indicates that our governing body can no longer be fiscally responsible. In reality, the prospect of ever balancing the budget is dim.

Section 1 Review (Answers)
1. Policy aimed at influencing the economy by regulating the amount of money in circulation for which the Federal Reserve System is responsible.
2. The Fed regulates monetary policy by increasing or decreasing the rate at which the money supply grows in the United States. It also regulates the amount of credit available and consequently interest rates.
3. Fiscal policy is determined by Congress and the president. It includes lowering or raising taxes, increasing or decreasing government spending, and targeting specific aspects of society that are malfunctioning.
4. Whenever the federal government spends more than it receives in tax revenues, it runs a budget deficit.
5. It is difficult for the government to reduce the deficit because citizens demand more and more expensive programs while resisting taxes. Answers might also mention defense spending and the fact that raising taxes is detrimental to a politician's career.

SECTION 2

Points to Stress
- The benefits-received principle of taxation.
- The ability to pay principle of taxation.
- Differences among progressive, regressive, and proportional tax systems.
- The major types of taxes.
- The manner in which taxes direct economic activity.

Kickoff Activity
As an introduction to Section 2, give the students five minutes in which to list as many reasons for paying taxes as possible. At the end of the allotted time, let volunteers read their lists aloud, and encourage the students to respond to one anothers' ideas.

Working with the Preview Questions
Have the students read the study questions, and let volunteers share their responses. Remind the students that they will find more detailed answers to these questions as they read the text. Then have the students keep these questions in mind as they read and take notes on Section 2.

Caption Answer A gasoline tax that is used to pay for highway construction and repair exemplifies the benefits-received principle.

The federal budget deficit is probably much higher than is actually reported. Each year, in an effort to make the deficit look smaller, Congress takes more and more government expenditures out of the official budget and puts them in a category called **off-budget items**. For example, the government removed all of the operating losses of the U.S. Postal Service from the official budget. Also, numerous government-sponsored enterprises are slowly but surely building up large amounts of debt that have not shown up in the official figures. The estimate for 1993 is over $1 trillion of such debt.

Many observers of the federal government's fiscal management strategies contend that the only way to end budget deficits is to pass a constitutional amendment requiring a balanced budget. Few observers, however, believe that such an amendment will soon be passed.

Section 1 Review

1. What is monetary policy? Who is responsible for the nation's monetary policy?
2. How does the Federal Reserve System regulate monetary policy?
3. How is fiscal policy carried out?
4. Briefly describe deficit spending.
5. **For critical analysis:** Why is it so difficult for our government to reduce the deficit?

Section 2

Systems of Taxation

Preview Questions

- What is the benefits-received principle of taxation?
- What is the ability-to-pay principle of taxation?
- What is the difference between progressive, regressive, and proportional tax systems?
- What are the major types of taxes?
- How do taxes direct economic activity?

Governments—federal, state, and local—have various methods of taxation at their disposal. The best known of these is the federal personal income tax system. At the state and local levels, property taxes make up the bulk of the taxes collected. In addition to these taxes, there are corporate income taxes, sales taxes, excise taxes, inheritance taxes, and gift taxes. About 85 percent of all federal, state, and local government revenues come from taxation. Figure 19–6 on page 471 lists the major taxes that the various levels of government use to raise revenue.

▲ Whenever we buy gasoline, we not only must pay for the gasoline, but also federal taxes on the gasoline. These taxes are used to pay for highway construction and repair. Which principle of taxation does this type of tax exemplify?

Principles of Taxation

Taxes can be justified according to one of three major principles.

Benefits-Received Principle Under the **benefits-received principle**, those who use a particular government service support it with taxes in proportion to the benefits they receive. Those who do not use the service do not pay taxes for it. For example, a gasoline tax to pay for highway construction and repair is based on this principle. Those who use the highways usually buy more gasoline, and therefore pay more in gasoline taxes.

A tax based on the benefits-received principle is useful in raising money to pay for a service used only by certain individuals. Many government services, however, such as national defense, benefit everyone equally. Also, there are circumstances in which those who most need certain services, such as the elderly and the poor, are the ones least able to pay taxes for them.

Ability-to-pay Principle Under the **ability-to-pay principle**, those with higher incomes pay more in taxes

TEACHING STRATEGIES

Introduction
Guide the students in reading the section introduction and studying figure 19–6, Major Taxes: What is the importance of each tax listed here? Do you pay this particular kind of tax? Why or why not? Who do you know who does pay this kind of tax?

Comprehension
Ask the students to identify other examples of taxes that are justified by the benefit-received principle.

Discussion Starter
Help the students discuss their responses to the fact that all property owners, including those without school-age children, pay taxes to support the local school system: Do you think this is fair? Why or why not? If not, to whom is it unfair? Should parents who pay to send their children to private schools also have to pay taxes that support public schools? Why or why not? Which principle of taxation applies here? Encourage a lively exchange of ideas in response to these questions.

Comprehension
Ask the students to identify specific examples of taxes that are justified by the sacrifice principle.

Discussion Starter
Let the students identify and discuss both advantages Which principle of taxation applies here? Encourage a lively exchange of ideas in response to these questions.and disadvantages of the proportional form of taxation.

Discussion Starter
Guide the students in discussing progressive taxation: Who is intended to benefit from this form of taxation? Why? How?

Figure Answer Since a proportional tax is based on a fixed percentage, students should understand that a total income of $650.00 would result in a total tax of $65.00.

This figure content is also featured on *West's American Government Videodisc* (see the index found in the *TRB*) and is available in the transparency package.

This figure content is also featured on *West's American Government Videodisc* (see the index found in the *TRB*) and is available in the transparency package.

Figure Answer Students should understand that since the actual percentage of taxes rises as income rises with the progressive tax system, the wealthy are more likely to feel unduly burdened by the progressive tax system.

Proportional Tax System

Income	Proportional Rate	Tax
First $100	10%	$10
Second $100	10%	$10
Third $100	10%	$10
Total Income: $300		Total Tax: $30

FIGURE 19–4 Proportional Tax System. This table illustrates the principle of proportional taxation. With the same proportional tax, how much tax would be paid on the total income of $650.00?

than those with lower incomes, regardless of the number of government services they use.

The Sacrifice Principle The third principle of taxation, the **sacrifice principle**, holds that the sacrifices people make to pay their taxes should be equitable. Generally, it is assumed that the sacrifices people make when paying taxes to the government become smaller as their incomes become larger. When a $100 tax is paid, a millionaire is surely sacrificing less than a person who earns $10,000 a year. The problem with this principle is determining how to make everyone's sacrifice equitable.

Forms of Taxation

There are three ways in which taxes can be classified, depending on their effects on those who are taxed.

Proportional Taxation **Proportional taxation** is a system by which taxpayers pay a fixed percentage on every dollar of income. When their incomes increase or decrease, the taxes they pay increase or decrease accordingly. If the proportional tax rate is 10 percent, you pay ten cents in taxes out of every dollar you earn. If you earn $1,000, you pay $100 in taxes; if you earn $1 million, you pay $100,000 in taxes. Figure 19–4 above illustrates the principle of proportional taxation.

Progressive Taxation In contrast to proportional taxation, **progressive taxation** means that the actual *percentage* of taxes, or tax rate, rises as income rises. The progressive system can be described as one in which the marginal tax rate increases. The term **marginal tax rate** refers to the rate paid on *additional* amounts of income. Figure 19–5 below illustrates the principle of progressive taxation.

Regressive Taxation As you can imagine, **regressive taxation** is the opposite of progressive taxation. In a regressive tax system, the rate of taxation decreases as income rises. The marginal rate falls and is usually below the average rate. For example, imagine that all government revenues were obtained from a 50 percent tax on food. Because the percentage of income spent on food falls as the total income rises, we also know that the percentage of total income that would be paid in taxes under such a system would likewise fall as income rises. This would be a regressive taxation plan.

Progressive Tax System

Income	Marginal Rate	Tax
First $100	10%	$10
Second $100	20%	$20
Third $100	30%	$30
Total Income: $300		Total Tax: $60

FIGURE 19–5 Progressive Tax System. This table illustrates the principle of progressive taxation. Which individuals in our society are most likely to feel that a progressive tax system is unfair?

Figure Answer Personal income tax, estate taxes, gift taxes, and corporate income taxes (up to $100,000 at the federal level) are progressive taxes, which means that the actual percentage of taxes rises as income rises.

This figure content is also featured on *West's American Government Videodisc* (see the index found in the *TRB*) and is available in the transparency package.

Major Taxes

Tax	Description	Type (Progressive, Regressive, or Proportional)
Personal Income	Tax paid as a percentage of income. This is the major source of revenue for the federal government. Many states and some local governments also levy personal income taxes.	Progressive at the federal level, but sometimes proportional at the state level.
Social Insurance (Social Security)	Taxes covered by the Federal Insurance Contributions Act (FICA). This is the second largest source of federal government revenue.	Proportional up to $55,500 in 1992; regressive above that.
Corporate Income	Tax paid to the federal government as a percentage of corporate profits. Some states also levy corporate income taxes.	At the federal level, progressive up to $100,000; proportional above that.
Excise	Tax paid by the consumer on the manufacture, use, or consumption of certain goods. The major federal excise taxes are on alcohol, tobacco, and gasoline. Some states also levy excise taxes.	Generally regressive.
Estate	Federal tax on the property of someone who has died. Some states also levy an estate tax.	Progressive; percentage of tax increases with the value of the estate.
Inheritance	Tax paid by those who inherit property from someone who has died. This is a state tax only.	Varies by state.
Gift	Tax paid by the person who gives a gift. This is a federal tax only.	Progressive; percentage increases with the value of the gift.
Sales	Tax paid on purchases. Almost all states, as well as many local governments, levy a sales tax. The rate varies from state to state and within states. Items that are taxed also vary from state to state. Some states tax clothing, but many states do not.	Generally regressive.
Property	State and local taxation of the value of property. Both real property, such as buildings and land, and personal property, such as stocks, bonds, and home furnishings, may be taxed.	Proportional; percentage is set by state and local governments.
Custom duties	Tax on imports that is paid by the importer.	Proportional.

▲ **FIGURE 19–6 Major Taxes.** The table above lists and describes the major taxes in this country. Which of the above taxes are progressive in nature?

Multidiscipline Strategies

Math Divide the class into several groups; have the members of each group work together to gather statistics on taxation in at least eight different countries in various parts of the world. Then have the group members organize, compare, and discuss the figures they have collected. Finally, have the group members select the most appropriate kind of graph in which to present their information and then work together in planning and drawing that graph.

Enrichment
Ask two or three volunteers to work together in investigating the background of the Wilson-Gorman Tariff Act: What motivated the proposal of individual income taxes? Who supported the bill? Who opposed it? Why? Have these volunteers write up their findings in a short report, and make their reports available to the other students in the class.

Extension
Ask the students to find out what the rates of this year's income taxes are. Then give the students a chance to explain how they found that information and to discuss their reactions to the rates.

Discussion Starter
Help the students discuss the changes in maximum tax rates since 1961: Why do you think these changes have been made? Who benefits from these changes? Do you agree with the trend reflected in these figures? Why or why not?

Discussion Starter
Focus the students' attention on the statement that the importance of personal income taxes has increased: Why do you think this has happened? Taking into account public attitudes toward income taxes, do you think this trend will continue? Why or why not?

Enrichment
Have one of the students read about income taxes collected during the Civil War: Where were the taxes collected? How were they collected? On what authority? What was the public response to these income taxes? Ask this student to present his or her findings to the class in a brief oral report.

Some examples of regressive taxes are sales taxes on food and clothing, the Social Security tax, and the excise tax on gasoline.

How Our Progressive Federal Income Tax System Evolved

The Constitution in Article I, Section 8 gives Congress the authority "to lay and collect taxes, duties, imposts and excises," but no reference was made to an income tax at the time the Constitution was drafted. In 1894, however, the Wilson-Gorman Tariff Act provided for individual income taxes of 2 percent on incomes above $4,000. The country knew about income taxes from the period during the Civil War, when $4.4 million of such taxes were collected. Nonetheless, the concept of income taxation set forth by the Wilson-Gorman Tariff Act was aggressively challenged and had to be settled by a Supreme Court decision in 1895. Finally, in 1913, the Sixteenth Amendment was passed, which reads as follows:

> The Congress shall have power to lay and collect taxes on incomes, from whatever source derived, without apportionment among the several states, and without regard to any census or enumeration.

Congress responded by passing Section 2 of the Underwood-Simmons Tariff Act of 1913, which provided for a 1 percent rate on taxable income with an exemption of $3,000 plus $1,000 more to a married head of household. This concept of exempting the first several thousand dollars of income from taxes has continued to the present time, in the form of personal exemptions and standard deductions.

The Underwood-Simmons Tariff Act also provided for a surtax (an additional tax) that was levied progressively on incomes over $20,000, with a maximum total tax rate of 7 percent on incomes over $500,000. These taxes may seem paltry in comparison to today's rates, but they were considered quite large in those times. The concept of progressiveness introduced in 1913 met with considerable debate, which continued for several years thereafter.

Undoubtedly, progressiveness is here to stay, at least in principle, but the progressive nature of our personal income tax system is much less obvious than it once was. Until 1961, the maximum tax rate was a whopping 91 percent; from 1961 through 1986, it was 50 percent. Subsequent to the Tax Act of 1990, it is now 31 percent.

Federal income taxes are the largest and the most important source of federal tax revenues. See Figure 19–7.

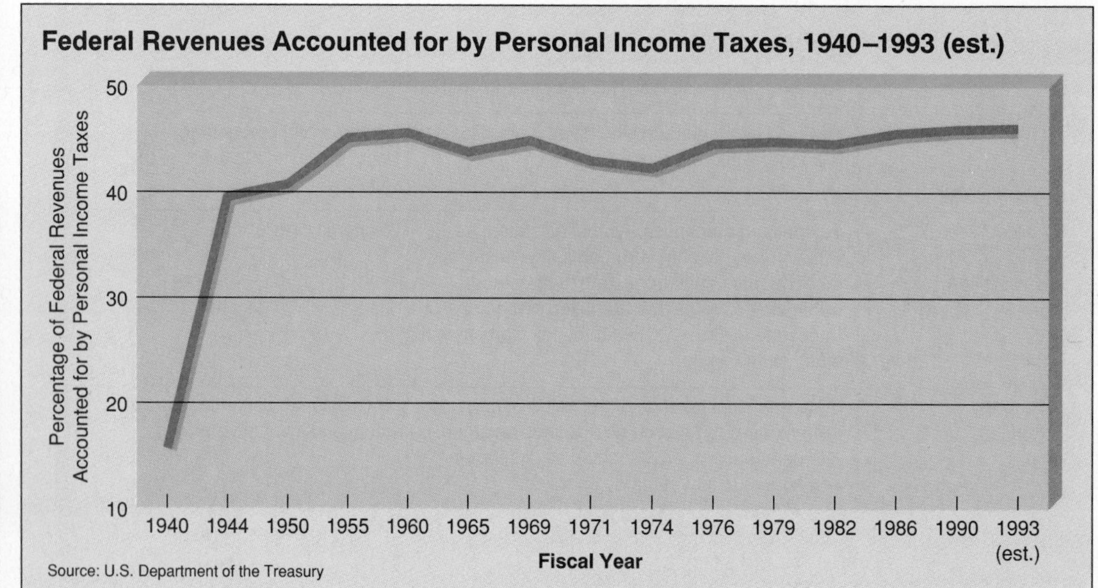

FIGURE 19–7 **Federal Revenues Accounted for by Personal Income Taxes, 1940–1993 (est.).** This graph shows the percentage of federal revenues that are accounted for by personal income taxes. During which period of time did this percentage show its most dramatic increase?

This figure content is also featured on *West's American Government Videodisc* (see the index found in the *TRB*).

Figure Answer The most dramatic increase occurred between the years of 1940 and 1944.

Enrichment
Have a group of students select some of the countries represented in figure 19–8, Tax Burdens in Selected Countries, and read about the government benefits citizens receive in those countries: How do the social services in those countries compare to the social services available in the United States? Are the differences in taxes paid reflected in differences in benefits received? Ask these students to discuss their findings with the rest of the class.

Federal Revenues Accounted for by Personal Income Taxes In 1940, individual income taxes accounted for 15.5 percent of federal revenues. Now, however, individual income taxes account for 46 percent of federal revenues.

Comparing the Tax Burden Across Countries

It may seem that the U.S. taxpayer is overburdened with taxes. After all, the average American worker works for the government well into the month of May before having earned enough to pay all federal, state, and local taxes for that year. But compared to workers in Denmark, Sweden, the Netherlands, the United Kingdom, Finland, Germany, and other countries, the American worker pays less in income taxes and social insurance payments. However, it should be noted that many of these countries provide a greater array of expensive social services, such as health care, child care, and higher education to all citizens. Figure 19–8 shows the tax burden of workers throughout the industrialized world.

Taxation as a Way of Directing Economic Activity

Taxation is more than a way for government to raise money; it is also a way in which the government can

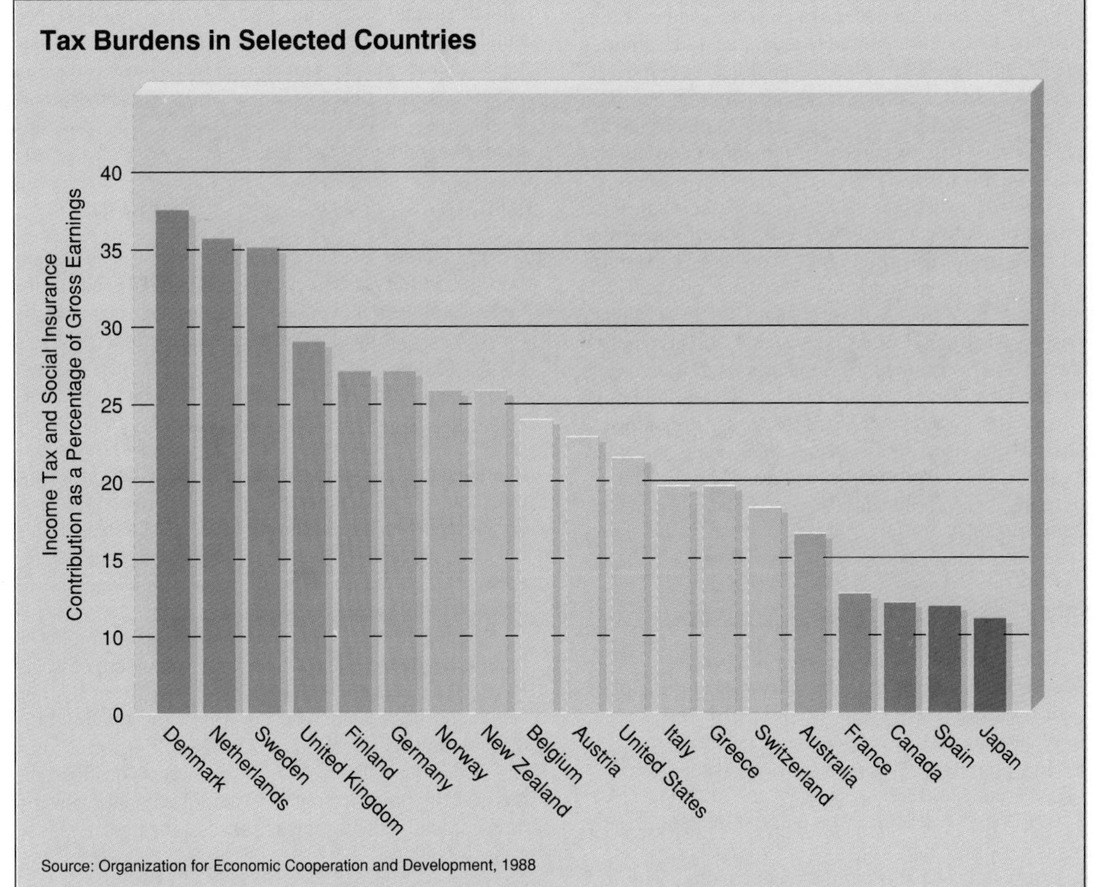

FIGURE 19–8 Tax Burdens in Selected Countries. This graph shows the income tax and social insurance contributions of workers in selected countries throughout the world. Why do you think the tax burdens are so much higher in Denmark, the Netherlands, and Sweden?

Figure Answer Students should understand that there are a variety of reasons why the tax burdens might be higher in these three countries. One of the most important of which is that these countries offer a greater array of expensive social services, such as national health care and child care and fully paid higher education.

Discussion Starter
Guide the students in considering "luxury taxes": What are these taxes? Are they an example of taxes used to discourage certain activities? Why or why not? What are the most recent changes made in federal luxury taxes? Why were these changes made?

Reteaching Strategies
1. Let the students work with partners to review and compare their notes. Encourage the students to refer to the text if necessary, and to make needed changes or additions to their own notes.
2. Have the students work in small groups to write three short paragraphs explaining the three different principles used to justify taxation.

Evaluation Strategies
1. Have the students write their answers to the Section 2 Review questions.
2. Have the students take the Section 2 Quiz found in the *TRB*.

Section 2 Review (Answers)
1. Under the benefits-received principle, those who use a particular service pay for it with taxes in proportion to the benefit they receive. Under the ability-to-pay principle, those with higher incomes pay more in taxes than those with lower incomes whether they use the services or not.
2. The sacrifice principle holds that the sacrifices people make to pay their taxes should be equitable.
3. Proportional taxation is a system by which taxpayers pay a fixed percentage of every dollar of income. Progressive taxation is a system in which the more you earn the more you pay in taxes, but in addition, the percentage taken out of each additional dollar earned rises. Regressive taxation is a system in which the rate of taxation decreases as income rises.
4. Progressive. You might explain that the federal income tax system is a modifed progressive system in that a number of deductions are allowed.
5. Taxes can be used to encourage or discourage certain activities by individuals and businesses according to the rates that apply.
6. Answers will vary, e.g., at higher and higher tax rates, people decide it is not worth their efforts to be working so much, so that there is less production in the economy. Also, some people argue that at higher and higher tax rates, people find it more profitable to cheat on their income tax by not reporting all of the income that they earn.

SECTION 3

Points to Stress
- The definition of poverty.
- Major income-maintenance programs designed by government to help the poor.

Kickoff Activity
Ask the students this question: What is poverty? Give them about five minutes in which to write their answers, and then encourage

direct how businesses and individuals use resources, as well as a means for regulating economic activity.

Taxes are commonly used to encourage certain activities by businesses and individuals. Often cities and states will temporarily reduce or eliminate taxes for a company as a way of persuading it to locate in a particular area. Governments at all levels encourage investment in their bonds by offering tax-free interest. Taxes are also used to direct resources toward investments that are desirable but costly. For example, many states encourage homeowners to insulate their homes by allowing insulation costs to be deducted from their income before calculating their state income taxes.

Taxes can also be used to discourage certain activities. Excise taxes, for example, are supposed to discourage the use of such items as cigarettes and gasoline. Customs duties are supposed to reduce sales of imported goods. Other taxes are used as penalties for certain actions. For example, a person withdrawing money from an Individual Retirement Account (IRA) before the age of 59½ must pay 10 percent of the amount withdrawn as a federal tax penalty.

Taxes can also be used to control the nature and growth of economic activity. This is done by adjusting tax rates and the distribution of taxes. Government officials must keep in mind, however, that individuals and businesses may react to these changes, so these officials must try to strike a balance between too many and too few taxes. For example, raising taxes for a state or city can actually decrease revenues if businesses and homeowners move away to escape high taxes. In contrast, a city can find itself short of funds if it grants too many tax reductions to try to attract business. As you can understand, this forces many cities into making some difficult decisions.

SECTION 2 REVIEW

1. What is the difference between the benefits-received principle and the ability-to-pay principle of taxation?
2. What is the sacrifice principle of taxation?
3. How do progressive, regressive, and proportional tax systems differ?
4. What type of system is the federal personal income tax system?
5. How can taxes be used to direct economic activity?
6. **For critical analysis:** How does people's behavior change when they are subjected to higher and higher tax rates on their income?

SECTION 3

The Government's Attempt at Eliminating Poverty

Preview Questions
- How is poverty defined?
- What are the major income-maintenance programs that the government has designed to help the poor?

Throughout the history of the world, mass poverty has been an accepted inevitability. This nation and others, however, particularly in the Western world, have sustained enough economic growth in the past several hundred years so that mass poverty can no longer be said to be a problem. As a matter of fact, the existence of poverty in the United States today is both bizarre and tragic. How can there still be so much poverty in a nation of so much abundance?

Defining Poverty

The income level that is used to determine who falls into the poverty category was originally based on the cost of a nutritionally adequate food plan designed by the U.S. Department of Agriculture for emergency or temporary use. The threshold was determined by multiplying the cost of the food plan by three, on the assumption that food expenses comprise approximately one-third of a poor family's income. In 1969 a federal interagency committee looked at the calculations of the threshold and decided to set new standards. Until then, annual revisions of the threshold level were based only on price changes in the food budget. After 1969 the adjustments were made on the basis of changes in the average of all prices.

The poverty threshold thus represents the amount of income needed to maintain a specified standard of living as of 1963, with the value increased yearly in relation to general price increases. For 1992, for example, the official poverty level for a family of four was over $14,000. It has increased since then in proportion to the increase in price averages. Additionally, the poverty threshold varies with family size and location.

Poverty Over Time

The official poverty level is based on gross income (income before taxes), including cash but not including them to compare and discuss their ideas.

Working with the Preview Questions
Let volunteers read the study questions aloud, and encourage the students to discuss their ideas in response to the questions. Then ask the students to keep these questions in mind as they read and outline Section 3.

Teaching Strategies

Introduction
Have the students read the section introduction independently. To encourage discussion, you might ask questions such as these: Why do you think mass poverty has been accepted as inevitable? What do you consider the reasons for the existence of so much poverty in a country as wealthy as ours?

Discussion Starter
Help the students consider the threshold income level used to define poverty: Why do you think the government calculates this income level? Who benefits from a governmental definition of poverty? How? Do you image that people who live just above that level feel poor? Why or why not?

Discussion Starter
Help the students discuss the groups that have traditionally been poor and the new groups that face rising rates of poverty: Why are members of each group so susceptible to poverty? What particular problems do members of each group face in overcoming poverty?

Comprehension
Ask several students to explain the significance of the changes that have occurred among single-parent families in the past three decades.

Discussion Starter
Focus the students' attention on that statement that 40 percent of all children in the United States are considered poor: What are the implications of this fact? What special problems does this fact raise now? What problems does it raise for the future? Why?

Extension
Ask the students to gather and discuss current statistics on the unemployment rate among youth, both nationally and locally.

Caption Answer Single-parent families have the potential for only one income and generally must also shoulder the cost of expensive child care in order to secure that income.

in-kind subsidies, such as food stamps and housing vouchers. (A subsidy is a transfer of a benefit. An in-kind subsidy is in the form of real things instead of money.) If we adjust poverty levels for such benefits, the percentage of the population that is below the poverty line drops dramatically.

The New Poor

Traditionally, the poorer segments of our population have been minorities, the elderly, and women. While these groups have recently experienced minor increases in income levels, poverty rates among people in particular subgroups show an alarming increase. These new groups can be identified as single-parent families, youths, and single elderly people.

Single-Parent Families Most single-parent families are headed by women. In the early 1960s the per capita income (income for each person) of white families headed by mothers was about 67 percent of two-parent families; by 1992, it had fallen to 58 percent. The income of African-American single-mother families was 61 percent of the income of two-parent families in the 1960s; now it has fallen to 48 percent. And not only do mother-only families have less income, but their numbers have increased dramatically. Whereas 10 percent of all families were headed by a single mother in the early 1960s, by 1992 this figure had jumped to 23 percent, which means that today nearly one out of every four families is headed by a mother only.

The natural result of this increase is the rising incidence of poverty among children. Today, children are 50 percent more likely than the rest of the population to be living in poverty. About 13 million children (some 40 percent of all children in the United States) are considered to be poor. Adding to the problem is the fact that children brought up in poverty are likely to grow up to be poor adults. For example, 36 percent of all girls from families that receive welfare end up on welfare as adults, compared to 9 percent of those from families that do not receive welfare.

Youths Among black and white youths, the unemployment rate has increased markedly. For African-American youths ages 16 to 24, the unemployment rate has increased from 13.4 percent in 1960 to an estimated 39.6 percent in 1992. Furthermore, young people (ages 16 to 24) in the 1990s earn less compared to older workers (aged 35 to 54) than they did twenty-five years ago.

The House Select Committee on Children, Youth and Family reported in 1989 that half of all African-American children in the United States live in poverty, compared with 42 percent of Hispanic children, 25 percent of all preschoolers, and 20 percent of all children. Its study also revealed that single-parent families are nine times

There has been a dramatic increase in the number of single-parent families in the last thirty years. Why do you think such families are more likely to live in poverty?

Discussion Starter
Guide the students in discussing the significance of the figures on poverty among elderly people: Why is poverty a particularly difficult problem for elderly people to cope with?

Comprehension
Let a volunteer explain why there is a lack of data on homeless people.

Enrichment
Have one of the students research and report on the deinstitutionalization of the mentally ill: What was this process? When and why did it take place? What effects has it had? What controversy arose as a result?

Extension
Ask the students to find out about local shelters: Where are shelters located? What services do they provide? Whom do they serve? How are they funded? Guide the students in discussing what they have learned.

Enrichment
Ask the students: Have you heard people complain that, by the time you retire, there will be no money left in the Social Security system? Do you think this could be true? Then have the students research the functioning of the Social Security system and the predictions made for its future. Engage the students in a discussion of their findings and of the conclusions they draw from those findings.

Discussion Starter
Guide the students in considering the fact that OASDI benefits are not based on need: Do you think this distribution of benefits is fair? Why or why not? Do you believe wealthy retirees should receive regular Social Security payments while other people their age have to continue working—and may still be living in poverty? Why or why not?

Enrichment
Let an interested volunteer research and report on the SSI pro-

Caption Answer Students should understand that shelters cannot solve the homeless problem, merely provide compassionate assistance. Long-term solutions would involve rehabilitative help such as mental health services and substance abuse counseling, career counseling, classes in parenting, etc.

more likely than two-parent families to have a gross annual income of less than $10,000.

Single Elderly People Even though the nation's welfare system has helped improve the income of the elderly, some have fallen through the cracks. This is particularly true for low-wage earners, widows of men with low incomes, and the unemployed single elderly. For example, about 25 percent of all single elderly are estimated to be living in poverty. Among African-American single elderly, the percentage is even higher.

The Homeless

The last ten years have brought a new awareness of the plight of the homeless and with it a new debate about how many there are and how they should be helped. Lack of information about the homeless has led to conflicting claims. While some government officials claim that the homeless are mostly mentally ill and few in number, people who work to help the homeless claim they number from two to three million. New research has revealed that most of the homeless are *not* mentally ill and are fewer in numbers than most homeless advocates claim. The nonpartisan research group Urban Institute estimated after a survey that there are about 600,000 homeless people in the U.S.; of those, about one-third are mentally ill. We do know, in addition, that about two-thirds of the homeless have serious personal problems that have contributed to their predicament. For example, recent studies show that over one-third are alcoholics and about one-fourth are either drug abusers or have been previously convicted of a serious crime.

A growing segment of the homeless population consists of entire families. About 20 percent of today's homeless are families, most of them young single women with children, who are housed in temporary shelters throughout the country. In response to the plight of the homeless, many shelters have been established around the nation providing short-term emergency needs such as hot meals and a bed for the night. For the homeless to be permanently helped, however, they need the transitional services offered by the shelters plus rehabilitative help (mental health services and substance-abuse counseling), classes in parenting, and assistance in getting employment and disability benefits.

Attacks on Poverty: Major Income-Maintenance Programs

There are a variety of income-maintenance programs designed to help the poor, a few of which are discussed below.

Social Security For the retired and the unemployed, certain social insurance programs provide income payments in prescribed situations. The best known is **Social**

Homeless shelters, such as this one in Boston, Massachusetts, provide much needed short-term care for the homeless. Do such shelters offer a long-term solution to our nation's homeless problem?

gram: Why was it established? Who introduced and supported the program? Who opposed it? Why? What were the original intentions of the program? How successful has it been? What does the future of the SSI program appear to be?

Discussion Starter
Encourage the students to consider the failure of the United States to effect a long-term decline in the rate of poverty: Why do you think there has been no significant decline? Do you think the rate of poverty *can* be reduced? Why or why not? What do you believe the government should be doing to reduce poverty? What do you believe individual citizens should be doing?

Reteaching Strategies
1. Let the students work in groups to review and revise their outlines of Section 3.
2. Have the students list what they consider to be the four most important facts about poverty in the United States. Then let the students compare and discuss their lists, either in groups or as a class.

Evaluation Strategies
1. Have the students write their answers to the Section 3 Review questions.
2. Have the students take the Section 3 Quiz found in the *TRB.*

Section 3 Review (Answers)
1. Poverty is defined by the poverty threshold. The poverty threshold represents an absolute measure of income needed to maintain a specified standard of living as of 1963, with the value increased yearly in relation to general increases in prices.
2. Single-parent families, youths, and single elderly people.
3. Social security, Supplemental Security Income, Aid to Families with Dependent Children, and food stamps.
4. Answers will vary, e.g., the government should not be involved because the problem would only be made worse in the long run if relief were available. Or, the government should provide more shelters for the homeless and expand the building of public housing. At the same time, churches and other organizations should also spend a larger share of their money on helping the homeless by providing food and shelter.

Security, which includes what has been called Old-age, Survivors, and Disability Insurance (OASDI). Social Security is essentially a program of obligatory saving financed from payroll taxes imposed on both employers and employees. Workers pay for Social Security while working and receive the benefits after retirement. When the insured worker dies before retirement, benefits go to the survivors, including widows and children. Special benefits provide for disabled workers. Over 90 percent of all employed persons in the United States are covered by OASDI.

Social Security was originally designed during the Great Depression in the 1930s to transfer income only to the poor elderly. It was intended to be a program that workers paid for themselves through their contributions. Today it is simply an **income transfer** between generations that is only roughly related to previous earnings. In other words, Social Security is a system in which income is transferred from Americans who work (the young through middle-aged) to those who are no longer working (retired persons). In this way, the relatively young subsidize the relatively old. One pays in when one is younger and receives payments when one is older.

Benefit payments from OASDI redistribute income to some degree. Benefit payments are not, however, based on the recipient's need. Participants' contributions give them the right to benefits even if they would be financially secure without them. Social Security is not really an insurance program, however, because people are not guaranteed that the benefits they receive will be in proportion with the contributions they made. Nor is Social Security a personal savings account. The benefits are legislated by Congress. In the future, Congress may not be as sympathetic toward older people as it has been; it could (and probably will have to) legislate for lower real levels of benefits instead of higher ones due to the increasing number of elderly. The average life span is increasing, which means that people will live longer after retirement and therefore collect more benefits.

Supplemental Security Income (SSI) and Aid to Families with Dependent Children (AFDC) Many people who are poor do not qualify for Social Security benefits. They are assisted through other programs. Starting in 1974, a federally financed and administered **Supplemental Security Income (SSI)** program was instituted. The purpose of SSI is to establish a nationwide minimum income for the aged, the blind, and the disabled.

Aid to Families with Dependent Children (AFDC) is a state-administered program, partially financed by federal grants. This program provides aid to impoverished families with dependent children.

Food Stamps **Food stamps** are government-issued coupons that can be used to purchase food. Food stamps are available for low-income individuals and families. Recipients must prove that they qualify by showing that they do not make very much money (or none at all). In 1964 about 367,000 Americans were receiving food stamps. In 1993 the estimate is over 23 million recipients. The annual cost of funding food stamps jumped from $860,000 to more than $15 billion. Workers who find themselves on strike and even some college students are eligible to receive food stamps.

A congressional committee estimated that by 1992 one in every 13 citizens were using food stamps. The food-stamp program has become a major part of the welfare system in the United States. It was started in 1964 and, in retrospect, seems to have been started mainly to benefit the nation's agricultural sector by increasing food-buying ability. The program has become a method of promoting better nutrition among the poor.

No Apparent Reduction in Poverty Rates

In spite of the numerous programs just mentioned and the hundreds of billions of dollars transferred to the poor, the officially defined rate of poverty in the United States has shown no long-run tendency to decline. It reached its low of around 11 percent in 1973, and its peak of over 15 percent in 1983. It fell in the late 1980s but started to rise in 1991 and 1992.

Section 3 Review

1. How is poverty defined for government purposes?
2. Which groups in society show the highest poverty rates?
3. What are the major income-maintenance programs designed by the government to help the poor?
4. **For critical analysis:** What do you think the federal government should do to ease the plight of the homeless in America? What other actions do you think can be taken by other groups of people?

TEACHING GOVERNMENT IN ACTION

Read

Introduce this feature by asking students to name the five health care issues which they feel are most important in the country today. Although student responses will vary, they should include mention of AIDS, drug and alcohol abuse, tobacco related deaths, and so on. Allow the students time to share all of their responses. Then explain to the students that as Surgeon General, it is Antonia Coello Novello's responsibility to help coordinate the efforts to battle these national (international) health problems. Then have the students read this profile to themselves.

Discuss

Use the following questions to help stimulate a discussion of this Government in Action feature. Who is Antonia Coello Novello? Why was she profiled in this American government text? In what ways does she differ from her predecessors as Surgeon General? In what ways do you think she is similar to her predecessors? What actions is Novello urging states to take in dealing with cigarettes? Why do you think she's urging these actions? How would you describe Novello's concerns as quoted here regarding the AIDS issue? What point does Novello make here regarding alcohol?

Analyze and Apply

This feature talks about both tobacco and alcohol as being health problems for our nation today. To expand this discussion, invite a health teacher from your school to speak to your class. He or she should discuss the physical, social, and legal consequences of smoking and drinking for teens. Students should have a list of questions prepared for this speaker. As a follow up activity, divide the class into groups and have each group prepare two posters. One poster's topic should be "Ten Reasons Not to Smoke." The other poster's topic should be "Ten Reasons Not to Drink."

Review

Use the following questions to review the content of this Government in Action profile. When did Antonia Coello Novello become Surgeon General of the United States? How is she unique among the people who have held this post? Where was Novello born? What are three health problems mentioned in this feature?

Think About It (Answers)

1. Answers will vary. Students should understand that the Surgeon General is the official spokesperson for the U.S. government on health issues, and does not make public declarations or warnings without the necessary or valid proofs.

See the Extended Case Study materials on AIDS found in the Resource Center at the back of this book.

GOVERNMENT IN ACTION

PROFILE

Antonia Coello Novello

Antonia Coello Novello, as Surgeon General of the United States, holds one of the most important medical posts in the nation. For example, it is through her office that the nation is made aware of the dangers of smoking, of drinking excessive alcohol, and of AIDS. In 1990 when she was sworn in, she became the nation's first Hispanic and also first female surgeon general.

Dr. Novello was born in Puerto Rico, went to school there, and received her medical degree in pediatrics from the University of Puerto Rico's School of Medicine in 1970. While she was working toward her medical degree, she was chosen Intern of the Year. She went on to do advanced degree work in public health at Maryland's Johns Hopkins University in 1982. She became medical advisor to Senator Orrin Hatch of Utah when he served on the U.S. Senate Committee on Labor and Human Resources. She later became the Deputy Director of the National Institute of Child Health and Human Development. While working there she specialized in the effects of AIDS on newborns and young children.

She is particularly concerned about the dangers of cigarette smoking. During the first meeting of a federal committee discussing smoking, Dr. Novello urged the states to enforce laws barring cigarette sales to minors. She believes that unless something is done, about five million of the children living today will die of smoking-related diseases.

Additionally, Novello is concerned about AIDS: ''AIDS is the only epidemic in the world where children will survive their parents,'' she said. ''By the year 2000, we might have as many as ten million children who are orphans of this epidemic. We have got to do the best we can for all children.'' (For more about AIDS, see the Extended Case Study in the Resource Center.)

Alcohol abuse also remains high on her priorities of problems that need to be solved, particularly among the nation's youth. In interview after interview she points out that alcohol ''is the only drug whose use has not been declining significantly.'' Alcohol-impaired driving remains one the of leading causes of death among our youth. ''Kids still think that drinking is cool, and that is what frightens me so much,'' she said in an interview in the *Saturday Evening Post* in 1991.

In that same interview she talked about the future: ''I want to be able to look back some day and say, 'I did make a difference,' whether it was to open the minds of people to think that a woman can do a good job, or whether it is the fact that so many kids out there think they could be me. Then all the headaches . . . will have been worth it.''

THINK ABOUT IT

1. How much importance should be given to the declaration of the surgeon general of the United States that smoking is injurious to one's health?

SECTION 4

Points to Stress

- Major federal environmental laws.
- The major provisions of the National Environmental Policy Act of 1969.
- The definition of global warming and the greenhouse effect and the federal government's response to these threats.

Kickoff Activity

Give the students five minutes in which to write their answers to this question: What are you doing to help clean up the environment? After all the students have finished writing, ask for volunteers to read their responses to the rest of the class.

Working with the Preview Questions

Read these four study questions to the class, and encourage the students to share their ideas in response to each. Then remind the students to keep these questions in mind as they read Section 4.

Teaching Strategies

Introduction

Ask one of the students to read the section introduction aloud. Then ask: What is our environment? What is our ecology? How are the two interrelated? Why do you think people have accepted such widespread destruction of our environment and our ecology? Do you think it is possible to reverse this trend of acceptance? If not, why not? If so, how?

Enrichment

Let an interested volunteer research the 1969 explosion of Union Oil's well near Santa Barbara: What were the results? How did the media cover the incident? How did the public respond? Have the volunteer write a short report of his or her findings, and distribute copies of the report to the other students.

Caption Answer Student answers will vary and can be used as a springboard for a discussion on the importance of our environment versus the cost to private businesses and consumers.

SECTION 4

Cleaning Up the Environment

Preview Questions

- What are some of the more recent major federal environmental laws? What did they set out to accomplish?
- What were the major provisions of the National Environmental Policy Act of 1969?
- What are global warming and the greenhouse effect? What has been the federal government's response to these problems?

When the Exxon supertanker *Valdez* struck Bligh Reef in the pristine, frigid waters of Prince William Sound in Alaska in 1989, it spilled a quarter of a million barrels (more than 10 million gallons) of crude oil into the water, causing the worst oil spill in North American history. Within a week the oil slick covered almost 1,000 square miles, killing and maiming marine animals, fish, and migratory birds. Within four weeks the slick had grown to 1,600 square miles and threatened wildlife living hundreds of miles to the southwest of the accident site. By the end of the summer of 1989, Exxon Corporation had already spent more than $1 billion on cleanup efforts but probably recovered less than one-fourth of the crude oil that had escaped from the hold of the *Valdez*. (See the Resource Center for original source materials on this case.) Two years later, in the winter of 1991, the world saw an oil spill ten to twenty times worse than the one that occurred in Alaska. This spill, however, was not an accident. It was created during the Persian Gulf War when Iraq opened the spigot on a Kuwaiti supertanker loading platform.

Oil spill disasters in the United States and elsewhere serve as constant reminders that human actions often create unwanted side effects—the destruction of our environment and of our ecology. Human beings emit pollutants into the air and the water every day. Each year the atmosphere of our planet receives 20 million metric tons of sulfur dioxide, 18 million metric tons of ozone pollutants, and 60 million metric tons (one metric ton is about 2,200 pounds) of carbon monoxide.

▲ This otter was one of the tragic casualties of the disaster that occurred in Alaska in 1989 when the Exxon *Valdez* spilled a quarter of a million barrels of crude oil into the water. What steps do you think our government should take to see that such disasters are averted in the future?

How the Government Has Addressed the Pollution Problem

Our country's government has been responding to pollution problems since before the American Revolution, when the Massachusetts Bay Colony issued regulations to try to stop the pollution of Boston Harbor. In the nineteenth century, states passed laws controlling water pollution after scientists and medical researchers convinced most policymakers that dumping sewage into drinking and bathing water caused disease. At the national level, the first Water Pollution Control Act in 1948 mandated research and assistance to the states, but little was done. In 1952, the first state air-pollution law was passed in Oregon. Again at the national level, the Air Pollution Control Act of 1955 gave some assistance to states and cities. Figure 19–9 on pages 480 and 481 lists the major landmarks of environmental legislation in the United States.

The National Environmental Policy Act The year 1969 marks perhaps the true start of federal government involvement in pollution controls. In that year, the conflict between oil interests and environmentalists literally erupted when a Union Oil Company's oil well exploded six miles off the coast of Santa Barbara, California,

Discussion Starter
Guide the students in carefully reading and discussing the chart, Major Federal Environmental Legislation: What is the importance of each act?

Enrichment
Ask several students to research and present an oral report on the current activities of the CEQ.

Enrichment
You might want to share with the students the following information about additional major federal environmental legislation.
1976 Toxic Substances Control Act—designed to screen new chemicals and ban or limit the use of those that present an unreasonable health risk.
1987 Clean Water Act Amendment—provides for a program of federal financial assistance to states for construction of 10,000 sewage treatment plants.
1973 Endangered Species Act—amended 1982, 1988; prohibits the import or trade in any product of an endangered or threatened species other than for scientific purposes.
1990 Oil Pollution Act—raised liability and compensation limits for tanker oil spills in U.S. waters; placed a 5-cent fee on each barrel of oil to create a trust fund for cleanup and damages beyond the spiller's $10 billion liability limit.

Figure Answer The first major federal environmental legislation was the Refuse Act of 1899. Students should understand that in 1899 the dumping of solid wastes into navigable waters was a much more obvious problem than issues of air quality or deforestation.

This figure content is also featured on *West's American Government Videodisc* (see the index found in the *TRB*) and is available in the transparency package.

Major Federal Environmental Legislation

Legislation	Description
1899 Refuse Act	Made it unlawful to dump refuse into navigable waters without a permit. A 1966 court decision made all industrial wastes subject to this act.
1955 Federal Water Pollution Control Act	Set standards for treatment of municipal water waste before discharge. Revisions to this act were passed in 1965 and 1967.
1963 Clean Air Act	Coordinated research and assisted state and local governments in establishing control programs.
1965 Clean Air Act Amendments	Authorized establishment of federal standards for automobile exhaust emissions, beginning with 1968 models.
1965 Solid Waste Disposal Act	Provided assistance to state and local governments for control programs and authorized research in this area.
1965 Water Quality Act	Authorized the setting of standards for discharges into waters.
1967 Air Quality Act	Established air quality regions, with acceptable regional pollution levels. Required local and state governments to implement approved control programs or be subject to federal controls.
1969 National Environmental Policy Act	Established Council for Environmental Quality for the purpose of coordinating all federal pollution control programs. Authorized the establishment of the Environmental Protection Agency to implement CEQ policies on a case-by-case basis.
1970 Clean Air Act Amendments	Authorized the Environmental Protection Agency to set national air pollution standards. Restricted the discharge of six major pollutants into the lower atmosphere. Required automobile manufacturers to reduce nitrogen oxide, hydrocarbon, and carbon monoxide emissions by 90 percent (in addition to the 1965 requirements) during the 1970s. Set aircraft emission standards. Required states to meet deadline for complying with EPA standards. Authorized legal action by private citizens to require EPA to enforce approved standards against undiscovered offenders.

FIGURE 19–9 Major Federal Environmental Legislation. The figure above lists and describes important pieces of federal environmental legislation. When was the first of these acts passed? With what was it concerned?

releasing 235,000 gallons of crude oil. The result was an oil slick that covered an area of eight hundred square miles, washing up on the city's beaches and killing plant life, birds, and numerous fish. Hearings in Congress revealed that the Interior Department did not know which way to go in the energy-environmental trade-off—allow more oil exploration with possible damage to the ecology or save the environment at all costs.

Congress did know, however, and passed the National Environmental Policy Act in 1969. This landmark legislation established, among other things, the Council on Environmental Quality (CEQ), and mandated that an

Enrichment
Have a small group of students learn more about the Clean Air Act of 1990, especially as it applies to your state and community: What programs have been instituted locally? What procedures have been altered or eliminated? Why? Ask these students to plan and make a bulletin board display showing how this act has affected local businesses and individuals.

Major Federal Environmental Legislation (continued)

Legislation	Description
1972 Federal Water Pollution Control Act Amendments	Set national water quality goal of restoring polluted waters to swimmable, fishable waters by 1983.
1972 Pesticide Control Act	Required that all pesticides used in interstate commerce be approved and certified as effective for their stated purposes. Required certification that they were harmless to humans, animal life, animal feed, and crops.
1974 Clean Water Act	Originally called the Safe Water Drinking Act, this law set (for the first time) federal standards for water suppliers serving more than twenty-five people, having more than fifteen service connections, or operating more than sixty days per year.
1976 Resource Conservation and Recovery Act	Encouraged conservation and recovery of resources. Put hazardous waste under government control. Disallowed the opening of new dumping sites. Required that all existing open dumps be closed or upgraded to sanitary landfills by 1983. Set standards for providing technical, financial, and marketing assistance to encourage solid waste management.
1977 Clean Air Act Amendments	Pushed deadline for automobile emission requirements ahead to 1981.
1980 Comprehensive Environmental Response, Compensation and Liability Act	Established a "superfund" to clean up toxic waste dumps.
1990 Clean Air Act	The most comprehensive legislation to date. This act mandated the following: the oldest coal-burning power plants must cut emissions by 40 percent to reduce acid rain; industrial emissions of 189 toxic chemicals must be reduced by 90 percent by the year 2000; production of CFCs must stop by the year 2002; controls on other factories and businesses intended to reduce smog in 96 cities to healthful levels by 2005. Utilities were granted "credits" to emit certain amounts of sulfur dioxide, and those that emit less than the maximum allowed can sell their credits to other polluters.

environmental impact statement be prepared for every recommendation, report on legislation, or major federal action that would significantly affect the quality of the environment. The act therefore gave citizens and public interest groups concerned with the environment a weapon against unnecessary and inappropriate use of our resources by government.

Clean Air Act of 1990 In 1990 a new amendment to the 1983 Clean Air Act was passed, which consisted of over one thousand pages of regulations on American industry.

One innovative aspect of this act was that Congress mandated formulas for new gasoline that will be used in cars in the smoggiest cities. Also, the act required

Service Learning Activity

There is a misconception that voluntarism in the United States is extinct. There are many active choices for young people to make in the areas of helping the poor and working to protect the environment. There are literally thousands of local organizations helping the needy that students may join. Students should contact local churches, the mayor's office, or check the Yellow Pages under "Social Service Agencies." Students can also volunteer to help local environmentalists with a vast array of tasks like recycling drives, prairie restoration, and habitat protection. Have students check the Yellow Pages under "Environmental, Conservation & Ecological Organizations." The Fish and Wildlife Service of the Department of the Interior, Environmental Action, Inc., World Wildlife Fund, and National Wildlife Federation all have offices in Washington, D.C. The Sierra Club is in San Francisco, and the National Audubon Society is in New York.

TEACHING CITIZENSHIP SKILLS AND RESPONSIBILITIES

Read
Introduce this feature by asking the students to read the title and then to share their own ideas on the subject: What are you doing now to be a waste-conscious consumer? Why are those steps important? What else do you think you could be doing? After a brief discussion, let several students participate in reading the feature aloud to the rest of the class.

Discuss
Pose questions such as these to help the students discuss the feature: What disposable items do you and your family use? What would it take to get you—and the other members of your family—to give up these throw-aways? What is the significance of the high output of garbage in this country? Where and how can people in your community recycle glass, metal, and paper? What products that use recycled paper are you familiar with? Where can those products be purchased? What are some examples of durable, long-lasting products? What are the benefits of buying such products? Where and how can you repair—or have repaired—small, simple appliances that might otherwise be thrown away? What are some of the local agencies that accept used clothing, furniture, and appliances? What do these agencies do with donated items? What kind of planning is required to avoid impulse purchases? What are the benefits of such planning?

Analyze and Apply
Ask the students to work in small groups to plan and produce radio spots advertising specific techniques for becoming waste-conscious consumers.

Review
Help the students review this feature by asking questions such as these: What problems do disposable items create? What are three specific things you can do to become a more waste-conscious consumer?

CITIZENSHIP SKILLS AND RESPONSIBILITIES

How to Be a Waste-Conscious Consumer

We live in what many people have called a "throwaway society." Much of what we buy is disposable—razors, plastic dishes and cups, diapers, newspapers, and even such items as cameras. Every year we throw away 25 billion styrofoam cups, over 2 billion razors, and 200 million automobile tires. Americans throw out ten times their weight in trash every year, or about a half ton (one thousand pounds) for every person. No other country in the world can match the United States' output of garbage on a per capita (per person) basis. The total amount of trash generated in the United States each day—400,000 tons—is overwhelming.

Each of us can take steps to be less wasteful. Being a waste-conscious consumer only requires awareness and a little extra effort at times. Here are some simple places to begin:

- **Recycle purchased goods packaged in recyclable materials.** Glass, aluminum, paper, and some plastics can be recycled; other kinds of plastics and styrofoam cannot. Look at the containers to see if they have been recycled and/or are recyclable.
- **Buy bulk.** Encourage your family to buy products in bulk or in family-size amounts. This reduces packaging wastes and also saves money.
- **Buy recycled paper products.** Napkins, bathroom tissue, paper towels, greeting cards, and stationery are all available now on recycled paper. If your grocers or stationers don't supply these products, ask them to start.
- **Purchase fresh fruits and vegetables.** Fresh produce is often more nutritious than packaged; it also requires less packaging.
- **Buy durable, long-lasting products.** These products won't wear out quickly, which means you'll be throwing away less often. (You get better quality and a better bargain, too—check ratings in *Consumer Reports* magazine before making a major purchase.)
- **Take care of what you own.** The better care you take, the longer your goods will last, and the less waste you will create.
- **Borrow or rent before you buy.** Don't buy something you will use only once or twice, such as special party supplies, unusual tools, or a sporting goods item that may only be a temporary interest. Borrow or rent the equipment or products to find out if you really need to own them.
- **Donate what you no longer need.** Goodwill, the Salvation Army, or a local church can find people who would be happy to make use of clothes or furniture that you no longer want or need.
- **Avoid impulse buying.** Plan your purchases so that you don't end up with things you don't really want or need. (This will also help you not to waste your income.)

TAKING ACTION

1. Make a list of ten ways that you could change your everyday activities to reduce the amount of waste you create.
2. Take a tour through a pharmacy or a supermarket and make a list of all the products that are packaged in nonrecyclable materials. Then think of ways in which those items could be packaged in a more waste-efficient manner. Summarize your findings.

Vocabulary
Let volunteers respond to these questions: What is global warming? Why is it a threat to our environment?

Comprehension
Have several students restate, in their own words, the ideas expressed by Udall.

Comprehension
Ask volunteers to identify fossil fuels, to explain the relationship between burning fossil fuels and the emission of carbon dioxide, and to describe the effects on the earth's atmosphere of deforestation and the burning of trees.

Extension
You might wish to ask a science or biology teacher from your school to speak to your class. He or she could discuss the scientific explanations for global warming and the greenhouse effect with your students. Students should prepare in advance a list of questions for the speaker.

that if by the year 2003 certain cities still experience dangerous levels of pollution that continue to destroy the ozone layer of our atmosphere, automobile emissions standards for cars driven in those cities will be drastically increased. Severe restrictions on potential cancer-causing air toxins were imposed, and severe restrictions on the total emissions of sulfur dioxide from electric utilities was mandated.

Global Warming

One of the most pressing concerns in the world today is the threat of **global warming**—the gradual increase in average temperature throughout the world. Not too many years ago, ironically, most environmental observers and concerned scientists were worried about a new ice age. In the June 24, 1974, issue of *Time* magazine, for example, the editor said that "the atmosphere has been growing gradually cooler for the past three decades. The trend shows no indication of reversing." Dr. Reid Bryson, a specialist in climatology, stated in 1980 that "the overall cooling trend is unmistakable, and in coming years it will profoundly affect agriculture, geopolitics, and human survival worldwide." As late as May 12, 1983, the editors of *Rolling Stone* magazine stated the following:

> For years now, climatologists have foreseen a trend toward colder weather—long range, to be sure, but a trend as inevitable as death. . . . According to one theory, all it would take is a single cold summer to plunge the earth into a sudden apocalypse of ice.

By the 1990s, however, scientists had determined that the earth was getting too warm. According to the National Academy of Sciences, "global environmental change [global warming] may well be the most pressing international issue of the next century . . . the future welfare of human society is . . . at risk."

Some observers believe there is a silver lining in the cloud of global warming. James R. Udall, a frequent contributor to *Audubon, National Wildlife,* and *Sierra* magazines, wrote:

> A century from now historians may conclude that the threat of global warming was the best thing that ever happened to the environment. Humanity has an enormous investment in a stable climate, and global warming gives us a compelling, selfish, economic incentive to change patterns of energy use that have proved so harmful to the environment.

The Greenhouse Effect and Global Warming

The **greenhouse effect** is the trapping of heat inside the earth's atmosphere, which is the result of pollution caused largely by the burning of fossil fuels and the emission of carbon dioxide (CO_2).

Discussion Starter
Help the students consider the fact that convincing data about the earth's warming is not yet available: Does this lack of data mean that no action should be taken to slow or reverse the warming of the earth? Why or why not?

Critical Thinking Skills
Guide the students in analyzing the need for reduction in the use of fossil fuels and the response of the American public to that need: Do you believe people understand the importance of reducing our use of fossil fuels? Why or why not? If not, how do you think people can be helped to appreciate that importance? Do you believe that people are willing to make basic life-style changes in order to improve the environment?

Discussion Starter
Have the students discuss the EPA's requirements for improved gas mileage in new cars: How effective are these requirements? What other methods could be used to reduce the emissions of carbon dioxide? Why do you believe those methods are not being more actively pursued? What additional steps—if any—do you think the EPA should be taking? Why?

Enrichment
Let two interested students gather figures on the destruction of the ozone layer during the past 10 years. Have these students prepare a chart or other visual display of their findings.

Discussion Starter
Encourage the students to consider and discuss the dangers posed by CFCs: What can and should consumers be doing in response to these dangers? Why?

Discussion Starter
Help the students discuss the need for U.S. aid to Brazil to help reduce rain forest destruction: Why do you think Brazil needs compensation for its loss of rain-forest profits? Whose responsibility is it to help Brazil in efforts to improve the world environment? Why? Encourage the students to express and support various points of view in this discussion.

Reteaching Strategies
1. Ask the students to choose partners; have them work together to list what they consider the six most important steps to be taken in cleaning up the environment.
2. Work with small groups of students. Help them use a map or globe to point out areas that now face—or could soon face—special environmental problems.

Evaluation Strategies
1. Have the students write their answers to the Section 4 Review questions.
2. Have the students take the Section 4 Quiz found in the *TRB*.

Section 4 Review (Answers)
1. It established the Council for Environmental Quality for the purpose of coordinating all federal pollution control programs.
2. The oldest active coal-burning plants must cut emissions by 40 percent; industrial emissions of 189 toxic chemicals must be reduced by 90 percent by the year

Scientists still deeply disagree over the extent and nature of global warming and the greenhouse effect. It may take another ten years before objective and completely convincing evidence is available that the earth is indeed warming.

Nevertheless, some of the most complex computer models of the world's climate, such as one at the National Center for Atmospheric Research, suggest that if the current rate of the greenhouse effect continues, by the year 2050 the earth's temperature will rise by three to nine degrees Fahrenheit. This would be an enormous change in temperature and would cause ecological changes that would result in dramatic social, economic, and political upheavals: The ice caps on mountain peaks would melt; coastal water levels would rise, which would flood many cities; forests would die; and farmland and crops would be severely stressed.

Most experts now agree that the greenhouse effect and the resulting global warming may well pose one of the most serious challenges to U.S. and world leaders in the coming decades. Scientists and policymakers agree that the problem must be addressed on a global scale. The discovery of severe environmental problems in Eastern Europe, plus China and India's continued reliance on coal as a major energy source, make the issue urgent. And because the United States, with only 5 percent of the world's population, produces 23 percent of the world's carbon dioxide, the responsibility for Americans is quite clear.

Perhaps most daunting is the fact that only drastic reductions in the use of fossil fuels and the increasing use of alternative energy sources will slow down, stop, and perhaps reverse the damage already done. Those energy sources (such as nuclear energy) are not currently cost-effective or safe, and new clean-energy sources and technologies have yet to be devised, much less put on line for use.

Depletion of the Ozone Layer

The ozone layer shields the earth from excessive ultraviolet radiation from the sun. In high doses, this radiation causes skin cancer, cataracts, and suppression of the human immune system as well as harming crops and wildlife.

In 1990 scientists discovered that the ozone layer is being destroyed much faster than was previously thought—there has been a 10 percent reduction since 1987 over Europe and North America. Over the polar regions, especially in Antarctica, 50 percent of the ozone layer has been lost, which has caused the so-called "holes" in the ozone shield. Industrial chemicals that contain chlorine—chloroflurocarbons (CFCs), halons, carbon tetrachloride, and methyl chloroform—are among the principal culprits in destroying the ozone molecules.

In 1987 fifty-six nations signed a treaty in Montreal, Canada, that requires them to cut the production and use of CFCs in half by the year 2000. The new data mentioned above, however, have increased pressure for a more rapid rate of elimination of this and other ozone-depleting chemicals. The United States, Japan, and several other countries support the complete elimination of chloroflurocarbons by the end of this century.

Stiffer federal laws in the U.S. now require special disposal and handling of equipment containing ozone-reducing chemicals that might leak into the atmosphere. They also call for the reduction of CFCs in widely used consumer products such as aerosol cans.

A related issue involves destruction of the rain forests of South America, Indonesia, Hawaii, and the northwestern United States. Concerned ecologists, politicians, and ordinary citizens have joined forces throughout the world to reduce the destruction of these forests, the greatest concentration of which is in Brazil. It has been argued that because green vegetation helps produce the right mix of gases in the air that we breathe, if we continue to destroy the rain forests we will suffer in the future. To date there has been little indication that the U.S. is willing to offer the Brazilian government economic incentives for reducing rain forest destruction.

SECTION 4 REVIEW

1. What did the National Environmental Policy Act of 1969 establish?
2. What were the major provisions of the Clean Air Act of 1990?
3. **For critical analysis:** Can we expect poor countries to have the same environmental concerns that the United States has? Explain.

2000; productions of CFCs must stop by the year 2005; severed restrictions on the total emissions of sulfur dioxide from electric utilities mandated.

3. Answers will vary, e.g., we cannot expect poorer nations to have the same environmental concerns that the United States has because they cannot afford such a luxury. Poorer nations are first concerned with the food, shelter, and material well being of their citizens.

TEACHING CHALLENGE TO THE AMERICAN DREAM

Read

Introduce this Challenge to the American Dream feature by having the students read and respond to the title: Why does our banking system need to be saved? Who should be responsible for saving the banking system? What methods should be used? After a brief discussion, let several students participate in reading the feature aloud to the rest of the class.

Discuss

Use questions such as these to encourage discussion of the feature: What do you remember about media coverage of the S&L crisis? How did you react to news of the problem? How did members of your family and others around you react? Why? Why do you think all thrifts and banks pay the same insurance premium? Do you believe that those who make risky investments on behalf of thrifts and banks are to blame for the crisis? Why or why not? If not, why not? If so, should they be held financially responsible? Why or why not? What changes—if any—do you believe are necessary to improve the functioning of our banking system?

Analyze and Apply

Let the students work in groups to investigate local savings and loan institutions: How many were in business (within a defined community) in 1975? How many have moved into the community since then? Which have failed? During what years? Ask the members of each group to create and display a chart that shows their findings.

Review

To help the students review this Challenge to the American Dream feature, ask questions such as these: How many thrifts failed each year during the second part of the 1980s? How did the method of government insurance for banks contribute to the S&L crisis?

You Decide (Answers)

1. Answers will vary, e.g., the bank officers are responsible because they made risky investments.

2. Answers will vary, e.g., insuring deposits up to $100,000 benefits a few richer Americans but is paid for by all Americans. The amount should be lowered.

CHALLENGE TO THE AMERICAN DREAM

Can the Government Save Our Banking System?

The savings and loan industry has been in continual crisis since the mid 1980s and the banking industry in general is not in good shape. Federal policymakers, however, weren't aware of an impending savings and loan (S&L) crisis prior to 1980. After all, for the past forty years, very few savings and loan associations—called *thrifts* in the banking industry—had failed. All this changed in 1980, when 35 thrifts failed. The number of failures tripled the following year and continued to increase until about 500 thrifts were failing every year. Public concern increased with the number of failures.

Senators and representatives began worrying that massive failures in the savings and loan industry might lead to a banking panic in the entire United States and might even threaten our international banking connections. The result was the 1987 Competitive Banking and Quality Act, which provided for $10.8 billion over three years to help the beleaguered Federal Savings and Loan Insurance Corporation (FSLIC).

That money turned out to be a drop in the bucket. Lobbyists for the thrift industry argued that much, much more was needed. One of the first national problems that the Bush administration had to deal with in 1989 was the potential rescue of depositors in failed savings and loans. With the backing of the administration, the Financial Institution Reform, Recovery, and Enforcement Act of 1989 (Thrift Bailout Act) was passed.

The Causes of the S & L Crisis

The government in effect insures most deposits today in the United States up to $100,000 through the Federal Deposit Insurance Corporation (FDIC). Thrifts and banks pay a small amount to the government for this insurance. Each bank pays the same amount, no matter how risky the investments they undertake. As a result of having such a good insurance deal, some savings and loan associations and banks decide to make risky, but potentially high-paying, investments. If those risky, high-paying investments do not pan out, the thrift or bank is vulnerable to trouble. But the depositors do not have to worry because of federal deposit insurance.

In effect, the managers of thrifts and banks who do this pay little of the costs if those high-risk, high-yielding investments go bad, but reap substantial rewards if they turn out well. Because most of them have gone bad, we have had numerous failures in the thrift and banking industries.

Because the Thrift Bailout Act of 1989 basically did not change the incentives facing the managers and owners of thrifts and banks, more trouble can be predicted for the future. Unless the cost of deposit insurance is higher when riskier investments are undertaken by thrifts and banks, many of them will continue to act recklessly. Be prepared for future bailout bills similar to the one that cost every man, woman, and child in the United States $2,000 in 1989. In other words, because the same incentive structure faces other types of American financial institutions, we can expect similar problems to arise and similar bailout bills to be passed by Congress.

The challenge to the American dream is to protect savers while at the same time removing the incentive for managers of financial institutions to take unnecessary risks simply because they know that the federal government will bail them out.

You Decide

1. Who is responsible for the increasing number of failed thrifts?
2. Most Americans have bank deposits of less than $20,000. Therefore, insuring deposits up to $100,000 benefits only a small percentage of Americans. Do you approve of the $100,000 ceiling on federally insured deposits? Why or why not?

Chapter Evaluation

To evaluate student mastery of chapter material, you might:

1. Use Chapter Test A from the *TRB*.
2. Use Chapter Test B from the *TRB*.
3. Construct your own test using items from the *West American Government Test Bank* found in the *TRB*.
4. Use the accompanying computerized test software to construct and print a customized chapter test.

Review Questions (Answers)

1. Monetary policy is policy aimed at influencing the economy by regulating the amount of money in circulation. If the country has a loose money policy, credit is inexpensive and abundant. If the country has a tight money policy, credit is expensive and in short supply.
2. The Federal Reserve System is a network of 12 regional banks that regulates banking and monetary policy in the United States.
3. Fiscal policy is the use of federal government revenues and expenditures by the president and Congress to influence the economy.
4. Whenever the federal government spends more than it receives in tax revenues, it runs a budget deficit. Every time a budget deficit occurs, the government issues U.S. treasury bonds which add to the public debt.
5. Benefits-received principle, whereby those who use a particular government service support it with taxes in proportion to the benefits they receive; ability-to-pay principle, whereby those with higher incomes pay more in taxes than those with lower incomes; and the sacrifice principle, whereby the sacrifices people make to pay their taxes should be equitable.
6. Proportional tax is a system by which taxpayers pay a fixed percentage of every dollar of income. Progressive tax means that the actual percentage of taxes or tax rate increases as income rises. A regressive tax is a system in which the rate of taxation decreases as income rises.
7. Personal income tax.
8. Single-parent families, youths, and single elderly people.
9. Social security is an income transfer between generations. Supplemental Security Income establishes a nationwide minimum

CHAPTER 19 REVIEW

Key Terms

ability-to-pay principle 469
Aid to Families with Dependent Children (AFDC) 477
benefits-received principle 469
budget deficit 466
business cycles 464
depressions 464
environmental impact statement 481
Federal Reserve System 459
fiscal policy 459
food stamps 477
global warming 483
greenhouse effect 483
in-kind subsidies 475
income transfer 477
inflation 461
loose monetary policy 459
marginal tax rate 470
monetary policy 459
national debt 466
off-budget items 469
progressive taxation 470
proportional taxation 470
public debt 466
recessions 464
regressive taxation 470
sacrifice principle 470
Social Security 476
Supplemental Security Income (SSI) 477
tight monetary policy 459
U.S. Treasury bonds 466

Summary

1. The basic tools that the federal government uses to manage the national economy are monetary policy and fiscal policy. Monetary policy, which is the responsibility of the Federal Reserve System, involves regulating the amount of money in circulation. The Federal Reserve is governed by a board of governors and is divided into geographic areas. In principle, Federal Reserve monetary policy is supposed to be countercyclical, which means it creates policies that run counter to the current business cycle. Fiscal policy, which is the responsibility of the president and Congress, consists of adjusting federal taxes and spending to affect the rate of growth of the total demand for goods and services in the economy. When the government spends more money than it receives in revenues, it runs a budget deficit. The total amount of money owed by the federal government is the public debt. In 1985 Congress passed the Gramm-Rudman-Hollings Deficit Reduction Act in an effort to require that Congress reduce and eventually eliminate the budget deficit. Despite two sets of revisions to this act, Congress has failed to meet its deficit reductions.

2. Eighty-five percent of all government revenues are raised by taxation. There are three principles to justify different levels of taxation: benefits received, ability to pay, and sacrifice. The three ways in which taxes can be imposed are according to proportional, progressive, or regressive systems. The federal personal income tax system is a progressive tax. A comparison of tax percentages among other countries in the world shows that the United States' tax rates are about in the middle range. Governments sometimes use taxes to direct economic activity. For example, excise taxes on cigarettes and alcohol can discourage their purchase and use.

3. The official poverty level is an absolute measure of income needed to maintain a specified standard of living as of 1963, with the value increased yearly in relation to general price increases. Traditionally, the poorer segments of our population have been minorities, the elderly, and women. Poverty rates among single-parent families, youths, and single elderly people are increasing. The 1990s has brought a new awareness of the plight of the homeless in our country. The major income-maintenance programs of the federal government are Social Security, Supplemental Security Income (SSI), Aid to Families with Dependent Children (AFDC), and food stamps.

4. The government has formal policies that deal with pollution in the environment. The National Environmental Policy Act of 1969 established the Council for Environmental Quality (CEQ) and mandated that environmental impact statements be prepared for every recommendation, report on legislation, or major federal action that would significantly affect the quality of the environment. One of the most pressing concerns in the world today is the threat of global warming. The greenhouse effect is the trapping of heat inside the earth's atmosphere, which is the result of pollution caused largely by the burning of fossil fuels and the emission of carbon dioxide. There are still deep disagreements among scientists over the extent and nature of global warming caused by the greenhouse effect. The destruc-

income for the aged, the blind, and the disabled. Aid to Families with Dependent Children provides aid to families in which dependent children do not have the financial support of the father. Food stamps are used to purchase food.
10. Answers will vary, e.g., the 1969 National Environmental Policy Act established the Council for Environmental Quality for the purpose of coordinating all federal pollution control programs. It also mandated that an environmental impact statement be prepared for every recommendation, report on legislation, or major federal action that would significantly affect the environment. The Clean Air Act of 1990 established many new regulations on American industry.

Questions for Thought and Discussion (Answers)
1. Answers will vary, e.g., the advantage is that these loans save many jobs. The disadvantage is that they cost the taxpayers and give businesses less incentive to work out their problems by themselves.
2. Answers will vary, e.g., the government should be required to have a balanced budget. An increasing amount of the national debt is owed to foreigners which means fewer interest payments are paid to Americans. As the federal government pays more and more in interest, it has less to spend on important needs of the country.
3. Answers will vary, e.g., the burden should be shared by federal, state, and local governments. No one level of government can handle such a big problem all by itself.

Social Studies Skills (Answers)
1. There is no difference between the percentage income tax paid on the first and third $100 earned.
2. The first $100 is taxed at 10 percent marginal rate, the third at 30 percent marginal rate. The third $100 is therefore taxed at a rate three times the tax rate of the first $100.
3. Average tax for $300 of income equals $60 ÷ $300, or 20 percent.

CHAPTER 19 REVIEW—Continued

tion of the ozone layer due to pollutants is another major threat to our environment.

Review Questions

1. What is monetary policy? What is the difference between a tight and a loose monetary policy?
2. Briefly describe the Federal Reserve System and how it functions.
3. What is fiscal policy?
4. How does the government accumulate a public debt?
5. What are the three principles of taxation?
6. What are the three types of tax systems and how do they differ?
7. What is the most important source of federal government revenues?
8. Which groups in society typically have the highest poverty rates?
9. What are the major income-maintenance programs designed by the government to help the poor and how do they work?
10. Briefly describe the major efforts on the part of the federal government to help solve the pollution problem.

Questions for Thought And Discussion

1. Our government has in the past provided loans to large businesses to save them from bankruptcy, which keeps them operating and saves thousands of jobs. What do you think are the pros and cons of such a policy?
2. Do you think the federal government should be required to have a balanced budget? Why or why not?
3. In your opinion, who should be held responsible for cleaning up the environment: businesses, the state governments, or federal taxpayers? Give reasons for your answer.

Improving Your Skills

Communication Skills

Recognizing Your Own Value Judgments

Students of government are often called upon to express their opinions on numerous subjects. Throughout this book, you have been learning how to think critically before expressing an opinion. Underlying this need to think critically is the need to recognize your own value judgments. Whether we are aware of it or not, each of us has a set of values and therefore a set of value judgments about everything that we consider. Our values are influenced by our parents, peers, schools, books we read, movies we see, religious beliefs, and countless other variables. Even though you may not be able to pinpoint or change these past influences, you can learn to be aware of them so they don't cloud your thinking about a certain issue. Not recognizing your own value judgments can close your mind to facts and reasoning.

The next time you find yourself reacting very positively or very negatively to an issue about which you do not have all the facts, stop and examine your value judgments. Ask yourself if they are clouding your judgment.

Writing

Re-read the section on the new poor on pages 475 through 476. Make a list of your value judgments concerning this issue.

Social Studies Skills

Working with Percentages and Averages

Look at Figure 19–4 and Figure 19–5 on page 470. Answer the following questions:

1. In Figure 19–4, what is the difference between the percentage income tax rate paid on the first $100 earned and on the third $100 earned?
2. In Figure 19–5, answer the same question as above.
3. What is the average rate of taxation for $300 of income earned in Figure 19–5?

Activities and Projects

1. Research the Clean Air Act of 1990. In your research, find the various estimates of the annual cost Americans will pay to conform to the act's requirements.
2. Research the latest scientific findings about global warming. Write a summary of your results.

CHAPTER INTRODUCTION

Instructional Objectives
By the end of the chapter students should be able to:
- Summarize the development of American foreign policy.
- Differentiate between the processes used by the president and Congress in making foreign and defense policies.
- Describe the structure and functions of the Departments of Defense and State.
- Identify the goals of American foreign policy and the methods used to achieve them.

Using the Keynote
As an introduction to Chapter 20, encourage the students to share and discuss their own ideas about foreign policy: What is it? Who makes it? What do you consider the guiding purpose of American foreign policy?

Then let the students read and respond to the quotation from Henry Kissinger: How do your ideas compare to those expressed by Kissinger? What do you think Kissinger meant by "the strength and ideals of freedom"? Why do you think he called this "a turbulent world"?

Introducing the Chapter
Read the introduction to the class, and guide the students in discussing it: Are you personally concerned with events throughout the world? Why or why not? If not, do you feel you should be? What examples can you cite of the entanglement of our everyday lives with those of other people around the world? Why are these interrelationships so important?

Previewing the Sections

Section 1 Have the students read the title of Section 1; then ask volunteers to find and read aloud the important subheadings and the title of the special feature in this section.
Section 2 Let the students glance through Section 2. Ask: Why does the foreign policy of the United States matter to you?
Section 3 Ask the students to page through Section 3, considering its content: What can you learn from the section title, the main headings, and the charts within this section?
Section 4 Let volunteers read aloud the title of Section 4, the main headings, the graph title, and the photo captions. Then ask: What do you already know about America's foreign policy goals?
Section 5 Have the students look through Section 5. Then have the students list three questions they expect to have answered as they read Section 5.

CHAPTER 20

Defense and Foreign Policy

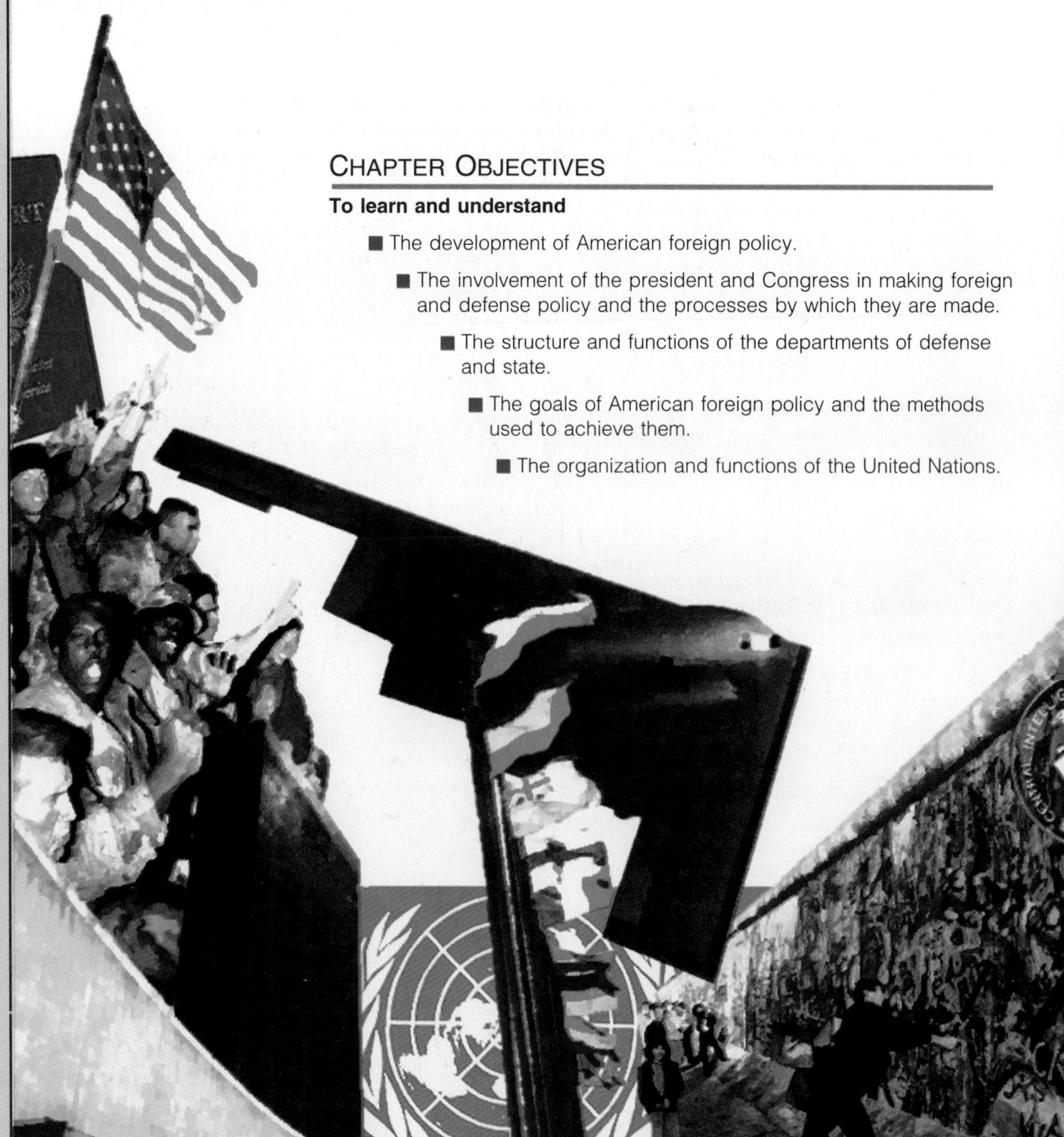

CHAPTER OBJECTIVES

To learn and understand

- The development of American foreign policy.
- The involvement of the president and Congress in making foreign and defense policy and the processes by which they are made.
- The structure and functions of the departments of defense and state.
- The goals of American foreign policy and the methods used to achieve them.
- The organization and functions of the United Nations.

West's American Government Assignment Guide

Activity Sheets
Basic Concepts 20 *TRB* (Reteaching)
Enrichment Activity 20 *TRB*
Building Social Studies Skills 20 *TRB*

Quizzes
Chapter 20 Section 1 Quiz *TRB*
Chapter 20 Section 2 Quiz *TRB*
Chapter 20 Section 3 Quiz *TRB*
Chapter 20 Section 4 Quiz *TRB*
Chapter 20 Section 5 Quiz *TRB*

Tests
Chapter 20 Test A *TRB*
Chapter 20 Test B *TRB*
Chapter 20 Test Bank *TRB*
Chapter 20 WESTEST Computerized Testing

SECTION 1

Points to Stress
- United States' isolationism and the reasons for abandoning.
- The cold war.
- Historical approaches of American foreign policy and the way they were developed.

Kickoff Activity
Have the students write short paragraphs in response to these questions: What is isolationism? What purposes is it intended to serve? When everyone has finished writing, encourage the students to compare and discuss their ideas. Point out to the students that they will learn more about isolationism as they study Section 1.

Working with the Preview Questions
Let volunteers read these study questions aloud; encourage the students to look through Section 1, pointing out the paragraphs that will probably be most important in answering each question. Then tell the students to keep these study questions in mind, noting complete answers, as they read Section 1.

Teaching Strategies

Introduction
Ask a volunteer to read the introductory paragraph aloud. Then give several students an opportunity to define *foreign policy* in their own words, and pose these questions for class discussion: Would it be possible for a nation to function without a foreign policy? Why or why not?

Comprehension
Invite volunteers to explain why the purpose of American foreign policy has always been to protect our national security.

Keynote

"The intent of American foreign policy is to promote, together with our allies, the strength and ideals of freedom in a turbulent world."

—— **Henry Kissinger (1923–) Former Secretary of State**

INTRODUCTION

Why are we as Americans concerned with what Henry Kissinger, national security advisor and secretary of state under President Nixon, called the turbulent world? Should we not be strictly concerned with our own internal affairs? For much of our nation's early history, America was relatively isolated from the rest of the world, but this is no longer true. Mass communication, transportation, world trade, and technology have entangled our everyday lives with the lives of other people around the world. Decisions about war, peace, and international trade are made jointly by many nations. Events happening in one corner of the world may affect the interests of all Americans. For example, when the country of Iraq invaded Kuwait in 1990, the war that resulted touched the lives of almost every American.

As Americans, we cannot ignore what is happening in the rest of the world. And as citizens of the world, we must learn more about international issues, and about how United States foreign policy affects this country's interests and influences global affairs.

SECTION 1

The Development of Our Foreign Policy

Preview Questions

- What is isolationism? Why was this policy abandoned by the United States?
- What was the Cold War?
- What have been some of the historical approaches of American foreign policy? How were these approaches developed?

Every nation has a **foreign policy**—some systematic and general plan that guides a country's attitudes and actions toward the rest of the world. Foreign policy includes all the economic, military, commercial, and diplomatic positions and actions a nation takes in its relationships with other countries. American foreign policy has been shaped by events and attitudes that have developed over a long period of time.

The History of American Foreign Policy

The basic purpose of American foreign policy has always been to protect the national security of the United States. **National security** means protecting the nation's freedom and independence from unwanted interference, threat, or takeover from other nations. Over the years our nation has worked to preserve national security in many ways. A brief look at the history of American foreign policy will help to explain how several approaches to foreign policy have evolved.

The Formative Years The nation's founders and our early presidents believed that **isolationism**—avoiding political involvement with other nations—was the best way to protect American interests. The young United States tried to stay out of other nations' conflicts, particularly European wars. The reason for this policy was not because America was uninterested in the fate of Europe. Rather, there was so much to be done here at home in building a new nation. We had many problems of our own, a huge continent to explore and settle, and two oceans separating us from most of the world. Also, the colonies were not yet strong enough to directly influence European developments. Our young nation instead set an example for a new political system that was so attractive it might naturally lead Europe to political reform.

Discussion Starter
Help the students discuss their responses to these questions: Is there any current interest in isolationism? What motivates such interest? Which political leaders are espousing it? How do you feel about isolationism—even limited isolationism?

Comprehension
Let volunteers answer this question: From what dangers were Washington and Jefferson attempting to protect the nation?

Enrichment
Ask a pair of students to learn more about the Monroe Doctrine: What foreign policy developments led to this proclamation? How did American political leaders respond? How did other nations respond? What was public opinion in response to the proclamation? Have these students share their findings in a brief oral report.

Vocabulary
Be sure the students can identify and define the verb on which the noun *intervention* is based.

Enrichment
Assign three groups of students to learn about Puerto Rico, Guam, and the Philippines as part of the United States' colonial empire: Under what circumstances did the United States gain control of that territory? How was the territory governed—and what changes took place in the means of governing? What is the current relationship between the United States and that area? Then have each group give a short report to the rest of the class.

When George Washington became president, the United States was still small, weak, and struggling to thrive and develop. In his farewell address in 1796, President Washington urged Americans "to steer clear of permanent alliances with any portion of the foreign world." President Thomas Jefferson later echoed this sentiment when he said that America wanted peace with other nations but "entangling alliances with none."

During the 1700s and 1800s, the United States generally stayed out of the conflicts and political issues in the rest of the world. From the beginning, however, the United States developed ties abroad through trade treaties and exchanges of diplomatic representatives with other nations.

Of course, staying completely isolated, even in that day and age, was not an easy thing to do. In the 1820s many European nations were expanding into Latin America. The United States saw Central and South America as its own backyard, and viewed European expansion as a threat to its economic and security interests. In a historic message to Congress in 1823, President James Monroe proclaimed what has become known as the **Monroe Doctrine**. In his message, President Monroe stated that the United States would not accept foreign intervention in the Western Hemisphere. He declared that the United States would look on "any attempt on [the part of other nations] to extend their system to any portion of this hemisphere as dangerous to our peace and security." In return, the United States would not meddle in European affairs.

Expansionism and the Beginning of Interventionism While Americans tried to avoid involvement in European affairs, they began expanding westward across the North American continent. This expansion led the United States into conflicts with other nations such as Mexico, France, Spain, and Great Britain, which held claims to lands to the south and west of the original thirteen colonies. Meanwhile, American traders were roaming the world in search of new markets and American businesses were expanding across the Pacific, beginning trade with Japan, China, and other Asian countries in the mid 1800s. Isolationism no longer seemed to fit America's role in a fast-changing world. The U.S. built up its military forces and began to take a greater role in international affairs.

The first real step toward **interventionism**, or direct involvement in foreign affairs, came with the Spanish-American War of 1898, when the United States fought to free Cuba from Spanish rule. The United States defeated Spain and gained control of several Spanish possessions, including Puerto Rico, Guam, and the Philippines. As a result, the United States now had a **colonial empire** and was acknowledged as a world power. (A colonial empire consists of numerous colonies—dependent countries or people that are given little ability to self-govern.)

To protect American interests in Asia, Secretary of State John Hay announced the Open Door Policy of 1899. For years, Japan and many European powers had struggled to gain trade advantages in this part of the world. The new policy opened Chinese markets to the world's leading trading nations. It allowed all countries, including the United States, equal trade and access to the region.

In the early 1900s, President Theodore Roosevelt adopted a policy that shifted the emphasis of the Monroe Doctrine. He proposed that the United States be allowed to invade Latin American countries when doing so was necessary to guarantee our country's own political and economic stability. Under what came to be known as the *Roosevelt Corollary to the Monroe Doctrine,* the United States began to police Latin America in the early 1900s and sent troops into several Latin American countries to help prevent domestic uprisings.

World Wars As World War I raged in Europe in 1914, isolationism was still a strong sentiment in the United States. For three years, the United States stayed out of the war. President Woodrow Wilson urged a policy of **neutrality**, in which a country does not take sides in an armed conflict. When American ships in international waters were attacked without reason by German submarines, however, the United States entered the war. President Wilson talked about the broad ideals that the United States represented and that had to be defended. He believed the United States had to enter—and win—the war to preserve our democratic system. It was the first time the United States took part in a full-scale war that arose from European disputes.

After World War I was won, the United States once again returned to a policy of isolationism. During the 1920s and 1930s most Americans wanted to avoid getting involved in European affairs. The United States refused to join the League of Nations, the new international diplomatic body proposed by President Woodrow Wilson. Most Americans seemed to want a return to a policy of isolationism.

This return to isolationism, however, was only temporary. Even though the United States initially tried to stay out of World War II and officially sought to remain

Discussion Starter
Guide the students in considering and discussing the Roosevelt Corollary to the Monroe Doctrine: Whose political and economic stability was to be guaranteed? How did the United States benefit from offering such a guarantee? What attitudes toward Latin America are implied by this Corollary? To what extent are the corollary—and the attitudes it implies—still in evidence today?

Enrichment
Ask a group of students to gather information about the history and achievements of the League of Nations. Have these students draw and display a chart or time line, summarizing their findings.

Enrichment
Let interested students research and report on the bombings of Hiroshima and Nagasaki at the end of World War II. Then encourage all the students to participate in a discussion of the bombings: What were the intended effects? What were the actual effects—both short-term and long-term? Do you believe the bombings can be justified? Why or why not?

Enrichment
Ask an interested volunteer to research and report on the purposes and effects of the Marshall Plan.

Caption Answer The sentiment for isolationism led Wilson to urge a policy of neutrality, keeping the United States out of the first world war for three years. At the end of the war, after successful U.S. involvement, this sentiment again plagued Wilson as he attempted to establish the League of Nations, only to have the Senate reject the proposal.

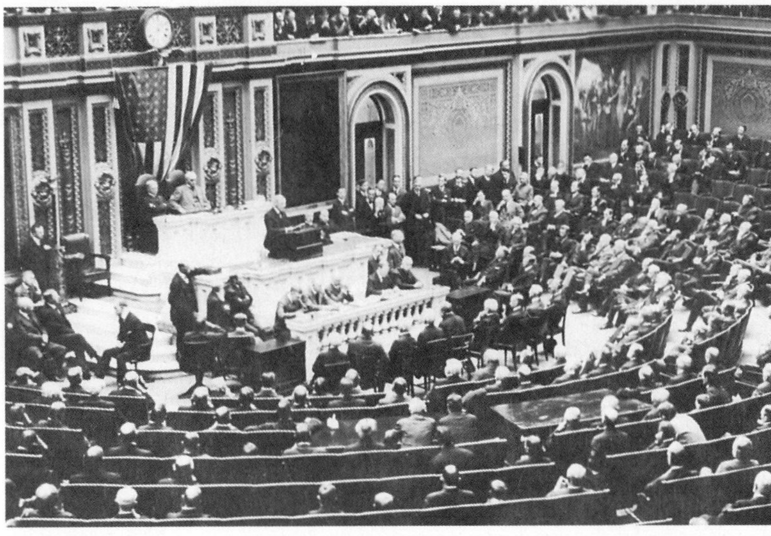

Woodrow Wilson, shown here reading the Armistice Treaty to Congress on November 11, 1918, was president during the First World War. How did the strong, national sentiment favoring isolationism affect Wilson's foreign policy both before and after the War?

neutral, most Americans realized that their nation might eventually be drawn into the war. When the Japanese attacked Pearl Harbor in 1941, the United States entered the war. The United States, in alliance with Australia, Great Britain, Canada, China, France, and the Soviet Union (the Allies) eventually fought Germany, Italy, and Japan, which were called the Axis countries. The war ended four years and millions of lives later when the United States dropped atomic bombs on the Japanese cities of Hiroshima and Nagasaki.

After World War II, the United States emerged with a dramatically different role in world affairs. The United States and the Soviet Union with its communist-dominated power structure, emerged as **superpowers**, countries so strong that their actions determined the direction of international peace and security. The United States decided to participate actively in the postwar resettlement of Europe. The **Marshall Plan**, named after then-Secretary of State George Marshall, was a massive program of economic recovery aid to the war-torn countries

These American soldiers, shown debarking from Coast Guard landing barges and storming a French beach under heavy fire, were a part of the historic D-Day Invasion of World War II. What new role did the United States assume following the end of World War II?

Caption Answer Following World War II, the United States, along with the Soviet Union, assumed the new role of "superpower." These two countries were so strong that their actions could determine the direction of international peace and security.

Vocabulary
Have the students define the term *communism:* What form of communism was practiced in the Soviet Union and Eastern Europe?

Vocabulary
Let the students check the meaning and derivation of the noun *bloc.* How are the words *bloc* and *block* related?

Enrichment
Encourage interested students to read about NATO as part of the Western bloc; let these students discuss the results of their research with the rest of the class.

Enrichment
Have a group of students read about the Berlin Wall and prepare a bulletin board display about its history.

Caption Answer Students should understand that both the Korean War and the War in Vietnam were fought to contain the spread of communism.

Multidiscipline Strategies

Science What are the reactions that produce the explosion and devastation of a nuclear weapon? How is that reaction used to create other forms of nuclear energy? Ask the students to explore the answers to one or both of these questions, using books and journal articles as resources. Then let the students work with partners or in small groups to summarize their findings, either in charts or in written reports.

◀ Although not a direct confrontation between the United States and the Soviet Union, the War in Vietnam evolved from Cold War pressures to contain communism. What other war was fought for similar reasons?

of Europe. This foreign aid program was started in 1948 and helped war-torn Europe recover rapidly.

The Cold War Unfortunately, the World War II alliance between the United States and the Soviet Union began to deteriorate quickly. The Soviet Union opposed American political and economic values. Many Americans thought that the Soviet Union and the spread of **communism** were a primary threat to democracy. Between 1945 and 1949, one after another, the countries of Eastern Europe—Hungary, Poland, Bulgaria, Romania, and Czechoslovakia—fell under Soviet domination, forming what became known as the **Communist bloc**. When communists, backed by the Soviets, tried to take over in Greece and Turkey, President Harry Truman sent American troops to help those countries. These actions were the beginning of a new foreign policy called **containment**, a policy to prevent the spread of communism by offering threatened nations U.S. military and economic aid.

In order to make the policy of containment effective, it was necessary to form an alliance of countries that needed protection. The United States initiated a policy of **collective security** involving the formation of mutual defense alliances with other nations. (This policy is discussed in the next to the last section of this chapter.) President Truman pledged military aid to any European nation threatened by communist expansion. Thus, the United States became the leader of the **Western bloc** of democratic nations that included France, Great Britain, Australia, Canada, Japan, the Philippines, and other countries in Western Europe and Latin America.

Britain's Prime Minister Winston Churchill established the tone for a new relationship between the Soviet Union and Western allies in his famous ''iron curtain'' speech in Fulton, Missouri, on March 5, 1946:

> An iron curtain has descended across the Continent. Behind that line all are subject in one form or another, not only to Soviet influence but to a very high . . . measure of control from Moscow.

The reference to an **iron curtain** described the political boundaries between the democratic countries in Europe and the Soviet-controlled communist countries in Eastern Europe. Almost all delusions of friendship between the Soviet Union and Western allies was over by 1949. These tensions became known as the **Cold War**, a state of hostility in which no fighting between nations actually occurs, but rather is a war of words, warnings, and ideologies, backed up by a constant readiness for military conflict. The term *iron curtain*, from Winston Churchill's speech in 1946, became even more appropriate in 1961, when the Soviets insisted that Berlin be split among the allies by the Berlin Wall, which separated East Berlin from West Berlin.

Although the Cold War was mainly a war of words and belief systems, the wars in Korea and Vietnam are examples of confrontations that grew out of the effort to contain communism.

The Arms Race and Deterrence The tensions induced by the Cold War led both the Soviet Union and the United States to try to surpass each other militarily. They began competing for more and better weapons, with greater destructive power. This phenomenon was commonly known as the arms race, which is supported by a policy of **deterrence**—of rendering ourselves and our allies so strong militarily that our very strength will deter

Critical Thinking Skills
Let the students analyze and discuss the theory of mutual assured-destruction: How sound is the concept underlying this theory? Do you believe MAD made sense during the Cold War? Do you believe it makes sense now? Why or why not? Encourage a lively exchange of ideas.

Discussion Starter
Let the students share and discuss their reactions to the possibility of nuclear war: How likely do you think we are to face a nuclear war in the next ten years? Why? How do you compare the dangers of a nuclear war with those of a conventional war? What dangers do you see of a conventional war leading to nuclear war? What do you feel should be done to avert the dangers of conventional and nuclear war?

Enrichment
Have a pair of students research and report on the U.S. boycott of the 1980 Olympic Games: Why was the decision to boycott the Games made? How did the public respond? What were the effects of the boycott?

Enrichment
Ask a small group of students to research the recent reunification of Germany: What benefits to the German people has the reunification produced? What problems has it created? How are those problems being approached? Have these students work together to write a report of their findings; make this report available to the rest of the class.

Caption Answer An arms race is the competition between nations in building more and deadlier weapons.

▲ The arms race began in earnest when Americans learned in 1949 that Russia had developed its own nuclear weaponry. What is an arms race?

(stop or discourage) any attack on us. It is essentially a policy of "building weapons for peace." Out of deterrence came the theory of **mutual-assured destruction (MAD)**, which means that if the forces of both nations were equally capable of destroying each other, neither would take a chance on war.

Nuclear Power and Détente The destructive power of nuclear weaponry has spread throughout the world. The United States, parts of the former Soviet Union, China, Britain, and several other countries all have the capability of detonating nuclear bombs. As nuclear capabilities expanded, so did the fear that nuclear conflict could destroy life on Earth as we know it in a matter of minutes. American leaders began to look for possibilities of easing the tensions of the Cold War. President Nixon and his Secretary of State, Henry Kissinger, spoke of a diplomatic concept called **détente**, which means a relaxation of tensions between communist and noncommunist nations. Nixon and Kissinger succeeded, to a limited degree, in bringing about détente by negotiating arms control treaties and trade agreements with the Soviet Union. They sought to increase contacts between the nations, thus creating economic, social, and scientific relationships that would ease tensions. The policy of détente was not limited to the Soviet Union, however. The Nixon administration also began negotiations to establish a new relationship with the People's Republic of China.

Détente Threatened In 1979 the Soviet Union invaded Afghanistan to stop the anti-government activities of Afghan troops. The Carter administration retaliated by restricting grain sales to the Soviet Union and by prohibiting Americans from participating in the Olympic Games held in Moscow in 1980. In 1981, the Polish communist regime, backed by the Soviets, crushed the growing labor union movement called Solidarity, which had demanded extensive economic, social, and political reforms. These and other events around the world once again brought about tense relations between the United States and the Soviet Union.

Under President Reagan, talk of détente was halted, and a harder line with the Soviet Union was adopted. During his first administration, Reagan vowed not to discuss further arms control agreements until the Soviet Union met certain conditions, among them the removal of troops from Afghanistan.

Thawing of the Cold War Beginning in the mid 1980s, the stranglehold that the Soviet Union had maintained for forty years over both the Communist bloc and its own people started to loosen. The major event that signaled the end of the Communist era occurred on November 9, 1989, when the Berlin Wall between East and West Berlin was torn down. The result was like a combination of the fall of the French Bastille and New Year's Eve—a revolution and a celebration. In a relatively short period of time, East Germany became reunited with West Germany and democracies were introduced in a number of Eastern European countries such as Poland and Czechoslovakia. The Soviet Union stopped trying to control that part of the world, focusing its efforts on maintaining unity at home in the face of a massive independence movement from the majority of the fifteen Soviet republics.

The Second Russian Revolution and the End of the Cold War

In August 1991, a number of disgruntled Communist Party leaders took illegal control of the Soviet Union's central government. Russian citizens raised up in revolt and defied those leaders. In particular, the democratically elected president of the Russian republic (the largest republic in the former Soviet Union), Boris Yeltsin, openly

TEACHING BUILDING SOCIAL STUDIES SKILLS

Read

Before the students read this Building Social Studies Skills feature, encourage them to discuss their own experiences with and reactions to TV news: Who watches TV news in your home? When? Which news shows do you find most informative? Most enjoyable? How often do you and your family members—or you and your friends—discuss what you have seen and heard on TV news broadcasts? What do you think you learn from such discussions? After this introductory discussion, ask several students to read the feature aloud to the rest of the class.

Discuss

Guide the students in discussing the content of this feature: Do you think watching TV news is the best way to learn about important world events? Why or why not? Is there one best way? If so, what is it? Why is it important to think critically about what you see and hear on TV news? How can each of these points and guidelines make you a more thoughtful and perceptive consumer of TV news? What recent examples can you cite of news stories that weren't as bad as they seemed when initially reported? Of news stories that were actually worse than the initial reports suggested?

Analyze and Apply

Divide the class into four or five groups. Have the members of each group select a specific event (from the school, the community, the state, or the nation) and present three different simulated newscasts on that event. Each newscast should present the story in a different light or from a different point of view. Help the other students discuss the differences among the three broadcasts presented by each group.

Review

Ask the students these questions to help them review this Building Social Studies Skills feature: Who has "processed" a TV news story before it reaches you? What is a trail balloon, and how is it used?

Extension

Have the students read about the current status of the republics of the former Soviet Union: What form of government has each established? With what success?

Reteaching Strategies

1. Have the students work with partners to write brief topic outlines of the material presented in Section 1.

2. Ask the students to work in small groups to draw simple time lines of the major events in the development of American foreign policy.

Evaluation Strategies

1. Have the students write their answers to the Section 1 Review questions.

2. Have the students take the Section 1 Quiz found in the *TRB.*

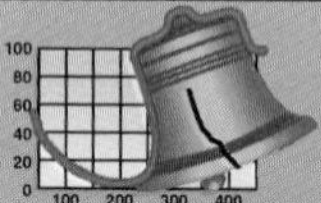

BUILDING SOCIAL STUDIES SKILLS

How to Watch TV News

Watching the news on television is usually the easiest (though not always the best) way to learn about important world events. As you watch the news, think about what you are seeing and hearing. Remember that by the time a news story reaches you, it has been "processed" several times.

Suppose tonight's feature story is about the Pentagon: first, information on the event has been issued by a Pentagon spokesperson; second, a reporter writes his or her version of the story; third, network editors edit the story; and fourth, the on-camera newscaster delivers it to the American public.

Keep a few points and guidelines in mind as you watch and listen to the TV news:

- Every day thousands of events occur throughout the world. News programs are relatively short and editors must choose a small number of these stories to report. The time they have to deliver the story is limited and decisions have to made about what to air in a short period of time.
- The day of the week often influences how the news is reported. Sunday is a slow day, so commentary on programs may be more inflated. On a slow Monday morning, reporters may exaggerate statements by officials so that there is something to report, which is sometimes called a *"Monday morning plant."* On Friday nights less will likely be reported because fewer people watch the news at that time.
- Sometimes a **trial balloon** is released, which is when an official "leaks" information about a proposal to find out what public reaction would be if it became policy. A "hostile leak" happens when an opponent of a policy proposal leaks information to the press to encourage hostile reactions to the proposal.
- Camera angles, the way in which a person is interviewed, and the time allotted can make a big difference in how the story appears to the public.
- Sometimes news stories aren't as bad as they seem when initially reported. Reporters, of course, want the story to seem more important so they will get more credit. In contrast, sometimes the worst stories are worse than reporters initially suggest. Experienced reporters are sometimes reluctant to fully discuss a problem because they fear they will lose access to important public officials.

PRACTICING YOUR SKILLS

1. Decide on one important topic to investigate. Watch one in-depth show on the topic, usually available on the Public Broadcasting Station (PBS) channel in your area or on a commercial network during a weekend talk show. Then watch the news about the same topic on a regular news show. Note any differences that you observe.
2. Try to listen to a news commentary on the same subject on a radio station, again probably on your local PBS affiliate. Note any differences you observe between the radio presentation of the news and the TV presentation.
3. Choose an important issue that is likely to continue in the news for several days. Take notes on the first news story you hear and record your reaction about the nature and seriousness of the event, the time given to the story, and the importance the news program seems to attach to the story. For the next several days, listen to as many other news stories as you can concerning that same issue. After several days, note how your opinion has changed, if at all.

Section 1 Review (Answers)
1. It was believed that avoiding political involvement with other nations was the best way to protect American interests. As America began to expand and become involved in foreign affairs, the policy of isolationism began to change to that of interventionism.
2. During the Cold War, the United States initiated a policy of collective security involving the formation of mutual defense alliances with other nations in order to make the policy of containment effective.
3. Détente means a relaxation of tensions between communist and noncommunist nations. President Nixon and Henry Kissinger succeeded to a limited degree, by negotiating arms control treaties and trade agreements with the Soviet Union and by increasing social and cultural contacts.
4. Answers will vary, e.g., the Cold War is completely over. The break-up of the Soviet Union officially ended the Cold War.

Caption Answer In an astoundingly short period of time following the destruction of the Berlin Wall, East and West Germany were reunited and many Eastern European countries moved toward democracy and freedom.

▲ These children, in what was then West Germany, helped to tear down the Berlin Wall in 1989. What changes followed in Germany and Eastern Europe?

defied the military troops in Moscow. This attempted coup was overthrown after three days in what has become known as the Second Russian Revolution, the first one occurring 74 years earlier when the communists established their power base. Within several weeks, the Communist Party in the Soviet Union lost virtually all of its power. Most of the 15 former Soviet republics declared their independence and the Union of Soviet Socialist Republics (U.S.S.R.) was in effect no more.

The political destruction of the other superpower in the world besides the United States in 1991 led to an almost immediate response from President Bush. He ordered the American nuclear arsenal throughout the world to be dramatically, drastically, and permanently reduced. He did this without any promise on the part of the leadership within the former Soviet Union that it would do the same. The reality was that the economic burden of maintaining in working order a huge nuclear arsenal was no longer possible for the impoverished former Soviet Union. Moreover, there was no longer a central authority that could require that large amounts of that nation's resources be devoted to building up its nuclear arms capacity.

Without question, the year 1991 will go down in history books as one of the most significant in modern times because of the total collapse of communism in the former Soviet Union and because of the true end to the Cold War, the arms race, and nuclear arms build-up in the United States and the former Soviet Union.

But even as the U.S. becomes the only superpower left and the former republics of the Soviet Union shift to more democratic styles of government, the United States foreign policy faces a problem: the fate of nuclear weapons in the new republics. The United States foreign policy of the foreseeable future also will have to deal with continuing problems in the Middle East, ethnic rivalries within the former Soviet Union and the former Soviet-bloc countries such as Yugoslavia, as well as a host of other problems throughout the world.

Section 1 Review

1. Why did the early United States develop a policy of isolationism? Why was this policy abandoned?
2. When and why did the United States initiate a policy of collective security?
3. What is the diplomatic concept of détente and how was it implemented between the United States and the Soviet Union during the Cold War?
4. **For critical analysis:** Given the international political climate today, do you think the Cold War is completely over? Why or why not?

Section 2

Foreign Policy Makers

Preview Questions

- What powers concerning foreign policy does the Constitution give to the president? What other foreign policy powers have developed over time?
- What role do cabinet members play in foreign policy and defense policy making?
- What other agencies are involved in shaping foreign policy?
- What are Congress's constitutional powers concerning foreign policy?

The Constitution provides for a partnership between Congress and the president in developing American

SECTION 2

Points to Stress
- Constitutional powers given to the president concerning foreign policy and the development of other foreign policy powers.
- The role played by cabinet members in foreign and defense policy making.
- The other agencies involved in the making of foreign policy.
- Constitutional powers of Congress concerning foreign policy.

Kickoff Activity
Ask the students to list at least five political leadership positions that carry with them strong influence over American foreign policy. After all the students have finished writing their lists, encourage them to share and discuss their ideas.

Working with the Preview Questions
Let volunteers read these study questions aloud. Then have the students work together to prepare an outline format, based on these questions. Ask all the students to follow that format as they read and outline Section 2.

Teaching Strategies

Introduction
Have a volunteer read the section introduction aloud. Then encourage discussion by posing questions such as these: Do you think the framers intended to create "an invitation to struggle for the privilege of directing American foreign policy"? Why or why not? What are the advantages of preventing the president from holding absolute power over the country's foreign policy? What are the disadvantages?

Comprehension
Ask the students to explain what treaties and executive agreements are, and to explain the distinction between the two.

Discussion Starter
Help the students consider the president's role in speaking for the nation: What are some recent examples? To what extent is this role ceremonial? To what extent is it substantive?

Comprehension
You may want to have the students recall (from Chapter 16) the details of these forms of presidential power.

Discussion Starter
Encourage the students to discuss the roles of various department heads in creating and carrying out foreign policy: Why do the secretary of state and the secretary of defense deal full time with foreign policy matters? Why are the Departments of Commerce, Agriculture, Treasury, and Energy now also involved in foreign policy?

Caption Answer The two roles defined by these responsibilities are those of commander in chief and chief dipomat.

foreign policy. The boundaries of each branch in this partnership were not, however, clearly spelled out. As one constitutional expert once observed, the Constitution created "an invitation to struggle for the privilege of directing American foreign policy" between the president and Congress. On many occasions, the president and Congress have in fact struggled over power in this area.

As commander in chief, however, the president has become chief foreign policy maker and assumes much of the decision-making power in the area of foreign policy. But the president is not alone in shaping our foreign policy; Congress, a number of officials, and a vast national security bureaucracy assist in shaping and checking the president's decisions. It is also important to remember that foreign policy is the sum of an entire country's attitudes and actions toward the external world.

Executive Branch

The president is granted specific powers by the Constitution in the area of foreign policy. Article II, Section 1 names the president commander in chief of the armed forces. As commander in chief, presidents oversee the military and guide defense policies. Starting with Abraham Lincoln, presidents have interpreted this role broadly and have sent American troops, ships, and weapons to trouble spots at home and around the world.

The Constitution also gives the president the power to make treaties, provided that two-thirds of the Senate approve. In addition to treaty-making powers, the president makes use of executive agreements—pacts between the president and the heads of other nations. These agreements do not require Senate approval. Furthermore, the Constitution gives the president certain diplomatic powers, such as the power to appoint ambassadors to represent our country in other nations, and the power to recognize foreign governments through receiving ambassadors.

The president also influences foreign policy as head of state. As a national symbol, the president represents the United States to the rest of the world. When a foreign policy issue or international question arises, the nation expects the president to make a formal statement.

The president also has a great deal of influence over foreign policy through many informal techniques, which include access to more information than any other governmental authority, combined with a strong, centralized administration that enables the chief executive to act quickly and decisively in an emergency. In addition, the president has budget-making powers and can influence the amount of funds allocated for different programs. The president can also influence public opinion to a greater extent than any other public official. Furthermore, the president's foreign policy responsibilities take on special significance because he has ultimate control over the use of nuclear weapons.

The Cabinet Members All members of the president's cabinet concern themselves with international problems and recommend policies to deal with them. As the U.S.'s power in the world has increased, and as economic factors have become more important, the departments of commerce, agriculture, treasury, and energy have become more involved in foreign policy decisions. The secretary of state and the secretary of defense, however, are the only cabinet members who concern themselves with foreign policy matters on a full-time basis.

Most presidents have relied heavily on the advice of their secretaries of state, who have traditionally been key advisors to the president on foreign policy matters. The secretary of state participates in the development of U.S. policies to respond to international events. The secretary meets with foreign ministers and heads of other governments; he or she represents the United States at international meetings and negotiations. For example, Secretary of State James Baker met with the Iraqi foreign

▲ The president is responsible for overseeing the military and controlling foreign policy. What two presidential roles are defined by these responsibilities?

Enrichment
Ask two students to research and report on the current secretaries of state and defense: What background, education, and training does each bring to the position? Why does each appear to have been appointed? What are each secretary's particular policy interests and attitudes? What has each accomplished thus far? What is each expected to accomplish?

Discussion Starter
Guide the students in considering both the purpose of the NSC and the date of its establishment: Why do you imagine the NSC was created? What need for such an organization was felt? By whom? Does this seem to be a continuing need? Why or why not?

Extension
Let the students research and then discuss the methods the CIA uses to gather intelligence: What concerns and controversies are associated with these methods? How does the CIA justify the use of such methods? What is your reaction to the CIA's use of these methods? What changes—if any—do you believe should be made? Why?

Cooperative Learning
Ask the students to form groups, and assign each group to learn more about one of these organizations: the Arms Control and Disarmament Agency; the USIA, especially the Voice of America; the U.S. AID; or the Peace Corps. Then give the members of each group an opportunity to share and discuss what they have learned with the rest of the class.

Caption Answer Much of its information is gathered from overt sources, such as radio broadcasts, newspapers, tourists, and satellite photography. Additionally, some of its information is gathered through secret activities.

minister, Tariq Aziz, in early 1991 in Geneva to discuss the United Nations deadline for the Iraqi withdrawal of forces from Kuwait. In that same year, he met with many Middle Eastern governments to try to put together a regional peace conference.

The secretary of defense advises the president on all aspects of United States military and defense policy, as well as supervises all the military activities of the American government and works to see that the decisions of the president as commander in chief are carried out. The secretary advises and informs the president on the nation's military forces, weapons, and bases, and works closely with the American military, especially the Joint Chiefs of Staff, in gathering and studying defense information. For example, Secretary of Defense Dick Cheney and General Colin Powell, chairman of the Joint Chiefs of Staff, worked together closely during the Persian Gulf War in 1991.

▲ The Central Intelligence Agency, where George Bush served as director in 1976 and 1977, is charged with coordinating American intelligence activities abroad. How does the CIA gather its information?

National Security Council The National Security Council (NSC) was established by the National Security Act of 1947. Its official function is "to advise the president with respect to the integration of domestic, foreign, and military policies relating to the national security."

The formal members of the NSC include the president, the vice president, the secretary of state, and the secretary of defense, but meetings are often attended by the chairperson of the Joint Chiefs of Staff, the director of the Central Intelligence Agency, and representatives of other departments. The special assistant for national security affairs, who is a member of the president's White House staff, is the director of the NSC. The special assistant informs the president, coordinates advice and information on foreign policy, and serves as a liaison with other officials.

Every president uses the NSC and its members in different ways and it can be as important and powerful as each president wants it to be. President Eisenhower made frequent use of the NSC, whereas President Kennedy convened it infrequently and on an informal basis. Henry Kissinger, President Nixon's powerful special assistant, played a major role—many would say *the* major role—in formulating American foreign policy during the Nixon administration. He was made secretary of state in Nixon's second term.

In the mid 1980s some members of the NSC were the focus of scandal because of their role in a secret operation to sell arms to Iran in exchange for the release of United States hostages held in Lebanon by pro-Iranian forces. The profits from these arms sales were diverted to the anti-government rebels, known as *contras,* who were fighting the Sandinista government of Nicaragua.

The NSC played a more traditional role when President Bush relied heavily on both Secretary of State James Baker and National Security Advisor Brent Scowcroft for advice during the Persian Gulf War of 1991.

Central Intelligence Agency The CIA was created after World War II to coordinate American intelligence activities abroad. The CIA provides the president and his advisors with up-to-date information about the political, military, and economic activities of foreign governments. Such information is called **intelligence**. The CIA gathers much of its intelligence from overt (open) sources, such as foreign radio broadcasts and newspapers, people who travel abroad, and satellite photographs. Other information is gathered from covert (secret) activities. The CIA has tended to operate autonomously, and the nature of its work, methods, and operating funds are kept secret.

Other Agencies There are several other government groups that help shape American foreign policy. The Arms Control and Disarmament Agency was formed in 1961 to study and develop policies to deal with the nuclear arms race. The United States Information Agency (USIA) works to strengthen communications and understanding between the United States and other nations.

TEACHING CITIZENSHIP SKILLS AND RESPONSIBILITIES

Read

Introduce this feature by helping the students discuss their own interest and involvement with foreign policy: Who do you think is in a position to exert influence on our nation's foreign policy? Why? What effect can you have on American foreign policy? How? After this introductory class discussion, let the students work in groups to read and discuss the Citizenship Skills and Responsibilities feature.

Discuss

Present the following questions for group discussion: Of the five methods named for influencing foreign policy, which do you believe is most effective? Which appeals most strongly to you? Why? Remind the groups to consider and discuss each of the listed organizations: What is this group's particular interest? How closely do the group's stated aims match your own interests and ideas regarding foreign policy? What is your level of interest in this particular organization? Why?

Analyze and Apply

Have the students continue working in their groups; ask each group to select one of the listed groups for further investigation: When, how, and why was it founded? What are its purposes, activities, and publications? Then have the group members work together to make a large chart showing the most important information about the organization, including the address and phone numbers. Post the groups' charts in public areas of the school (hallways, lobbies, etc.) so that other students can read them.

Review

Ask questions such as these to help the students review this Citizenship Skills and Responsibilities feature: What are two of the organizations that study and act on foreign policy issues? What are the particular interests of those two organizations?

Discussion Starter

Help the students discuss Congress's powers in the field of foreign policy: How does each of these powers enable Congress to influence and guide American foreign policy? Is Congress limited to reacting to the president, or does Congress have some initiative of

CITIZENSHIP SKILLS AND RESPONSIBILITIES

How to Influence American Foreign Policy

You may try to influence foreign policy by communicating with your congressional officials or with the White House. You can also lobby, demonstrate, and join with others who share your views. Some organizations in which you might find such people include the following:

- ACCESS
  1730 M St. NW, Suite 605
  Washington, DC 20036
  (202) 785-6630

A nonprofit clearinghouse of information on international security and peace issues.

- American Friends Service Committee
  Peace Education Division
  1501 Cherry St.
  Philadelphia, PA 19102
  (215) 241-7000

An activist group that works for peace, justice, and equality. Worldwide programs are based on the conviction that nonviolent solutions can be found to problem situations.

- Amnesty International USA
  National Office
  322 Eighth Avenue
  New York, NY 10001
  (212) 807-8400

An international group that investigates human rights abuses and lobbies for the release of political prisoners throughout the world. For more about Amnesty International, see the Citizenship Skills and Responsibilities feature in Chapter 26.

- The Center for Defense Information
  1500 Massachusetts Ave. NW
  Washington, DC 20005
  (202) 862-0700

Studies the defense budget, weapons systems, and troop levels to educate the public.

- The Brookings Institute
  1775 Massachusetts Ave. NW
  Washington, DC 20036
  (202) 797-6000

Conducts research on public policy issues in the social sciences, particularly economics, government, and foreign affairs.

- Committee for National Security
  1601 Connecticut Ave. NW
  Washington, DC 20009
  (202) 745-2450

Informs Americans about national security and arms control issues and encourages citizen participation in the debate on U.S. military and foreign policy.

It is best known for running Voice of America, a round-the-clock radio program that is translated into approximately forty different languages. The Agency for International Development (AID) gives financial and technical help to other countries. The Peace Corps sends American volunteers to work on development and education projects in other countries.

Congressional Powers

Although the executive branch takes the lead in foreign policy matters, Congress also has some power over foreign policy. Remember that Congress alone has the power to declare war. It also has the power to appropriate funds to build new weapons systems and to equip American armed forces. The Senate has the power to approve or reject treaties and the appointment of ambassadors. In 1973, Congress passed the War Powers Act (over President Nixon's veto), which limits the president's use of troops in military action without congressional approval. Presidents since then, however, have not interpreted the act to mean that Congress must be consulted before military action is taken. Presidents Ford, Carter, Reagan, and Bush all ordered military action and then its own? Encourage the students to explain and support their opinions.

Enrichment

Assign one of the students to research and report on the Congressional debate of Bush's authority to deploy troops in the Persian Gulf: What questions and issues were raised? How was the final decision reached? How did the public react to the debate and the decision?

Reteaching Strategies

1. Ask the students to choose partners with whom to review and revise their outlines of Section 2.
2. Work with small groups of students. Help them discuss their responses to this question: How are the powers of the executive and legislative branches of government balanced on the creation and execution of foreign policy?

Evaluation Strategies

1. Have the students write their answers to the Section 2 Review questions.
2. Have the students take the Section 2 Quiz found in the *TRB.*

Section 2 Review (Answers)

1. The president is commander in chief of the armed forces. The president also has the power to make treaties and executive agreements and diplomatic powers.
2. All cabinet members assist at times, but the secretaries of state and defense concern themselves with foreign policy matters on a full-time basis. The National Security Council and the CIA also assist the president.
3. Congress has the power to declare war and the power to appropriate funds to build new weapons systems. The Senate has the power to approve or reject treaties and the appointment of ambassadors.
4. Presidents have used their power as commander-in-chief to order military actions. This has become a more and more accepted power of the president. It is accepted that he or she has the power to commit troops and weapons in times of emergency. The 1973 War Powers Act recognizes these facts.

- Clergy and Laity Concerned
  198 Broadway, Room 302
  New York, NY 10038
  (212) 964-6730

Deals with all foreign policy issues.

- National Commission for Economic Conversion and Disarmament
  Box 15025
  Washington, DC 20003
  (202) 462-0091

Promotes greater awareness about the ties between disarmament, economic planning, and the military economy through citizen forums and publications.

- The Fellowship of Reconciliation
  523 N. Broadway
  Upper Nyack, NY 10960
  (914) 358-4601

Fosters public education and nonpartisan discussion of foreign policy issues by publishing books and pamphlets.

- Institute for Policy Studies
  1601 Connecticut St. NW
  Washington, DC 20009
  (202) 234-9382

The Institute for Policy Studies does research and public education on public policy issues.

- World Policy Institute
  77 United Nations Plaza, 5th Floor
  New York, NY 10017
  (212) 490-0010

Conducts research and provides information on global issues, including disarmament, peacekeeping, new international economic order, human rights, and social justice. Promotes scholarship and coursework on the above topics at colleges and universities throughout the country.

Taking Action

1. Write to three of the organizations listed above and ask for information about their objectives and activities. Write a one-sentence summary of what each organization does and how it operates.
2. Pick a foreign policy issue that interests you, such as the independence of the former Soviet republics, human rights violations in other countries, or control of poverty in Africa or Latin America. Write a letter to the organization listed above that seems most appropriate to the cause. Ask what the organization is doing in this area and how you can help.

informed Congress after the fact. After President Bush had deployed troops to the Persian Gulf, Congress debated his authority to do so, but then voted to give him authority to wage war there in 1991.

Several congressional committees are directly concerned with foreign affairs. The most important are the Armed Services Committee and the International Relations Committee in the House, and the Armed Services Committee and the Foreign Relations Committee in the Senate. There are other committees in Congress that indirectly deal with matters such as oil, agriculture, imports, and others that influence foreign policy.

Section 2 Review

1. What are the constitutional powers of the president concerning foreign policy?
2. What individuals and agencies assist the executive branch in foreign policy matters?
3. What constitutional powers does Congress have concerning foreign policy?
4. **For critical analysis:** If Congress has the sole right to declare war, how is it possible for presidents to involve American armed forces in military actions without congressional approval?

SECTION 3

Points to Stress
- The structure and functions of the Department of State.
- Responsibilities of the foreign service.
- Basic features of the Department of Defense.

Kickoff Activity
Ask the class this question: What are some of the jobs held by people who work for the Department of State? Give the students five minutes in which to list as many job titles as possible. At the end of the allotted time, encourage the students to compare and discuss their lists.

Working with the Preview Questions
Have the students read these three study questions, and encourage volunteers to suggest possible answers. Then ask the students to keep these study questions in mind as they read Section 3.

Teaching Strategies

Introduction
After the students have read the brief section introduction, you might encourage discussion with questions such as these: Why are the main responsibilities for carrying out foreign policy assigned to cabinet departments? Why do you imagine the Department of State was the first executive

Caption Answer The goal of the department is to ensure the security and well-being of the United States.

SECTION 3

The Departments of State and Defense

Preview Questions

- What is the structure of the Department of State? What are its functions?
- What are the responsibilities of the foreign service?
- What is the basic job of the Department of Defense?

Although the president and Congress have the ultimate power to make foreign policy, two departments in the executive branch are primarily responsible for carrying out foreign policy: The Department of State, which is the oldest and largest of all the executive departments; and the Department of Defense, formed in 1949 from the Department of War and Navy.

Department of State

The Department of State is, in principle, the agency most directly concerned with foreign affairs. The overall goal of the department is to ensure the security and well-being of the United States. The Department of State maintains diplomatic relations with nearly two hundred independent nations around the world and with the United Nations. It informs the president about international issues, negotiates treaties with foreign governments, and protects the interests of Americans who are traveling or conducting business abroad.

▲ As secretary of state, James Baker headed the federal department most directly concerned with foreign affairs. What is the goal of the Department of State?

Structure The department employs about 24,000 employees and staffs embassies and consulates around the world. It is organized into specialties, or regional bureaus, one for each of the five major geographic regions of the world: The Middle East, Africa, Latin America, Asia, and Europe. Other bureaus, such as the Bureau of Human Rights and Humanitarian Affairs, the Bureau of Intelligence and Research, and the Bureau of Economic and Business Affairs, have more broadly defined responsibilities.

The secretary of state has several assistants. The most important is the deputy secretary of state, who directs the department when the secretary is not present. Various undersecretaries advise the secretary on issues such as foreign economic policy, relations with developing nations, educational and cultural affairs, and military arms exports.

The Foreign Service The **foreign service** conducts most of the United States' relations with other countries. Its responsibilities include maintaining embassies, consulates, and other U.S. offices around the world; negotiating agreements with nations; and maintaining cordial relations with foreign governments and people. More than 4,200 men and women represent the United States in hundreds of locations throughout the world. To become a foreign service officer (FSO), college graduates must first perform well on the civil service exam. They are then trained in special federal government schools in the skills of diplomacy. In their service abroad, foreign service officers are assigned to either an American embassy or to an American consulate.

An **embassy** is the office of an ambassador to a foreign nation. Embassies are located in the capital cities of foreign countries. The primary purpose of an embassy is to facilitate diplomatic communications between governments. They keep the State Department informed about the internal politics and foreign policies of the host government, and keep the host government informed about the official policies of the American government.

department? Why do you think it is now the largest?

Enrichment
Ask a volunteer to learn more about these five major geographic areas. Let this volunteer share his or her findings with the rest of the class, using a map to identify the areas and explaining the main focus of each regional bureau.

Discussion Starter
Encourage the students to discuss the work of FSOs: Who do you imagine would be interested in a career as a Foreign Service Officer? What advantages—and disadvantages—would probably be associated with a career in the foreign service? Does becoming an FSO interest you? Why or why not?

Extension
Ask the students to explain (or find out) how American travelers in foreign countries might use the American embassies.

Enrichment
Allow each student to choose a foreign country (or assign a different country to each student); have the students identify and read about the American ambassador to that country: What is the ambassador's background and training? When and why was the ambassador appointed to this post? How visible and active has the ambassador been in the country to which he or she has been posted? How widely are the ambassador's statements and activities covered in the American media? Ask the students to summarize their findings in brief written reports, to be made available to other members of the class.

Discussion Starter
Help the students discuss the functions of American consulates: Who is most likely to make use of a consulate's services? Why? How?

Caption Answer The Department of Defense was established by the National Security Act of 1947 and replaced the War Department and the Navy Department. Until 1947, the marines were under the jurisdiction of the Navy Department.

Discussion Starter
Guide the students in discussing the formation of the Department of Defense: What do you think prompted the formation of the department in the year 1947? What are the advantages of a single jurisdiction for all the activities of the American military? What—if any—are the disadvantages?

The Marines, shown here training at boot camp, are just a part of our nation's armed forces. When did the Marines come under the jurisdiction of the Department of Defense?

An **ambassador** heads each embassy and is a personal representative of the president of the United States. He or she reports to the president through the secretary of state. If the ambassador is absent from an embassy, the **chargé d'affaires**, a lower ranking foreign-service official, may temporarily assume the duties. Ambassadors are assisted by one or more diplomatic secretaries and a counselor, a high-ranking foreign service officer who advises the ambassador on matters of international law and diplomatic practice. An embassy staff usually includes political, military, and economic **attachés**, or aides, plus interpreters, clerks, and intelligence officials, among others.

An American **consulate** is the office of the **consul**, who is assigned to promote American business interests in foreign cities. The consul and his or her staff handle questions and problems from individuals and companies about business requirements, transportation, and interpretation of foreign laws. Consuls also protect the welfare of U.S. citizens living or traveling abroad, as well as issue **passports**, certificates that entitle their holders to the privileges accorded to them by international custom and treaties. No American citizen can legally leave the country without a passport, except for trips to Canada, Mexico, and a few other nearby countries that admit people who do not hold a valid passport.

In some cases, to travel abroad it is necessary to obtain another document called a **visa**, a special document of admission issued by the government of the country the person wishes to enter. Visas are issued by consulates in other countries.

Department of Defense

The Department of Defense (DOD) is the principal executive department that establishes and carries out defense policy and protects our national security. The Department of Defense was established by the National Security Act of 1947 to bring all of the various activities of the American military under the jurisdiction of a single department headed by a civilian secretary of defense. It replaced two older cabinet-level military departments, the War Department and the Navy Department.

The Department of Defense supervises the armed forces of the United States and gives advice to the president on military and defense matters. The DOD also works to ensure that the decisions of the president as commander in chief are carried out.

Structure There are three military departments within the DOD: the departments of the Army, Navy, and Air Force.

Each of these branches is headed by a civilian secretary who is assisted by senior military officers. The U.S. Marine Corps, which is under the jurisdiction of

TEACHING GOVERNMENT IN ACTION

Read
Before the students begin to read the Profile, let volunteers respond to these questions: What is the Joint Chiefs of Staffs? What is the job of the Chairman of the Joint Chiefs of Staff? Who is General Colin Powell? How did he become familiar to many Americans? Then ask the students to read the Profile to themselves.

Discuss
Guide the students in discussing the Profile by posing questions such as these: Do you consider it significant that no African American before Powell has been head of the Joint Chiefs? Why or why not? How do you think the environment in which Powell grew up influenced his outlook and his attitudes? Why do you think Powell writes "Stay in school" on every letter he sends to a child? How do you think Powell's experiences in Vietnam have influenced his work since then?

Analyze and Apply
Have the students work in groups to plan and write letters to General Colin Powell—or to others who work in public service. Ask the members of each group to work together on a single letter—planning the information and questions to be included, composing the letter, and preparing a neat, correct letter for mailing. Be sure the students have a chance to read and share the responses that come to their letters.

Review
Ask the students these review questions: Where did Colin Powell grow up? What seems to be the most important thing he learned as a student as New York's City College? What was his importance during the Persian Gulf War?

GOVERNMENT IN ACTION

PROFILE

General Colin Powell

General Colin Powell, along with then Secretary of Defense Dick Cheney, speaks to the press during the 1991 Persian Gulf War.

Colin Powell is the first black officer and the youngest man to chair the Joint Chiefs of Staff, the principle military advisors to the president. During the Persian Gulf War in 1991, he played a major role in the United States' success and helped restore the country's confidence in its military system. In a variety of senior posts during the 1980s, he helped rebuild the military forces that performed so well in the Persian Gulf. After the war, lawmakers immediately began proposing to make him a five-star general for his brilliant leadership.

Colin Powell is the son of Maud and Luther Powell, both of whom immigrated from Jamaica in their early twenties, and met at a picnic in the Bronx of New York City. The general was born in Harlem, but his family moved to the South Bronx when he was three. Some attribute Powell's ability to communicate effectively with many types of people to both the strong bonds in his family's Jamaican immigrant community, and to his upbringing in New York's diversified neighborhoods. He grew up among African Americans, Hispanics, Jews, Poles, Italians, and many other racial and ethnic groups.

Powell preaches the gospel of hard work because that is what he learned at home. His father worked long hours as a shipping clerk

the Navy, maintains its own leadership and identity. Congress determines how each branch of the armed forces will be organized and governed. Moreover, the top leaders of the Department of Defense, such as the secretary, are all required to be civilians.

Joint Chiefs of Staff The top ranking officers of each of the armed forces are known together as the Joint Chiefs of Staff (JCS). The Joint Chiefs of Staff is made up of the chief of staff of the Army, the chief of staff of the Air Force, and the chief of naval operations. The commandant of the Marine Corps also attends the JSC meetings. The chairperson of the Joint Chiefs of Staff is appointed by the president for a two-year term.

The Joint Chiefs of Staff serve as key military advisors to the president, the secretary of defense, and the National Security Council. They are responsible for handing down the president's orders to the nation's military units, preparing strategic plans, and recommending military actions. They also propose military budgets, new weapons systems, and military regulations. For example, the Joint Chiefs of Staff may propose developing a new missile or forming a special military unit.

Selective Service System There are two methods used to recruit citizens to serve in the armed forces. The first method is the volunteer enlistment system. Any person who has a high school diploma may enlist after fulfilling

Think About It (Answers)

1. Answers will vary, e.g., ambition, dedication, loyalty.

2. Answers will vary, e.g., some people may choose a career in public service because they have a desire to serve the country in some way. Others may choose a career in public service because they want the kind of security it offers.

Enrichment

Let one of the students identify the current members of the JCS and make a chart identifying those individuals.

Extension

Let volunteers find and share answers to these questions: Where and how can you enlist in the armed forces? What are some of the benefits that may be associated with enlisting in a branch of the military?

Extension

Ask all the students to interview men and women who remember the draft: How did they react to the draft at the time? Looking back, have their opinions about the draft changed? If so, how? Give the students an opportunity to share and discuss what they have learned from these interviews.

Critical Thinking Skills

Guide the students in analyzing the restrictions placed on women in the military: On what assumptions are these restrictions based? Do you consider those assumptions valid? Why or why not? How would you define the term *combat?* Do you believe women should be allowed to participate in combat? Why or why not? Should they be required to participate in combat? Why or why not?

in the garment industry and his mother was a seamstress. Powell's parents, along with other relatives, gave the children a strong sense of security and discipline.

At New York's City College, Powell received average grades, but discovered an enduring passion for the importance of education. Even now, when he gets some three hundred letters a day, he tries to answer the ones from children personally, always writing on the bottom line, "Stay in school."

After college, Powell chose the Reserve Officers Training Corps (ROTC). The Army sent him many places, and each helped shape and expand his view of the world. At Fort Devens, Massachusetts, he met Alma Johnson, a speech pathologist, who was later to become his wife and mother of their three children, on a blind date. In Vietnam, where Powell learned firsthand the horrors of war, he won a Purple Heart after stepping on a Viet Cong booby trap and a Soldier's Medal for pulling two fellow soldiers out of a burning helicopter.

After fourteen years on active duty, Powell was named a White House fellow in 1972 and assigned to work for both Frank Carlucci, who was then deputy director of the Office of Management and Budget, and for Caspar Weinberger, then budget director. He moved back and forth between military and political jobs, rising rapidly through the ranks, making contacts, and developing his administrative skills. He served as national security advisor during President Ronald Reagan's last year in office in 1988. In October, 1989, President George Bush named him to head the Joint Chiefs of Staff, which made him the first black in the nation's history to sit at the table where the gravest decisions of war and peace are made. During the Persian Gulf War, Will Ball, the former secretary of the Navy said, "Colin Powell is a big reason why the president and secretary of defense showed the kind of confidence they did in the military leadership."

THINK ABOUT IT

1. What personal attributes do you think would lead to a successful career in public service? Explain your answer.
2. Why do you think some people choose careers in public service? Explain your answer.

the requirements. The second method, known as the **draft**, is the selection of persons for compulsory military duty and was used from 1940 until 1973 in the United States. The official name for this compulsory system is the Selective Service System.

Although the draft was suspended in 1973, it was not repealed. This means that all males between the ages of 18 and 26 are eligible for **conscription** (enrollment for compulsory military service) if they are called to serve. Any male citizen must still register with the Selective Service upon reaching his eighteenth birthday in case a military draft is needed during a national emergency.

Although women are not eligible to be drafted, they may volunteer to serve in any branch of the armed services. Women comprise over 11 percent of the U.S. military. By law, they are excluded from combat roles but in recent years have been performing more and more tasks that would expose them to risk in the event of war. In the U.S. invasion of Panama, 170 women were flown in, including a captain of military police who led her platoon against armed Panamanian defense forces. In the Persian Gulf War of 1991, women served as military police, helicopter pilots, and intelligence gatherers.

The increasing role of women has reawakened a debate about the proper role of women in the military, specifically whether the services should exclude them from combat. Defense officials say that any change would have to come from Congress. A New York Times/

Discussion Starter
As the students study the table, National Defense Spending as a Percentage of Total Outlays, 1940–1996 (est.), encourage them to share their reactions to the portion of the federal budget devoted to defense: What does this percentage indicate about our national interests and priorities?

Figure Answer The sharpest rises occurred in the early 1940s and the early 1950s.

Discussion Starter
Encourage the students to consider and discuss the "peace dividend": Do you think a peace dividend will ever really be available for spending? Why or why not? If not, why not? If so, how do you think it should be spent?

Enrichment
Let two or three students research the military reserves: Who serves in the reserves? Why? What are their duties? What are the benefits of being a reservist? What part did reservists play in the Persian Gulf War? How were they treated when they returned to civilian life? Ask the volunteers to present a short oral report of their findings.

Discussion Starter
Help the students consider the kinds of budget cuts proposed by Cheney after the Persian Gulf War: What are the advantages of such budget cuts? Who stands to benefit from them? What are the disadvantages? Who is likely to suffer? What alternatives to such cuts can you suggest?

Reteaching Strategies
1. Have the students form small groups; guide each group of students in discussing their responses to the Preview Questions at the beginning of Section 3.
2. Let the students work in pairs to write, in their own words, definitions of these terms: *FSO, embassy, ambassador, consul, passport, visa.*

Evaluation Strategies
1. Have the students write their answers to the Section 3 Review questions.
2. Have the students take the Section 3 Quiz found in the *TRB.*

Section 3 Review (Answers)
1. The overall goal of the Department of State is to ensure the security and well-being of the United States.
2. The foreign service is made up of officials from the State Department who serve in foreign countries and conduct relations with other countries.
3. The top ranking officers of the armed forces make up the Joint Chiefs of Staff. They act as military advisors to the president, the secretary of defense, and the NSC. They convey the president's orders to the military, prepare military budgets and strategic plans, and recommend military actions.
4. Answers will vary, e.g., the founders probably believed they could avoid more wars this way. Ci-

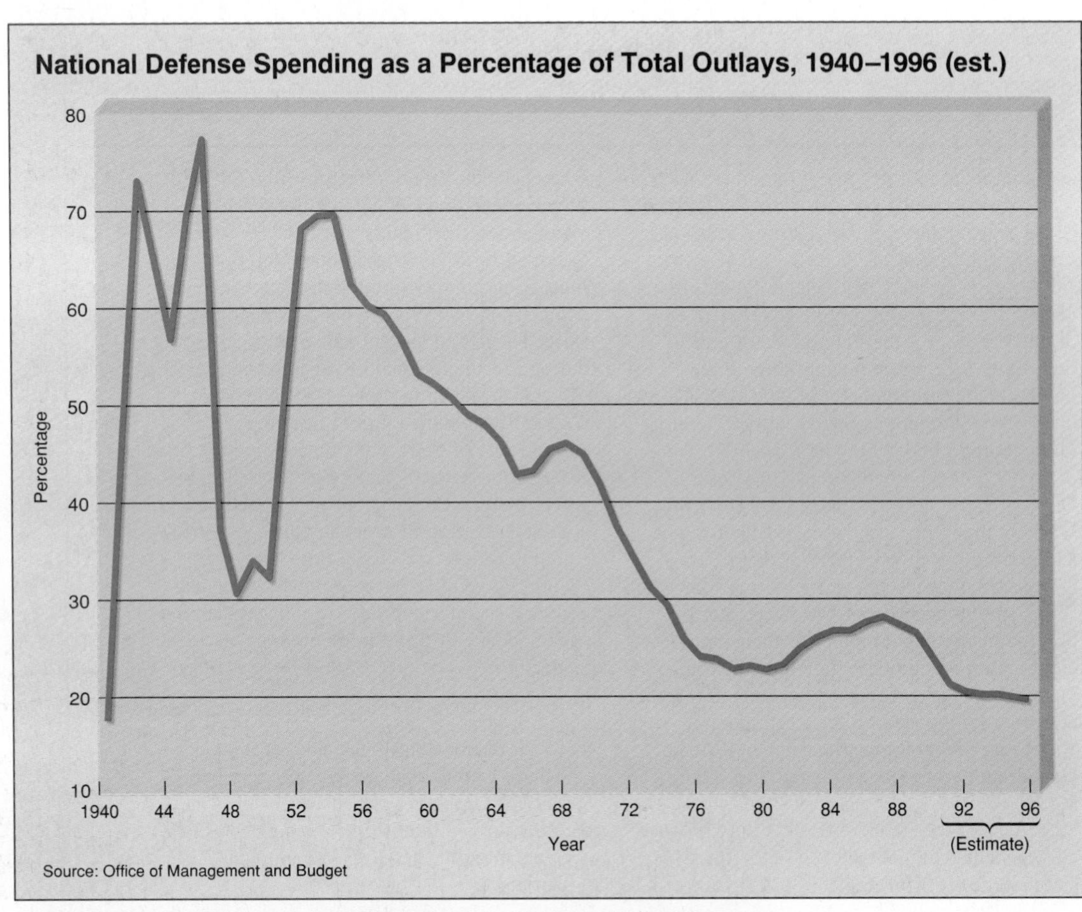

FIGURE 20–1 National Defense Spending as a Percentage of Total Outlays, 1940–1996 (est.). The above line graph depicts United States expenditures for defense as a percentage of total outlays. What two periods saw the sharpest rises in these percentages?

CBS poll in 1990 showed that seven out of ten Americans say women in the armed forces should be allowed to serve in combat units if they wish to do so.

Defense Spending As Figure 20–1 above illustrates, over the years defense spending has accounted for a large portion of federal expenditures.

The military budget as a percentage of total income of the United States started growing under the Carter administration and increased rapidly under the Reagan administration. During the first year of the Bush administration in 1989, the fall of the Berlin Wall and with it the iron curtain and the Cold War brought about a call for decreased military spending on the part of the United States. Members of Congress, political scientists, and concerned citizens started talking about the "peace dividend" that would soon arise with the decreased need for the United States to spend so heavily for military hardware. There was an immediate reduction in the total number of men and women in the armed services. A long-range plan calling for a 25 percent reduction in armed services personnel was also outlined.

Unfortunately, for the American citizen and for the world, the euphoria lasted less than a year because of the invasion of Kuwait by Iraq. In preparation for the allied liberation of Kuwait, the United States decided to send hundreds of thousands of U.S. military personnel, including those on active reserve—civilians who train vilian leaders would be more likely to try negotiation and diplomatic means first. The founders wanted war powers only to be exercised at the discretion of and for the purposes of the people's elected leaders.

SECTION 4

Points to Stress

- The primary goals of American foreign policy.
- The definition of diplomacy and what it involves.
- Reasons for foreign aid provided by the United States.
- Reasons for alliances built throughout the world by the United States.
- The major alliances.
- The manner in which trade measures can be used as a foreign policy tool.

Kickoff Activity

Have the students write short paragraphs in response to these questions: Can world peace be achieved in your lifetime? Why or why not? After all the students have completed their paragraphs, ask several students to read theirs to the rest of the class, and encourage a brief discussion of the students' ideas.

Working with the Preview Questions

Let the students read these questions and share their responses. Then remind the students that they will find more complete answers as they study Section 4; ask them to keep the study questions in mind as they read the section and write brief outlines of it.

Teaching Strategies

Introduction

Ask one of the students to read the section introduction to the rest of the class. Then encourage the students to discuss their responses to these questions: Why do you think the goals of American foreign policy have remained fixed? How and why do you think the specifics of that policy have changed?

Enrichment

Let a group of interested volunteers read about the production of nuclear weapons: Which countries have already produced such weapons? Which countries have not yet produced nuclear weapons but have—or nearly have—the capability? Ask the volunteers to prepare a chart of this information and share it with the class; encourage all the students to discuss their reactions to the information in the chart.

Discussion Starter

Help the students discuss the foreign policy goal of supporting human rights: Why do most Americans consider this an important foreign policy goal? What methods should be used to achieve this goal? Do you believe that the United States ever uses inappropriate methods in attempting to assure human rights? Encourage the students to explain their responses.

regularly and who are available in case of emergency. Talk of a peace dividend quickly disappeared; in its place was discussion of the costs of replacing all the missiles, planes, and other equipment lost in the Persian Gulf War. In the first few weeks of the war, the U.S. fired over 300 Tomahawk missiles, each of which cost $1.2 million.

After the war, Secretary of Defense Dick Cheney went back to work on the congressionally mandated 25 percent military reduction by drawing up plans to close thirty-one major military bases, shutting down weapons productions lines, and reducing the overall size of the armed forces. His plans drew immediate fire from local officials and members of Congress whose districts were affected by the cuts.

SECTION 3 REVIEW

1. What is the primary responsibility of the Department of State?
2. What is the foreign service?
3. Who are the persons that make up the Joint Chiefs of Staff, and what is their function?
4. **For critical analysis:** Why do you think the founders made sure that the military would always be subordinate to civilian leaders?

SECTION 4

American Foreign Policy Goals and the Methods Used to Achieve Them

Preview Questions:

- What are the main goals of American foreign policy?
- What is diplomacy and what does it involve?
- Why has the United States provided foreign aid to other countries?
- Why has the United States built alliances throughout the world?
- What are the major alliances?
- How can trade measures be used as a foreign policy tool?

United States foreign policy includes the goals our nation wants to achieve in the world and the techniques and strategies used to achieve them. The specifics of American foreign policy may change with new situations and new administrations, but the fundamental objectives and goals have remained fixed.

American foreign policy as a whole is guided by the overall purpose of promoting national security, or keeping the nation safe from attack or harm. Every aspect of our foreign policy is related to the need to maintain the United States as a free and independent nation, secure from unwanted external influence.

The United States has worked toward this overall purpose by setting policies to achieve several goals.

World Peace One of the most important foreign policy goals of the United States is world peace. The security of the United States, as well as that of other nations, is best protected when nations stay out of wars. Alternatives to military conflict offer the best hope for maintaining true peace. There is also less likelihood that countries will be drawn into war and that nuclear weapons will be used.

In working toward this goal, American leaders cooperate and negotiate with other countries, form alliances, and send aid to other countries when needed.

Economic Prosperity Economic prosperity for the United States is an important goal of American foreign policy. A nation must be economically strong in order to be secure. Economic prosperity also depends on free and open trade with other countries. Because our nation is not self-sufficient in a number of natural resources, such as oil, we must be able to obtain those resources from other nations. American businesses also need other countries to buy their products. Because other nations trade with the United States, it is important that those nations also be economically strong.

Human Rights **Human rights** are the basic necessities and freedoms to which all people, as human beings, are naturally entitled. History is full of examples of how violations of human rights have threatened world peace. Revolutions often break out when governments deny human rights to their own people. Often other nations are drawn in to help resolve the conflicts. The United States supports human rights by publicly criticizing human rights violations committed by other nations, and by providing food, medical supplies, and other types of aid to people of other nations in times of emergency, such as famine or earthquake. Such help is provided for humanitarian reasons and it also contributes to maintaining political stability throughout the world.

Discussion Starter
Help the students discuss the withholding of food as a method of showing American disapproval: How effective do you think this method has been in promoting democracy? Do you think it is a method that Americans should use to promote democracy in other countries? Why or why not?

Discussion Starter
Encourage the students to discuss their responses to questions such as these: What attitudes do our grants of foreign aid convey? Should these attitudes be reevaluated? Should our policy of granting foreign aid be reconsidered? Why or why not?

Enrichment
Let a small group of volunteers research major summit meetings of the past two decades: What were the purposes of each? The results? Ask the volunteers to make and display a chart that summarizes their findings.

Caption Answer Primarily, nations that support our foreign policy goals, and that are allies, receive American foreign aid.

Foreign aid has long been a tool of American foreign policy. Here, following the Persian Gulf War, Kurdish refugees wait in line for food at a U.S. sponsored refugee camp. Which nations are most likely to receive foreign aid from the United States?

Democracy Another American foreign policy goal has been to encourage democratic forms of government in some parts of the world. American foreign policy has supported the democratic rights of people in other nations and has lent support to nations striving toward democracy, such as Romania, Hungary, and Poland in the late 1980s. When the central Soviet government started repressing the independence movements of democratically elected governments in the former Soviet republics in 1991, the United States felt compelled to show its disapproval by withholding food and other aid that was promised to the Soviet Union. Promoting democratic ideals is another way of protecting American security.

Tools of American Foreign Policy

As you have seen, the major goal of American foreign policy is to protect national security. The United States uses several tools to achieve this and other foreign policy goals. These tools include diplomacy, defense, foreign aid, alliances and pacts, and trade agreements.

Diplomacy **Diplomacy** is the total process of political relations with other countries, including the settling of differences and conflicts through peaceful means. It is the most important tool of American foreign policy. Many other foreign policy tools such as alliances and trade agreements fall under the heading of diplomacy. True diplomacy involves working with people through various forms of compromise and negotiation. When issues or disagreements between nations arise, each nation usually sends representatives, known as diplomats, to speak with diplomats from other nations about the issues. Diplomatic relations are often carried out by the Department of State, but sometimes there is a **summit meeting**, in which the president meets with other heads of state. For example, a summit meeting between President Bush, former Soviet President Mikhail Gorbachev, and other European leaders in Paris in 1990 led to the signing of a charter to cut military arsenals in Europe.

Foreign Aid Economic aid to other countries has been an American foreign policy tool for over 50 years. It began with the Lend-Lease Program of the early 1940s, in which we gave nearly $50 billion in food, munitions, and other supplies to our allies in World War II. Since that time, as shown in Figure 20–2, the United States has given billions of dollars to other countries in the form of foreign aid. Most aid is in the form of grants, not loans that must be repaid. In total dollars, the United States supplies more foreign aid than any other nation, but as

Comprehension
Let volunteers comment on the Marshal Plan by answering these questions: How did European countries benefit from the Marshal Plan? How did the United States benefit?

Enrichment
Have volunteers research and report on the U.S. support given to Afghanistan and Nicaragua.

Vocabulary
Ask the student to identify and define the verb (and noun) on which the noun *alliance* is based: How does understanding this verb help you understand the meaning of *alliance?*

Figure Answer Students should understand that during the first half of the decade, expenditures were rising steadily only to experience a marked drop-off during the second half of the 1980s. Expenditures began to rise sharply again in the last months of the decade.

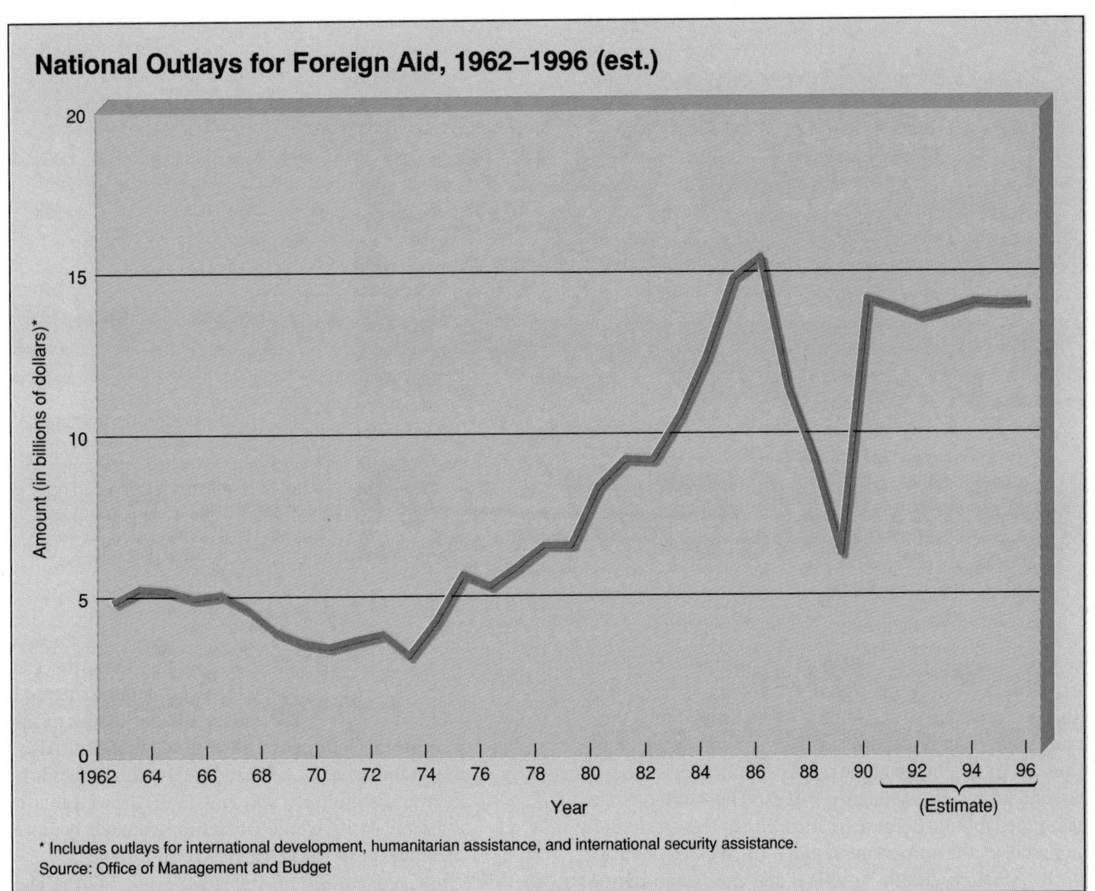

▲ **FIGURE 20–2 National Outlays for Foreign Aid, 1962–1996.** The above line graph depicts the United States' expenditures for foreign aid in billions of dollars since 1962. From looking at this graph, how would you describe the 1980s in terms of foreign aid expenditures?

a percentage of our national budget, our foreign aid is not as great as other industrialized nations such as Japan.

After World War II, the Marshall Plan promoted economic recovery in Europe. Under the Marshall Plan, the United States gave billions of dollars to sixteen Western European nations between 1948 and 1952. This aid helped with Western Europe's remarkable postwar economic recovery and increased its ability to trade with the U.S.

American foreign aid goes primarily to nations that support our foreign policy goals. Aid has been given to prevent the establishment of governments with political ideals contrary to our own, and to help countries fight against aggression. For example, the United States gave money and weapons to groups fighting the Soviet-backed government in Afghanistan in the 1980s. It also provided military support for the *contras,* the group fighting the Sandinista government in Nicaragua. The United States also gives economic aid to establish friendly relations with nations. Most of our economic aid programs are administered by the independent Agency for International Development (AID) in close cooperation with the departments of state and agriculture. Military aid is channeled through the Defense Department.

Alliances American foreign policy is also based on the concept of security through alliances and pacts. An **alliance** is a group of nations or individuals joined together

Multidiscipline Strategies

Geography Where are the world's major supplies of oil? How much oil is available within the United States? In countries the United States considers its allies? In countries with which the United States may not have friendly relationships? Have the students work with partners to research the answers to these questions. Encourage the students to research how much oil Americans consume as well. Then ask the partners to draw world maps, showing the locations of major oil supplies; guide the students in discussing the implications of their findings.

Vocabulary
As the students consider the term *multilateral treaties,* you might ask them to identify and define the root and the prefix in the adjective *multilateral.*

Enrichment
Assign a pair of students to research answers to these questions: In what ways was NATO unable to deal with the Middle Eastern conflict? What caused this inability? What basic changes are being suggested—or put into effect—for NATO? Why?

Caption Answer United States foreign aid can take many forms, including food, munitions, other supplies, or straight economic/monetary aid.

Discussion Starter
Guide the students in discussing the Rio Pact: Why do you think that, unlike NATO, the Rio Pact members have not set up a military organization? What does this imply about the relationships among OAS members? What does it imply about at least some OAS members and non-OAS countries?

Enrichment
Have one of the students read more about the Anzus Pact: Against what background was the pact formed? What problems or disagreements have strained relationships among the members? What is the current status of the Anzus Pact? Ask this student to prepare and present a brief report to the rest of the class.

The Contras, the group fighting the Sandinista government in Nicaragua, were the recipients of extensive military aid, including high-tech military equipment as shown here. What other forms might U.S. foreign aid take?

for a common purpose, whether it be military, economic, or political. A **mutual defense alliance** is a military alliance formed among countries when they feel a common threat to their security. Under such an alliance nations become allies and pledge to support each other in case of an attack by enemy forces. The United States has signed mutual defense treaties with at least 42 nations included in the important regions of Western Europe, North America, South America, and the island nations of the South Pacific. They are **multilateral treaties** in that they are international treaties signed by a group of several nations.

- *North Atlantic Treaty Organization (NATO)* After World War II, the United States and leaders of Western European nations gathered in Washington to create the North Atlantic Treaty Organization (NATO). NATO was originally composed of the United States, Canada, Great Britain, France, Italy, Portugal, the Netherlands, Belgium, Luxumbourg, Denmark, Norway, and Iceland. Greece and Turkey joined the alliance in 1952, West Germany in 1955, and Spain in 1982.

  The chief objective of NATO was the collective defense of Western Europe, particularly against Soviet aggression. NATO's military forces were set up to be the first line of defense for Western Europe. By the 1990s, as relations between the Western nations and the republics from the ex-Soviet Union improved, NATO members agreed that NATO must redefine its role in broader terms as more of a partner of these new republics. Also, the inability of NATO to deal with the Middle Eastern conflict in 1990 and 1991 showed that it must recast its whole operation to make it more meaningful in today's new world alliances.
- *The Organization of American States (OAS)* The Rio Pact, also called the Inter-American Treaty of Reciprocal Assistance, was signed in 1947. This pact formalized the long-standing cooperation among the nations of the Western Hemisphere. It committed the United States to defend 32 countries of Latin America. Unlike NATO, the members of the Rio Pact have not set up an international military organization.

  In 1948, members of the Rio Pact established the Organization of American States (OAS). The goals of the OAS are to promote economic development and strengthen peace and security in the Western hemisphere, to prevent or to peacefully negotiate conflicts, and to seek solutions for political, judicial, and economic problems.
- *Anzus Pact* The Anzus Pact of 1951 is a defense pact that unites Australia, New Zealand, and the United States. It commits these countries to come to one another's aid in case of attack. The U.S.

TEACHING GOVERNMENT IN ACTION

Read

Introduce this Government in Action Profile by encouraging the students to discuss what they already know about Nelson Mandela. After the discussion, ask the students to read the Profile independently.

Discuss

Use questions such as these to guide the students in discussing the Profile: Who are some of the other leaders of the ANC? With what ANC activities are you familiar? What has been the purpose of those activities? Which American civil rights leaders used tactics similar to those Mandela used? What is the reference made in the name "Black Pimpernel"? Why was he released? How do you imagine Mandela felt when, after 27 years, he left the prison?

Analyze and Apply

Have the students work in small groups to research and discuss the current situation of the ANC, Mandela, and other anti-apartheid leaders in South Africa.

Review

To help the students review this Government in Action Profile, ask questions such as these: What is the central goal of the African National Congress? When and why was Nelson Mandela sentenced to life imprisonment? When was he released?

Think About It (Answers)

1. Answers will vary. Perhaps a majority of Black South Africans consider the whites a "foreign" element on their land and are fighting for political freedom. They are also fighting for economic liberty, as did the American revolutionaries. Like Washington's efforts to increase colonial unity, Mandela realizes the necessity of getting the Black South Africans to overcome tribal jealousies and distrust.

GOVERNMENT IN ACTION

PROFILE

Nelson Mandela

Nelson Rolihlahla Mandela was born in 1918 into the royal family of the Xhosa-speaking Tembu people in South Africa. Educated at a Methodist school, he became a lawyer and in 1944 joined the African National Congress (ANC), an organization dedicated to nonviolent protest of South Africa's racial segregation laws. In 1948, when the nationalist (whites only) party assumed power and legalized the apartheid policy of racial separation, Mandela led a campaign of civil disobedience. He headed the ANC's youth wing in the early 1950s and became a deputy president in 1952. In 1953, as white oppression of blacks and other nonwhites grew, Mandela was ''banned'' (legally restricted) for five years. Three years later, he was accused of treason and underwent a trial that lasted until 1961, when he was acquitted. Soon after, he set up the ANC's military wing and went underground, winning the name ''Black Pimpernel.''* He was arrested in August, 1962, convicted of incitement and sentenced to five years in jail. While in prison, he was charged with sabotage and treason along with the rest of the ANC high command, and in 1964 was sentenced to life imprisonment.

Mandela made a final statement from the dock of the treason trial. ''I have cherished the ideal of a democratic and free society,'' he said then, ''in which all persons live together in harmony and with equal opportunities. It is an ideal which I hope to live for, and to see realized. But, my Lord, if need be, it is an ideal for which I am prepared to die.'' He was not photographed or quoted for the duration of his prison term.

For many who believed that peace would be possible among South Africans, the release of Nelson Mandela from prison seemed the first step. On February 11, 1990, the man-turned-myth stepped out of his prison gate, hand in hand with his wife Winnie, and walked a few steps before ducking into a car to escape the shouts of the world's press.

Mandela didn't waste any time getting down to business. ''We have waited too long for freedom, and we can wait no longer,'' declared Mandela in his first public utterance in twenty-seven years. ''Now is the time to intensify our struggle.''

*The allusion here is to *The Scarlet Pimpernel,* a book by Baroness Orczy, which related the swashbuckling stories of the elusive Sir Percy Blakency in France in the 1800s.

THINK ABOUT IT

1. How do you think Nelson Mandela compares with the leaders of the American Revolution?

Discussion Starter
Help the students discuss the importance of free-trade pacts with American neighbors, Canada and Mexico: How do Canadians view the United States? How do Mexicans view us? Why? What attitudes do Americans often exhibit toward these neighbors?

Section 4 Review (Answers)
1. World peace, economic prosperity, human rights, and democracy throughout the world.
2. Diplomacy is the total process of political relations with other countries, including settling differences of opinions and conflicts through peaceful means.
3. Foreign aid has been given to prevent the establishment of governments with political ideals contrary to our own, and to help countries fight against aggression.
4. To provide for mutual defense and security.
5. Trade measures are used to get other countries to buy American goods, which helps economic prosperity, and to get trade partners to support our other foreign policy goals.
6. Answers will vary. e.g., the United States depends on other countries for resources, so it must be concerned with internal politics that would prevent the United States from obtaining those needed resources. Also, the United States has to worry about a renegade country's ability to wage nuclear war.

Enrichment
Ask a small group of interested volunteers to research and report on the economic sanctions against South Africa: What specific situations led to the institution of sanctions? What were the main arguments in favor of sanctions? Who supported sanctions? Why? What were the main arguments against sanctions? Who opposed them? Why? What is the current status of those sanctions? What changes are anticipated? Let these volunteers report their findings to the rest of the class, and encourage all the students to discuss the appropriateness and the effectiveness of these sanctions.

Reteaching Strategies
1. Let the students work in small groups to review and, if necessary, revise their outlines of Section 4.
2. Ask the students to use their own words in writing definitions of these terms: *human rights, diplomacy, alliance, sanctions.*

Evaluation Strategies
1. Have the students write their answers to the Section 4 Review questions.
2. Have the students take the Section 4 Quiz found in the *TRB.*

has entered into bilateral treaties, treaties between two nations, with Spain, Japan, the Philippines, and the Republic of Korea.

Trade Measures Another foreign policy tool involves the terms under which the United States trades with other countries. Two aims of American trade measures are to get other countries to buy American goods, which helps bolster economic prosperity, and to get trade partners to support our other foreign policy goals. Trade terms include agreements about how much of a foreign product will be allowed to be sold in the United States and which tariffs, or taxes, the products will be subject to. For example, the United States negotiated a free-trade agreement with Canada during the latter part of the 1980s, an agreement that started to take effect during the 1990s. A similar agreement is being negotiated with Mexico.

Sometimes the United States punishes other nations through the withdrawal of trade benefits. **Economic sanctions** are measures of withholding trade benefits, supplies or economic aid to pressure a foreign government to cease certain activities. They are sometimes used by American leaders when they are dealing with governments that are following policies the United States does not approve of. For example, when the Soviet Union sent troops to Afghanistan in 1979, the United States showed its disapproval by refusing to sell wheat to the Soviets. In 1982 President Reagan ordered a ban on the use of American technology to build a natural gas pipeline in the Soviet Union in protest against the Soviet Union's role in restraining a nationwide trade union in Poland. In 1986, Congress initiated and passed a bill instituting economic sanctions against South Africa to pressure that nation into ending apartheid, their legal system of racial segregation. In 1990, President Bush imposed severe economic sanctions against Iraq in an effort to force Iraq's leader, Suddam Hussein, to withdraw his forces from Kuwait.

Defense On a number of occasions, the United States has used military force to achieve foreign policy goals. In addition to the five occasions when the United States declared war, American troops have been used abroad without declarations of war many times, which is what happened in both the Korean War and the Vietnam War. In 1989, American forces overthrew Panama's president, Manuel Noriega. President Bush said the invasion was to protect American interests, especially the Panama Canal, and to rid Panama of a corrupt leader. In 1991, the United States used military force in Iraq when its leader refused to withdraw military forces from Kuwait.

SECTION 4 REVIEW

1. What are the major American foreign policy goals?
2. What is diplomacy?
3. Why does the United States provide foreign aid to other nations?
4. Why has the United States built a network of alliances?
5. How are trade measures used as a tool of foreign policy?
6. **For critical analysis:** In 1991, the United States government claimed that it needed to wage war against Iraq in order to liberate Kuwait. Do you think the United States should be concerned with the internal politics of Middle Eastern countries, or any other country in the world for that matter? Give reasons for your answer.

SECTION 5

The United Nations

Preview Questions

- When and why was the United Nations formed?
- What are the purposes and principles outlined in the U.N. Charter?
- What are the functions of the General Assembly and the Security Council?

The United Nations (U.N.) is a name that was first adopted by those nations allied in opposition against Germany, Italy, and Japan during World War II. The name became prominent worldwide when the Declaration of the United Nations was signed by twenty-six countries on January 4, 1942. In the late summer and fall of 1944, diplomats from the United States, the United Kingdom, the Soviet Union, and China held talks in Washington, D.C., with the goal of a permanent organization in mind. In April 1945, forty-six nations attended the United Nations Conference on International Organization in San Francisco. Those countries plus five others became the original members of the United Nations and signed the Charter of the United Nations on June 26 of that year. (See the Resource Center.)

The U.N. Charter

The Charter of the United Nations, signed in 1945, consists of a preamble and articles similar to the preamble

SECTION 5

Points to Stress

- The time of and reasons for the creation of the United Nations.
- The purposes and principles outlined in the U.N. Charter.
- The functions of the General Assembly and the Security Council.

Kickoff Activity

Write the name, *The United Nations,* on the chalkboard; ask the students to list at least eight words and phrases that the name brings to mind. After all the students have finished writing their lists, encourage volunteers to share their ideas.

Working with the Preview Questions

Let volunteers read the three study questions aloud, and allow volunteers to share their responses. Then have the students read Section 5 independently, keeping these questions in mind.

Teaching Strategies

Introduction

After the students have read the section introduction, encourage discussion by asking these questions: How—if at all—does information about this early division alter your concept of the United Nations? Do you think that division (between the Allies and the Axis powers) is still reflected in the U.N.? Do you believe that other divisions are reflected in the U.N.? If so, what divisions? If not, why not?

Discussion Starter

Encourage the students to share their ideas in response to these questions: How does the Charter of the United Nations differ from the Constitution of the United States? Why do you think the U.N. Charter is so precise? What do the details and precision in the Charter imply about the founders of the U.N.?

Cooperative Learning

Let the students work in groups to study and discuss the purposes and principles presented in the U.N. Charter.

Vocabulary

Let volunteers define both the verb *deliberate* and the adjective *deliberative.*

Extension

Ask the students to recall and discuss current or recent sessions of the U.N. General Assembly: What kind of media coverage do these sessions usually get? Why?

Caption Answer The four purposes of the United Nations are: to preserve world peace, to encourage nations to be just in their actions toward each other, to help nations to cooperate in solving their problems, and to serve as an agency through which nations can work toward these three goals.

and articles of the United States Constitution. The charter outlines the purposes, structure, and powers of the United Nations. It differs from the U.S. Constitution in that it has 111 articles, compared to the Constitution's 7 articles. The preamble expresses the guiding spirit of the organization; the charter lists four purposes and seven principles.

The Four Purposes:

1. To preserve world peace.
2. To encourage nations to be just in their actions toward each other.
3. To help nations to cooperate in solving their problems.
4. To serve as an agency through which nations can work toward these three goals.

The Seven Principles:

1. All members have equal rights.
2. Each member is expected to carry out its duties under the charter.
3. Each member agrees to the principle of settling disputes peacefully.
4. Each member agrees not to use force or threat of force against other nations except in self-defense.
5. Each member agrees to help the U.N. in every action it takes to carry out the purposes of the charter.
6. The U.N. agrees to act on the principle that the nonmember states have the same duties as member states to preserve world peace and security.
7. The U.N. accepts the principle of not interfering in the internal affairs—domestic problems—of member nations, so long as these actions do not harm other nations.

The Organization of the U.N.

The United Nations has a complex structure as set forth in its charter. It is built around six principal organs:

1. The General Assembly
2. The Security Council
3. The Economic and Social Council
4. The Trusteeship Council
5. The International Court of Justice
6. The Secretariat

Figure 20–3 on the next page shows the basic organizational structure of the United Nations.

The General Assembly The General Assembly is the only body, or organ, within the U.N. in which all members are represented. Each member has one vote, but may send as many as five representatives. Important questions are decided by a majority vote or by a **supermajority vote** of two-thirds, depending on the importance of the matter.

The General Assembly is a **deliberative organ**, which means it deliberates on, or discusses and decides, important issues. It is a type of town meeting in which the "towns" are represented by the member nations of the world. This international town meeting is held once a year at the U.N. permanent headquarters in New York City, on the East River in midtown Manhattan, and usually takes place in September.

The regular assembly meetings last for three months beginning on the third Tuesday in September. Special sessions may be called, usually to discuss important world issues concerning peacekeeping and finances.

The Security Council The Security Council has the primary responsibility for maintaining international

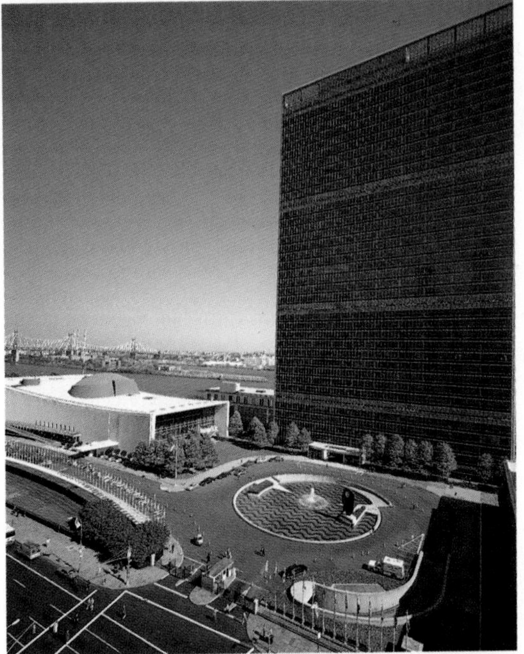

▲ The United Nations is headquartered in this complex in New York City. What are the four purposes of the United Nations?

Discussion Starter
Guide the students in studying and discussing the chart, The United Nations System: Into what major groups is the U.N. divided? How are those groups related to one another? Which group or groups form the center of power?

Discussion Starter
Guide the students in discussing the Security Council: What do you think is the purpose of having five permanent members on the council? Why do you think these specific countries are the permanent members? Do you think that the system of maintaining permanent members should be changed? Why or why not? Do you think that the countries selected for permanent membership should be changed? Why or why not?

Comprehension
Ask volunteers to explain the fact that the Security Council may, in some cases, call for the use of force: How can this be reconciled with the U.N.'s purposes and principles?

Enrichment
Have each student research one of the battle zones into which the U.N. Security Council has sent military observer teams: What were the causes of conflict in each case? How were the observers received? How effective were they? Then give the students an opportunity to share and discuss their findings.

Figure Answer Students should understand that much like the town meetings that are held in New England wherein each citizen has the opportunity to speak up and be heard, a meeting of the General Assembly allows the representatives of each nation to stand and speak up and be heard by the representatives from the other nations of the world.

This figure content is also featured on *West's American Government Videodisc* (see the index found in the *TRB*) and is available in the transparency package.

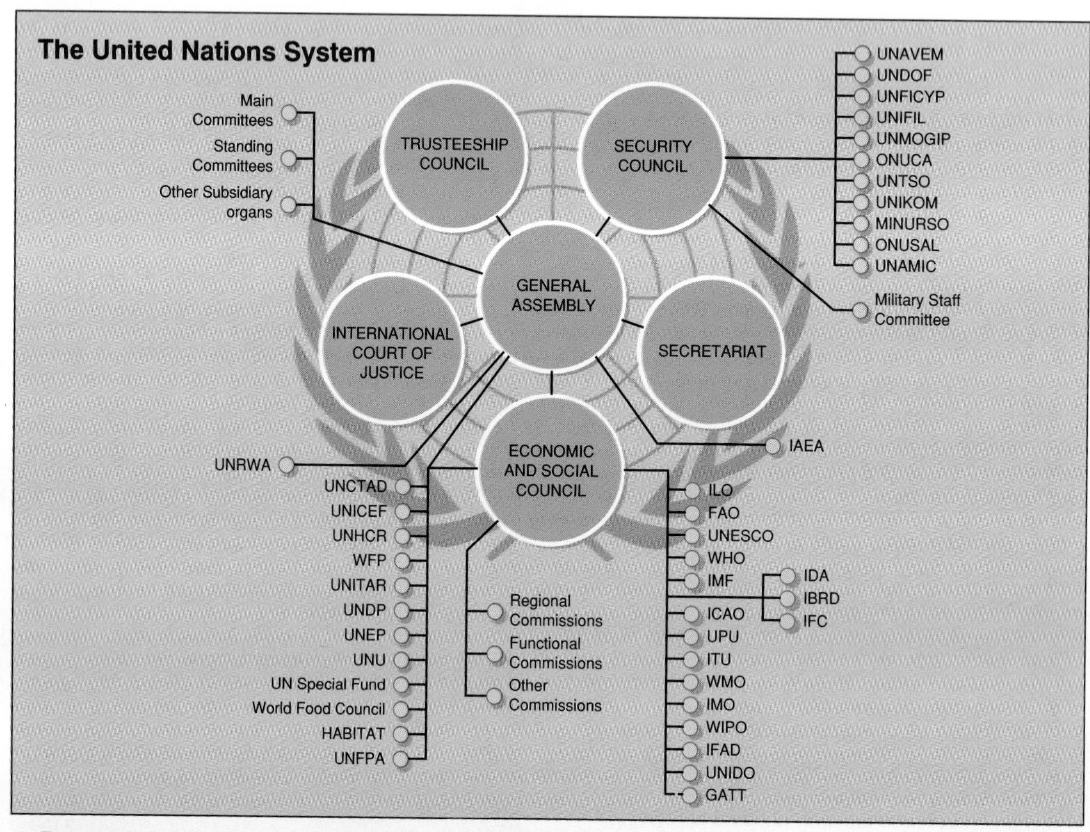

▲ FIGURE 20–3 **The United Nations System.** This chart shows the basic structure of the U.N. How is a meeting of the General Assembly similar to a town meeting?

peace. Originally the council consisted of eleven members: five permanent (France, the United Kingdom, the Soviet Union (now Russia), the United States, and China[1]) and six nonpermanent that were elected by the General Assembly for two-year terms. In 1965, the Charter was amended to enlarge the council to fifteen members by allowing for four more nonpermanent nations. Currently, five nonpermanent members must come from African and Asian countries, one from Eastern European countries, two from Latin American countries, and two from Western European and other countries.

Members of the U.N. agree to carry out the decisions of the Security Council, which in effect can decide the course of action that the U.N. should take in settling an international dispute. Any one of the five permanent members, though, can veto a Security Council decision.

Under certain circumstances when clear-cut aggression has occurred, the Security Council may call for military action by asking U.N. members to contribute military personnel to a U.N. peacekeeping force. Such an event occurred in the 1950s, when North Korean military forces attacked South Korea. Because of the temporary absence of the representative from the Soviet Union, the Security Council was able to immediately deal with the situation. Even after the Soviet representative returned to the council and blocked that body's peacekeeping actions in Korea, the General Assembly took over and adopted the ''Uniting for Peace

1. Originally Nationalist China, later changed to People's Republic of China on October 25, 1971.

Discussion Starter
Encourage the students to discuss the 1991 bombings of Iraq: Do you believe the United States would have proceeded with these bombings, even without the backing of the United Nations? Why or why not?

Reteaching Strategies
1. Let the students work with partners to review and discuss the content of Section 5; have the partners write a brief topic outline of the section.
2. Ask the students to form small groups in which to discuss the organization of the United Nations, referring to the chart on pages 512–513 as necessary. Then have the group members work together to write a paragraph describing that organization.

Evaluation Strategies
1. Have the students write their answers to the Section 5 Review questions.
2. Have the students take the Section 5 Quiz found in the *TRB.*

Section 5 Review (Answers)
1. All members have equal rights; each member is expected to carry out its duties under the charter; each member agrees to the principle of settling disputes peacefully; and each member agrees not to use force or threat of force against other nations except in self-defense; each member agrees to help out the U.N.; the U.N. agrees to deal with nonmember states the same as member states; and the U.N. agrees to the principle of noninterference in members' domestic affairs.
2. To deliberate, discuss, and decide important issues.
3. To maintain international peace.
4. Answers will vary, e.g., this system is not fair because countries vary a great deal in size, strength, and the amount they contribute. You might point out to the students that the General Assembly represents the countries of the entire world. For important questions a two-thirds majority vote is required. Even then these votes are not legally binding. The real power of the U.N. rests in the hands of the Security Council.

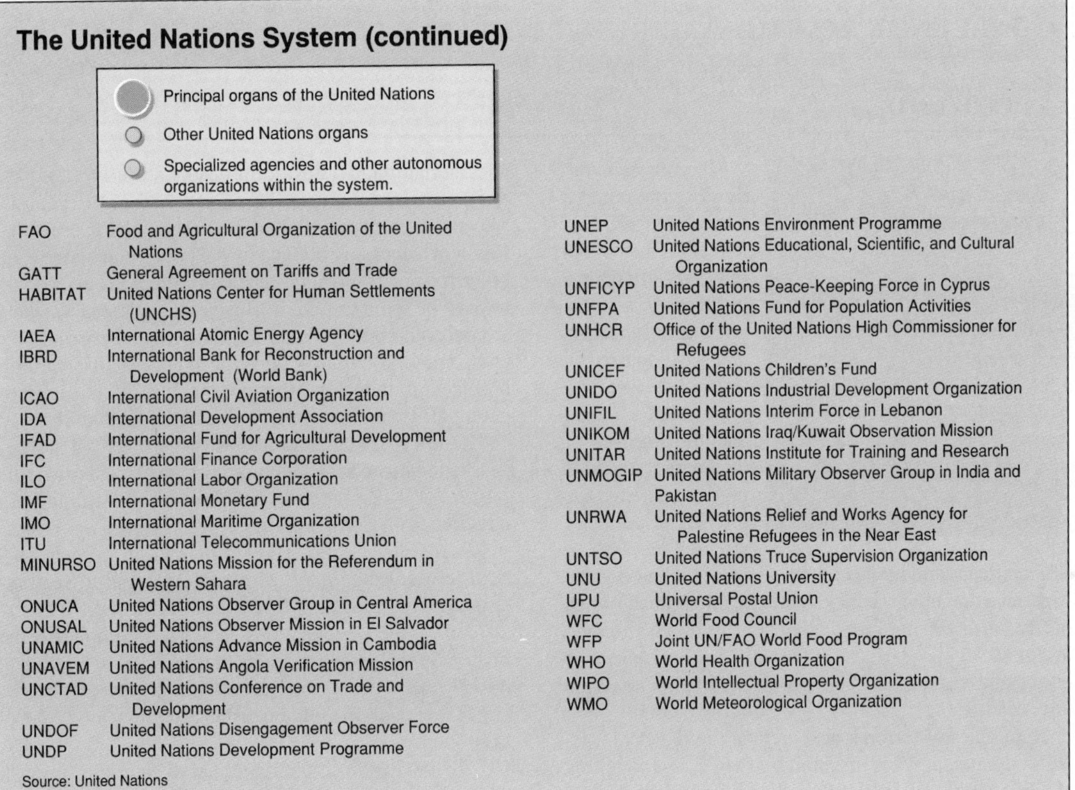

The United Nations System (continued)

Principal organs of the United Nations
Other United Nations organs
Specialized agencies and other autonomous organizations within the system.

FAO	Food and Agricultural Organization of the United Nations
GATT	General Agreement on Tariffs and Trade
HABITAT	United Nations Center for Human Settlements (UNCHS)
IAEA	International Atomic Energy Agency
IBRD	International Bank for Reconstruction and Development (World Bank)
ICAO	International Civil Aviation Organization
IDA	International Development Association
IFAD	International Fund for Agricultural Development
IFC	International Finance Corporation
ILO	International Labor Organization
IMF	International Monetary Fund
IMO	International Maritime Organization
ITU	International Telecommunications Union
MINURSO	United Nations Mission for the Referendum in Western Sahara
ONUCA	United Nations Observer Group in Central America
ONUSAL	United Nations Observer Mission in El Salvador
UNAMIC	United Nations Advance Mission in Cambodia
UNAVEM	United Nations Angola Verification Mission
UNCTAD	United Nations Conference on Trade and Development
UNDOF	United Nations Disengagement Observer Force
UNDP	United Nations Development Programme
UNEP	United Nations Environment Programme
UNESCO	United Nations Educational, Scientific, and Cultural Organization
UNFICYP	United Nations Peace-Keeping Force in Cyprus
UNFPA	United Nations Fund for Population Activities
UNHCR	Office of the United Nations High Commissioner for Refugees
UNICEF	United Nations Children's Fund
UNIDO	United Nations Industrial Development Organization
UNIFIL	United Nations Interim Force in Lebanon
UNIKOM	United Nations Iraq/Kuwait Observation Mission
UNITAR	United Nations Institute for Training and Research
UNMOGIP	United Nations Military Observer Group in India and Pakistan
UNRWA	United Nations Relief and Works Agency for Palestine Refugees in the Near East
UNTSO	United Nations Truce Supervision Organization
UNU	United Nations University
UPU	Universal Postal Union
WFC	World Food Council
WFP	Joint UN/FAO World Food Program
WHO	World Health Organization
WIPO	World Intellectual Property Organization
WMO	World Meteorological Organization

Source: United Nations

Resolution'' proposed by the United States. It allowed U.N. forces to remain until the conflict was over.

The Security Council has sent in military observer teams to several battle zones in Cyprus, the Congo, and the Middle East. It has developed small military forces that are positioned between the opposing forces. They are not to engage in combat, but rather to separate the hostile forces by creating a neutral area.

The most recent important actions of the United Nations and the Security Council involved the severe economic sanctions imposed on Iraq after its invasion of Kuwait in August 1990. When those economic sanctions did not force Iraq's president Saddam Hussein to withdraw his occupational forces from Kuwait, the Security Council voted to allow the use of force by coalition countries. Led by the United States, these countries, with the backing of the United Nations, proceeded to bomb Iraqi targets in and out of Kuwait beginning on January 16, 1991. The result was the complete defeat of the Iraqi military 100 days later and the withdrawal of Iraqi forces from Kuwait. The U.N. further made an effort to oversee the destruction of Iraq's chemical, biological, and nuclear weapon stockpiles.

SECTION 5 REVIEW

1. Name the seven principles of the United Nations.
2. What is the main purpose of the General Assembly?
3. What is the main responsibility of the Security Council?
4. **For critical analysis:** Every member nation of the U.N. has an equal vote in the General Assembly. Do you think this one-nation one-vote system is fair? Give reasons for your answer.

TEACHING CHALLENGE TO THE AMERICAN DREAM

Read

Begin by having the students read and discuss the title of this Challenge to the American Dream feature: What is terrorism? When and where is it conducted? What are the purposes of terrorism? Its effects? What do you think can and should be done about terrorism? Encourage all the students to contribute to this discussion. Then have volunteers read the Challenge to the American Dream feature aloud to the rest of the class.

Discuss

Help the students discuss the feature by posing questions such as these: Do you agree that terrorism is the "ultimate violation of human rights"? Why or why not? When is a bombing, hijacking, kidnapping, murder, or armed attack an act of terrorism rather than a simple crime? What sets terrorism apart from other crimes? How and why do you imagine terrorists who support different political causes are able to work together? Why do you think Pan Am decided to refuse to allow Iraqis holding Iraqi passports to fly on its planes? Do you consider the decision fair? To whom? Why? Do you believe that there are any causes that might justify terrorism? If so, what are those causes? If not, why not?

Analyze and Apply

Ask the students to work in small groups, planning and presenting short skits about people reacting to news of terrorism. Each skit should show both negative and positive reactions to such news.

Review

To help the students review this special feature, ask questions such as these: What is terrorism? What challenge does terrorism pose to the American dream?

CHALLENGE TO THE AMERICAN DREAM

Terrorism

Terrorism is defined as the random use of staged violence at infrequent intervals to achieve political goals. International terrorism has occurred in virtually every region of the world and the number of incidents is increasing. Terrorism has directly or indirectly affected the lives of all Americans and has become a serious challenge to the American dream of security, freedom, and human rights. In fact, terrorism has been called the "ultimate violation of human rights" because terrorist actions are aimed at killing and harming innocent people, mainly for attention to a "cause."

Examples of terrorist acts include the attacks on Israeli Olympic athletes in Munich in 1972, the hijacking of TWA flight 847 in 1985, and the seizure of the *Achille Lauro,* an Italian cruise ship in 1986. In 1991, Iraq threatened worldwide terrorism against the United States and its allies when the war in the Persian Gulf began.

Terrorist methods include bombings, hijackings, kidnappings, murders, and armed attacks on foreign embassies. Whatever their methods, terrorists destabilize international relations and are dangerous and difficult for nations to control.

It is believed that terrorist groups are linked through international networks that supply arms, money, supplies, and training. They represent many different ethnic, religious, political, and nationalist policies. Nations thought to be engaged in state-sponsored terrorism include Iraq, Iran, Libya, and Syria. However, you should not believe that terrorism is confined to the Middle East. Other groups that have been accused of terrorist activity include the Irish Republican Army (IRA), Italy's Red Brigade, and even some environmental groups, such as Earth First. Even nonpolitical criminal groups have turned to terrorist tactics to achieve their goals.

Terrorism is taking its toll both in the United States and internationally. Beside the deaths, suffering, and psychological and emotional pain inflicted on its victims, terrorism restricts diplomatic efforts and trade efforts. Political leaders are blamed by the public and blame each other for not controlling terrorism. Precious tax dollars have to be spent to fight it. Businesspeople and travelers are delayed and restricted by searches and precautions, and sometimes unfairly questioned because of their ethnic background. For example, the FBI started investigating all Iraqi Americans living in the United States in 1990 and 1991. Pan American Airways (now out of business) announced at the beginning of the war in the Middle East in 1991 that it would not allow Iraqis holding Iraqi passports to fly on its planes.

The United States' general policy toward terrorism is to refuse to negotiate with terrorists, and to seek international agreements that punish offenders. Political differences between nations, however, complicate the matter. Some believe that acts of terrorism are legitimate if they are for a just cause. Terrorism is viewed by some as a foreign policy tool of resistance to unwanted control or influence.

The challenge to the American dream is to prevent the actions of the few—the terrorists and the governments that support them—from infringing on the psychological and physical welfare of all Americans, and on the civil liberties of those who may be linked by birth and nationality to terrorist groups, but not involved in any way in their actions.

You Decide

1. What do you think could be done to prevent state-sponsored terrorism?
2. Do you agree with the United States policy not to negotiate with terrorists? If so, how might your opinion change if a family member or friend were a victim of a terrorist action, such as a plane hijacking?
3. How could the rising incidents of terrorism lead to the civil rights violations of innocent people?

You Decide (Answers)

1. Answers will vary, e.g., the United States could use trade measures to pressure those foreign governments involved.

2. Answers will vary, e.g., the United States should not negotiate with terrorists because it would only encourage those terrorists and others to use terroristic tactics in the future. If they achieve what they want, their tactics work, and they will use them again.

3. Answers will vary, e.g., as the incidents of terrorism increase, the security measures employed become stricter. Travelers will be delayed and restricted by searches and precautions. People of certain ethnic groups may be unfairly treated.

Chapter Evaluation

To evaluate student mastery of chapter material, you might:

1. Use Chapter Test A from the *TRB.*

2. Use Chapter Test B from the *TRB.*

3. Construct your own test using items from the *West American Government Test Bank* found in the *TRB.*

4. Use the accompanying computerized test software to construct and print a customized chapter test.

Observable Mastery

Divide students up into groups of five. Provide to each a current foreign policy issue that they will research. Be sure that the issue is one on which they will be able to find material. Have each student cover one of the following as it pertains to American foreign policy and their issue: The president, Congress, Department of State, Department of Defense, and the United Nations. Students should group oral reports demonstrating the specific foreign policy operations related to their issues. Inform students that they are to look for policy disagreements among the institutions responsible for foreign policy.

CHAPTER 20 REVIEW

Key Terms

alliance 507
ambassador 501
attachés 501
chargé d'affaires 501
Cold War 492
collective security 492
colonial empire 490
communism 492
Communist bloc 492
conscription 503
consul 501
consulate 501
containment 492
deliberative organ 511
détente 493
deterrence 492
diplomacy 506
draft 503
economic sanctions 510
embassy 500
foreign policy 489
foreign service 500
human rights 505
intelligence 497
interventionism 490
iron curtain 492
isolationism 489
Marshall Plan 491
Monroe Doctrine 490
multilateral treaties 508
mutual defense alliance 508
mutual-assured destruction 493
national security 489
neutrality 490
passports 501
summit meeting 506
super-majority vote 511
superpowers 491
trial balloon 494
visa 501
Western bloc 492

Summary

1. Every nation has a foreign policy—some systematic and general plan that guides a country's attitudes and actions toward the rest of the world. American foreign policy has been shaped by historical events and attitudes. The nation's founders and early presidents believed that isolationism was the best way to protect American interests. As America expanded and became more involved in world events, it moved away from isolationism and toward interventionism. After the nation became involved in World War I and World War II, the United States emerged as a superpower. Then the wartime alliance between the Soviet Union and the United States deteriorated into the Cold War. The tension brought on by the Cold War led to the arms race. The political demise of the Soviet Union effectively ended the Cold War in the 1990s.

2. The Constitution provides for a partnership between Congress and the president in developing foreign policy, but on many occasions the president and Congress struggle over power in this area. The president's constitutional powers in foreign affairs involve serving as commander in chief, making treaties with other nations, and appointing ambassadors. The president relies on the secretary of state, the secretary of defense, and other members of the National Security Council for advice. The constitutional powers given to Congress in the area of foreign policy include the power of the Senate to confirm the president's diplomatic appointments, and the power to ratify all treaties. The Congress as a whole has the sole power to declare war.

3. The departments of state and defense are responsible for carrying out foreign and defense policy on a day-to-day basis. The Department of State maintains diplomatic relations with nearly two hundred nations around the world. It informs the president on international issues, negotiates treaties, and protects the interests of Americans traveling or conducting business abroad. The Department of Defense is the principal executive department that establishes and carries out defense policy and protects our national security. The top-ranking officers of each of the armed forces are known together as the Joint Chiefs of Staff, the chairperson of which is appointed by the president.

4. The nation's overall foreign policy goal is to protect our national security. Other objectives include world peace, economic prosperity, human rights, and democracy. The tools of American foreign policy include diplomacy, foreign aid, alliances, trade measures, and defense.

5. In April 1945, forty-six allied nations attended the United Nations Conference on International Organization in San Francisco. The United Nations was started on June 26 of that year, with the purpose of preserving world peace, encouraging just actions between nations, and helping nations solve their problems. Some of its guiding principles are that all members have equal rights, that each member agrees to settle disputes peacefully,

Review Questions (Answers)

1. To protect the national security of the United States.
2. Avoiding political involvement with other nations was thought to be the best way to protect American interests. As the nation expanded and began developing ties abroad, however, the policy was gradually abandoned.
3. In 1898, the United States became involved in the Spanish-American War and fought to free Cuba from Spanish rule. To protect American interests in Asia, **Secretary of State John Hay announced the Open Door** Policy of 1899 opening Chinese markets to the world's leading trading nations. The United States began to police Latin America in the early 1900s. The United States became involved in World Wars I and II.
4. After World War II, the alliance between the United States and the Soviet Union began to deteriorate. As the countries of Eastern Europe began to fall under Soviet dominion, the United States began a policy of containment.
5. The president is commander-in-chief of the armed forces. The president has the power to make treaties and has certain diplomatic powers such as the power to appoint ambassadors. The president is assisted by cabinet members, especially the secretaries of state and defense, the National Security Council, and the CIA.
6. Congress has the power to declare war. It has the power to appropriate funds for weapon systems and to equip the armed forces. It has the power to reject or approve treaties and the appointment of ambassadors.
7. The goal of the Department of State is to ensure the security and well-being of the United States. The Department of Defense is the principal executive department that establishes and carries out defense policy and protects national security. The Joint Chiefs of Staff serve as key military advisors to the president, the secretary of defense and the National Security Council.
8. The volunteer enlistment system and the draft.
9. World peace, economic prosperity, human rights, and democracy throughout the world.
10. Diplomacy is the total process of political relations with other countries, including the settling of differences and conflicts through peaceful means.
11. To support nations which support our foreign policy goals, to prevent the establishment of governments with political ideals contrary to our own, and to help other countries fight aggression.
12. They serve as collective defense and pledge to support each other.
13. To get other countries to buy American goods and to get trade partners to support our other foreign policy goals.
14. To preserve world peace, to encourage nations to be just in their actions toward each other, to help nations to cooperate in solving problems, and to serve as an agency through which nations can work toward these three goals.
15. Each member: (1) has equal rights; (2) is expected to carry out its duties; (3) agrees to the princi-

CHAPTER 20 REVIEW—Continued

and that the U.N. not interfere in the internal affairs of member nations. The most important principal organs of the United Nations are the General Assembly, which is a deliberative body, and the Security Council, which is responsible for maintaining international peace.

Review Questions

1. What is the basic purpose of American foreign policy?
2. Describe the original policy of isolationism and why it was abandoned.
3. Briefly describe the United States' increasing involvement in world affairs since 1898.
4. Briefly describe the Cold War.
5. What are the president's foreign policy-making powers as granted by the Constitution? Who assists him in this area?
6. What are the constitutional powers given to Congress in the area of foreign policy?
7. What responsibilities do the Department of State and the Department of Defense have in foreign policy? What other agencies are involved in foreign policy decisions?
8. What two methods have been used to recruit citizens to serve in the armed forces?
9. What are the main foreign policy goals of the United States?
10. What is diplomacy?
11. Why has the United States provided foreign aid to other nations?
12. How are alliances used to achieve American foreign policy goals?
13. How are trade measures used to achieve foreign policy goals?
14. Why was the United Nations formed?
15. What are the seven principles of the United Nations as listed in the charter?
16. What are the two most important bodies within the United Nations?
17. Who are the members of the Security Council of the United Nations?
18. Name two ways in which you can attempt to influence American foreign policy.
19. Name two examples of terrorism.

Questions for Thought and Discussion

1. Think of at least one foreign policy issue for which the president and Congress might hold different views. Which branch do you think would be most influential in determining policy for that particular issue? Why?
2. Do you think the president or Congress should have a more dominant role in foreign policy affairs? Give reasons for your answer.
3. What do you think would be the consequences for the rest of the world if the United States returned to the policy of isolationism and withdrew from world affairs?
4. Do you think international trade measures and economic policy should be used to serve foreign policy goals? Why or why not?
5. It has been said that the United States is the only superpower left in the world. Explain your reasons for agreeing or disagreeing with this statement.
6. During the war in the Persian Gulf, anti-war demonstrators argued that the United States had too many pressing problems at home—inadequate health care for the poor, a failing educational system, and urban deterioration—to be spending billions of dollars to bomb another country. Do you believe that this is a valid argument against U.S. military involvement elsewhere? Explain why or why not.

Improving Your Skills
Communication Skills

Determining Fallacies in Reasoning

Students of government must often analyze or evaluate statements and viewpoints. Part of this skill involves recognizing fallacies in reasoning. A *fallacy* is a false idea or error, which can take the form of an unsound or unsupported argument, an error in facts, or an inaccurate conclusion.

When analyzing a statement or viewpoint for fallacies, follow these guidelines:

- **Read or listen to the statement carefully.** Try to pinpoint the main idea and the conclusion.

ple of settling disputes peacefully; (4) agrees not to use force except in self-defense; (5) agrees to help the U.N. in its actions. The U.N. agrees (6) to deal with nonmember states the same as member states, and (7) agrees to the principle of noninterference in members' domestic affairs.
16. The General Assembly and the Security Council.
17. **France, United Kingdom, Russia, United States, and China are permanent members; ten nonpermanent members elected by the General Assembly for two-year terms.**
18. Communicate with congressional officials or the White House. Join together with others who share your view.
19. Answers will vary, e.g., attacks on Israeli Olympic athletes in Munich in 1972, and seizure of the *Achille Lauro,* an Italian cruise ship.

Questions for Thought and Discussion (Answers)
1. Answers will vary, e.g., the president and Congress would be likely to disagree on the interpretation of the War Powers Resolution. The president would probably be most influential in this area.
2. Answers will vary, e.g., the president and Congress should both take an active part in foreign policy making, but the president should have the dominant role. After all, the president is elected by everyone whereas each member of Congress is elected only by a small part of the country.
3. Answers will vary, e.g., weak countries would be exploited by more powerful countries without the United States.
4. Answers will vary, e.g., both trade measures and economic policy are legitimate means that might prevent military actions.
5. Answers will vary, e.g., since its break-up into independent republics, the Soviet Union is no longer the superpower that the United States is due to economic and political problems within that country.
6. Answers will vary, e.g., this is not a valid argument because if the security and economic well-being of the nation is threatened, then no other domestic problem compares.

Social Studies Skills (Answers)
1. One way would be to order the data on the basis of income with highest average household income listed first, then the rest in declining order of average household income. The other way these data could be sequenced is on the basis of average household income in ascending order.
Figure 20–2
2. In chronological order by year, starting with 1962.
3. No, the sequencing order would not change.

Pages 489–495
1. The information is sequenced in chronological order starting with isolationism after the founding of the nation.
2. The information could have been ordered in terms of discussing periods of isolationism, then periods of wars.

CHAPTER 20 REVIEW—Continued

- **Ask yourself how the conclusion was reached.** The following list describes some of the most common fallacies to look for.

1. No real connection between the information presented and the conclusion.
2. Only one cause is identified when there are many.
3. Correlation is mistaken for causation. (See page 318).
4. The evidence used is irrelevant or only vaguely connected to the information presented.
5. More information is needed to support the conclusion.
6. The conclusion is not based on facts but on the argument that "everyone thinks so."

Writing

Read the statements below. Using the list above, write a short description of which fallacies apply to each of the statements.

- It is wrong for the United States to intervene in the affairs of troubled countries. We have too many problems with crime, education, and poverty in our own country.
- Public opinion overwhelmingly opposed the president's actions in Nicaragua. This proves that he was ill advised by his foreign policy team.
- The reason for intervention in the Persian Gulf in 1990 and 1991 was because of the danger that the world price of oil would be controlled by Iraq.

Social Studies Skills

Sequencing Data and Information

Part of understanding the world around you requires that you be able to put data and information in some kind of logical order. This is called *sequencing*. For example, if you read three articles on the AIDS epidemic, each one treating a different aspect of the problem, you would need to sequence the information from the three sources in order to make sense of it. When dealing with numbers—data—you have to be able to sequence such information in a way that tells you something. Often this is done for you in the form of a graph, such as Figure 20–1, which shows you how defense spending, expressed as a percentage of total federal government outlays, has changed throughout the years. These data have been sequenced for you in *chronological order,* starting from 1940 on. Data can be sequenced in many different ways. Assume that you have a table with data on average household income for each of the fifty states. One way to sequence the data is by state in alphabetical order.

1. What are at least two other ways the data could be sequenced?

Now look at Figure 20–2 on page 507 and answer these questions:

2. In what way is the data sequenced for you on the graph?
3. Would the sequencing change if the horizontal axis showed only five-year intervals?

Now skim through Section 1 in this chapter (pages 489 to 495):

1. How is the information on the history of foreign policy sequenced?
2. What other way could this information be sequenced?

Activities and Projects

1. Choose one of the last five presidents and write a report on his major foreign policy accomplishments and mistakes. Include a list and brief description of each of his closest foreign policy advisors.
2. Prepare a poster of pictures and articles that illustrate the nation working toward one of its major foreign policy goals.
3. Write a list of all the qualifications you think an ambassador to a Middle Eastern country should have. Prepare a script of all the questions you would ask the individual if you were the president considering his or her appointment.
4. Stage a debate on one of the following statements: (1) Women should be allowed to serve in combat roles in the military; (2) The president should not be allowed to order military action without prior congressional approval; (3) The Cold War is over.
5. Choose a goal of U.S. foreign policy and show with historical evidence what the U.S. has done in the last twenty years to achieve that goal.

Working with the Videodisc

The text below is from Professor Roger LeRoy Miller's introduction for the motion segment for Unit 8:

Today, there are over 80,000 separate government entities in these United States. Our system of federalism has allowed for this proliferation of government entities. Over 70 percent of all government employees work for local and state governments and much of the activity of government is carried on at the state and local level.

In the following video segment you will see how a typical state government operates. There are, of course, differences across the states, but the similarities are much more numerous. Additionally, there are many similarities between the way that all state governments operate and the way the federal government operates.

To access this segment, use the bar code below or the videodisc index found in the *TRB*.

Frame 33000

UNIT EIGHT

State and Local Governments

Unit Contents

CHAPTER INTRODUCTION

Instructional Objectives

By the end of the chapter students should be able to:

- Characterize the nature of state constitutions.
- Describe the state legislative structure and process.
- Summarize the process of a bill becoming a law at the state level.
- Discuss the following forms of direct democracy at the state level; the initiative, the referendum, and the recall.

Using the Keynote

Introduce Chapter 21 by reading aloud the John Adams quotation and ask: Do you agree with Adams's assessment of this resolution? Why or why not? Why do you think Adams expressed this attitude? Has he been proved correct?

Introducing the Chapter

Let volunteers read the Introduction aloud. Then guide the students in discussing the content by posing questions such as these: What examples can you cite of the continuing process of the creation of local units of government? What does the word *pluralism* mean? How does the prefix *hyper-* affect the meaning of the word (in *hyperpluralism*)? What are your most common contacts with state and local government? How aware are you—and other citizens—of these contacts? Why?

Previewing the Sections

Section 1 Ask for volunteers to read aloud the title of Section 1, the main headings, the titles of the figures, and the photo captions.

Section 2 Have the students page through Section 2. Then ask the students to complete the following sentence: As I study Section 2, I expect to. . . .

Section 3 Let the students look through Section 3. Ask: How do the main headings relate to the section title?

Section 4 As the students browse through Section 4, let volunteers read aloud the section title and the main headings. Ask: How might state legislatures differ from Congress?

Section 5 Ask the students to glance at Section 5. Ask: What does the chart on page 541 indicate about the content of the section?

Section 6 Have the students skim through Section 6, paying particular attention to the section title and the main headings.

CHAPTER 21

State Constitutions and Legislative Processes

CHAPTER OBJECTIVES

To learn and understand

- The nature of state constitutions.
- The state legislative structure and process.
- The organization of state legislatures.
- How a bill becomes a law at the state level.
- State forms of direct democracy: the initiative, the referendum, and the recall.

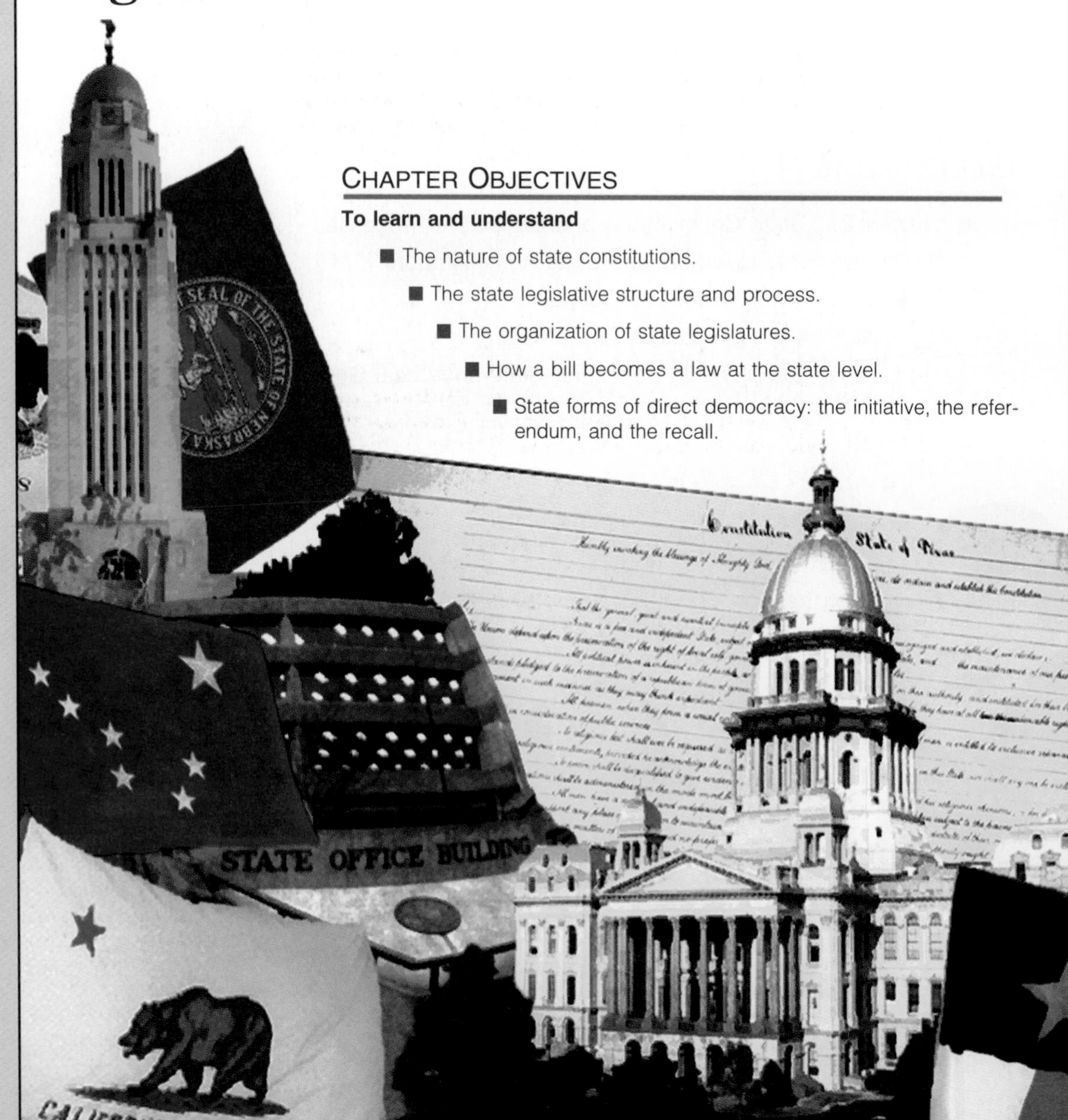

West's American Government Assignment Guide

Activity Sheets
Basic Concepts 21 *TRB* (Reteaching)
Enrichment Activity 21 *TRB*
Building Social Studies Skills 21 *TRB*

Quizzes
Chapter 21 Section 1 Quiz *TRB*
Chapter 21 Section 2 Quiz *TRB*
Chapter 21 Section 3 Quiz *TRB*
Chapter 21 Section 4 Quiz *TRB*
Chapter 21 Section 5 Quiz *TRB*

Tests
Chapter 21 Test A *TRB*
Chapter 21 Test B *TRB*
Chapter 21 Test Bank *TRB*
Chapter 21 WESTEST Computerized Testing

Social Studies Tool Kit Software
Chapter 21 Activity

Keynote

"Yesterday, the greatest question was decided which ever was debated in America, and the greater perhaps never was, nor will ever be decided among men. A resolution was passed without one dissenting colony, "that these United Colonies are, and of right ought to be, free and independent States."

—— **John Adams**
(1735–1826) Second President of the United States

INTRODUCTION

In the opening quote, John Adams used key words from the Resolution of Independence passed on July 3, 1776. His reference to independent states was extremely accurate, for the fifty states in this nation are in many ways independent. Each has its own constitution, its own judiciary, and its own legislature. In this chapter you will see the elements of those constitutions and legislative processes.

In 1787, the federal government was created according to a deliberate plan. The thirteen states obviously had to be included in the system. So, too, did the large number of local units of governments that existed at that time. After 1787, however, the remaining states, cities, and other local forms of government were not created so systematically. The process has not yet ended; new local governmental units are still being created all the time.

The system as it exists today with more than eighty thousand separate government units in the United States has been called **hyperpluralism**, a word that simply means our government is so fragmented that it is difficult to make decisions and to take action. Now, of course, many things do get done. The government provides roads, hospitals, schools, social programs, and police protection, among many other things. In fact, each of you comes into contact with state and local government workers almost every day of your life.

Not surprisingly, the number of civilian employees in state and local governments has been increasing. By 1998, it is estimated that almost 15 million Americans will work directly for state and local governments. A knowledge of how these governments operate is relevant for you and every other citizen, for these are the governments with which you will have the most direct contact during your life.

SECTION 1

The U.S. Constitution and the State Constitutions

Preview Questions

- What are the powers that the U.S. Constitution gives to state governments?
- Why are state constitutions typically long and detailed compared to the U.S. Constitution?
- What major elements do state constitutions contain?
- How can a state constitution be revised?

We live in a federal system in which there are fifty separate state governments and one federal government. The U.S. Constitution gives a broad range of powers to state governments; it also prohibits state governments from engaging in certain activities. The U.S. Constitution never explicitly defines the powers of the states; rather, state powers were simply reserved, which means that states may do anything that the Constitution does not prohibit them from doing, or that is not expressly delegated to the federal government.

The major reserved powers of the states include the power to spend and regulate **intrastate commerce**, that is, commerce within a given state. The states also have general **police power**, meaning they can protect their citizens by passing and enforcing laws in the areas of public safety (through traffic laws, for example), health and welfare (through immunization and child-abuse

SECTION 1

Points to Stress
• Powers and limitations placed on state governments.
• The reasons for long and detailed state constitutions.
• Major elements contained in state constitutions.
• Manner in which a state constitution can be revised.

Kickoff Activity
Ask the students to list similarities between your state constitution and the U.S. Constitution; give them about five minutes to complete this activity. Then ask volunteers to read their lists aloud, and encourage the students to compare and discuss their ideas.

Working with the Preview Questions
Go over these study questions with the students; remind them that these questions can help them recognize the key information presented in Section 1. Then have the students keep these questions in mind while reading and taking notes on the section.

Teaching Strategies

Introduction
Let volunteers read the section introduction aloud, and have the students look up and reread the Tenth Amendment found in the Resource Center. Then give several students an opportunity to restate, in their own words, the quotation from Article VI of the Constitution from page 524, and encourage the students to explain its meaning and discuss its impact.

Enrichment
You might point out to students the fact that, in practice, police power is concurrently held by the states and the federal government, which has such agencies as the FBI, the DEA, and the special agents of the treasury department.

Discussion Starter
Help the students consider the difference in length and detail between the U.S. Constitution and most state constitutions: What do you think accounts for this extreme difference? What were the intentions of the framers of the U.S. Constitution? How were they different from the background and the intentions of those who wrote most state constitutions?

Discussion Starter
Encourage the students to share their ideas about the period of time when people lost confidence in state legislatures: What do you think accounts for this loss of confidence? How do you think the trend was reversed? What trend in confidence—growth or loss—can you identify now within your own state? Why?

Discussion Starter
Help the students consider and discuss the distinctions between constitutional law and statutory law. Begin by letting volunteers explain, in their own words, the difference between the two kinds of law. Then ask: How did the framers and their situation differ from the authors of state constitutions? Why do you think the authors of state constitutions were so prone to confuse the two kinds of law? What problems has that confusion created?

Caption Answer Students should remember that many of the founders were uneasy with the notion of an overly strong national government and felt that as many powers as possible should be reserved to the states. Remind students, however, that nationalized police do exist in many countries such as France (discussed in Chapters 4 and 26).

▲ General police power is one of the major powers reserved to the states in the United States Constitution. Why do you think the founding fathers chose to give this power to the states rather than to the national government?

laws), and morality (laws against pornography). The police power of the states should not be confused with the protective functions performed by police departments. The regulation of public safety is only one of the many police powers of the states, which include regulating sanitation in restaurants, setting the minimum legal age for smoking, etc.

Restrictions on state and local governmental activity are implied by the Constitution in Article VI, Paragraph 2:

> This Constitution, and the Laws of the United States, which shall be made in Pursuance thereof; and all Treaties made, or which shall be made, under the Authority of the United States, shall be the Supreme Law of the Land; and the Judges in every State shall be bound thereby, any Thing in the Constitution or Laws of any State to the Contrary notwithstanding.

The paragraph states that the Constitution is the supreme law of the land, and no state or local law can conflict with the Constitution, with laws made by the United States Congress, or with treaties entered into by the federal government. Judicially, the U.S. Supreme Court has been the final judge of conflicts arising between the federal and state governments.

State Constitutions

The United States Constitution is a model of brevity. State constitutions, in contrast, are typically models of excessive length and detail. For over two hundred years, the U.S. Constitution has endured as a binding body of law, with only twenty-seven amendments thus far. Such is not the case with state constitutions. Texas has had five constitutions; Louisiana has had eleven; Georgia has had nine; South Carolina has had seven; and Alabama, Florida, and Virginia have had six each. Many have been amended numerous times. In Texas, for example, 487 amendments have been submitted to the voters and 339 of those amendments have been adopted. The number of amendments that voters may be asked to approve in one election sometimes numbers in the hundreds. Over an 84-year period ending in 1985, the citizens of Alabama, for example, were asked to approve 656 amendments—of which they adopted 452.

Figure 21–1 on pages 524–25 provides general information on the constitutions of the various states.

Why State Constitutions Are Long The length and mass of detail of many state constitutions reflect the loss of popular confidence in state legislatures between the end of the Civil War and the early 1900s. During that period, forty-two states adopted or revised their constitutions. Constitutions that were adopted before or after that period are shorter and contain fewer restrictions on the powers of state legislatures.

An equally important reason for the length and detail of state constitutions is that the constitution framers at the state level had a difficult time distinguishing between constitutional law and statutory law. (Remember from Chapter 18 that statutory law is law made by legislatures such as the Congress of the United States or the legislatures of the various states.) Many laws that are clearly statutory have been put into state constitutions. For example, South Dakota has in its state constitution the authorization for a cordage and twine plant at the state penitentiary. The Texas constitution includes a pay schedule for state legislators. When legislators want a raise, the constitution must be amended. The Alabama

Extension
Have the students (or several volunteers) bring in copies of your state constitution. Ask the students to identify the six parts of state constitutions and to compare the text's general description of each part with that specific part of your state's constitution.

Discussion Starter
Have the students discuss the separation of powers provided for in state constitutions: What do you think accounts for the fact that every state constitution provides for that separation? Why do you think some states include the distribution-of-powers clause in their constitutions? Why do you think other states felt secure in merely implying that separation of powers? Which did the authors of your state constitution do?

constitution includes a thirteen-and-a-half-page amendment establishing the "Alabama Heritage Trust Fund." An article of the California constitution discusses the tax-exempt status of the Huntington Library and Art Gallery. Obviously, the U.S. Constitution contains no such details. It leaves to the Congress the nuts-and-bolts activity of making specific statutory laws.

Typical Form and Content

State constitutions are similar in terms of their overall structure to the U.S. Constitution. They include the following:

1. A preamble.
2. A bill of rights.
3. An outline of the framework of government.
4. A listing of state powers and responsibilities.
5. A provision for local government.
6. An amending clause that details the methods of formal constitutional change.

The Preamble Most state constitutional preambles are similar to the one in the U.S. Constitution, in that they begin with "We, the people . . . do ordain and establish. . . ." The majority of states refer to some principle of divine guidance, something that the U.S. Constitution does not do.

Bill of Rights Often called a declaration of rights, every state has a section that spells out the civil liberties and rights of its citizens. The majority of state constitutions were adopted prior to the ratification of the Fourteenth Amendment to the U.S. Constitution, which protects individuals' rights against overbearing state governments. Consequently, while there was good reason for extensive bills of rights in state constitutions prior to July 9, 1868, today most of them add little to their citizens' civil liberties and rights beyond those in the U.S. Constitution. Some, however, do offer specific protections such as a ban against discrimination based on sex, or the right to organize labor unions.

Framework of Government A typical state constitution establishes the structure for the legislative, executive, and judicial branches of government. Through what is known as a distribution-of-powers clause, about 50 percent of the states provide for the separation of powers. In the remaining states, the separation of powers is implied from the constitution as a whole, similar to the way such separation of powers is implied in the U.S. Constitution.

Governmental Functions Some state constitutions specify in precise detail what the state government's activities may be; other states are more loose in their delegation of government duties. Most state constitutions restrict the state government's powers over taxation and finance. Most also make public education a state responsibility.

Local Governments The majority of state constitutions explain in detail the structure and power of local governments. (Local governments are under the authority of state governments.) In certain states, however, some cities and counties are allowed to conduct their affairs without state interference. (See Chapter 25 for more details on local government.)

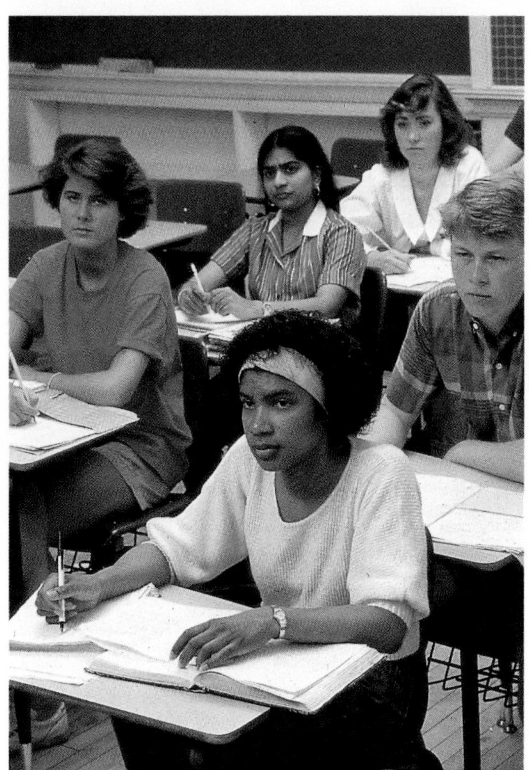

▲ Public education is spelled out as a state responsibility in most state constitutions. What other levels of government also are responsible for public education?

Caption Answer The responsibility for public education encompasses all major levels of government from the broad national policies of the federal government to the more rigid guidelines and criteria established by state governments to the actual nuts and bolts working administration of local school districts.

Discussion Starter
Guide the students in studying and discussing the table, General Information on State Constitutions: What specific facts do you find about your state constitution? Which of those facts do you find most interesting? Surprising? Why? How do the facts about your state constitution compare to those about the constitutions of other states? How do you account for the similarities? For the differences?

General Information on State Constitutions

State or Other Jurisdiction	Number of Constitutions*	Dates of Adoption	Effective Date of Present Constitution	Estimated Length (number of words)	Number of Amendments: Submitted to Voters	Number of Amendments: Adopted
Alabama	6	1819, 1861, 1865, 1868, 1875, 1901	Nov. 28, 1901	174,000	656	452
Alaska	1	1956	Jan. 3, 1959	13,000	28	20
Arizona	1	1911	Feb. 14, 1912	28,876 (a)	187	104
Arkansas	5	1836, 1861, 1864, 1868, 1874	Oct. 30, 1874	40,720 (a)	156	71 (b)
California	2	1849, 1879	July 4, 1879	33,350	756	449
Colorado	1	1876	Aug. 1, 1876	45,679	227	108
Connecticut	4	1818(c), 1965	Dec. 30, 1965	9,564	24	23
Delaware	4	1776, 1792, 1831, 1897	June 10, 1897	19,000	(d)	115
Florida	6	1839, 1861, 1865, 1868, 1886, 1968	Jan. 7, 1969	25,100	63	41
Georgia	10	1777, 1789, 1798, 1861, 1865, 1868, 1877, 1945, 1976, 1982	July 1, 1983	25,000 (a)	11 (e)	10
Hawaii	1 (f)	1950	Aug. 21, 1959	17,453 (a)	85	77
Idaho	1	1889	July 3, 1890	21,500	183	103
Illinois	4	1818, 1848, 1870, 1970	July 1, 1971	13,200	7	3
Indiana	2	1816, 1851	Nov. 1, 1851	9,377 (a)	65	36
Iowa	2	1846, 1857	Sept. 3, 1857	12,500	48	45 (g)
Kansas	1	1859	Jan 29, 1861	11,865	107	80 (g)
Kentucky	4	1792, 1799, 1850, 1891	Sept. 28, 1891	23,500	54	2
Louisiana	11	1812, 1845, 1852, 1861, 1864, 1868, 1879, 1898, 1913, 1921, 1974	Jan 1, 1975	36,146 (a)	24	15
Maine	1	1819	March 15, 1820	13,500	181	153 (h)
Maryland	4	1776, 1851, 1864, 1867	Oct. 5, 1867	41,134	227	195
Massachusetts	1	1780	Oct. 25, 1780	36,690 (a, i)	141	116
Michigan	4	1835, 1850, 1908, 1963	Jan. 1, 1964	20,000	41	15
Minnesota	1	1857	May 11, 1858	9,500	203	109
Mississippi	4	1817, 1832, 1869, 1890	Nov. 1, 1890	23,500	124	54
Missouri	4	1820, 1865, 1875, 1945	March 30, 1945	42,000	100	62
Montana	2	1889, 1972	July 1, 1973	11,866 (a)	17	10

*The constitutions referred to in this table include those Civil War documents customarily listed by the individual states.
(a) Actual word count.
(b) Eight of the approved amendments have been superseded and are not printed in the current edition of the constitution. The total adopted does not include five amendments that were invalidated.
(c) Colonial charters with some alterations served as the first constitutions in Connecticut (1638, 1662) and in Rhode Island (1663).
(d) Proposed amendments are not submitted to the voters in Delaware.
(e) Estimated length of the printed constitution, which includes only provisions of statewide applicability. Local amendments comprise most of the total constitution.
(f) As a kingdom and a republic, Hawaii had five constitutions.
(g) The figure given includes amendments approved by the voters and later nullified by the state supreme court in Iowa (three), Kansas (one), Nevada (six), and Wisconsin (two).
(h) The figure does not include one amendment approved by the voters in 1967 that is inoperative until implemented by legislation.

▲ **FIGURE 21–1 General Information on State Constitutions.** As you can see from looking at the table on these pages, most state constitutions are quite wordy and many have a large number of amendments. Why are state constitutions so long?

Figure Answer There are a number of reasons for the length of state constitutions. Many reflect the loss of popular confidence in state legislatures in the late 1800s and early 1900s. Another reason is that many state constitutions include very specific statutory laws. Still another reason, which will be dealt with later, is the popularity of constitutional initiatives to amend state constitutions in many states.

Extension

You might ask volunteers to obtain and read a copy of your state's constitution. These students should outline the constitution and present their findings to the class in the form of a poster.

General Information on State Constitutions (continued)

State or Other Jurisdiction	Number of Constitutions*	Dates of Adoption	Effective Date of Present Constitution	Estimated Length (number of words)	Number of Amendments: Submitted to Voters	Number of Amendments: Adopted
Nebraska	2	1866, 1875	Oct. 12, 1875	20,048 (a)	276	183
Nevada	1	1864	Oct. 31, 1864	20,770	165	100 (g)
New Hampshire	2	1776, 1784	June 2, 1784	9,200	271 (j)	141 (j)
New Jersey	3	1776, 1844, 1947	Jan. 1, 1948	17,086	48	36
New Mexico	1	1911	Jan. 6, 1912	27,200	213	104
New York	4	1777, 1822, 1846, 1894	Jan 1, 1895	80,000	270	203
North Carolina	3	1776, 1868, 1970	July 1, 1971	11,000	30	24
North Dakota	1	1889	Nov. 2, 1889	31,000	208 (k)	119 (k)
Ohio	2	1802, 1851	Sept. 1, 1851	36,900	241	142
Oklahoma	1	1907	Nov. 16, 1907	68,800	254 (l)	114 (l)
Oregon	1	1857	Feb. 14, 1859	25,965	347	174
Pennsylvania	5	1776, 1790, 1838, 1873, 1968(m)	1968(m)	21,675	24 (m)	19 (m)
Rhode Island	2	1842(c)	May 2, 1843	19,026 (a, i)	84	44
South Carolina	7	1776, 1778, 1790, 1861, 1865, 1868, 1895	Jan 1, 1896	22,500 (n)	628 (o)	454 (o)
South Dakota	1	1889	Nov. 2, 1889	23,300	178	92
Tennessee	3	1796, 1835, 1870	Feb. 23, 1870	15,300	55	32
Texas	5	1845, 1861, 1866, 1869, 1876	Feb. 15, 1876	62,000	487	339
Utah	1	1895	Jan. 4, 1896	17,500	121	73
Vermont	3	1777, 1786, 1793	July 9, 1793	6,600	206	49
Virginia	6	1776, 1830, 1851, 1869, 1902, 1970	July 1, 1971	18,500	19	16
Washington	1	1889	Nov. 11, 1889	29,400	139	76
West Virginia	2	1863, 1872	April 9, 1872	25,600	96	59
Wisconsin	1	1848	May 29, 1848	13,500	161	118 (g)
Wyoming	1	1889	July 10, 1890	31,800	90	51
American Samoa	2	1960, 1967	July 1, 1967	6,000	13	7
No. Mariana Islands	1	1977	Oct. 24, 1977	—	—	—
Puerto Rico	1	1952	July 25, 1952	9,281 (a)	6	6

(i) The printed constitution includes many provisions that have been annulled. The length of effective provisions is an estimated 24,122 words (12,490 annulled) in Massachusetts and 11,399 words (7,627 annulled) in Rhode Island.
(j) The constitution of 1784 was extensively revised in 1792. Figures show proposals and adoptions since 1793, when the revised constitution became effective.
(k) The figures do not include submission and approval of the constitution of 1889 itself and of Article XX; these are constitutional questions included in some counts of constitutional amendments and would add two to the figure in each column.
(l) The figures include one amendment submitted to and approved by the voters and subsequently ruled by the supreme count to have been illegally submitted.
(m) Certain sections of the constitution were revised by the limited constitutional convention of 1967. Eighteen amendments have been proposed and adopted since 1968.
(n) Of the estimated length, approximately two-thirds is of general statewide effect; the remainder is local amendments.
(o) Of the 628 proposed amendments submitted to the voters, 130 were of general statewide effect and 496 were local; the voters rejected 83 (12 statewide, 71 local). Of the remaining 543, the General Assembly refused to approve 100 (22 statewide, 78 local), and 443 (96 statewide, 347 local) were finally added to the constitution.

Source: *Book of the States*, 1988–89 (Lexington, Kentucky: Council of State Governments, 1990).

Discussion Starter
As the students read that some states require regular constitutional conventions, encourage discussion by asking these questions: What attitude toward the state constitution does such a requirement imply? What do you think motivates that attitude?

Enrichment
Let an interested volunteer research the answers to these questions and report to the rest of the class: When was the last constitutional convention called in your state? Why and how was it called? What were the results of the convention? When is the next constitutional convention in your state anticipated? Why?

Figure Answer The most common method is through a two-thirds majority vote of the state legislature.

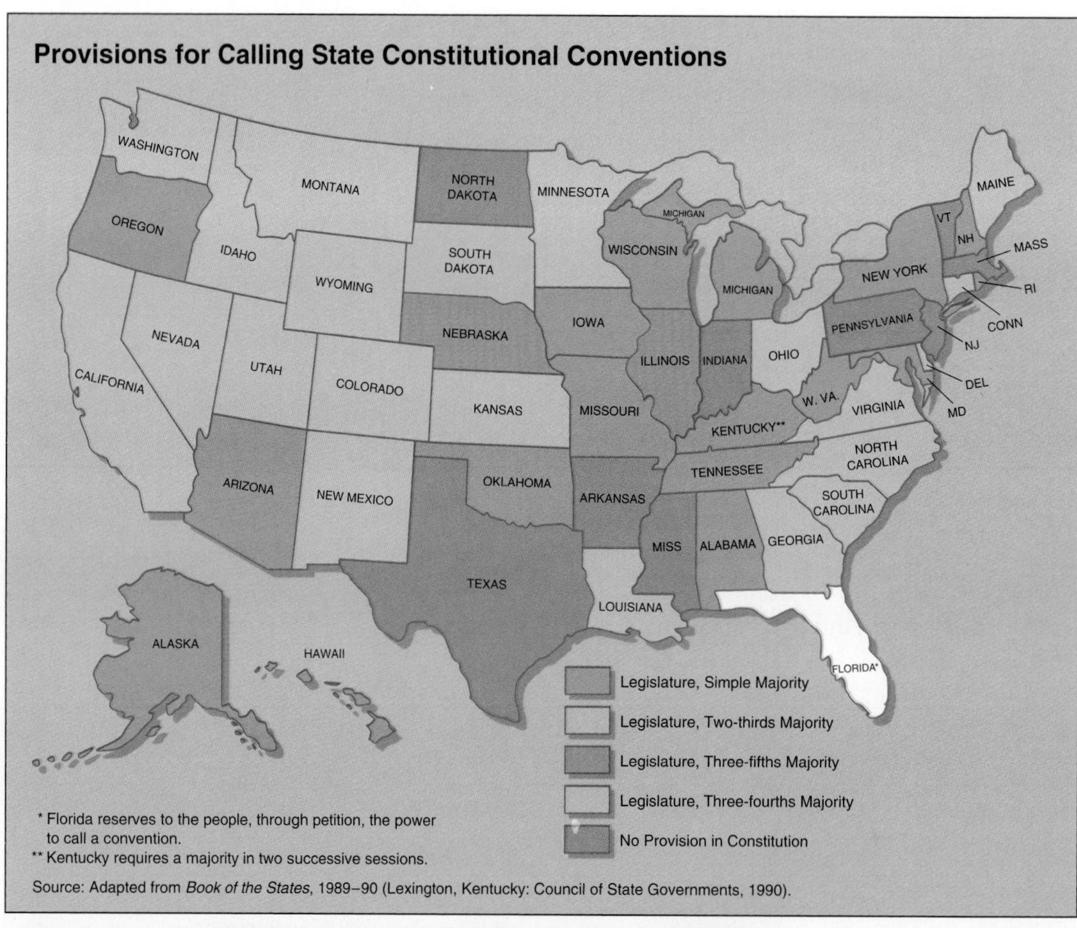

FIGURE 21–2 Provisions for Calling State Constitutional Conventions. As you can see from the map above, there are a variety of methods used among the states for calling state constitutional conventions. What is the most common method? Which method does your state employ?

Amending State Constitutions

There are three ways for proposing amendments that are included in the fifty state constitutions: by constitutional convention, by legislative activity, or by popular demand. The most commonly used method has been by convention.

State Constitutional Conventions By the beginning of the 1990s, almost 250 state constitutional conventions had been used to write an entirely new constitution, or to attempt to amend an existing one. This is not surprising, because four-fifths of all state constitutions expressly allow for such conventions. Some states, such as Illinois, New York, Ohio, and Michigan, require that such conventions be called periodically to consider whether changes are needed, and if so to propose them. Figure 21–2 above shows how a constitutional convention must be called in each of the states.

Proposing Amendments Amendments to state constitutions are made in two ways: by the legislature and by initiative petition.

- **By the legislature** All states authorize legislatures to propose constitutional amendments. Usu-

TEACHING BUILDING SOCIAL STUDIES SKILLS

Read

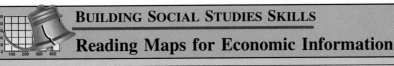

Before the students begin reading the Building Social Studies Skills feature, allow them to discuss their own interest in and experiences with maps that show economic information: What kinds of economic information are you most likely to find recorded on maps? Why? How have you used maps that present economic information? How easy did you find it to read and understand such maps? Why? After the discussion, let the students read the feature on their own.

Discuss

Use questions such as these to help the students discuss the feature: What are the advantages of presenting certain kinds of economic information on a map rather than on a chart or graph? What are those kinds of information that are best presented on a map? What are the guidelines for reading a map? How will following each of the guidelines here help you read an economic map accurately?

Analyze and Apply

Divide the class into groups, and have the members of each group select one kind of economic information that can be effectively shown on a map. Then let the group members gather that information about your state and draw their own map, showing the information they have gathered. Display all the groups' maps, and give the students an opportunity to examine and discuss the other groups' work.

Review

Ask these questions to help the students review the Building Social Studies Skills feature: What is economic information? What can an economic map help you understand?

Practicing Your Skills (Answers)

1. 26 percent.
2. 22 percent.
3. No, the very low tax states are found on both the east and west coasts, and in the northern and southern parts of the country.

BUILDING SOCIAL STUDIES SKILLS

Reading Maps for Economic Information

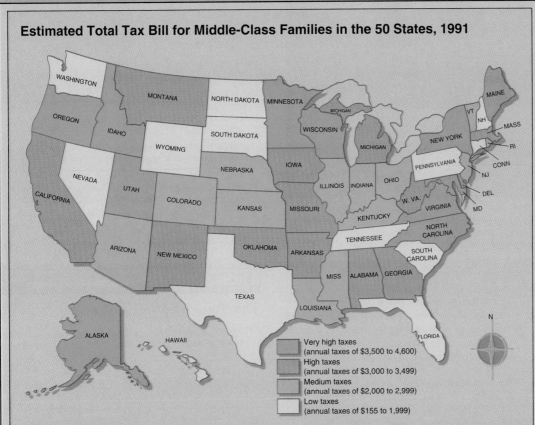

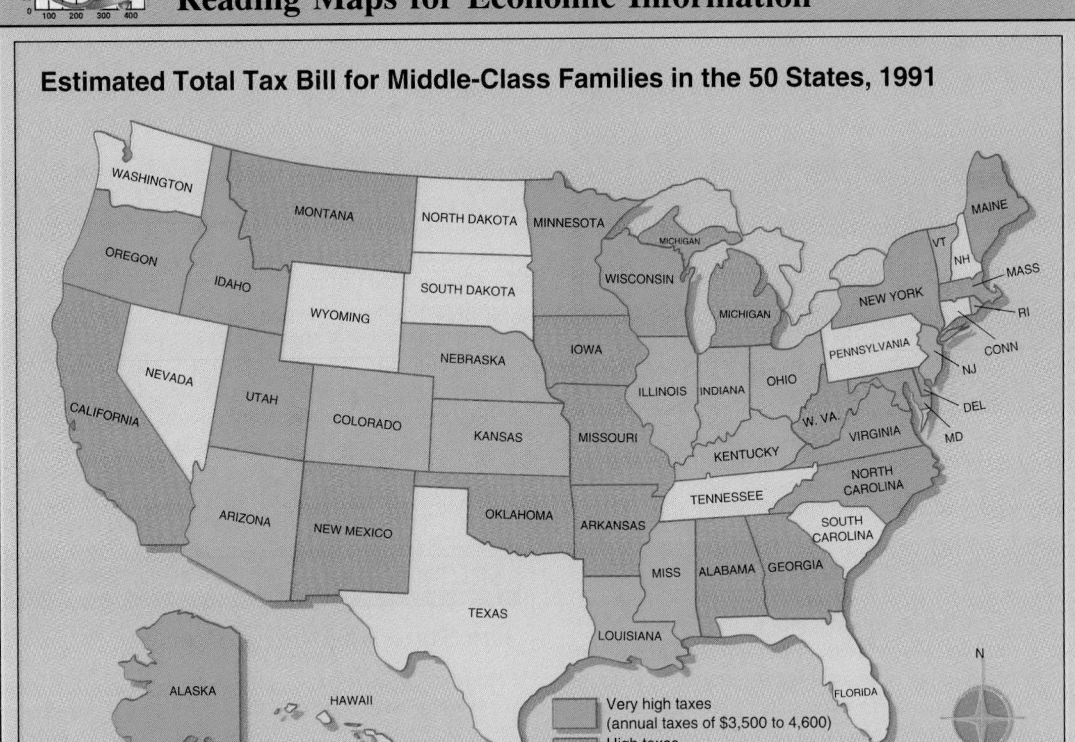

Economic information comprises a wide variety of subjects: international trade, distribution of resources, business, transportation, agriculture, manufacturing. It can also include information about unemployment rates, rates of economic growth, and costs of living.

One method of finding economic information is by reading and interpreting special-purpose maps such as economic maps, which communicate specific sets of economic data.

To accurately read an economic map, use the map reading skills you learned on page 290. Then determine the kind of economic information on the map you are studying, and use these data to help you draw conclusions about the information presented.

PRACTICING YOUR SKILLS

Study the map above.

1. What percentage of states qualify as having "low taxes"?
2. What percentage of states qualify as having "very high taxes"?
3. Is there any geographic pattern to where the low-tax states are concentrated?

Comprehension
Ask volunteers to explain the purpose of requiring an extraordinary majority for passage of constitutional amendments.

Discussion Starter
Encourage the students to share and discuss their responses to the constitutional initiative: What advantages do you think this procedure offers? What disadvantages might be associated with it? Then ask: Does our state constitution provide for the constitutional initiative? Do you think it should? Why or why not?

Caption Answer Students should understand that the constitutional initiative process is one of the few remaining examples of direct democracy extant in this country.

Reteaching Strategies
1. Let the students work in small groups to compare and discuss the notes they have taken on Section 1. Encourage individual students to revise their notes as necessary.
2. Have the students work with partners to write a list of important constitutional facts for your state.

Evaluation Strategies
1. Have the students write their answers to the Section 1 Review questions.
2. Have the students take the Section 1 Quiz found in the *TRB*.

Section 1 Review (Answers)
1. The powers to spend and to regulate intrastate commerce and police power.
2. The U.S. Constitution is short, whereas state constitutions are typically of excessive length and detail.
3. A preamble, a bill of rights, an outline of the framework of government, a listing of state powers and responsibilities, a provision for local government, and an amending clause that details the methods of formal constitutional change.
4. By constitutional convention, by legislative activity, or by popular demand.
5. Answers will vary, e.g., there has been a loss of confidence in state legislatures. Getting provisions into a state's constitution makes them much more difficult to change. Also, the writers had a difficult time distinguishing between constitutional law and statutory law.

SECTION 2

Points to Stress
- Reasons for bicameralism in state legislatures.
- Criticism of bicameralism.
- The importance of *Baker* v. *Carr* and *Reynolds* v. *Sims.*

Kickoff Activity
Give the students five minutes in which to list as many facts as possible about your state legislature. En-

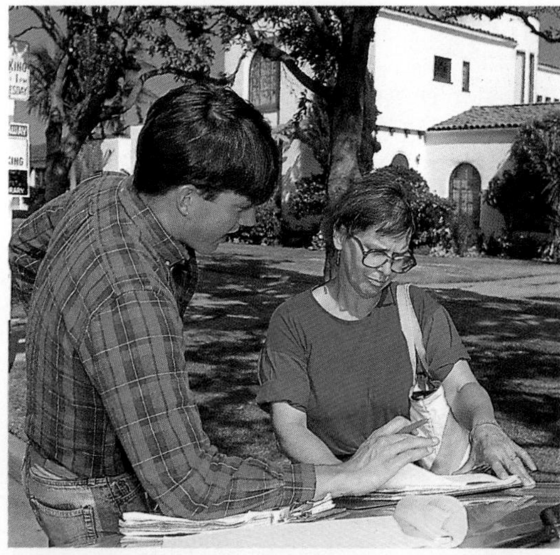

▲ Citizens can propose constitutional amendments through petitions in 17 states including California. Are constitutional initiatives examples of representative democracy or direct democracy?

ally an **extraordinary majority** of votes, which will typically be two-thirds or three-fifths of the total number of legislators, is required to propose an amendment. In some states a proposed amendment has to be passed in two successive sessions of the legislature.

- **The constitutional initiative** Among the states, seventeen (Arizona, Arkansas, California, Colorado, Florida, Illinois, Massachusetts, Michigan, Missouri, Montana, Nebraska, Nevada, North Dakota, Ohio, Oklahoma, Oregon, and South Dakota) have a unique feature in their constitutions called the **constitutional initiative**. This is a process that allows citizens to propose a constitutional amendment through petitions signed by a required number of registered voters. This initiative allows citizens to place a proposed amendment on the ballot without calling a whole constitutional convention. The number of signatures required to get a constitutional initiative on the ballot varies from state to state, usually between 5 and 10 percent of the total number of votes cast in the last gubernatorial election. The states that have used the initiative process most often are California and Oregon.

Ratification No matter which method of proposal is used, all states except Delaware require an amendment to be ratified by a majority of the voters in the general election. (In Delaware, a constitutional amendment must receive a two-thirds vote by the state legislature in two consecutive sessions.) In the states in which voter approval is required, proposals coming from the legislature are adopted far more often than those that originated by initiative.

Section 1 Review

1. What are some powers reserved to the states?
2. What are the differences between the U.S. Constitution and most state constitutions?
3. What six major elements does each state constitution contain?
4. How can state constitutions be amended?
5. **For critical analysis:** Why do you think so many state constitutions contain what is obviously statutory law, which might better be dealt with directly by the state legislatures?

Section 2

The State Legislative Process

Preview Questions

- Why have state legislatures followed the national lead of bicameralism?
- Why is bicameralism criticized?
- What is the importance of the decisions in *Baker* v. *Carr* and *Reynolds* v. *Sims*?

During the early years of the American republic, the legislative branch was clearly more important than the executive and judicial branches of state government. Most state constitutions mention the legislative branch first. It was initially regarded as the primary method for putting state constitutional law into action. Today, however, the state legislature has lost much of its glow. Governors—the states' chief executives—have emerged as the leaders of the people in legislative affairs. Nonetheless, state legislatures are important forces in state politics and state governmental decision making. The task of these assemblies is to develop and pass laws on such matters as taxes, business and commerce regulation, and funding for school systems and welfare payments. Allocation of state funds and program priorities are vital issues to residents and communities in every state.

courage them to include facts about the number of houses, the distinction between the houses, the number of legislators, and so on. At the end of the allotted time, encourage the students to compare and discuss their lists.

Working with the Preview Questions
Go over these study questions with the class, and encourage volunteers to share their responses. Then remind the students to keep these questions in mind as they read Section 2.

Teaching Strategies

Introduction
Ask one of the students to read the section introduction aloud. Then ask the class about the role of the governor in your state: Has the governor emerged as the leader in legislative affairs? If so, what specific evidence can you cite? If not, why not?

Comprehension
Ask the students to explain how bicameral legislatures add to the checks and balances on the exercise of governmental power.

Discussion Starter
Encourage the students to discuss the states' desire to be "just like Washington, D.C.": What advantages are associated with functioning in the same way as the national Congress? What disadvantages might also be associated with that practice? Why?

Critical Thinking Skills
Guide the students in analyzing the argument that a single-house legislative system allows the responsibility for action to be more clearly assigned: To what extent can this argument be considered valid? Why? What problems remain, even with a unicameral system, in assigned responsibility for action taken—or not taken—by the legislature? Why do you think this criticism of bicameralism is frequently applied to state legislatures—but rarely to the U.S. Congress?

Caption Answer The following are criticisms of the bicameral plan: Passing the buck is too easy because of the difficulty of assigning blame. Interest groups can more easily kill proposed legislation because it is only necessary to kill it in one of the two houses. Conference committees are accused of being too powerful and of occasionally operating irresponsibly.

Enrichment
Assign two or three students to research the success of the unicameral system in Nebraska. Let these students present the information they have gathered to the rest of the class, and then encourage all the students to participate in comparing your state legislature with Nebraska's.

Extension
Have the students identify the size of your state legislature: How does it compare to other states? What reasons can you find to explain the size of the legislature?

Most state legislatures, such as the North Carolina legislature shown here, are bicameral. What do critics of bicameral legislatures point to as problems with this system?

Bicameral Systems

Bicameralism—a legislative system made up of two houses—exists in all state legislatures except Nebraska, which instituted a unicameral (one house) plan in 1937. Unicameral legislatures did exist in Pennsylvania (1776 to 1790), Georgia (1777 to 1789), and Vermont (1777 to 1836).

There are many reasons why bicameral legislatures prevail: they add to the checks and balances on the exercise of governmental power; they are consistent with the idea of limited government (discussed in Chapter 2); and they follow the pattern of the federal government as laid out in the U.S. Constitution. This desire to be "just like Washington, D.C." was a major reason that Pennsylvania and Georgia abandoned their single-house legislatures.

Criticisms of Bicameralism Even though bicameralism is clearly the rule in state legislatures, many experts criticize the system. Under a bicameral plan, "passing the buck" for legislative failures is easy; placing the blame is difficult. Additionally, interest groups can more easily kill proposed legislation in a bicameral system; all they have to do is squelch it in one of the two houses. As with the federal government, a bicameral state legislature requires a conference committee (discussed in Chapter 14) to resolve differences in proposed legislation. Some experts argue that these conference committees constitute a "third house" that occasionally operates irresponsibly.

By contrast, those who support unicameralism argue that a single-house legislature would be more responsible for its actions, and that a unicameral body would increase the prestige (and salaries) of state legislators. They would also be able to give more full-time service to their respective states. The experience in Nebraska since 1937 appears to confirm this. According to some studies, a typical legislator in Nebraska seems to be of higher caliber, and has become more responsive to her or his constituents than legislators under the old bicameral system.

In spite of the arguments, however, tradition remains on the side of bicameralism. The general public's lack of interest in the issue of unicameralism gives it little chance to come up for a vote.

The Sizes of the Two Houses The size of state legislatures varies dramatically. In the lower houses of representatives, 40 members sit in Alaska, 41 in Delaware, and 42 in Nevada; but 203 sit in Pennsylvania and 400 sit in New Hampshire.[1] There is less diversity in the

1. New Hampshire developed a strong dislike of government beyond its towns' borders when it was ruled directly from England as a royal colony. Its house of representatives has at least one member for each town regardless of population. It is the third-largest legislature in the English-speaking world, topped only by Congress and the British House of Commons.

Enrichment
Ask one of the students to research and report to the rest of the class on the apportionment provisions in your state's constitution. Also have the student report on recent reapportionment attempts: When were such attempts made? Why? With what success?

Comprehension
As the students read about the Court's decision in *Reynolds* v. *Sims,* ask them to explain how this division of houses in state bicameral legislatures differs from the division within the U.S. Congress.

Vocabulary
Let a volunteer remind the rest of the class of the definition and derivation of *gerrymandering.*

Caption Answer
Changes that resulted from *Reynolds* v. *Sims* included completely new constitutions in some states, numerous constitutional amendments in others, and a general movement to modernize the state legislatures.

This case is excerpted in the *West's American Government Handbook of Selected Court Cases.*

states' upper houses. These vary from 20 seats in Alaska to 67 in Minnesota.

Apportionment

Apportioning Seats **Apportionment** is the system by which seats are distributed among the districts in a state. Each state's constitution provides for apportionment—some on the basis of districts with equal populations, some on the basis of geographical area, and some on the basis of other economic factors. In almost all cases, however, population is at least one of the major bases for distributing legislative seats. As with the federal government, state legislators have often attempted to use **reapportionment** as a way to guarantee that one district remains in Republican party hands or one district remains in Democratic party hands. Reapportionment occurs when population increases, decreases, or shifts within a state. Usually reapportionment has to occur every ten years, within two years after the census is taken, as outlined in the U.S. Constitution.

Baker* v. *Carr For years rural areas were able to dominate state legislatures because geography instead of population was used as the primary means of setting districts. This meant that areas with few citizens had as much power as areas with many more citizens. This practice came to an end in 1962, when the Supreme Court ruled in *Baker* v. *Carr* that federal courts could properly hear cases in which citizens claimed that the pattern of legislative apportionment in their state denied them equal protection of the law under the Fourteenth Amendment.

Reynolds* v. *Sims In a landmark case in 1964, *Reynolds* v. *Sims,* the U.S. Supreme Court changed the rules governing the election of state legislators even further. The Court said that every state electoral district for both houses of the state legislatures had to be drawn with equal populations. Until 1964, state legislatures were controlled by rural, less populated sections of each state, causing rural overrepresentation and therefore urban underrepresentation. But as the Court said in 1964:

> Legislators represent people, not trees or acres. [They] are elected by voters, not farms or cities. . . . [T]he seats in both houses of a bicameral state legislature must be apportioned on a population basis.

For the first time after *Reynolds* v. *Sims,* urban, minority, and suburban populations were able to influence state legislatures in a way that had never been possible. Not surprisingly, the new reapportioned legislatures often drafted and adopted completely new state constitutions. In other states, numerous constitutional amendments were passed to streamline and modernize many parts of the state government. An important aspect of this modernization was the trend toward full-time professional legislators, as well as the hiring of expert legislative assistants.

Creative Map Making

Gerrymandering (discussed in Chapter 12) is an example of creative map making, where legislative districts are drawn in order to guarantee that one political party maintains control of a particular voting district. Figure

◀ The Supreme Court ruling in *Reynolds* v. *Sims* that all electoral districts had to be drawn with equal populations led to increased representation for urban, suburban, and minority populations. This change is reflected in the growing number of minority legislators such as these. What other reforms in state legislatures were prompted by the *Reynolds* v. *Sims* decision?

TEACHING CITIZENSHIP SKILLS AND RESPONSIBILITIES

Read

Begin by encouraging the students to discuss their own ideas about—and possible experiences with—witnessing crimes: Have you ever seen a crime taking place? Do you know anyone who has? If you did witness a crime, what do you imagine you would feel like doing? What do you think you should do? Why? After this discussion, ask two or three of the students to read the Citizenship Skills and Responsibilities feature aloud to the rest of the class.

Discuss

Stimulate a class discussion of the feature by posing questions such as these: Why are people likely to want to forget about a crime they have witnessed? What is wrong with ignoring a crime? For whom can this kind of action cause problems? Does your community have a 9-1-1–line? What kinds of help can you get by calling 9-1-1? If you don't have 9-1-1, what number should you call for police or ambulance assistance? When you answer police questions, why is it important to avoid exaggeration and personal commentary? What attitude toward appearing in court do many people have? What is your own attitude? Why?

Analyze and Apply

Ask the students to visit a local court during a day when one or more minor criminal cases are being heard. (Or arrange for the class to go to court together.) Instruct the students to sit quietly and watch carefully, taking notes if possible, and then to write up a log of what took place in court. After the visits, encourage the students to compare and discuss what they saw and heard: What actually goes on in court? How does it compare to the court scenes you often see on TV shows or in movies?

Caption Answer Students should understand that people often fear the police or retaliation by criminals. Many people also fear the repercussions of their involvement with the legal system.

Review

Use these questions to help the students review the Citizenship Skills and Responsibilities feature: What is the first thing you should do if you witness a crime? What should you tell the police about a crime you have witnessed? If you are called to testify in court, how should you answer attorneys' questions?

CITIZENSHIP SKILLS AND RESPONSIBILITIES

Witnessing a Crime

▲ Helping law enforcement officials is one of the responsibilities each of us as citizens share. Why do you think many people seek to avoid this responsibility?

Witnessing a crime can be a frightening and intimidating experience. The first reaction is often to run away and forget about it. As a citizen, however, you have a responsibility to help enforce law and order in your community, which in this case may involve identifying yourself as a witness to a crime. If you run away from this responsibility, it may be more difficult to prosecute the criminal, leaving him or her free to commit more crimes and harm more victims in your community. Offering your account as a witness can help make your community and neighborhood a safer place to live.

If you witness a crime, find the nearest phone and call the police immediately, which you can usually do by dialing 911. If the victim needs medical attention, call an ambulance first (also usually by dialing 911). Give the time, place, and the nature of the crime. While you wait for the police or ambulance to arrive, try to remember as many specific details as possible about the crime, the perpetrator (the person who committed the crime), and any vehicle involved. When the police arrive, answer all their questions in as much detail as you can. Do not leave out any details, even if you think they are not important. Also, do not exaggerate or add any personal commentary. If you are asked to sign a testimony, be sure to read what the officer has written and check it for accuracy before you sign.

Chances are you will not be contacted again. You may, however, be called to testify in court. Again, answer the questions as completely and honestly as possible. Do not leave out details and do not exaggerate. The attorney for the defendant will probably cross-examine you. Remember that you are not on trial and do not need to defend yourself. She or he may ask you questions that sound confusing or accusatory, but remember that she or he is only trying to do a job, and is probably trying to bring out any inconsistencies or weaknesses in your testimony. If you answer honestly, directly, briefly, and to the point, you should have no problem. You will have fulfilled your responsibility as a citizen. Remember that crime affects all of us and that each of us is responsible for doing what we can to help keep our communities safe.

TAKING ACTION

1. See if there is a "crime alert" program in your neighborhood. If there is, obtain information on how it works and how you and your household can participate.
2. Many newspapers have a local section that lists the reported crimes in your area. If your newspaper has this regular section, read it for several weeks in a row. Note what percentage of the crimes reported were actually witnessed by someone.
3. The next time you attend a school sporting event with a friend, have each of you spend ten minutes observing what is happening in the crowd around you. The following morning, write down what you observed. Compare your observations with those of your friend. Try to determine why differences might exist in your observations.

Discussion Starter
Guide the students in considering the map, Proposed Sixty-Ninth Assembly District in California: What aspects of this proposal make it a clear example of gerrymandering?

Figure Answer Gerrymandering is attempted so that legislative districts can be drawn in order to guarantee one political party control of a particular voting district and, therefore, control of that district's seat in the legislature.

This figure content is also featured on *West's American Government Videodisc* (see the index found in the *TRB*) and is available in the transparency package.

Reteaching Strategies
1. Have the students form small discussion groups in which to share their responses to the Preview Questions at the beginning of Section 2.
2. Let the students work with partners to write two paragraphs: one explaining the advantages of a unicameral legislature, the other explaining the advantages of a bicameral legislature.

Evaluation Strategies
1. Have the students write their answers to the Section 2 Review questions.
2. Have the students take the Section 2 Quiz found in the *TRB*.

Section 2 Review (Answers)
1. They have followed the pattern of the U.S. Constitution; bicameralism adds checks and balances on the exercise of governmental power and is consistent with the idea of limited government.
2. Urban, more populated, minority, and suburban areas of states benefitted through increased representation.
3. The Court ruled that every state electoral district for both houses of the state legislatures had to be drawn with equal populations.
4. Answers will vary, e.g., with efficient committees and strict organization, such legislatures can be effective.

SECTION 3

Points to Stress
• Length of terms and salaries for members of each house in state legislatures.
• The time and duration of state legislative sessions.
• The distinction between partisan and nonpartisan elections.

Kickoff Activity
Ask the students to spend five minutes listing the names of as many current state legislators as possible. Then encourage the students to compare and discuss their lists.

Caption Answer Generally speaking, state legislators are paid much less than are members of the U.S. Congress.

Proposed Sixty-Ninth Assembly District in California

▲ FIGURE 21–3 **Proposed 69th Assembly District in California.** Although the proposed assembly district above does not exactly resemble a salamander, as did the original gerrymander, it has obviously been drawn for political purposes. Why is such gerrymandering attempted?

21–3 shows how a proposed district was gerrymandered in California. This particular example of gerrymandering was done in an unsuccessful attempt to create a Democratic district in Orange and Los Angeles counties in California.

In spite of continuing attempts to gerrymander, in most states (with the exception of a few rural states) the state legislatures fairly represent the population. Most of the real political power in state politics has moved from the countryside to the cities and suburbs. This shift in political power throughout the states was reflected during the early 1990s when state legislatures in California, Texas, Florida, and other states had to redraw congressional districts for the U.S. House of Representatives in Washington, D.C.

SECTION 2 REVIEW

1. Why have all states but one adopted bicameral legislatures?
2. Which population groups within the states have benefited most from the Supreme Court's decisions in *Baker* v. *Carr* and *Reynolds* v. *Simms*?
3. How have *Baker* v. *Carr* and *Reynolds* v. *Simms* changed the way states are apportioned?
4. **For critical analysis:** Do you think it is possible for a state house of representatives with hundreds of members in it, such as in New Hampshire, to be an effective legislative body? Why or why not?

SECTION 3

State Legislators

Preview Questions
- What are the typical terms of office of state legislators?
- What is the difference between a partisan and nonpartisan election?

State legislators have been criticized as being less professional and less qualified than those in the U.S. Congress. The reality is that most state legislators are paid relatively little and given relatively fewer resources to work with. In almost twenty states legislators are paid less than $10,000 per year. Figure 21–4 on pages 534–35 shows how well your state legislators are paid.

The low salaries for state legislators are partially explained by the fact that, while members of the U.S. Congress have regular, year-round jobs as congressmen or congresswomen, state legislators by contrast, serve actively for erratic periods—full time for a few months and at odd times for the remainder of their terms. This means that state legislators often have other jobs and look upon their legislative duties as a sideline. In some states, such as California and New York, however, there is a trend toward making the job of legislator a full-time and adequately paying job, as well as increasing funding for legislative staff and providing research assistants.

About 40 percent of all state legislators are lawyers or farmers; many others are business executives. Most state legislators move on to other jobs in government

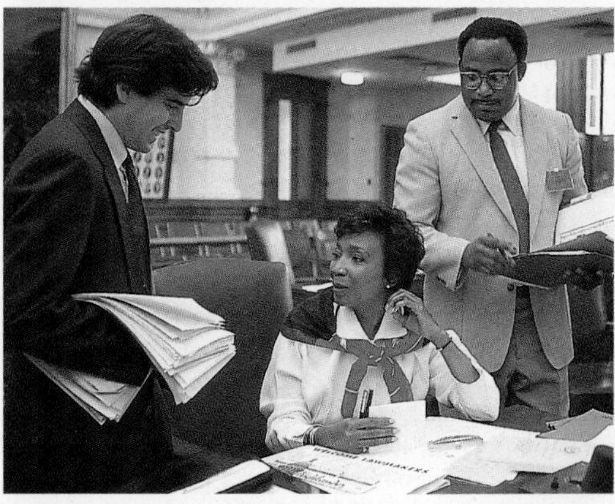

▲ Eddie Bernice Johnson is a member of the Texas State Senate. On average, are state legislators paid like their federal counterparts?

Working with the Preview Questions
Have the students read these study questions and then glance through Section 3, noting where they expect to find the answer to each question. Remind the students to keep these questions in mind as they read and take notes on the section.

Teaching Strategies

Introduction
Have the students read the section introduction, and guide them in studying figure 21–5, Characteristics of State Legislatures. Ask them to locate and consider the information about your state. Then help them consider the information about all the other states: What range of figures can you identify for each category? Where does your state fit within this range? What do you believe accounts for the wide differences among states?

Discussion Starter
Help the students consider the trend toward making the state legislator's position a full-time job: What are the advantages of this trend to legislators? To voters? What disadvantages might each group face because of this trend?

TEACHING GOVERNMENT IN ACTION

Read
As an introduction to this Government in Action feature, you might engage the students in a brief discussion of lobbying: What is lobbying? What do you know about lobbying in our state capital? Conclude the discussion by asking volunteers to read the Government in Action feature aloud to the rest of the class.

Discuss
Guide the students' discussion of the feature with questions such as these: What are the effects of a rapid rise in the number of lobbyists? Are state legislatures "unsophisticated citizen assemblies"? What is the meaning of the title of this feature, The "Congressionalization" of State Legislatures?

Analyze and Apply
Have the students work in groups to investigate the activities of specific lobbying groups in your state capital. Ask the members of each group to prepare and present a chart or written report on their findings.

Review
Ask the students these review questions: What is one of the reasons for the growth of lobbying at the state level? What is one of the problems people associate with lobbying at the state level?

Think About It (Answers)
1. Answers will vary, e.g., state legislators will be more influenced by special interest groups and grow dependent on them for campaign finance.
2. Answers will vary, e.g., state legislatures will become increasingly influenced by pressure groups.

CASE STUDY

The "Congressionalization" of State Legislatures

GOVERNMENT IN ACTION

In the past decade there has been an explosion of lobbyists at the state level, both in numbers and in the range of types. For example, the number of registered lobbyists in Iowa more than doubled between 1984 and 1992.

There are many reasons for this surge in state lobbyists. Deregulation by the federal government has given states a greater role in the regulation of business, banking, consumer affairs, and the environment, which means lobbyists will exert more influence on state legislators to support their causes. For example, the prospect that the state might institute new regulations on automobile rentals in Florida prompted car-rental companies to hire more than forty lobbyists in Tallahassee in 1990. Another reason for greater state lobbying is the drying up of federal funds. With funding for many programs now in the hands of the states, lobbyists have even more reason to seek support in state legislatures.

Some observers believe this proliferation of lobbyists at the state level is fundamentally altering the character of state legislatures, which for a long time were regarded as unsophisticated citizen assemblies. Some believe that candidates for state offices will increasingly turn to lobbyists for money, which will lead to some of the campaign finance problems seen on the national level.

THINK ABOUT IT

1. Is there anything wrong with having more lobbyists working in state governments? Explain.
2. How could the increase in state lobbyists alter the character of state legislatures?

and the private sector after serving their term. In other words, there is a higher rate of turnover among state legislators, compared to the lengthy careers of members of the U.S. Congress.

Terms of State Legislators

You can see in Figure 21–4 that legislators serve either two-year or four-year terms. As with the U.S. Congress, state senators are often elected for longer terms than are state representatives. In all but four states—Alabama, Louisiana, Maryland, and Mississippi—representatives are chosen for two-year terms. In any given year, more than 25 percent of the 7,500 state legislators in the country are serving their first term in office.

The Election Process

In every state, legislators are chosen by popular vote. Typically, candidates for the state legislature are nominated in party primaries (discussed in Chapter 10). The general election is typically partisan—held along political party lines—pitting a Democratic party candidate for representative or senator against a Republican party candidate. In a few states, including Delaware, legislative candidates are chosen in conventions. (In Nebraska's unicameral system, candidates are nominated in nonpartisan primaries in which no party affiliation is used for candidates.)

Most states have elections for state legislators in November in even-numbered years. The exceptions are Louisiana, Mississippi, New Jersey, and Virginia, in which elections are held in odd-numbered years. In Louisiana elections are held in October of odd-numbered years. In those four states, the goal has been to separate state and local issues from national politics. One result has been relatively lower voter turnout for elections in those four states than in the other forty-six states, in which both national and state elections are held at the same time.

When the Legislature Meets

Most states have annual legislative sessions. You can see from Figure 21–4, however, that there are some exceptions. Texas is the largest state whose legislature still meets **biennially** (every two years). In the 1990s

Extension
Ask the students to recall (or find out) how legislators are chosen in your state: How efficiently does this system seem to run? What are its main advantages? What are the disadvantages associated with this particular system?

Discussion Starter
Help the students consider the interest of some states in separating their political issues from national politics: Why do you imagine these states want to make this kind of break? Who benefits from separating state and local politics from national politics? How do those groups and individuals benefit? What disadvantages might be associated with this kind of separation? Why?

Figure Answer New Hampshire has the most seats in its House of Representatives with 400. As pointed out in the footnote on page 549, New Hampshire's House of Representatives has at least one member for each town, regardless of population. With 400 members, it is the third largest legislature in the English-speaking world, topped only by the U.S. Congress and the British House of Commons.

Characteristics of State Legislatures

	Seats in Senate	Length of Term	Seats in House	Length of Term	Years Sessions Are Held	Salary[1]
Alabama	35	4	105	4	annual	$ 10 (d)
Alaska	20	4	40	2	annual	22,140
Arizona	30	2	60	2	annual	15,000
Arkansas	35	4	100	2	odd	7,500[2]
California	40	4	80	2	even	40,816
Colorado	35	4	65	2	annual	17,500
Connecticut	36	2	151	2	annual	16,760
Delaware	21	4	41	2	annual	23,282
Florida	40	4	120	2	annual	21,684
Georgia	56	2	180	2	annual	10,000
Hawaii	25	4	51	2	annual	27,000
Idaho	42	2	84	2	annual	30 (d)
Illinois	59	—[3]	118	2	annual	35,661
Indiana	50	4	100	2	annual	11,600
Iowa	50	4	100	2	annual	16,600
Kansas	40	4	125	2	annual	52 (d)
Kentucky	38	4	100	2	even	100 (d)
Louisiana	39	4	105	4	annual	16,800[2]
Maine	35	2	151	2	even	7,500[4]
Maryland	47	4	141	4	annual	25,000
Massachusetts	40	2	160	2	annual	30,000
Michigan	38	4	110	2	annual	45,450
Minnesota	67	4	134	2	odd	26,395
Mississippi	52	4	122	4	annual	10,000
Missouri	34	4	163	2	annual	22,414

[1] Salaries annual unless otherwise noted as (d), per day, or (b), biennium (per two-year period).
[2] Plus per day.
[3] Terms vary from two to four years.
[4] For odd year, $4,000 for even year.
[5] Unicameral legislation.

▲ **FIGURE 21–4 Characteristics of State Legislatures.** This table examines state legislatures. Which state has the most seats in its legislature?

Enrichment
Ask one of the students to research answers to these questions: How often does your state legislature meet in regular sessions? When? Is there a limit on the number of days for each regular session? If so, what is that limit? How can special sessions be called? When were the most recent special sessions? With what issues did the legislators deal during those special sessions? Does your state allow for a veto session? If so, how often has it been used in the past two decades? Let the volunteer prepare and present a chart summarizing the answers to these questions.

Characteristics of State Legislatures (continued)

	Seats in Senate	Length of Term	Seats in House	Length of Term	Years Sessions Are Held	Salary[1]
Montana	50	—[3]	100	2	odd	52,13 (d)
Nebraska[5]	49	4	—	—	annual	12,000
Nevada	21	4	42	2	odd	104 (d)
New Hampshire	24	2	400	2	annual	200 (b)
New Jersey	40	—[3]	80	2	annual	35,000
New Mexico	42	4	70	2	annual	75 (d)
New York	61	4	150	2	annual	57,500
North Carolina	50	4	120	2	odd	11,124
North Dakota	53	2	100	2	odd	90 (d)
Ohio	33	4	99	2	annual	31,659
Oklahoma	48	4	101	2	annual	32,000
Oregon	30	2	60	2	odd	11,868
Pennsylvania	50	4	203	2	annual	47,000
Rhode Island	50	2	100	2	annual	5 (d)
South Carolina	46	4	124	2	annual	10,000
South Dakota	35	2	70	2	annual	4,267
Tennessee	33	4	99	2	odd	16,500
Texas	31	4	150	2	odd	7,200[2]
Utah	29	4	75	2	annual	65 (d)
Vermont	30	2	150	2	odd	6,750
Virginia	40	4	100	2	annual	18,000
Washington	49	4	98	2	annual	17,900
West Virginia	34	4	100	2	annual	6,500
Wisconsin	33	4	99	2	annual	32,239
Wyoming	30	4	64	2	annual	75 (d)

[1] Salaries annual unless otherwise noted as (d), per day, or (b), biennium (per two-year period).
[2] Plus per day.
[3] Terms vary from two to four years.
[4] For odd year, $4,000 for even year.
[5] Unicameral legislation.
Source: Adapted from *Book of the States*, 1989-90 (Lexington, Kentucky: Council of State Governments, 1990)

Developing Skills for the Information Age

Actions of state legislatures receive media coverage from national news sources when legislation is pending that might have nation-wide ramifications, such as a bill outlawing abortion. Everyday business is left to regional or local news organizations.

One of the criticisms of local news agencies is that they do not have qualified political reporters on staff. Have students arrange to interview writers and editors who are responsible for political coverage in local papers. The same may be done for television and radio stations which cover local and state politics. Encourage students to read as many stories as possible before they conduct their interview. Students need to prepare questions in advance, dealing with the following areas: Educational background, prior experience, sources of information, opinions on the legislature, quality of readership, and ways to improve political coverage. Students should complete an essay in support of or against the quality of local political coverage.

Reteaching Strategies

1. Let the students work in groups to review and revise the notes they have taken on Section 3.

2. Have the students work with partners to write, in their own words, definitions of these terms: *partisan primaries, non-partisan primaries, special session, veto session.*

Evaluation Strategies

1. Have the students write their answers to the Section 3 Review questions.

2. Have the students take the Section 3 Quiz found in the *TRB.*

Section 3 Review (Answers)

1. Most states have elections for state legislatures in November of even-numbered years.

2. Most state legislatures meet annually.

3. Answers will vary according to the pay scale in your state and student attitudes. Note that it is often argued that the greater the pay the less a legislator is likely to be influenced by money from interest groups.

SECTION 4

Points to Stress

- The legislative leaders in your state.
- The types of committees used by state legislatures and their importance.

Kickoff Activity

As an introduction to Section 4, have the students create quick organizational charts showing their understanding of the organization of their state legislature. When all the students have completed their charts, let them work briefly in small groups to compare and discuss their ideas.

Working with the Preview Questions

After the students have read and briefly discussed these study questions, instruct them to read Section 4 and take notes, keeping these questions in mind.

Teaching Strategies

Introduction

Let the students read this brief section introduction. Then encourage discussion by asking questions such as these: How do you think the organization of our state legisla-

Kentucky, Minnesota, Montana, Nevada, North Carolina, North Dakota, Oregon, Tennessee, and Vermont also began meeting on a biennial basis. In California the legislature runs a continuous two-year session.

Over three-fourths of the states have limited their regular sessions to a specific number of days, ranging from 20 to 180. Other states effectively limit the length of sessions by paying legislators in such a way that their payment expires after a stated period.

In addition to regular sessions, the governors of most states may call legislators into a **special session**, which allows the state legislature to take up urgent matters such as revising the budget or eliminating a special tax.

Eight states allow a type of special session called a **veto session** to be held soon after each regular session. In Connecticut, Hawaii, Louisiana, Missouri, New Jersey, Utah, Virginia, and Washington, legislators can reconsider bills vetoed by the governor and attempt to override the governor's veto, if enough popular support within the legislature exists. (See Chapter 23 for more information on the governor's veto power.)

Section 3 Review

1. When do most states hold their general elections?
2. How often do the legislatures in most states meet?
3. **For critical analysis:** Do you think the legislators in your state are being paid too little? Too much? What difference do you think it would make if their salaries were changed? Give reasons for your answers.

SECTION 4

How the Legislature Is Organized

Preview Questions

- Who are the leaders in a state legislature?
- What types of committees are used by state legislatures? Why are they important?

Most state legislatures are organized in a manner similar to the U.S. Congress. They use presiding officers, committee systems, and legislative aides.

The Officers

Normally, those who preside over the sessions of state legislative chambers are powerful political figures. In all states except Nebraska, the lower house of the legislature elects its own presiding officer, known as the **speaker**. In the majority of states the popularly elected **lieutenant governor** is the president of the senate. (There are fifteen states in which the lieutenant governor does not double as the president of the senate. In these states the senators choose their own presiding officers.)

The powers of the presiding officers are basically the same in all states. Speakers appoint committees, as do most presidents of the senates. Presiding officers in most states have the ability to control the business in that chamber. They decide to which committee a bill will go, and which bills will be considered on the floor. They enforce the rules during debate, and control who speaks in debates. Typically, because the speaker of the house is a political leader, he or she has more weight than the president of the senate. This is because the president of the senate is usually a lieutenant governor who has been chosen by the people rather than by the members of the senate.

The Committee System

There are three types of committees used in state legislatures: standing, joint, and interim.

Standing Committees Most of the work of state legislatures is done through **standing committees** in each house, also referred to as permanent committees. Standing committees sort out the bills that should reach the floor for debate, and inform each chamber's members what business has been carried on within the committees. Standing committees are normally organized around areas such as education, local government, highways, and the environment. The number of standing committees varies from nine in Alaska to over thirty in other states. The number of members per committee varies from ten to forty, with the average being about twelve.

It is in standing committees that proposed bills are given the closest attention. A committee may amend or rewrite a bill, or ignore it altogether (which is the usual procedure, because 500 to several thousand bills are typically introduced in state legislatures).

Because standing committees do the most important work of the legislature, a good committee assignment is quite desirable. Legislators wage political battle in order to be assigned to a good committee. Seniority and political influence are the major factors in determining assignments, which are usually made by the speaker of the house or the president of the senate. Speakers may use committee appointments to repay political debts incurred ture is similar to that of the U.S. Congress?

Comprehension
Let volunteers identify the speaker and the lieutenant governor of your state.

Vocabulary
Ask one of the students to explain the meaning of the phrase *has more weight:* In what sense does the speaker of the house usually have more weight than the president of the Senate?

Enrichment
Have a group of volunteers prepare and display a chart of the standing committees in your state legislature.

Discussion Starter
Focus the students' attention on the fact that some bills introduced into the state legislature may be completely ignored: What is your reaction to this fact? Why do you think bills that will undoubtedly be ignored are nonetheless introduced? Who benefits from such activities? Who loses time—and money—as a result? Should restrictions be made on the introduction of bills into the state legislature? Why or why not?

Extension
Have the students find and discuss the answers to these questions: Does your state legislature include joint committees? If so, what functions do those committees serve? How do state joint committees compare to the joint committees of the U.S. Congress?

Extension
Ask the students to find out whether your state legislature uses interim committees. If not, why not? If so, when and for what particular purposes?

Caption Answer Answers will vary, e.g., this system of organization has proven to be a rational way to organize the workload.

Most state legislatures are organized in a manner similar to the United States Congress with presiding officers, committee systems, and legislative staffs. Why do you think these similarities exist?

during campaigns for the speakership. Special interest groups may lobby hard to get a favorite legislator assigned to an important committee that affects their clients.

Joint Committees **Joint committees** are another form of standing committees, but these are made up of members of both chambers of the legislature. Massachusetts, Maine, and Connecticut have used joint committees effectively for years. (Maine and Connecticut use *only* joint committees.) Over 50 percent of state legislatures have one or more joint committees. Joint committees in all bicameral legislatures have to be set up to deal with the problems of administering certain legislative details, such as reconciling and making identical the two versions of the same bill before it is sent to the governor to be signed.

Interim Committees Because state legislatures are not continuously in session, the use of **interim committees** has become more popular. Interim committees study particular problems while the state legislature is out of session, and report their findings and recommendations to the next session. Some states have emergency boards that are similar to interim committees. Oregon, for example, has an emergency board that has specific power over state budget matters when the legislature is not in session.

Multidiscipline Strategies

Math How accurately is the diversity of our state's population reflected by the membership of our state's legislature? Have the students work in groups to gather information in response to this question. Let the group members work together to decide what specific questions on this topic they want to answer and then to collect information in answer to those questions. Finally, ask the group members to present their information in a graph to be displayed to the rest of the class.

Discussion Starter
Guide the students in considering the increase in staff size that has taken place in most state legislatures: Why do you think staff size has increased so markedly over the past three decades? What are the advantages of these increases in staff service? What possible disadvantages might be associated with the increases?

Reteaching Strategies
1. Let the students work in small groups to review and revise the organizational charts they drew for the Kickoff Activity to include important committees. Then have the group members work together to plan and draw a new chart showing the organization of your state legislature.
2. Ask the students to work with partners in going over the notes they took on Section 4. Remind the students to refer to the text to resolve any questions, and encourage them to make additions or corrections to their own notes.

Evaluation Strategies
1. Have the students write their answers to the Section 4 Review questions.
2. Have the students take the Section 4 Quiz found in the *TRB*.

Section 4 Review (Answers)
1. The lower house elects its speaker, and in the majority of states, a popularly elected lieutenant governor is the president of the Senate.
2. Standing committees are permanent and do most of the work. They are organized around areas such as education, highways, and the environment. Joint committees are made up from both chambers of the legislature. Interim committees study particular problems while the state legislature is out of session.
3. Answers will vary, e.g., as legislators have increased the size of their staffs, they have been better able to tailor their efforts to meet the specific needs of their constituents.

SECTION 5

Points to Stress
- The steps necessary for a bill to become a state law.
- The sources of bills at the state level.
- The number of bills introduced each year at the state level.

Kickoff Activity
Pose this question to the students: How is the process by which a bill becomes law different in your state from that process in the U.S. Congress? Give the students five minutes to write their answers to this question; then encourage them to compare and discuss their ideas.

Working with the Preview Questions
Have the students read and discuss these study questions. Then ask them to use these questions as a guide in writing outlines of Section 5.

Legislative Assistance

As mentioned before, an important aspect of most state legislatures is the use of legislative aides. In an attempt to help legislators understand the complexity of the legislation needed, legislative councils were used from 1930 to 1965. These councils were made up of experts who provided research for the legislators. Their role has been that of fact finders.

Since 1965, however, individual legislators have increased their staff size. Legislative aides now regularly do the research and analytical services that were once provided by legislative councils.

Additionally, most state legislatures have bill-drafting services, which attempt to prevent loopholes in proposed legislation. They also attempt to change bills so as to avoid future potential trouble in the courts. Bill-drafting agencies typically operate between state legislative sessions.

Section 4 Review

1. What officer normally presides over a state lower house? Upper house?
2. What types of committees are used by state legislatures? Why are they important?
3. **For critical analysis:** Why do you think state legislatures gradually stopped using legislative councils in favor of their own legislative aides?

Section 5

How a State Bill Becomes Law

Preview Questions

- What are the necessary steps for a bill to become law in a state legislature?
- Which groups of people suggest bills to state legislators?
- How many bills are introduced each year at the state level?

Legislatures exist to make laws. The lawmaking machinery in the state legislatures is similar to that used in Congress. Figure 21–5 shows how an idea becomes first a bill and eventually a law in one state. (This procedure is similar to the one discussed in Chapter 14.)

As you can see, a bill becomes a law at the state level after going through an elaborate process, just as happens with bills in the U.S. Congress. A bill must pass first to a house committee and then to the whole house for a vote. Next it normally goes to a senate committee and then is voted on by the full senate. Finally, if it has survived thus far, it lands on the governor's desk for signature. But just as in the U.S. Congress, few bills make it through this process very easily. Most do not reach the finish line.

During any legislative session, thousands of bills are introduced. It has been estimated that approximately one hundred thousand bills are introduced in the fifty state legislatures in any one calendar year. But the number of bills introduced in any one state varies dramatically. New York might have twenty-five times more bills introduced than a state such as Utah.

When the governor signs a bill, it becomes a law in that state. In all states except North Carolina, the governor may also choose to veto a bill. When this happens, legislators can attempt to override the veto by passing the bill again with a majority vote in each house, but in most cases the governor's veto normally holds. Less than 5 percent of all vetoed bills are overridden in state legislatures.

Where State Bills Come From

At the national level, the source of bills in either house of Congress is congressional members themselves. The same is true with state legislators. Thus, with both legislative bodies, legislators are the source of legislation. Only a legislator may actually introduce a bill in the house or senate of a state legislature. In reality, however, it is the lobbyists who will often suggest to legislators that certain bills be introduced. Additionally, the governor, similar to the president of the United States, is another major source of ideas for potential bills. Finally, administrators in state and local government agencies may suggest various bills to legislators.

Section 5 Review

1. Who may introduce a bill in a state legislature?
2. Who are the people who suggest bills to state legislators?
3. How many bills are introduced at the state level each year?
4. What percentage of vetoed bills are overridden by state legislators?
5. **For critical analysis:** How do you think our system of democracy would be affected if citizens could directly introduce bills at the state level?

Teaching Strategies

Introduction
Let a volunteer read the brief section introduction aloud, and guide the students in studying the figure, How a State Bill Becomes a Law. Focus attention on each step in the process: What makes this step in the process significant? What are the options for the next step in the process? What particular problems might supporters—or opponents—of a bill face at each stage?

Cooperative Learning
Divide the class into groups, and have the members of each group explore the specific process through which a bill must pass in your state legislature in order to become a law. Ask the group members to record the process in a chart, a table, or a brief written report.

Extension
You may want to have the students find the answers to these questions: How many bills were introduced in your state legislature during the last session? Of those bills, how many became laws?

Enrichment
Ask a volunteer to research and report the answers to these questions: Why does the governor of North Carolina have no veto power? How is the balance of power between the executive branch and the legislative branch maintained without that veto?

Reteaching Strategies
1. Work with small groups of students as they review the answers they wrote to the question posed in the Kickoff Activity: How would you revise your answer now? What have you learned about the functioning of your state legislature?
2. Let the students work in groups to review and revise their outlines of Section 5.

Evaluation Strategies
1. Have the students write their answers to the Section 5 Review questions.
2. Have the students take the Section 5 Quiz found in the *TRB.*

Section 5 Review (Answers)
1. Only a legislator can actually introduce a bill in the legislature.
2. Lobbyists, the governor, and agencies of state and local government.
3. It has been estimated that approximately 100,000 bills are introduced in the 50 state legislatures in one year.
4. Less than 5 percent.
5. Answers will vary, e.g., the system would be too complicated and time-consuming if people directly introduced legislation. People can suggest legislation to their legislators.

Figure Answer Students should understand that the role of the conference committee at the state level is similar to that at the national level, where members from both houses meet to iron out differences between the House and Senate versions of similar bills so that one bill can be approved by both houses.

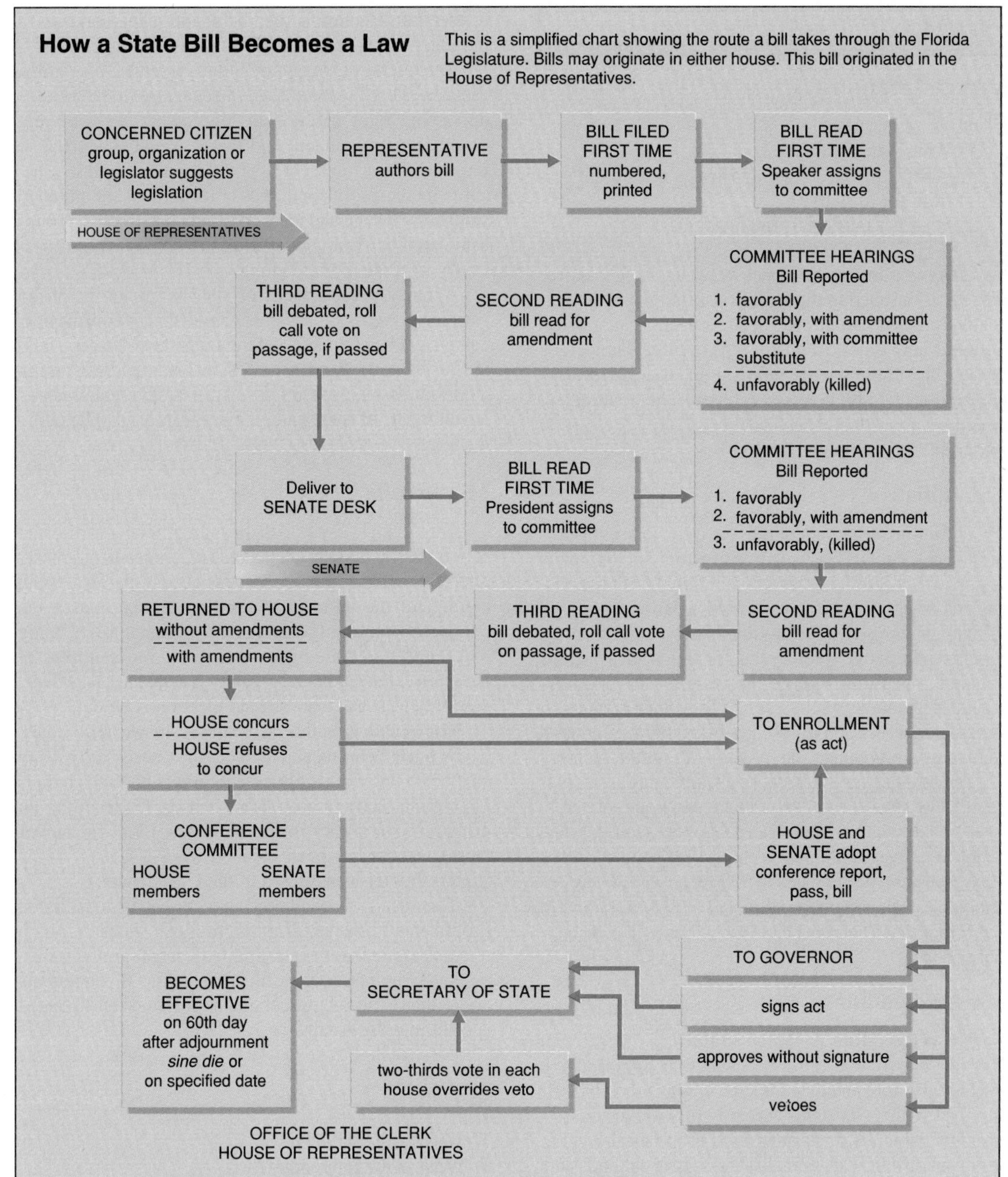

▲ **FIGURE 21–5 How a State Bill Becomes a Law.** The flow chart above describes the general process through which a state bill becomes a law. As you can see, this chart has been modeled on the process in the Florida legislature. What is the function of the conference committee in this process?

SECTION 6

Points to Stress
- The definition of the initiative.
- The definition of referendum and its difference from the initiative.
- The purpose of the recall.

Kickoff Activity
Ask the students to write short paragraphs explaining the concept of direct democracy. When everyone has finished writing, have volunteers read their answers aloud, and encourage the students to compare and discuss their ideas about direct democracy.

Working with the Preview Questions
Have a volunteer read the three study questions aloud; let the students discuss what they already know in response to each. Then ask the students to keep these questions in mind as they read and take notes on Section 6.

Teaching Strategies

Introduction
After the students have read the section introduction, encourage a brief discussion: Why do you think voters want to feel that they have some direct control of their government?

Extension
Ask the students to recall (or research) answers to these questions: Is the referendum used in our state? If so, how? What are some examples of its recent use? If not, why not?

Critical Thinking Skills
Encourage the students to analyze the argument that use of the referendum weakens legislative responsibility: How could the referendum do that? Do you think it actually does? What relationship—if any—can you identify between this weakening of legislative responsibility and the growing popularity of referendum-use among citizens?

Reteaching Strategies
1. Have the students work with partners to review their notes on Section 6. Remind them to refer to the text to resolve any questions.
2. Work with small groups of students, guiding them in discussing responses to this question: How does direct democracy work in our state?

Evaluation Strategies
1. Have the students write their answers to the Section 6 Review questions.
2. Have the students take the Section 6 Quiz found in the *TRB.*

Section 6 Review (Answers)
1. A method available to voters for proposing new laws which bypasses legislatures. The first step usually involves circulating a petition to place an issue on the ballot so that it can be voted on by the people of the state.

SECTION 6

Direct Democracy

Preview Questions
- What is the initiative?
- What is the referendum? How is it different from the initiative?
- For what purpose is the recall used?

There is a major difference between the legislative process as outlined in the U.S. Constitution and the legislative process as outlined in the various state constitutions. Many states exercise a type of direct democracy through the initiative, the referendum, and the recall—procedures that allow voters to control the government directly. Direct democracy at the state level was first started in Oregon before the 1920s.

The Initiative

The **initiative** lets citizens bypass legislatures by proposing new statutes or changes in government for citizen approval. It is similar to the constitutional initiative discussed on page 528, but is used for new laws, as opposed to changing the state constitution. Most states that allow for citizen initiatives require that the initiative's backers circulate a petition to place the issue on the ballot. A certain percentage of the registered voters in the last gubernatorial election must sign the petition. If enough signatures are obtained, the issue is put on the ballot.

Twenty-one states use the legislative initiative, typically those states in which political parties are relatively weak and in which nonpartisan groups are strong. Some major initiatives that have been passed include a 1982 Massachusetts requirement that voters approve any future nuclear plant construction; and a 1990 initiative in California that limits the number of terms a legislator can serve.

The Referendum

The **referendum** is similar to the initiative, except that the issue (or constitutional change) is proposed first by the legislature and then directed to the voters for their approval. Thirty-six states currently provide for the referendum, which is most often used at the local level to approve local school bond issues and to amend state constitutions. In a number of states that provide for the referendum, a bill passed by the legislature may be "put on hold" by obtaining petitions with the required number of signatures from voters who oppose it. A statewide referendum election is then held, and if the majority of the voters disapprove of the bill, it is no longer valid.

The referendum was not initially intended for regular use. Indeed, it has been used infrequently in the past. Its opponents argue that it is an unnecessary check on representative government and that it weakens legislative responsibility. In recent years, the referendum has become increasingly popular as citizens have attempted to control their state and local governments. Interest groups have been active in sponsoring the petition drives necessary to force a referendum.

A fairly regular focus of state referenda has been various versions of an amendment that would bestow equal rights on women. Referendum elections were held in Florida and Nevada in 1978, in Iowa in 1980, and in Vermont in 1986 on proposals for a state equal rights amendment. In each state, the proposal was rejected by the voters.

The Recall

The **recall**—a vote to dismiss an official—is directed at public officials who are deemed incompetent or grossly unethical in their conduct. Voters may circulate a petition calling for the removal of such an official, and if the petition obtains a sufficient number of signatures (usually that number is quite high—it may be, for example, 25 percent of the number of votes cast in the last gubernatorial election), then a recall election is held.

The recall is authorized mainly in western states. Being placed on a recall ballot does not necessarily mean an elected person is guilty of anything, although charges of criminal activity are often a reason for recalling an official. So far, only former governor Lynn Frazier of North Dakota has been recalled from office, in 1922. (Later, Frazier was elected to the U.S. Senate.)

The recall is often used as a threat to legislators. Proponents of the recall in the fourteen states in which it exists argue that the possibility of recall prevents outrageously inappropriate official behavior. Its opponents argue that it makes officeholders prey to well-financed special interest groups.

SECTION 6 REVIEW

1. What is the initiative?
2. What is the referendum?
3. When is a recall used?
4. **For critical analysis:** How do you think the existence of the initiative, the referendum, and the recall affects the political behavior of state officials?

2. A method similar to the initiative, except that the issue is proposed first by the legislature and then directed to the voters for their approval.
3. When public officials are deemed incompetent or grossly unethical in their conduct.
4. Answers will vary, e.g., each one gives the voters more power and might cause the legislators to heed the wishes of the voters more carefully and diligently.

TEACHING CHALLENGE TO THE AMERICAN DREAM

Read

Introduce this feature by having the students read and respond to the Challenge to the American Dream title: How long do some legislators retain their positions in state legislatures? What problems are associated with such long stays? What benefits might also be associated with lengthy stays? After this introductory discussion, ask the students to listen as volunteers read the Challenge to the American Dream feature aloud.

Discuss

Ask questions such as these to guide the students in discussing the feature: Why do you think incumbents are so regularly reelected? What is the "old boy" network? How do lobbyists "invest" in legislators? Who benefits from such investments? Does public opinion in your state seem to support limitations on the terms served by legislators?

Analyze and Apply

Have all the students work together to interview local voters on term limits for state legislators. The students should plan and prepare a specific interview form, decide who should be interviewed, conduct the interviews according to their plan, and then organize the information they gather. Encourage the students to publish their findings in a school newspaper.

Review

Ask questions such as these to help the students review this Challenge to the American Dream feature: Which state legislators are most likely to keep their positions for 20 years or more? What is one of the major arguments in favor of term limitations for state legislators? What is one of the major arguments against such term limitations?

You Decide (Answers)

1. Answers will vary, e.g., to break up the "old-boy" networks in legislatures and not give legislatures a chance to become dependent on lobbyists.
2. Lobbyists will have more influence on the naiveté of new legislators. It will upset the balance between the legislature and the governor.
3. Answers will vary, e.g., yes, the same arguments apply because the same negative influences by special interest groups affect legislatures at all levels of government.
4. Answers will vary, e.g., there should not be term limitations at any level. The people should be the judge of whether or not an incumbent should be reelected.

CHALLENGE TO THE AMERICAN DREAM

Limiting Lengthy Stays in the State Legislature

In the United States Congress, incumbents are reelected more than 90 percent of the time, leading to very lengthy stays in the federal legislature. The situation is not exactly the same in state legislatures. Those who do not hold leadership positions in state legislatures generally leave within ten years and move on to another career. Those who hold leadership positions—party leaders and committee chairpersons—often keep their seats for twenty years or more.

The voters in California struck at the heart of the professional state legislature by approving with a 52 percent majority Proposition 140 in 1990. That initiative sets strict limits on the number of years any state officeholder, from governor to superintendent of education, can serve. Anyone whose office calls for a four-year term (including all forty state senators) will be allowed to serve only two terms. The eighty state assemblypersons who are elected for two-year terms can hold office for three terms only. Once a state officeholder has finished his or her time, he or she will not be allowed to return to the same office.

Those who supported Proposition 140 claimed that it would clean up the "old-boy network" that dominated the California state legislature. They were right. Immediately after Proposition 140 was passed, the majority floor leader of the lower body, Tom Hannighan, announced his retirement. The assembly speaker *pro tem,* Michael Roos, indicated he was considering retirement. The speaker of the assembly, Willie Brown, estimated that 40 percent of his colleagues would retire when their terms were up. In addition, approximately 700 of the legislature's 2500 staff members were expected to retire.

Lobbyists responded to the proposition immediately, claiming that they were losing their "investments"—long-time incumbents with whom they had developed working relationships and who understood their particular interests.

Those against Proposition 140 argued that the success of the initiative would help rather than hinder special interests and their lobbyists. Skillful lobbyists will now be able to exploit the inexperience of novice politicians, of which there will be many due to the term limitations. Others argue that term limitations will upset the balance of power between the governor and the legislature. According to this argument, only an experienced legislator aided by a savvy research staff can offset the tremendous power that the governor holds. Still others point out that legislators who have a limited time in office may waste more of the public's money because they don't have to worry about future consequences.

California was not the first state to have its citizens approve term limitation for its legislators. Oklahoma and Colorado had already done the same. The trend may be strengthened by the national debate over term limitation for representatives and senators in Washington, D.C.

With or without term limits, it is apparent that citizens are looking to take steps to ensure that elected representatives do indeed reflect the wishes and attitudes of their constituents. As you've learned in this chapter, term limits is only one of the steps currently being considered around the country. You read in Section 3 of this chapter that there is also a trend toward making the job of state legislator a full-time, adequately compensated position. The challenge to the American dream is to have experienced but dedicated state legislators run each government with the public good in mind at all times.

You Decide

1. What are the arguments in favor of term limitation?
2. What are the arguments against term limitation?
3. Do you think the same arguments can apply at the state and national levels?
4. Do you think there should be term limitation for every elected government official at all levels—local, state, and federal? Why or why not?

Observable Mastery

Divide the class into five groups for the purpose of conducting research and presenting information to the class on your state legislature. Assign to each group one of the following areas for study: The nature of your state's constitutions, your state legislative structure and process, the organization of your state legislature, how a bill becomes a law at your state level, and examples of the initiative, referendum, and/or recall in your state.

Students can present the information orally, or if time does not allow, they may create visuals to reflect their findings that can be displayed in the classroom.

Chapter Evaluation

To evaluate student mastery of chapter material, you might:

1. Use Chapter Test A from the *TRB*.
2. Use Chapter Test B from the *TRB*.
3. Construct your own test using items from the *West American Government Test Bank* found in the *TRB*.
4. Use the accompanying computerized test software to construct and print a customized chapter test.

Review Questions (Answers)

1. The power to spend and to regulate intrastate commerce and the general police power.
2. The length reflects the loss of popular confidence in state legislatures between the end of the Civil War and the early 1900s. Also framers at the state level had difficulty distinguishing between constitutional law and statutory law and many statutory laws were put into constitutions.
3. A preamble; a bill of rights; an outline of the framework of government; a listing of state powers and responsibilities; a provision for local government; an amendment clause that details the methods of formal constitutional change.
4. By constitutional convention, by legislative activity, or by popular initiative.
5. States follow the national pattern; they add to the checks and balances on the exercise of governmental power; and they are consistent with the idea of limited government.
6. Critics argue that a unicameral legislature would be more responsible for its action. Interest groups can more easily kill proposed legislation in a bicameral legislation. Legislators in a unicameral legislature could give more full-time service.

CHAPTER 21 REVIEW

Key Terms

apportionment 530
biennially 533
constitutional initiative 528
extraordinary majority 528
hyperpluralism 521
initiative 540
interim committees 537
intrastate commerce 521
joint committees 537
lieutenant governor 536
police power 521
reapportionment 530
recall 540
referendum 540
speaker 536
special session 536
standing committees 536
veto session 536

Summary

1. The U.S. Constitution reserves powers to the state, which means states may do anything that the Constitution does not prohibit them from doing, or that is not expressly reserved for the federal government. No state or local law may be in conflict with the U.S. Constitution, with laws made by the United States Congress, or with treaties entered into by the federal government. State constitutions are typically lengthy and detailed. They usually include a preamble, a bill of rights, an outline of the framework of government, a listing of the state's powers and responsibilities, a provision for local government, and an amending clause that details the methods of formal constitutional change.

2. Bicameralism exists in all state legislatures except Nebraska, which has a unicameral legislature. The size of state legislatures varies dramatically. Each state's constitution provides for a system of apportionment—how seats are distributed among the districts of a state. A long-standing pattern of rural overrepresentation ended with the Supreme Court decision *Baker* v. *Carr* (1962). Since that case, the Court has consistently held that the Fourteenth Amendment's equal protection clause requires that electoral districts in each state contain equal numbers of persons.

3. Most state legislators are paid relatively little and are given few resources with which to work. They serve either two-year or four-year terms. In every state, legislators are chosen by popular vote. Most states have annual legislative sessions, but some meet biennially.

4. Most state legislatures are organized in a manner similar to the U.S. Congress. In all states except Nebraska, the lower house of the legislature elects its own presiding officer, known as the speaker. In a majority of states, the popularly elected lieutenant governor is president of the senate. As in Congress, a major share of the legislature's work is done in committees.

5. The lawmaking machinery in the state legislatures is similar to that used in Congress.

6. Many states exercise direct democracy through several methods. The initiative technique lets citizens bypass legislatures by proposing new statutes or changes in government for citizen approval. The referendum is an issue that is first proposed by the legislature and then directed to the voters for their approval. The recall is a petition by the citizens calling for the removal of a public official deemed incompetent or grossly unethical in conduct.

Review Questions

1. What are the major powers reserved to the states?
2. Why are most state constitutions long and detailed?
3. Which basic elements are included in each state's constitution?
4. What are the three ways in which a state constitution may be amended?
5. Why are all but one of the fifty state legislatures bicameral?
6. What are the criticisms of bicameralism?
7. How was the imbalance between urban and rural representation in state districts resolved?
8. What are the terms and salaries of your state legislators?
9. Who are the presiding officers in the state legislatures? What are their chief powers?
10. Briefly describe the functions and importance of the three types of committees used in state legislatures.

7. *Baker* v. *Carr* and *Reynolds* v. *Sims* ensured that every state electoral district for both houses had to be drawn with equal populations.
8. Answers will vary according to your state.
9. Answers will vary according to your state.
10. Most of the work is done in permanent standing committees based on subject areas. Joint committees are another form of standing committee, but are made up of members from both chambers. Interim committees study particular problems.
11. They allow the voters to bypass state legislatures if need be.
12. Phone the police, usually by dialing 9-1-1. If the victim needs medical attention, call an ambulance. Remember as many specific details as possible. Answer questions by the police in as much detail as you can, but do not exaggerate.
13. Answers will vary, e.g., those for term limitations argue that it will break up the "old boy" network. Those against term limitations argue that it would help rather than hinder special interests, that it will upset the balance between the governor and the legislature, and that legislators may waste the public's money even more.

Questions for Thought and Discussion (Answers)

1. Answers will vary, e.g., every state needs its own constitution because every state has its own needs. The framework of government and the states' powers and responsibilities have to be set forth in a written constitution.
2. Answers will vary by state.
3. Answers will vary, e.g., legislators might feel they are working long hours, but accomplishing very little. They might feel their hard work goes unappreciated because of the numerous complaints from constituents. They may need to seek other forms of employment in order to support themselves and their families.
4. Answers will vary by state.

Social Studies Skills (Answers)

1. All states but two on the left-hand side of the map have some provision in the state constitution for calling for a state constitutional convention. The majority of states in the West require a two-thirds majority.
2. There is no easily discernible pattern to the way the states on the right-hand side of the map are colored. Thus, there is no way to easily describe their similarities or differences.

CHAPTER 21 REVIEW—Continued

11. What functions do the initiative, the referendum, and the recall serve?
12. What are the main actions you should take if you witness a crime?
13. What are the arguments for and against limitations of terms in the state legislature?

Questions for Thought and Discussion

1. Do you think every state needs its own constitution? Why or why not?
2. What qualifications do you think are important for a state legislator? To what issues and problems do you think a legislator in your state should pay particular attention?
3. The turnover rate of state legislators is fairly high due to the low salary and part-time nature of their work. What might be some other reasons for this high turnover rate? How might this problem be solved?
4. Does your state use the legislative initiative? If so, how often and for what purposes has it been used? What have been some of the more recent initiatives? Do you think that the initiative process is truly a form of direct democracy?

Improving Your Skills

Communication Skills

Seeing Both Sides of an Issue

Whether you are doing research, writing a report, debating a question, or discussing a problem, it is often important to see both sides of an issue. It is easy to become blind to other points of view after you have firmly made up your mind. If you have ever been in a position in which you felt as though someone refused to listen to your side of the story, then you know how counterproductive this can be. Sometimes it is difficult to admit, even to ourselves, that there is another side to an issue. Usually, however, there is at least one other side to the story, and it never hurts to find out as much as you can about it. You have nothing to lose by listening to your opponent; doing so will either cause you to change your position, help to strengthen your own arguments, or allow you to understand the other side more clearly.

Writing

Choose an issue on which you have taken a strong position. That issue may be gun control, capital punishment, abortion, or a state or local issue that is currently in the news. Research an opposing view of the issue as thoroughly as possible and write a report on that position. When you have finished, evaluate how you now feel about the issue. Does your position remain unchanged? Do you feel even more strongly than before that your position is correct? Or do your feelings remain the same but you now have a clearer understanding of the other side? Include your impressions in your report.

Social Studies Skills

Comparing Similarities and Differences

Look at the political map on page 526. Examine the states on the left half of the map (that is, including Texas, Oklahoma, Kansas, Nebraska, South Dakota, and North Dakota, plus those states to their left.) What is the main similarity among them that you can glean from reading the map, if any?

Now look at the economic map on page 527. Examine the other states on the right side of this map. Is there any way to easily describe their differences or similarities using the information provided on the map? Explain your answer.

Activities and Projects

1. Write a brief description of your state constitution, including its main principles and its history.
2. Think of a state-sponsored program that is important to you. Imagine that funds for the program are going to be cut, and you are a lobbyist who must convince a state legislator to oppose the funding cut for that program. Write a script that spells out your argument as if you were presenting it to the legislator.
3. Prepare a bulletin board display in the form of an organization chart that shows the different members and committees of your state legislature.

CHAPTER INTRODUCTION

Instructional Objectives

By the end of the chapter students should be able to:

• Describe the features of the modern office of governor.
• Outline the many roles of the governor.
• Discuss the powers of the governor.
• Identify the other state administrators and their principle functions.

Using the Keynote

Let one of the students read aloud the quotation from Sophocles, and encourage discussion by posing questions such as these: What is meant here by the word *governor?* Can—or should—a governor be expected to know what is best for the state? If so, how? If not, why not? What kind of reasons might a governor have for fearing to follow the course that is best for the state? Why do those fears evoke the speaker's contempt? When Sophocles refers to "the man who sets private friendship above the public welfare," is he referring only to government officials? Why or why not?

Then focus the students' attention on the quotation as a whole, and ask several students to rephrase the statement in their own words.

Introducing the Chapter

Give the students time to read the Introduction independently. Then guide a brief class discussion by asking these questions: How do you respond to the evaluation of the governor as quoted by de Tocqueville? How do you think that evaluation compares to one that might be made of the authority and power of your state's current governor?

Previewing the Sections

Section 1 Let the students look through Section 1; ask a volunteer to read aloud the section title and the main headings. Ask: What can you conclude about the topics covered in this section?
Section 2 Ask volunteers to read aloud from Section 2 the section title, the main headings, and the photo captions. Ask: How do you think the roles of governors may vary from state to state? Why?
Section 3 Have the students page through Section 3, noting especially the section title, the main headings, the organizational chart, and the special feature. Let the students consider what they hope to learn in studying this section.
Section 4 Instruct the students to glance through Section 4, paying particular attention to the main headings and subheadings and the photographs. Then guide the students in briefly discussing what they already know about other state administrators and what they hope to learn about that subject.

CHAPTER 22

Governors and State Administrators

CHAPTER OBJECTIVES

To learn and understand

- The features of the present-day office of governor.
- The many roles of the governor.
- The powers of the governor.
- The other state administrators and their principal functions.

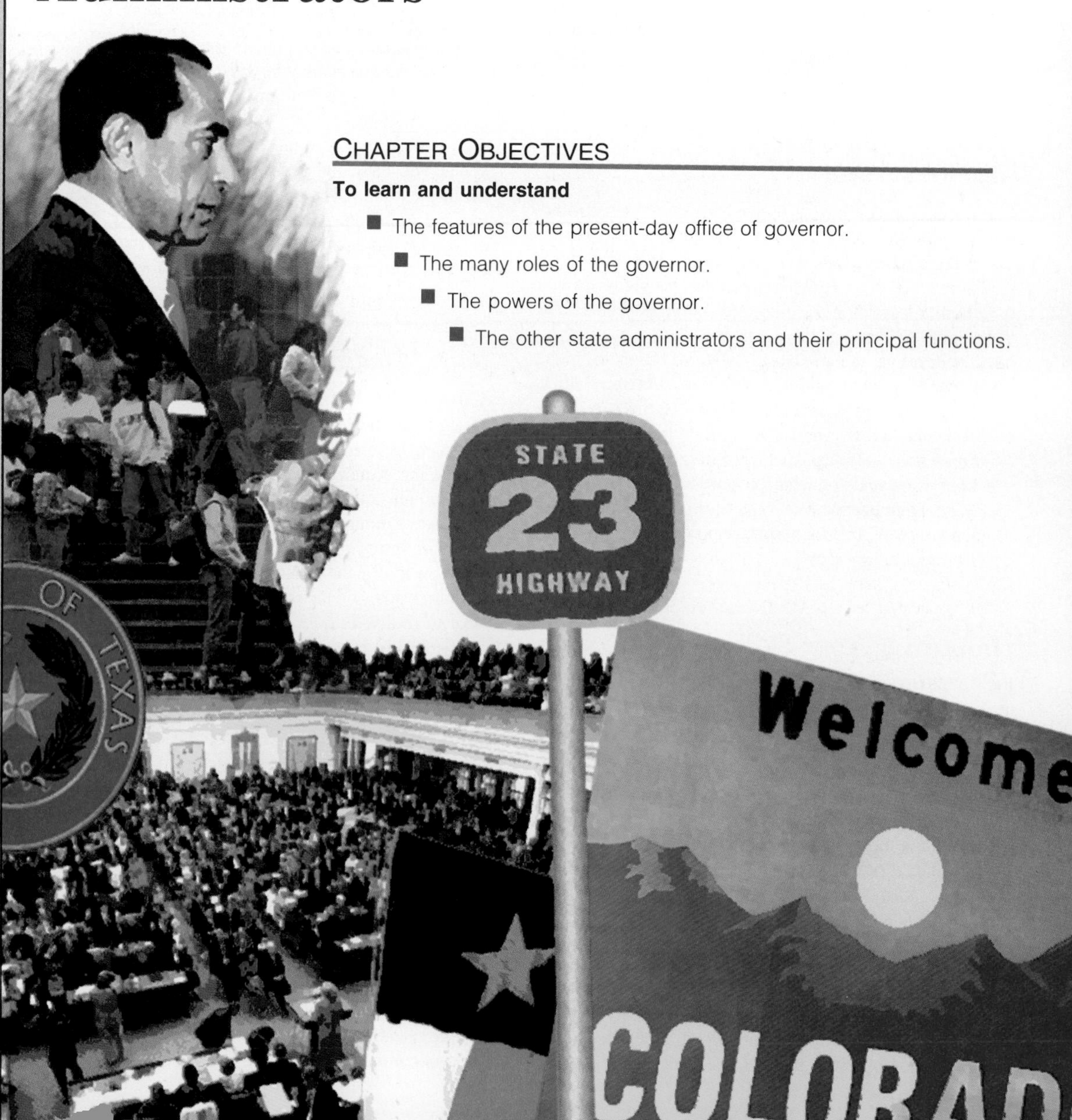

West's American Government Assignment Guide

Activity Sheets
Basic Concepts 22 *TRB* (Reteaching)
Enrichment Activity 22 *TRB*
Building Social Studies Skills 22 *TRB*
Quizzes
Chapter 22 Section 1 Quiz *TRB*
Chapter 22 Section 2 Quiz *TRB*
Chapter 22 Section 3 Quiz *TRB*
Chapter 22 Section 4 Quiz *TRB*

Tests
Chapter 22 Test A *TRB*
Chapter 22 Test B *TRB*
Chapter 22 Test Bank *TRB*
Chapter 22 WESTEST Computerized Testing
Social Studies Tool Kit Software
Chapter 22 Activity

Keynote

"I have nothing but contempt for the kind of governor who is afraid, for whatever reason, to follow the course that he knows is best for the state; and as for the man who sets private friendship above the public welfare—I have no use for him either."

—— **Sophocles**
(495–406 B.C.) Greek Playwright

INTRODUCTION

When the Greek dramatist Sophocles wrote the above statement more than 2000 years ago, he expressed a sentiment that remains with us today. Whoever takes over the governorship of a state must do what is best for that state and seek the highest level of public welfare for its citizens. State governors have not always had the ability to do so, however, as one political observer found out in the 1800s.

In 1831 the French political writer Alexis de Tocqueville was interviewing an American politician. The American told de Tocqueville that "the governor counts for absolutely nothing and is paid only $1,200."[1] Clearly the office of the governor has changed since the 1830s. Indeed, just about every period of social reform in American history is associated with politicians who were governors. The policies of Governor Al Smith of New York helped pave the way for the New Deal that President Franklin D. Roosevelt put into effect during the Great Depression of the 1930s. Governor Terry Sanford of North Carolina became a civil rights moderate in a Southern state during this country's modern civil rights movement. During the 1970s, Governor Jerry Brown of California took stands on consumerism, women's rights, and the environment that made him a symbol of that era.

The governorship often serves as a stepping stone to the U.S. Senate or even to the presidency—former Governor Jimmy Carter of Georgia became president (1977–1981) as did former Governor Ronald Reagan of California (1981–1989). In all, six of our nation's presidents in this century have been former governors.

The reason that the political writer, Alexis de Tocqueville, said that governors counted for absolutely nothing in 1831 was because, at that time, governors were just one of a large number of elected state officials. Most states had been following the tradition of President Andrew Jackson, which held that the more state officials people elected, the more direct and more representative government would be.

But even before Jackson, there was no great love of state governors. The colonists had suffered under the royal governors, and the memories of this experience could be seen in the first state constitutions. No authority was given to the chief state executive. The governor was not even elected by the people. In every state except Massachusetts and New York, the legislature appointed the governor, and then only for a one-year term.

SECTION 1

The Modern Governor

Preview Questions

- What are the formal and informal qualifications for being a governor?
- What is the selection process and length of service for governors?
- How may a governor be removed from office?

Today a governor is the chief executive officer in each of the fifty states. The most populous states have given their governors great control over the state executive branch. Even a few less populated states, such as Alaska and Hawaii, have made provisions for strong governors.

1. As quoted in *State Government* (52), Summer 1979, p. 95.

SECTION 1

Points to Stress
- Qualifications for governor, both formal and informal.
- The selection process and length of service for governors in your state.
- The manner in which a governor may be removed from office in your state.

Kickoff Activity
Ask the students this question: How many governors of our state—current and past—can you name? Give them about five minutes in which to write their lists; then ask volunteers to read their lists aloud. Encourage the students to compare their lists and suggest changes where necessary.

Working with the Preview Questions
After the students have read these three study questions, encourage volunteers to suggest answers, based on what they already know. Then guide the students in working together to prepare an outline format based on these three questions. Have all the students follow this format as they read and outline Section 1.

Teaching Strategies

Introduction
Read this brief section introduction aloud to the class. Then stimulate discussion by asking: What do you think has motivated some states to make their governors more powerful than other states' governors? What do you think has motivated the states that have granted fewer powers to their governors? Into which group do you believe your own state falls? Why?

Extension
Ask the students to identify the specific formal qualifications for the post of governor in your state. You might want students to list these on a chart comparing them with the formal qualifications for the presidency.

Cooperative Learning
Let the students form small groups in which to discuss the current governor of your state: How does he or she meet each of these informal requirements? Does your governor fail to meet any of these informal requirements? If so, why do you think your governor nonetheless succeeded in being elected?

Discussion Starter
Guide the students in discussing the specific procedures for selecting the governor of your state: What are the advantages of the system used in your state? What problems might be associated with that system? Do you believe the system your state uses should be altered in any way? If so, how? If not, why not?

Enrichment
Ask a small group of volunteers to gather current information on the term limits for governors in all 50 states. Have these volunteers present the information in a chart or on a map.

Enrichment
Assign a pair of students to research and report on Governor Orval Faubus of Arkansas: What was his background before being

Caption Answer Student answers may vary, but should express an understanding of the importance of the media in today's elections because most voters will base their opinion of the candidate's ability on the image he or she presents through the media.

Qualifications

The formal qualifications for the governor of most states are simple. He or she has to be an American citizen and has to be of a certain age, usually no younger than 25 or 30. Most states require that the governor has lived in the state for at least five years. Finally, a candidate for governor must be a qualified voter (satisfied the state's age and length of residency requirements).

These formal qualifications for governor do not even exist in Kansas and Ohio. In some states, such as California, Massachusetts, Ohio, and Wisconsin, one can become governor at the age of 18.

Because millions of men and women satisfy the formal requirements to become governor, the *informal* requirements are what truly determine who will be elected. No handbook is available to outline such qualifications, but they certainly include name familiarity, political experience, skill in relating to the media, and voter appeal, in terms of personal demeanor and personality.

To become governor, a person must first win a major party's nomination and then follow through by winning the majority of votes in the general election. The combination of personal characteristics that allows such events to occur can be summed up as the informal qualifications for governor.

The Selection Process

Today every state selects its governor by popular vote. In forty-six states a **plurality** (at least one more vote than that received by any other candidate, which may or may not be a majority of the total vote) is all that is needed for a candidate to be elected. In Arizona, Georgia, and Louisiana, if no candidate obtains a majority of votes (more than 50 percent), there is a run-off election between the two candidates with the most votes. In the absence of a majority in Mississippi, the winner is chosen by the lower chamber of the legislature. Finally, in Vermont in a similar situation the choice is made by both chambers.

Major party candidates are usually nominated in primaries, although conventions are sometimes used. In Washington state, nominees are chosen by caucus and then a primary is used to determine the final candidates.[2]

The Length of Service

Gone are the one-year terms of office that were so popular in the early days of this nation. Forty-seven states now have the governor serve for a minimum of four years. New Hampshire, Rhode Island, Arkansas, and Vermont have two-year terms.

Many states place limits on the number of terms that a governor may serve. Kentucky, New Mexico, and Virginia, for example, essentially prevent a second full term; they allow the governor to serve additional terms, but not consecutively. In twenty-seven states, governors may

2. Only three states—Connecticut, Utah, and Virginia—still use the convention method for nominating gubernatorial candidates.

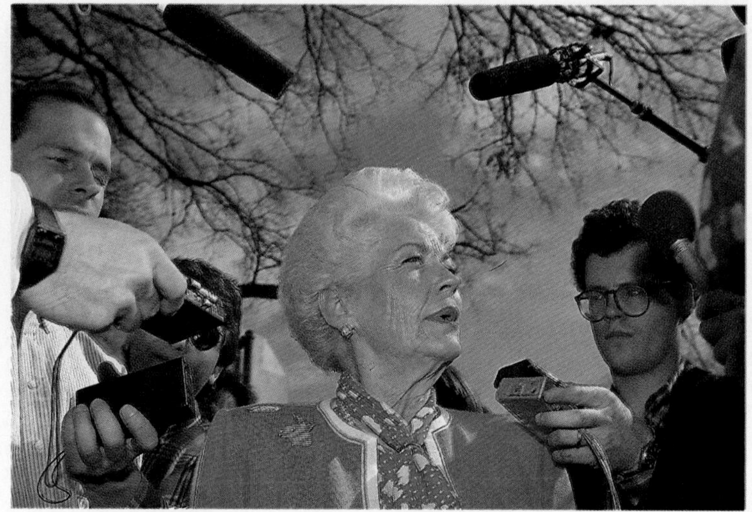

Media skills are an important informal qualification for the office of governor. Here, Governor Ann Richards of Texas is shown speaking with reporters on the campaign trail. Why do you think media skills are so important?

elected governor? What were the most important aspects of his record as governor? Why was he re-elected so many times? What does his repeated re-election imply about the attitudes and interests of Arkansas' voters?

Enrichment
Let two or three volunteers gather information in response to these questions: In the history of our state, which governors have left office before the end of the elected term? Under what circumstances? By whom was each replaced? Ask the volunteers to prepare and present a chart that shows their findings.

Discussion Starter
Help the students discuss their responses to these questions: What is the purpose of impeachment? Whom is it intended to protect? Why? Why do you think Oregon has no provision for impeachment of its governor? Does this lack of impeachment powers leave any groups or individuals "unprotected"? Why or why not?

Discussion Starter
Stimulate class discussion by posing questions such as these: What is the purpose of a recall? What specific actions do you imagine might motivate voters to initiate a recall action? Why?

Discussion Starter
Guide the students in considering the office of governor and its attractions: Who do you think is attracted to seeking the office of governor? Why? Do you believe the office should hold a strong appeal for a wider range of citizens? If not, why not? If so, what should be done to attract more—and more diverse—citizens to seek the office?

serve two consecutive terms. Nineteen states have a two-term limit. Governors who choose to run for a second term almost always win. The power of incumbency is great at virtually all levels of government.

The all-time record for gubernatorial service is held by Governor George Clinton of New York, who held office from 1777 to 1795 and from 1801 to 1804. He did this by winning seven three-year terms. The modern record goes to Orval Faubus who was governor of Arkansas from 1955 to 1967—six consecutive two-year terms.

In the Event of Death or Removal

The governorship may become vacant because of the death or incapacity of the governor. Also governors may resign in order to take over an important cabinet position at the request of the president, or to become a U.S. senator. Some governors have been removed legally by either impeachment or recall.

Every state's constitution provides for a successor if the governorship becomes vacant. In forty-three states, the second in command—the lieutenant governor—takes over. In a few states, such as Maine, New Hampshire, New Jersey, and West Virginia, the president of the state senate takes over. In three states—Arizona, Oregon, and Wyoming—the state secretary of state becomes governor.

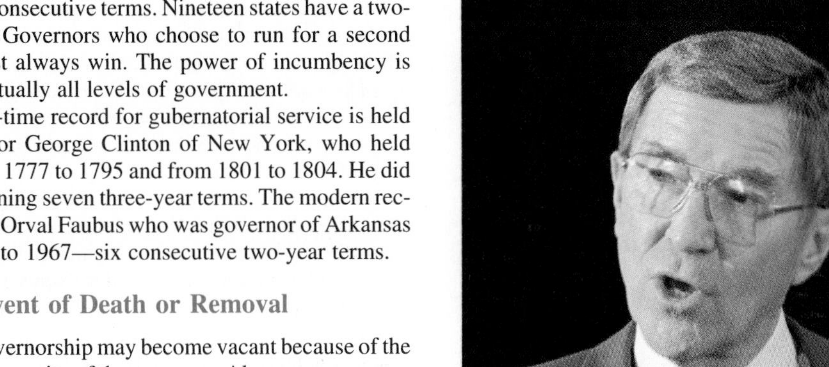

▲ Evan Mecham is one of only 5 governors to have been impeached in the 20th century. How does impeachment of the chief executive at the state level compare with impeachment of the president?

Impeachment As with impeachment proceedings at the national level, removing the governor in this manner usually requires an indictment by the lower chamber, a trial by the upper chamber (in which the senators are the jury members and the state supreme court justices are the judges), and conviction. Often the chief justice of the state supreme court presides at the trial.

Only Oregon does not allow the removal of the governor by impeachment. Impeachment is not impossible, but it is infrequent. Governor Evan Mecham of Arizona was impeached and removed from office in 1988 when he was convicted on criminal charges of campaign finance mishandling and lending $80,000 of state money to his car dealership. (He was later acquitted of felony charges.) In the twentieth century only four other governors have been removed in such a manner.[3]

The Recall About 25 percent of the states provide for removal of the governor by recall. By signing petitions, voters in these states can require a special election to determine whether or not the governor (or other state officials) can be removed before the term expires. Only one governor—Lynn J. Frazier of North Dakota—has been removed in this manner, in 1921.

The Question of Pay

The annual salaries that are paid to governors range from a low of $35,000 in Arkansas to a high of $130,000 in New York, but a governor's salary is not his or her only compensation.

Governors in all states except Arizona, Massachusetts, Rhode Island, and Vermont are provided with an official residence. Additionally, all governors are given extremely generous expense accounts so that in fact most of their daily expenditures are paid for by state taxpayers.

Dollars and cents, however, are not what lure great Americans to the office of governor. Honor, prestige, and a sense of public duty are what propel some of the nation's greatest leaders into the governorship.

3. William Salzer of New York in 1913; James E. Ferguson of Texas in 1917; J. C. Walton of Oklahoma in 1923; and Henry S. Johnston of Oklahoma in 1929.

Caption Answer Students should understand that the processes are very similar.

Reteaching Strategies
1. Let the students work in small groups to review Section 1 by reviewing and comparing their outlines. Encourage individual students to make corrections or additions to their outlines if necessary.
2. Ask pairs of students to work together, using their own words to define these terms: *plurality, incumbency, lieutenant governor.*

Evaluation Strategies
1. Have the students write their answers to the Section 1 Review questions.
2. Have the students take the Section 1 Quiz found in the *TRB.*

Section 1 Review (Answers)

1. The formal requirements are that he or she has to be an American citizen and be of a certain age, usually 25 or 30. The informal requirements are what actually determine who can become governor. They have consisted of such qualifications as religion, name familiarity, political experience, race, skill in relating to the media, and voter-appealing personality.

2. Four years.

3. Removing the governor by impeachment, which usually requires an indictment by the lower chamber, a trial by the upper chamber, and conviction. Additionally, about 25 percent of the states provide for removal of the governor by recall.

4. Answers will vary, e.g., political experience is the most important informal qualification. If the candidate has no political experience, he or she will spend the term trying to learn the ropes and gain the needed experience.

SECTION 2

Points to Stress

- The responsibilities of the governor as chief executive.
- The way that governors fulfill their roles as chief legislator and policy maker.
- The other roles fulfilled by the governor.

Kickoff Activity

Instruct the students to list at least six tasks undertaken by the governor of your state. When everyone has finished writing, encourage the students to compare and discuss their lists.

Working with the Preview Questions

Let volunteers read these study questions aloud, and encourage the students to share their ideas about responses. Then remind the students that they will find more complete answers to the study questions as they read Section 2; have them read the section independently, keeping the questions in mind.

Teaching Strategies

Introduction

After the students have read the section introduction, ask them to recall recent news coverage of your governor's activities: Which of these roles do you think the governor was filling in each case?

Comprehension

Let volunteers explain how the election of other office-holders in the executive branch limits the governor's power.

Enrichment

Let a small group of volunteers research recent examples in which your state's governor has been held responsible for developments—both positive and negative—over which he or she actually had very little control. Ask the volunteers to share their findings with the rest of the class, and encourage all the students to discuss their reactions to each development.

SECTION 1 REVIEW

1. What is the difference between the formal and informal qualifications one must meet in order to become governor?
2. What is the typical length of service for governors?
3. What are the ways a governor can be removed from office?
4. **For critical analysis:** What do you think is the most important informal qualification for becoming governor? What makes that qualification more important than the others?

SECTION 2

The Governor's Many Roles

Preview Questions

- As chief executive, what are the governor's responsibilities?
- How do governors carry out their roles as chief legislator and policymaker?
- What other roles do governors play?

Just as the president of the United States has numerous roles, including those spelled out by the U.S. Constitution and those that have evolved through custom, so, too, does the governor have certain roles. Each governor may be referred to as his or her state's chief executive, chief legislator and policymaker, chief political party leader, and chief spokesperson. These many roles may require the governor to appear at the dedication of a new state building one hour, give a high school lecture on civics the next hour, lunch with a visiting foreign dignitary the following hour, and then fly to Tokyo to lobby a Japanese automobile maker to locate a new manufacturing plant in the state.

The Chief Executive

As with the federal government, the executive branch of any state is responsible for carrying out the laws passed by the state legislature. The governor is the state's chief executive. He or she must take whatever steps are necessary to make sure that the executive branch administers the state's laws. In some situations the governor's actual control over the executive branch is limited by the fact that many other officeholders within that branch are also elected, rather than appointed by the governor.

The governor's job within the executive branch also involves settling disputes between the different departments and agencies. Whenever a scandal occurs, even though it may be many levels removed from the governorship, the governor is often blamed by the public. No matter how strong or weak the governor's actual control over the executive branch may be, the public almost always holds the governor responsible for anything that happens. The reverse of this is that the governor benefits when something good happens, even if he or she had nothing to do with it.

The Chief Legislator and Policymaker

Again, just as the president of the United States proposes legislation to the Congress, so too do governors recommend legislation to state legislatures. They typically do this by having a state legislator introduce desired bills. Even though most governors lack formal legislative powers, an aggressive governor can have a powerful influence on the legislative process.

Another way of viewing the governor as chief legislator is that he or she is chief policymaker. While running for office, governors often propose numerous ideas during their campaigns. A candidate might argue that the state's school system should be changed. He or she might campaign on a platform of having a new program to help the homeless. Once elected, such candidates then must attempt to enlist the help of the legislature to put their proposed policies into effect.

The Chief Political Party Leader

Because almost all governors run for office on either the Democratic or Republican ticket, they become the state leader for that political party when they are elected, and are the voice of the party when in office. In this role, the governor is expected to attend political party dinners, campaign for party candidates in local elections, and speak frequently at party functions, particularly those that involve raising money. Each governor is expected to participate in the annual meeting of governors from the same party, at either the Democratic or the Republican Governors' Conference.

All of this is sound in theory, but not always true in reality. On occasion, governors have had little influence

TEACHING CITIZENSHIP SKILLS AND RESPONSIBILITIES

Read
Introduce this Citizenship Skills and Responsibilities feature by asking the following questions: How many of you have your driver's license? Would you describe driving as a right for all citizens or as a privilege for some citizens? Why? Allow the students time to share their responses, then ask a volunteer to read this feature aloud to the class.

Discuss
Stimulate a discussion of this material by asking the following questions: What is the purpose of traffic laws? What type of information is usually indicated on a traffic ticket? What can happen to those who ignore traffic tickets?

Analyze and Apply
To help students analyze and apply this feature content, you might wish to invite a state trooper or local police officer to speak to your class regarding driver safety and traffic laws. Encourage the speaker to discuss the consequences of failing to take action on a traffic citation and of driving while under the influence of alcohol or drugs.

Review
Use the following questions to review student understanding of this feature: What can happen if you ignore a traffic ticket? If you receive a traffic ticket, what steps can you take? What is the purpose of traffic laws?

Reteaching Strategies
1. Have each student write a brief topic outline of Section 2.
2. Work with small groups of students; guide them in reviewing and discussing the various roles of the governor of your state.

Evaluation Strategies
1. Have the students write their answers to the Section 2 Review questions.
2. Have the students take the Section 2 Quiz found in the *TRB.*

Section 2 Review (Answers)
1. As chief executive, the governor is responsible for carrying out the laws passed by the state legislature.
2. Governors propose legislation to state legislators.
3. As chief party leader, the governor is the state voice of the party while in office. He or she is expected to attend and speak to party functions, and attend the annual meeting of governors from the same party.
4. He or she speaks to people outside the state regarding federal issues or multi-state issues.
5. Answers will vary, e.g., a governor's role as chief political party leader might come into conflict with the roles of chief executive or legislator if the party's needs conflicted with the general population's needs.

CITIZENSHIP SKILLS AND RESPONSIBILITIES

Responsible Driving and Traffic-Law Violations

Contrary to one old saying, laws, particularly when they are traffic laws, are *not* meant to be broken. Traffic laws are created for one purpose only: to make driving a safer experience. As a responsible citizen, you have a duty to obey all traffic laws in your community and those in other locations whenever you are driving. If individuals didn't follow traffic laws, driving would be much more dangerous. Indeed, deaths on the highway remain a serious problem in this country, but there are many more deaths per passenger miles driven in countries in which the citizens do not obey traffic laws as well as we do.

If you do violate a traffic law and are pulled over by police personnel, then you have a duty and responsibility to follow your state's procedures. Traffic tickets are issued by state and local authorities to motorists who ignore or abuse their responsibilities and violate traffic laws. The ticket usually indicates the type, location, and date of the offense, and when the offender should appear in court. Ignoring a traffic ticket can result in an increase in the fine or even arrest.

If you receive a traffic ticket, you have two choices. Usually, you can just mail in a check or money order in the amount specified on the ticket (if your state allows this). If you feel you were unfairly ticketed, however, you can choose to appear in court at the time and location specified on the ticket. You may plead not guilty, or you may plead guilty and explain the special circumstances that influenced your action. For example, you might protest a ticket for an illegal left turn if the "No Left Turn" sign had been painted over with graffiti. The judge will listen to your argument and then make a decision, which could be no penalty, reduced penalty, or full penalty.

TAKING ACTION

1. Obtain a copy of the fines for various traffic-law violations in your state. Write a paragraph describing why the most expensive fines are so costly.
2. Write a description of what might occur if each city in your state were able to make up its own traffic laws.

over the party nominations of other state and local officials. Additionally, whenever a governor becomes unpopular or an embarrassment to his or her party, he or she loses influence very rapidly.

The Chief Spokesperson for the State

When the governor speaks to people outside the state, he or she often plays the role of spokesperson for the state's citizens and businesses. Governors, for example, may speak out in favor of a federal government grant for highway construction or for aid to the schools. They often do this by traveling to Washington, D.C., to argue their case before the appropriate federal officials. When problems affect several states, such as pollution or water shortages, governors represent their own states in multistate negotiations. Finally, it is governors who travel to other countries to plead the case for foreign economic investment in their states.

SECTION 2 REVIEW

1. As chief executive, what are the governor's responsibilities?
2. How do governors perform their role as chief legislator?
3. How do governors perform their role as chief party leader?
4. How do governors perform their role as chief spokesperson?
5. **For critical analysis:** Do you think there are situations when the various roles a governor plays might come into conflict? Give a possible example to explain your answer.

SECTION 3

Points to Stress
- The most important executive powers of the governor.
- Budgetary powers possessed by governors.
- Legislative and judicial powers allowed governors.

Kickoff Activity
Give the students five minutes in which to list as many differences as possible between the powers held by the governor of your state and the powers held by the president of the United States. At the end of the allotted time, have several of the students read their lists aloud, and encourage a brief class discussion.

Working with the Preview Questions
Guide the students in reading and considering these three study questions. Then remind the students to keep these questions in mind as they read and take notes on Section 3.

Teaching Strategies

Introduction
Let the students read this brief section introduction independently, then help them review the purposes of the system of checks and balances: How do the powers of the governor fit into this system?

Vocabulary
Ask several students to explain, in their own words, the differences between the *executive* and *the chief executive.*

Enrichment
Have an interested volunteer research and report on the 1990 situation in Massachusetts (or a similar situation) in which a governor attempted to restrict the lieutenant governor's access to power.

SECTION 3

The Powers of the Governor

Preview Questions
- What are the most important executive powers of governors?
- What budgetary powers do governors possess?
- What are governors' legislative and judicial powers?

Each state's constitution bestows certain explicit powers on the governor, just as the U.S. Constitution does on the president. The specific executive, legislative, and judicial powers of the governor are all part of the checks and balances system.

State Executive Powers

The U.S. Constitution states that the president of the United States is "the executive" of the federal government. Most state constitutions, in contrast, describe their governors as the "chief executive" in state government. The difference between *the* and *chief* may not seem like much, but it is. No one legally shares supreme executive power with the president of the United States. In many states, though, executive power may be shared among several executive officers who are often also popularly elected.

No popularly elected executive in the state government can be directly controlled by the governor, at least not very easily. This may be especially true with the lieutenant governor. There have been particularly trying times when the governor of one political party has been voted into office while the lieutenant governor—the equivalent of the vice president—was from the opposing political party. This occurred in California in 1978, Missouri in 1980, and Iowa in 1982 and 1986. In such situations, the governor may even be unwilling to travel out of the state in order to keep the lieutenant governor from seizing power during the governor's absence. In 1990, for example, Massachusetts Governor Michael Dukakis postponed a trip abroad because he feared his lieutenant governor would use too much of her power in his absence. In twenty-two states, the lieutenant governor must run for office with the governor.

A state's chief executive must seek cooperation whenever there is a divided executive branch. Cooperation is certainly more difficult when important state officials, such as the attorney general and the secretary of state, are not of the same political party as the governor.

Figure 22–1 on page 551 shows the executive branch of a typical state. Imagine how difficult it would be for you as governor if all of the elected officials shown were not from your party.

In at least several states the governor has great power over the executive branch. In these few states, such as New Jersey and Tennessee, the state constitutions have created an executive branch with only one or very few elected officials. Additionally, the governor in these states has the power to appoint numerous department and agency heads.

Appointment and Removal Powers One of the most important executive powers of the governor is the power to appoint and remove state officials. Whenever a governor can appoint her or his own department and agency heads, that governor is more likely to be able to coordinate policies and be more powerful. A governor who can reward supporters by appointing them to important department and agency positions will have a greater chance of success in carrying out her or his policies. One way to judge a governor's power is to see whether that governor can in fact select and appoint loyal and competent assistants.

One factor that can potentially reduce a governor's ability to appoint loyal followers is the requirement in most states that major appointees be confirmed by the state senate, which is part of the system of checks and balances. Some legislatures also set qualifications that appointees must meet in order to assume office. In those states in which there is vigorous two-party competition, legislatures often require that a specified number of members of each commission or board be from each party. The result is that the governor must appoint members of the opposite party during her or his administration.

The reality is that fewer than one-fifth of the state governors appoint secretaries of state, attorney generals, auditors, treasurers, controllers, and superintendents of public instruction. Some states have hundreds of state agencies; even with strong appointment powers, no governor could administer so many state agencies effectively.

The governor's ability to remove appointed administrators from office is controlled by many of the same rules of appointment. Most state constitutions as well as state laws place numerous restrictions on the governor's power to fire state employees. These restrictions have a cost. Many governors have found themselves rendered

Extension
Ask the students to recall (or find out) whether the lieutenant governor runs with the governor in your state.

Comprehension
Have the students explain the importance of the powers to appoint and remove state officials; let volunteers give examples of both kinds of power in your state.

Cooperative Learning
Let the students work in groups to study the chart, Typical State Executive Branch. Then have the group members work together to research and draw a similar chart showing the specific organization of the executive branch in your state.

Enrichment
Assign a group of interested students to gather information in response to these questions: Who holds the major administrative positions in our state government? What was the process by which each of those individuals was selected? Then have these students prepare a bulletin board display about their findings.

Discussion Starter
Guide the students in discussing and evaluating the leadership of your governor. Then encourage the students to identify current or recent governors from around the country who have shown outstanding leadership: What sets these governors apart?

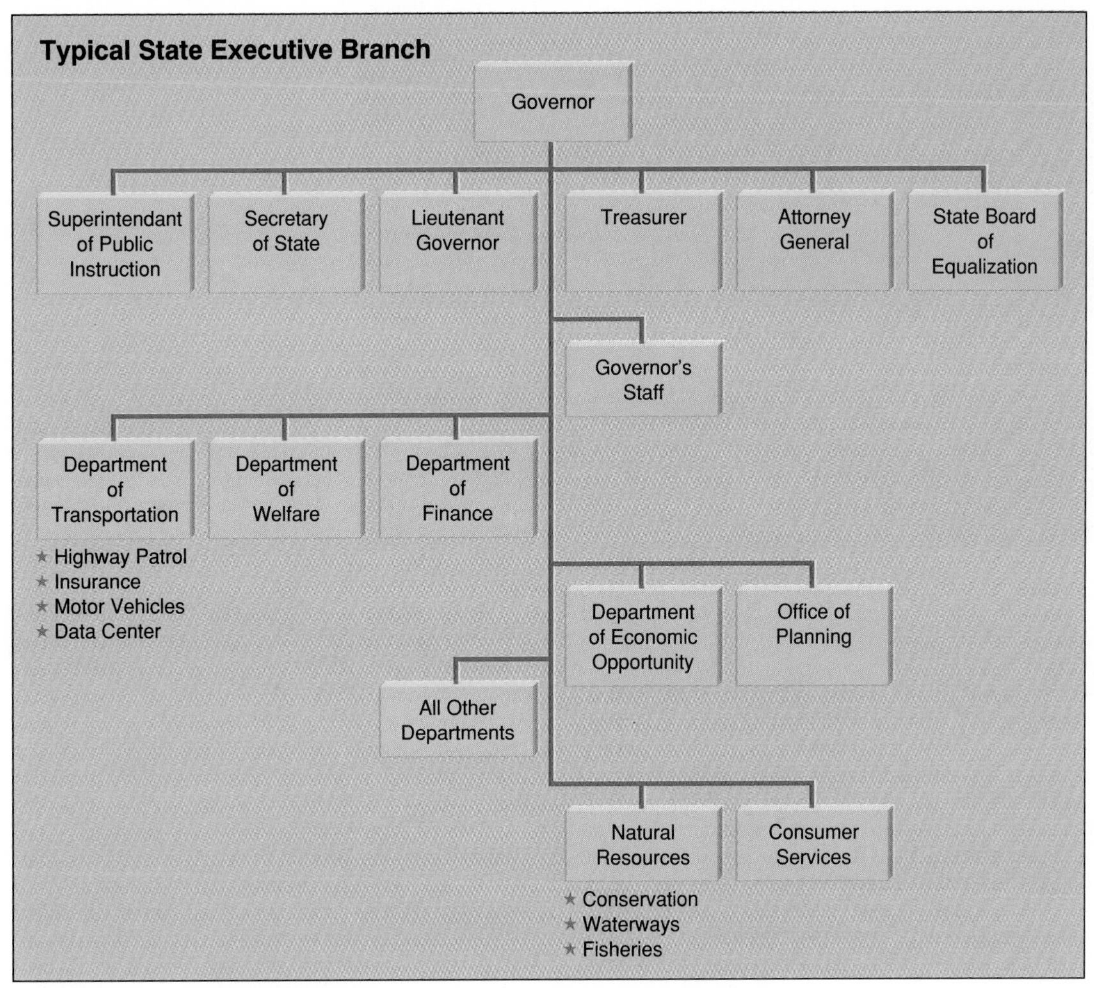

▲ FIGURE 22–1 **Typical State Executive Branch.** The above organizational chart depicts a typical state executive branch. How does this organizational chart compare with the organizational chart for the executive branch of the federal government on page 404?

ineffective by their inability to rid themselves of incompetent subordinates.

Administering Laws As chief administrator, the governor is expected to make sure that all the laws passed by the state legislature are faithfully executed. Of course, no governor alone can accomplish such a task. Some states follow the U.S. Constitution by giving the governor the power to require department heads to submit annual written reports on the status of the laws that relate to their departments. The actual work of carrying out the state's laws is undertaken by thousands of individuals who make up the state's executive branch.

Some state agencies are subject to the governor's direct control. Others are not, but rather are headed by elected officials. Sometimes a governor finds that he or she has difficulty supervising the state Department of Justice if it is run by a state attorney general who was elected by the voters and is from another party.

Governors sometimes can be effective leaders in spite of serious obstacles. They do this in a variety of ways, such as appealing to the public, using their talents of

Figure Answer Students should understand that although the typical state executive branch has many departments, there are, generally speaking, fewer major departments than at the federal level. Additionally, students should understand that unlike the president's cabinet, many directors of state departments are elected.

FYI

State constitutions grant different types and degrees of power to governors. States have been ranked according to the formal powers granted to the governor by Thad Beyle in *Politics in the American States,* Virginia Gray et al., eds. Among those states assigned weak status were Florida, Mississippi, New Hampshire, Texas, and North Carolina.

Some of the states ranked moderate were Arkansas, Colorado, Delaware, Indiana, Maine, Virginia, and Wisconsin.

Strong states included California, Illinois, Massachusetts, New York, Ohio, Tennessee, and Utah. The rankings reflect budget powers, appointive powers, tenure potential, and veto powers.

Comprehension
Ask volunteers to explain why this nation's first governors had virtually no budgetary powers. Why do modern governors need such powers? How do they use those powers?

Enrichment
Have two or three students research the specific budget process used in your state; then ask them to explain the process to the rest of the class.

Enrichment
Allow interested students to work together in researching and discussing control over the National Guard: In what instances have governors refused to comply with a president's orders for National Guard participation? Why? With what results?

Discussion Starter
Help the students discuss their responses to a governor's use of the "power of the purse" to influence the attitudes and actions of department heads: Do you consider this use of the governor's powers legitimate? Effective? Fair? Why or why not?

Caption Answer Answers will vary, but students should understand that when performing ceremonial functions, the governor acts for all the people of the state.

Like the president, governors spend time performing ceremonial functions. Here Governor Mario Cuomo of New York congratulates five Special Olympics participants. Are a governor's ceremonial functions important?

persuasion, and working through their own political parties.

Power of the Purse In the early years of this nation, governors had virtually no budgetary powers. In most states today, in contrast, planning and carrying out the budget is a significant responsibility for the governor. Just as the president of the United States prepares an annual budget, so too do many governors prepare annual or biannual budgets. After the governor finishes the budget, it is sent to the legislature for approval.

The governor's budget can be seen as a political plan of action. She or he clearly emphasizes which programs have high priority by the amount of money that is allocated to those programs. Whenever the governor and the majority in the legislature are of different political parties, disputes will often arise about the governor's proposed budget.

Many astute governors can use their budget-making powers to effectively control state administration. Imagine, for example, that a governor is having trouble with the head of the department of public instruction. That department head has been popularly elected and is from the other political party. The governor certainly cannot fire that person, nor can she or he control that person very easily. But, the governor can use the budget-making power of the office to reduce the amount of money going to that department. The "power of the purse" often has profound effects on a department head's attitude.

Once a budget is authorized by the legislature, most governors possess the power to control the pattern of expenditures through executive agencies and departments. Governors often have the power to decide which expenditures will be made in a particular year. A governor may withhold the funding for a particular project if she or he is not satisfied with the way the project is progressing.

Power Over the Militia The governor is the commander in chief of the armed forces of the state, which used to be called the state militia. Legislation at the close of World War I created the National Guard, which is made up of state units under the control of the governor. Whenever there is a national emergency or a war, the president of the United States can "nationalize" the National Guard and put it under the power of the United States Armed Forces. President Bush did this in August, 1990, in Operation Desert Shield, when Iraq invaded Kuwait.

Except in times of national emergency, the governor commissions officers in the National Guard. He or she can call them out to suppress riots or to help in emergencies such as floods, earthquakes, and natural disasters. The National Guard was called to help when Mount St. Helens erupted in Washington state in 1980, in Alaska when the *Exxon Valdez* oil tanker spilled oil in 1989, during the San Francisco Bay Area earthquake in California in 1989, and again in response to the Los Angeles riots in 1992.

Comprehension
You may want to give the students an opportunity to recall and explain the governor's role as chief legislator in recommending legislation.

Extension
Ask the students to recall (or find out) what specific powers your governor has in calling special sessions and specifying matters to be considered during such sessions.

Discussion Starter
Encourage the students to share and discuss their ideas in response to this question: Why is the threat of a governor's veto generally less effective than the threat of a president's veto?

Caption Answer The president can nationalize the National Guard whenever there is a war or other national emergency.

The governor is commander in chief of his or her state's National Guard units. How can this power be superseded by the president?

Most governors delegate military matters to an adjunct general, and place little importance on their role as commander in chief. Sometimes governors have filled the National Guard units with officers selected on a political basis. As long as those selected are trained, no harm is necessarily done, but if they are untrained, some National Guard units may be ineffective during state emergencies.

In some states, the state police report directly to the governor.

Legislative Powers

In the role of chief state legislator, the governor has specific legislative powers that include the ability to call special legislative sessions, the power to veto legislation, and the power to recommend legislation, which you have already read about.

Calling Special Legislative Sessions In the 1990s a number of governors had to call special sessions to solve large state budget deficit problems. In calling the special legislative sessions, the governors were exercising one of their legislative powers.

Every state gives the governor the power to call a special session of the legislature. This power is usually exclusively held by the governor. In those rare states that allow the legislature to call itself into special session, the power is rarely exercised.

About 50 percent of the states allow the governor to specify the matters that may be taken up by the legislature at the special session. In some states, constitutions do not allow the legislature to consider any other matters except those for which the session was called.

Power to Veto Legislation The veto power of the president of the United States gives him immense leverage. The simple threat of a presidential veto often means the legislation will not be passed by Congress. The threat of a governor's veto is not necessarily as effective. Every state except North Carolina has given the governor the power to veto legislation. In some states, however, the time after the legislature passes a bill and when the governor must veto it is short. It is three days in Iowa, Minnesota, New Mexico, North Dakota, and Wyoming. In a number of other states it is only six or seven days. If the governor does not veto a measure during the designated period, it normally becomes law.

- **Pocket veto** The president of the United States has a **pocket veto**. If he refuses to sign a bill and Congress adjourns within ten working days after the bill has been submitted, the bill is killed for that session of Congress. In most states the opposite is true—bills that the governor neither signs nor vetoes after the legislature has adjourned become law without her or his signature. Thirteen states do have some form of pocket veto, however.

Multidiscipline Strategies

Literature Governors attract a lot of attention as chief state executive, and some of them have lived quite colorful and interesting lives. Encourage students to read a biography or autobiography of a governor. Students should write a precis of the book for extra credit. Porter McKeever wrote *Adlai Stevenson: His Life and Legacy,* Morrow; Harry Williams wrote *Huey Long,* Bantam Books; and Robert McElvaine wrote *Mario Cuomo: A Biography,* Scribner's. Many other well-written biographies are available, from which your students can pick.

Comprehension
Ask the students to recall and explain what a line-item veto is and how it is used.

Extension
Have the students recall (or find out) whether the governor of your state has the power of a line-item veto. If so, with what restrictions? If not, what movement is there toward granting the governor that power?

Discussion Starter
Guide the students in discussing a governor's power to pardon: In what kinds of cases do you think a pardon is most frequently granted? Why? Do you believe a governor should be granted sole pardoning power? Why or why not?

Discussion Starter
You may want to help the students discuss some aspects of capital punishment: Does your state use this form of punishment? Why or why not? What do you think of capital punishment? Do you consider it effective? Legal? Ethical? Why or why not?

Caption Answer Most governors can issue pardons, reprieves, and paroles.

The time periods are usually longer than the ten days given to the president. In Oklahoma it is a 15-day period; in Florida it is a 15-day period, and in Michigan it is 14 days.

- **Line-item veto** In forty-three states, the governor has some provision for a **line-item veto**, which allows the governor to veto a particular item in a bill with which he or she disagrees, while signing the rest of the bill into law. A bill may therefore be passed with parts of it vetoed by the governor. This power is not available to the president of the United States, although presidential line-item veto has been requested (albeit unsuccessfully) by both President Reagan and President Bush.

In most states, the line-item veto is restricted to items in **appropriation bills**, which determine how much should be spent in various categories. This bill appropriates sums of money to be spent in specific areas of government, such as on public housing and highways. In twelve states the governor can reduce the amount of the appropriation, but not completely. Nineteen states give the governor the ability to use the line-item veto on more than just appropriations.

Line-item vetoes are typically used to reduce extravagant appropriations. They also can be used by a governor who wishes to punish lawmakers who have opposed his or her programs.

No governor has absolute veto power. In all states (except those thirteen in which there is some form of a pocket veto), a governor's veto can be overridden by the legislature, usually with a two-thirds vote of the full membership of each chamber. About 5 percent of all state bills are vetoed by governors. Less than 10 percent of such vetoes are overridden.

Judicial Powers

The governor's judicial powers are usually restricted to **clemency proceedings**, which involve the showing of mercy toward those convicted of a crime. In this area there are three actions that most governors can take: pardons, reprieves, and paroles.

Pardon The governors of the royal colonies also acted as **chancellors**, that is, triers of fact who decided judicial problems on the basis of the concept of fairness rather than specific laws. This role of the royal colonial governor has evolved into the present-day governor's judicial power to grant pardons. A **pardon** is the release from the penalty for a criminal offense.

Today's busy governors rarely examine more than the most notorious criminal cases. When he or she believes that a conviction is wrong or a penalty too harsh, the governor may grant a full or conditional pardon. Some states require that the governor work with a state pardon board. Others require that a governor's pardon be ratified by a council or by the state senate. Even in states in which the governor has sole pardoning power, there are state advisory pardon boards that investigate the cases and make recommendations.

The record for the highest number of pardons is held by Governor Miriam "Ma" Ferguson of Texas, who during her term from 1925 to 1927 pardoned almost four thousand convicted felons—about five a day!

Similar to the pardon is the governor's power to **commute**, or reduce, the sentence imposed by a court. Governors have commuted many death sentences to the lesser sentence of life imprisonment.

Reprieve A **reprieve** is a postponement of the carrying out of a criminal sentence, and is typically given for a specified short period of time. Criminals sentenced to die can often obtain a governor's reprieve to allow their lawyers more time to appeal their case because, for example, new evidence that may prove their innocence has been discovered. In 1991, for example, Governor L. Douglas

▲ During her term during the 1920s, Governor Miriam Ferguson of Texas pardoned almost 4000 convicted felons. What other judicial powers do most governors have?

TEACHING BUILDING SOCIAL STUDIES SKILLS

Read

Before the students start reading this Building Social Studies Skills feature, encourage a brief discussion of memory and its importance: Why is having a good memory important? In what sense is having a good memory a result of habit? What do you do when you want to remember important names or other significant information? How did you learn—or make up—the memory techniques you use? What interesting or unusual techniques for improving memory do your friends or family members use? With what success? After the discussion, let several volunteers participate in reading the feature aloud.

Discuss

Help the students discuss this special feature: Why is memory especially important when you speak, write, take tests, or study? In what other particular situations do you consider having a good memory especially important? Why? Why is each of the guidelines here important? Which of these guidelines have you tried? Which do you use regularly? Which do you anticipate trying soon? Why?

Analyze and Apply

Have the students form small groups. Ask the members of each group to select a subject on which to practice memory-improving techniques—a list of facts about a specific current event, a speech or skit they plan to present, a school test, a textbook chapter, or some other subject relevant to all the group members. Then guide them in working together to discuss and apply the specific memory-improving guidelines from this feature to the subject they have chosen.

Review

Ask questions such as these to help the students review this Building Social Studies Skills feature: Why should you study subjects that are different (rather than similar) one after the other? What are mnemonics?

BUILDING SOCIAL STUDIES SKILLS

Improving Your Memory

The ability to remember facts, dates, and comments accurately is important for success in school and for success in most careers. It is important to understand that you can improve your memory, much as you can improve any skill. Whether you are speaking, writing, taking a test, or studying, improving your memory is beneficial. The following guidelines can help you remember better:

- **Arouse your interest in the material.** Keep an open mind about the material. You are more likely to forget what you don't agree with. Tell yourself that you will remember what you are learning and feel confident that you will remember.
- **Search for the organization of ideas.** Use summaries, headings, and categories to synthesize and group ideas.
- **Learn what you read or hear.** Try to accurately learn and understand the material.
- **Personalize the information.** Try to relate it to something in your life.
- **Quiz yourself.** Recite the material from memory immediately after reading or hearing it, or else simply ask yourself about what you just read or heard.
- **Reinforce learning and remembering.** Use note-taking, discussing with friends, drawing, and reciting out loud to help you remember what you just learned.
- **Study in twenty- to forty-minute intervals.** Take short breaks between study periods. This helps keep comprehension and memory at peak levels.
- **Learn mnemonics.** Special memorizing systems called mnemonics (pronounced ni-ˈmän-iks) can help you memorize long lists. For example, if you needed to memorize a list of the following four states—Florida, Arizona, California, and Texas—you could create your own mnemonic by using the first letters of the states to spell FACT. Just remembering FACT can help you remember the names of those states.

PRACTICING YOUR SKILLS

1. During two successive weekends, watch the same political talk show on TV. During the first week just watch the program the way you normally would. The next day write a paragraph of what the show was about.
2. During the following week's show, use the tips provided above as you watch the show. The next day again write a summarizing paragraph.
3. Compare the two paragraphs. Which is a more accurate representation of the information?

Critical Thinking Skills
Have the students consider and analyze the power of reprieve, particularly in the example of Wilder's 1991 granting of a reprieve to Giarratano: Does this use of the reprieve grant a governor higher judicial power than the Supreme Court holds? Why or why not?

Enrichment
Let a small group of interested volunteers research and discuss with the class Bush's 1988 publicity campaigns exploiting the image of Dukakis as being too lenient on convicted criminals: How was this image developed? What issues other than the "soft on crime" question were involved in this campaign? How did media critics respond to the publicity campaign? Why? How did voters respond to it? Why?

Reteaching Strategies
1. Ask the students to work with partners to review—and if necessary revise—the notes they have taken on Section 3.
2. Help the students work in small groups to discuss the powers of your state's governor: How do those powers compare with the powers of the president?

Evaluation Strategies
1. Have the students write their answers to the Section 3 Review questions.
2. Have the students take the Section 3 Quiz found in the *TRB.*

Section 3 Review (Answers)
1. Appointment and removal of department and agency heads, administering laws, power over the militia, and preparing the annual budget.
2. The ability to call special legislative sessions, the power to veto legislation, and the power to recommend legislation.
3. The power to pardon, to reprieve, and parole.
4. Answers will vary, e.g., the disadvantage would be that the governor and lieutenant governor might be working at cross-purposes. A possible advantage might be that both parties are represented in the executive branch of the state.

Caption Answer Forty-three states have lieutenant governors.

SECTION 4

Points to Stress
- The major executive officers found in most states.
- The method of selection and primary responsibilities of the major executive officers found in most states.

Kickoff Activity
Give the students several minutes in which to write lists answering this question: Other than that of the governor, what are the major executive offices in our state government? When all the students have finished writing, let volunteers read their lists aloud, and encourage the students to compare their ideas.

Working with the Preview Questions
Have the students read these two study questions aloud, and encourage interested students to share

Wilder of Virginia spared the life of Joseph M. Giarratano Jr., a Norfolk fisherman convicted and sentenced to death for the murder of a woman and her daughter. Governor Wilder gave Giarratano a chance for a second trial after the United States Supreme Court rejected the convicted murderer's final appeal the previous year.

Parole If a governor believes that a convicted felon has served enough prison time, that governor may request early parole. **Parole** is the release of a prisoner prior to the end of his or her court-determined sentence.

Few governors enjoy exercising their clemency powers. Applications for pardons, reprieves, and paroles are numerous. In recent years, a governor who exercises such powers may be accused of "being soft on crime." This is exactly what happened to Massachusetts Governor Michael Dukakis when he ran for president against George Bush in 1988. Dukakis had allowed some convicted criminals to leave jail on weekends for the purpose of getting work experience. One of them committed murder. In publicity campaigns, Bush exploited the image of Dukakis being too lenient on convicted criminals. It is not surprising that most states have full-time boards or staffs to handle these problems, instead of directly involving the governor in each one of them.

SECTION 3 REVIEW

1. What are the executive powers of the governor?
2. What are the legislative powers of the governor?
3. What are the judicial powers of the governor?
4. **For critical analysis:** What do you think are the advantages and disadvantages of having a governor and lieutenant governor from different political parties?

SECTION 4

Other State Administrators

Preview Questions
- What are the major executive officers found in most states?
- How are these officers selected and what are their primary responsibilities?

The governor in most states shares his or her executive powers with a number of other state administrators. Only in Maine, New Jersey, and Tennessee is the governor the only popularly elected executive branch officer. It is difficult to accurately list which of the other state officers are the most important. Not only do the powers of each of the other executive officers differ from state to state, but they differ depending upon the administration within each state. One governor may give his or her lieutenant governor many responsibilities; the next may not use the lieutenant governor at all.

The Lieutenant Governor

Forty-three states have a **lieutenant governor**. This is a position similar to the vice president of the United States, although many lieutenant governors have more real power than does the vice president. In only one of those forty-three states is the lieutenant governor not elected by the people. In Tennessee the speaker of the senate is also the lieutenant governor.

As mentioned previously in this chapter, the lieutenant governor normally succeeds the governor whenever he or she dies, is incapacitated, resigns, or is impeached and convicted. In many states, the lieutenant governor presides over the state senate.

▲ Joanell Dyrstad is lieutenant governor for the state of Minnesota. Do all states have a lieutenant governor?

what they already know in response to each. Then remind the students to keep these questions in mind, looking for more detailed answers, as they read Section 4.

Teaching Strategies

Introduction

Let a volunteer read the brief section introduction aloud to the rest of the class. Then let the students discuss their ideas in response to these questions: How do you think the fact of being the only popularly elected executive officer affects a governor's powers? A governor's attitudes and actions? Why do you think there is so much variety in the powers and responsibilities granted to various executive officers in different states?

Comprehension

Ask the students to recall and briefly explain the powers of the vice president.

Extension

Have the students find and discuss the answers to these questions: Who is the lieutenant governor of our state? What powers and responsibilities does our lieutenant governor have? What are some specific examples of the ways in which the current lieutenant governor has used his or her powers? If there is no lieutenant governor, why doesn't our state have one?

Discussion Starter

Help the students discuss the various methods by which attorney generals are selected: What are the implications of these different ways of achieving this office?

Cooperative Learning

Ask the students to work in groups; have the members of each group select one attorney general who has gained wide publicity from his or her office and then used that publicity as the basis for a campaign for governor. Let the group members work together to research that person's background and career; then encourage them to discuss what they have learned.

Individuals who seek the position of lieutenant governor often regard it as a stepping stone to the governorship. After all, no one wants to become a career lieutenant governor because of the few responsibilities that the position carries. In thirty-eight states the lieutenant governor is not even a member of the governor's cabinet. The most a lieutenant governor usually can expect to do is to serve on boards and commissions and to take over when the governor is physically absent from the state. In a few states, however, the lieutenant governor does have quite a bit of power. For example, many observers of Texas politics believe that the lieutenant governor and the speaker of the Texas House have more power than does the governor.[4]

The Attorney General

Forty-three states have popularly elected attorney generals. In Alaska, Hawaii, New Hampshire, New Jersey, and Wyoming the governor appoints the attorney general. In Tennessee, the state supreme court makes the appointment, and in Maine the attorney general is appointed by the legislature. The **attorney general** is the legal advisor to the governor, to all other executive officers, and to all legislators. (Occasionally, a state attorney general will give legal advice to local officials.) Each state attorney general acts as the chief state prosecutor in criminal proceedings and as the state defender whenever the state finds itself defending a lawsuit.

Much of the work of a state attorney general involves writing opinions that have to do with the interpretation of the state constitution and of laws passed by the legislature. When the governor's office or legislature asks for a written opinion from the attorney general's office, it may want to know whether its actions are constitutionally legal. The attorney general's opinions often have the force of law unless they are successfully challenged in court.

In the last several decades, some individuals have used the office of the attorney general as a stepping stone to the governorship. They have undertaken widely publicized campaigns against organized crime, big business, organized labor, or consumer fraud in order to impress state political party officials. The publicity these attorney generals obtain often improves their chances of being selected to run in the next gubernatorial election.

▲ In 43 states including Colorado, where Gayle Norton (shown above) is the attorney general, the attorney general is elected. What does an attorney general do?

The Secretary of State

All states except Alaska, Hawaii, and Utah have an office of the secretary of state. In Delaware, Maryland, New Jersey, New York, Oklahoma, Pennsylvania, Texas, and Virginia the governor appoints the secretary of state. In Maine, New Hampshire, and Tennessee the post is filled by the legislature. In the rest of the states, the post is elected by the voters.

The secretary of state's job is mostly routine. He or she is the official custodian of records, the keeper of the "great seal" of the state, and supervisor of all elections. State law guides most of the actions of the secretary of state. He or she can seldom affect policy, but in some states the secretary does have certain policy-making powers. For example, in Illinois the secretary of state has much legislative say in the area of drinking and driving. Additionally, in some states the secretary of state is next in the order of succession if the governor cannot fulfill his or her term of office.

4. It is interesting to note that although Warren G. Harding was lieutenant governor of Ohio, he ran unsuccessfully for governor. Nonetheless, he was still elected president of the United States in 1920 by the largest number of popular votes up to that time.

Caption Answer The attorney general is legal advisor to the governor and all other executive officers and to all legislators. Much of an attorney general's work involves writing opinions dealing with the interpretation of the state constitution and of laws passed by the legislature.

Extension

Ask the students to find and discuss answers to these questions: Does your state have a secretary of state? If so, who holds that office now? How was he or she selected? What are the main responsibilities of your secretary of state? What policy-making powers does your secretary of state hold?

Discussion Starter
Guide the students in considering the duties of treasurer: What are the responsibilities of a state's treasurer? Given those responsibilities, which method of selecting a treasurer seems most appropriate? Why?

Vocabulary
Have the students use dictionaries to compare the definitions of these three nouns: *auditor, controller, comptroller.* In what sense are all three words the same? What different shades of meaning can the three words have?

Discussion Starter
Help the students discuss the office of chief school administrator: Why is this such an important office? Whom does your state's chief school administrator affect directly? Indirectly? What do you consider the most appropriate means of selecting a chief school administrator? Why?

Caption Answer While the powers of the superintendent of public instruction may vary from state to state, many have some form of legislative power in that they can either formally or informally propose legislation for educational programs.

Cooperative Learning
Let the students work in groups to share and discuss responses to these questions: What are the powers of the head of public education in our state? How does he or she influence what happens to you and to other students in your school system? What control do voters in your state have over the activities of the head of public education?

Extension
Let the students work together to identify and explore all the major agencies in your state: What is the purpose of each agency? How does it function?

Reteaching Strategies
1. Have the students form small discussion groups in which to share their responses to the Preview Questions at the beginning of Section 4.
2. Let the students work with partners to write brief job descriptions for these offices within your state: attorney general, treasurer, auditor.

Evaluation Strategies
1. Have the students write their answers to the Section 4 Review questions.
2. Have the students take the Section 4 Quiz found in the *TRB.*

Section 4 Review (Answers)
1. In addition to the governor, a lieutenant governor, an attorney general, a secretary of state, and a treasurer.
2. They are popularly elected or appointed.
3. The responsibilities of the lieutenant governor vary, depending on the governor. The attorney general is the legal advisor to the governor. The secretary of state is the official custodian of records. The treasurer makes payments for payrolls and other state expenses.
4. Answers will vary, e.g., it is believed that governors and lieutenant governors from the same party and with the same ideas will work better together.

The Treasurer

The office of the treasurer exists in forty-seven states. From this office the financial matters of the government are carried out. In thirty-eight states, the treasurer is popularly elected. In Alaska, Michigan, New Jersey, New York, and Virginia the governor appoints the treasurer. The legislature appoints the treasurer in Maine, Maryland, New Hampshire, and Tennessee. In the remaining three states the duties of the treasurer are taken care of by another department, and the head of that department is appointed by the governor. The state treasurer's main responsibility is to make payments for payrolls and other state expenses. In some states the treasurer also collects taxes.

Many states find themselves with surplus monies during certain times of the year, particularly just after state income taxes are due. The state treasurer's job in this situation is to invest the surplus monies in order to make sure that the state obtains interest on these extra funds. In this capacity, the state treasurer becomes a money manager. He or she usually invests the surplus funds in bonds issued by the federal government and sometimes in bonds issued by local governments and even by private corporations.

The Auditor

Most states have an office of the **auditor**, sometimes called the office of the state **controller**, or the state **comptroller**. Because states' constitutions do not allow the spending of state money without legislative authorization, some state official has to verify that the legislature has actually approved each amount spent. Thus the state auditor possesses the power to authorize those payments that are provided by law. In some cases, the auditor must certify that a state expenditure is legal before the state treasurer can release the funds. In other states, the state auditor must also examine what happens after the expenditures are made. In other words, the state auditor will make sure that the spending was in accord with the law.

The Superintendent of Public Instruction

Every state has a chief school administrator, or a superintendent of public instruction, who oversees all public school instruction. Sometimes this person is known as the commissioner of education, and often shares authority with the state board of education.

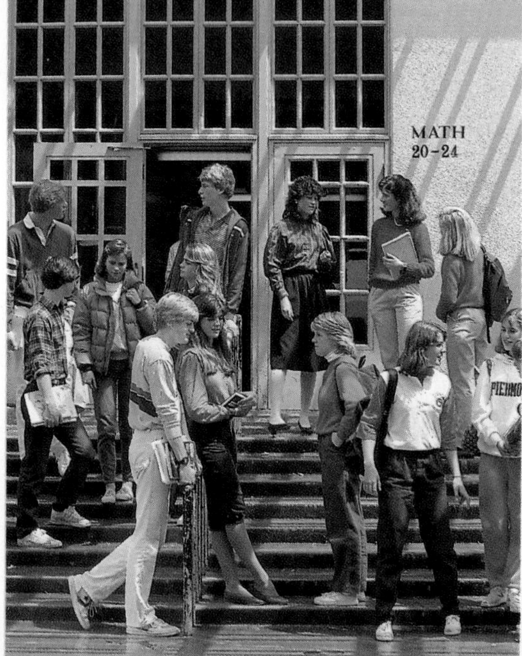

▲ Every state has a superintendent of public instruction, or chief school administrator, who is responsible for overseeing public schools within the state. Does a superintendent of public instruction have any legislative authority?

The powers of the state head of public education vary dramatically. In some states such as Texas, the office of the superintendent of public instruction has great control over which textbooks are used in the state schools. In other states, there is relatively no control over textbooks. Some of the other powers of the superintendent of public instruction are:

- To implement all education programs instituted by law and the state legislature.
- To propose legislation for education programs.
- To mandate a course of study for public instruction and conduct and supervise state competency testing.
- To coordinate technical assistance to all school districts.
- To enforce and audit all programs in education set by the legislature, such as minimum days and special education requirements.
- To control state-financed programs in higher education.
- To inform the public on the quality of public education in the state, including both weaknesses and strengths.
- To work with the federal government in the area of special education grants.

TEACHING CHALLENGE TO THE AMERICAN DREAM

Read

As an introduction to this Challenge to the American Dream feature, you might encourage the students to share and discuss their responses to these questions: What do you think the relationships between national politics and state politics are? What do you think they should be? Do you believe that the election of your state's governor should be linked to the election of your nation's president? Why or why not? How do you think the timing of elections affects the relationship between state and national politics? After the discussion, allow volunteers to read the feature aloud to the rest of the class.

Discuss

Help the students discuss the content of the feature and their reactions to it: What is the difference between the gubernatorial elections held in 1920 and those held in 1988?What accounts for that difference? Who would want to weaken the influence of national politics over state politics? Why? Who would want to maintain the stronger influence of national politics? Why? How fully do you think state politics can be isolated from national politics? Who is responsible for low voter participation in off-year gubernatorial elections? What can or should be done to improve voter participation?

Analyze and Apply

How can improving voter awareness and participation help solve the problems posed by the influence of national politics over state politics? What can you do to improve awareness and increase participation among local voters? Let the students work in groups to discuss their responses to these questions and then to plan and carry out a voter-involvement campaign.

Review

Pose questions such as these to help the students review this Challenge to the American Dream feature: How are state officials trying to isolate themselves from national politics? What is one of the main problems with holding state elections during off-presidential election years?

You Decide (Answers)

1. Answers will vary, e.g., state elections should be isolated from national elections. The issues and problems are separate, so the state should not necessarily follow the national pattern.

2. Answers will vary, e.g., during a presidential election year, voters are influenced by the prominence of the national campaign. If there is a personal relationship between the president and a governor, the governor could obtain more federal funds for his or her state.

Other Officers and Agencies

The offices previously discussed are the most significant ones in the state administration. There are hundreds of other offices, however; many were created by state constitutions, others were created by the legislatures. The list below gives a sample of the many state offices that now exist.

- Department of Health
- Department of Natural Resources
- Department of Revenue
- Department of Motor Vehicles
- Department of Consumer Services
- Department of Highway Safety
- Department of Labor and Employment Security
- Department of Professional Regulation
- Department of Water Management
- Department of Transportation
- Board of Prisons and Parole
- Board of Agriculture
- Board of Medical Examiners

SECTION 4 REVIEW

1. What are the major executive officers found in most states?
2. How are these officers normally selected?
3. What are the primary duties of these officers?
4. **For critical analysis:** Almost half the states now require that governors and lieutenant governors run for office as a team. Why do you think these states have adopted this requirement? Explain.

CHALLENGE TO THE AMERICAN DREAM

Off-Year Election of Governors

Increasingly, state elected officials, including the governor, are isolating themselves from national politics. This isolation results from electing their governors and other executive officials in off–presidential election years. For example, in 1920, a presidential election year, only twelve states did not have gubernatorial elections. In 1988, also a presidential election year, thirty-six states did not have gubernatorial elections.

The purpose behind this shift has been to weaken the influence of national politics over state politics. For example, if a Democratic candidate is running for governor during a presidential election year when the Democratic candidate for president is obviously going to achieve a landslide victory, the Democratic gubernatorial candidate will have a much better chance of winning. This is called the **coattail effect**. But if the governor's race is two years later, the presidential election will have little influence.

Some argue that state politics should be isolated from national politics. In a system of federalism, state governments are as important as the federal government. Therefore, state officials should be elected on their own merits, not on the popularity of a presidential candidate.

This is a valid argument, but a major problem with separating gubernatorial elections from presidential elections is less voter participation. On average, only 75 percent of the voters who vote during the presidential election years vote during off–presidential election years.

You Decide

1. Do you think it is more important to have gubernatorial elections isolated from presidential elections at the expense of voter participation, or is it more important to increase voter participation in state elections by having the governor and the president elected during the same year? Explain your answer.
2. Why would citizens voting at the state level be influenced by who is running for president?

Observable Mastery
Place the name of your governor on the board. Have students supply the following information in order to compile a personal and power profile on the governor. Age, political experience, margin of victory in last election, political party, years left in term, salary, and any miscellaneous personal background.

Then have students complete the following: Roles of the governor, powers of the governor, other executive officials with whom the governor shares responsibility. Students should have a visual depiction of the person and powers of the governor when they are done.

Chapter Evaluation
To evaluate student mastery of chapter material, you might:
1. Use Chapter Test A from the *TRB.*
2. Use Chapter Test B from the *TRB.*
3. Construct your own test using items from the *West American Government Test Bank* found in the *TRB.*
4. Use the accompanying computerized test software to construct and print a customized chapter test.

Review Questions (Answers)
1. They are popularly elected.
2. Four years.
3. In 43 states, the lieutenant governor takes over. In the other states, either the president of the Senate or the secretary of state takes over.
4. Impeachment is done by the legislature, while recalls are done by voters.
5. As chief executive, the governor is responsible for carrying out the laws. As chief legislator, the governor recommends legislation and proposes ideas during their campaign. As chief political party leader, the governor is the voice of the party. As chief spokesperson, the governor speaks for the state's citizens and businesses regarding

CHAPTER 22 REVIEW

Key Terms

appropriation bills 554
attorney general 557
auditor 558
coattail effect 559
chancellors 554
clemency proceedings 554
commute 554
comptroller controller 558
lieutenant governor 556
line-item veto 554
pardon 554
parole 556
plurality 546
pocket veto 553
reprieve 554

Summary

1. The governor is the chief executive officer in each of the fifty states. Most states have given their governors a great deal of control. Every state selects its governor by popular vote. Most governors serve four-year terms, while a few still serve two-year terms. In forty-three states, succession falls first to the lieutenant governor, in four states to the president of the senate, and in three to the secretary of state. The governor may be removed by impeachment in every state but Oregon and by recall in about 25 percent of the states.

2. A governor's roles in office include that of chief executive, chief legislator and policymaker, chief political party leader, and chief spokesperson.

3. In most states, executive power is shared among several officers. Important executive powers of the governor include appointing and removing officials, administering laws, planning and carrying out the budget, and commanding the National Guard. The specific legislative powers of the governor include the ability to call special legislative sessions, the power to veto legislation, and the power to recommend legislation. The governor's judicial powers are restricted to those of clemency proceedings.

4. There are several other major executive offices in every state. The leaders of these offices are usually popularly elected. They include the lieutenant governor, attorney general, secretary of state, treasurer, auditor, and superintendent of public instruction.

Review Questions

1. How do governors assume their office?
2. What is the normal length of term for a governor?
3. In most states, who succeeds the governor if he or she dies or cannot fulfill his or her term of office?
4. What is the difference between impeachment and recall?
5. Briefly describe each of the roles performed by a governor.
6. What are the governor's executive powers?
7. Why are the governor's powers of appointment and removal important?
8. Briefly describe the legislative and judicial powers of the governor.
9. What other major executive offices are found in most states today?
10. If you believe that a traffic ticket was improperly given to you, what should you do?
11. Why have most states chosen to hold gubernatorial elections during years when there is no presidential election?

Questions for Thought and Discussion

1. The governorship is considered by many to be an excellent preparation for the presidency. In what ways do you think it would prepare someone for the presidency? In what ways do you think it would not?
2. What are the advantages and disadvantages of the line-item veto? Do you think the president should have this power? Why or why not?
3. What formal qualifications must a candidate meet to run for governor in your state? What additional qualifications would you recommend?
4. What are the possible advantages of having the governor and lieutenant governor be from different parties? What are the disadvantages?

national issues or issues involving other states.
6. Administering laws, the power of the purse, the power over the militia.
7. A governor who can reward supporters by appointing them to important department and agency positions will have a greater chance of success in carrying out his or her policies.
8. The governor may call special sessions of the legislature. He or she has the power to veto legislation. The governor's judicial powers are the pardon, reprieve, and parole.
9. Lieutenant governor, attorney general, secretary of state, and treasurer.
10. You can appear in court at the time and location specified on the ticket and plead not guilty.
11. To avoid the "coattail effect" and to weaken the influence of national politics over state politics.

Questions for Thought and Discussion (Answers)
1. Answers will vary, e.g., the governor would gain experience in executive, legislative, and judicial powers which are, in some ways, similar to the roles played by the president. State issues, however, are very different from national issues.
2. Answers will vary, e.g., line-item vetoes can be used to reduce extravagant appropriations. The president should also have this power. Currently, because the president does not have this power, he or she cannot specifically eliminate requested legislation and spending without vetoing an entire bill. Therefore, special interest groups are able to pass numerous pieces of legislation that would not otherwise be passed.
3. Answers will vary according to your state. Informal qualifications include political experience, skill in dealing with the media, and voter appeal in terms of personality and personal appearance.
4. Answers will vary, e.g., being from different parties, they might better represent all the voters. They may not, however, be able to work together as a team.

Social Studies Skills (Answers)
1. Answers will vary, but students should want to look at what happened to the volume of first class mail after the price increase, the speed of delivery after the price increase, and the change in the percentage of letters lost or misdelivered.
2. Answers will vary, but students will want to see what happens to key state services, the effectiveness of the state legislation, and the popularity of the governor after his or her request.
3. Answers will vary, but students will want to examine how the governor reacts to the criticism, how the popularity ratings of the governor and that of the lieutenant governor change, and what happens in the next election.

CHAPTER 22 REVIEW—Continued

Improving Your Skills

Communication Skills

Using an Almanac

Knowing where to look for information can save you hours of searching. If you are looking for up-to-date information about people, places, or events that is contained in a single volume, an almanac is often a good place to start.

An almanac is published yearly, and contains facts about states, towns, counties, cities, government agencies, population, major events, and many other subjects. There are also specialized almanacs such as state almanacs or almanacs of statistics.

Writing

Using an almanac, find out the following information about your state government and write a brief report:

1. The names of the governor and lieutenant governor.
2. When the state constitution was ratified.
3. The number of years in the governor's term.
4. The annual salary of the governor.
5. The number of members in the upper legislative house.
6. The number of members in the lower legislative house.
7. The salaries of your state legislators.
8. The number of members on the state supreme court.
9. The annual salaries of the state supreme court justices.

Social Studies Skills

Decision Making and Predicting the Consequences of Decisions

Policymakers, government officials, and indeed all types of bureaucrats must make decisions, the consequences of which may be important for many individuals. At the national level, decision makers must decide issues with consequences that might affect millions of people in many countries. Before you can make proper decisions yourself, you should be aware of the steps in decision making:

1. Define what you need or want or must do.
2. Examine all of the resources you have available to help you make the decision.
3. Identify the choices you actually have.
4. Gather as much information as you can effectively use.
5. Evaluate and compare your decision options.
6. Make your decision.

Evaluation of the consequences of your own decisions is often quite easy. If you choose to study more for one course than for another, you'll be able to see if the extra studying pays off. But policymakers in government can not so easily determine the consequences of many of their decisions. In the following examples, write down how you would evaluate the consequences of the following decisions:

1. The U.S. Postal Service decides to raise the price of sending a first-class letter by 50 percent.
2. The governor of your state asks the state legislature to cut 15 percent of all state spending by next year.
3. The lieutenant governor starts publicly criticizing the governor.

Activities and Projects

1. From a reference book in your library that deals with your state government, find an organizational chart and a budget chart for your state. Determine from the chart and your readings which agencies and commissions overlap in their responsibilities.
2. Write to a current or former state executive asking for a response to a question on a current issue. Report the executive's response back to the class.
3. Interview a current or former executive in your state. Find out about his or her office and experiences. Report on the interview for the class.
4. Prepare an organizational chart of your state's elected officials. Describe their terms, responsibilities, and relationships to each other.
5. Prepare a biography of your governor that tells his or her life history, political background, and accomplishments in office.

CHAPTER INTRODUCTION

Instructional Objectives

By the end of the chapter students should be able to:

• Describe the organization of state court systems.
• Specify the various methods by which judges are selected.
• Explain how life and property are protected through the enforcement of state criminal laws.
• Discuss the prosecution of those charged with crimes.
• Characterize the sentencing of those convicted of crimes.

Using the Keynote

As an introduction to Chapter 23, engage the students in a brief discussion of justice: How would you define the word *justice?* How important is justice to you? To other citizens? Why?

Follow the discussion by reading aloud the Keynote Quotation. Encourage the students to restate the quotation in their own words and to discuss their understanding of and their reaction to the ideas presented: Are there always conflicting interests within a society? Why do conflicting interests need to be accommodated? Can or should citizens expect more than a "tolerable accommodation" of those interests? Why or why not?

Introducing the Chapter

Ask one of the students to read the Introduction aloud to the rest of the class. Guide the students in beginning to consider the state court system by asking questions such as these: To whom are the state courts and their functions important? Why? Why is it important for you—and other students—to understand how the state courts work?

Previewing the Sections

Section 1 Let the students glance through Section 1, paying particular attention to the main headings, the figure title, and the photo captions.
Section 2 Ask for volunteers to read aloud the section title, the main headings, and the map title in Section 2. Then ask the students: What powers and responsibilities do judges have?
Section 3 Have the students page through Section 3. Ask: How does the law affect your life?
Section 4 Let volunteers find and read aloud the section title, the main headings, and the photo captions in Section 4. Then help the students discuss what they expect to learn as they study this section.
Section 5 Ask the students to look through Section 5, noting especially the section title, the main headings, and the photograph. Then have the students list at least three facts relating to sentencing and prisons with which they are already familiar.

CHAPTER 23

The State Courts

CHAPTER OBJECTIVES

To learn and understand

- The organization of state court systems.
- The various methods by which judges are selected.
- The ways in which state criminal laws are passed and enforced.
- The prosecution and sentencing of those charged with and convicted of crimes.

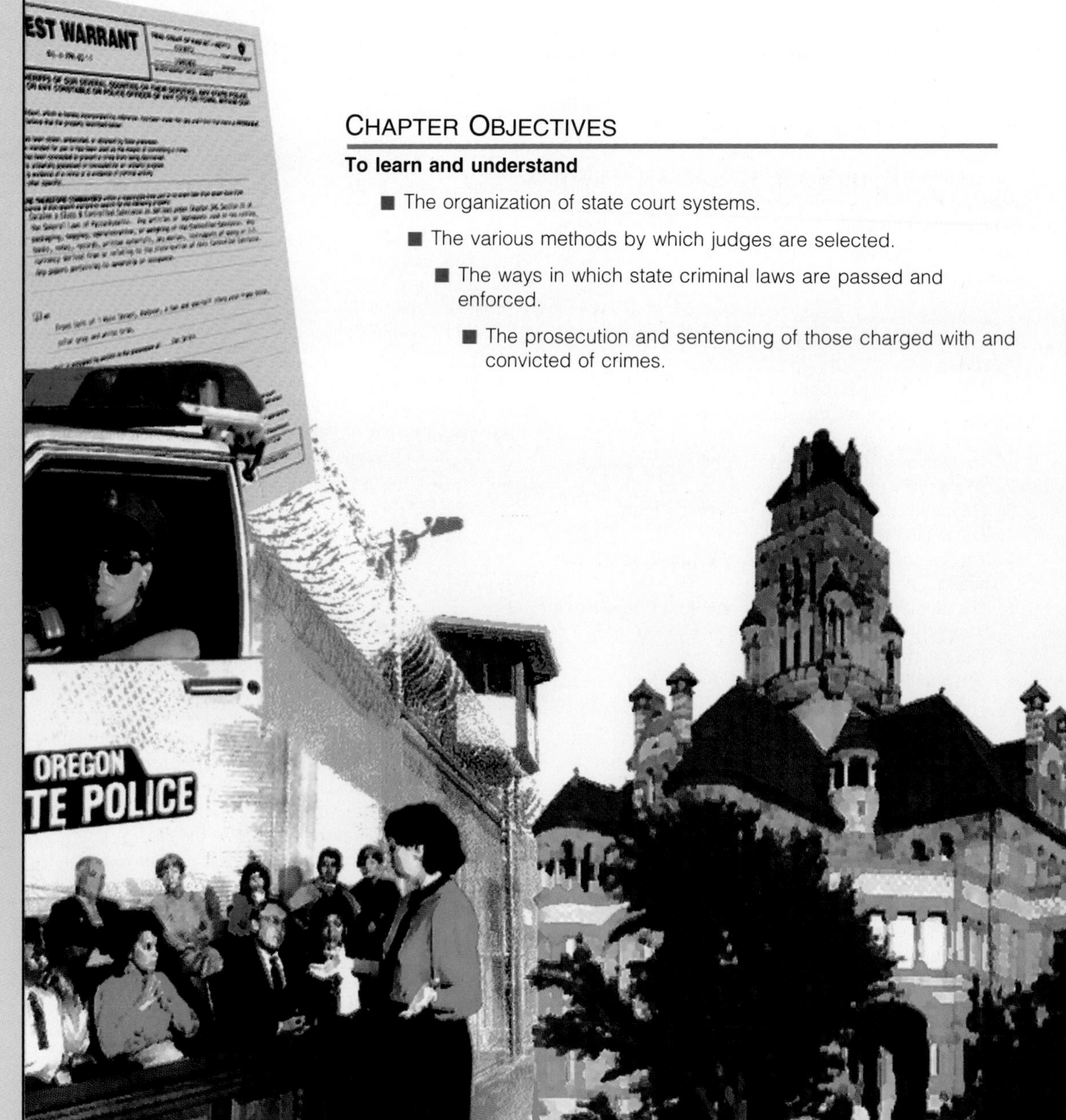

West's American Government Assignment Guide

Activity Sheets
Basic Concepts 23 *TRB* (Reteaching)
Enrichment Activity 23 *TRB*
Building Social Studies Skills 23 *TRB*
Quizzes
Chapter 23 Section 1 Quiz *TRB*
Chapter 23 Section 2 Quiz *TRB*
Chapter 23 Section 3 Quiz *TRB*
Chapter 23 Section 4 Quiz *TRB*
Chapter 23 Section 5 Quiz *TRB*

Tests
Chapter 23 Test A *TRB*
Chapter 23 Test B *TRB*
Chapter 23 Test Bank *TRB*
Chapter 23 WESTEST Computerized Testing
Social Studies Tool Kit Software
Chapter 23 Activity

Keynote

"Justice, I think, is the tolerable accommodation of the conflicting interests of society".

—— **Learned Hand**
(1872–1961) American Jurist

INTRODUCTION

Judge Learned Hand talked about justice in this chapter's opening quote. He realized that the people in any society will have conflicts with each other. They will then seek justice. Justice is dispensed in the court system that has existed since the beginning of this country.

In Chapter 18 you learned about the federal court system. The overwhelming majority of judicial disputes, however, are settled in state courts. There are fifty state court systems, none of which is exactly like another. All have the same purpose, however: to decide disputes between individuals, or between individuals and government, or to determine the guilt or innocence of those accused of committing a crime.

SECTION 1

A Typical State Court System

Preview Questions

- How are state court systems organized?
- What are the different types of state courts?
- What types of cases does each one hear?

Every state has a different court system, but most systems are organized around three levels of courts. Any person who is involved in a lawsuit typically has the opportunity to plead the case before a **trial court**. That is the first level. If that person loses the case, he or she usually has the opportunity to appeal the decision to two other levels of courts, called **appellate courts** (also called **review courts**). Appellate courts only listen to cases and reconsider decisions of trial courts. In most states a case proceeds first through a trial court with an automatic right to review by the state's appellate court; then, if necessary, the case goes to the state's highest review court.

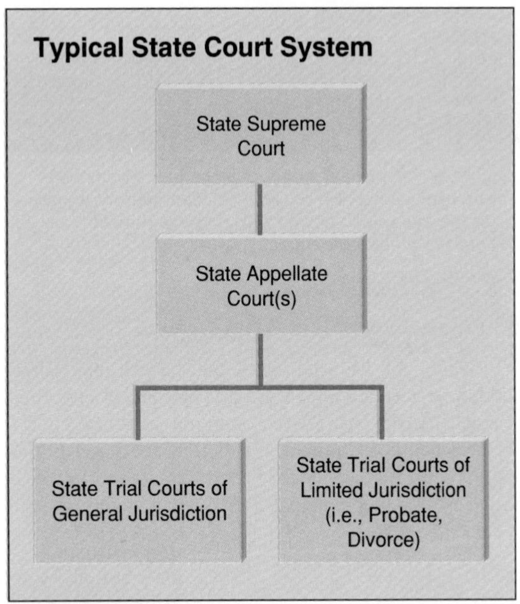

▲ **FIGURE 23–1 Typical State Court System.** As you can see from the organizational chart above, a typical state court system is similar to the federal court system discussed in chapter 18. What is meant by the term *jurisdiction* as it is used in this figure?

Figure 23–1 above shows the three tiers of a typical state court system.

Each court has certain powers of **jurisdiction**, which, if you remember from Chapter 18, means that each court has a certain amount of power to decide cases. Courts with **limited jurisdiction** can only hear particular types of cases; courts with **general jurisdiction** can hear virtually all cases.

SECTION 1

Points to Stress
- The organization of state court systems.
- The different types of state courts and the types of cases they hear.

Kickoff Activity
Give the students five minutes in which to list at least two facts they already know about the state court system. At the end of the allotted time, encourage the students to compare and discuss their lists.

Working with the Preview Questions
Go over these study questions with the class, allowing volunteers to share their responses. Then have the students read Section 1 independently, taking notes in response to these questions.

Teaching Strategies

Introduction
After the students have read the section introduction, let volunteers review the distinctions between the meanings of these terms, especially as used to identify courts: *trial, appellate (appeal), review.* Then guide the students in studying and discussing figure 23–1, Typical State Court System.

This figure content is also featured on *West's American Government Videodisc* (see the index found in the *TRB*) and is available in the transparency package.

Figure Answer Jurisdiction as used in this figure refers to the powers of individual courts to decide cases based on the subject matter of each case.

Vocabulary
Let volunteers define the adjectives *inferior* and *minor* as they are used here; be sure the students do not connect the concept of "unimportant" with the terms *special inferior trial courts* or *minor judiciary courts*.

Caption Answer Justices of the peace are best known for conducting marriage ceremonies. Students should understand, however, that they also handle minor disputes and those crimes punishable by small fines or short jail terms.

Enrichment
Ask an interested volunteer to research the history of JPs in your state and, if appropriate, to collect a few stories about the activities of interesting or unusual JPs. Then let the volunteer write up a short report to be shared with the rest of the class.

Caption Answer General jurisdiction trial courts have the authority to hear and decide cases in nearly every subject matter.

Extension
Ask the students to identify the name used for general-jurisdiction trial courts in your state.

Extension
Ask the students to find and read news stories about current cases that are going to be appealed or that are already before an appellate court. Encourage the students to share the information they have gathered from these news stories and to discuss how such news items help them understand the uses of courts of appeal.

Reteaching Strategies
1. Let the students work in groups to review Section 1 by going over their notes together. Remind the students to refer to the text if necessary and to make any needed corrections in their own notes.
2. Have the students work with partners to write their own definitions of these terms: *trial court, appellate court, jurisdiction, JP, magistrate.*

Evaluation Strategies
1. Have the students write their answers to the Section 1 Review questions.
2. Have the students take the Section 1 Quiz found in the *TRB*.

▲ One of the earliest courts of limited jurisdiction was the justice court which was presided over by a justice of the peace as shown here. For what function are justices of the peace best known?

Limited-Jurisdiction Trial Courts

Every state has trial courts that have limited jurisdiction in certain subject areas. They are often called special inferior trial courts, or minor judiciary courts. Typical courts of limited jurisdiction are domestic relations courts, which handle only divorces and child custody cases; local municipal courts, which mainly handle traffic cases; probate courts, which handle the administration of wills and estate settlement problems; and small claims and justice courts. (For more about small claims courts, see the *Citizenship Skills and Responsibilities* feature in this chapter.) Typically, the minor judiciary courts do not keep complete written records of trial proceedings.

Justice Courts One of the earliest courts of limited jurisdiction was the **justice court**, presided over by a **justice of the peace**, or JP. In the early days of this nation, JPs were found everywhere in the country. One of the most famous JPs was Judge Roy Bean, the "hanging judge" of Langtry, Texas, who presided over his court at the turn of this century.

Today, in more than half the states, justice courts no longer exist. JPs still serve a useful function in some cities and in rural areas where they are usually popularly elected. JP courts, for example, still exist in Texas counties. The subject matter that can be brought before JPs is limited to minor disputes between private individuals or companies, or only those crimes punishable by small fines or short jail terms. JPs are best known, however, for conducting marriage ceremonies.

Magistrate Courts The equivalent of a county JP in the city is a **magistrate**. **Magistrate courts** have the same limited jurisdiction as do justice courts in rural settings. Magistrates are often popularly elected for short terms.

▶ General jurisdiction trial courts may also be called county courts, district courts, superior courts, or circuit courts. These courts meet in court houses such as the one shown here. What type of authority do general jurisdiction trial courts have?

Section 1 Review (Answers)

1. Trial courts, appellate courts, and state supreme courts.

2. They have jurisdictions that are limited to certain subject matters.

3. They can hear virtually all types of cases.

4. Answers will vary, e.g., the appeal might take an inordinate amount of time and clog the judicial system for others.

SECTION 2

Points to Stress

- The three major ways in which judges are selected.
- The pros and cons of popularly elected judges.
- The Missouri Plan.

Kickoff Activity

What are the essential attributes of a good judge? Let the students write short lists in response to this question. When everyone has finished writing, ask volunteers to read their lists aloud; encourage the students to discuss and defend their ideas.

Working with the Preview Questions

Go over these three study questions with the class. Then guide the students in writing an outline format based on the questions. Have the students use this format to write outlines of Section 2.

Teaching Strategies

Introduction

Let one of the students read aloud the brief section introduction. Then encourage the students to discuss their responses to these questions: Which method of selection do you think is most likely to result in judges with the attributes you consider essential? (See the Kickoff Activity above.) Why?

Discussion Starter

Help the students consider the concept of judicial responsibility: To whom should judges be responsible? How would you define *judicial responsibility?* Do you believe the definition has changed over the course of our country's history? Why or why not?

General-Jurisdiction Trial Courts

Trial courts that have general jurisdiction may be called county courts, district courts, superior courts, or circuit courts. The name in Ohio is Court of Common Pleas; the name in New York is Supreme Court; the name in Massachusetts is Trial Court. (The actual court names sometimes do not correspond with what the court does.) General-jurisdiction trial courts have the authority to hear and decide cases in nearly every subject matter.

In trial courts, the parties to a controversy may dispute the particular facts, which law should be applied to those facts, and how that law should be applied. If a party is entitled to and requests a trial by jury, the appropriate issues will be tried before a jury in the trial courts, not in the appellate courts.

Courts of Appeal and Review

Every state has at least one court of review, or appellate court. The function of these courts is mostly limited to hearing appeals. Appeals courts normally only review the records of the trial courts and determine whether the judgments of the trial courts were correct. No jury and no witnesses are present during an appeal.

These intermediate appellate, or review, courts are often called the courts of appeals. The highest court of the state is usually called the supreme court.[1] Appellate courts try few cases.

Appellate courts look at questions of law and procedure, but not usually questions of fact. The decisions of each state's highest court on all questions of state law are final, unless overruled by the Supreme Court of the United States.

SECTION 1 REVIEW

1. What are the three tiers of state court systems?
2. What are limited jurisdiction courts?
3. What are general jurisdiction courts?
4. **For critical analysis:** How do you think the right of appeal might interfere with guarantees of a fair and speedy trial?

1. In New York the state supreme court is called the court of appeals. In Texas and Oklahoma there are two "highest" appellate courts. In Texas, for example, the state district court decisions can be appealed to either the Texas Supreme Court or to the Texas Court of Criminal Appeals.

SECTION 2

How Judges Are Selected

Preview Questions

- What are the three major ways in which judges are selected?
- What are the pros and cons of popularly electing judges?
- What is the Missouri Plan?

There are over 16,000 judges sitting in state and municipal courts today. These judges obtained their posts through one of three major methods of selection: popular election, gubernatorial appointment, or selection by the legislature.

History of Judicial Selection

During the colonial period, governors and their councils made virtually all judicial appointments. Modifications to this rule were made in the first state constitutions. Georgia, however, was the only state to provide for the popular election of judges. The citizens of Georgia began to grow suspicious of the control that wealthy businesspeople and landowners had over the general population. Their idea was that the best place to ensure judicial responsibility was at the ballot box—an idea that became more and more prevalent in the twentieth century, as most states gradually moved to the popular election of judges.

Judicial Selection Today

Governors appoint some state judges in about one-fourth of the states today. In Delaware, Massachusetts, and New Hampshire, governors appoint all judges. In the other states that use gubernatorial appointment, the governor appoints most of them.

An alternative option for judicial appointment, rarely used today, is selection by the legislature. The state legislatures in Connecticut, Rhode Island, South Carolina, and Virginia appoint some or all of their judges. In all remaining states, judges are to some extent popularly elected.

Note that in some states, even though judges are nominally popularly elected in theory, they usually have first been appointed to fill a vacant seat, then run for office as an incumbent. In Minnesota, for example, incumbents are reelected most of the time and usually run unopposed.

TEACHING CITIZENSHIP SKILLS AND RESPONSIBILITIES

Read

Before the students begin reading this Citizenship Skills and Responsibilities feature, let them share their own knowledge about—and perhaps experiences with—small claims court: What is the purpose of a small claims court? Whom are small claims courts intended to serve? Have you or any of your family members ever been to small claims court? If so, why and with what results? Based on what you now know, do you anticipate that you will ever use a small claims court? Why or why not? After a short discussion, have the students read the feature independently.

Discuss

Use questions such as these to guide the students in discussing the Citizenship Skills and Responsibilities feature: Why might each of the examples at the beginning of the feature lead you to a small claims court? What other examples can you think of? Under what circumstances is it wise to avoid paying a lawyer for his or her advice? Why? Why is checking with the clerk of the small claims court an essential first step? How will sitting in on several small claims proceedings help you? What does it mean that "the small claims court does not act as a collection agency"? Why is it important to understand this fact before you file suit? What is "winning by default"?

If you were preparing to go to small claims court, do you think you would consult with a friend who was a lawyer? Do you think you would pay for a consultation with a lawyer? Why or why not? How could your presentation of inaccuracies prejudice your case? What kind of language and style should you use in a demand letter? What does it mean to "settle the case out of court"? Why is it important to have written evidence of any attempts to settle out of court?

CITIZENSHIP SKILLS AND RESPONSIBILITIES

The Small Claims Court

Someday you may think you were cheated by your former landlord because you didn't get your security deposit returned when you moved out. Or perhaps a dry cleaner may ruin your best clothes and not want to pay you for the damages. Or someone may owe you money and refuse to repay you. Rather than paying for a lawyer, you may be able to take advantage of a small claims court to remedy these situations. In most states today you have the right to use the services of small claims courts when the amount in dispute is less than $5,000.

How These Courts Work

The first thing you do is ask the clerk of the small claims court in your area whether the court can handle your case. Make sure that the court has jurisdiction over the person or business you wish to sue, and that you have the correct business name and address of the company or individual being sued. Usually, the defendant must live, work, or do business within the area of the court's jurisdiction.

Remember that courts often require strict accuracy; if you cannot provide exact information, the suit will be thrown out. Also, the small claims court is not a collection agency. If you are filing suit against a firm that no longer is in business, you may have a very difficult time collecting.

While you are at the courthouse, it might prove helpful to sit in on a few proceedings. This will give you an idea of what to expect when your day in court arrives.

Once you file suit, a summons goes out to the defending party. When a company receives the summons, it may decide to resolve the issue out of court. About one-fourth of all cases for which summonses are issued are settled out of court.

Preparing for Trial

When you attend the trial, you should have on hand all necessary and pertinent receipts, canceled checks, written estimates, contracts, and any other form of documented evidence that you can show the judge. Explain the entire story in chronological order (the order in which events occurred) with supporting evidence to show the judge exactly what happened. Make sure that your dates are accurate (remember that inaccuracies can discredit your case). Also, make sure you have a copy of your ''demand letter,'' which should be no more than two double-spaced, typewritten pages, and should clearly summarize both the facts of the case and your demands of the other party. It is important that you hand this letter to the judge on trial day. It will not only present your version of the story, but also will demonstrate that you are taking a reasonable approach to the situation.

What Happens in Court

The judge generally will let you present your case in simple language without the help of a lawyer. In fact, in some states neither the plaintiff nor the defendant is allowed to have a lawyer present. You may receive the judge's decision immediately or by notice within a few weeks.

If your opponent tries to settle the case out of court, make sure his or her proposed offer is written down so that it can be upheld if the offer is withdrawn. You should sign these written documents and file them with the court so that the agreement can be legally enforced. It is best to have your opponent appear with you before the judge to outline the settlement terms. Generally, if you win or if you settle out of court, you should be able to get your opponent to pay for the court costs, which vary greatly depending on the state.

The table on the following page provides information on small claims courts.

TAKING ACTION

1. Go to your local small claims court and obtain the necessary forms for filing suit.
2. Listen to at least one small claims court proceeding and answer the following questions:

- How much money was sought for damages?
- Was the judge understanding of the plaintiff's problems? Was the judge understanding of the defendant's position?
- Did you agree with the judge's rulings?

Analyze and Apply

Let the students work in small groups to discuss what they have learned about small claims court: Who uses this court? How are those people served by the court? What kinds of results are usually achieved? Then have the group members work together to write a short story or a skit about people involved in a small claims suit.

Review

Ask the students review questions such as these: What is one example of a suit that might be made in small claims court? What is the maximum amount for which you can sue in small claims court in our state?

Characteristics of Small Claims Courts in Selected States

State	Maximum Amount of Suit	Lawyers Allowed?	Who Can Appeal? Plaintiff	Who Can Appeal? Defendant	Initial Cost*
Alabama	$5,000	yes	yes	yes	$0–$1,000, $26; $1,001–$5,000, $44
Arizona	$1,000	no	yes	yes	$3
California	$2,000	no	no	yes	$6
Colorado	$2,000	no	yes	yes	$17
Connecticut	$1,500	yes	no	no	$20
District of Columbia	$2,000	yes	yes	yes	$1 + serving fee
Florida	$2,500	yes	yes	yes	$0–$100,$41; $101–$2,500, $50
Georgia	$3,000	yes	yes	yes	$0–$300, $38; $301–$3,000, $38
Illinois	$15,000	no	yes	yes	$0–$250, $20; $251–$500, $30; $501–$2,500, $40; $2,501–$15,000, $85
Indiana	$3,000	yes	yes	yes	$29
Iowa	$2,000	yes	yes	yes	$17 + serving fees
Kansas	$1,000	no	yes	yes	$0–$500, $10; $501–$1,000, $30
Kentucky	$1,500	yes	yes	yes	$22.85
Louisiana	$2,000	yes	no	no	$43.50
Maine	$1,400	yes	yes	yes	$20 per defendant
Maryland	$2,500	yes	yes	yes	$5 + serving fee
Massachusetts	$1,500	yes	no	yes	$0–$500, $16.25; $500–$1,500, $21.25
Michigan	$1,500	no	no	no	$0–$600, $10 + serving fee; $601–$1,500, $20 + serving fee
Minnesota	$2,000	yes	yes	yes	$500–$999.99, $19 + recording fee of $15; $1,000–$2,000, $24 + recording fee of $15
Mississippi	$1,000	yes	yes	yes	1 party, $32; 2 parties, $40
Missouri	$1,000	yes	yes	yes	$0–$99.99, $5 + fees; $100–$1,000, $10 + serving fees
New Jersey	$1,000	yes	yes	yes	$4.10
New York	$2,000	yes	judge; yes arbitrator, no	yes no	$19
North Carolina	$1,500	yes	yes	yes	$19 + serving fees
Ohio	$1,000	yes	yes	yes	$17
Oklahoma	$1,500	yes	yes	yes	$37 + serving fees
Pennsylvania	$5,000	yes	yes	yes	$1–$500, $16, $501–$2,000, $22; $2,001–$5,000, $42
South Carolina	$1,000	yes	yes	yes	$30
Tennessee	$10,000	yes	yes	yes	$42.75
Texas	$5,000	yes	yes	yes	$45
Virginia	$7,000	yes	yes	yes	$12
Wisconsin	$1,000	yes	yes	yes	$18 + serving fees
Wyoming	$750	yes	yes	yes	$13

*In some states, the initial cost will vary, depending on the amount of the claim. In Alabama, for example, if the claim in dispute is between $0 and $1,000, the initial cost (for filing fees, etc.) will be $26; if the claim is between $1,000 and $5,000, the initial cost will be $44.

Discussion Starter
As the students consider the "pros" of popular election of judges, you might pose questions such as these: What is the relationship between popular interests and the law? In what kinds of situations might popular interests conflict with the law? Which are judges intended to serve? Why?

Comprehension
Let several students explain how being a political activist and a strong partisan might conflict with being a fair judge. Encourage the students to recall or make up examples of specific conflicts that could result.

Critical Thinking Skills
Encourage the students to analyze the interests of political party organizations, lawyers' organizations, and special interest groups in supporting the popular election of judges: What do you think motivates each of these groups in supporting popular elections? How important is the support such groups provide? Who might oppose the popular election of judges? Why? Do you think such elections should continue? Why or why not?

Caption Answer The two other major methods of selection for state judges are popular election and selection by the legislature.

Popular Election—Pros and Cons

Over three-fourths of all judges sitting in state and municipal courts today are popularly elected. In Alabama, Michigan, Mississippi, Oregon, Texas, Washington, and Wisconsin, for example, all judges are popularly elected, except for municipal court judges, who are usually appointed by their respective city councils.

The Pros Advocates of popular election claim that these judges are just as competent as those chosen by any other method. Presumably, elected judges also make decisions that are more in line with popular desires and interests than appointed judges. Finally, the popular election of judges prevents governors or the dominant party in the legislature from building up a "party machine" by rewarding loyal followers with judgeships.

The Cons Those who oppose the popular election of judges in partisan races point out that political bosses and party machines control the nominations and elections. Virtually the only way for a judge to be truly popularly elected is for that person to be a political activist and a strong partisan; otherwise, he or she will not get the endorsement of the local party. During the heat of an election, voters may not give sufficient consideration to the legal expertise of a particular judicial candidate. Additionally, highly qualified individuals who find playing politics distasteful may never seek a judicial office. Finally, elected judges may make decisions with an eye to reelection rather than on the merits of each case.

As the debate goes on, what is sure is that all moves to abandon the current system of popular election have failed. Political party organizations, state bar associations, lawyers' groups, and special interest groups have all vigorously supported the popular election of judges. For political parties, such elections offer an opportunity to reward faithful party loyalists. For special interest groups, they offer an opportunity to influence election results through campaign contributions. State bar associations and other lawyers' groups support popular elections because they can attempt to control elections by controlling candidate nominations.

The Missouri Plan—An Alternative?

Is it possible to combine the appointment and election processes to select judges? Yes, say the American Bar Association and the President's Commission on Law Enforcement and Administration of Justice. The American Bar Association recommends that judges (other than magistrates) be nominated by a special judicial nominating committee and appointed by the governor. Once this is done, appointees are approved or rejected at a general election after serving an initial term of three years and subsequent terms every ten years.

Multidiscipline Strategies

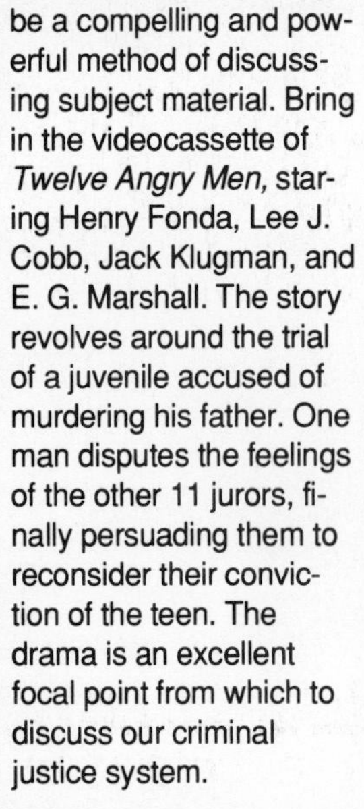

Drama Fiction can often be a compelling and powerful method of discussing subject material. Bring in the videocassette of *Twelve Angry Men*, staring Henry Fonda, Lee J. Cobb, Jack Klugman, and E. G. Marshall. The story revolves around the trial of a juvenile accused of murdering his father. One man disputes the feelings of the other 11 jurors, finally persuading them to reconsider their conviction of the teen. The drama is an excellent focal point from which to discuss our criminal justice system.

In New Hampshire, the governor appoints all judges including those for the supreme court. This is an example of gubernatorial appointment powers. What are the two other major methods of selection for state judges?

Enrichment
Ask a volunteer to research and report on the President's Commission on Law Enforcement and Administration of Justice: What is it? What purposes is it intended to serve? What are its accomplishments?

Comprehension
Help the students study and discuss the map, Selection of Judges: What does this map tell about our state? About neighboring states? About trends within the country?

Discussion Starter
As the students consider the Missouri Plan, ask them to identify both its advantages and its disadvantages. Then encourage the students to express and defend their own reactions to the plan.

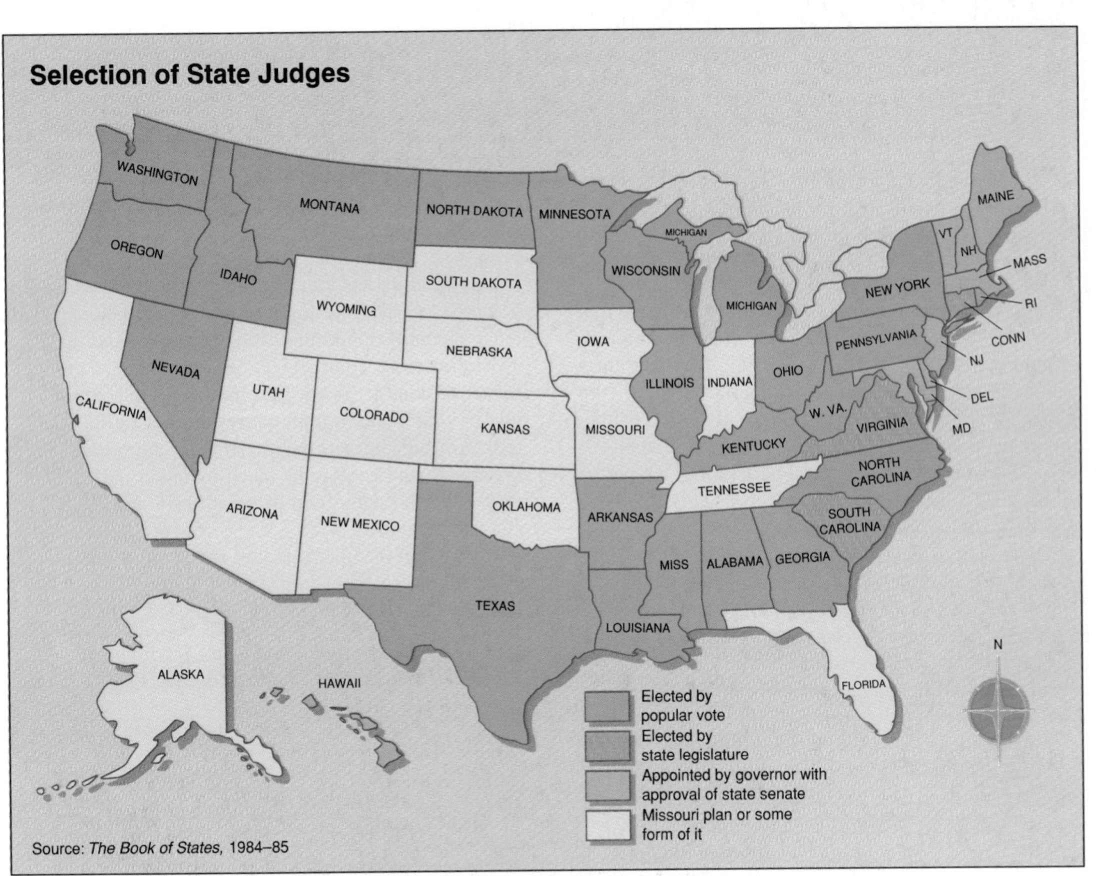

▲ **FIGURE 23–2 Selection of State Judges.** By looking at the map above, you can see which method for the selection of state judges is used in your state. Which of the methods shown on the map is recommended by the American Bar Association and the President's Commission on Law Enforcement and Administration of Justice?

Figure Answer The Missouri Plan is recommended by the American Bar Association and the President's Commission on Law Enforcement and Administration of Justice. This plan calls for judges to be nominated by a special judicial nominating committee and appointed by the governor. Each judge is then subject to approval or rejection at a general election held after an initial term of three years and every ten years during subsequent terms.

This plan has been offered for over seventy years by the American Bar Association. A version of the plan was used in California in 1934. Missouri has followed the plan since adopting its new constitution in 1947. It has therefore been labeled the **Missouri Plan**.

In Missouri the governor appoints all seven justices of the state's supreme court, and the thirty-two judges of the state court of appeals.[2] Certain other trial court judges, such as those sitting in the Kansas City metropolitan area, are also appointed. The governor is required to make these appointments from a list of names recommended by a judicial nominating commission made up of members of the state bar association, private citizens, and at least one sitting judge.[3]

After the appointed jurist is in office at least one year, she or he must have her or his name appear on the next general election ballot. The voters decide whether or not the judge should be kept. If the voters say yea, the judge serves a regular term and then seeks further terms in later general elections. If the voters say nay, the governor makes a new appointment in the same manner as before.

2. Often the term *judge* is used to refer to those who preside over trial courts and the term *justice* for those who preside over appellate courts.

3. The term *sitting* judge distinguishes judges who are currently active in the judicial system, as opposed to those who are not. Most retired judges retain their title as judge for the rest of their lives even though they are not sitting judges.

TEACHING BUILDING SOCIAL STUDIES SKILLS

Read
Introduce this Building Social Studies Skills feature with a brief discussion during which the students share what they already understand about contracts: What is a contract? Who can enter into a contract? What are the usual purposes for entering into a contract? After the discussion, ask two or three students to read the feature aloud to the rest of the class.

Discuss
To help the students discuss the new information presented here about contracts, ask questions such as these: How are an airline ticket, a guarantee on your stereo, and an agreement with your mechanic contracts? Why are written contracts preferable to verbal contracts? In what circumstances might a verbal contract be sufficient? Why is it necessary to understand the terms of a contract? Under what circumstances should you have a lawyer evaluate a contract before you sign it? Why? What are some examples of contracts that, for various reasons, may not be legally binding? What are some examples of breached contracts?

Analyze and Apply
Let the students work with partners to plan and write up simple contracts. Then have each pair of students present their contract to the rest of the class for evaluation: Who will agree to sign the contract? Why?

Review
Ask questions such as these to help the students review this Building Social Studies Skills feature: What is a contract? What is consideration? What is a breached contract?

Enrichment
Let one of the students research the impeachment procedure for judges in your state. When have judges been impeached? Why? With what results? Ask the student to present his or her findings in a brief oral report to the rest of the class.

Reteaching Strategies
1. Ask the students to work with partners to compare and, if necessary, revise their outlines of Section 2.
2. Let the students work in small groups to discuss the Missouri Plan; suggest that the group members draw simple sketches showing all the steps involved in carrying out this plan.

Evaluation Strategies
1. Have the students write their answers to the Section 2 Review questions.
2. Have the students take the Section 2 Quiz found in the *TRB*.

Section 2 Review (Answers)
1. Governors appoint about one-fourth of state judges. In the remaining states, they are, to some extent, popularly elected. Rarely, they are selected by the legislature.
2. The pros are that elected judges make decisions that are more in line with popular desires, and that the popular election of

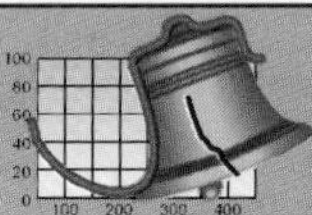

BUILDING SOCIAL STUDIES SKILLS
Understanding Contracts

A contract is a legal agreement made between two or more people or groups of people. Throughout your life, you will be involved with many contracts such as rental agreements, insurance plans, or real estate contracts. Even an airline ticket, a guarantee on your stereo, or an agreement with a mechanic to fix your brakes is a contract. Contracts contain a promise either to perform or to refrain from certain actions. They may be either written or verbal, although a written contract is more easily enforceable. In many cases, the law requires written contracts.

A contract contains several parts. First, the party writing the contract makes an offer, usually involving the exchange of goods or services. For example, a health club offers an individual the use of its facilities. The second part of the contract is the recipient's acceptance of the offer. Most contracts are enforceable only if each party receives something of value, which is called **consideration**. For example, the health club in the contract receives an initiation fee and monthly fees. The customer in turn gets use of the club's facilities. Each party must understand and accept the terms of the contract. After the terms of the contract have been fulfilled, the contract is completed.

There are a number of ways in which a contract may be broken. The offer, the acceptance, and the consideration must all be included in the deal. If one or more of these parts is left out, the contract is not legally binding and can be voided. The contract must be agreed to, without force or bribery, by persons of legal age and sound mind. If all of these conditions are not met, the contract can be canceled. A breached contract is one that has been violated, or one in which one or both parties did not fulfill the terms of the contract. Legal action to enforce a breached contract may be taken by either party. It may either be settled out of court or the injured party can sue for damages.

Always remember that you need to fully understand all parts of any contract that you are asked to sign.

PRACTICING YOUR SKILLS

1. Ask your parents or adult friends to show you a contract, such as a car rental agreement, and identify the three main parts discussed above.
2. Write down a summary of the three main parts in the contract.

Even though California and Missouri were the first states to adopt this hybrid form of appointment and election, some form of the Missouri Plan has been adopted in a number of the states for at least some judges, as you can see in Figure 23–2 on page 569.

Removal of Judges

Virtually all judges are appointed or elected for a fixed term from six to twelve years. At the end of their term they are either reelected or reappointed, or else they leave the bench.

If a state judge is acting improperly, that judge can be impeached. Every state except Oregon provides for the impeachment process that you read about in the previous chapter. Impeachment by the legislature is a procedure seldom used; only when gross misconduct has occurred will a legislature attempt to remove a judge through impeachment and conviction. In most cases there is no remedy for lesser faults such as neglect of duty or infirmity caused by age and illness. The state has to wait until the unfit judge either dies, resigns, retires, or fails to win reelection.

Judges can in certain states and under certain circumstances be recalled. Sometimes judges may be removed when a legislature directs the governor to do so.

The most recent trend has been to establish boards of judicial qualifications to evaluate judges and remove them if necessary. In 1960, for example, a commission of judicial performance was established in California that consists of private citizens, attorneys, and several sitting judges. It receives complaints and holds hearings for those judges accused of improper or unfair conduct. Over three-fourths of the states now use a similar board or commission. Whenever such boards ask a judge to leave and that judge refuses, the commission may take the case judges prevents governors or the dominant party from building up a "party machine." The cons are that political bosses and party machines control nominations and elections. It is also argued that highly qualified individuals who find playing politics distasteful will not run and that elected judges may make decisions with an eye to re-election rather than the merits of the case.

3. Judges would be nominated by a special judicial nominating committee and appointed by the governor. Appointees would then be approved or rejected at a general election after serving an initial term of three years and subsequent terms every ten years.

Caption Answer Answers will vary according to your state.

4. Answers will vary, e.g., the Missouri plan is best for the public. The governor must first make the appointment, but it is from a list made up of the nominating commission which consists of members of the state bar association, private citizens, and at least one sitting judge. The voters can decide whether or not the appointed judge should be re-elected or not.

SECTION 3

Points to Stress

- The place where state crimes are defined.
- Mandatory sentencing and victim compensation laws.
- Those responsible for the administration of criminal laws.
- The role of state police in this process.

Kickoff Activity

Have one of the students read the section title aloud. Then ask the students to list at least five words or phrases that express their responses to the title. After all the students have completed their lists, encourage volunteers to share and explain what they have written.

Working with the Preview Questions

Let the students read and briefly discuss their initial responses to these study questions. Then instruct the students to keep the questions in mind, looking for more detailed answers, as they read Section 3.

Teaching Strategies

Introduction

Ask a volunteer to read the section introduction aloud. Then encourage the students to discuss their responses to these questions: How does crime affect you and your family?

Discussion Starter

Ask the students to discuss their responses to questions such as these: What are the advantages of mandatory sentencing? Why is a system of mandatory sentencing most often applied to drug-related crimes? Do you think there are any disadvantages associated with mandatory sentencing? If so, what are they?

▲ California voters removed state Chief Justice Rose Bird from office in 1986. What are the methods for removal of judges in your state?

to the state supreme court, which may then take whatever disciplinary action it deems necessary.

Section 2 Review

1. What are the major methods used to select judges?
2. What are the pros and cons of popularly elected judges?
3. How does the Missouri Plan arrive at a compromise between appointment and election of judges?
4. **For critical analysis:** Which method for selecting judges do you think is best for the general public? Explain your answer.

Section 3

Protection of Life and Property

Preview Questions

- Who defines what the state crimes are?
- What are mandatory sentencing and victim compensation laws?
- Who enforces most criminal laws? Does every state have a state police force?

Crime has become a major problem in our society. In a typical year in the 1990s between 12 and 13 million serious crimes are reported to the police. About a million and a half of those are violent crimes: murder, rape, robbery, and aggravated assault. The remainder are property crimes including burglary and motor vehicle theft. In such a typical year, about $15 billion of property is stolen, of which approximately 30 percent is recovered. Crime rates have usually been higher in urban areas. In the 1990s, however, crime has grown fastest in suburbs and rural areas. While crime is not confined to any particular group, young people between the ages of 15 and 24 commit more violent crimes than those in any other age group. And while males commit six times as many crimes as females, in recent years the crime rate has grown fastest among women. In public opinion polls, Americans mention crime as the first or second most important problem facing our country.

The protection of life and property is for the most part the responsibility of state and local governments. After all, the federal government has only limited jurisdiction over most crimes. The majority of crimes are actions that violate state laws. Over 90 percent of all employees in the criminal justice system are paid with state and local funds.

State Criminal Laws

Remember from Chapter 18 that crimes are offenses against society as a whole, even though in each case the crime may be committed against one or more individuals. Because crimes are offenses against society, they are prosecuted by a public official, not by the victims.

Crimes are defined by state statutes, which are laws enacted by state legislatures. The crimes of murder, rape, assault, burglary, and the sale and use of certain drugs are prohibited by the state criminal code.

There are wide discrepancies throughout the 50 states with respect to the definition of specific crimes and the penalties for being convicted of committing them. Many states have the death penalty for certain types of homicide; others do not have the death penalty at all.

Mandatory Sentencing A number of legislatures have introduced **mandatory sentencing**, which is a system of fixed terms of imprisonment for specific crimes. Mandatory sentencing is part of state law, which is written by elected legislators. Particularly with respect to drug-related crimes, there is an increasing tendency of legislatures to impose mandatory sentencing.

Victim Compensation Laws Some states provide for compensation—usually monetary—to victims of serious

TEACHING GOVERNMENT IN ACTION

Read

Begin by letting volunteers respond to questions such as these: What is a minor? How are the rights of minors different from the rights of adults? What is the purpose of distinguishing between minors and adults? What do you know about the rights and privileges of minors in court? After a short discussion, let the students read this Government in Action feature independently.

Discuss

Use questions such as these to guide a discussion of the feature: How were Gerald Gault's rights violated by the police? How were his parents' rights violated? What does it mean to be "declared a delinquent"? What is your reaction to the sentence Gerald was given? Why do you think it was so harsh? Why do you think it was so different from a sentence that would have been handed down to an adult? What can you learn from studying the chart of a typical juvenile court process? What happens at each step in this process? What are the options at each step? Why do you think the Supreme Court reached its decision in the *Gault* case? What is the significance of this decision?

Analyze and Apply

Let the students work in groups to research the answers to these questions: What is the legal definition of a juvenile? Who decides whether a defendant will be tried as a juvenile or as an adult? How is that decision reached? What are the possible consequences of that decision? After the group members have completed their research, let them discuss their findings and consider responses to these ques-

GOVERNMENT IN ACTION

CASE STUDY

Protecting the Rights of Minors

Gerald Gault, age 15, was accused of making an obscene phone call to a neighbor. He was taken into custody while his parents were at work. The police did not bother to notify Mr. and Mrs. Gault of what had happened to their son. Gerald was placed in a detention center. When his frantic parents finally learned that he was in custody, they were simply told that there would be a hearing the next day. No one mentioned the nature of the complaint against Gerald.

The complaining neighbor, Mrs. Cook, did not attend Gerald's hearing; instead, a police officer testified about what Mrs. Cook told him. Gerald denied making the obscene remarks, and blamed the call on a friend. No lawyers were present and no record was made of what was said at the hearing. (A juvenile court hearing does not have a jury.) The judge ruled that the evidence weighed against Gerald. Gerald was declared a delinquent and sentenced to a state reform school until age 21. Any adult found guilty of the same crime would have been sent to a county jail for no longer than sixty days.

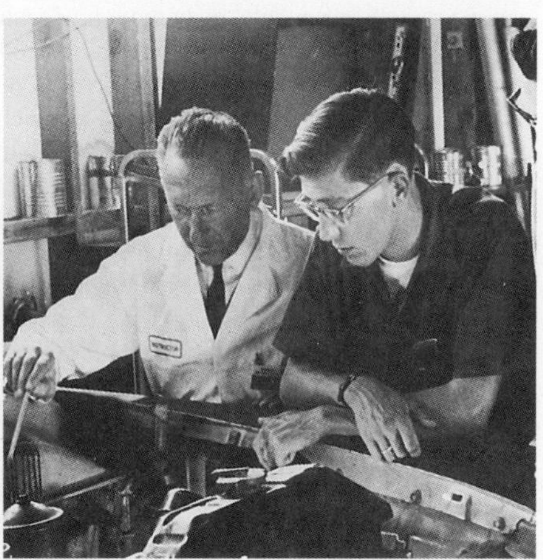

▲ Gerald Gault is shown here studying automotive repair at a Job Corps center. In 1964, a juvenile court in Arizona ordered then 15-year-old Gault to be confined to a state industrial school for a maximum of six years for allegedly making an obscene telephone call. In 1967, however, the U.S. Supreme Court ruled that the juvenile court proceeding had denied Gault due process of law.

The figure on the next page shows a typical juvenile court process.

The legal process for juveniles is just as complicated, if not more so, as the process for adults. But adults have always had the right to a jury trial and the right to a lawyer. Gerald Gault's parents believed that he had been mistreated by not being granted the same rights that an adult would have. Their case went all the way to the U.S. Supreme Court, which ruled that juveniles are in fact entitled to many of the same rights as adults. Specifically, the justices held that juveniles charged with a delinquent act are entitled to be informed of the charges against them, to confront and cross-examine witnesses, to remain silent, and to be represented by an attorney.

The *Gault* decision (1967) gave young people accused of a crime many of the same rights as adults, but not all. Not until 1970 did the Supreme Court decide that juveniles charged with a criminal act must be found "delinquent by proof beyond a reasonable doubt." Juveniles still do not have the right to a jury trial or bail.

THINK ABOUT IT

1. What would have been your reaction had you been in Gerald Gault's situation?
2. Do you think that juveniles should have the right to a trial by jury? If so, should it be a jury of their peers as it is with adults? What might be the advantages and disadvantages of such jury trials?
3. Do you think that an adult could ever be convicted on the basis of hearsay testimony from a police officer who simply explained what the alleged victim had told him or her? Why or why not?

tions: Should the method of distinguishing between juveniles and adults in the court system be revised? If not, why not? If so, how?

Review

To help the students review this Government in Action feature, ask these questions: What rights were denied to Gerald Gault? What is the significance of the *Gault* decision?

Think About It (Answers)

1. Answers will vary.

2. Answers will vary, e.g., juveniles should have a right to a jury of their peers. The advantage is that juveniles would be treated fairly just like adults. The disadvantage is that it would cost more tax dollars, take more time, and perhaps not deal with the special problems of minors.

3. Answers will vary, e.g., this would not happen to an adult because of the many rights of the accused.

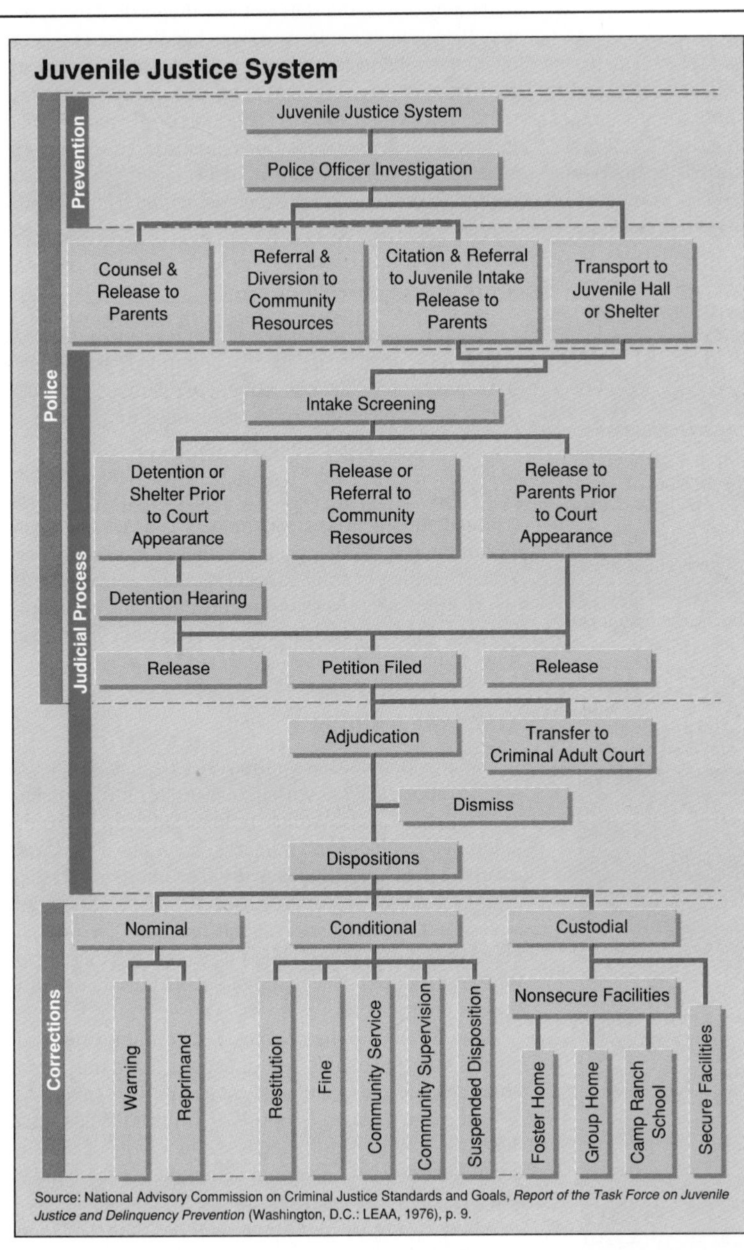

Source: National Advisory Commission on Criminal Justice Standards and Goals, *Report of the Task Force on Juvenile Justice and Delinquency Prevention* (Washington, D.C.: LEAA, 1976), p. 9.

Discussion Starter
As the students consider extradition, let them discuss their ideas in response to these questions: What cases—if any—can you imagine in which you personally would oppose extradition? What would motivate your opposition?

Extension
Ask the students to identify the title, the powers, and the responsibilities of your state's police system.

Caption Answer In two-thirds of the states, state police have the general authority to enforce all state laws. In the remaining states, the state police have authority only to handle special aspects of motor vehicle law. State troopers might also be responsible for state regulations regarding fish and game, liquor or drug laws, and protecting the governor.

Discussion Starter
Encourage discussion by asking the students these questions: What do you think makes Americans suspicious of a police force that is not locally controlled? How can the definition of "locally controlled" vary from community to community? Do you believe that this attitude is more true of Americans than of other people around the world? Why or why not?

Enrichment
Have a volunteer read about the involvement of your state's National Guard units in international wars and national conflicts during this century. Let the volunteer prepare a chart or bulletin board display summarizing that information.

Enrichment
Ask an interested volunteer to research and report on the 1970 confrontation at Kent State University: Who was involved in the protest demonstration? Why had the National Guard been called onto the campus? What controversies surrounded the shootings? When and how did the parents of the slain students sue? What were the results of those suits?

Reteaching Strategies
1. Work with small groups of students as they discuss their responses to the Preview Questions.
2. Have the students work with partners to plan and write one-paragraph responses to this question: Why is crime a major problem?

Evaluation Strategies
1. Have the students write their answers to the Section 3 Review questions.
2. Have the students take the Section 3 Quiz found in the *TRB*.

Section 3 Review (Answers)
1. A system of fixed terms of imprisonment for specific crimes.
2. Laws that require compensation to victims of serious criminal offenses.
3. It is a legal procedure by which a criminal who has fled to another state is returned to the state in which he or she committed the crime.
4. Answers will vary, e.g., one benefit would be that all criminals committing the same crimes would be treated equally. It would cut down on discrimination. One cost

criminal offenses such as assault. In other states, such as Utah and Mississippi, a judge in a state court can force a criminal to compensate the victims of a crime. That means that the criminal must pay money to the victims of his or her crime.

Extradition **Extradition** is the legal procedure by which a criminal who has fled to another state is returned to the state in which he or she committed the crime. Extradition laws are expressly stated in Article IV of the U.S. Constitution. In most cases, the return of the fugitive is a routine matter, but there have been cases when requests for extradition have been contested. These are usually cases where racial or political equality may be at stake, or cases that involve separation and divorce, such as one parent leaving the state and refusing to provide financial support for a dependent child.

The State Police

Most criminal laws are enforced by municipal police departments. Nonetheless, state police forces can be found in all states except Hawaii. The notion of state police originated with the famous Texas Rangers, who organized in 1835 during the Texas revolution. In 1865 Massachusetts established a system of state constables. Both Arizona and New Mexico at the turn of the century created border patrols modeled after the Texas Rangers. In 1903 Connecticut established a small state force and in 1905 Pennsylvania did the same.

Today, two-thirds of the states have state police who have general authority to enforce all state laws. In the remaining states, the state police (often called the Highway Patrol) have authority only to handle special aspects of motor-vehicle law enforcement. In some instances, state troopers are responsible for making sure that state regulations with respect to game and fish are not violated. In others, state troopers enforce liquor and drug laws. In some states such as Arkansas, Idaho, Oregon, and Washington, the state police are charged with the duty of protecting the governor.

▼ State police forces can be found in all states except Hawaii. Here, officers of the California Highway Patrol operate a sobriety checkpoint on New Year's Eve. What type of authority do state police officers have?

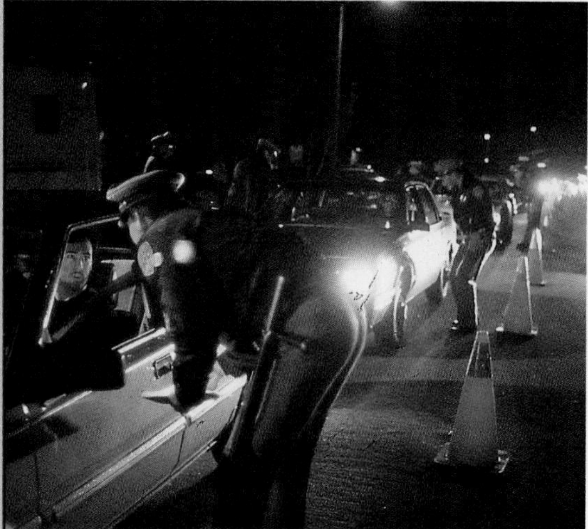

State Police Jurisdiction

Americans have a history of being suspicious of any police force that is not locally controlled. This makes state police jurisdiction difficult to define. The state police are almost uniformly prohibited from enforcing the laws of local governments unless they are invited to do so.

In those states having a state police force with general criminal jurisdiction, state troopers can act anywhere within the state limits whenever state laws are violated. Whenever the governor so requests, state police are usually required to assist state administrators and regulatory agencies such as those concerned with public health and school attendance.

The State Militia

You read about state militias in Chapter 22. The organized and better-known part of the state militia is called the National Guard, which is financed largely by the federal government and trained to meet those standards set up by the United States Army. The unorganized state militia is normally composed of all able-bodied adult males, and, in some states, adult females. The unorganized militia is seldom called up either for training or for duty. It could conceivably be called in the event of serious emergencies.

The history of the organized state militia (the National Guard) is mainly one of actions taken during national emergencies. National Guard units were called into federal service during World War I, World War II, and the Korean War. Most recently, certain parts of the National Guard were called into action during the conflict with Iraq in 1990 and 1991.

On occasion, the performance of the National Guard has reflected poor supervision and perhaps poor training.

would be that judges would have less discretion to take particular circumstances into consideration.

SECTION 4

Points to Stress

- The role of the department of justice in your state.
- The job of the prosecuting attorney.
- The typical criminal process by which individuals are prosecuted.

Kickoff Activity

Ask the students to write definitions of these two words: *prosecute* and *persecute.* When everyone has finished writing, let several students read their definitions aloud, and encourage the students to discuss the differences between the two words.

Working with the Preview Questions

Go over these three study questions with the class. Then instruct the students to keep the questions in mind as they read and take notes on Section 4.

Teaching Strategies

Introduction

Let one of the students read the section introduction aloud to the rest of the class. Then encourage the students to discuss their responses to this question: Why is prosecuting offenders an essential aspect of the legal system?

Discussion Starter

As the students consider the job of a district attorney, encourage discussion with questions such as these: Why is this such a highly political office? Who benefits from the political aspects of this position? How? What disadvantages might be associated with the political nature of the office? Why?

In 1970, four students were killed by overreacting national guardsmen at Kent State University during a protest of the United States' invasion of Cambodia. The parents of those students who died sued the governor of Ohio and several guardsmen. In contrast, guardsmen who served during the Middle East crisis in 1990 and 1991 provided valuable and highly skilled labor power.

SECTION 3 REVIEW

1. What is mandatory sentencing?
2. What are victim compensation laws?
3. How does extradition work?
4. **For critical analysis:** What do you think would be the costs and benefits of a uniform set of criminal laws?

SECTION 4

Prosecuting Offenders

Preview Questions

- Who presides over the department of justice in every state?
- What is the job of a prosecuting attorney?
- What is the typical process by which individuals suspected of committing a crime are prosecuted?

State laws are created by the legislature and enforced by state and local police personnel. When state laws have been violated and the suspected violator is apprehended, prosecution follows. Prosecuting offenders is the job of the state departments of justice, the prosecuting attorneys, and others.

The State Departments of Justice

Every state has an attorney general, usually popularly elected, who presides over some type of justice department. During the time the attorney general is in office, he or she cannot continue to engage in private legal practice. The attorney general handles lawsuits in which the state and its officials are a party, and also deals with local prosecutors. In Alaska, Delaware, and Rhode Island, there are no local prosecutors so the responsibility of handling local government lawsuits is centralized at the state level. Even in the other states, local prosecutors may often ask the attorney general for advice.

The Prosecuting Attorney

Those who are suspected of violating state law are normally arrested by local police departments. The prosecution of those suspects is then handled by a local **prosecuting attorney**, or PA, who works for the government. His or her title is often **district attorney**, or DA, or county attorney. The PA or DA acts on behalf of the people. He or she often names suspected criminals so that they can be brought before a grand jury.

The position of district attorney is highly political, and is normally an elective office. District attorneys are highly visible individuals who often launch political careers when they engage in effective anticrime campaigns.

District or county attorneys do not simply prosecute violators of state law. They also assist police personnel in uncovering crimes, defend officials in the counties in which they work, and also advise county officials and the minor court judges on legal issues.

The major job of the district attorney is to determine which individuals the police have apprehended should be charged with a crime. District attorneys wield great power throughout a suspect's criminal proceedings. They even confer with judges about what the sentencing should be if there is a conviction.

The Criminal Process

Throughout any criminal proceedings, there are numerous safeguards designed to guarantee the rights of individuals against the state. Not all criminal proceedings are exactly alike, but the following steps generally occur in most criminal cases.

Arrest Unless an individual is caught while actually committing a crime, a **warrant** must be issued for his or her arrest. A warrant is an order issued by a magistrate that authorizes a police officer to make an arrest. Before a warrant may be issued, there must be **probable cause** for suspecting that the individual in question has in fact committed a crime. For example, if a policeman sees a person with a pistol in his or her belt standing outside a convenience store, this may be probable cause. Arrest may sometimes be made without a warrant if there is no time to get one, but the action of the arresting officer is still judged by the standard of probable cause.

Indictment Individuals must be formally charged with having committed specific crimes before they can be brought to trial. This charge is called an **indictment** if issued by a **grand jury**, which consists of twelve to

Discussion Starter

As the students consider safeguards to guarantee the rights of individuals against the state, you may want to raise these discussion questions: What concerns have been raised in recent years regarding too much interest in the rights of defendants and too little interest in the rights of victims? What arguments are presented in favoring of protecting victims' rights? In favor of protecting defendants' rights? Can both be protected? Why or why not? Which do you believe should take precedence? Why?

Vocabulary

Ask the students to define *probable:* Where does *probable* lie on the spectrum between possible cause and certainty?

Discussion Starter

Focus the students' attention on the fact that arrests can be made without a warrant under certain conditions: Why are warrants usually required? How could this exemption from the requirement be misinterpreted? Misused? Do you think the exemption should be altered? Why or why not?

Critical Thinking Skills
Ask the students to evaluate and discuss the evidence presented here about grand jury hearings. What purposes are grand juries intended to serve? What purposes do they appear actually to be serving? What are the benefits of the current grand jury system? What problems does it involve? Do you believe the use of grand juries should be continued? Why or why not?

Comprehension
Let the students suggest other kinds of questions that might be raised in *voir dire:* What would the purpose of these questions probably be?

Discussion Starter
Guide the students in considering the requirement that a jury's verdict be unanimous: What is the purpose of this requirement? How well does this practice serve the intended purpose? What problems might be involved with this practice? Do you think justice could be served if the requirement were changed to allow ten of the twelve jurors to agree? Nine of the twelve? Seven?

Reteaching Strategies
1. Assign the students partners; have the partners review Section 4 by comparing and discussing the notes they have taken. As they work, encourage the students to make any necessary corrections or additions to their notes.
2. Have the students use their own words in writing definitions of these terms: *warrant, indictment, arraignment, grand jury, petit jury.*

Evaluation Strategies
1. Have the students write their answers to the Section 4 Review questions.

Caption Answer Before a warrant may be issued, there must be probable cause for suspecting that the individual in question has in fact committed a crime.

Extension
Work with the students to arrange for a local public defender to visit the class. Ask the public defender to speak briefly about his or her work; then allow time for the students to ask questions. (You may want to help the students plan interesting and appropriate questions.)

Comprehension
Let the students respond to these questions: Is bail always granted? Why not? Does the refusal to grant bail indicate anything about the defendant's guilt or innocence?

Discussion Starter
Encourage the students to discuss the differences between a bench trial and a jury trial: What would probably motivate a defendant to choose a bench trial? A jury trial?

Caption Answer The Sixth Amendment of the Constitution guarantees every accused person the right to a trial by an impartial jury. Only if the accused waives this right can a bench trial be held.

▲ Normally, for the police to make an arrest, as shown above, a warrant must be issued. What circumstance is required for the issuance of a warrant?

twenty-three citizens. During a grand jury hearing the prosecutor, perhaps the district attorney or one of the assistant district attorneys, will attempt to show the grand jury that the evidence is sufficient to indict the individual in question. The grand jury then weighs the evidence. If the majority of the grand jurors believes that the evidence is sufficient to hold the person for trial, it votes for the formal indictment.

Even though the grand jury is intended to act as a check on the power of the prosecutor, it usually does whatever the prosecutor recommends. Ninety-eight percent of all cases brought before grand juries result in a formal indictment. The average grand jury spends no more than five to ten minutes reviewing each case.

States are not required to use grand juries, and about half of the states do not use them. In those states, the prosecutor brings the evidence before a magistrate. If the magistrate agrees, she or he issues an **information**, a formal accusation that will cause the suspect to be arraigned.

▼ In a bench trial, as shown here, only the judge decides whether the defendant is guilty or not guilty. Can an accused person be forced to have a bench trial?

Arraignment Upon indictment, the suspect, or defendant, is arraigned.[4] **Arraignment** is a method by which a defendant comes before the judge, who then reads the formal charges listed in the indictment or information. The defendant, or his or her lawyer, then enters a plea of guilty or not guilty.

The Right to Counsel The defendant has the right to an attorney of his or her own choosing. If the defendant cannot obtain an attorney, a court-appointed lawyer, usually called a **public defender**, is assigned to the case.

In criminal cases there is typically a **preliminary hearing**, which is used by a magistrate to ensure that the defendant has been informed of and understands his or her rights and why the arrest was made. Once the magistrate determines that the defendant has been given "due process," then the magistrate will set bail. The setting of bail allows the accused to be out of jail until a jury renders its verdict.

The Trial The Sixth Amendment to the United States Constitution guarantees to every accused person a speedy and public trial by an impartial jury. Not everyone accused may want to have a jury trial, in which case a **bench trial** is held. In a bench trial, only the judge hears the evidence and decides whether the defendant is guilty or not guilty.

If a jury trial is requested, the individuals who sit on that jury are part of a **trial jury** (also called a **petit jury**), as opposed to a grand jury. A petit jury determines guilt or innocence, whereas a grand jury does not. Petit juries normally consist of twelve persons, although budget considerations have forced many states to reduce jury members to as few as six.

Jury Selection The names of potential jurors are usually selected from voter registration lists, home owner-

4. The state is the plaintiff (the prosecuting party) in a criminal trial. In civil trials, the plaintiff may be an individual or a business.

2. Have the students take the Section 4 Quiz found in the *TRB*.

Section 4 Review (Answers)

1. The prosecuting attorney represents the state.

2. After the arrest is made, the person is formally indicted, or charged. Upon indictment, the defendant is arraigned, where he or she comes before a judge who then reads the formal charges. The defendant pleads guilty or not guilty. There is then a preliminary hearing, and if a trial is requested, there is a trial by jury or bench trial.

3. The grand jury weighs the evidence and decides whether or not it is sufficient to hold the person for trial.

4. Answers will vary, e.g., the person should be disqualified if he or she has ever had anything to do with the defendant or has already made up his or her mind regarding the defendant's guilt.

SECTION 5

Points to Stress

- Plea bargaining and the reasons for its common usage.
- The types of sentences that may be imposed on an individual convicted of a crime.
- Probation and parole.

Kickoff Activity

Write the word *prison* on the chalkboard. Let the students read the word silently and then list at least six words or phrases the word brings to mind. When all the students have finished writing, give several volunteers an opportunity to read their lists aloud.

Working with the Preview Questions

Let volunteers read the study questions aloud, and invite interested students to share their initial responses. Then have the students use these questions to develop main headings for a topic outline. Let the students use these main headings as aides in writing their own outlines of Section 5.

Teaching Strategies

Introduction

After the students have read the section introduction, guide them in a brief discussion of what they already understand about plea bargaining. Encourage them to recall (or bring in) news articles about cases that ended in plea bargaining: What kinds of crimes were involved? What was the result for the accused in each case?

Discussion Starter

Guide the students in considering and discussing the arguments for and against plea bargaining: Which do you find more convincing? What alternatives to plea bargaining do you believe should be considered?

Extension

Have the students gather news stories about all four categories of sentences—prison, fine, treatment, and community service. Let the students discuss the news stories and compare the cases in which different sentences were handed down.

ship lists, and sometimes from driver's license lists in a particular location. When the judge, prosecutor, and defense attorneys examine prospective jurors to ensure that their judgment will be impartial, the process is called ***voir dire***, a French phrase meaning "to speak the truth." Usually *voir dire* consists of questions asked orally to individual prospective jurors, in order to determine whether that person could render a fair judgment.

Jury's Verdict In most states, the jury's verdict must be unanimous; everyone must agree that the accused is guilty. Exceptions are sometimes made for minor criminal cases in which only a majority vote is required.

When a jury cannot agree on a verdict, it is called a **hung jury**, and the judge declares a mistrial. A new trial with a new jury may be held, or the prosecutor may simply drop the charges against the defendant.

The current judicial trend is toward fewer and fewer jury trials because of their cost and time. The explosion of crimes committed in the United States has made it virtually impossible for everyone accused of a crime to obtain a jury trial. Therefore, more and more prosecuting attorneys are making deals with accused persons, who agree to plead guilty to a lesser crime.

SECTION 4 REVIEW

1. Who does a prosecuting attorney represent?
2. What are the steps involved in a typical criminal proceeding?
3. What is the job of the grand jury? Why is it important?
4. **For critical analysis:** What would be some reasons why you would disqualify a prospective juror?

SECTION 5

Sentencing and Prisons

Preview Questions

- What is plea bargaining? Why is it so common?
- What types of sentences may be imposed on an individual convicted of a crime?
- What is probation? What is parole?

Many cases never come to trial. Among the cases that do reach trial, a mid-trial agreement may be made between the defendant, the prosecuting attorney, and the judge. About 90 percent of all cases are settled before or during the trial through a process known as plea bargaining.

Plea Bargaining

In a **plea bargaining** arrangement, the defendant agrees to plead guilty, usually to a lesser charge than the prosecutor originally brought. Let's say, for example, that John Smith has been charged with armed robbery, which carries a maximum sentence of 20 years. Smith's attorney may relate to Smith that the prosecutor will reduce the charge to simple robbery, which carries a maximum of only five years in prison, in exchange for a guilty plea to the reduced charge. Smith knows for certain that he will receive a maximum of only five years in prison if he agrees. The prosecutor is willing to plea bargain in order to reduce the number of cases coming to trial in the extremely crowded courts, and to be assured that the case will result in a guilty plea.

Proponents of plea bargaining believe that defendants are given greater power in the legal process. In reality, however, a major reason for plea bargaining is that it reduces the stress on our overloaded judicial system. Opponents of plea bargaining argue that reducing the charge allows individuals to avoid properly paying for their crimes. Some argue that plea bargaining makes a mockery of the law because criminals can bargain for reduced sentences.

Sentencing

Whether through plea bargain or through a full trial, a sentence must be imposed if a defendant is found guilty. After the verdict is known, a judge will pronounce a **sentence**, which is the penalty imposed on anyone convicted of a crime. A sentence often involves a specific period of time to be spent in prison. It may also involve the payment of a fine, a requirement for therapeutic treatment, or a certain number of hours that must be spent in community service.

Juries often make recommendations concerning sentencing in criminal trials. Judges are not legally required to follow a jury's recommendation, although in some states, judges rarely disregard a jury's sentence. Judges may be guided by their personal views of the defendant, by recommendations from the prosecuting attorney and other court aides, by recommendations from social service administrators, and by state laws.

Determinate and Indeterminate Sentences Determinate sentences are fixed sentences for a particular

Discussion Starter
Help the students examine both the advantages and the disadvantages of determinate sentencing. Then ask them: Do you think the current trend toward determinate sentencing is healthy? Why or why not?

Cooperative Learning
Ask the students to work in groups to learn more about prison overcrowding: What problems does it cause? Who suffers as a result? Why has the overcrowding of prisons become such a serious and widespread situation? What suggestions for solutions have been made? What do you think should be done about prison overcrowding?

Caption Answer A sentence may also involve the payment of a fine, a requirement for therapeutic treatment, or a certain number of hours of community service.

Reteaching Strategies
1. Let the students work with partners to review Section 5 by comparing and discussing their section outlines. Remind the students to make corrections or additions to their own outlines as needed.
2. Have groups of students work together to review the steps in the criminal justice process from arrest to sentencing. Ask the group members to draw a flow chart showing all the steps.

Evaluation Strategies
1. Have the students write their answers to the Section 5 Review questions.
2. Have the students take the Section 5 Quiz found in the *TRB*.

Section 5 Review (Answers)
1. Plea bargaining is an arrangement in which the defendant agrees to plead guilty, usually for a lesser charge than the prosecutor originally brought. It reduces the number of cases on our overloaded judicial system, but reducing the charge allows individuals to avoid properly paying for their crimes.
2. Determinate sentences are fixed sentences for a particular crime. Indeterminate sentences mean there may be a maximum or minimum number of years, depending on whether the convicted criminal demonstrates "good behavior" and seems rehabilitated. The trend is toward more determinate sentencing.
3. Probation is an alternative to a jail sentence, in which a person is allowed to go free provided he or she maintains good behavior and is supervised by a probation officer. Parole is a supervised period which occurs after imprisonment.
4. Answers will vary, e.g., probation is punishment, although not as severe as imprisonment. It is giving the defendant a second chance.

For those found guilty of a crime, the sentence may involve a specific period of time to be spent in prison. What other penalties may be imposed as a sentence or a part of a sentence?

crime. A state law may say, for example, that anyone convicted of armed robbery must serve twenty years behind bars. When those twenty years are completed, the offender has to be released.

Indeterminate sentences mean there may be a maximum or minimum number of years, depending on whether the convicted criminal demonstrates good behavior and seems rehabilitated and ready to return to society.

The trend today is toward determinate sentencing. For some crimes this kind of sentencing is mandatory.

Probation

Probation is an alternative to a jail sentence for some convicted offenders. Under probation, a judge may suspend a convicted criminal's sentence and allow him or her to go free, provided he or she maintains good behavior and is supervised by a probation officer. Historians believe that Massachusetts was the first state to authorize probation in 1836.

Because of overcrowded prisons, about one-third of all persons tried and convicted today are placed on probation. The largest number of individuals placed on probation are juveniles who are convicted in juvenile court.

Parole

When individuals are allowed to leave prison before the end of their sentence, they are said to be on **parole**. Historically, parole was used as a reward for good behavior. Today, by contrast, parole is typically used to reduce overcrowding in prisons. The difference between probation and parole is that parole occurs after imprisonment, whereas probation occurs before or in place of imprisonment. Parole is often used in conjunction with indeterminate sentencing.

Parole, as we know it now, has only existed since the late 1800s, when Ohio, in 1884, became the first state to parole inmates of state prisons. Today all states have parole as an option. In some states, however, particularly in some Southern states, parole is less frequent and more difficult to obtain.

Section 5 Review

1. What is plea bargaining? What arguments have been made for and against it?
2. What is the difference between determinate and indeterminate sentencing? Currently, which type of sentencing is more popular?
3. What is the difference between probation and parole?
4. **For critical analysis:** Do you think probation is punishment or is it a way to let a criminal go free? Explain your answer.

TEACHING CHALLENGE TO THE AMERICAN DREAM

Read
Before the students read this Challenge to the American Dream feature, encourage them to discuss what they now know and feel about capital punishment: Why is capital punishment used in this country? In what other countries is it used? Which countries do not permit capital punishment? How do your family members and other adults around you seem to regard capital punishment? What is your own opinion of capital punishment? Why? Encourage the students to present and support various responses to these questions. Then have volunteers read the feature aloud to the class.

Discuss
Use questions such as these to help the students discuss the feature: What do the adjectives *random* and *arbitrary* mean? What is the significance of the Supreme Court's applying these words to describe the imposition of the death penalty? In what ways could the death penalty be viewed as violating the Eighth Amendment? The Fourteenth Amendment? Do you believe it does violate either or both of these amendments? Why or why not? What do you think society's need for justice is? How—if at all—can the administration of the death penalty satisfy that need? Is capital punishment a barbaric act? If not, why not? If so, might it nonetheless be justified? If so, how? What do you think accounts for the trend of increasing support for imposition of the death penalty?

Analyze and Apply
Have the students work together to gather and organize information on community attitudes toward capital punishment. Let them work together to compose a questionnaire eliciting responses about some—or all—of the issues raised in this feature. Then have them create and follow a plan for using the questionnaire to collect information. Finally, let the students organize the information and discuss what conclusion can be drawn.

Review
Ask questions such as these to help the students review this Challenge to the American Dream feature: What is one of the main arguments in favor of the death penalty? What is one of the main arguments against it?

You Decide (Answers)
1. Answers will vary, e.g., capital punishment is not cruel and unusual for first degree murder as long as it is administered fairly. The writers of the Constitution did not view it as cruel and unusual. They forbade not the taking of life, but the taking of life "without due process of law."
2. Answers will vary, e.g., even when states were executing fewer death-row inmates, the violent crime rates continued to rise. This is not a good measure of whether or not capital punishment is a deterrent. Besides, the real issue is not deterrence but whether justice permits or even requires the death penalty.

CHALLENGE TO THE AMERICAN DREAM

The Question of Capital Punishment

The Eighth Amendment of the U.S. Constitution prohibits cruel and unusual punishment. Until a Supreme Court decision in 1972, the death penalty was not considered cruel and unusual. Indeed, a number of states had imposed the death penalty for a variety of crimes and allowed juries to decide when the condemned could be sentenced to death.

Many people believed that the imposition of the death penalty was random and arbitrary. For example, 53 percent of all persons executed from 1930 to 1965 were African American, even though African Americans constituted less than 10 percent of the population.

A 1972 decision by the Supreme Court stated that the death penalty, as then applied, violated the Eighth and Fourteenth Amendments. It ruled that capital punishment is not necessarily cruel and unusual if the criminal has murdered or attempted to murder someone. In its opinion, however, the Court requested that the states make more precise laws so that the death penalty would be applied more consistently. A majority of states have followed this instruction. The laws in these states now define exactly which crimes are punishable by death.

Capital punishment remains one of the most debated aspects of our criminal justice system. Those who support it maintain that it serves as a deterrent to serious crime and satisfies society's need for justice. Those opposed to the death penalty do not believe it has any deterrent value and hold that it constitutes a barbaric act in civilized society.

The challenge to the American dream is to balance the need to punish and deter serious crimes against the public's reluctance to take a person's life.

You Decide

1. Do you think capital punishment is cruel and unusual, and therefore in violation of the U.S. Constitution? Why or why not?
2. In spite of the fact that more states are executing death-row prisoners, violent crime rates have continued to rise. What do you think this indicates about the role of capital punishment in deterring crime?

CHAPTER 23 REVIEW

Key Terms

appellate courts 563
arraignment 576
bench trial 576
consideration 570
district attorney 575
extradition 574
general jurisdiction 563
grand jury 575
hung jury 577
indictment 575
information 576
jurisdiction 563
justice court 564
justice of the peace 564
limited jurisdiction 563
magistrate 564
magistrate courts 564
mandatory sentencing 571
Missouri Plan 569
parole 578
petit jury 576
plea bargaining 577
preliminary hearing 576
probable cause 575
probation 578
prosecuting attorney 575
public defender 576
review courts 563
sentence 577
trial courts 563
trial jury 576
***voir dire* 577**
warrant 575

Observable Mastery
Provide students with a fictional criminal suspect and begin at the time of arrest. Have students take turns completing the next step in the criminal process, providing the important details of each step. Be sure students include the warrant for arrest, indictment, arraignment, right to counsel and the preliminary hearing, the judge and how he or she got his or her job, the trial and jury, the verdict, and sentencing. Students should also include relevant issues like plea bargaining, mandatory sentencing, victim crime compensation laws, extradition, parole, and the opportunity for appeal. Through this exercise students can demonstrate an understanding of the entire criminal law process.

Chapter Evaluation
To evaluate student mastery of chapter material, you might:
1. Use Chapter Test A from the *TRB*.
2. Use Chapter Test B from the *TRB*.
3. Construct your own test using items from the *West American Government Test Bank* found in the *TRB*.
4. Use the accompanying computerized test software to construct and print a customized chapter test.

Review Questions (Answers)
1. Trial court, appellate court, and the state supreme court.
2. Courts of limited jurisdiction can hear only special cases.
3. Courts of general jurisdiction can hear virtually all cases.
4. Governors appoint about one-fourth of judges, and in most remaining states judges are to some extent popularly elected.
5. The pros for popular election are that the judges make decisions that are more in line with the public's wishes. It also prevents governors or the dominant party from building up a "party machine" by rewarding loyal followers. The cons are that the only way a judge can be elected is to be politically active and a strong partisan. They may make decisions with an eye to reelection rather than on the merits of each case. Highly qualified individuals who don't want to play politics may never seek judicial office.
6. Judges are nominated by a special judicial nominating committee and appointed by the governor. Appointees are then approved or rejected at the general election after serving an initial term of three years and subsequent terms every ten years.
7. Mandatory sentencing is a system of fixed terms of imprisonment for specific crimes.

CHAPTER 23 REVIEW—Continued

Summary

1. Every state has a different court system, but most systems are organized around three levels of courts: the trial courts of general and limited jurisdiction, the courts of appeals, and the supreme court. Limited jurisdiction means that courts can hear only certain types of cases. General jurisdiction means that courts can hear virtually all cases. Every state has at least one court of review, or appellate court.

2. State judges are selected by the governor, by the legislature, or by the people. The Missouri Plan is a selection process that combines the processes of executive appointment and popular election. Judges are normally elected for a fixed term. During their terms in office, judges may be impeached and, if convicted, removed from office.

3. Crimes are defined by state statutes, which are laws enacted by state legislatures. A number of legislatures have introduced mandatory sentencing, which fixes sentencing for certain crimes. Some states provide for victim compensation. Most criminal laws are enforced by municipal police departments. All states except Hawaii have a state police system.

4. Every state has an attorney general who presides over some type of department of justice. The prosecution of criminal suspects is normally handled by a local prosecuting attorney. Typically, criminal proceedings begin with arrest, followed by indictment, arraignment, and a trial.

5. Most criminal cases are settled by a plea bargaining arrangement in which the defendant agrees to plead guilty, usually to a lesser charge than the prosecutor originally brought. A sentence is the penalty imposed on anyone convicted of a crime. Probation is an alternative to a jail sentence, which involves subjecting the violator to certain rules and placing him or her under the supervision of a probation officer. Parole occurs when prisoners are allowed to leave prison before the end of their prison sentence and are placed under supervision.

Review Questions

1. What are the three tiers of the state court system?
2. What is meant by limited jurisdiction?
3. What is meant by general jurisdiction?
4. What are the methods by which judges are selected?
5. What are the arguments for and against the popular election of judges?
6. Briefly describe the Missouri Plan.
7. What is mandatory sentencing?
8. What are victim compensation laws?
9. What is the job of a prosecuting attorney?
10. Briefly describe the steps in a typical criminal proceeding.
11. What is plea bargaining? Why is it used so often?
12. What types of sentences can be imposed on those convicted of crimes?
13. What is the difference between probation and parole?
14. Who may use a small claims court and for what purpose?
15. What are the arguments for and against capital punishment?

Questions for Thought and Discussion

1. Do you think plea bargaining is a good way to remedy the problem of crowded courts and prisons? Why or why not?
2. Why is the right to appeal a case important?
3. Should appeals be restricted? If so, to what extent?
4. How are judges selected in your state? How do you think judges should be selected in your state?
5. What qualifications do you think are important in a state judge?
6. Should criminals be given alternatives to prison sentences? If so, what type of criminals should be offered this and what should the alternatives be?

Improving Your Skills
Communication Skills

Determining the Reliability of Information

Learning to judge the reliability of information is important to your lifelong learning, both in school and out. Information that is reliable is clear and accurate. When trying to assess the reliability of written or spoken information, ask yourself the following questions:

8. Victim compensation laws provide compensation, usually money, to victims of serious criminal offenses.
9. The prosecution of suspects on behalf of the people.
10. After arrest, the person must be formally charged, or indicted. Upon indictment, the suspect is arraigned, which is the method by which the suspect comes before the judge who reads the formal charges. The defendant pleads guilty or not guilty. Typically, there is a preliminary hearing and if the person requests a jury trial, a jury is selected and there is a jury trial. If not, there is a bench trial.
11. Plea bargaining is an arrangement by which the defendant agrees to plead guilty to a lesser charge than the prosecutor originally brought. It is used often to assure the case will result in a guilty plea and to reduce the number of cases coming to trial.
12. Determinate sentencing calls for a specified period of time for a specific crime. Indeterminate sentencing calls for a minimum and maximum number of years, depending on good behavior and rehabilitation. The defendant might also receive probation.
13. Probation is in place of imprisonment. Parole is used after imprisonment.
14. In most states you may use small claims court when the amount is less than $5,000.
15. Answers will vary, e.g., those who support it maintain that it serves as a deterrent to serious crime and satisfies society's need for justice. Those opposed do not believe it has any deterrent value and is cruel and unusual punishment.

CHAPTER 23 REVIEW—Continued

- What is the background or qualifications of the person presenting the information? Is he or she an expert in a particular area?
- What are the biases or value judgments of the writer or speaker?
- Is the information based on primary or secondary sources?
- Which fallacies, if any, are present in the line of reasoning?
- Is the person confusing correlation with causation?
- What evidence is presented to support the argument? Are there alternative explanations that are being ignored? Is the information oversimplified?

Writing

Read the following excerpted article and answer each of the above questions when possible.

Energy Piracy
Forbes, October 14, 1991 p. 235.

Energy markets have been relatively trouble-free since President Reagan decontrolled oil prices in 1981, letting markets work their magic. But trouble looms as hungry lobbyists circle around a fat new package of energy pork, which is thinly justified by the quaint notion that energy is the one industry best left to Soviet-style Central planning.

The federal government is contemplating requiring Detroit to produce more electric cars, ostensibly to help the "greenhouse effect." But electric cars require electric power plants, which already account for one-third of all hydrocarbon emissions, while cars account for only one-fourth. And those costly car batteries end up as tons of toxic waste. The principal beneficiaries of a forced switch to electric cars would be the electric utility lobby.

Proponents of a federal energy policy also argue that we need to reduce our vulnerability to a disturbance in world oil supplies. But it is impossible to escape global shocks to world trade, whether a country imports oil or not. In both 1980 and 1990, Britain, which is self-sufficient in oil, sank into deep recession; Japan, which imports virtually all nonnuclear power, was unscathed.

There is no more justification for central planning in the energy market than there is in the copper market. World oil reserves are larger than ever, and vast areas of the globe may soon open to exploration. In a world of rapidly improving technology, the worst thing we could do would be to stifle innovation and flexibility with rigid rules, and their inevitable political favoritism.

So, next time someone tells you that this country badly needs a federally supported and mandated energy policy, ask him or her: Who would be the real beneficiary?

Social Studies Skills

Working with Flow Charts

Look at the flow chart on page 573.

1. What process is being depicted?
2. What are the three immediate possibilities that exist after the intake screening?
3. What can happen to the arrested minor just prior to adjudication (i.e., prior to going before a juvenile court judge for a hearing, judgment, and sentencing)?

Activities and Projects

1. Research the state prisons in your state to find out about problems such as poor facilities, overcrowding, or lack of funds. Devise a plan that would solve these problems. Write a letter to the governor that tells how you see the problems and offers your proposed solutions.
2. Interview a prosecutor, judge, or defense attorney about the court system in your state. Find out about how the courts are organized and the kinds of cases each court handles. Report the results of the interview back to the class.
3. Prepare a bulletin board display of the state court system in your state.
4. Stage a debate on one of the following statements: (1) Capital punishment should be abolished. (2) Poverty causes crime. (3) Gun control laws would reduce crime. (4) Prisons should be dehumanizing. (5) Crime victims should participate in sentencing.
5. Interview a state or local police officer to find out what he or she thinks is the most pressing criminal problem today and how the problem could be solved. Present your findings to the class.

Questions for Thought and Discussion (Answers)

1. Answers will vary, e.g., it is a way to unburden the overburdened system, but should not be used for serious or violent crimes.
2. Answers will vary, e.g., it allows another court to review a case if there are unresolved questions.
3. Answers will vary, e.g., appeals should be restricted to a set of guidelines that would point to any discrepancies during the trial.
4. Answers will vary according to your state.
5. Answers will vary, e.g., judges should be fair, reasonable, and intelligent.
6. Answers will vary, e.g., criminals accused of minor nonviolent offenses should be given the alternative of community service time.

Social Studies Skills (Answers)

1. The juvenile justice system.
2. (a) Detention, (b) release or referral to community resources, and (c) release to parents.
3. Transfer to criminal adult court.

CHAPTER INTRODUCTION

Instructional Objectives

By the end of the chapter students should be able to:

- Discuss the legality of local government.
- Identify the basic functions of local government.
- Describe the operation and organization of local governmental units.
- Characterize the governing of municipalities.

Using the Keynote

As an introduction to Chapter 24, ask one of the students to read aloud the quotation from Macaulay. Then guide a brief discussion of the quotation by posing questions such as these: What is happiness? In what sense does our government keep you happy? Is it reasonable to expect a government to make you happy? What kinds of governmental powers are implied by Macaulay's statement? How relevant to today's government do you consider the statement? Why?

Introducing the Chapter

Let a volunteer read the Introduction to the rest of the class. Encourage the students to discuss their ideas in response to these questions: Do you agree that the best government is the government closest to home? Why or why not? How do others around you—family members, adult acquaintances, and friends—seem to feel on this question? How do their attitudes affect yours? Do you believe that most citizens know more about our national government or our local government? Why?

Previewing the Sections

Section 1 Have volunteers read aloud the section title, the two main headings, the map, and the photo captions in Section 1. Then encourage the students to consider what they will learn in reading this section: What do you already know about the legality of local government? What do you expect to learn about it?

Section 2 Let the students look through Section 2 on their own, paying particular attention to the main headings. Ask them: What have you already learned from these headings about various units of local government? What else do you hope to learn as you read Section 3?

Section 3 Have the students glance through Section 3, and ask for volunteers to read aloud the main headings and the chart titles. Then ask the students to list at least four questions they expect to have answered as they study this section.

CHAPTER 24

Local Government

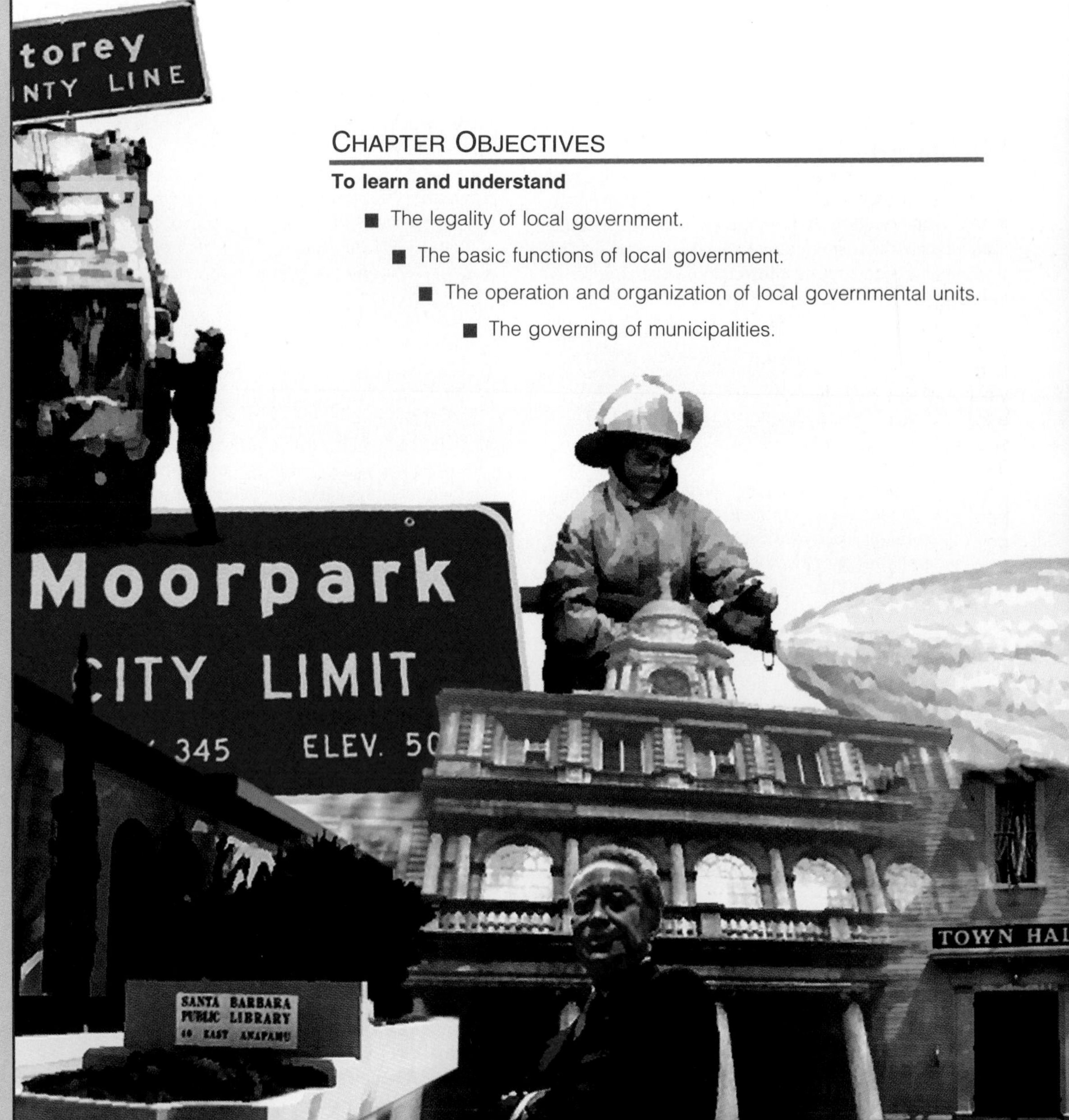

CHAPTER OBJECTIVES

To learn and understand

- The legality of local government.
- The basic functions of local government.
- The operation and organization of local governmental units.
- The governing of municipalities.

West's American Government Assignment Guide

Activity Sheets
Basic Concepts 24 *TRB* (Reteaching)
Enrichment Activity 24 *TRB*
Building Social Studies Skills 24 *TRB*

Quizzes
Chapter 24 Section 1 Quiz *TRB*
Chapter 24 Section 2 Quiz *TRB*
Chapter 24 Section 3 Quiz *TRB*

Tests
Chapter 24 Test A *TRB*
Chapter 24 Test B *TRB*
Chapter 24 Test Bank *TRB*
Chapter 24 WESTEST Computerized Testing

Keynote

"That is the best government which desires to make the people happy, and knows how to make them happy."

—— **Lord Thomas Babington Macaulay (1800–1859) English Historian and Politician**

INTRODUCTION

According to the English historian Lord Macaulay in the opening quote, the best governments are ones that work to make the people happy. For most individuals, the best government is the government closest to home, which is their local government.

Some of the oldest governments in our country are local governments. Long before the states were formed, cities and towns provided government services to their residents. Then, after each state adopted its own constitution, certain powers and responsibilities were formally granted to local government units.

For most individuals, local governments play a personal role in the American political system. Local governments provide water, sewage, garbage collection, and police and fire protection services to residents in cities, towns, and rural areas. For this reason, many people have contact with local governments on a continual basis.

SECTION 1

The Legality and Functions of Local Government

Preview Questions

- What is the relationship between state and local governments?
- What are the major functions of local government?
- What is the largest expense for most local governments?

The U.S. Constitution does not mention local governments. Thus, states have full authority in establishing local governments and in defining their powers and responsibilities. Consequently, every local government is a creation of its parent state. The state can create a local government and the state can terminate the right of a local government to exist. Indeed, states have often abolished entire counties, school districts, cities, and special districts. Since World War II, almost 20,000 school districts have gone out of existence or were consolidated with other school districts.

Dillon's Rule

Because local governments are legal creations of the state, for many years it seemed that the state government could dictate everything the local governments did. The narrowest possible view of the legal status of local governments follows **Dillon's rule**, outlined by John F. Dillon in his *Commentaries on the Law of Municipal Corporations* in 1811. He stated that municipal corporations—called **municipalities**—possess only those powers that the states expressly grant to them. Cities governed under Dillon's rule have thus been dominated by the state legislature. Those cities wishing to obtain the status of a municipal corporation have simply petitioned the state legislature for a charter, which typically has been extremely narrow. That is, the city has limited powers to tax and make laws.

The Home-Rule Movement

In a revolt against state legislative power over municipalities, the home-rule movement began. The movement was based on **Cooley's rule**, derived from an 1871 decision (*People* v. *Hurlbut*) by Michigan Judge Thomas Cooley, who stated that cities should be able to rule from home, or to govern themselves. Since 1900, about four-

SECTION 1

Points to Stress
- The relationship between state and local governments.
- The home-rule movement.
- The major functions of local government.
- The largest expense for most local governments.

Kickoff Activity
Have the students list at least six services that local governments provide for their citizens. When all the students have finished writing, let volunteers read their lists loud. Encourage the students to identify and discuss the services that benefit them personally.

Working with the Preview Questions
Let the students read these three study questions and identify the paragraphs within Section 1 where they expect to find the answers. Then have the students keep these questions in mind as they read the section independently.

Teaching Strategies

Introduction
After the students have read the section introduction, you might pose these questions for discussion: What is the significance of the fact that the Constitution does not provide for any local governments? What specific examples can you cite of local governments being abolished? What happened to cause the termination of those governments?

Comprehension
Ask the students to explain, in their own words, Dillon's Rule. Then let volunteers explain its significance.

Extension
Have the students recall or research the answers to these questions: Do you live in a home-rule city or a general-law city? When and why was it established as such?

Discussion Starter
Encourage the students to discuss their responses to these questions: Why is education such a major expense for local governments? Who benefits when public schools provide a good education? How do those people benefit?

Extension
Ask the students to learn about and discuss any special methods their school district has used to raise money.

Discussion Starter
Help the students consider and discuss the decisions made about their local police force: Who makes decisions about the activities of our police officers? What is the response of the public to recent decisions about such questions as how many officers are needed, how officers should be armed, and how officers should patrol given neighborhoods? In what ways do local citizens try to influence these decisions? With what success?

Caption Answer Usually state and federal taxes pay some of the educational cost, but the bulk of the funding comes via local tax payers.

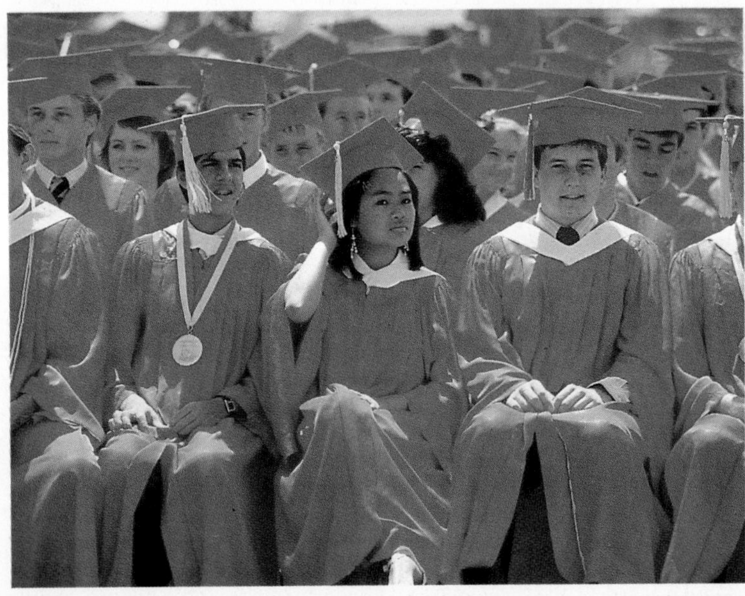

Education is the single largest expense of most local governments. Who provides the funding for public education?

fifths of all states have allowed **municipal home rule**, but only on issues in which no state interests are involved.

A municipality must choose to become a **home-rule city**; otherwise, it operates as a **general-law city**. In the latter case, the state passes certain general laws relating to cities of different sizes, which are designated as first-class cities, second-class cities, or towns. Once a city, by virtue of its population, receives such a ranking, it follows the general law put down by the state for that city size. Only if it chooses to be a home-rule city can it avoid such state government restrictions. In most states, only cities with populations of 2,500 or more can choose home rule.

Take a ride through your local community. As you look around, think about how much of what you see is provided by your local government. You will pass schools, police cars, fire stations, libraries, parks, golf courses, parking lots, sports arenas, garbage trucks, hospitals, and other facilities that are maintained and operated by your city. The services that cities and counties provide are so extensive that it is difficult to catalog all of them.

Education

Schools are one service provided by local government with which you've probably become quite familiar. Education is the single largest expense of most local governments. About 45 percent of local government budgets goes toward funding for public schools.[1]

You've probably heard people in your community talking about problems or issues in the schools. Maybe you even have some concerns and opinions of your own about how your local government runs the school system. Many local citizens are concerned about public schools because the schools affect the whole community. The school system is responsible for educating young people who will one day work in the community and become its leaders. Usually, state and federal taxes pay some educational costs, but local taxpayers often provide most of the money and make the key decisions regarding the operation of the public schools.

Police and Fire Protection

Police protection is the second largest expense of most American cities, and fire protection is third. Most local communities are very concerned about how crime is being controlled by the local police force. Local governments must decide how many police officers a community needs, how these officers will be armed, and which areas they will patrol.

1. Education is becoming more of a state issue, however, given that states on average now expend about 25 percent of their budgets on elementary and secondary education expenditures.

Vocabulary
Ask volunteers to explain what is meant by this term: *public welfare.*

Extension
Ask the students to identify any cities that seem disorganized or run down: What do you think has happened to contribute to these problems? How are the cities trying to solve those problems?

Enrichment
Let an interested volunteer research the life and accomplishments of Benjamin Banneker, who contributed to the planning and surveying of Washington, D.C. Have the student prepare a bulletin board display about Banneker.

Enrichment
Ask a pair of students to research and report on the current work of The National Capital Planning Commission.

Caption Answer Police protection is the second largest expense for most American cities.

Fire protection varies with the size of the community. If you live in a small town, your fire department may be staffed by volunteers. If you live in a large city, your fire department is probably staffed by full-time professionals.

Public Welfare

Although federal and state governments pay part of the cost of public welfare, the share that local governments pay continues to rise. Public welfare includes payments to the poor and needy. For the big cities, public welfare is one of the largest expenditures. New York City, for example, has 4 percent of the nation's population but 17 percent of the nation's low-income population, which means that more people in New York City need assistance than in other parts of the country.

One obstacle to local government funding of public-welfare programs is that city expenditures are growing faster than revenues, which means that the cities are spending more money than they take in. Cities are finding that they have more needy to take care of at ever higher costs.

City Planning and Zoning

Without planning, cities would probably develop haphazardly. Potential results could be industrial plants built downtown, railroads running through the heart of a city, skyscrapers shutting out sunlight on narrow streets, main roads built too far apart or too close together, and public buildings inaccessible to those who need them. Maybe you live in a city, or have visited one, that seems disorganized, run-down, or in which it is impossible to find your way around. For these reasons, most cities have seen the need to create order out of random growth, and have established planning agencies or commissions to plan how cities will grow.

Washington, D.C., is one of the few cities that began as and has remained a planned city. In 1790 Congress decided to build the nation's capital along the Potomac River. President Washington assigned the job of laying out the city to a French engineer named Major Pierre-Charles L'Enfant (1754–1825). He designed the city in a grid with streets running east to west named according to the alphabet, and streets running north to south named by number. He also planned for wide streets, scenic parks, graceful turning circles, and large areas to be reserved for public buildings. At first, both L'Enfant and his plan were dismissed as being too extravagant, but later his original plan was restudied and has been followed fairly closely through the years. Today, the National Capital Planning Commission guides the development of our nation's capital city.

In certain areas of almost any community there are only residential houses of a particular kind or areas that are only retail stores. Signs and billboards are normally only in certain areas and are similar in size. These aspects

The cost of fire protection is the third largest expense for most American cities. What is the second largest expense?

Comprehension
Guide the students in studying the map of Washington, D.C. Ask: What makes this plan appealing? Also encourage students who have visited Washington to describe their impressions of the city.

Figure Answer The development of Washington, D.C. is guided by the National Capitol Planning Commission.

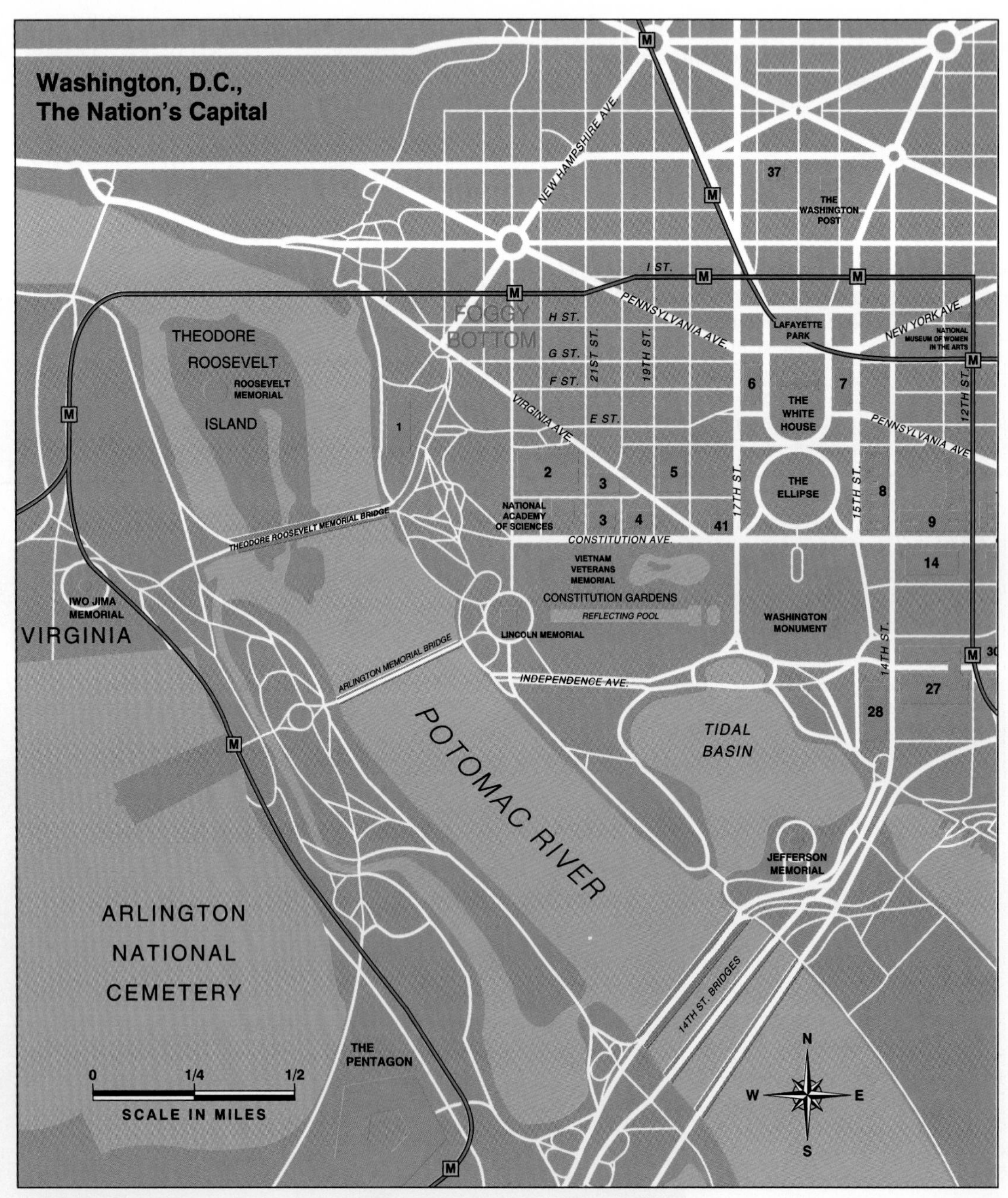

▲ **FIGURE 24–1 Map of Washington, D.C.** Washington, D.C. was planned by a French engineer named Major Pierre-Charles L'Enfant, who designed the city in a grid with streets running east to west named according to the alphabet and streets running north to south named by number. Washington, D.C. remains a planned city. Who guides the development of Washington, D.C. today?

Multidiscipline Strategies

Geography Provide students with as many maps of the various units of government that influence their lives as possible. Bring in U.S., state, county, school district, township, and village maps. Have students examine each map legend and scale. It would be particularly useful if the state map had counties, county map had townships, and township map had cities or even precincts.

Encourage students to discuss the types of services expected from each unit of government. Direct students to the various governmental units that share a border with theirs. Is there a fundamental difference in or duplication of services?

An additional activity would encompass completing a value-mapping exercise based on the population of counties. Students could shade counties based on population values. Have students speculate as to why certain counties are heavily populated, while others are moderate or low in population. Encourage students to think in terms of geography, transportation, and economics. This data may be acquired from *The World Almanac and Book of Facts.*

TEACHING CITIZENSHIP SKILLS AND RESPONSIBILITIES

Read

Before the students begin reading this Citizenship Skills and Responsibilities feature, introduce the subject of garbage and encourage the students to discuss what they already know about it: What garbage-related problems are facing our community, our country, and our planet? What government-sponsored programs are designed to deal with these problems? What can private groups and individuals do about our garbage problems? What are you doing? Why? After this introductory discussion, let the students read the feature independently.

Discuss

Stimulate a discussion of the feature by asking questions such as these: Why is American production of garbage so high? What does all this garbage imply about our activities and our attitudes? What changes do people need to make in their daily lives in order to reduce this production of garbage? How does recycling work? What problems does it solve—or help solve? Does your community have curbside pickup for recycling? If so, how long has this service been in place and how successful has it been? If not, are any groups now working to establish this service? Why can each of the guidelines Duncan suggested be useful in starting a recycling program?

Analyze and Apply

Encourage the students to agree on the best way to put into practice some of the suggestions in this feature; they might begin a recycling program at the school, or support an existing effort in the community, or even work to start a new recycling program in the community.

Review

Ask questions such as these to help the students review the feature: What garbage-related problems do city and town governments face? How can recycling help solve those problems?

CITIZENSHIP SKILLS AND RESPONSIBILITIES

Recycling in Your Community

We are fast becoming a nation of city dwellers. As people move to the cities, they bring their garbage with them. The amount of waste generated by U.S. residences and businesses increased by two and a half times between 1960 and 1992, from about 82 million tons to over 200 million tons. This places a demanding and costly burden on city and town governments.

Most cities have chosen to bury or burn their garbage, but landfill space is becoming more expensive, and rising costs are straining municipal budgets. While most Americans believe that proper waste disposal is crucial to a clean, safe environment, many people have a "not-in-my-backyard" attitude about dealing with waste. They do not want landfills near their homes because they worry about odors, contamination of water and soil, rodents, and other environmental problems.

One option that local governments have turned to is recycling—the re-processing of waste—such as newspapers, aluminum, and glass, into usable materials. Some experts believe that recycling could reduce the amount of our nation's trash by at least 30 percent.

One good way of promoting recycling in your community is by starting a "curbside recycling" program. In Marin County, California, a woman rallied volunteers in her community, met with local garbage collectors, and started a curbside program. As a result of her efforts, Gloria Duncan began a program in which homeowners set out buckets of sorted recyclable material along with the garbage.

If you want to start a recycling program in your areas, here are some guidelines that Duncan used:

1. **Find your allies.** You will need to look for volunteers and experts in your community who are willing to help you in your efforts. These people could include municipal waste disposal administrators, environmentalists, business people, senior citizens, and legal professionals.
2. **Let the media know.** Contact newspapers, radio stations, television stations, and city magazines. Be sure the public knows your concerns and what you are trying to accomplish. To raise awareness of recycling issues, Duncan and her Solid Waste Management Committee put on an elaborate gourmet dinner, the "Garbage Gala," for four hundred people at the recycling center. All decorations used for the event were made from recycled materials.
3. **Be professional.** Be businesslike with the people you talk to. Reach out to as many people as you

Recycling is one way all of us can help protect and preserve our environment.

Comprehension
Ask the students to identify variously zoned areas in your community.

Discussion Starter
Help the students consider both the advantages and the disadvantages of zoning. Then encourage the students to share and discuss their own opinions of zoning.

Discussion Starter
Give the students an opportunity to discuss recreational and cultural activities in their own community: What recreational and cultural programs does our local government provide? How well do these programs seem to meet the needs of the community's citizens? How much influence do you and other citizens feel you have over the programs that are offered? What—if anything—do you do to influence the decisions that are made about these programs? What else could you do?

Caption Answer Student answers will vary but might mention such programs as organized sports programs, cultural programs, museums, zoos, public parks, and convention centers.

Citizenship Skills and Responsibilities

Recycling in Your Community (Continued)

can, but remember that they will take you more seriously if you have a professional attitude.

4. **Go to City Hall.** Consult with local political leaders. Explain your goals and ask for advice on how to achieve them. Come up with a plan and present it. Be thorough and persistent. Duncan's group was turned down at first, settled for partial funding for a study the second time, and on the third try received the support it wanted.

For help in starting a recycling program, call the National Recycling Coalition at 202-659-6883, the Environmental Protection Agency Hotline at 800-424-9346, or the Environmental Defense Fund recycling number 800-CALL-EDF.

Taking Action

1. Divide your class into groups. Have each group devise steps to start recycling in your town.

of the community are often regulated by zoning boards or planning agencies. **Zoning** is the method that cities use to regulate the way property, such as land and buildings, are used. Through zoning practices, a city strives for order.

Generally, a zoning ordinance classifies each portion of land in the city as part of one of three zones: residential, commercial, or industrial. Each of these is divided into subzones. For example, one residential zone might be designated for single-family homes (houses), while another would allow apartment houses. Zoning ordinances also place limits on the height and area of structures, the distances they must be set back from other property lines, and other restrictions on land use. Nearly every major city in the United States is zoned today. (One notable exception is Houston, Texas, which only has privately contracted deed restrictions. Some critics of zoning point out that Houston is nonetheless no different than any other large city that has zoning.)

Recreational and Cultural Activities

As Americans, our leisure time has increased (compared to the 19th century) and cities have responded with recreational and cultural programs. Local governments offer community programs such as football, baseball, swimming, ice skating, and dancing. They also maintain city zoos and museums, and help build arenas, sports facilities, and convention centers.

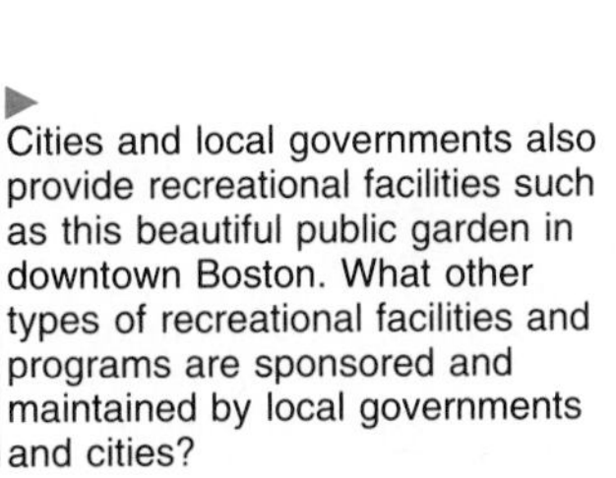

Cities and local governments also provide recreational facilities such as this beautiful public garden in downtown Boston. What other types of recreational facilities and programs are sponsored and maintained by local governments and cities?

FYI

"All politics is local" and "think globally, act locally," are two popular expressions. These expressions are especially true concerning waste removal and disposal. Local units of government are finding it increasingly difficult and expensive to dispose of vast amounts of trash in an environmentally sound fashion.

In the past, local governments buried, burned, or even dumped trash in the oceans. These methods of disposal are no longer acceptable, and local governments nationwide are searching for alternatives. About 83 percent of the trash in landfills can be reused. On average 41 percent is paper, 18 percent yard waste, 9 percent metal, 8 percent glass, and 7 percent plastic. Some of the more hopeful alternatives include reduction, recycling/reuse, and waste-as-energy schemes. Some states, Illinois for example, reduced the amount of garbage by passing laws prohibiting lawn waste in landfills. Instead, the waste is composted and used as fertilizer.

Reteaching Strategies

1. Let the students work with partners to review and revise the notes they have taken on Section 1.

2. Have the students work in groups to discuss how zoning can be used to control the development of a town or city. Then ask the group members to sketch a map of an imaginary city, showing how zoning could be used to make the city attractive to both residents and businesses.

Evaluation Strategies

1. Have the students write their answers to the Section 1 Review questions.

2. Have the students take the Section 1 Quiz found in the *TRB*.

Section 1 Review (Answers)

1. It was based on Cooley's rule which stated that cities should be allowed to govern themselves.

2. Schools, police and fire protection, public welfare, city planning and zoning, recreation and cultural activities.

3. Education.

4. Answers will vary, e.g., it would be haphazardly built, with industrial and residential buildings in the same areas.

SECTION 2

Points to Stress

- The functions of county government.
- The organization of county government.
- Major problems of county governments.
- The manner in which municipalities are created.
- The definition of special districts.

Kickoff Activity

Give the students five minutes in which to lists as many facts as possible about their own county (or parish or borough) government. (If you are in Connecticut or Rhode Island, ask the students to write about their understanding of why the state has no counties.) At the end of the allotted time, encourage the students to compare and discuss their lists.

Caption Answer Student answers will vary but can include maintaining records for deaths, marriages, property ownership, registering voters, preparing ballots, supervising elections, and any number of other police or regulatory services.

SECTION 1 REVIEW

1. Briefly describe the home-rule movement.
2. What services do local governments provide?
3. Which services normally constitute the largest single expense in a typical big city?
4. **For critical analysis:** What might happen in a city without any zoning laws?

SECTION 2

How Local Governments Operate

Preview Questions

- What are the typical functions of county government?
- How are county governments organized?
- What are the major problems of county governments?
- How are municipalities created?
- What are special districts?

Local governmental units fall into four major categories: counties, municipalities, towns and townships, and special districts.

Counties

If you look at a map of your state, you can see that it is divided into **counties** of different sizes and shapes. A county is a major local government unit that typically administers community services such as roads, schools, and law enforcement. State governments created counties to assist them in carrying out state laws. Organized county governments are found in every state except Connecticut and Rhode Island. In Louisiana, counties are called **parishes**, and in Alaska, they are called **boroughs**.

There are over three thousand counties in the United States, which vary greatly in both size and population. San Bernardino County in California is the largest geographically, with 20,102 square miles, and New York County in New York is the smallest, with less than 22 square miles. Los Angeles County has over eight million residents, while Loving County in Texas has only ninety-one. Some states have a large number of counties, such as Texas with its 254 counties. Others have only a few, such as Delaware and Hawaii, each of which has only three.

County governments also vary a great deal in importance. In rural areas and in the South, county governments have become major providers of services. In these areas, early settlements were spread over large areas with few towns and villages. One town in the county became the county seat, where the county government resided. In the New England states, in contrast, people settled in towns and townships, which became the important units of local government.

Recently, in some metropolitan areas, county governments have taken over some of the functions once handled by city governments. The government of Dade County, Florida, for example, administers water, transportation, and other services in Miami. In many other areas, however, the importance of counties has declined, and there have even been attempts to abolish them.

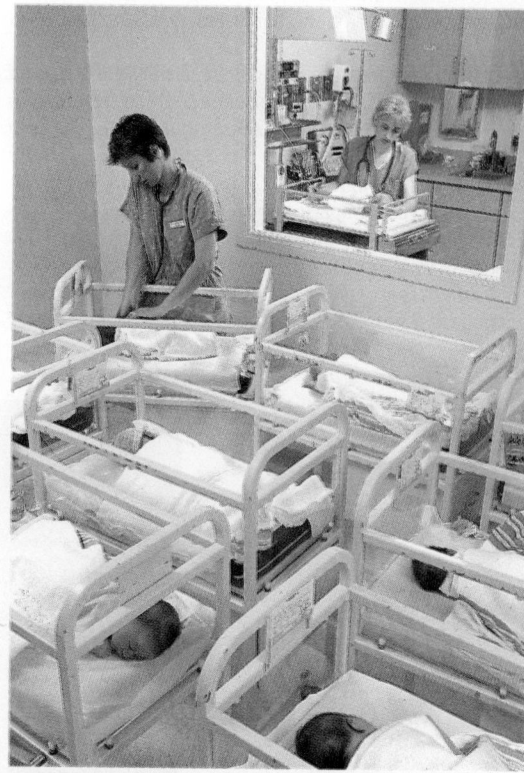

▲ Maintaining a record of births is one of the many responsibilities and functions of county government. What are some of the other responsibilities and functions of county governments?

Working with the Preview Questions
Have volunteers read these study questions aloud, and encourage the students to discuss their own ideas in response to each. Explain that they will find more detailed answers as they read Section 2. Then have them read the section, taking notes in the form of topic outlines.

Teaching Strategies

Vocabulary
Ask the students to use dictionaries to check the derivation and the related definitions of the noun *county*.

Extension
Have the students recall or research information about their own state and county: Into how many counties is our state divided? What is the name of our county? What are its boundaries? What and where are our neighboring counties?

Discussion Starter
Encourage the students to examine and discuss the specific advantages that might be associated both with county governments taking over from municipalities and with the declining importance of counties. Then ask: Can you see either of these processes developing in our area? How? With what results?

Comprehension
Let volunteers explain the importance of the record-keeping services provided by county governments.

Extension
Ask the students to investigate and discuss the specific services provided by your county government.

Extension
If possible, help the students arrange to have a member of your county board visit the classroom and speak to the students about his or her work.

Caption Answer Students should understand that the federal government is also involved in the operation of all airports as the Federal Aviation Administration regulates air travel.

Functions of County Government The responsibilities and functions of a county are usually determined by the state constitution and state laws. Typically, counties provide record-keeping services for their communities. They maintain records of births, deaths, marriages, and property ownership. They also register voters, prepare ballots, supervise elections, and keep election records on behalf of state governments.

Most counties also provide a number of police and regulatory services. Some counties have a county sheriff's department that maintains jails and other correctional facilities. Many counties have their own court systems, and may issue permits and licenses such as for hunting, fishing, and marriage. Other services might include operating airports, hospitals, and transportation systems; collecting taxes; and maintaining parks and libraries.

Organization of County Government Because state laws differ, the organization of county governments differs from one state to another. Most counties are governed by a **county board**, which may also be known as a board of commissioners, a board of supervisors, or a board of chosen freeholders. The men and women of these boards are almost always elected. They are usually chosen from districts in the county, rather than on an at-large basis. Their term of office is usually four years but can run as long as eight. County boards range in size from a few members to over 50.

The smaller county boards are usually known as boards of commissioners. They have from three to seven members who generally serve full time and hold no other public office during the time they are on the board. These officials may be elected at-large or by districts.

Another kind of county board is a board of supervisors, which typically has an average of 15 or more members. County supervisors are elected from townships (discussed on page 594) and are often supervisors for their respective townships as well.

The powers of these boards are generally both legislative and executive. Legislative powers may involve the passing of health and zoning ordinances. The most important legislative functions, however, are those dealing with finances, such as collection of taxes, appropriation of funds, and fixing the salaries of those who work for the county. Executive powers may involve the appointment of certain county officers and employees, and the administration of courts, jails, hospitals, roadways, welfare programs, and elections.

Many county governments operate airports such as the one shown here. What other levels of government might be involved in the operation of airports?

Cooperative Learning
Divide the class into eight small groups, and have each group investigate one of these elected officials in your county: sheriff, district attorney, superintendent of schools, clerk, auditor, treasurer, assessor, coroner. Let the group members work together to find out who holds that office, what specific duties that individual undertakes, and how he or she was elected. Then ask each group to report its findings to the rest of the class.

Discussion Starter
Encourage the students to discuss their ideas about the lack of effective leadership in county government: Is the confusion and inefficiency a necessary result of the lack of a single executive leader? Why or why not? What are some of the possible solutions to these problems related to leadership? Which solution do you think would be most effective? Why?

Discussion Starter
Help the students compare the three different plans—county manager, chief administrator, and elected chief executive: What are the advantages and disadvantages of each plan? Which seems most likely to be widely effective? Why?

Caption Answer The county sheriff maintains the jail and serves as the police official in unincorporated areas of the county.

County sheriff's officers answer to an elected county sheriff. What are the responsibilities of an elected county sheriff?

Elected Officials Most boards share their powers and responsibilities with other elected officials. These officials and their duties include:

- *Sheriff*—maintains the jail and serves as the police official in unincorporated areas of the county.
- *District Attorney*—prosecutes criminal cases on behalf of the state and county.
- *Superintendent of Schools*—chief administrator for the county's elementary and secondary schools. (In some states superintendents are appointed by a school board.)
- *County Clerk*—registers and records documents such as deeds, mortgages, birth and death certificates, and divorce decrees.
- *Auditor*—keeps financial records and authorizes payments to meet county obligations.
- *Treasurer*—keeps county funds and authorizes payments from these funds.
- *Assessor*—sets value on taxable property in the county.
- *Coroner*—investigates violent deaths and those not witnessed by a doctor.

Special Boards and Commissions In some counties, special boards may be elected or appointed to perform specific tasks. They commonly include the school board, the board of health, the hospital board, the library board, and the planning board.

Changing County Government

Counties have developed in diverse ways throughout our nation's history. Some of their unusual characteristics have come to be perceived as problems. Some politicians and citizens believe that county governments are outmoded, and point out the need for change. According to these people, several problem areas are in need of reform.

Leadership One of the biggest problems is the absence of real executive leadership. The confusing mass of elected county officials makes it impossible for the average citizen to learn which county official is responsible for what. Inefficiency, waste, inaction, and an unresponsive government are often the result.

- **The county-manager plan** In an effort to provide more effective leadership, some larger counties have reorganized themselves and now have a county manager, county executive, or chief administrator. Under the **county-manager plan**, the elected county board remains the legislative, policy-making arm of county government. The county manager, who is hired by and responsible to the county board, is the board's chief executive. The board makes legislation and decides policy, while the manager administers these laws and executes these policies. More than 50 counties around the country have adopted this plan.

- **The chief administrator plan** The **chief administrator plan** is a limited version of the county manager plan. The chief administrative officer (CAO) differs from the county manager because he or she shares responsibilities in certain key areas with the county board or with other individuals. In some areas, such as budgets and appointments, the CAO has little or no power. Perhaps because it is a less radical change, this plan has become more popular, and over 500 counties currently use it.
- **Elected chief executive plan** Another variation on the county manager plan is the **elected chief executive plan**. The executive officer is elected directly by the voters and works with the county board. Nearly sixty counties today have this kind of system.

The Weakness of the Counties The relative weakness of the counties in relation to the states is another problem. Most state constitutions severely restrict the powers of county boards. County officials often cannot respond effectively to modern problems because they have limited abilities to tax, spend, and legislate.

Recognizing the need for more local independence, over half the states have now provided for home rule. This means that states allow the counties to decide the details of their own governmental structures, subject to the approval of the local voters. This step toward reform has been offered to some 1,500 counties in the nation, but only about 100 have taken advantage of it.

Municipalities

When the first census was taken in 1790, only 5.1 percent of the 3,929,214 people living in the United States lived in **urban areas**, or areas that are highly populated. In the early 1800s, with the advent of large-scale manufacturing and the invention of farming machines that reduced the need for manual labor, people began to move to the new urban industrial and transportation centers. Cities grew rapidly. By 1860, the urban population had multiplied thirty times. By 1900, 39.7 percent of the population lived in cities. In 1990, this figure reached 77 percent and is still rising.

This shift from rural to urban society in the United States has meant dramatic changes in government. If you have ever lived or stayed on a farm or in the country, you know that you cannot always depend on government services to pick up your garbage, send snow plows when you need them, or put a stop sign on your corner. But in the city, the relationships between people living in close proximity are far more complex than those among people living on neighboring farms. Urban residents place more demands on government to provide services and protection. The larger the population, the greater the need and expenses of services.

Urban areas with their own units of government are called municipalities. Depending on local custom or state laws, municipalities are known as cities, towns, boroughs, or villages. Each municipality is created by the state, which has complete authority and control over all local government within the municipal borders. State constitutions and statutes contain a large number of provisions relating to municipal government.

Incorporation Cities and towns develop local governments when they are granted special legal status by the state legislature through **incorporation**. When a city becomes incorporated, it actually becomes a legal municipal corporation. Each state sets out in its constitution

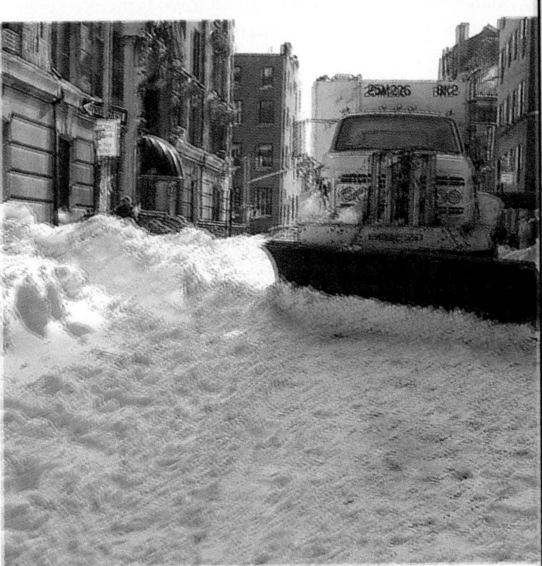

▲ Urban residents place demands on government to provide services such as keeping the streets cleared of snow. What are urban areas with their own units of government called?

Discussion Starter
Encourage the students to discuss their ideas in response to this question: What is behind the reluctance of county governments to assume more power from state governments?

Discussion Starter
Pose questions such as these for discussion: What evidence do you see of the move to urban areas? How does this growth of cities affect individuals? How does it affect governments? Have you seen any evidence of a counter-movement toward exurban living? If so, what examples can you cite?

Comprehension
Let several students explain the importance of the relationship between larger populations and more expensive government services. Why is an understanding of this relationship important?

Extension
Ask one of the students to find and report the date of incorporation of your city or town (or of the nearest city or town).

Caption Answer Urban areas with their own units of government are called municipalities. Incorporated cities and towns are legal municipal corporations.

Extension
Have the students find and list the requirements for municipal incorporation in your state.

Discussion Starter
Help the students discuss the advantages and disadvantages of municipal corporation: What arguments would you expect to hear on both sides during a campaign to collect signatures on a petition requesting incorporation?

Enrichment
Let a pair of volunteers research the history of town meetings within a specific New England town: When was the first town meeting held? Have they been held on a regular basis since then? What trends in participation can be discerned? Have the volunteers prepare and present a brief oral report summarizing their findings.

Enrichment
Ask an interested student to read about the federal land surveys conducted in the 1780s: What areas were surveyed? Why? By whom? How were the surveys used? Have the student write a short report of his or her findings, to be shared with the rest of the class.

Extension
Ask the students to recall or find the answers to these questions: Do you live in an unincorporated area? Are there unincorporated areas near our community? You may want to assign one of the students to draw and display a local map showing unincorporated areas.

Caption Answer Each resident of a town is invited to participate in the annual town meeting. Normally, however, few residents show up unless a high-interest item is on the agenda.

or statutes what a community must do to become a municipal corporation. Most states require that a certain number of persons live in an area before incorporation can take place.

A state does not choose which cities or towns to incorporate; rather, the citizens of the city or town must submit a petition with a certain number of signatures to a public official, usually a judge. In most states, an election is held to obtain voter approval for the city to be declared a municipal corporation.

The difference between counties and municipalities is in how and why they are created. Counties are established by the state and exist to serve the state's administrative needs. Municipalities, in contrast, are established at the request of their residents, largely because of concentrations of populations and the services they need.

New England Towns and Townships

Towns and townships are not quite the same thing, although they can be grouped together.

The New England Town The **New England town** is not to be confused with the word *town* used as just another name for a city. A New England town typically consists of one or more urban settlements and the surrounding rural areas. In Maine, Massachusetts, New Hampshire, Vermont, and Connecticut, city and county governments are combined into one town government. Consequently, counties have little importance in New England. In Connecticut, counties are simply a way to mark geographical boundaries.

From the New England town comes the tradition of the annual **town meeting**, at which direct democracy was (and continues to be) practiced. Town meetings in Vermont date back to 1749, forty-two years before it became a state. Each resident of a town is summoned to the annual meeting at the town hall. Those who attend the meeting levy taxes, pass laws, elect town officials, and appropriate money for different activities.

Normally, few residents show up for town meetings today unless a high-interest item is on the agenda or unless a family's member wants to be elected to office. The town meeting takes a full day or longer, and few citizens can set aside such a large amount of time. Because of the declining interest in town meetings, many New England towns have adopted a **town manager system**, in which the voters elect three **selectmen** who then appoint a professional town manager. Selectmen (and

▲ Town meetings take place in town halls such as this one in Massachusetts. Which town residents can participate in town meetings?

women) take care of overseeing the town manager's work. The town manager in turn appoints other officials.

Townships **Townships** operate somewhat like counties. They perform the same functions that counties would do otherwise. Several dozen townships may exist within a county. Indiana, Iowa, Kansas, Michigan, Minnesota, New Jersey, New York, Ohio, Pennsylvania, and Wisconsin all have numerous townships.

A township differs from a New England town in that it is meant to be a rural government rather than a city government. Moreover, townships are never the principal unit of local government, as are New England towns. The boundaries of most townships are based on federal land surveys of the 1780s, which mapped land into six-mile squares (townships) that were then subdivided into thirty-six blocks of one square mile each called sections. Along the boundaries of each section a road was built.

Although townships have few functions left to perform in many parts of the nation, they are still politically important in others. In some metropolitan areas, townships are the political units that provide most public

Comprehension
Guide the students in studying and discussing figure 24–2: With which of these special districts are you familiar? Which kinds of special districts seem surprising to you? Which special districts do we have in our state? How are the functions of other special districts carried out in our communities?

Figure Answer Student answers will vary according to the composition of your district.

This figure content is also featured on *West's American Government Videodisc* (see the index found in the *TRB*).

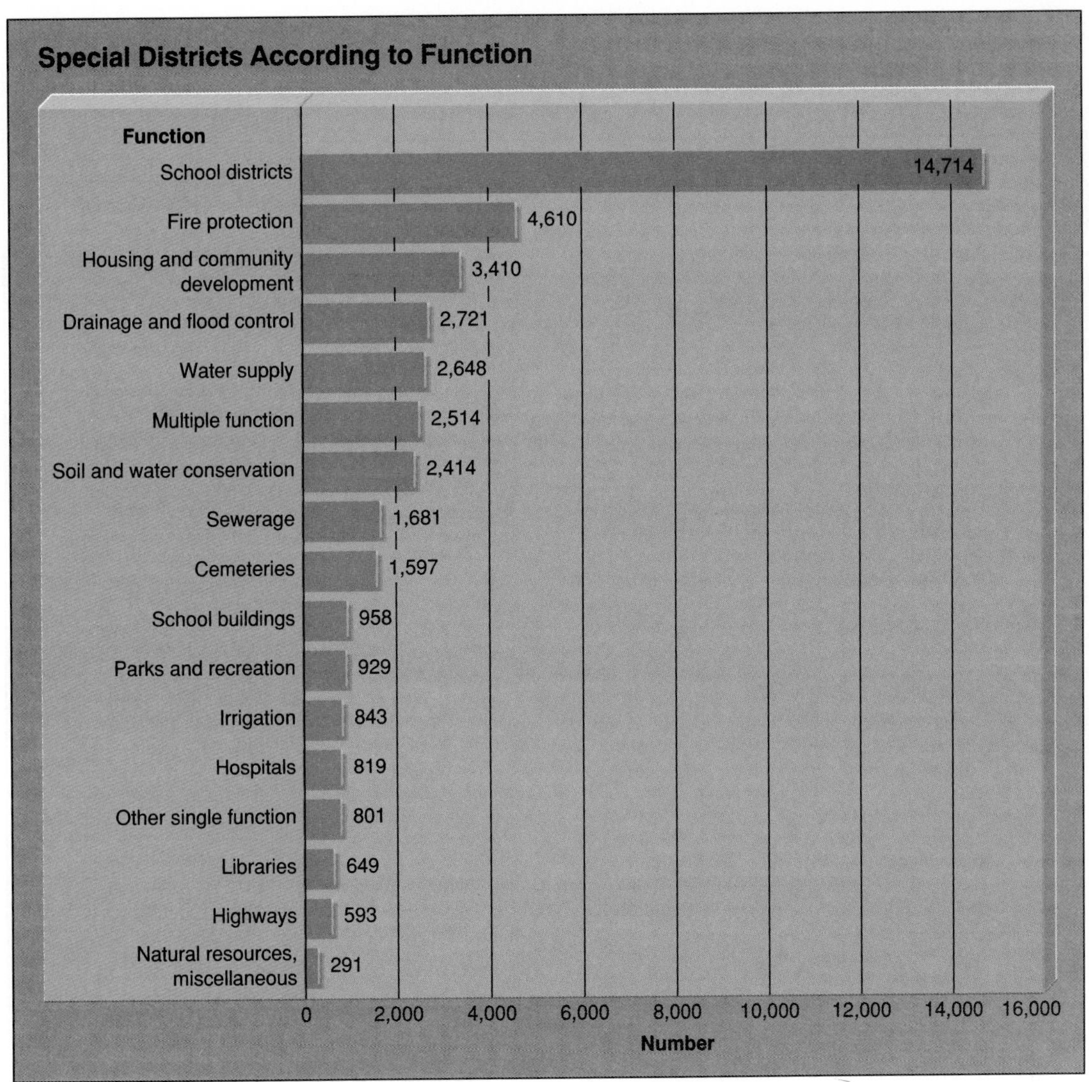

▲ **FIGURE 24–2 Special Districts According to Function.** As you can see from the figure above, the most common form of special districts are school districts. How many schools make up your district?

services to residents who live in **unincorporated areas**, which are areas outside the geographical boundaries of a municipality.

Special Districts

The most common form of local government is the special district, which includes school districts. There are more than 44,000 special districts, of which slightly less than 15,000 are school districts. Special districts are one-function governments that are usually created by the state legislature and governed by a board of directors. In addition to school districts, there are districts for fire protection (the second most common kind of district), as well as districts for mosquito control, cemeteries, sewers, garbage collection, and numerous other concerns.

TEACHING GOVERNMENT IN ACTION

Read

Before reading this Government in Action feature, ask the students to consider not only the direct costs of enforcing the laws against illegal drug use and abuse, but the indirect costs, as well. Ask students to name as many of these side effects as possible and list them on the blackboard. (A partial list would include health care costs from accidents caused by drug abuse, treatment and recovery costs, costs to businesses from time lost, social welfare costs due to unemployment, and the cost to society of its human resources.) When you feel students have gained an appreciation of the enormous costs to society caused by illegal drug use and abuse, have volunteers read this selection aloud to the rest of the class.

Discuss

To stimulate a class discussion of this feature ask the following: How are state and local officials involved in the war on drugs? How has the war on drugs burdened our court system? What specific steps would you recommend to make the war against drugs more effective?

Analyze and Apply

Ask a representative from the police department, social services, or the health department to speak to the class about local efforts to fight the war against drugs. Ask students to prepare two or three questions in advance (questions should pertain to the specific department invited to speak).

Review

Ask students the following questions to review the content of this Government in Action feature: Who enforces state laws against illegal drugs? What other crimes are commonly related to illegal drug use? How are civil court cases affected by police prosecution of drug related cases? What kind of drug use has been decreased by the current war against drug use? According to the feature, what specific substances show a decline in use, especially among high school students?

Think About It (Answers)

1. As demonstrated with Prohibition, it is very difficult to enforce a legal ban on an activity without citizen support for that ban. Other difficulties involve coordination of federal, state, and local programs for enforcement and the impact on the judicial and penal systems.

2. Answers will vary, but should reflect the knowledge that health education aimed at fostering voluntary compliance with the law must be a key part of any attempt to curtail drug and alcohol abuse.

Reteaching Strategies

1. Let the students work in small groups to review and discuss their outlines of Section 2. Remind individual students to make any necessary corrections to their work.

2. Let the students work with partners to correct and add to the list of county facts they wrote in the Section 2 Kickoff Activity.

GOVERNMENT IN ACTION

CASE STUDY

Waging the War on Drugs

The problem of illegal drugs is widespread in the United States. While federal legislation and money spent on the war against illegal drugs get all the headlines, however, most of the costs associated with the war on drugs are faced at the local level. It is local police forces that are involved in upholding state laws against illegal drugs.

The number of robberies, violent acts, and murders associated with illegal drugs are hard to estimate. In some major cities, authorities estimate that over half of all homicides are drug-related, typically due to ''turf'' wars and drug deals gone awry. In many cities, drug users steal and commit assaults in order to obtain money to satisfy their expensive drug habits.

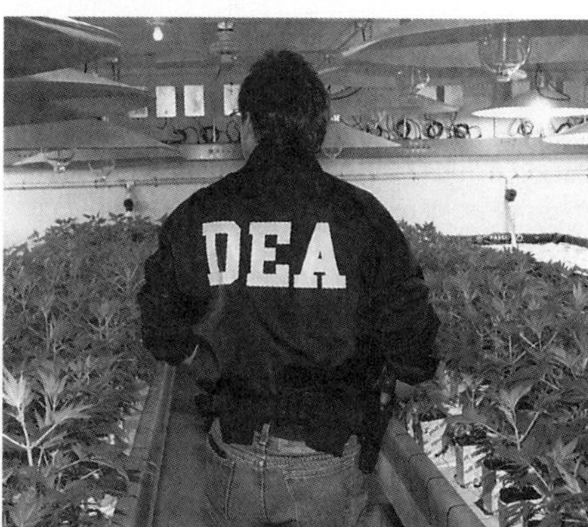

Current attempts at stopping drug sales and use have resulted in over 1.1 million drug-related arrests per year. The courts have also found themselves increasingly burdened by the increased police activity with respect to illegal drugs. Court calendars are overflowing. Because of speedy-trial statutes for criminal cases, virtually all drug cases get on the docket (court agenda) before civil cases. Civil lawsuits—those involving private parties rather than the state—often take two, three, four, and sometimes five years to get to court.

There are basically three major views of how the United States should regulate illegal drugs. The most liberal view argues for complete legalization. The most conservative view is that even harsher penalties and a higher degree of law enforcement are needed to eliminate illegal drug use. The middle view advocates increased education and regulation, and perhaps decriminalizing certain ''soft'' drugs such as marijuana. Currently ten states have decriminalized the possession of small amounts of marijuana for personal use.

While evidence does not indicate that the current drug war has reduced the amount of criminal activity associated with illegal drugs, there is some evidence that the casual use of illegal drugs has declined. For several years in a row, the government has reported that the use of cocaine among high school students has decreased. Certainly the use of all mind-altering drugs, including alcohol and nicotine, is currently on a downward trend. Americans seemed to be realizing more and more that the human body was not meant to consume many, if any, mind-altering drugs and still remain healthy. The amount of alcohol consumed per person in the United States has continued to decline since 1985.

(For more information, see the Extended Case Studies in the Resource Center at the end of this book.)

THINK ABOUT IT

1. What are the difficulties always faced by any government that attempts to make certain activities or goods illegal?
2. What kind of advice would you give to a new mayor in your city with respect to the war on drugs?

Evaluation Strategies

1. Have the students write their answers to the Section 2 Review questions.

2. Have the students take the Section 2 Quiz found in the *TRB.*

Section 2 Review (Answers)

1. Functions are determined by the state constitution or state laws. Typically, they provide record-keeping services, register voters, prepare ballots, and supervise elections. Most provide a number of police and regulatory services.

2. Some are outmoded and in need of change. One of the biggest problems is the absence of real executive leadership.

3. Urban areas with their own units of government. Special legal status by the state legislature.

4. One-function governments that are usually created by the state legislature and governed by a board of directors.

5. Answers will vary, e.g., an incorporated city can tax its citizens more to provide them with more government services.

SECTION 3

Points to Stress

- The major forms of city government.
- Important features of the forms of city government.

Kickoff Activity

What is a city manager? What is a mayor? Give the students time to write short answers in response to these introductory questions. When everyone has finished writing, ask for volunteers to read their responses aloud. Encourage a brief discussion, and remind the students that they will learn more about these positions as they study Section 3.

Working with the Preview Questions

Go over the study questions with the class; let interested volunteers share their initial responses to each question. Then ask the students to take notes in response to these questions as they read Section 3.

Teaching Strategies

Introduction

After the students have read the section introduction, encourage them to discuss what they already know about the four types of municipal representative governments: Which towns and cities can you identify as using these various governmental forms?

Vocabulary

Let a volunteer explain the meaning of the phrase *collectively responsible* as used in point 3 under the commission plan.

Comprehension

Ask the students about functions of a mayor in the commission plan: What ceremonial duties does a mayor in this form of government probably undertake?

Discussion Starter

Guide the students in discussing the position of the mayor in the council-manager plan: Why do you think the office of mayor is retained in this system?

Special districts may also be referred to as authorities, boards, or corporations. Figure 24–2 on page 595 shows the different kinds of districts.

One important feature of special districts is that they cut across geographical and governmental boundaries. Sometimes special districts cut across state lines, such as the Port of New York Authority, which was established by an interstate compact between New Jersey and New York. A mosquito-control district may cut across both municipal lines and county lines. A metropolitan transit district may provide bus service to dozens of municipalities and to several counties.

Except for school districts, the typical citizen is not very aware of most special districts. Indeed, most citizens do not know what governmental unit provides their weed control, mosquito control, water supplies, or sewage services. Part of the reason for the low profile of special districts is that most administrators are appointed, not elected, and therefore receive little public attention.

Section 2 Review

1. How are the functions of county governments determined? What do county governments typically do?
2. What are some problems with county governments?
3. What are municipalities? What does incorporation mean?
4. What are special districts?
5. **For critical analysis:** What do you think would be the advantages and disadvantages of incorporation for a city?

Section 3

How Municipalities Are Governed

Preview Questions

- What are the major forms of municipal government?
- What are the important features of each municipal government plan?

Of the many types of municipal representative governments, most operate according to four basic systems: the commission plan, the council-manager plan, the mayor-administrator plan, and the mayor-council plan.

The Commission Plan

The **commission plan** of municipal government consists of a commission of three to nine members who have both legislative and executive powers. A commission government is organized as follows:

1. Executive and legislative powers are concentrated in a small group of individuals, who are elected at-large on a (normally) nonpartisan ballot.
2. Each commissioner is individually responsible for heading a particular municipal department, such as the department of public safety.
3. The commission is collectively responsible for passing ordinances and controlling spending.
4. The mayor is selected from the members of the commission (the mayoral position is only ceremonial).

Figure 24–3 on page 598 shows a typical commission plan. The commission plan originated in Galveston, Texas, in 1901, and had its greatest popularity during the first twenty years of this century. It appealed to municipal government reformers, who looked upon it as a type of business organization that would eliminate what they saw as built-in problems in long ballots and partisan municipal politics. Unfortunately, giving both legislative and executive power to a small group of individuals means that there are no checks and balances on administration and spending. Also, since the mayoral office is ceremonial, there is no provision for strong leadership. Not surprisingly, only about one hundred cities today use the commission plan: Tulsa, Salt Lake City, Mobile, Topeka, and Atlantic City are a few of them.

The Council-Manager Plan

In the **council-manager plan** of municipal government, an elected city council appoints a professional manager who acts as the chief executive. He or she is typically called the **city manager**. In principle, the manager is simply there to see that the general directions of the city council are carried out. In practice, he or she often makes many decisions and policies. The important features of the council-manager plan are as follows:

1. The council or commission consists of five to seven members, elected at-large on a nonpartisan ballot.
2. A professionally trained manager can hire and fire subordinates and is responsible to the council.
3. The mayor may be chosen from within the council or from outside, but he or she has no executive

Discussion Starter
Encourage the students to discuss their ideas about the council-manager plan: Why do you think it is so widely used in smaller cities? Why do you think it is not more popular in large cities?

Comprehension
Ask the students to explain the role of the mayor in the mayor-administrator plan of municipal government: How does vesting political leadership in this elected official affect the functioning of the government? Why does it make that kind of difference?

Figure Answer Under the commission plan of municipal government, the mayor's role is ceremonial.

This figure content is also featured on *West's American Government Videodisc* (see the index found in the *TRB*) and is available in the transparency package.

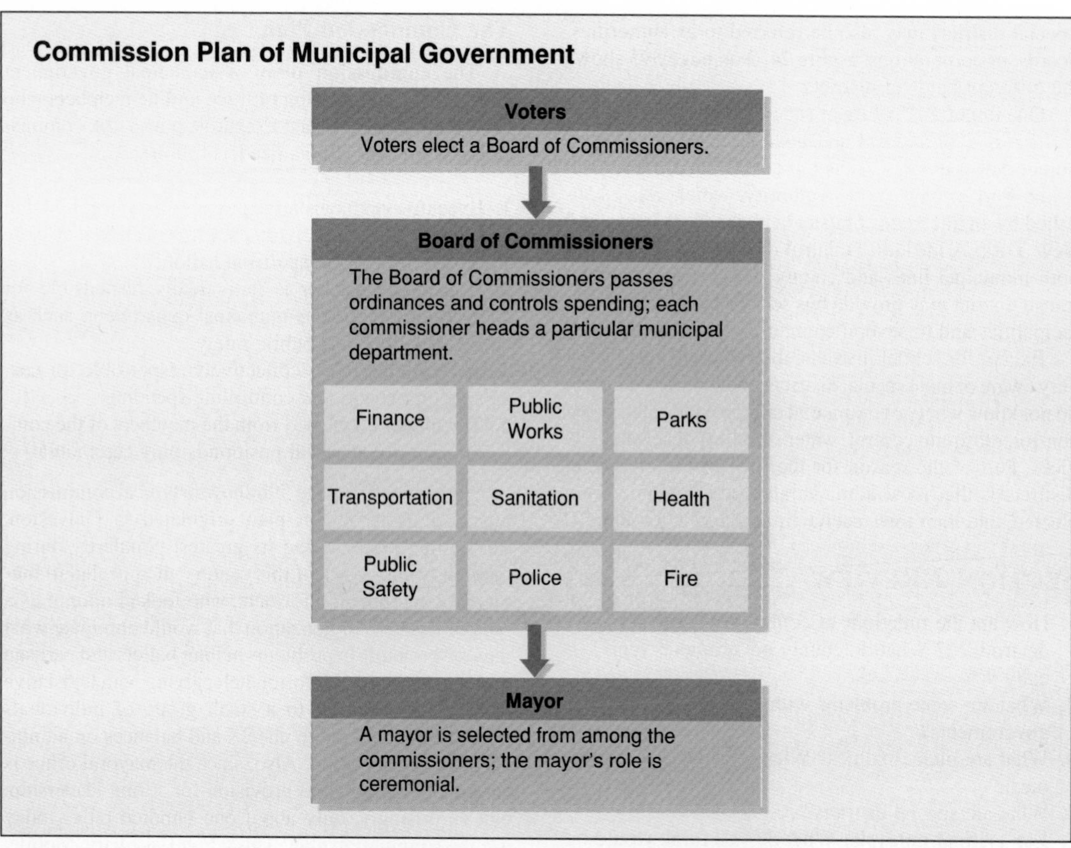
Commission Plan of Municipal Government
Voters
Voters elect a Board of Commissioners.
Board of Commissioners
The Board of Commissioners passes ordinances and controls spending; each commissioner heads a particular municipal department.
Finance
Public Works
Parks
Transportation
Sanitation
Health
Public Safety
Police
Fire
Mayor
A mayor is selected from among the commissioners; the mayor's role is ceremonial.

▲ **FIGURE 24–3 Commission Plan of Municipal Government.** The figure above shows the organization of a municipal government according to the commission plan. According to this plan, what type of role does the mayor assume?

function. As with the commission plan, the mayor's position is largely ceremonial. The city manager works for the council and not the mayor (unless, of course, the mayor is part of the council).

Figure 24–4 on the next page shows the council-manager plan of government.

Today about two thousand cities use the council-manager plan. About one-third of the cities with populations above 5,000 and about one-half of the cities with populations above 25,000 operate with this type of plan. Only four large cities of more than 500,000 people—Cincinnati, Dallas, San Antonio, and San Diego—have adopted the plan.

The major defect of the council-manager plan, as with the commission plan, is that there is no strong executive leadership. It is therefore not surprising that large cities rarely use such a plan. The council-manager plan is also considered undemocratic because the executive—the city manager—is not elected by the people, but rather is appointed by the council.

The Mayor-Administrator Plan

The **mayor-administrator plan** is often used in large cities where there is a strong mayor. It is similar to the council-manager plan, except that the mayor is an elected chief executive and as such has powers of political leadership. The mayor appoints an administrative officer whose function is to free the mayor from routine administrative tasks, such as personnel direction and budget supervision.

Extension
Have the students recall (or research) and discuss the answers to these questions: Which of the four plans does your city (or the city closest to you) use? How well does that governmental plan seem to meet the needs of the citizens?

Discussion Starter
Encourage the students to identify and discuss the advantages and disadvantages of both the strong mayor-council plan and the weak mayor-council plan.

Figure Answer Under the council-manager plan of municipal government, the city manager is responsible for carrying out policy, directing city departments, and functions as the city's chief executive.

This figure content is also featured on *West's American Government Videodisc* (see the index found in the *TRB*) and is available in the transparency package.

Council-Manager Plan of Municipal Government

Voters
Voters elect a city council, and in some cities a mayor.

City Council
The city council makes policy and employs a city manager to enact policy.

Mayor
The mayor either is elected by the voters or is a city council member elected by the council; the mayor's role is largely ceremonial.

City Manager
The city manager, usually a professionally trained administrator, is appointed by the city council to carry out policy, direct all city departments (i.e., finance, public works, parks, transportation, sanitation, health, public safety, police, fire), and hire and fire all city workers. The manager is the city's chief executive.

▲ FIGURE 24–4 **Council-Manager Plan of Municipal Government.** The figure above outlines the council-manager plan. Under this plan, who is responsible for carrying out policy?

The Mayor-Council Plan

The **mayor-council plan** of municipal government is the oldest and most widely used. The mayor is an elected chief executive and the council is the legislative body. Virtually all councils are unicameral (except in Everett, Massachusetts). A council typically has five to nine members, except in very large cities such as Chicago, which has fifty members. Council members are popularly elected for four- to six-year terms.

▲ David Dinkins, shown here, is the mayor of New York City. What type of mayor-council plan is used in New York City?

Within the mayor-council plan, there are subplans known as the strong-mayor type or the weak-mayor type.

The Strong Mayor-Council Plan In the **strong mayor-council plan**, the mayor is the chief executive and has almost complete control over hiring and firing employees and preparing the budget. The mayor plays a strong role in the formation of city policies, and usually serves a four-year term. The strong-mayor system is most often found in large cities such as New York and San Francisco.

The Weak Mayor-Council Plan The **weak mayor-council plan** completely separates executive and legislative functions. The mayor is elected as chief executive officer; the council is elected as the legislative body. This traditional separation of powers allows for checks and balances on spending and administration. The mayor has only limited powers and little control over staffing and budget, and is often elected for a two-year term. This

Caption Answer New York City, like many large cities, uses the strong mayor-council plan.

Discussion Starter
As the students consider the functioning of political machines, ask questions such as these: How and why did the machines help immigrants new to the big cities of the United States? Who helps new immigrants today? How? Do you think today's new immigrants might appreciate having some of the services offered by the old political machines? Why or why not?

Figure Answer The strong mayor-council system is most often found in large cities such as New York and San Francisco.

The figure content is also featured on *West's American Government Videodisc* (see the index found in the *TRB*) and is available in the transparency package.

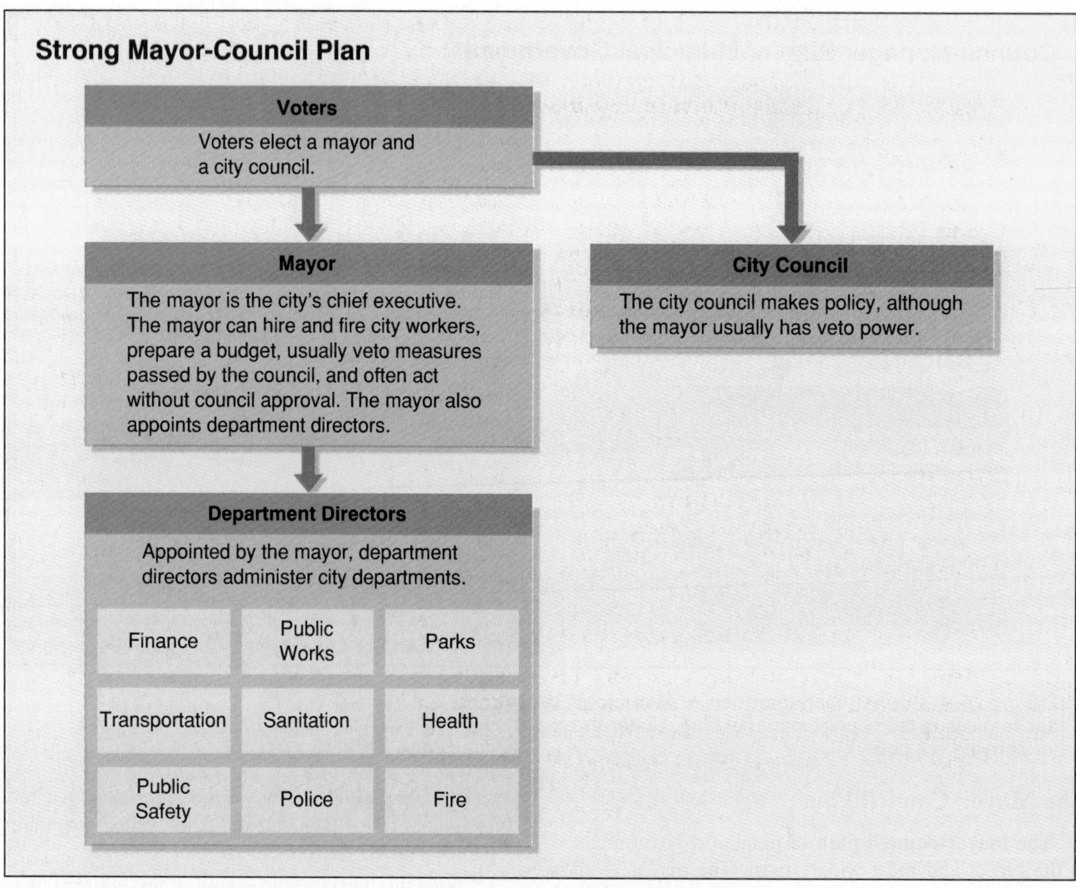

Strong Mayor-Council Plan
Voters
Voters elect a mayor and a city council.
Mayor
The mayor is the city's chief executive. The mayor can hire and fire city workers, prepare a budget, usually veto measures passed by the council, and often act without council approval. The mayor also appoints department directors.
City Council
The city council makes policy, although the mayor usually has veto power.
Department Directors
Appointed by the mayor, department directors administer city departments.
Finance
Public Works
Parks
Transportation
Sanitation
Health
Public Safety
Police
Fire

▲ **FIGURE 24–5 Strong Mayor-Council Plan.** As you can see from the organization chart above, under the strong mayor-council plan, the voters elect both the mayor and the city council. In what type of city is the strong mayor-council system most often found?

plan is often found in small or medium-sized cities; in some small cities, in fact, the office of mayor is only a part-time position.

About 50 percent of all American cities use some form of the mayor-council plan. Most recently the mayor-council plan has lost ground to the council-manager plan in small and medium-sized cities.

Figure 24–5 above, and 24–6 on page 602 show the two forms of the mayor-council plan.

A Question of Patronage—Or City Machines?

In the late nineteenth and early twentieth centuries, many major cities were run by "the machine." This was a political organization in which each city block within the municipality had an organizer, each neighborhood had a political club, and each district had a leader. All of these parts of the machine had a boss—such as Richard Daley in Chicago, Edward Crump in Memphis, or Tom Pendergast in Kansas City.

The machine emerged in the 1840s, when the first waves of European immigrants came to the United States to work in urban factories. When those individuals, who often lacked the ability to communicate in English, needed help, the machine was there to help them. The urban machine forged a strong political institution by relying on the support of the dominant ethnic groups. In this way, the machine could keep its boss (usually the mayor) in office year after year.

TEACHING BUILDING SOCIAL STUDIES SKILLS

Read

Introduce this Building Social Studies Skills feature by encouraging the students to share their current understanding of percentages: What are percentages? How are they usually used? How can you convert decimal numbers into percentages? How can you convert fractions into percentages? After a brief discussion, let volunteers read the feature aloud to the rest of the class.

Discuss

Pose questions such as these to guide the students in discussing the Building Social Studies Skills feature: What is the purpose of a sales tax? Who pays sales taxes? Who computes them? How can percentages be converted to decimals? How can percentages be converted to fractions? Why is it important to understand the distinction between changes in percent and changes in actual numbers? Why is it important to recognize the difference between the two when you are reading statistics? How can you be sure you understand what the figures in a table or chart represent?

Analyze and Apply

Let the students work in groups to practice figuring and using percentages. Have the group members create a simple survey form with at least six different questions; then have the group members gather survey responses from at least 25 people. Instruct the students to prepare tables showing the results of their surveys in both actual numbers and percentages. Display all the groups' charts, and encourage the students to examine and discuss all the survey information.

Review

Ask the students to review questions such as these: What does percent mean? Suppose you know that 275 students voted for a particular student council candidate; what else do you have to know in order to figure what percentage of the vote that candidate received?

Practicing Your Skills (Answers)

1. Motor vehicles had the highest recovery rate (67 percent).
2. Currency had the lowest recovery rate (4 percent).
3. 16.75 times greater (or 1,675 percent greater).

Note: Many students will incorrectly work #3—they will figure 67 percent – 5 percent = 62 percent for the "greater" answer. You can't subtract percentages.

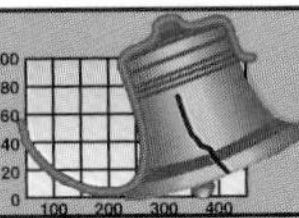

BUILDING SOCIAL STUDIES SKILLS

Figuring and Using Percentages

Throughout any text on American government, you are presented with many statistics, the most important of which are percentages. Percentages are often used to indicate how much of the American population is living in poverty, or how many people voted for a particular candidate.

Percentages indicate a certain number of parts per hundred. Certain expenses, such as tax rates, are determined in percentages. For example, when you buy a $20 book with a 7 percent sales tax, you have to add 7 cents in tax for every dollar you pay for the book. The calculation for this would be .07 × $20 = $1.40, which makes the total cost of the book $21.40.

Percentages can either be expressed as percentages, using the percent sign (%), or as decimals. In the calculation above, 7% was changed to .07, both of which mean 7 parts out of 100. The decimal equivalent of a percent is found by moving the decimal point two places to the left and dropping the percent sign. To change decimals to percentages, move the decimal point two places to the right and add the percent sign.

Percentages are used to figure out certain portions of a number. Say you are told, for example, that of the 400 people who voted in a recent local election, 300 voted for the Democratic candidate. You can calculate the percentage of people who voted for the Democrat in the following way: divide the number of those who voted Democrat by the total number of those who voted. The calculation would be 300 ÷ 400 = .75, or 75 percent.

In the same example, if you were told that 75 percent of the voters voted for the Democratic candidate, you can determine how many votes that candidate got if you know the total number who voted. In this case you would multiply .75 by 400 to get 300.

Remember that there is a difference between changes in *percent* and changes in *actual numbers.* For instance, a doubling of a percentage is not equivalent to increasing the total number twofold. When you are reading statistics, it's best to know whether you are actually reading about changes in percentages or changes in the actual number.

PRACTICING YOUR SKILLS

The table below gives the values of stolen property and the amounts recovered in a recent year. On a separate sheet of paper, calculate the percentages of the total amounts that were recovered. Then answer the questions below.

1. Which category of stolen property had the highest recovery rate?
2. Which category had the lowest?
3. How much greater is the highest recovery rate than the lowest recovery rate?

Property Stolen and Recovered

Type of Property	Value Stolen	Amount Recovered	Percentage Recovered
Motor Vehicles	$6 billion	$4 billion	
Firearms	$100 million	$10 million	
Currency	$1 billion	$40 million	
Televisions and Stereos	$1 billion	$50 million	

Enrichment
Let one of the students research and report on Richard J. Daley: How did he develop his position as an important city boss? What methods did he use as mayor? What were his most important accomplishments? Who benefitted from his activities and attitudes? How?

Extension
Ask the students to investigate and discuss any machine politics in your city or area: Was your community ever run by a political machine? When? With what successes and problems? What vestiges—if any—of that political machine can be seen in local government today?

Reteaching Strategies
1. Have pairs of students work together to review Section 3 by comparing and discussing the notes they have taken. Remind the students to refer to the text for clarification if necessary.
2. Work with small groups of students; help them identify and discuss their own form of municipal government.

Evaluation Strategies
1. Have the students write their answers to the Section 3 Review questions.
2. Have the students take the Section 3 Quiz found in the *TRB*.

Section 3 Review (Answers)
1. The commission plan, the council-manager plan, the mayor-administrator plan, and the mayor-council plan.

Figure Answer Department directors are appointed by the city council under this plan.

This figure content is also featured on *West's American Government Videodisc* (see the index found in the *TRB*) and is available in the transparency package.

Multidiscipline Strategies

Art Have the students work together to find and share political cartoons or caricatures of as many different political machine bosses as possible. As the students share and discuss these cartoons, ask them to explain, in detail, what they can learn about each boss from the cartoons. Then have them follow up the cartoons by reading about the reputation and activities of each boss. Finally, encourage interested students to draw and display their own cartoons of machine bosses.

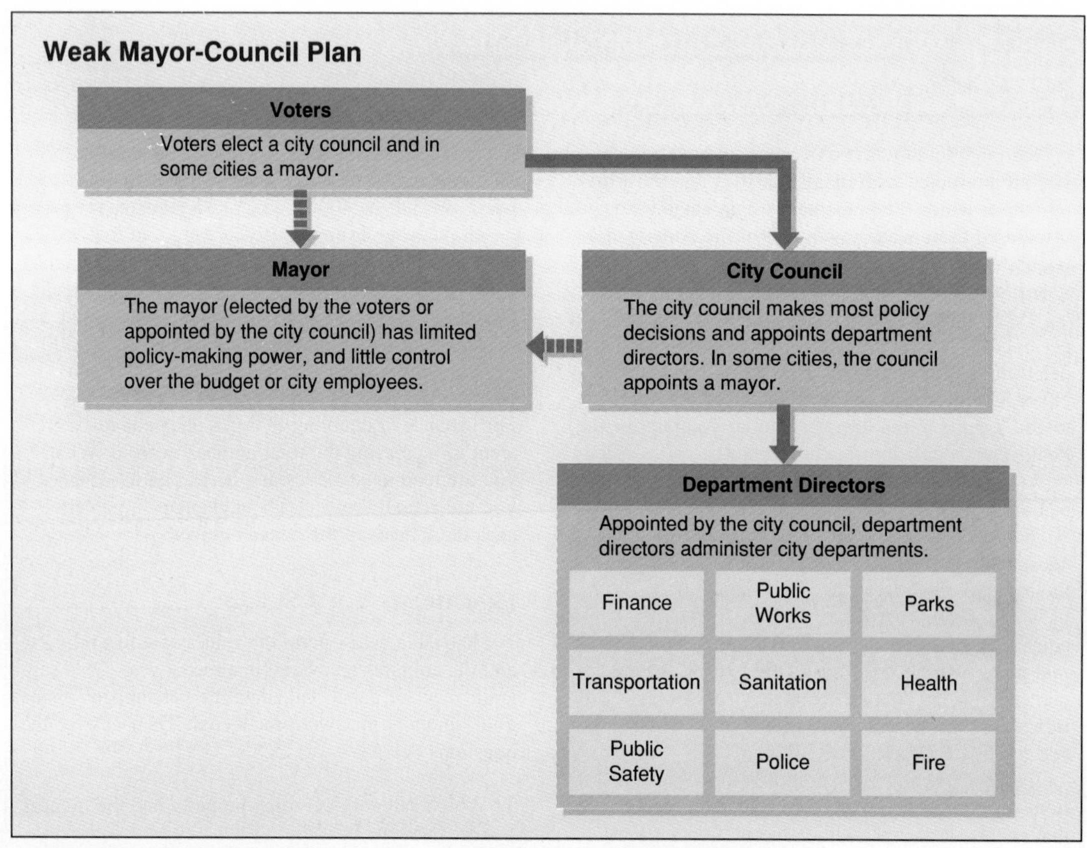

Weak Mayor-Council Plan
Voters
Voters elect a city council and in some cities a mayor.
Mayor
The mayor (elected by the voters or appointed by the city council) has limited policy-making power, and little control over the budget or city employees.
City Council
The city council makes most policy decisions and appoints department directors. In some cities, the council appoints a mayor.
Department Directors
Appointed by the city council, department directors administer city departments.
Finance
Public Works
Parks
Transportation
Sanitation
Health
Public Safety
Police
Fire

▲ **FIGURE 24–6 Weak Mayor-Council Plan.** The organization chart above is for the weak mayor-council plan. Under the weak mayor-council system, who is responsible for appointing department directors?

The machine was oiled by patronage. The party in power was often referred to as the patronage party. Loyal voters were rewarded with deliveries of Thanksgiving turkeys or coal at Christmas in return for their continued support for machine candidates. The power of the machine lay in its ability to control votes, and the votes of new urban immigrants from Europe or from rural America were especially crucial.

When the last of the big-city bosses, Mayor Richard Daley of Chicago, died in December 1976, an era that had lasted well over one hundred years died with him. The big-city machine had already begun to be in serious trouble in the 1960s, when community activists organized to work for municipal government. Soon a government of administrators began to appear. Fewer offices were elective, and more were appointive—presumably filled by professionals who had no political axes to grind, payoffs to make, or patrons to please.

SECTION 3 REVIEW

1. What are the major types of municipal representative governments?
2. Which types of city government are most common and why?
3. What is patronage? How did the machine use patronage in city politics?
4. **For critical analysis:** If you lived in a large city with serious social and economic problems, which plan of municipal government do you think would be most effective in dealing with these problems? Explain your answer.

2. The mayor-council plan is the oldest and most widely used.
3. Patronage is rewarding faithful party workers and followers with government employment and contracts. The power of the machine lay in its ability to control votes and support through patronage.
4. Answers will vary, e.g., the strong-mayor council plan because the city would need strong executive leadership.

TEACHING CHALLENGE TO THE AMERICAN DREAM

Read
Before the students read this Challenge to the American Dream feature, help them review all the units of local government: How do these units overlap? What problems do you think this overlapping can cause? After a brief discussion, ask one of the students to read the feature aloud to the rest of the class.

Discuss
Guide a class discussion of the feature by posing questions such as these: What are the benefits of consolidation? What kinds of problems do you think consolidation might cause? Why do you think functional consolidations are usually the most successful? What other examples of functional consolidation can you suggest? What do you think made the Metro consolidation such a success? Do you think it would work as well elsewhere? Why or why not? What does it mean to have advisory power only? What can make advisory power especially effective? Why do some political forces still oppose consolidation at the county and local levels? What do opponents of consolidation feel they might lose?

Analyze and Apply
Let the students work in groups to research and discuss consolidations that have taken place in your area or that are being suggested. Ask the group members to analyze the effectiveness of each consolidation and the probability of success of each suggestion. Then encourage the various groups to share and discuss their findings with the rest of the class.

Review
To help the students review this Challenge to the American Dream feature, ask questions such as these: What is consolidation? What are functional consolidations? What are COGs?

You Decide (Answers)
1. Answers will vary, e.g., as new communities rose up, they wanted to rule themselves.
2. Answers will vary, e.g., small communities that would like the assistance of larger units.
3. Answers will vary, e.g., those in leadership positions would be most reluctant to give up or share their positions.

CHALLENGE TO THE AMERICAN DREAM

Can Overlapping Governmental Units Be Avoided?

There are over eighty thousand separate and often overlapping governmental units within the United States. For example, there may be a division of the *county* government that concerns itself with water and sewage. Within that county there may be multiple *municipalities* that also concern themselves with water and sewage. This type of overlap exists throughout most of the United States. Consequently, it would seem that any attempt to reduce this confusion must involve some type of consolidation.

Consolidation

Consolidation is defined as the joining of two or more governmental units to form a single unit. Typically, a state constitution or a state statute will designate consolidation procedures.

Consolidation is often recommended for metropolitan-area problems, but to date few consolidations have actually been put into practice. The most successful consolidations have been **functional consolidations**—particularly of the police, health, and welfare departments of a city and a county. Functional consolidations group agencies according to the main job, or function, they perform. In some cases, functional consolidation is a satisfactory alternative to the complete consolidation of governmental units. The most successful form of functional consolidation was started in 1957 in Dade County, Florida. The county, now called Metro in government circles, is a union of twenty-six municipalities, each of which has its own governmental entity. The county government that oversees the municipalities operates under a home-rule charter. The county, or Metro, has authority to furnish water, planning, mass transit, and police services, and to set minimum standards of performance by all agencies. The governing body of Metro is an elected thirteen-member board of county commissioners, which appoints a county manager and a county attorney.

Councils of Governments (COGs)

Another type of consolidation is **councils of governments** (COGs), voluntary organizations of counties and municipalities that attempt to tackle areawide problems. COGs are an alternative means of treating major regional problems that various communities are unwilling to tackle on a consolidated basis either by full consolidation or functional consolidation of governmental units. More than two hundred COGs have been established since 1966. The impetus for their establishment was and continues to be federal government grants.

Generally the power of COGs is advisory only. Each member unit simply selects its council representatives, who report back to the unit after COG meetings. Nonetheless, today there are several COGs that have begun to have considerable influence on regional policy. These include the Metropolitan Washington Council of Governments, the Supervisors' Inter-County Commission in Detroit, and the Association of Bay Area Governments in San Francisco.

The challenge to the American dream is to continue to increase the amount of consolidation at the county and local levels in order to make local government more efficient.

You Decide

1. How do you think the United States ended up with so many governmental units?
2. Who among those in government do you think would be most likely to initiate consolidation?
3. Functional consolidation seems like a good idea, yet very few governments have agreed to use it. What political forces do you think might oppose functional consolidation of city and county departments?

Observable Mastery

The object of this Observable Mastery is for your students to create a complete local government profile based on the chapter's material. Provide students with their tasks in advance so they can work on visuals that can be displayed in the classroom.

Have students determine if their city is based on home-rule or general-city incorporation. Under county organization have them determine if they have a county-manager, chief administrator, or elected-chief executive model. Is the municipality operated by commission, council-manager, mayor-administrator, or mayor-council, weak or strong, plan? What special township districts exist? Finally, is there evidence of patronage? All of this should be diagrammed, with actual names if possible.

Chapter Evaluation

To evaluate student mastery of chapter material, you might:

1. Use Chapter Test A from the *TRB*.
2. Use Chapter Test B from the *TRB*.
3. Construct your own test using items from the *West American Government Test Bank* found in the *TRB*.
4. Use the accompanying computerized test software to construct and print a customized chapter test.

Review Questions (Answers)

1. Dillon's rule states that municipal governments may possess only those powers that the states expressly grant to them. Cooley's rule states that cities should be able to rule from home, or govern themselves.
2. Schools, police and fire protection, public welfare, city planning and zoning, and recreational and cultural activities.
3. Zoning is the method that cities use to regulate the way property, such as land and buildings, are used. A city uses zoning for orderly growth.
4. Record-keeping services, registering voters, preparing ballots, and supervising elections.

Chapter 24 Review

Key Terms

boroughs 590
chief administrator plan 593
city manager 597
commission plan 597
consolidation 603
Cooley's rule 583
council-manager plan 597
councils of government 603
counties 590
county board 591
county-manager plan 592
Dillon's rule 583
elected chief executive plan 593
functional consolidations 603
general-law city 584
home-rule city 584
incorporation 593
mayor-administrator plan 598
mayor-council plan 599
municipal home rule 584
municipalities 583
New England town 594
parishes 590
selectmen 594
strong mayor-council plan 599
town manager system 594
town meeting 594
townships 594
unincorporated areas 595
urban areas 593
weak-mayor council plan 599
zoning 589

Summary

1. The Constitution makes no mention of local governments; consequently, every local government is a creation of the state. Since 1900, about four-fifths of all states have allowed municipal home rule.

2. Local governments provide many important services, including education, police and fire protection, public welfare, city planning and zoning, and recreational and cultural activities.

3. Every state except Connecticut and Rhode Island is divided into counties. Counties vary widely in size, population, and importance. The responsibilities and functions of a county are usually determined by the state constitution and state laws. Most counties are governed by a county board. Most boards share their powers and responsibilities with other elected officials. Many people believe that county governments are outmoded and point out the need for reform. Urban areas with their own units of government are called municipalities. Cities and towns develop local governments when they are granted special legal status by the state legislature through incorporation. Townships perform the same functions as a county. Special districts are units of government created to deal with a special function of government such as garbage collection.

4. The major forms of municipal representative government are the commission plan, the council-manager plan, the mayor-administrator plan, and the mayor-council plan. There have been a number of attempts at reducing the confusion and overlap of governmental units. Consolidation is the union of two or more governmental units to form a single unit, and is often recommended for metropolitan-area problems. The most successful consolidations have been functional consolidations—particularly of city and county police, health, and welfare departments. Councils of government are voluntary organizations of counties and municipalities that attempt to tackle areawide problems.

Review Questions

1. What is the difference between Dillon's rule and Cooley's rule?
2. What are the major functions of local government?
3. What is zoning? Why is it important to a city?
4. Name several functions of counties.
5. What are some problems with county governments? How have some counties attempted to deal with these problems?
6. How is a municipality formed? From where does the authority to form a municipality come?
7. How do the towns of New England differ from the townships in other parts of the country?
8. Why are special districts created?
9. Briefly describe the types of municipal governments. What are the disadvantages and advantages of each?
10. What is machine politics?

5. Lack of effective leadership which leads to inefficiency, waste, and inaction. Some larger counties now have a county manager, county executive, or chief administrator.
6. Each municipality is created by the state. Cities and towns develop local governments when they are granted special legal status by the state legislature through incorporation.
7. A New England town typically consists of one or more urban settlements and the surrounding urban areas. Citizens practice direct democracy at town meetings.
8. To govern one issue such as a school district, sewers, garbage collection, or numerous other concerns.
9. The commission plan consists of a commission of three to nine members who have both legislative and executive powers. The council-manager plan consists of a professional manager who acts as chief executive and a council. The mayor-administrator plan is similar to the council-manager plan but the chief executive, the mayor, is elected. The mayor-council plan consists of a mayor and council, both popularly elected. One advantage of the commission plan is that it eliminates long ballots and partisan municipal politics. The disadvantages are that there are no checks and balances and no strong leadership. The council-manager plan has similar advantages and disadvantages. The mayor-administrator plan, as well as the mayor-council plan, both have the advantage of separating the chief executive from the legislative body. The disadvantage of these two plans is that they result in a long ballot.
10. Political organization in which each city block has an organizer, each neighborhood has a political club, each district a leader, and all these parts of the machine have a boss. Faithful party workers were rewarded with government employment and contracts.
11. (1) Find allies for help, (2) Contact media for publicity, (3) Be professional, (4) Consult with City Hall.
12. They attempt to tackle areawide problems.

CHAPTER 24 REVIEW—Continued

11. List four guidelines that you can use to start a recycling program in your community.
12. What function do councils of government provide?

Questions for Thought and Discussion

1. What is an important issue in your community that you would like to bring before the city council for action? What kind of action would you recommend that the council take?
2. Do you think the New England style of direct democracy would work in your community? Why or why not?
3. How do you think that reducing the size of local governments would affect those governments' abilities to serve the people?
4. Which plan of government does your city or town use? How well do you think that plan works? If you do not think it works well, which other plan would you recommend?
5. Compare and contrast the different types of municipal governments outlined in this chapter. Choose the one you believe most effective and explain your choice.
6. Which functions of government do you think would be easiest to consolidate?

Improving Your Skills

Communication Skills

Working in Groups

You have been or probably will be in many situations in which you will work with a group of other people. You may join a group working together to fight pollution in your community, serve on a student council or government board, or collaborate with others on a group project for school. Keep the following tips in mind when you join a group:

- Remember that you are only one member of the group. Do not dominate, but do not be afraid to contribute your opinion.
- Listen to everything others have to say. Distinguish in your mind between fact and opinion and between the important and unimportant. Ask questions if you do not understand or need more information.
- Stay focused on the goal or goals of the group.
- When it is your turn to speak, speak clearly, with proper enunciation, pronunciation, and grammar. Do not speak too quickly or too slowly.
- If people do not seem to understand each other, it may be because words sometimes mean different things to different people. It could also be that people are perceiving the situation differently. Be sure to clarify for everyone what the issue under discussion is exactly.

Writing

Write a script about a group working together who ignore all of the above tips. Role play the script with other members of your class.

Social Studies Skills

Working with Charts and Percentages

Look at the chart in Figure 24–2 on page 595. Answer these questions:

1. What percentage of the total number of special districts does the number of school districts represent?
2. What percentage of the total number of special districts does the number of fire protection districts represent?

Activities and Projects

1. Imagine that you are in charge of developing a form of government for a city of 25,000 people. Prepare a plan that tells which form of government you would use, and the responsibilities that would be given to each government official. Present the plan to the class.
2. Choose an issue in your community about which you are concerned, such as aid to the homeless. Research the issue and write a letter to a top city official addressing the issue.
3. Attend a city or county council meeting. Take notes on the procedures and report back to the class.
4. Attend a school board meeting. Write an outline of the major issues in your school district.
5. Invite a city official to your class to speak about his or her responsibilities and roles in the community.

Questions for Thought and Discussion (Answers)

1. Answers will vary.
2. Answers will vary, e.g., it would not work because there are too many people. There is also a lack of interest in most political decisions.
3. Answers will vary, e.g., reducing the size would make the local system more efficient.
4. Answers will vary.
5. Answers will vary, e.g., the council-manager plan works best because the manager is a professional manager and not a politician. The voters are still able to popularly elect the council members.
6. Answers will vary, e.g., mass transit services, water, and garbage services.

Social Studies Skills (Answers)

1. The total number of special districts listed is 42,192; school districts are 14,714. Therefore, school districts represent 14,714 ÷ 42,192, or 34.87 percent.
2. 10.93 percent.

CHAPTER INTRODUCTION

Instructional Objectives
By the end of the chapter students should be able to:
• Summarize the powers and limitations of state and local taxing.
• List the contributions from the federal government.
• List the amount and classify the patterns of state and local spending.

Using the Keynote
Begin by asking the students to define and discuss these two terms: *federalism* and *feudalism.* Then let a volunteer read the Sternlieb quotation aloud, and encourage the students to explain, in their own words, Sternlieb's idea. In what sense is our community a hodgepodge of responsibilities and taxing powers? How are the problems of one unit of local government compounded by being surrounded by other governmental units, all facing the same kinds of problems?

After the students have explained and considered the quotation, encourage them to express their own opinions: Do you agree with Sternlieb? Why or why not?

Introducing the Chapter
Have one of the students read the Introduction aloud. Then encourage a brief discussion by posing questions such as these: Why has the federal government shifted much of the financial responsibility for services onto cities and states? Do you think members of the tax-paying public are aware of this shift? How aware should they be? How have the awareness and the attitudes of citizens contributed to the frustration felt by many state and local officials? What resolution of this difficult situation can you foresee?

Previewing the Sections

Section 1 Ask the students to spend several minutes looking at Section 1. From this brief look, what can you conclude about the content of the section?
Section 2 Let volunteers read aloud the section title, the main headings, the figure titles, and the special feature titles in Section 2. Then ask the students: What do you already know about taxation? What do you expect to learn about taxation and other sources of government revenue as you study this section?
Section 3 Have the students page through Section 3, paying particular attention to the section title, the figure title, the main headings, and the bold-faced key terms. Give the students an opportunity to share their current understanding of those terms and to identify the specific vocabulary words that are still unclear to them.
Section 4 Instruct the students to look through Section 4. Then have the students list at least three specific questions they expect to have answered as they read this section.

CHAPTER 25

Paying for State and Local Government

CHAPTER OBJECTIVES

To learn and understand

- The limitations of state and local powers of taxation.
- How the federal government contributes financially to state and local governments.
- The priorities and patterns of state and local spending.

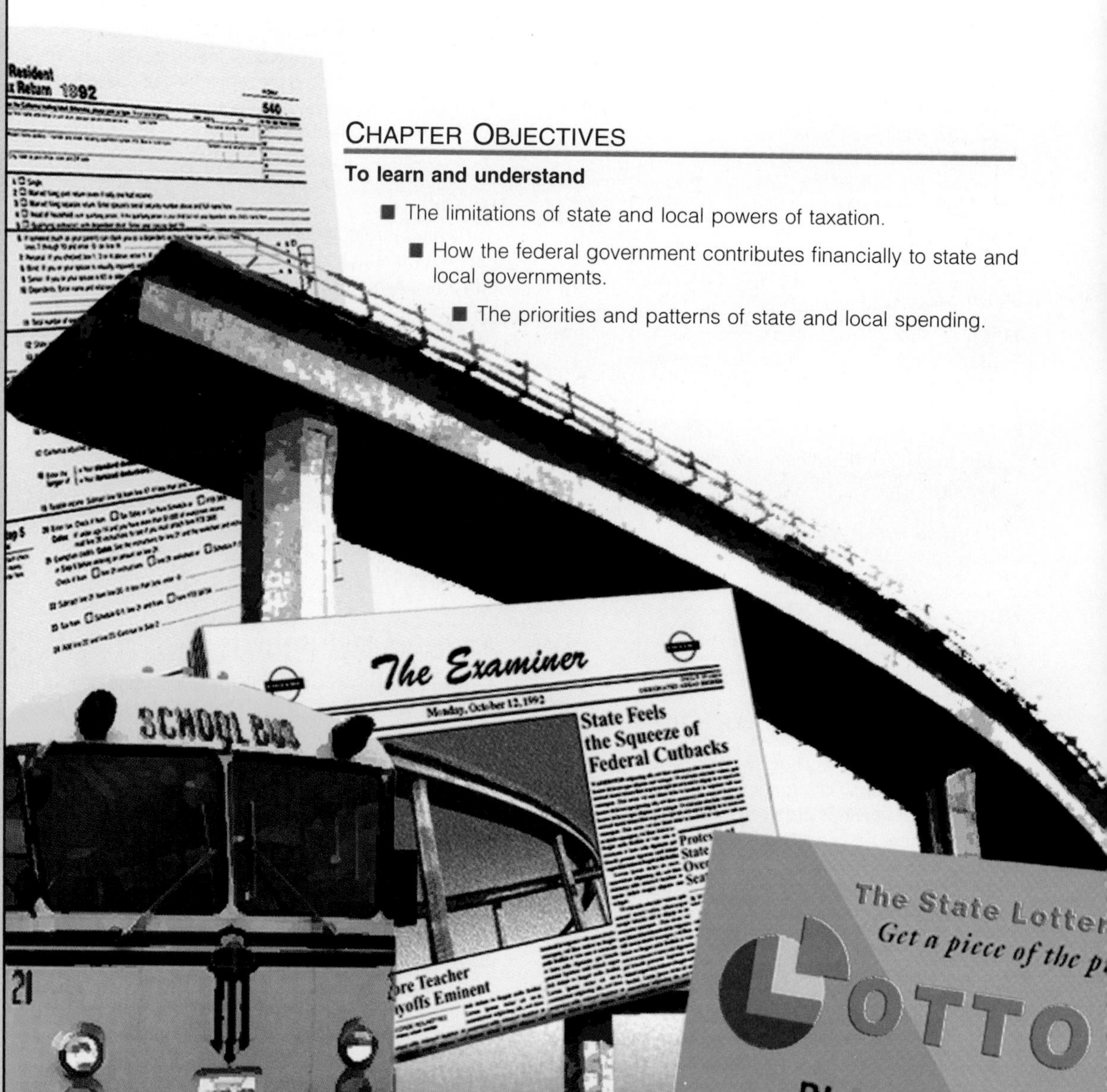

West's American Government Assignment Guide

Activity Sheets
Basic Concepts 25 *TRB* (Reteaching)
Enrichment Activity 25 *TRB*
Building Social Studies Skills 25 *TRB*

Quizzes
Chapter 25 Section 1 Quiz *TRB*
Chapter 25 Section 2 Quiz *TRB*
Chapter 25 Section 3 Quiz *TRB*

Tests
Chapter 25 Test A *TRB*
Chapter 25 Test B *TRB*
Chapter 25 Test Bank *TRB*
Chapter 25 WESTEST Computerized Testing

Social Studies Tool Kit Software
Chapter 25 Activity

Keynote

"We don't have New Federalism, we have New Feudalism, where every community fends for itself with a hodgepodge of responsibilities and taxing powers."

—— **George Sternlieb**
(1923–) Urban Specialist and Professor Emeritus of Public Policy at Rutgers University

INTRODUCTION

George Sternlieb's quote above echoes the frustrations many state and local officials have felt in recent years as the federal government has shifted a heavier financial burden and responsibility to the cities and states. At the same time, public demands for better city and state services have become enormous.

State and local governments spend over one trillion dollars per year. The money for such budgets has to come from somewhere. State governments have a large number of sources of revenue, while local governments have fewer. One of the most important of these sources is the taxes all of us pay in one form or another. There are limitations, however, on the types of taxes that state and local governments can use.

SECTION 1

Limitations on State and Local Taxation

Preview Questions

- What limits does the Constitution place upon the taxing powers of state and local governments?
- What other limitations are placed on state and local taxing power?

There are basically two types of limitations on state and local powers of taxation—those that come from the federal government and those that come from the state governments themselves. Of course, no state or local government can exceed the taxing power given to the federal government by the U.S. Constitution. Additionally, because local governments obtain their taxing power from state governments, their taxing powers are limited by not only state constitutions, but also by laws passed by state legislatures.

U.S. Constitutional Limitations

Within the U.S. Constitution only a few limitations are placed on state and local taxing powers. These limitations apply to agencies of the federal government, interstate commerce, and due process.

Agencies of the Federal Government U.S. Supreme Court Chief Justice John Marshall said that "the power to tax involves the power to destroy." In his famous 1819 decision, *McCulloch* v. *Maryland* (discussed in detail in Chapter 4), Marshall put to rest any hope of state governments being able to tax an agency of the federal government. That Supreme Court decision still stands today and prevents states from taxing the operations, land, buildings, or any other aspect of the federal government.

Interstate Commerce Article I, Section 10, Clause 2 of the Constitution states that "no State shall . . . lay any Imposts [taxes] or Duties on Imports or Exports. . . ." Furthermore, Clause 3 states that "no State shall . . . lay any Duty of Tonnage. . . ." Clause 2 prevents the states from taxing both imports into the United States and exports to other countries. Clause 3 prevents the states from taxing ships according to their cargo capacity.

The Supreme Court has said that the U.S. Constitution gives Congress, not the states, the power to regulate interstate and foreign trade. Therefore, the states

SECTION 1

Points to Stress
- Limits placed on the taxing powers of the state and local governments by the federal Constitution.
- Other limitations placed on state and local taxing power.

Kickoff Activity
Ask the students to write short paragraphs in response to these questions: Do your state and local governments have the power to tax federal land or federal buildings within their areas? Why or why not? When everyone has finished writing, let the students compare and discuss their responses.

Working with the Preview Questions
Ask volunteers to read these study questions aloud; then ask other volunteers to identify the main headings that indicate where information in response to each question can be found. Have the students keep the questions in mind as they read and take notes on Section 1.

Teaching Strategies

Introduction
After the students have read the introductory paragraph, help them discuss the limitations on state and local taxation powers: How do these limitations contribute to the frustration of state and local officials?

Comprehension
Let the students identify examples of agencies of the national government within your state: What losses does your state face by being unable to tax these agencies?

Discussion Starter
Help the students discuss the limitations that the Constitution places on state and local taxing of interstate commerce: Why do you think these limitations were included in the Constitution? Do you believe they still make sense today? Why or why not?

Comprehension
Encourage the students to suggest other examples of reasonable and unreasonable classifications for the purpose of collecting taxes.

Caption Answer Students should understand that as Marshall pointed out, "The power to tax involves the power to destroy." If states were allowed to tax aspects of the federal government, they could, in effect, destroy these aspects within their state borders by taxing them out of existence.

Extension
Have the students research and discuss the specific limitations on taxing powers that are included in your state constitution.

Discussion Starter
Help the students consider the tax-exempt status of religious organizations, museums, operas, and cemeteries: What is the purpose of these exemptions? Who benefits as a result of the exemptions? Who suffers? Do you believe that states can afford to maintain such exemptions? Why or why not?

Reteaching Strategies
1. Ask the students to work with partners, using their notes to review together the information presented in Section 1. Remind the students to refer to the text to resolve any questions; also encourage them to revise their notes as necessary.
2. Work with small groups of students. Guide them in discussing and revising the paragraphs they wrote during the Kickoff Activity for this section.

Evaluation Strategies
1. Have the students write their answers to the Section 1 Review questions.
2. Have the students take the Section 1 Quiz found in the *TRB*.

Section 1 Review (Answers)
1. The limitations that come from the federal government by the Constitution, and from the state governments by their constitutions.
2. The limitations apply to agencies of the federal government, interstate commerce, and due process.
3. Answers will vary, e.g., Marshall meant that a state's power to tax property or agencies of the federal government would allow them to undermine the authority of the national government.

▲ The Supreme Court decision in *McCullough* v. *Maryland* forbids states from taxing the operations, land, buildings, or any other aspect of the federal government. Why do you think the Supreme Court felt it was necessary to deny states this power?

cannot pass laws that prevent imports from being brought into their respective states. The states cannot tax such imports either.

Due Process The due process clause of the Fourteenth Amendment to the U.S. Constitution can be used to limit the power of state and local governments to impose taxes. Under the due process clause, taxes must be imposed and administered fairly and not be so great as to be the equivalent of seizing property. For example, your local government could not pass a property tax that was so high that only a few people could afford to pay it and the rest would therefore have to forfeit their property.

The due process clause also forbids unreasonable classifications for the purpose of collecting taxes. It is reasonable to collect a tax on smokers by taxing cigarettes. It is reasonable to collect a tax on the users of automobiles by taxing gasoline. It is unreasonable, however, to make only blond-haired citizens pay a state income tax and to let everyone else live tax free.

State Constitutional Limitations

Each state has constitutional limitations on the taxing power of that state. Additionally, each state constitution puts limits on the taxing power of local governments. Virtually all state constitutions indicate that all taxes must be uniformly applied, and applied for public purposes only.

All states normally exempt religious organizations, museums, operas, and cemeteries from taxation. (This means that these organizations do not have to pay state and local taxes.) Some state constitutions set maximum rates for different taxes such as those on cigarettes. Others prohibit certain kinds of taxes such as a tax on any personal income.

SECTION 2

Points to Stress

- The major types of taxes used at the state and local level.
- The tax that produces the largest amount of revenue among most states.
- The tax that produces the largest amount of revenue among local governments.
- The principal nontax sources of revenue for state and local governments.

Kickoff Activity

How do your state and local governments raise money? Ask the students to list at least five revenue-raising activities in response to this question. When all the students have written their lists, let several volunteers read theirs aloud and encourage a brief discussion.

Working with the Preview Questions

Go over these four study questions with the class. Then ask the students to use these questions in writing the main headings for an outline of Section 2. Have them fill in their outlines as they read the section.

SECTION 1 REVIEW

1. What are the two basic limitations on state and local taxation powers?
2. What restrictions does the federal Constitution place on state and local taxing powers?
3. **For critical analysis:** What did John Marshall mean when he said "the power to tax involves the power to destroy?" Explain your answer.

SECTION 2

Sources of State and Local Revenues

Preview Questions

- What are the major types of taxes used at the state and local levels?
- Which tax produces the largest amount of revenue in most states?
- Which tax produces the largest amount of revenue for local governments?
- From which principal nontax sources do state and local governments draw revenues?

There are three sources of state and local revenues: taxes, nontax revenues, and intergovernmental transfers.

Types of Taxes

There is a large variety of taxes that are assessed at all levels of government. In Chapter 19 you learned about some of these taxes, which include the following:

- Personal income tax
- Corporate income tax
- Excise tax
- Estate tax
- Inheritance tax
- Sales tax
- Property tax

Personal Income Tax These are taxes paid on personal income each year. Seven states have no personal income tax system: Florida, Nevada, South Dakota, Texas, Washington, Wyoming, and Alaska. The other 43 states have assessed taxes on personal income at rates from as low as .4 percent in Iowa to as high as 12 percent in Massachusetts.

Corporate Income Tax Corporations pay taxes on their profits in all but five states—Nevada, South Dakota, Texas, Washington, and Wyoming. In the other 45 states they pay rates from as low as one percent in Alaska and Arkansas to as high as 10.5 percent in North Dakota and 12.25 percent in Pennsylvania.

Excise Tax When there are special taxes paid by the consumer for the use and consumption of certain goods they are called **excise taxes**. A number of states collect excise taxes on cigarettes, gasoline, alcoholic beverages, and telephone use. There is very little uniformity in how much each state collects in excise taxes on cigarettes and gasoline.

Cigarette taxes per pack of 20 are the lowest in tobacco-growing states—North Carolina (5 cents), South Carolina (7 cents), Virginia (2.5 cents), and Kentucky (3 cents). The high cigarette-tax states are California, Connecticut, Illinois, Iowa, Minnesota, Nevada, New Jersey, New York, North Dakota, Washington, and Wisconsin.

Estate and Inheritance Taxes When someone dies, some states levy a tax on the value of the property (estate) that the deceased leaves behind. Some states, either in addition or instead of the estate tax, assess a tax on those who inherit property from someone who has died. The inheritance tax does not exist at the federal level, but the estate tax does. All such taxes are called **death taxes**.

Sales Tax There is no sales tax at the federal level. Only five states have no general sales tax: Alaska, Delaware, Montana, New Hampshire, and Oregon. Sales taxes in other states range from a low of 3 percent in Colorado and North Carolina to a high of 8.25 percent in parts of California. Local sales taxes are tacked on to state sales taxes in many cities. In New York City, for example, the local sales tax adds another 4.25 percent to the 4 percent state sales tax, bringing total sales tax on each dollar spent in New York City to 8.25 cents.

Property Tax The majority of states impose a tax on the value of property. Virtually every municipality uses the property tax to raise the majority of its revenues. The most well-known property tax is that levied on the value of real estate—land and the houses or buildings on it. A number of states collect taxes on personal property, such

Teaching Strategies

Introduction

Read the brief section introduction aloud, and let the students discuss what they already know about the distinctions between taxes, nontax revenues, and intergovernmental transfers.

Discussion Starter

Focus the students' attention on the choice made by seven states not to tax personal income: Why do you think these states avoid taxing personal income? What are the benefits to the state in declining to tax personal income? What problems might this decision raise for the state? Does your state levy taxes on personal income? Do you think it should? Why or why not?

Extension

Help the students recall (or research) and discuss answers to these questions: What is the rate of taxation on personal income in your state? The rate of taxation on corporate profits?

Discussion Starter

Encourage the students to discuss their reactions to special taxes on cigarettes: What is the rationale for these taxes? Do you consider them fair? Why or why not?

Discussion Starter

Let the students discuss their ideas in response to these questions: What is the justification for estate and inheritance taxes? Do you think such taxes should be levied? Why or why not?

Extension

Have the students recall (or research) and discuss the answers to these questions: Are local taxes added to our state sales tax? If so, what percent? What is the total percentage we pay in sales tax?

Comprehension
Guide the students in reading and comparing the two pie graphs in The Importance of Taxes at the State and Local Levels.

This figure content is also featured on *West's American Government Videodisc* (see the index found in the *TRB*) and is available in the transparency package.

Discussion Starter
Ask the students to consider the difference between the federal and the state governments in percentage of revenues collected from personal income tax: What do you think accounts for this difference? Why don't states raise their revenues by levying higher income taxes?

Figure Answer Students should understand that property taxes are the most important form of tax for local governments but, at the state level, are not as important as sales taxes.

FYI

Adam Smith wrote the *Wealth of Nations* in 1776 which spelled out his philosophy of capitalism. In the book he also addressed the criteria for a successful tax structure. Smith's criteria are surprisingly relevant to today's circumstances. First, Smith felt a tax ought to be fair, meaning one ought to pay in proportion to income. Second, there should be clarity and certainty to taxation. Everyone should have information on tax rates and method of payment. The tax should not be arbitrary, meaning that standards be applied and maintained. Third, the tax should be easy to pay and easy to collect. Related to this is the idea that taxes should not be so onerous as to discourage business activity or labor. An example of easy payment and collection is federal taxes that are automatically drawn from one's paycheck. Finally, a tax should be easy to administer, so that collection costs do not negate tax revenues. Share these criteria with students and evaluate the current sources of taxation using them as a guide.

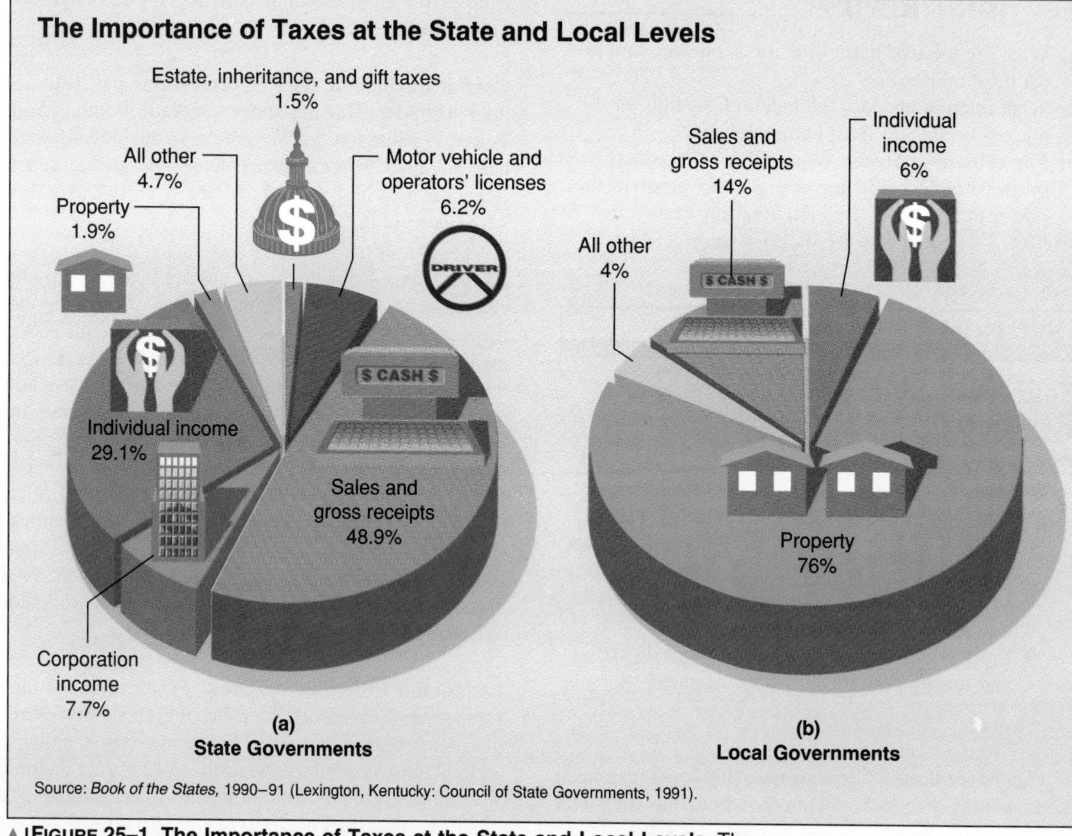

▲ FIGURE 25–1 **The Importance of Taxes at the State and Local Levels.** The graphs above show the importance of each type of tax for both state and local governments. How important are property taxes to each of these levels of government?

as motor vehicles, business machines, boats, trailers, and trucks.[1]

The Importance of Each Tax

The pie charts above in Figure 25–1 show the percentages of the various kinds of taxes raised by state and local governments.

By far the most important tax for most states is the general sales tax, which is a tax levied as a proportion of the retail price of any good when it is sold. The most important tax at the local level is the property tax, which accounts for over three-fourths of all local taxes raised.

Whereas the federal government obtains more than 44 percent of its total revenues from personal income taxes, states obtain less than 15 percent from this type of tax. There is tremendous variation in the amounts of state and local taxes collected.

The highest taxes are paid by residents in Connecticut, District of Columbia, Massachusetts, and New Jersey. The lowest taxes are paid by residents of Mississippi and Utah.

State Nontax Revenues

Some state and local governments operate businesses from which they receive revenues. Like the federal government, states also borrow.

1. Personal property consists of things that can be moved; real property is immovable.

Enrichment
Have a pair of interested volunteers research the services provided to citizens by the high-taxing states and by the low-taxing states: What is the relationship between taxes collected and services delivered? Let the volunteers report their findings to the rest of the class, and encourage all the students to discuss the implications of these findings.

Discussion Starter
Focus the students' attention on the businesses operated by state and local governments: Do you imagine that these businesses face private-sector competition? Why or why not? If not, is this arrangement fair to the citizens?

Enrichment
Let a small group of students investigate the amount of money collected locally from parking and traffic fines: How much is collected each year? How is that money spent? Ask the students to summarize their findings in a chart to be displayed in the classroom.

Caption Answer Student answers will vary according to your city.

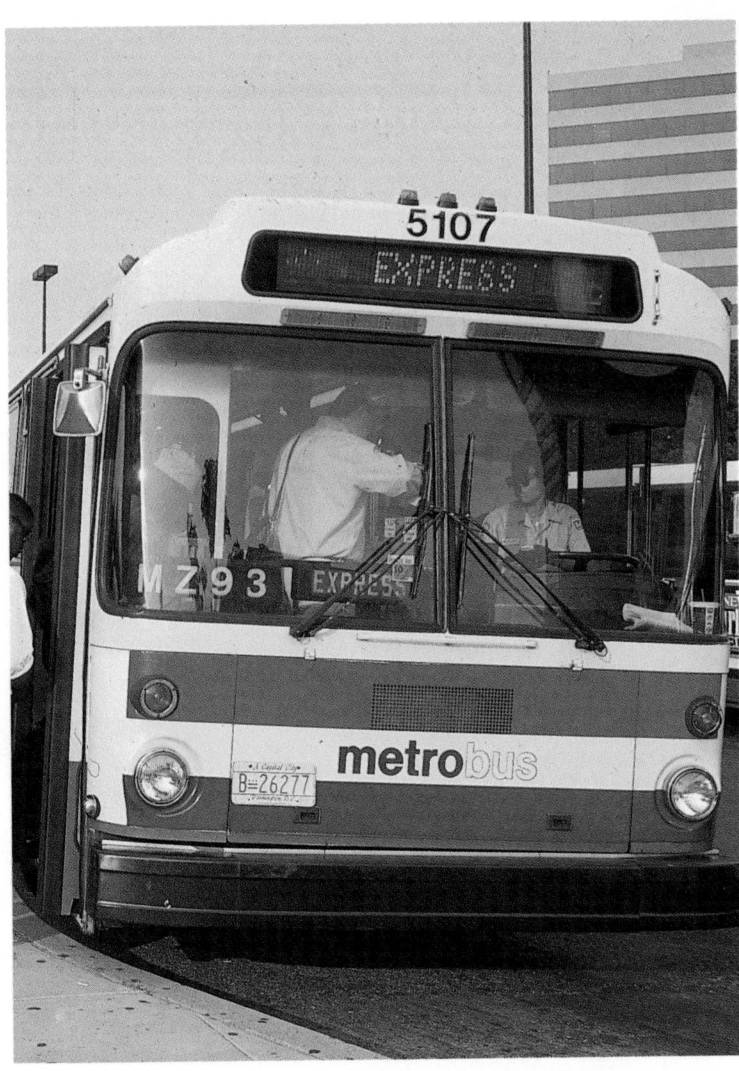

A number of cities own and operate their own bus systems. Does your city own and operate its own bus system?

Government-Operated Businesses State and local governments operate toll bridges and toll roads. Some states, particularly Washington, operate ferries. Alaska has had numerous businesses including a slaughterhouse and a phone company. The state of North Dakota markets Dakota-made flour. The state of California operates a railroad line in San Francisco. Eighteen states, including Idaho, Maine, Utah, West Virginia, and Montana operate liquor stores.

A number of cities own and operate their own water systems, bus systems, and electric power companies. A number of cities operate warehouses, office buildings, and wharfs. Whenever these government-operated businesses make a profit, the profits constitute a source of revenue that can be used for other state and local expenditures.

Less important nontax sources of revenues include fines accessed in state and local courts, as well as interest on investments.

Borrowing Sometimes states and cities find that they cannot pay for all of their expenditures, and are forced

TEACHING GOVERNMENT IN ACTION

Read

As an introduction to this Government in Action feature, let the students discuss their own ideas about and reactions to state lotteries: Does our state run a lottery? Why or why not? Do you think it should? Why or why not? Have you or your friends or family members ever played in a state-run lottery? How often? With what success?What do you think the chances are that any one person will win a big jackpot in a state-run lottery? In addition to the pay-offs, what advantages do you see in the lotteries? What disadvantages do you associate with them? After this discussion, ask for volunteers to read the feature aloud.

This figure content is also featured on *West's American Government Videodisc* (see the index found in the *TRB*).

Discuss

Use questions such as these to guide a class discussion of the feature: Do you think most lottery players are familiar with the statistics on the chance of winning a big jackpot? Why do you think people continue to play the lottery, in spite of the poor odds? How do a lottery's small pay-offs influence players? Do most people who win small amounts actually receive more money than they spend on playing the lottery? Who is responsible for the fact that poorer families spend a higher percentage of their income on lottery tickets than richer families? Do you think that state governments have the right or the responsibility to restrict the sale of lottery tickets? Why or why not? Do you know anyone (or have you read about anyone) who has played South Dakota's VLT or who has participated in Oregon's legalized betting? Do you consider the Michigan lottery ad informative? Why or why not?

Analyze and Apply

Ask the students to work with partners or in small groups to gather information about the money collected from lotteries within your state (or, if your state has no lottery, another specific state): How much money has the state-run lottery raised in each of its years of existence? Of that money, how

GOVERNMENT IN ACTION

CASE STUDY

State-Run Lotteries on the Rise

In 1964, the first modern state lottery was started in New Hampshire. From 1984 to 1992, thirty-two states, as well as the District of Columbia, had taken in a total of almost \$100 billion in state lottery revenues. In 1992 alone, the estimate was almost \$22 billion in lottery revenues. In 1975 the per-person ticket sales in the states that had lotteries was only \$23; by 1992 it had jumped to \$129 per person. The chart below shows how lottery sales increased over a period of fifteen years.

Sometimes states hold super lotteries that generate tremendous revenues. In 1991, for example, the state of New York held a super lottery that had a \$90 million jackpot. Ticket sellers sold 61 million tickets in ten days—more than 21,000 a minute in the period just prior to the drawing. When a Florida lottery jackpot reached \$106 million, the rate of ticket sales toward the end reached 44,000 tickets a minute and lottery officials were pleading on TV for the public to remain calm.

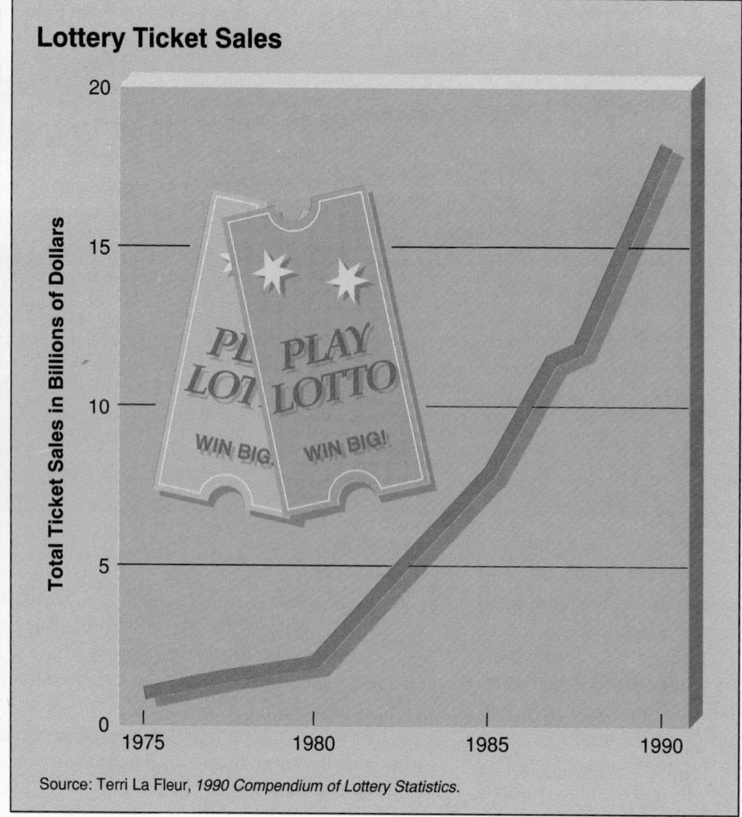

much has gone directly into state funds? How much has been spent on the expenses of running the lottery? Was the lottery established to raise money for a specific purpose? If so, what is that purpose, and how successful has the lottery been in raising money for it? When the students have completed their research, encourage them to compare and discuss their findings.

Review

Ask the students these review questions about the Government in Action feature: About how much money did state lotteries raise in 1992? In what sense do state lotteries represent a regressive tax system?

Think About It (Answers)

1. Answers will vary, e.g., there is no real difference. Lotteries have just become more acceptable as states find they need more and more revenue.

2. Answers will vary, e.g., the only benefits would be those they receive back from the government in the form of services. In some states, part of lottery-ticket profits are used to pay for public education.

It might be surprising that so many people invest so much in a game that offers such a small chance of winning. Chances of winning a big jackpot are about 13 million to 1 (compare these odds with the chances of being killed by lightning during a thunderstorm, which are about 400,000 to 1).

Some argue that state lotteries, even though voluntary, represent a regressive tax system. (Remember from Chapter 19, that in a regressive tax system, the percentage of income tax paid decreases as income increases.) The reason it is called regressive is that poorer families spend a higher percentage of their income on lottery tickets than richer families. According to one study, the true tax rate on lottery purchases is higher than the total tax on cigarettes or alcohol. In other words, the average lottery expenditure seems to be about the same, no matter what a person's income is. That means that the tax on those expenditures, expressed as a percentage of income, falls as income increases. In California, for example, average yearly lottery expenditures fall from 1.5 percent of income in the lowest-income class (under $10,000) to less than .01 percent of income in the $50,000 to $60,000 class.

Nonetheless, lotteries probably will be around for a long time because they are an attractive way to obtain needed revenues. They represent a revenue source that was not used prior to 1964. Most observers believe that virtually every state in the nation will have a lottery by the year 2010.

In addition to the lottery, more and more states are seeking revenues from allowing other forms of legalized gambling. The video lottery terminal (VLT) looks and sounds like other video arcade games. Instead of playing a video game, however, participants play poker, blackjack, and bingo. If participants win, they do not get their money immediately, but rather the VLT prints out a receipt that allows them to collect the money elsewhere. South Dakota first started operating these machines under the state lottery system in 1989. In the first nine months of legalization, South Dakota VLTs took in $127 million from 3,800 machines, which is about $180 per person in the state, or four times the revenues they were receiving from the state lottery. In Oregon, there is legalized betting on professional football. People bet on their favorite team to beat or tie the "point spread," or number of points by which the favored team is expected to win.

In 1975 the federal government lifted its ban against advertising lotteries on TV and radio. Every state that currently has a lottery is using increasingly clever advertising to sell it. In Michigan, for example, a TV ad shows a man in a convenience store who says he would never play the lottery because he would have a better chance of being struck by lightning. At that instant he is struck by a bolt out of the blue. He then says, "One ticket, please."

Although the rate of increase in lottery ticket sales slowed in 1991 and 1992, lotteries remain a popular way for states to generate revenue. It appears that what is for citizens a 13-million-to-1 long shot has become for many states a sure thing.

Think About It

1. There are laws against gambling in almost every state in the nation. Why, then, do states have legal lotteries? In other words, what might be the difference between gambling in a state-run lottery and any other type of gambling?
2. If lottery ticket sales represent a form of regressive taxes, what are the benefits that the poor receive from these implicit taxes?

TEACHING CITIZENSHIP SKILLS IN ACTION

Read
Before the students begin reading this Building Citizenship Skills feature, encourage a brief discussion by asking questions such as these: What is community action? What purposes does it serve? What local groups engage in community action? Who are local community action leaders? After the students have shared and discussed their ideas, ask them to read the feature independently.

Discuss
Pose questions such as these to help the students discuss the feature: What would you want to do in response to each situation described in the first paragraph? Whom would you contact for help? When you are trying to organize citizens for community action, why is it important to focus on citizens who are directly affected? What can you do to raise their awareness of the problem you perceive and the solution you support? What are some examples of specific public hearings you might attend? Why is it important to encourage all group members to attend? How can organizing a letter-writing campaign improve the effectiveness of written protests? Why is attracting attention to your group important? What guidelines should you keep in mind when preparing press releases?

Analyze and Apply
Work with the students to identify and discuss various public hearings to be held in your area. Then ask the students to attend at least one public hearing and to discuss how it was conducted and what it accomplished.

Review
To help the students review this Building Citizenship Skills feature, ask them questions such as these: How should you start organizing a community action group? What are two decisions that members of a community action group need to make?

Comprehension
Let volunteers respond to these questions: What are bonds? How do they work? Whom are they intended to benefit?

Reteaching Strategies
1. Let the students work with partners to compare and discuss the outlines they have written of Section 2.
2. Work with small groups of students, helping them discuss their responses to these questions: Which state and local taxes affect you? How?

CITIZENSHIP SKILLS AND RESPONSIBILITIES

Organizing for Community Action

Every week decisions are made in your community that directly affect your local environment and daily life. Getting involved in local government is a good way to learn where you stand politically, and a good place to develop skills for community action. Suppose you read in the newspaper that the city planning board has decided to demolish the oldest neighborhood in town, where your grandparents' Victorian-style apartment building still stands, to make room for a fish cannery. Suppose you hear that the city plans to cut down all the trees lining your street to widen the road. Suppose you see on the news that the police department has decided to reduce police patrols in your neighborhood, even though burglaries and violent crimes have risen dramatically and you feel unsafe.

Some decisions may be difficult to fight because of the many demands placed on local government, but if enough citizens are in opposition, government officials can be persuaded. After all, in a democracy, government officials are responsible to everyone. Here are some steps you can take to influence the decisions of your local government.

1. **Organize a group.** Gather together the people in your community who also oppose the government action. Start with your friends and plan a meeting. Tell them to talk with their friends and neighbors and invite them all to come. Also invite anyone who can speak knowledgeably about your cause. Conduct the meeting as an open forum and let everyone express their opinion.
2. **Attend public hearings.** Urge all the members of your group to attend. Present your opinions in a clear, straightforward manner.
3. **Decide on your exact goals.** Having decided on your goals, come up with a plan of action. Give your group a name and appoint a leader. Announce the purpose of your group to public officials involved. Organize activities to express your views.
4. **Attract attention.** Write press releases and send them to local TV stations, radio stations, and newspapers. Be direct and give good reasons for your opinions. Be sure to emphasize the importance of your cause to the community.
5. **Start a petition drive.** Circulate petitions around your neighborhood through your group members and get as many signatures as possible. Submit the petitions to the appropriate public officials.

TAKING ACTION

1. Choose a local problem in which you have a strong interest. Follow newspaper reports on this problem for two weeks. Then write down the way you would organize community action to solve this problem.
2. Put at least one of your steps into action.

to borrow by issuing state and municipal bonds. State and local governments choose to sell bonds in order to complete many large projects. The building of highways, bridges, dams, schools, and government buildings are often paid for through this kind of borrowing.

Many states have found that they have had to borrow on a grand scale as their expenditures have greatly exceeded their revenues. For example, in 1991 California found itself with a projected budget shortfall—a negative difference between projected spending and estimated revenues—of almost $13 billion. Other states that have run into fiscal trouble in the 1990s include Connecticut, Florida, Michigan, Maryland, Massachusetts, New Jersey, Pennsylvania, and Virginia.

Often state and local governments can easily sell bonds to cover their deficits because the interest earned by the purchasers is exempt from federal income taxes.

Intergovernmental Transfers

An increasingly important source of revenue for state and local governments is the receipt of funds from the federal government. In the next section you will read

Evaluation Strategies
1. Have the students write their answers to the Section 2 Review questions.
2. Have the students take the Section 2 Quiz found in the *TRB*.

Section 2 Review (Answers)
1. Personal income tax, corporate income tax, excise tax, sales tax, property tax, and estate and inheritance taxes.
2. Generally, state governments are most dependent on sales taxes and cities are most dependent on property taxes.
3. Government-operated businesses and borrowing.
4. Answers will vary, e.g., everything bought should be taxed equally. Alternatively, it is not fair to tax necessaries such as food and prescription drugs. Such a tax is especially hard on the poor, for whom these items constitute a greater share of total income then they do for the rich.

Caption Answer Student answers will vary but might include toll bridges, ferries, the state-run slaughterhouse and phone company in Alaska, Dakota made flour in North Dakota, state run liquor stores in 18 states, and water, bus, and electric power companies.

SECTION 3

Points to Stress
- The methods by which the national government returns nationally collected tax dollars to state and local governments.
- The manner in which those methods differ.

Kickoff Activity
Ask the students to read the title of Section 3. Then ask them this question: How freely does Uncle Sam grant money to state and local governments? Give the students five minutes in which to write responses—including explanations of their ideas—to the question. At the end of the allotted time, let several volunteers read their responses aloud.

Working with the Preview Questions
Have the students read and consider these two study questions. Then ask them to keep the questions in mind as they study Section 3.

Teaching Strategies

Introduction
Let a volunteer read the section introduction aloud to the rest of the class. Help the students study and discuss figure 25–2, Declining Federal Contribution to State and Local Governments: What trend does the chart show? What are the implications of that trend?

Extension
Ask the students to identify and discuss local projects that have been financed by categorical grants: How have these projects benefitted local citizens? Would the projects have been possible without grants? Why or why not?

This turnpike in Massachusetts is just one example of a government-operated business. What other types of government-operated businesses exist around the nation?

about how the federal government gives money back to the states.

SECTION 2 REVIEW

1. What are the major taxes used at the state and local levels?
2. Which tax produces the largest amount of revenue for the states? For the local governments?
3. What are the major sources of nontax revenues?
4. **For critical analysis:** Some people argue that some items such as food and prescription drugs should be exempt from sales tax because they are necessities. Others argue that sales taxes from such items are important sources of revenue, and that everyone should contribute to the government's revenue base. Which side do you agree with? Give reasons for your answer.

SECTION 3

Money from Uncle Sam

Preview Questions
- What are the methods by which the federal government distributes federal tax dollars to state and local governments?
- How do these methods differ?

Today, the federal government collects over 60 percent of all tax dollars. As part of our system of cooperative federalism, the federal government gives a significant amount of the funds collected from these taxes back to the states (which give to the local governments). In fiscal year 1992, the federal government distributed almost $110 billion, although this amount represents a decline over earlier years. Figure 25–2 on the next page shows the pattern of federal contributions over a period of thirty years.

There are basically three separate methods by which the federal government returns federal tax dollars to state and local governments: categorical grants-in-aid, block grants, and general grants-in-aid (also called general revenue sharing).

Categorical Grants

The concept of a federal government grant-in-aid was derived from a 1902 law providing that revenues from the sale of federally owned lands were to be shared with certain states and territories for irrigation and land reclamation. Such grants are tied to specific categories of government spending. They are therefore called **categorical grants**. Others include the establishment of agricultural extension programs, highway construction, vocational education, and maternal and child health. During Roosevelt's first two terms in office, categorical grants increased from $200 million to $3 billion per year.

The number and scope of the categorical grants expanded further as part of the Great Society program of President Lyndon Johnson during the 1960s. Grants became available in the fields of education, pollution control, conservation, recreation, and highway construction

Discussion Starter
Encourage the students to discuss their responses to these questions: In what sense are project grants an improvement over categorical grants? In what sense do project grants present further disadvantages?

Enrichment
Let a volunteer research and report on Reagan's 1982 State of the Union Address: What were the most important features of the "new federalism" he proposed? How did Congress and the public respond to his proposals?

This figure content is also featured on *West's American Government Videodisc* (see the index found in the *TRB*).

Figure Answer Federal contributions to state and local spending were at their highest in 1980.

Multidiscipline Strategies

Literature Have students read Henry David Thoreau's essay *Civil Disobedience.* Thoreau was an advocate of not paying taxes if the money was to be used in support of unjust causes. "But, if I deny the authority of the state when it presents its tax-bill, it will soon take and waste all my property . . ." wrote Thoreau. Have students discuss whether or not they agree with Thoreau's position, and what would happen if citizens decided to act like him. When, if ever, would a citizen have the right to not pay taxes? Are there times today, as with the Mexican War or slavery discussed by Thoreau, when a citizen has an obligation to not pay taxes? Thoreau wrote, "I simply wish to refuse allegiance to the state, to withdraw and stand aloof from it effectually." Should citizens have that right to "stand aloof" from the state? The entire essay or excerpts could be utilized in order to discuss this topic.

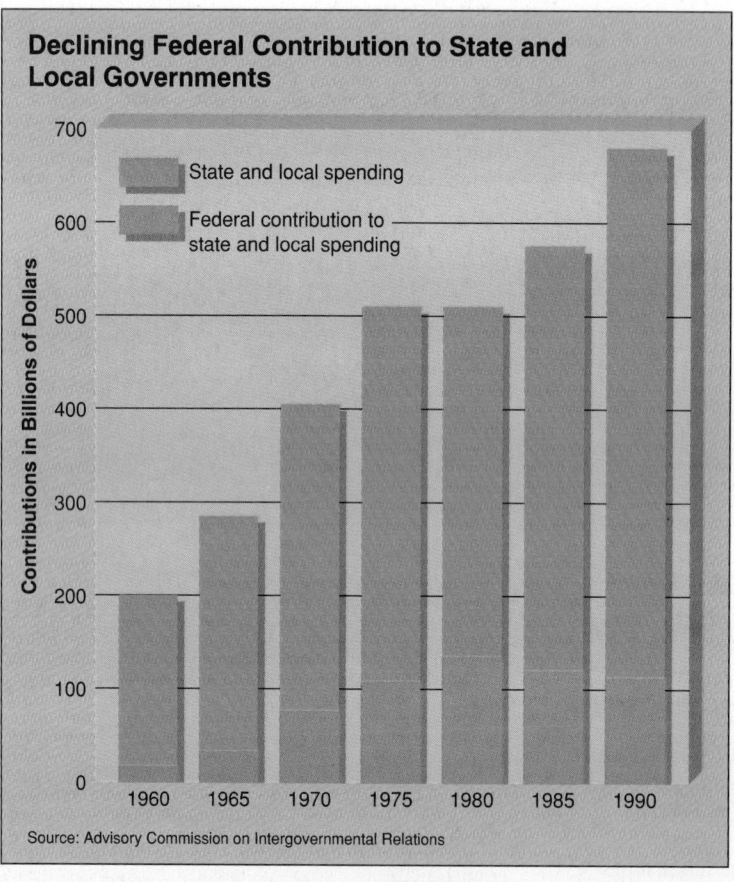

FIGURE 25–2 Declining Federal Contribution to State and Local Governments. As you can see from looking at this bar graph, state and local governments are having to spend an increasing amount of money to fund their programs. According to this chart, in what year was the federal contribution to state and local spending at its highest?

and maintenance. For some of the categorical grant programs, the state and local governments must contribute the same amount of money offered by the federal government, which is called **matching funds**. For other types of programs, the funds are awarded according to a formula that takes into account the relative wealth of the state. This is a process known as **equalization**.

Although all state and local officials, as well as their congressional representatives, enjoy taking credit for the results of projects funded by categorical grants, many would prefer to get the money with fewer restrictions. Local officials argue, for example, that the materials specified as suitable for a federally subsidized highway project in the South are not the best ones for roads in the North. It can be argued, however, that these specifications are necessary to raise local standards and practices to a uniform level. In general, categorical grants have remained under fairly tight control by Congress.

In a move to bypass the states, Congress established the **project grant** approach, which allows state and local agencies to apply directly for assistance to local offices that administer federal funds. In this way, the funds can be directly placed where—in the eyes of Congress—they are most needed.

Block Grants

Although they did not originate with him, **block grants** were an important part of President Ronald Reagan's "new federalism" program, which he outlined in his first State of the Union Address in 1982. Block grants are federal funds that are transferred to state and local governments to provide broad support in areas such as health care and criminal justice.

Comprehension
Have the students explain the differences between categorical grants and block grants.

Critical Thinking Skills
Guide the students in assessing the various kinds of federal aid to state and local governments: For local projects in your community, which do you think provides the most effective assistance? Why?

Discussion Starter
Encourage the students to discuss their own ideas about revenue-sharing: Should revenue-sharing programs be revised? To state governments? To local governments? Why or why not?

Reagan supported block grants as an alternative to categorical grants, partly because it is politically easier to reduce block grants than it is to reduce categorical grants. A categorical grant affects one particular group. That group is often willing to spend considerable effort and resources to prevent a budget cut from affecting its funds. A block grant, however, affects many programs in one general area. For the grant recipients, then, it is politically more difficult to muster the necessary opposition to prevent a budget cut.

Supporters of block grants argue that they are necessary to reduce the kind of waste that has occurred under categorical grants. Opponents argue that block grants reduce overall federal aid, that state and local officials are not as capable of administering programs as are federal officials, and that state and local officials do not have sufficient information about, or interest in, the people who are supposed to benefit from the programs. In addition, critics say, a block-grant approach to federalism contributes to increasing inequality among the states and is potentially harmful to the poor, because state legislatures are less likely than the federal government to spend funds on social welfare programs.

General Grants-in-Aid, or Revenue Sharing

In an effort to move away from the federal government's involvement with categorical grants, the Nixon administration in 1972 asked Congress to remit to state and local governments a certain percentage of federal tax revenues each year, on a more or less automatic basis, with few strings attached. Under this arrangement, one-third of the funds went to the states and two-thirds were sent directly to local governments. It is clear that the major impetus behind revenue sharing was President Nixon's desire to reduce the role of the federal government while increasing that of state and local governments. Revenue sharing grew for several years and then started to decline. One reason for the decline of revenue sharing relative to other types of assistance was the exclusion of state governments from the program in 1980. Although some argue that revenue-sharing funds were wasted on unimportant problems, many mayors and county officials saw the funds as a way to pay for needed facilities and to reduce the local tax burden. The budget crisis confronting the federal government in the mid-1980s led Congress to abolish revenue sharing to local governments at the end of 1986. There has been some talk during the 1990s, however, of reviving the revenue-sharing program.

Federal Grants Carry Strings Attached

The federal government rarely gives federal grants without imposing more regulations on state and local affairs. For example, it forced all states to lower the speed limit on their roads to 55 miles per hour by enacting the Emergency Highway Conservation Act of 1974. This act prohibited federal funding for highway construction in states that had a speed limit greater than 55. (Congress then passed a law in 1987 that allowed states to raise highway speed limits to 65 miles per hour on most rural interstate highways.) The federal government used a similar tactic in 1984 to impose a nationwide minimum

▲ Although all state and local officials need and appreciate the federal funding they receive for projects such as the bridge construction shown here, these funds do not come without strings attached. How is the 55 m.p.h. speed limit an example of the type of strings that are often attached to federal funds?

Caption Answer The Emergency Highway Conservation Act of 1974 prohibited federal funding for highway construction in states that had a speed limit greater than 55. Because all states needed these funds, all states were forced to impose the 55 m.p.h. speed limit.

TEACHING BUILDING SOCIAL STUDIES SKILLS

Read

Introduce this Building Social Studies Skills feature by engaging the students in a brief discussion of their own experiences in reading tables and charts: Where do you most often find tables and charts? What kinds of information do they typically present? How does the format help make the information easier to understand and use? After this discussion, let one of the students read the feature aloud to the rest of the class.

Discuss

Help the students consider and discuss the feature by asking questions such as these: How do charts and tables help make it easier to compare figures and recognize relationships? How can each of the guidelines here help you read and understand statistical tables and charts?

Analyze and Apply

Let the students work in groups to study and discuss a variety of statistical tables and charts. Have all the group members bring in tables or charts from periodicals, journals, and books. Then ask the group members to work together, following the feature guidelines to study and understand all the tables and charts.

Review

Ask the following questions to help the students review this Building Social Studies Skills feature: What are statistics? What is the first step in reading a statistical table?

Practicing Your Skills (Answers)

1. Conterminous means "having a common boundary, or being contiguous." Thus, the conterminous United States is all of those states that border one another, which means it does not include Hawaii or Alaska. Hence, the balance of conterminous United States means the population in all areas that are not within 50 miles of coastal areas of the conterminous United States.

2. The total population living within 50 miles of coastal shorelines in 1940 was 60.5 million, in 1990 132.5 million or a difference of 72 million. This represents a 119 percentage change.

3. The result is the total conterminous United States.

Reteaching Strategies

1. Let the students work in small groups to discuss their responses to the Preview Questions at the beginning of Section 3.

2. Ask the students to reread and revise the responses they wrote to the Kickoff Activity question at the beginning of this section.

Evaluation Strategies

1. Have the students write their answers to the Section 3 Review questions.

2. Have the students take the Section 3 Quiz found in the *TRB*.

Section 3 Review (Answers)

1. Categorical grants-in-aid, and block grants.

2. Categorical grants are federal funds that are distributed to states

BUILDING SOCIAL STUDIES SKILLS

Reading Statistical Tables

Statistics are numerical data. Tables help organize large amounts of data so that they can be analyzed more easily. It makes it easier to make comparisons and see relationships. Reading statistical tables involves scanning groups of numbers in rows and columns. Follow these guidelines:

- Read the title and subtitle and any other labels to identify what types of data are being presented.
- Check to see in what quantities each category of statistics is presented. Values may vary, so look closely. Often, a note in parentheses will indicate whether numbers are meant to indicate thousands, millions, tons, dollars, or other units.
- Examine the statistics in each row and column and look for comparisons and relationships. Note differences and similarities.
- Read footnotes, if any are presented. They will sometimes explain any deviations in the presentation of data or any recording procedures that have changed. A blank space usually means that no figures were available or no activity took place.

PRACTICING YOUR SKILLS

Study the table below and answer the following questions:

1. What does *conterminous* mean? (Check your dictionary.) What does "balance of conterminous U.S." mean?
2. What was the total increase of population living within fifty miles of the coastal shoreline in the United States from 1940 to 1990? What percentage change did that represent?
3. When you add the total population in coastal areas and the "balance of conterminous U.S.," what is the result?

Population in Coastal Areas, 1940–1990

Year	Population of the Conterminous United States (in Millions)	Total Population Within 50 Miles of U.S. Coasts (in Millions)	Resident Populations of Counties Within 50 Miles of U.S. Shorelines (in Millions)				Population of the Balance of the Conterminous United States (in Millions)
			Atlantic Ocean	Pacific Ocean	Great Lakes	Gulf of Mexico	
1940	131.7	60.5	29.9	7.5	18.9	4.2	71.2
1950	150.7	73.5	34.6	11.5	21.8	5.6	77.2
1960	178.5	92.7	41.7	16.8	26.4	7.8	85.7
1970	202.3	108.5	48.2	21.5	29.3	9.5	93.8
1980	225.2	118.5	50.7	25.4	29.8	12.6	106.7
1990	250.4	132.5	56.4	30.7	30.3	15.1	117.9

Source: *Statistical Abstract of the United States.* Washington, D.C.: U.S. Government Printing Office, 1991.

for specific purposes and in specified ways. Block grants are fixed amounts of money given to local or state governments by the federal government to be used for general purposes.
3. Answers will vary, e.g., yes, the loss of federal revenues has affected my city because we have fewer job training programs and fewer federal benefits for special programs in our schools.

SECTION 4

Points to Stress
• The largest three categories of state expenditures in percentage terms.
• The largest three local expenditures in percentage terms.
• Two important growth areas in state and local budgets.

Kickoff Activity
As an introduction to this section, let the students read the section title and the first two study questions. Give the students about five minutes in which to list their best guesses in response to the questions about state and local government expenditures. When they have all finished writing, let the students compare and discuss their ideas; remind them that, as they study Section 4, they will find accurate answers to these questions.

Working with the Preview Questions
Let the students read all three study questions. Ask them to keep these questions in mind as they read and take notes on Section 4.

Teaching Strategies

Introduction
Ask one of the students to read the introductory paragraph aloud. Then guide the students in studying the two figures, State Expenditures and Local Expenditures. Encourage the students to share and discuss their reactions to the categories and percentages listed in each table.

Extension
Ask the students to find out how much your state spends on prisons: How has that level of spending changed over the past decade? What trend has developed? What are the implications of that trend?

Figure Answer 15.5 percent of total state spending is devoted to highways.

This figure content is also featured on *West's American Government Videodisc* (see the index found in the *TRB*) and is available in the transparency package.

Discussion Starter
Encourage the students to discuss the public's support of punishment, rather than rehabilitation, for convicted criminals: What do you think accounts for this change in attitude? Do you agree that punishment should be emphasized? Why or why not?

drinking age of 21. Congress passed a law that withheld up to 15 percent of federal highway funding from any state that did not raise its drinking age to 21 by the end of 1987.

SECTION 3 REVIEW

1. By what methods does the federal government return federal tax dollars to state and local governments?
2. Briefly describe each of these methods.
3. **For critical analysis:** How do you think the loss of federal revenues since 1986 has affected your city or town, if at all?

SECTION 4

State and Local Government Spending

Preview Questions

- What are the largest three categories of state expenditures?
- What are the largest three categories of local expenditures?
- What are two important growth areas in state and local budgets?

Figure 25–3 on the right shows state expenditures for the latest year for which data are available. Figure 25–4 on the next page shows the same data for local governments. If you look at the tables carefully, you will notice a clear pattern. Both state and city expenditures are concentrated in the areas of education, public welfare, highways, and health and hospitals. Education is the biggest category of expenditure, particularly at the local level. This expenditure pattern stands in sharp contrast to the spending of the federal government, which allocates only about four percent of its budget to education.

Several areas of spending have become a cause for growing concern in state budgets. Among these areas are prisons and education.

The High Cost of Prisons

State and local governments are almost entirely responsible for housing our prison population (over one million Americans). The estimated total prison budget for 1992 is $25 billion, of which the federal government is providing less than $2 billion. While prison maintenance represents an average of only four percent of state spending, some states such as Michigan spend over seven percent of its budget on prisons. On the whole, spending on prisons has grown between 13 and 15 percent per year since 1986.

Even though the number of reported crimes is actually declining, public opinion on how criminals should be treated is shifting away from rehabilitation and toward punishment, which means longer prison terms. In addition to the one million inmates already in prison across the nation, over 2,500 new inmates are introduced every week. In one year alone, this number is enough to fill five average-sized prisons. Prison expansion is

State Expenditures (in Percentages)

Spending Category	Percentage of Total Spending
Education	26.66
Public welfare	21.04
Highways	15.51
Health and hospitals	10.28
Interest on general debt	4.32
Natural resources	3.80
Corrections	2.46
Financial administration	2.03
General control	1.67
Social insurance administration	1.63
Police	1.48
General public building	.59
Air transportation	.30
Housing and urban renewal	.28
Water transport and terminals	.24
Libraries	.10
Other	7.61

Source: The Tax Foundation, *Facts and Figures on Government Finance*, 1990.

▲ **FIGURE 25–3 State Expenditures.** The table above shows the major categories of state expenditures. What percentage of state funds are expended for highways?

Enrichment
Assign a group of interested volunteers to research the emphasis that has been placed on improving education: What specific programs have been put into place? With what success? What national efforts are being made to improve education? How are your state and local governments responding to this trend? Let these volunteers discuss their findings with the rest of the class.

Reteaching Strategies
1. Have the students work in small groups to review and revise the notes they took while reading Section 4.
2. Work with small groups of students to review and discuss the information presented in the two tables, State Expenditures and Local Expenditures.

Evaluation Strategies
1. Have the students write their answers to the Section 4 Review questions.
2. Have the students take the Section 4 Quiz found in the *TRB*.

Caption Answer Students should understand that education costs are growing at an alarming rate, doubling from 100 billion to almost 200 billion per year during the 1980s.

Section 4 Review (Answers)
1. Education, public welfare, highways, health and hospitals, and interest on the general debt.
2. Education, public welfare, and health and hospitals.
3. It has increased dramatically.
4. Answers will vary, e.g., the federal government has reduced aid in many areas. The policy has shifted to one that asserts state and local governments should be more responsible for education.

Discussion Starter
Guide the students in considering the equalization of education spending throughout a state: What problems are caused when spending is not equal in all areas of a state? How does equalizing that spending help solve those problems? Why do you think some states have had to be forced to equalize education spending? What response do you think this process evokes from state officials and citizens? Why?

Figure Answer Police funding accounts for 5.08 percent of total local spending as compared with 1.48 percent of total state spending.

This figure content is also featured on *West's American Government Videodisc* (see the index found in the *TRB*) and is available in the transparency package.

Local Expenditures (in Percentages)

Spending Category	Percentage of Total Spending
Education	44.88
Public welfare	7.06
Health and hospitals	6.78
Highways	5.66
Police	5.08
Interest on general debt	3.84
Sewerage	3.72
General control	2.58
Fire protection	2.44
Parks and recreation	2.42
Housing and urban renewal	1.80
Sanitation (other than sewerage)	1.44
Financial administration	1.26
General public building	1.25
Corrections	.89
Air transportation	.76
Libraries	.72
Natural resources	.64
Water transport and terminals	.30
Parking facilities	.21
Other	6.27

Source: The Tax Foundation, *Facts and Figures on Government Finance*, 1990.

▲ FIGURE 25–4 **Local Expenditures.** The table above shows the major categories for local expenditures. What percentage of total local spending is devoted to police? How does this compare with state expenditures?

expensive—housing each inmate in new prisons costs up to $25,000 per year.

Education

One of the biggest items in every state and local budget is education. During the 1980s and 1990s, there has been a big emphasis on improving education, particularly in low-income districts. Consequently, state and local spending on elementary and secondary schools doubled in the 1980s from less than $100 billion to almost $200 billion per year.

In the past, local governments have borne the brunt of all the costs of public schooling. Since the 1970s, however, state governments have taken on a greater share of total spending. The states now account for up to half of all public school spending. This occurs through aid to local districts.

▲ One of the biggest expenses faced by state and local governments is the cost of education. How have education costs grown?

Section 4 Review

1. List five major spending categories at the state level.
2. List three major spending categories at the local level.
3. What has happened to state and local spending on prisons in the past decade?
4. **For critical analysis:** While the state governments have had to take on increasing responsibility for financing local public schools, the federal government has actually reduced such aid. Why do you think the federal government has reduced its assistance to education?

The federal government has reduced spending on education because of the large federal government deficit.

TEACHING CHALLENGE TO THE AMERICAN DREAM

Read

Before the students begin reading this Challenge to the American Dream feature, help them review and discuss the financial problems that face cities and states. Then let several volunteers participate in reading the feature aloud to the rest of the class.

Discuss

Stimulate a class discussion of the feature by asking questions such as these: How have presidents justified the shifting of large parts of the financial burden from the federal government to state and city governments? What effects has this shift had? Which do you consider the most powerful sources of pressure to spend? Why? Why do you think the states have obliged themselves to balance their budgets, while the federal government has not made such a commitment? What short-term effects will cutting back services and laying off state workers have on state finances? What will the long-term effects be? Why do you think the number of state workers has risen so rapidly? What problems may be associated with that rise?

Analyze and Apply

Have groups of students work together to discuss their responses to the issues raised in this Challenge to the American Dream feature. What is one step that local citizens can and should take to help alleviate these problems? Encourage the students to discuss their ideas and agree on an answer to that question. Once they have agreed, let them work together to write a letter to the editor of a local newspaper, presenting their idea.

Review

Let the students respond to these review questions: How did the policies of Presidents Carter and Reagan contribute to the current financial crisis facing our state and city governments? Which groups are pressuring state and local governments to spend more and more money?

You Decide (Answers)

1. Answers will vary, e.g., states should not be allowed to operate at a deficit because they might run up huge deficits they would be unable to repay.

2. Answers will vary, e.g., yes, because the pressures to spend will increase as people demand more services.

CHALLENGE TO THE AMERICAN DREAM

Cities and States in Need

All across the United States, state and local governments have been stricken with financial crises. The immediate cause of the problems seemed to begin with the nation's economic downturn in the late 1980s, but conditions have been worsening over the past decade. What state and city public officials are now facing is the combined effect of several long-term trends:

- Beginning with President Carter's administration and accelerating under President Reagan's "new federalism," the federal government has shifted a heavier financial burden to the states and cities, cutting or eliminating federal grants for housing, education, mass transportation, and public works projects. In the late 1970s, the federal government provided 25 percent of state and local budgets. It now provides less than 17 percent.
- The public is increasingly resistant to new or higher taxes, partly because it believes government is not spending money wisely. Several states have passed initiatives to limit or roll back taxes, and several other states have ousted officials who raised taxes.
- The pressures to spend are enormous. Much of the pressure comes from the public's increasing demand for better schools, harsher punishment of criminals, and better care for the increasing numbers of elderly people. Other pressures come from the growing number of federal rules and regulations that often place new responsibilities on states and cities without giving them sufficient money to carry out the rules. Still other pressures come from the courts, which have forced states to build new prisons to ease overcrowding, or to make changes in education programs.

Unlike the federal government, which can and does operate at a deficit, all states except Vermont are legally bound to have balanced budgets. This leaves states with options of limiting spending or raising taxes, although recently states have often violated the law by running deficits. In the early 1990s, governors of northeastern states such as New York, Massachusetts, and Rhode Island called for severe cutbacks in education, health, and other services and the layoff of thousands of state workers to reduce those states' mounting deficits.

The search for additional revenue sources continues at all levels of government. As pointed out in this chapter, many states have instituted lotteries in order to obtain more revenues. One state has even instituted something called the **value-added tax**, or VAT, which is a tax on the value increase of a company's product. A VAT is a tax on the difference between the costs that go into producing a product and the revenues received from selling the product.

No matter what additional taxes are used in various states and municipalities, a fiscal crisis will be a problem for the United States for many years to come. The number of state employees almost everywhere has increased much faster than the population. In the decade of the 1980s, for example, state and local government employment increased over ten times faster than the population increased in the state of New York. There is no way that such increases in government employment can be handled without taxpayers paying a larger percentage of their income to the government.

The challenge to the American dream is to supply and improve state and local government services wherever such improvement is needed, and to pay for these improvements in a way that does not overburden voters and cause them to revolt.

You Decide

1. Should states be allowed to operate with a deficit? Why or why not?
2. Do you think states and cities will be forced to raise taxes? Why or why not?

Observable Mastery
Place "State" and "Local" on a horizontal axis of a chart on the blackboard. Place "tax revenue sources" and "expenditures" on the vertical axis of the chart. Have students come up and fill in the chart, providing the major sources of revenue for both state and local government.

Students should then complete the chart by filling in the major areas of expenditures for both state and local government. Be sure to reinforce the idea that although revenue sources are very different for state and local governments, the top four areas of expenditures are the same.

Chapter Evaluation
To evaluate student mastery of chapter material, you might:
1. Use Chapter Test A from the *TRB*.
2. Use Chapter Test B from the *TRB*.
3. Construct your own test using items from the *West American Government Test Bank* found in the *TRB*.
4. Use the accompanying test software to construct and print a customized chapter test.

Review Questions (Answers)
1. Limitations apply to agencies of federal government, interstate commerce, and due process.
2. Sales tax and individual income tax.
3. Property tax is the major tax at the local level.
4. Government-operated businesses and borrowing as well as fines and interest on investments.
5. Categorical grants and block grants.
6. Education.
7. Education.
8. Organize a group. Write press releases about your goals and send them to local TV stations and newspapers. Start a petition drive.
9. The federal government has shifted more of the financial burden to states and localities. The public

CHAPTER 25 REVIEW

Key Terms

block grants 616
categorical grants 615
death taxes 609
equalization 616
excise taxes 609
matching funds 616
project grant 616
value-added tax 621

Summary

1. The federal government and the state governments place limitations on state and local powers of taxation. The U.S. Constitution prevents states from taxing the operations, land, buildings, or any other aspect of the federal government. It prohibits states from regulating and taxing interstate and foreign trade, and the due process clause requires state and local governments to impose and administer taxes fairly. It also forbids unreasonable classifications for the purpose of collecting taxes. Each state also has constitutional limitations on the taxing power of that state and its local governments.

2. Major state and local taxes include the personal income tax, corporate income tax, excise tax, estate tax, inheritance tax, sales tax, and property tax. The most important tax at the state level is sales tax. The most important tax at the local level is property tax. Some state and local governments operate businesses from which they receive revenues. States and cities also borrow by issuing state and municipal bonds.

3. The federal government returns federal tax dollars to state and local governments in three ways. Categorical grants-in-aid are funds for specific purposes or programs. Block grants transfer federal funds to state and local governments to provide broad support in areas such as health care and criminal justice. Revenue sharing occured when a certain percentage of tax income each year was remitted to state and local governments.

4. A breakdown of state government expenditures shows that spending on education, public welfare, highways, and health and hospitals uses about 75 percent of the entire state government budget. At the local level, education uses about 45 percent of local budgets. Public welfare, health and hospitals, highways, and police use up another 25 percent of local budgets. Two areas of growing concern in state and local spending are the increased spending levels on prisons and on education.

Review Questions

1. What limits does the U.S. Constitution place on the taxing abilities of state and local governments?
2. Which are the two major taxes used at the state level?
3. What is the most important tax used at the local level?
4. What types of nontax revenues do state and local governments receive?
5. What are the methods by which the federal government returns federal tax dollars to the states?
6. What is the largest single category of government spending at the state level?
7. What is the largest single category of government spending at the local level?
8. What steps can you take to persuade others that action about a certain issue should be taken in your community?
9. Why have states and cities developed fiscal crises?

Questions for Thought and Discussion

1. It is argued by some that revenue sharing is better than grants-in-aid because grants-in-aid give too much power to the federal government. Others favor them, fearing that revenue sharing encourages waste, corruption, and inefficiency. Give reasons for both arguments.
2. Many people argue that schools are in dire need of improvement and that the nation's future is at risk because schools are performing poorly. If state fiscal conditions worsen in the years ahead, school budgets are unlikely to escape without cutbacks. How do you think this conflict can be solved? What do you think are some of the causes for the breakdown in the school system?
3. In which areas, if any, do you think your local government spends too much money? Too little money? Give reasons for your answers.

is increasingly resistant to new or higher taxes. The pressures to spend are enormous.

Questions for Thought and Discussion (Answers)

1. Answers will vary, e.g., the argument for revenue sharing rather than grants-in-aid includes the belief that local and state governments better know their particular needs and should be given flexibility in spending. The argument against revenue sharing includes the belief that states and localities will be more wasteful and careless with federal money if it is not earmarked for specific purposes.
2. Answers will vary, e.g., communities, parents, and students will have to help in solving the school crisis. Some school systems have deteriorated because of lack of appropriate funding and over burdening of some schools by too many students.
3. Answers will vary according to your local government.
4. Answers will vary, e.g., they should not depend on federal money because they are setting themselves up for a crisis when the money is not there. It also makes them dependent on the federal government, which may make stipulations about how the money must be spent.
5. Answers will vary, e.g., these taxes are fairly easy to collect. Alternatives to reliance on these taxes include business enterprises, lotteries, and other types of taxes as sources of revenue.
6. Answers will vary, e.g., they should be allowed to raise money through business enterprises. The people are receiving a service for fees rather than simply paying taxes.

Social Studies Skills (Answers)

1. (a) A pie chart; (b) A bar chart.
2. Student charts will vary.
3. With a pie chart, any way is acceptable. With a bar chart either in descending or ascending order would be most appropriate.
4. Answers will vary, but for a bar chart ascending and descending ordering easily shows the relative importance of a category.

CHAPTER 25 REVIEW—Continued

4. Do you think state and local governments should depend on the federal government for a major share of their revenues? Why or why not?
5. Why do you think states rely so heavily on sales taxes? Why do you think cities rely so heavily on property taxes? What kinds of alternatives would you propose to reduce heavy reliance on these taxes?
6. Do you think state and local governments should be allowed to raise money through business enterprises? Why or why not?

Improving Your Skills

Communication Skills

Using Context Clues to Determine Word Meanings

In your reading and studies, you will occasionally come across words you do not recognize. If you do not know the meaning of a word, you may not fully understand the passage you are reading. One way to find the meaning of unfamiliar words is to look them up in the dictionary. Another way is to carefully examine the way the word is used in context. A careful reader may find many clues to the meaning of a word in surrounding words and sentences, and in the main idea of the writing.

Writing

Read the following sentences. Use context clues to determine the meanings of the underlined words. Then write your own definition of each of the words. Check your definitions against the dictionary for accuracy.

> The conventional view is that the burgeoning of the American nation-state occurred hand in hand with the shrinkage in the role and power of the individual American states. Certainly from the 1930s to the 1960s state governments declined in relative importance. Governors and state legislatures wallowed in mediocrity. Social and economic problems seemed to be susceptible only to national solutions. The states came to be widely regarded as historical anomalies, of no particular significance in a new, thoroughly nationalized society.

Social Studies Skills

Working with Sequencing Data and Statistical Tables

Statistical tables are one of the many ways to sequence data and information. The way that the data are sequenced is often up to the person who is presenting the data. For example, the data on state and local expenditures presented in Figure 25–3 on page 619 and Figure 25–4 on page 620 are sequenced in *decreasing* order of expenditures (except for the last, catch-all category of "Other"). The data could have also been presented in *increasing* order of expenditures.

1. What is at least one other way the data could have been presented? (Hint: Look at the other figures in this chapter.)
2. Once you have chosen another way of presenting the same data, sketch out how this other presentation would look.
3. Do you have choices in how you order the data with this other way of presentation?
4. If your answer to question 3 above is yes, give reasons why you would want the data presented in one order rather than another.

Activities and Projects

1. Imagine that you are a lobbyist for a particular program whose funds have been cut. Develop an oral argument to present to the legislature that will convince your state legislators to restore the program's funding.
2. Obtain a copy of your state budget. Analyze the budget to determine the items on which your state spends the most money. Write a paragraph on each of the top three items that tells why you think your state spends the most money in these areas.
3. If your state has a lottery, get the statistics showing the growth in revenues collected since the lottery began. Then find out what percentage of these revenues has gone to finance public education. Is this percentage increasing or decreasing?
4. Write a paragraph or two summarizing how your state compares to other states with respect to the amount of state and local taxes collected and the manner in which those taxes are collected.

Working with the Videodisc

The text below is from Professor Roger LeRoy Miller's introduction for the motion segment for Unit 9:

Fast-changing technology permitted the world's first ever live television coverage of an enemy bombing at the beginning of this decade. The "enemy" was the coalition forces headed by the United States and the bombing targets were in Baghdad, Iraq. The TV coverage was provided by CNN and its American reporters and a satellite transmission system. Also, thanks to instantaneous news, in the 1990s we were able to watch the demise of the Soviet Union and the rise of 15 independent republics, this all having occurred after most of Eastern Europe moved down the road to democracy. In recent years, many formally authoritarian nondemocratic governments have taken dramatic steps toward democracy, but it's important to understand, however, the numerous differences among even the most democratic political systems.

In this last video segment, you will see some of the British Parliament in action. Although similar in nature, the British parliamentary system still seems quite foreign to Americans used to our own way of governing ourselves. Finally, the tremendous changes in the former Soviet Union are illustrated by a few clips from the legislature in Moscow not that many years ago.

The watchword in the way other countries govern themselves is simply change, and there's bound to be plenty of that in the years ahead.

To access this segment, use the bar code below or the videodisc index found in the *TRB.*

UNIT NINE

Other Nations

Unit Contents

CHAPTER INTRODUCTION

Instructional Objectives
By the end of the chapter students should be able to:
- Describe the nature of the constitutional monarchy in Great Britain.
- Characterize the French system of government.
- Characterize the Japanese system of government.
- Differentiate among the economic systems.
- Identify the main characteristics of the American economy.
- Identify the main characteristics of Marxian economics and discuss the converging of the world's political systems.

Using the Keynote
Before the students start reading Chapter 26, encourage them to explain their ideas about these phrases: *economic freedom* and *political freedom.* What does each phrase mean? How important is the concept expressed by each phrase? How can these freedoms be achieved? Who has them? Who strives for them? Why?

Then let one of the students read aloud the Friedman quotation.

Introducing the Chapter
Use questions such as these to stimulate a brief class discussion: In what ways are people alike all around the world? What similarities in basic needs and interests unite all the people of the world? In what ways are people in various parts of the world different? How do cultural traditions, governments, and economic systems divide people from different parts? How do you react to such differences? Why? After the discussion, let volunteers read the Introduction aloud.

Previewing the Sections

Section 1 Let the students page through Section 1. Ask the students to identify the aspects of British government about which they expect to learn.
Section 2 Ask the students to look through Section 2: What do the headings in this section tell you about the content?
Section 3 Have volunteers read aloud the section title, the main headings, and the artwork captions in Section 3. Ask: What are three facts you already know about the subjects covered in this section?
Section 4 Allow the students to browse through Section 4. Ask: What do you expect to learn as you study Section 4?
Section 5 Ask volunteers to go through Section 5. Then ask: Which of the key terms presented in these headings are familiar to you?
Section 6 Have the students look through Section 6. Ask: What do you already know about the topics covered in this section?

CHAPTER 26

Comparing Governments and Economic Systems

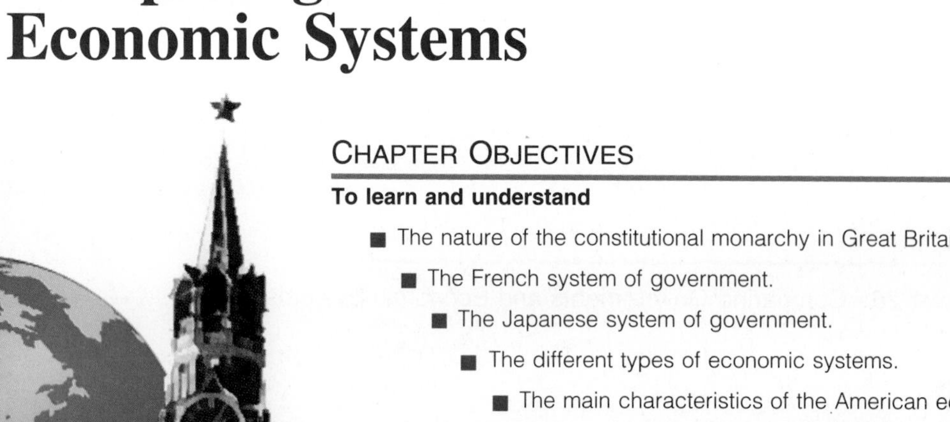

CHAPTER OBJECTIVES

To learn and understand
- The nature of the constitutional monarchy in Great Britain.
- The French system of government.
- The Japanese system of government.
- The different types of economic systems.
- The main characteristics of the American economy.
- The main characteristics of Marxian economics and the converging of the world's political systems.

West's American Government Assignment Guide

Activity Sheets
Basic Concepts 26 *TRB* (Reteaching)
Enrichment Activity 26 *TRB*
Building Social Studies Skills 26 *TRB*
Quizzes
Chapter 26 Section 1 Quiz *TRB*
Chapter 26 Section 2 Quiz *TRB*
Chapter 26 Section 3 Quiz *TRB*
Chapter 26 Section 4 Quiz *TRB*
Chapter 26 Section 5 Quiz *TRB*
Chapter 26 Section 6 Quiz *TRB*
Tests
Chapter 26 Test A *TRB*
Chapter 26 Test B *TRB*
Chapter 26 Test Bank *TRB*
Chapter 26 WESTEST Computerized Testing

Keynote

"Economic freedom is . . . an indispensable means toward the achievement of political freedom."

—— Milton Friedman
(1912–) American Economist

INTRODUCTION

One glimpse at a news broadcast reveals that there are massive and mystifying differences among governments around the world. Custom, religion, tradition, dress, and language all seem to differ greatly from culture to culture. The titles and powers of those in office vary from nation to nation. The lawmaking bodies have various forms and the economic systems are often very different. The people in other countries have widely differing ideas of what government should do.

Not all governments would agree with Milton Friedman's opening quote. The extent to which other peoples have true economic and political freedom varies dramatically from country to country throughout the world. The downfall in the late 1980s and early 1990s of the political and economic systems that have greatly restricted political freedom has certainly driven this point home to the rest of the world.

As you learned in Chapter 4, governments can be grouped into several distinct types such as unitary, federal, and confederal. You also learned the difference between parliamentary and presidential systems, and the differences between dictatorial and democratic rule. This chapter will present a more specific examination of several other governments in the world: Great Britain, France, and Japan.

This chapter takes a comparative approach in discussing other governments and economic systems. By comparing these governments and economic systems with our own, you should gain an insight into the complexities involved in our political and economic dealings with these countries.

Additionally in this chapter, we will look at the role technology plays in shaping a new world order. Because news and information can be almost instantaneously transmitted throughout the world, political leaders are subject now, more than ever, to the influence of world public opinion.

SECTION 1

Great Britain

Preview Questions

- What are the main characteristics of the British political system?
- What are the similarities and differences between the British and American political systems?
- What is the function of the monarchy in Great Britain today?
- How does the British Parliament operate?

Many principles of the political system in the United States originated in England. For this reason, Americans are inclined to think that the government of Great Britain is similar to our own. While both the United States and Great Britain are democracies, there are fundamental differences between the two.

Constitutional Monarchy

The United States is a republic, a country in which the sovereign power is held by the voters and is exercised by elected representatives who are responsible to the people. Great Britain, in contrast, is a monarchy, in which sovereignty lies with the **hereditary ruler**, someone who rules because he or she was the son or daughter of a previous ruler. The monarchy falls to the oldest son or daughter of the current monarch. The new monarch then holds the title of King or Queen.

The laws and customs that define the powers of the monarch have evolved throughout history. English monarchs once ruled with absolute power, but since the 1800s, the powers of the monarch have decreased significantly. The Queen's duties today as head of state are mainly ceremonial, such as "opening" the sessions of

SECTION 1

Points to Stress
- The main characteristics of the British political system.
- Similarities and differences between the British and American systems.
- The function of the monarchy in Great Britain today.
- Operations of the British Parliament.

Kickoff Activity
Give the students five minutes in which to list as many differences as possible between our political system and the system in great Britain. At the end of the allotted time, give the students a chance to share and discuss their lists.

Working with the Preview Questions
Ask a volunteer to read these study questions aloud. Encourage interested students to share their initial responses. Then have the students keep these study questions in mind as they read and take notes on Section 1.

Teaching Strategies

Introduction
After the students have read the brief section introduction, encourage them to identify and discuss the various ties of history and of political principles: How did the relationship between the colonies and England affect the development of our country and of our government? What are the current relationships between the United States and Great Britain?

Vocabulary
Ask volunteers to define these terms and give examples to clarify their explanations: *sovereign power, sovereignty.*

Extension
As the students consider the importance of the monarch in England, encourage them to discuss the media coverage given to the Queen and to other members of the royal family. You might have students bring in newspaper and magazine stories about the Queen and her family; if possible, have students share some articles from British publications. How seriously do members of the public take the ceremonial roles of the monarch and her family members? What does the royal family seem to represent to the people of Great Britain? To people here? Why?

Discussion Starter
Guide the students in considering the governmental role of the British monarch: What role does the Queen play? Who bears the costs of supporting the Queen and her family "in royal style"? Why do you believe the British system nonetheless retains its monarch? Do you believe the British people will relegate the monarch to a less visible—and less expensive—position? Do you think they should? Why or why not?

Vocabulary
Ask the students to refer to dictionaries to find the definitions of the noun *constitution:* Which definitions are given first? Do you find this surprising?

Discussion Starter
Focus the students' attention on the fact that many Parliamentary practices have evolved through tradition, rather than being prescribed in a written document: Do you think this makes it easier for Parliament to change its practices than for the U.S. Congress to make such changes? Why or why not?

Comprehension
Ask the students to explain the significance of the term *fusion of pow-*

Caption Answer Students should understand that as a modern constitutional monarchy, Great Britain has put the real powers of the government in the hands of Parliament and the prime minister. The Queen's role in this constitutional monarchy is ceremonial.

▲ As the reigning monarch of Great Britain, Queen Elizabeth II, shown here, is a symbol of national unity and political continuity. Why is it said that the British monarch reigns but does not rule?

Parliament or giving her royal assent to a treaty already passed by Parliament. The Queen nominally appoints the prime minister and the cabinet that together make up the British government, but she appoints only those people who have been selected by the majority of the House of Commons. She does not have the power to dismiss the prime minister and cannot veto acts of Parliament. All acts of the British government, however, are formally carried out in the name of the Queen even though the real power of the government is exercised by the prime minister and other high officials.

Thus, as has often been said, the British monarch today reigns but does not rule. Nonetheless, the British monarchy is a cherished tradition and a symbol of national unity and continuity.

Unwritten Constitution Because the powers and duties of the monarch are limited by Britain's unwritten constitution, the monarch is known as a **constitutional monarch**. As you know, the American system is governed by a single written constitution. Great Britain has no constitution in our sense of the word because it is a whole body of agreements, some written and some unwritten. Written parts of the British constitution are based on the Magna Carta (1215), the 1689 Bill of Rights, the Reform Bill of 1832, laws passed by Parliament, and various charters. It also incorporates judicial decisions through the years that make up British common law.

The unwritten part has derived from custom and usage—practices that have gained acceptance over time. There is no written document, for example, that describes the process by which the lower house of Parliament chooses or dismisses the prime minister. The practice has instead evolved through tradition. The U.S. Constitution, in contrast, spells out how the office of the presidency is to be filled.

Because there is no single document setting forth the structure and operation of government, the British constitution changes as that nation's needs change. The rules may be changed without a complicated amendment process; an old provision may be simply removed or replaced by a majority vote of Parliament. This flexibility has allowed the British constitution to adapt to changing times while the British tradition remains stable.

Parliament

The central institution of the British government is the national legislature, known as **Parliament**. Like our own Congress, Parliament is a bicameral legislature: It is made up of the House of Commons and the House of Lords. Unlike Congress, however, the British Parliament (like all parliamentary systems) is based on the *fusion* of powers rather than the *separation* of powers. It manages both the legislative and the executive powers of the nation. Parliament's legislative powers include passing and changing laws; its executive power includes choosing the prime minister, who is the majority party leader in the House of Commons, and the cabinet that will serve the prime minister.

The House of Commons The **House of Commons** is the legislative branch that consists of elected officials. This lower house, known as "the Commons," is the more powerful of the two houses. Its 635 members, known as **Members of Parliament**, or MPs, are popularly elected from geographic districts.

The Commons meets in Westminster, the ancient and grand building located on the Thames River in London. On each side of the high-ceilinged chamber, originally ers and to contrast it with the American practice of *separating powers.*

Enrichment
Let a group of volunteers work together to learn about Britain's most recent prime ministers: Who were they? To what party did each belong? How did each come to power? What were the most important policies and accomplishments of each? What caused each to leave office? Ask these volunteers to prepare a written or oral report about the prime ministers.

Extension
Have the students read about—or, if possible, watch (on C-SPAN) or listen to coverage of—the House of Commons in session: How would you compare a meeting of the House of Commons with a meeting of the House of Representatives? What differences strike you? How are the two similar?

Enrichment
Have an interested volunteer research the various titles of hereditary peers: Who takes precedence over whom? What is the correct form of address used to holders of these titles? How are individuals with these titles regarded in modern society? Let the volunteer prepare and present a chart summarizing his or her findings.

Comprehension
To check the students' comprehension, ask them: In what ways—if at all—does the House of Lords act as a check or balance on the powers of the House of Commons?

Comprehension
Let volunteers respond to these questions: To whom are members of the American cabinet responsible? Why? To whom are members of the British cabinet responsible? Why?

Extension
If possible, play for the students (or have them listen to radio presentations of) recordings made during "question hour." Then let the students discuss their reactions to the way the session is conducted.

Caption Answer The British prime minister is elected by the majority party in the House of Commons.

designed for only 350 members, there are five rows of benches for each party, and a large open space in the center with a raised chair at one end for the presiding officer, known as the speaker. Leaders of each party sit in the front rows on each side facing each other. The MPs sitting in the remaining rows are known as the "back benchers." In the center of the chamber is an open space. The chamber is, in every sense of the word, a political arena.

Any MP is allowed to introduce legislation, but most measures are introduced by the government, which is made up of the prime minister and the cabinet collectively. The bill is then debated and sent to one of the eight standing committees that review the bills and prepare them for final consideration by the full chamber. Committees in the House of Commons are not like committees in Congress, which specialize in areas such as agriculture or armed services. Rather, they are general committees that consider bills on a wide range of subjects. After the committee prepares the bills for final consideration, they are sent to the floor, where a vote is taken. They need a simple majority vote for passage.

British Prime Minister John Major is shown here with former Prime Minister Margaret Thatcher. Who elects the British prime minister?

House of Lords The upper chamber of Parliament is known as the **House of Lords**, which is an aristocratic body of persons who have mostly inherited their titles. There are over seven hundred **hereditary peers** with titles such as *baron, viscount, earl,* and *duke.* (Peers are members of the nobility who became so by birth; hence they are called hereditary peers.) The other members are appointed for life by the Queen, including two archbishops, and nine specially appointed **law lords**, which are the British equivalent of a Supreme Court. There are also life peers, chosen for honored careers in arts, politics, science, or business, who hold this title for their entire lives and cannot pass the title on to their children. Usually, there are only about one hundred members in attendance at sessions of the House of Lords.

The House of Lords was once a powerful branch of the British government, but today it has little real authority over legislation. If the House of Lords defeats a bill passed in the Commons, the Commons need only pass it a second time in the next session of the Commons to make the bill into law. The House of Lords may amend legislation, but any changes it makes can be canceled by the Commons.

The Government

As you have learned, there is no separation of legislative and executive powers in the British government. The majority party in the House of Commons elects one of their members as leader of the executive branch, known as the **prime minister**. He or she[1] selects other members of Parliament to become **ministers** to form a cabinet. Each minister is also the head of an executive department, much like the American cabinet. (Unlike members of the American cabinet, however, British ministers are also legislators.) Together, the prime minister and cabinet make up the "government," which is the equivalent of our presidential administration. Americans talk about the Bush administration, while the British speak of the Major government, after John Major.

The prime minister and the cabinet must always maintain the support of the majority of the House of Commons, and are accountable to them. Unlike members of the U.S. Congress or presidential cabinet, almost every day, during what is called the "question hour," the British cabinet ministers appear in the Commons to answer questions about their area of responsibility. Any MP may ask a question about any relevant subject. Questions will usually concern a certain government program or a cabinet minister who is the subject of criticism in the press.

Usually, the ministers answer questions to the satisfaction of the members of their own party, but if the

1. In 1979 Margaret Thatcher became the first woman to hold the post.

Discussion Starter
Guide the students in discussing the circumstances under which elections can be called in Britain: What are the advantages—and disadvantages—to the party in power? To the party not in power?

Enrichment
Have two groups of volunteers research and report on Britain's major parties, the Labour Party and the Conservative Party: What are the major policy interests of each?

Critical Thinking Skills
Encourage the students to analyze the means by which British voters choose their elected officials: What factors do they consider? How do those factors compare with those the American voters consider? Which approach would you expect to result in a legislative body that better represents the interests and needs of the voting public? Why?

Cooperative Learning
Divide the class into five groups. Assign each group to research the delivery of one of these services to citizens in Great Britain: education, police and fire protection, housing, public health, street maintenance. Then let the members of each group share and discuss their findings with the rest of the class.

Reteaching Strategies
1. Ask the students to work with partners, reviewing and comparing their notes. Remind individual students to make any needed corrections or additions to their own notes.
2. Work with small groups of students to review the ideas they listed during the Kickoff Activity at the beginning of this section. Help the group members work together in revising and adding to their lists.

Evaluation Strategies
1. Have the students write their answers to the Section 1 Review questions.
2. Have the students take the Section 1 Quiz found in the *TRB*.

Section 1 Review (Answers)
1. The United States' constitution is written, while the British constitution is unwritten in the sense that it is not contained in one document

questions and answers cause the government to lose support of some party members, the ministers may ''bolt'' to the opposition. If the government loses enough support, it may fail to win a **vote of confidence**—a wish to retain the existing government—and be forced to resign. Parliament is then dissolved and the government must run for reelection.

Elections and Political Parties

Although there is no fixed date for British elections, a general election must be held at least once every five years, and may take place anytime within that period. The prime minister decides when a general election will take place. He or she generally will call for one when conditions seem to indicate that the prime minister's party will gain seats in the House of Commons.

Elections can, however, take place under other circumstances, such as when the government loses a vote of confidence as mentioned above. Thus, although MPs are elected to five-year terms, the Parliament of which they are a member may be dissolved before then, and they must run for reelection.

Much like the United States, Parliament is organized according to political parties. The party that wins the most seats in a parliamentary election gets to form the government, and the next largest party is known as the **opposition**. Leaders of the opposition appoint their own potential cabinet members, who ''shadow'' particular members of the ruling cabinet. If the opposition party should gain a majority in Parliament, this so-called shadow cabinet would then become the government.

Also like the United States, two major political parties have dominated British politics since World War II. They are the Labour Party and the Conservative Party. The Labour Party gets much of its support from working people, particularly those who belong to the country's strong labor unions. The Conservative Party relies mostly on support from the middle and upper classes. Each of the two major parties has held the government several times since 1940. Several other smaller parties, such as the Social and Liberal Democratic Party, have some support.

Parties are more disciplined and organization is much stricter in Britain than in the United States. MPs are expected to support the government on all major votes. In general elections, voters tend to choose candidates almost solely by party label, not on the basis of issue positions, personality, or individual qualifications.

Local Government

Great Britain has a **unitary government**, which holds national law to be supreme, and centralizes governmental power at the national level. This is in contrast to the system in the United States, in which governmental power is shared between the federal government and the

As in the United States, it is the people of Great Britain who are responsible for electing their representatives. How often are British elections held?

Caption Answer Students should understand that a general election must be held at least once every five years but may take place more frequently. The prime minister decides when a general election will take place. General elections are also held following a loss by the government in a vote of confidence.

but exists in several written and unwritten forms.
2. The monarchy in Great Britain today is largely ceremonial.
3. While the U.S. Congress is based on the separation of powers, the British Parliament is based on the fusion of powers. It manages both the executive and legislative powers of the nation.
4. The prime minister and cabinet. To govern Great Britain, much as both the executive and legislative branches together govern the United States. As a unitary government the prime minister and Parliament also have direct authority over county and local governments.
5. Answers will vary, e.g., the president of the United States should have as much direct contact with Congress as the prime minister does with Parliament, as in the "question hour."

SECTION 2

Points to Stress

- Changes reflected in the present French Constitution.
- Powers of the French president and how they differ from those of the U.S. president.
- The roles of the prime minister and cabinet in the French government.
- The manner in which local units are governed in France.

Kickoff Activity
In what ways is the government of France similar to our government? Give the students about five minutes to list their ideas in response to that question. When the time is up, ask several of the students to read their lists aloud.

Working with the Preview Questions
Have the students read these four study questions, and let volunteers point out the main headings that indicate where the answers will be found. Ask the students to use these questions as guidelines as they read and write topic outlines of Section 2.

Teaching Strategies

Introduction
Ask one of the students to read the introductory paragraphs aloud. Then encourage the students to recall and discuss the main issues, events, and effects of the French Revolution. You might refer students back to the Government In Action Case Study in Chapter 2.

Discussion Starter
Ask the students to consider the effects of having 20 different governments in 12 years: How do you think these changes affected the daily lives of French citizens? How do you imagine the changes affected their attitudes? Why?

Caption Answer Student answers may vary, but might suggest that a combination of France's long history of powerful monarchs and the failure of the Fourth Republic, which had a weaker central government, led to the strong French presidency today.

state governments. Local governments in Great Britain are controlled by the central government; local units serve only the purposes set out for them by Parliament.

County boroughs and **administrative councils** are the major local governmental units in Great Britain. Members of these units are popularly elected, but do not have their own revenue-raising powers. They depend on the national government for most public funds. Local government is responsible for services such as education, police and fire protection, housing, public health, and street maintenance.

SECTION 1 REVIEW

1. Describe the basic difference between the British and United States constitutions.
2. What is the function of the monarchy in Great Britain today?
3. What are the major differences between the United States Congress and the British Parliament?
4. Who makes up the government in Great Britain? What are the functions of that government?
5. **For critical analysis:** Do you think there are any elements of the British system which, if adopted by the United States, would improve our system of government? Give reasons for your answer.

SECTION 2

France

Preview Questions

- How has the present French constitution changed the French system of government?
- What are the powers of the French president? How do they differ from those of the United States president?
- What role do the prime minister and the cabinet play in French government?
- How are local units governed in France?

France has been an important European nation for centuries. Ruled under an absolute monarchy for almost one thousand years, it changed into a democracy after the French revolution and the resulting Declaration of 1789.

Like Great Britain, the French democracy is a unitary government; like the United States, it is a republic with a written constitution. Despite these similarities, however, the French government has its unique characteristics.

The Constitution

Since 1791, France has had five republics, each under a different constitution. The Fourth Republic had serious problems and lasted for only twelve years until it was dissolved in 1958. Two critical problems were that the chief executive was weak while the legislature exercised very strong power, and the Parliament was divided by many competing political parties. Therefore, no one party was ever able to obtain enough support to be able to rule the government. As a result, France had twenty different governments under seventeen prime ministers during the period from 1946 to 1958.

The Constitution of the Fifth Republic is the current constitution and has been in effect since 1958. This latest constitution was designed with the central purpose of creating a strong and stable government. The old parliamentary system was retained, but was combined with a strong president.

The French President

The constitution of 1958 transformed the French president into a key figure in French politics, with some powers that far exceed the powers of the United States president.

▲ François Mitterand, as the president of France, has some powers that exceed the powers of the president of the United States. Is there anything in France's history to suggest why its constitution would call for such a strong president?

Discussion Starter
Ask the students to discuss what might happen in our country if the president, like the president of France, were empowered to bypass the legislative branch of government and take votes directly to the people.

Comprehension
Let volunteers explain how the powers of the French president to act in any situation that poses "a grave and immediate" threat compare to the powers of the American president during time of war.

Discussion Starter
Encourage the students to share and discuss their responses to these questions: How are members of the French cabinet like members of the U.S. cabinet? How are they different?

Discussion Starter
Help the students consider the fact that, after leaving the cabinet, French ministers may not return to their seats in Parliament: What do you think is the purpose of this restriction? How do you believe it affects the career interests and activities of French ministers?

Enrichment
Let a group of interested volunteers work together to learn about the current prime minister and cabinet in France: Who are they? What are their interests and policy goals? Ask the volunteers to write a short report, to be shared with the rest of the class.

Discussion Starter
Encourage the students to share their responses to the restricted legislative powers of the French Parliament: What is the likely purpose of these restrictions? Who benefits from them? How?

The president of France is the only nationally elected official in the country and serves a seven-year term (which may soon become five years). The constitution gives the president the power to appoint the prime minister and other high officials, as well as the power to negotiate treaties and act as commander in chief of the military.

Two other significant constitutional powers are available to the French president that do not exist in the British or American systems. One gives the president the power to bypass Parliament completely. He or she may call for a national referendum. The other power gives the president the right to take complete control of the government in times of grave emergency. Basically, he or she can then undertake virtually any necessary action to suit the gravity of the national emergency.

Whenever the French president does not like the way his or her legislative program is being treated in the lower house—called the **National Assembly**—he or she can ask for new elections. This is known as dissolving the Parliament.

The Government: The Prime Minister and Cabinet

The president and the prime minister and his or her cabinet are often referred to as "the government," as is done in Britain. Both the prime minister and his or her cabinet are allowed to have executive and legislative powers simultaneously. The French president picks the prime minister, in contrast to the way the legislature does in Britain. Then the prime minister picks his or her own cabinet members. These individuals head various executive departments such as foreign affairs and finance. They are called ministers, just as in Britain. Cabinet members can be chosen from the Parliament (and then must resign), but usually are from the business, legal, or cultural worlds outside of politics. Many are career civil servants who have specialized in the area in which they are appointed, such as agriculture or the arts.

In spite of the fact that cabinet members are not members of Parliament, they still control the course of bills as they are taken through the legislature. In other words, the prime minister and cabinet determine the legislative agenda. They introduce bills and sit in the National Assembly. In fact, all taxing and spending bills must originate from the cabinet. When the president is not happy with the popularity of his or her prime minister, the president can fire the person and put someone else in place who may do a job that is better accepted by the French electorate.

The Legislature

Parliament has two houses, the National Assembly and the Senate. As in the U.S., the Senate is considered the upper house. The Assembly consists of 491 deputies; the Senate has 305 senators.

The French Parliament is limited in its lawmaking powers by the constitution, which specifically outlines

The lower house of the French legislature is called the National Assembly. What type of powers does the French president have over the National Assembly?

Caption Answer The French president has the power to choose the prime minister and to dissolve the National Assembly.

Extension
Encourage the students to learn more about the powers and responsibilities of the president and the prime minister of France: How do the two offices differ? Do you believe the same person could be suited for either job?

Cooperative Learning
Divide the class into four groups, and assign each group one of the French presidents who served under the current constitution. Ask the group members to work together in researching the background and policy interests of that prime minister and in reporting to the rest of the class.

Enrichment
Let a pair of interested students read about the Communist Party in France: What is its history? How broad is its support? How has it changed in response to recent events in the former Soviet Union and in Eastern Europe? Ask these students to present their findings in a bulletin board display.

Discussion Starter
Guide the students in considering the effects of the central government on schools in France: How do you react to the example of the fifth-graders, all doing the same thing at the same time? How does their education system compare to that of the United States? What—if anything—do you think the United States might learn from France in regard to education? What—if anything—do you think France might learn from the United States?

the subjects that may be legislated. These areas include education, criminal justice, social welfare, civil rights, and administration of local communities. The subjects *not* listed are the sole area for which the government is able to enact laws by decree, that is, without approval of the Parliament.

Parliament has little authority over the budget and may not reduce revenues or raise expenditures.

Similar to the American system, all bills must be approved by both houses in France and then signed by the president. Also similar to the U.S. system, there are permanent, or standing, committees in both houses, all with a number of subcommittees. In the U.S., all such subcommittees are highly specialized. But in France, they are closer to the British subcommittees, which are responsible for general areas. If the Assembly and the Senate pass different versions of a bill, the prime minister appoints a joint committee to resolve the differences. (The somewhat similar process occurs in the U.S. system.) If this appointed committee cannot resolve the issues in dispute, the prime minister can ask the Assembly to vote on the bill. If it does so and the president signs the bill, it becomes law.

Elections and Political Parties

All parties can nominate candidates for the presidency. To be elected, a candidate must win a majority vote. If no candidate wins a clear majority, a second runoff election is held two weeks later. In this election, only the two candidates with the most votes run, and the winner is named president. There is no limit on the number of terms a president may serve.

Since the formation of the Fifth Republic in 1958, there have been four presidents, the first one being World War II hero General Charles de Gaulle. He remained in power until 1969. Then Georges Pompidou was elected and died in office in 1974. Valery Giscard d'Estaing was elected that year and stayed until 1981, when François Mitterand took over.

Members of the Assembly are popularly elected from single-member districts for five-year terms, unless new elections are called sooner. Senate members are chosen by a body composed mostly of elected officials in the country's ninety-six geographical governmental divisions called **departments**. Senators serve nine-year terms, and one-third of the seats are up for election every three years.

As with all democracies, France has many political parties. For many years, the most important party was the Rally for the Republic, popularly known as the

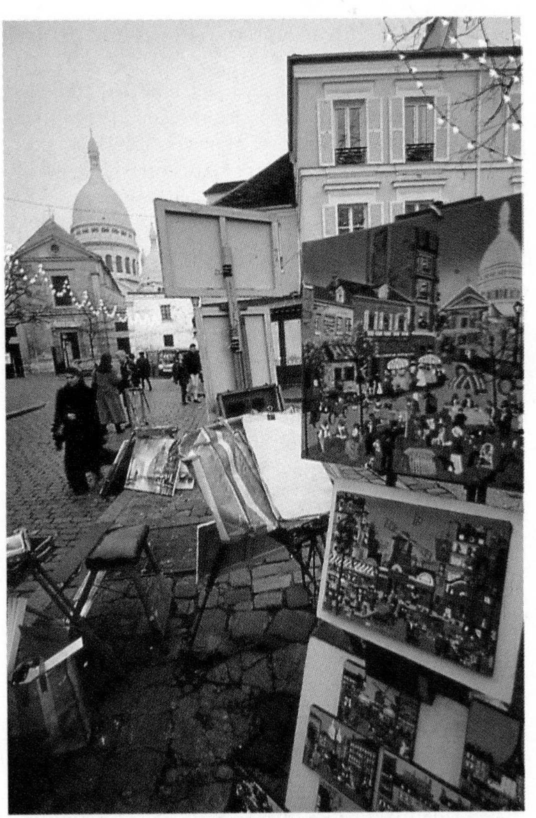

▲ France has a unitary form of government. What does this mean for the people in the cities and towns of France?

Gaullists. The Socialist Party became the most important in the 1980s and early 1990s. This is the party to which Mitterand belongs. The National Front, an extreme right-wing party, began capturing more support in the 1990s. It is headed by Jean LePen, who believes in severely restricting immigration. Except for supporters of the Communist Party, the French do not tend to identify strongly with political parties and voters may shift parties from election to election. Different parties, however, do attract broad groups of people. For example, the Socialist Party consists mainly of salaried workers and government bureaucrats.

Local Government

The central government in Paris has long controlled all local government with an iron fist. This has been possible because France has a unitary system of gov-

Caption Answer Students should understand that under a unitary form of government the cities and towns have no local government units and are controlled by the central government, in this case by cabinet ministers in Paris.

Reteaching Strategies
1. Let the students work in small groups to discuss and review the content of Section 2, as they have noted it in their outlines. Encourage the group members to refer to the text to resolve any questions, and remind the students to make necessary corrections to their own outlines.
2. Have the students work with partners to review, revise, and extend the lists they wrote as part of the Kickoff Activity at the beginning of this section.

Evaluation Strategies
1. Have the students write their answers to the Section 1 Review questions.
2. Have the students take the Section 1 Quiz found in the *TRB.*

Section 2 Review (Answers)
1. To appoint the prime minister, negotiate treaties, and act as commander-in-chief of the military. The president also has the power to send a vote directly to the voters for approval in the national referendum. The president may also act single-handedly in times of emergency.
2. The prime minister and cabinet in France are not chosen by the legislature. The president chooses the prime minister who in turn appoints cabinet ministers, usually skilled civil servants and experts in their field.
3. The constitution limits the lawmaking powers of the French Parliament to certain areas including education, criminal justice, and social welfare.
4. The government is highly centralized and most features of local government are controlled by the cabinet ministries in Paris.
5. Answers will vary, e.g., this does not mean that France has an unstable government. It may have had an unstable government in the past, but today it is just as stable as any government in the Western world.

SECTION 3

Points to Stress
- The Japanese constitution and how it compares with the U.S. Constitution.
- The make-up of the two houses of the national legislature in Japan.
- The make-up of the executive branch and the method of selecting the prime minister.

Kickoff Activity
Give the students five minutes in which to list their ideas in response to this question: How is the system of government in Japan similar to ours? When all the students have completed their lists, ask several volunteers to share their responses with the rest of the class.

Working with the Preview Questions
Go over the Preview Questions with the class. Then have the students work together to write the main headings, based on these questions, for a topic outline of Section 3. Instruct the students to follow this outline format as they read and take notes on the section.

ernment, which affords little power to the subnational government units.

As stated above, France is divided into departments. Each department is run by a commissioner, an official appointed by the national government. The local governments carry out the policies of the central government in areas such as police protection and improvement of roads. Nonetheless, the central government still dominates local affairs in a way that would shock Americans. For example, we are used to local authority over our schools. In France, the Ministry of Education almost completely controls the subjects that every public school student takes, when he or she takes them, and what textbook will be used.

In 1981, President Mitterand declared that the powers of the local units would be enlarged. The changes have been resisted, however, and few significant changes have taken place.

Even with its unitary system, every city in France still has its important office of the mayor headed by a person who was popularly elected as mayor. The mayor is responsible for all of the infrastructure of the city—local park maintenance, street cleaning, local traffic police, and so on, without controlling the budget.

Section 2 Review

1. What are the special powers of the French president?
2. How do the functions of the French prime minister and cabinet compare to those of the British prime minister and cabinet?
3. What limits are placed on the French Parliament's powers?
4. How does the French unitary form of government operate?
5. **For critical analysis:** The current French government is on its fifth republic. Does this mean that it should be considered an unstable government? Why or why not?

Section 3

Japan

Preview Questions
- How does the modern Japanese constitution compare with ours?
- What is the structure of Japan's legislature?
- How is the prime minister chosen?

Prior to the end of World War II, Japan had been governed by royal rulers for over a century and a half. These rulers, called *mikados*, were absolute monarchs. Their will was carried out by military dictators, noble families, and warriors. True democracy has been known to Japan only since 1947, when the occupying American forces prepared a constitution for that country.

Today the political system in Japan resembles a combination of those which exist in Great Britain and France. Similar to that of France, the form of government is unitary, meaning it is centralized in the national government in Tokyo. It is similar to that of Great Britain in being a constitutional monarchy with a figurehead monarch, the emperor.

The Japanese Constitution

Actually, the constitution created by the American forces under General Douglas MacArthur after World War II was not the first constitution the country had known. Under Emperor Mutsuhito, a constitution was adopted toward the end of the nineteenth century. Even though that constitution created a legislature, it was, of course, the emperor and his cabinet who retained virtually all power.

The current constitution specifies that political power is derived from the people of Japan. This should be contrasted to the power that the emperors previously wielded, which was considered to be divine. Just as in America, today the Japanese express their will by voting secretly in popular elections. The Japanese constitution contains a preamble that is similar to the preamble in the American constitution and, essentially, states that the people shall act through their duly elected representatives in their national legislature.

Bill of Rights The modern Japanese constitution, like the American one, has a bill of rights. The rights in the Japanese bill of rights, however, are even more extensive than those in the American counterpart. The rights of freedom of speech, freedom of the press, and freedom of religion exist in both constitutions. The Japanese went further, though, when they created the right of equality of the sexes and the right to work.

No More Wars Prior to their defeat in World War II, the military held tremendous power within the Japanese system. Given that the Americans had just defeated the Japanese, it is not surprising that the occupying army insisted that an anti-war clause be written into the constitution. In this way, the Americans believed they could

Teaching Strategies

Introduction
After the students have read the section introduction, encourage volunteers to share what they know about Japan's royal rulers and the society over which they reigned. Then ask: Why do you think the Japanese government has retained a role, albeit ceremonial, for the emperor? What is the attitude of the Japanese people toward their emperor?

Discussion Starter
Help the students consider the origin of the Japanese constitution: How important is the source of this constitution? Why is the Japanese constitution so similar to ours? How might the spirit of the two documents differ? Why?

Discussion Starter
Encourage the students to share their ideas in response to these questions: Why do you think the equality of the sexes is established in the Japanese constitution? Why was it not included in our Constitution?

Extension
You may want to have the students research the stance taken by Japan during the Persian Gulf War in 1991: How did the antimilitary clause in the Japanese constitution affect Japan's position and the relationship between Japan and the United States?

Comprehension
Help the students continue to compare the Japanese system with the American system: In our system, who has the power to make treaties, raise funds, and make appropriations? Why?

Discussion Starter
Let the students share and discuss their responses to questions such as these: Which parliamentary house in another country do you think is most like the Japanese House of Councilors? In what respects are they similar? How do you account for that similarity? In what respects are they different?

Caption Answer The House of Representatives, the lower house of the National Diet, has the most power of the two houses, including the power to elect the prime minister.

Extension
Have the students recall (or research) the customs and traditions of Japanese society: How do these customs and traditions affect the conduct of the modern Japanese Diet?

Discussion Starter
Encourage the students to consider the history of Japan as they respond to this question: Why do you think there is no separation between the executive and legislative branches of the Japanese government?

ensure that the Japanese government would never again be in a position to wage war. The constitution states that Japan "forever renounces war as a sovereign right of the nation and the threat or use of force as a means of settling any international disputes." It goes on to state further that no military forces will ever be maintained.

Some now argue that we went too far in forcing this clause onto the Japanese, and that we have unfairly limited the sovereignty of that nation. Consequently, since the middle 1950s Japan has been allowed to maintain a self-defense force. The issue of defense became even more important when coalition forces (mainly from Europe and America) were involved in a war against Iraq after that country invaded Kuwait in 1990. Many Japanese criticized their current government because it did not send any military forces to the Middle East to help the coalition.

Law Making in the Japanese System

Through its constitution, Japan has a parliament that is called the **National Diet**. It consists of two houses—the House of Councilors and the House of Representatives. Just as in the United States, the House of Representatives is considered the lower house; nonetheless, it has more power than the so-called upper house, the House of Councilors. As with the British system, parliament elects a prime minister, who in turn chooses an eighteen-member cabinet. The prime minister and his cabinet are the executive branch, but because they are chosen from the legislative branch, there is no clear separation of powers as in the American system.

The House of Representatives The more than five hundred representatives in the lower (but more powerful) house are elected by the people from multi-membered districts. The House of Representatives can make treaties and appropriations, and raise funds. It also has the unique power to topple the government. That is to say, it can force the prime minister and his cabinet to resign. This is done, as in Britain, through a vote of "no confidence."

Most bills must be passed by both houses. If the upper house, however, does not pass a bill, the House of Representatives can override this "negative" vote by passing the bill for a second time by a two-thirds majority.

The House of Councilors There are 252 seats in the House of Councilors. Councilors are elected from specific districts or from the nation as a whole. Councilors serve six-year terms. As in the House of Lords in Britain, the House of Councilors has little power. Observers of

▲ Prime Minister Miyazawa of Japan is also a member of the National Diet. Which of the two houses of the National Diet is responsible for electing the prime minister?

the Japanese government claim that the House of Councilors, nonetheless, serves an important advisory role.

The Notion of Consensus When Americans first observe how the British legislature conducts itself, they are often shocked. Legislators may make "catcalls" during a speech by the prime minister, joke behind his or her back, and so on. The speeches by the legislators are often full of humor. A Japanese person might feel the same shock when observing how the American Congress works, since in comparison to the Diet, the U.S. Congress is quite noisy with many heated debates. The difference has to do with tradition, culture, and history. The Japanese have a tradition of broad agreement on issues, sometimes called rule by consensus. If, for example, the party in power wants legislation that the minority party strongly opposes, the majority party will rarely go forward with that legislation. Rather, a compromise will be sought.

Legislation in the National Diet is often introduced by the government—the prime minister and his cabinet—and by the bureaucracy through the cabinet. In any event, members of the government party are expected to vote with the government even if they do not agree with the proposed legislation. If they strongly disagree, nor-

Discussion Starter
Encourage a discussion of the Japanese bureaucracy: How are bureaucrats generally regarded in this country? What do you think accounts for the regard and respect granted to members of the Japanese bureaucracy? Who do you think benefits from the Japanese bureaucratic system? How?

Discussion Starter
As the students finish reading about the bureaucracy within the Japanese government, encourage them to share their responses to these questions: Do the bureaucrats of Japan appear to feel they are running their country? Do you think they actually are? Why or why not?

Caption Answer Students should understand that the Japanese bureaucracy has played an important role in Japanese success. The bureaucracy's careful long-range planning and power in advising and directing Japanese corporate activities have been very important to Japan's economic success.

Multidiscipline Strategies

Language Arts Have the students work in pairs to select and read a Japanese short story or novel. Let the partners discuss the work, paying particular attention to depictions of daily life and to the influence of societal traditions on the characters. Then ask the partners: What do you consider a central theme of this work? What familiar American short story or novel presents the same (or a similar) theme? Let the partners review the American work and discuss the similarities and differences between the Japanese and American works.

mally they do not vote. The reality is that most of the legislation proposed by the government's party ends up, in one form or another, becoming law.

The Prime Minister and His Cabinet

As stated before, the prime minister is chosen by the Diet and is a member of the Diet. Of the eighteen members of his or her cabinet, at least half must be from the Diet. In reality, virtually all members of the Japanese government's cabinet are also legislators. Sometimes an important member of the bureaucracy is chosen by the prime minister to become part of the cabinet. As with the U.S. cabinet, the Japanese cabinet includes the heads of various ministries (executive departments) such as agriculture and forestry, education, labor, health and welfare, justice, and foreign affairs. Much of the job of the cabinet involves pushing government-sponsored legislation through the Diet. If the prime minister is not satisfied with the progress of the legislation that his or her government has proposed, he or she may dissolve the House of Representatives. Then new elections are called. Consequently, not all members of the House of Representatives are allowed to serve a full four-year term.

In keeping with the consensus tradition, virtually no dissent is allowed within the cabinet. That is to say, if a cabinet member disagrees with what the prime minister is doing, that cabinet member must resign.

The All-Powerful Bureaucracy

While the bureaucracy is sometimes considered the fourth branch of government in the United States, in Japan it can truly be said to have taken on a much more serious and important role. The federal bureaucracy in America has relatively little to do with making government policy. Not so in Japan. Some students of Japanese politics even argue that bureaucrats are an important ruling force in the country.

Some of the best and the brightest of those who complete college in Japan decide to enter the bureaucracy. They are not attracted by the pay, for the pay scale in the government in Japan (as in virtually all other developed countries) is relatively low. In other words, top-ranked college graduates in Japan can almost always earn higher incomes if they go into private business. But a Japanese government bureaucrat is highly regarded in that society. Such jobs carry prestige, which overcomes the relatively low salary scale.

To show how much confidence legislators have in the bureaucracy, they write legislation in a very general way. They leave it up to the bureaucracy to fill in the details of rulemaking and implementation. Some bureaucracies make important policy decisions with respect to interest rates and the availability of credit. Other powerful bureaucracies decide which industries to help and which not to help.

In America, the head of a government agency may meet infrequently, if at all, with the Congress. Just the opposite situation exists in the Japanese system. There, politicians have frequent meetings with the heads of different agencies. Although career bureaucrats in Japan do not particularly like politicians who interfere, the bureaucrats accept the need to justify their actions to the legislators.

In recent years, Japan has become an economic power, exporting many products, including these automobiles. What role do you think the bureaucracy plays in Japan's economic success?

TEACHING CITIZENSHIP SKILLS AND RESPONSIBILITIES

Read
Before the students begin reading this Citizenship Skills and Responsibilities feature, engage them in a brief discussion about human rights: What are human rights? What are your personal interests in human rights? How do you feel about supporting human rights for others in this country? Around the world? What do you know about Amnesty International? What kinds of work does it do? How? Then let one or two volunteers read the feature aloud to the rest of the class.

Discuss
Guide a discussion of the feature by posing questions such as these: What is your personal response to information about people being tortured and illegally imprisoned? What is the significance of the fact that Amnesty International won the Nobel Peace Prize? Do you know which musicians support Amnesty International or similar causes? How does this information affect your attitude toward the musicians? Why do you think Amnesty International focuses on individual cases rather than on whole groups? How would you evaluate the means by which Amnesty International seeks to achieve its goals?

Analyze and Apply
Ask the class to divide into four or five groups. Have the members of each group work together to gather information on Amnesty International's objections to specific practices in the United States. Then let the group members discuss their findings: Do you agree that these practices violate human rights? What can you do to make a difference in your own country?

Review
Use these questions to help the students review the Citizenship Skills and Responsibilities feature: What is Amnesty International? What are two of this organization's goals? What are two of the methods Amnesty International uses in trying to achieve those goals?

CITIZENSHIP SKILLS AND RESPONSIBILITIES

How to Support Human Rights

There are still many places in the world where men, women, and children are being illegally imprisoned and tortured. These people aren't guilty of any crime except being born a different color, practicing a different religion, speaking a different language, or having different political views from the people who are torturing them. If you are interested in learning more about struggles for human rights around the world, a good place to start is with Amnesty International.

Amnesty International was founded in 1961 to organize the world to take a stand against human rights injustices. In 1977 it won the Nobel Peace Prize for "defending human dignity against violence and subjugation." In 1986 Amnesty International enlisted the support of rock musicians to bring the human rights message to American youth; their "Conspiracy of Hope" tour boosted national action. Each year it has enlisted more people to support its cause.

Today, Amnesty International has grown into a worldwide network of over 700,000 people with branches in many countries and more than 100 researchers who compile the latest information on torture and state-supported abuses of human rights. As of 1992, Amnesty International had taken on more than 31,000 individual cases and was a key factor in the release of almost 2,000 political prisoners. Other goals are to ensure prompt and fair trials for political prisoners and to end torture and executions. It attempts to achieve these goals through publicity, lobbying, legal aid, and letter-writing campaigns that focus on the cases of specific individuals.

To become a member, send whatever donation you can. The suggested membership fees are $25, or $15 for students and senior citizens. If you are interested, write to Amnesty International USA, 322 Eighth Avenue, New York, NY 10001, or telephone 212-807-8400.

TAKING ACTION

1. Do further research on three specific cases in which Amnesty International has recently been involved. Report back to the class on your findings and your assessment of the organization.
2. Research human rights violations in a particular country in which you are interested.
3. Research the history of apartheid in South Africa.

Enrichment
Have an interested volunteer research and give a short oral report on Japan's LDP: How and by whom was it founded? What are the major policies it espouses? Who have the most important LDP leaders been? What changes has the LDP undergone in recent years? Why?

Critical Thinking Skills
Help the students consider and analyze the fact that Japan, France, and Great Britain all have highly centralized governments, whereas the United States does not: What features do the three smaller countries share in contrast to the United States? Which of these features might help account for their choice of a highly centralized government? Why?

Reteaching Strategies
1. Ask the students to form small discussion groups. Then have the group members compare and review their outlines of Section 3; encourage the students to improve their notes if necessary.
2. Have pairs of students work together to write two short paragraphs: one explaining the similarities between the American and Japanese systems of government, the other explaining the differences.

Evaluation Strategies
1. Have the students write their answers to the Section 3 Review questions.
2. Have the students take the Section 3 Quiz found in the *TRB*.

Section 3 Review (Answers)
1. An anti-military clause forbidding maintenance of a military force was written into the Japanese Constitution at the insistence of America.
2. Laws are made in the House of Representatives, the lower house of the National Diet, where the rule of consensus operates to forge legislative compromises.
3. Strong private interest groups form coalition political parties, such as the LDP, that elect the Prime Minister through control of the House of Representatives.
4. Answers will vary and may include such points as the rule of consensus, which encourages unity; a high respect for public service; and a highly educated, technical civil service bureaucracy.

SECTION 4

Points to Stress
• Characteristics of command economies and their relation to market systems.
• Characteristics of a capitalistic economic system.
• Characteristics of a mixed economic system.

Kickoff Activity
Ask the students to write short paragraphs in response to these questions: What is an economic system? What examples can you give? After all the students have finished writing, encourage several volunteers to share their paragraphs for class discussion.

One Dominant Political Party

Japan has a multi-party system because it is a democracy. Nonetheless, one political party has dominated the scene since the mid-1950s. It is the Liberal-Democratic Party, or LDP. The LDP has several factions, each headed by a powerful political leader within the Diet. When one of those leaders is chosen as prime minister, he or she will normally choose as cabinet members only those who have been loyal to his or her ideas.

In spite of the differences in political viewpoints among the factions of the LDP, as a whole it has been pro-American. The LDP is considered a rather conservative party. Consequently, most opposition parties are generally on the other end of the political spectrum. The most powerful opposition party is the Socialist Party. Its main rallying point is opposition to the LDP's pro-American stand.

The Japanese Government's Role in the Economy

The Japanese government takes many strong stands regarding the economy as a whole. It has, for example, prohibited almost all labor immigration until recently. It gives tax breaks to Japan's large agricultural sector and prevents competition from other countries. For example, as late as 1992, it would not allow any importation of rice from the United States in order to protect its own rice farmers.

Because the Japanese economy has done so well under its current form of government, many observers in the United States have argued that what the Japanese government does for the economy might provide a model for other nations.

Section 3 Review

1. What did America force Japan to include in its constitution after World War II?
2. How does the National Diet make laws?
3. How do political parties influence who will be prime minister in Japan?
4. **For critical analysis:** Japan is an economic power in the world today. What aspect of its government system might have helped cause this situation?

Section 4

Types of Economic Systems

Preview Questions

- What is a command economic system? How does it compare to a market system?
- What is a capitalist economic system?
- What is a mixed economic system?

An **economic system** is the way in which a nation uses its resources to satisfy its people's needs and wants. A nation's economic system and its government are closely related.

If you were to make a list of your personal goals and compare it with the list made by a person of your age in parts of Africa, the People's Republic of China, North Korea, or Sweden, the lists probably would be very different. One of the reasons the lists would be different is that each of these nations has a different economic system. Remember, however, that no matter which economic system a country uses, every country faces the same challenge of satisfying the needs and wants of its citizens with its capability to generate goods and services.

Economists have identified three types of modern economic systems: command, or controlled; market, or capitalist; and mixed. Remember as you read this section that the economic systems described are pure, or ideal, types. They are economic models, not examples of how economies actually function. Most economic systems today are mixed. The United States, for example, has a mixed economy, but it is said to have a market economy because it mainly responds to the market. China also has a mixed economy, but it is said to have a command economy because almost all economic activity there is planned by the government.

Command, or Controlled, System

In a pure **command economic system**, the individual has little, if any, influence over how the basic economy functions. Government controls the means of producing what people want—land, labor, and **capital** (machines, factories, tools)—and therefore makes all decisions about their use. This is why this form of economic system is also called a controlled economy. The terms socialism and **communism** are also applied to command economies.

The government may be one person, a small group of leaders, or a group of central planners in a government agency. These people choose how resources are to be used at each stage in production and decide the distribution of goods, services, and even labor. The government, through a series of regulations about the kinds and amount of education available to different groups, guides people into certain jobs.

During the Middle Ages in Europe, the command economy was the major economic system. The land-

Working with the Preview Questions
Go over these three study questions with the class, and let the students identify the main headings that indicate where the response to each question is presented. Then ask the students to keep the questions in mind while they read and take notes on Section 4.

Teaching Strategies

Introduction
Let a volunteer read the section introduction aloud. Then encourage a brief discussion by posing questions such as these: What differences would you expect if you were to compare your goals with those of someone your age in North Korea? In Sweden? Why would you expect to find such differences? What similarities would you expect? Why? How do you think governmental systems and economic systems affect the daily lives and aspirations of people? In what respects are people around the world alike, no matter what governmental or economic systems they live under?

Vocabulary
Ask volunteers to define the terms *socialism* and *communism:* How are the two systems alike? What are the most important differences between them?

Discussion Starter
Guide the students in considering the successes of the command economy in Europe during the Middle Ages: Why do you think this system worked at that place and in that time? What has changed since then? Do you think it could work, in the same form, in any part of the world now? Why or why not?

Comprehension
Let volunteers answer these questions: Why are the neighborhood examples, in which a homeowner pays a student to mow the lawn or shovel snow, such good illustrations of the market system? What might happen if several students competed to mow lawns in a given neighborhood? How would the market system operate then?

Figure Answer Students should understand that consumers help to fund the government through taxes, while benefitting from government programs and spending in the form of wages, transfer payments, and interest.

Discussion Starter
Encourage the students to consider some other issues related to a market system: In a pure market economy, what happens to people who, for various reasons, cannot work? What happens if people do not want to work in service jobs that might be considered unattractive?

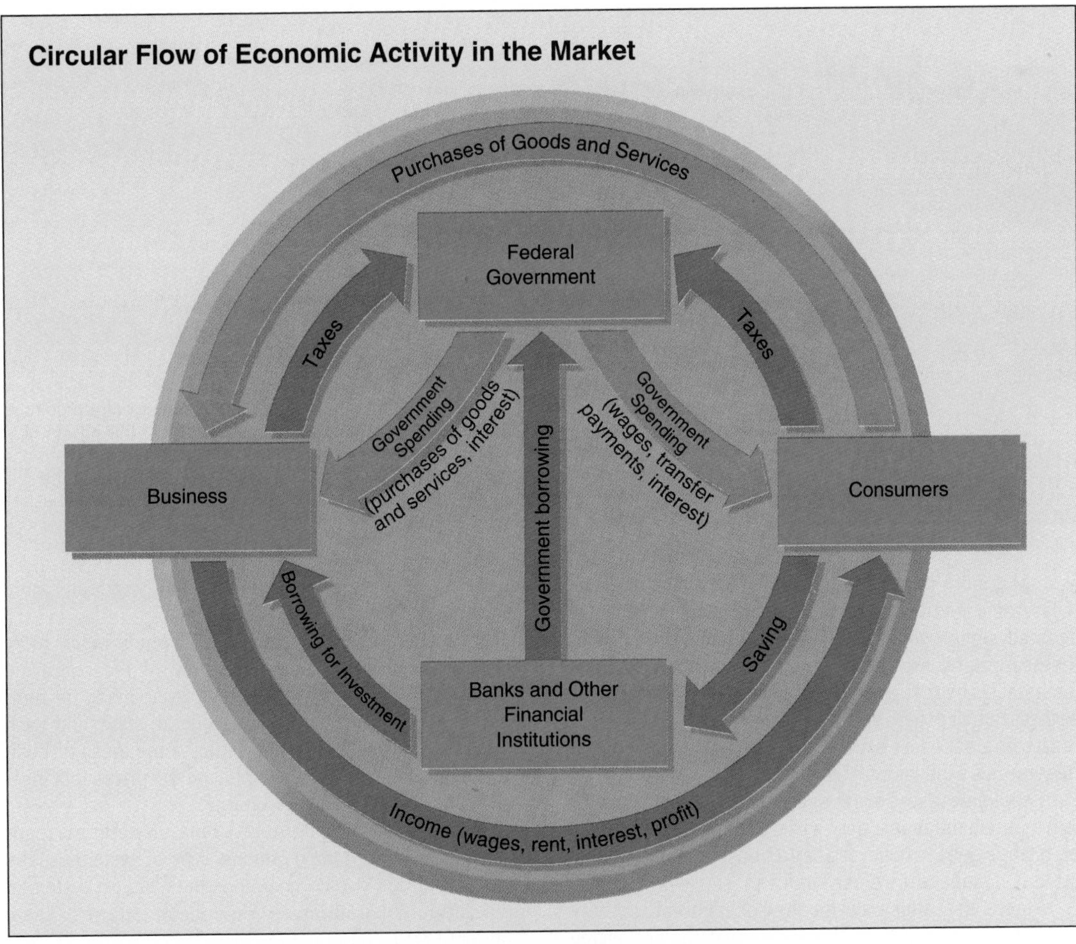

FIGURE 26–1 Circular Flow of Economic Activity in the Market. The figure above shows the flow of economic activity through the market in a capitalist system. According to this figure, what is the relationship between consumers and the federal government?

holder of each manor decided what and how much to produce, who should produce each good or service, how, and for whom.

Market, or Capitalist, System

The opposite of a command economic system is a **market economic system**, otherwise known as **capitalism**. In a pure market economy system, government does not intervene: Individuals own the means of production and decide for themselves who to work for, how to work, and how to spend their income. These decisions are made through the free interaction of individuals looking out for their own best interests in the market. **Market** in this sense is not a place; rather, it is the activity of buying and selling goods and services. In a market economy, buyers and sellers can freely choose to do business with those who best satisfy their needs and wants. The exchange of goods and services may take place in a worldwide market for a good such as crude oil, or it may take place in a neighborhood where a homeowner pays a student to mow lawns, or shovel snow.

In a pure market economic system, producers of goods and services decide how to use their resources based solely on the trends of the market; government planning has no part in these decisions. Suppose, for

Comprehension
Ask volunteers to identify other examples of regulation in the American economy.

Discussion Starter
Help the students consider the kind of mixed economy in use in the People's Republic of China: What advantages do you think might be associated with this economy? How do you think the economy might affect the personal satisfaction and interests of the citizens? What disadvantages do you think are associated with the economy? In your opinion, do the advantages outweigh the disadvantages—or do the disadvantages outweigh the advantages? Why?

Caption Answer The central government plans how to use the farms' resources and sets production targets for the farms.

Reteaching Strategies
1. Let the students work with partners to compare and discuss the notes they have taken on Section 4. Have them refer to the text to resolve any questions, and remind them to correct their own notes if necessary.
2. Work with the students in small groups; help them discuss their concept of daily life under all three economic systems.

Evaluation Strategies
1. Have the students write their answers to the Section 4 Review questions.
2. Have the students take the Section 4 Quiz found in the *TRB.*

Section 4 Review (Answers)
1. In a command system, the government controls the means of production—land, labor, and capital. In a market economy, individuals own the means of production and make the decisions.
2. Mixed economies.
3. Answers will vary, e.g., it becomes easier to make comparisons as even mixed economic systems tend toward either command or market systems.

The Chinese system of agriculture depends largely on the efforts of workers, such as these, on collective farms. How does the central government control the activity of collective farms?

example, more people begin buying the compact discs (CDs) of a particular musical group. This increase in demand signals to the record company that it should invest more resources—time, money, effort—into producing CDs by that group. If, however, CD sales are low for a particular group, the company will not produce more of the group's CDs, because buyers have signaled that they do not want more.

People are also free in a pure market economic system to sell their labor as they wish. They may take, refuse, or change jobs whenever they choose, assuming that there is a demand for their labor.

Figure 26–1 illustrates the flow of economic activity through the market in the capitalist system. The inside arrows show individuals selling the means of production to businesses, who use them to produce goods and services. The flow of money from businesses to individuals in the form of rent, wages, interest and profits, and its return to businesses as consumer spending, is illustrated on the outside of the figure.

Mixed Economic System

We just explained theoretical economic systems; it is doubtful whether these economic systems ever existed in their pure form. They are useful models for analyzing existing systems, however. Today, almost all economic systems are what economists call mixed economies. A **mixed economy** contains characteristics of both a command economy and a pure market economy. The mix will vary so that any one economic system leans more toward one type than another.

The United States, for example, tends much more toward the market system than toward the command system. All decisions are not, however, made by individuals reacting to the market. Federal, state, and local governments make laws regulating some areas of business. Among these, for example, are the prices that electric utility companies may charge.

The People's Republic of China, in contrast, tends much more toward the command type of system usually called communism. For example, the Chinese system of agriculture is based largely on collective farms. These are large farms in which the land, buildings, and equipment are owned by the government. Central government planners make decisions about how to use these resources, such as how many acres or hectares of wheat or sugar beets to plant and harvest. Hundreds of individuals may work together on one collective farm to meet the production targets the government has set. The Chinese economy also has some limited characteristics of the market system. Some Chinese farmers are allowed small plots of land to grow crops or livestock to use themselves or to sell for whatever price the market will bring. No central planner decides what and how much the farmers should grow on their personal plots or how or to whom they should sell, or at what prices.

Economists classify economies according to which pure system their activities most resemble. As a result, the United States is said to have a market economy, and the People's Republic of China, North Korea, and Viet-

SECTION 5

Points to Stress

- The role of government in the American economy.
- The freedoms needed for entrepreneurship to flourish.
- The major causes of economic competition.

Kickoff Activity

What do you consider the most important advantages of living under the American economic system? Pose this question for the class, and give the students five minutes in which to list their responses. At the end of the allotted time, encourage the students to share and discuss their ideas.

Working with the Preview Questions

Have the students read these three study questions, and encourage interested students to share their initial responses. Remind the students that they will find more detailed responses as they study Section 5; ask the students to keep these questions in mind as content guidelines while they read the section.

Teaching Strategies

Introduction

After the students have read the section introduction, encourage a short discussion by asking questions such as these: Why are all six of these characteristics essential to a pure market economy? How are the characteristics interrelated?

Comprehension

Let several students restate Smith's ideas about the "invisible hand" of competition in their own words.

Discussion Starter

Focus the students' attention on the growing role of government during the past century: How has this growth affected our economic system? Do government regulation of businesses and government provision of public services "chip away" at our capitalist system? Do you believe it is necessary to restrict the growth of government in order to maintain capitalism? Why or why not?

Vocabulary

Let volunteers respond to these questions: What is enterprise? What is free enterprise?

Caption Answer Students should understand that *free enterprise* refers to the individual's freedom to own and control their own business and compete in the marketplace.

nam are said to have a command economy. No two economies, however, even if they share many of the same characteristics, are exactly the same.

SECTION 4 REVIEW

1. What is the main difference between a market economy and a command economy?
2. What type of economic system do most nations have today?
3. **For critical analysis:** If every economic system in the world is a mixed system, then why do we make a distinction between command economies and market economies?

SECTION 5

Characteristics of the American Economy

Preview Questions

- What role does government play in the American economy?
- What freedoms are needed for entrepreneurship to flourish?
- What is one of the main causes of economic competition?

A pure market economic system has six major characteristics: little or no government control, freedom of enterprise, freedom of choice, private property, profit incentive, and competition. These characteristics are interrelated, and to varying degrees all are present in the American economy. The role of government, however, is much greater than it would be if the United States had a pure market system. Since our nation's founding, government involvement in individual economic choices has grown greatly. As the role of government grows, it can influence the degree to which individuals can freely exercise their economic freedoms and rights.

Capitalism

In his book *The Wealth of Nations,* Adam Smith in 1776 described a system in which government has little to do with economic activity. He said that individuals left on their own would work for their own self-interests; in doing this, he argued, they would be guided as if by an "invisible hand" of competition to achieve the maximum good for society.

Smith's idea of the ideal economic system is called capitalism, another name for the market system. Economists argue whether capitalism in its pure form, as Smith describes it, has ever existed. Certainly today, capitalism as practiced in the United States differs from Smith's original idea. Capitalism today would be best defined as an economic system in which private individuals own the means of production. As a result, they have the right to use those means in any way they choose within the limits of the law. In other words, individuals have a voice in how they use their labor and the things they own to produce income. In our society, however, the law sets certain restrictions on these rights.

The Role of Government Smith did see the need for government to intervene in some areas. He believed that government should provide for the national defense and eliminate any business practices that limited trade. Government was also needed to issue money, tax people for public works, and settle legal disputes. The founders of the new United States were influenced by Smith and others who believed in as little government control as possible. Many aspects of this philosophy were written

▼ Small business owners, such as this grocer, are a vital part of our system of free enterprise. What does the term *free enterprise* mean?

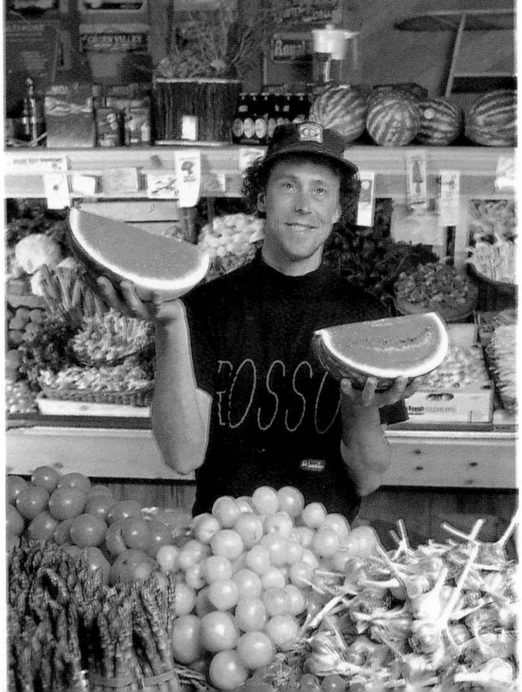

TEACHING BUILDING SOCIAL STUDIES SKILLS

Read

Encourage a brief introductory discussion by asking the students questions such as these: What is a mathematical mean? What is a mathematical median? How are the two different? Why is it important to understand those differences? After the discussion, let the students take turns in reading the Building Social Studies Skills feature aloud to the rest of the class.

Discuss

Use questions such as these to help the students discuss the feature: What do you learn when you find the average income in an occupation that interests you? Would you expect to earn that specific income if you chose that career? Why or why not? What are the meanings of the noun *average?* What does a mean figure tell you? What does it not tell you? What does a median figure tell you? What does it not tell you? What do you consider the best uses of means? Of medians?

Analyze and Apply

Have the students work with partners or in small groups. Let the groups collect and discuss articles from newspapers and news magazines in which average figures are reported. Then let each pair or group of students select one of the articles and research the actual range of figures from which that average was calculated: What appears to have been calculated—the mean or the median?

Review

Ask the students these review questions about the Building Social Studies Skills feature: What is a mean? How is it calculated? What is a median? How is it figured?

BUILDING SOCIAL STUDIES SKILLS

Understanding Mean and Median

Average, percent, actual number, mean, median—these are all terms used with statistics. Throughout this textbook, you have been reading and using statistics. Some are mentioned within the text, and some are used in graphs and tables. Researchers use statistics to indicate to what extent different characteristics, such as occupations, income, amounts of money spent on various budget items, and so on, are present in different populations. Population, as statisticians use the term, can be a group of people, businesses, or branches of government.

You may not realize it, but the data that statisticians gather can be helpful to you in making your own decisions. For example, when you are trying to choose a career, it would be useful to know the average income in the occupations that interest you. If you are thinking of becoming a construction worker or actor, it would also be useful to find out the average number of weeks in a year that the typical construction worker or actor is employed. You can also turn your own information into statistics. For example, in planning a budget, you might want to decide on the average percentages of income that you are willing to pay for items such as food.

Averages: Mean and Median

Important information is often summarized in averages. People, however, sometimes use the word *average* when they should really use the terms *mean* or *median.* Researchers use means and medians to give an overall view of a population or to summarize various statistics.

Mean The mean is the average of a series of items. It is found by adding the items and then dividing by the number of items in the series. The list of numbers below gives the weekly salaries of seven students in one class who all have part-time, after-school jobs. You can find the mean salary by adding the weekly wages and then dividing by the number of students.

$ 10
41
49
53
57
$210 ÷ 5 = $42

The mean weekly salary for these students is $42.

Median Sometimes using the mean to interpret a set of statistics can be misleading. This is especially true if one or two numbers in the series are much larger than the others. A median can be more accurate.

The median is the midpoint in any series of numbers arranged in order. For example, in the list of

into the Constitution. The new government would deal mainly with national defense and keeping peace, and would limit its powers over individual economic choices. Since the 1880s, the role of government—federal, state, and local—has increased significantly in the United States, especially in the areas of regulating business and providing public services.

Freedom of Enterprise The American economy is also called the **free enterprise system**. This term emphasizes the fact that individuals are free to own and control the means of production. For example, if you decide to go into business for yourself, your abilities and resources will help you decide the good or service to produce, the quantity, and the methods of production. Of course, there is no guarantee that you or any entrepreneur will succeed; in fact, you may lose all your money. Thus, the freedom to make money includes the risk of losing it.

There are certain legal limits to freedom of enterprise, however. According to the law, you cannot make, sell, or buy anything illegal. Certain industries such as prescription drug manufacturers are regulated by law. State governments require professionals such as lawyers and physicians to pass examinations before they can be licensed to practice. In most states, teenagers must be 16 years old before they can legally work, and then laws set limits on how many hours they can work. And all

Practicing Your Skills (Answers)

1. 6.1 percent mean.
2. 6.9 percent median.
3. While the mean provides an average figure, an unusually large but atypical piece of data can give misleading results. The median is a mid-value datapoint.

Comprehension

Let the students compare the position of the small business owner in the free enterprise system and in a command economy.

Discussion Starter

Guide the students in discussing the limits to freedom of enterprise: Do you believe these restrictions are necessary? Why or why not? Can you envision a society in which free enterprise would function successfully—and no such restrictions would be needed? If not, why not? If so, how would you describe that society?

Extension

Let the students share and discuss their responses to this question: How do you personally exercise your freedom of choice in our economic system?

Discussion Starter

Help the students consider the property owned by the U.S. government: What purpose do you believe this government ownership serves? What are the alternatives? Do you think changes should be made? If so, what and why? If not, why not?

salaries on page 642, $49 is the median weekly wage. The number of students that earn more than $49 a week is equal to the number that earn less than $49 a week.

In this case, the mean of the series, $42, is smaller than the median, $49. This is because one of the students earns $10 a week, less than a quarter of any other student's salary. This one small salary pushes the mean much lower than it would be if only the other four salaries were averaged.

PRACTICING YOUR SKILLS

The table below shows the percentage rates of unemployment in different countries in 1990.

1. Calculate the mean unemployment rate in the countries other than the U.S.
2. Calculate the median rate of unemployment in these countries.
3. Explain the importance of mean and median in using data.

Unemployment Rates in Selected Countries, 1990

Country	Rate of Unemployment	Country	Rate of Unemployment
United States	5.5	Germany	5.2
Canada	8.1	Italy	7.0
Australia	6.9	Netherlands	8.0
Japan	2.1	Sweden	1.5
France	9.2	United Kingdom	6.9

Source: Department of Labor, Bureau of Labor Statistics

governments—federal, state, and local—require individuals and businesses to pay taxes.

Freedom of Choice Freedom of choice is the other side of freedom of enterprise. Freedom of choice means that buyers make the decisions about what should be produced. The success or failure of a good or service in the marketplace depends on whether individuals freely choose to buy it. People buy or do not buy a particular group's CDs. The record company, in reality, may choose to continue making CDs with the group anyway, even though it knows it will not make a lot of profit. Normally, though, the group will not be asked to record another album.

Private Property **Private property** is simply the items owned by individuals or groups rather than by government. Individual rights to private property are guaranteed by the U.S. Constitution. You as an individual are free to buy whatever you can afford whether it is land, a business, a home, an automobile, and so on. You can also control how, when, and by whom your property is used. If you own a business, you can keep any **profit** you make. Profit is the money left over after all the costs of production, distribution, and taxes have been paid.

Within the United States, government at all levels controls some property. Parks, firefighting and police equipment, military bases, and post offices are some examples of government-owned property.

Discussion Starter
As the students discuss the profit incentive, you might ask them: What are other kinds of incentives? Other than profit, what motivates people to work? Are those incentives as important as profit? More important? Why or why not?

Enrichment
Let a small group of volunteers work together to research answers to these questions: Which industries have been regulated by the federal government? Why? With what results? Have the volunteers present their findings in an oral report, and encourage all the students to discuss the implications of this regulation.

Caption Answer Student answers will vary, but might include military bases, fire and police equipment, school facilities, etc.

Discussion Starter
Guide the students in discussing the example in which competition drives the price of personal computers down: Is this the result that invariably reaches consumers? Why or why not?

Reteaching Strategies
1. Ask the students to form small groups in which to discuss and compare their responses to the Preview Questions at the beginning of Section 5.
2. Have the students write paragraphs in response to these questions: Which of the six characteristics of a pure market economy is most important to you? Why?

Evaluation Strategies
1. Have the students write their answers to the Section 5 Review questions.
2. Have the students take the Section 5 Quiz found in the *TRB.*

Section 5 Review (Answers)
1. Little or no government control, freedom of enterprise, freedom of choice, private property, profit incentive, and competition.
2. A system in which the government has little to do with economic activity. Individuals left on their own would work for their own self interests, and in so doing, would be guided by an "invisible hand" of competition to achieve the maximum good for society.
3. The term emphasizes the fact that individuals are free to own and control the means of production.
4. It ensures that no one company has complete control over the price of a particular product.
5. Answers will vary, e.g., without the existence of private property rights, people could not be rewarded for improving property and therefore they would have little incentive to invest in anything. Investment is necessary for economic growth.

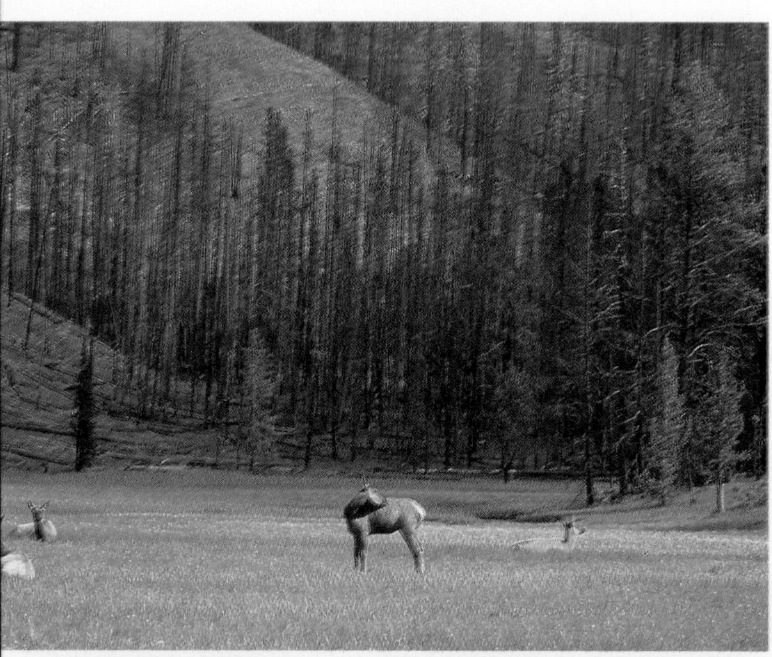

While individual rights to private property are guaranteed by the U.S. Constitution, government at all levels also controls some property, such as Yellowstone National Park shown here. What other examples of government-owned property can you name?

Profit Incentive Whenever a person invests time, know-how, money, and other capital resources in a business, that investment is made with the idea of making a profit. The desire to make a profit is called the **profit incentive**, and it is mainly this hope that motivates people to produce things that others want to buy. After all, if no one buys what a seller produces, there will be no profit, only losses. For example, if you went into business mowing lawns, you would expect to make enough money to cover your expenses and make some profit. This desire for profit is your incentive.

Competition **Competition** is the rivalry among producers or sellers of similar goods to win more business by offering the lowest prices or best quality. In many industries, competition requires a large number of independent buyers and sellers to ensure that no one company has complete control over the price of a particular product. If one company attempts to raise its prices, potential customers can simply go to one of the many other sellers. In the ideal world, this is how competition would work. In practice, however, the federal government over the past one hundred years has had to regulate some business practices in an attempt to make sure that competition continues to exist.

It is the opportunity to make a profit that encourages competition. Suppose that only one business makes a particular product such as a personal computer. Because potential buyers would have no alternative seller to turn to, the computer company could charge as much as people who really want a personal computer would be willing to pay. Then suppose a second company enters the market with a similar computer at a lower price. Now the two businesses would have to compete for buyers, which would force computer prices down.

Section 5 Review

1. What are the six major characteristics of a pure market economy?
2. How did Adam Smith define capitalism?
3. Why is the American economy also called a free enterprise system?
4. Why is competition important in our economy?
5. **For critical analysis:** Why is the existence of private property critical to a capitalist economic system?

SECTION 6

Points to Stress

- The key theories of Karl Marx.
- Historical results of applying Marxist theories in the former Soviet Union.
- Modern China's attempt to change its command socialist system.

Kickoff Activity

Write the term *Communist countries* on the chalkboard, and ask the students what that term brings to mind. Give them five minutes to list words and phrases suggested to them by the term. When the time is up, encourage the student to compare and discuss their lists.

Working with the Preview Questions

Go over the three study questions with the class. Then have the students work together to use these questions in writing main headings for a topic outline. Have the students read Section 6 and use the planned main headings in outlining the section.

Teaching Strategies

Introduction

Ask one of the students to read the section introduction aloud to the rest of the class. Then encourage volunteers to answer these questions: What does *converging* mean? Why can the 1990s be called "the era of converging political and economic systems"? Also, ask the students to recall hearing the breaking news about the end of authoritarian communist regimes and the collapse of the former Soviet Union: How did you react to those news stories? What were the reactions of your family members and friends? Why did these news stories evoke such reactions? How do you think these changes affect the daily lives of citizens in Eastern Europe and the former Soviet Union? How do the changes affect us here in the United States?

SECTION 6

Converging Political and Economic Systems

Preview Questions

- What were Karl Marx's key theories?
- What was the result of applying Marxist theories to the former Soviet Union?
- How has modern China attempted to change its command socialist system?

The 1990s can definitely be called the era of converging political and economic systems. The world witnessed one of the most comprehensive fundamental changes in the structure of a political and economic system in a major part of the world. Specifically, starting at the end of 1989 and culminating in August of 1991, we witnessed the virtual wholesale elimination of the authoritarian communist regimes in Albania, Bulgaria, Czechoslovakia, East Germany (now united with West Germany), Hungary, Poland, Romania, and Yugoslavia. In addition, the summer of 1991 witnessed the Second Great Russian Revolution in which the central authority for the fifteen republics of the former Soviet Union completely collapsed. Soon thereafter the Baltic states of Latvia, Estonia, and Lithuania declared their independence and were recognized by governments worldwide. On Christmas day, 1991, the Soviet Union as a political entity disappeared. In its place was instituted the loosely formed Commonwealth of Independent States consisting of 11 former Soviet republics.

At no other time in history has such a large number of people lived through such a complete political and economic change in such a short period of time.

The Roots of Communism and Socialism

Much of today's socialist political and economic theory, and especially that associated with the former Soviet Union, has its origins in the works of a man named Karl Marx. Karl Marx was a political writer who developed a number of socialist theories that are still adhered to in some parts of the world, particularly the People's Republic of China. In 1867 Marx wrote a book called *Das Kapital.* In that book he discussed what he called the labor theory of value. According to his theory, the value of things produced depends on the human labor time spent producing them. Marx claimed that workers spent part of the day working to cover the cost of maintaining themselves and their family and that they were only paid wages equal to this subsistence amount of

The resignation of Mikhail Gorbachev in 1991 was the final official act of the Soviet Union. What has replaced the Soviet Union?

Caption Answer In the place of the former Soviet Union is a loosely formed commonwealth of independent states consisting of eleven former Soviet republics.

TEACHING GOVERNMENT IN ACTION

Read

Introduce this Government in Action feature by reminding the students of the familiar statement that the world is growing smaller. Then ask them: In what sense is this statement true? How does technology contribute to this "shrinking" of the globe? What are some of the implications of our smaller world? After a brief introductory discussion, have volunteers read the feature aloud.

Discuss

Help the students discuss the feature by asking questions such as these: Why do you think totalitarian governments have existed over such a long period of time? What do you consider the significance of the recent growth of democratic governments? How do people use "low-tech" information transmission systems—including, for example, photocopy machines in the former Soviet Union—to preserve and share records? What are the effects of those activities? How does knowledge of democratically elected governments affect the attitudes and activities of people living under totalitarian governments? Why?

Analyze and Apply

Let the students work in groups to discuss how the flow of information from democratic countries would affect the feelings, ideas, and attitudes of people in totalitarian countries. Then have each student write a short sketch or draw a picture or cartoon to illustrate the impact of such information on the lives of individuals.

Review

Help the students review the Government in Action feature by asking these questions: How have forms of government changed around the world during the past century? How does the technological revolution in telecommunications affect the propaganda used by totalitarian governments?

Think About It (Answers)

1. Answers will vary, but should reflect the knowledge that access to technology that spreads information (television, radio, FAX machines, printing technologies) is still not available to the general population. Also, the governments in these countries are very powerful.

2. A strong, democratic tradition of self-government was well established in this country before the development of communication technology. Indeed, it may be that the development of technology was a direct result of the political and economic freedoms enjoyed in democratic countries.

GOVERNMENT IN ACTION

CASE STUDY

Technology versus Totalitarianism?

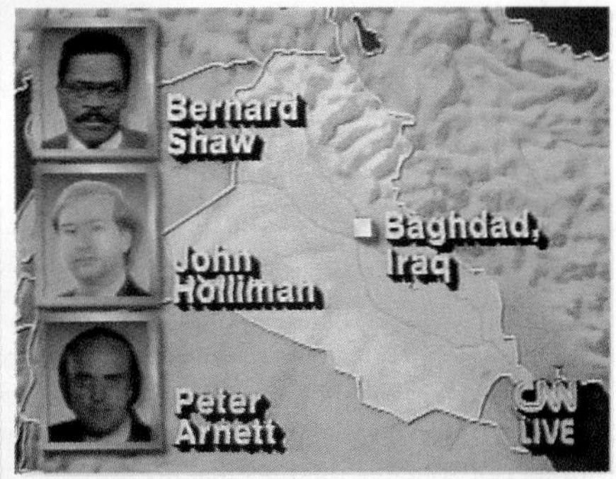

News services, such as the Cable News Network, have proven to be important and nearly instantaneous sources for news throughout the world.

Since the beginning of time there have been totalitarian governments throughout the world. Since the beginning of time there have been dictators, absolute monarchs, and in general, those who ruled without the consent of the governed. A comparison of today with the world a hundred years ago, however, does yield a definite observation—there are fewer totalitarian governments today than ever before in the history of the world. In particular, just a few short years ago the former Union of Soviet Socialist Republics was governed by a non-democratic set of rulers.

Why the big change? One possible answer lies, perhaps, in the age of technology. More specifically, the answer may possibly lie in the age of modern telecommunications. Today, with the proliferation of satellite transmission, relatively inexpensive radio and television receivers, relatively inexpensive portable radio and television transmitters, as well as worldwide telephone service, it is no longer possible to keep the ''masses in the dark.'' Even more ''low-tech'' information transmission systems prevent information from being squelched. Desktop publishing and fax machines guarantee that the truth in print can be easily disseminated.

What does all this mean for totalitarian governments? It means that they have a difficult time keeping their people ignorant about the way of life in countries with democratically elected governments. It means that totalitarian governments, which usually rule over relatively poor citizens, cannot prevent those very citizens from learning about the material comforts that are experienced in other parts of the world.

Propaganda utilized by totalitarian governments has less force than it used to because of the technological revolution in telecommunications. Alternative views to the ''government line'' are now readily available to a growing percentage of the world's citizenry. Take the example of Saddam Hussein, who claimed, when he invaded Kuwait in 1990, that he was simply doing so to ''protect the people from a bad government.'' When news reports showing Iraqi soldiers looting and carrying away private and government property from Kuwait were seen throughout the world, Hussein's propaganda no longer seemed credible. Consider also that when hard-line communists took over the government in the former Soviet Union in August 1991, the world immediately knew what was happening. The opposition to that illegal change in government was broadcast not only to the people in the former Soviet Union but to the rest of the world.

THINK ABOUT IT

1. As of the first part of the 1990s, only a few major nondemocratic regimes remained in the world, including the People's Republic of China, North Korea, and Vietnam. Why has the increased availability of information about the benefits of democracy not changed those regimes?
2. Communication was extremely crude and difficult during the birth of this nation. How did we end up with a democracy, nonetheless?

Enrichment
Have one of the students research the life and accomplishments of Karl Marx and then write a short report on Marx, to be shared with other students in the class.

Discussion Starter
Guide the students in considering Marx's principle, "from each according to his ability, to each according to his needs." What is the appeal of this principle? To whom might it be especially attractive? Who would probably be uninterested in a system based on this principle? What is your reaction to Marx's principle? Why?

Cooperative Learning
Let the students form small groups, and ask each group to select one of the former satellite countries as a subject for research. Have the group members work together to learn how the chosen country became a satellite of the Soviet Union, how its government and economy functioned during that period, and what has happened in that country during recent years. Then have the members of each group present a short report to the rest of the class.

Extension
Encourage the students to gather and discuss evidence to show the failure—or success—of the "Great Experiment."

Caption Answer Student answers will vary. Students might express an understanding that this was a symbolic way for the people to revenge themselves against the oppressive leaders of the past.

Statues of communist leaders such as Joseph Stalin, shown here, were razed throughout the former Soviet Union. Why do you think the people were so quick to destroy these symbols?

income. The rest of the day they in effect worked without pay, creating surplus value, what he called a source of wealth and profit for those who own the means of production. Those who own the means of production are called capitalists.

Among other things, Marx argued that there would be economic crises in capitalist countries. He thought such crises would eventually cause the collapse of capitalism and the rise of socialism and then eventually ideal communism, which he defined as a situation in which the government would wither away completely. In communism, Marx forsaw a final state of existence in which the principal ''from each according to his ability, to each according to his needs'' would guide all economic decisions. Many of Marx's ideas were put into political and economic practice by the former Soviet Union, many countries in Eastern Europe, the People's Republic of China, and Vietnam.

The Failure of Communism

While is is possible to argue abstractly the merits of Marxist thought, the world has provided information about the reality of such thought. In particular, the ideas of Marx as applied in the former Soviet Union and its Eastern-bloc satellites did not yield major benefits for the average citizen. The so-called socialist ''Great Experiment'' lasted in the ex-Soviet Union for 74 years and

Following the break-up of the Soviet Union, Russian President Boris Yeltsin emerged as one of the most powerful political figures in that part of the world. What challenges do Yeltsin and the other leaders of the Commonwealth of Independent States face?

Caption Answer These leaders face many challenges, not the least of which are to confront the instability that has resulted from the collapse of the Soviet government, to revive their economies, and to establish enduring political systems.

Discussion Starter
Help the students discuss the statement Churchill is rumored to have made: How would you state Churchill's idea? Do you agree with the statement? Why or why not?

Enrichment
Ask a pair of students to research and report on China's Civil War: What were the major issues? Who were the important leaders? What were the immediate results of the war? The long-term results?

Caption Answer The Communist Party has ruled the People's Republic of China since 1949.

Vocabulary
Let volunteers explain the meaning of *an iron fist:* What does it mean that Mao ruled with an iron fist?

Discussion Starter
Encourage the students to discuss China's "coastal open cities" and "special economic zones": What do you think motivated their establishment? What purposes are they intended to serve? What future do you think they have? Why?

Reteaching Strategies
1. Let the students work with partners, using their outlines to review the content of Section 6. Remind the students to refer to the text if necessary and to make any needed corrections to their own outlines.
2. Work with small groups of students, helping them discuss their responses to this question: What future do you think communism has in the People's Republic of China?

Evaluation Strategies
1. Have the students write their answers to the Section 6 Review questions.
2. Have the students take the Section 6 Quiz found in the *TRB.*

In June of 1989, a popular movement for democracy in the People's Republic of China was openly crushed by government tanks and soldiers. How long has the People's Republic of China been under communist rule?

in its satellite countries for a little over 40 years. For most researchers, that is a sufficient time period during which to determine whether the ''experiment'' worked. It did not.

All of the former communist countries in Eastern Europe and in what was the Soviet Union are now attempting in various ways to revitalize their economies and democratize their political systems. While the future of the Commonwealth of Independent States within the former Soviet Union is unknown (and in fact that loose confederation of nations may not even exist when you read this), one thing is certain: the challenges that face the people and political representatives are enormous. New political and economic structures will surely emerge. Some forms of central command and socialism will undoubtedly remain, but certainly not very much. Former Prime Minister Winston Churchill of Britain was once rumored to have said that democracy was the worst system known to civilization, but the best of all the alternatives. The same could probably be said about capitalism as an economic system.

What About China?

While command socialism fell apart in the former Soviet Union and Eastern Europe, it continued in force in the People's Republic of China.

After the communists emerged victorious in China's Civil War following World War II, they instituted an economic system similar in nature to the one in the former Soviet Union. Central planning from the capital, Beijing, occurred not only with respect to deciding all economic questions but also in deciding all political questions. The Communist Party has ruled since 1949. From that time until his death in 1976, Chairman Mao ruled with an iron fist. In 1978 a new leader, Deng Xiaoping, took over power. On the economic front, Deng did decentralize Chinese industry to some extent. He also allowed some foreign investment. The result has been an increase in Chinese living standards.

Politically, though, there has been relatively little movement towards democracy.

The Results of Centralized Control An interesting comparison can be made between the more open, market-oriented economies in Taiwan and Hong Kong and the centralized, command economy in mainland China. In 1950 the average income per person of China and Taiwan was about the same. Hong Kong had a little more. By 1992, the average income in Taiwan was 30 times that of mainland China and in Hong Kong 35 times more.

Creating Special Economic Zones The Chinese leadership was aware of this great difference in income between its centrally planned command socialist economy and the market economies just next door. In 1979, Deng Xiaoping designated fourteen cities along China's coast as ''coastal open cities,'' with extra freedoms and tax breaks for foreign trade and investment. Additionally, five ''special economic zones'' were created with even more free market privileges.

The result has been a boom in the coastal arc stretching from Hainan Island in the southwest through Guangdong Province, adjacent to Hong Kong, and on to Fujian

TEACHING CHALLENGE TO THE AMERICAN DREAM

Read
Begin by having the students read the title question of this Challenge to the American Dream feature. Encourage a brief discussion in response to that title: What are the major problems facing the world today? Do you believe those problems can be solved? Do you believe that people should attempt to solve them? Why or why not? Do you believe your attitude—and the attitudes of other people your age—makes a difference in the solutions to those problems? After the students have had an opportunity to share and compare their ideas, let them read the feature independently.

Discuss
Use questions such as these to guide a discussion of the Challenge to the American Dream feature: Who is being affected by the AIDS epidemic? How? How do the problems of crime and drugs in this country influence the way you lead your life? How do they affect your family members, your friends, and your neighbors? Does war—or the threat of war—pose a problem for people around the world? What do you consider the most positive developments in our modern society? Why? How hopeful do you think you—and other Americans—should be? Why? What do you think you and your contemporaries can do to help solve the problems the world faces now—and the further problems that may develop during your lifetime?

Analyze and Apply
Let the students work with partners or in small groups to discuss and clarify their own attitudes toward the world's problems. Then have each student plan, prepare, and present a work—such as a poem, a painting, a dance, a video, or a song—expressing his or her attitude.

Review
Ask the students these review questions: What are two of the major problems facing the world today? What are two of the most positive recent developments in American society?

You Decide (Answers)
1. Answers will vary, e.g., on the whole the benefits outweigh the costs because the average American is much better off.
2. Answers will vary, e.g., nuclear proliferation. If nuclear weapons are used the other problems will suddenly become insignificant.
3. Answers will vary, e.g., it seems that people would rather read and hear about catastrophes and problems than good news. This philosophy probably affects textbooks as well as newspapers, magazines, and television.

CHALLENGE TO THE AMERICAN DREAM

Can We Ever Solve the World's Problems?

After reading this text, you may get the impression that the world's problems are insurmountable. After all, the AIDS epidemic seems to be increasing worldwide; the drug and crime problem in the United States is getting worse, not better; and war is definitely not something in the past for it has happened as recently as 1991 (and maybe even more recently by the time you read this book). Moreover, throughout the previous pages in this text, you have read about many other problems in the United States and throughout the world.

There is another side to all this negativity, however. Just look at what has happened in the United States in only two hundred years. We went from being an almost purely agricultural society to one in which agriculture occupies less than 3 percent of the population. At the same time, the standard of living of the average American has skyrocketed. Indeed, what well-to-do people had available at the beginning of this nation's history would be considered a relatively low standard of living today.

Even though we read about epidemics, health problems, pollution, and cancer-causing food additives and toxins, the average life expectancy in the United States continues to rise.

Even though we continue to read about increasing crime rates in the United States, the average American is actually safer than he or she was in the major cities of the world several hundred years ago.

Even though we read about horrible plane crashes, the average flyer on an airplane is over one hundred times safer than someone driving the same distance in a car, and three or four times safer than the average airplane passenger was thirty years ago.

While it is true that the AIDS epidemic is a horrible scourge on humanity, it has only been around for little more than a decade and medical science has already started to find potential cures.

While it is true that some indicators of educational achievement are not very heartwarming, the average American today is many times more educated than he or she was several hundred years ago or even fifty years ago. Indeed, so many Americans are becoming educated that four years of college has become accepted as an educational standard.

Even though environmental problems continue to grow, more Americans than ever before have begun to make changes in the way they live, in what they buy, and in how they view the environment. This *greening* of America reflects a positive trend for saving the environment.

Think about how much leisure time Americans have today compared to the past. The average work week is 37.5 hours in the United States. Several hundred years ago it exceeded 60 hours a week.

Nonetheless, do not go too far in looking at the positive side of everything. There are numerous challenges to the American dream just as there are numerous challenges to the dream of worldwide peace, prosperity, and equality for all. Concerned, educated, and dedicated Americans will always be needed to understand and help solve the many challenges that exist now and the many new ones that will exist in the future.

You Decide

1. On the whole, do you think that the benefits of economic progress in the United States have outweighed the costs? Why or why not?
2. Of all the challenges that face our society today, which ones do you think need the most urgent attention? Why?
3. Some people say bad news sells and good news does not. Therefore, all we hear about are problems. Do you agree? Why or why not? Is it possible that this philosophy affects textbooks also?

Section 6 Review (Answers)

1. Karl Marx introduced the labor theory (value of things depends on human time spent developing them); surplus value (value created beyond subsistence level of human beings); historical necessity of economic crises.
2. The collapse of command socialism in the Communist bloc countries discredited the economic theories of Communism.
3. The 1992 average income was 30–35 times lower in Mainland China than in Hong Kong or Taiwan.
4. Answers will vary. Not necessarily, since capitalist economies still face severe problems providing for all their citizens; or, yes, since the countries with the highest standards of living are primarily capitalist or mixed economies.

Chapter Evaluation

To evaluate student mastery of chapter material, you might:
1. Use Chapter Test A from the *TRB.*
2. Use Chapter Test B from the *TRB.*
3. Construct your own test using items from the *West American Government Test Bank* found in the *TRB.*
4. Use the accompanying computerized test software to construct and print a customized chapter test.

Review Questions (Answers)

1. The U.S. Constitution is written while the British constitution is unwritten in the sense that it is a whole body of agreements, some written and some unwritten.
2. It manages both the legislative and executive powers of the nation.
3. The prime minister and cabinet.
4. The power to appoint the prime minister, to negotiate treaties, and to act as commander-in-chief of the military. The French president also has the power to send a vote directly to the people for approval and to take whatever action he deems necessary in any situation that "poses a grave and immediate" threat to the nation.
5. The prime minister is not chosen by the legislature.
6. The constitution specifically outlines the subjects that may be legislated.
7. Parties are more disciplined and organization is much stricter in Great Britain and France than in the United States. During recent years, four major parties have emerged in France as compared to two in the United States.
8. They are both under the direct authority of the national government.
9. A denial of the Japanese emperor's divine right to rule, investment of power in the individual,

Province, which is opposite Taiwan. Fujian Province, for example, with 30 million people was one of China's poorest provinces in the 1970s. Yet industrial output has increased seven times from 1990 to 1992.

Section 6 Review

1. What were some of the socialist ideas introduced by Karl Marx?
2. What event occurred in the last few years that changed many people's view of communism?
3. How has mainland China fared economically compared to Taiwan and Hong Kong?
4. **For critical analysis:** Can the failure of command socialism and communism in the former Soviet Union be equated to the triumph of capitalism?

Chapter 26 Review

Key Terms

administrative councils 631
capital 638
capitalism 639
command economic system 638
communism 638
competition 644
constitutional monarch 628
county boroughs 631
departments 633
economic system 638
free enterprise system 642
hereditary ruler 627
heredity peers 629
House of Commons 628
House of Lords 629
law lords 629
market 639
market economic system 639
Members of Parliament 628
ministers 629
mixed economy 640
National Assembly 632
National Diet 635
opposition 630
Parliament 628
prime minister 629
private property 643
profit incentive 644
unitary government 630
vote of confidence 630

Summary

1. Great Britain is a democratic constitutional monarchy. It has no constitution in our sense of the word but rather has a whole body of agreements, some written and some unwritten. Since the 1800s the monarch has served mainly a ceremonial function. The British Parliament is a bicameral legislature made up of the House of Commons, which has most of the power, and the House of Lords. The majority party in the House of Commons elects one of its members as the prime minister, who in turn selects other members to form the cabinet. Great Britain has a unitary form of government, which means powers are centralized at the national level.

2. The French democratic government operates under a written constitution that was adopted in 1958 and that created a mixed parliamentary/presidential system. The president is the most powerful governmental figure and is the only nationally elected official. The French Parliament consists of the National Assembly and the Senate. The president chooses the prime minister, who in turn appoints cabinet members. The French government is unitary and highly centralized.

3. Japan's constitution was set down by the occupying American forces and went into effect in 1947. Japan's legislature has a parliament of two houses, called the National Diet, in which the upper house is the House of Councilers, and the lower house is the House of Representatives. The House of Representatives has the most power. It consists of more than five hundred members chosen from 130 election districts. The upper house has 252 members. Legislation is normally introduced by the bureaucracy or the government in power rather than by the legislators themselves. The prime minister is a member of the Diet; he or she selects the cabinet, half of whose members must be from the Diet. Japan has a multiparty system with one dominant party, the Liberal Democratic Party (LDP).

4. An economic system is the way in which a nation uses its resources to satisfy its people's needs and wants.

and an anti-military clause are key points of the Japanese constitution.
10. The Japanese legislature is the National Diet, composed of the upper House of Councilors with very little actual power, and the lower House of Representatives. Members to the House of Representatives are directly elected by the nation.
11. The prime minister, who is a member of the National Diet, heads both the combined executive and legislative branches of government.
12. In a command system, government controls the means of production and makes most of the decisions about their use, while in a market system price and production are determined by the laws of supply and demand.
13. They contain characteristics of both a command and a pure market economy.
14. Little or no government control, freedom of enterprise, freedom of choice, private property, profit incentive, and competition.
15. He viewed the government as having little to do with economic activity. Individuals acting in their own self interests would be guided by an "invisible hand" of competition to achieve the maximum good for society.
16. Individuals are free to own and control the means of production.
17. The desire to make a profit is a key element in capitalism.
18. Marx predicted the collapse of capitalistic economies and the eventual rise of a pure communistic economy.
19. The governments and economies of most of the world's communist countries collapsed between 1989 and 1991.
20. The Communist Party has ruled in China since 1949. Very recently, it has been experimenting with mixed market economies in "special economic zones."
21. The goals of Amnesty International include: to defend human dignity against violence and subjugation; to ensure prompt and fair trials for political prisoners; and to end torture and executions.

Questions for Thought and Discussion (Answers)

1. Answers will vary, e.g., the British monarch is a very old and comfortable custom with the British people. He or she provides them a needed ceremonial head of the nation of whom they are proud. Most Americans would be opposed to an American monarch because the notion defies our political traditions.
2. Answers will vary, e.g., the United States should have a ceremonial head to free the president's time for more serious business. The Congress should maintain closer contact with the executive.
3. Answers will vary, e.g., in the long run the economy would be healthier. In the short run many who benefit from government intervention would suffer and would not allow it to happen.

CHAPTER 26 REVIEW—Continued

In a command economic system, the government controls the means of production and the individual has very little influence over how the economy functions. In a market economic system, government does not intervene: Individuals own the means of production and make decisions based on the trends of the market. Today, almost all economic systems are mixed economies; some contain more characteristics of a command economy and some more closely resemble a market economy.

5. A pure market economic system has six major characteristics: little or no government control, freedom of enterprise, freedom of choice, private property, profit incentive, and competition. In the United States, the government's role in the economy is much greater than it would be if it were a pure market system. Capitalism is defined as an economic system in which private individuals own the means of production.

6. Many of the former centrally planned socialist and communist countries in Eastern Europe and the former Soviet Union (and the People's Republic of China) based their economic theories on the works of Karl Marx, whose most important book was *Das Kapital,* written in 1867. Marx outlined his labor theory of value and talked about capitalists exploiting the surplus value of the workers. He predicted the eventual failure of capitalism. He believed that socialism and communism would ultimately prevail. The break-up of the former Soviet Union and its satellite countries has proven Marx to be incorrect. China remains a socialist country, but is gradually opening up larger and larger parts to capitalism.

Review Questions

1. What is the difference between the United States Constitution and the British Constitution?
2. How does the British Parliament differ from the United States Congress?
3. What is meant by the term *government* in Great Britain?
4. What are the powers of the French president?
5. Why is the French parliamentary system unique?
6. What limits the French Parliament's lawmaking powers?
7. What is the difference between American, British, and French political parties?
8. What is the similarity between the French and British local governments?
9. What are the key aspects of the Japanese constitution?
10. How is the Japanese legislature formed?
11. Who performs the executive functions of government in Japan and are they separate from the legislative branch?
12. Briefly describe the command and market economic systems.
13. Why are most economies considered mixed?
14. List the six major characteristics of a pure market economic system.
15. Briefly describe Adam Smith's idea of competition and how he viewed the role of government in the economy.
16. Why is the United States called a free enterprise system?
17. What role does profit play in capitalism?
18. What were some of the predictions that Marx made?
19. What happened to most of the world's communist countries between 1989 and 1991?
20. How is China governed?
21. Describe the goals of Amnesty International.

Questions for Thought and Discussion

1. Why do you think Great Britain continues to have a monarch even though his or her role is now mainly ceremonial? How do you think most American people would react to a monarch in this country?
2. What, if any, features of other nations' governments do you think should be incorporated into our government? Give reasons for your answer.
3. Some people think that the United States' government should play no role in the economy and that we should work toward a pure free-enterprise economy. What do you think the benefits of such an arrangement would be? What would be the problems?

Improving Your Skills
Communication Skills

Determining the Strength of an Argument

Whether you are doing research, debating an issue, or listening to the argument of a friend, teacher, or sales-

Observable Mastery
Have students prepare a chart which compares and contrasts the governmental organization of Great Britain, Japan, France, and the United States. Major characteristics such as legislative structure and powers, executive power, method of selection, and terms of office should be included. Provide for a miscellaneous section that could include historical facts and important personalities.

This can be done as a class or in groups. If you choose to conduct this exercise in groups each group could complete a chart on one nation, or each group could do all nations, and the results could be compared. Display the finished products in the classroom.

CHAPTER 26 REVIEW—Continued

person, it is important to be able to determine the strength of an argument. It is sometimes easy to be persuaded by an overbearing writer or speaker, by flowery language, or by the manner in which the argument is presented. To assess the strength of an argument, you must look past these elements to examine the evidence and the reasons that the argument uses as a basis.

This skill is also critical when you are presenting an argument. Just presenting an opinion is not enough. You also must support your argument with evidence and sound reasoning. Ask these questions to determine the strength of your own or another's arguments:

- Is the argument stated in the clearest and most understandable way?
- What evidence, if any, is used to support the argument? Is the evidence relevant and accurate?
- What reasons are presented for making the argument? Do they directly relate to the issue?
- Are there enough reasons and evidence to support the argument, or are more needed?
- Has important evidence been left out that would weaken or disprove the argument?
- Would an unbiased person hearing the argument, evidence, and reasons be convinced?

Writing Exercise

Listen to a speech or debate, taking notes on what you hear. After the event, review your notes and write out answers to the questions above. Then write a paragraph explaining your opinion on the strengths of the arguments presented.

Social Studies Skills

Comparing Similarities and Differences

In your study of other governments and economic systems, you cannot help but make comparisons of both the similarities and differences. Also, it is natural to compare what is new and different with what you already know. Specifically, you might automatically compare the parliamentary system of Britain with the way the United States political system operates. When you read about command socialism in China, you might automatically compare it to the more-or-less decentralized capitalist system in the United States.

Consider the British and the French political systems. Reread the sections on them before you answer the following questions.

1. In what ways is the selection of the prime minister the same or different?
2. What are the similarities between the French Senate and the British House of Lords? What are the differences?
3. Does the prime minister in each country have about the same amount of power? If the answer is no, explain your answer.
4. Explain the similarities and differences between the way in which a national law becomes effective in each country.
5. The two systems are both called parliamentary. Does that mean they are the same? If your answer is no, explain your answer.

Activities and Projects

1. Create a bulletin board display that compares the main features of the governments discussed in this chapter.
2. Research the political system of a country not discussed in this chapter, such as Mexico, South Africa, or India. Write a report comparing the government of the country to that of the United States.
3. Find a person in your community who is originally from another country. Interview that person to get his or her impressions on the differences and similarities between the governmental and economic systems in his or her native country and in the United States. Find out his or her opinions about which systems work better, and what kinds of experiences he or she has had with either government.

THE RESOURCE CENTER

CONTENTS

Original Source Documents

Constitution of the United States of America*

The Preamble

We the People of the United States, in Order to form a more perfect Union, establish Justice, insure domestic Tranquility, provide for the common defence, promote the general Welfare, and secure the Blessings of Liberty to ourselves and our Posterity, do ordain and establish this Constitution for the United States of America.

The Preamble declares that "We the People" are the authority for the Constitution (unlike the Articles of Confederation, which derived their authority from the states). The Preamble also sets out the purposes of the Constitution.

Article I. (Legislative Branch)

The first part of the Constitution is called Article I; it deals with the organization and powers of the lawmaking branch of the national government, the Congress.

Section 1. Legislative Powers

All legislative Powers herein granted shall be vested in a Congress of the United States, which shall consist of a Senate and House of Representatives.

Section 2. House of Representatives

Clause 1: Composition and Election of Members. The House of Representatives shall be composed of Members chosen every second Year by the People of the several States, and the Electors in each State shall have the Qualifications requisite for Electors of the most numerous Branch of the State Legislature.

Each state has the power to decide who may vote for members of Congress. Within each state, those who may vote for state legislators may also vote for members of the House of Representatives (and, under the Seventeenth Amendment, for U.S. senators). When the Constitution was written, nearly all states limited voting rights to white male property owners or taxpayers at least twenty-one years old. Subsequent amendments granted voting power to African-American men, all women, and eighteen-year-olds.

Clause 2: Qualifications. No Person shall be a Representative who shall not have attained to the Age of twenty five Years, and been seven Years a Citizen of the United States, and who shall not, when elected, be an Inhabitant of that State in which he shall be chosen.

Each member of the House must (1) be at least twenty-five years old, (2) have been a U.S. citizen for at least seven years, and (3) be a resident of the state in which she or he is elected.

Clause 3: Apportionment of Representatives and Direct Taxes. Representatives [and direct Taxes][1] shall be apportioned among the several States which may be included within this Union, according to their respective Numbers [which shall be determined by adding to the whole Number of free Persons, including those bound to Service for a Term of Years, and excluding Indians not taxed, three fifths of all other Persons].[2] The actual Enumeration shall be made within three Years after the first Meeting of the Congress of the United States, and within every subsequent Term of ten Years, in such Manner as they shall by Law direct. The Number of Representatives shall not exceed one for every thirty Thousand, but each State shall have at Least one Representative; and until such enumeration shall be made, the State of New Hampshire shall be entitled to chuse three, Massachusetts eight, Rhode Island and Providence Plantations one, Connecticut five, New York six, New Jersey four, Pennsylvania eight, Delaware one, Maryland six, Virginia ten, North Carolina five, South Carolina five, and Georgia three.

*The spelling, capitalization, and punctuation of the original have been retained here. Brackets indicate passages that have been altered by amendments to the Constitution.

[1]Modified by the Sixteenth Amendment.
[2]Modified by the Fourteenth Amendment.

A state's representation in the House is based on the size of its population. Population is counted in each decade's census, after which Congress reapportions House seats. Since early in this century, the number of seats has been limited to 435.

Clause 4: Vacancies. When vacancies happen in the Representation from any State, the Executive Authority thereof shall issue Writs of Election to fill such Vacancies.

The "Executive Authority" is the state's governor. When a vacancy occurs in the House, the governor calls a special election to fill it.

Clause 5: Officers and Impeachment. The House of Representatives shall chuse their Speaker and other Officers; and shall have the sole Power of Impeachment.

The power to impeach is the power to accuse. In this case, it is the power to accuse members of the executive or judicial branch of wrongdoing or abuse of power. Once a bill of impeachment is issued, the Senate holds the trial.

Section 3. The Senate

Clause 1: Term and Number of Members. The Senate of the United States shall be composed of two Senators from each State [chosen by the Legislature thereof],[3] for six Years; and each Senator shall have one Vote.

Every state has two senators, each of whom serves for six years, and has one vote in the upper chamber. Since the Seventeenth Amendment in 1913, all senators are elected directly by voters of the state during the regular election.

Clause 2: Classification of Senators. Immediately after they shall be assembled in Consequence of the first Election, they shall be divided as equally as may be into three Classes. The Seats of the Senators of the first Class shall be vacated at the Expiration of the second Year, of the second Class at the Expiration of the fourth Year, and of the third Class at the Expiration of the sixth Year, so that one third may be chosen every second Year; [and if Vacancies happen by Resignation, or otherwise, during the Recess of the Legislature of any State, the Executive thereof may make temporary Appointments until the next Meeting of the Legislature, which shall then fill such Vacancies].[4]

One-third of the Senate's seats are open to election every two years (unlike the House, all of whose members are elected simultaneously).

[3]Repealed by the Seventeenth Amendment.
[4]Modified by the Seventeenth Amendment.

Clause 3: Qualifications. No Person shall be a Senator who shall not have attained to the Age of thirty Years, and been nine Years a Citizen of the United States, and who shall not, when elected, be an Inhabitant of that State for which he shall be chosen.

Every senator must be at least thirty years old, a citizen of the United States for a minimum of nine years, and a resident of the state in which he or she is elected.

Clause 4: The Role of the Vice President. The Vice President of the United States shall be President of the Senate, but shall have no Vote, unless they be equally divided.

The vice-president presides over meetings of the Senate but cannot vote unless there is a tie. The Constitution gives no other official duties to the vice-president.

Clause 5: Other Officers. The Senate shall chuse their other Officers, and also a President pro tempore, in the Absence of the Vice President, or when he shall exercise the Office of President of the United States.

When the vice-president is absent, the Senate votes for one of its members to preside; this person is usually called the president pro tempore because of the temporary situation of the position.

Clause 6: Impeachment Trials. The Senate shall have the sole Power to try all Impeachments. When sitting for that Purpose, they shall be on Oath or Affirmation. When the President of the United States is tried, the Chief Justice shall preside: And no Person shall be convicted without the Concurrence of two thirds of the Members present.

The Senate conducts trials of officials that the House impeaches. The Senate sits as a jury, with the vice-president presiding if the president is not on trial.

Clause 7: Penalties for Conviction. Judgment in Cases of Impeachment shall not extend further than to removal from Office, and disqualification to hold and enjoy any Office of honor, Trust, or Profit under the United States: but the Party convicted shall nevertheless be liable and subject to Indictment, Trial, Judgment, and Punishment, according to Law.

On conviction on impeachment charges, the Senate can only force an official to leave office and prevent him or her from holding another office in the federal government. The individual, however, can still be tried in a regular court.

Section 4. Congressional Elections: Times, Manner, and Places

Clause 1: Elections. The Times, Places and Manner of holding Elections for Senators and Representatives, shall be prescribed in each State by the Legislature thereof; but the Congress may at any time by Law make or alter such Regulations, except as to the Places of chusing Senators.

Congress set the Tuesday after the first Monday in November in even-numbered years as the date for congressional elections. In states with more than one seat in the House, Congress requires that representatives be elected from districts within each state. Under the Seventeenth Amendment, senators are elected at the same places as other officials.

Clause 2: Sessions of Congress. [The Congress shall assemble at least once in every Year, and such Meeting shall be on the first Monday in December, unless they shall by Law appoint a different Day.][5]

Congress has to meet every year at least once. The regular session now begins at noon on January 3 of each year, subsequent to the Twentieth Amendment, unless Congress passes a law to fix a different date. Congress stays in session until its members vote to adjourn. Additionally, the president may call a special session.

Section 5. Powers and Duties of the Houses

Clause 1: Admitting Members and Quorum. Each House shall be the Judge of the Elections, Returns, and Qualifications of its own Members, and a Majority of each shall constitute a Quorum to do Business; but a smaller Number may adjourn from day to day, and may be authorized to compel the Attendance of absent Members, in such Manner, and under such Penalties as each House may provide.

Each chamber may exclude or refuse to seat a member-elect.

The quorum rule requires that 218 members of the House and 51 members of the Senate be present in order to conduct business. This rule is normally not enforced in the handling of routine matters.

Clause 2: Rules and Discipline of Members. Each House may determine the Rules of its Proceedings, punish its Members for disorderly Behaviour, and, with the Concurrence of two thirds, expel a Member.

The House and the Senate may adopt their own rules to guide their proceedings. Each may also discipline its members for conduct that is deemed unacceptable. No member may be expelled without a two-thirds majority.

Clause 3: Keeping a Record. Each House shall keep a Journal of its Proceedings, and from time to time publish the same, excepting such Parts as may in their Judgment require Secrecy; and the Yeas and Nays of the Members of either House on any question shall, at the Desire of one fifth of those Present, be entered on the Journal.

The journals of the two houses are published at the end of each session of Congress.

Clause 4: Adjournment. Neither House, during the Session of Congress, shall, without the Consent of the other, adjourn for more than three days, nor to any other Place than that in which the two Houses shall be sitting.

Congress has the power to determine when and where to meet, provided, however, that both houses meet in the same city. Neither house may recess in excess of three days without the consent of the other.

Section 6. Rights of Members

Clause 1: Compensation and Privileges. The Senators and Representatives shall receive a Compensation for their services, to be ascertained by Law, and paid out of the Treasury of the United States. They shall in all Cases, except Treason, Felony and Breach of the Peace, be privileged from Arrest during their Attendance at the Session of their respective Houses, and in going to and returning from the same; and for any Speech or Debate in either House, they shall not be questioned in any other Place.

Congressional salaries are to be paid by the U.S. Treasury rather than by the members' respective states. The original salaries were $6 per day; in 1857 they were $3,000 per year. Both representatives and senators currently are paid $125,100 each year.

Members cannot be arrested for things they say during speeches and debates in Congress. This immunity applies to the Capitol Building itself and not to their private lives.

Treason is defined in Article III, Section 3. A felony is any serious crime. A breach of the peace is any indictable

[5]Changed by the Twentieth Amendment.

offense less than treason or a felony. Members cannot be arrested for anything they say in speeches or debates in Congress.

Clause 2: Restrictions. No Senator or Representative shall, during the Time for which he was elected, be appointed to any civil Office under the Authority of the United States, which shall have been created, or the Emoluments whereof shall have been encreased during such time; and no Person holding any Office under the United States, shall be a Member of either House during his Continuance in Office.

During the term for which a member was elected, he or she cannot concurrently accept another federal government position.

Section 7. Legislative Powers: Bills and Resolutions

Clause 1: Revenue Bills. All Bills for raising Revenue shall originate in the House of Representatives; but the Senate may propose or concur with Amendments as on other Bills.

All tax and appropriation bills for raising money have to originate in the House of Representatives. The Senate, though, often amends such bills and may even substitute an entirely different bill.

Clause 2: The Presidential Veto. Every Bill which shall have passed the House of Representatives and the Senate, shall, before it becomes a Law, be presented to the President of the United States; If he approve he shall sign it, but if not he shall return it, with his Objections to the House in which it shall have originated, who shall enter the Objections at large on their Journal, and proceed to reconsider it. If after such Reconsideration two thirds of that House shall agree to pass the Bill, it shall be sent together with the Objections, to the other House, by which it shall likewise be reconsidered, and if approved by two thirds of that House, it shall become a Law. But in all such Cases the Votes of both Houses shall be determined by Yeas and Nays, and the Names of the Persons voting for and against the Bill shall be entered on the Journal of each House respectively. If any Bill shall not be returned by the President within ten Days (Sundays excepted) after it shall have been presented to him, the Same shall be a Law, in like Manner as if he had signed it, unless the Congress by their Adjournment prevent its Return in which Case it shall not be a Law.

When Congress sends the president a bill, he or she can sign it (in which case it becomes law) or send it back to the house in which it originated. If it is sent back, a two-thirds majority of each house must pass it again for it to become law. If the president neither signs it nor sends it back within ten days, it becomes law anyway, unless Congress adjourns in the meantime.

Clause 3: Actions on Other Matters. Every Order, Resolution, or Vote to which the Concurrence of the Senate and House of Representatives may be necessary (except on a question of Adjournment) shall be presented to the President of the United States; and before the Same shall take Effect, shall be approved by him, or being disapproved by him, shall be repassed by two thirds of the Senate and House of Representatives, according to the Rules and Limitations prescribed in the Case of a Bill.

The president must either sign or veto everything that Congress passes, except votes to adjourn and resolutions not having the force of law.

Section 8. The Powers of Congress

Clause 1: Taxing. The Congress shall have Power To lay and collect Taxes, Duties, Imposts and Excises, to pay the Debts and provide for the common Defence and general Welfare of the United States; but all Duties, Imposts and Excises shall be uniform throughout the United States;

Duties are taxes on imports and exports. Impost is a generic term for tax. Excises are taxes on the manufacture, sale, or use of goods.

Clause 2: Borrowing. To borrow Money on the credit of the United States;

Congress has the power to borrow money, which is normally carried out through the sale of U.S. treasury bonds on which interest is paid. Note that the Constitution places no limit on the amount of government borrowing.

Clause 3: Regulation of Commerce. To regulate Commerce with foreign Nations, and among the several States, and with the Indian Tribes;

This is the Commerce Clause, which gives to the Congress the power to regulate interstate and foreign trade. Much of the activity of Congress is based on this clause.

Clause 4: Naturalization and Bankruptcy. To establish a uniform Rule of Naturalization, and uniform Laws on the subject of Bankruptcies throughout the United States;

Only Congress may determine how aliens can become citizens of the United States. Congress may make laws with respect to bankruptcy.

Clause 5: Money and Standards. To coin Money, regulate the Value thereof, and of foreign Coin, and fix the Standard of Weights and Measures;

Congress mints coins and prints and circulates paper money. Congress can establish uniform measures of time, distance, weight, etc. In 1838 Congress adopted the English system of weights and measurements as our national standard.

Clause 6: Punishing Counterfeiters. To provide for the Punishment of counterfeiting the Securities and current Coin of the United States;

Congress has the power to punish those who copy American money and pass it off as real. Currently, the fine is up to $5,000 and/or imprisonment for up to fifteen years.

Clause 7: Roads and Post Offices. To establish Post Offices and post Roads;

Post roads include all routes over which mail is carried—highways, railways, waterways, and airways.

Clause 8: Patents and Copyrights. To promote the Progress of Science and useful Arts, by securing for limited Times to Authors and Inventors the exclusive Right to their respective Writings and Discoveries;

Authors' and composers' works are protected by copyrights established by copyright law, which currently is the 1978 Copyright Act. Copyrights are valid for the life of the author or composer plus fifty years. Inventors' works are protected by patents, which vary in length of protection from three and a half to seventeen years. A patent gives a person the exclusive right to control the manufacture or sale of her or his invention.

Clause 9: Lower Courts. To constitute Tribunals inferior to the supreme Court;

Congress has the authority to set up all federal courts, except the Supreme Court, and to decide what cases those courts will hear.

Clause 10: Punishment for Piracy. To define and punish Piracies and Felonies committed on the high Seas, and Offences against the Law of Nations;

Congress has the authority to prohibit the commission of certain acts outside U.S. territory and to punish certain violations of international law.

Clause 11: Declaration of War. To declare War, grant Letters of Marque and Reprisal, and make Rules concerning Captures on Land and Water;

Only Congress can declare war, although the president, as commander in chief, can make war without Congress's formal declaration. Letters of marque and reprisal authorized private parties to capture and destroy enemy ships in wartime. Since the mid-nineteenth century, international law has prohibited letters of marque and reprisal, and the United States has honored the ban.

Clause 12: The Army. To raise and support Armies, but no Appropriation of Money to that Use shall be for a longer Term than two Years;

Congress has the power to create an army; the money used to pay for it must be appropriated for no more than two-year intervals. This latter restriction gives ultimate control of the army to civilians.

Clause 13: Creation of a Navy. To provide and maintain a Navy;

This clause allows for the maintenance of a navy. In 1947 Congress created the air force.

Clause 14: Regulation of the Armed Forces. To make Rules for the Government and Regulation of the land and naval Forces;

Congress sets the rules for the military mainly by way of the Uniform Code of Military Justice, which was enacted in 1950 by Congress.

Clause 15: The Militia. To provide for calling forth the Militia to execute the Laws of the Union, suppress Insurrections and repel Invasions;

The militia is known today as the National Guard. Both Congress and the president have the authority to call the National Guard into federal service.

Clause 16: How the Militia is Organized. To provide for organizing, arming, and disciplining the Militia, and for governing such Part of them as may be employed in the Service of the United States, reserving to the States respectively, the Appointment of the Officers, and the Authority of training the Militia according to the discipline prescribed by Congress;

This clause gives Congress the power to "federalize" state militia (National Guard). When called into such service, the National Guard is subject to the same rules that Congress has set forth for the regular armed services.

Clause 17: Creation of the District of Columbia. To exercise exclusive Legislation in all Cases whatsoever, over such District (not exceeding ten Miles square) as may, by Cession of particular States, and the Acceptance of Congress, become the Seat of the Government of the United States, and to exercise like Authority over all Places purchased by the Consent of the Legislature of the State in which the Same shall be, for the Erection of Forts, Magazines, Arsenals, dock-Yards, and other needful Buildings;—And

Congress established the District of Columbia as the national capital in 1791. Virginia and Maryland had granted land for the District, but Virginia's grant was returned because it was believed it would not be needed. Today, the District is sixty-nine miles square.

Clause 18: The Elastic Clause. To make all Laws which shall be necessary and proper for carrying into Execution the foregoing Powers, and all other Powers vested by this Constitution in the Government of the United States, or in any Department or Officer thereof.

This clause—the Necessary and Proper Clause, or the Elastic Clause—grants no specific powers, and thus it can be stretched to fit different circumstances. It has allowed Congress to adapt the government to changing needs and times.

Section 9. The Powers Denied to Congress

Clause 1: Question of Slavery. The Migration or Importation of such Persons as any of the States now existing shall think proper to admit, shall not be prohibited by the Congress prior to the Year one thousand eight hundred and eight, but a Tax or duty may be imposed on such Importation, not exceeding ten dollars for each Person.

"Persons" referred to slaves. Congress outlawed the slave trade in 1808.

Clause 2: Habeas Corpus. The privilege of the Writ of Habeas Corpus shall not be suspended, unless when in Cases of Rebellion or Invasion the public Safety may require it.

A writ of habeas corpus is a court order directing a sheriff or other public officer who is detaining another person to "produce the body" of the detainee so the court can assess the legality of the detention.

Clause 3: Special Bills. No Bill of Attainder or ex post facto Law shall be passed.

A bill of attainder is a law that inflicts punishment without a trial. An ex post facto law is a law that inflicts punishment for an act that was not illegal when it was committed.

Clause 4: Direct Taxes. [No Capitation, or other direct, Tax shall be laid, unless in Proportion to the Census or Enumeration herein before directed to be taken.][6]

A capitation is a tax on a person. A direct tax is a tax paid directly to the government, such as a property tax. This clause was intended to prevent Congress from levying a tax on slaves per person and thereby taxing slavery out of existence.

Clause 5: Export Taxes. No Tax or Duty shall be laid on Articles exported from any State.

Congress may not tax any goods sold from one state to another or from one state to a foreign country. (Congress does have the power to tax goods that are bought from other countries, however.)

Clause 6: Interstate Commerce. No Preference shall be given by any Regulation of Commerce or Revenue to the Ports of one State over those of another: nor shall Vessels bound to, or from, one State, be obliged to enter, clear, or pay Duties in another.

Congress may not treat different ports within the United States differently in terms of taxing and commerce powers. Congress may not tax goods sent from one state to another. Finally, Congress may not give one state's port a legal advantage over those of another state.

Clause 7: Treasury Withdrawals. No Money shall be drawn from the Treasury, but in Consequence of Appropriations made by Law; and a regular Statement and Account of the Receipts and Expenditures of all public Money shall be published from time to time.

Federal funds can be spent only as Congress authorizes. This is a significant check on the president's power.

[6]Modified by the Sixteenth Amendment.

Clause 8: Titles of Nobility. No Title of Nobility shall be granted by the United States: And no Person holding any Office of Profit or Trust under them, shall, without the Consent of the Congress, accept of any present, Emolument, Office, or Title, of any kind whatever, from any King, Prince, or foreign State.

No person in the United States may be bestowed a title of nobility such as a duke or duchess. This clause also discourages bribery of American officials by foreign governments.

Section 10. Those Powers Denied to the States

Clause 1: Treaties and Coinage. No State shall enter into any Treaty, Alliance, or Confederation; grant Letters of Marque and Reprisal; coin Money; emit Bills of Credit; make any Thing but gold and silver Coin a Tender in Payment of Debts; pass any Bill of Attainder, ex post facto Law, or Law impairing the Obligation of Contracts, or grant any Title of Nobility.

Prohibiting state laws "impairing the Obligation of Contracts" was intended to protect creditors. (Shays's Rebellion—an attempt to prevent courts from giving effect to creditors' legal actions against debtors—occurred only one year before the Constitution was written.)

Clause 2: Duties and Imposts. No State shall, without the Consent of the Congress, lay any Imports or Duties on Imports or Exports, except what may be absolutely necessary for executing its inspection Laws; and the net Produce of all Duties and Imposts, laid by any State on Imports or Exports, shall be for the Use of the Treasury of the United States; and all such Laws shall be subject to the Revision and Controul of the Congress.

Only Congress can tax imports. Further, the states cannot tax exports.

Clause 3: War. No State shall, without the Consent of Congress, lay any Duty of Tonnage, keep Troops, or Ships of War in time of Peace, enter into any Agreement or Compact with another State, or with a foreign Power or engage in War, unless actually invaded, or in such imminent Danger as will not admit of delay.

A duty of tonnage is a tax on ships according to their cargo capacity. No states may effectively tax ships according to their cargo unless Congress agrees. Additionally, this clause forbids any state to keep troops or warships during peacetime or to make a compact with another state or foreign nation unless Congress so agrees. States can, in contrast, maintain a militia, but its use has to be limited to internal disorders that occur within a state—unless, of course, the militia is called into federal service.

Article II. (Executive Branch)

Section 1. The Nature and Scope of Presidential Power

Clause 1: Four-Year Term. The executive Power shall be vested in a President of the United States of America. He shall hold his Office during the Term of four Years, and, together with the Vice President, chosen for the same Term, be elected, as follows.

The president has the power to carry out laws made by Congress, called the executive power. He or she serves in office for a four-year term after election. The Twenty-second Amendment limits the number of times a person may be elected president.

Clause 2: Choosing Electors From Each State. Each State shall appoint, in such Manner as the Legislature thereof may direct, a Number of Electors, equal to the whole Number of Senators and Representatives to which the State may be entitled in the Congress; but no Senator or Representative, or Person holding an Office of Trust or Profit under the United States, shall be appointed an Elector.

The "Electors" are more commonly known as the "electoral college." The president is elected by electors—that is, representatives chosen by the people—rather than by the people directly.

Clause 3: The Former System of Elections. [The Electors shall meet in their respective States, and vote by Ballot for two Persons, of whom one at least shall not be an Inhabitant of the same State with themselves. And they shall make a List of all the Persons voted for, and of the Number of Votes for each; which List they shall sign and certify, and transmit sealed to the Seat of the Government of the United States, directed to the President of the Senate. The President of the Senate shall, in the Presence of the Senate and House of Representatives, open all the Certificates, and the Votes shall then be counted. The Person having the greatest Number of Votes shall be the President, if such Number be a Majority of the whole Number of Electors appointed; and if there be more than one who have such Majority, and have an equal Number of Votes, then the

House of Representatives shall immediately chuse by Ballot one of them for President; and if no Person have a Majority, then from the five highest on the List the said House shall in like Manner chuse the President. But in chusing the President, the Votes shall be taken by States, the Representation from each State having one Vote; A quorum for this Purpose shall consist of a Member or Members from two thirds of the States, and a Majority of all the States shall be necessary to a Choice. In every Case, after the Choice of the President, the Person having the greater Number of Votes of the Electors shall be the Vice President. But if there should remain two or more who have equal Votes, the Senate shall chuse from them by Ballot the Vice President.][7]

The original method of selecting the president and vice-president was replaced by the Twelfth Amendment. Apparently, the framers did not anticipate the rise of political parties and the development of primaries and conventions.

Clause 4: The Time of Elections. The Congress may determine the Time of chusing the Electors, and the Day on which they shall give their Votes; which Day shall be the same throughout the United States.

Congress set the Tuesday after the first Monday in November every fourth year as the date for choosing electors. The electors cast their votes on the Monday after the second Wednesday in December of that year.

Clause 5: Qualifications for President. No person except a natural born Citizen, or a Citizen of the United States, at the time of the Adoption of this Constitution, shall be eligible to the Office of President; neither shall any Person be eligible to that Office who shall not have attained to the Age of thirty five Years, and been fourteen Years a Resident within the United States.

The president must be a natural-born citizen, be at least thirty-five years of age when taking office, and have been a resident within the United States for at least fourteen years.

Clause 6: Succession of the Vice President. [In Case of the Removal of the President from Office, or of his Death, Resignation or Inability to discharge the Powers and Duties of the said Office, the same shall devolve on the Vice President, and the Congress may by Law provide for the Case of Removal, Death, Resignation or Inability, both of the President and Vice President, declaring what Officer shall then act as President, and such Officer shall act accordingly, until the Disability be removed, or a President shall be elected.][8]

This former provision provided for the method by which the vice-president was to succeed to the presidency, but its wording is ambiguous. It was replaced by the Twenty-fifth Amendment.

Clause 7: The President's Salary. The President shall, at stated Times, receive for his Services, a Compensation, which shall neither be encreased nor diminished during the Period for which he shall have been elected, and he shall not receive within that Period any other Emolument from the United States, or any of them.

The president maintains the same salary during each four-year term. Moreover, she or he may not receive additional cash payments from the government. Originally set at $25,000 per year, it is currently $200,000 a year plus a $50,000 taxable expense account.

Clause 8: The Oath of Office. Before he enter on the Execution of his Office, he shall take the following Oath or Affirmation: ''I do solemnly swear (or affirm) that I will faithfully execute the Office of President of the United States, and will to the best of my Ability, preserve, protect and defend the Constitution of the United States.''

The president is ''sworn in'' prior to beginning the duties of the office. Currently, the taking of the oath of office occurs on January 20, following the November election. The ceremony is called the inauguration. The oath of office is administered by the chief justice of the United States Supreme Court.

Section 2. Powers of the President

Clause 1: Commander in Chief. The President shall be Commander in Chief of the Army and Navy of the United States, and of the Militia of the several States, when called into the actual Service of the United States; he may require the Opinion, in writing, of the principal Officer in each of the executive Departments, upon any Subject relating to the Duties of their respective Offices, and he shall have Power to grant Reprieves and Pardons for Offences against the United States, except in Cases of Impeachment.

The armed forces are placed under civilian control because the president is a civilian, but still commander in chief of the military. The president may ask for the help

[7]Changed by the Twelfth Amendment.

[8]Modified by the Twenty-fifth Amendment.

of the heads of each of the executive departments (thereby creating the Cabinet). The Cabinet members are chosen by the president with the consent of the Senate, but they can be removed without Senate approval.

The president's clemency powers extend only to federal cases. In those cases, he or she may grant a full or conditional pardon, or reduce a prison term or fine.

Clause 2: Treaties and Appointment. He shall have Power, by and with the Advice and Consent of the Senate, to make Treaties, provided two thirds of the Senators present concur; and he shall nominate, and by and with the Advice and Consent of the Senate, shall appoint Ambassadors, other public Ministers and Consuls, Judges of the supreme Court, and all other Officers of the United States, whose Appointments are not herein otherwise provided for, and which shall be established by Law; but the Congress may by Law vest the Appointment of such inferior Officers, as they think proper, in the President alone, in the Courts of Law, or in the Heads of Departments.

Many of the major powers of the president are identified in this clause, including the power to make treaties with foreign governments (with the approval of the Senate by a two-thirds vote) and the power to appoint ambassadors, Supreme Court justices, and other government officials. Most such appointments require Senate approval.

Clause 3: Vacancies. The President shall have Power to fill up all Vacancies that may happen during the Recess of the Senate, by granting Commissions which shall expire at the end of their next Session.

The president has the power to appoint temporary officials to fill vacant federal offices without Senate approval if the Congress is not in session. Such appointments expire automatically at the end of Congress's next term.

Section 3. Duties of the President

He shall from time to time give to the Congress Information of the State of the Union, and recommend to their Consideration such Measures as he shall judge necessary and expedient; he may, on extraordinary Occasions, convene both Houses, or either of them, and in Case of Disagreement between them, with Respect to the Time of Adjournment, he may adjourn them to such Time as he shall think proper; he shall receive Ambassadors and other public Ministers; he shall take Care that the Laws be faithfully executed, and shall Commission all the Officers of the United States.

Annually, the president reports on the state of the union to Congress, recommends legislative measures, and proposes a federal budget. The State of the Union speech is a statement not only to Congress but also to the American people. After it is given, the president proposes a federal budget and presents an economic report. At any time he or she so chooses, the president may send special messages to Congress while it is in session. The president has the power to call special sessions, to adjourn Congress when its two houses do not agree for that purpose, to receive diplomatic representatives of other governments, and to ensure the proper execution of all federal laws. The president further has the ability to empower federal officers to hold their positions and to perform their duties.

Section 4. Impeachment

The President, Vice President and all civil Officers of the United States, shall be removed from Office on Impeachment for, and Conviction of, Treason, Bribery, or other high Crimes and Misdemeanors.

Treason denotes giving aid to the nation's enemies. The definition of high crimes and misdemeanors is usually given as serious abuses of political power. In either case, the president or vice-president may be accused by the House (called an impeachment) and then removed from office if convicted by the Senate. (Note that impeachment *does not mean removal, but rather the state of being accused of treason or high crimes and misdemeanors.)*

Article III. (Judicial Branch)

Section 1. Judicial Powers, Courts, and Judges

The judicial Power of the United States, shall be vested in one supreme Court, and in such inferior Courts as the Congress may from time to time ordain and establish. The Judges, both of the supreme and inferior Courts, shall hold their Offices during good Behaviour, and shall, at stated Times, receive for their Services a Compensation, which shall not be diminished during their Continuance in Office.

The Supreme Court is vested with judicial power, as are the lower federal courts that Congress creates. Federal judges serve in their offices for life unless they are impeached and convicted by Congress. The payment of federal judges may not be reduced during their time in office.

Section 2. Jurisdiction

Clause 1: Cases Under Federal Jurisdiction. The judicial Power shall extend to all Cases, in Law and Equity, arising under this Constitution, the Laws of the United States, and Treaties made, or which shall be made, under their Authority;—to all Cases affecting Ambassadors, other public Ministers and Consuls;—to all Cases of admiralty and maritime Jurisdiction;—to Controversies to which the United States shall be a Party;—to Controversies between two or more States; [—between a State and Citizens of another State;—][9] between Citizens of different States;—between Citizens of the same State claiming Lands under Grants of different States, [and between a State, or the Citizens thereof, and foreign States, Citizens or Subjects.][10]

The federal courts take on cases that concern the meaning of the U.S. Constitution, all federal laws, and treaties. They also can take on cases involving citizens of different states and citizens of foreign nations.

Clause 2: Cases for the Supreme Court. In all Cases affecting Ambassadors, other public Ministers and Consuls, and those in which a State shall be a Party, the supreme Court shall have original Jurisdiction. In all the other Cases before mentioned, the supreme Court shall have appellate Jurisdiction, both as to Law and Fact, with such Exceptions, and under such Regulations as the Congress shall make.

In a limited number of situations, the Supreme Court acts as a trial court and has original jurisdiction. These cases involve a representative from another country or involve a state. In all other situations, the cases must first be tried in the lower courts and then can be appealed to the Supreme Court. Congress may, however, make exceptions. Today the Supreme Court acts as a trial court of first instance on rare occasions.

Clause 3: The Conduct of Trials. The Trial of all Crimes, except in Cases of Impeachment, shall be by Jury; and such Trial shall be held in the State where the said Crimes shall have been committed; but when not committed within any State, the Trial shall be at such Place or Places as the Congress may by Law have directed.

Any person accused of a federal crime is granted the right to a trial by jury in a federal court in that state in which the crime was committed. Trials of impeachment are an exception.

Section 3. Treason

Clause 1: The Definition of Treason. Treason against the United States, shall consist only in levying War against them, or, in adhering to their Enemies, giving them Aid and Comfort. No Person shall be convicted of Treason unless on the Testimony of two Witnesses to the same overt Act, or on Confession in open Court.

Treason is the making of war against the United States or giving aid to its enemies.

Clause 2: Punishment. The Congress shall have Power to declare the Punishment of Treason, but no Attainder of Treason shall work Corruption of Blood, or Forfeiture except during the Life of the Person attainted.

Congress has provided that the punishment for treason range from a minimum of five years in prison and/or a $10,000 fine to a maximum of death. "No Attainder of Treason shall work Corruption of Blood" prohibits punishment of the traitor's heirs.

Article IV. (Relations Among the States)

Section 1. Full Faith and Credit

Full Faith and Credit shall be given in each State to the public Acts, Records, and judicial Proceedings of every other State. And the Congress may by general Laws prescribe the Manner in which such Acts, Records and Proceedings shall be proved, and the Effect thereof.

All states are required to respect one another's laws, records, and lawful decisions. There are exceptions, however. A state does not have to enforce another state's criminal code. Nor does it have to recognize another state's grant of a divorce if the person obtaining the divorce did not establish legal residence in the state in which it was given.

Section 2. Treatment of Citizens

Clause 1: Privileges and Immunities. The Citizens of each State shall be entitled to all Privileges and Immunities of Citizens in the several States.

A citizen of a state has the same rights and privileges as the citizens of another state in which he or she happens to be.

Clause 2: Extradition. A Person charged in any State with Treason, Felony, or other Crime, who shall flee from Justice, and be found in another State, shall on Demand of the executive Authority of the State from which he fled, be delivered up, to be removed to the State having Jurisdiction of the Crime.

Any person accused of a crime who flees to another state must be returned to the state in which the crime occurred.

[9] Modified by the Eleventh Amendment.
[10] Modified by the Eleventh Amendment.

Clause 3: Fugitive Slaves. [No Person held to Service or Labour in one State, under the Laws thereof, escaping into another, shall, in Consequence of any Law or Regulation therein, be discharged from such Service or Labour, but shall be delivered up on Claim of the Party to whom such Service or Labour may be due.][11]

This clause was struck down by the Thirteenth Amendment, which abolished slavery in 1865.

Section 3. Admission of States

Clause 1: The Process. New States may be admitted by the Congress into this Union; but no new State shall be formed or erected within the Jurisdiction of any other State; nor any State be formed by the Junction of two or more States, or Parts of States, without the Consent of the Legislatures of the States concerned as well as of the Congress.

Only Congress has the power to admit new states to the union. No state may be created by taking territory from an existing state unless the state's legislature so consents.

Clause 2: Public Land. The Congress shall have Power to dispose of and make all needful Rules and Regulations respecting the Territory or other Property belonging to the United States; and nothing in this Constitution shall be so construed as to Prejudice any Claims of the United States, or of any particular State.

The federal government has the exclusive right to administer federal government public lands.

Section 4. Republican Form of Government

The United States shall guarantee to every State in this Union a Republican Form of Government, and shall protect each of them against Invasion; and on Application of the Legislature, or of the Executive (when the Legislature cannot be convened) against domestic Violence.

Each state is promised a form of government in which the people elect their representatives, called a republican form. The federal government is bound to protect states against any attack by foreigners or during times of trouble within a state.

Article V. (Methods of Amendment)

The Congress, whenever two thirds of both Houses shall deem it necessary, shall propose Amendments to this Constitution, or on the Application of the Legislatures of two thirds of the several States, shall call a Convention for proposing Amendments, which, in either Case, shall be valid to all Intents and Purposes, as Part of this Constitution, when ratified by the Legislatures of three fourths of the several States, or by Conventions in three fourths thereof, as the one or the other Mode of Ratification may be proposed by the Congress; Provided that no Amendment which may be made prior to the Year One thousand eight hundred and eight shall in any Manner affect the first and fourth Clauses in the Ninth Section of the First Article; and that no State, without its Consent, shall be deprived of its equal Suffrage in the Senate.

Constitutional Amendments may be proposed by either of two ways: a two-thirds vote of each house (Congress) or by majority vote at a convention called by Congress at the request of two-thirds of the states. Ratification of amendments may be carried out in two ways: by the legislatures of three-fourths of the states or by the voters in three-fourths of the states. No state may be denied equal representation in the Senate.

Article VI. (National Supremacy)

Clause 1: Existing Obligations. All Debts contracted and Engagements entered into, before the Adoption of this Constitution shall be as valid against the United States under this Constitution, as under the Confederation.

During the Revolutionary War and the years of the Confederation, Congress borrowed large sums. This clause pledged that the new federal government would assume those financial obligations.

Clause 2: Supreme Law of the Land. This Constitution, and the Laws of the United States which shall be made in Pursuance thereof; and all Treaties made, or which shall be made, under the Authority of the United States, shall be the supreme Law of the Land; and the Judges in every State shall be bound thereby, any Thing in the Constitution or Laws of any State to the Contrary notwithstanding.

This is typically called the Supremacy Clause; it declares that federal law takes precedence over all forms of state law. No government, at the local or state level, may make or enforce any law that conflicts with any provision of the Constitution, acts of Congress, treaties, or other rules and regulations issued by the president and his or her subordinates in the executive branch of the federal government.

Clause 3: Oath of Office. The Senators and Representatives before mentioned, and the Members of the several

[11]Repealed by the Thirteenth Amendment.

State Legislatures, and all executive and judicial Officers, both of the United States and of the several States, shall be bound by Oath or Affirmation, to support this Constitution; but no religious Test shall ever be required as a Qualification to any Office or public Trust under the United States.

Every federal and state official must take an oath of office promising to support the U.S. Constitution. Religion may not be used as a qualification to serve in any federal office.

Article VII. (Ratification)

The Ratification of the Conventions of nine States shall, be sufficient for the Establishment of this Constitution between the States so ratifying the Same.

Nine states were required to ratify the Constitution. Delaware was the first and New Hampshire the ninth.

Done in Convention by the Unanimous Consent of the States present the Seventeenth Day of September in the Year of our Lord one thousand seven hundred and Eighty seven and of the Independence of the United States of America the Twelfth. In witness whereof we have hereunto subscribed our Names,

Go. WASHINGTON
Presid't. and deputy from Virginia

Attest
WILLIAM JACKSON
Secretary

DELAWARE
Geo. Read
Gunning Bedfordjun
John Dickinson
Richard Basset
Jaco. Broom

MASSACHUSETTS
Nathaniel Gorham
Rufus King

CONNECTICUT
Wm. Saml. Johnson
Roger Sherman

NEW YORK
Alexander Hamilton

NEW JERSEY
Wh. Livingston
David Brearley.
Wm. Paterson.
Jona. Dayton

PENNSYLVANIA
B. Franklin
Thomas Mifflin
Robt. Morris
Geo. Clymer
Thos. FitzSimons
Jared Ingersoll
James Wilson.
Gouv. Morris

NEW HAMPSHIRE
John Langdon
Nicholas Gilman

MARYLAND
James McHenry
Dan of St. Thos. Jenifer
Danl. Carroll.

VIRGINIA
John Blair
James Madison Jr.

NORTH CAROLINA
Wm. Blount
Richd. Dobbs Spaight.
Hu. Williamson

SOUTH CAROLINA
J. Rutledge
Charles Cotesworth Pinckney
Charles Pinckney
Pierce Butler.

GEORGIA
William Few
Abr. Baldwin

Articles in addition to, and amendment of the Constitution of the United States of America, proposed by Congress and ratified by the Legislatures of the several states, pursuant to the Fifth Article of the original Constitution.

Amendments to the Constitution of the United States

The Bill of Rights[12]

Amendment I. Religion, Speech, Assembly, and Politics

Congress shall make no law respecting an establishment of religion, or prohibiting the free exercise thereof; or abridging the freedom of speech, or of the press; or the right of the people peaceably to assembly, and to petition the Government for a redress of grievances.

Congress may not create an official church or enact laws limiting the freedom of religion, speech, the press, assembly, and petition. These guarantees, like the others in the Bill of Rights (the first ten amendments), are not absolute—each may be exercised only with regard to the rights of other persons.

Amendment II. Militia and the Right to Bear Arms

A well regulated Militia, being necessary to the security of a free State, the right of the people to keep and bear Arms, shall not be infringed.

[12]On September 25, 1789, Congress transmitted to the state legislatures twelve proposed amendments, two of which, having to do with Congressional representation and Congressional pay, were not adopted. The remaining ten amendments became the Bill of Rights.

To protect itself, each state has the right to maintain a volunteer armed force. States and the federal government regulate the possession and use of firearms by individuals.

Amendment III. The Quartering of Soldiers

No Soldier shall, in time of peace be quartered in any house, without the consent of the Owner, nor in time of war, but in a manner to be prescribed by law.

Before the Revolutionary War, it had been common British practice to quarter soldiers in colonists' homes. Military troops do not have the power to take over private houses during peacetime.

Amendment IV. Searches and Seizures

The right of the people to be secure in their persons, houses, papers, and effects, against unreasonable searches and seizures, shall not be violated, and no Warrants shall issue, but upon probable cause, supported by Oath or affirmation, and particularly describing the place to be searched, and the persons or things to be seized.

Here the word warrant *means "justification" and refers to a document issued by a magistrate or judge indicating the name, address, and possible offense committed. Anyone asking for the warrant, such as a police officer, must be able to convince the magistrate or judge that an offense probably has been committed.*

Amendment V. Grand Juries, Self-incrimination, Double Jeopardy, Due Process, and Eminent Domain

No person shall be held to answer for a capital, or otherwise infamous crime, unless on a presentment or indictment of a Grand Jury, except in cases arising in the land or naval forces, or in the Militia, when in actual service in time of War or public danger; nor shall any person be subject for the same offence to be twice put in jeopardy of life or limb; nor shall be compelled in any criminal case to be a witness against himself, nor be deprived of life, liberty, or property, without due process of law; nor shall private property be taken for public use, without just compensation.

There are two types of juries. A grand jury considers physical evidence and the testimony of witnesses, and decides whether there is sufficient reason to bring a case to trial. A petit jury hears the case at trial and decides it. "For the same offence to be twice put in jeopardy of life or limb" means to be tried twice for the same crime. A person may not be tried for the same crime twice or forced to give evidence against herself or himself. No person's right to life, liberty, or property may be taken away except by lawful means, called the due process of law. Private property taken for use in public purposes must be paid for by the government.

Amendment VI. Criminal Court Procedures

In all criminal prosecutions, the accused shall enjoy the right to a speedy and public trial, by an impartial jury of the State and district wherein the crime shall have been committed, which district shall have been previously ascertained by law, and to be informed of the nature and cause of the accusation; to be confronted with the witnesses against him; to have compulsory process for obtaining witnesses in his favor, and to have the assistance of counsel for his defence.

Any person accused of a crime has the right to a fair and public trial by a jury in the state in which the crime took place. The charges against that person must be so indicated. Any accused person has the right to a lawyer to defend him or her and to question those who testify against him or her, as well as the right to call people to speak in his or her favor at trial.

Amendment VII. Trial by Jury in Civil Cases

In Suits at common law, where the value in controversy shall exceed twenty dollars, the right of trial by jury shall be preserved, and no fact tried by jury, shall be otherwise re-examined in any Court of the United States, than according to the rules of the common law.

A jury trial may be requested by either party in a dispute in any case involving more than $20. If both parties agree to a trial by a judge without a jury, the right to a jury trial may be put aside.

Amendment VIII. Bail, Cruel and Unusual Punishment

Excessive bail shall not be required, nor excessive fines imposed, nor cruel and unusual punishments inflicted.

Bail is that amount of money that a person accused of a crime may be required to deposit with the court as a guar-

antee that she or he will appear in court when requested. The amount of bail required or the fine imposed as punishment for a crime must be reasonable compared with the seriousness of the crime involved. Any punishment judged to be too harsh or too severe for a crime shall be prohibited.

Amendment IX.
The Rights Retained by the People

The enumeration in the Constitution, of certain rights, shall not be construed to deny or disparage others retained by the people.

Many civil rights that are not explicitly enumerated in the Constitution are still hailed by the people.

Amendment X.
Reserved Powers of the States

The powers not delegated to the United States by the Constitution, nor prohibited by it to the States, are reserved to the States respectively, or to the people.

Those powers not delegated by the Constitution to the federal government or expressly denied to the states belong to the states and to the people. This clause in essence allows the states to pass laws under its "police powers."

Amendment XI
(Ratified on February 7, 1795).
Suits Against States

The Judicial power of the United States shall not be construed to extend to any suit in law or equity, commenced or prosecuted against one of the United States by Citizens of another State, or by Citizens or Subjects of any Foreign State.

This amendment has been interpreted to mean that a state cannot be sued in federal court by one of its citizens, by a citizen of another state, or by a foreign country.

Amendment XII
(Ratified on June 15, 1804).
Election of the President

The Electors shall meet in their respective states, and vote by ballot for President and Vice-President, one of whom, at least, shall not be an inhabitant of the same State with themselves; they shall name in their ballots the person voted for as President, and in distinct ballots the person voted for as Vice-President, and they shall make distinct lists of all persons voted for as President, and of all persons voted for as Vice-President, and of the number of votes for each, which lists they shall sign and certify, and transmit sealed to the seat of the government of the United States, directed to the President of the Senate;—The President of the Senate shall, in the presence of the Senate and House of Representatives, open all the certificates and the votes shall then be counted;—The person having the greatest number of votes for President, shall be the President, if such number be a majority of the whole number of Electors appointed; and if no person have such majority, then from the persons having the highest numbers not exceeding three on the list of those voted for as President, the House of Representatives shall choose immediately, by ballot, the President. But in choosing the President, the votes shall be taken by States, the representation from each State having one vote; a quorum for this purpose shall consist of a member or members from two-thirds of the States, and a majority of all States shall be necessary to a choice. [And if the House of Representatives shall not choose a President whenever the right of choice shall devolve upon them, before the fourth day of March next following, then the Vice-President shall act as President, as in the case of the death or other constitutional disability of the President.][13]—The person having the greatest number of votes as Vice-President, shall be the Vice-President, if such number be a majority of the whole number of Electors appointed, and if no person have a majority, then from the two highest numbers on the list, the Senate shall choose the Vice President; a quorum for the purpose shall consist of two-thirds of the whole number of Senators, and a majority of the whole number shall be necessary to a choice. But no person constitutionally ineligible to the office of President shall be eligible to that of Vice-President of the United States.

The original procedure set out for the election of president and vice-president in Article II, Section 1, resulted in a tie in 1800 between Thomas Jefferson and Aaron Burr. It was not until the next year that the House of Representatives chose Jefferson to be president. This amendment changed the procedure by providing for separate ballots for president and vice-president.

Amendment XIII
(Ratified on December 6, 1865).
Prohibition of Slavery

Section 1.

Neither slavery nor involuntary servitude, except as a punishment for crime whereof the party shall have been duly

[13]Changed by the Twentieth Amendment.

convicted, shall exist within the United States, or any place subject to their jurisdiction.

Some slaves had been freed during the Civil War. This amendment freed the others and abolished slavery.

Section 2.
Congress shall have power to enforce this article by appropriate legislation.

Amendment XIV (Ratified on July 9, 1868). Citizenship, Due Process, and Equal Protection of the Laws

Section 1.
All persons born or naturalized in the United States, and subject to the jurisdiction thereof, are citizens of the United States and of the State wherein they reside. No State shall make or enforce any law which shall abridge the privileges or immunities of citizens of the United States; nor shall any State deprive any person of life, liberty, or property, without due process of law; nor deny to any person within its jurisdiction the equal protection of the laws.

Under this provision, states cannot make or enforce laws that take away rights given to all citizens by the federal government. States cannot act unfairly or arbitrarily toward, or discriminate against, any person.

Section 2.
Representatives shall be apportioned among the several States according to their respective numbers, counting the whole number of persons in each State, excluding Indians not taxed. But when the right to vote at any election for the choice of electors for President and Vice President of the United States, Representatives in Congress, the Executive and Judicial officers of a State, or the members of the Legislature thereof, is denied to any of the male inhabitants of such State, being [twenty-one][14] years of age, and citizens of the United States, or in any way abridged, except for participation in rebellion, or other crime, the basis of representation therein shall be reduced in the proportion which the number of such male citizens shall bear to the whole number of male citizens twenty-one years of age in such State.

Section 3.
No person shall be a Senator or Representative in Congress, or elector of President and Vice President, or hold any office, civil or military, under the United States, or under any State, who having previously taken an oath, as a member of Congress, or as an officer of the United States, or as a member of any State legislature, or as an executive or judicial officer of any State, to support the Constitution of the United States, shall have engaged in insurrection or rebellion against the same, or given aid or comfort to the enemies thereof. But Congress may by a vote of two-thirds of each House, remove such disability.

This provision forbade former state or federal government officials who had acted in support of the Confederacy during the Civil War to hold office again. It limited the president's power to pardon those persons. Congress removed this "disability" in 1898.

Section 4.
The validity of the public debt of the United States, authorized by law, including debts incurred for payment of pensions and bounties for services in suppressing insurrection or rebellion, shall not be questioned. But neither the United States nor any State shall assume or pay any debt or obligation incurred in aid of insurrection or rebellion against the United States, or any claim for the loss or emancipation of any slave, but all such debts, obligations and claims shall be held illegal and void.

Section 5.
The Congress shall have power to enforce, by appropriate legislation, the provisions of this article.

Amendment XV (Ratified on February 3, 1870). The Right to Vote

Section 1.
The right of citizens of the United States to vote shall not be denied or abridged by the United States or by any State on account of race, color, or previous condition of servitude.

No citizen can be refused the right to vote simply because of race or color or because that person was once a slave.

Section 2.
The Congress shall have power to enforce this article by appropriate legislation.

[14]Changed by the Twenty-sixth Amendment.

Amendment XVI
(Ratified on February 3, 1913).
Income Taxes

The Congress shall have power to lay and collect taxes on incomes, from whatever source derived, without apportionment among the several States, and without regard to any census or enumeration.

This amendment allows Congress to tax income without sharing the revenue so obtained with the states according to their population.

Amendment XVII
(Ratified on April 8, 1913).
The Popular Election of Senators

The Senate of the United States shall be composed of two Senators from each State, elected by the people thereof, for six years; and each Senator shall have one vote. The electors in each State shall have the qualifications requisite for electors of the most numerous branch of the State legislatures.

When vacancies happen in the representation of any State in the Senate, the executive authority of such State shall issue writs of election to fill such vacancies: *Provided,* That the legislature of any State may empower the executive thereof to make temporary appointments until the people fill the vacancies by election as the legislature may direct.

This amendment shall not be so construed as to affect the election or term of any Senator chosen before it becomes valid as part of the Constitution.

This amendment modified portions of Article I, Section 3, that related to election of senators. Senators are now elected by the voters in each state directly. When a vacancy occurs, either the state may fill the vacancy by a special election, or the governor of the state involved may appoint someone to fill the seat until the next election.

Amendment XVIII
(Ratified on January 16, 1919).
Prohibition.

Section 1.
After one year from the ratification of this article the manufacture, sale, or transportation of intoxicating liquors within, the importation thereof into, or the exportation thereof from the United States and all territory subject to the jurisdiction thereof for beverage purposes is hereby prohibited.

Section 2.
The Congress and the several States shall have concurrent power to enforce this article by appropriate legislation.

Section 3.
This article shall be inoperative unless it shall have been ratified as an amendment to the Constitution by the legislatures of the several States, as provided in the Constitution, within seven years from the date of the submission hereof to the States by the Congress.[15]

This amendment made it illegal to manufacture, sell, and transport alcoholic beverages in the United States. It was ended by the Twenty-first Amendment.

Amendment XIX
(Ratified on August 18, 1920).
Women's Right to Vote.

The right of citizens of the United States to vote shall not be denied or abridged by the United States or by any State on account of sex.

Congress shall have power to enforce this article by appropriate legislation.

Women were given the right to vote by this amendment, and Congress was given the power to enforce this right.

Amendment XX
(Ratified on January 23, 1933).
The Lame Duck Amendment

Section 1.
The terms of the President and Vice President shall end at noon on the 20th day of January, and the terms of Senators and Representatives at noon on the 3d day of January, of the years in which such terms would have ended if this article had not been ratified; and the terms of their successors shall then begin.

This amendment modified Article I, Section 4, Clause 2, and other provisions relating to the president in the Twelfth Amendment. The taking of the Oath of Office was moved from March 4 to January 20.

---

[15]The Eighteenth Amendment was repealed by the Twenty-first Amendment.

Section 2.
The Congress shall assemble at least once in every year, and such meeting shall begin at noon on the 3d day of January, unless they shall by law appoint a different day.

Congress changed the beginning of its term to January 3. The reason the Twentieth Amendment is called the Lame Duck Amendment is because it shortens the time between when a member of Congress is defeated for reelection and when he or she leaves office.

Section 3.
If, at the time fixed for the beginning of the term of the President, the President elect shall have died, the Vice President elect shall become President. If a President shall not have been chosen before the time fixed for the beginning of his term, or if the President elect shall have failed to qualify, then the Vice President elect shall act as President until a President shall have qualified; and the Congress may by law provide for the case wherein neither a President elect nor a Vice President elect shall have qualified, declaring who shall then act as President, or the manner in which one who is to act shall be selected, and such person shall act accordingly until a President or Vice President shall have qualified.

This part of the amendment deals with problem areas left ambiguous by Article II and the Twelfth Amendment. If the president dies before January 20 or fails to qualify for office, the presidency is to be filled in the order given in this section.

Section 4.
The Congress may by law provide for the case of the death of any of the persons from whom the House of Representatives may choose a President whenever the rights of choice shall have devolved upon them, and for the case of the death of any of the persons from whom the Senate may choose a Vice President whenever the right of choice shall have devolved upon them.

Congress has never created legislation subsequent to this section.

Section 5.
Sections 1 and 2 shall take effect on the 15th day of October following the ratification of this article.

Section 6.
This article shall be inoperative unless it shall have been ratified as an amendment to the Constitution by the legislatures of three-fourths of the several States within seven years from the date of its submission.

Amendment XXI (Ratified on December 5, 1933). The Repeal of Prohibition.

Section 1.
The eighteenth article of amendment to the Constitution of the United States is hereby repealed.

Section 2.
The transportation or importation into any State, Territory, or possession of the United States for delivery or use therein of intoxicating liquors, in violation of the laws thereof, is hereby prohibited.

Section 3.
This article shall be inoperative unless it shall have been ratified as an amendment to the Constitution by conventions in the several States, as provided in the Constitution, within seven years from the date of the submission hereof to the States by the Congress.

The amendment repealed the Eighteenth Amendment but did not make alcoholic beverages legal everywhere. Rather, they remained illegal in any state that so designated them. Many such "dry" states existed for a number of years after 1933. Today, there are still "dry" counties within the United States, in which alcoholic beverages are illegal.

Amendment XXII (Ratified on February 27, 1951). Limitation of Presidential Terms.

Section 1.
No person shall be elected to the office of the President more than twice, and no person who has held the office of President, or acted as President, for more than two years of a term to which some other person was elected President shall be elected to the office of President more than once. But this Article shall not apply to any person holding the office of President when this Article was proposed by the Congress, and shall not prevent any person who may be holding the office of President, or acting as President, during the term within which this Article becomes operative from holding the office of President or acting as President during the remainder of such term.

Section 2.
This article shall be inoperative unless it shall have been ratified as an amendment to the Constitution by the legislatures of three-fourths of the several States within seven years from the date of its submission to the States by the Congress.

No president may serve more than two elected terms. If, however, a president has succeeded to the office after the halfway point of a term in which another president was originally elected, then that president may serve for more than eight years, but not to exceed ten years.

Amendment XXIII (Ratified on March 29, 1961). Presidential Electors for the District of Columbia.

Section 1.
The District constituting the seat of Government of the United States shall appoint in such manner as the Congress may direct:

A number of electors of President and Vice President equal to the whole number of Senators and Representatives in Congress to which the District would be entitled if it were a State, but in no event more than the least populous State; they shall be in addition to those appointed by the States, but they shall be considered, for the purposes of the election of President and Vice President, to be electors appointed by a State; and they shall meet in the District and perform such duties as provided by the twelfth article of amendment.

Section 2.
The Congress shall have power to enforce this article by appropriate legislation.

Citizens living in the District of Columbia have the right to vote in elections for president and vice-president. The District of Columbia has three presidential electors, whereas before this amendment it had none.

Amendment XXIV (Ratified on January 23, 1964). The Anti-Poll Tax Amendment.

Section 1.
The right of citizens of the United States to vote in any primary or other election for President or Vice President, for electors for President or Vice President, or for Senator or Representative in Congress, shall not be denied or abridged by the United States, or any State by reason of failure to pay any poll tax or other tax.

Section 2.
The Congress shall have power to enforce this article by appropriate legislation.

No government shall require a person to pay a poll tax in order to vote in any federal election.

Amendment XXV (Ratified on February 10, 1967). A Presidential Disability and Vice Presidential Vacancies.

Section 1.
In case of the removal of the President from office or of his death or resignation, the Vice President shall become President.

Whenever a president dies or resigns from office, the vice-president becomes president.

Section 2.
Whenever there is a vacancy in the office of the Vice President, the President shall nominate a Vice President who shall take office upon confirmation by a majority vote of both Houses of Congress.

Whenever the office of the vice-presidency becomes vacant, the president may appoint someone to fill this office, provided Congress consents.

Section 3.
Whenever the President transmits to the President pro tempore of the Senate and the Speaker of the House of Representatives his written declaration that he is unable to discharge the powers and duties of his office, and until he transmits to them a written declaration to the contrary, such powers and duties shall be discharged by the Vice President as Acting President.

Whenever the president believes she or he is unable to carry out the duties of the office, she or he shall so indicate to Congress in writing. The vice-president then acts as president until the president declares that she or he is again able to properly carry out the duties of the office.

Section 4.
Whenever the Vice President and a majority of either the principal officers of the executive departments or of such other body as Congress may by law provide, transmit to the President pro tempore of the Senate and the Speaker of the House of Representatives their written declaration that the President is unable to discharge the powers and duties of his office, the Vice President shall immediately assume the powers and duties of the office as Acting President.

Thereafter, when the President transmits to the President pro tempore of the Senate and the Speaker of the House of Representatives his written declaration that no inability exists, he shall resume the powers and duties of his office unless the Vice President and a majority of either the principal officers of the executive department or of such other body as Congress may by law provide, transmit within four days to the President pro tempore of the Senate and the Speaker of the House of Representatives their written declaration that the President is unable to discharge the powers and duties of his office. Thereupon Congress shall decide the issue, assembling within forty-eight hours for that purpose if not in session. If the Congress, within twenty-one days after receipt of the latter written declaration, or, if Congress is not in session, within twenty-one days after Congress is required to assemble, determines by two-thirds vote of both Houses that the President is unable to discharge the powers and duties of his office, the Vice President shall continue to discharge the same as Acting President; otherwise, the President shall resume the powers and duties of his office.

Whenever the vice president and a majority of the members of the Cabinet believe that the president cannot carry out his or her duties, they shall so indicate in writing to Congress. The vice president shall then act as president. When the president believes that she or he is able to carry out her or his duties again, she or he shall so indicate to the Congress. If, though, the vice president and a majority of the Cabinet do not agree, Congress must decide by a two-thirds vote within three weeks who shall act as president.

Amendment XXVI (Ratified on July 1, 1971). The Eighteen Year Old Vote.

Section 1.
The right of citizens of the United States, who are eighteen years of age or older, to vote shall not be denied or abridged by the United States or by any State on account of age.

No one over eighteen years of age can be denied the right to vote in federal or state elections by virtue of age.

Section 2.
The Congress shall have power to enforce this article by appropriate legislation.

Amendment XXVII (Ratified on May 7, 1992). Congressional Compensation Changes.

No law, varying the compensation for the services of the Senators and Representatives, shall take effect, until an election of Representatives shall have intervened.

An intervening congressional election is required before any changes in congressional compensation may be instituted.

The Magna Carta (1215)

The Magna Carta is the ''great charter'' of English civil liberties. King John signed it at Runnymede on June 15, 1215. His barons forced him to do so. The document, which is excerpted below, consists of sixty-three clauses, which protect the rights of the church, the feudal lords, the lords' subtenants, and the merchants. Royal privileges, the administration of justice, and the behavior of royal officials are also covered in the document.

John, by the grace of God, king of England, lord of Ireland, duke of Normandy and Aquitaine, count of Anjou, to all his archbishops, bishops, abbots, earls, barons, justiciars, foresters, sheriffs, stewards, servants, and all bailiffs and faithful men, health. * * *

Chapter 1

First, we grant to God, and by this our present charter we confirm, for us and our heirs forever, that the English church be free, and have its rights whole and its liberties unimpaired; * * * We have granted to all free men of our realm, for ourself and our heirs forever, all these underwritten liberties to have and to hold, for themselves and their heirs, from us and our heirs.

Chapter 20

A free man shall not be amerced for a small offense unless according to the measure of the offense, and for a great offense he shall be amerced according to the greatness of the offense, saving his tenement, and the merchant in the same manner, saving his merchandise, and the villein shall be amerced in the same manner, saving his tools of husbandry, if they fall into our mercy, and none of the aforenamed mercies shall be imposed except by the oath of reputable men of the vicinage.

Chapter 21

Earls and barons shall not be amerced but by their equals, and only according to the measure of the offense.

Chapter 28

No constable, or other bailiff of ours, shall take the corn or chattels of anyone, unless he forthwith pays money for them, or can have any respite by the good will of the seller.

Chapter 30

No sheriff or bailiff of ours, or any other, shall take horses and carts of any free man for carrying, except by the will of the free man.[1]

Chapter 31

Neither we nor our bailiffs will take any wood for our castles, or other of our works, except by consent of the man whose wood it is.

Chapter 32

We will not hold the lands of those who are convict of felony, except for one year and one day, and then the lands shall be returned to the lords of the fees.

Chapter 38

No bailiff in future shall put anyone to law by his mere word, without trustworthy witnesses brought forward for it.

Chapter 39

No free man shall be seized, or imprisoned, or disseised, or outlawed, or exiled, or injured in any way, nor will we enter on him or send against him except by the lawful judgment of his peers, or by the law of the land.

Chapter 40

We will sell to no one, or deny to no one, or put off right or justice.

Chapter 41

All merchants shall have safe conduct and security to go out of England or come into England, and to stay in, and go through England, both by land and water, for buying or selling, without any evil tolls, by old and right customs, except in time of war; and if they be of the land at war against us, and if such shall be found in our land, at the beginning of war, they shall be attached without loss of person or property, until it be known by us or our chief justiciar how the merchants of our land are treated who are found then in the land at war with us; and if ours be safe there, others shall be safe here.[2]

Chapter 46

All barons who have founded abbeys, whence they have charters of the kings of England, or ancient tenure, shall have their custody while vacant, as they ought to have it.

1. In 1216 the chapter was modified to say that the horses and carts should not be taken unless the owner received a specified amount of money. In 1217 a chapter was inserted that prohibited bailiffs from taking carts from the demesne of a cleric, a knight, or a lady. In 1225 chapters 30 and 31 from the Charter of 1215 and the new chapter were combined into a single chapter.

2. In 1216 the words "unless formerly they have been publicly prohibited" were inserted after "All merchants."

Chapter 53

We will have the same respite, and in the same way, about exhibiting justice of deforesting or maintaining the forests, which Henry our father, or Richard our brother afforested, and of the wardship of the lands which are of another's fee, of which thing we have hitherto had the wardship, by reason of the fee, because someone held of us by military service, and of the abbeys which were founded on the fee of another than our own, in which the lord of the fee says he has the right; and when we return, or if we stay from our journey, we will afford full justice to those who complain of these things.

Chapter 54

No one shall be seized or imprisoned for the appeal of a woman about the death of any other man but her husband.

Chapter 60

All these aforesaid customs and liberties which we have granted to be held in our realm, as far as belongs to us, towards our own, all in our realm, both clergy and lay, shall observe, as far as belongs to them, towards their own.

Chapter 63

Wherefore we will and firmly order that the English church should be free, and that the men of our realm should have and hold all the aforenamed liberties, rights, and grants, well and in peace, freely and quietly, fully and completely, for them and their heirs, from us and our heirs, in all things and places, forever, as is aforesaid. It is sworn both by us, and on the part of the barons, that all these aforesaid shall be kept in good faith and without ill meaning. Witnesses, the abovenamed and many others. Given by our hand, in the meadow which is called Runnymede, between Windsor and Staines, on the fifteenth day of June, in the seventeenth year of our reign.

Source: William Stubbs, ed., *A Translation of Such Documents as Are Unpublished in Dr. Stubbs' Select Charters* (n.d.), pp. 187–197.

Mayflower Compact (1620)

The Mayflower Compact was entered into by the adult male Pilgrims in the cabin of the Mayflower *on November 11, 1620. The forty-one men who signed it agreed to establish a preliminary government. The compact bound the signers to a government by majority rule during the time they knew they had to wait for a royal charter. Many view this compact as the first step in the development of democracy in America.*

In the name of God, Amen. We, whose names are underwritten, the loyal subjects of our dread sovereign lord King James, by the grace of God, of Great Britain, France, and Ireland, king, defender of the faith, &c. Having undertaken for the glory of God, and advancement of the Christian faith, and the honor of our king and country, a voyage to plant the first colony in the northern parts of Virginia, do by these presents, solemnly and mutually, in the presence of God and one another, covenant and combine ourselves together into a civil body politic, for our better ordering and preservation and furtherance of the ends aforesaid; and by virtue hereof do enact, constitute, and frame such just and equal laws, ordinances, acts, constitutions, and officers, from time to time, as shall be thought most meet and convenient for the general good of the colony; unto which we promise all due submission and obedience. In witness whereof we have hereunto subscribed our names at Cape Cod the eleventh of November, in the reign of our sovereign lord King James, of England, France, and Ireland, the eighteenth, and of Scotland, the fifty-fourth, anno Domini, 1620.

Mr. John Carver	Digery Priest
Mr. William Bradford	Thomas Williams
Mr. Edward Winslow	Gilbert Winslow
Mr. William Brewster	Edmund Margesson
Isaac Allerton	Peter Brown
Miles Standish	Richard Bitteridge
John Alden	George Soule
John Turner	Edward Tilly
Francis Eaton	John Tilly
James Chilton	Francis Cooke
John Craxton	Thomas Rogers
John Billington	Thomas Tinker
Joses Fletcher	John Ridgdale
John Goodman	Edward Fuller
Mr. Samuel Fuller	Richard Clark
Mr. Christopher Martin	Richard Gardiner
Mr. William Mullins	Mr. John Allerton
Mr. William White	Thomas English
Mr. Richard Warren	Edward Doten
John Howland	Edward Liester
Mr. Steven Hopkins	

Source: Ben Perley Poore, ed., *The Federal and State Constitutions, Colonial Charters, and Other Organic Laws of the United States*, vol. 1 (1878), p. 931.

Declaration of Independence (1776)

The Declaration of Independence was adopted by the Second Continental Congress on July 4, 1776. It was the formal mechanism by which the thirteen American colonies justified their separation from Britain. The formal signing of the declaration took place on August 2, 1776.

IN CONGRESS, JULY 4, 1776
THE UNANIMOUS DECLARATION of the thirteen united STATES OF AMERICA

WHEN in the Course of human events, it becomes necessary for one people to dissolve the political bands which have connected them with another, and to assume among the powers of the earth, the separate and equal station to which the Laws of Nature and of Nature's God entitle them, a decent respect to the opinions of mankind requires that they should declare the causes which impel them to the separation.

We hold these truths to be self-evident, that all men are created equal, that they are endowed by their Creator with certain unalienable Rights, that among these are Life, Liberty and the pursuit of Happiness. That to secure these rights, Governments are instituted among Men, deriving their just powers from the consent of the governed; That whenever any Form of Government becomes destructive of these ends, it is the Right of the People to alter or to abolish it, and to institute new Government, laying its foundation on such principles and organizing its powers in such form, as to them shall seem most likely to effect their Safety and Happiness. Prudence, indeed, will dictate that Governments long established should not be changed for light and transient causes; and accordingly all experience hath shown, that mankind are more disposed to suffer, while evils are sufferable, than to right themselves by abolishing the forms to which they are accustomed. But when a long train of abuses and usurpations, pursuing invariably the same Object evinces a design to reduce them under absolute Despotism, it is their right, it is their duty, to throw off such Government, and to provide new Guards for their future security.

Such has been the patient sufferance of these Colonies; and such is now the necessity which constrains them to alter their former Systems of Government. The history of the present King of Great Britain is a history of repeated injuries and usurpations, all having in direct object the establishment of an absolute Tyranny over these States. To prove this, let Facts be submitted to a candid world.

He has refused his Assent to Laws, the most wholesome and necessary for the public good.

He has forbidden his Governors to pass Laws of immediate and pressing importance, unless suspended in their operation till his Assent should be obtained; and when so suspended, he has utterly neglected to attend to them.

He has refused to pass other Laws for the accommodation of large districts of people, unless those people would relinquish the right of Representation in the Legislature, a right inestimable to them and formidable to tyrants only.

He has called together legislative bodies at places unusual, uncomfortable, and distant from the depository or their public records, for the sole purpose of fatiguing them into compliance with his measures.

He has dissolved Representative Houses repeatedly, for opposing with manly firmness his invasions on the rights of the people.

He has refused for a long time, after such dissolutions, to cause others to be elected; whereby the Legislative powers, incapable of Annihilation, have returned to the People at large for their exercise; the State remaining in the mean time exposed to all the dangers of invasion from without, and convulsions within.

He has endeavored to prevent the population of these States; for that purpose obstructing the Laws for Naturalization of Foreigners; refusing to pass others to encourage their migration hither, and raising the conditions of new Appropriations of Lands.

He has obstructed the Administration of Justice, by refusing his Assent to Laws for establishing Judiciary powers.

He has made Judges dependent on his Will alone, for the tenure of their offices, and the amount and payment of their salaries.

He has erected a multitude of New Offices, and sent hither swarms of Officers to harrass our people, and eat out their substance.

He has kept among us, in times of peace, Standing Armies, without the Consent of our legislatures.

He has affected to render the Military independent of and superior to the Civil power.

He has combined with others to subject us to a jurisdiction foreign to our constitution, and unacknowledged by our laws; giving his Assent to their Acts of pretended Legislation:

For quartering large bodies of armed troops among us;

For protecting them, by a mock Trial, from punishment for any Murders which they should commit on the Inhabitants of these States;

For cutting off our Trade with all parts of the world;

For imposing Taxes on us without our Consent;

For depriving us in many cases, of the benefits of Trial by Jury;

For transporting us beyond Seas to be tried for pretended offences;

For abolishing the free System of English Laws in a neighbouring Province, establishing therein an Arbitrary government, and enlarging its Boundaries so as to render it at once an example and fit instrument for introducing the same absolute rule into these Colonies;

For taking away our Charters, abolishing our most valuable Laws, and altering fundamentally the Forms of our Governments;

For suspending our own Legislatures, and declaring themselves invested with power to legislate for us in all cases whatsoever.

He has abdicated Government here, by declaring us out of his Protection and waging War against us.

He has plundered our seas, ravaged our Coasts, burnt our towns, and destroyed the lives of our people.

He is at this time transporting large Armies of foreign Mercenaries to complete the works of death, desolation and tyranny, already begun with circumstances of Cruelty and perfidy scarcely paralleled in the most barbarous ages, and totally unworthy the Head of a civilized nation.

He has constrained our fellow Citizens taken Captive on the high Seas to bear Arms against their Country, to become the executioners of their friends and Brethren, or to fall themselves by their Hands.

He has excited domestic insurrections amongst us, and has endeavored to bring on the inhabitants of our frontiers, the merciless Indian Savages, whose known rule of warfare, is an undistinguished destruction of all ages, sexes and conditions.

In every state of these Oppressions We have Petitioned for Redress in the most humble terms. Our repeated Petitions have been answered only by repeated injury. A Prince, whose character is thus marked by every act which may define a Tyrant, is unfit to be the ruler of a free people.

Nor have We been wanting in attentions to our British brethren. We have warned them from time to time of attempts by their legislature to extend an unwarrantable jurisdiction over us. We have reminded them of the circumstances of our emigration and settlement here. We have appealed to their native justice and magnanimity, and we have conjured them by the ties of our common kindred to disavow these usurpations, which would inevitably interrupt our connections and correspondence. They too have been deaf to the voice of justice and consanguinity. We must, therefore, acquiesce in the necessity, which denounces our Separation, and hold them, as we hold the rest of mankind, Enemies in War, in Peace Friends.—

WE, THEREFORE, the REPRESENTATIVES of the UNITED STATES OF AMERICA, in General Congress, Assembled, appealing to the Supreme Judge of the world for the rectitude of our intentions, do, in the Name, and by Authority of the good People of these Colonies, solemnly publish and declare, That these United Colonies are, and of Right ought to be FREE AND INDEPENDENT STATES; that they are Absolved from all Allegiance to the British Crown, and that all political connection between them and the State of Great Britain, is and ought to be totally disolved; and that as Free and Independent States, they have full Power to levy War, conclude Peace, contract Alliances, establish Commerce, and to do all other Acts and Things which Independent States may of right do. And for the support of this Declaration, with a firm reliance on the protection of Divine Providence, we mutually pledge to each other our Lives, our Fortunes and our sacred Honor.

John Hancock
Button Gwinnett
Lyman Hall
Geo. Walton
Benj. Harrison
Thos. Nelson, Jr.
Francis Lightfoot Lee
Carter Braxton
Lewis Morris
Richd. Stockton
Jno. Witherspoon
Fras. Hopkinson
Wm. Hooper
Joseph Hewes
John Penn
Edward Rutledge
Thos. Heyward, Jr.
Thomas Lynch, Jr.
Arthur Middleton
Samuel Chase
Wm. Paca
Thos. Stone
Charles Carroll of Carrollton
George Wythe
Richard Henry Lee
Th. Jefferson
Robt. Morris
Benjamin Rush

Benj. Franklin
John Morton
Geo. Clymer
Jas. Smith
Geo. Taylor
James Wilson
Geo. Ross
Caesar Rodney
Geo. Read
Tho. M: Kean
Wm. Floyd
Phil. Livingston
Frans. Lewis
John Hart
Abra. Clark
Josiah Bartlett
Wm. Whipple
Saml. Adams
John Adams
Robt. Treat Paine
Elbridge Gerry
Step. Hopkins
William Ellery
Roger Sherman
Sam. Huntington
Wm. Williams
Oliver Wolcott
Matthew Thornton

Articles of Confederation (1781–1789)

The Articles of Confederation were in effect the first constitution of the United States, formally joining all the colonies under a centralized government. They were submitted to the Continental Congress in 1776, adopted the next year, but not ratified by all the states until 1781. They remained in force until the ratification of the U.S. Constitution in 1788.

To all to whom these Presents shall come, we the undersigned Delegates of the States affixed to our Names send greeting

Whereas the Delegates of the United States of America in Congress assembled did on the fifteenth day of November in the Year of our Lord One Thousand Seven Hundred and Seventy-seven, and in the Second Year of the Independence of America agree to certain articles of Confederation and perpetual Union between the States of Newhampshire, Massachusetts-bay, Rhode-island, and Providence Plantations, Connecticut, New York, New Jersey, Pennsylvania, Delaware, Maryland, Virginia, North-Carolina, South-Carolina and Georgia in the Words following, viz.

Articles of Confederation and perpetual Union between the States of Newhampshire, Massachusetts-bay, Rhodeisland and Providence Plantations, Connecticut, New-York, New-Jersey, Pennsylvania, Delaware, Maryland, Virginia, North-Carolina, South-Carolina and Georgia.

Article I

The stile of this confederacy shall be "The United States of America."

Article II

Each State retains its sovereignty, freedom and independence, and every power, jurisdiction and right, which is not by this confederation expressly delegated to the United States, in Congress assembled.

Article III

The said States hereby severally enter into a firm league of friendship with each other, for their common defense, the security of their liberties, and their mutual and general welfare, binding themselves to assist each other, against all force offered to, or attacks made upon them, or any of them, on account of religion, sovereignty trade or any other pretence whatever.

Article IV

The better to secure and perpetuate mutual friendship and intercourse among the people of the different States in this Union, the free inhabitants of each of these States, paupers, vagabonds and fugitives from justice excepted, shall be entitled to all privileges and immunities of free citizens in the several States; and the people of each State shall have free ingress and regress to and from any other State, and shall enjoy therein all the privileges of trade and commerce, subject to the same duties, impositions and restrictions as the inhabitants thereof respectively, provided that such restrictions shall not exceed so far as to prevent the removal of property imported into any State, to any other State of which the owner is an inhabitant; provided also that no imposition, duties or restriction shall be laid by any State, on the property of the United States, or either of them.

If any person guilty of, or charged with treason, felony, or other high misdemeanor in any State, shall flee from justice, and be found in any of the United States, he shall upon demand of the Governor or Executive power, of the State from which he fled, be delivered up and removed to the State having jurisdiction of his offense.

Full faith and credit shall be given in each of these States to the records, acts and judicial proceedings to the courts and magistrates of every other State.

Article V

For the more convenient management of the general interests of the United States, delegates shall be annually appointed in such manner as the legislature of each State shall direct, to meet in Congress on the first Monday in November, in every year, with a power reserved to each State, to recall its delegates, or any of them, at any time within the year, and to send others in their stead, for the remainder of the year.

No State shall be represented in Congress by less than two, nor by more than seven members; and no person shall be capable of being a delegate for more than three years in any term of six years; nor shall any person, being a delegate, be capable of holding any office under the United States, for which he, or another for his benefit receives any salary, fees or emolument of any kind.

Each state shall maintain its own delegates in a meeting of the States, and while they act as members of the committee of the States.

In determining questions in the United States, in Congress assembled, each State shall have one vote.

Freedom of speech and debate in Congress shall not be impeached or questioned in any court, or place out of Congress, and the members of Congress shall be protected in their persons from arrests and imprisonments, during the time of their going to and from, and attendance on Congress, except for treason, felony, or breach of the peace.

Article VI

No State without the consent of the United States in Congress assembled, shall send any embassy to, or receive any embassy from, or enter into any conference, agreement, alliance or treaty with any king, prince or state; nor shall any person holding any office or profit or trust under the United States, or any of them, accept of any present, emolument, office or title of any kind whatever from any king, prince or foreign state; nor shall the United States in Congress assembled or any of them, grant any title of nobility.

No two or more States shall enter into any treaty, confederation or alliance whatever between them, without the consent of the United States in Congress assembled, specifying accurately the purposes for which the same is to be entered into, and how long it shall continue.

No State shall lay any imposts or duties, which may interfere with any stipulations in treaties, entered into by the United States in Congress assembled, with any king, prince or state, in pursuance of any treaties already proposed by Congress, to the courts of France and Spain.

No vessels of war shall be kept up in time of peace by any State, except such number only, as shall be deemed necessary by the United States in Congress assembled, for the defence of such State, or its trade; nor shall any body of forces be kept up by any State, in time of peace, except such number only, as in the judgement of the United States, in Congress assembled, shall be deemed requisite to garrison the forts necessary for the defence of such State; but every State shall always keep up a well regulated and disciplined militia, sufficiently armed and accoutered, and shall provide and constantly have ready for use, in public stores, a due number of field pieces and tents, and a proper quantity of arms, ammunition and camp equipage.

No State shall engage in any way without the consent of the United States in Congress assembled, unless such State be actually invaded by enemies, or shall have received certain advice of a resolution being formed by some nation of Indians to invade such State, and the danger is so imminent as not to admit of a delay, till the United States in Congress assembled can be consulted: nor shall any State grant commissions to any ships or vessels of war, nor letters of marque or reprisal, except it be after a declaration of war by the United States in Congress assembled, and then only against the kingdom or state and the subject thereof, against which war has been so declared and under such regulations as shall be established by the United States in Congress assembled, unless such State be infested by pirates, in which case vessels of war may be fitted out for that occasion, and kept so long as the danger shall continue, or until the United States in Congress assembled shall determine otherwise.

Article VII

When land-forces are raised by any State for the common defence, all officers of or under the rank of colonel, shall be appointed by the Legislature of each State respectively by whom such forces shall be raised, or in such manner as such State shall direct, and all vacancies shall be filled up by the State which first made the appointment.

Article VIII

All charges of war, and all other expenses that shall be incurred for the common defence or general welfare, and allowed by the United States in Congress assembled, shall be defrayed out of a common treasury, which shall be supplied by the several States, in proportion to the value of all land within each State, granted to or surveyed for any person, as such land and the buildings and improvements thereon shall be estimated according to such mode as the United States in Congress assembled, shall from time to time direct and appoint.

The taxes for paying that proportion shall be laid and levied by the authority and direction of the Legislatures of the several States within the time agreed upon by the United States in Congress Assembled.

Article IX

The United States in Congress assembled, shall have the sole and exclusive right and power of determining on peace and war, except in the cases mentioned in the sixth article—of sending and receiving ambassadors—entering into treaties and alliances, provided that no treaty of commerce shall be made whereby the legislative power of the respective States shall be restrained from imposing such imposts and duties on foreigners, as their own people are subjected to, or from prohibiting the exportation or importation of any species of goods or commodities whatsoever—of establishing rules for deciding in all cases, what captures on land or water shall be legal, and in what manner prizes taken by land or naval forces in the service of the United States shall be divided or appropriated—of granting letters of marque and reprisal in times of peace—appointing courts for trial of piracies and felonies committed on the high seas and establishing courts for receiving and determining finally appeals in all cases of captures, provided that no member of Congress shall be appointed a judge of any of the said courts.

The United States in Congress assembled shall also be the last resort on appeal in all disputes and differences now subsisting or that hereafter may arise between two or more States concerning boundary, jurisdiction or any other cause whatever; which authority shall always be exercised in the manner following. Whenever the legislative or executive authority or lawful agent of any State in controversy with another shall present a petition to Congress, stating the matter in question and praying for a hearing, notice thereof shall be given by order of Congress to the legislative or executive authority of the other State in controversy, and a day assigned for the appearance of the parties by their lawful agents, who shall then be directed to appoint by joint consent, commissioners or judges to constitute a court for hearing and determining the matter in question: but if they cannot agree, Congress shall name three persons out of each of the United States, and from the list of such persons each party shall alternately strike out one, the petitioners beginning, until the number shall be reduced to thirteen; and from that number not less than seven, nor more than nine names as Congress shall direct, shall, in the presence of Congress be drawn out by lot, and the persons whose names shall be so drawn or any five of them, shall be commissioners or judges, to hear and finally determine the controversy, so always as a major part of the judges who shall hear the cause shall agree in the determination: and if either party shall neglect to attend at the day appointed, without showing reasons, which Congress shall judge sufficient, or being present shall refuse to strike, the Congress shall proceed to nominate three persons out of each State, and the Secretary of Congress shall strike in behalf of such party absent or refusing; and the judgment and sentence of the court to be appointed, in the manner before prescribed, shall be final and conclusive; and if any of the parties shall refuse to submit to the authority of such court, or to appear or defend their claim or cause, the court shall nevertheless proceed to pronounce sentence, or judgment, which shall in like manner be final and decisive, the judgment or sentence and other proceedings being in either case transmitted to Congress, and lodged among the acts of Congress for the security of the parties concerned: provided that every commissioner, before he sits in judgment, shall take an oath to be administered by one of the judges of the supreme court of the State where the cause shall be tried, "well and truly to hear and determine the matter in question, according to the best of his judgment, without favour, affection or hope of reward:" provided also that no State shall be deprived of territory for the benefit of the United States.

All controversies concerning the private right of soil claimed under different grants of two or more States, whose jurisdiction as they may respect such lands, and the States which passed such grants are adjusted, the said grants or either of them being at the same time claimed to have originated antecedent to such settlement of jurisdiction, shall on the petition of either party to the Congress of the United States, be finally determined as near as may be in the same manner as is before prescribed for deciding disputes respecting territorial jurisdiction between different States.

The United States in Congress assembled shall also have the sole and exclusive right and power of regulating the alloy and value of coin struck by their own authority, or by that of the respective States.—fixing the standard of weights and measures throughout the United States.—regulating the trade and managing all affairs with the Indians, not members of any of the States, provided that the legislative right of any State within its own limits be not infringed or violated—establishing and regulating post-offices from one State to another, throughout all the United States, and exacting such postage on the papers passing thro' the same as may be requisite to defray the expenses of the said office—appointing all officers of the land forces, in the service of the United States, excepting regimental officers—appointing all the officers of the naval forces, and commissioning all officers whatever in the service of the United States—making rules for the government and regulation of the said land and naval forces, and directing their operations.

The United States in Congress assembled shall have authority to appoint a committee, to sit in the recess of Congress, to be denominated "a Committee of the States," and to consist of one delegate from each State; and to appoint such other committees and civil officers as may be necessary for managing the general affairs of the United States under their direction—to appoint one of their number to preside, provided that no person be allowed to serve in the office of president more than one year in any term of three years; to ascertain the necessary sums of money to be raised for the service of the United States, and to appropriate and apply the same for defraying the public expenses—to borrow money or emit bills on the credit of the United States transmitting every half year to the respective States an account of the sums of money so borrowed or emitted,—to build and equip a navy—to agree upon the number of land forces, and to make requisitions from each State for its quota, in proportion to the number of white inhabitants in such State; which requisition shall be binding, and thereupon the Legislature of each State shall appoint the regimental officers, raise the men and cloath, arm and equip them in a soldier like manner, at the expense of the United States; and the officers and men so cloathed, armed and equipped shall march to the place appointed, and within the time agreed on by the United States in Congress assembled; but if the United States in Congress assembled shall, on consideration of circumstances judge proper that any State should not raise men, or should raise a smaller number than its quota, and that any other State should raise a greater number of men than the quota thereof, such extra number shall be raised, officered, cloathed, armed and equipped in the same manner as the quota of such State, unless the legislature of such State shall judge that such extra number cannot be safely spared out of the same, in which case they shall raise officer, cloath, arm and equip as many of such extra number as they judge can be safely spared. And the officers and men so cloathed, armed, and equipped, shall march to the place appointed, and within the time agreed on by the United States in Congress assembled.

The United States in Congress assembled shall never engage in a war, nor grant letters of marque and reprisal in time of peace, nor enter into any treaties or alliances, nor coin money, nor regulate the value thereof, nor ascertain the sums and expenses necessary for the defence and welfare of the United States, or any of them, nor emit bills, nor borrow money on the credit of the United States, nor appropriate money, nor agree upon the number of vessels of war, to be built or purchased, or the number of land or sea forces to be raised, nor appoint a commander in chief of the army or navy, unless nine States assent to the same: nor shall a question on any other point, except for adjourning from day to day be determined, unless by the votes of a majority of the United States in Congress assembled.

The Congress of the United States shall have power to adjourn to any time within the year, and to any place within the United States, so that no period of adjournment be for a longer duration than the space of six months, and shall publish the journal of their proceedings monthly, except such parts thereof relating to treaties, alliances or military operations, as in their judgment require secresy; and the yeas and nays of the delegates of each State on any question shall be entered on the journal, when it is desired by any delegate; and the delegates of a State, or any of them, at his or her request shall be furnished with a transcript of the said Journal, except such parts as are above excepted, to lay before the Legislatures of the several States.

Article X

The committee of the States, or any nine of them, shall be authorized to execute in the recess of Congress, such of the powers of Congress as the United States in Congress assembled, by the consent of nine States, shall from time to time think expedient to vest them with; provided that no power be delegated to the said committee, for the exercise of which, by the articles of confederation, the voice of nine States in the Congress of the United States assembled is requisite.

Article XI

Canada acceding to this confederation, and joining in the measures of the United States, shall be admitted into, and entitled to all the advantages of this Union: but no other colony shall be admitted into the same, unless such admission be agreed to by nine States.

Article XII

All bills of credit emitted, monies borrowed and debts contracted by, or under the authority of Congress, before the assembling of the United States, in pursuance of the present confederation, shall be deemed and considered as a charge against the United States, for payment and satisfaction whereof the said United States, and the public faith are hereby solemnly pledged.

Article XIII

Every State shall abide by the determinations of the United States in Congress assembled, on all questions which by this confederation are submitted to them. And the articles of this confederation shall be inviolably observed by every State, and the Union shall be perpetual; nor shall any alteration at any time hereafter be made in any of them; unless such alteration be agreed to in a Congress of the United States, and be afterwards confirmed by the Legislatures of every State.

And whereas it has pleased the Great Governor of the world to incline the hearts of the Legislatures we respectively represent in Congress, to approve of, and to authorize us to ratify the said articles of confederation and perpetual union. Know ye that we the undersigned delegates, by virture of the power and authority to us given for that purpose, do by these presents, in the name and in behalf of our respective constituents, fully and entirely ratify and confirm each and every of the said articles of confederation and perpetual union, and all and singular the matters and things therein contained: and we do further solemnly plight and engage the faith of our respective constituents, that they shall abide by the determinations of the United States in Congress assembled, on all questions, which by the said confederation are submitted to them. And that the articles thereof shall be inviolably observed by the States we re[s]pectively represent, and that the Union shall be perpetual.

In witness whereof we have hereunto set our hands in Congress.

Done at Philadelphia in the State of Pennsylvania the ninth day of July in the year of our Lord one thousand seven hundred and seventy-eight, and in the third year of the independence of America.

On the part and behalf of the State of New Hampshire

JOSIAH BARTLETT, JOHN WENTWORTH, Junr., August 8th, 1778.

On the part and behalf of the State of Massachusetts Bay

JOHN HANCOCK, SAMUEL ADAMS, ELBRIDGE GERRY, FRANCIS DANA, JAMES LOVELL, SAMUEL HOLTEN.

On the part and behalf of the State of Rhode Island and Providence Plantations

WILLIAM ELLERY, HENRY MARCHANT, JOHN COLLINS.

On the part and behalf of the State of Connecticut

ROGER SHERMAN, SAMUEL HUNTINGTON, OLIVER WOLCOTT, TITUS HOSMER, ANDREW ADAMS.

On the part and behalf of the State of New York

JAS. DUANE, FRA. LEWIS, WM. DUER, GOUV. MORRIS.

On the part and in behalf of the State of New Jersey, Novr. 26, 1778

JNO. WITHERSPOON, NATHL. SCUDDER.

On the part and behalf of the State of Pennsylvania

ROBT. MORRIS, DANIEL ROBERDEAU, JONA. BAYARD SMITH, WILLIAM CLINGAN, JOSEPH REED, 22d July, 1778.

On the part & behalf of the State of Delaware

THO. M'KEAN, Feby. 12, 1779. JOHN DICKINSON, May 5th, 1779 NICHOLAS VAN DYKE.

On the part and behalf of the State of Maryland

JOHN HANSON, March 1, 1781. DANIEL CARROLL, Mar. 1, 1781.

On the part and behalf of the State of Virginia

RICHARD HENRY LEE, JOHN BANISTER, THOMAS ADAMS, JNO. HARVIE, FRANCIS LIGHTFOOT LEE.

On the part and behalf of the State of No. Carolina

JOHN PENN, July 21st, 1778. CORNS. HARNETT, JNO. WILLIAMS.

On the part & behalf of the State of South Carolina

HENRY LAURENS, WILLIAM HENRY DRAYTON, JNO. MATHEWS, RICHD. HUTSON, THOS. HEYWARD, Junr.

On the part & behalf of the State of Georgia

JNO. WALTON, 24th July, 1778. EDWD. TELFAIR, EDWD. LANGWORTHY.

Federalist Papers No. 10 and No. 51 (1787/1788)

During the battle over ratification of the U.S. Constitution in 1787 and 1788, Alexander Hamilton, James Madison, and John Jay wrote a series of eighty-five political essays favoring the adoption of the document. James Madison wrote, among others, two of the most famous—Number 10 and Number 51. Number 10, considered a classic in political theory, deals with the nature of groups, or factions, as he called them. His view, favoring a large republic, is presented in Number 51.

The Federalist No. 10

James Madison, November 22, 1787

TO THE PEOPLE OF THE STATE OF NEW YORK.

Among the numerous advantages promised by a well constructed Union, none deserves to be more accurately developed than its tendency to break and control the violence of faction. The friend of popular governments, never finds himself so much alarmed for their character and fate, as when he contemplates their propensity to this dangerous vice. He will not fail therefore to set a due value on any plan which, without violating the principles to which he is attached, provides a proper cure for it. The instability, injustice and confusion introduced into the public councils, have in truth been the mortal diseases under which popular governments have every where perished; as they continue to be the favorite and fruitful topics from which the adversaries to liberty derive their most specious declamations. The valuable improvements made by the American Constitutions on the popular models, both ancient and modern, cannot certainly be too much admired; but it would be an unwarrantable partiality, to contend that they have as effectually obviated the danger on this side as was wished and expected. Complaints are every where heard from our most considerate and virtuous citizens, equally the friends of public and private faith, and of public and personal liberty; that our governments are too unstable; that the public good is disregarded in the conflicts of rival parties; and that measures are too often decided, not according to the rules of justice, and the rights of the minor party; but by the superior force of an interested and over-bearing majority. However anxiously we may wish that these complaints had no foundation, the evidence of known facts will not permit us to deny that they are in some degree true. It will be found indeed, on a candid review of our situation, that some of the distresses under which we labor, have been erroneously charged on the operation of our governments; but it will be found, at the same time, that other causes will not alone account for many of our heaviest misfortunes; and particularly, for that prevailing and increasing distrust of public engagements, and alarm for private rights, which are echoed from one end of the continent to the other. These must be chiefly, if not wholly, effects of the unsteadiness and injustice, with which a factious spirit has tainted our public administrations.

By a faction I understand a number of citizens, whether amounting to a majority or minority of the whole, who are united and actuated by some common impulse of passion, or of interest, adverse to the rights of other citizens, or to the permanent and aggregate interests of the community.

There are two methods of curing the mischiefs of faction: the one, by removing its causes; the other, by controlling its effects.

There are again two methods of removing the causes of faction: the one by destroying the liberty which is essential to its existence; the other, by giving to every citizen the same opinions, the same passions, and the same interests.

It could never be more truly said than of the first remedy, that it is worse than the disease. Liberty is to faction, what air is to fire, an aliment without which it instantly expires. But it could not be a less folly to abolish liberty, which is essential to political life, because it nourishes faction, than it would be to wish the annihilation of air, which is essential to animal life, because it imparts to fire its destructive agency.

The second expedient is as impracticable, as the first would be unwise. As long as the reason of man continues fallible, and he is at liberty to exercise it, different opinions will be formed. As long as the connection subsists between his reason and his self-love, his opinions and his passions will have a reciprocal influence on each other; and the former will be objects to which the latter will attach themselves. The diversity in the faculties of men from which the rights of property originate, is not less an insuperable obstacle to a uniformity of interests. The protection of these faculties is the first object of Government. From the protection of different and unequal faculties of acquiring property, the possession of different degrees and kinds of property immediately results: and from the influence of these on the sentiments and views of the respective proprietors, ensues a division of the society into different interests and parties.

The latent causes of faction are thus sown in the nature of man; and we see them every where brought into different degrees of activity, according to the different circumstances of civil society. A zeal for different opinions concerning religion, concerning Government and many other points, as well of speculation as of practice; an attachment to different leaders ambitiously contending for pre-eminence and power; or to persons of other descriptions whose fortunes have been interesting to the human passions, have in turn divided mankind into parties, inflamed them with mutual animosity, and rendered them much more disposed to vex and oppress each other, than to co-operate for their common good. So strong is this propensity of mankind to fall into mutual animosities, that where no substantial occasion presents itself, the most frivolous and fanciful distinctions have been sufficient to kindle their unfriendly passions, and excite their most violent conflicts. But the most common and durable source of factions, has been the various and unequal distribution of property. Those who hold, and those who are without property, have ever formed distinct interests in society. Those who are creditors, and those who are debtors, fall under a like discrimination. A landed interest, a manufacturing interest, a mercantile interest, a monied interest, with many lesser interests, grow up of necessity in civilized nations, and divide them into different classes, actuated by different sentiments and views. The regulation of these various and interfering interests forms the principal task of modern Legislation, and involves the spirit of party and faction in the necessary and ordinary operations of Government.

No man is allowed to be a judge in his own cause; because his interest would certainly bias his judgment, and, not improbably, corrupt his integrity. With equal, nay with greater reason, a body of men, are unfit to be both judges and parties, at the same time; yet, what are many of the most important acts of legislation, but so many judicial determinations, not indeed concerning the rights of single persons, but concerning the rights of large bodies of citizens, and what are the different classes of legislators, but advocates and parties to the causes which they determine? Is a law proposed concerning private debts? It is a question to which the creditors are parties on one side, and the debtors on the other. Justice ought to hold the balance between them. Yet the parties are and must be themselves the judges; and the most numerous party, or, in other words, the most powerful faction must be expected to prevail. Shall domestic manufactures be encouraged, and in what degree, by restrictions on foreign manufactures? are questions which would be differently decided by the landed and the manufacturing classes; and probably by neither, with a sole regard to justice and the public good. The apportionment of taxes on the various descriptions of property, is an act which seems to require the most exact impartiality; yet, there is perhaps no legislative act in which greater opportunity and temptation are given to a predominant party, to trample on the rules of justice. Every shilling with which they over-burden the inferior number, is a shilling saved to their own pockets.

It is in vain to say, that enlightened statesmen will be able to adjust these clashing interests, and render them all subservient to the public good. Enlightened statesmen will not always be at the helm: Nor, in many cases, can such an adjustment be made at all, without taking into view indirect and remote considerations, which will rarely prevail over the immediate interest which one party may find in disregarding the rights of another, or the good of the whole.

The inference to which we are brought, is, that the *causes* of faction cannot be removed; and that relief is only to be sought in the means of controlling its *effects.*

If a faction consists of less than a majority, relief is supplied by the republican principle, which enables the majority to defeat its sinister views by regular vote: It may clog the administration, it may convulse the society; but it will be unable to execute and mask its violence under the forms of the Constitution. When a majority is included in a faction, the form of popular government on the other hand enables it to sacrifice to its ruling passion or interest, both the public good and the rights of other citizens. To secure the public good, and private rights, against the danger of such a faction, and at the same time to preserve the spirit and the form of popular government, is then the great object to which our enquiries are directed: Let me add that it is the great desideratum, by which alone this form of government can be rescued from the opprobrium under which it has so long labored, and be recommended to the esteem and adoption of mankind.

By what means is this object attainable? Evidently by one of two only. Either the existence of the same passion or interest in a majority at the same time, must be prevented; or the majority, having such co-existent passion or interest, must be rendered, by their number and local situation, unable to concert and carry into effect schemes of oppression. If the impulse and the opportunity be suffered to coincide, we well know that neither moral nor religious motives can be relied on as an adequate control. They are not found to be such on the injustice and violence of individuals, and lose their efficacy in proportion to the number combined together; that is, in proportion as their efficacy becomes needful.

From this view of the subject, it may be concluded, that a pure Democracy, by which I mean, a Society, consisting of a small number of citizens, who assemble and administer the Government in person, can admit of no cure for the mischiefs of faction. A common passion or interest will, in almost every case, be felt by a majority of the whole; a communication and concert results from the form of Government itself; and there is nothing to check the inducements to sacrifice the weaker party, or an obnoxious individual. Hence it is, that such Democracies have ever been spectacles of turbulence and contention; have ever been found incompatible with personal security, or the rights of property; and have in general been as short in their lives, as they have been violent in their deaths. Theoretic politicians, who have patronized this species of Government, have erroneously supposed, that by reducing mankind to a perfect equality in their political rights, they would, at the same time, be perfectly equalized and assimilated in their possessions, their opinions, and their passions.

A republic, by which I mean a government in which the scheme of representation takes place, opens a different prospect, and promises the cure for which we are seeking. Let us examine the points in which it varies from pure democracy, and we shall comprehend both the nature of the cure and the efficacy which it must derive from the union.

The two great points of difference, between a democracy and a republic, are, first, the delegation of the government, in the latter, to a small number of citizens, elected by the rest; secondly, the greater number of citizens, and greater sphere of country, over which the latter may be extended.

The effect of the first difference is, on the one hand, to refine and enlarge the public views, by passing them through the medium of a chosen body of citizens, whose wisdom may best discern the true interest of their country, and whose patriotism and love of justice, will be least likely to sacrifice it to temporary or partial considerations. Under such a regulation, it may well happen, that the public voice, pronounced by the representatives of the people, will be more consonant to the public good, than if pronounced by the people themselves, convened for the purpose. On the other hand the effect may be inverted. Men of factious tempers, of local prejudices, or of sinister designs, may by intrigue, by corruption, or by other means, first obtain the suffrages, and then betray the interest of the people. The question resulting is, whether small or extensive republics are most favorable to the election of proper guardians of the public weal, and it is clearly decided in favor of the latter by two obvious considerations.

In the first place, it is to be remarked that, however small the republic may be, the representatives must be raised to a certain number, in order to guard against the cabals of a few; and that however large it may be, they must be limited to a certain number, in order to guard against the confusion of a multitude. Hence, the number of representatives in the two cases not being in proportion to that of the constituents, and being proportionally greatest in the small republic, it follows, that if the proportion of fit characters be not less in the large than in the small republic, the former will present a greater option, and consequently a greater probability of a fit choice.

In the next place, as each Representative will be chosen by a greater number of citizens in the large than in the small Republic, it will be more difficult for unworthy candidates to practise with success the vicious arts, by which elections are too often carried; and the suffrages of the people being more free, will be more likely to center on men who possess the most attractive merit, and the most diffusive and established characters.

It must be confessed, that in this, as in most other cases, there is a mean, on both sides of which inconveniences will be found to lie. By enlarging too much the number of electors, you render the representative too little acquainted with all their local circumstances and lesser interests; as by reducing it too much, you render him unduly attached to these, and too little fit to comprehend and pursue great and national objects. The Federal Constitution forms a happy combination in this respect; the great and aggregate interests being referred to the national, the local and particular, to the state legislatures.

The other point of difference is, the greater number of citizens and extent of territory which may be brought within the compass of Republican, than of Democratic Government; and it is this circumstance principally which renders factious combinations less to be dreaded in the former, than in the latter. The smaller the society, the fewer probably will be the distinct parties and interests composing it; the fewer the distinct parties and interests, the more frequently will a majority be found of the same party; and the smaller the number of individuals composing a majority, and the smaller the compass within which they are placed, the more easily will they concert and execute their plans of oppression. Extend the sphere, and you take in a greater variety of parties and interests; you make it less probable that a majority of the whole will have a common motive to invade the rights of other citizens; or if such a common motive exists, it will be more difficult for all who feel it to discover their own strength, and to act in unison with each other. Besides other impediments, it may be remarked, that where there is a consciousness of unjust or dishonorable purposes, communication is always checked by distrust, in proportion to the number whose concurrence is necessary.

Hence it clearly appears, that the same advantage, which a Republic has over a Democracy, in controlling the effects of faction, is enjoyed by a large over a small Republic—is enjoyed by the Union over the States composing it. Does this advantage consist in the substitution of Representatives, whose enlightened views and virtuous sentiments render them superior to local prejudices, and to schemes of injustice? It will not be denied, that the Representation of the Union will be most likely to possess these requisite endowments. Does it consist in the greater security afforded by a greater variety of parties, against the event of any one party being able to outnumber and oppress the rest? In an equal degree does the increased variety of parties, comprised within the Union, increase this security? Does it, in fine, consist in the greater obstacles opposed to the concert and accomplishment of the secret wishes of an unjust and interested majority? Here, again, the extent of the Union gives it the most palpable advantage.

The influence of factious leaders may kindle a flame within their particular States, but will be unable to spread a general conflagration through the other States: a religious sect, may degenerate into a political faction in a part of the Confederacy but the variety of sects dispersed over the entire face of it, must secure the national Councils against any danger from that source: a rage for paper money, for an abolition of debts, for an equal division of property, or for any other improper or wicked project, will be less apt to pervade the whole body of the Union, than a particular member of it; in the same proportion as such a malady is more likely to taint a particular county or district, than an entire State.

In the extent and proper structure of the Union, therefore, we behold a Republican remedy for the diseases most incident to Republican Government. And according to the degree of pleasure and pride, we feel in being Republicans, ought to be our zeal in cherishing the spirit, and supporting the character of Federalists.

Publius

The Federalist No. 51

James Madison, February 6, 1788

TO THE PEOPLE OF THE STATE OF NEW YORK.

To what expedient then shall we finally resort for maintaining in practice the necessary partition of power among the several departments, as laid down in the constitution? The only answer that can be given is, that as all these exterior provisions are found to be inadequate, the defect must be supplied, by so contriving the interior structure of the government, as that its several constituent parts may, by their mutual relations, be the means of keeping each other in their proper places. Without presuming to undertake a full development of this important idea, I will hazard a few general observations, which may perhaps place it in a clearer light, and enable us to form a more correct judgment of the principles and structure of the government planned by the convention.

In order to lay a due foundation for that separate and distinct exercise of the different powers of government, which to a certain extent, is admitted on all hands to be essential to the preservation of liberty, it is evident that each department should have a will of its own; and consequently should be so constituted, that the members of each should have as little agency as possible in the appointment of the members of the others. Were this principle rigorously adhered to, it would require that all the appointments for the supreme executive, legislative, and judiciary magistracies, should be drawn from the same fountain of authority, the people, through channels, having no communication whatever with one another. Perhaps such a plan of constructing the several departments would be less difficult in practice than it may in contemplation appear. Some difficulties however, and some additional expense, would attend the execution of it. Some deviations therefore from the principle must be admitted. In the constitution of the judiciary department in particular, it might be inexpedient to insist rigorously on the principle; first, because peculiar qualifications being essential in the members, the primary consideration ought to be to select that mode of choice, which best secures these qualifications; secondly, because the permanent tenure by which the appointments are held in that department, must soon destroy all sense of dependence on the authority conferring them.

It is equally evident that the members of each department should be as little dependent as possible on those of the others, for the emoluments annexed to their offices. Were the executive magistrate, or the judges, not independent of the legislature in this particular, their independence in every other would be merely nominal.

But the great security against a gradual concentration of the several powers in the same department, consists in giving to those who administer each department, the necessary constitutional means, and personal motives, to resist encroachments of the others. The provision for defense must in this, as in all other cases, be made commensurate to the danger of attack. Ambition must be made to counteract ambition. The interest of the man must be connected with the constitutional rights of the place. It may be a reflection on human nature, that such devices should be necessary to control the abuses of government. But what is government itself but the greatest of all reflections on human nature? If men were angels, no government would be necessary. If angels were to govern men, neither external nor internal controls on government would be necessary. In framing a government which is to be administered by men over men, the great difficulty lies in this: You must first enable the government to control the governed; and in the next place oblige it to control itself. A dependence on the people is no doubt the primary control on the government; but experience has taught mankind the necessity of auxiliary precautions.

This policy of supplying by opposite and rival interests, the defect of better motives, might be traced through the whole system of human affairs, private as well as public. We see it particularly displayed in all the subordinate distributions of power; where the constant aim is to divide and arrange the several offices in such a manner as that each may be a check on the other; that the private interest of every individual, may be a sentinel over the public rights. These inventions of prudence cannot be less requisite in the distribution of the supreme powers of the state.

But it is not possible to give to each department an equal power of self defense. In republican government the legislative authority, necessarily, predominates. The remedy for this inconveniency is, to divide the legislature into different branches; and to render them by different modes of election, and different principles of action, as little connected with each other, as the nature of their common functions, and their common dependence on the society, will admit. It may even be necessary to guard against dangerous encroachments by still further precautions. As the weight of the legislative authority requires that it should be thus divided, the weakness of the executive may require, on the other hand, that it should be fortified. An absolute negative, on the legislature, appears at first view to be the natural defense with which the executive magistrate should be armed. But perhaps it would be neither altogether safe, nor alone sufficient. On ordinary occasions, it might not be exerted with the requisite firmness; and on extraordinary occasions, it might be prefidiously abused. May not this defect of an absolute negative be supplied, by some qualified connection between this weaker department, and the weaker branch of the stronger department, by which the latter may be led to support the constitutional rights of the former, without being too much detached from the rights of its own department?

If the principles on which these observations are founded be just, as I persuade myself they are, and they be applied as a criterion, to the several state constitutions, and to the federal constitution, it will be found, that if the latter does not perfectly correspond with them, the former are infinitely less able to bear such a test.

There are moreover two considerations particularly applicable to the federal system of America, which place that system in a very interesting point of view.

First. In a single republic, all the power surrendered by the people, is submitted to the administration of a single government; and usurpations are guarded against by a division of the government into distinct and separate departments. In the compound republic of America, the power surrendered by the people, is first divided between two distinct governments, and then the portion allotted to each, subdivided among distinct and separate departments. Hence a double security rises to the rights of the people. The different governments will control each other; at the same time that each will be controlled by itself.

Second. It is of great importance in a republic, not only to guard the society against the oppression of its rulers; but to guard one part of the society against the injustice of the other part. Different interests necessarily exist in different classes of citizens. If a majority be united by a common interest, the rights of the minority will be insecure. There are but two methods of providing against this evil: The one by creating a will in the community independent of the majority, that is, of the society itself, the other by comprehending in the society so many separate descriptions of citizens, as will render an unjust combination of a majority of the whole, very improbable, if not impracticable. The first method prevails in all governments possessing an hereditary or self appointed authority. This at best is but a precarious security; because a power independent of the society may as well espouse the unjust views of the major, as the rightful interests, of the minor party, and may possibly be turned against both parties. The second method will be exemplified in the federal republic of the United States. While all authority in it will be derived from and dependent on the society, the society itself will be broken into so many parts, interests and classes of citizens, that the rights of individuals or of the minority, will be in little danger from interested combinations of the majority. In a free government, the security for civil rights must be the same as for religious rights. It consists in the one case in the multiplicity of interests, and in the other, in the multiplicity of sects. The degree of security in both cases will depend on the number of interests and sects; and this may be presumed to depend on the extent of country and number of people comprehended under the same government. This view of the subject must particularly recommend a proper federal system to all the sincere and considerate friends of republican government: Since it shows that in exact proportion as the territory of the union may be formed into more circumscribed confederacies or states, oppressive combinations of a majority will be facilitated, the best security under the republican form, for the rights of every class of citizens, will be diminished; and consequently, the stability and independence of some member of the government, the only other security, must be proportionally increased. Justice is the end of government. It is the end of civil society. It ever has been, and ever will be pursued, until it be obtained, or until liberty be lost in the pursuit. In a society under the forms of which the stronger faction can readily unite and oppress the weaker, anarchy may as truly be said to reign, as in a state of nature where the weaker individual is not secured against the violence of the stronger: And as in the latter state even the stronger individuals are prompted by the uncertainty of their condition, to submit to a government which may protect the weak as well as themselves: So in the former state, will the more powerful factions or parties be gradually induced by a like motive, to wish for a government which will protect all parties, the weaker as well as the more powerful. It can be little doubted, that if the state of Rhode Island was separated from the confederacy, and left to itself, the insecurity of rights under the popular form of government within such narrow limits, would be displayed by such reiterated oppressions of factious majorities, that some power altogether independent of the people would soon be called for by the voice of the very factions whose misrule had proved the necessity of it. In the extended republic of the United States, and among the great variety of interests, parties and sects which it embraces, a coalition of a majority of the whole society could seldom take place on any other principles than those of justice and the general good; and there being thus less danger to a minor from the will of the major party, there must be less pretext also, to provide for the security of the former, by introducing into the government a will not dependent on the latter; or in other words, a will independent of the society itself. It is no less certain than it is important, notwithstanding the contrary opinions which have been entertained, that the larger the society, provided it lie within a practicable sphere, the more duly capable it will be of self government. And happily for the *republican cause,* the practicable sphere may be carried to a very great extent, by a judicious modification and mixture of the *federal principle.*

Publius

Anti-Federalist Writings (1787–1788)

Those who opposed the ratification of the United States Constitution were called the Anti-Federalists to show their opposition to the Federalists, who were in favor of the Constitution's ratification. Many of the Anti-Federalists' writings were published under pen names, just as were some of the writings of the Federalists.

Because the original Constitution (without its amendments) did not contain a bill of rights, many Anti-Federalist writers were opposed to ratification as is evidenced by the excerpt below, written by an unknown Anti-Federalist.

The truth is, that the rights of individuals are frequently opposed to the apparent interests of the majority—For this reason the greater the portion of political freedom in a form of government the greater the necessity of a bill of rights—Often the natural rights of an individual are opposed to the presumed interests or heated passions of a large majority of democratic government; if these rights are not clearly and expressly ascertained, the individual must be lost; and for the truth of this I appeal to every man who has borne a part in the legislative councils of America. In such government the tyranny of the legislative is most to be dreaded.

—A (Maryland) Farmer in the Maryland Gazette, *April 1788.*

Because the United States was so large a territory, many Anti-Federalists did not believe that it could be governed by one national government. They believed that it would not be a government by the will of the people and, therefore, it would become arbitrary. Robert Yates of New York, using the pen name Brutus, presented these ideas in the following excerpt:

In every free government, the people must give their assent to the laws by which they are governed. This is the true criterion between a free government and an arbitrary one. The former are ruled by the will of the whole [the people], expressed in any manner they may agree upon; the latter by the will of one, or a few. If the people are to give their assent to the laws, by persons chosen and appointed by them, the manner of the choice and the number chosen must be such, as to possess, be disposed, and consequently qualified to declare the sentiments of the people; for if they do not know, or are not disposed to speak the sentiments of the people, the people do not govern, but the sovereignty is in a few. Now, in a large-extended country, it is impossible to have a representation, possessing the sentiments, and of integrity, to declare the minds of the people . . . .

—Brutus, October 1787

Monroe Doctrine (1823)

The Monroe Doctrine is a statement about U.S. foreign policy prepared by John Quincy Adams, and presented by President James Monroe to the Congress on December 2, 1823. The goal of the doctrine was to prevent European involvement in Latin America's new republics.

Fellow citizens of the Senate and House of Representatives:

Many important subjects will claim your attention during the present session, of which I shall endeavor to give, in aid of your deliberations, a just idea in this communication. I undertake this duty with diffidence, from the vast extent of the interests on which I have to treat and of their great importance to every portion of our Union. I enter on it with zeal from a thorough conviction that there never was a period since the establishment of our revolution when, regarding the condition of the civilized world and its bearing on us, there was greater necessity for devotion in the public servants to their respective duties, or for virtue, patriotism, and union in our constituents.

Meeting in you a new Congress, I deem it proper to present this view of public affairs in greater detail than might otherwise be necessary. I do it, however, with peculiar satisfaction, from a knowledge that in this respect I shall comply more fully with the sound principles of our government. The people being with us exclusively the sovereign, it is indispensable that full information be laid before them on all important subjects, to enable them to exercise that high power with complete effect. If kept in the dark, they must be incompetent to it. We are all liable to error, and those who are engaged in the management of public affairs are more subject to excitement and to be led astray by their particular interests and passions than the great body of our constituents, who, living at home in the pursuit of their ordinary avocations, are calm but deeply interested spectators of events and of the conduct of those who are parties to them. To the people every department of the government and every individual in each are responsible, and the more full their information the better they can judge of the wisdom of the policy pursued and of the conduct of each in regard to it. From their dispassionate judgment much aid may always be obtained, while their approbation will form the greatest incentive and most gratifying reward for virtuous actions and the dread of their censure the best security against the abuse of their confidence. Their interests in all vital questions are the same, and the bond, by sentiment as well as by interest, will be proportionably strengthened as they are better informed of the real state of public affairs, especially in difficult conjunctures. It is by such knowledge that local prejudices and jealousies are surmounted, and that a national policy, extending its fostering care and protection to all the great interests of our Union, is formed and steadily adhered to. . . .

At the proposal of the Russian imperial government, made through the minister of the emperor residing here, a full power and instructions have been transmitted to the minister of the United States at St. Petersburg to arrange by amicable negotiation the respective rights and interests of the two nations on the northwest coast of this continent. A similar proposal had been made by his imperial Majesty to the government of Great Britain, which has likewise been acceded to. The government of the United States has been desirous by this friendly proceeding of manifesting the great value which they have invariably attached to the friendship of the emperor and their solicitude to cultivate the best understanding with his government. In the discussions to which this interest has given rise and in the arrangements by which they may terminate the occasion has been judged proper for asserting, as a principle in which the rights and interests of the United States are involved, that the American continents, by the free and independent condition which they have assumed and maintain, are henceforth not to be considered as subjects for future colonization by any European powers. . . .

It was stated at the commencement of the last session that a great effort was then making in Spain and Portugal to improve the condition of the people of those countries, and that it appeared to be conducted with extraordinary moderation. It need scarcely be remarked that the result has been so far very different from what was then anticipated. Of events in that quarter of the globe, with which we have so much intercourse and from which we derive our origin, we have always been anxious and interested spectators. The citizens of the United States cherish sentiments the most friendly in favor of the liberty and happiness of their fellow men on that side of the Atlantic. In the wars of the European powers in matters relating to themselves, we have never taken any part, nor does it comport with our policy so to do. It is only when our rights are invaded or seriously menaced that we resent injuries or make preparation for our defense. With the movements in this hemisphere we are of necessity more immediately connected, and by causes which must be obvious to all enlightened and impartial observers. The political system of the allied powers is essentially different in this respect from that of America. This difference proceeds from that which exists in their respective governments; and to the defense of our own, which has been achieved by the loss of so much blood and treasure, and matured by the wisdom of their most enlightened citizens, and under which we have enjoyed unexampled felicity, this whole nation is devoted. We owe it, therefore, to candor and to the amicable relations existing between the United States and those powers to declare that we should consider any attempt on their part to extend their system to any portion of this hemisphere as dangerous to our peace and safety. With the existing colonies or dependencies of any European power, we have not interfered and shall not interfere. But with the governments who have declared their independence and maintained it, and whose independence we have, on great consideration and on just principles, acknowledged, we could not view any interposition for the purpose of oppressing them, or controlling in any other manner their destiny, by any European power in any other light than as the manifestation of an unfriendly disposition toward the United States. In the war between those new governments and Spain, we declared our neutrality at the time of their recognition, and to this we have adhered, and shall continue to adhere, provided no change shall occur which, in the judgment of the competent authorities of this government, shall make a corresponding change on the part of the United States indispensable to their security.

The late events in Spain and Portugal show that Europe is still unsettled. Of this important fact no stronger proof can be adduced than that the allied powers should have thought it proper, on any principle satisfactory to themselves, to have interposed by force in the internal concerns of Spain. To what extent such interposition may be carried, on the same principle, is a question in which all independent powers whose governments differ from theirs are interested, even those most remote, and surely none more so than the United States. Our policy in regard to Europe, which was adopted at an early stage of the wars which have so long agitated that quarter of the globe, nevertheless remains the same, which is, not to interfere in the internal concerns of any of its powers; to consider the government *de facto* as the legitimate government for us; to cultivate friendly relations with it, and to preserve those relations by a frank, firm, and manly policy, meeting in all instances the just claims of every power, submitting to injuries from none. But in regard to those continents, circumstances are eminently and conspicuously different. It is impossible that the allied powers should extend their political system to any portion of either continent without endangering our peace and happiness; nor can anyone believe that our southern brethren, if left to themselves, would adopt it of their own accord. It is equally impossible, therefore, that we should behold such interposition in any form with indifference. If we look to the comparative strength and resources of Spain and those new governments, and their distance from each other, it must be obvious that she can never subdue them. It is still the true policy of the United States to leave the parties to themselves in the hope that other powers will pursue the same course.

Seneca Falls Declaration (1848)

The Seneca Falls Declaration, a "declaration of sentiments," was issued at an important women's rights convention held at Seneca Falls, New York in July, 1848. The convention was organized by Elizabeth Cady Stanton and Lucretia Mott.

We hold these truths to be self-evident; that all men and women are created equal; that they are endowed by their Creator with certain inalienable rights; that among these are life, liberty, and the pursuit of happiness; that to secure these rights governments are instituted, deriving their just powers from the consent of the governed. . . .

Now, in view of this entire disfranchisement of one-half the people of this country, their social and religious degradation, in view of the unjust laws above mentioned, and because women do feel themselves aggrieved, oppressed, and fraudulently deprived of their most sacred rights, we insist that they have immediate admission to all the rights and privileges which belong to them as citizens of the United States.

[*Excerpt*]

Emancipation Proclamation (1862)

President Abraham Lincoln issued the Emancipation Proclamation on September 23, 1862, in order to gain world support for the Union cause. The document stated that after January 1, 1863, all slaves in the rebel states would be free. The proclamation did not apply to the border states of Delaware, Kentucky, Maryland, and Missouri, nor to that part of the Confederacy already occupied by Northern troops, such as Tennessee and parts of Virginia and Louisiana.

By the President of the United States of America:
A PROCLAMATION

Whereas, on the twenty-second day of September, in the year of our Lord one thousand eight hundred and sixty-two, a proclamation was issued by the president of the United States, containing, among other things, the following, to wit:

"That on the first day of January, in the year of our Lord one thousand eight hundred and sixty-three, all persons held as slaves within any state or designated part of a state, the people whereof shall then be in rebellion against the United States, shall be then, thenceforward and forever, free; and the executive government of the United States, including the military and naval authority thereof, will recognize and maintain the freedom of such persons and will do no act or acts to repress such persons, or any of them, in any efforts they may make for their actual freedom.

"That the executive will, on the first day of January aforesaid, by proclamation, designate the states and parts of states, if any, in which the people thereof, respectively, shall then be in rebellion against the United States; and the fact that any state, or the people thereof, shall on that day be in good faith represented in the Congress of the United States, by members chosen thereto at elections wherein a majority of the qualified voters of such states shall have participated, shall, in the absence of strong countervailing testimony, be deemed conclusive evidence that such state, and the people thereof, are not then in rebellion against the United States."

Now, therefore, I, Abraham Lincoln, president of the United States, by virtue of the power in me vested as commander in chief of the army and navy of the United States, in time of actual armed rebellion against the authority and government of the United States, and as a fit and necessary war measure for suppressing said rebellion, do, on this first day of January, in the year of our Lord one thousand eight hundred and sixty-three, and in accordance with my purpose so to do, publicly proclaimed for the full period of one hundred days from the day first above mentioned, order and designate as the states and parts of states wherein the people thereof, respectively, are this day in rebellion against the United States, the following, to wit:

Arkansas, Texas, Louisiana (except the parishes of St. Bernard, Plaquemines, Jefferson, St. John, St. Charles, St. James, Ascension, Assumption, Terre Bonne, Lafourche, St. Mary, St. Martin, and Orleans, including the city of New Orleans), Mississippi, Alabama, Florida, Georgia, South Carolina, North Carolina, and Virginia (except the forty-eight counties designated as West Virginia, and also the counties of Berkeley, Accomac, Northampton, Elizabeth City, York, Princess Ann, and Norfolk, including the cities of Norfolk and Portsmouth), and which excepted parts are for the present left precisely as if this proclamation were not issued.

And by virtue of the power and for the purpose aforesaid, I do order and declare that all persons held as slaves within said designated states and parts of states are, and henceforward shall be, free; and that the executive government of the United States, including the military and naval authorities thereof, will recognize and maintain the freedom of said persons.

And I hereby enjoin upon the people so declared to be free to abstain from all violence, unless in necessary self-defense; and I recommend to them that, in all cases when allowed, they labor faithfully for reasonable wages.

And I further declare and make known that such persons, of suitable condition will be received into the armed service of the United States to garrison forts, positions, stations, and other places and to man vessels of all sorts in said service.

And upon this act, sincerely believed to be an act of justice, warranted by the Constitution upon military necessity, I invoke the considerate judgment of mankind and the gracious favor of Almighty God.

In witness whereof, I have hereunto set my hand and caused the seal of the United States to be affixed.

Done at the city of Washington this first day of January, in the year of our Lord one thousand eight hundred and sixty-three, and of the independence of the United States of America the eighty-seventh.

By the President:
William H. Seward, Abraham Lincoln
Secretary of State.

Pledge of Allegiance (1892)

The Pledge of Allegiance, a solemn oath of allegiance to the United States, has been attributed to Francis Bellamy, a Baptist minister.

I pledge allegiance to the Flag of the United States of America and to the Republic for which it stands, one Nation under God,* indivisible, with liberty and justice for all.

*The words "under God" were added in 1954.

The American's Creed (1917)

The American's Creed, composed by William Tyler Page in 1917, is a statement of our common political values. It is a set of beliefs about the proper role of government and the dignity of the individual. It attempts to show the consensus of Americans' values and beliefs. The values expressed are individualistic, democratic, and egalitarian.

Composed in 1917 by William Tyler Page (1868–1942).

"I believe in the United States of America as a government of the people, by the people, for the people; whose just powers are derived from the consent of the governed; a democracy in a Republic; a sovereign Nation of many sovereign States; a perfect Union, one and inseparable; established upon those principles of freedom, equality, justice, and humanity for which American patriots sacrificed their lives and fortunes.

"I therefore believe it is my duty to my country to love it; to support its Constitution; to obey its laws; to respect its flag; and to defend it against all enemies."

Brown v. *Board of Education of Topeka (1954)*

The landmark Supreme Court case Brown *v.* Board of Education of Topeka *overturned the "separate but equal doctrine" established by the 1896 case of* Plessy *v.* Ferguson. *At the time of this decision, the Supreme Court was led by Chief Justice Earl Warren.*

In approaching this problem, [w]e must consider public education in the light of its full development and its present place in American life throughout the Nation. Only in this way can it be determined if segregation in public schools deprives these plaintiffs of the equal protection of the laws.

Today, education is perhaps the most important function of state and local governments. Compulsory school attendance laws and the great expenditures for education both demonstrate our recognition of the importance of education to our democratic society. It is required in the performance of our most basic public responsibilities, even service in the armed forces. It is the very foundation of good citizenship. Today it is a principal instrument in awakening the child to cultural values, in preparing him for later professional training, and in helping him to adjust normally to his environment. In these days, it is doubtful that any child may reasonably be expected to succeed in life if he is denied the opportunity of an education. Such an opportunity, where the state has undertaken to provide it, is a right which must be made available to all on equal terms.

We come then to the question presented: Does segregation of children in public schools solely on the basis of race, even though the physical facilities and other 'tangible' factors may be equal, deprive the children of the minority group of equal educational opportunities? We believe that it does.

To separate [African Americans] from others of similar age and qualifications solely because of their race generates a feeling of inferiority as to their status in the community that may affect their hearts and minds in a way unlikely ever to be undone.

We conclude that in the field of public education the doctrine of 'separate but equal' has no place. Separate educational facilities are inherently unequal. Therefore, we hold that the plaintiffs and others similarly situated for whom the actions have been brought are, by reason of the segregation complained of, deprived of the equal protection of the laws guaranteed by the Fourteenth Amendment. This disposition makes unnecessary any discussion whether such segregation also violates the Due Process Clause of the Fourteenth Amendment.

Because these are class actions, because of the wide applicability of this decision, and because of the great variety of local conditions, the formulation of decrees in these cases presents problems of considerable complexity. On reargument, the consideration of appropriate relief was necessarily subordinated to the primary question—the constitutionality of segregation in public education. We have now announced that such segregation is a denial of the equal protection of the laws.

[*Excerpts*]

The Preamble to the Charter of the United Nations

Just as the United States is governed by the rules set forth in the Constitution, so too is the United Nations governed by the rules set forth in the Charter of the United Nations drafted and put into force in 1945. The U.N. Charter, like the Constitution, begins with a preamble that expresses the spirit of the organization.

We the peoples of the United Nations determined

to save succeeding generations from the scourge of war, which twice in our lifetime has brought untold sorrow to mankind, and

to reaffirm faith in fundamental human rights, in the dignity and worth of the human person, in the equal rights of men and women and of nations large and small, and

to establish conditions under which justice and respect for the obligations arising from treaties and other sources of international law can be maintained, and

to promote social progress and better standards of life in larger freedom,

and for these ends

to practice tolerance and live together in peace with one another as good neighbors, and

to unite our strength to maintain international peace and security, and

to ensure, by the acceptance of principles and the institution of methods, that armed force shall not be used, save in the common interest, and

to employ international machinery for the promotion of the economic and social advancement of all peoples,

have resolved to combine our efforts to accomplish these aims.

Accordingly, our respective governments, through representatives assembled in the city of San Francisco, who have exhibited their full powers found to be in good and due form, have agreed to the present Charter of the United Nations and do hereby establish an international organization to be known as the United Nations.

Annotated Table of Legal Cases

How to Read Legal Case Citations and Find Court Decisions

Court decisions are recorded and published in various places. When a court case is mentioned, the notation used to refer to, or to cite, it denotes where the published decision can be found.

State courts of appeal decisions are usually published in two places, the state reports of that particular state and the more widely used *National Reporter System* published by West Publishing Company. Some states no longer publish their own reports. The *National Reporter System* divides the states into the following geographic areas: Atlantic (A. or A.2d, where 2d refers to second series), South Eastern (S.E. or S.E.2d), South Western (S.W. or S.W.2d), North Western (N.W. or N.W.2d), North Eastern (N.E. or N.E.2d), Southern (So. or So.2d), and Pacific (P. or P.2d).

Federal trial court decisions are published unofficially in West's *Federal Supplement* (F.Supp.), and opinions from the circuit courts of appeal are reported unofficially in West's *Federal Reporter* (F. or F.2d). Opinions from the United States Supreme Court are reported in the *United States Reports* (U.S.), the *Lawyer's Edition of the Supreme Court Reports* (L.Ed.), West's *Supreme Court Reporter* (S. Ct.), and other publications. The *United States Reports* is the official edition of the United States Supreme Court decisions published by the federal government. Many early decisions are missing from these volumes. An unofficial and more complete edition of Supreme Court decisions, the *Lawyer's Edition of the Supreme Court Reports,* is published by the Lawyers Cooperative Publishing Company of Rochester, New York. West's *Supreme Court Reporter* is an unofficial edition of decisions dating from October 1882. These volumes contain headnotes and brief editorial statements of the law involved in the case.

State courts of appeal decisions are cited by giving the name of the case; the volume, name, and page number of the state's official report (if the state publishes its own reports); the volume, unit, and page number of the *National Reporter;* and the volume, name, and page number of any other selected reporter. Federal court citations are also listed by giving the name of the case and the volume, name, and page number of the reports.

Table of Court Cases

■ ***Afroyim* v. *Rusk* (1967)**	A civil rights/citizenship case in which the Court ruled that all citizens have "a constitutional right to remain a citizen in a free country unless [they] voluntarily relinquish that citizenship." Part of the Nationality Act of 1940 was declared unconstitutional because it provided for the automatic expatriation of any American citizen who voted in a foreign election.
■ ***Baker* v. *Carr* (1962)**	A Fourteenth Amendment/apportionment case in which the Court ruled that state legislatures had to be apportioned to provide equal protection under the law.
■ ***Barron* v. *Mayor of Baltimore* (1833)**	A civil rights/Bill of Rights case in which the Court ruled that the Bill of Rights applied only to the national government, not to the state governments.
■ ***Betts* v. *Brady* (1942)**	A rights of the accused/right to an attorney case in which the Court held that criminal defendants were not automatically guaranteed the right to have a lawyer present when they were tried in court, except in capital cases (overturned in *Gideon* v. *Wainright*).
■ ***Bigelow* v. *Virginia* (1975)**	A freedom of speech/advertising case involving so-called commercial speech in which the Court held that the state cannot prohibit newspaper advertising of abortion services.
■ ***Board of Education of Westside Community Schools* v. *Mergens* (1990)**	A separation of church and state case in which the Court ruled in favor of a Christian Bible club that wanted to meet on school grounds after regular school hours in Omaha, Nebraska.
■ ***Brandenburg* v. *Ohio* (1969)**	A free speech/national security decision in which the Court narrowed its definition of seditious speech so that advocating the use of force is legal unless such advocacy "is directed to inciting or producing imminent lawless action and is likely to produce such action."

Table of Court Cases—*Continued*

■ ***Branzburg* v. *Hayes* (1972)**	A freedom of speech/confidentiality case in which the Court held that the First Amendment grants no special privileges to reporters. They must therefore respond to questioning during a valid criminal trial or investigation.
■ ***Brown* v. *Board of Education* (1955)**	A civil rights case in which the Court asked for rearguments concerning the way in which the states should implement civil rights decisions including its 1954 decision *Brown* v. *Board of Education of Topeka.* The Court indicated that the lower courts must ensure that African Americans be admitted to schools on a nondiscriminatory basis "with all deliberate speed."
■ ***Brown* v. *Board of Education of Topeka* (1954)**	A civil rights case that established that public schools' segregation of races violated the equal protection clause of the Fourteenth Amendment.
■ ***Burstyn* v. *Wilson* (1952)**	A freedom of press case involving the motion picture industry in which the Court held that "liberty of expression by means of motion pictures is guaranteed by the First and Fourteenth Amendments." Nonetheless, the Court held that prior censorship of films by local and state authorities may be constitutional under certain circumstances, usually involving obscenity.
■ ***Cox* v. *New Hampshire* (1941)**	A freedom of assembly case in which the Court ruled that sixty-eight Jehovah's Witnesses had violated the statute prohibiting parading without a permit and further upheld the right of a municipality to control its public streets.
■ ***De Jonge* v. *Oregon* (1937)**	A freedom of assembly case involving a man convicted for holding a public meeting that was sponsored by the Communist Party. The Court overturned his conviction, ruling that the Oregon law restricted too much the rights of free speech and assembly. This case put the right of assembly on equal footing with the rights of free speech and press.
■ ***Dennis* v. *United States* (1951)**	A free speech and national security case in which the Court ruled that the Smith Act—a law against seditious speech—could be applied to members of the Communist Party.
■ ***Dillon* v. *Gloss* (1921)**	A case ruling that allows Congress to place a "reasonable time limit" on the ratification process for amendments to the United States Constitution.
■ ***Dred Scott* v. *Sandford* (1857)**	A civil rights/citizenship case in which the Court declared that slaves were not citizens of any state or of the United States. (The Court also declared unconstitutional the Missouri Compromise because it deprived a person of his property [his slave] without due process of law.)
■ ***Engel* v. *Vitale* (1962)**	The so-called Regents' Prayer Case, in which the Court outlawed even the voluntary saying of a nondenominational prayer written by the New York State Board of Regents. An important separation of church and state case.

Table of Court Cases—*Continued*

■ ***Escobedo* v. *Illinois* (1964)**	A rights of the accused/right to counsel case in which the Court overturned the conviction of Danny Escobedo, who had been arrested by Chicago police in connection with the murder of his brother-in-law. Escobedo's request to see his lawyer had been refused even though the lawyer was in the police station trying to see Escobedo during his questioning.
■ ***Everson* v. *Board of Education* (1947)**	A First Amendment/establishment clause case in which the Court ruled in favor of tax-supported busing of students who attended parochial schools.
■ ***Feiner* v. *New York* (1951)**	A freedom of assembly case in which the Court upheld a conviction for unlawful assembly because the police had acted to preserve public order. Feiner, during a speech in Syracuse, New York, verbally attacked President Harry S Truman and the mayor of Syracuse. When the police were called, the crowd was on the verge of attempting to stop Feiner from speaking.
■ ***Ford* v. *Wainwright* (1986)**	An Eighth Amendment/capital punishment case in which the Court ruled that the U.S. Constitution bars states from executing convicted killers who have become insane while waiting on death row.
■ ***Frontiero* v. *Richardson* (1973)**	A civil liberties/gender classification case in which the Court ruled against any sex discrimination based on ''romantic paternalism.''
■ ***Furman* v. *Georgia* (1972)**	An Eighth Amendment/capital punishment case in which the Court struck down Georgia's laws allowing the death penalty because the laws gave too much discretion to juries and judges in deciding whether capital punishment should be imposed.
■ ***Gannet Company* v. *De Pasquale* (1979)**	A freedom of press/gag order case in which the Court held that if a judge found a reasonable probability that news publicity would harm a defendant's right to a fair trial, the court could impose a gag rule: ''Members of the public have no constitutional right under the Sixth and Fourteenth Amendments to attend criminal trials.''
■ ***Gibbons* v. *Ogden* (1824)**	For the first time, the national government's power over commerce was defined in an expansive way. In effect, the power of the national government to regulate commerce has no limitations other than those specifically found in the Constitution.
■ ***Gideon* v. *Wainwright* (1963)**	A rights of the accused/right to counsel case in which the Court said that persons who can demonstrate that they are unable to afford to have a lawyer present and are accused of felonies must be given a lawyer at the expense of the government.
■ ***Gitlow* v. *New York* (1925)**	A free speech/bad-tendency rule case that allows First Amendment freedoms to be curtailed if there is a possibility that such expression might lead to some evil. In this case, a member of a left-wing group was convicted of violating New York State's criminal anarchy statute when he published and distributed materials urging the violent overthrow of the U.S. government.

Table of Court Cases—*Continued*

Case	Description
■ ***Gregg*** **v.** ***Georgia*** **(1976)**	An Eighth Amendment/capital punishment case in which the Court indicated for the first time that the death penalty does not "invariably violate the Constitution."
■ ***Griswold*** **v.** ***Connecticut*** **(1965)**	A civil liberties/right to privacy case in which the Court overthrew a Connecticut law that effectively prohibited the distribution of contraceptives. In the case Justice William O. Douglas claimed that the First, Third, Fourth, Fifth, and Ninth Amendments created "penumbras, formed by emanations from those guarantees that help give them life and substance," and went on to talk about zones for privacy that are guaranteed by these rights.
■ ***Hazelwood School District*** **v.** ***Cathy Kuhlmeier*** **(1988)**	A First Amendment/freedom of speech and press case in which the Court held that school officials may impose reasonable restrictions on the speeches of students, teachers, and other members of the school community.
■ ***Hoyt*** **v.** ***Florida*** **(1961)**	A civil rights/gender classification case in which the Court ruled as constitutional a law that required men to serve on juries, but allowed women to choose whether or not they wished to serve.
■ ***Kaiser Aluminum and Chemical Co. (United Steelworkers of America)*** **v.** ***Weber*** **(1979)**	A civil rights/reverse discrimination case in which a union apprenticeship program that used a racial quota was deemed legal even if it violated the words of the Civil Rights Act of 1964 because it did not violate the spirit. Essentially, any form of reverse discrimination—even explicit quotas—is permissible provided that it is the result of legislative, executive, or judicial findings of past discrimination.
■ ***Katz*** **v.** ***United States*** **(1967)**	A Fourth Amendment/wiretapping case in which the Court overturned Katz's conviction for transmitting betting information across state lines from a public phone booth in Los Angeles. The FBI had placed recording devices outside the booth without a warrant.
■ ***Klopfer*** **v.** ***North Carolina*** **(1967)**	A Sixth Amendment/right to a speedy trial case in which the Court first held that the Sixth Amendment's guarantee applies to the states because of the Fourteenth Amendment.
■ ***Lemon*** **v.** ***Kurtzman*** **(1971)**	An excessive entanglement case in which the Court held that the establishment clause was designed to prevent sponsorship, financial support, and active involvement of the government in religious activity. The Court did not allow a Pennsylvania law that provided for financial payments to private schools to cover their costs for textbooks, some teachers' salaries, and other teaching materials for nonreligious courses only.
■ ***Louisiana*** **v.** ***Resweber*** **(1947)**	An Eighth Amendment cruel and unusual punishment case in which the Court held that a convicted murderer could be subjected to a second electrocution after the first one failed to work properly.

Table of Court Cases—*Continued*

■ ***Lynch* v. *Donnelly* (1984)**	A separation of church and state case in which the Court said that the city of Pawtucket, Rhode Island, could include a nativity scene in its holiday display because the scene formed part of an ensemble with Santa's sleigh and reindeer and a Christmas tree.
■ ***Mapp* v. *Ohio* (1961)**	A rights of the accused/exclusionary rule case in which the Court overturned the conviction of Dollree Mapp for possession of obscene materials because police had found pornographic books in her apartment after searching it without a warrant despite her verbal refusal to let them in.
■ ***Marbury* v. *Madison* (1803)**	The Court ruled for the first time an act of Congress unconstitutional, thereby establishing the principle of judicial review.
■ ***McCollum* v. *Board of Education* (1948)**	A ''release time'' program case in which the Court would not allow such a program in Champaign, Illinois, because school classrooms were being used for religious purposes.
■ ***McCulloch* v. *Maryland* (1819)**	The Court's ruling upheld the constitutionality of a creation of the Bank of the United States and denied to the states the power to tax it because ''the power to tax involves the power to destroy.'' The ruling clarified the doctrine of implied powers of the national government.
■ ***Miller* v. *California* (1973)**	A freedom of speech/obscenity case in which the Court created a formal list of requirements as a legal test of obscenity. They are that (1) the average person finds that it violates contemporary community standards; (2) the work taken as a whole appeals to prurient interest in sex; (3) the work shows patently offensive sexual conduct; and (4) the work lacks serious redeeming literary, artistic, political, or scientific merit.
■ ***Minersville School District* v. *Gobitis* (1940)**	A free exercise of religion/flag salute case in which the Court held that because the flag was a symbol of national unity, requiring that it be saluted was not an infringement on the free exercise of religion.
■ ***Miranda* v. *Arizona* (1966)**	A rights of the accused/right to remain silent case in which a mentally disturbed suspect, Ernesto Miranda, had been arrested, questioned for two hours, and confessed to the crime of kidnapping and rape. His conviction was reversed by the Court on the basis of the Fifth and Sixth Amendments. Now people are read their rights, including the right to remain silent.
■ ***Mueller* v. *Allen* (1983)**	An excessive entanglement case in which the Court upheld a Minnesota tax law giving parents a state income-tax deduction for the cost of textbooks, transportation for elementary and secondary schoolchildren, and tuition whether the children go to private or public schools.
■ ***Murray* v. *Giarratano* (1989)**	An Eighth Amendment/capital punishment case in which the Court held that indigent death-row inmates have no constitutional right to a lawyer for a second round of state court appeals.

Table of Court Cases—*Continued*

■ ***Myers*** **v.** ***United States*** **(1926)**	The presidential removal power case in which the Court held unconstitutional an 1876 law that required Senate consent before the president could dismiss a postmaster.
■ ***Near*** **v.** ***Minnesota*** **(1931)**	A freedom of press/prior restraint case in which a Minnesota law prohibiting the publication of malicious and scandalous newspapers or magazines was held to be invalid because it constituted unconstitutional prior restraint in violation of the First and Fourteenth Amendments.
■ ***New York Times*** **v.** ***United States*** **(1971)**	A freedom of press/prior restraint case involving the publication of sensitive government documents relating to the government's policy in Vietnam from 1945 to 1967. The U.S. government attempted to suspend the publication of the so-called *Pentagon Papers,* but the Court held that the government could only prosecute after publication, not before.
■ ***In re Oliver*** **(1948)**	A Sixth Amendment/right to a public trial case in which the Court ruled that not only must a trial be speedy, but it also must be held in public.
■ ***Penry*** **v.** ***Lynaugh*** **(1989)**	An Eighth Amendment/capital punishment case in which the Court held that mentally retarded persons may be executed for murder.
■ ***Plessy*** **v.** ***Ferguson*** **(1896)**	A civil rights case in which the Court ruled that state laws enforcing segregation by race were constitutional when accommodations were equal as well as separate. (Subsequently overturned by *Brown* v. *Board of Education of Topeka.*)
■ ***Powell*** **v.** ***Alabama*** **(1932)**	A Sixth Amendment right to counsel case in which the Court ruled that the accused has a right to a lawyer in capital punishment cases.
■ ***Powell*** **v.** ***McCormack*** **(1969)**	A congressional qualifications case in which the Court ruled that the House of Representatives could not exclude any elected member who met the Constitution's requirements for citizenship, residence, and age.
■ ***Reed*** **v.** ***Reed*** **(1971)**	A civil rights/gender classification case in which the Court ruled against an Idaho law that gave fathers preferences over mothers in taking care of their children's estates.
■ ***Regents of the University of California*** **v.** ***Bakke*** **(1978)**	A civil rights/reverse discrimination case in which the Court allowed the University of California, Davis Campus, School of Medicine to admit students on the basis of race if the school's aim is to combat the effects of past discriminations. The Court held, nonetheless, that Bakke must be admitted to the medical school because its admissions policy had used race as the *sole* criterion for a limited number of "minority" positions.
■ ***Reynolds*** **v.** ***Sims*** **(1964)**	A congressional reapportionment case in which the Court ruled that both chambers of a state legislature must be apportioned with equal populations in each district. This "one-person, one-vote" principle had already been applied to congressional districts in *Wesberry* v. *Sanders.*

Table of Court Cases—*Continued*

■ ***Reynolds* v. *United States* (1879)**	A free exercise of religion case in which the Court held that Reynolds, a Mormon living in Utah who had been convicted of polygamy, had violated federal law. The Court ruled that polygamy was a crime and therefore could not be excused as religious practice. Hence, people are free to believe and worship as they wish so long as their conduct does not violate laws that protect the safety, health, or morals of the community.
■ ***Richmond* v. *Croson* (1989)**	A civil rights/reverse discrimination case in which the Court ruled that any program that favors blacks over whites has to be judged by the same constitutional test applicable to any law that favors whites over blacks.
■ ***Richmond Newspapers, Inc.* v. *Virginia* (1980)**	A freedom of press/gag order case in which the Court ruled that actual trials must be opened to the public except under unusual circumstances.
■ ***Robinson* v. *California* (1962)**	A Eighth Amendment/no cruel and unusual punishment case in which the Court ruled that the Fourteenth Amendment extends the Eighth Amendment to the states. Here the Court struck down a California law that defines drug addiction as a crime to be punished rather than an illness to be treated.
■ ***Rochin* v. *California* (1952)**	A due process of law/procedural due process case, sometimes referred to as "the stomach pumping case," in which a suspected illegal drug user was taken to a hospital and administered a liquid that forced him to vomit. Morphine capsules thereby recovered were used to convict him of violating the state's narcotics laws. The Court overruled the conviction, holding that it violated the Fourteenth Amendment's guarantee of procedural due process.
■ ***Roe* v. *Wade* (1973)**	A privacy case in which the Court ruled that state antiabortion laws were unconstitutional except when they applied to the last three months of pregnancy.
■ ***Rostker* v. *Goldberg* (1981)**	A civil rights/gender classification case in which the Court upheld the U.S. government selective service law that requires only men to register for the draft.
■ ***Schenck* v. *United States* (1919)**	A free speech case involving the clear and present danger test in which the Court upheld the Espionage Act of 1917, which made it a crime to encourage resistance to the military draft. The Court said that a person who encourages draft resistance during a war is a "clear and present danger."
■ ***Smith* v. *Allwright* (1944)**	A voting rights case in which the Court declared that the white primary was a violation of the Fifteenth Amendment. The Court reasoned that the political party was actually performing a state function in holding a primary election and therefore not acting as a private group.
■ ***South Carolina* v. *Katzenback* (1966)**	A voting rights case in which the Court held that Congress had acted correctly by passing the Voting Rights Act as a way to implement the Fifteenth Amendment guarantee of the right to vote to every citizen of the United States regardless of race, color, or previous condition of servitude.

Table of Court Cases—*Continued*

■ ***Stone* v. *Graham* (1980)**	A separation of church and state case in which the Court would not allow a Kentucky law that required the Ten Commandments to be posted in all public classrooms.
■ ***Teitel Film Corporation* v. *Cusack* (1968)**	A freedom of press/motion picture case in which the Court held that the government can ban a film if at a judicial hearing it is proven to be obscene.
■ ***Thornhill* v. *Alabama* (1940)**	A freedom of speech/picketing case in which the Court held that picketing was a form of expression protected by the First and Fourteenth Amendments. Nonetheless, picketing may be prevented if it is set in a background of violence, and even peaceful picketing may be controlled if it is being done for an illegal purpose.
■ ***United States* v. *Nixon* (1974)**	A presidential executive privilege case in which the Court ruled that President Nixon had to hand over secret tapes containing his Oval Office conversations while in the White House. The Court ruled that executive privilege could not be used to prevent evidence from being heard in criminal proceedings.
■ ***Walz* v. *New York City Tax Commission* (1970)**	A separation of church and state case in which the Court ruled that tax exemptions for churches do not violate the First Amendment, but rather show the state's "benevolent neutrality" toward religion.
■ ***Wesberry* v. *Sanders* (1964)**	A Fourteenth Amendment/congressional districting case in which the Court ruled that the state of Georgia's formation of congressional districts created such huge population differences that they violated the Constitution. This case was the basis of the Court's ruling later requiring one person, one vote.
■ ***West Virginia Board of Education* v. *Barnette* (1943)**	A free exercise of religion/flag salute case in which the Court held that laws requiring a flag salute were an unconstitutional interference with the free exercise of religion.
■ ***Wilkinson* v. *Jones* (1987)**	A freedom of speech and press/cable TV case in which the Court held that state government cannot regulate independent cable programming. The case involved a Utah law prohibiting the cable broadcast of indecent material between 7 A.M. and midnight.
■ ***Yates* v. *United States* (1957)**	A free speech and national security case in which the Court said that merely advocating the overthrow of a government is not illegal, because such speech only addresses people's belief as opposed to causing them to undertake actions against the government.
■ ***Zorach* v. *Clauson* (1952)**	A "release time" case in which the Court upheld a New York City program because that program required religious classes to be held in private places and not on school campuses.

Extended Case Studies

Immigration Reform and Control Act of 1986 and Amnesty

Introduction

In 1986 Congress passed the first major revision of the nation's immigration policy in twenty years. The Immigration Reform and Control Act of that year contained several controversial provisions. One provided amnesty and legal status for illegal aliens who could prove they had lived continuously in the U.S. since at least January 1, 1982. Another provision granted amnesty to agricultural workers who were employed for 90 days in the twelve-month period preceding May 1, 1986. A third section made it illegal for all U.S. employers to hire illegal aliens knowingly. Penalties were stiff, ranging from $250 to $10,000 for each alien on the payroll.

A Source Document:
Excerpts from the Immigration and Control Act of 1986

§ 1255a. Adjustment of status of certain entrants before Jan. 1, 1982, to that of person admitted for lawful residence

(a) Temporary resident status. The Attorney General shall adjust the status of an alien to that of an alien lawfully admitted for temporary residence if the alien meets the following requirements:

(1) Timely application. (A) During application period. Except as provided in subparagraph (B), the alien must apply for such adjustment during the 12-month period beginning on a date (not later than 180 days after the date of enactment of this section [enacted Nov. 6, 1986]) designated by the Attorney General.

* * * *

(C) Information included in application. Each application under this subsection shall contain such information as the Attorney General may require, including information on living relatives of the applicant with respect to whom a petition for preference or other status may be filed by the applicant at any later date under section 204(a) [8 USCS § 1154(a)].

(2) Continuous unlawful residence since 1982. (A) In general. The alien must establish that he entered the United States before January 1, 1982, and that he has resided continuously in the United States in an unlawful status since such date and through the date the application is filed under this subsection.
(B) Nonimmigrants. In the case of an alien who entered the United States as a nonimmigrant before January 1, 1982, the alien must establish that the alien's period of authorized stay as a nonimmigrant expired before such date through the passage of time or the alien's unlawful status was known to the Government as of such date.

* * * *

(3) Continuous physical presence since enactment. (A) In general. The alien must establish that the alien has been continuously physically present in the United States since the date of the enactment of this section [enacted Nov. 6, 1986].
(B) Treatment of brief, casual, and innocent absences. An alien shall not be considered to have failed to maintain continuous physical presence in the United States for purposes of subparagraph (A) by virtue of brief, casual, and innocent absences from the United States.
(C) Admissions. Nothing in this section shall be construed as authorizing an alien to apply for admission to, or to be admitted to, the United States in order to apply for adjustment of status under this subsection.

Media Reports

The bill will go down in history as the largest amnesty program for illegal aliens in modern history—also the longest and one of the more generous. But was it a success? That is still a lingering question in the minds of many. No one argues that it was perfect, not even Senator Alan Simpson of Wyoming, co-sponsor of the bill. ''There will never be a perfect bill, any more than there are perfect children, perfect marriages, or perfect crimes,'' he said. Below is a sample of some of the media articles at the time.

U.S. Border Control: Holes in the Policy?
Los Angeles Times, *February 10, 1992.*

In the last several days, news stories in San Diego and Los Angeles came together, quite coincidentally, to remind us how difficult—perhaps even impossible—it is to stop the flow of illegal migrant workers from Mexico into this country. All of the stories involve what is arguably the federal government's most unappreciated agency, the U.S. Immigration and Naturalization Service. It is surely the most underfunded and overworked.

Of course the U.S.-Mexican border has been open so long to the flow of people and goods that it can never be completely closed. Nor should it be—for the only long-term solution to illegal migration is free and open trade that eventually equalizes economic opportunity in the two countries. But meanwhile the flow of people across the line must be better regulated so it is not the chaotic, and often dangerous, free-for-all it is now.

Source: Copyright, 1992, *Los Angeles Times.* Reprinted by permission.

Why Amnesty Failed
by Jason DeParle
The Washington Monthly, *April 1988, p. 11.*

Eva has a problem. She's lived in Chicago for eight years as an illegal immigrant. The new immigration law that took effect last May gives her the chance to shed that illegal status for a work permit and eventual citizenship. But Eva lacks the paper trail she needs to prove her history of U.S. residence. She lacks the hundreds of dollars it would cost her to apply. And she lacks the faith that immigration authorities won't deport her children, who didn't begin arriving from Mexico until 1984, two years after the amnesty cut-off date. "If I give them the names of my children," she says, "they'll take them."

As the year-long legalization program draws to a close, there are hundreds of thousands of Evas: illegal immigrants too poor, confused, or afraid to capitalize on its one-time offer. When the program kicked off last May, immigration officials predicted that between 2 million and 3.9 million people would register. But as March began only a million had come forward, and head-counters have consistently deflated their final prediction, which has now sagged to only 1.35 million. To spur a last-minute surge, sombrero-topped immigration officials have been Texas two-stepping from one photo op to another, broadcasting Spanish jingles and attending burrito bakes. They've even begun placing flyers in the bags of tortillas sold in grocery stores, urging people to apply. But all the salsa in San Diego won't coax forth the number of illegals the law was intended to help.

Source: Reprinted by permission from *The Washington Monthly.* Copyright by The Washington Monthly Company, 1611 Connecticut Avenue, NW, Washington D.C., 20009. (202) 462-0128.

As the end of the year approached and the legalization program drew to a close, some wanted to buy more time and asked Congress to extend the deadline for a year.

Slamming the Golden Door
Newsweek, *May 9, 1988, p. 18.*

A last-minute push to extend the amnesty program for six months died in the Senate last week when amnesty's original sponsor, Wyoming Republican Alan Simpson, jumped ship to join Texas's Phil Gramm in leading the fight against it. The bill's backers wanted the extension to reach more aliens who were still afraid to apply, but then accepted the INS argument that the law was sufficiently understood. "This is it," said Simpson. "It's a one-time shot. If you want to live the dream, you have to do it by midnight, May 4. It will never come again." The rush to register, which had been speeding up for months, was expected to become a stampede this week. Even so, the slow pace in the early months of the program meant the final total of aliens registered would be well below the original INS prediction of 2 million or more.

Nobody knows how many illegal residents there are; estimates of the underground population run from 4.5 million to 7 million or more. Immigrant activists worried that many aliens, particularly in Asian communities, still didn't understand the law and hadn't applied. And from now on, warns Leonel Castillo, a former INS commissioner still active in immigration affairs in Houston, "those who did not qualify for amnesty are going to have to hide much more cleverly and do much more dangerous things to stay out of reach."

Source: From *Newsweek,* May 9, 1988;

Conclusion

The amnesty program passed by Congress in 1986 remains as one of Congress's most obvious admissions that America is indeed a land of immigrants. Undoubtedly there will be other amnesty programs as the Congress attempts to deal with similar problems in the future.

Analysis Questions

1. What does the heading of the section of the Act reproduced above mean when it states "adjustment of status of certain entrants"?
2. Why does the Act require "continuous unlawful residence since 1982"?
3. In the quote from the article in the *Washington Monthly,* did the author, Jason DeParle, believe the program was working? Why or why not?
4. Why was there an attempt to extend the time period during which the amnesty program was to remain in effect?

The AIDS Epidemic

Introduction

One of the most serious medical, social, and economic problems facing the United States and the world today involves the disease called acquired immune deficiency syndrome (AIDS). AIDS has become a worldwide epidemic. Experts estimate that by the year 2000, 40 million individuals will be infected with the human immunodeficiency virus (HIV) that normally causes AIDS. Further, it is estimated that in America several million individuals will be infected by HIV by the same year. Already, well over 100,000 Americans have died from AIDS.

Media Reports

The following article was taken from a domestic media source.

The AIDS Disaster

by Steven Findlaw

U.S. News & World Report, *June 17, 1991, p 22.*

How many will die? Will a cure or vaccine be found? Will the health-care system become overwhelmed? These questions have no precise answers. Science and modern medicine may eventually triumph over AIDS, but the best guess of most scientists is that neither a cure nor a vaccine will be found by the end of the century. In the meantime, it is clear that the last thing America should treat AIDS with is complacency. In all likelihood, the spread of HIV and the death toll will rise steeply in the decade ahead, tempered only by the effectiveness of local responses, including education and prevention efforts. By the year 2000, the World Health Organization projects that 40 million people worldwide will be infected with HIV, including an appalling 10 million children. Five to 10 million people could die of the disease, including a projected 500,000 in the United States. San Francisco might lose 4 percent of its population in the 1990s to AIDS; New York, 2 to 3 percent. Some cities in East and Central Africa could lose 15 percent.

At the same time, more and more of the faces of AIDS in the United States will be black or brown, many poor and disenfranchised. In a few years, minorities will account for much more than half of all new cases. "Nowhere do I see any planning for the future of what will be a complex and expensive disease to treat," says William Haseltine of Harvard's Dana-Farber Cancer Institute.

If, by most standards, the AIDS epidemic will become harder to combat in the decade ahead, it could become easier in one respect: More at-risk groups may support testing for HIV. When the AIDS antibody test became available in 1985, gay groups and many public-health officials counseled people to avoid it lest they invite discrimination. The discouragement proved remarkably effective: The Centers for Disease Control estimates that 75 percent of the 1 million to 1.5 million HIV-infected persons in the United States do not know they are infected. But beginning in 1989, some gay leaders and public-health experts—despite the persistence of

HIV-based discrimination—started changing their minds about routine testing, particularly for groups like hospital patients, clients at sexual-disease clinics, health-care workers, newborns and pregnant women.

Source: Copyright, June 17, 1991, *U.S. News & World Report.*

A Foreign Media Source

Sometimes a different "slant" on a problem can be gleaned from reading the foreign media. Specifically, it is easy for Americans to get magazines and newspapers published in Britain and other English-speaking countries. In the example below, *The Economist* magazine, published in London, talks about the problem of AIDS in Africa.

An African Example

The Economist
September 21, 1991, p. 24.

For a small, poor country like Uganda, AIDS causes troubles that existing medical and social services cannot cope with. Uganda was the first African country openly to acknowledge that it had an AIDS epidemic. Just how big an epidemic is still unknown, but certainly it is vast. One estimate puts the number of people infected with HIV at 1m [million], 11% of the adult population. Some projections based on such figures suggest that Uganda will have 22m people in 2015, one-third of whom will be infected; without AIDS, the population might have been around 37m.

The effects of AIDS on village life are devastating. Young couples may die within a few years or even months of each other, leaving behind orphans and parents whom normally they would care for. Instead, the elderly find themselves forced to care for their sick children and grandchildren. Foreign aid workers and local charities alike are straining their resources to build orphanages and old peoples' homes. The traditional family structure may begin to break up.

The economic consequences of the epidemic are considerable. Beside the direct loss of hard-working young adults, many people have to stay away from work to care for relatives. A less obvious burden is that of funerals, which professionals in Kampala worry about constantly. Ugandans are buried in their traditional villages, and it is customary for all the dead person's colleagues to attend the funeral. This can mean that entire government departments are absent for days at a time, attending funerals in far-flung parts.

Efforts to prevent AIDS run up against a basic problem: it is hard in Uganda, as anywhere else, to make people believe that what they do now will have consequences in several years' time, especially when they receive conflicting advice. Witch-doctors, often trusted more than modern doctors, may explain AIDS as the result of curses. Phoney cures abound. A year ago President Daniel arap Moi of Kenya claimed Kemron, a type of interferon created by a Kenyan-Japanese-American research team, as a miracle cure. Many people in Africa still believe him, though there is no proof that it works.

Educators have more than ignorance to contend with. Women may refuse to listen to advice at all if it involves talking about sex. Men, who may consider venereal disease almost a mark of pride, see the use of condoms as unmasculine. There is also apathy. Uganda has undergone 20 years of war, looting and terror. It suffers from terrible endemic diseases, which in some areas still kill more people than AIDS. Many do not see why they should change sexual habits just because of another disease; arguments that would be compelling elsewhere can be weak in a society inured to death.

The spread of information too is difficult. Newspapers are few, and nearly 60% of Ugandans are illiterate anyway. Noreen Kaleeba, director of the AIDS Support Organisation (TASO) in Kampala, believes that the only effective way of teaching people how to avoid AIDS is one-to-one counselling, with a special African twist. TASO goes to villages to find local story-tellers responsible for recounting village history and brings them to Kampala, where they are trained about AIDS, and sent back to incorporate their new knowledge into their tales. The result may not be undiluted scientific truth—embellishment is a traditional part of African story-telling—but success, measured in questionnaires showing how many people now use condoms, is much higher than it was in the past.

For all its difficulties, the fact that Uganda does anything at all is testimony to the qualities of its president, Yoweri Museveni. Halting the spread of AIDS requires a willingness to admit that the problem exists. Many other African governments, notably Kenya's, have refused to acknowledge its extent. In

Uganda, honesty about AIDS was possible in the atmosphere of political openness and press freedom that followed the end of a civil war. Other countries may require political upheavals before they too acknowledge their plight.

Source: © 1991 *The Economist Newspaper Ltd.* Reprinted with permission.

Conclusion

AIDS is one of the most momentous problems we face today. There is hope that a vaccine soon will be developed. In the meantime, the United States and the world will have to pay the price of this deadly disease. That price includes illness, tragedy, and enormous medical and social costs.

Analysis Questions

1. In your reading of the excerpt from the *U.S. News and World Report* article, do you get the impression that the author thinks AIDS will be cured in the near future? Explain your answer.
2. About how many Americans who are HIV infected know they are so infected?
3. What are some of the problems that African countries have in solving the AIDS problem?
4. Why is the spread of information difficult in Uganda and in other African countries?

The War on Drugs

Introduction

America's fight against the sale and use of illegal drugs takes on greater proportions every year. It has been estimated that federal, state, and local spending on the war on drugs exceeds $30 million annually. Some argue that the war against illegal drugs should only be a part of the war against all harmful drugs, including alcohol and nicotine, two of this country's most significant causes of death and illness.

The Federal Government's Response

For many years the federal government has been deeply involved in the war on drugs. As part of President Bush's campaign against the war on drugs he commissioned a National Drug Control Strategy. The following is the letter that he wrote to the Speaker of the House when he submitted the National Drug Control Strategy in 1989.

The White House
Washington, September 5, 1989

Dear Mr. Speaker:

Consistent with section 1005 of the Anti-Drug Abuse Act of 1988 (21 U.S.C. 1504), I am today pleased to transmit my Administration's 1989 National Drug Control Strategy for congressional consideration and action.

This report is the product of an unprecedented national effort over many months. America's fight against epidemic illegal drug use cannot be won on any single front alone; it must be waged *everywhere*—at every level of Federal, State, and local government and by every citizen in every community across the country. Accordingly, we have conducted a thorough, intensive, and unflinching review of Federal anti-drug efforts to date. And we have solicited advice and recommendations from hundreds of interested and involved anti-drug leaders outside the Federal Government. The result is a comprehensive blueprint for new direction and effort—and for success in the near- and long-term future.

I am especially grateful for the valuable contributions made during this process by Members of Congress, with whom we consulted broadly as our strategy was being conceived and formulated these past 6 months. I ask that this spirit of bipartisan cooperation now be extended to the difficult but necessary work that lies ahead: full swift funding and implementation of the many proposals and initiatives contained in this report. On behalf of those Americans most directly suffering from the scourge of drugs—and all the many more who must be further protected from it—I ask for your help and support.

Sincerely,
George Bush

The Honorable Thomas S. Foley
Speaker of the House of Representatives
Washington, D.C. 20515

Media Reports

In any one week, countless newspapers, magazines, and other media sources run articles on the war on drugs. In the following excerpt you can read how effective the president's war on drug abuse has been.

Cocaine Use Jumps Despite Bush's War Against Drug Abuse

The Greenville News
December 19, 1991, p. 17.

WASHINGTON (AP)—After three years of the Bush administration's war against drugs, cocaine use increased this year and drug-related visits to hospital emergency rooms jumped, according to studies made available Wednesday.

Administration drug policy officials pointed to some good news in the statistics: Younger people seem to be turning against drugs, so the drug-use figures should decline in the future.

But for now, "The problem seems to be collapsing into groups within our society who can least afford the problems caused by their addiction: older and inner city addicts," said Bob Martinez, director of the Office of National Drug Control Policy.

* * * *

Overall, the household survey found that current use of any illicit drug—at least once in the previous month—has fallen steadily, from 14.5 million in 1988 to 12.6 million this year.

For cocaine, however, past month use rose from 1.6 million last year to 1.9 million this year. That still remained far below the 2.9 million who said they had used cocaine within the previous month in 1988.

The overwhelming bulk of the increase this year was among people age 35 and older, while monthly cocaine use among people 12–34 has dropped steadily from 2.5 million in 1988 to 1.37 million this year, the survey found.

That, the finding that past-month use of any illicit drug by people under age 35 declined steadily from 12.2 million in 1988 to 9.2 million this year and that the decline has been pronounced among adolescents is "very good news," said Martinez.

"It means that we are shutting down the pipeline into drug addiction, especially among young Americans," he said.

At the same time, Americans 35 and older increased their use of all illicit drugs, especially cocaine and marijuana.

"This dramatically points out one of the sad lessons of the drug war—once you start to use drugs, it's very hard to get off and stay off," Martinez said.

The findings prompted criticism from Rep. Charles B. Rangel, D-N.Y. and the chairman of the House Select Committee on Narcotics, who said the findings were incomplete, but said they "indicate that we are not turning the corner on the drug problem, as the administration has been saying for the last year."

Media Reports—A Different View

Not everyone believes that "getting tough" on drugs is the way to solve the problem. Indeed, there are some who argue for legalization of certain drugs that are now illegal. One of them is a U.S. federal judge.

U.S. Judge: Legalize Drugs

By David Lyons
The Miami Herald, *Thursday, November 28, 1991, p. 2B.*

Reflecting the frustration of fellow judges inundated by cocaine and marijuana cases, a South Florida federal judge has publicly called for the legalization of drugs.

U.S. District Judge James C. Paine made the stunning statement last week during a luncheon meeting of the Federal Bar Association in Miami.

"I know there are a lot of people who do not agree," Paine said Wednesday in an interview from his West Palm Beach office. "I just think it's kind of inevitable."

Paine, 67, is regarded widely as a conservative in South Florida legal circles. But after 12 years on the bench, presiding over an unabated flood of drug cases in his courtroom, he said it is time to find other ways to combat the drug problem.

"I'd say I've held this viewpoint for three or four years," Paine said. "I'd been thinking about it for quite a long time."

Before a shocked audience of about 50 people, Judge Paine made these points:

- Federal courts were not designed—and cannot accommodate—"every case involving crack cocaine or all of the drug-related cases in which local police make an arrest on every day of each week."

- Criminal caseloads in the federal courts have exploded.
- The prohibition of alcohol—sold to the public as "an economic and moral bonanza"—was a failure. As with the war on alcohol in the 1920s, the war on drugs benefited smugglers and "the forces of big government."
- Illegal drugs breed more crime, stronger drugs and the abuse of civil liberties.

Paine isn't the first judge to urge legalization. Two years ago, U.S. District Judge Robert W. Sweet of New York made similar remarks.

Source: Reprinted with the permission of *The Miami Herald.*

Conclusion

The human and economic costs of drug abuse continue to plague American society. The reality, though, is that most Americans do not abuse drugs of any kind, even alcohol and nicotine. Indeed, alcohol consumption per capita has been declining since 1985. Tobacco addiction has decreased even more dramatically: Back in the 1950s, fully 60 percent of American adults were smokers. Today that number is less than 29 percent. Also, it appears that casual use of cocaine and marijuana declined somewhat in the late 1980s and early 1990s. Some observers believe that educational programs against abuse of all drugs have started to have an effect in America.

Analysis Questions

1. When you compare the first newspaper article with George Bush's hopes expressed in his letter, what conclusions can you reach? Explain your answer.
2. What are the arguments that counter the federal judge's call for legalizing drugs?
3. What steps do you think you can take to help in the war on drugs?

Exxon Valdez

Introduction

The fate of the oil tanker *Exxon Valdez* begins, perhaps, when a captain with too much alcohol in his blood turns over the command of his tanker to an unqualified third mate. The mate sends contradictory orders to the engine room and the vessel is impaled on Bligh Reef, causing millions of gallons of oil to gush from the mangled hull. The supposedly impossible has happened. And it couldn't have happened at a worse time in a worse place, threatening and eventually killing thousands of birds, eagles, sea otters, and other marine life teeming along the jagged coast of Prince William Sound in Alaska. By the middle of the week, Exxon, owner of the wounded tanker, admits that the largest oil spill in U.S. history is spreading out of control.

Media Reports

The *Exxon Valdez* disaster dominated news stories for many weeks following the spill. The following excerpts present a timely view of this environmental tragedy and its aftermath.

Alaska Oil Spill May Be Largest in U.S. Waters

By Maura Dolan and Ronald B. Taylor
Los Angeles Times, *March 25, 1989, p. 1.*

A Long Beach-bound Exxon oil tanker ran aground on a reef Friday and spilled up to 12 million gallons of crude oil into Alaska's Prince William Sound, a pristine Pacific waterway rich in wildlife, fisheries and tourist attractions. It is shaping up as the nation's largest oil spill ever.

The *Exxon Valdez,* a 987-foot tanker owned by Exxon Shipping Co., rammed the Bligh Reef about 25 miles from the city of Valdez, the northernmost ice-free port in the United States at, 12:30 a.m.

"This is the largest oil spill in U.S. history, and it unfortunately took place in an enclosed water body with numerous islands, channels, bays and fiords," Richard Golob, publisher of the Golob Oil Pollution Bulletin, told the Associated Press.

Source: Copyright 1989, *Los Angeles Times.* Reprinted by permission.

It's Nature's Turn to Repair the Damage

Newsweek, *September 18, 1989, p. 50.*

The slick is gone from the gray-green waters of Alaska's southern coast, the place that has become known to millions of Americans as Pristine Prince

William Sound. The 11 million-gallon sea of petroleum that came boiling up from the tanks of the *Exxon Valdez* has long since broken up into floating ponds; the ponds reduced to puddles; the puddles in turn eroded into sticky, amorphous globs of tar or whipped by waves into the frothy emulsion known as mousse. Some has evaporated; 2.6 million gallons have been recovered and returned to their owner, Exxon; and a substantial fraction has washed ashore. The slick is gone—and by the end of this week the army of out-of-work fishermen, volunteer housewives and fortune seekers that Exxon mobilized for the fantastic task of scrubbing more than 1,000 miles of rocks will be gone, too, departing just ahead of the storms of the early Alaskan autumn. Exxon, a billion dollars poorer and, it is to be hoped, a little wiser, is going home; and what it leaves behind, it leaves to the lonely wind, the rippling tide and the slow but inexorable processes of tort law.

Drop by Drop: A Box Score

Oil spilled: **10,836,000 gallons**

Shoreline contaminated by oil: **1,090 miles**

Shoreline treated by Exxon: **1,087 miles**

Shoreline still needing cleaning, according to the state: **At least 1,000 miles**

Number of dead birds: **33,126**
of dead eagles: **138**
of dead otters: **980**

Cost of cleanup to Exxon: **$1.28 billion (after-tax cost; insurance companies will reimburse Exxon $400 million)**

People involved in cleanup: **12,000**

Vessels and planes used in cleanup: **1,385**

Oil recovered: **2,604,000 gallons (est.)**

Waste from oil cleanup: **24,000 tons**

Lawsuits filed against Exxon: **145**

Sources: Exxon, U.S. Fish and Wildlife Service, Alaska Department of Environmental Conservation

Source: From *Newsweek*, September 18, 1989.

Secret Studies Put Spill Damage at $15 Billion

By Michael Parrish
Los Angeles Times*, October 8, 1991, p. A1.*

Unpublished studies by state and federal researchers contend that the true cost of environmental damage from the *Exxon Valdez* oil spill in Alaska could be as high as $15 billion, according to experts familiar with the secret reports.

The figure stands in dramatic contrast to the $1.125-billion settlement that Exxon Corp. agreed to last week to settle criminal and civil complaints brought by the state of Alaska and the federal government.

Nobel laureate economists connected with the studies include Robert M. Solow of MIT on the Alaska team, James Tobin of Yale University on the federal team and Kenneth J. Arrow of Stanford University and George Stigler of the University of Chicago, both doing research for Exxon.

The state team's estimates range from $3 billion to as high as $15 billion for damages to Prince William Sound, though there are some indications that they have begun to focus on a much narrower range. Federal researchers apparently see a range of $4 billion to $10 billion. Exxon spokesman Lance Lamberton declined comment on anything having to do with Exxon's studies.

Source:

Other Source Materials

Even while Exxon and other groups were cleaning up in the aftermath of this tremendous oil spill, the courts and government agencies were investigating the captain and the company. A transcript of the marine radio discussion between the man in charge of the ship, Captain Joseph Hazelwood, and the head of the Coast Guard for the area encompassing Valdez Harbor, Commander Steve McCall, was widely broadcast. The following is part of that conversation reproduced in Art Davidson's *In the Wake of the Exxon Valdez* (Sierra Club Books, San Francisco, 1990, pp. 19–20.)

MCCALL: *Exxon Valdez,* this is the captain of the port, Commander McCall. Do you have any more of an estimate as to your situation at this time? Over.

HAZELWOOD: Oh, not at the present, Steve . . . but we are working our way off the reef . . . the vessel has been holed. Right now we're trying to steer off the reef. And we'll get back to you as soon as we can.

MCCALL: Roger on that. You know, we've got all our planned mechanisms in place to give you what assistance we can. . . . Take it, take it slow and easy and, you know, I'm telling you the obvious, but . . . take it slow and easy and we are getting help out as fast as we can.

HAZELWOOD: Okay. We're in pretty good shape right now stabilitywise. We're just trying to extract her off the shoal here and you can probably see me on your radar. And once I get underway I'll let you know.

MCCALL: Roger. Yeah. Another thing, now again, before you make any drastic attempt to get underway you make sure you don't . . . start doing any ripping. You got a rising tide. You got another about an hour and a half worth of tide in your favor. Once you hit the max I wouldn't recommend doing much wiggling. Over.

HAZELWOOD: Okay. Yeah, I think . . . the major damage has kind of been done. We've kind of . . . rolled over it and we're just kind of hung up in the stern here. We'll just drift over it and I'll get back to you. We'll be standing by. *Exxon Valdez,* clear.

Conclusion

On September 30, 1991, a settlement among Exxon, the State of Alaska, and the U.S. Department of Justice was announced. The settlement called for Exxon to pay $900 million in civil damages and an additional $100 million, if needed, for environmental cleanup. Exxon further had to pay $25 million in criminal penalties and $100 million in criminal restitution. This settlement was approved by the U.S. District Court on October 8, 1991.

Captain Hazelwood was acquitted of criminal charges. Some say the polluted area will never be the same.

Analysis Questions

1. How much money did the Exxon Corporation spend on cleaning up the oil spill? (Note that there are two estimates in the source materials. Make sure you indicate from which source your estimate comes.)
2. One of the sources claims that 145 law suits were filed against Exxon. Write down a list of the people, companies, and groups that might have sued Exxon and the reasons they would have done so.
3. Reread the marine radio conversation between Captain Hazelwood and Commander McCall. How would you characterize the tone of their conversation in light of the enormity of the event?

PRESIDENTS AND VICE PRESIDENTS OF THE UNITED STATES

1 GEORGE WASHINGTON

Born: February 22, 1732
Died: December 14, 1799
Dates in office: 1789–1797
Profession before presidency: Planter
Political party: None
State of birth: Virginia

George Washington took his oath of office as the first president of the United States on the balcony of Federal Hall on Wall Street in New York City. Understanding the precedent-setting role of his position, Washington acted cautiously as president, working to flesh out the framework of government that was described in the Constitution.

***Vice president:* John Adams**
(see John Adams's listing under Presidents)

2 JOHN ADAMS

Born: October 30, 1735
Died: July 4, 1826
Dates in office: 1797–1801
Profession before presidency: Lawyer
Political party: Federalist
State: Massachusetts

On at least two occasions, John Adams went against popular public opinion. As a lawyer, Adams defended the British soldiers who killed three Americans at the Boston Massacre in 1770, feeling a mob mentality was taking over the colony. As president, Adams ignored public sentiment for war with France and instead coaxed France to accept neutrality rights at sea with the United States in exchange for most-favored-nation status.

***Vice president:* Thomas Jefferson**
(see Jefferson's listing under Presidents)

3 THOMAS JEFFERSON

Born: April 13, 1743
Died: July 4, 1826
Dates in office: 1801–1809
Profession before presidency: Planter
Political party: Democratic-Republican
Home state: Virginia

Not known for his eloquence, Thomas Jefferson was the ''silent member'' of the Continental Congress. He used his writing skills to draft the Declaration of Independence at age 33. During Jefferson's first term as president, he approved the purchase of the vast Louisiana Territory for a paltry $15 million dollars. However, he had originally sent his negotiators to buy only West Florida and New Orleans.

***Vice president:* Aaron Burr**
Home state: New Jersey
Political party: Democratic-Republican
Profession: Lawyer

***Vice president:* George Clinton**
Home state: New York
Political party: Democratic-Republican
Profession: Lawyer

4 JAMES MADISON

Born: March 16, 1751
Died: June 28, 1836
Dates in office: 1809–1817
Profession before presidency: Lawyer
Political party: Democratic-Republican
Home state: Virginia

The shortest and slightest president, James Madison stood about 5 feet 4 inches and weighed just 100 pounds.

Madison contributed to the ratification of the Constitution with his co-authored *Federalist* essays. According to Daniel Webster, "Madison had as much to do as any man in framing the Constitution, and as much to do as any man in administering it."

Vice president: **George Clinton**
Home state: New York
Political party: Democratic-Republican
Profession: Lawyer

Vice president: **Elbridge Gerry**
Home state: Massachusetts
Political party: Democratic-Republican
Profession: Importer and shipper

5 JAMES MONROE

Born: April 28, 1758
Died: July 4, 1831
Dates in office: 1817–1825
Profession before presidency: Lawyer
Political party: Democratic-Republican
Home state: Virginia

James Monroe faced a nation's fears that Spain might attempt to retake its former colonies in Latin America and that Russia might extend its claims in Alaska to the Oregon Territory. He consequently declared to Congress in 1823 a warning to European nations about intervention in the Western Hemisphere. The message came to bear his name: the Monroe Doctrine.

Vice president: **Daniel D. Tompkins**
Home state: New York
Political party: Democratic-Republican
Profession: Lawyer

6 JOHN QUINCY ADAMS

Born: July 11, 1767
Died: February 23, 1848
Dates in office: 1825–1829
Profession before presidency: Lawyer
Political party: Democratic-Republican
Home state: Massachusetts

John Quincy Adams was the only president who was the son of a president. Adams ambitiously proposed a strong program sponsored by the federal government to link the sections of the nation with highways and canals, to create a national university, and to build an astronomical observatory. The programs were largely passed over by Congress, however. Adams obtained only the extension of the Cumberland Road into Ohio and the construction of the Chesapeake and Ohio Canal.

Vice president: **John C. Calhoun**
Home state: South Carolina
Political party: Democratic-Republican
Profession: Lawyer

7 ANDREW JACKSON

Born: March 15, 1767
Died: June 8, 1845
Dates in office: 1829–1837
Profession before presidency: Lawyer
Political party: Democratic
Home state: South Carolina

As a major general in the War of 1812, Andrew Jackson became a national hero due to his victory over the British at New Orleans. More than any president who came before him, Jackson was elected by the popular vote of common citizens. Later, as president, he recommended eliminating the electoral college.

Vice president: **John C. Calhoun**
Home state: South Carolina
Political party: Democratic-Republican
Profession: Lawyer

Vice president: **Martin Van Buren**
(see Van Buren's listing under Presidents)

8 MARTIN VAN BUREN

Born: December 5, 1782
Died: July 24, 1862
Dates in office: 1837–1841
Profession before presidency: Lawyer
Political party: Democratic
Home state: New York

Only about 5 feet 6 inches tall, Martin Van Buren, the "Little Magician," was elected vice president on Andrew Jackson's ticket in 1832. He won the presidency in 1836. A severe economic slump plagued Van Buren's term. Over nine hundred banks closed across the country. Many of Van Buren's deflationary measures contributed to the prolonged depression.

***Vice president:* Richard M. Johnson**
Home state: Kentucky
Political party: Democratic
Profession: Lawyer

9 William H. Harrison

Born: February 9, 1773
Died: April 4, 1841
Dates in office: 1841
Profession before presidency: Lawyer
Political party: Whig
Home state: Virginia

William H. Harrison was the last president born a British subject. His presidency lasted exactly one month. He caught a cold, which turned into pneumonia, while delivering his inaugural address. Shortly before he died, he spoke his last words: "I wish you to understand the true principles of the government. I wish them carried out. I ask nothing more."

***Vice president:* John Tyler**
(see Tyler's listing under Presidents)

10 John Tyler

Born: March 29, 1790
Died: January 18, 1862
Dates in office: 1841–1845
Profession before presidency: Soldier
Political party: Whig
Home state: Virginia

As vice president, John Tyler took the office of president upon the death of William H. Harrison. He became known as "a president without a party" after the Whigs expelled him for failing to go along with them on their plan to establish a national bank. Nevertheless, Tyler was able to enact much positive legislation. For example, his "Log Cabin" Bill allowed settlers to claim and later purchase 160 acres of land before it was put on the public market.

11 James K. Polk

Born: November 2, 1795
Died: June 15, 1849
Dates in office: 1845–1849
Profession before presidency: Lawyer
Political party: Democratic
Home state: North Carolina

James K. Polk was a candidate committed to the nation's "Manifest Destiny," the belief that the United States was divinely destined to rule from sea to sea. He urged reannexation of Texas and reoccupation of Oregon. He also favored acquiring California. These views plunged Polk and the United States into, among other things, the Mexican War. This conflict lasted from 1846 to 1848, when the border between the two countries was fixed at the Rio Grande.

***Vice president:* George M. Dallas**
Home state: Pennsylvania
Political party: Democratic
Profession: Lawyer

12 Zachary Taylor

Born: November 24, 1784
Died: July 9, 1850
Dates in office: 1849–1850
Profession before presidency: Soldier
Political party: Whig
Home state: Virginia

Zachary Taylor was nicknamed "Old Rough and Ready" from his days as a general in the Mexican War. President Taylor was a former slave owner who told the Southern states that threatened secession that he would personally lead the Union army against them if any of them tried to secede. Taylor's only son, Richard, served in the Civil War as a general in the Confederate army.

***Vice president:* Millard Fillmore**
(see Fillmore's listing under Presidents)

13 MILLARD FILLMORE

Born: January 7, 1800
Died: March 8, 1874
Dates in office: 1850–1853
Profession before presidency: Lawyer
Political party: Whig
Home state: New York

Millard Fillmore embraced the compromise between slave and free states that Zachary Taylor had opposed. Called the Compromise of 1850, it included bills that admitted California as a free state; settled the Texas boundary; granted territorial status to New Mexico; approved the controversial Fugitive Slave Act, which required the federal government to assist in returning escaped slaves to their masters; and abolished slave trade in the District of Columbia.

14 FRANKLIN PIERCE

Born: November 23, 1804
Died: October 8, 1869
Dates in office: 1853–1857
Profession before presidency: Lawyer
Political party: Democratic
Home state: New Hampshire

Franklin Pierce entered the presidency on the heels of tragedy. Just two months before he took office, he and his wife saw their eleven-year-old son killed in a train wreck. Then the tranquility of the years after the Compromise of 1850 ended when Senator Stephen Douglas proposed the Kansas-Nebraska Act, which said in part that the residents of the new territories could decide the slavery question themselves. The result was a rush into Kansas, where southerners and northerners battled in a prelude to the Civil War.

***Vice president:* William R. King**
Home state: North Carolina
Political party: Democratic
Profession: Lawyer

15 JAMES BUCHANAN

Born: April 23, 1791
Died: June 1, 1868
Dates in office: 1857–1861
Profession before presidency: Lawyer
Political party: Democratic
Home state: Pennsylvania

James Buchanan was the only president who never married. He served at a frightful time for the fast-dividing nation. Buchanan misread the political realities of his time. He thought that the problems between North and South could be solved constitutionally through the Supreme Court. In his inaugural address, he said that the Supreme Court was about to settle the situation "speedily and finally."

***Vice president:* John C. Breckinridge**
Home state: Kentucky
Political party: Democratic
Profession: Lawyer

16 ABRAHAM LINCOLN

Born: February 12, 1809
Died: April 15, 1865
Dates in office: 1861–1865
Profession before presidency: Lawyer
Political party: Republican
Home state: Kentucky

Abraham Lincoln constantly reminded the world that the issues of the Civil War involved more than North versus South, slave versus free. At Gettysburg, he proclaimed "that this nation, under God, shall have a new birth of freedom—and that government of the people, by the people, for the people shall not perish from the earth." On January 1, 1863, Lincoln issued the Emancipation Proclamation, which declared slaves free within states controlled by the Confederacy. He was assassinated on Good Friday, April 14, 1865, by John Wilkes Booth at Ford's Theatre in Washington, D.C.

Vice president: **Hannibal Hamlin**
Home state: Maine
Political party: Republican
Profession: Lawyer

Vice president: **Andrew Johnson**
(see Andrew Johnson's listing under Presidents)

17 ANDREW JOHNSON

Born: December 29, 1808
Died: July 31, 1875
Dates in office: 1865–1869
Profession before presidency: Tailor
Political party: National Union
Home state: North Carolina

To Andrew Johnson fell the task of reconstructing the nation after the Civil War and Abraham Lincoln's death. Johnson restored legal rights to the Southern states swiftly, since in his view they had never technically left the Union (because the Union was indissoluble). Johnson faced impeachment by the House when he allegedly violated the Tenure of Office Act by wrongly dismissing the secretary of war. He was tried by the Senate and acquitted by one vote.

18 ULYSSES S. GRANT

Born: April 27, 1822
Died: July 23, 1885
Dates in office: 1869–1877
Profession before presidency: Soldier
Political party: Republican
Home state: Ohio

Ulysses S. Grant became commander of all Union armies in March 1864. Robert E. Lee formally surrendered to Grant at Appomattox, Virginia, on April 9, 1865. As president, Grant clashed with speculators, whose attempt to corner the gold market greatly disrupted American business. Grant realized his shortcomings as president. He said, "It was my fortune, or misfortune, to be called to the office of Chief Executive without any previous political training."

Vice president: **Schuyler Colfax**
Home state: New York
Political party: Republican
Profession: Deputy auditor

Vice president: **Henry Wilson**
Home state: New Hampshire
Political party: Republican
Profession: Shoe factory owner

19 RUTHERFORD B. HAYES

Born: October 4, 1822
Died: January 17, 1893
Dates in office: 1877–1881
Profession before presidency: Lawyer
Political party: Republican
Home state: Ohio

Rutherford B. Hayes won the most disputed election in American history. Hayes's election depended upon disputed electoral votes in Louisiana, South Carolina, and Florida. He needed every electoral vote from those states to win; a panel established by Congress determined that Hayes did indeed win the election: 185 electoral votes to 184 over Governor Samuel J. Tilden of New York.

Vice president: **William A. Wheeler**
Home state: New York
Political party: Republican
Profession: Lawyer

20 JAMES A. GARFIELD

Born: November 19, 1831
Died: September 19, 1881
Dates in office: 1881
Profession before presidency: Lawyer
Political party: Republican
Home state: Ohio

On July 2, 1881, James A. Garfield was strolling in a Washington, D.C., railroad station. He was shot in the back by Charles Guiteau, a man who had been rebuffed by the president for an appointment to a diplomatic post following the election. Garfield lay wounded in the White House for weeks. Alexander Graham Bell, the inventor of the telephone, designed an electrical device in an attempt to find the bullet still lodged in the president. On September 6, Garfield, seemingly recuperating, was taken to a New Jersey resort. He died there on September 19.

Vice president: **Chester A. Arthur**
(See Arthur's listing under Presidents)

21 CHESTER A. ARTHUR

Born: October 5, 1829
Died: November 18, 1886
Dates in office: 1881–1885
Profession before presidency: Lawyer
Political party: Republican
Home state: Vermont

Chester A. Arthur was appointed by President Grant as collector of the port of New York in 1871. He was responsible for collection of about 75 percent of the nation's duties from ships that landed within his jurisdiction. The customhouse was riddled with scandal, including the proven charge that employees were expected to kick back part of their salaries to the Republican Party. As president, Arthur sought to rid himself of machine politics. In 1883, Congress passed the Pendleton Act, which protected employees against removal from their jobs for political reasons.

22 GROVER CLEVELAND

Born: March 18, 1837
Died: June 24, 1908
Dates in office: 1885–1889; 1893–1897
Profession before presidency: Lawyer
Political party: Democratic
Home state: New Jersey

Grover Cleveland was the only president to leave the White House and return for a second term four years later. After his defeat by Benjamin Harrison in 1888, Cleveland returned to his law practice in New York City, seemingly retired from active political life. In his second term, the nation faced a great depression. When railroad workers went on strike in Chicago, Cleveland said, "If it takes the entire army and navy of the United States to deliver a postcard in Chicago, that card will be delivered."

Vice president: **Thomas A. Hendricks**
Home state: Ohio
Political party: Democratic
Profession: Lawyer

23 BENJAMIN HARRISON

Born: August 20, 1833
Died: March 13, 1901
Dates in office: 1889–1893
Profession before presidency: Lawyer
Political party: Republican
Home state: Ohio

Benjamin Harrison was the grandson of William H. Harrison, the nation's ninth president. Benjamin Harrison signed the Sherman Anti-Trust Act in 1890, the first of the antitrust laws to curb the abuse of monopolies that conspired to restrict trade. Harrison was defeated for reelection in 1892 by Grover Cleveland, the man he had triumphed over four years earlier.

Vice president: **Levi P. Morton**
Home state: Vermont
Political party: Republican
Profession: Businessman and banker

24 GROVER CLEVELAND

(See earlier entry)

Vice president: **Adlai E. Stevenson**
Home state: Kentucky
Political party: Democratic
Profession: Lawyer

25 WILLIAM McKINLEY

Born: January 29, 1843
Died: September 14, 1901
Dates in office: 1897–1901
Profession before presidency: Lawyer
Political party: Republican
Home state: Ohio

During William McKinley's term, the United States intervened in the Spanish-American War and destroyed the Spanish fleet outside Santiago harbor in Cuba, captured Manila, in the Philippines, and occupied Puerto Rico. McKinley followed public opinion in annexing the acquired territories (except Cuba). McKinley was assassinated in 1901. He was shot while standing in a receiving line at a Pan American Exposition in Buffalo, New York.

***Vice president:* Garret A. Hobart**
Home state: New Jersey
Political party: Republican
Profession: Lawyer

***Vice president:* Theodore Roosevelt**
(see Theodore Roosevelt's listing under Presidents)

26 THEODORE ROOSEVELT

Born: October 27, 1858
Died: January 6, 1919
Dates in office: 1901–1909
Profession before presidency: Author
Political party: Republican
Home state: New York

Theodore Roosevelt was not quite forty-three years old when he took over as president for the slain William McKinley. Roosevelt was a charismatic man who led the American people and Congress toward progressive reforms and a strong foreign policy. Roosevelt staunchly defended the right by the United States to use military force, if necessary, to defend the principles of the Monroe Doctrine. His famous words were "Speak softly and carry a big stick; you will go far."

***Vice president:* Charles W. Fairbanks**
Home state: Ohio
Political party: Republican
Profession: Lawyer

27 WILLIAM H. TAFT

Born: September 15, 1857
Died: March 8, 1930
Dates in office: 1909–1913
Profession before presidency: Lawyer
Political party: Republican
Home state: Ohio

William H. Taft was appointed a federal circuit judge at thirty-four years old. He always would prefer law to politics. Nevertheless, he rose politically through presidential appointments and was nominated as Theodore Roosevelt's Republican successor in 1908. Taft was uncomfortable as president. After he was defeated for reelection, he was appointed chief justice of the Supreme Court of the United States by President Warren G. Harding. He considered the appointment his greatest honor. "I don't even remember being President," he said.

***Vice president:* James S. Sherman**
Home state: New York
Political party: Republican
Profession: Lawyer

28 WOODROW WILSON

Born: December 29, 1856
Died: February 3, 1924
Dates in office: 1913–1921
Profession before presidency: Educator
Political party: Democratic
Home state: Virginia

Woodrow Wilson's campaign slogan for reelection in 1916 was "He kept us out of war." But after his election, Wilson knew that the United States could not remain neutral in the world war. On April 2, 1917, he asked Congress to declare war on Germany. Early the next year, Wilson set forth his famous Fourteen Points, the only basis, he insisted, on which lasting peace could be made. The armistice was signed on November 11, 1918.

***Vice president:* Thomas R. Marshall**
Home state: Indiana
Political party: Democratic
Profession: Lawyer

29 WARREN G. HARDING

Born: November 2, 1865
Died: August 2, 1923
Dates in office: 1921–1923
Profession before presidency: Editor
Political party: Republican
Home state: Ohio

Warren G. Harding was a master of the great phrase, and this, combined with his handsome looks, won him a landslide election in 1920. Harding appeared to be on his way to carrying out his campaign promise of "less government in business and more business in government" when word got to him that some of his friends were using their official positions for their own gain. Harding said, "My friends, they're the ones keeping me walking the floor nights." Harding died in office of a heart attack while in San Francisco in 1923. A historians' poll in 1962 ranked him, along with Ulysses S. Grant, as the worst of the presidents.

***Vice president:* Calvin Coolidge**
(see Coolidge's listing under Presidents)

30 Calvin Coolidge

Born: July 4, 1872
Died: January 5, 1933
Dates in office: 1923–1929
Profession before presidency: Lawyer
Political party: Republican
Home state: Vermont

Calvin Coolidge's father, a notary public, administered his son the oath of office at their family home upon learning of the death of President Warren G. Harding. Coolidge quickly became a popular president, known for his dry wit. Once, a woman sitting next to him at a dinner party confided that she had bet that she could get at least three words from him in conversation. "You lose," he quietly responded.

***Vice president:* Charles G. Dawes**
Home state: Ohio
Political party: Republican
Profession: Lawyer

31 Herbert C. Hoover

Born: August 10, 1874
Died: October 20, 1964
Dates in office: 1929–1933
Profession before presidency: Engineer
Political party: Republican
Home state: Iowa

Herbert C. Hoover gained international attention during World War I by leading the distribution of food and supplies to war-torn Europe. He was the secretary of commerce under Presidents Harding and Coolidge before being nominated for president in 1928. Hoover became a scapegoat for the depression that plagued the nation after the stock market crash of 1929. Under the later Truman and Eisenhower administrations, Hoover was appointed to head the commissions that reorganized the executive departments.

***Vice president:* Charles Curtis**
Home state: Kansas
Political party: Republican
Profession: Lawyer

32 Franklin D. Roosevelt

Born: January 30, 1882
Died: April 12, 1945
Dates in office: 1933–1945
Profession before presidency: Lawyer
Political party: Democratic
Home state: New York

Franklin D. Roosevelt became president in the midst of the Great Depression. He declared in his inaugural address, "The only thing we have to fear is fear itself." He pledged that his primary task was to put people back to work. By 1935, the nation's economy had recovered somewhat, but Roosevelt's New Deal policies were being criticized increasingly by American businessmen and bankers. Roosevelt was elected to three more terms, the most for any president. After the bombing of Pearl Harbor, Roosevelt directed the United States into World War II.

***Vice president:* John N. Garner**
Home state: Texas
Political party: Democratic
Profession: Lawyer

***Vice president:* Henry A. Wallace**
Home state: Iowa
Political party: Democratic
Profession: Writer and editor

***Vice president:* Harry S Truman**
(see Truman's listing under Presidents)

33 Harry S Truman

Born: May 8, 1884
Died: December 26, 1972
Dates in office: 1945–1953
Profession before presidency: Businessman
Political party: Democratic
Home state: Missouri

Harry S Truman was only vice president for a few weeks when President Franklin D. Roosevelt died on April 12, 1945. As president, Truman made some of the most important decisions in history. He ordered the atomic bomb to be dropped on two cities in Japan at the close of World War II. In June 1945, he witnessed the signing of the Charter of the United Nations. Truman won a close election in 1948 over Republican Thomas Dewey and proudly displayed an early edition of the *Chicago Tribune* that proclaimed otherwise: ''Dewey Defeats Truman.''

***Vice president:* Alben W. Barkley**
Home state: Kentucky
Political party: Democratic
Profession: Lawyer

34 Dwight D. Eisenhower

Born: October 14, 1890
Died: March 28, 1969
Dates in office: 1953–1961
Profession before presidency: Soldier
Political party: Republican
Home state: Texas

Dwight D. Eisenhower was the commanding general for the Allied forces in Europe in World War II. As president, he concentrated on maintaining world peace. Eisenhower sent federal troops to Little Rock, Arkansas, to ensure compliance with the federal court order to desegregate the schools. He pointed to peace as his administration's legacy. ''The United States never lost a soldier or a foot of ground in my administration. We kept the peace,'' he said.

***Vice president:* Richard M. Nixon**
(see Nixon's listing under Presidents)

35 John F. Kennedy

Born: May 29, 1917
Died: November 22, 1963
Dates in office: 1961–1963
Profession before presidency: Author
Political party: Democratic
Home state: Massachusetts

John F. Kennedy was the youngest president to die. He was assassinated in Dallas, Texas, in November 1963. Kennedy won a close election over Richard M. Nixon, due in part to Kennedy's performance in a series of televised debates. He was the first Roman Catholic president. At his inauguration, he declared, ''Ask not what your country can do for you—ask what you can do for your country.''

***Vice president:* Lyndon B. Johnson**
(see Lyndon B. Johnson's listing under Presidents)

36 Lyndon B. Johnson

Born: August 27, 1908
Died: January 22, 1973
Dates in office: 1963–1969
Profession before presidency: Teacher
Political party: Democratic
Home state: Texas

Lyndon B. Johnson's ''Great Society'' program became the agenda for his administration. Aid to education, attack on disease, Medicare, urban renewal, war on poverty, and the removal of obstacles to the right to vote were many of the recommendations that Johnson sent to Congress. The escalating Vietnam War was Johnson's downfall; controversy over the war fueled protests at home. Johnson declined to seek reelection in 1968.

***Vice president:* Hubert H. Humphrey**
Home state: South Dakota
Political party: Democratic
Profession: Pharmacist, teacher

37 Richard M. Nixon

Born: January 9, 1913
Dates in office: 1969–1974
Profession before presidency: Lawyer
Political party: Republican
Home state: California

Richard M. Nixon succeeded in bringing an end to the Vietnam War and improving relations with the Soviet Union and China. His election in 1968 was a political comeback. He had been defeated for the presidency in 1960 and for governor of California in 1962. Nixon's presidency ended in the Watergate scandal, in which a break-in of the Democratic headquarters during the 1972 reelection campaign was tied to his administration. Faced with the prospect of impeachment, Nixon resigned on August 9, 1974. He was the only president to resign the office.

***Vice president:* Spiro T. Agnew**
Home state: Maryland
Political party: Republican
Profession: Lawyer

***Vice president:* Gerald R. Ford**
(see Ford's listing under Presidents)

38 Gerald R. Ford

Born: July 14, 1913
Dates in office: 1974–1977
Profession before presidency: Lawyer
Political party: Republican
Home state: Nebraska

In September 1974, Gerald R. Ford granted former president Nixon "a full, free and absolute pardon for all offenses against the United States which he has committed or may have committed or taken part in" during his term in office. Gradually, Ford chose a presidential cabinet of his own. Ford won the Republican nomination for president in 1976 but lost the election to Jimmy Carter. At his inauguration, President Carter began: "For myself and for our nation, I want to thank my predecessor for all he has done to heal our land."

***Vice president:* Nelson A. Rockefeller**
Home state: Maine
Political party: Republican
Profession: Businessman

39 James E. Carter, Jr.

Born: October 1, 1924
Dates in office: 1977–1981
Profession before presidency: Businessman
Political party: Democratic
Home state: Georgia

James E. ("Jimmy") Carter, Jr., began campaigning for the presidency in December 1974. His two-year campaign gained momentum, and he was a first-ballot nominee of the Democratic Party. Carter established a national energy program during his administration and sought to improve the environment. His greatest foreign policy accomplishment was the Camp David agreement of 1978 between Egypt and Israel.

***Vice president:* Walter F. Mondale**
Home state: Minnesota
Political party: Democratic
Profession: Lawyer

40 Ronald W. Reagan

Born: February 6, 1911
Dates in office: 1981–1989
Profession before presidency: Actor
Political party: Republican
Home state: Illinois

As president of the Screen Actors Guild, Ronald W. Reagan became tangled in disputes involving communism. His political views subsequently changed from liberal to conservative. As president, Reagan obtained legislation to stimulate economic growth, curb inflation, increase employment, and strengthen national defense. His ''peace through strength'' foreign policy is credited as one of the reasons for the collapse of the Communist bloc shortly after his second term.

Vice president: **George H. W. Bush**
(see Bush's listing under Presidents)

41 GEORGE H. W. BUSH

Born: June 12, 1924
Dates in office: 1989–1993
Profession before presidency: Businessman
Political party: Republican
Home state: Massachusetts

George H. W. Bush pledged a return to traditional American values and aimed to make America ''a kinder and gentler nation.'' Bush's handling of the brief Persian Gulf War in 1991 increased his popularity. One of Bush's primary domestic goals was to put an end to ''the scourge of drugs'' that racked the nation.

Vice president: **J. Danforth Quayle**
Home state: Indiana
Political party: Republican
Profession: Lawyer

42 WILLIAM J. B. CLINTON

Born: August 19, 1946
Dates in office: 1993–
Profession before presidency: Governor of Arkansas
Political Party: Democrat
Home State: Arkansas

Running a campaign that focused on change, William Jefferson Blythe Clinton was swept into the presidency in an election that saw the first upturn in voter turnout since the election of John F. Kennedy. On election night he spoke at a victory rally in Little Rock, Arkansas and said, ''My fellow Americans, with high hopes and brave hearts, in massive numbers, the American people have voted to make a new beginning.''

Vice president: **Albert Gore, Jr.**
Home state: Tennessee
Political Party: Democrat
Profession: Journalist

SUPREME COURT CHIEF JUSTICES AND ASSOCIATE JUSTICES SINCE 1789

*Each justice is listed along with a notation of the president who nominated him or her and the home state of the justice. (** indicates chief justices)*

Chief Justice John Jay

****John Jay, 1789–1795**
George Washington
New York

John Rutledge, 1789–1791
George Washington
South Carolina

William Cushing, 1789–1810
George Washington
Massachusetts

James Wilson, 1789–1798
George Washington
Pennsylvania

John Blair, 1789–1796
George Washington
Virginia

Robert H. Harrison, 1789–1790
George Washington
Maryland

James Iredell, 1790–1799
George Washington
North Carolina

Thomas Johnson, 1791–1793
George Washington
Maryland

William Paterson, 1793–1806
George Washington
New Jersey

Chief Justice John Rutledge

****John Rutledge, 1795[a]**
George Washington
South Carolina

Samuel Chase, 1796–1811
George Washington
Maryland

[a]John Rutledge served as Chief Justice from August, 1795, until he was rejected in December of the same year.

Chief Justice Oliver Ellsworth

****Oliver Ellsworth, 1796–1799**
George Washington
Connecticut

Bushrod Washington, 1798–1829
John Adams
Virginia

Alfred Moore, 1799–1804
John Adams
North Carolina

Chief Justice John Marshall

****John Marshall, 1801–1835**
John Adams
Virginia

William Johnson, 1804–1834
Thomas Jefferson
South Carolina

Henry Brockholst Livingston, 1806–1823
Thomas Jefferson
New York

Thomas Todd, 1807–1826
Thomas Jefferson
Kentucky

Joseph Story, 1811–1845
James Madison
Massachusetts

Gabriel Duval, 1812–1835
James Madison
Maryland

Smith Thompson, 1823–1843
James Monroe
New York

Robert Trimble, 1826–1828
John Quincy Adams
Kentucky

John McLean, 1829–1861
Andrew Jackson
Ohio

Henry Baldwin, 1830–1844
Andrew Jackson
Pennsylvania

James M. Wayne, 1835–1867
Andrew Jackson
Georgia

Chief Justice Roger B. Taney

****Roger B. Taney, 1836–1864**
Andrew Jackson
Maryland

Philip P. Barbour, 1836–1841
Andrew Jackson
Virginia

John Catron, 1837–1865
Andrew Jackson
Tennessee

John McKinley, 1837–1852
Martin Van Buren
Alabama

Peter V. Daniel, 1841–1860
Martin Van Buren
Virginia

Samuel Nelson, 1845–1872
John Tyler
New York

Levi Woodbury, 1845–1851
James K. Polk
New Hampshire

Robert C. Grier, 1846–1870
James K. Polk
Pennsylvania

Benjamin R. Curtis, 1851–1857
Millard Fillmore
Massachusetts

John A. Campbell, 1853–1861
Franklin Pierce
Alabama

Nathan Clifford, 1858–1881
James Buchanan
Maine

Noah H. Swayne, 1862–1881
Abraham Lincoln
Ohio

Samuel F. Miller, 1862–1890
Abraham Lincoln
Iowa

David Davis, 1862–1877
Abraham Lincoln
Illinois

Stephen J. Field, 1863–1897
Abraham Lincoln
California

Chief Justice Salmon P. Chase

****Salmon P. Chase, 1864–1873**
Abraham Lincoln
Ohio

William Strong, 1870–1880
Ulysses S. Grant
Pennsylvania

Joseph P. Bradley, 1870–1892
Ulysses S. Grant
New Jersey

Ward Hunt, 1872–1882
Ulysses S. Grant
New York

Chief Justice Morrison R. Waite

****Morrison R. Waite, 1874–1888**
Ulysses S. Grant
Ohio

John M. Harlan, 1877–1911
Rutherford B. Hayes
Kentucky

William B. Woods, 1880–1887
Rutherford B. Hayes
Georgia

Stanley Matthews, 1881–1889
James A. Garfield
Ohio

Samuel Blatchford, 1881–1893
Chester A. Arthur
New York

Horace Gray, 1882–1902
Chester A. Arthur
Massachusetts

Lucius Q. C. Lamar, 1888–1893
Grover Cleveland
Mississippi

Chief Justice Melville W. Fuller

****Melville W. Fuller, 1888–1910**
Grover Cleveland
Illinois

David J. Brewer, 1889–1910
Benjamin Harrison
Kansas

Henry B. Brown, 1890–1906
Benjamin Harrison
Michigan

George Shiras, Jr., 1892–1903
Benjamin Harrison
Pennsylvania

Howell E. Jackson, 1893–1895
Benjamin Harrison
Tennessee

Edward D. White, 1894–1910
Grover Cleveland
Louisiana

Rufus W. Peckham, 1895–1909
Grover Cleveland
New York

Joseph McKenna, 1898–1925
William McKinley
California

Oliver W. Holmes, 1902–1932
Theodore Roosevelt
Massachusetts

William R. Day, 1903–1922
Theodore Roosevelt
Ohio

William H. Moody, 1906–1910
Theodore Roosevelt
Massachusetts

Horace H. Lurton, 1909–1914
William H. Taft
Tennessee

Charles E. Hughes, 1910–1916
William H. Taft
New York

Chief Justice Edward D. White

****Edward D. White, 1910–1921**
William H. Taft
Louisiana

William Van Devanter, 1911–1937
William H. Taft
Wyoming

Joseph R. Lamar, 1911–1916
William H. Taft
Georgia

Mahlon Pitney, 1912–1922
William H. Taft
New Jersey

James C. McReynolds, 1914–1941
Woodrow Wilson
Tennessee

John H. Clarke, 1916–1922
Woodrow Wilson
Ohio

Louis D. Brandeis, 1916–1939
Woodrow Wilson
Massachusetts

Chief Justice William H. Taft

****William H. Taft, 1921–1930**
Warren G. Harding
Connecticut

George Sutherland, 1922–1938
Warren G. Harding
Utah

Pierce Butler, 1922–1939
Warren G. Harding
Minnesota

Edward T. Sanford, 1923–1930
Warren G. Harding
Tennessee

Harlan F. Stone, 1925–1941
Calvin Coolidge
New York

Chief Justice Charles E. Hughes

****Charles E. Hughes, 1930–1941**
Herbert C. Hoover
New York

Owen J. Roberts, 1930–1945
Herbert C. Hoover
Pennsylvania

Benjamin N. Cardozo, 1932–1938
Herbert C. Hoover
New York

Hugo L. Black, 1937–1971
Franklin D. Roosevelt
Alabama

Stanley F. Reed, 1938–1957
Franklin D. Roosevelt
Kentucky

Felix Frankfurter, 1939–1962
Franklin D. Roosevelt
Massachusetts

William O. Douglas, 1939–1975
Franklin D. Roosevelt
Connecticut

Frank Murphy, 1940–1949
Franklin D. Roosevelt
Michigan

Chief Justice Harlan F. Stone

****Harlan F. Stone, 1941–1946**
Franklin D. Roosevelt
New York

James F. Byrnes, 1941–1942
Franklin D. Roosevelt
South Carolina

Robert H. Jackson, 1941–1954
Franklin D. Roosevelt
New York

Wiley B. Rutledge, 1943–1949
Franklin D. Roosevelt
Iowa

Harold H. Burton, 1945–1958
Harry S Truman
Ohio

Chief Justice Frederick M. Vinson

****Frederick M. Vinson, 1946–1953**
Harry S Truman
Kentucky

Tom C. Clark, 1949–1967
Harry S Truman
Texas

Sherman Minton, 1949–1956
Harry S Truman
Indiana

Chief Justice Earl Warren

****Earl Warren, 1953–1969**
Dwight D. Eisenhower
California

John M. Harlan, 1955–1971
Dwight D. Eisenhower
New York

William J. Brennan, Jr., 1956–1990
Dwight D. Eisenhower
New Jersey

Charles E. Whittaker, 1957–1962
Dwight D. Eisenhower
Missouri

Potter Stewart, 1958–1981
Dwight D. Eisenhower
Ohio

Byron R. White, 1962–
John F. Kennedy
Colorado

Arthur J. Goldberg, 1962–1965
John F. Kennedy
Illinois

Abe Fortas, 1965–1969
Lyndon B. Johnson
Tennessee

Thurgood Marshall, 1967–1991
Lyndon B. Johnson
New York

Chief Justice Warren E. Burger

****Warren E. Burger, 1969–1986**
Richard M. Nixon
Minnesota

Harry A. Blackmun, 1970–
Richard M. Nixon
Minnesota

Lewis F. Powell, Jr., 1972–1987
Richard M. Nixon
Virginia

Chief Justice William H. Rehnquist

****William H. Rehnquist, 1972–**
Richard M. Nixon
Arizona

John Paul Stevens, 1975–
Gerald R. Ford
Illinois

Sandra Day O'Connor, 1981–
Ronald W. Reagan
Arizona

Antonin Scalia, 1986–
Ronald W. Reagan
Virginia

Anthony M. Kennedy, 1988–
Ronald W. Reagan
California

David H. Souter, 1990–
George H. W. Bush
Maine

Clarence Thomas, 1991–
George H. W. Bush
Mississippi

State Atlas

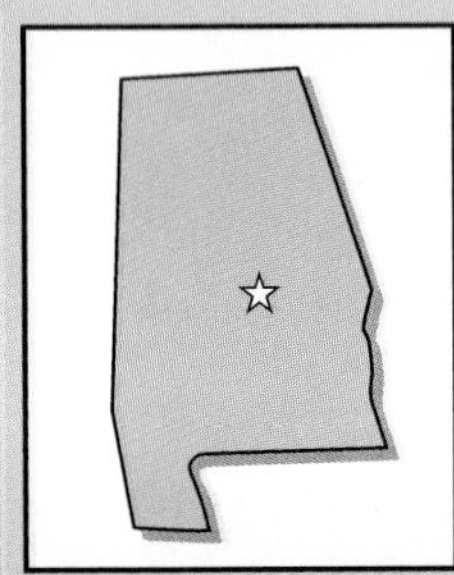

Alabama

Originally the name for "tribal town," the territory of Alabama was later the home of the Alabama, or Alibamon, Indians of the Creek confederacy.

Capital: Montgomery
Size: 51,705 sq. mi. (132,365 sq. km)
Population: 4,062,608
Order admitted: 22
Date admitted: December 14, 1819
Number of U.S. Congressional Districts: 7
Number of Registered Voters: 2,375,444
No party registration

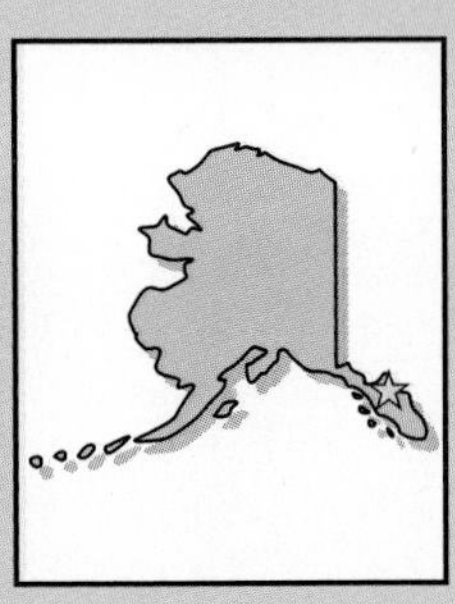

Alaska

The Russians adopted the word meaning "great lands" or "land that is not an island" from the Aleutian word alakshak.

Capital: Juneau
Size: 591,004 sq. mi. (1,512,970 sq. km)
Population: 551,947
Order admitted: 49
Date admitted: January 3, 1959
Number of U.S. Congressional Districts: 1 At Large
Number of Registered Voters: 306,264
Number of Democrats: 58,913 (19%)
Number of Republicans: 64,622 (21%)
Number of unaffiliated and minor parties: 182,729 (60%)

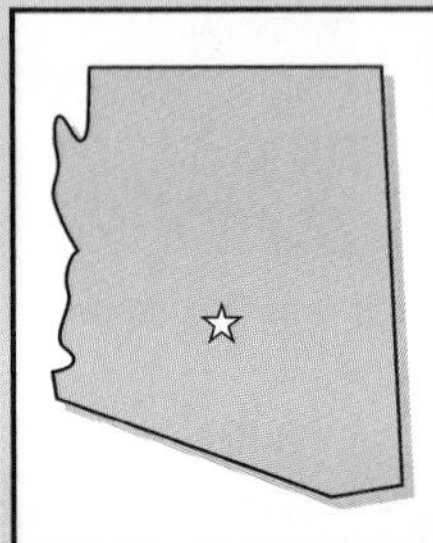

Arizona

The Spanish coined the name either from the Pima Indian word meaning "little spring place" or from the Aztec ari-zuma, *meaning "silver-bearing."*

Capital: Phoenix
Size: 114,000 sq. mi. (291,840 sq. km)
Population: 3,667,985
Order admitted: 48
Date admitted: February 14, 1912
Number of U.S. Congressional Districts: 6
Number of Registered Voters: 1,863,418
Number of Democrats: 779,351 (42%)
Number of Republicans: 871,073 (47%)
Number of unaffiliated and minor parties: 212,994 (11%)

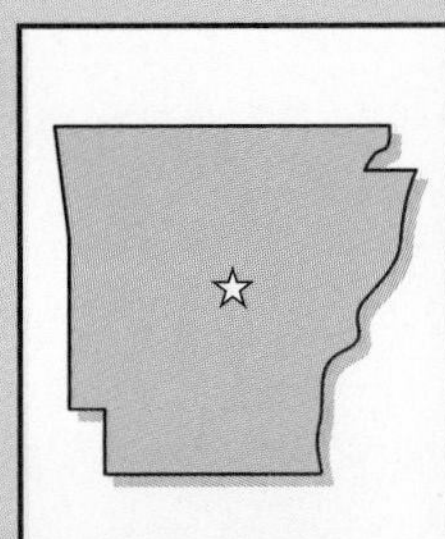

Arkansas

Once the territory of the Siouan Quapaw (downstream people), Arkansas *is the French derivative of this Indian name.*

Capital: Little Rock
Size: 53,187 sq. mi. (136,159 sq. km)
Population: 2,362,239
Order admitted: 25
Date admitted: June 15, 1836
Number of U.S. Congressional Districts: 4
Number of Registered Voters: 1,150,414
No party registration

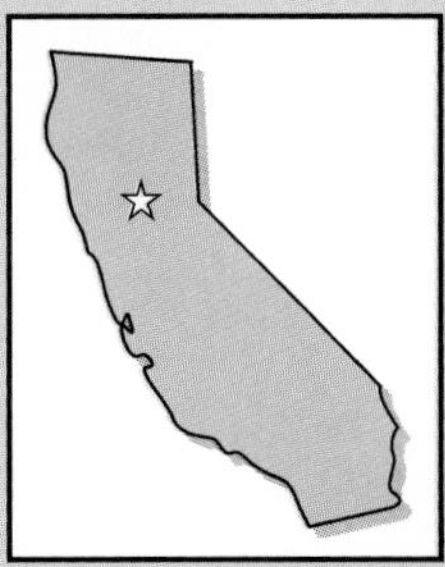

CALIFORNIA

The name of a fictitious earthly paradise in Las Serges de Esplandian, *a sixteenth-century Spanish romance. It is believed that Spanish conquistadors named this state.*

Capital: Sacramento
Size: 158,706 sq. mi. (406,287 sq. km)
Population: 29,839,250
Order admitted: 31
Date admitted: September 9, 1850
Number of U.S. Congressional Districts: 52
Number of Registered Voters: 13,478,027
Number of Democrats: 6,671,747 (50%)
Number of Republicans: 5,290,202 (39%)
Number of unaffiliated and minor parties: 1,516,078 (11%)

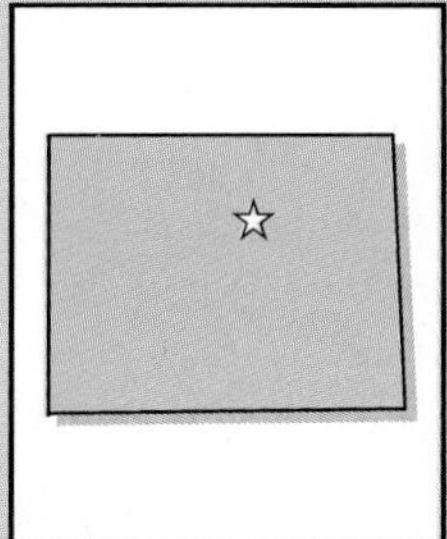

COLORADO

A Spanish word for "red." The name Colorado *first referred to the Colorado River.*

Capital: Denver
Size: 104,091 sq. mi. (266,473 sq. km)
Population: 3,307,912
Order admitted: 38
Date admitted: August 1, 1876
Number of U.S. Congressional Districts: 6
Number of Registered Voters: 1,921,653
Number of Democrats: 598,041 (31%)
Number of Republicans: 653,464 (34%)
Number of unaffiliated and minor parties: 670,148 (35%)

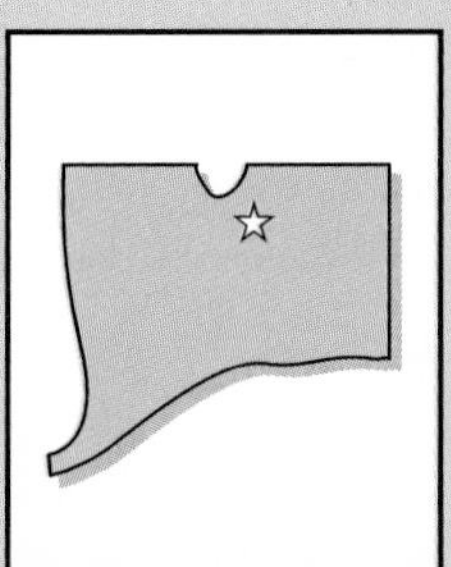

CONNECTICUT

The Algonquin and Mohican Indian word for "long river place."

Capital: Hartford
Size: 5,018 sq. mi. (12,846 sq. km)
Population: 3,295,669
Order admitted: 5
Date admitted: January 9, 1788
Number of U.S. Congressional Districts: 6
Number of Registered Voters: 1,700,871
Number of Democrats: 667,523 (39%)
Number of Republicans: 461,374 (27%)
Number of unaffiliated and minor parties: 534,595 (34%)

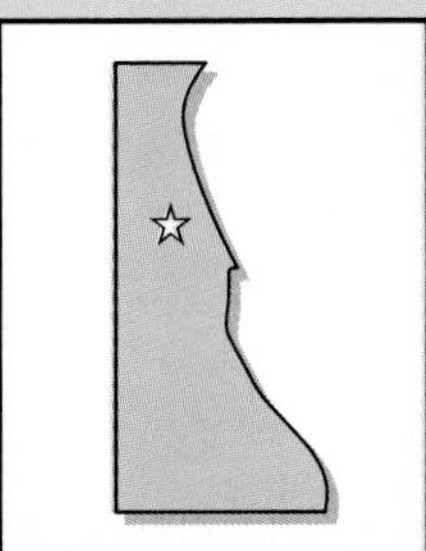

DELAWARE

This version of the name of Lord De La Warr, a governor of Virginia, was first used to name the Delaware River and later adopted by the Europeans to rename the local Indians, originally called the Lenni-Lenape.

Capital: Dover
Size: 2,044 sq. mi. (5,233 sq. km)
Population: 668,696
Order admitted: 1
Date admitted: December 7, 1787
Number of U.S. Congressional Districts: 1 At Large
Number of Registered Voters: 298,246
Number of Democrats: 127,197 (42%)
Number of Republicans: 112,524 (37%)
Number of unaffiliated and minor parties: 58,525 (20%)

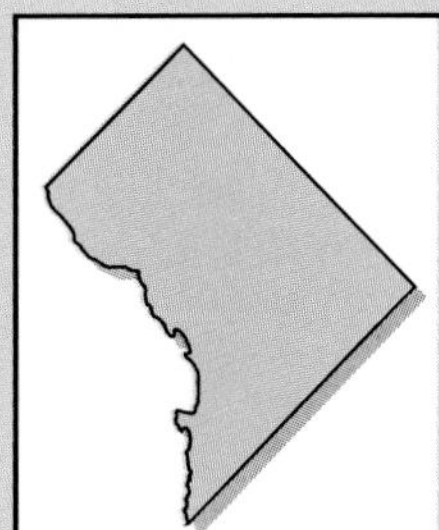

DISTRICT OF COLUMBIA

Named for Christopher Columbus in 1791.

The city of Washington is coextensive with the District of Columbia.
Size: 69 sq. mi. (177 sq. km)
Population: 604,000
Became seat of the federal government: June 10, 1800
Number of U.S. Congressional Districts: 1 At Large
Number of Registered Voters: 308,105

DISTRICT OF COLUMBIA,
Continued
Number of Democrats: 233,313 (76%)
Number of Republicans: 26,677 (9%)
Number of unaffiliated and minor parties: 48,115 (16%)

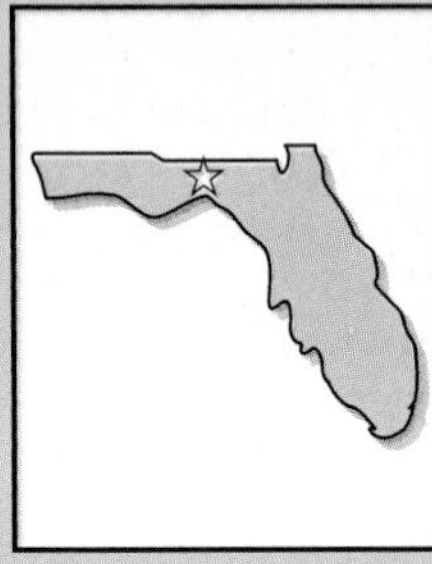

FLORIDA

In his search for the "Fountain of Youth," Ponce de Leon named this region "flowery Easter" or "feast of flowers" on Easter Sunday, 1513.

Capital: Tallahassee
Size: 58,644 sq. mi. (150,180 sq. km)
Population: 13,003,362
Order admitted: 27
Date admitted: March 3, 1845
Number of U.S. Congressional Districts: 23
Number of Registered Voters: 6,031,161
Number of Democrats: 3,149,747 (52%)
Number of Republicans: 2,448,488 (41%)
Number of unaffiliated and minor parties: 432,926 (7%)

GEORGIA

Named for King George II of England, who granted James Oglethorpe a charter to found the colony of Georgia in 1732.

Capital: Atlanta
Size: 58,910 sq. mi. (150,810 sq. km)
Population: 6,508,419
Order admitted: 4
Date admitted: January 2, 1788
Number of U.S. Congressional Districts: 11
Number of Registered Voters: 2,772,816
No party registration

HAWAII

Commonly believed to be an English adaptation of the native word for "homeland," hawaiki *or* owhyhee.

Capital: Honolulu
Size: 6,471 sq. mi. (16,566 sq. km)
Population: 1,115,274
Order admitted: 50
Date admitted: August 21, 1959
Number of U.S. Congressional Districts: 2
Number of Registered Voters: 453,389
No party registration

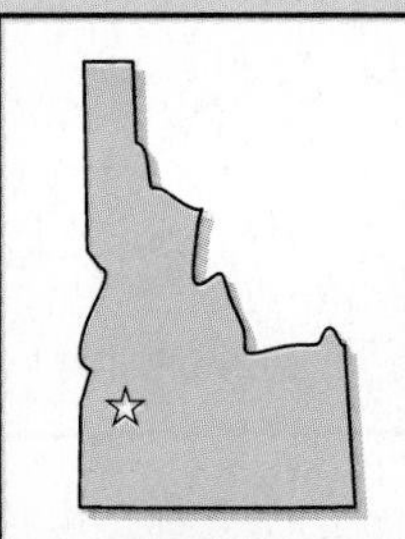

IDAHO

A named coined by the state meaning "gem of the mountains" or "light on the mountains." Originally the name Idaho *was to be used for the Pike's Peak mining territory in Colorado, and later for the mining territory of the Pacific Northwest. Others believe the name derives from the Kiowa Apache word for the Comanche.*

Capital: Boise
Size: 83,564 sq. mi. (213,924 sq. km)
Population: 1,011,986
Order admitted: 43
Date admitted: July 3, 1890
Number of U.S. Congressional Districts: 2
Number of Registered Voters: 540,247
No party registration

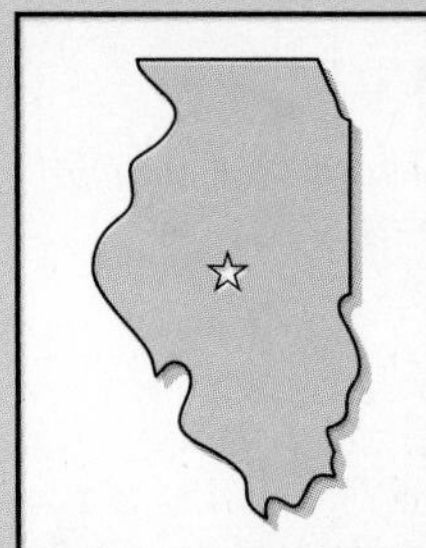

ILLINOIS

From the French version of the Algonquin word meaning "men" or "soldiers," Illini.

Capital: Springfield
Size: 57,871 sq. mi. (148,150 sq. km)
Population: 11,466,682
Order admitted: 21
Date admitted: December 3, 1818
Number of U.S. Congressional Districts: 20
Number of Registered Voters: 6,031,858
No party registration

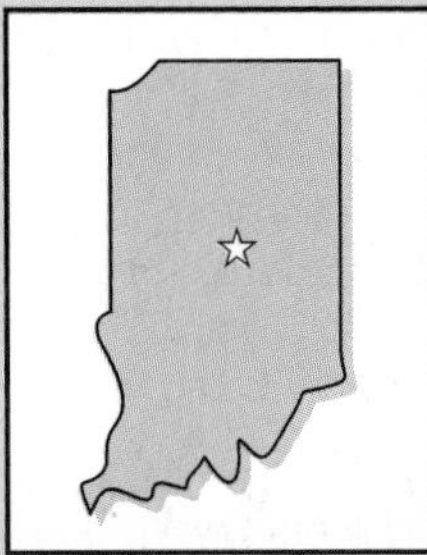

INDIANA

English-speaking settlers named the territory to mean "land of the Indians."

Capital: Indianapolis
Size: 36,413 sq. mi. (93,217 sq. km)
Population: 5,564,228
Order admitted: 19
Date admitted: December 11, 1816
Number of U.S. Congressional Districts: 10
Number of Registered Voters: 2,764,768
No party registration

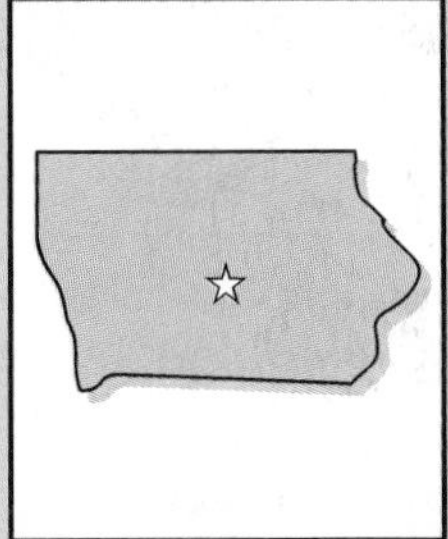

IOWA

The Sioux word for "one who puts to sleep" or "beautiful land."

Capital: Des Moines
Size: 56,275 sq. mi. (144,064 sq. km)
Population: 2,787,424
Order admitted: 29
Date admitted: December 28, 1846
Number of U.S. Congressional Districts: 5
Number of Registered Voters: 1,580,160
Number of Democrats: 599,704 (38%)
Number of Republicans: 496,193 (31%)
Number of unaffiliated and minor parties: 484,263 (31%)

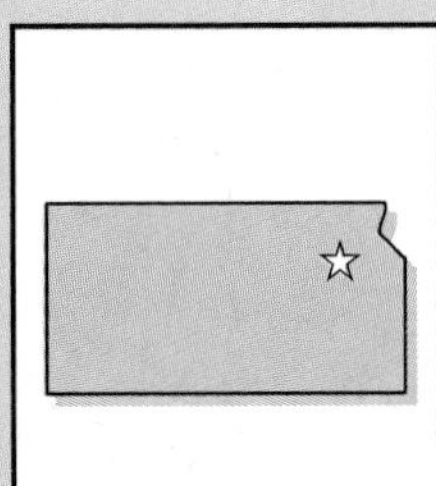

KANSAS

Derived from the Sioux word for those who lived south (the "south wind people") of their territory, which was mainly Wisconsin, Iowa, Minnesota, and North and South Dakota.

Capital: Topeka
Size: 82,277 sq. mi. (210,629 sq. km)
Population: 2,485,600
Order admitted: 34
Date admitted: January 29, 1861
Number of U.S. Congressional Districts: 4
Number of Registered Voters: 1,204,574
Number of Democrats: 358,331 (30%)
Number of Republicans: 530,628 (44%)
Number of unaffiliated and minor parties: 315,615 (26%)

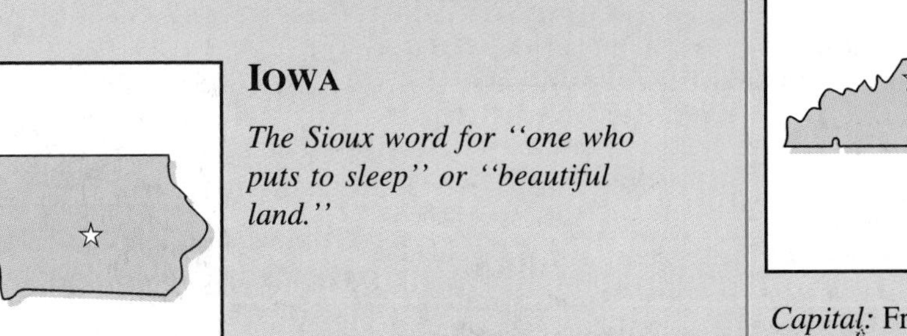

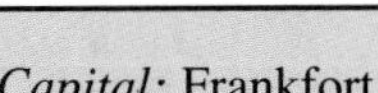

KENTUCKY

Originally the term for the Kentucky Plains in Clark County, Kentucky *is believed to derive from the Indian word meaning "dark and bloody ground," "meadow land," or "land of tomorrow."*

Capital: Frankfort
Size: 40,409 sq. mi. (103,447 sq. km)
Population: 3,698,969
Order admitted: 15
Date admitted: June 1, 1792
Number of U.S. Congressional Districts: 6
Number of Registered Voters: 1,854,315
Number of Democrats: 1,249,312 (67%)
Number of Republicans: 547,932 (30%)
Number of unaffiliated and minor parties: 57,071 (3%)

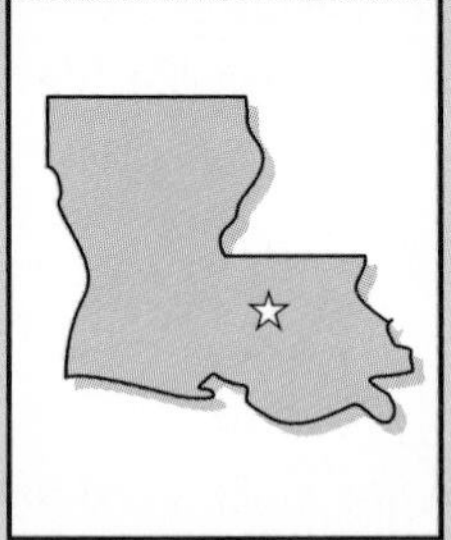

LOUISIANA

Present-day Louisiana is just a fraction of the territory that was named for the French King Louis XIV by Sieur de La Salle.

Capital: Baton Rouge
Size: 47,752 sq. mi. (122,245 sq. km)
Population: 4,238,216
Order admitted: 18
Date admitted: April 30, 1812
Number of U.S. Congressional Districts: 7
Number of Registered Voters: 2,169,099
Number of Democrats: 1,605,967 (74%)
Number of Republicans: 385,422 (18%)
Number of unaffiliated and minor parties: 177,710 (8%)

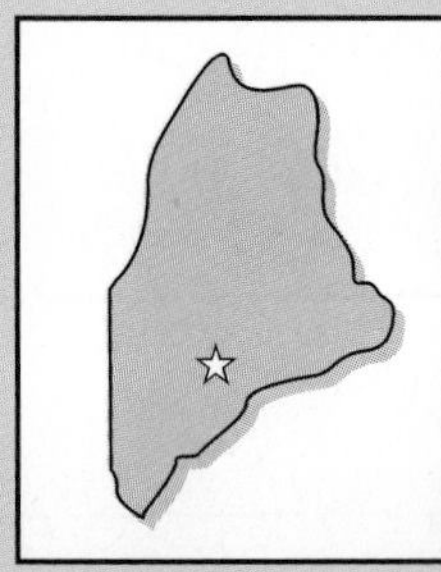

MAINE

Originally a French territory, Maine *was the ancient French word for "province." It is also believed that it refers to the mainland, as distinct from the many islands off the state's coast.*

Capital: Augusta
Size: 33,265 sq. mi. (85,158 sq. km)
Population: 1,233,223
Order admitted: 23
Date admitted: March 15, 1820
Number of U.S. Congressional Districts: 2
Number of Registered Voters: 824,658
Number of Democrats: 272,089 (33%)
Number of Republicans: 246,277 (30%)
Number of unaffiliated and minor parties: 306,292 (37%)

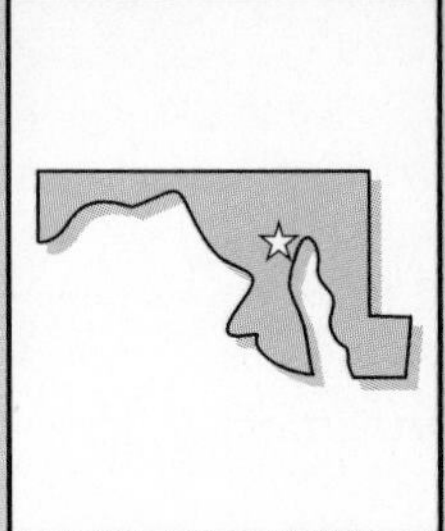

MARYLAND

Named for Queen Henrietta Maria, wife of Charles I of England.

Capital: Annapolis
Size: 10,460 sq. mi. (26,778 sq. km)
Population: 4,798,622
Order admitted: 7
Date admitted: April 28, 1788
Number of U.S. Congressional Districts: 8
Number of Registered Voters: 2,123,209
Number of Democrats: 1,341,857 (63%)
Number of Republicans: 613,714 (29%)
Number of unaffiliated and minor parties: 167,638 (8%)

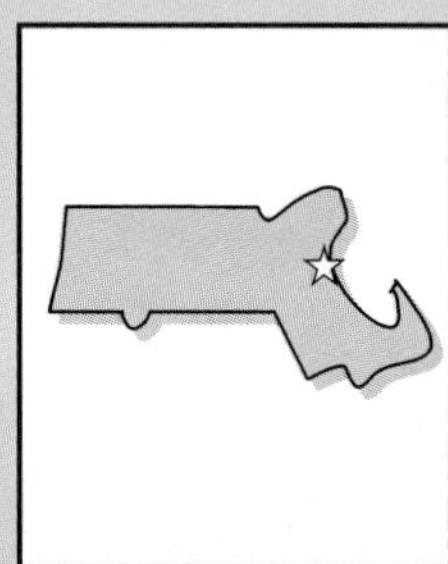

MASSACHUSETTS

The name of the Indian tribe that lived near Milton, Massachusetts, meaning "large hill place."

Capital: Boston
Size: 8,284 sq. mi. (21,207 sq. km)
Population: 6,029,051
Order admitted: 6
Date admitted: February 6, 1788
Number of U.S. Congressional Districts: 10
Number of Registered Voters: 3,213,763
Number of Democrats: 1,342,239 (42%)
Number of Republicans: 441,982 (14%)
Number of unaffiliated and minor parties: 1,429,582 (44%)

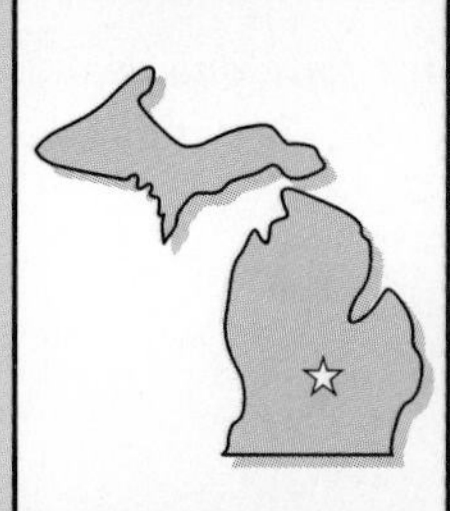

MICHIGAN

Believed to be from the Chippewa word micigama, *meaning "great water," after Lake Michigan, although Alouet defined it in 1672 as designating a clearing.*

Capital: Lansing
Size: 58,527 sq. mi. (151,584 sq. km)
Population: 9,328,784
Order admitted: 26
Date admitted: January 26, 1837
Number of U.S. Congressional Districts: 16
Number of Registered Voters: 5,892,001
No party registration

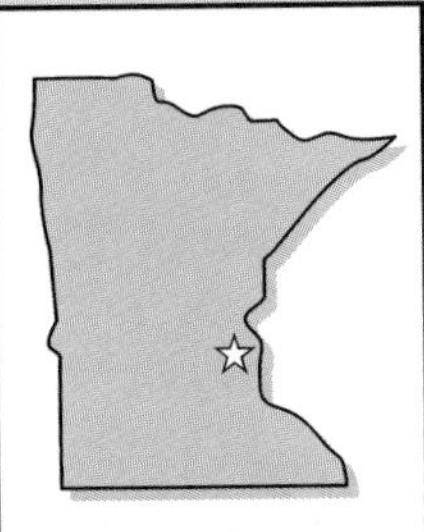

MINNESOTA

Named from the Sioux description of the Minnesota River, "sky-tinted water" or "muddy water."

Capital: Saint Paul
Size: 86,614 sq. mi. (221,732 sq. km)
Population: 4,387,029
Order admitted: 32
Date admitted: May 11, 1858
Number of U.S. Congressional Districts: 8
Number of Registered Voters: 2,830,649
No party registration

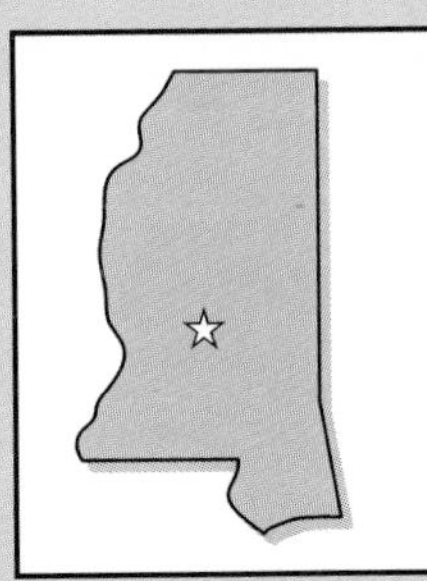

MISSISSIPPI

Most likely derived from the Chippewa words mici *(great) and* zibi *(river), it was first written by La Salle's lieutenant Henri de Tonti as "Michi Sepe."*

Capital: Jackson
Size: 47,689 sq. mi. (122,084 sq. km)
Population: 2,586,443
Order admitted: 20
Date admitted: December 10, 1817
Number of U.S. Congressional Districts: 5
Number of Registered Voters: 1,592,992
No party registration

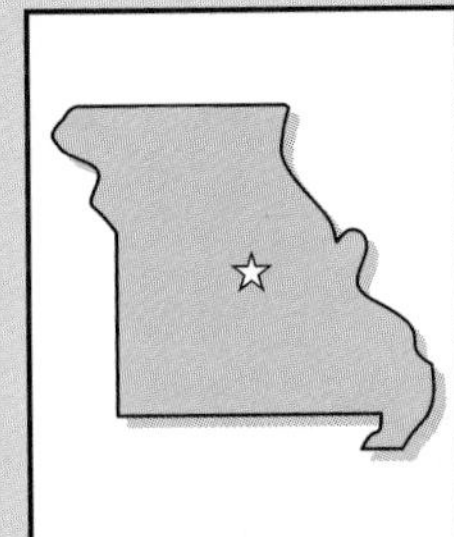

MISSOURI

Meaning "muddy water," this state is named after an Algonquin Indian tribe.

Capital: Jefferson City
Size: 69,697 sq. mi. (178,424 sq. km)
Population: 5,137,804
Order admitted: 24
Date admitted: August 10, 1821
Number of U.S. Congressional Districts: 9
Number of Registered Voters: 2,747,000
No party registration

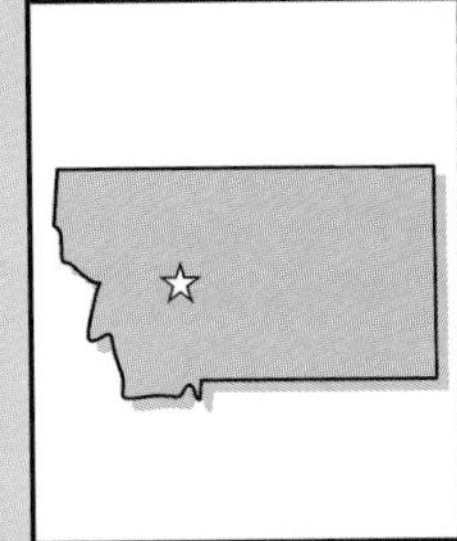

MONTANA

Derived from the Latin word meaning "mountainous."

Capital: Helena
Size: 147,046 sq. mi. (376,438 sq. km)
Population: 803,655
Order admitted: 41
Date admitted: November 8, 1889
Number of U.S. Congressional Districts: 1
Number of Registered Voters: 435,900
No party registration

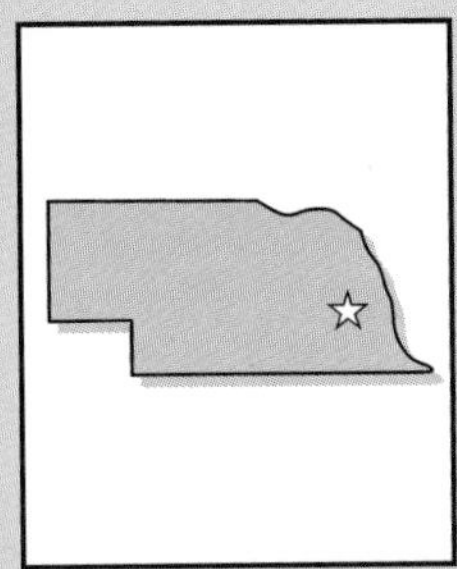

NEBRASKA

Descriptive of the Platte River, Nebraska *is from the Omaha or Otos Indian word for "broad water" or "flat river."*

Capital: Lincoln
Size: 77,355 sq. mi. (198,029 sq. km)
Population: 1,584,617
Order admitted: 37
Date admitted: March 1, 1867
Number of U.S. Congressional Districts: 3
Number of Registered Voters: 890,579
Number of Democrats: 374,023 (42%)
Number of Republicans: 449,335 (50%)
Number of unaffiliated and minor parties: 67,221 (8%)

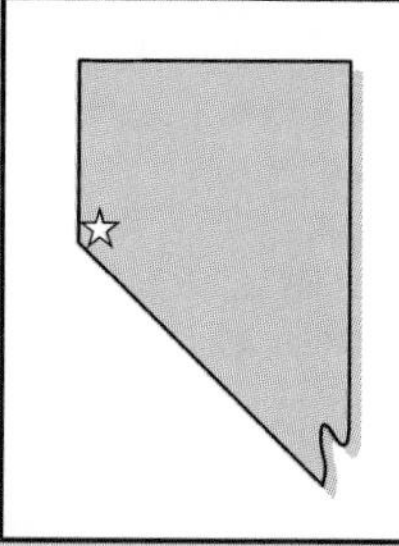

NEVADA

Spanish word meaning "snow-clad."

Capital: Carson City
Size: 110,561 sq. mi. (283,036 sq. km)
Population: 1,206,152
Order admitted: 36
Date admitted: October 31, 1864
Number of U.S. Congressional Districts: 2
Number of Registered Voters: 364,965
Number of Democrats: 166,497 (46%)
Number of Republicans: 160,930 (44%)
Number of unaffiliated and minor parties: 37,537 (10%)

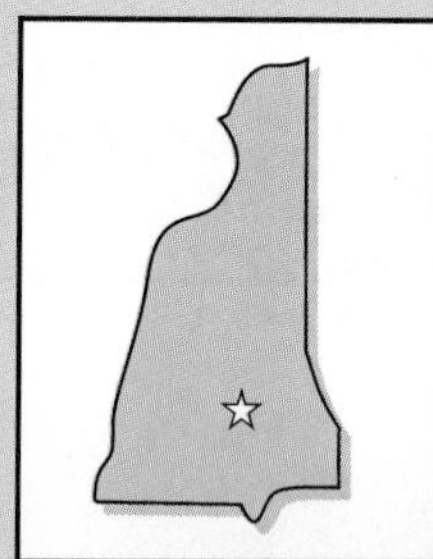

NEW HAMPSHIRE

Captain John Mason named this colony for his home county in England in 1629.

Capital: Concord
Size: 9,279 sq. mi. (23,754 sq. km)
Population: 1,113,915
Order admitted: 9
Date admitted: June 21, 1788
Number of U.S. Congressional Districts: 2
Number of Registered Voters: 658,716
Number of Democrats: 192,217 (29%)
Number of Republicans: 253,972 (39%)
Number of unaffiliated and minor parties: 202,527 (31%)

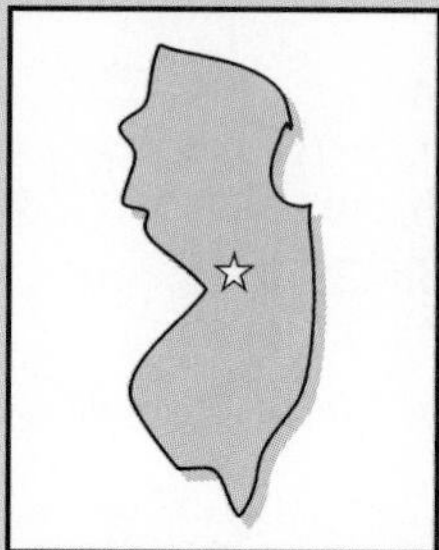

NEW JERSEY

Named after the Isle of Jersey in England by John Berkeley and Sir George Carteret.

Capital: Trenton
Size: 7,787 sq. mi. (19,935 sq. km)
Population: 7,748,634
Order admitted: 3
Date admitted: December 18, 1787
Number of U.S. Congressional Districts: 13
Number of Registered Voters: 3,705,175
Number of Democrats: 1,199,098 (32%)
Number of Republicans: 787,822 (21%)
Number of unaffiliated and minor parties: 1,718,255 (46%)

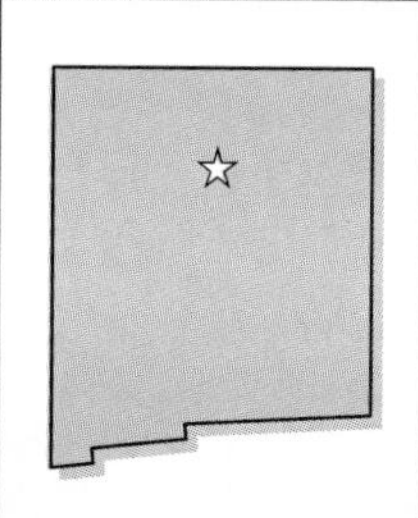

NEW MEXICO

Named by the Spanish for the territory north and west of the Rio Grande.

Capital: Santa Fe
Size: 121,593 sq. mi. (311,278 sq. km)
Population: 1,521,779
Order admitted: 47
Date admitted: January 6, 1912
Number of U.S. Congressional Districts: 3
Number of Registered Voters: 658,374
Number of Democrats: 387,441 (59%)
Number of Republicans: 233,616 (35%)
Number of unaffiliated and minor parties: 37,317 (6%)

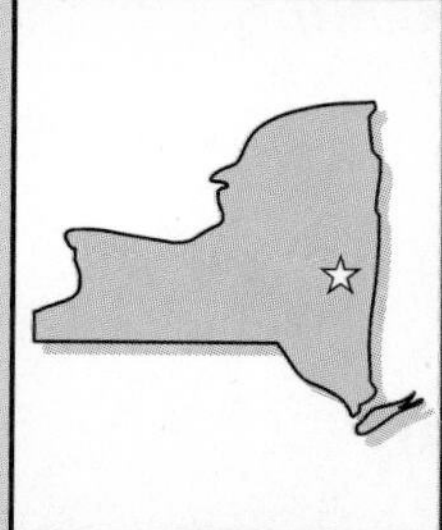

NEW YORK

Originally named New Netherland, New York was later named after the Duke of York and Albany, who received a patent to the region from his brother Charles II of England and captured it from the Dutch in 1664.

Capital: Albany
Size: 52,735 sq. mi. (135,002 sq. km)
Population: 18,044,505
Order admitted: 11
Date admitted: July 26, 1788
Number of U.S. Congressional Districts: 31
Number of Registered Voters: 8,201,532

Number of Democrats: 3,884,984 (47%)
Number of Republicans: 2,620,288 (32%)
Number of unaffiliated and minor parties: 1,696,260 (21%)

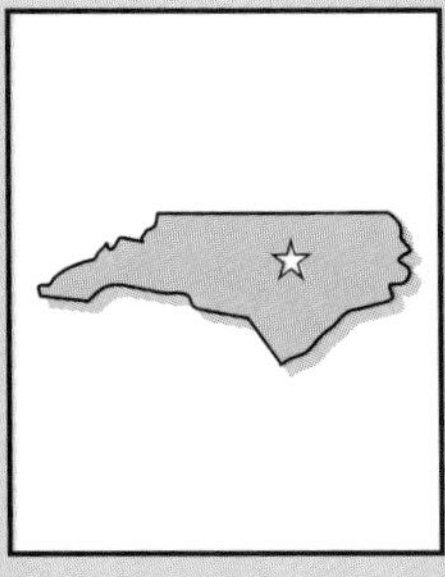

NORTH CAROLINA

From the Latin name Carolus, *meaning "Charles." The colony was originally given to Sir Robert Heath by Charles I and was to be called Province of Carolana. Carolana was divided into North and South Carolina in 1710.*

Capital: Raleigh
Size: 52,669 sq. mi. (134,833 sq. km)
Population: 6,657,630
Order admitted: 12
Date admitted: November 21, 1789
Number of U.S. Congressional Districts: 12
Number of Registered Voters: 3,347,635
Number of Democrats: 2,132,379 (64%)
Number of Republicans: 1,029,892 (31%)
Number of unaffiliated and minor parties: 185,364 (6%)

NORTH DAKOTA

From the Sioux word meaning "friend" or "ally."

Capital: Bismarck
Size: 70,702 sq. mi. (180,997 sq. km)
Population: 641,364
Order admitted: 39
Date admitted: November 2, 1889
Number of U.S. Congressional Districts: 1 At Large
Number of Registered Voters: No state voter registration

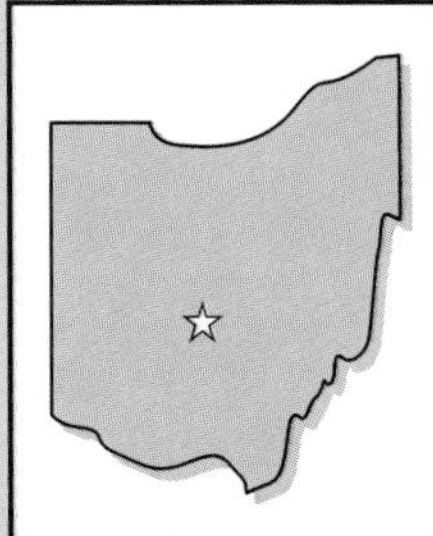

OHIO

From an Iroquois Indian word variously meaning "great," "fine," or "good river."

Capital: Columbus
Size: 44,787 sq. mi. (114,655 sq. km)
Population: 10,887,325
Order admitted: 17
Date admitted: March 1, 1803
Number of U.S. Congressional Districts: 19
Number of Registered Voters: 5,833,653
Number of Democrats: 1,879,405 (32%)
Number of Republicans: 1,270,446 (22%)
Number of unaffiliated and minor parties: 2,683,802 (46%)

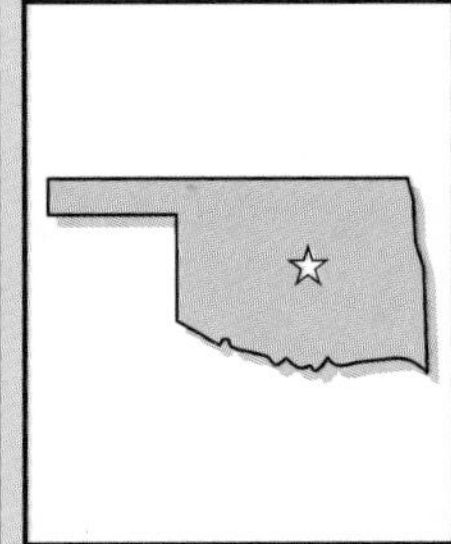

OKLAHOMA

The Choctaw Indian word meaning "red man," which was coined by the Reverend Allen Wright, a Choctaw-speaking Indian.

Capital: Oklahoma City
Size: 69,956 sq. mi. (179,087 sq. km)
Population: 3,157,604
Order admitted: 46
Date admitted: November 16, 1907
Number of U.S. Congressional Districts: 6
Number of Registered Voters: 2,010,684
Number of Democrats: 1,305,291 (65%)
Number of Republicans: 656,714 (33%)
Number of unaffiliated and minor parties: 48,697 (2%)

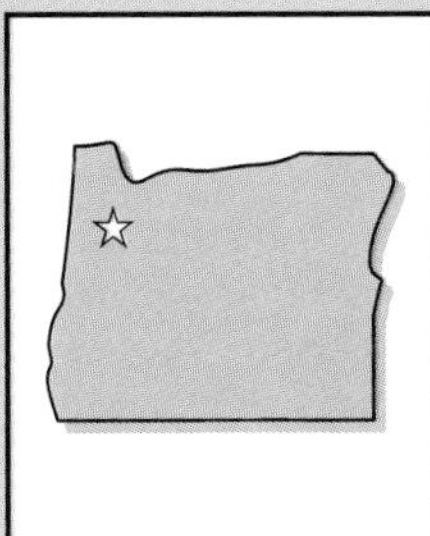

OREGON

One theory maintains that it may have been a variation on the name of the Wisconsin River, called Ouaricon-sint *on a French map dated 1715. Later, Major*

OREGON, *Continued*
Robert Rogers named a river "called by the Indians Ouragon" in his request to seek a Northwest Passage. Another theory derives the word from the Algonquin wauregan, *meaning "beautiful water."*

Capital: Salem
Size: 97,073 sq. mi. (248,507 sq. km)
Population: 2,853,733
Order admitted: 33
Date admitted: February 14, 1859
Number of U.S. Congressional Districts: 5
Number of Registered Voters: 1,476,500
Number of Democrats: 692,100 (47%)
Number of Republicans: 570,933 (39%)
Number of unaffiliated and minor parties: 213,467 (14%)

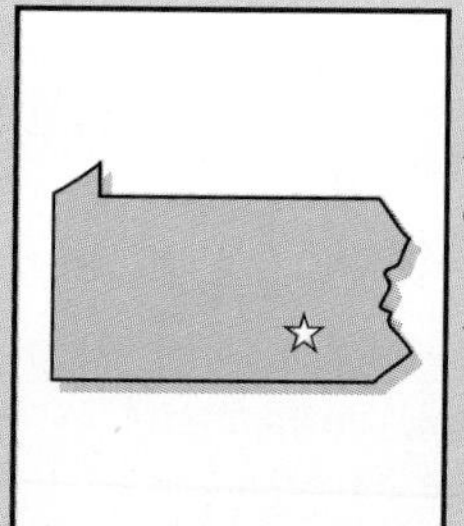

PENNSYLVANIA

Named after the colony's founder, the Quaker William Penn. The literal translation is "Penn's woods."

Capital: Harrisburg
Size: 46,043 sq. mi. (118, 870 sq. km)
Population: 11,924,710
Order admitted: 2
Date admitted: December 12, 1787
Number of U.S. Congressional Districts: 21
Number of Registered Voters: 5,659,189
Number of Democrats: 2,907,156 (51%)
Number of Republicans: 2,476,222 (44%)
Number of unaffiliated and minor parties: 275,811 (5%)

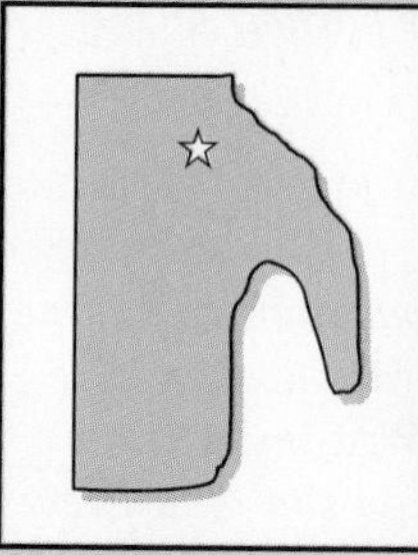

RHODE ISLAND

Possibly named by Giovanni de Verrazano, who charted an island about the size of an island of the same name in the Mediterranean. Another theory suggests Rhode Island was named Roode Eylandt by Dutch explorer Adrian Block because of its red clay.

Capital: Providence
Size: 1,212 sq. mi. (3,103 sq. km)
Population: 1,005,984
Order admitted: 13
Date admitted: May 29, 1790
Number of U.S. Congressional Districts: 2
Number of Registered Voters: 536,773
No party registration

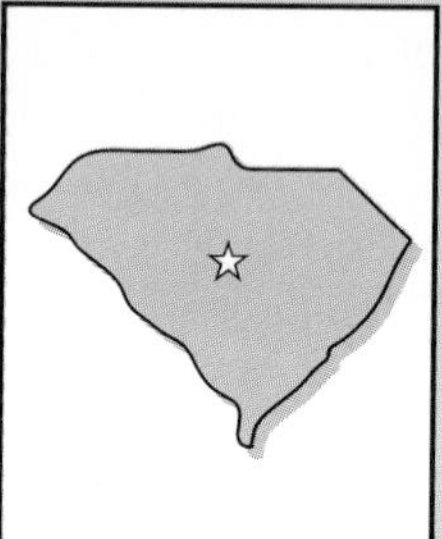

SOUTH CAROLINA

See *North Carolina.*

Capital: Columbia
Size: 31,113 sq. mi. (79,649 sq. km)
Population: 3,505,707
Order admitted: 8
Date admitted: May 23, 1788
Number of U.S. Congressional Districts: 6
Number of Registered Voters: 1,360,082
No party registration

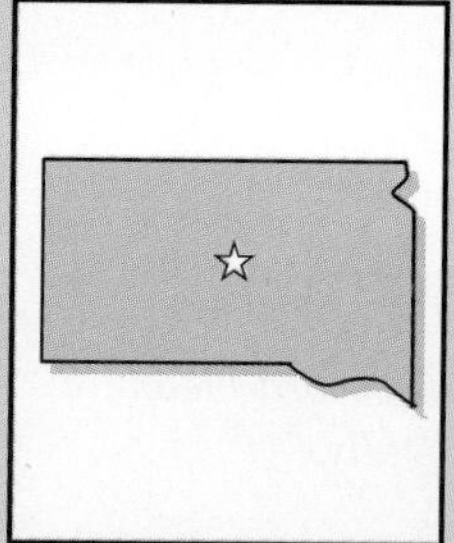

SOUTH DAKOTA

See *North Dakota.*

Capital: Pierre
Size: 77,116 sq. mi. (197,417 sq. km)
Population: 699,999
Order admitted: 40
Date admitted: November 2, 1889
Number of U.S. Congressional Districts: 1 At Large
Number of Registered Voters: 420,351
Number of Democrats: 180,181 (43%)
Number of Republicans: 207,036 (49%)
Number of unaffiliated and minor parties: 33,134 (8%)

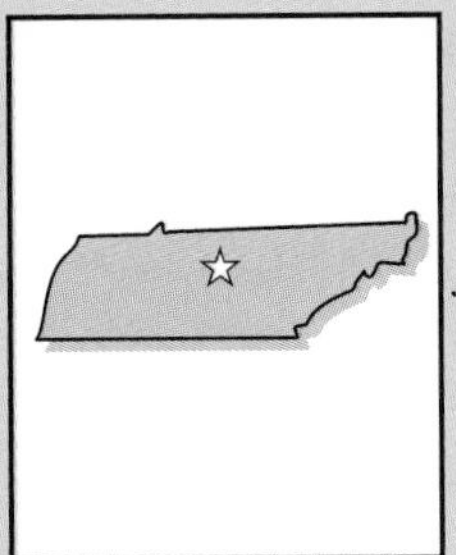

TENNESSEE

The state of Franklin, or Frankland, from 1784 to 1788, it was finally named after the Cherokee villages called tanasi *on the Little Tennessee River.*

Capital: Nashville
Size: 42,144 sq. mi. (107,889 sq. km)
Population: 4,896,641
Order admitted: 16
Date admitted: June 1, 1796
Number of U.S. Congressional Districts: 9 At Large
Number of Registered Voters: 2,460,968
No party registration

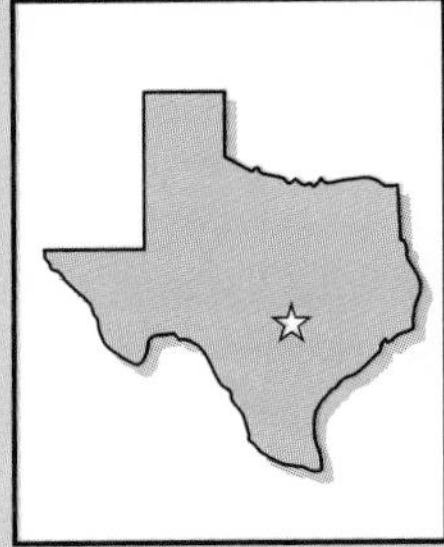

TEXAS

Also written texias, tejas, *and* teysas, Texas *is a variation on the Caddo Indian word for "friend" or "ally."*

Capital: Austin
Size: 266,807 sq. mi. (691,030 sq. km)
Population: 17,059,805
Order admitted: 28
Date admitted: December 29, 1845
Number of U.S. Congressional Districts: 30
Number of Registered Voters: 7,701,499
No party registration

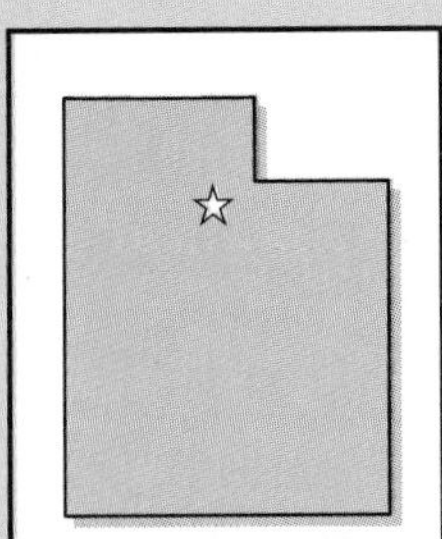

UTAH

Meaning "upper" or "higher." Utah *is derived from a name used by the Navajos (Utes) to designate a Shoshone tribe.*

Capital: Salt Lake City
Size: 84,899 sq. mi. (217,341 sq. km)
Population: 1,727,784
Order admitted: 45
Date admitted: January 4, 1896
Number of U.S. Congressional Districts: 3
Number of Registered Voters: 780,555
No party registration

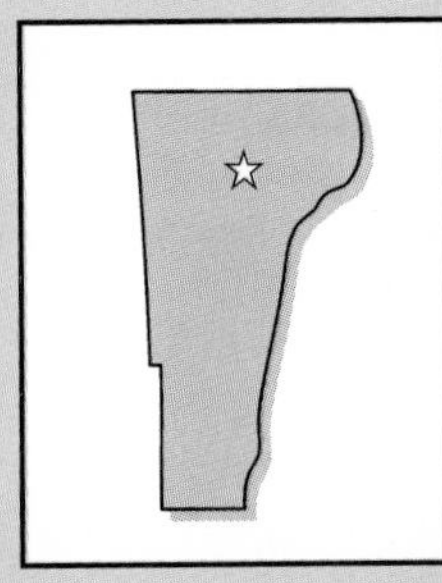

VERMONT

It is believed Samuel de Champlain coined the name from the French words vert *(green) and* mont *(mountain). Later, Dr. Thomas Young proposed this name when the state was formed in 1777.*

Capital: Montpelier
Size: 9,614 sq. mi. (24,612 sq. km)
Population: 564,964
Order admitted: 14
Date admitted: March 4, 1791
Number of U.S. Congressional Districts: 1 At Large
Number of Registered Voters: 350,349
No party registration

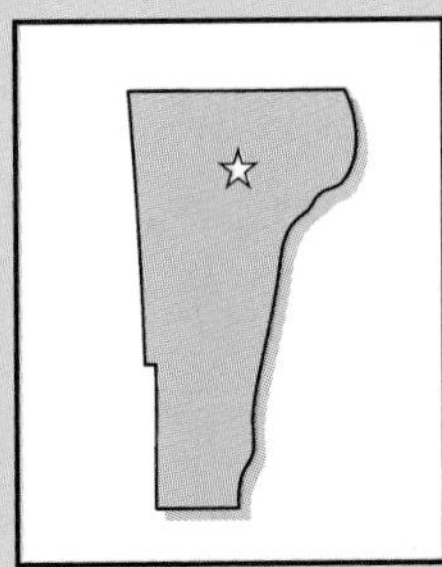

VIRGINIA

Named for the Virgin Queen of England, Queen Elizabeth I, by Sir Walter Raleigh, who first visited its shores in 1584.

Capital: Richmond
Size: 40,767 sq. mi. (104,364 sq. km)
Population: 6,216,568
Order admitted: 10
Date admitted: June 25, 1788
Number of U.S. Congressional Districts: 11
Number of Registered Voters: 2,735,339
No party registration

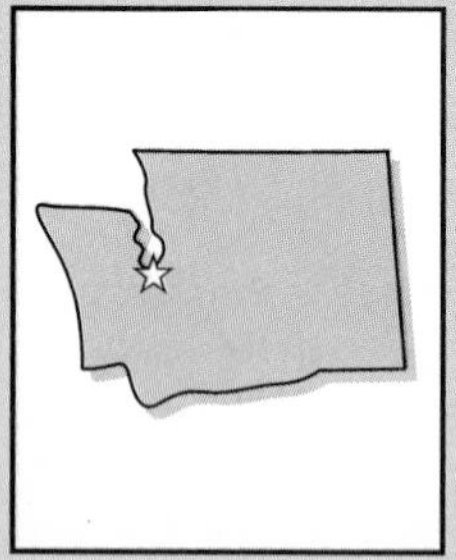

WASHINGTON

Originally named the Territory of Columbia, it was changed to Washington *in honor of the first U.S. President because of the already existing District of Columbia.*

Capital: Olympia
Size: 68,139 sq. mi. (174,436 sq. km)
Population: 4,887,941
Order admitted: 42
Date admitted: November 11, 1889
Number of U.S. Congressional Districts: 9
Number of Registered Voters: 2,225,101
No party registration

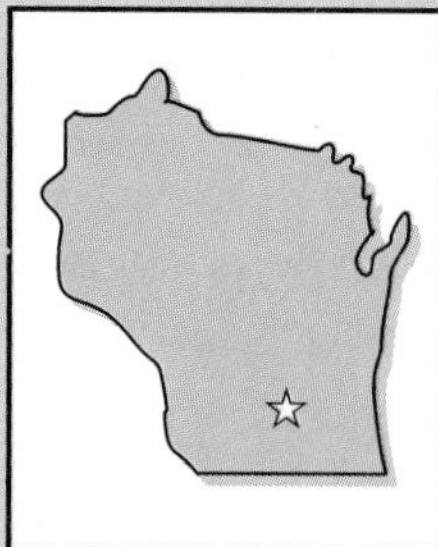

WISCONSIN

A Chippewa word that was spelled Ouisconsin *and* Mesconsing *by early explorers. Wisconsin was formally named by Congress when it became a state.*

Capital: Madison
Size: 56,153 sq. mi. (145,436 sq. km)
Population: 4,906,745
Order admitted: 30
Date admitted: May 29, 1848
Number of U.S. Congressional Districts: 9
Number of Registered Voters: No state voter registration

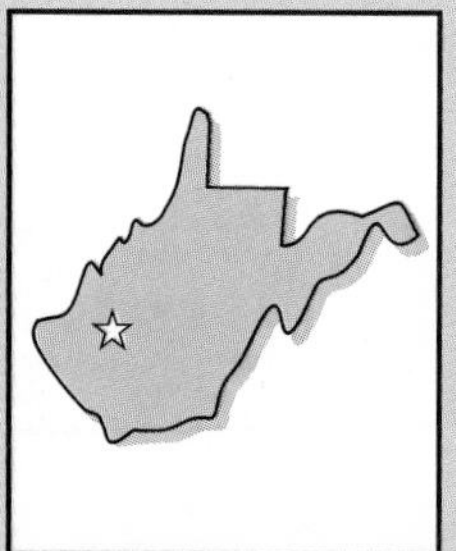

WEST VIRGINIA

Named when this area refused to secede from the Union in 1863.

Capital: Charleston
Size: 24,231 sq. mi. (62,031 sq. km)
Population: 1,801,625
Order admitted: 35
Date admitted: June 20, 1863
Number of U.S. Congressional Districts: 3
Number of Registered Voters: 884,839
Number of Democrats: 585,755 (66%)
Number of Republicans: 275,556 (31%)
Number of unaffiliated and minor parties: 23,528 (3%)

WYOMING

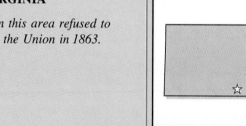

The Algonquin word meaning "large prairie place," the name was adopted from Wyoming Valley, Pennsylvania, the site of an Indian massacre. It was widely known from Thomas Campbell's poem "Gertrude of Wyoming."

Capital: Cheyenne
Size: 97,809 sq. mi. (250,391 sq. km)
Population: 455,975
Order admitted: 44
Date admitted: July 10, 1890
Number of U.S. Congressional Districts: 1 At Large
Number of Registered Voters: 222,331
Number of Democrats: 77,140 (35%)
Number of Republicans: 125,900 (57%)
Number of unaffiliated and minor parties: 19,291 (9%)

U.S. AND WORLD MAPS

MAP OF THE UNITED STATES

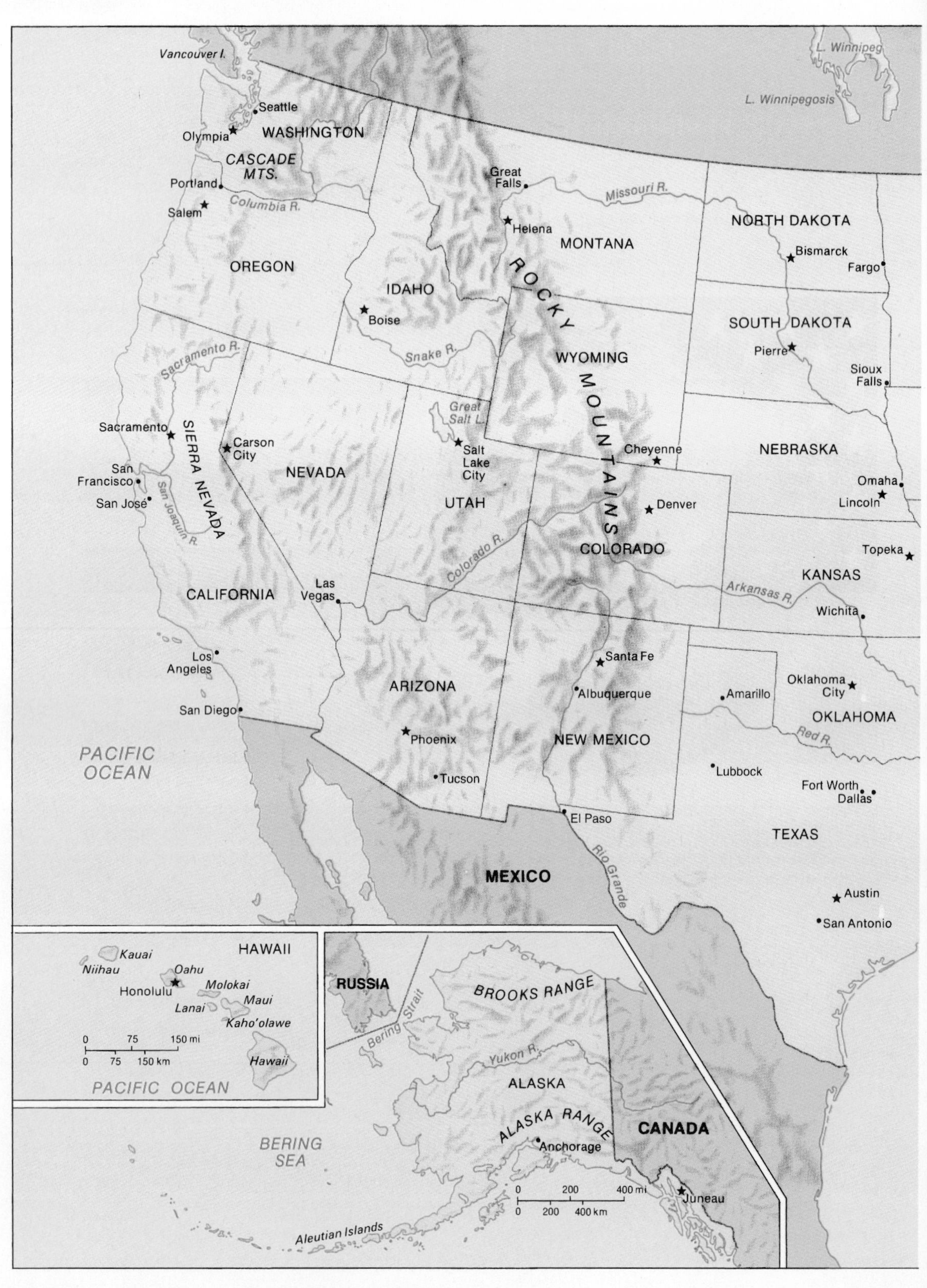

The United States
CANADA
L. Nipigon
L. of the Woods
MINNESOTA
L. Superior
MICHIGAN
L. Huron
St. Lawrence R.
MAINE
Augusta
Burlington
Montpelier
NEW HAMPSHIRE
Champlain
Portland
Concord
Manchester
Boston
VERMONT
Connecticut R.
MASSACHUSETTS
Albany
Providence
RHODE ISLAND
CONNECTICUT
Hartford
L. Ontario
Buffalo
NEW YORK
WISCONSIN
St. Paul
Minneapolis
L. Michigan
Milwaukee
Madison
Lansing
L. St. Clair
Detroit
L. Erie
New York
Newark
Trenton
IOWA
Des Moines
Chicago
Cleveland
PENNSYLVANIA
Philadelphia
Harrisburg
Pittsburgh
NEW JERSEY
OHIO
Columbus
INDIANA
ILLINOIS
Baltimore
Dover
DELAWARE
Washington
Annapolis
Indianapolis
Springfield
Cincinnati
WEST VIRGINIA
DISTRICT OF COLUMBIA
MARYLAND
Kansas City
St. Louis
Jefferson City
Frankfort
Louisville
Ohio R.
Charleston
Richmond
Norfolk
KENTUCKY
VIRGINIA
MISSOURI
APPALACHIAN MTS.
Cumberland R.
ATLANTIC OCEAN
Raleigh
Tennessee R.
NORTH CAROLINA
Nashville
Charlotte
ARKANSAS
TENNESSEE
SOUTH CAROLINA
Memphis
Little Rock
Mississippi R.
Columbia
Atlanta
Charleston
MISSISSIPPI
Birmingham
ALABAMA
GEORGIA
LOUISIANA
Jackson
Montgomery
Tallahassee
Jacksonville
Baton Rouge
Houston
New Orleans
FLORIDA
Tampa
Orlando
0 150 300 mi
0 150 300 km
L. Okeechobee
Miami
GULF OF MEXICO
BAHAMAS
CUBA
HAITI

MAP OF THE WORLD

The World

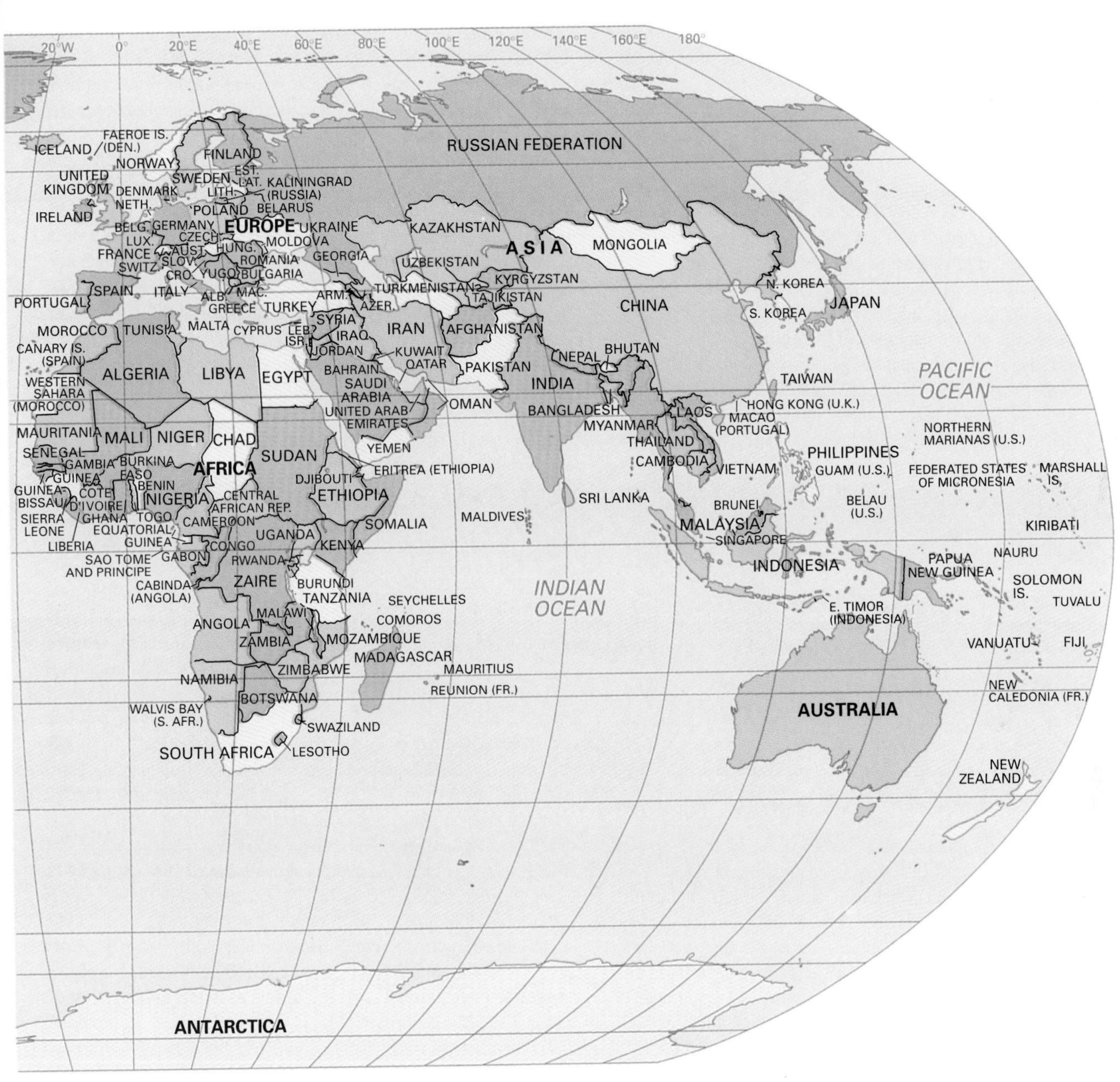

ALB. –ALBANIA
ARM. –ARMENIA
AUST. –AUSTRIA
AZER. –AZERBAIJAN
BELG. –BELGIUM
CRO. –CROATIA
CZECH. –CZECHOSLOVAKIA
(DEN.) –DANISH
EST. –ESTONIA
ISR. –ISRAEL
LAT. –LATVIA
LEB. –LEBANON
LITH. –LITHUANIA
LUX. –LUXEMBOURG
MAC. –MACEDONIA
NETH. –NETHERLANDS
SLOV. –SLOVENIA
(S. AFR.) –SOUTH AFRICAN
SWITZ. –SWITZERLAND
(U.K.) –BRITISH
YUGO. –YUGOSLAVIA

GLOSSARY

ability-to-pay principle A taxation principle under which those with higher incomes pay more in taxes than those with lower incomes, regardless of the number of government services they use.

abridging Depriving or diminishing.

absentee ballot A vote that is mailed in by the voter, rather than cast at the polls.

absolute monarchs Monarchs who have complete and unlimited power. (Compare with *constitutional monarchs.*)

absolute monarchy A government in which rulers hold complete and unlimited power.

acid rain Rain that contains a high concentration of acid-forming chemicals, usually caused by pollution from industrial smokestacks being released into the atmosphere and combining with water vapor.

acquittal The delivery of a defendant from a criminal charge usually by a verdict of not guilty.

act of admissions A bill passed by Congress that admits a state into the Union.

administrative assistant A person hired to manage a lawmaker's office, supervise his or her schedule, and give advice. (Administrative assistants also work for other types of professionals.)

administrative councils Local government units in Great Britain.

affirmative action Job hiring policies that allow special considerations for traditionally disadvantaged groups (such as women or racial minorities) in an effort to overcome the present effects of past discrimination.

agenda A list or program of goals to be accomplished. In government, agenda setting usually involves deciding which public policy questions will be debated, considered, or carried out.

agents of political socialization Groups of people who influence the political opinions of others.

Aid to Families with Dependent Children (AFDC) A social program, funded in part by the federal government and administered by the state, that provides financial assistance to impoverished families with children.

alien One who is not a citizen of the state or nation in which she or he lives.

allegiance Loyalty and service to one's country and government.

alliance Association of two or more nations joined together for mutual benefit.

ambassador A diplomat of high rank who represents his or her government to a foreign country.

amendments Written changes or additions to a law or body of laws, such as the United States Constitution.

American's Creed The principles set forth in the Declaration of Independence, which include natural rights, limited government, equality under the law, and government by consent of the governed.

amnesty A governmental grant of pardon to a large group of individuals.

Anti-Federalists A political group that opposed the adoption of the Constitution because of the document's centralist tendencies and that attacked the framers of the Constitution for failing to include a bill of rights.

appellate courts Courts that review decisions reached by lower (usually trial) courts.

appellate jurisdiction Authority of a court to review decisions reached by lower courts.

apportionment Distribution and assignment of seats in a legislative body among electoral districts; the assignment, based on state population, of the 435 seats of the U.S. House of Representatives.

appropriation The authorization of money for a specific purpose; money approved by the legislature as funding for the activities of another branch of government.

appropriation bill A bill that formally sets aside money for a specific purpose.

armistice A temporary agreement between opponents to stop fighting (also called a *cease-fire*).

arraignment A preliminary court proceeding in which the defendant hears the charges and enters his or her plea.

assembly A gathering of people for a common purpose.

at large The election of an official by the voters of an entire governmental unit such as a state or county, rather than by voters of a subdivision of that area.

attaché Member of an embassy staff who serves in a particular capacity.

attorney general Head of the Department of Justice who is appointed by the president and is a member of the president's cabinet.

auditor One who examines records or accounts to check their accuracy.

Australian ballot A secret ballot that is prepared, distributed, and tabulated by government officials at public expense. The method was introduced to the United States from Australia in 1888 and replaced an open ballot.

authoritarian A concentration of power in a leader who is not constitutionally responsible to the people.

authority The power to influence thought, opinion, and behavior. (Legal authority can be defined as the power to make and enforce laws.)

autocracy A government in which the power and authority is in the hands of a single person.

bad-tendency rule The doctrine holding that speech, religious practice, or other First Amendment freedoms may be permissibly curtailed if such expressions might lead to some "evil."

bail Money that a prisoner may be required to deposit with a court to obtain his or her release and to guarantee that he or she will appear in court at a designated time.

balance the ticket A method by which a presidential candidate chooses a vice presidential candidate who possesses complementary characteristics and thus improves the chances of winning an election.

ballot A printed voting form.

bandwagon effect A propaganda technique that attempts to persuade people to support a candidate or issue because large numbers of other people are supposedly doing so.

bankruptcy The state of being legally unable to pay debts.

bench trial A trial before a judge, without a jury.

benefits-received principle A system of taxation in which those who use a particular government service support it with taxes in proportion to the benefits they receive from it.

biased sample A polling sample that does not accurately represent the population.

bicameral legislature A legislature made up of two chambers or parts. The United States has a bicameral legislature, composed of the House of Representatives and the Senate. (Compare with *unicameral legislature.*)

biennially An event that occurs once every two years.

bills Proposed laws.

bills of attainder Legislative acts that inflict punishment on particular persons or groups without granting them the right to a trial.

blanket primary A primary in which all candidates' names are printed on the same ballot, regardless of party affiliation. In a blanket primary, voters may choose candidates from more than one party.

block grants A type of funding program in which the federal government gives money to state and local governments to use in broadly defined areas of public policy, such as criminal justice or mental health.

boroughs Administrative subunits of a city. In Alaska, a borough is the equivalent of a county.

boycott An organized refusal by consumers to buy specific goods, usually in protest against certain conditions of production or manufacturing.

budget Spending plan for government submitted by the president to Congress in January of each year.

budget deficit When the federal government spends more than it receives.

burden of proof The obligation that rests with the prosecution to prove whether a defendant is guilty of a crime.

bureaucracy A large organization that is structured hierarchically to carry out specific functions.

bureaucrats Those employed by bureaucracies.

business cycle A cycle of economic activity consisting of recession, recovery, growth, and decline.

busing (for integration) A system of transporting public school students from the neighborhoods where they live to schools in other areas. The aim of busing is to eliminate school segregation based on residential patterns.

cabinet An advisory group selected by the president to assist with decision making. A cabinet is traditionally composed of the heads of the executive departments and other officers whom the president may choose to appoint.

calendar A schedule of the order in which bills will be taken up by committee or on the floor.

Calendar of General Orders A schedule that lists bills to be considered by a legislative body, such as the Senate.

campaign manager An individual hired by a candidate to be in charge of the candidate's election campaign.

canvasses The door-to-door solicitations of votes or survey of public opinion throughout a specific area.

capital Any kind of property (such as machines, buildings, tools, or money) used to produce other goods and services.

capital cases Criminal cases in which the sentence might involve the death penalty.

capitalism An economic system in which the individuals own the factors of production and have the right to use those resources in any way they choose within the limits of the law (also called a *market system* or a *free enterprise system*).

card stacking A propaganda technique that emphasizes all the favorable arguments supporting an issue or candidate but does not address the negative arguments.

case law A history of cases that, when taken together, form precedents for later judicial decisions.

casework A form of social work in which members of Congress directly involve themselves in the problems and needs of individual citizens.

caseworkers Members of congressional staffs who manage the numerous requests for help from constituents.

categorical grants Federal grants-in-aid to states or local governments for use on very specific programs or projects.

caucuses Closed meetings of party leaders to select party candidates or decide on policy.

cease-fire See *armistice.*

censorship The suppression of material (such as books, plays, music, and so on) deemed objectionable on moral, political, or other grounds.

censure An official reprimand of a legislator by his or her peers.

census An official count of the population of a city, state, or nation. A census is performed for the whole United States every ten years.

chancellors Judges in colonial times who resolved judicial disputes on the basis of fairness rather than on specific laws.

chargé d'affaires Member of an embassy who ranks below the ambassador and who may temporarily assume the duties of the ambassador.

charter A document issued by a government that grants rights to a person, group of persons, or a corporation to carry on a certain activity.

checks and balances A major principle of American government in which each of the three branches is given the means to check (to restrain or balance) the actions of the others.

chief administrator plan A plan for county government in which a chief administrative officer shares responsibilities in certain key areas with the county board or with other individuals.

chief diplomat The role of the president in recognizing and interacting with foreign governments.

chief executive Head of the executive branch of government.

chief of staff The person who directs the president's office in the White House and serves as presidential adviser.

city manager An official appointed by an elected city council to administer city government.

civil disobedience The activity of nonviolent protest used to draw attention to certain laws and issues.

civil law The body of laws that regulate disputes between private citizens over noncriminal matters, such as contractual agreements, domestic relations, and business practices.

civil liberties Individual rights protected by the Constitution against the powers of the government.

civil rights Constitutionally guaranteed rights and freedoms of Americans.

civil rights movement A political and social movement that began in the 1950s and organized blacks, whites, and people of other races to end the policies of segregation. It sought to establish equal opportunities in the political and economic sectors and to end policies that erected barriers against people because of race.

civil service The term used for the system governing the civilian employees of the government and generally for those who obtained employment through the merit system.

Civil Service Commission The central personnel agency of the federal government.

civil service examination An employment examination given as part of the civil service system to ensure that government jobs go only to qualified people.

clear and present danger The rule or test, first proposed by Justice Oliver Wendell Holmes, which holds that free speech cannot be limited unless it clearly endangers the society the government is designed to protect.

clemency proceedings Proceedings in which a governor may grant a pardon or reprieve for those convicted of a crime.

clerk of the House A non-member staff officer of the House of Representatives.

closed primaries The most widely used primary system, in which voters may only nominate candidates from the party with which they are registered.

cloture A limiting of debate by a legislature in order to get an immediate vote on the question being discussed.

cloture rule A Senate rule that imposes a one-hour limit on the amount of time a senator may speak about a bill or issue.

coalitions Alliances of political groups that cooperate to gain a majority vote.

coattail effect The influence a popular or unpopular candidate for top office can have on voter support of other candidates of the same party.

Cold War The ideological, political, and economic impasse that existed between the United States and the Soviet Union after World War II.

collective security The policy of forming international defense alliances to increase the security of each member nation.

colonial empire A group of colonized nations held under the rule of a single imperial power.

command economic system An economic system in which the government controls the factors of production and makes all decisions about their use.

commerce clause The section of the Constitution that grants Congress the power to regulate trade among the states and with foreign countries.

commercial speech Advertising statements that describe products; have some degree of First Amendment protection.

commission plan A plan for municipal government that consists of a commission of three to nine members who have both legislative and executive powers.

committee of the whole A procedure that the House of Representatives uses to expedite its business by creating itself into one large committee.

common law A body of law that originated in England in which individual judges decided cases in accordance with prevailing customs. As similar decisions were applied to similar cases, a legal standard developed for the nation. Common law forms the basis of the American legal system.

common law marriage When a man and a woman continuously live together as husband and wife for a certain period of time, such as seven years, they are considered to have entered into a common law marriage which is treated the same as all other marriages.

communism Economic and political system based on the theories of Karl Marx. In such a system, the entire economy is based on collective ownership and government control of property and the means of production. Individuals are expected to contribute to the economy according to their ability and are given income according to their needs. Also an economic and political system implemented in countries such as China and, until recently, the Soviet Union, in which the state controls the production and distribution of goods and the government is directed by a single authoritarian leader or party.

Communist bloc A group of countries that fell under Soviet rule after World War II.

commute To reduce a criminal sentence imposed by a court of law.

competition Rivalry among producers or sellers of similar goods to increase sales and profits.

comptroller (also controller) An officer who audits accounts and supervises the financial affairs of a corporation or governmental body.

concurrent jurisdiction A sharing of legal authority between federal and state courts.

concurrent majority A principle advanced by John C. Calhoun that states that democratic decisions should be made only with the agreement of all segments of society affected by the decision. Without their agreement, a decision should not be binding on those whose interests it violates.

concurrent powers Powers held by both the federal and state governments in a federal system.

concurrent resolutions Congressional measures that deal with matters requiring the action of the House and Senate, but for which a law is not needed. They are intended to express an opinion or an official policy. Concurrent resolutions must be passed by both chambers of Congress, but do not require the president's signature and do not have the force of law.

concurring opinion A statement written by a justice who agrees (concurs) with the court's decision, but for reasons different from the majority opinion.

confederal system A league of independent sovereign states, joined together by a central government that has only limited powers over them.

confederation A league of independent states that are united only for the purpose of achieving common goals.

conferees Members of a conference committee.

conference committee A special joint committee appointed to reconcile differences when a bill passes the two houses of Congress in different forms.

conference report A report submitted by a conference committee after it has drafted a single version of a bill.

congressional district The geographic area within a state that is served by one representative in Congress.

congressional immunity A privilege set out in the Constitution that guarantees freedom of speech to members while they are conducting congressional business. Protects the freedom of legislative debate.

conscription Compulsory enrollment in the armed services.

consensus General agreement among the citizenry on an issue.

consent Permission and agreement of the governed.

consent of the governed The principle that government is based on the will of the people and as such can be abolished by the people.

conservatives Those with a set of political beliefs that includes a limited role for government, support for traditional values, and preference for the status quo.

consideration That which each party receives of value when signing a contract.

consolidation The joining of two or more governmental units to form one unit.

constituents The voters in a legislator's home district.

constitutional initiative A process that allows citizens to propose a constitutional amendment through petitions signed by a required number of registered voters.

constitutional monarchy A government in which kings or queens share governmental power with elected lawmakers.

consul A member of the American consulate whose job is to promote American business interests in foreign cities.

consulate Office of the consul.

containment A U.S. diplomatic policy first adopted by the Truman administration to keep communist power contained within its existing boundaries and thus "build situations of strength" around the globe.

contempt Disrespect for or willful disobedience of the rules or orders of a court or legislative body.

contempt of Congress Disrespect for or willful disobedience of Congress.

contiguous Adjoining.

controller See *comptroller.*

convening The formal opening of each term of Congress. The Twentieth Amendment of the Constitution reset the date at January 3 of each odd-numbered year unless Congress sets another date.

Cooley's rule Derived from an 1871 decision by Michigan Judge Thomas Cooley, who stated that cities should be able "to rule from the home," that is, to govern themselves instead of being governed by the state government.

cooperative federalism The theory that the states and the federal government should cooperate in solving problems.

copyright The exclusive legal right of a person to publish, reproduce, or sell his or her own literary, musical, or artistic creations.

council-manager plan A plan for municipal government in which an elected city council appoints a professional manager who acts as the chief executive.

Council of Economic Advisors A staff agency in the executive office that advises the president on measures to maintain stability in the nation's economy. The council helps the president prepare an annual economic report for Congress and develops economic plans and budget recommendations for maintaining employment, production, and purchasing power.

councils of governments Voluntary political organizations of counties and municipalities concerned with areawide problems, formed to coordinate multiple governmental units.

counties Governmental units set up by the state to administer state law and business at the local level. Counties are drawn up by area, rather than by rural or urban criteria.

county board The governing body of a county, elected by voters to carry out county business.

county boroughs A local governmental unit in Great Britain.

county-manager plan Plan for county government in which policies are made by an elected body and are carried out by a manager hired by and responsible to that body.

Credentials Committee A committee that convenes at each political party's national convention to inspect the claims of prospective delegates and determine which may participate.

criminal law A body of law that defines crimes and determines punishment for committing them. The government is the prosecutor in criminal cases since crimes are against the public order.
currency power The power granted to Congress by the Constitution to coin money and regulate its value.

death taxes Estate and inheritance taxes levied by the state.
decentralization The shifting of power from the federal government to state and local governments.
***de facto* segregation** Racial segregation that occurs not as a result of deliberate intentions but because of previous social and economic conditions and residential patterns.
***de jure* segregation** Racial segregation that occurs because of laws or administrative decisions by public agencies.
delegated, expressed, or enumerated powers Those powers directly granted to the federal government by the Constitution as stated in Article I, Section 8.
delegates People who are authorized to speak, vote, or otherwise act on behalf of others. (Representatives from state political parties to a national party convention serve as *delegates* to that convention.)
deliberative organ Deliberates, discusses, and decides important issues.
democracy A system of government in which the people have ultimate political authority. The word is derived from the Greek *demos* (people) and *kratia* (authority).
denaturalization The loss of citizenship through due process of law. Often used for those who used fraud or deception in the naturalization process or for those who are thought to be obstructing the functions of government.
Dennison Rule An 1861 ruling by the U.S. Supreme Court that upheld the right of the governor of Ohio to refuse an extradition request by the governor of Kentucky for a ''free man of color'' on charges that he had helped a slave escape to freedom.
departments A French term for geographic divisions for the purpose of establishing local governments.
deportation Legal process by which a nation returns aliens to their country of origin.
depressions Major slowdowns of economic activity characterized by high unemployment and business downturns and failures.
détente A French word used to refer to the relaxation of tensions between the United States and the Soviet Union under the administration of President Richard Nixon.
deterrence The United States policy adopted after World War II of using the threat of massive retaliation to discourage aggression by its enemies.
dictatorship A form of government in which absolute power is exercised by a single person who has usually obtained his or her power by the use of force.
Dillon's rule A principle outlined by John F. Dillon's *Commentaries on the Law of Municipal Corporations* (1911), which states that municipal corporations possess only those powers that the states expressly grant to them.
diplomacy The process by which states establish and maintain political relations with each other through such means as treaties, agreements, and alliances.
diplomat A person who carries out the means of diplomacy on behalf of his or her native country.
direct democracy A system of government in which political decisions are made by the people themselves rather than by elected representatives. This form of government was widely practiced in ancient Greece.
direct primary An election within a party in which the voters select the candidates who will run on the party ticket in the subsequent general election.
direct tax A tax that must be paid by the person on whom it is levied.
disenfranchise To deprive voters of the ability to vote.
dissenting opinion A statement written by a justice in which he or she dissents from the conclusion reached by the majority of the court. The justice expounds his or her own views about the case.
district attorney An attorney who initiates and conducts legal action on behalf of the state, especially in criminal proceedings.
diversity of citizenship A legal concept that applies to cases arising between citizens of different states, or between a foreign country and citizens of a state or of different states.
divine right theory A theory that the right to rule by a king or a queen was derived directly from God rather than from the consent of the people.
division of powers A basic principle of federalism provided in the U.S. Constitution, by which powers are divided between units of government (such as the federal and state governments), on a geographic basis.
doctrine A particular position, policy, or principle.
doubling time The rate at which a population will double, e.g., every five years or every thirty years.
draft Compulsory service in the military.
draft registration The process by which 18-year-old males are required to present themselves as available for the draft should a draft be enacted.
dual citizenship The condition of being a citizen of two sovereign nations or of both a state and a nation.
dual federalism A system of government in which both the federal and state governments maintain diverse but sovereign powers.
due process clause The constitutional guarantees set out in the Fifth and Fourteenth Amendments to the Constitution that government will not illegally or arbitrarily deprive a person of life, liberty, or property. (Also called **due process of law**.)

economic sanctions Refusal to trade with a foreign nation as a means of expressing disapproval of that nation's political or economic policies.

economic system The way in which a nation uses its resources to satisfy people's needs and wants.

elastic clause Article I, Section 8 of the Constitution, which gives Congress the power to make all laws "necessary and proper" to carry out its functions.

elected chief executive plan A plan for county government in which the executive officer, such as a mayor, is elected directly by the voters and works with the county board.

electoral college The group of electors who are selected by the voters in each state to officially elect the president and vice president. The number of electors in each state is equal to the number of each state's representatives in both houses of Congress.

electoral college system A unique American institution, created by the Constitution, providing for the selection of the president by electors chosen by the state parties, subject to the laws of each state.

electorate All the citizens entitled to vote in a given election.

electors Those individuals chosen early in the presidential election year by state laws and political party apparatus. The electors cast ballots for the president and vice president in order to make the formal selection of president and vice president.

embassy The official residence and offices of an ambassador.

enabling act A law passed by Congress that allows a territory to draw up a constitution and become eligible for statehood.

enemy aliens Citizens of those nations with which the United States is at war.

enumerated powers See *delegated, expressed, or enumerated powers.*

environmental impact statement A statement mandated by the Environmental Policy Act that must show the costs and benefits of federal actions that could significantly affect the quality of the environment.

equal employment opportunity A goal of the 1964 Civil Rights Act to end discrimination based on race, color, religion, sex, or national origin in conditions of employment and to promote employers to foster equal job opportunities.

equalization A method for adjusting the amount of money that a state must supply to receive federal funds, which takes into account the wealth of the state and its ability to tax its citizens.

equal protection clause Clause in the Fourteenth Amendment that forbids any state to deny to any person within its jurisdiction the equal protection of the laws. This is the major constitutional restraint on the power of governments to discriminate against persons because of race, national origin, or sex.

espionage The practice of spying to obtain information about the plans and activities of a foreign power.

establishment clause A part of the First Amendment that prohibits the establishment of a church officially supported by the federal government. It has been applied to prevent government aid to religious schools, prayer in public schools, and the teaching of religious fundamentalist theories of creation (as opposed to scientific theories of evolution).

evolutionary theory A theory that holds that government evolved over time as families first joined together into clans and then into tribes: Out of the tribes a leader emerged, which eventually gave rise to the gradual establishment of government.

excessive entanglement theory A rule applied by the Supreme Court to maintain the separation of church and state. To be constitutional, government aid to religious school groups must meet three requirements: (1) the purpose must be clearly secular; (2) it must neither advance nor inhibit religion; and (3) it must avoid excessive entanglement of government and religion.

excise taxes A tax levied on certain actions, such as the manufacture or sale of certain commodities such as tobacco or liquor within a country.

exclusionary rule The rule that any illegally obtained evidence cannot be used at the court trial of the person from whom the evidence was seized. The rule is based upon the Supreme Court interpretation of the Fourth and Fourteenth Amendments.

exclusive jurisdiction A court's authority to hear cases that fall outside the legal scope of other courts.

executive agreements Binding international agreements made between chiefs of state that do not require legislative sanction.

executive authority A person with strong and wide-reaching administrative powers who oversees the executive branch of a system.

Executive Office of the President (EOP) Nine staff agencies that assist the president in carrying out major duties. Established by President Franklin D. Roosevelt by executive order under the Reorganization Act of 1939.

executive order A rule or regulation issued by a chief executive (such as a president or governor) that has the effect of law.

executive privilege The right of the president (or other officials named by the president) to refuse to appear before, or to withhold information from, a legislative committee on the grounds that revealing the information in question may threaten national security.

expatriation The act of voluntarily renouncing (giving up) citizenship in one's nation of origin.

exports Goods that a nation produces and sells to other nations.

ex post facto Criminal laws that made certain acts a crime and then punished people for committing the acts before the laws were passed. Ex post facto laws are prohibited by the Constitution.

expressed powers See *delegated, expressed, or enumerated powers.*

expulsion The forced removal of a member of Congress for misconduct.

extradition A process by which fugitive suspected criminals are returned to the jurisdiction of the prosecuting state.

extraordinary majority A majority that is greater than 50 percent plus one. The U.S. Constitution, for example, requires extraordinary majorities of two-thirds of the House and Senate for Congress to propose a Constitutional Amendment.

factions Groups or cliques within a larger group.

federal budget The federal government's itemized plan for the expenditure of funds over a certain period of time.

federal government A term that refers to the central or national government, particularly in the United States.

federal question Arises whenever the cause of action of a plaintiff is based at least in part on the United States Constitution, a treaty, or a federal law. Federal questions can be addressed only by the federal judiciary.

Federal Reserve System The central bank of the United States. "The Fed" was established in 1913 and is led by a board of governors.

federal system A form of government in which a written constitution provides for a separation of powers between a central government and several regional governments. This separation is established by an authority superior to both the central and regional governments, such as a written document. In the United States, the division of powers between the federal government and the fifty states is explained by the Constitution.

Federalists Those who favored a strong central government and the new Constitution.

felonies Serious criminal offenses punishable by imprisonment. The penalties range from one year in prison to death.

"fighting words" Words that when uttered by a public speaker are so inflammatory that they could provoke the average listener to violence.

filibuster Unlimited debate to halt action in the Senate.

First Continental Congress The first gathering of delegates from twelve of the thirteen colonies for the purpose of drafting a federal constitution. The Congress was held in Philadelphia in 1774.

fiscal policy The discretionary adjustments of government expenditures and/or taxes in order to achieve national economic goals, such as high employment and price stability.

fiscal year The twelve-month period that is determined for bookkeeping or accounting purposes. The government's fiscal year runs from October 1 through September 30.

food stamps Government-issued coupons that can be used to purchase food.

force theory A theory of the origins of government that holds that when strong persons or groups conquered territories, they forced everyone living in those territories to submit to their will.

foreign policy A nation's political and economic goals with respect to other nations; the techniques and strategies used to achieve those goals.

foreign service The cadre of officials in the State Department who serve in foreign countries.

franchise The legal right to vote. The franchise was extended to African Americans by the Fifteenth Amendment, to women by the Nineteenth Amendment, and to all citizens ages eighteen and over by the Twenty-Sixth Amendment.

franking privilege A privilege that allows members of Congress to send material through the mail by substituting their facsimile signature (frank) for postage.

free enterprise system See *capitalism.*

free exercise clause The provision of the First Amendment that guarantees the free exercise of religion.

fugitive An individual wanted for committing a crime who has fled from prosecution.

full faith and credit clause Article VI, Section I of the Constitution, which requires states to recognize one another's laws and court decisions. It ensures that rights established under deeds, wills, contracts, and other civil documents in one state will be honored by other states.

functional consolidations The cooperation of two or more units of local government in providing services to their inhabitants.

Fundamental Orders of Connecticut America's first written constitution which called for a representative assembly, made up of elected representatives from each town to serve in that assembly and to make laws. It also called for the popular election of a governor and judges.

fundamental rights Those basic rights necessary for the concept of an ordered liberty such as voting and freedom of religion.

fund-raisers Events paid for by candidates staged in order to raise funds for campaign costs.

gag orders Orders issued by judges that restrict publication of news about a trial in progress or a pretrial hearing in order to protect the accused's rights to a fair trial.

gender gap The difference in political opinions between men and women. A term used to describe the difference in the percentages of votes cast for a particular candidate by women and by men. The term was widely used after the 1980 election and brought up again before the 1992 election.

general election Regularly scheduled statewide elections at which voters make the final selection for public officeholders.

general jurisdiction The authority of a court to decide all matters that come before it.

generalization An oversimplification that doesn't hold true in every specific case.

general-law city A city operating under state laws that apply to all local government units of a similar type.

gerrymandering The practice of redrawing legislative district boundary lines to obtain voting advantages for a political party or group.

glittering generalities A propaganda method that uses broad, sweeping statements that sound impressive but have little real meaning.

global warming The gradual increase in average climatic temperatures throughout the world.

government The institutions and processes through which public policies are made for a society.

government bonds Certificates bought by individuals and companies as a means of loaning money to the government. In exchange for borrowing the money, the government promises to repay buyers the full amount of the loan, plus interest, at a later time.

government corporation An agency of government that is run as a business enterprise. Such an agency is established when the activity is primarily commercial, produces revenue, and requires greater flexibility than permitted in most government agencies.

grand jury A jury, consisting of six to twenty-three persons, that hears criminal charges against individuals and determines whether there is enough evidence to justify holding a trial.

grandfather clause A method used by Southern states to exempt whites from state taxes and literacy laws as a means of denying the franchise to black voters. The clause allowed anyone who could prove that his grandfather had voted before 1867 to vote in current elections.

green vote A vote from those who favor stronger laws to protect and preserve the environment.

greenhouse effect The trapping of heat inside the earth's atmosphere, which is a result of pollution caused largely by the burning of fossil fuels and the emission of carbon dioxide.

grievances Complaints.

habeas corpus An order designed to prevent illegal arrests and imprisonments; it demands that a prisoner be brought before the court and that the detaining officer show why the prisoner should not be released.

hereditary peers Members of the British nobility who become so by birth. There are over 700 hereditary peers with titles such as baron, viscount, earl, and duke. These are all members of the House of Lords.

hereditary ruler Someone who rules because he or she is the son or daughter of a previous ruler.

home-rule city A city with a charter that allows local voters to frame, adopt, and amend their own charter.

hopper The wooden box in the House of Representatives into which new bills are dropped.

horizontal federalism The rules laid out in the Constitution that prevent any one state from setting itself apart from the others by, for example, creating its own foreign policy.

House of Commons The lower and more powerful house of Parliament in Great Britain.

House of Lords The upper chamber of Parliament in Great Britain.

House Rules Committee A permanent committee of the House of Representatives that provides the rules under which bills can be considered, debated, and amended.

human rights Term referring to the rights and privileges of all human beings. These rights are stated in the Declaration of Independence as life, liberty, and the pursuit of happiness. They are guaranteed and protected by the Bill of Rights.

hung jury A jury that cannot agree unanimously on a verdict.

hyperpluralism A form of pluralism in which government is so decentralized and authority so fragmented that nothing is accomplished.

ideologues A term applied to individuals whose political opinions are very strong, either at the liberal or conservative extremes.

ideology A set of beliefs about the nature of people and the institutions of government.

illegal aliens Individuals who enter the United States without a legal permit or who enter as tourists and stay longer than their tourist status allows.

image building A process of molding a candidate's image to meet the particular needs of the campaign by using public and private opinion polls and other media-related devices.

immigrants People who move to a new country for the purpose of establishing permanent residency and becoming citizens.

immunity Protection against being brought to trial for certain actions.

impeachment A formal charge brought against a public official for misconduct or wrongdoing in office.

implied powers The powers of the federal government that are implied by the expressed powers in the Constitution, particularly in Article I, Section 8.

impoundment The process by which the president can refuse to spend money that Congress has appropriated for a certain purpose.

incarceration Imprisonment.

income transfer The transfer of income from one group to another, as with the farm program, and the transfer from one generation to another, as occurs in the social security program.

incorporation The process of setting up a city through the granting of a charter by the state.

incorporation theory The view that most of the protections of the Bill of Rights are incorporated into the Fourteenth Amendment's protection against infringement from state governments.

incumbent An official who is presently holding office.

independent executive agencies Federal agencies with a specific function that report directly to the president.

independent regulatory agencies Responsible for a specific type of public policy. Their function is to create and implement rules that regulate private activity and protect the public interest in a particular sector of the economy.

independents Voters who do not regularly identify themselves with a political party or support candidates of a particular party.

indictment A formal finding by a grand jury that there is sufficient evidence against a particular person to warrant a criminal trial.

indirect democracy See *representative democracy.*

indirect tax A tax levied on an individual or business but passed on to another party for payment.

inflation A general increase in prices.

information A statement issued by a prosecutor that there is enough evidence to bring the accused person to trial, without the use of a grand jury.

inherent powers The powers of the federal government which, although not expressly granted by the Constitution, belong to it by virtue of its role as the government of a sovereign state.

initiative A procedure by which voters can propose a change in state and local laws by means of gathering signatures on a petition and submitting it to the legislature for approval.

in-kind subsidies Assistance that is given in forms other than cash, such as food stamps.

institutions Organizations and establishments in a society that are devoted to the promotion of a particular cause. Some of the institutions in our government are the legal system, Congress, and the social welfare system.

intelligence Information gathered about the capabilities and intentions of foreign governments.

interdependence The condition of individuals, organizations, and nations being dependent upon one another.

interest group An organized group of individuals sharing common objectives who actively attempt to influence policy through lobbying, the publication of public opinion polls, and other methods.

interim committees Legislative committees that function between legislative sessions. Such committees study particular issues and report their findings in the next legislative session.

interstate commerce Trade between two or more states.

interstate compact An agreement between two or more states to cooperate on a policy or problem. Minor compacts are made without congressional approval, but any compact that tends to increase the power of the contracting states relative to other states or relative to the federal government generally requires the consent of Congress.

interventionism A political policy of changing or preserving the internal political affairs of foreign nations.

intrastate commerce Trade among different regions in the same state.

iron curtain Described the political boundaries between the democratic countries in Europe and the Soviet-controlled communist countries in Eastern Europe.

iron triangle Term used for a three-way alliance between legislators, bureaucrats, and interest groups to make or preserve policies that benefit their respective individual interests.

isolationism A political policy of noninvolvement in world affairs.

joint committees Legislative committees composed of members from both houses of Congress.

joint resolutions Legal measures, similar to bills, passed by Congress and signed by the president that have the force of law.

judicial activism A doctrine that advocates an active role for the Supreme Court in enforcing the Constitution and in using judicial review. An activist court takes a broad view of the Constitution and involves itself in legislative and executive matters.

judicial circuits The twelve courts that hear appeals from district courts located within their respective circuits.

judicial implementation The process by which court decisions are translated into policy.

judicial restraint A doctrine that holds that the Supreme Court should rarely use its power of judicial review or otherwise intervene in the political process.

judicial review The power of the courts to determine the constitutionality of the actions of the executive, legislative, and judicial branches of government. First established in *Marbury v. Madison* (1803).

junkets Trips by members of Congress to gather information about proposed legislation, such as a new trade bill.

jurisdiction The power of a court to try and decide certain cases.

jury duty The responsibility of all citizens, if called, to serve on a jury for a criminal trial.

jus sanguinis The "law of the blood," as grounds for American citizenship, states that a child born on foreign soil becomes an American citizen at birth if at least one of the parents is a U.S. citizen, and if that citizen has lived in the United States for at least ten years after the age of 14.

jus soli The "law of the soil," as grounds for American citizenship, states that all persons born in the United States are American citizens.

justice court A local court that hears minor civil and criminal cases, performs marriages, and legalizes documents.

justice of the peace A local judicial official who presides over the activities of the justice court.

keynote speaker A person of national renown chosen to speak and rouse enthusiasm at a political party's national convention.

Kitchen Cabinet The name given to a president's unofficial advisors who help him with policy and decisions. The name was coined during Andrew Jackson's presidency.

labor force All individuals over 16 who are working or who are actively looking for a job.

law clerk Recent law school graduates who work for justices by performing much of the research and preliminary drafting necessary for the justices to form an opinion.

law lords Nine members of the House of Lords in Great Britain. They are the equivalent of a British Supreme Court.

legal tender Legitimate currency for trade or purchasing.

legislative assistants Aides to lawmakers who make sure that the lawmakers are well informed about the bills they must deal with.

legislative correspondents Aides to lawmakers who handle their correspondence.

legislative director Aide to lawmakers who directs and manages the lawmaker's staff.

legislative power The authority to make laws.

legislature A government body primarily responsible for the making of laws.

legitimacy The legal authority of the officials, acts, and institutions of government, conferred by the people on the grounds that the government's actions are an appropriate use of power and that the government is a legally constituted authority.

libel Defamation of character in writing.

liberalism A political ideology whose advocates prefer an active government in dealing with human needs, support individual rights and liberties, and place a priority on social needs over military needs.

liberals Those who hold a set of political beliefs that includes the advocacy of active government intervention to improve the welfare of individuals, support for civil rights, and political change.

lieutenant governor A state official who acts as governor should the governor be absent from the state, become disabled, or die. He or she may act as president of the state senate.

life expectancy How many years a certain group of people is expected to live.

limited government A form of government based on the principle that government should perform only the functions that the people have given it the power to perform.

limited jurisdiction The authority of a court to hear only specific kinds of cases.

line-item veto A power used by an executive branch to veto one or more provisions of a bill while allowing the remainder of the bill to become law.

line organizations Government or corporate groups that provide direct services or products for the public.

literacy tests A voting requirement once used by Southern states that demanded that citizens prove they could read in order to qualify to vote. Primarily used to deny African Americans the right to vote, literacy tests are now outlawed.

lobbying All the efforts by individuals or organizations to affect the passage, defeat, or contents of legislation. The term comes from the lobby of the legislature itself, where petitioners used to corner legislators and speak about their concerns.

lobbyist A person who usually acts as an agent for a group that seeks to bring about the passage or defeat of legislative bills, to influence their content, or to influence administrative actions.

loose constructionists Those who believe that the Constitution should be interpreted loosely and who give broad definitions to the powers of the federal government.

loose monetary policy A policy designed to stimulate the economy by making credit inexpensive and widely available.

Madisonian Model The model of government devised by James Madison in which the powers of the government are separated into three branches: executive, legislative, and judicial.

magistrate A local judicial official with limited jurisdiction.

magistrate court A lower court in a small town or city.

Magna Carta The great charter that King John of England was forced to sign in 1215 as protection against the absolute powers of the monarchy. It included such fundamental rights as trial by jury and due process of law.

majority floor leader The chief spokesperson of the majority party in the Senate who directs the legislative program and sets the party strategy.

majority leader The leader of the majority party in the House. The majority leader of the House is elected by the caucus of party members to act as spokesperson for the party and to keep the party together.

majority opinion The written statement of the views of the majority of judges in support of a decision made by the court on which they preside.

majority party The party that holds over half the seats in the legislature.

majority rule A political system in which a majority determines the outcome of elections. A simple majority requires 50 percent plus one of the vote, whereas an extraordinary majority requires more than 50 percent plus one of the vote.

malapportionment A condition that results when, based on population and representation, the voting power of citizens in one district becomes more influential than the voting power of citizens in another district.

mandatory preference poll A type of primary election in which delegates are required to vote for the candidate chosen by the voters at the national convention.

mandatory sentencing A system by which specific crimes carry fixed terms of imprisonment.

marginal tax rate The percentage of additional dollars that must be paid in income taxes. The marginal tax rate is applied to the highest tax bracket only.

market The activity of buying and selling goods and services.

market economic system The opposite of a command economic system; otherwise known as capitalism.

markup sessions Meetings in which congressional conference committee members decide which changes, if any, should be made on a bill.

Marshall Plan A massive program of economic recovery for the nations of Europe after World War II. Named after former Secretary of State George C. Marshall, Jr., who had that post from 1947 to 1949.

mass media The technical means of communication (especially radio, newspapers, and television) designed to reach, inform, and often influence large numbers of people.

matching funds The funds a state must pay (or "match") when issued many categorical grants. Some programs require states to raise only 10 percent of the funds; others require an even share.

Mayflower Compact A document that stated that laws were to be made for the general good of the people, drawn up by Pilgrim leaders in 1620 on the voyage of the *Mayflower.*

mayor-administrator plan A plan for city government used in large urban areas in which the mayor plays a prominent political role. The mayor appoints a chief administrative officer whose function is to free the mayor from routine administrative tasks.

mayor-council plan A plan for city government in which the mayor is an elected chief executive and the council is the legislative body.

Members of Parliament Normally the elected officials of the House of Commons in Great Britain, but may also include the appointed members of the House of Lords.

merit The standard qualifications and performance criteria used to hire and promote government employees.

merit system The system used to select, promote, and retain government employees based on competitive exams and performance reviews.

minimum wage The minimum hourly wage that workers must be paid as determined by the federal government.

ministers Cabinet members in a parliamentary government.

minor party A political party that is less widely supported in a governmental system. In the United States any party other than one of the two major parties (Republican and Democratic) is considered a minor party.

minority floor leader The party officer in the Senate who commands the minority party's policies and directs its legislative program and strategy.

minority leader The leader of the minority party in the House.

minority party The party with fewer members in each house of Congress.

Miranda Rules The 1966 Supreme Court ruling that criminal suspects must be informed of their constitutional rights at the time of arrest.

Missouri Plan A method of selecting judges in which judges are first nominated by a special committee and then appointed by the governor. After serving an initial term, the judicial appointment is either confirmed or rejected at the general election.

mistrial A trial that is canceled because the judge believes it has not been fair in some way.

mixed economy An economic system that contains characteristics of both a command economy and a pure market economy. The mix may vary so that any economic system may lean more toward one pure type than another.

moderates People with political views that are in the middle ground between liberal and conservative.

monarchy A system of government ruled by a hereditary monarch (a king or a queen).

monetary policy Changes in the rate of growth of the money supply and in the availability of credit.

monopoly An industry or company that has total control over the sale of a product or service and does not face competition.

Monroe Doctrine The policy statement included in President Monroe's 1823 annual message to Congress, which set out three principles: (1) European nations should not establish new colonies in the Western Hemisphere; (2) European nations should not intervene in the affairs of independent nations of the Western Hemisphere; and (3) the United States should not interfere in the affairs of European nations.

multilateral treaties Treaties among three or more nations.

multiparty system An electoral system in which three or more political parties compete for public offices.

municipal home rule The power vested in a local unit of government to draft or change its own charter and to manage its own affairs.

municipalities Local units of government that have the authority to govern urban or city areas.

mutual-assured destruction (MAD) A theory that held that as long as the United States and the Soviet Union both had nuclear forces that were large, invulnerable, and somewhat equal, then neither nation would take the chance of waging war with the other.

mutual defense alliance An agreement among allied nations to support one another in case of an attack by enemy forces.

name calling A propaganda method that attaches a negative or unpopular label to a person to discredit that person's public image.

nation An area within a particular geographic boundary within which an organized government makes and enforces laws without the approval of a higher authority.

National Assembly The lower house of the French legislature.

national convention The meeting held by each major party every four years to select presidential and vice presidential candidates, to choose a national committee, to write a party platform, and to conduct party business.

national debt The total amount of money the national government owes as a result of borrowing and interest on borrowing. This occurs when the government exceeds its budget and spends more funds than it collects.

National Diet Through its constitution, Japan has a Parliament that is called the National Diet. It consists of two houses—the House of Councilors and the House of Representatives.

national party chairperson Individual who directs the work of the party national committee.

national party committee The political party leaders who direct party business during the time between the national party conventions. The group leads the party's national organization.

national security The nation's protection from unwanted interference, threat, or takeover from other nations. A sense of freedom and independence for the nation.

National Security Council (NSC) A council that advises the president on domestic and foreign matters concerning the safety and defense of the nation. This staff agency of the Executive Office was established by the National Security Act of 1947.

nationalists Individuals who feel strong loyalty and devotion to their nation.

nationality Membership in a particular nation or country.

natural aristocracy Officials whom President Thomas Jefferson placed in the executive bureaucracy.

natural rights Rights that do not come from governments but are inherent within every single man, woman, and child by virtue of the fact that he or she has been born and is a human being.

naturalization The legal process by which an individual born a citizen of one country becomes a citizen of another.

naturalized citizens Citizens from other countries who legally become American citizens. The naturalization process involves meeting certain requirements of residency, literacy, and acceptance of the principles of American government.

Navigation Acts Restrictions placed on colonial activity from 1651 to 1750 by Great Britain, which include the condition that only English ships could be used for trade within the British Empire.

necessary and proper clause Article I, Section 8, of the Constitution, which gives Congress the power to make all laws ''necessary and proper'' for the federal government to carry out its responsibilities.

negative campaign advertising Advertising in a political campaign aimed at discrediting and damaging the opposing candidate.

neutral competency Federal bureaucrats are expected to exhibit neutral competency, which means that they are supposed to apply their technical skills to their jobs without regard to political issues.

neutrality A position of not being aligned with either side in a dispute or conflict, such as a war.

New Deal A program ushered in by the Roosevelt administration in 1933 designed to help the United States out of the Great Depression. It included many government spending and public assistance programs, in addition to thousands of regulations of economic activity.

New England town A governmental unit in the New England states that combines the roles of city and county governments. ''Town'' includes a central village and surrounding rural areas, and practices direct democracy.

new federalism A plan to limit the federal government's role in regulating state governments, in order to give the states increased power to decide how they should spend all government revenues.

no contest A plea in a criminal case in which the defendant neither admits or denies the charges. The principal difference between a plea of guilty and a plea of no contest is that the latter may not be used against the defendant in a civil action.

nominating convention An official meeting of a political party to choose its candidates and select delegates.

nomination A party's naming and endorsing of a particular person as a candidate for public office.

nonpartisan elections Elections held without the participation of political parties to fill certain offices, such as judicial, city, or school board positions.

nonresident aliens Aliens who expect to stay in a foreign country for a short, specified time.

Northwest Ordinance A 1787 congressional act that established a basic pattern for how states should govern new territories north of the Ohio River.

obscenity A form of speech that is not protected under the First Amendment. A work that taken as a whole appeals to a prurient interest in sex by depicting sexual conduct as specifically defined by legislation or judicial interpretation in a patently offensive way, and that lacks serious literary, artistic, political, or scientific value.

off-budget items A category outside an official budget.

office-group ballot A ballot on which candidates are listed according to the office for which they are running.

Office of Management and Budget (OMB) Assists the president in preparing the proposed annual budget, which the president must submit to Congress in January of each year.

old-age pensions Retirement plans giving people money after they stop working.

one-party system An electoral system in which only one political party exists, is legal, or has any chance of winning elections.

open primary A direct primary in which voters may cast ballots without having to declare their party orientation.

opinion The statement of a court or judge concerning the decision reached in a case. It expounds the law as applied to the case and details the reasons on which the judgment was based.

opposition The next largest party in a parliamentary government, next to the ruling party. Leaders of the opposition appoint their own potential cabinet members, who ''shadow'' particular members of the ruling cabinet, and hope to some day replace them.

oral arguments The verbal arguments presented by opposing counsel.

original jurisdiction The legal authority of a court to hear the first presentation of a case.

oversight function The power of Congress to follow up on laws it has passed to ensure that they are being properly enforced and administered.

pardon The act of granting a prisoner release from punishment. A pardon can be granted by a president or a governor before or after a criminal conviction.

parishes A term used in Louisiana to describe administrative units of local government.

Parliament The name of the national legislative body in countries governed by a parliamentary system, as in England and France.

parliamentary democracy A form of democracy in which the executive leadership (which usually consists of a prime minister and his or her cabinet) is chosen by and responsible to a democratically elected parliament.

parole The release of a prisoner before the completion of his or her prison sentence.

partisan elections Elections in which candidates running for office are identified by their political parties.

partisan politics Politics in support of a particular party's ideology.

partisan preference The preference of one party over another by voters or legislators.

party identification Linking oneself to a particular party.

party platform The document drawn up by each party at the national convention that outlines the policies and positions of the party. The platform is submitted to the entire convention for approval.

party ticket A list of candidates for various offices that belong to one political party.

party-column ballot A form of ballot used in general elections in which candidates are listed in one column under their respective party names. This ballot emphasizes voting along party lines rather than for particular individuals.

passports Government-issued certificates that identify a person as a citizen of that government's country and authorize the person to travel abroad.

patent A license granted to an inventor that gives exclusive rights to manufacture and sell the invention for a specified period of time.

patronage A system of rewarding party faithfuls and workers with government employment and contracts.

peer group A group of people who share relevant social characteristics such as age and economic status. Peer groups play an important role in shaping individual attitudes and beliefs.

peers Individuals who are one's equals.

petit jury A group of up to twelve persons who hear the facts of a civil or criminal case in a court of law and give a verdict; also called *trial jury.*

petition A request that individuals submit to government officials. The petition may involve government policy or it may be a request to become a citizen.

picketing A form of protest in which workers on strike publicly march in an attempt to raise public awareness of a certain controversy and to persuade consumers not to deal with the employer until the strike is settled.

pigeonhole Filing a bill away or putting it aside for no further action. The term is borrowed from the old-time desks in committee rooms of Congress that had small compartments or "pigeonholes" for filing papers.

plain folks A method of propaganda that attempts to attract people to a political figure by portraying him or her as just an average American.

plaintiff A person who files suit in a court of law.

planks Issues or beliefs that make up a political party's platform.

plea bargaining Agreements between a prosecutor and a defense attorney whereby a defendant pleads guilty to a lesser charge in exchange for a lighter sentence. The prosecutor is willing to plea bargain in order to move the case through an extremely crowded court and to be ensured that the case will result in a guilty plea.

plurality A situation in which a candidate wins an election by receiving more votes than the others but does not necessarily win a majority. Most federal, state, and local laws allow for elections to be won by a plurality vote.

pocket veto A special veto power used by the chief executive after the legislature has adjourned. Bills that are not signed by the chief executive die after a specified period of time and must be reintroduced if Congress wishes to reconsider them.

police power The authority of the states to legislate for the protection of the health, safety, and welfare of the people.

policy voting When people vote for candidates who share their stand on certain key issues.

political action committee (PAC) A committee that is established by and represents the interests of corporations, labor unions, or special interest groups. PACs raise money and give donations to campaigns on behalf of the groups they represent.

political consultants Professionals hired by a political candidate to devise strategy, create campaign themes, and manage the image building of a candidate's political campaign.

political machines Organizations within a political party that control elections by granting favors in exchange for votes or money.

political participation The ways in which individuals can participate in the political process, such as by voting, serving on juries, helping with political campaigns, and running for a political office.

political party A group of organized citizens with a broad set of common beliefs who join together to elect candidates to public office and determine public policy.

political patronage A system of appointing people to political positions on the basis of service to the party rather than on any qualifications or merits.

political philosophy A set of notions or ideas about how people should be governed.

political socialization The process by which individuals develop political beliefs and form opinions about political issues. Important forces in this process include the family and the educational system.

politics The authoritative allocation of resources for a society;

the process of deciding who gets what, when, and how in a society.

poll tax A special tax that had to be paid before voting. The Twenty-Fourth Amendment outlawed the poll tax in federal elections, and in 1966 the Supreme Court declared it unconstitutional in all elections.

popular vote A vote cast by someone other than an elector; the number of actual votes cast in an election.

porkbarrel Appropriations for local projects that improve legislators' popularity in their own districts.

power The possession of control, authority, or influence over others.

power of recognition The power of the executive branch to accept the legal existence of another country's government.

preamble An introductory statement to an official document that usually explains the document's goals and purposes.

precedent A court rule that sets a standard for subsequent legal decisions in similar cases.

precincts The smallest voting districts at the local level.

preference poll A type of primary election in which voters may cast separate votes for candidates and for convention delegates.

preferred-position doctrine A Supreme Court test that requires that limitations be applied to the First Amendment only to avoid imminent, serious, and important evils.

preliminary hearing A court hearing at which evidence is submitted and testimony heard to determine whether there is enough reason to continue with court proceedings.

president of the Senate The role given by the Constitution to the vice president of the United States. As presiding officer, he or she may call on members to speak, put questions to a vote, and may cast a vote only in the event of a tie.

president *pro tempore* The temporary presiding officer of the Senate in the absence of the vice president.

presidential democracy A democracy in which the people elect both the president and the legislature. (Compare with *parliamentary democracy.*)

press conferences Scheduled interviews with the media.

press secretary A member of the White House staff who holds press conferences for reporters and lets people know what the president thinks about current national and international issues.

pressure groups Private organizations that use persuasion and pressure to see that laws are passed in favor of their interests.

preventive detention Holding accused felons without bail if judges feel that the suspect, if released, will commit another crime.

primaries Elections held before a general election in which candidates from the same party compete for the party nomination.

prime minister The chief executive in a parliamentary system who is elected by the legislature from among its own members.

principle of federalism A system of government in which the power to govern is shared by a central (or federal) government and state governments, as outlined in a written constitution.

prior restraint The restraining of an action before it has actually occurred. Government censorship of documents or broadcasts before they are published or aired is an example of prior restraint.

private bills A legislative measure that applies only to certain persons or places, rather than to the nation as a whole.

private property Goods owned by individuals or groups rather than by government.

privileges and immunities clause A section of the Constitution that requires states not to discriminate against one another's citizens in such areas as legal protection, access to the courts, freedom to travel, and property rights.

probable cause Sufficient evidence to believe that a crime has been committed. Reasonable grounds for issuing a search warrant against an individual, his or her home, or personal possessions.

probation The suspension of a criminal sentence by a judge on the grounds that the individual maintain good behavior and be supervised by a probation officer for a specified period of time.

procedural due process A provision in the Constitution that states that the law must be carried out in a fair and orderly manner.

processes Procedures.

profit The amount of money left over after all the expenses of running a business have been paid.

profit incentive The desire to make money that motivates people to produce, buy, and sell goods and services.

progressive taxation A system of taxation in which individuals pay a higher percentage of additional tax dollars as income rises. In this way, the marginal tax rate exceeds the average tax rate.

Prohibition The fourteen-year era (from 1920 to 1933) during which it was illegal in the United States to manufacture, transport, or consume intoxicating beverages. Prohibition began with the Eighteenth Amendment and was repealed by the Twenty-First Amendment.

project grants Assistance grants that state and local agencies can apply for directly, so that funds can be allocated to where they are needed.

propaganda The spreading of ideas, information, or rumor for the purpose of helping or injuring an institution, a cause, or a person.

proportional taxation A system of taxation in which the tax *rate* remains constant regardless of a person's income.

proportionality A concept of the "just war theory," which states that the good that might be achieved by winning a war must clearly outweigh the harm that may be done.

prosecuting attorney The official who represents the government and initiates and carries out legal proceedings.

prototype A model.

psychoactives A term that applies to all drugs that affect the mind such as alcohol, nicotine, caffeine, marijuana, opiates, and cocaine.

public bills A legislative measure that applies to the nation as a whole.

public debt See *national debt.*

public defender The attorney appointed to represent a defendant in a criminal case should the defendant be unable to hire an attorney.

public-interest groups Groups that are formed with the broad goal of working for the "public good."

public opinion Opinions and attitudes shared by significant numbers of people on social and political issues.

public opinion poll A random survey to discover popular views on matters of public importance.

public policies Policies that affect the public at large. Public policies are typically carried out by the legislative and executive branches of local, state, and federal government.

pure speech The freely voiced, peaceful expression of thoughts, ideas, or opinions, at home or in public.

quorum The minimum number of legislators who must be present for a legislative body to conduct business.

quota A rule enforced by the government that states that a certain number of jobs, promotions, or other types of selections must be given to members of certain groups.

radical left Persons on the extreme left side of the political spectrum who do not believe in working within the established political processes to achieve their goals and who often want to destroy the established governmental system.

random sample A cross-section of a population that has been polled on a specific issue.

ratification Formal approval or final consent of a constitution, constitutional amendment, or treaty.

ratings system A system by which interest groups evaluate (rate) the performance of legislators based on how the legislators have served the interest groups.

rational-basis test A method used by the Supreme Court to ensure equal legal protection to all individuals. It applies to suspected discrimination situations that affect diverse individuals.

reactionaries People who resist change much more strongly than do either moderates or conservatives. Reactionaries not only do not want society to change, they are willing to actively fight against social change.

realigning election An election in which the electorate turns away from the dominant party and replaces it with a new dominant party.

reapportionment The redrawing of legislative district lines, usually after a census is taken, in accordance with population changes indicated by the census.

recall A procedure that allows voters to dismiss an elected official from a state or local office before the official's term is expired.

recall election An election that gives citizens the power to remove an elected official from office before the end of his or her term.

recesses Periods of time during which a legislative or judicial body is not in session.

recessions Periods of time in which the rate of economic growth is consistently lower than usual.

record vote (also **roll-call vote**) A method of voting in a legislature in which legislators call out their votes on an issue. A computer records each vote electronically and display boards show how each member has voted.

referendum A form of direct democracy in which legislative or constitutional measures are first decided upon by the legislature and then presented to the voters for approval.

refugees People who must flee from danger in their native countries and find residence outside their homeland.

registration Entering one's name onto a list of eligible voters. Registration requires meeting certain age, residency, and citizenship requirements.

regressive taxation A system of taxation in which individuals pay a lower percentage of tax dollars as income rises. In this way, the marginal tax rate is less than the average tax rate.

released time The time students are given away from regular public school classes to attend religious instruction sessions.

repeal To rescind or do away with legislation.

representative assembly A law-making body that is composed of individuals who represent the population.

representative democracy (also **indirect democracy**) A system of democracy in which the people elect representatives who work within government on behalf of the people. (Compare with *direct democracy.*)

representative government A government in which the people, by whatever means, choose a limited number of individuals to determine policy for all citizens.

representatives Officials who are elected to a legislative office for a specific time for the purpose of determining policy for all citizens.

reprieve A postponement of a criminal sentence imposed by a court of law. The president or governor has the power to grant reprieves and usually does so for humanitarian reasons.

reprimand An official reproach used by Congress for a member guilty of misconduct.

republic The name given to a nation in which the supreme power rests in those who are entitled to vote and is exercised by elected representatives who are responsible to voters and who govern according to law. (Compare with *representative democracy.*)

republican form of government A system of government in which the supreme power rests with the voters, who elect representatives to operate the government for them.

reserved powers Powers that are neither granted to the federal government nor expressly forbidden to the states and are therefore retained by the states or by the people.

residency A requirement that a person live within a state for a specified period of time in order to qualify to vote.

resident aliens People who have immigrated to the United States to establish permanent residence.

resulting powers The accumulation of several expressed powers that results in a certain power of the federal government.

revenue bills Bills that involve the raising of money for the government. According to the Constitution, revenue bills must originate in the House of Representatives.

revenue-sharing program A program in which the federal government allocated funds to states and cities with virtually no strings attached. Recipient governments could use the funds in any way they saw fit.

reverse discrimination The assertion that affirmative action programs that require preferential treatment or quotas discriminate against those who have no minority status.

review courts See *appellate courts.*

revolution The popular overthrow of an established government or political system and its replacement with a new system of government. Famous revolutions include the American (1775–83), the French (1789–99), Russian [February Revolution (March 17, 1917) and October Revolution (November 7, 1917)], and the Second Russian Revolution, which occurred in August of 1991.

rider An amendment or provision attached to a bill that is not related to the subject of the bill.

roll-call vote See *record vote.*

rule of law A basic principle of government that accompanies constitutional supremacy which states that government shall be carried out according to established law, and that both those who govern and those who are governed will be bound by this law.

run-off election A repeat election between the two front runners in a prior election when no candidate has received a majority of votes. Run-off elections are usually held in places where the law requires a majority vote.

sabotage A destructive act intended to hinder a nation's defense efforts.

sacrifice principle A principle of taxation that holds that the sacrifices people make to pay their taxes should be fair.

samples Small numbers of people who represent a cross-section of the total population that has been polled on a specific issue.

sampling error The level of confidence in the findings of a public opinion poll.

search warrant An order issued and authorized by a judge that gives police the power to search a specific place in connection with a particular crime.

searches and seizures The methods used by law enforcement officials to look for and collect the evidence they need to convict individuals suspected of crimes as referred to in the Fourth Amendment.

secession The act of formally withdrawing from membership in an alliance; the withdrawal of a state from the federal union.

Second Continental Congress The congress of the colonies that met in 1775 to assume the powers of a central government and establish an army.

seditious speech Speech intended to promote resistance to lawful authority and that especially advocates the violent overthrow of a government.

segregation The enforced separation, often by discriminatory means, of racial, ethnic, or other groups from the rest of the population in education, housing, or other areas.

select committees Temporary legislative committees established for a special purpose.

selectmen Individuals chosen by a township to serve on the local board and manage the daily affairs of the town.

self-incrimination Providing damaging information or testimony against oneself in a court of law.

self-nomination Announcing one's own desire to run for public office.

senatorial courtesy An unwritten rule that an executive appointment to a certain state must first be approved by the senators of that state.

seniority An unwritten rule followed in both houses of Congress that specifies that members with longer terms of continuous service will be given preference when committee chairpersons and holders of other significant posts are selected.

sentence The punishment imposed by a court of law on an individual who is found guilty of a crime.

separate-but-equal doctrine A doctrine long held by the Supreme Court, which declared that segregation in schools and public accommodations did not imply the superiority of one race over another. It held that the Equal Protection Clause of the Fourteenth Amendment did not forbid racial segregation as long as the facilities for blacks were equal to those provided for whites. The doctrine was overturned in the *Brown v. Board of Education* decision of 1954.

sessions Regular periods of time during which legislative bodies assemble and conduct business.

shield laws Laws that protect reporters in courts of law against disclosing their sources and revealing other confidential information.

simple resolution Legislation that deals with matters affecting only one house of Congress and is passed by that house alone.

single-member district system A method of election in which only one candidate can win election to each office.

single-member districts Electoral districts from which single officeholders are chosen by voters.

slander The public utterance of a statement that holds a person up for contempt, ridicule, or hatred and thus damages the person's reputation.

social conflict Friction between groups within a society. Sometimes social conflict is resolved by violence, other times by the judicial system, and other times by changes in customs and traditions.

social contract theory A theory of society that states that individuals voluntarily agree to create an organized society in order to secure mutual protection and welfare. A theory derived from Hobbes, Locke, and Rousseau.

Social Security A government insurance program of obligatory saving financed from payroll taxes imposed on both employers and employees. Workers pay for the benefits while working and receive the benefits after they retire.

socioeconomic factors Social and economic factors such as age, income, education, and occupation.

Solid South A term used to describe the tendency of the southern states to vote Democratic after the Civil War.

solidarity Mutual agreement within a group.

sovereignty The supreme and independent authority that a government possesses within its own territory.

speaker The presiding officer in the lower house of a state legislature.

Speaker of the House The presiding officer in the House of Representatives, always a long-time member of the majority party and often the most powerful and influential member of the House.

special election An election held whenever an issue must be decided before the next regular election is held.

special sessions Unscheduled sessions of Congress ordered by the president.

speech plus A verbal expression of opinions, ideas, or beliefs combined with some sort of action such as marching or demonstrating.

split-ticket voting The act of voting for candidates from more than one political party in the same election.

spoils system An arrangement under which the political party that wins an election gives government jobs to its own party members.

sponsor A legislator who drafts and proposes bills.

Stamp Act An act passed by the British Parliament in 1765 which placed the first direct tax on the colonies. The Stamp Act required the use of tax stamps on all legal documents, newspapers, pamphlets, playing cards, and certain business agreements.

standing committees Permanent committees within the House or Senate that consider bills within a subject area.

standing vote A method of voting in the legislature in which those who favor a measure and those who oppose it are required to stand up to show their vote.

State of the Union Address An annual message from the president to Congress in which a legislative program is proposed. The message is aimed not only at Congress but to the American people and to the world.

status quo The existing state of affairs.

statutory law A law passed by a legislature.

straight-ticket voting The act of voting exclusively for candidates of the same party in an election.

straw poll A survey of opinions taken to estimate the strength of opposing candidates or the popularity of a proposed law.

strict constructionists Those who believe that the Constitution should be interpreted strictly and feel that the federal government should have only those powers specifically named in the Constitution.

strong mayor-council plan A plan for city government in which the mayor is the chief executive and has almost complete control over hiring and firing employees and preparing the budget.

subcommittees Divisions of larger committees that deal with a particular part of the committee's policy area.

subpoena A legal writ that requires a person to give a testimony in court.

substantive due process The Constitutional requirement that the laws used in accusing and convicting persons of crimes must be fair.

succession The legal procedure by which government leaders succeed the presidency should the president die, become disabled, or be removed from office.

suffrage See *franchise.*

suffragists Those who advocated for women's right to vote.

summit meeting A conference between the heads of two or more nations.

summons A notice that calls on a defendant to appear in court.

super-majority vote Used by the General Assembly of the United Nations. Important questions are decided by a majority vote or by a super-majority vote of two-thirds, depending on the importance of the matter.

superpowers The nations with the greatest economic and military power.

Supplemental Security Income (SSI) A government program that establishes a minimum income for the aged, the blind, and the disabled.

supremacy clause Article VI, Section 2 of the Constitution, which establishes the Constitution and federal laws as superior to all state and local legislation.

suspect classification A test used by the Supreme Court to determine if the classification of individuals based on race, national origin, or sex has in any way denied those individuals equal protection of the law.

symbolic speech The expression of beliefs, opinions, or ideas through forms other than speech or print.

teller vote A method of voting in a legislature in which those who favor a measure and those who oppose it are required to walk down an aisle to show their vote.

tenure The period of time during which a public official holds office.

term See *tenure.*

testimonials A propaganda technique that involves persuading people to support an issue or candidate because well-known individuals, such as a prominent government official or famous entertainers, offer such support.

third parties Political parties other than the two major parties, usually composed of dissatisfied groups that have split from the major parties.

Three-Fifths Compromise A compromise reached during the Constitutional Convention in which it was agreed that three-fifths of all slaves were to be counted both for tax purposes and for representation in the House of Representatives.

tight monetary policy A policy designed to slow the economy by making credit expensive and in short supply.

tolerance A fair and objective attitude toward those whose opinions, race, religion, and nationality differ from one's own.

totalitarian A ruler who rules without the consent of the governed.

town manager system A system adopted by some New England towns in which voters elect selectmen who then appoint professional town managers.

town meeting A traditional form of New England town government at which direct democracy is practiced.

townships Local government units that are subdivisions of counties and have similar governing procedures.

tracking polls Polls that track public opinion of candidates on nearly a daily basis as election day approaches.

trade and product organizations Organizations that usually support policies that benefit business in general and work toward seeking policy goals that benefit their particular membership.

transfer A propaganda technique that involves associating a candidate with a respected person, group, or symbol.

treason Article III, Section 3 of the Constitution states that treason "shall consist in levying war against (the United States), or in adhering to their enemies, giving them aid and comfort."

treaty A formal agreement between the governments of two or more countries.

trial balloon The practice of testing public reaction to a new idea by unofficially publicizing it.

trial courts A court of original jurisdiction that hears civil and criminal cases.

trial jury See *petit jury.*

two-party system A political system in which two strong and established parties compete for political offices.

tyranny The arbitrary or unrestrained exercise of power by an oppressive individual or government.

unanimous Being of one mind; agreement.

unanimous opinion Agreement by all judges on the same court decision.

unconstitutional Contrary to constitutional provisions and so invalid.

undocumented aliens illegal aliens.

unicameral legislature A legislature with only one legislative body. (Compared with *bicameral legislature.*)

unincorporated areas Areas not located within municipal boundaries.

unitary government A centralized governmental system in which local or subdivisional governments exercise only those powers given to them by the central government.

unitary system A centralized governmental system in which local or subdivisional governments exercise only those powers given to them by the central government.

United States Treasury Bonds See *government bonds.*

urban areas Highly populated communities.

value-added tax A tax on the difference between the costs that go into producing a product and the revenues received from selling the product.

veto A latin word meaning "I forbid"; the refusal by an official, such as the president or governor, to sign a bill into law.

veto power A constitutional power that enables the chief executive (president or governor) to reject legislation and return it to the legislature with reasons for the objection. This prevents or delays the bill from becoming law.

veto session A session in which state legislators can consider bills vetoed by the governor and attempt to override the governor's veto, if enough popular support within the legislature exists.

visa A permit to enter another country, issued from the country one wishes to enter.

voice vote A method of voting in a legislature.

voir dire A French phrase meaning "to speak the truth"; refers to the process by which prospective jurors are examined to ensure their judgments will be impartial.

vote of confidence Support from the parliament for the existing government.

voter turnout The percentage of eligible citizens who actually take part, or "turn out" in the election process.

waive To relinquish or give up.

War Powers Act The law passed in 1973 that spells out the conditions under which the president can commit troops to war without congressional approval.

wards The local units of a party organization.

warrant An order issued by a court authorizing a public official to proceed in a specified manner, such as a search warrant.

weak mayor-council plan Plan for city government in which the mayor is elected as chief executive officer; the council is elected as the legislative body. The mayor has only limited powers and little control over staffing and budgeting, and is often elected for a two-year term.

Western Bloc The democratic nations that emerged victorious after World War II, led by the United States.

whips Assistant floor leaders who aid the majority and minority floor leaders.

whistle-blower A government employee who calls public attention to fraud, mismanagement, or waste in his or her own agency or department.

White House Press Corps A group of reporters assigned to cover the presidency full time.

winner-take-all system A system in which the presidential candidate who wins the preference vote in a primary automatically wins the support of all the delegates chosen in the primary.

writ of certiorari A written order issued by a higher court to a lower court to send up the record of a case for review.

writ of mandamus A written order issued by a court commanding an official of the government to perform a specified lawful duty or act.

write-in candidate Someone who will campaign without being listed on the ballot, and will ask voters to write his or her name on the ballot on election day.

zoning The method by which local governments regulate how property may be used.

INDEX

M

O

P

T

X

Y

Z

Statesman/Lynn Dobson; **Chapter 22** Mario Cuomo/Office of the Govenor of New York; Seal/State of Texas; Texas Legislature/Austin American Statesman/Lynn Dobson; Welcome to Colorado sign/State of Colorado; **Chapter 23** Prison/PhotoEdit/Mary Kate Denny; Oregon State Police/Photo Researchers; Jury/Stock Boston/Billy Barnes; Court House/Texas Department of Highways and Public Transportation; **Chapter 24** Garbage Collector/Stock Boston/Frank Siteman; Firefighter/Stock Boston/Martin Rogers; Town Hall/Stock Boston/Philip Jon Bailey; Mayor Dinkins/City Hall/Sygma/A. Tannenbaum; **Chapter 25** Freeway/Stock Boston/Joe Sohm; **Unit Nine** Japanese Diet/Ministry of Foreign Affairs, Japan; Boris Yeltsin/Black Star/Klaus Reisenger; John Major/British Tourist Authority; Houses of Parliament/British Tourist Authority; Money/Comstock (ID# 5622); François Mitterand/Sygma/T. Orban; **Chapter 26** Boris Yeltsin/Black Star/Klaus Reisenger; John Major/British Tourist Authority; Houses of Parliament/British Tourist Authority; Money/Comstock (ID# 5622)

Intext Photo Credits

4 Barbara Alper, Stock, Boston, Inc.; **5** (left) David R. Frazier, Photo Researchers; **5** (right) Gabor Demjen, Stock, Boston, Inc.; **6** Christopher Morris, Black Star; **7** Susan McCartney, Photo Researchers; **8** The Granger Collection, New York; **9** Bettman; **11** cartoonist: Don Addis, Creators Syndicate; **12** Farrell Grehan, Photo Researchers; **15** F. Hibon, Sygma; **17** P. Durand, Sygma; **18** Dennis Brack, Black Star; **24** The Granger Collection, New York; **25** (top) Bettmann; **25** (bottom) Bettmann; **27** The Granger Collection, New York; **28** The Granger Collection, New York; **29** The Granger Collection, New York; **31** The Granger Collection, New York; **31** (inset) The Granger Collection, New York; **32** The Granger Collection, New York; **32** (inset) Bettmann; **33** The Granger Collection, New York; **39** The Granger Collection, New York; **41** The Granger Collection, New York; **42** Bettmann; **43** The Granger Collection, New York; **46** (left) The Granger Collection, New York; **46** (middle) The Granger Collection, New York; **46** (right) Photo Researchers; **48** Linda Barlett, Photo Researchers; **53** Dennis Brack, Black Star; **57** Sal Di Marco Jr., Black Star; **59** Photo Researchers; **61** (top) The Granger Collection, New York; **61** (bottom) Norman Rockwell Museum; **63** The Granger Collection, New York; **64** The Granger Collection, New York; **68** J. Langevin, Sygma; **70** Bettmann; **71** John Troha, Black Star; **76** Sygma; **79** by Marlette for New York Newsday; **80** Bob Daemmrich, Stock, Boston, Inc.; **85** Joe Sohm/Chromosohm, Stock Boston, Inc.; **87** Michael Sullivan, Black Star; **87** (inset) Fred Ward, Black Star; **89** Bettmann; **92** Bettmann; **93** Harry Wilks, Stock, Boston, Inc.; **94** Bettmann; **95** Bettmann; **96** D. B. Owen, Black Star; **96** (inset) Photo Researchers; **97** Mitch Kezar, Black Star; **104** Mitch Kezar, Black Star; **106** (top) Bettmann; **106** (bottom) Bettmann; **108** Tom McHugh, Photo Researchers; **110** Bettmann; **112** Martin Rogers, Stock, Boston, Inc.; **112** (inset) Mike Maple, Woodfin Camp & Associates; **113** Bettmann; **114** Mike Mazzaschi, Stock, Boston, Inc.; **115** Bettmann; **117** J. P. Laffont, Sygma; **118** Sidney Harris; **120** M. Grecco, Stock, Boston, Inc.; **123** Steve Leonard, Black Star; **124** Matt Slothhower, Black Star; **130** Billy E. Barnes, Stock, Boston, Inc.; **131** Handlesman, New Yorker Magazine; **132** Larry Mulvehill, Photo Researchers; **134** AP/Wide World Photos; **135** Hans Halberstadt, Photo Researchers; **137** Billy E. Barnes, Stock, Boston, Inc.; **139** S. Elbez, Sygma; **140** Flip Schulke, Black Star; **141** Bettmann; **142** Elliott Erwitt, Magnum Photos; **143** Bettmann; **144** Spencer C. Grant, Photo Researchers; **144** (inset) Lee Lockwood, Black Star; **146** Black Star; **148** Paul Sakuma, Sygma; **149** Bob Daemmrich, Stock, Boston, Inc.; **151** Stacy Pick, Stock, Boston, Inc.; **157** Bettmann; **158** Sue Bennett; **159** Joe Sohm/Chromosohm, Stock, Boston, Inc.; **164** Bob Daemmrich, Stock, Boston, Inc.; **165** Bob Fitch, Black Star; **166** (top) Bettmann; **170** Don Milici; **172** Ira Wyman, Sygma; **176** Clint Wilson; **177** Owen Franken, Sygma; **182** (top) Bob Daemmrich, Stock, Boston, Inc.; **182** (bottom) Dennis Brack, Black Star; **183** P. Durand, Sygma; **184** A. Tannenbaum, Sygma; **185** Dennis Brack, Black Star; **186** Barry Thumma, AP/Wide World; **187** Bob Daemmrich, Stock, Boston, Inc.; **191** Bettmann; **193** (top) Bettmann; **193** (bottom left) Bettmann; **193** (bottom right) Bettmann; **196** H. Charles Laun, Photo Researchers; **196** Campbell, Sygma; **197** The Granger Collection, New York; **198** Shelly Katz, Black Star; **199** Bob Daemmrich, Stock, Boston, Inc.; **201** (left) Bob Daemmrich, Stock, Boston, Inc.; **201** (right) R. Maiman, Sygma; **202** Dennis Brack, Black Star; **208** (top) John Troha, Black Star; **208** (bottom) United Features Syndicate; **211** Charles Gupton, Stock, Boston, Inc.; **212** Sygma; **215** J. L. Atlan, Sygma; **215** (inset) Sygma; **217** (left) Bettmann; **217** (right) Bettmann; **220** Lisa Quinones, Black Star; **221** (left) Bettmann; **221** (right) P. F. Gero, Sygma; **224** Dennis Brack, Black Star; **225** Dennis Brack, Black Star; **226** Mark Richards, Photo Edit; **229** Dennis Brack, Black Star; **234** Library of Congress; **235** Bettmann; **237** Dennis Brack, Black Star; **240** (left) Bettmann; **240** (right) R. Malman, Sygma; **245** Rick Browne, Stock, Boston, Inc.; **247** (top) Bettmann; **247** (bottom) Bob Daemmrich, Stock, Boston, Inc.; **249** Bettmann; **253** (top) Rick Friedman, Black Star; **253** (bottom) Tom Zimberoff, Sygma; **254** R. Prigent, Sygma; **255** J. L. Atlan, Sygma; **256** Bettmann; **262** (top) Bingham, Bettmann; **262** (bottom) Bettmann; **264** The Granger Collection, New York; **265** Bettmann; **266** The Granger Collection, New York; **267** Bettmann; **269** Stayskal, Tampa Tribune; **271** James Kamp, Black Star; **275** Bettmann; **277** Bob Daemmrich, Stock, Boston, Inc.; **284** Dennis Brack, Black Star; **285** Dennis Brack, Black Star; **287** Bettmann; **289** Rob Nelson, Black Star; **290** The Office of the Senator Robert Dole; **295** Tannenbaum, Sygma; **297** Bettmann; **298** Dennis Brack, Black Star; **299** Ron Sachs, Sygma; **301** Dennis Brack, Black Star; **302** The Office of Senator Mikulski; **305** G. Mathieson, Sygma; **306** Shelly Katz, Black Star; **314** Billy E. Barnes, Stock, Boston, Inc.; **315** Herblock, Washington Post; **316** (top) Joe McNally, Sygma; **316** (bottom) Diane M. Lowe, Stock, Boston, Inc.; **317** The Granger Collection, New York; **322** Rob Lawlor, Philadelphia Daily News; **324** J. A. Atlan, Sygma; **327** Arthur Grace, Stock, Boston, Inc.; **329** Sygma; **326** Dennis Brack, Black Star; **334** Dennis Brack, Black Star; **336** James Kamp, Black Star; **337** (top) R. Sachs, Sygma; **337** (bottom) Dennis Brack, Black Star; **340** House of Representatives; **341** Senator Bentsen's Office; **343** House of Representatives; **345** AP/Wide World Photos; **347** Ron Sachs, Sygma; **349** Carl Hjelte, Black Star; **356** (top) Dennis Brack, Black Star; **356** (bottom) The Granger Collection, New York; **357** The Granger Collection, New York; **358** Sygma; **359** Owen Franken, Stock, Boston, Inc.; **360** The Granger Collection, New York; **361** The Granger Collection, New York; **365** Baldev, Sygma; **366** The Granger Collection, New York; **367** Dennis Brack, Black Star; **368** Ralph Dunagin, reprinted with special permission of NAS, Inc.; **369** Sygma; **370** Rick Friedman, Black Star; **372** Christopher Brown, Stock, Boston, Inc.; **373** (left) Dennis Brack, Black Star; **373** (right) Bettmann; **378** Dennis Brack, Black Star; **379** Christopher Morris, Black Star; **382** Bettmann; **383** Bettmann; **385** Dennis Brack, Black Star; **386** Bettmann; **387** Bettmann; **388** Black Star; **389** Bettmann; **394** Bettmann; **397** J. P. Laffont, Sygma; **401** NAS, Inc.; **402** Ted Thai, Sygma; **405** Andy Levin, Photo Researchers; **409** Phil Huber, Black Star; **410** J. P. Laffont, Sygma; **411** Edward Madigan's Office; **415** (top) Sygma; **415** (bottom) Peter Menzel, Stock, Boston, Inc.; **418** Philadelphia Enquirer; **421** Bettmann; **425** Hutchings, Photo Researchers; **432** Ellis Herwig, Stock, Boston, Inc.; **434** Billy E. Barnes, Stock, Boston, Inc.; **437** Tony Korody, Sygma; **439** Sygma; **440** Collection of the Curator/Supreme Court; **441** Robert Clayton Burns, Hood Museum of Art; **446** O. Franken, Sygma; **448** Sachs, Sygma; **452** Sydney Harris; **453** The Supreme Court Historical Society/ National Geographic Society; **462** Photo Researchers; **463** Bettmann; **465** Dennis Brack, Black Star; **466** (top) Bettmann; **466** (bottom) Trevor, Albuquerque Journal; **467** R. Maiman, Sygma; **469** Bob Daemmrich, Stock, Boston, Inc.; **475** Janice Rubin, Black Star; **476** Andy Levin, Photo Researchers; **478** Andy King, Sygma; **479** B. Nation, Sygma; **482** Photo Researchers; **483** Wayne Stayskal, Tampa Tribune; **485** G. Mathieson, Sygma; **491** (top) Black Star; **491** (bottom) Bettmann Archives; **492** J. P. Fizet, Sygma; **493** Alain Nogues, Sygma; **495** J. Langevin, Sygma; **496** Sygma; **497** Black Star; **500** Bettmann; **501** Bob Krist, Black Star; **502** Bettmann; **506** Bettmann; **508** Sygma; **509** Peter Turnley, Black Star; **511** Photo Researchers; **514** Sygma; **522** David Frazier, Photo Researchers; **523** Kevin Horan, Stock, Boston, Inc.; **528** P. M. Grecco, Stock, Boston, Inc.; **529** Charles Gupton, Stock, Boston, Inc.; **530** Bob Daemmrich, Stock, Boston, Inc.; **531** Spencer Grant, Stock, Boston, Inc.; **532** Bob Daemmrich, Stock, Boston, Inc.; **537** Austin-American Statesman; **541** Bob Daemmrich, Stock, Boston, Inc.; **546** Bob Daemmrich, Stock, Boston, Inc.; **547** Bettmann; **552** Governor Cuomo's Office; **553** Greg Smith, Stock, Boston, Inc.; **554** Archives Division Texas State Library; **555** John DeVisser, Black Star; **556** Lt. Governor Dyrstad's Office; **557** Colorado Attorney General's Office; **558** Jim Sugar, Black Star; **559** Bettmann; **564** (top) Rick Friedman, Black Star; **564** (bottom) Bob Daemmrich, Stock, Boston, Inc.; **568** William Johnson, Stock, Boston, Inc.; **571** Bettmann; **572** AP/Wide World Photos; **574** Spencer Grant, Photo Researchers; **576** (top) Tannenbaum, Sygma; **576** (bottom) David Woo, Stock, Boston, Inc.; **578** Fabricius, Stock, Boston, Inc.; **579** Paul Hamann, Sygma; **584** Ellis Herwig, Stock, Boston, Inc.; **585** Sacramento Bee, Stock, Boston, Inc.; **588** Evatt, Sygma; **589** Richard Palsey, Stock, Boston, Inc.; **590** Jim Pickerell, Stock, Boston, Inc.; **591** Tom Zimberoff, Sygma; **592** Bob Daemmrich, Stock, Boston, Inc.; **593** Tom Sobolik, Black Star; **594** Frederik Bodin, Stock, Boston, Inc.; **608** John Coletti, Stock, Boston, Inc.; **611** Mark Burnett, Stock, Boston, Inc.; **615** John Coletti, Stock, Boston, Inc.; **617** (left) Neal McVay, Stock, Boston, Inc.; **617** (right) Greg Cranna, Stock, Boston, Inc.; **620** Rob Nelson, Black Star; **621** J. L. Atlan, Sygma; **628** Tim Graham, Sygma; **629** Bettmann Archives; **630** Ron Watts, Black Star; **631** T. Orban, Sygma; **632** Alain Nogues, Sygma; **633** B. Annebioque, Sygma; **635** Yamaguchi, Sygma; **636** P. Perrin, Sygma; **637** Jeff Kravitz, Sygma; **640** Kirschenbaum, Stock, Boston, Inc.; **641** McVay, Stock, Boston, Inc.; **644** Carey, Sygma; **645** Sygma; **646** Sygma; **647** (top) P. Le Segratain, Sygma; **647** (bottom) Klaus Reisinger, Black Star; **648** J. Langevin, Sygma; **649** Patrick Forden, Sygma; **710** George Washington/The Bettmann Archive; John Adams/The Bettmann Archive; Thomas Jefferson/The Bettmann Archive; James Madison/ The Bettmann Archive; **711** James Monroe/The Bettmann Archive; John Quincy Adams/The Bettmann Archive; Andrew Jackson/The Bettmann Archive; Martin Van Buren/The Bettmann Archive; **712** William H. Harrison/The Bettmann Archive; John Tyler/The Bettmann Archive; James K. Polk/The Bettmann Archive; Zachary Taylor/The Granger Collection, New York; **713** Millard Fillmore/The Bettmann Archive; Franklin Pierce/The Bettmann Archive; James Buchanan/The Bettmann Archive; Abraham Lincoln/The Bettmann Archive; **714** Andrew Johnson/ The Granger Collection, New York; Ulysses S. Grant/The Bettmann Archive; Rutherford B. Hayes/The Granger Collection, New York; James A. Garfield/The Bettman Archive; **715** Chester A. Arthur/The Bettmann Archive; Grover Cleveland/The Bettmann Archive; Benjamin Harrison/The Granger Collection, New York; William McKinley/The Granger Collection, New York; **716** Theodore Roosevelt/The Bettmann Archive; William H. Taft/ The Bettmann Archive; Woodrow Wilson/The Bettmann Archive; Warren G. Harding/The Bettmann Archive; **717** Calvin Coolidge/ The Bettmann Archive; Herbert C. Hoover/The Bettmann Archive; Franklin D. Roosevelt/The Bettmann Archive; **718** Harry S Truman/The Bettmann Archive; Dwight D. Eisenhower/The Bettmann Archive; John F. Kennedy/The Bettmann Archive; Lyndon B. Johnson/The Bettmann Archive; **719** Richard M. Nixon/ The Bettmann Archive; Gerald R. Ford/The Bettmann Archive; James E. Carter, Jr./The Bettmann Archive; Ronald W. Reagan/ The Granger Collection, New York; **720** George H. W. Bush/The Granger Collection, New York; William J. B. Clinton/Bettmann; **721** John Jay/The Bettmann Archive; John Rutledge/The Granger Collection, New York; Oliver Ellsworth/The Bettmann Archive; John Marshall/The Bettmann Archive; **722** Roger B. Taney/The Granger Collection, New York; Salmon P. Chase/The Bettmann Archive; Morrison R. Waite/The Bettmann Archive; **723** Melville W. Fuller/The Bettmann Archive; Edward D. White/The Bettmann Archive; William H. Taft/The Bettmann Archive; **724** Charles E. Hughes/The Bettmann Archive; Harlan F. Stone/ The Bettmann Archive; Frederick M. Vinson/The Bettmann Archive; Earl Warren/The Bettmann Archive; **725** Warren E. Burger/The Bettmann Archive; William H. Rehnquist/Sygma.